GERMAN LAW ACCESSIBLE

Kruse/Tute

Corporate Criminal Liability in Germany

Preface

The genesis of this handbook lies in a shared experience we encountered early on in practising in the field of white-collar criminal law. Repeatedly, in discussions with colleagues and in our day-to-day work, we noticed a gap: despite the growing significance of corporate criminal liability in the German legal system, there is a striking lack of comprehensive, practice-oriented literature on this subject in the English language. What was particularly notable was that this observation was not ours alone. In conversations with peers from various fields – whether in law firms, corporations, or universities – we also encountered a recurring sense of need: practitioners working across borders and legal systems are looking for accessible and well-structured resources that can help them navigate this complex area of German Law in English.

This handbook is our response to that need. It aims to provide legal professionals – both in Germany and abroad – with a clear and reliable overview of the principles of German criminal law as they relate to corporate conduct and liability. We did not want to simply translate legal terms or statutory provisions. Instead, our goal has been to contextualise and convey these principles in a way that resonates with the realities of international legal practice.

The fact that this handbook brings together contributions from a wide range of authors is, in itself, telling. It reflects the fact that many colleagues from different backgrounds shared our perception and were willing to lend their expertise to this project. Their involvement stands as further evidence of how relevant and practically pressing the topic of corporate criminal liability has become.

We hope this handbook will serve as both a guide and a reliable reference tool for all those engaging with German corporate criminal law – whether in cross-border matters, in-house legal departments, or academic contexts. At the same time, we hope to contribute to the ongoing international discourse on corporate accountability, and to shed light on the distinctive contours of the German legal tradition in this evolving field.

Finally, we are very grateful to all contributing authors for their expertise and collaborative spirit, to Lukas Danner for his consistently helpful support, and to the C.H.Beck Verlag for including this handbook in the 'German Law Accessible' series – particularly Dr. Roland Klaes, Dr. Klaus Winkler, and Dr. Jonathon Watson for their support, and above all Aleksandra Hadzic, whose dedication proved essential in bringing this work to completion.

Frankfurt, December 2025

Dr. Björn Kruse LL.M.
Christoph Tute

List of authors

Adrian Baldewein is a lawyer specializing in criminal law and data protection law and a certified external data protection officer at Lilie Ihwas Rechtsanwälte in Frankfurt/Main. He primarily works in areas of white-collar and corporate criminal law, criminal tax law and data protection (criminal) law. He advises and defends individuals and companies at all stages of proceedings, including complex, large-scale proceedings and internal investigations. Additionally, he represents companies and individuals against data protection authorities in cases of violations of the General Data Protection Regulation and the Federal Data Protection Act. *[Chapter 16 – Data protection (criminal) law]*

Laura Borgel is a partner in the Frankfurt office of the law firm Feigen Graf. She advises and represents both individual clients and corporates across the entire spectrum of commercial criminal law, the law regarding tax offences and regulatory offences. Handelsblatt has repeatedly noted Laura Borgel to be one of Germany's top lawyers in the field of commercial criminal law. Additionally, she was honoured by the JUVE editorial team as a 'rising star in commercial and criminal tax law' (JUVE 2023/24). Dr Laura Borgel studied law in Hamburg and Oxford and business in Vallendar. *[Chapter 5 – Confiscation]*

Florian Domjan (born Opper) is partner at Beukelmann Müller Partner, a law firm specialising in white-collar crime. Prior to his admission to the bar, he served for several years as a public prosecutor in a department of the Munich I Public Prosecutor's Office that focused on white-collar crime, where he handled numerous large-scale cases. He was subsequently appointed as a criminal judge, presiding over cases in the areas of white-collar and narcotics criminal law. Drawing on his judicial experience, he advises and defends individuals, companies, and corporate bodies in white-collar and tax criminal matters, with a further focus on preventive compliance in areas such as labour law, social security, and foreign trade law. He studied law at the Julius Maximilian University of Würzburg, specialising in business and European law. *[Chapter 14 – Money laundering]*

Tillmann Gessert is a partner and certified lawyer for criminal law at Rettenmaier Frankfurt. From 2014 to 2016, he gained experience as a research assistant at Freshfields Bruckhaus Deringer LLP in Frankfurt. Before joining Rettenmaier Frankfurt, he completed his legal clerkship at the Frankfurt Higher Regional Court, with a criminal law focus. Since 2017, he has been working as a criminal defence lawyer, advising and defending individuals, companies in all areas of commercial and tax criminal law. For his work, he has been recognised by Legal500, Best Lawyers and others. *[Chapter 23 – Foreign trade law]*

Bernd Groß has been a partner at the criminal law firm Feigen Graf since 2007. His area of practice includes commercial and tax law criminal defence of individuals as well as criminal law advice and representation of companies – also in an international context. He specializes in banking, capital market, tax and environmental criminal law – in particular in connection with advice in cum/ex and cum/cum proceedings as well as investigations into money laundering, fraud and so-called 'greenwashing'. The legal journal JUVE 2024/2025 refers to him as the 'chief strategist in criminal tax law'. *[Chapter 2 – Principles of corporate responsibility and strategies; Chapter 13 – Tax]*

Mathias Grzesiek is a specialist lawyer in the field of criminal law and partner at Rosinus | Partner Rechtsanwälte in Frankfurt, advising on complex economic and IT criminal law matters. He studied law and earned his doctorate in criminal law at Goethe University Frankfurt before completing a clerkship at the Higher Regional Court Frankfurt with a criminal-law focus. Over the past years he has built expertise in white-collar crime and IT-related defence work, particularly in the healthcare sector. As editor of the Strafrecht-Digital blog and a lecturer in criminology at Goethe University Frankfurt, he shapes both academic and professional discussions. *[Chapter 17 – IT criminal law]*

Laura Hainlein is an in-house lawyer specialized in compliance. She began her career in the automotive sector and now works in the mechanical engineering sector as a Senior Compliance Manager. Over the years, she has developed specific expertise in internal investigations and whistleblower management. Laura Hainlein is a Certified Compliance Officer (Universität St. Gallen) and holds a Master of Laws (LL.M.) in 'Business Law and Compliance'. In addition, she also teaches courses at Universities of Applied Sciences, focusing on general compliance, internal investigations, and whistleblower management. She is a member at the Deutsches Institut für Compliance e.V. (DICO) where she organizes and conducts training sessions on internal investigations and whistleblower systems. *[Chapter 7 – Whistleblower systems as part of the CMS]*

Laura Harandt-Wüst is an in-house lawyer specializing in criminal law and internal investigations. She currently serves as Head of the Group Case Management & Investigation Office at Fresenius, where she leads complex internal investigations with a particular focus on cross-border and international matters. In this role, she has also been responsible for managing the company's whistleblower reporting channel, reinforcing Fresenius' commitment to transparency and compliance. Prior to joining Fresenius in 2020, she advised clients on criminal and corporate criminal liability matters at an international law firm. Dr. Harandt-Wüst studied law at Goethe University Frankfurt, where she earned her doctorate and completed her legal clerkship. Her legal training included a posting at the German Embassy in Santiago de Chile. *[Chapter 8 – Internal investigations]*

Chad Heimrich is specialized in white-collar criminal defence and extradition and currently Counsel at Knauer Rechtsanwälte in Frankfurt. After his law studies at Westfälische Wilhelms-University in Münster, he obtained an LL.M. at Queen Mary University in London, where he particularly focused on EU and international criminal law. He completed his legal clerkship at a law firm specialized in criminal law and at the German Bar Association in Brussels. In his current practice, Chad Heimrich regularly represents national and international entities and their managers in white-collar and extradition matters. He also frequently publishes in the field of EU criminal law. *[Chapter 9 – International cooperation in criminal matters]*

Christoph Henckel is a salary partner at EVEN Rechtsanwälte in Hamburg and specializes in white-collar criminal defence and criminal tax law. He studied law at Bucerius Law School in Hamburg and Georgetown University Law Center in Washington, DC and completed his doctorate with a thesis on procedural rules for plea bargaining. He advises and defends individuals and companies at all stages of proceedings, including compliance matters and internal investigations. He regularly publishes on issues of white-collar criminal, criminal tax and criminal procedure law. *[Chapter 25 – Protection of commercially valuable information]*

Jeanie Henn is a senior public prosecutor at the public prosecutor's office in Mannheim where she works in the special department for white-collar crime. Before joining the judiciary, Dr. Henn worked for several years as an attorney in the antitrust department of a leading business law firm. Her current practice focuses on criminal tax law as well as corruption and fraud in the health care sector. Dr. Henn is the author of various professional articles and has several years of experience as a speaker. *[Chapter 10 – Corruption]*

Mayeul Hiéramente is a specialist lawyer in criminal law. He is active in the defence of individuals and companies and advises in all areas of white-collar and tax criminal law. He is particularly interested in cross-border cases and the associated exchange across different (legal) traditions and specialist disciplines (Mutual Legal Assistance, Extraditions). He is the editor and author of a commentary on the German Trade Secrets Act published by Beck. *[Chapter 25 – Protection of commercially valuable information]*

Saleh R. Ihwas is a specialist lawyer for criminal law and a certified external data protection officer. His predominant focus is in areas of white-collar and corporate criminal law, data protection (criminal) law and internet criminal law. He defends and advises individual defendants as well as companies at all stages of proceedings. His advisory work to these companies includes the conduct of internal investigations as well as the representation in complex scope proceedings. He also represents companies and individuals against data protection authorities in cases of violations of the General Data Protection Regulation and the Federal Data Protection Act. Dr. Ihwas is a lecturer at the German FernUniversität Hagen and regularly publishes on the topics of criminal law and data protection law. *[Chapter 16 – Data protection (criminal) law]*

Lucas Jürss is a partner at the Düsseldorf office of the law firm tdwe, where he acts as a certified specialist lawyer for criminal law. He advises and represents both individual clients as well as corporations in commercial criminal law, tax criminal law, and compliance matters. Dr. Lucas Jürss is recognized by WirtschaftsWoche and Handelsblatt/Best Lawyers (Ones to Watch) as an outstanding lawyer in the fields of white-collar crime, tax criminal law, and corporate governance & compliance. Additionally, he serves as a member of the Human Rights Committee of the German Federal Bar Association. Dr. Lucas Jürss studied law in Hamburg, including a period abroad in Paris, and completed his doctorate at the Free University of Berlin with a thesis on director liability for fines imposed on stock corporations. *[Chapter 11 – Fraud and subsidy fraud]*

Pedram Karami has been a licensed attorney since 2017. He possesses extensive expertise in representing individuals and companies in criminal and regulatory offence proceedings. Before founding KARAMI Legal, Dr. Karami worked for several years with major international law firms in Frankfurt and Paris. His legal proficiency spans a wide range of areas, including tax criminal law, medical device law, pharmaceutical criminal law, environmental criminal law, as well as corruption, fraud, and money laundering. A particular focus of Dr. Karami's practice lies in advising startups and medium-sized enterprises. Through his in-depth legal counsel, Dr. Karami helps companies navigate complex regulatory frameworks and develop effective compliance strategies to ensure sustainable success. *[Chapter 6 – Compliance management systems]*

Karolina Kessler specialises in white-collar criminal law and is a partner at Tsambikakis & Partner Rechtsanwälte mbB. She advises and defends companies and private individuals in complex white-collar criminal law proceedings. She has particular expertise in the field of medical criminal law. Hospital groups, healthcare facilities and pharmaceutical manufacturers as well as managing directors, physicians and pharmacists rely on Dr. Kessler's foresight and broad expertise when it comes to advice and in all phases of criminal proceedings. Dr Kessler regularly publishes on topics of white-collar criminal law and medical criminal law and is regularly listed by Handelsblatt and WirtschaftsWoche as a highly recommended lawyer for white-collar criminal law. *[Chapter 21 – Criminal liability in medical practice under German law]*

Peter Klormann is a partner in the Frankfurt office of international law firm Sullivan & Cromwell LLP. He advises on a wide range of M&A transactions as well as general corporate law, corporate governance and securities law matters. Peter has also worked on a number of significant capital markets transactions, for both investors and issuers, and related compliance matters. He has advised listed companies on their implementation of capital markets compliance systems and regularly represents clients in proceedings with the German Federal Financial Supervisory Authority (BaFin). He earned his law degree and doctorate from the Ruprecht-Karls-University of Heidelberg, as well as an LL.M. from the University of Chicago. *[Chapter 22 – Capital markets laws]*

Anna-Elisabeth Krause-Ablaß is a lawyer in the Frankfurt office of the law firm Flick Gocke Schaumburg. She has 14 years of experience as a national public prosecutor and a European Delegated Prosecutor. Anna now advises both individual clients and corporates on all questions of white-collar crime and criminal tax law and conducts internal investigations. She finished her legal studies at the University of Bonn and her doctoral thesis on European Corporate Law at the University of Duesseldorf and the Institut suisse de droit comparé in Lausanne/Switzerland. *[Chapter 2 – Principles of corporate responsibility and strategies]*

Björn Kruse is a specialist lawyer in criminal law (*Fachanwalt für Strafrecht*) and partner at ARKTIK Legal in Frankfurt. He advises on complex national and international criminal cases, with a particular focus on tax criminal law, cybercrime, money laundering, corruption and corporate criminal liability. His practice also includes representation in INTERPOL Red Notice cases and extradition proceedings, where he regularly acts in cross-border contexts. At ARKTIK Legal, he is also working on complex commercial disputes involving criminal law – particularly those concerning fraud, insolvency-related offences, or shareholder conflicts that call for parallel civil and criminal defence strategies. He studied law at Goethe University Frankfurt, where he also earned his doctorate in criminal law. He also accomplished an LL.M. in international criminal law at the University Campus of the United Nations in Turin (Italy). *[Introduction; Chapter 4 – § 30 OWiG; Chapter 18 – Supply chain due diligence]*

Moritz Lange is a partner in the Frankfurt office of the law firm Feigen Graf. He is considered a 'very experienced criminal defence lawyer' (Legal 500 2024) and a 'specialist for cum-ex' (JUVE 2023/24). Further he was recognised by Juve Verlag as a 'rising star in commercial and criminal tax law' and in the elite group of the '40 under 40' lawyers in 2023. Dr Moritz Lange finished his legal studies at the University of Tübingen with a focus on tax law and his doctoral thesis at the Goethe University in Frankfurt am Main. *[Chapter 3 – Fundamentals of criminal proceedings]*

Sophie-Charlotte Lipp is a lawyer in the Frankfurt office of the law firm Feigen Graf. She advises and represents both individual clients as well as corporates in white-collar crime and criminal tax law. Sophie-Charlotte Lipp, M.A., finished her legal and business studies at EBS University in Wiesbaden and at IE University in Madrid. *[Chapter 3 – Fundamentals of criminal proceedings]*

Manuel Lorenz is a specialist lawyer for criminal law, white-collar and corporate criminal law. He defends individuals and companies in all commercial, tax and environmental criminal proceedings as well as administrative offence proceedings. His practice also focuses on providing liability-reducing advice to companies and employees, particularly in the environmental and waste sector, as well as conducting internal investigations to clarify possible legal violations in companies. Dr. Manuel Lorenz is a member of the board of the Koblenz Bar Association, lecturer at the University of Trier in the areas of commercial and fiscal criminal law as well as European and international criminal law, lecturer at the Environmental Institute Offenbach for environmental criminal law and the criminal liability of companies and persons in environmental law. Dr. Manuel Lorenz publishes regularly in the field of environmental criminal law as well as on topics of general commercial criminal law. [*Chapter 20 – Environmental criminal law, product criminal law, and food criminal law*]

Maximilian Müller is a partner of Beukelmann Müller Partner, a white-collar crime specialist practice. He specialises in business and tax crimes and advises and defends private individuals, companies and management. Proceedings of international relevance and extradition cases form a pillar of his work. Maximilian studied law at the University of Lausanne in Switzerland, at LMU Munich in Germany and at Trinity College Dublin in Ireland. He is an Accredited Specialist Lawyer for Criminal Law and Certified Consultant for Tax Criminal Law. Maximilian co-founded the international lawyers' network association Global Criminal Law Counsel (GCLC) and is an active member of the International Bar Association (IBA), the American Bar Association (ABA), the European Criminal Bar Association (ECBA) and the European Fraud and Compliance Lawyers (EFCL). The German Federal Bar Association (Bundesrechtsanwaltskammer, BRAK) called him to be a member of both the Committee for Criminal Procedural Law and the Committee for European Law. Moreover, he is a member of the Committee for Accredited Specialist Lawyers for Criminal Law of the Munich Bar Association. *[Chapter 14 – Money laundering]*

Dominic Reitner has been an associate at Feigen Graf since 2022. One of his main areas of practice is the defence of individuals and companies in criminal tax proceedings – particularly in the context of VAT carousels and cum/ex investigations. He studied law and basics of economics in Wiesbaden and Kingston (Ontario). His dissertation analyses the judicial approach concerning the determination of tax evasion intend. *[Chapter 13 – Tax]*

Tony Rostalski is a specialist criminal lawyer and compliance expert based in Cologne. With his law firm, ROSTALSKI Wirtschaftsstrafrecht & Compliance, he advises and defends individuals and companies at all stages of white-collar and regulatory investigations and proceedings. He has extensive experience defending against allegations of fraud, breach of trust, corruption, cartel offences, insider trading, money laundering, export control and sanctions violations, environmental offences, tax offences (including voluntary self-disclosures), as well as healthcare and employment-related offences. This includes defence against freezing and seizure of assets. Beyond defence work, Rostalski conducts internal investigations in corporate and public-sector compliance proceedings – particularly in the context of reports under the German Whistleblower Protection Act (HinSchG) – and advises on crisis response and reputation management. He has extensive experience building practical compliance management systems (ISO 37301) and anti-bribery management systems (ISO 37001) for companies and public authorities, including enterprise risk assessments, policy development, training, whistleblower systems, and third-party due diligence. His compliance advisory work also covers technology regulation – especially the EU AI Act and the GDPR. Rostalski additionally serves as an ombudsperson (*Vertrauensanwalt*) for companies and government bodies. *[Chapter 23 – Foreign trade law]*

Ricarda Schelzke is a specialist lawyer for criminal law at GvW Graf von Westphalen in Frankfurt. She advises and defends individuals and companies in white-collar criminal matters, constitutional law, and the laws of professional conduct. Before joining GvW Graf von Westphalen, she was a lawyer at Freshfields and in prestigious criminal law firms. Dr. Schelzke studied at the Bucerius Law School in Hamburg and at the University of California – Law San Francisco in the US. She serves on the board of the Wirtschaftsstrafrechtliche Vereinigung (WisteV) as well as on the constitutional committee of the Deutscher Anwaltverein and regularly publishes on issues of white-collar criminal, constitutional and criminal procedure law. *[Chapter 19 – Criminal labour law]*

Sören Schomburg is specialized in white-collar criminal defence and extradition and is a partner of Knauer Rechtsanwälte in Berlin. After his studies at Humboldt-Universität in Berlin and King's College in London, he completed his legal clerkship at the German Ministry of Foreign Affairs and a law firm in Tokyo. Today, he represents national and international entities and their managers in white-collar matters as well as in extradition and has authored numerous specialist publications on commercial criminal law, INTERPOL and on the European Arrest Warrant. He is a member of the advisory board of the European Criminal Bar Association and was part of an expert group working on the reform of the German Act on International Mutual Assistance in Criminal Matters. *[Chapter 9 – International cooperation in criminal matters]*

Max Schwerdtfeger is a partner at EVEN Rechtsanwälte in Hamburg and specializes in white-collar criminal defence. Max studied law at Passau University, the University of Western Australia in Perth and holds a Ph.D. from Bucerius Law School, Hamburg. Max defends and advises individuals and companies in all areas of white-collar and tax criminal law. He is a lecturer in white-collar criminal law and the law of parliamentary inquiry committees at the University of Hamburg. *[Chapter 11 – Fraud and subsidy fraud]*

Peter-Jan Solka is a salary partner at EVEN Rechtsanwälte in Hamburg and specializes in white-collar criminal defence. Peter-Jan studied law at Bucerius Law School in Hamburg and the University of New South Wales in Sydney, Australia. He represents both individuals and companies with a special focus on defending against public confiscation claims, frequently publishes specialist articles and is regularly recommended in leading publications. *[Chapter 5 – Confiscation]*

Andrea Soprano is a Counsel at Baker McKenzie Rechtsanwaltsgesellschaft mbH in Frankfurt, specializing in restructuring and insolvency law. Andrea studied law and international business law at the University of Erlangen-Nuremberg, where she also earned her doctorate degree. Her practice focuses on advising German and international companies, shareholders, creditors, and other stakeholders on all aspects of restructuring and insolvency law. She regularly advises company management on legal risks and insolvency filing obligations, as well as financial institutions and investors on financial restructuring and insolvency proceedings, on trustee structures and on M&A transactions arising from the crisis or insolvency, both on the seller and the buyer side. Andrea is also a co-author of several publications in her field. She is a member of Distressed Ladies – Women in Restructuring e.V. *[Chapter 15 – Insolvency]*

Timm Sperber is a prosecutor at the public prosecutor's office in Mannheim, where he works in the special department for white-collar crime. He studied law in Heidelberg, Montpellier and Berlin. He then attended the postgraduate program of the College of Europe in Bruges on a scholarship and graduated with a Master's degree (LL.M. Eur). Before joining the judiciary, he worked as a legal officer at the Federal Ministry for the Environment, Nature Conservation, Construction and Nuclear Safety in Berlin. His current practice focuses on criminal tax law as well as corruption and fraud in the health care sector. *[Chapter 10 – Corruption]*

Christoph Tute is a specialist lawyer for criminal law and partner at the Frankfurt-based law firm schilling tute. He advises and defends corporations and individuals in all areas of white-collar criminal law and criminal tax law, with his practice focusing particularly on breach of trust, as well as corruption, money laundering, tax evasion, environmental offences, and confiscation of assets. He studied law with a focus on criminal law in Munich and Lisbon and completed his legal clerkship in Berlin. He serves as treasurer on the board of the Wirtschaftsstrafrechtliche Vereinigung e.V. (WisteV) and regularly publishes articles and holds lectures on German and international white-collar criminal law and corporate compliance topics. *[Introduction; Chapter 12 – Breach of trust]*

Sarah Zinndorf is a lawyer at Gleiss Lutz in Frankfurt, specializing in European and German competition law with a particular focus on the digital economy. She advises clients on merger control, cooperation and distribution contracts, cartel proceedings and litigation, abuse of dominance as well as competition law compliance. She has been recognized several times by Handelsblatt/Best Lawyers for her expertise in competition law. Sarah studied at the Ruprecht-Karls-University of Heidelberg (Dr. iur.) and the Complutense University of Madrid, and was previously a visiting scholar at the University of Chicago Law School. As part of her legal clerkship, she worked for the European Commission (DG Competition). *[Chapter 24 – Competition law]*

Summary table of contents

Preface V
List of authors VII
List of abbreviations XXIII
Abbreviations of cited works XXXIX
Weblinks to English translations XLIX

CHAPTER 1
INTRODUCTION

A. Conceptual framework 1
B. Scope and approach 2
C. Overview 3

CHAPTER 2
PRINCIPLES OF CORPORATE RESPONSIBILITY AND STRATEGIES

A. Criminal liability of companies 7
B. Criminal liability of company employees and management 13
C. Companies' procedural status during criminal proceedings 18
D. Strategies of corporate defence 23

CHAPTER 3
FUNDAMENTALS OF CRIMINAL PROCEEDINGS

A. Introduction 31
B. The parties to criminal proceedings 33
C. Organisation and jurisdiction of criminal courts 34
D. Sequence of criminal proceedings 37
E. Execution proceedings 53

CHAPTER 4
§ 30 OWIG

A. Introduction 58

B. Regulatory fine imposed on legal persons and on partnerships (§ 30 OWiG) . 59
C. Sanctions and confiscation of financial benefits 72
D. Independent proceedings (§ 30 sub. 4 OWiG)............................ 76
E. Seizure of assets (§ 30 sub. 6 OWiG)....................................... 77
F. Procedural obstacles 77
G. Procedure in case of legal succession (§ 30 sub. 2a OWiG).................. 80
H. Jurisdiction and responsible authority..................................... 80
I. Summary and outlook 82

CHAPTER 5
CONFISCATION

A. Introduction: purpose and legal bases of confiscation 84
B. Overview on the systematics of the law on confiscation..................... 85
C. The principle: confiscation from persons involved in the offence 88
D. § 73b StGB: confiscation from third parties 94
E. §§ 73d and 73e StGB, § 459g sub. 5 StPO: 'objections' against confiscation (deduction of expenditure, lapsing, proportionality) 100
F. Procedural principles 105

CHAPTER 6
COMPLIANCE MANAGEMENT SYSTEMS

A. Introduction 112
B. Legal obligations to implement CMS in Germany......................... 113
C. Substantive design of CMS... 116
D. Common CMS pillars 127
E. Legal and regulatory challenges to CMS 129
F. Conclusion 129

CHAPTER 7
WHISTLEBLOWER SYSTEMS AS PART OF THE CMS

A. General introduction: whistleblowing and whistleblower protection in Germany 132
B. Requirements of the German HinSchG.. 135
C. Further legal frameworks.. 153

D. Excursus: grievance mechanism according to the German Due Diligence Supply Chain Act (LkSG) 156

E. First steps for the set-up of a whistleblower system according to HinSchG ... 156

CHAPTER 8
INTERNAL INVESTIGATIONS

A. Introduction 160

B. Legal and factual obligations to conduct internal investigations 161

C. Basic principles governing the internal investigation process 163

D. Cooperating with authorities 166

E. Investigation steps 167

CHAPTER 9
INTERNATIONAL COOPERATION IN CRIMINAL MATTERS

A. Introduction: legal bases of international cooperation in criminal matters ... 186

B. Extradition 188

C. Mutual legal assistance 202

D. Transfer of sentenced persons 214

E. Execution of fines 216

CHAPTER 10
CORRUPTION OFFENCES

A. General remarks 220

B. The legal framework 221

C. Types of corruption offences 223

D. Compliance: how to prevent corruption 242

CHAPTER 11
FRAUD AND SUBSIDY FRAUD

A. Introduction 244

B. Practical relevance 245

C. The offence of fraud under § 263 StGB 247

D. The offence of subsidy fraud under § 264 StGB 264

CHAPTER 12
BREACH OF TRUST

A. Introduction 270
B. Elements of the crime 270
C. Commission of and complicity in a breach of trust 284
D. Legal consequences 285
E. Most relevant cases 285
F. Conclusion 291

CHAPTER 13
TAX

A. Introduction: criminal tax law in the judiciary's focus 294
B. Substantive criminal tax law 295
C. Procedural law relating to criminal tax law 313
D. Law on regulatory tax offences 317

CHAPTER 14
MONEY LAUNDERING

A. Introduction: the fight against money laundering 324
B. Repressive approach: § 261 StGB 326
C. The German Money Laundering Act 332
D. Conclusion 349

CHAPTER 15
INSOLVENCY

A. Management's duties during the crisis of the company 353
B. Management's duties after insolvency has occurred 359
C. Management's criminal liability in the context of insolvency 365
D. Characteristics of German insolvency proceedings 368
E. Pre-insolvency reorganisation proceedings (StaRUG) 373
F. Applicable law, jurisdiction and recognition of StaRUG and insolvency proceedings 377

CHAPTER 16
DATA PROTECTION (CRIMINAL) LAW

A. Introduction 380
B. European data protection law and German criminal law 381
C. Liabilities within thc GDPR 385
D. Liabilities within the BDSG 395
E. Conclusion 408

CHAPTER 17
IT CRIMINAL LAW

A. The phenomenon of cybercrime and its significance for IT criminal law 410
B. Fundamentals of IT criminal law 412
C. Typical offences in IT criminal law 416
D. Practice of IT criminal law 426

CHAPTER 18
SUPPLY CHAIN DUE DILIGENCE

A. Disclaimer: legal status as of October 2025 436
B. Introduction 437
C. The developement of business and human rights 439
D. Regulatory content of the LkSG 442
E. Conclusion 465

CHAPTER 19
CRIMINAL LABOUR LAW

A. Introduction 468
B. Withholding of social security contributions 469
C. Work safety 476
D. Illegal employment 481
E. Collective labour law 488
F. Procedural peculiarities 491

CHAPTER 20
ENVIRONMENTAL CRIMINAL LAW, PRODUCT CRIMINAL LAW, AND FOOD CRIMINAL LAW

A. Environmental criminal law ... 498
B. Product criminal law ... 512
C. Food criminal law ... 520

CHAPTER 21
CRIMINAL LIABILITY IN MEDICAL PRACTICE UNDER GERMAN LAW

A. Introduction ... 528
B. Criminal law risks in connection with medical treatment ... 529
C. Economic criminal law in medicine ... 539
D. Offences concerning medicinal products and pharmaceuticals ... 553

CHAPTER 22
CAPITAL MARKETS LAWS

A. Introduction ... 558
B. Market abuse regime ... 562
C. Further compliance obligations ... 575
D. Marketing of financial instruments ... 580

CHAPTER 23
FOREIGN TRADE LAW

A. Introduction ... 586
B. Corporate criminal liability in foreign trade law ... 587
C. Principles of AWG compliance ... 597
D. Selected practical problems ... 599

CHAPTER 24
COMPETITION LAW

A. Introduction ... 610
B. Prohibition of agreements restricting competition (§ 1 GWB, Art. 101 TFEU) 612
C. Abuse control: abuse of dominance and other levels of market power (§§ 18, 19, 19a, 20 GWB, Art. 102 TFEU) ... 620

D. Public and private enforcement 628

E. Merger control 640

F. Actions subsequent to sector inquiries 646

CHAPTER 25
PROTECTION OF COMMERCIALLY VALUABLE INFORMATION

A. Introduction 650

B. Violation of confidentiality obligations 652

C. Protection of trade secrets and intellectual property 659

D. Illegal access to secret information 672

Glossary 677
German – English 677
English – German 685

Index 693

List of abbreviations

I. General abbreviations

ABC	anti-bribery and corruption
AG	1. Aktiengesellschaft 2. Die Aktiengesellschaft (journal) 3. Amtsgericht (local court)
AI	artificial intelligence
AL	Arbeit und Leistung (journal)
alt.	Alternative
AMLA	Anti-Money Laundering Authority
AMLC	Committee on Anti Money Laundering
ArbG	Arbeitsgericht (labour court)
ArbRAktuell	Arbeitsrecht Aktuell (journal)
ARP	Arbeitsschutz in Recht und Praxis (journal)
Art.	Article
BAG	Bundesarbeitsgericht (Federal Labour Court)
BAGE	Entscheidungen des Bundesarbeitsgerichts (collection of decisions of the BAG)
BayObLG	Bayerisches Oberstes Landesgericht (Higher Regional Court of Bavaria)
BayObLGSt	Entscheidungen des Bayerischen Obersten Landesgerichts in Strafsachen (collection of decisions of the BayObLG in criminal matters)
BayVGH	Bayerischer Verwaltungsgerichtshof (Higher Administrative Court of Bavaria)
BB	Betriebs-Berater (journal)
BeckRS	beck-online.RECHTSPRECHUNG (database collection of decisions)
BER	block exemption regulation
BFH	Bundesfinanzhof (Federal Fiscal Court)
BFHE	Entscheidungen des Bundesfinanzhofs (collection of decisions of the BFH)
BGBl.	Bundesgesetzblatt (Federal Law Gazette)
BGH	Bundesgerichtshof (Federal Court of Justice)
BGHSt	Entscheidungen des Bundesgerichtshofes in Strafsachen (collection of decisions of the BGH in criminal matters)
BGHZ	Entscheidungen des Bundesgerichtshofes in Zivilsachen (collection of decisions of the BGH in civil matters)
BR-Drs.	Bundesratsdrucksache (German Bundesrat publication)
BSG	Bundessozialgericht (Federal Social Court)
BSGE	Entscheidungen des Bundessozialgerichts (collection of decisions of the BSG)
BT-Drs.	Bundestag Drucksache (German Bundestag publication)

BVerfG	Bundesverfassungsgericht (German Federal Constitutional Court)
BVerfGE	Entscheidungen des Bundesverfassungsgerichts (collection of decisions of the BVerfG)
BVerwG	Bundesverwaltungsgericht der Bundesrepublik Deutschland (German Federal Administrative Court)
BVerwGE	Entscheidungen des Bundesverwaltungsgerichts (collection of decisions of the BVerwG)
BVwG	Bundesverwaltungsgericht der Republik Österreich (Austrian Federal Administrative Court)
CAP	corrective action plan
CB	Compliance Berater (journal)
CC	Abteilung Cybercrime (Department for cybercrime at BKA)
CCF	Commission for the Control of Interpol's Files
CCZ	Corporate Compliance Zeitschrift (journal)
CDU	Christlich Demokratische Union Deutschlands (Christian Democratic Union of Germany)
cf.	confer
CFD	contracts for difference
CFI	Court of First Instance
CFSP	Common Foreign and Security Policy
Ch.	Chapter
CJEU	Court of Justice of the European Union
CMS	Compliance Management System
CO	compliance officer
COSO	Committe of Sponsoring Organisations
CRR	Capital Requirements Regulation
CSR	corporate social responsibility
CSU	Christlich-Soziale Union in Bayern (Christian Social Union in Bavaria)
D&O	directors and officers
DB	Der Betrieb (journal)
DDoS	distributed denial of service
DNFBPS	designated non-financial bodies and professions
DoS	denial-of-service
DRG	Diagnosis Related Group
DStR	Deutsches Steuerrecht (journal)
DStRE	Deutsches Steuerrecht – Entscheidungsdienst (journal)
e.g.	*exempli gratia*
EAW	European Arrest Warrant
EC	European Community
ECJ	European Court of Justice
ECN	European Competition Network
ECtHR	European Court of Human Rights
ed.	editor

Ed.	Edition (beck-online)
edn	edition
EDPs	European Delegated Prosecutors
eds	editors
EEA	European Economic Area
EEIG	European Economic Interest Grouping
EFTA	European Free Trade Association
EIO	European Investigation Order
EL	Ergänzungslieferung (supplement of a loose-leaf edition)
EPPO	European Public Prosecutor's Office
ESG	environmental, social and governance
ESMA	European Securities and Markets Authority
et al.	*et alia*
et seq.	*et sequentia*
et seqq.	*et sequentia*
etc.	*et cetera*
EU	European Union
EUR	euro
EURIBOR	Euro Interbank Offered Rate
EUStA	Europäische Staatsanwaltschaft (European Public Prosecutor's Office)
EuZW	Europäische Zeitschrift für Wirtschaftsrecht (journal)
EWIV	Europäische wirtschaftliche Interessensvereinigung
FATF	Financial Action Task Force on Money Laundering
FCJ	Federal Court of Justice
FCPA	US Foreign Corrupt Practices Act
FDI	foreign direct investment
FD-StrafR	Fachdienst Strafrecht (Criminal law Department)
FG	Finanzgericht (fiscal court)
FHArbSozR	Fundheft für Arbeits- und Sozialrecht (journal)
FIU	Financial Intelligence Unit
fn.	footnote
FNA	Federal Network Agency
FRG	Federal Republic of Germany
GA	Goltdammer's Archiv für Strafrecht (journal)
GAFA	Google, Apple, Facebook, Amazon
GAFAM	Google, Apple, Facebook, Amazon, Microsoft
GbR	Gesellschaft bürgerlichen Rechts (civil law partnership)
GC	General Court
G-DRG-System	German Diagnosis Related Group System
GenStA	Generalstaatsanwaltschaft (German General Public Prosecutor's Office)
GewArch	Gewerbearchiv – Zeitschrift für Gewerbe- und Wirtschaftsverwaltungsrecht (journal)

GmbH	Gesellschaft mit beschränkter Haftung (limited liability company/'Ltd.')
GmbH & Co. KG	Gesellschaft mit beschränkter Haftung & Compagnie Kommanditgesellschaft (Limited Partnership with Limited Company as general partner)
GRUR	Gewerblicher Rechtsschutz und Urheberrecht (journal)
GRUR-Int	Gewerblicher Rechtsschutz und Urheberrecht – Internationaler Teil (journal)
GRUR-RS	Gewerblicher Rechtsschutz und Urheberrecht – Digitale Rechtssprechungssammlung (journal)
GWR	Gesellschafts- und Wirtschaftsrecht (journal)
half-sent.	half sentence (Halbsatz)
i.a.	inter alia
i.c.w.	in connection with
i.e.	*id est*
ICN	International Competition Network
ICP	Internal Compliance Programmes
IPO	initial public offering
JA	Juristische Arbeitsblätter (journal)
JIT	Joint Investigation Teams
JuS	Juristische Schulung (journal)
JZ	Juristenzeitung (journal)
K&R	Kommunikation & Recht (journal)
KG	1. Kammergericht (Court of Appeal in Berlin) 2. Kommanditgesellschaft (Limited partnership)
KGaA	Kommanditgesellschaft auf Aktien
KMU	kleine und mittlere Unternehmen
KommJur	Kommunaljurist (journal)
KritV	Kritische Vierteljahresschrift für Gesetzgebung und Rechtswissenschaft (journal)
LAG	Landesarbeitsgericht (higher labour court)
LG	Landgericht (regional court)
lit.	*litera*
LMRR	Lebensmittel-Rechtsprechung (journal)
MCC	medical care centre
MDR	Monatsschrift für Deutsches Recht (journal)
MittdtPatA	Mitteilungen der deutschen Patentanwälte (journal)
MLA	mutual legal assistance
MMR	MultiMedia und Recht – Zeitschrift für IT-Recht und Recht der Digitalisierung (journal)
MPR	Medizin Produkte Recht (journal)
MSchrKrim	Monatsschrift für Kriminologie und Strafrechtsreform (journal)
MTF	multilateral trading facility
NAC	National Central Bureau
NAP	national action plan

NCA	national competition authorities
NCB	National Central Bureau
Newsdienst Compliance	Corporate Compliance Zeitschrift – Newsdienst Compliance (journal)
NIS	network information security
NJOZ	Neue Juristische Online-Zeitschrift (journal)
NJW	Neue Juristische Wochenschrift (journal)
NJW-RR	Neue Juristische Wochenschrift – Rechtsprechungs-Report (journal)
NKC	Nationale Kooperationsstelle Cybercrime (National Point of Contact for Anti-Cybercrime Cooperation)
no.	number
NStZ	Neue Zeitschrift für Strafrecht (journal)
NStZ-RR	Neue Zeitschrift für Strafrecht – Rechtsprechungs-Report (journal)
NVwZ	Neue Zeitschrift für Verwaltungsrecht (journal)
NZA	Neue Zeitschrift für Arbeits- und Sozialrecht (journal)
NZA-RR	Neue Zeitschrift für Arbeits- und Sozialrecht – Rechtsprechungs-Report (journal)
NZG	Neue Zeitschrift für Gesellschaftsrecht (journal)
NZI	Neue Zeitschrift für Insolvenz- und Sanierungsrecht (journal)
NZKart	Neue Zeitschrift für Kartellrecht (journal)
NZS	Neue Zeitschrift für Sozialrecht (journal)
NZWiSt	Neue Zeitschrift für Wirtschafts-, Steuer- und Unternehmensstrafrecht (journal)
öAT	Zeitschrift für das öffentliche Arbeits- und Tarifrecht (journal)
OECD	Organisation for Economic Cooperation and Development
oHG	offene Handesgesellschaft (general partnership)
OJ	Official Journal
OLG	Oberlandesgericht (higher regional court)
OTF	organized trading facility
OVG	Oberverwaltungsgericht (higher administrative court)
p.	page
para.	paragraph
PHI	private health insurance
PinG	Privacy in Germany (journal)
PStR	Praxis Steuerstrafrecht (journal)
R&D	research and development
R&D BER	research and development block exemption regulations
RAK	Rechtsanwaltskammer (bar association)
RdA	Recht der Arbeit (journal)
RefE	Referentenentwurf (draft bill/legislative proposal)
RegE	Regierungsentwurf (government draft)
RIW	Recht der Internationalen Wirtschaft (journal)
RL	Richtlinie

RPM	resale price maintenance
RRP	recommended retail price
SCCF	Statute of the Commission for the Control of Interpol's Files
SE	Societas Europaea
SEI	Stop Ecocide International
sent.	sentence
SHI	statutory health insurance
SIEC	significant impediment to effective competition
SIRENE	Supplementary Information Request at the National Entries
SIS	Schengen Information System
SKK	Sonderkommission Kartellbekämpfung (Special unit for combating cartels)
SMEs	small and medium-sized enterprises
SPA	special prorate agreement
SPD	Sozialdemokratische Partei Deutschlands (Social Democratic Party of Germany)
StA	Staatsanwaltschaft (German Public Prosecutor's Office)
StraFo	Strafverteidiger Forum (journal)
StV	Strafverteidiger (journal)
sub.	subsection
TCLR	Transnational Criminal Law Review
TOMs	technical and organizational measures
TTBER	technology transfer block exemption regulations
UK	United Kingdom
UKuR	Ukraine-Krieg und Recht (journal)
UN	United Nations
US	United States
var.	Variante (variant)
VAT	value added tax
VBER	vertical agreements block exmeption regulations
VG	Verwaltungsgericht (administrative court)
VGH	Verwaltungsgerichtshof (higher administrative court)
VO	Verordnung (Regulation)
Vor.	Vorbemerkung (preliminary notes)
VuR	Verbraucher und Recht (journal)
WD	Wissenschaftliche Dienste (Research Services of the German Bundestag)
WiJ	Journal der Wirtschaftsstrafrechtlichen Vereinigung e.V. (journal)
WiRO	Wirtschaft und Recht in Osteuropa (journal)
wistra	Zeitschrift für Wirtschafts- und Steuerstrafrecht (journal)
WM	Zeitschrift für Wirtschafts- und Bankrecht (journal)
WRP	Wettbewerb in Recht und Praxis (journal)
WuW	Wirtschaft und Wettbewerb (journal)

ZAC	Zentrale Ansprechstellen Cybercrime (Central Cybercrime Contact Points)
ZAR	Zeitschrift für Ausländerrecht und Ausländerpolitik (journal)
ZD	Zeitschrift für Datenschutz (journal)
ZGR	Zeitschrift für Unternehmens- und Gesellschaftsrecht (journal)
ZHR	Zeitschrift für das gesamte Handels- und Wirtschaftsrecht (journal)
ZInsO	Zeitschrift für das gesamte Insolvenz- und Sanierungsrecht (journal)
ZIP	Zeitschrift für Wirtschaftsrecht (journal)
ZIS	Zeitschrift für Internationale Strafrechtsdogmatik (journal)
ZRP	Zeitschrift für Rechtspolitik (journal)
ZStW	Zeitschrift für die gesamte Strafrechtswissenschaft (journal)
ZWH	Zeitschrift für Wirtschaftsstrafrecht und Haftung im Unternehmen (journal)

II. Abbreviation of German legislation

AbfVerbrG	Abfallverbringungsgesetz	Waste Shipment Act
AEntG	Arbeitnehmerentsendegesetz	Posted Workers Act
AGG	Allgemeines Gleichbehandlungsgesetz	General Act on Equal Treatment
AktG	Aktiengesetz	Stock Corporation Act
AMG	Arzneimittelgesetz	Medicinal Products Act
AO	Abgabenordnung	Fiscal Code
ArbSchG	Arbeitsschutzgesetz	Occupational Safety and Health Act
ArbZG	Arbeitszeitgesetz	Act on Working Hours
AStBV (St) 2025	Anweisungen für das Straf- und Bußgeldverfahren (Steuer)	Guidelines for criminal proceedings and proceedings on regulatory offences (tax)
AtG	Atomgesetz	Atomic Energy Act
AufenthG	Aufenthaltsgesetz	Residence Act
AÜG	Arbeitnehmerüberlassungsgesetz	Act on Temporary Agency Work
AWG	Außenwirtschaftsgesetz	German Foreign Trade and Payments Act
AWV	Außenwirtschaftsverordnung	German Foreign Trade and Payments Ordinance
BÄO	Bundesärzteverordnung	Federal Medical Regulation
BauFordSiG	Bauforderungssicherungsgesetz	German Act on the Protection of Construction Claims
BauPG	Bauproduktengesetz	Construction Products Act
BaustellV	Baustellenverordnung	Ordinance regarding construction sites
BBG	Bundesbeamtengesetz	Federal Civil Service Act
BDSG	Bundesdatenschutzgesetz	Federal Data Protection Act
BeamtStG	Beamtenstatusgesetz	Civil Servant Status Act

BetrVG	Betriebsverfassungsgesetz	Works Constitution Act
BGB	Bürgerliches Gesetzbuch	German Civil Code
BImSchG	Bundes-Immissionsschutzgesetz	Federal Immission Control Act
BImSchV	Bundes-Immissionsschutzverordnung	Federal Immission Control Regulation
BiostoffV	Biostoffverordnung	Ordinance on Biological Agents
BNatSchG	Bundes-Naturschutzgesetz	Federal Nature Conservation Act
BORA	Berufsordnung für Rechtsanwälte	Rules of Professional Practice for Lawyers
BörsG	Börsengesetz	German Stock Exchange Act
BpO	Betriebsprüfungsordnung	Tax Audit Code
BRAO	Bundesrechtsanwaltsordnung	Federal Code for Lawyers
BVerfGG	Bundesverfassungsgerichtsgesetz	Federal Constitutional Court Law
ChemG	Chemikaliengesetz	Chemicals Act
DCGK	Deutscher Corporate Governance Kodex	German Corporate Governance Codex
DesignG	Designgesetz	Design Act
DRiG	Deutsches Richtergesetz	German Judiciary Act
EStDV	Einkommensteuer-Durchführungsverordnung	Income Tax Implementation Ordinance
EStG	Einkommensteuergesetz	Income Tax Act
EWIVAG	EWIV-Ausführungsgesetz	Act to implement the EEC regulation on the European Economic Interest Grouping
FGO	Finanzgerichtsordnung	Code of Procedure for Fiscal Courts
FinDAG	Gesetz über die Bundesanstalt für Finanzdienstleistungsaufsicht	Act Establishing the Federal Financial Supervisory Authority
GebrMG	Gebrauchsmustergesetz	Utility Model Act
GenG	Genossenschaftsgesetz	Cooperative Societies Act
GeschGehG	Geschäftsgeheimnisgesetz	Act on the Protection of Trade Secrets
GewO	Gewerbeordnung	German Trade Regulation Act
GG	Grundgesetz	German Basic Law
GmbHG	Gesetz betreffend die Gesellschaften mit beschränkter Haftung	Act on Limited Liability Companies
GOÄ	Gebührenordnung für Ärzte	German Medical Fee Index
GPSG	Geräte- und Produktsicherheitsgesetz	German Equipment and Product Safety Act
GVG	Gerichtsverfassungsgesetz	Courts Constitution Act
GWB	Gesetz gegen Wettbewerbsbeschränkungen	Act Against Restraints of Competition
GwG	Geldwäschegesetz	German Money Laundering Act
HalblSchG	Halbleiterschutzgesetz	Semiconductor Protection Act
HGB	Handelsgesetzbuch	Commercial Code
HinSchG	Hinweisgeberschutzgesetz	Whistleblower Protection Act
HwO	Handwerksordnung	Law on the Organisation of Skilled Trades

IFG	Informationsfreiheitsgesetz	German Freedom of Information Act
IfSG	Infektionsschutzgesetz	Infection Protection Act
InsO	Insolvenzordnung	German Insolvency Code
IRG	Internationales Rechtshilfegesetz	Act on International Mutual Assistance in Criminal Matters
JArbSchG	Jugendarbeitsschutzgesetz	Young Persons' Protection in Employment Act
JGG	Jugendgerichtsgesetz	Youth Courts Act
KAGB	Kapitalanlagegesetzbuch	German Capital Investment Code
KHEntgG	Krankenhausentgeltgesetz	Hospital Remuneration Act
KHG	Krankenhausfinanzierungsgesetz	Hospital Financing Act
KrWG	Kreislaufwirtschaftsgesetz	Closed Substance Cycle Waste Management Act
KSG	Bundes-Klimaschutzgesetz	German Climate Protection Act
KStG	Körperschaftssteuergesetz	Corporate Income Tax Act
KWG	Kreditwesengesetz	German Banking Act
KWKG	Kraft-Wärme-Kopplungsgesetz	Combined Heat and Power Act (CHP Act)
LFGB	Lebensmittel- und Futtermittelgesetzbuch	German Food, Commodities and Feed Code
LkSG	Lieferkettensorgfaltspflichtgesetz	Act on Corporate Due Diligence Obligations in Supply Chains
LSpG	Lebensmittelspezialitätengesetz	Food Specialities Act
MarkenG	Markengesetz	Trademark Act
MBO-Ä	Musterberufsordnung für Ärzte	Medical Practitioners' Model Code of Conduct
MilchMargG	Milch- und Margarinegesetz	Milk and Margarine Act
MiLoG	Mindestlohngesetz	Act Regulating a General Minimum Wage
MPBetreibV	Medizinprodukte-Betreiberverordnung	Ordinance on the Operation of Medical Devices
MPDG	Medizinprodukte-Durchführungsgesetz	Medical Device Law Implementation Act
MPG	Medizinproduktegesetz	German Medical Devices Act
MuSchG	Mutterschutzgesetz	Maternity Protection Act
NIS2UmsuCG	NIS2 Umsetzungs- und Cybersicherheitsstärkungsgesetz	NIS2 Implementation Act
NLPosV	Netto-Leerverkaufspositionsverordnung	German Regulation on Net Short Selling
ÖLG	Öko-Landbaugesetz	Organic Farming Act
OWiG	Gesetz über Ordnungswidrigkeiten	German Act on Regulatory Offences
PartGG	Partnerschaftsgesellschaftsgesetz	Act on Partnership Companies of Members of Independent Professions
PatG	Patentgesetz	Patent Act
ProdSG	Produktsicherheitsgesetz	Product Safety Act
PublG	Publizitätsgesetz	German Disclosure Act

RDG	Rechtsdienstleistungsgesetz	Act on Out-of-Court Legal Services
RefE HinSchG	Referentenentwurf eines Gesetzes für einen besseren Schutz hinweisgebender Personen sowie zur Umsetzung der Richtlinie zum Schutz von Personen, die Verstöße gegen das Unionsrecht melden	Draft of a law for better protection of whistleblowers and on the implementation of the Directive on the protection of persons who report violations of Union law
RiFlEtikettG	Rindfleischettiketierungsgesetz	Beef Labelling Act
RistBV	Richtlinien für das Strafverfahren und das Bußgeldverfahren	Instructions on Criminal Procedure and Administrative Fines Procedure
RpflG	Rechtspflegergesetz	Judicial Officers Act
RVG	Rechtsanwaltsvergütungsgesetz	German Attorney Remuneration Law
SAG	Sanierungs- und Abwicklungsgesetz	German Act on the Recovery and Resolution of Credit Institutions
SchwarzArbG	Schwarzarbeitsbekämpfungsgesetz	Act to Combat Undeclared Work and Unlawful Employment
SEAG	SE-Ausführungsgesetz	German SE Implementation Act
SGB	Sozialgesetzbuch	German Social Code
SortSchG	Sortenschutzgesetz	Plant Variety Protection Act
SprAuG	Sprecherausschussgesetz	Executives' Committee Act
StaRUG	Unternehmensstabilisierungs- und restrukturierungsgesetz	Act on the Stabilisation and Restructuring Framework for Businesses
StGB	Strafgesetzbuch	German Criminal Code
StimmRMV	Stimmrechtsmitteilungsverordnung	Voting Rights Notification Regulation
StPO	Strafprozessordnung	Code of Criminal Procedure
StrEG	Gesetz über die Entschädigung für Strafverfolgungsmaßnahmen	Act regarding Compensation for Wrongful Prosecution
StrlSchG	Strahlenschutzgesetz	Radiation Protection Act
StVollstrO	Strafvollstreckungsordnung	Law on Enforcement of Criminal Sentences
SubVG	Subventionsgesetz	German Subsidies Act
TabStG	Tabaksteuergesetz	Tobacco Tax Act
TDDDG	Telekommunikation-Digitale Dienste-Datenschutz-Gesetz	Telecommunications Digital Services Data Protection Act
TierSchG	Tierschutzgesetz	Animal Welfare Act
UmwG	Umwandlungsgesetz	Transformation Act
UrhG	Urheberrechtsgesetz	Act on Copyright and Related Rights
UStG	Umsatzsteuergesetz	Value Added Tax Act
UWG	Gesetz gegen den unlauteren Wettbewerb	Act Against Unfair Competition
VAG	Versicherungsaufsichtsgesetz	German Insurance Supervision Act
VermAnlG	Vermögensanlagegesetz	German Capital Investment Act
VerpackG	Verpackungsgesetz	Packaging Act
VerSanG	Verbandssanktionengesetz	Corporate Sanctions Act

VIG	Verbraucherinformationsgesetz	Consumer Information Act
VVG	Versicherungsvertragsgesetz	Insurance Contracts Act
WeinG	Weingesetz	Wine Act
WHG	Wasserhaushaltsgesetz	Federal Water Act
WiStG	Wirtschaftsstrafgesetz 1954	Economic Offences Act 1954
WpAV	Wertpapierhandelsanzeigeverordnung	Securities Trading Notification Regulation
WpHG	Wertpapierhandelsgesetz	Securities Trading Act
WpPG	Wertpapierprospektgesetz	Securities Prospectus Act
WRegG	Wettbewerbsregistergesetz	Competition Register Act
WRV	Weimarer Reichsverfassung	Weimar Constitution
ZAG	Zahlungsdiensteaufsichtsgesetz	Payment Services Supervision Act
ZPO	Zivilprozessordnung	Code of Civil Procedure

III. German authorities and ministries

BAFA	Bundesamt für Wirtschaft und Ausfuhrkontrolle	Federal Office of Economics and Export Control
BaFin	Bundesanstalt für Finanzdienstleistungsaufsicht	Federal Financial Supervisory Authority
BfJ	Bundesamt für Justiz	Federal Office of Justice
BKA	Bundeskriminalamt	Federal Criminal Police Office
BKartA	Bundeskartellamt	Federal Cartel Office
BMAS	Bundesministerium für Arbeit und Soziales	Federal Ministry of Labour and Social Affairs
BMJV	Bundesministerium der Justiz und für Verbraucherschutz	Federal Ministry of Justice and Consumer Protection
BMWE	Bundesministerium für Wirtschaft und Energie	Federal Ministry for Economic Affairs and Energy
BSI	Bundesamt für Sicherheit in der Informationstechnik	Federal Office for Information Security
DICO	Deutsches Institut für Compliance	German Institute for Compliance
LKA	Landeskriminalamt	State Criminal Police Office

IV. EU Regulations and Directives

AEUV	Vertrag über die Arbeitsweise der Europäischen Union	Treaty on the Functioning of the European Union
Crimean Annexation Regulation	Regulation (EU) No 269/2014 concerning restrictive measures in respect of actions undermining or threatening the territorial integrity, sovereignty and independence of Ukraine	VO (EU) 269/2014 über restriktive Maßnahmen bzgl. der Souveränität der Ukraine

CRIM-MAD	Market Abuse Directive (Directive 2014/57/EU on criminal sanctions for market abuse)	Marktmissbrauchsrichtlinie
CSDDD	Corporate Sustainability Due Diligence Directive	Europäische Lieferkettenrichtlinie
CSRD	Corporate Sustainability Reporting Directive (Directive (EU) 2022/2464)	CSR-Richtlinie
Damages Directive	Directive 2014/104/EU	EU-Schadensersatzrichtlinie
Directive 2016/943/EU	Directive (EU) 2016/943 on the protection of undisclosed know-how and business information (trade secrets) against their unlawful acquisition, use and disclosure	Geschäftsgeheimnis-Richtlinie
DMA	Digital Markets Act	Gesetz über digitale Märkte
DORA	Regulation on Digital Operational Resilience for the Financial Sector	Verordnung über die Betriebsstabilität digitaler Systeme des Finanzsektors
DSA	Digital Services Act	Gesetz über digitale Dienste
Dual-Use Regulation	EU Regulation 2021/821 on dual use goods	Dual-Use-Verordnung
EAW Framework Decision	Council Framework Decision 2002/584/JHA of 13.06.2002 on the European arrest warrant and the surrender procedures between Member States	EuHb-Rahmenbeschluss (Rahmenbeschluss 2002/584/JI über den Europäischen Haftbefehl und die Übergabeverfahren zwischen den Mitgliedstaaten)
ECHR	European Convention on Human Rights	Europäische Menschenrechtskonvention
ECN+ Directive	Directive (EU) 2019/1 to empower the competition authorities of the Member States to be more effective enforcers and to ensure the proper functioning of the internal market	ECN+-Richtlinie
E-Evidence Regulation	Regulation (EU) 2023/1543 on European Production Orders and European Preservation Orders for electronic evidence in criminal proceedings and for the execution of custodial sentences following criminal proceedings	e-Beweismittelsicherungs-Verordnung
EIO Directive	Directive 2014/41/EU on the European Investigation Order in criminal matters	EEA-RL (Richtlinie 2014/41/EU über die Ermittlungsanordnung in Strafsachen)
EPPO Regulation	Regulation 2017/1939/EU implementing enhanced cooperation on the establishment of the European Public Prosecutor's Office	EuStA-VO (Verordnung (EU) 2017/1939 zur Durchführung einer Verstärkten Zusammenarbeit zur Errichtung der Europäischen Staatsanwaltschaft)
EU Merger Regulation	Regulation (EC) No 139/2004	Fusionskontrollverordnung

EU Money Laundering Regulation	Regulation (EU) 2024/1624 on the prevention of the use of the financial system for the purposes of money laundering or terrorist financing	Geldwäsche-Verordnung
EU-US Data Privacy Framework	Commission Implementing Decision EU 2023/1795 on the adequate level of protection of personal data under the EU-US Data Privacy Framework	Durchführungsbeschlusses (EU) 2023/1795 der Kommission über die Angemessenheit des Schutzniveaus für personenbezogene Daten nach dem Datenschutzrahmen EU-USA
Framework Decision on Mutual Recognition of Financial Penalties	Framework Decision 2005/214/JHA on the application of the principle of mutual recognition to financial penalties	Rahmenbeschluss 2005/214/JI über die Anwendung des Grundsatzes der gegenseitigen Anerkennung von Geldstrafen und Geldbußen
Framework Decision on the Mutual Recognition to Judgments in Criminal Matters	Council Framework Decision 2008/909/JHA of 27 November 2008 on the application of the principle of mutual recognition to judgments in criminal matters imposing custodial sentences or measures involving deprivation of liberty for the purpose of their enforcement in the European Union (OJ L 327, 5.12.2008, S. 27–46).	Rahmenbeschluss 2008/909/JI des Rates vom 27. November 2008 über die Anwendung des Grundsatzes der gegenseitigen Anerkennung auf Urteile in Strafsachen, durch die eine freiheitsentziehende Strafe oder Maßnahme verhängt wird, für die Zwecke ihrer Vollstreckung in der Europäischen Union
FSR	Foreign Subsidies Regulation	Drittstaatsubventionen-Verordnung
GDPR	General Data Protection Regulation (Regulation (EU) 2016/679)	DSGVO (Datenschutzgrundverordnung)
Insolvency Regulation	Regulation (EU) 2015/848 on insolvency proceedings	Insolvenz-Verordnung
IVDR	In-vitro Diagnostics Medical Device Regulation (Regulation (EU) 2017/746)	IVD-VO (In-vitro-Diagnostika-Verordnung)
MAR	Market Abuse Regulation (Regulation (EU) No 596/2014 on market abuse)	Marktmissbrauchsverordnung
MDR	Medical Device Regulation (Regulation (EU) 2017/745)	MP-VO (Medizinprodukte-Verordnung)
MiFID II	Market in Financial Instruments Directive (Directive 2014/65/EU on markets in financial instruments)	MiFID II (EU-Finanzinstrumenterichtlinie)
NIS2 Directive	Directive (EU) 2022/2555 on measures for a high common level of cybersecurity accross the Union	NIS-2-Richtlinie (Richtlinie (EU) 2022/2555 über Maßnahmen für ein hohes gemeinsames Cybersicherheitsniveau in der Union)
PIF Directive	Directive (EU) 2017/1371 on the fight against fraud to the Union's financial interests by means of criminal law	PIF-Richtlinie (Richtlinie (EU) 2017/1371 über die strafrechtliche Bekämpfung von gegen die finanziellen Interessen der Union gerichtetem Betrug)
Prospectus Regulation	Regulation (EU) 2017/1129 on the prospectus to be published when securities are offered to the public or admitted to trading on a regulated market	EU-Prospektverordnung

Russia Sanctions Regulation	Council Regulation (EU) No 833/2014 concerning restrictive measures in view of Russia's actions destabilising the situation in Ukraine	Russland-Sanktionen-Verordnung
SFDR	Sustainable Finance Disclosures Regulation (Regulation (EU) No 2019/2088)	EU-Offenlegungsverordnung
Short Selling Regulation	Regulation (EU) No 236/2012 on short selling and certain aspects of credit default swaps	Leerverkaufsverordnung
Sixth Anti-Money Laundering Directive	Directive (EU) 2024/1640 on the mechanisms to be put in place by Member States for the prevention of the use of the financial system for the purposes of money laundering or terrorist financing	Sechste EU-Geldwäscherichtlinie
TEU	Treaty on European Union	Vertrag über die Europäische Union
TFEU	Treaty on the Functioning of the European Union	Vertrag über die Arbeitsweise der Europäischen Union
Transparency Directive	Directive 2004/109/EC on the harmonization of transparency requirements in relation to information about issuers whose securities are admitted to trading on a regulated market	Transparenz-Richtlinie
Union Customs Code	Regulation EU (No) 952/2013 laying down the Union Customs Code	EU-Zollkodexverordnung
Waste Shipments Regulation	Regulation (EC) No 1013/2006 on shipments of waste	Abfallverbringungs-Verordnung (Verordnung (EG) Nr. 1013/2006 über die Verbringung von Abfällen)
WB Directive	EU Directive on the protection of persons who report breaches of Union law (Directive (EU) 2019/1937)	Hinweisgeber-Richtlinie

V. International Conventions and Treaties

1957 European Convention	European Convention on Extradition	Europäisches Auslieferungsübereinkommen (EurAuslÜbk)
1959 Mutual Assistance Convention	1959 European Convention on Mutual Assistance in Criminal Matters	Europäisches Übereinkommen über die Rechtshilfe in Strafsachen (EuRhÜbk)
2000 EU Mutual Assistance Convention	Convention on Mutual Assistance in Criminal Matters between EU Member States	Übereinkommen über die Rechtshilfe in Strafsachen zwischen den Mitgliedstaaten der Europäischen Union (EU-RhÜbk)
Additional Protocol to the Convention on the Transfer of Sentenced Persons	Additional Protocol to the Convention on the Transfer of Sentenced Persons	Zusatzprotokoll zum Übereinkommen über die Überstellung verurteilter Personen (Überstellungs-Übereinkommen-ZProt)

CCC	Council of Europe's Convention on Cybercrime	Cybercrime-Konvention
CFR	Charter of Fundamental Rights of the European Union	EU-Grundrechte-Charta
CISA	Convention Implementing the Schengen Agreement	Schengener Durchführungsübereinkommen (SDÜ)
Council of Europe Convention on the Transfer of Sentenced Persons	Council of Europe Convention on the Transfer of Sentenced Persons	Übereinkommen über die Übersetellung verurteilter Personen (Überstellungs-Übeinkommen)
ECHR	European Convention on Human Rights	Europäische Menschenrechtskonvention
MLAT EU-US	Agreement on Mutual Legal Assistance between the United States of America and the European Union	Abkommen zwischen den Vereinigten Staaten von Amerika und der Europäischen Union über Rechtshilfe (RHÜ EU-US)
MLAT Germany-US	Treaty Between the United States of America and the Federal Republic of Germany on Mutual Legal Assistance in Criminal Matters	Vertrag zwischen der Bundesrepublik Deutschland und den Vereinigten Staaten von Amerika über die Rechtshilfe in Strafsachen (RhV DE/USA)
Surrender Agreement EU/IS-NO	Agreement between the European Union and the Republic of Iceland and the Kingdom of Norway on the surrender procedure between the Member States of the European Union and Iceland and Norway	Übereinkommen zwischen der Europäischen Union und der Republik Island und dem Königreich Norwegen über das Übergabeverfahren zwischen den Mitgliedstaaten der Europäischen Union und Island und Norwegen
TCA	EU-UK Trade and Cooperation Agreement	Handels- und Kooperationsabkommen EU/UK
US-Germany Extradition Treaty	Treaty between the United States of America and the Federal Republic of Germany concerning Extradition	Auslieferungsvertrag zwischen der Bundesrepublik Deutschland und den Vereinigten Staaten von Amerika (AuslV D-USA)
US-Germany Extradition Treaty	1978 Treaty between the United States of America and the Federal Republic of Germany concerning Extradition	Auslieferungsabkommen vom 20. 06. 1978 zwischen der Bundesrepublik Deutschland und den Vereinigten Staaten von Amerika

Abbreviations of cited works

Adick/Bülte FiskalStrafR	Adick/Bülte, Fiskalstrafrecht, 2nd edn 2019 (cited as Adick/Bülte FiskalStrafR/author's name).
Altmeppen	Altmeppen, Gesetz betreffend die Gesellschaften mit beschränkter Haftung: GmbHG, 11th edn 2023 (cited as Altmeppen/author's name).
ARR WirtschaftsStrafR-HdB	Achenbach/Ransiek/Rönnau (eds), Handbuch Wirtschaftsstrafrecht, 6th edn 2023 (cited as ARR WirtschaftsStrafR-HdB/author's name).
Auernhammer	Eßer/Kramer/von Lewinski (eds), DSGVO/BDSG – Datenschutz-Grundverordnung/Bundesdatenschutzgesetz und Nebengesetze, 8th edn 2023 (cited as Auernhammer).
Auer-Reinsdorff/Conrad IT- und DatenschutzR-HdB	Auer-Reinsdorff/Conrad (eds), Handbuch IT- und Datenschutzrecht, 3rd edn 2019 (cited ad Auer-Reinsdorff/Conrad IT- und DatenschutzR-HdB/author's name).
BBB	Bechtold/Bosch/Brinker, EU-Kartellrecht, 4th edn 2023.
BDW	Baeck/Deutsch/Winzer, Arbeitszeitgesetz, 4th edn 2020.
Bechtold/Bosch	Bechtold/Bosch, GWB, 11th edn 2025.
BeckFormB Strafverteidiger	Hamm/Leipold (eds), Beck'sches Formularbuch für den Strafverteidiger, 6th edn 2018 (cited as BeckFormB Strafverteidiger/author's name).
BeckOGK	beck.online Grosskommentar (cited as BeckOGK/author's name, online edition, date and year).
BeckOK ArbR	Rolfs/Giesen/Meßling/Udsching (eds), BeckOK Arbeitsrecht (cited as BeckOK ArbR/author's name, online edition, date and year).
BeckOK AußenWirtschaftsR	Niestedt (ed), BeckOK Außenwirtschaftsrecht (cited as BeckOK AußenWirtschaftsR/author's name, online edition, date and year).
BeckOK BGB	Hau/Poseck (eds), BeckOK BGB (cited as BeckOK BGB/author's name, online edition, date and year).
BeckOK DatenschutzR	Wolff/Brink (eds), BeckOK Datenschutzrecht (cited as BeckOK DatenschutzR/author's name, online edition, date and year).
BeckOK GeschGehG	Fuhlrott/Hiéramente (eds), BeckOK GeschGehG, (cited as BeckOK GeschGehG/author's name, online edition, date and year).
BeckOK GG	Epping/Hillgruber (eds), BeckOK Grundgesetz (cited as BeckOK GG/author's name, online edition, date and year).
BeckOK GmbHG	Ziemons/Jaeger/Pöschke (eds), BeckOK GmbHG (cited as BeckOK GmbHG/author's name, online edition, date and year).

BeckOK HinSchG	Colneric/Gerdemann (eds), BeckOK HinSchG (cited as BeckOK HinschG/author's name, online edition, date and year).
BeckOK OWiG	Graf (ed), BeckOK OWiG (cited as BeckOK OWiG/author's name, online edition, date and year).
BeckOK PatR	Fitzner/Kubis/Bodewig/Metzger (eds), BeckOK Patentrecht (cited as BeckOK PatR/author's name).
BeckOK StGB	von Heintschel-Heinegg/Kudlich (eds), BeckOK StGB (cited as BeckOK StGB/author's name, online edition, date and year).
BeckOK StPO	Graf (ed), BeckOK StPO mit RiStBV und MiStra (cited as BeckOK StPO/author's name, online edition, date and year).
BeckOK UmweltR	Giesberts/Reinhardt (eds), BeckOK Umweltrecht (cited as BeckOK UmweltR/author's name).
BeckOK UStG	Weymüller, BeckOK UStG (cited as BeckOK UStG/author's name, online edition, date and year).
BeckOK VwGO	Posser/Wolff/Decker, BeckOK VwGO (cited as BeckOK VwGO/author's name, online edition, date and year).
BeckRA-HdB	Hamm, Beck'sches Rechtsanwalts-Handbuch, 12th edn 2022 (cited as BeckRA-HdB/author's name).
BHPR Antikorruptions-Compliance	Busch/Hoven/Pieth/Rübenstahl (eds), Antikorruptions-Compliance, 1st edn 2020.
BHS Compliance-Officer	Bürkle/Hauschka/Schieffer, Der Compliance Officer, 2nd edn 2024 (cited as BHS Compliance-Officer/author's name).
Börner UmweltStrafR	Börner, Umweltstrafrecht, 1st edn 2020.
Brettel/Schneider WirtschaftsStrafR	Brettel/Schneider, Wirtschaftsstrafrecht, 3rd edn 2021.
Bürkle Compliance	Bürkle, Compliance in Versicherungsunternehmen, 3rd edn 2020 (cited as Bürkle Compliance/author's name).
Callies/Ruffert	Callies/Ruffert (eds), EUV/AEUV, 6th edn 2022 (cited as Callies/Ruffert/author's name).
Dannecker/Meyer	Dannecker/Meyer (eds), Unternehmenssanktionen in der Europäischen Union, 1st edn 2023 (cited as Dannecker/Meyer/author's name).
Delmas-Marty	Delmas-Marty (ed), Corpus Juris: Introducing Penal Provisions for the Purpose of the Financial Interests of the European Union, 1997.
Dieners Gesundheitswesen-Compliance-HdB	Dieners, Handbuch Compliance im Gesundheitswesen, 4th edn 2022 (cited as Dieners Gesundheitswesen-Compliance-HdB/author's name).
Diergarten/Fraulob	Diergarten/Fraulob, Geldwäsche, 1st edn 2019.
Dreier/Schulze	Dreier/Mantz/Raue/Specht-Riemenschneider, Urheberrechtsgesetz, 8th edn 2025 (cited as Dreier/Schulze/author's name).

Ehmann/Selmayr	Ehmann/Selmayr, Datenschutz-Grundverordnung, 3rd edn 2024 (cited as Ehmann/Selmayr/author's name).
Eidam Unternehmen und Strafe	Eidam, Unternehmen und Strafe, 5th edn 2018.
EnzEuR XI	Böse (ed), Enzyklopädie Europarecht, Band 11: Europäisches Strafrecht, 2nd edn 2021 (cited as EnzEuR XI/author's name).
Erbs/Kohlhaas	Erbs/Kohlhaas, Strafrechtliche Nebengesetze (cited as Erbs/Kohlhaas/author's name, supplement number, month and year).
ErfK	Müller-Glöge/Preis/Schmidt (eds), Erfurter Kommentar zum Arbeitsrecht, 25th edn 2025 (cited as ErfK/author's name).
EuArbRK	Franzen/Gallner/Oetker, Kommentar zum europäischen Arbeitsrecht, 5th edn 2024 (cited as EuArbRK/author's name).
Fischer	Fischer/Anstötz/Lutz, Strafgesetzbuch: StGB, 72nd edn 2025 (cited as Fischer/author's name or only Fischer).
FormB-ArbR	Hümmerich/Lücke/Mauer, Arbeitsrecht, 10th edn 2022.
Franzheim/Pfohl Umwelt-StrafR	Franzheim/Pfohl, Umweltstrafrecht – Eine Darstellung für die Praxis, 2nd edn 2001.
FS Feigen	Livonius/Graf/Wolter/Zöller, Strafverteidigung im Wirtschaftsleben: Festgabe für Hanns W. Feigen, 1st edn 2014. (cited as FS Feigen/author's name).
FS Merkel	Bublitz/Bung/Grünewald/Magnus/Putzke/Scheinfeld, Recht-Philosophie – Literatur – Festschrift für Reinhard Merkel zum 70. Geburtstag, 1st edn 2020 (cited as FS Merkel/author's name).
FS Schiller	Lüderssen/Volk/Wahle, Festschrift für Wolf Schiller zum 65. Geburtstag am 12. Januar 2014, 1st edn 2014. (cited as FS Schiller/author's name).
GJW	Graf/Jäger/Wittig, Wirtschafts- und Steuerstrafrecht, 3rd edn 2024 (cited as GJW/author's name).
GJW	Graf/Jäger/Wittig, Wirtschafts- und Steuerstrafrecht, 3rd edn 2024 (cited as GJW/author's name)
GKR ArbStrafR-HdB	Gercke/Kraft/Richter, Arbeitsstrafrecht, 3rd edn 2021 (cited as GKR ArbStrafR-HdB/author's name).
Glaser	Glaser, Geldwäsche (§ 261 StGB) durch Rechtsanwälte und Steuerberater bei der Honorarannahme, 1st edn 2009.
Göhler	Göhler, Gesetz über Ordnungswidrigkeiten: OWiG, 19th edn 2024 (cited as Göhler/author's name).
Gola/Heckmann	Gola/Heckmann (eds), DS-GVO – BDSG, 3rd edn 2022 (cited as Gola/Heckmann/author's name).
Gola/Schomerus BDSG	Gola/Schomerus (eds), BDSG, 12th edn 2015 (cited as Gola/Schomerus BDSG/author's name).

GPKGB Int. Rechtshilfeverkehr	Grützner/Pötz/Kreß/Gazeas/Brodowski (eds), Internationaler Rechtshilfeverkehr in Strafsachen (cited as GPKGB Int. Rechtshilfeverkehr/author's name, supplement number, month and year).
Grigoleit	Grigoleit, AktG – Aktiengesetz, 2nd edn 2020 (cited as Grigoleit/author's name).
Grüneberg	Ellenberger/Götz/Grüneberg/Herrler/von Pückler/Retzlaff/Siede/Sprau/Thorn/Weidenkaff/Weidlich/Wicke (eds), Bürgerliches Gesetzbuch, 84th edn 2025 (cited as Grüneberg/author).
GTZ	Gercke/Temming/Zöller, Heidelberger Kommentar Strafprozessordnung, 7th edn 2023 (cited as GTZ/author's name).
Hackner/Schierholt Int. Rechtshilfe	Hackner/Schierholt (eds), Internationale Rechtshilfe in Strafsachen, 4th edn 2023.
Handel Meldestellenbeauftragte	Handel, Meldestellenbeauftragte, 1st edn 2023.
HdB-EuStrafR	Sieber/Satzger/von Heintschel-Heinegg (eds), Europäisches Strafrecht, 2nd edn 2014 (cited as HdB-EuStrafR/author's name).
HdLexEU	Bergmann, Handlexikon der Europäischen Union, 6th edn 2022 (cited as HdLexEU/author's name).
Herzog	Herzog (ed), Geldwäschegesetz: GwG, 5th edn 2023 (cited as Herzog/author's name).
HK-DS-GVO/BDSG	Sydow/Marsch (eds), DS-GVO – BDSG, 3rd edn 2022 (cited as HK-DS-GVO/BDSG/author's name).
HK-KapMarktStrafR	Park, Kapitalmarktstrafrecht, 6th edn 2024 (cited as HK-KapMarktStrafR/author's name).
HK-OWiG	Gassner/Seith, Ordnungswidrigkeitengesetz, 3rd edn 2025 (cited as HK-OWiG/author's name).
HK-StrafR	Dölling/Duttge/König/Rössner (eds), Gesamtes Strafrecht, 5th edn 2022 (cited as HK-StrafR/author's name).
HKV Computer- und InternetStrafR	Hilgendorf/Kusche/Valerius (eds) Computer- und Internetstrafrecht, 3rd edn 2023.
HKV StrafR-HdB VI	Hilgendorf/Kudlich/Valerius, Handbuch des Strafrechts, Band 6: Strafrecht Allgemeiner Teil II, 1st edn 2021 (cited as HKV StrafR-HdB VI/author's name).
HML Corporate Compliance	Hauschka/Moosmayer/Lösler, Corporate Compliance, 3rd edn 2016 (cited als HML Corporate Compliance/author's name).
Höchstetter	Höchstetter, Der Nachweis im mindestlohnrechtlichen Sanktionsverfahren, 1st edn 2020.
Hoeren/Münker	Hoeren/Münker, GeschGehG, 1st edn 2021 (cited as Hoeren/Münker/author's name).
HOK	Harte-Bavendamm/Ohly/Kalbfus, GeschGehG, 2nd edn 2024 (cited as HOK/author's name).
HSH MMR-HdB	Hoeren/Sieber/Holznagel, Handbuch Multimedia-Recht, 62nd edn 2024 (cited as HSH MMR-HdB/author's name).

Hüls/Reichling	Hüls/Reichling, Heidelberger Kommentar Steuerstrafrecht, 3rd edn 2025 (cited as Hüls/Reichling/author's name).
IBP Compliance	Inderst/Bannenberg/Poppe, Compliance, 3rd edn 2017.
JJR	Joecks/Jäger/Randt (eds), Steuerstrafrecht, 9th edn 2023 (cited as JJR/author's name).
KassKomm	Körner/Krasney/Mutschler/Rolfs (eds), Kasseler Kommentar Sozialversicherungsrecht (cited as KassKomm/author's name, supplement number, month and year).
KBFW	Kremer/Bachmann/Favoccia/von Werder, Deutscher Corporate Governance Kodex, 9th edn 2023 (cited as KBFW/author's name).
Kipker Cybersecurity-HdB	Kipker, Cybersecurity, 2nd edn 2023, Handbook (cited as Kipker Cybersecurity-HdB/author's name).
KK-OWiG	Mitsch, Karlsruher Kommentar zum Gesetz über Ordnungswidrigkeiten: OWiG, 6th edn 2025 (cited as KK-OWiG/author's name).
KKS	Kollmer/Klindt/Schucht (eds), Arbeitsschutzgesetz, 4th edn 2021 (cited as KKS/author's name).
KK-StPO	Barthe/Gericke, Karlsruher Kommentar zur Strafprozessordnung, 9th edn 2023 (cited as KK-StPO/author's name).
Klein	Klein, Abgabenordnung: AO, 18th edn 2024 (cited as Klein/author's name).
KMW DatenschutzsanktionenR-HdB	Klaas/Momsen/Wybitul (eds), Datenschutzsanktionenrecht, 1st edn 2023 (cited as KMW DatenschutzsanktionenR-HdB/author's name).
Koch	Koch, Aktiengesetz, 19th edn 2025.
Kochheim Cybercrime	Kochheim, Cybercrime und Strafrecht in der Informations- und Kommunikationstechnik, 2nd edn 2018.
Köhler/Feddersen	Köhler/Bornkamm/Feddersen/Alexander/Odörfer/Scherer, UWG, 43rd edn 2025 (cited as Köhler/Feddersen/author's name).
Kohlmann	Kohlmann (ed), Steuerstrafrecht (cited as Kohlmann/author's name, supplement number, month and year).
Koreng/Lachenmann DatenschutzR-FormHdB	Koreng/Lachenmann (eds), Formularhandbuch Datenschutzrecht, 4th edn 2025 (cited as Koreng/Lachenmann DatenschutzR-FormHdB/author's name).
Kreikebohm/Dünn SGB IV	Kreikebohm/Dünn (eds), SGB IV, 4th edn 2022 (cited as Kreikebohm/Dünn SGB IV/author's name).
Krell UmweltStrafR	Krell, Umweltstrafrecht, 1st edn 2017.
Krenberger/Krumm	Krenberger/Krum, OWiG, 8th edn 2024 (cited as Krenberger/Krum/author's name).
Kubis/Tödtmann Vorstand-HdB	Kubis/Tödtmann, Arbeitshandbuch für Vorstandsmitglieder, 3rd edn 2022 (cited as Kubis/Tödtmann Vorstand-HdB/author's name).

Kühling/Buchner	Kühling/Buchner, DS-GVO BDSG, 4th edn 2024 (cited as Kühling/Buchner/author's name).
Laue/Kremer Neues DatenschutzR	Laue/Kremer (eds), Das neue Datenschutzrecht in der betrieblichen Praxis, 2nd edn 2019 (cited as Laue/Kremer/author's name).
Lenz Produkthaftung	Lenz, Produkthaftung, 2nd edn 2022. (cited as Lenz Produkthaftung/author's name).
Letzien Internationale Korruption	Letzien, Internationale Korruption und Jurisdiktionskonflikte, 1st edn 2017.
LKH	Lackner/Kühl/Heger (eds), StGB, 30th edn 2023 (cited as LKH/author's name).
LK-StGB	Leipziger Kommentar Strafgesetzbuch: StGB Vol. 1: §§ 1-18, 13th edn 2020 Vol. 6: §§ 69-79b, 14th edn 2024 Vol. 16: §§ 284-305a, 13th edn 2023 Vol. 18: §§ 323a-330d, 13th edn 2021 (cited as LK-StGB/author's name).
LTZ	Leipold/Tsambikakis/Zöller (eds), AnwaltKommentar StGB, 3rd edn 2020 (cited as LTZ/author's name).
MAH AgrarR	Dombert/Witt (eds), Münchener Anwaltshandbuch Agrarrecht, 3rd edn 2022 (cited as MAH AgrarR/author's name).
MAH ArbR	Moll (ed.), Münchener Anwaltshandbuch Arbeitsrecht, 6th edn 2025 (cited as MAH ArbR/author's name).
MAH MedR	Clausen/Schroeder-Printzen (eds), Münchener Anwaltshandbuch Medizinrecht, 3rd edn 2020 (cited as MAH MedR/author's name).
MAH Strafverteidigung	Knauer/Müller/Schlothauer, Münchener Anwaltshandbuch Strafverteidigung, 3rd edn 2022 (cited as MAH Strafverteidigung/author's name).
MAH WirtschaftsStrafR	Volk/Beukelmann, Münchener Anwaltshandbuch Verteidigung in Wirtschafts- und Steuerstrafsachen, 3rd edn 2020 (cited as MAH WirtschaftsStrafR/author's name).
Matt/Renzikowski	Matt/Renzikowski, Strafgesetzbuch: StGB, 2nd edn 2020 (cited as Matt/Renzikowski/author's name).
Mayer Untreue	Materialien zur Strafrechtsreform, Vol. 1: Gutachten der Strafrechtslehrer, 1954 (cited as Mayer Untreue).
Michalke Umweltstrafsachen	Michalke (ed.), Umweltstrafsachen, 3rd edn 2021.
MLL Managerhaftung-HdB	Melot de Beauregard/Lieder/Liersch, Managerhaftung, 1st edn 2022 (cited as MLL Managerhaftung-HdB/author).
Momsen/Grützner WirtschaftsSteuerStrafR-HdB	Momsen/Grützner, Wirtschafts- und Steuerstrafrecht, 2nd edn 2020 (cited as Momsen/Grützner WirtschaftsSteuerStrafR-HdB/author's name).
Moosmayer Compliance	Moosmayer, Compliance, 4th edn 2024.
Moosmayer/Lösler Corporate Compliance	Moosmayer/Lösler, Corporate Compliance, 4th edn 2024 (cited as Moosmayer/Lösler Corporate Compliance/author's name).

MüKoAktG	Münchener Kommentar zum Aktiengesetz: AktG Vol. 2: §§ 76-117, MitbestG, DrittelbG, 6th edn 2023 (cited als MüKoAktG/author's name).
MüKoGmbHG	Münchener Kommentar zum Gesetz betreffend die Gesellschaften mit beschränkter Haftung: GmbHG Vol. 1: §§ 1-34, 5th edn 2025 Vol. 2: §§ 35-52, 4th edn 2023. (cited as MüKoGmbHG/author's name).
MüKoStGB	Münchener Kommentar zum Strafgesetzbuch: StGB Vol. 1: §§ 1-37, 5th edn 2024 Vol. 2: §§ 38-79b, 4th edn 2020 Vol. 3: §§ 80-184k, 4th edn 2021 Vol. 4: §§ 185-262, 4th edn 2021 Vol. 5: §§ 263-297, 4th edn 2022 Vol. 6: §§ 298-358, 4th edn 2022 Vol. 7: Nebenstrafrecht I, JGG, AMG, AntiDopG, BtMG, GÜG, NpSG, TPG, TFG, GenTG, TierSchG, BNatSchG, VereinsG, VersammlG, 4th edn 2022 Vol. 8: Nebenstrafrecht II: MarkenG, UrhG, UWG, GeschGehG, AO, SchwArbG, AÜG, BetrVG, AktG, AWG, BauFoSiG, BörsG, DepotG, GenG, GewO, GmbHG, HGB, InsO, KWG, SanktDG, WpHG, TTDSG, TMG, 4th edn 2023 (cited as MüKoStGB/author's name).
MüKoStPO	Münchener Kommentar zur Strafprozessordnung Vol. 1: §§ 1-150 StPO, 2nd edn 2023 Vol. 2: §§ 151-332 StPO, 2nd edn 2024 Vol. 3: §§ 333-499 StPO, 2nd edn 2024 Vol. 4: GVG, EGGVG, GDolmG, EMRK, EGStPO, EGStGB, ZSHG, StrEG, JGG, G 10, AO, 2nd edn 2025 (cited as MüKoStPO/author's name).
MüKoUWG	Münchener Kommentar zum Lauterkeitsrecht Vol. 1: §§ 1-7 UWG, 3rd edn 2020 Vol. 2: §§ 8-20 UWG, 3rd edn 2022. (cited as MüKoUWG/author's name).
Müller-Gugenberger WirtschaftsStrafR-HdB	Müller-Gugenberger (ed.), Wirtschaftsstrafrecht, 8th edn 2024 (cited as Müller-Gugenberger WirtschaftsStrafR-HdB.
NK-BDSG	Simitis, Bundesdatenschutzgesetz, 7th edn 2011 (cited as NK-BDSG/author's name).
NK-DatenschutzR	Simitis/Hornung/Spiecker gen. Döhmann (eds), Datenschutzrecht, 2nd edn 2025 (cited as NK-DatenschutzR/author's name).
NK-ProdR	Ehring/Taeger (eds), Produkthaftungs- und Produktsicherheitsrecht, 1st edn 2022 (cited as NK-ProdR/author's name).
NK-RechtshilfeR	Ambos/König/Rackow (eds), Rechtshilferecht in Strafsachen, 2nd edn 2020 (cited as NK-RechtshilfeR/author's name).
NK-StGB	Kindhäuser/Neumann/Paeffgen/Saliger (eds), Strafgesetzbuch, 6th edn 2023 (cited as NK-StGB/author's name).
NK-WSS	Leitner/Rosenau (eds), Wirtschafts- und Steuerstrafrecht, 2nd edn 2022 (cited as NK-WSS/author's name).

NSH	Noack/Servatius/Haas, GmbH-Gesetz, 23rd edn 2022 (cited as NSH/author's name).
Paal/Pauly	Paal/Pauly (eds), DS-GVO BDSG, 3rd edn 2021 (cited as Paal/Pauly/author's name).
Park Durchsuchung	Park, Durchsuchung und Beschlagnahme, 5th edn 2022.
Pechstein/Nowak/Häde	Pechstein/Nowak/Häde (eds), Frankfurter Kommentar EUV/GRC/AEUV, 2nd edn 2023 (cited as Pechstein/Nowak/Häde/author's name).
Peters/Bröckers	Peters/Bröckers (eds), Vermögensabschöpfung im Strafverfahren, 1st edn 2019 (cited as Peters/Bröckers/author's name).
Petri ArbStrafR	Petri, Arbeitsstrafrecht, 3rd edn 2021.
Prütting	Prütting, Medizinrecht, 7th edn 2024 (cited as Prütting/author's name).
Rengier StrafR AT	Rengier, Strafrecht Allgemeiner Teil, 16th edn 2024.
Reufels/Soltysiak WhistleblowingR	Reufels/Soltysiak, Das neue Whistleblowing-Recht, 1st edn 2023.
Richardi BetrVG	Richardi (ed), Betriebsverfassungsgesetz, 17th edn 2022 (cited as Richardi BetrVG/author's name).
Rotsch Criminal Compliance	Rotsch, Criminal Compliance, 1st edn 2015 (cited as Rotsch Criminal Compliance/author's name).
Roxin/Greco StrafR AT I	Roxin/Greco, Strafrecht Allgemeiner Teil, Band 1: Grundlagen: Der Aufbau der Verbrechenslehre, 5th edn 2020.
Roxin StrafR AT II	Roxin, Strafrecht Allgemeiner Teil, Band 2: Besondere Erscheinungsformen der Straftat, 1st edn 2003.
Sack Umweltschutz-Strafrecht	Sack, Umweltschutz-Strafrecht, 49th edn 2023.
Saliger UmweltStrafR	Saliger, Umweltstrafrecht, 2nd edn 2020.
Saliger/Tsambikakis MedStrafR-HdB	Saliger/Tsambikakis (eds), Strafrecht der Medizin, 1st edn 2022 (cited as Saliger/Tsambikakis MedStrafR-HdB/author's name).
Schmidt-Salzer Entscheidungssammlung Produkthaftung	Schmidt-Salzer, Entscheidungssammlung Produkthaftung – Mit einer Einführung und Urteilsanmerkungen, 2nd edn 1976.
Schmitt/Köhler	Schmitt/Köhler (eds), Strafprozessordnung, 68th edn 2025 (cited as Schmitt/Köhler/author's name).
Schomburg/Lagodny	Schomburg/Lagodny (eds), Internationale Rechtshilfe in Strafsachen = International Cooperation in Criminal Matters, 6th edn 2020 (cited as Schomburg/Lagodny/author's name).
Schrader	Schrader, Die Strafbarkeit des Verteidigers wegen Geldwäsche (§ 261) durch Annahme bemakelter Honorarmittel, 2008.
Sharma	Sharma, Data Privacy and GDPR Handbook, 1st edn 2019.
Sosnitza/Meisterernst	Sosnitza/Meisterernst, Lebensmittelrecht (cited as Sosnitza/Meisterernst/author's name, supplement number, month and year).
Spindler/Schuster	Spindler/Schuster, Recht der elektronischen Medien, 4th edn 2019 (cited as Spindler/Schuster/author's name).
SSW StGB	Satzger/Schluckebier/Werner (eds), Strafgesetzbuch (StGB), 6th edn 2024 (cited as SSW StGB/author's name).

Streinz/Kraus LebensmittelR-HdB	Streinz/Kraus (eds), Lebensmittelrechts-Handbuch (cited as Streinz/Kraus LebensmittelR-HdB/author's name, supplement number, month and year).
Streinz/Meisterernst	Streinz/Meisterernst (eds), BasisVO/LFGB, 2nd edn 2025 (cited as Streinz/Meisterernst/author's name).
Taeger/Gabel	Taeger/Gabel (eds), DSGVO – BDSG – TTDSG, 4th edn 2022 (cited as Taeger/Gabel/author's name).
Thüsing Beschäftigtendatenschutz	Thüsing, Beschäftigtendatenschutz und Compliance, 3rd edn 2021 (cited as Thüsing Beschäftigtendatenschutz/author's name).
Thüsing HinSchG	Thüsing, Hinweisgeberschutzgesetz: HinSchG, 1st edn 2024 (cited as Thüsing HinSchG/author's name).
TK StGB	Eisele et al. (eds), Tübinger Kommentar Strafgesetzbuch, 31st edn 2025 (cited as TK StGB/author's name).
Ullenboom	Ullenboom, Praxisleitfaden Vermögensabschöpfung, 2nd edn 2021.
Ulsenheimer/Gaede ArztStrafR	Ulsenheimer/Gaede/Biermann/Bock/Dießner, Arztstrafrecht in der Praxis, 6th edn 2021 (cited as Ulsenheimer/Gaede ArztStrafR/author's name).
Wessing/Dann Korruptionsverfahren	Wessing/Dann, Deutsch-Amerikanische Korruptionsverfahren, 1st edn 2013 (cited as Wessing/Dann Korruptionsverfahren/author's name).
Winkler Strafbarkeit des Strafverteidigers	Winkler, Die Strafbarkeit des Strafverteidigers jenseits der Strafvereitelung. Zugleich ein Beitrag zur Auslegung des § 261 StGB, 1st edn 2005.
WJS WirtschaftsStrafR-HdB	Wabnitz/Janovsky/Schmitt, Handbuch des Wirtschafts- und Steuerstrafrechts, 6th edn 2025 (cited as WJS WirtschaftsStrafR-HdB/author's name).
WRW LkSG	Wagner/Ruttloff/Wagner (eds), Das Lieferkettensorgfaltspflichtengesetz in der Unternehmenspraxis, 1st edn 2022 (cited as WRW LkSG/author's name).

Weblinks to English translations

German legislation

AGG – Allgemeines Gleichbehandlungsgesetz	**General Act on Equal Treatment**	https://www.gesetze-im-internet.de/englisch_agg
AktG – Aktiengesetz	**Stock Corporation Act**	https://www.gesetze-im-internet.de/englisch_aktg
AO – Abgabenordnung	**Fiscal Code**	https://www.gesetze-im-internet.de/englisch_ao
ArbSchG – Arbeitsschutzgesetz	**Occupational Safety and Health Act**	https://www.gesetze-im-internet.de/englisch_arbschg
AWG – Außenwirtschaftsgesetz	**Foreign Trade and Payments Act**	https://www.gesetze-im-internet.de/englisch_awg
BDSG – Bundesdatenschutzgesetz	**Federal Data Protection Act**	https://www.gesetze-im-internet.de/englisch_bdsg/englisch_bdsg.html
BGB – Bürgerliches Gesetzbuch	**German Civil Code**	https://www.gesetze-im-internet.de/englisch_bgb/
DCGK – Deutscher Corporate Governance Kodex	**German Corporate Governance Codex**	https://www.dcgk.de//files/dcgk/usercontent/en/download/code/220627_German_Corporate_Governance_Code_2022.pdf
FinDAG – Gesetz über die Bundesanstalt für Finanzdienstleistungsaufsicht	**Act Establishing the Federal Financial Supervisory Authority**	https://www.bafin.de/SharedDocs/Veroeffentlichungen/EN/Aufsichtsrecht/Gesetz/findag_aktuell_en
GeschGehG – Geschäftsgeheimnisgesetz	**Act on the Protection of Trade Secrets**	https://www.gesetze-im-internet.de/englisch_geschgehg
GG – Grundgesetz der Bundesrepublik Deutschland	**Basic Law of the Federal Republic of Germany**	https://www.gesetze-im-internet.de/englisch_gg
GmbHG – Gesetz über die Gesellschaften mit beschränkter Haftung	**Act on Limited Liability Companies**	https://www.gesetze-im-internet.de/englisch_gmbhg
GVG – Gerichtsverfassungsgesetz	**Courts Constitution Act**	https://www.gesetze-im-internet.de/englisch_gvg
GWB – Gesetz gegen Wettbewerbsbeschränkungen	**Act Against Restraints of Competition**	https://www.gesetze-im-internet.de/englisch_gwb
GwG – Geldwäschegesetz	**Money Laundering Act**	https://www.bafin.de/SharedDocs/Veroeffentlichungen/EN/Aufsichtsrecht/Gesetz/GwG_en.html?nn=8379954
HGB – Handelsgesetzbuch	**Commercial Code**	https://www.gesetze-im-internet.de/englisch_hgb
HinSchG – Hinweisgeberschutzgesetz	**Whistleblower Protection Act**	https://www.gesetze-im-internet.de/englisch_hinschg
IFG – Informationsfreiheitsgesetz	**Freedom of Information Act**	https://www.gesetze-im-internet.de/englisch_ifg

InsO – Insolvenzordnung	**Insolvency Code**	https://www.gesetze-im-internet.de/englisch_inso
IRG – Internationales Rechtshilfegesetz	**Act on International Mutual Assistance in Criminal Matters**	https://www.gesetze-im-internet.de/englisch_irg
KWG – Kreditwesengesetz	**German Banking Act**	https://www.bafin.de/SharedDocs/Downloads/EN/Aufsichtsrecht/dl_kwg_en.html?nn=8379954
LkSG – Lieferkettensorgfaltspflichtgesetz	**Act on Corporate Due Diligence Obligations in Supply Chains**	https://www.csr-in-deutschland.de/SharedDocs/Downloads/EN/act-corporate-due-diligence-obligations-supply-chains.pdf?__blob=publicationFile
OWiG – Gesetz über Ordnungswidrigkeiten	**Act on Regulatory Offences**	https://www.gesetze-im-internet.de/englisch_owig
SchwarzArbG – Schwarzarbeitsbekämpfungsgesetz	**Act to Combat Illegal Employment**	https://www.gesetze-im-internet.de/englisch_schwarzarbg/englisch_schwarzarbg.html
StGB – Strafgesetzbuch	**Criminal Code**	https://www.gesetze-im-internet.de/englisch_stgb
StPO – Strafprozessordnung	**Code of Criminal Procedure**	https://www.gesetze-im-internet.de/englisch_stpo
UmwG – Umwandlungsgesetz	**Transformation Act**	https://www.gesetze-im-internet.de/englisch_umwg
UWG – Gesetz gegen den unlauteren Wettbewerb	**Act Against Unfair Competition**	https://www.gesetze-im-internet.de/englisch_uwg/index.html
VAG – Versicherungsaufsichtsgesetz	**German Insurance Supervision Act**	https://www.bafin.de/SharedDocs/Downloads/EN/Aufsichtsrecht/dl_vag_en_va.html?nn=8379954
WpHG – Wertpapierhandelsgesetz	**German Securities Trading Act**	https://www.bafin.de/SharedDocs/Veroeffentlichungen/EN/Aufsichtsrecht/Gesetz/WpHG_en.html?nn=8379954

EU legal documents, official journals etc.

EUR-Lex	https://eur-lex.europa.eu/homepage.html

CHAPTER 1
INTRODUCTION

Table of contents

A. Conceptual framework 1
B. Scope and approach 2
C. Overview 3

A. Conceptual framework

The commercial exchange of goods and services has long since transcended national borders and takes place on a global scale. In contrast, the law – and particularly criminal law as a subfield – continues to follow predominantly national rules and regulations. 1

Even when national legislation is influenced by international developments, particularly by European Union directives and regulations, such supranational or international norms rarely have direct effect. They generally require implementation into national law, usually leaving the domestic legislature a degree of discretion in their transposition. 2

This presents both linguistic and structural challenges for legal practitioners: German (criminal) law is codified in the German language. 3

The Federal Ministry of Justice provides unofficial English translations for some of the most relevant texts.[1] These translations can provide a certain support when working internationally, translating and presenting specific provisions. However, they are merely unofficial translations and the German version is always authoritative. As much as these translations are helpful, certain legal concepts may have been incorporated in that process that may not be applicable, at least not in the specific case. They can, therefore, easily mislead – especially when the English wording feels more familiar than it should – and should always be used with caution and reservation. 4

After all, many legal – and even more so: doctrinal – terms are often rooted in centuries-old legal traditions for which no precise equivalents exist in English, necessitating more detailed explanations of the terminology. 5

Such explanations face challenges particularly in view of the multitude of statutory provisions and the characteristics of the German legal tradition. 6

Legal practitioners from all jurisdictions might intuitively expect the existence of a criminal code. The fact that regulatory offences (*Ordnungswidrigkeiten*), which fall below the threshold of criminal liability, are also sanctioned is likewise expected. However, what surprises many: under German law, legal persons are sanctioned through regulatory offences – not criminal convictions. 7

The reason why a sanction imposed on legal persons cannot be considered a criminal penalty under the Criminal Code is, in short, that legal persons lack the capacity for guilt. In the German legal tradition, shaped by early religious thought, 'guilt' is a fundamental 8

---

[1] See, for example, the Criminal Code at: https://www.gesetze-im-internet.de/englisch_stgb/; for links to further translations → Weblinks to English translations.

prerequisite for criminal liability – one that presupposes moral agency and can, therefore, only be attributed to natural persons.

9 Decades of debate over the establishment of a genuine 'corporate criminal law', as a distinct third pillar alongside individual criminal law and regulatory offence law, appeared to culminate in 2020 in a draft Act on Corporate Sanctions (*Verbandssanktionengesetz*). However, this draft legislation ultimately failed and has so far not been revisited. This exemplifies the intricate and lengthy interaction between academic discourse, practical necessities and policy decisions – often ultimately subject to rather short-term political considerations.

10 It is hardly reasonable to expect even the more or less invested observer from abroad to follow this process in detail. Accordingly, the often-heard assertion that Germany has no 'corporate criminal law' may come as a surprise.

11 Given these complexities, this handbook provides structured guidance for practitioners navigating German corporate criminal liability. It is designed for two primary audiences: German legal practitioners who interact with international colleagues and business partners, and foreign professionals who wish to understand and apply German criminal law – whether working on international matters, conducting cross-border investigations, or ensuring compliance in multinational operations.

B. Scope and approach

12 The growing importance of corporate criminal liability in German law has not been matched by corresponding English-language resources for practitioners. Given Germany's position as a major trading nation and its extensive international business relations, this lack of accessible literature represents a significant practical challenge. This handbook seeks to address that shortcoming.

13 Aimed primarily at legal practitioners, this handbook prioritises straightforward, accessible presentation over complex academic discourse. This approach reflects the belief that practical utility – rather than theoretical comprehensiveness – best serves practitioners working across different legal systems and languages with the goal of achieving as much clarity across jurisdictions as possible.

14 However, the approach taken here goes beyond mere translation of German legal terminology. Writing as German legal practitioners, the authors have sought to explain and situate German concepts within the broader context of international business practice and comparative legal understanding.

15 The handbook employs German legal terminology throughout, with English explanations provided where necessary. Key German terms are retained (such as *Ordnungswidrigkeiten* and *Anknüpfungstat*) wherever these concepts lack precise English equivalents and are essential for effective communication with German legal practitioners and authorities. A comprehensive glossary of German legal terms and their English explanations is provided to assist readers (→ Glossary).

16 The legal framework presented reflects the state of German law as of October 2025. Given the dynamic nature of this field – particularly with ongoing legislative discussions surrounding the reform of corporate sanctions – practitioners should verify current developments for matters arising after this date.

17 While this handbook covers the most significant areas of corporate criminal liability, it does not purport to be exhaustive. The selection of topics reflects those offences and regulatory areas that, in the publishers' experience, are most frequently encountered

in practice and most relevant to businesses operating internationally or with German operations.

It should also be emphasised that the effective handling of corporate criminal issues often relies on professional judgment, practical experience, and informal practices that cannot be conclusively covered in writing. This handbook is, therefore, intended not as a substitute for, but as an invitation to, dialogue with practitioners experienced in German corporate criminal law. **18**

Where relevant, Chapters include practical guidance on strategic considerations, compliance measures, and interaction with German authorities. Furthermore, the authors also address the international dimensions of German corporate criminal law, including mutual legal assistance and cross-border investigations. **19**

This handbook aims to function as both a practical working tool and a reference source for legal professionals dealing with German corporate criminal law across various contexts. Additionally, it seeks to advance understanding of how German approaches to corporate responsibility interact with broader international regulatory trends. **20**

C. Overview

As mentioned in → mn. 8, criminal responsibility is, in principle, limited to **natural persons**. However, this does not mean that corporate misconduct goes unsanctioned. Under the framework of German regulatory offence law (*Ordnungswidrigkeitenrecht*), **legal entities** can be subjected to significant monetary sanctions and confiscation if certain conditions are met. Central to this mechanism is the requirement of an attributive act – typically, a criminal or regulatory violation committed by a managerial or supervisory individual within the company. Only when such an act, known as a so-called *Anknüpfungstat* (underlying act), is established and can be imputed to the corporation under § 30 of the *Gesetz über Ordnungswidrigkeiten* (Regulatory Offences Act), does corporate liability come into play. **21**

This indirect model of attribution underscores the continued relevance of individual culpability as the gateway to holding companies accountable. It is precisely this intricate relationship between personal misconduct and corporate sanction that this handbook seeks to explain. **22**

In addition to the Criminal Code and the Regulatory Offences Act, a vast and complex array of criminal and regulatory provisions embedded within sector-specific legislation exists. The provisions of this so-called ancillary criminal law (*Nebenstrafrecht*) that are most relevant to corporate conduct in Germany will be explained in the course of this handbook. **23**

With that in mind, this handbook is structured into a general and a special part. **24**

The **general part** outlines the fundamental principles of corporate liability (→ Ch. 2) and the German criminal procedure (→ Ch. 3). The understanding developed in these Chapters will be helpful in comprehending how sanctions against companies arise and are structured (→ Ch. 4). A key element of corporate sanctions – and one that can have similarly severe implications for those affected – is a judicial order for the confiscation of assets and proceeds derived from offences (→ Ch. 5). **25**

Well-structured compliance management systems (→ Ch. 6) serve to prevent misconduct or, at the very least, to ensure its timely detection and can be taken into account favourably when determining sanctions. An effective compliance management system **26** should also include a whistleblowing mechanism (→ Ch. 7), which allows employees to report internal violations. If corporate officers become aware of misconduct through such a system or a whistleblower report, the matter will typically be subject to internal investigations (→ Ch. 8). Given the international orientation of this handbook, an introduction to mutual legal assistance in criminal matters is included (→ Ch. 9).

27 The **special part** of the handbook then addresses individual offences and categories of offences under both core and ancillary criminal law. As stated above, such offences, when committed by certain individuals, are the key requirement for monetary sanctions against legal entities and for a confiscation of profits. A comprehensive understanding of the underlying offences is, therefore, crucial to the evaluation of corporate criminal liability.

28 Diverging standards of social adequacy mean that corruption issues are particularly relevant in cross-border matters (→ Ch. 10). The offences of fraud (→ Ch. 11) and breach of trust (→ Ch. 12) are classic elements of German criminal practice and, due to their broad definitions, entail low thresholds for criminal liability. The same applies to tax offences (→ Ch. 13), which are especially pertinent in international business contexts e.g. involving import and export duties.

29 Where illicit gains have been generated, caution is required in handling such assets, as liability for money laundering may arise (→ Ch. 14). Insolvency proceedings also involve strict rules for the handling of remaining assets, with criminal consequences for violations (→ Ch. 15).

30 More recent and increasingly important areas of criminal law relate to data protection (→ Ch. 16), information technology (→ Ch. 17), and due diligence obligations in supply chains (→ Ch. 18).

31 By contrast, fields such as labour law (→ Ch. 19), environmental and product liability (→ Ch. 20), medical and pharmaceutical law (→ Ch. 21), and capital markets (→ Ch. 22) appear more traditional, yet remain practically relevant in criminal matters.

32 The geopolitical situation of the last years has led to a growing importance of foreign trade law and the sanctions it provides for (→ Ch. 23). Competition and antitrust law (→ Ch. 24) are particularly significant for large international corporations.

33 Finally, the protection of trade secrets (→ Ch. 25) is addressed – a topic which, like many of the aforementioned areas, has been heavily influenced by EU legislation in recent years.

CHAPTER 2
PRINCIPLES OF CORPORATE RESPONSIBILITY AND STRATEGIES

Bibliography: Adam/Schmidt/Schumacher, Nulla poena sine culpa – Was besagt das verfassungsrechtliche Schuldprinzip?, NStZ 2017, 7; Bachmann, Interne Ermittlungen – ohne Grenzen?, ZHR 180 (2016), 563; Ballo, Beschlagnahmeschutz im Rahmen von Internal Investigations – Zur Reichweite und Grenze des § 160a StPO, NZWiSt 2013, 46; Beukelmann, Strafbarkeit des Aufsichtsrats, NJW-Spezial 2009, 152; Bittmann, Das Gesetz zur Reform der strafrechtlichen Vermögensabschöpfung in der Rechtsprechung – Teil 1/2, NStZ 2019, 383; Bott/Kollhoff, Kurz und klarstellend: zur Nebenklagebefugnis von Unternehmen, StraFo 2019, 413; Dinter, Akteneinsichtsrecht und Interessenkonflikte – zu Regelungsdefiziten bei der Sanktionierung von Unternehmen, NStZ 2023, 7; Greco/Caracas, Internal investigations und Selbstbelastungsfreiheit, NStZ 2015, 7; Greeve, Privatisierung behördlicher Ermittlungen, StraFo 2013, 89; Groß/Wenzl, DB Sonderausgabe Nr. 02/2017, 97; Kämpfer/Travers/Schwerdtfeger, Unternehmensverteidigung unter Geltung des Verbandssanktionengesetzes, NZG 2020, 848; Knauer, Der Regierungsentwurf zur Einführung eines Gesetzes zur Sanktionierung von verbandsbezogenen Straftaten – großer Wurf oder bittere Pille?, NStZ 2020, 441; Kraft/Winkler, CCZ 2009, 29, CCZ 2009, 29; Kusnik, Wenn die Staatsanwaltschaft im Unternehmen ermittelt: Abläufe und Verhaltensleitlinien bei einer Durchsuchung der Geschäftsräume, CCZ 2015, 22; Lindemann/Sommer, Die strafrechtliche Geschäftsherrenhaftung und ihre Bedeutung für den Bereich der Criminal Compliance, JuS 2015, 1057; Minoggio, Das Schweigerecht der juristischen Person als Nebenbeteiligte im Strafverfahren, wistra 2003, 121; Mosbacher/Dierlamm, Betriebsangehöriger als Überwachungsgarant – Anm. zu BGH, Urteil vom 17. 7. 2009 – 5 StR 394/08, NStZ 2010, 268; Nietsch, Legal Privilege und interne Untersuchungen in den USA und dem Vereinigten Königreich – Rechtsvergleichende Überlegungen zur möglichen Regelung des Vertraulichkeitsschutzes von internen Untersuchungen –, CCZ 2019, 49; Pörtge, Die unternehmerische Ermessensentscheidung über Verteidigung oder Kooperation, CCZ 2020, 65; Raum, Die Verwertung unternehmensinterner Ermittlungen, StraFo 2012, 395; Richter II, Sockelverteidigung *Voraussetzung, Inhalte und Grenzen der Zusammenarbeit von Verteidigern verschiedener Beschuldigter, NJW 1993, 2152; Rieks, Die Nebenklage – Terra Incognita des Wirtschaftsstrafverfahrens, NStZ 2019, 643; Rönnau/Hohn, Die Festsetzung (zu) hoher Vorstandsvergütungen durch den Aufsichtsrat – ein Fall für den Staatsanwalt?, NStZ 2004, 113; Rübenstahl, Zur „regelmäßigen" Garantenstellung des Compliance Officers, NZG 2009, 1341; Rudkowski, Die Aufklärung von Compliance-Verstößen durch „Interviews", NZA 2011, 612, Sahan/Altenburg, Der „faktische Nicht Geschäftsführer", NZWiSt 2018, 161; Schünemann, Die aktuelle Forderung eines Verbandsstrafrechts – Ein kriminalpolitischer Zombie, ZIS 1/2014 p. 10; Schwerdtfeger, Untreuestrafbarkeit und Aufsichtsrat, NZWiSt 2018, 266; Theile, Compliance und Strafrecht, JuS 2017, 913; Trüg, Die Implikationen unterschiedlicher Formen der Unternehmensverteidigung – am Beispiel idealtypischer Modelle, NStZ 2020, 130; Trüg, Die Verteidigung von Unternehmen, NZWiSt 2022, 106; van Cleve, Ausstrahlungswirkung privatrechtlicher Vergleiche auf Einziehungsentscheidungen, NZWiSt 2023, 218; Wagner/Spemann, Organhaftungs- und Strafbarkeitsrisiken für Aufsichtsräte, NZG 2015, 945; Welke/Wenzel, Auskunft auf Verlangen? – Praktischer Umgang mit Auskunftsersuchen staatlicher Ermittlungsbehörden im Unternehmen, BB 2021, 1737; Winkler, BVerfG zu Jones Day – wie sicher sind die Ergebnisse einer internen Untersuchung?, StraFo 2018, 464.

Table of contents

A. Criminal liability of companies ... 7
I. Basic principle: no criminal liability of companies in Germany ... 7
II. Possibilities of sanctioning companies in a criminal law context ... 8
1. Corporate fine ... 8
a) Requirements ... 8
b) Legal consequences ... 8
c) Enforcing corporate fines ... 9
2. Confiscation ... 9
a) Overview ... 9
b) Requirements ... 9
c) Amount of confiscation and restrictions ... 10
d) Duty of the authorities to confiscate ... 10
III. Further consequences of criminal investigations for companies ... 11
IV. Summary ... 12
B. Criminal liability of company employees and management ... 13
I. Criminal liability of a company's executive bodies ... 13
II. Criminal liability of the company's de facto managers ... 14
III. Criminal liability of the members of the company's supervisory board ... 14
IV. Criminal liability of the compliance officer ... 15
V. Accountability of executive bodies and employees with supervisory duties under regulatory offences law ... 15
VI. Excursus: aiding and abetting of offences committed by customers through acts related to a particular occupation or profession ... 17
VII. Summary ... 18
C. Companies' procedural status during criminal proceedings ... 18
I. Position and rights of companies as a party to confiscation proceedings or involvement as a secondary party (quasi-accused status) ... 18
II. Status and rights of companies as victims of a criminal offence ... 20
III. Status and rights of companies in other cases ... 21
IV. Excursus: surrender and information obligations/legal privilege in Germany ... 21
V. Summary ... 22
D. Strategies of corporate defence ... 23
I. Starting point: determination of the facts ... 23
II. Determination of the company's interests ... 24
III. Identification of possible defence approaches ... 24
1. Case scenario 1: defence at the factual level ... 25
2. Case scenario 2: defence at the level of the legal situation ... 25
3. Case scenario 3: defence at the level of sentencing/admission to offence ... 25
IV. Determination of a defence strategy ... 26
V. Approach to employees ... 27
1. Accused employees ... 28
2. Potential witnesses ... 29
3. Other employees ... 29
VI. Summary ... 30

1 Criminal liability in the corporate context is gaining in importance in Germany. While top managers were rarely ever the focus of public prosecutors' investigations 20 years ago,

and companies to an even lesser extent, the criminalisation of top executives and corporates has increased over the past few years. It is a fact that only a very small proportion of pre-trial proceedings result in an indictment and a public trial. Most investigations end in a different manner.[1] However, the psychological barriers for law enforcement authorities to conduct investigations against corporate leaders and large companies have seen a sharp drop over the past two decades.

At the same time, the need for companies to clarify and resolve criminal matters themselves has grown significantly in recent years. Topics such as company-wide purges, good corporate citizenship, internal investigations and compliance have become fads that have not only led to a flourishing consultancy market but have also opened up a new dimension of dealing with criminal offences in a corporate context.[2] **2**

This chapter provides an overview of the criminal liability of companies (→ mn. 4 et seqq.) and their representatives (→ mn. 34 et seqq.) under German law. Furthermore, we will address the procedural status of companies during criminal proceedings as well as the rights and obligations they are subject to (→ mn. 58 et seqq.). At the same time, we will also outline options for the defence of companies against investigative measures (→ mn. 81 et seqq.). For an in-depth analysis of the various areas of economic criminal law, please refer to the following chapters. **3**

A. Criminal liability of companies

Germany has no separate statutory provisions for the criminal liability of legal persons. Therefore, companies cannot be charged with a criminal offence in Germany (→ mn. 5). However, numerous case scenarios exist where criminal investigations are also directed against a company, so that the company's status in the criminal proceedings is ultimately comparable to that of an accused person (→ mn. 6 et seqq.). Moreover, criminal proceedings against company employees commonly have a serious impact on inherent corporate interests, for example as a consequence of search measures or media coverage, which means that companies themselves also have an interest *per se* in playing an active role in these criminal proceedings (→ mn. 23 et seqq.). Depending on the case scenario, companies are accorded various rights and obligations that may permit, if not compel, their participation in the criminal proceedings (→ mn. 32 et seq.). **4**

I. Basic principle: no criminal liability of companies in Germany

In contrast to many other jurisdictions, corporate criminal law is not part of the German legal system.[3] This is due to the fact that German criminal law is shaped by the dogmatic principle that any sanctions must be based on the degree of a perpetrator's personal guilt. Since personal guilt is only attributable to natural persons and not to companies, the German system arrives at the conclusion that companies, as legal entities, cannot commit crimes.[4] **5**

---

[1] MAH WirtschaftsStrafR/Minoggio § 8 mn. 96.

[2] Trüg NZWiSt 2022, 106 (107) et seq.

[3] BeckOK StGB/Momsen/Laudien, 62. Ed. 1.8.2024, StGB § 14 mn. 31.

[4] BeckOK StGB/Momsen/Laudien, 62. Ed. 1.8.2024, StGB § 14 mn. 31; Schünemann ZIS 1/2014, p. 10; Adam/Schmidt/Schumacher NStZ 2017, 7 (on the principle of culpability in general).

II. Possibilities of sanctioning companies in a criminal law context

6 Even though a company itself cannot commit a criminal offence and can therefore not assume the formal status of the accused in criminal proceedings, the law enforcement authorities have two options to ultimately direct criminal proceedings (also) against the company itself: for one, there is the option of imposing a corporate fine on a company if its employees have committed criminal offences within the overall corporate context (→ mn. 7 et seqq.). Secondly, the criminal proceedings may be geared towards depriving the company of any gains from its offending by way of confiscation (→ mn. 12 et seqq.).

1. Corporate fine

7 First of all, companies can be prosecuted and sanctioned by way of monetary fines for regulatory offences committed by their management (*Verbandsgeldbuße*), § 30 OWiG. A corporate fine is, strictly speaking, not a penalty but rather a regulatory fine. A company may become subject to a regulatory fine if one of its managers has committed a criminal offence that is related to the company. Chapter C.II. 'Status and rights of companies as victims of a criminal offence' (→ mn. 64 et seqq.) addresses the topic of corporate fines in greater detail. The following therefore provides only a brief overview of the requirements and legal consequences of corporate fines.

a) Requirements

8 The basic requirement for the imposition of a regulatory fine on a company is that a member of its executive bodies or one of its managers has committed a criminal or regulatory offence. The person who committed the criminal or regulatory offence does not necessarily need to be identified during the proceedings against the company. The authorities may also impose an 'anonymous' regulatory fine if it has been determined that an offence was committed by *any* executive or manager of the company.[5] A further option is utilising a nexus to offences committed abroad, provided that German criminal law or German regulatory offences law applies to such offences.[6]

9 In addition, the criminal or regulatory offence must have been related to the company's operations and the company must have been enriched by the offence. In other words: the offence must have been committed 'in connection with the management or governance of the company'. Breaches of duty that have no connection to the commercial activity pursued by the business or the company are excluded.[7]

b) Legal consequences

10 The legal consequence of § 30 OWiG is the imposition of a fine on a legal entity. For criminal offences, this fine may be up to 10 million EUR in the case of intent and up to 5 million EUR in the case of negligence. If, on the other hand, the offence is a regulatory offence, the maximum fine that can be imposed will be determined by the maximum regulatory fine imposable for the regulatory offence concerned. Moreover, the amount of the fine may be increased, without limitation, by the amount of the economic benefit (net profit) which the company derived from the criminal offence.[8]

---

[5] KK-OWiG/Rogall OWiG § 30 mn. 119 et seq.
[6] KK-OWiG/Rogall OWiG § 30 mn. 88.
[7] KK-OWiG/Rogall OWiG § 30 mn. 90.
[8] KK-OWiG/Mitsch OWiG § 17 mn. 119.

c) Enforcing corporate fines

11 Unlike in the case of criminal offences committed by natural persons which the law enforcement authorities are obligated to prosecute, the decision to impose a fine in accordance with § 30 OWiG is left to the discretion of the prosecuting authority. Since the imposition of a fine is not a mandatory consequence of a criminal offence, in practice it is often the result of a **negotiated agreement** between the public prosecutor's office and the company. This applies in particular to any anonymous fines, where the perpetrator is not individually identified by name in the regulatory fine notice. Even though the company suffers a financial disadvantage as a result of such a negotiated fine, accepting such a fine enables the relevant company to avoid a trial that would otherwise attract a great deal of publicity and be, in all likelihood, harmful to its reputation. For this reason, the imposition of a fine pursuant to § 30 OWiG for a company-related offence is often the outcome that the company's defence lawyers would aim for (also see → mn. 96 et seq., → mn. 98 et seqq.).

2. Confiscation

12 If a company has benefitted financially from someone's criminal offence, it may be deprived of this financial advantage by means of confiscation (*Einziehung*). Such confiscation, which does not constitute a penalty under German law,[9] is not a capped amount. For a detailed description, please see → mn. 58 et seqq. The following therefore serves merely as an overview of the requirements and legal consequences of confiscation:

a) Overview

13 Confiscation is a measure *sui generis* that has no punitive character under German law.[10] It aims to disgorge all assets obtained by way of or for a criminal offence, regardless of whether these assets were obtained by participants in the criminal offence or by third parties who were not involved in the offence. A disgorgement order therefore does not necessarily include a judicial determination of guilt on the part of any company employee. Instead, it only follows the principle that crime should not pay off. Nobody should be allowed to benefit financially from an offence. Unlike the decision to impose a fine, the confiscation is not at the discretion of the law enforcement authorities but is a mandatory legal consequence of a crime (also see → mn. 22).

b) Requirements

14 As previously explained, under German law companies are incapable of committing criminal offences themselves. Therefore, criminal disgorgement at companies follows the rules of criminal disgorgement at so-called **third parties**. The legal basis for criminal disgorgement at third parties is § 73b sub. 1, 2 StGB.

15 § 73b sub. 1, 2 StGB essentially addresses two case scenarios:

- firstly, cases where the company directly obtained crime proceeds and the perpetrator acted on behalf of the third party (so-called 'representation cases'[11], § 73b sub. 1 no. 1 StGB), and

---

[9] BVerfG 10.2.2021– 2 BvL 8/19, NJW 2021, 1222 mn. 103.
[10] BVerfG 10.2.2021 – 2 BvL 8/19, NJW 2021, 1222.
[11] TK StGB/Eser/Schuster StGB § 73b mn. 3.

- secondly, cases where crime proceeds were transferred to the company by another person and the third party acted in bad faith (so-called 'transfer cases'[12], § 73b sub. 1 no. 2b StGB).

16 In the first case, the requirement is that the company has received crime proceeds because the perpetrator of the criminal offence was acting 'on behalf of' the company. This would be the case if the perpetrator acted – even if only de facto – in the interest of the third party at the time of or in connection with their participation in the offending.[13] It is, however, not required that this participant actually be an employee of the company.

17 In the second case, the requirement is that someone has transferred crime proceeds to the company's accounts. This might be the case, for example, if the crime proceeds were originally paid to a subsidiary and only later transferred to the accounts of the parent company.[14]

18 Should one of the above case scenarios present itself, the law enforcement authorities may confiscate any monies obtained by the company.

c) Amount of confiscation and restrictions

19 The determination of the disgorgement amount takes place in two steps. Firstly, it must be determined what assets were obtained through the offending ('assets obtained'). In a second step, certain expenses may be deducted from this amount:

- 'Assets obtained' essentially correspond to (the value of) all crime profits received directly or transferred to a third party, which – even if only temporarily – became part of the company's assets.
- Expenses may be deducted from the 'assets obtained' if they have a factual and temporal connection to the offence and have not been deliberately spent in its preparation.

20 Criminal disgorgement with regard to crime proceeds is precluded where the proceeds have been paid back to the injured party or there has been some kind of settlement (*Vergleich*) with the injured party.[15] This provision is intended to encourage companies to agree on appropriate compensation with the victims of their criminal offending.

21 Lastly, criminal disgorgement may be limited by considerations of proportionality under § 459g StPO. In this context, any subsequent loss of crime profits (*Entreicherung*) for example can be taken into account.

d) Duty of the authorities to confiscate

22 As the law enforcement authorities are legally bound to order confiscation against a company that has become enriched[16], it must be assumed that whenever a company benefits from the criminal offending of one of its employees, this company will be formally involved in the criminal proceedings as a party to the confiscation proceedings (*Einziehungsbeteiligte*) (further details under → mn. 58 et seqq.). This involvement as a party to the confiscation proceedings may be averted by reaching a settlement with the victim of the criminal offence at an early stage or by repaying all amounts related to the offence. Framing the confiscation scenario is therefore often one of the foremost tasks of the corporate defence (see → mn. 91 et seqq. for further details).

---

[12] MüKoStGB/Joecks/Meißner StGB § 73b mn. 15.

[13] LG Bonn 18.3.2020 – 62 KLs – 213, Js 41/19 – 1/19, BeckRS 2020, 13619 mn. 1408.

[14] See for legal entities as third parties according to § 73b StGB BeckOK StGB/Heuchemer, 62. Ed. 1.8.2024, StGB § 73b mn. 2.

[15] RegE BT-Drs. 18/9525, 69; Bittmann NStZ 2019, 383 (396); van Cleve NZWiSt 2023, 218 (221) et seq.

[16] TK StGB/Eser/Schuster StGB § 73 mn. 28; MüKoStGB/Joecks/Meißner StGB § 73 mn. 46; see also for the exceptions § 421 StPO.

III. Further consequences of criminal investigations for companies

However, even if neither the imposition of a corporate fine nor a potential confiscation against the company is in the offing and the company therefore has no formal status in these proceedings that is similar to that of an accused person, the company's interests may be seriously affected in the event of investigations into its managers and employees. Against this background, the following aspects in particular must be taken into account, as they will necessarily result in a company having to consider what kind of active role it will play in any criminal proceedings against its own staff:[17] 23

- **reputation/public image.** Criminal proceedings against corporate staff often attract a great deal of publicity and may involve measures such as searches of the company's business premises. The company's active participation in the investigation may help to avert any such measures (by voluntarily handing over documents, for example) or to influence public perception.[18] 24
- **duty to furnish information and to surrender documents or materials.** Even if neither the imposition of a corporate fine nor confiscation is under consideration, law enforcement authorities often approach companies to establish the facts. This applies, in particular, to large-scale proceedings. This frequently involves comprehensive requests for information and the surrender of documents being sent to the legal departments, which means that data and information must be handed over.[19] In addition, the company may be requested to name witnesses, give access to its premises for on-site visits or comply with other requests. In these cases, the company often assumes the role of a coordinator. In doing so, it is required to comply with its statutory surrender and information obligations while at the same time ensuring that the proceedings progress in an orderly fashion. Particularly in cases of complex large-scale proceedings involving multiple agencies[20], it must be ensured that communication with the various agencies is consistent and that different contact persons do not provide differing information as a result of differing levels of knowledge. 25
- **non-criminal consequences.** If a staff member of a company is convicted of a company-related criminal offence, this may also have consequences outside criminal law, not only for the manager or employee but also for the company, such as the conviction being recorded in the central business register or the competition register, which may restrict the company's ability to participate in public tenders.[21] Other conceivable measures are the revocation of existing business licences (such as a licence to operate a banking business) or particularly in the finance or food sector – the public 'naming and shaming' of offenders via supervisory announcements.[22] These non criminal consequences may in fact have a greater and more serious impact on a company than the imposition of a corporate fine or confiscation. By getting involved early on and endeavouring to frame the criminal proceedings, these consequences may be averted to a certain degree (for instance under § 125 GWB or, at the very least, may be mitigated. 26
- **working atmosphere.** How a company deals with employees who are involved in criminal proceedings can have a significant impact on both working atmosphere and cor- 27

---

[17] Regarding the various aspects, see FS Feigen/Groß p. 67 (77 et sqq.).

[18] Cf. Kusnik CCZ 2015, 22 (23, 25); MAH WirtschaftsStrafR/Minoggio § 8 mn. 137.

[19] Instructive: Welke/Wenzel BB 2021, 1737 (1741).

[20] As is the case, for example, for industrial accidents, which are usually investigated by the prosecutor's office, various insurers as well as supervisory authorities.

[21] Cf. § 2 WRegG (*Wettbewerbsregistergesetz*, Competition Register Act) regarding the requirements for entry of offences into the register and the legal consequences of such recording, §§ 123, 124 GWB; MAH WirtschaftsStrafR/Kempf/Schilling/Oesterle § 10 mn. 25 et seq.

[22] Cf. § 125 WpHG.

porate culture.[23] Again, it is advisable to develop a positioning and a strategy early on in order to ensure the consistent and transparent handling of the pending proceedings.

28 – **prevention of future criminal offending and potential follow-on proceedings.** Depending on the type of criminal offence, there is a risk of repeat offending and follow-on proceedings. Companies must therefore analyse whether this is an organisational/ongoing problem or an isolated case and whether, going forward, further preventive measures need to be taken.[24]

29 – **recourse/personnel decisions.** In the context of criminal proceedings, oftentimes the necessity arises to reconsider personnel decisions or to examine recourse claims.[25] This applies all the more so whenever the allegations cast doubt on whether the staff member can remain in the company's employment or if the company itself was the victim of the employee's offending, as would be the case if the employee has embezzled company funds. Again, the company must involve itself closely with the criminal proceedings, or even conduct its own investigations alongside the criminal investigations, in order to fulfil this task.

30 – **non-criminal obligations to investigate and to act.** In some cases, criminal offences committed by employees give rise to investigation and reporting obligations outside the sphere of criminal law. This is conceivable, for example, if the company subsequently becomes aware that tax returns filed in previous years were in fact incorrect. This would require the submission of corrected tax returns. Similarly, investigation obligations under corporate law may also play a role, as the company management might be obliged to follow up on the allegations made in order to prevent any further damage to the company or to enforce recourse claims.[26] Whenever any such non-criminal obligations to investigate and to act exist, the company must ensure that these are duly met. As a rule, this requires active involvement with the criminal proceedings.

31 – **cost control.** Lastly, a company may be affected by criminal proceedings through shouldering the associated expenses (e.g. for the defence of the relevant employees or internal investigations). Particularly in cases where internal investigations are considered necessary, this may entail significant costs.

IV. Summary

32 Even though there is no corporate criminal law in Germany, more and more companies are involved in criminal proceedings for the prosecution of white-collar crime, as the imposition of a corporate fine or an order for confiscation against a company are conceivable options. A company's role in these cases is comparable to that of the accused person in criminal proceedings.

33 What is more, even in cases where the company does not have a status that is similar to that of a person charged with a criminal offence, it may be seriously impacted by the proceedings, for instance if the law enforcement authorities involve the company in the investigation of the facts or if the media coverage of the criminal proceedings also affects the company. In these cases too, the company would be well advised to take an active role in the proceedings to influence the outcome of the proceedings in its own interest by putting up a solid corporate defence.

---

[23] Cf. MüKoGmbHG/Fleischer GmbHG § 43 mn. 191; Moosmayer Compliance mn. 144 et seq.

[24] Cf. regarding increased supervisory obligations in case of offences, which might be repeated in future: GJW/Niesler OWiG § 130 mn. 45 et seq.; KK-OWiG/Rogall OWiG § 130 mn. 68.

[25] MAH WirtschaftsStrafR/Minoggio § 8 mn. 128, 143.

[26] MAH WirtschaftsStrafR/Minoggio § 8 mn. 143; Trüg NZWiSt 2022, 106 (108).

B. Criminal liability of company employees and management

34 As outlined above, the sanctioning of or confiscation against a company is always based on the commission of a criminal offence by an executive body or a staff member of the company. A number of aspects that are specific to German law must be taken into account when considering criminal liability of employees in the corporate context:

I. Criminal liability of a company's executive bodies

35 As is the case in practically every other legal system, the members of a company's management are primarily accountable for any **criminal offences they themselves have committed** by their own acts. This includes, for example, fraud (§ 263 StGB), embezzlement (§ 266 StGB), bribery (§ 334 StGB), tax evasion by way of submitting incorrect or incomplete information (§ 370 sub. 1 no. 1 AO), balance sheet fraud (§ 331 HGB) or insider trading (§ 119 sub. 3 no. 1 WpHG) in conjunction with Art. 14 lit. a Regulation (EU) 596/2014 (Market Abuse Regulation).

36 In addition, members of management boards may also be criminally liable for offences committed by an **employee** of the company. This is due to the fact that under German law, crimes can also be committed by omission, cf. § 13 StGB.[27] Under § 13 StGB, a person may be held liable for failure to act if that person has an obligation to act (*Garantenstellung*). With regard to corporate crimes, the management needs to be particularly mindful of two case scenarios: firstly, the management has a duty to intervene if it becomes aware that an employee has committed company-related criminal offences (*allgemeine Geschäftsherrenhaftung*).[28] In these cases, the management's duty to act arises from the fact that the company's operations may give rise to an increased risk of offending.[29] Secondly, the management has a duty to intervene if its previous acts have created a dangerous situation, for example by launching a product that subsequently proves to be harmful (prior conduct contrary to one's duty).

37 Whenever a duty to act exists under the above criteria, there is a need to ascertain exactly who would be subject to this duty, particularly with regard to executive bodies consisting of more than one person. In principle, in the case of a **collegiate body** with different areas of responsibility (i.e. the management board of a public limited company under German law (*Aktiengesellschaft*)), each member is primarily responsible for his or her respective portfolio.[30] However, criminal liability can no longer be attributed along the portfolio lines within a board consisting of several members if cross-policy issues are at stake or if a decision is taken jointly (*Gremienentscheidung*). In the event of material transactions in particular, such as product recalls that affect the entire company across all divisions, the responsibility lies with every member of the board.[31] The same applies in crises or extraordinary situations.[32] Moreover, this principle also generally applies to the implementation of compliance structures, provided that there is a clear allocation of responsibilities for compliance stipulated in the internal rules of procedure.[33]

---

[27] LKH/Heger StGB § 13 mn. 4.
[28] Rotsch Criminal Compliance/Dannecker § 5 mn. 22.
[29] BGH 6.7.1990 – 2 StR 549/89, NJW 1990, 2560 (2562).
[30] Kubis/Tödtmann Vorstand-HdB/Taschke/Zapf § 12 mn. 38.
[31] BGH 6.7.1990 – 2 StR 549/89, NJW 1990, 2560.
[32] Kubis/Tödtmann Vorstand-HdB/Taschke/Zapf § 12 mn. 42.
[33] Kubis/Tödtmann Vorstand-HdB/Taschke/Zapf § 12 mn. 40.

38 Also, in the practice of criminal defence, it has been observed that the investigating authorities have a tendency to initiate proceedings, by default, against the members of a company's executive bodies registered in the trade register whenever the suspicion of a company-related criminal offence arises, even where there is no indication that these members contributed in any way to the offending. In some cases, the authorities might resort to this approach because the real perpetrator is not known and they are simply looking for someone who can be identified by name and against whom the proceedings can be directed. In other cases, the initiation of criminal proceedings is based on an inadequate understanding of criminal responsibilities or the assumption that the management must have been aware of the offending. One other aspect is that, in general, companies take investigations against their executive bodies very seriously. The authorities can leverage this fact to prevail on a company to agree to a settlement, for example. Depending on what exactly the background of the initiation of criminal proceedings is, an effective defence in many of these cases would be to highlight the fact that the relevant executive board member was not actually involved in the offending.

II. Criminal liability of the company's de facto managers

39 Criminal liability may also extend to any de facto directors of a company (*Strohgeschäftsführer*), who are subject to the same obligations under criminal law as duly appointed managers.[34] De facto directors may become liable for offences linked to the function of a managing director (§ 14 sub. 3 StGB).[35] It is therefore not possible to avoid criminal responsibility by managing a company's business without being formally appointed. More specifically, de facto managing directors are also obliged to submit tax returns correctly and on time. They may also become liable for embezzlement to the detriment of the company's assets.[36]

III. Criminal liability of the members of the company's supervisory board

40 Criminal investigations may also focus on supervisory board members, as they are capable of committing certain offences under economic criminal law. First of all, a number of special offences exist that can essentially only be committed by members of the supervisory board or the executive officers/management of a company. These offences include but are not limited to § 331 HGB (incorrect presentation), § 399 AktG (false information) and § 404 AktG (violation of the duty to maintain confidentiality).

41 Moreover, members of the supervisory board may become liable for **embezzlement** if the supervisory board, in the course of its supervisory activities, discovers acts of the executive board that could cause the company **financial loss**. Depending on the facts of the specific case, the supervisory board would most likely be obliged to assert claims for damages against the management board. Should a member of the supervisory board violate this obligation, this could constitute embezzlement.[37] Furthermore, embezzlement

[34] WJS WirtschaftsStrafR-HdB/Raum, 5th edn 2020, Ch. 4 mn. 20; Sahan/Altenburg NStZ 2018, 161.
[35] Sahan/Altenburg NZWiSt 2018, 161.
[36] Sahan/Altenburg NZWiSt 2018, 161.
[37] WJS WirtschaftsStrafR-HdB/Raum, 5th edn 2020, Ch. 4 mn. 56; Wagner/Spemann NZG 2015, 945 (946).

may also have been committed if the supervisory board fails to prevent a member of the management board from committing a company-related criminal offence.[38] Moreover, supervisory board members may also be liable for embezzlement if the remuneration they grant to the members of the management board is not in line with company interests.[39]

It is also important to note that each member of the supervisory board is liable under criminal law for any decisions that result in unlawful financial losses, even if such decisions are taken by the supervisory board as a whole. Once a decision has been taken unanimously, each member of the supervisory board is deemed to be an accomplice pursuant to § 25 sub. 2 StGB. In the event of a majority vote, it is not only the voting members that may be deemed perpetrators but also any non-voting members. According to the case law of the Federal Court of Justice (*Bundesgerichtshof*), the non-voting members are only free of criminal liability if they have taken all legally permissible measures to prevent such a decision from being adopted.[40] This can even go so far as to require any member of the supervisory board who votes against such a decision to resign his or her mandate or inform the authorities.[41] 42

IV. Criminal liability of the compliance officer

At present, it is highly controversial whether compliance officers are actually liable for prosecution if they fail to prevent company-related offending. Those who subscribe to this point of view stress that compliance officers have a responsibility (derived from the company management) for the prevention of criminal offences.[42] In their view, compliance officers are responsible for preventing the company's employees from violating corporate or statutory rules.[43] This obligation extends to monitoring, communication and escalation.[44] In order to minimise legal uncertainty within the company, it is therefore advisable to clearly define the respective areas of responsibility.[45] 43

V. Accountability of executive bodies and employees with supervisory duties under regulatory offences law

Furthermore, persons who are entrusted with the management of employees by virtue of their position (as a member of an executive body) or by virtue of a mandate run the risk of committing a regulatory offence if they fail to properly supervise their subordinates. 44

Under § 130 OWiG, the intentional or negligent failure to fulfil business-related supervisory duties constitutes a **regulatory offence** if an employee commits a business-related criminal or regulatory offence and the commission of this offence would have at least been made more difficult if a supervisory measure had been taken. More specifically, the following should be noted: 45

---

[38] OLG Karlsruhe 4.9.2008 – 4 U 26/06, AG 2008, 900 (902); Schwerdtfeger NZWiSt 2018, 266 (267).

[39] BGH 21.12.2005 – 3 StR 470/04, NStZ 2006, 214; Rönnau/Hohn NStZ 2004, 113 (120 et seq.).

[40] BGH 6.7.1990 – 2 StR 549/89, NJW 1990, 2560.

[41] Beukelmann NJW-Spezial 2009, 152.

[42] NK-WSS/Burchard StGB § 13 mn. 36 et seq.; Rübenstahl NZG 2009, 1341 (1343); Mosbacher/Dierlamm NStZ 2010, 268 (269).

[43] Kraft/Winkler CCZ 2009, 29 (31).

[44] Lindemann/Sommer JuS 2015, 1057 (1062).

[45] Lindemann/Sommer JuS 2015, 1057 (1062).

46 § 130 OWiG is the **central compliance rule** under German law.[46] The purpose of this provision is to close forensic criminal liability loopholes resulting from the fact that, as a result of decentralisation and delegation of tasks, the company's senior management itself usually does not act but rather delegates the performance of its obligations to subordinate staff.[47] For this reason, § 130 OWiG stipulates that directors must take certain supervisory measures and provides for sanctions if they fail to do so.

47 The specific measures to be taken by a manager to prevent any infringements of the provisions in force at the relevant company depend on the circumstances of the individual case.[48] In any event, however, the supervisory measure that was not performed must have been reasonable and legally permissible if it had, in fact, been performed. In principle, proper supervision includes management duties, organisational obligations, selection obligations and monitoring obligations. The management is required to **organise** staff properly and to allocate responsibilities, clearly structuring and documenting the various areas of responsibility.[49] This includes keeping staff effectively **informed** of all the duties assigned to them. However, establishing a dedicated compliance department is not mandatory. Nevertheless, having a compliance department in place usually demonstrates that compliance with the rules applicable to the company is taken seriously.[50] The **obligation to select** entails that the management must ensure the careful selection of reliable staff and, if applicable, subordinate supervisors in accordance with the requirements of the specific job.[51] The higher the risk potential of the position to be filled, the higher are the requirements for the selection obligation. Finally, adequate supervision and **monitoring of staff** is required. Where there are actual indications that an employee has breached the rules, the manager is required to intervene and to verify whether such a breach has in fact occurred. Should this in fact be the case, it is the responsibility of the manager to issue a warning and, if necessary, impose **penalties** under labour law.

48 § 130 OWiG requires the supervisor to take the **necessary** supervisory measures. The criterion of necessity means that, when choosing from several equally appropriate measures, the supervisor may choose that one that is the least burdensome.[52] In this respect, there are no excessively strict requirements.[53] Furthermore, the supervisory measures required by the management must be **reasonable**. Only those measures that are legally permissible can be deemed reasonable.[54]

49 Apart from establishing that a requisite supervisory measure has been intentionally or negligently omitted, the imposition of a sanction pursuant to § 130 OWiG also requires a nexus with a breach of rules, i.e. the commission of a criminal offence or a regulatory offence by a person to be supervised who violated operational obligations. In addition, the violation must be **business-related**. Only those obligations that are imposed on the management are business-related.[55] The requisite business-related nature is deemed to exist if the violation was committed by an employee in the course of his or her work activities. Likewise, obligations that apply to all and sundry are not business-related, which means

---

[46] Theile JuS 2017, 913 (914).
[47] KK-OWiG/Rogall § 130 mn. 4.
[48] BGH 25.6.1985 – KRB 2/85, NStZ 1986, 34.
[49] HK-KapMarktStrafR/Eggers ch. 14.1. mn. 2.
[50] KK-OWiG/Rogall § 130 mn. 58; HK-KapMarktStrafR/Eggers, ch. 14.1. mn. 2.
[51] KK-OWiG/Rogall § 130 mn. 42.
[52] KK-OWiG/Rogall § 130 mn. 40; NK-WSS/Gräfin von Galen/Schaefer OWiG § 130 mn. 34.
[53] Leitner/Rosenau/Gräfin v. Galen/Schaefer OWiG § 130 mn. 55.
[54] BGH 11.3.1986 – KRB 8/85, wistra 1986, 222 (223).
[55] GJW/Niesler OWiG § 130 mn. 62.

they cannot constitute a qualified breach of rules either (such as generally refraining from committing offences that are unrelated to the company).[56]

An **intentional** offence under § 130 OWiG is deemed to have been committed if the supervisor is aware that he or she should and could take certain supervisory measures but fails to do so. However, only in very rare cases would the law enforcement authorities be able to prove this. That said, they would still have the option of proving a **negligent** lack of supervision, for which the requirements are much lower. 50

Failure to comply with one's supervisory obligation constitutes a regulatory offence and is subject to a fine pursuant to § 130 sub. 3 OWiG. On the one hand, the amount of the fine depends on whether the breach of supervisory duty was committed intentionally or negligently. On the other hand, it is dependent on whether the infringement committed by the employee constitutes a criminal offence or a regulatory offence. In the event of intentional breaches of supervision resulting in a violation in the form of a criminal offence, the maximum fine is 1 million EUR (§ 130 sub. 3 sent. 1 OWiG. In the case of negligent breaches of supervision resulting in a criminal offence, the maximum amount is reduced to 500,000 EUR (§ 17 sub. 2 OWiG). If, on the other hand, the violation committed by the employee constitutes a regulatory offence, and not a criminal offence, the maximum amount of the fine for the breach of supervision is determined by the maximum regulatory fine imposable for the specific breach of duty (§ 130 sub. 3 sent. 3 OWiG). In the event of negligent breaches of supervisory obligations, the maximum amount referred to in § 17 sub. 2 OWiG will be halved. 51

VI. Excursus: aiding and abetting of offences committed by customers through acts related to a particular occupation or profession

Another issue that arises in connection with company-related criminal offences is the question of exactly when a company employee would be liable of participating in a criminal offence (committed, for instance, by a customer) if the employee's actions have no criminal relevance of their own – the employee is only 'doing his job' – but de facto the employee is embroiled in the commission of a criminal offence (through acts related to his occupation or profession). This would be the case, for example, if a bank employee helped a customer to transfer money to an offshore jurisdiction. 52

According to case law, the bank employee bears criminal liability in these cases if he is aware of the principal offender's decision to commit the offence and his contribution to the offence has a reinforcing effect while his actions relinquish their routine character and must be interpreted as 'solidarisation' with the principal offender and no longer as neutral acts. The employee may then be liable as an aider and abetter, if he or she considered it possible that a criminal offence would be committed on the basis of his or her actions.[57] The legal situation applies accordingly to advisors (e.g. tax advisors or lawyers) who support their clients in committing a crime through actions that de facto are neutral in themselves. This would be the case, for example, with a tax advisor who submits a tax return for his client even though he knows that this will lead to a tax evasion. 53

[56] GJW/Niesler OWiG § 130 mn. 63.

[57] BGH 22.1.2014 – 5 StR 468/12, NZWiSt 2014, 139; BGH 21.12.2016 – 1 StR 112/16, wistra 2017, 270.

VII. Summary

54 The criminal liability of the executive bodies and employees of any company always also depends on the specific role and the associated obligations of the relevant employee. Particularly in those cases where the employee is accused of having failed to act, it must be examined in detail whether the employee was in fact under any duty to act. Likewise, if it is alleged that several persons participated in the commission of a criminal offence, it must be examined how the individual employee contributed to the offence.

55 More specifically, when initiating criminal proceedings against the executive bodies of a company, the authorities have to bear in mind that, due to the customary delegation of power within companies, these bodies are unlikely to have been the actors and can therefore not be held criminally liable. Nevertheless, companies and their executive bodies should brace themselves for the possibility that the investigating authorities may often be unwilling to terminate any proceedings against accused executive body members before the conclusion of the entire proceedings (by way of imposing a corporate fine, for example).

C. Companies' procedural status during criminal proceedings

56 Due to the mechanisms and reasons described under 'Possibilities of sanctioning companies in a criminal law context' (→ mn. 6 et seqq.), companies in Germany would in all likelihood be affected by investigations concerning criminal offences committed by their employees in a corporate environment.

57 The rights and obligations of a company and its opportunities to exert influence during criminal proceedings depend on the company's specific role during the proceedings. Against this backdrop, three procedural positions of the company may be distinguished, each offering different opportunities for exerting influence:

I. Position and rights of companies as a party to confiscation proceedings or involvement as a secondary party (quasi-accused status)

58 Insofar as the public prosecutor's office proceeds on the assumption that the commission of a criminal offence would require the imposition of a regulatory fine or confiscation against the company, the relevant company would be involved in the criminal proceedings as a so-called confiscating party or secondary party (*Einziehungs- oder Nebenbeteiligte*). The company's status is then similar to that of an accused in criminal proceedings (*beschuldigtenähnliche Stellung*).[58]

59 From the time when the law enforcement authorities consider involving a company as a party to confiscation proceedings or as a secondary party, the company has rights that are similar to that of an accused person during the investigation. For example, the company has the right to inspect files in order to gain information on the status of the investigation.[59] Furthermore, the company has the right to be heard and to make state-

[58] § 427 sub. 1 StPO; KK-StPO/Schmidt/Scheuß StPO § 424 mn. 16.
[59] § 428 sub. 1 StPO in conjunction with § 147 sub. 1 StPO; Dinter NStZ 2023, 7 (8).

ments.[60] Where a company is a party to confiscation proceedings or a secondary party, defence records as well as any correspondence with the company's defence counsel cannot be seized, as is the case for accused persons.[61] The question whether – and if so, to what extent – a right to remain silent may be derived from the status of a secondary party is subject to controversy.[62]

Following completion of the investigation proceedings, the prosecutor's office exam- 60
ines whether sufficient probability exists that the requirements for a corporate fine or confiscation have been met. If this is the case, any further proceedings may take one of two courses:

- the company may participate as a party to the confiscation proceedings or a secondary 61
  party in a public trial (main proceedings) against its employees (**joined proceedings** under §§ 424 sub. 1 and 444 sub. 1 sent. 1 StPO. In these cases, the company is essentially a 'co-indictee'[63] and must be summoned to attend the trial in accordance with § 444 sub. 2 sent. 1 StPO. By operation of § 444 sub. 2 sent. 2 StPO in conjunction with § 427 sub. 1 sent. 1 StPO, the company will be accorded the rights and powers of an accused person (*Beschuldigter*) or a defendant (*Angeklagter*), depending on the status of the proceedings. Accordingly, the company may, through its counsel, request that evidence be taken, summon witnesses and make statements in its defence.[64] The company is entitled to a legal adviser, cf. §§ 422 sub. 2 sent. 2, 428 StPO.[65]
- following completion of its investigations, the prosecutor's office may decide to conduct 62
  a separate procedure – often in writing and thus non-public – against the company (so-called objective proceedings). During such a trial, the prosecutor's office itself may issue, for example, a regulatory fine notice imposing a corporate fine (cf. § 30 sub. 4 sent. 1 OWiG).[66] Moreover, independent confiscation proceedings may be conducted against the company if the authorities are unable to identify a specific person to be prosecuted for the criminal offence. Again, these proceedings may be conducted in writing and thus with the public being excluded. However, it is mandatory for separate confiscation proceedings (cf. § 435 sub. 1 sent. 1 StPO) to be brought before a court; the prosecutor's office itself cannot issue a confiscation order under its own authority (in contrast to imposing a corporate fine).

Oftentimes, companies wish to avoid any involvement in public trials and are therefore 63
keen to avert the initiation of any such proceedings against themselves or their employees. In these cases, discussions with the prosecutor's office as well as choosing the right defence strategy can create opportunities to influence the outcome of the proceedings as early as during the preliminary investigations. In many instances, a solution can be found in conjunction with the prosecutor's office that results in the termination of the criminal proceedings against the company's employees, with a regulatory fine notice or a confiscation order only being issued in written proceedings (for greater details see → mn. 96 et seq., → mn. 98 et seqq.).

---

[60] MüKoStPO/Langlitz/Scheinfeld StPO § 426 mn. 2.

[61] MAH WirtschaftsStrafR/Kempf/Schilling/Oesterle § 10 mn. 175.

[62] NK-WSS/Gräfin von Galen/Schaefer OWiG § 30 mn. 80; Minoggio wistra 2003, 121; regarding the status of the debate as to whether the right to remain silent under ordinary law is also anchored in the constitutional principle of *nemo tenetur*: KK-OWiG/Rogall OWiG § 30 mn. 209.

[63] Cf. MüKoStPO/Langlitz/Scheinfeld StPO § 444 mn 2.

[64] Cf. MüKoStPO/Langlitz/Scheinfeld StPO § 427 mn 4.

[65] For further details, see Wessing/Dann Korruptionsverfahren/Wessing § 6 mn. 51.

[66] Krenberger/Krumm OWiG § 30 mn. 60 et seq.

II. Status and rights of companies as victims of a criminal offence

64 Likewise, if a company has suffered damage or loss as a consequence of criminal offences committed by its staff or third parties, this company has various options to become involved in the criminal proceedings. The nature of any potential participation depends on the offence committed and the interests of the company. In principle, there are three options to gain formal participation:

65 – Firstly, to the extent that claims for damages will be asserted, the aggrieved company may also assert these types of civil-law claims in criminal proceedings as part of adhesion proceedings (*Adhäsionsverfahren*) under § 403 sent. 1 StPO. In this case, the company will participate in a public trial against the accused employee in the capacity of an ancillary plaintiff (*Adhäsionskläger*). The company has the right to be represented by counsel and to file motions in court.

66 – Secondly, where specific criminal offences, which are listed exhaustively in the relevant statutory provision, have been committed, the company may join the criminal proceedings as a private accessory prosecutor (*Nebenkläger*). In proceedings in the area of economic criminal law, this would primarily be an option if industrial property rights, copyrights or trade secrets, as stated in § 395 sub. 1 no. 6 StPO, have been violated.[67] In contrast to the adhesion proceedings under §§ 403 et seq. StPO, private accessory prosecution (*Nebenklage*) is admissible independent of the assertion of any civil-law claims.[68] Private accessory prosecutors have the right to inspect files (§ 406e StPO). In addition, § 397 StPO bestows a wide range of procedural rights on private accessory prosecutors, such as the right to ask questions, to make statements or to move for the admission of evidence; they must be involved and heard to the same extent as the prosecution and, provided that the requirements of §§ 400 et seq. StPO are met, have the power to appeal.

67 – Thirdly, companies may participate in criminal proceedings as secondary aggrieved parties within the meaning of § 438 StPO if items are to be confiscated (§§ 73, 73b, 74–74b StGB) to which they hold *in rem* rights. The decision to permit this type of participation is made *ex officio*. The secondary aggrieved party (*Nebenbetroffene*) has the same rights as a party to the confiscation proceedings (§ 438 sub. 3 StPO in conjunction with § 427 sub. 1 StPO).

68 Even if a company does not seek any formal status as an ancillary plaintiff or a private accessory prosecutor, it has the right to information regarding the status of the proceedings by way of file access, provided it can demonstrate a legitimate interest (§ 406e StPO). Such a legitimate interest is deemed to exist if the file access serves to preserve civil-law interests warranting protection, such as the assertion of or the defence against civil-law claims.[69] File access is a reliable option for companies to obtain certainty with regard to the status and outcome of the investigations.[70] Furthermore, companies may also make statements, or propose that evidence be taken, to advance the progress of the investigations, even if they are not formally involved in the proceedings.

---

[67] See BeckOK StPO/Weiner, 49. Ed. 1.10.2023, § 395 mn 22; regarding companies' entitlement to private accessory prosecution: Bott/Kollhoff StraFo 2019, 413.

[68] Rieks NStZ 2019, 643 (644).

[69] Momsen/Grützner WirtschaftsSteuerStrafR-HdB/Klahold/Berndt § 10 mn. 22.

[70] Momsen/Grützner WirtschaftsSteuerStrafR-HdB/Klahold/Berndt § 10 mn. 25.

III. Status and rights of companies in other cases

Where the requirements for the imposition of a corporate fine or for confiscation against a company have not been met, and the company itself has not suffered any damage or loss through the offences, it will not be formally involved in the criminal proceedings as a party. **69**

That said, the company may nevertheless be the subject of coercive measures, such as searches. Legal remedies would be available against any such measures, as they have a direct impact on the company itself.[71] Moreover, the company may be the subject of the prosecution's requests for information and surrender of documents (for greater details, see → mn. 74 et seqq.). **70**

Particularly in cases where complex facts must be investigated and appraised or the prosecutor's office investigates several employees of a company, the company will often have a coordinating function (see → mn. 23 et seqq.). In fact, information requests along with the examination of witnesses or on-site visits may be coordinated via the company. In addition, the company can assist the employees concerned in gathering factual information required for their defence. **71**

Independent of the specific involvement through measures or requests from the prosecutor's office, the company may also actively obtain information regarding the status of the investigations and follow the proceedings. For instance, the company may apply for permission to inspect files as a third party within the meaning of § 475 StPO. For this purpose, a legitimate interest in the inspection of files must be demonstrated. Such an interest may result, for example, from the examination of recourse claims against employees or the wish to improve the in-house compliance system in line with insights gained during the investigations.[72] The company may also decide to issue a statement regarding the allegations against its employees, which may be expedient if the company wishes to protect its employees and formulate defensive positions that apply to all staff. **72**

However, given that it is not a party to the proceedings, the company would not benefit from any formal legal positions – such as protection from seizure and the right to remain silent – in these cases.[73] Likewise, the company would not be able to formally participate in a trial. **73**

IV. Excursus: surrender and information obligations/legal privilege in Germany

As the German understanding of legal privilege differs considerably from the Anglo-American concept, foreign companies in particular oftentimes misconceive the legal grounds and limits of freedom from seizure as well as the extent of surrender and information obligations in Germany in this area.[74] **74**

It should be noted that any documents in the possession of a company must usually be surrendered at the law enforcement authorities' request. These authorities have the power to secure any such documents. Even where these documents have been drawn up by lawyers or constitute correspondence with lawyers, they are, in many cases, not protected from seizure. More specifically, the following should be noted: **75**

---

[71] Cf. e.g. § 98 sub. 2 sent. 2 StPO; § 304 et seqq. StPO.

[72] BT-Drs. 14/1484, 26; Momsen/Grützner WirtschaftsSteuerStrafR-HdB/Klahold/Berndt § 10 mn. 25; compare also with further examples: MüKoStPO/Singelnstein StPO § 475 mn. 16.

[73] Cf. regarding protection from seizure: MüKoStPO/Hauschild § 97 mn 29.

[74] Regarding privileges under US law, see Nietsch CCZ 2019, 49 (50) et seq.

76 German criminal procedural law grants comparatively wide-ranging investigative powers to law enforcement authorities. For instance, at the authorities' request, companies are required to surrender evidence (§§ 95 et seq. StPO). Moreover, companies in their role as third parties (§ 103 StPO) may be subjected to searches, during which documents may be seized or secured as evidence (§ 94 StPO). Provided they are lawful, any requests for information and surrender of documents by the investigating authorities must be answered truthfully and within the time limits set by the prosecutor's offices.[75] Otherwise, the company would be liable to further searches; also, coercive measures may be taken against company executives.[76]

77 The investigative powers of the law enforcement authorities are limited by the so-called legal privilege: lawyers (except in-house counsel)[77] and defence counsel have the right to refuse testimony (§ 53 sub. 1 no. 2, 3 StPO). In addition, the prohibition of seizure extends to **defence records as well as any correspondence** between **lawyer and accused** (§§ 97 sub. 1, 148 StPO).

78 As companies are, technically, not accused persons under German law (see → mn. 5), this provision therefore needs to be construed accordingly to reflect the corporate context. It is arguably the prevailing legal view that any documents prepared by the defence lawyer may only be protected from seizure if the company advised by such lawyer could, based on objective criteria, possibly be involved as a secondary party or a party to confiscation proceedings and would therefore have a **status that is similar to that of an accused person**.[78] Whether this is in fact the case must be assessed on a case-by-case basis. As it stands, the requirements for the degree of suspicion are yet to be clarified[79]; however, the mere concern that court proceedings may be initiated does not suffice.[80] A status that is similar to that of an accused person will in any case be deemed to exist if this is insinuated in a file note concerning the verification of suspicions or in a search warrant.[81]

79 Subsequent problems may arise if documents – which may originate from in-house investigations – have to be surrendered to the law enforcement authorities. On the one hand, there is the possibility that any such documents will be disclosed to the other parties in civil proceedings by granting file access.[82] On the other hand, disclosure vis-à-vis the law enforcement authorities may be interpreted as a privilege waiver from a US perspective, foregoing the protection of confidentiality that would apply in the USA.[83] For this reason, companies should seek legal advice to ensure that any surrender of documents is fully compliant with the law and is given maximum protection.

V. Summary

80 Depending on a company's status, its rights and obligations during criminal proceedings may differ greatly. If the company has a quasi-accused status, its position during criminal proceedings is largely comparable to that of an accused person. It would therefore have comprehensive rights to information and protection but would, on the other

[75] Regarding the handling of any such requests: Welke/Wenzel BB 2021, 1737 et seq.
[76] Cf. § 95 sub. 2 StPO; LG Limburg 18.02. 2019 – 1 Qs 5/19, NZWiSt 2019, 158.
[77] MüKoStPO/Hauschild § 97 mn. 39.
[78] Cf. MüKoStPO/Hauschild § 97 mn. 29.
[79] MAH WirtschaftsStrafR/Kempf/Schilling/Oesterle § 10 mn. 179.
[80] BVerfG 27.6.2018 – 2 BvR 1405/17, 2 BvR 1780/17, NJW 2018, 2385 (2390) mn. 95; KK-StPO/Greven StPO § 97 mn. 14b.
[81] MAH WirtschaftsStrafR/Kempf/Schilling/Oesterle § 10 mn. 175.
[82] Knauer NStZ 2020, 441 (446).
[83] On this issue see Nietsch CCZ 2019, 49 (53) et seq.

hand, be formally involved as a party to the criminal proceedings and might thus be required to participate in a public trial. That said, companies as the aggrieved party also have wide-ranging participatory rights. What is more, irrespective of any formal status as a secondary party or aggrieved party, companies may be actively involved by requesting file access, making statements and assuming coordinating tasks.

D. Strategies of corporate defence

In light of the above, companies will generally have an interest in being actively **81**
involved in criminal proceedings that are directed against their executive bodies or employees or – by derivation – against themselves. For this purpose, companies must develop a strategy to handle the investigations.

Obviously, this strategy will largely depend on the specific circumstances, such as the **82**
nature of the allegations, the company's specific interests or the attitude of its contacts at the relevant authorities. 'Kit-set' solutions are therefore out of the question. While an exhaustive presentation of all conceivable defence strategies is beyond the scope of this chapter, the following provides a rough overview of the fundamental approaches and the key decision parameters when devising a corporate defence strategy.

I. Starting point: determination of the facts

At the commencement of investigations, the corporate defender must, first of all, con- **83**
duct a strategic analysis to ascertain the risk situation of the company he or she advises.[84] This requires, first and foremost, identifying the company's interests. Only once the interests of the company as well as the potential interests of other parties involved have been defined, may a strategy be devised that would afford the greatest chances of success in terms of achieving the desired goal.[85]

To be able to conduct this analysis, it is, first of all, necessary to understand the facts **84**
of the case. This must not be confused with the commonly propagated performance of a so-called internal investigation during which the company – mostly in light of corporate-law considerations – conducts its own complete investigation of the facts in parallel with the official investigations.[86] Instead, the material objective elements of a problematic set of facts must, first of all, be recognised in order to assess both the risk situation and the available options for action.[87]

Against this background, the assessment of the facts includes the alleged facts, the per- **85**
sons and periods potentially involved as well as any evidence available to prove this set of circumstances. Furthermore, an initial analysis of the legal situation should be performed (is the alleged conduct, if it happened as alleged and this can be proven, punishable?).

Based on such an assessment of the facts, it must then be determined which addi- **86**
tional information would be required for the proper defence (or in view of other legal obligations) and in which form such information can be gathered. Whenever new infor-

---

84 MAH WirtschaftsStrafR/Minoggio § 8 mn. 127.
85 Trüg NZWiSt 2022, 106 (108); Kämpfer/Travers/Schwerdtfeger NZG 2020, 848 (850 et seq.).
86 Cf. Groß/Wenzl DB 2017, 97; Ballo NZWiSt 2013, 46 et seq.; Park Durchsuchung mn. 1073.
87 Bachmann ZHR 180 (2016), 563 et seqq.; Trüg NZWiSt 2022, 106 (111).

mation regarding the set of facts has been obtained, the strategy must be reviewed and, if required, adjusted.

87 Moreover, it is vital to ensure that any legal breaches that may become apparent as part of the analysis of the facts are immediately and effectively stopped (so-called stop-the-breach) with a view to both the present and the future, to avoid any further risk exposure of the parties involved.[88]

II. Determination of the company's interests

88 Subsequently, the defence team must explore – generally in close consultation with company representatives – which positions the company considers particularly important in its specific situation.[89] This may differ greatly from company to company and industry to industry. Companies operating on the capital market, for instance, may be keen to arrive at an understanding with the investigating authorities as soon as possible in order to safeguard their reputation, even if their chances of putting up a successful defence are very good. Other companies (for example in the B2B sector) are less concerned with public opinion but may be very eager to avoid an entry in the central business or competition register if public contracts account for a large share of their order volume. Some companies may be highly cost-sensitive or place great stock on sanctioning delinquent staff to the greatest extent possible in the sense of a zero-tolerance policy. Global companies would have to consider the spillover effect on other countries (if the breach is not restricted to Germany, for example). When weighing up the various parameters to be taken into consideration when defining a company's interests, the criteria discussed under → mn. 23 et seqq. should always be kept in mind: reputation/public image, costs, working atmosphere, recourse claims, potential non-criminal consequences and sanctions, statutory obligations to investigate, furnish information and surrender documents, prevention of breaches/follow-on proceedings in both the present and the future, as well as personnel decisions.

89 Also, during the analysis it must be ensured that the interests of the company management are not commingled with the interests of the company. Particularly in cases where allegations are (also) being levelled against the company management, precautions must be taken to make sure that the company's interests can be properly ascertained, if necessary, by involving someone who is not subject to any allegations.[90]

III. Identification of possible defence approaches

90 Along with the facts of the matter and the company's interests, the defence team must also consider the chances of success in light of the situation as it presents itself in order to determine the best possible approach to the defence. Again, it is obvious that the possible defence approaches are ultimately as diverse as the potential facts and company interests

---

[88] Cf. Trüg NZWiSt 2022, 106 (115); regarding the establishment of a 'criminal-law-proof organisational structure', see BeckRA-HdB/Knigge/Junker/Pischelt/Reinhart § 49 mn. 89.

[89] Trüg NZWiSt 2022, 106 (108) on the determination of a company's interests during criminal proceedings.

[90] Trüg NZWiSt 2022, 106 (109); MAH WirtschaftsStrafR/Minoggio § 8 mn. 126.

involved. However, if some schematisations were required, three recurring basic case scenarios[91] may be identified:

1. Case scenario 1: defence at the factual level

First of all, cases are conceivable where a breach – assuming it was in fact committed – would constitute a criminal offence or a regulatory offence but the facts of the matter, as ascertained by the investigating authorities, appear to be contestable. This may be the case if, in fact, no breach was committed and the investigating authorities are operating on the basis of incorrect assumptions regarding the actual facts. It may also be the case if there are compelling indications that the authorities are unable to prove that any such breach has been committed, for example because all the evidence is located abroad. **91**

In these cases, the defence can concentrate primarily on the factual level, clarifying the individual elements of the factual situation or pointing out any gaps in the evidentiary reasoning if applicable. However, within the corporate context, this type of defence often leads to further problems that require clarification, such as the question to what extent the company itself must investigate the facts or the scope of its obligations to furnish information and surrender documents.[92] As a rule, this requires a holistic view that includes all these aspects in its analysis. **92**

Various case scenarios, where the company is a party to confiscation proceedings, constitute a special form of defence. As confiscation is precluded in cases where a settlement has been reached with the victim of a criminal offence or where any profits derived from the offending have been repaid,[93] the company may still take action – such as repayment – during the investigations to ensure that the prerequisites for its involvement in the criminal proceedings cease to apply permanently. **93**

2. Case scenario 2: defence at the level of the legal situation

Furthermore, against the backdrop of an ever more complex law, the number of cases where the facts have been resolved (or can readily be clarified) but where the legal situation is unclear or contentious is increasing. **94**

For instance, an authority may regard a certain conduct as a punishable violation of fair competition whereas the company is operating under the assumption that the very same conduct constitutes permissible competitive behaviour. In these cases, the defence would focus on the level of substantive law. It should also be noted that such case scenarios oftentimes lend themselves to a consensual termination of the proceedings, as neither party wishes to run the risk of losing a public trial.[94] **95**

3. Case scenario 3: defence at the level of sentencing/admission to offence

Lastly, there are cases where the breach can (presumably) be proven and would, from all angles, constitute a prosecutable regulatory or criminal offence. In all of these cases, **96**

---

91 However, in complex white-collar crime cases in particular, a mixed scenario will generally present itself, so that the aforementioned defence approaches would not be applicable in their pure form but would rather serve as guidance for the defence focus.

92 MAH WirtschaftsStrafR/Minoggio § 8 mn. 129 refers to an impending 'investigative frenzy' that may also harm the company.

93 → mn. 13 et seqq.

94 Regarding termination subject to the imposition of conditions as a possible solution for cases where the legal situation is unclear, see, e.g., LG Bonn 28.2.2001 – 27 AR 2/01, NStZ 2001, 375.

the defence would primarily focus on the 'measure of punishment' (i.e. the amount of a corporate fine and the limitation of its consequences for both the company and its staff). In this context, the company and its defence team are in a position to endeavour – for example through comprehensive internal investigations or the willingness to cooperate in other ways or through reparations – that an appropriate result be achieved.[95]

97 However, whenever an internal investigation is carried out against this background and its results are passed on to the authorities, it must be ensured that this approach is always coordinated with the investigating authorities and that the comprehensive investigation also includes any incriminating facts and circumstances to avoid the impression that the company influences witnesses or intends to 'fabricate' its own set of facts. After all, if the promise of cooperation or investigation by a company proves to be mere lip service, this may lead to greater irritation on the part of the investigating authorities than if the company had not promised any cooperation in the first place. Again, the central issue is fair and reliable communication, which is strongly recommended in any case, irrespective of the choice of defence strategy.[96]

IV. Determination of a defence strategy

98 Once the above parameters – facts of the case, company's interests, possible defence approaches – have been analysed, the best defence strategy and the objective of the defence can be determined on this basis. This strategy may range from complete and over-compliant cooperation with the investigating authorities (particularly in case scenario 3 → mn. 97 et seq.) to the refusal of any kind of cooperation with the investigating authorities (particularly in case scenario 1 → mn. 92 et seqq.).[97]

99 In these cases, the company's interests must be conflated with the company's obligations (e.g. its legal obligations to investigate and to rectify) along with an analysis of the risk situation and possible defence approaches to develop a sensible strategy. The company must comply with its legal obligations in any case, otherwise new risks would arise in the future. While certain defence approaches may be likely to lead to success (e.g. flat-out denial) but conflict with the company's best interests (e.g. the wish for clarification/resolution), the defence team must weigh up their pros and cons.

100 In any case, the determination of a defence strategy always requires some predictions: what is the likelihood that the allegations can be sufficiently proven if the company does not cooperate? What will the effect be if the company cooperates to a limited or unlimited extent? What effect would a difference in behaviour have on any fine that may be imposed? Which behaviour should be chosen in order to avert any consequences outside criminal law? How can coercive measures be avoided to the greatest extent possible? What impact does the conduct of the defence have on the company's reputation?[98]

101 Moreover, these predictions must not ignore the beliefs and preferences of the investigating authorities: for instance, on the authorities' side, a prosecutor may be in charge of the case who, as a matter of principle, rejects the company's own contributions to clarifica-

---

[95] Trüg NZWiSt 2022, 106 (110) calls this a 'tiered incentive system' to avoid the full measure of sanctioning.

[96] Trüg NZWiSt 2022, 106 (109).

[97] p. 67 (82); Pörtge CCZ 2020, 65 (67 et seq.); regarding the conflicting goals of corporate defence, see Kämpfer/Travers/Schwerdtfeger NZG 2020, 848 (854 et seq.).

[98] FS Schiller/Hart-König p. 281 (308 et seq.), with further comments concerning a company's reputation.

tion and resolution and only ever wants to question witnesses himself.[99] In contrast, other prosecutors hold out the prospect of a significant reduction in sanctions or practicable all-encompassing solutions in return for cooperation during the investigations. Open, fair and early communication is required to understand the beliefs and perceptions of the investigating authorities. In this context, it is of paramount importance that nothing is promised to the investigating authorities that cannot (or should not) be delivered.[100]

In any case, the company's interests and the defence approach must always be assessed **102**
in light of the realities. For instance, if the evidence against the company is overwhelming, it may be unrealistic to categorically deny all allegations and thereby try to avoid any sanctions whatsoever. Accordingly, the corporate defender will have to reconcile all available information in such a manner that the defence strategy chosen would, realistically, be able to achieve the desired defence objective. The potential defence objectives may range from the discontinuation of the investigations through to comprehensive solutions (e.g. termination of the proceedings against employees while at the same time imposing a corporate fine on the company) up to the most lenient sentence possible for both the company and its employees.[101]

It should also be noted that, once a fundamental defence strategy or a fundamental **103**
defence style has been defined, it does not need to be strictly adhered to in its purest form. Instead, the defence lawyer generally needs to reconcile any conflicting goals in order to achieve a good balance.[102] While it may make sense to surrender documents to avert any imminent search of the company premises, even if the company denies any allegations and therefore, in principle, 'does not cooperate', occasionally the corporate defender will have to insist that the investigating authorities do not overstep legal boundaries, full cooperation notwithstanding. An example of this approach would be restricting seizure to only those documents that are relevant to the proceedings.[103]

However, irrespective of these situational nuances, it should be noted that the selection **104**
of a cooperative defence style will (almost always) be the right choice from the perspective of a corporate defender. That said, a cooperative attitude must not be confused with the total relinquishment of one's own positions. Quite commonly, the expectation of the investigating authorities in these cases is that the commission of a legal breach is not disputed, neither from a factual nor a legal perspective.[104] It is then up to the defence to communicate to the authorities that, in particular, the exchange of legal arguments does not equate to a confrontational defence strategy but is readily compatible with an otherwise cooperative stance.

V. Approach to employees

In this context, the company must pay particular attention to how it treats its employ- **105**
ees, with the correct approach depending on the role of the specific employees and the defence strategy chosen.

---

[99] MAH WirtschaftsStrafR/Minoggio § 8 mn. 135.
[100] Groß/Wenzl DB 02/2017, 97 (98).
[101] Trüg NZWiSt 2022, 106 (109).
[102] FS Feigen/Groß p. 67 (82); Dannecker/Meyer/Groß p. 4 et seq.; see also Trüg NStZ 2020, 130 et seq.
[103] FS Feigen/Groß p. 67 (82); Dannecker/Meyer/Groß p. 4 et seq.; see also Trüg NStZ 2020, 130 et seq.
[104] Dannecker/Meyer/Groß p. 4 et seq.

1. Accused employees

106 First of all, the company must contemplate how to treat **accused employees**. Often companies wish to support these employees to a certain degree, particularly if the allegations are unfounded or the investigations are also directed against the company. In these cases, the coordination of the defence approach through the cooperation between the corporate defender and the defence lawyers of the accused employees, the development of a joint line of defence and the avoidance of any inconsistencies in the conduct of the defence always serve as a solid base for the best possible defence (collaborative defence).[105] More specifically, a collaborative defence may counter any attempt by the investigating authorities to pit the individual persons involved against each other.[106] It also enables the defence team to share the work load whenever complex sets of circumstances and legal matters need to be processed during large-scale white-collar crime proceedings.[107] What is more, the large number of persons involved in these types of proceedings often require enormous logistical effort. The requisite organisational and content-related coordination of the defence is the responsibility of the company's defence counsel.[108]

107 In these cases, it is also important that the company refrains from communicating directly with the employees involved, but solely via the respective lawyers, to avoid any faux pas, such as giving rise to the impression on the part of the investigating authorities that the employees are being influenced. Furthermore, these cases also require an examination as to whether – despite the common line of defence – the company should take measures outside criminal law, such as stipulating repayment provisos if bonuses, etc. continue to be paid.

108 In other cases, it may be in line with the company's interests to deliberately distance itself from the accused employees in order to be able to conduct a successful purge[109] (*Selbstreinigung*) and minimize reputational risks.[110] In such cases, there would be no coordination with the defence. Also, the company may take measures against the relevant employees under employment law. However, in order to arrive at an informed decision, the company would have to consider the potential consequences that distancing itself from its employees could have on the further course of the criminal proceedings: would this result in some employees rejecting an all-encompassing solution and the proceedings then being dragged out, which would attract a great deal of publicity?[111]

109 Problems may also arise if the company is dependent on the accused employees for its investigation of the facts. Only where very strict requirements are met will information obtained through interviews with employees be protected from seizure by the investigating authorities.[112] In addition, conflicts between the company's interest in a clarification of the facts and the relevant employee's procedural right to remain silent may arise in these cases. While this procedural right, due to its very nature, does not apply within the

---

[105] Wessing/Dann Korruptionsverfahren/Wessing § 6 mn. 53; regarding terminology also see Richter II NJW 1993, 2152 et seq.

[106] Wessing/Dann Korruptionsverfahren/Wessing § 6 mn. 52.

[107] Wessing/Dann Korruptionsverfahren/Wessing § 6 mn. 56.

[108] Momsen/Grützner WirtschaftsSteuerStrafR-HdB/Klahold/Berndt § 10 mn. 61.

[109] In some areas of German regulatory or criminal law, a company has the chance to reduce the penalty by going through a successful purge, which most often also includes to distance itself from or to release employees who have committed crimes.

[110] Cf. Trüg NStZ 2020, 130 (132).

[111] Cf. MAH WirtschaftsStrafR/Minoggio § 8 mn. 143.

[112] Cf. Trüg NZWiSt 2022, 106 (112); BVerfG NJW 2018, 2385 et seq.; Winkler StraFo 2018, 464 et seq.; see also → mn. 75 et seqq.

relationship between employer and employee[113], it would de facto be subverted if employees were required to incriminate themselves during internal interviews, thus running the risk of being reported to the investigating authorities. Against this background, it is highly contentious whether the company would be subject to a disclosure obligation under employment law during pending criminal proceedings against an employee and, if so, whether evidence obtained in this manner would actually be inadmissible in a criminal court.[114] Another aspect that needs to be taken into consideration is the possibility that prosecutor's offices may take a critical view of employees being questioned by their employer or being involved in a clarification of the facts, as they may be unduly influenced by the respective company.[115]

Whenever a company intends to approach an employee for the purpose of clarifying 110
the facts, the employee's defence lawyer or legal adviser must always be involved. In addition, prior consultation with the prosecutor's office is also required. It is arguably best practice to advise employees as to their potential right to remain silent in analogy with §§ 53 and 55 StPO prior to questioning them.

2. Potential witnesses

Likewise, the aforementioned problems also arise when approaching employees who 111
may have been **witnesses** to the offences, as this may lead to self-incrimination by at-risk witnesses on the one hand and unwanted interference with the course of the prosecution's investigations on the other. Again, it is necessary to involve a representative of the witnesses, to advise any witnesses regarding their rights and to consult the prosecutor's office beforehand.

3. Other employees

However, even if employees are neither accused nor witnesses to the criminal offences 112
in question, a company would be well advised to judiciously communicate the status and progress of the criminal proceedings to its staff, since transparent communication may pre-empt uncertainties, for example in the aftermath of a search, and ensure that staff are able to arrive at a correct understanding of the company's position. This may also counter any deterioration of the morale within the company. Moreover, it would avoid creating the impression within the staff that criminal offences are not taken seriously ('tone from the top').[116] Particularly in cases where follow-up measures are required in response to criminal proceedings (increased monitoring, review of corporate processes, additional compliance measures), these measures must be communicated throughout the company to ensure their effective implementation.[117]

More specifically, the company must communicate the stance it has adopted vis-à-vis 113
the accused employees as carefully as possible, given that other staff will be very mindful

---

[113] Cf. Schmitt/Köhler/Schmitt StPO § 136 mn. 7a; Raum StraFo 2012, 395 (398); LG Hamburg 12.06.1984 – RReg. 4 St 240/83, MDR 1984, 867; LAG Baden-Württemberg 21.1.1962 – 4 Sa 81/61, DB 1963, 1055; OLG Karlsruhe 6.9.1988 – 1 Ss 68/88, NStZ 1989, 287; Rudkowski NZA 2011, 612 (613). Regarding the inadmissibility of unlawfully obtained evidence: Greco/Caracas NStZ 2015, 7 (8 et seq.); Greeve StraFo 2013, 89 (94).

[114] LG Hamburg 12.6.1984 – RReg. 4 St 240/83, MDR 1984, 867; LAG Baden-Württemberg 21.1.1962 – 4 Sa 81/61, DB 1963, 1055; OLG Karlsruhe 6.9.1988 – 1 Ss 68/88, NStZ 1989, 287; Rudkowski NZA 2011, 612 (613).

[115] MAH WirtschaftsStrafR/Minoggio § 8 mn. 142.

[116] MüKoGmbHG/Fleischer GmbHG § 43 mn. 191; Moosmayer Compliance mn. 144 et seq.

[117] Moosmayer Compliance mn. 5, mn. 348.

of its treatment of these employees. This is a challenging balancing act. On the one hand, companies that distance themselves from an accused employee may be criticised for having 'abandoned' this employee. It is therefore important to proceed with maximum openness and transparency. Only when the reasons why some of their colleagues have been dismissed have been clearly communicated to the remaining staff can any potential massive demotivation throughout the workforce be avoided over the medium term. On the other hand, companies that retain an accused employee may be criticised for being too lenient.[118]

VI. Summary

114 The choice of the right defence strategy depends on various parameters and must be determined on a case-by-case basis. If and when required, the chosen strategy may need to be adjusted over the course of the proceedings whenever new information comes to light. To arrive at a suitable defence strategy, all facts must be assessed, the company's interests must be defined and all possible defence approaches must be identified. Keeping close contact with the investigating authorities will be necessary in order to be able to take their positions and beliefs into consideration throughout the entire decision-making process.

115 As a rule, the company should therefore address both the risks and any potential (including non-criminal) consequences of criminal proceedings in order to be able to avert any negative consequences early on and in the best possible manner. Even if the company itself is not directly affected by the criminal proceedings, it will often be advisable to actively follow the proceedings and the employees concerned and to work towards a speedy and efficient resolution.

[118] Regarding the entire issue: FS Feigen/Groß p. 67 (81); MAH WirtschaftsStrafR/Wessing § 12 mn. 177.

CHAPTER 3
FUNDAMENTALS OF CRIMINAL PROCEEDINGS

Table of contents

A. Introduction 31
B. The parties to criminal proceedings 33
C. Organisation and jurisdiction of criminal courts 34
  I. German court system 34
  II. Types of courts with original jurisdiction 35
    1. Original subject-matter jurisdiction 35
    2. Venue 36
    3. Schedule of responsibilities 36
D. Sequence of criminal proceedings 37
  I. Preliminary investigation 37
    1. Commencement of preliminary investigation 37
    2. Rights and obligations of the parties involved 38
    3. Law of evidence 39
    4. Coercive measures 40
    5. Legal remedies 41
    6. Completion of preliminary investigation 41
      a) Indictment 41
      b) Termination pursuant to § 170 sub. 2 StPO 42
      c) Termination for discretionary reasons 43
        aa) Termination pursuant to § 153 StPO 43
        bb) Termination pursuant to § 153a StPO 44
      d) Other options for termination 44
  II. Interlocutory proceedings 45
  III. Trial 45
    1. Preparation of the main hearing 46
    2. Chronology of the main hearing 46
    3. Content of judgment 49
    4. Conclusion of the trial 50
  IV. Legal remedies 50
    1. Complaint 51
    2. Appeal on points of fact and law 52
    3. Appeal on points of law 52
E. Execution proceedings 53
  I. Execution of the sentence 54
  II. Costs of the proceedings 54
  III. Compensation 55

A. Introduction

The aim of the German system of criminal proceedings is to achieve legal peace by affirming and enforcing the state's right to impose punishment should this right arise in individual cases.[1] The state's right to impose punishment is a manifestation of the state's 1

[1] Schmitt/Köhler/Schmitt StPO Einleitung mn. 2, 4.

monopoly on the use of force, and serves to bolster the right of access to justice for anyone harmed by a criminal offence.[2] The state is under an obligation to investigate potential criminal offences and, where applicable, to pursue and punish the perpetrator. Criminal proceedings therefore encompass both the investigation of potentially punishable sets of facts by the law enforcement authorities as well as the entire course of the court proceedings, including the execution of the sentence.[3]

2 Criminal proceedings are always based on a substantive legal relationship that forms the subject matter of a decision. Substantive criminal law determines what specific conduct fulfils all the constituent elements of a penal provision, and under which circumstances a penalty should be imposed, and to what extent.[4] The core provisions of German criminal law are, first and foremost, compiled in the special part of the Criminal Code (*Strafgesetzbuch*, StGB), such as embezzlement in § 266 StGB and money laundering in § 261 StGB. There are, however, a number of additional laws that contain criminal provisions. These laws are often referred to as supplementary penal provisions and include, for example, tax evasion under § 370 AO.

3 Criminal proceedings are governed by detailed statutory provisions, with the Code of Criminal Procedure (*Strafprozessordnung*, StPO) and the Courts Constitution Act (*Gerichtsverfassungsgesetz*, GVG) being the most important legal sources. The StPO contains, inter alia, rules for the entire investigation, the court proceedings in the first instance, any appeal proceedings, confiscation proceedings, execution of the sentence, as well as the costs of the criminal proceedings. The provisions of the StPO assign comprehensive rights and obligations to the parties involved in criminal proceedings. The GVG complements the StPO with general procedural rules that apply before the ordinary courts, such as the courts' subject matter jurisdiction. Moreover, the StGB and the German Basic Law (*Grundgesetz*, GG) also contain important provisions concerning criminal proceedings. The general part of the StGB stipulates rules regarding the time-barring by limitation and the specific penalties. The Basic Law sets the boundaries for investigative measures in criminal proceedings and protects the person that is being investigated through the fundamental rights set forth in its articles.

4 This chapter will outline the fundamentals of criminal proceedings in Germany, highlighting the special aspects that apply to companies as potential secondary parties to these proceedings whenever this is of particular relevance. First of all, we will describe the parties to criminal proceedings (→ mn. 6 et seqq.) as well as the organisation and competencies of the various courts (→ mn. 11 et seqq.). This will be followed by an overview of the course that criminal proceedings take (→ mn. 24 et seqq.), explaining the principal fundamentals of the investigations, the trial and the appeal proceedings. The discussion will close with a brief overview of the execution proceedings.

5 The role of the injured party in the proceedings (§ 374 to 406l StPO) as well as the security proceedings under §§ 423 et seq. StPO and the summary proceedings under §§ 417 et seq. StPO, both of which are special forms of proceedings, are not explained in greater detail in this chapter.

[2] MüKoStPO/Kudlich StPO Einleitung mn. 1.
[3] Schmitt/Köhler/Schmitt StPO Einleitung mn. 58, 59.
[4] MüKoStPO/Kudlich StPO Einleitung mn. 3.

B. The parties to criminal proceedings

The main parties in German criminal proceedings are the accused person and his defence counsel on the one hand and the prosecutor's office on the other.[5] In addition, there may also be secondary parties who participate in the proceedings either in the public interest or to avert potential legal prejudice for themselves. This may include the injured party, fiscal authorities in criminal tax proceedings as well as secondary parties to confiscation proceedings or secondary parties to regulatory fine proceedings, whose involvement is limited to specific parts or decisions within the proceedings.[6] Furthermore, witnesses, interpreters and experts, for example, play an indirect role. **6**

The accused (*Beschuldigter*) is the person charged with a criminal offence.[7] Depending on the stage of the proceedings, the accused is also referred to as the indicted accused (*Angeschuldigter*) or the defendant (*Angeklagter*), § 157 StPO. Only natural persons can be the accused in German criminal proceedings. A natural person is a human being in his or her capacity as a legal subject, i.e. an entity capable of having rights and obligations.[8] **7**

Being legal persons and associations of persons, companies cannot be charged with a criminal offence in Germany. However, they can be secondary parties to the proceedings, which gives them a position that is similar to that of an accused person.[9] The involvement as a secondary party can be triggered by two different sets of circumstances: as a result of impending confiscation (§ 424 StPO) or as a result of an impending fine (§ 444 StPO). These situations often arise in the area of economic criminal law when employees or executive bodies of a company are the accused in criminal proceedings and the company faces confiscation or a fine as a consequence of these criminal offences. **8**

The defence counsel represents the interests of the accused person in criminal proceedings and is therefore under an obligation to highlight any and all circumstances or legal factors in the accused person's favour.[10] Defence counsels are usually lawyers, § 138 sub. 1 StPO. The accused person can choose to be represented by defence counsel at any stage of the proceedings (§ 137 sub. 1 StPO, counsel of one's own choice). In cases of mandatory defence under §§ 140 and 141 StPO, representation by defence counsel is prescribed by law. Mandatory defence is required, for example, when the accused person is charged with criminal offences that carry a minimum term of imprisonment of one year or for cases that are tried, in the first instance, before a higher regional court (*Oberlandesgericht*), regional court (*Landgericht*) or a court that includes lay judges (*Schöffengericht*), § 141 sub. 2 no. 1 and 2 StPO. Secondary parties to the proceedings also have the right to be represented by a lawyer at every stage of the proceedings (§ 428 sub. 1 sent. 1 StPO, § 444 sub. 2 sent. 2 in conjunction with § 428 sub. 1 sent. 1 StPO). Moreover, where the factual and legal situation is particularly difficult, representation by a lawyer may be necessary, and this lawyer will then be appointed by the court *ex officio* (§ 428 sub. 2 StPO, § 444 sub. 2 sent. 2 in conjunction with § 428 sub. 2 StPO). **9**

The prosecutor's office is the institution that conducts the proceedings against the accused person and, with the assistance of other law enforcement authorities, investigates the set of facts (§§ 160 sub. 1 and 161 sub. 1 StPO). At the end of the investigation, the prosecutor's office either indicts the accused person or terminates the proceedings. This also **10**

---

[5] Schmitt/Köhler/Schmitt StPO Einleitung mn. 72.
[6] Schmitt/Köhler/Schmitt StPO Einleitung mn. 73.
[7] MüKoStPO/Kudlich StPO Einleitung mn. 280.
[8] Grüneberg/Ellenberger BGB § 1 mn. 1.
[9] BVerfG 27.6.2018 – 2 BvR 1405/17, 2 BvR 1780/17, NJW 2018, 2385.
[10] BGH 17.9.1964 – III ZR 2015/63, NJW 1964, 2402.

follows from the principle of *ex officio* prosecution (so-called principle of legality), which prescribes that the prosecutor's office is both entitled and obligated to step in and investigate all prosecutable criminal offences in order to bring public charges, provided that sufficient factual indications exist that a criminal offence has been committed. During the trial, the prosecutor's office presents the case until the court has passed its judgment. Throughout the entire proceedings, the prosecutor's office is the representative of the public's interest in the prosecution of criminal offences.[11] Each individual investigation has a prosecutor assigned to it, who is responsible for conducting the proceedings. Prosecutor's offices are usually divided into several divisions; if and when required, they form special prosecutor's offices for particular focus areas, such as commercial criminal matters.

C. Organisation and jurisdiction of criminal courts

11 In Germany, the local courts (judges sitting alone and benches including lay judges), the regional courts (criminal panels as well as criminal chambers for particularly serious crimes) and the higher regional courts (criminal senates) make up the criminal court system.

12 Criminal courts that consist of the requisite number of professional judges and, where applicable, honorary lay judges (*Schöffen*) conduct the trial and, at the end of the proceedings, pronounce their judgment. Judges arrive at their decision independently (Art. 97 GG). If a court consists of several judges, one of them is designated the presiding judge. The presiding judge has the power to direct the formal course of the proceedings; this power is further fleshed out in various individual provisions. More specifically, the presiding judge opens and closes the proceedings, takes measures to adjourn the hearing, presides over the taking of evidence and the examination of witnesses and, in doing so, does not require the consent of the other judges. Instead, the presiding judge takes his measures as of right, unless they touch directly on the verdict.[12]

13 The jurisdiction and organisation of the criminal courts is subject to comprehensive statutory provisions.

I. German court system

14 Apart from the constitutional jurisdiction, independent courts of five non-constitutional subject areas exist in Germany: the ordinary courts (*ordentliches Gericht*), the labour courts (*Arbeitsgericht*), the administrative courts (*Verwaltungsgericht*), the fiscal courts (*Finanzgericht*) and the social security courts (*Sozialgericht*) (Art. 95 para. 1 GG). The ordinary courts have jurisdiction in criminal matters, § 13 GVG. The local courts (*Amtsgericht*), regional courts (*Landgericht*), higher regional courts (*Oberlandesgericht*) and the Federal Court of Justice (*Bundesgerichtshof*, BGH) exercise the judicial authority of the ordinary courts, § 12 GVG. The Federal Court of Justice is the highest of the courts of ordinary jurisdiction, Art. 95 para. 1 GG. In the hierarchy of the ordinary courts, the higher regional courts are directly subordinated to the Federal Court of Justice. Each German *Land* has at least one higher regional court, with the total number of higher

---

[11] Schmitt/Köhler/Schmitt StPO Einleitung mn. 87.
[12] Schmitt/Köhler/Schmitt StPO § 238 mn. 3, 4 et seqq.

regional courts in Germany being 24. Several regional court districts exist within the judicial district of each higher regional court. Most regional courts are located in the major cities of the respective *Land*. Every regional court district, in turn, consists of several local court districts.

II. Types of courts with original jurisdiction

A distinction is made between subject-matter jurisdiction (*ratione materiae*) and venue (*ratione loci*). Subject-matter jurisdiction relates to the question which judicial body at which court has original jurisdiction and authority to hear a particular criminal case. Potential judicial bodies at the local court are judges sitting alone and benches that include lay judges. The judicial bodies at the regional courts of original jurisdiction are the major criminal panels (*große Strafkammern*) and the criminal chambers for particularly serious crimes (*Schwurgerichte*). The judicial body at higher regional courts is the *Strafsenat* (criminal senate). Venue is the legally proper place where a case should be heard. 15

1. Original subject-matter jurisdiction

As a rule, the local court has jurisdiction if, in the specific case, the imposition of a fine or a sentence of imprisonment of no more than four years is to be expected (§ 24 sub. 1 no. 2 GVG) and neither the regional court nor the higher regional court has special jurisdiction (§ 24 sub. 1 no. 1 GVG), and unless the prosecutor's office presses charges before the regional court because of the elevated degree of vulnerability of the victim of the criminal offence or the particular significance or scale of the case (§ 24 sub. 1 no. 3 GVG). To this extent, the prosecutor's office has some discretionary scope within which to decide whether or not to bring public charges at the end of its investigation. 16

As a judicial body, criminal judges (*Strafrichter*) (sitting alone) at the local court have jurisdiction for misdemeanours (*Vergehen*) prosecuted by way of private criminal action, or if a term of imprisonment of no more than two years is to be expected (§ 25 GVG). Misdemeanours are unlawful acts for which the regular minimum punishment laid down by law is a fine or less than one year's imprisonment (§ 12 sub. 2 StGB). Crimes (*Verbrechen*) are all unlawful acts for which the regular minimum punishment laid down by law is imprisonment for a term of no less than one year (§ 12 sub. 1 StGB). Misdemeanours that can be prosecuted by way of private action are listed exhaustively in § 374 sub. 1 StPO; these offences are of limited relevance in the area of economic criminal law and include, for example, trespass (§ 123 StGB) and bodily harm (§ 223 StGB). The criminal judge possesses the full punitive power of the local court and can therefore impose imprisonment of up to four years. This is based on the consideration that aspects may emerge over the course of the trial that necessitate the imposition of a higher sentence than was originally expected at the time when the public charges were brought. In this way, the need for conducting the entire trial once again before a higher court can be averted. The judicial body that is made up by one criminal judge sitting alone consists in a professional judge. 17

The bench that includes lay judges is the next higher judicial body after the criminal judge sitting alone and has jurisdiction when the criminal matter falls under the jurisdiction of the local courts but is not within the competence of a criminal judge sitting alone (§ 28 GVG). Accordingly, the bench that includes lay judges has jurisdiction if the criminal matter adjudicated is a crime or a misdemeanour that would likely attract imprisonment of more than two years. This specific judicial body always consists in one professional judge and two lay judges, § 29 sub. 1 GVG. Upon the application of the prosecutor's office, 18 the bench that includes lay judges can be made up of two professional judges and two lay judges whenever this proves necessary in view of the scope of the criminal matter (§ 29 sub. 2 GVG). Lay judges are honorary judges, i.e. they have no legal training and are not qualified to hold judicial office in a professional capacity (§ 31 GVG). They fully participate in the main hearing and have the same voting rights as professional judges, § 30 sub. 1 GVG. However, they take no part in any decisions made outside the courtroom, § 30 sub. 2 GVG.

19 The major criminal panels (*große Strafkammern*) at the regional courts, as adjudicating bodies of first instance, have jurisdiction over all serious criminal offences (crimes) that do not fall under the jurisdiction of the local court or the higher regional court, as well as jurisdiction over all criminal matters where a sentence of imprisonment exceeding four years, or placement of the accused person in a psychiatric hospital, is to be expected (§ 74 sub. 1 GVG). This specific judicial body is composed of three professional judges and two lay judges, § 76 sub. 1 no. 2 GVG.

20 In its capacity as a criminal chamber for particularly serious crimes (*Schwurgericht*), the criminal panel may have original jurisdiction at the regional court and, as such, would have the authority to adjudicate any crime listed in § 74 sub. 2 GVG, the majority of which result in the death of another. Likewise, the criminal panel may have original jurisdiction over business crimes in its capacity as the *Wirtschaftsstrafkammer* in accordance with § 74c GVG, or in its capacity as the court division dealing with crimes against the state (*Staatsschutzkammer*) under the terms of § 74a GVG. The *Wirtschaftsstrafkammer* has, inter alia, jurisdiction over the criminal offences of money laundering, fraud and embezzlement whenever the assessment of these offences requires special commercial and business expertise (§ 74c sub. 1 no. 6 GVG).

21 Pursuant to § 120 GVG, the higher regional court has jurisdiction over serious crimes against the state or if the prosecution is conducted by the Federal Prosecutor General (*Generalbundesanwalt*).

2. Venue

22 The rules regarding venue are contained in §§ 7 to 21 StPO, with venue at place of commission (§ 7 StPO), venue at domicile or habitual residence (§ 8 StPO) and venue at place of apprehension (§ 9 StPO) being the primary venues. In the event that more than one court has local jurisdiction, the prosecutor's office has the option of choosing the venue where it intends to bring charges. Charges are mostly brought at the venue at the place of commission (§ 7 StPO), as this is the most efficient approach in terms of examining witnesses, who are generally likely to be residents of that locality, or with regard to inspecting the actual place where the offence was committed. The offence is deemed to have been committed at the place where the perpetrator acted or where the result being sought by the offence was achieved (§ 9 StGB). In the event that multiple venues would apply (concurrence of venue) and the indictment is pending before several courts, the court which first opened the investigation takes precedence, § 12 StPO.

3. Schedule of responsibilities

23 Every criminal court has several judicial bodies at the same hierarchical level. In other words: there are several criminal judges, benches that include lay judges, criminal panels and criminal senates. The question which judicial body has judiciary authority for the specific proceedings is decided on the basis of the schedule of responsibilities at the relevant court. This schedule is comparable to by-laws and stipulates, on the one hand, which judges are part of which judiciary body and, on the other, which judiciary body has jurisdiction. Jurisdiction cannot be influenced or altered (Art. 101 para. 1 sent. 2 GG).

D. Sequence of criminal proceedings

Criminal proceedings consist of two parts: the main proceedings and the execution proceedings. 24

I. Preliminary investigation

The main proceedings commence with the preliminary investigation, also known as preparatory proceedings (§§ 158 et seq. StPO). During the preliminary investigation, it is determined whether there is sufficient cause to bring public charges at the competent court, § 170 StPO. 25

1. Commencement of preliminary investigation

The prosecutor's office is obligated to initiate a preliminary investigation if initial suspicions exist that a criminal offence has been committed. In accordance with § 152 sub. 2 StPO, an initial suspicion exists if there are sufficient factual indications that a criminal offence has been committed. This requires that the prosecutor's office receives notice of any such suspicions. This may happen in one of two ways: the law enforcement authorities are either alerted to a suspected criminal offence by someone filing a criminal complaint (*Strafanzeige*) or a demand for prosecution (*Strafantrag*), or the prosecutor's office itself becomes aware of a suspected criminal offence, for example over the course of its investigations in another case. The prosecutor's office is then under an *ex officio* obligation to investigate any such suspicion (§ 160 sub. 1 StPO). 26

A criminal complaint represents the notification of the law enforcement authorities to a set of facts which, in the opinion of the complainant, gives rise to the need for prosecution.[13] Every citizen has the right to lodge a criminal complaint with regard to a criminal offence, § 158 sub. 1 StPO. A criminal complaint can either be made in writing or verbally. The complainant does not need to be identified, the complaint can also be lodged anonymously. The filing of a criminal complaint obligates the law enforcement authorities to examine the set of facts that form the subject matter of the complaint.[14] Criminal complaints can also be lodged together with a demand for prosecution. A demand for prosecution is an official statement in which the eligible applicant states that he requests criminal prosecution.[15] In contrast to the criminal complaint, demands for prosecution cannot be lodged verbally. Instead, they must be filed in writing with the prosecutor's office or a court or stated for the record with another authority, § 158 sub. 2 StPO. Certain offences under German criminal law can only be prosecuted if the injured party lodges a demand for prosecution, § 77 StGB. Offences that are only prosecuted upon application by the victim fall into two categories: absolute and relative offences. They 27

---

[13] Schmitt/Köhler/Köhler StPO § 158 mn. 1, 2.
[14] Schmitt/Köhler/Köhler StPO § 158 mn. 1, 2.
[15] Schmitt/Köhler/Köhler StPO § 158 mn. 3.

differ in that the former will only be prosecuted upon application, whereas the latter can also be prosecuted *ex officio* if a special public interest in prosecution exists. If they are prosecuted upon application, the applicant must have met certain requirements at the time the offence was committed (such as the requirement of being a family member of the perpetrator).[16] A special public interest is generally deemed to exist if the legal peace has been disturbed beyond the injured party's sphere of life, thus making prosecution an actual concern for the public at large.[17]

2. Rights and obligations of the parties involved

28 As required by § 160 sub. 1 StPO, the prosecutor's office is obligated to investigate the entire set of facts during the preliminary proceedings. In doing so, the prosecutor's office must ascertain not just incriminating but also any exonerating circumstances, as required by § 160 sub. 2 StPO. In its investigations, the prosecutor's office is authorised to demand information from any and all government agencies and to either conduct investigations itself or have them conducted by the agencies and officials of the police service (§§ 161 sub. 1 and 163 sub. 1 StPO). The prosecutor's office usually turns a large part of the investigations to be conducted over to the officers of the police service.

29 In the standard scenario, the accused person is unaware that he is the subject of an investigation. These proceedings are, as a rule, classified. However, the principle of due process demands that the accused person be questioned regarding any allegations made during the preliminary proceedings before the investigations are closed (§ 163a sub. 1 StPO). For this purpose, the law enforcement authorities will summon the accused person for questioning. As opposed to a summons from the police, the accused person is required to comply with a summons from the prosecutor's office (§ 163a sub. 3 StPO). The examination may be conducted by the police authorities (§ 163a sub. 4 in conjunction with § 136 StPO), by the prosecutor's office (§ 163a sub. 3 in conjunction with § 136 StPO) or an examining judge (*Ermittlungsrichter*, § 162 sub. 1 in conjunction with § 136 StPO). At the commencement of any examination, the accused person must be informed of the offences he is charged with, § 136 sub. 1 sent. 1 StPO. He must then be advised of his right to remain silent, § 136 sub. 1 sent. 2 StPO. The accused person is under no obligation to comment on the allegations, thereby potentially incriminating himself. This follows from the principle of freedom from self-incrimination under Art. 1 para. 1 in conjunction with Art. 2 para. 1 GG that states that no accused person is required to incriminate himself or to testify against himself.[18]

30 At this point of the preliminary proceedings, defence counsel, if any, may already play a role. It is common that anyone being accused consults with a lawyer before making a first statement vis-à-vis the law enforcement authorities regarding any allegations, § 137 StPO. The accused person must be informed about this option prior to the examination, § 136 sub. 1 sent. 2 StPO. Defence counsel will then communicate with the law enforcement authorities and represent the rights and interests of the accused person as early as during the preliminary proceedings. Defence counsel has the right to be present during any questioning of the accused person, § 136 sub. 1 sent. 2 StPO, and to inspect the investigation file, § 147 sub. 1 StPO.

31 Because of their special position, which is similar to that of an accused person, secondary parties to the proceedings have the same rights and obligations during the preliminary investigations as the accused person. Where, during the preliminary proceedings, the

---

[16] Fischer/Fischer/Lutz StGB § 77 mn. 2.
[17] MüKoStGB/Hardtung, 4th edn 2021, StGB § 230 mn. 25.
[18] Schmitt/Köhler/Schmitt StPO Einleitung mn. 29a.

law enforcement authorities become aware of aspects that would indicate the possible involvement of secondary parties, any potential secondary parties must be heard (§ 426 sub. 1 StPO and § 444 sub. 2 sent. 2 in conjunction with § 426 sub. 1 StPO). Furthermore, defence counsel retained by a secondary party also has the right to inspect the relevant files, § 147 sub. 1 StPO.

3. Law of evidence

As part of their investigation of the factual situation during the preliminary proceed- 32
ings, the law enforcement authorities gather the necessary evidence. Of particular relevance as evidence are the witness testimony (*Zeugenaussage*, §§ 48 et seq. StPO), expert testimony (*Sachverständigenaussage*, §§ 72 et seq. StPO), documentary evidence (§§ 249 et seq. StPO) as well as evidence by inspection (§§ 86 et seq. StPO).

Witnesses are persons who provide information about their perception of the facts in 33
criminal proceedings that are not being conducted against them.[19] As a rule, any person is capable of being a witness, even (small) children. Witnesses are obligated to appear before the court (§§ 48 sub. 1 and 51 StPO) and the prosecutor's office (§ 161a sub. 1 sent. 1 and sub. 2 StPO) when summoned. Like the accused person, witnesses are under no obligation to comply with summons for a questioning by the police. Witnesses are obligated to give evidence regarding the subject matter of the examination, § 48 sub. 2 StPO. They are under a duty to tell the truth and must be so instructed before their examination, § 57 StPO. False witness testimony before a court is punishable under §§ 153 et seq. StGB. There are, however, statutory exceptions that set out when a witness may refuse to give evidence. Witnesses must also be instructed about these exceptions before their testimony. In accordance with § 52 StPO, one of these exceptions concerns relatives of the accused person, such as spouses (no. 1) or children (no. 3). Where a witness has not been instructed about his right to refuse testimony as per § 52 StPO and he incriminates the accused person, this testimony cannot be used in the proceedings. Moreover, the witness also has the right to refuse to answer questions if this would put him, or a relative, at risk of being prosecuted for a criminal offence (§ 55 sub. 1 StPO). Pursuant to § 53 StPO, a further exception from the duty to give evidence relates to those who are subject to a professional duty of confidentiality, such as defence counsel (no. 2) and doctors (no. 3). Witnesses also have the right to be advised by legal counsel, § 68b StPO.

Expert testimony usually consists in an expert opinion prepared by an appointed 34
expert that contains information regarding facts or empirical principles.[20] Experts have a degree of expertise in their field of specialty that the law enforcement authorities and the courts generally do not possess.

Documentary evidence encompasses documents of any kind that can be read out and 35
are capable of functioning as evidence by virtue of their mental/intellectual/conceptual content.[21]

Evidence by inspection relates to proof that can be discerned by the senses, such as 36
seeing or hearing. In general, this includes all proof that is not witness or expert testimony or documentary evidence.[22] Examples of evidence by inspection are photos and video recordings.

---

[19] Schmitt/Köhler/Schmitt StPO Vorbemerkungen zu § 48 mn. 1.
[20] Schmitt/Köhler/Schmitt StPO Vorbemerkungen zu § 72 mn. 1, 7.
[21] Schmitt/Köhler/Schmitt StPO § 249 mn. 2.
[22] Schmitt/Köhler/Schmitt StPO § 86 mn. 1.

4. Coercive measures

37 So-called coercive measures may prove necessary over the course of the preliminary proceedings to ensure that the proceedings can be conducted and to obtain and seize evidence. Measures that have a particularly severe impact on the personal freedom of the accused person are referred to as coercive measures. These measures are therefore the subject of special statutory provisions. The most important coercive measures are searches (*Durchsuchung*, §§ 102, 103 and 105 StPO), seizures (*Beschlagnahme*, §§ 94 sub. 2 and 98 StPO) and pre-trial detention (*Untersuchungshaft*, §§ 112 and 125 StPO).

38 In contrast to any other investigative measures, coercive measures cannot be ordered by the law enforcement authorities themselves. Instead, they are subject to the requirement of judicial authority, which means that coercive measures require a formal order made by an independent judge (cf. §§ 98, 105 and 125 StPO). This is intended to protect the fundamental rights of the accused person that may be impacted by such a measure. However, in cases of imminent danger, specific coercive measures, such as searches under § 105 StPO or seizures under § 98 StPO, may be ordered by the prosecutor's office and, at a subordinated level, by its investigating officers, e.g. the police authorities. Imminent danger is present if the judge's order cannot be obtained without jeopardising the purpose of the measure being pursued.[23]

39 Searches of the accused person's premises serve for the discovery of evidence or the apprehension of the accused person, § 102 StPO. These searches may include the accommodation and the possessions of the accused person and even extend to a body search of the accused person, § 102 StPO.

40 Pursuant to § 103 sub. 1 sent. 1 StPO, a search may only be conducted in relation to anyone other than the accused person if this is done in order to apprehend the accused person or to pursue leads or to seize certain items. Furthermore, there must be factual indications that the accused person, the leads or the items being sought are located on the premises to be searched (§ 103 sub. 1 sent. 2 StPO). Companies are quite frequently the subject of search measures under §§ 103 and 105 StPO. In the standard scenario, their employees are accused of criminal offences, and the search is carried out to pursue leads and to seize certain items that are presumably located at the company's premises. In addition, the company may also be affected by the search measure as a secondary party.

41 Seizure is ordered if an item that could potentially serve as evidence in the investigation is not voluntarily surrendered, § 94 sub. 2 StPO. In such a case, seizure constitutes the formal taking possession of the particular item by transferring it into official custody.[24] § 97 StPO stipulates a prohibition of seizure of certain items which include, first and foremost, written communications and records of the defence counsel of the accused person (§ 97 sub. 1 no. 1 and 2, § 53 sub. 1 no. 3 and § 148 StPO).

42 Pre-trial detention is the coercive measure with the greatest impact on the accused person's personal freedom. It is ordered either to ensure that the accused person will be present during the criminal proceedings or to guarantee the proper determination of facts by the law enforcement authorities. Pre-trial detention may only be ordered if there is a strong suspicion that the accused person committed the offence, and there is a reason for detaining the suspect in custody which is based on fact (§ 112 sub. 1 sent. 1 StPO). A strong suspicion exists if there is a high probability that the accused person was either the perpetrator of or a participant in a criminal offence.[25] Potential reasons for arrest in accordance with § 112 sub. 2 StPO are flight, flight risk and suppression of evidence. The

---

[23] Schmitt/Köhler/Schmitt StPO § 98 mn. 6.
[24] Schmitt/Köhler/Schmitt StPO Vorbemerkungen zu § 94 mn. 3.
[25] Schmitt/Köhler/Schmitt StPO § 112 mn. 5.

mere fact that the accused person has a domicile abroad does not constitute a reason for arrest.[26] Also, pre-trial detention must be proportionate to the significance of the matter and the penalty to be expected (§ 112 sub. 1 sent. 2 StPO).

5. Legal remedies

There are no legal remedies to prevent preliminary proceedings from being initiated **43** and conducted. With regard to investigative measures ordered by the prosecutor's office or the law enforcement authorities, the accused person has the option of petitioning the court to decide on the measures (§ 98 sub. 2 sent. 2 StPO). The legal remedy in the form of a complaint may be an option to avert investigative measures ordered by the court, § 304 sub. 1 StPO. By operation of § 304 sub. 1 and sub. 2 StPO, anyone who is affected by such a measure, that is to say: whose rights have been violated, has the necessary standing to lodge a complaint. Accordingly, in the event of an unlawfully ordered search, anyone within the meaning of § 103 sub. 1 sent. 2 StPO who is subject to a search has standing to lodge a complaint.

6. Completion of preliminary investigation

When the prosecutor's office has concluded its investigation, it records the closing of **44** its investigation in the investigation file by way of a concluding memorandum (§ 169a StPO). At this time at the latest, defence counsel must be granted unrestricted access to the file in accordance with § 147 sub. 2 StPO.

The prosecutor's office will then decide whether to indict the accused person or to **45** terminate the proceedings.

a) Indictment

If the investigation has discovered sufficient cause to bring public charges, the prose- **46** cutor's office is obligated to indict the accused person (§ 170 sub. 1 StPO). Probable cause is deemed to be sufficient cause. Pursuant to §§ 170 sub. 1 and 203 StPO, probable cause exists if the probability that the accused person committed the offence, and will therefore be convicted, is greater than an acquittal.[27] Public charges will be brought by submitting the bill of indictment to the competent court. § 200 StPO specifies the content a bill of indictment is required to have. A bill of indictment must state the name of the accused person, the offence, time and place of its commission, the statutory characteristics of the offence and the penal provisions to be applied as well as the evidence, the trial court and the name of the defence counsel. If the prosecutor's office, during the preliminary proceedings, arrives at the conclusion that a secondary party should also be involved in the proceedings, as such a party might be subject to a fine or to confiscation, this must also be included in the bill of indictment as well as the legal and factual reasons therefor.[28]

A petition for a summary penalty order (*Strafbefehl*) as per § 407 StPO is a special **47** type of indictment. During these proceedings, the legal consequences of an offence that qualifies as a misdemeanour and falls within the purview of a criminal judge sitting alone or a bench that includes lay judges, can be determined without need for a hearing. These proceedings serve both the interests of the criminal courts by easing their case load and the interest of the accused person, as the proceedings can be disposed of quickly,

[26] Schmitt/Köhler/Schmitt StPO § 112 mn. 17a.
[27] BGH 22.4.2023 – StB 3/03, BeckRS 2003, 4494.
[28] Schmitt/Köhler/Schmitt StPO § 424 mn. 5, 6, § 444 mn. 4.

cost-efficiently and without the public impact of a hearing.[29] The legal consequences of the offence that may be imposed by a summary penalty order are set forth in § 407 sub. 2 StPO and include fines, cautions subject to reservation of punishment, driving bans and confiscation. Imprisonment of up to one year may be imposed if this sentence is suspended on probation and the accused person has a defence lawyer. Should the accused person disagree with the summary penalty order, he can object within two weeks from service of the summary penalty order (§ 410 StPO). Unless this objection is inadmissible, the court will set a trial date.

48 With the submission of the bill of indictment, the matter becomes pending before the court and the prosecutor's office passes the control over the proceedings on to the court.[30] The subject matter of the court proceedings is predetermined, as the court's decision will relate solely to the offence specified in the indictment, § 155 StPO.

b) Termination pursuant to § 170 sub. 2 StPO

49 As required by § 170 sub. 2 StPO, the prosecutor's office will terminate the preliminary proceedings if it does not have sufficient cause to bring public charges.

50 This may be due to procedural reasons if an impediment to prosecution exists. Potential impediments to prosecution are, for example, the statute of limitations for prosecution of crimes pursuant to §§ 78 et seq. StGB or if the perpetrator has not yet reached the age of criminal responsibility required by § 19 StGB. The statute of limitations for prosecution results in a criminal offence no longer being punishable, § 78 sub. 1 StGB. By operation of § 78a StGB, the limitation period commences upon completion of the offence, no later however than upon the result of the offence being realised. The length of the limitation period depends on the severity of the potential penalty and is set forth in § 78 sub. 3 StGB. For instance, the prosecution of criminal offences liable to a term of imprisonment greater than one year, but no more than five years, is time-barred after five years (§ 78 sub. 3 no. 4 StGB). Some supplementary penal provisions stipulate special limitation periods, for example for tax evasion in § 370 AO. Limitation periods may be interrupted and will start over from the beginning after each interruption, § 78c StGB. However, prosecution becomes time-barred at the latest upon expiry of double the time period of the statutory limitation period (absolute limitation), § 78c sub. 3 StGB. Pursuant to § 78b StGB, the limitation period may be suspended, which will toll the running of the statute of limitations. Thereafter, the limitation period recommences from when it stopped and will not start again from the very beginning.

51 For factual reasons, sufficient cause to bring public charges may be absent, either in cases where the accused person did not commit the offence, or it can simply not be proven that he committed the offence. The proceedings may be terminated for legal reasons if the act committed by the accused person is, in actuality, not a criminal offence. Moreover, the prosecutor's office may terminate the preliminary proceedings in part, provided that such termination relates to a severable act. However, any such termination does not result in double jeopardy (*ne bis in idem*), meaning that the proceedings can be resumed at any time.

52 As required by § 170 sub. 2 sent. 2 StPO, the prosecutor's office will notify the accused person of the procedural termination if he has already been questioned (order terminating proceedings). Where the preliminary proceedings were initiated by a demand for prosecution, the prosecutor's office will formally notify the petitioner of the termination. Under § 171 StPO, the petitioner has two weeks to lodge an objection to this notification.

---

[29] Schmitt/Köhler/Schmitt StPO Vorbemerkungen zu § 407 mn. 1.
[30] Schmitt/Köhler/Schmitt StPO Einleitung mn. 60b.

c) Termination for discretionary reasons

Furthermore, the prosecutor's office has the option to terminate the proceedings in accordance with the principle of discretionary prosecution. In this case, the proceedings would be terminated without trial. It would be politic to refer to scenarios like these as 'to refrain from prosecuting lesser offences' or 'to refrain from bringing public charges'. Termination for discretionary reasons may be proposed to the prosecutor's office by the accused person himself or his defence counsel. This is often the case in practice and benefits the accused person as, in this way, a trial may be avoided. In economic and criminal tax law matters in particular, termination under § 153a StPO (non-prosecution subject to imposition of conditions and directions) is the most relevant scenario for this type of termination. 53

aa) Termination pursuant to § 153 StPO. In accordance with § 153 sub. 1 StPO, the prosecutor's office may, with the approval of the court, refrain from prosecution if the subject matter of the proceedings is a misdemeanour, the perpetrator's culpability is deemed to be low, and there is no public interest in the prosecution of the offence. 54

Misdemeanours are unlawful acts for which the regular minimum punishment is a fine or imprisonment for a term of less than one year (§ 12 sub. 2 StGB). Embezzlement under § 266 StGB and money laundering under § 261 StGB are misdemeanours, for example. 55

The perpetrator's culpability is deemed to be low if it is clearly below the average, compared to the same misdemeanours committed by others, and punishment at the very bottom end of the range of potential penalties therefore appears appropriate.[31] This decision must be made in consideration of the criteria used for sentencing, § 46 sub. 2 StGB, which include the manner in which the offence was committed, the consequences of the offence that are attributable to the perpetrator, the degree of breach of duty, the perpetrator's motives, the perpetrator's conduct after the deed, as well as other aspects that relate to the degree of culpability on the part of the perpetrator. As a rule, it is favourable if the perpetrator has no prior convictions[32] and there are explainable reasons for the commission of the offence.[33] Where offences against property have been committed, the amount of loss or damage caused by the wrongdoing is a material factor[34], i.e. negligible harm also equates to a lesser degree of wrongdoing. The same applies in the case of tax offences with regard to the amount of tax evaded.[35] Voluntary efforts to make good the harm caused (reparation) also have a positive effect. For offences against property, this may be achieved, for example, by providing material compensation, i.e. by repaying the proceeds from the offence. 56

If culpability is deemed to be low, there is generally no public interest in prosecution. However, in individual cases, public interest in prosecution may exist if, for example, the injured party is a public figure or the offence had unusual consequences, and the public at large is therefore affected by the specific criminal offence.[36] 57

In accordance with § 153 sub. 1 sent. 2 StPO, the prosecutor's office may, even without the approval of the court, refrain from prosecution if the misdemeanour is not subject to an increased minimum sentence and if the consequences ensuing from the offence are minor. Consequences are generally deemed to be minor in cases of petty offences. The value threshold for offences against property is roughly 50 EUR.[37] 58

---

[31] Schmitt/Köhler/Schmitt StPO § 153 mn. 4.
[32] BGH 8.10.2014 – 1 StR 350/14, BeckRS 2014, 21422.
[33] MüKoStGB/Maier, 4th edn 2020, StGB § 46 mn. 205.
[34] MüKoStGB/Maier StGB § 46 mn. 256.
[35] MüKoStGB/Maier StGB § 46 mn. 256.
[36] MüKoStGB/Hardtung StGB § 230 mn. 25.
[37] Schmitt/Köhler/Schmitt StPO § 153 mn. 17.

59 The termination of the proceedings under the terms of § 153 StPO does not entail costs on the part of the accused person. Termination under § 153 StPO by the prosecutor's office does not result in double jeopardy.

60 **bb) Termination pursuant to § 153a StPO.** § 153a StPO enables the prosecutor's office to terminate the proceedings subject to the imposition of conditions and directions. This requires that the offence committed qualifies as a misdemeanour and that the conditions and directions are apt to eliminate the public interest in criminal prosecution and that the degree of culpability does not present an obstacle thereto, § 153a sub. 1 sent. 1 StPO. In addition, both the court and the accused person must agree to termination subject to the imposition of conditions and directions. As a rule, the prosecutor's office is free in determining the conditions and directions. § 153a sub. 1 sent. 2 StPO contains a catalogue of conditions and directions that may be considered, such as the condition to make specific reparation to compensate for the harm caused by the offence (§ 153a sub. 1 sent. 2 no. 1 StPO). This is the most common case in practice. The assessment of the degree of culpability is based on the criteria mentioned in § 153 StPO. In contrast to the low degree of culpability that is assumed for the application of § 153 StPO, the application of § 153a StPO is based on a medium degree of culpability.[38] Apart from the criteria stated in § 153 StPO, in economic and criminal tax law matters, voluntary disclosure (self-reporting) may also be a reason for termination in accordance with § 153a StPO.[39]

61 The consent of the accused person is given by declaration vis-à-vis the prosecutor's office. The prosecutor's office determines the conditions and directions for this purpose and sets a deadline by which the accused person would have to consent. It should be noted that the accused person's consent does not constitute an admission of guilt.[40]

62 With regard to compliance with conditions and directions, the accused will be set a time limit within which to comply with the conditions and directions and which, in the cases under § 153a sub. 1 sent. 3 StPO, is a maximum of six months; a different time limit applies to cases under § 153a sub. 1 sent. 2 no. 4 and 6 StPO. As an exception, § 153a sub. 1 sent. 4 StPO permits the extension of this time limit.

63 Once the accused person has fully complied with all his obligations, the offence can no longer be prosecuted as a misdemeanour (*ne bis in idem*), § 153a sub. 1 sent. 5 StPO. However, if he fails to comply with his obligations, the criminal proceedings will continue (§ 153a sub. 1 sent. 6 StPO).

d) Other options for termination

64 The proceedings may be terminated in accordance with § 154f StPO if the absence of the accused person prevents the opening or the conduct of the trial for a prolonged period of time. This would be the case, for example, if the accused person cannot be questioned because his whereabouts are unknown or if he moved, address unknown, after his questioning, and it is therefore not possible to present him with the bill of indictment, as required by § 201 StPO.

65 Termination pursuant to § 153c sub. 2 StPO may be required for offences committed abroad if, for example, the perpetrator has already been convicted in the US and the penalty that would in all likelihood be imposed in Germany would be of little consequence after imputation of the foreign sentence.

66 The Code of Criminal Procedure and supplementary penal provisions contain further reasons for a termination of the proceedings, which will not be discussed in detail here.

---

[38] Schmitt/Köhler/Schmitt StPO § 153a mn. 7.
[39] MüKoStPO/Peters StPO § 153a mn. 15.
[40] MüKoStPO/Peters StPO § 153a mn. 22.

The relevant rules are set forth in §§ 153b et seq. StPO and, for instance, in § 399 AO for criminal tax matters.

II. Interlocutory proceedings

67 After the preliminary proceedings and the indictment follow the interlocutory proceedings, also known as opening proceedings (§§ 199 et seq. StPO). During the interlocutory proceedings, the court examines the allegations of the prosecutor's office and decides whether to allow the indictment to proceed to trial (§ 199 sub. 1 StPO). During the interlocutory proceedings, the accused person (*Beschuldigter*) is referred to as the indicted accused (*Angeschuldigter*).

68 At this stage, the control over the proceedings has already passed from the prosecutor's office to the trial court. The court informs the indicted accused of the bill of indictment and requests that he states, within a certain time limit, whether he wishes to request that specific evidence be taken prior to the opening of the trial or whether he has any objections to the opening of the trial (§ 201 sub. 1 sent. 1 StPO). If the indicted accused is not yet represented by defence counsel, even though the requirements for mandatory defence are met, the court must appoint a counsel for the defence (§ 141 StPO).

69 When deciding whether to open the trial in accordance with § 199 sub. 1 StPO, the court examines whether probable cause exists.[41] Should probable cause exist, the court will order that the case proceeds to trial, § 203 StPO. The content of this order is prescribed by § 207 StPO. Pursuant to § 206 StPO, the court is not bound by the application of the prosecutor's office. The court may also order amendments subject to which it admits the indictment for trial, § 207 sub. 2 StPO. The order opening the trial brings about pendency (*lis pendens*).[42] The indicted accused has no legal remedy against this order, § 210 sub. 1 StPO. However, should the court, after examination of probable cause, arrive at the conclusion that, for legal or factual reasons, an acquittal is to be expected, it will order that the case does not proceed to trial (§ 204 StPO). Under § 210 sub. 2 StPO, the prosecutor's office has the remedy of an immediate complaint against such an order.

70 If the court determines that a procedural impediment exists, it will terminate the proceedings by order in accordance with § 206a StPO.

71 Moreover, pursuant to §§ 153 sub. 2 and 153a sub. 2 StPO, the court can terminate the proceedings for discretionary reasons before the main hearing by order if the respective statutory requirements for termination have been met and both the prosecutor's office and the accused person agree.

III. Trial

72 Once the court orders that the case proceed to trial, the main proceedings commence (§§ 213 et seq. StPO). This stage of the proceedings concerns the preparation of the main hearing (*Hauptverhandlung*). The main hearing generally ends with a judgment, § 260 StPO.

73 The main proceedings (trial) can be divided into two parts: the preparation of the main hearing and the main hearing itself. During the main proceedings, the accused indictee (*Angeschuldigter*) is referred to as the defendant (*Angeklagter*).

---

[41] Schmitt/Köhler/Schmitt StPO § 203 mn. 2.

[42] Schmitt/Köhler/Schmitt StPO Einleitung mn. 63.

1. Preparation of the main hearing

74 The preparations of the main hearing are governed by §§ 213 to 225 StPO. The presiding judge sets the date for the main hearing, § 213 StPO. In complex cases before the regional court or the higher regional court, where the main hearing is likely to last longer than ten days, the presiding judge is required to coordinate with both defence counsel and the prosecutor's office regarding the procedural steps of the main hearing before setting a hearing date.

75 The court summons the defendant (§ 216 StPO) and defence counsel (§ 218 StPO) to appear at the main hearing. There must be a period of no less than one week between the defendant being served with the summons and the commencement of the main hearing (§ 217 StPO). Any secondary parties to regulatory fine proceedings must also be summoned to the main hearing (§ 444 sub. 2 sent. 1 StPO). Pursuant to § 429 sub. 1 StPO, any secondary parties to confiscation proceedings will be informed of the date of the main hearing by service of process, advising these secondary parties that the case may also be heard in their absence, that they may appoint a lawyer to represent them and that the court will decide on confiscation against them (§ 429 sub. 3 StPO). There is, however, no need to serve a summons on secondary parties to confiscation proceedings.[43] That said, the court may order the personal appearance of secondary parties to confiscation proceedings (§ 426 sub. 2 sent. 1 StPO). The relevant parties are obligated to comply with any such order. If a secondary party to confiscation proceedings fails to appear without sufficient excuse, the court may order his compulsory attendance, provided that the relevant party has been informed of this possibility beforehand (§ 427 sub. 2 sent. 2 StPO).

76 Should the main hearing take place before a regional court or higher regional court, the composition of the court must be communicated no later than at the commencement of the main hearing, § 222a StPO.

2. Chronology of the main hearing

77 The main hearing is conducted in the uninterrupted presence of those appointed to adjudicate as well as the prosecutor and a registrar of the court registry office, § 226 sub. 1 StPO. Said registrar records the minutes during the main hearing (§ 271 sub. 1 sent. 1 StPO). It follows from the principle of public trial under Art. 6 ECHR and § 169 sub. 1 sent. 1 GVG that the hearing must be public. This serves the general public's interest in being informed and ensures that anyone who wishes to attend the main hearing is granted access to it.[44] Secondary parties to the proceedings have the same rights as the defendant during the main hearing (§§ 427 sub. 1 and 444 sub. 2 sent. 2 in conjunction with § 427 sub. 1 StPO).

78 Where persons who are unable to speak and/or understand German are to appear at a hearing, § 185 sub. 1 sent. 1 GVG requires that an interpreter be called in.

79 The course of the main hearing is prescribed, in detail, by law. The court must not deviate in any way from this sequence.

80 The hearing commences upon the matter being called (§ 243 sub. 1 sent. 1 StPO). The matter is called by the presiding judge in the courtroom. This is followed by the judge establishing whether the defendant and his defence counsel have appeared and whether any evidence required has been procured or, more specifically, whether the witnesses and experts summoned have appeared (§ 243 sub. 1 sent. 2 StPO). There is no need to establish the presence of the prosecution, as this is presupposed. Thereafter, any witnesses present

[43] Schmitt/Köhler/Schmitt StPO § 430 mn. 1.

[44] Schmitt/Köhler/Schmitt GVG § 169 mn. 1.

must leave the courtroom, § 243 sub. 2 sent. 1 StPO. They are not allowed to attend the main hearing before giving testimony.

The defendant is required to attend the main hearing and must not leave the hearing, § 231 StPO. No main hearing is conducted against a defendant who fails to appear, § 230 sub. 1 StPO. If the defendant fails to appear, without sufficient excuse, the court must issue an order to bring him before the court or issue an arrest warrant, provided that this is necessary in order to conduct the main hearing (§ 230 sub. 2 StPO). Exceptions from the duty to attend are set out in §§ 232 to 235 StPO. **81**

§ 48 sub. 1 StPO obligates witnesses to appear for their examination and give their testimony, unless one of the exemptions specified by law applies. **82**

The defendant is then questioned as to his personal circumstances (§ 243 sub. 2 sent. 2 StPO). The defendant is obligated to identify himself, so that the court can determine whether the defendant is identical to the person named in the bill of indictment. Apart from establishing his identity, the determination of the defendant's personal data also serves to establish whether the procedural requirements, such as his ability to stand trial, have been met.[45] The defendant is also questioned about his personal circumstances, in particular his prior personal history, job history, education and work, as well as his family and financial situation, since this information might be of relevance for the assessment of the offence as well as sentencing. However, in light of the above-mentioned principle of freedom from self-incrimination (→ mn. 29), the defendant is not required to provide any such details if he does not wish to. **83**

Following the questioning regarding the defendant's personal circumstances, the prosecutor reads out the bill of indictment (§ 243 sub. 3 sent. 1 StPO). This is when the public and any lay judges are, for the first time, informed about the subject matter of the proceedings and the allegations against the defendant. In addition, the presiding judge announces, as required by § 243 sub. 4 sent. 1 StPO, whether any verbal or written discussions under §§ 202a and 212 StPO took place prior to the main hearing insofar that they related to the possibility of reaching an understanding in accordance with § 257c StPO. This also applies even if these discussions failed to render a result.[46] These obligations serve the transparency requirement that is to ensure that any such discussions are always disclosed during the public hearing, leaving no room for any informal or uncontrollable conduct that would circumvent the procedural principles of criminal law.[47] **84**

The defendant is then instructed as to his right to remain silent (§ 243 sub. 5 sent. 1 StPO). If he agrees to make a statement, the presiding judge will question him with regard to the matter itself (§§ 243 sub. 5 sent. 2 and 136 StPO). The defendant's statement is referred to as an 'entry of appearance' and will be taken into account as evidence in reaching a verdict, even if it is not formally part of the taking of evidence and precedes it. In the event of complex proceedings before the regional court or the higher regional court, the defendant's defence counsel will have the opportunity, upon petition, to make a statement on behalf of the defendant, § 243 sub. 5 sent. 3 StPO. **85**

This is followed by the taking of evidence (§§ 244 to 257 StPO). The taking of evidence is generally the most comprehensive part of the main hearing. All evidence gathered by the law enforcement authorities during the preliminary proceedings as well as any new evidence must be assessed by the court at the time of the main hearing (so-called principle of immediacy). This requires the court to extend *ex officio* the taking of evidence to all facts and evidence that are of relevance for the decision (§ 244 sub. 2 StPO) in order to establish the truth. Making reference to evidence from the preliminary proceedings is not **86**

---

45 Schmitt/Köhler/Schmitt StPO § 243 mn. 11.

46 Schmitt/Köhler/Schmitt StPO § 243 mn. 18a.

47 BVerfG 19.3.2013 – BvR 2628/10, 2 BvR 2883/10, 2 BvR 2155/11, NJW 2013, 1058.

permissible. This has far-reaching implications for witnesses and experts: even if a witness or an expert has been questioned during the preliminary proceedings, they must once again be questioned in person by the court during the course of the main hearing, § 250 sent. 1 StPO. This examination must not be replaced by the reading out of the minutes of the prior examination, § 250 sent. 2 StPO. Exceptions from this rule only apply if, for example, the witness or the expert has in the meantime passed away, or the witness or the expert cannot be reasonably expected to appear in court given the distance they would have to travel and also considering the relevance of their testimony (§§ 251 sub. 1 no. 3 StPO and 251 sub. 2 no. 2 StPO). Witnesses will be questioned by the presiding judge. The presiding judge then permits his associate judges, the lay judges, the prosecutor as well as the defendant and his defence counsel to question the witness, § 248 sent. 2 StPO. Once their examination is completed, witnesses and experts are dismissed by the presiding judge. They are not permitted to leave the court before being dismissed (§ 248 sent. 1 StPO). For the purpose of taking their content into evidence, documents are read out during the main hearing, § 249 sub. 1 sent. 1 StPO. Likewise, statements in accordance with § 256 sub. 1 StPO may also be read out. This includes, for example, any declarations by public authorities contained in certificates or expert opinions (§ 256 sub. 1 no. 1 letter a StPO). Other evidence, such as video recordings, is inspected in the courtroom. After the hearing of each individual piece of evidence, the defendant has the right to make a statement regarding any specific piece of evidence, § 257 sub. 1 StPO.

87 Also, the prosecutor's office as well as the defendant and his defence counsel have the right to submit a motion to take evidence. A motion to take evidence (*Beweisantrag*) within the meaning of § 244 sub. 4 sent. 1 StPO exists if the petitioner earnestly requested that evidence about an alleged concrete fact concerning the question of culpability or sentencing be taken by means of a precisely designated piece of evidence and the motion indicates why that designated piece of evidence is purported to be able to prove the alleged fact. As a general rule, the court must grant any such motion. Only in a few exceptional cases prescribed by law may the court deny such a motion by way of an order (§ 244 sub. 3 sent. 2 and 3, sub. 4 and 5 StPO). This is the case, for example, if the fact to be proven is of no relevance to the decision (§ 244 sub. 3 sent. 3 no. 2 StPO) or if the evidence is entirely unsuited (§ 244 sub. 3 sent. 3 no. 4 StPO).

88 § 265 sub. 1 StPO requires judicial notice if, as a consequence of the same set of facts being given a different legal assessment or new facts emerging during the main hearing, the defendant is now being tried for a different offence than the offence stated in the indictment. This duty to notify serves to enable the effective defence of the accused person.[48] If it transpires that another offence under procedural law has been committed, that is to say: another set of facts applies, conviction is possible in the same proceedings by way of a supplementary charge, provided that the defendant agrees (cf. § 266 StPO).

89 The taking of evidence will conclude, once all evidence has been heard. After the taking of evidence has been concluded, the parties present their closing arguments, § 258 sub. 1 StPO. The prosecutor is the first to present his closing argument. He evaluates the outcome of the hearing from both a factual and a legal perspective, followed by his application. The prosecutor's application may be for an acquittal or for a conviction, with the imposition of a specific sentence. This is followed by defence counsel presenting his closing argument. Like the prosecutor, defence counsel will generally also evaluate the outcome of the hearing and submit his specific application.

90 Thereafter, the defendant must, expressly and unambiguously, be given the opportunity to have the last word, § 258 sub. 2 StPO. This provides the defendant with yet another

[48] Schmitt/Köhler/Schmitt StPO § 265 mn. 1, 2.

chance to make a statement with regard to the matter itself before the court reaches a verdict, in order to present his view on the matter and any factors that he considers favourable or mitigating.[49] In doing so, the defendant must not be restricted, neither with regard to length nor content of his statement. Only in cases where the defendant abuses his right to have the last word, for example by constantly repeating himself or making incongruous remarks, the presiding judge may caution the defendant.[50] The last word cannot be transferred and cannot be exercised by defence counsel. The defendant may decline to have the last word.[51]

After the defendant has had the last word, both the professional and honorary judges **91** leave the courtroom to deliberate on the judgment. As part of these deliberations, the judges will vote, with a majority of two thirds of the votes required to arrive at a judgment (§ 263 sub. 1 StPO). The exact course of deliberation and voting is prescribed in §§ 192 et seq. GVG. All deliberations are subject to confidentiality (§ 45 DRiG (*Deutsches Richtergesetz*, German Judiciary Act)).

The presiding judge will then pronounce judgment by reading out the operative part **92** of the judgment and the key reasons for the verdict (§ 268 sub. 2 sent. 1 and 2 StPO).

3. Content of judgment

The standard scenario is that the defendant is either convicted or acquitted. This is **93** entirely based on the court's belief and certitude arrived at under the terms of § 261 StPO. In accordance with the principle of the judge's free evaluation of evidence, the court is required to reach a determination solely on the basis of personal conviction – within the parameters of logic and arbitrariness – and not in concordance with any fixed rules of evidence.[52] As required by § 264 StPO, the defendant is acquitted when either his innocence has been proven or his guilt cannot be established from any legal perspective. A conviction is pronounced by stating the legal designation of the offence and the sentence. The sentence is the actual penalty, based on the measure of culpability. The provision of § 46 StGB, which sets out the principles of sentencing, plays an important role in this process. Depending on the penal provision violated, the court can either impose imprisonment or a fine.

A distinction is made between fixed-term imprisonment and life imprisonment (§§ 38 **94** and 39 StGB). Fixed-term imprisonment ranges from a minimum term of one month to a maximum term of 15 years. Where the term of imprisonment is less than one year, it may be suspended on probation, § 56 StGB. This requires the expectation that the conviction alone will serve as a warning to the convicted and that the convicted will refrain from committing any offences, without need for exposure to a correctional facility. This expectation takes into account the personality of the convicted, his behaviour after the offence, his living circumstances and the effect that the suspension on probation would in all likelihood have on him, § 56 sub. 1 StGB. As an exception under § 56 sub. 2 StGB, a term of imprisonment of over to two years may also be suspended on probation if, in addition to the requirements of § 56 sub. 1 StGB, the overall assessment of the offence and the personality of the convicted suggest that special circumstances apply. This should also include the consideration of any endeavours on the part of the convicted to make good the harm caused by his action(s) (§ 56 sub. 2 sent. 2 StGB).

---

49 MüKoStPO/Niehaus StPO § 258 mn. 16a.
50 Schmitt/Köhler/Schmitt StPO § 258 mn. 26.
51 MüKoStPO/Niehaus StPO § 258 mn. 16b.
52 MüKoStPO/Kudlich StPO Einleitung mn. 200 et seqq.

95 If the sentence is a fine, the fine is imposed by determining both the number of penalty units and the amount of each penalty unit, for example: '30 penalty units at 500 EUR each' (§ 260 sub. 4 sent. 3 StPO). The number of penalty units reflect the measure of culpability. For a low degree of culpability, the number of penalty units would be low. Conversely, a high degree of culpability attracts a high number of penalty units. The maximum number of penalty units that can be imposed is 360 (§ 40 sub. 1 StGB). The amount per penalty unit depends on the personal and financial circumstances of the perpetrator. The perpetrator's net income usually serves as the basis for this assessment. Pursuant to § 40 sub. 2 StGB, penalty units can range from 1 EUR to 30,000 EUR.

96 In addition to the primary sentence, § 44 StGB permits the ordering of a driving ban if the criminal offence was committed during or in connection with the operation of a motor vehicle, and a driving ban appears to be necessary in order to have an effect on the perpetrator or to defend the legal order, or this would make the imposition of a term of imprisonment and its execution avoidable.

97 Furthermore, confiscation under §§ 73 to 75 StGB also has a punitive character, provided that it is ordered solely against the perpetrator or a participant in a criminal offence[53] (for more detailed information → Ch. 5).

4. Conclusion of the trial

98 The main hearing ends with the pronouncement of the judgment, § 260 StPO. After the pronouncement, the defendant must be instructed with regard to the legal remedies, § 35a StPO.

IV. Legal remedies

99 If applicable, the trial is followed by the appeal proceedings, §§ 296 et seq. StPO. The available remedies against the judgment are the appeal on points of fact and law (§§ 312 et seq. StPO and the appeal on points of law (§§ 333 et seq. StPO). Only the prosecutor's office and the accused person are entitled to file legal remedies (§ 296 sub. 1 StPO). This concludes the main proceedings.

100 There are various ways – so-called legal remedies – to proceed against court decisions. Of primary relevance are the complaint, the appeal on points of fact and law, and the appeal on points of law. A complaint can be filed to appeal against orders and rulings of the court, such as search warrants. If a party to the trial believes that the judgment of the court of first instance is unjust or wrong, this party can file an appeal to have this judgment reviewed by a higher court (appeal on points of fact and law or appeal on points of law only). The filing of an appeal on points of fact and law or an appeal on points of law stops the judgment from becoming final and absolute (§§ 316 sub. 1 and 343 sub. 1 StPO). This means that the judgment will not have a legal effect. The appellate proceedings on points of fact and law and on points of law alone differ in that the appellate proceedings on points of fact and law serve as a second trial and thus lead to a comprehensive re-hearing of the subject matter defined in the court order to proceed to trial[54], whereas the proceedings relating to the appeal on a point of law focus on a purely legal review of the judgment and the underlying proceedings[55].

---

[53] Schmitt/Köhler/Köhler StPO Vorbemerkungen zu § 421 mn. 2.
[54] MüKoStPO/Quentin StPO Vor §§ 312 et seqq. mn. 1.
[55] MüKoStPO/Knauer/Kudlich StPO Vor § 333 mn. 1.

In accordance with § 296 StPO, the prosecutor's office and the accused person are entitled to file legal remedies. Pursuant to § 297 StPO, defence counsel may file the relevant legal remedies on behalf of the accused person. Secondary parties to the proceedings also have appellate rights in the appeal proceedings on points of fact and law or solely on points of law (§§ 431 and 444 sub. 2 sent. 2 in conjunction with § 431 StPO). **101**

In addition to these three important legal remedies, there is the notice of objection to a summary penalty order, reinstatement to one's former position and the constitutional complaint. **102**

1. Complaint

Complaints in criminal proceedings distinguish between the ordinary complaint (*Beschwerde*) under §§ 304 et seq. StPO and the immediate complaint (*sofortige Beschwerde*) under § 311 StPO. **103**

The ordinary complaint as per § 304 sub. 1 StPO may be lodged against any orders issued by the courts of original jurisdiction or during appeal proceedings as well as any rulings of the presiding judge, the judge during the preliminary proceedings or any commissioned or requested judge. Any judicial measures that have a direct impact on the course of the proceedings, the procedural powers or the legal position of a person can therefore be contested by way of a complaint. Said measures must be distinguished from mere notices, instructions or preparatory measures.[56] **104**

By virtue of § 304 sub. 1 and 2 StPO, anyone whose rights are affected by the contested measure, either under procedural or substantive law, has the standing to lodge a complaint.[57] Pursuant to § 306 sub. 1 StPO, the complaint must be lodged with the court that issued the contested decision. The law stipulates neither a time limit for lodging a complaint nor the requirement to file a statement of grounds for the complaint. The latter is, however, permissible and generally advisable.[58] Where the court considers the complaint to have merit, it is required under the terms of § 306 sub. 2 StPO to redress the complaint, meaning that the court itself will decide on the matter by way of a separate order. Otherwise, the complaint must be submitted to the court hearing the complaint no later than within three days, § 306 sub. 2 sent. 2 StPO. Complaints against the orders of local courts are heard by the regional court (§ 73 GVG) and complaints against regional court orders are heard by the higher regional court (§ 121 sub. 1 no. 2 GVG). **105**

The immediate complaint differs from the ordinary complaint in that it must be lodged within one week (§ 311 sub. 2 StPO) and that the court itself is not permitted to amend the contested order (§ 311 sub. 3 sent. 1 StPO).[59] Accordingly, as opposed to the ordinary complaint, the court is not authorised to set aside, amend or supplement the contested decision, except if the principle of due process would otherwise be violated. Instead, the matter must immediately be submitted to the court that has jurisdiction to decide about the complaint.[60] The immediate complaint is only admissible in rare special cases provided for by law, for example under § 210 sub. 2 StPO. **106**

---

[56] MüKoStPO/Neuheuser StPO § 304 mn. 10.
[57] Schmitt/Köhler/Schmitt StPO § 304 mn. 6.
[58] Schmitt/Köhler/Schmitt StPO § 306 mn. 7.
[59] Schmitt/Köhler/Schmitt StPO § 311 mn. 1.
[60] MüKoStPO/Neuheuser StPO § 311 mn. 9.

2. Appeal on points of fact and law

107 Upon an appeal on points of fact and law (*Berufung*), a judgment may be judicially reviewed both from a legal and a factual perspective. The court where this type of appeal is heard is the second trial court. This means that new facts and evidence may be introduced during the appeal proceedings, § 323 sub. 3 StPO. § 312 StPO permits this type of appeal against all orders of a local court, i.e. orders pronounced by a judge sitting alone or by a bench that includes lay judges. Judgments of the regional courts and the higher regional courts, on the other hand, cannot be challenged by this type of appeal but only by an appeal on points of law. Appeals on points of fact and law are heard by the minor criminal panel (*kleine Strafkammer*) of the regional court (§ 74 sub. 3 and § 76 sub. 1 sent. 1 GVG), which is composed of a presiding judge and two lay judges. If the trial court of original jurisdiction has imposed a fine of less than 15 penalty units (sent. 1), the proceedings have been terminated or the defendant was acquitted and the prosecutor's office had applied for the imposition of a fine of more than 30 penalty units (sent. 2), the appellate proceedings will only take place if the court accepts the appeal (§ 313 sub. 1 StPO). However, under § 313 sub. 2 StPO, the court is obligated to accept the appeal unless is it manifestly without merit.

108 The appeal on fact and law must be lodged within one week from the pronouncement of the judgment, either in writing or for the record of the registry of the court that pronounced the challenged judgment, § 314 sub. 1 StPO. For the record of the registry means that the appeal may be lodged verbally at the court's registry, provided that the registry then records the lodging of the appeal in writing. As a rule, the appeal on fact and law applies to the entire judgment, § 318 sent. 2 and § 327 StPO. However, the appeal on fact and law may be restricted to certain points, such as the sentence (§ 318 sub. 1 StPO). In this case, the appellate court would review only the sentence and not the entire judgment.

109 The statement of grounds for appeal may be submitted within one week after expiry of the deadline for the lodging of the appeal on fact and law, § 317 StPO. Other than for appeals on fact and law subject to acceptance for adjudication, the law does not require that a statement of grounds for the appeal be submitted. Nevertheless, a statement of grounds is always advisable, as the court and the appellee are, in this way, advised at an early stage, albeit on a preliminary basis, about the direction and scope of the appellate matter, so that any legal or factual issues can be addressed in the run-up to the new trial.

110 During the appellate proceedings, the main appeal hearing takes place; its structure is based on that of the main hearing during the trial of the first instance (§§ 324 sub. 1 sent. 1 and 243 sub. 1 StPO).

111 The appeal proceedings on fact and law conclude with a judgment. If the appellate court upholds the judgment of the court of the first instance, it will dismiss the appeal on fact and law on the merits. However, if it considers the judgment of the court of first instance to be mistaken, the appellate court sets this judgment aside and decides on the merits (§ 328 sub. 1 StPO). In doing so, the appellate court must observe the prohibition of *reformatio in peius* pursuant to § 331 sub. 1 StPO, meaning that, if it was only the defendant who appealed, the judgment of the first instance must not be altered to the detriment of the defendant in terms of the type and severity of the legal consequences of the offence.

3. Appeal on points of law

112 By way of an appeal on points of law (*Revision*), a judgment can be judicially reviewed from a legal perspective. Unlike the appeal on both fact and law, the appellate proceedings on points of law do not constitute a new trial. Instead, the judgment is only reviewed as to

whether procedural or substantive law has been violated (§ 337 sub. 1 StPO). This review is limited to the written judgment. Procedural law has been violated if an act that is prescribed by law has either been omitted or performed incorrectly or was, in its entirety, impermissible. A number of procedural breaches that are grounds for appeal on points of law are expressly set out in § 338 StPO, such as a judge participating in reaching the verdict after having been challenged for bias (§ 338 no. 3 StPO). With regard to the violation of substantive law, the appellate court not only examines whether substantive law has been applied correctly to the set of facts ascertained but also whether the determinations in the written judgment are free of any lacunas, contradictions as well as contraventions of the principles of logic or empirical principles. In accordance with §§ 333 and 335 sub. 1 StPO, an appeal on points of law is admissible against the judgments of the local courts, i.e. judges sitting alone and benches that include lay judges, and of the regional court, i.e. criminal panels as well as criminal chambers for particularly serious crimes, and against the judgments of the higher regional court. The higher regional court has jurisdiction over appeals on points of law against judgments of the local court as the court of first instance and for appellate judgments of the regional court. The higher regional court is composed of three judges (§§ 116 and 122 sub. 1 GVG). The Federal Court of Justice has jurisdiction over appeals on points of law against first-instance judgments of the regional courts and judgments of the higher regional court. The Federal Court of Justice makes its decisions as a panel consisting of five judges, §§ 130 and 135 sub. 1 GVG. Appeals on points of law must be lodged with the court that pronounced the judgment appealed against within one week of pronouncement, either in writing or for the record of the court registry (§ 341 sub. 1 StPO). Appeals on points of law must be accompanied by a statement of grounds. In the statement of grounds, the appellant must state the extent to which he contests the judgment and applies for it to be quashed, and must provide the grounds for his applications, § 344 StPO. More specifically, § 344 sub. 2 sent. 1 StPO requires that the appellant state whether the judgment is contested because of the violation of a procedural provision (procedural objection) or because the violation of any other legal provisions (substantive objection).[61] The time limit for filing the statement of grounds is one month after expiry of the time limit for submitting the appeal on points of law, § 345 sub. 1 StPO. Written statements of grounds for appeal on points of law must be signed by defence counsel or a lawyer, § 345 sub. 2 StPO.

If the appeal on points of law has merit, the court sets aside the judgment (§ 354 sub. 1 **113** and sub. 2 StPO). The appellate court itself either decides pursuant to § 354 sub. 1 StPO on the matter or remits the matter to a different adjudicating body of the lower court (§ 354 sub. 2 StPO). The lower court is bound by the legal assessment of the appellate court (§ 358 sub. 1 StPO). § 354 sub. 1a, 1b and 3 and §§ 354a and 355 StPO apply to various special situations, which will not be addressed here, as they are of little relevance.

E. Execution proceedings

The main proceedings are followed by the execution proceedings, §§ 449 et seq. StPO. **114** The execution proceedings are comprised of all other decisions, measures and orders that take place after the court's judgment.

[61] MüKoStPO/Knauer/Kudlich StPO § 344 mn. 57.

I. Execution of the sentence

115 Where a prison term has been imposed, the execution of the sentence relates to the proceedings from the judgment becoming final and absolute until the beginning of the imprisonment. This not only includes any and all measures and orders for the execution of the sentence, but also the amendment (cf. § 495a StPO) as well as the time-limited (cf. § 455 StPO) or the final setting aside (cf. 456 StPO) of a decision issued by a criminal court.[62] In respect of fines, the entire collection process forms part of the execution of the sentence.

116 The prosecutor's office has subject matter jurisdiction over the execution of the sentence, § 451 StPO. In this case, the local jurisdiction depends on the court of the first instance (§ 143 sub. 1 GVG and § 7 sub. 1 of the Law on Enforcement of Criminal Sentences (*Strafvollstreckungsordnung*, StVollstrO)). The *Strafvollstreckungskammer*, i.e. the chamber of the court for the execution of prison sentences, has jurisdiction to issue subsequent court orders in matters concerning the enforcement of imprisonment (§ 462a sub. 1 StPO). Legal venue is the chamber in whose district the penal institution is located where the convicted person is being held at the time the court is seized of the case, § 462a sub. 1 sent. 1 StPO.

117 The prerequisite for the commencement of the execution of the sentence is the existence of a judgment that has formally become final and absolute (formal legal force), § 449 StPO. Formal legal force means that the decision cannot be contested by the parties to the proceedings (at least not with an ordinary legal remedy) and that it cannot be altered as part of these proceedings.[63] It is not only judgments in the narrower sense that may be subject to execution but also all other enforceable court decisions that substitute for judgments.[64]

118 Execution of the sentence must be initiated, without undue delay, once the decision has become final and non-appealable. A reprieve of no more than four months may only be granted to avoid substantial prejudice that cannot be reconciled with the purpose of the penalty, § 456 StPO. The execution of the sentence may be suspended if the convicted person is ill or pregnant, § 455 StPO. In cases of extradition or expulsion, the authorities can abstain from execution of the sentence altogether, § 456a StPO.

119 For the execution of a term of imprisonment, the competent authority summons the convicted person to serve his sentence and, at the same time, requests that the relevant penal institution admit the convicted person. Should the convicted person fail to present himself, the enforcement agency may, on its own initiative, issue an order requiring the convicted person's appearance or an arrest warrant (§ 457 sub. 2, sub. 3 in conjunction with § 131 sub. 1 StPO). The provisions of the Court-Fee Collection Ordinance (*Justizbeitreibungsordnung*) apply to fines and are supplemented and, in part, modified by §§ 459a et seq. StPO.

II. Costs of the proceedings

120 Pursuant to § 464a sub. 1 sent. 1 StPO, the costs of the proceedings are comprised of the fees and expenses of the public treasury. The fees are the standard amounts fixed for the individual instances.[65] They depend on the penalty imposed. Expenses are based

---

[62] Schmitt/Köhler/Schmitt StPO Vorbemerkungen zu §§ 449 et seqq. mn. 1.
[63] Schmitt/Köhler/Schmitt StPO Einleitung mn. 163, 164.
[64] Schmitt/Köhler/Schmitt StPO § 449 mn. 1.
[65] MüKoStPO/Grommes StPO § 464a mn. 3.

on the actual monetary amounts expended and may only be charged in certain legally prescribed cases.

The costs of the proceedings also include any costs incurred in the preparation of the indictment along with the costs of the execution of the sentence, § 464a sub. 1 sent. 2 StPO. **121**

Every judgment, every summary penalty order and every decision terminating an investigation must determine the party who must bear the costs of the proceedings, § 464 sub. 1 StPO. **122**

To the extent that he has been convicted, the defendant must bear the costs of the proceedings, including his own expenses, such as the costs of court-assigned defence counsel, § 465 sub. 1 StPO. In addition, the defendant must bear the costs and expenses of the injured party in connection with the adhesion proceedings, § 472a StPO. **123**

In accordance with § 467 sub. 1 StPO and § 204 StPO, the costs of the proceedings and the indicted accused's necessary expenses must be borne by the public purse if the indicted accused is acquitted, if the case has been dismissed or if the court terminates the proceedings. Mandatory exceptions from this principle apply if the indicted accused caused extra costs or expenses through fault of his own (§ 467 sub. 2 StPO) or, by pretending that he committed the offences that he was accused of, or he caused the indictment (§ 467 sub. 3 sent. 1 StPO). An important optional exception from the payment of process costs by the indicted accused applies if the indicted accused made statements that were untruthful or withheld material exonerating circumstances (§ 467 sub. 3 sent. 2 no. 1 StPO), if a procedural impediment is the only reason why the indicted accused is not convicted for a criminal act (§ 467 sub. 3 sent. 2 no. 2 StPO) or if the court terminates the proceedings pursuant to a provision that affords the court discretion in this respect (§ 467 sub. 4 StPO). **124**

The costs of an unsuccessful legal remedy must be borne by whoever lodged the remedy (§ 473 sub. 1 sent. 1 StPO). A legal remedy is deemed to be unsuccessful if it was dismissed as either inadmissible or without merit or if it, ultimately, results in the same or materially the same outcome for the appellant.[66] **125**

If the prosecutor's office withdraws charges brought and terminates the proceedings, the necessary expenses are usually borne by the public treasury, § 467a StPO. Conversely, where the proceedings were already terminated before the formal conclusion of the investigation, no entitlement to a reimbursement of costs arises. **126**

III. Compensation

Those prosecuted have, in principle, several options to claim compensation. **127**

Where unlawful measures were imposed and government bodies were at fault, the person prosecuted has a compensatory claim based on dereliction of official duty (§ 839 BGB and Art. 34 GG). **128**

§ 198 sub. 1 sent. 1 GVG provides for monetary damages if the court proceedings are excessively long.[67] **129**

The Act regarding Compensation for Wrongful Prosecution (*Gesetz über die Entschädigung für Strafverfolgungsmaßnahmen*, StrEG) provides for compensation if a conviction is quashed or reduced after the case was reopened or after it has become final and absolute (§ 1 StrEG).[68] If the accused person is acquitted or the proceedings are terminated or the court refuses to proceed the case to trial, as required by § 2 StrEG the **130**

---

[66] Schmitt/Köhler/Schmitt StPO § 437 mn. 6.

[67] MüKoStPO/Kreicker GVG § 198 mn. 6 et seq.; Schmitt/Köhler/Schmitt GVG § 198 mn. 1.

[68] MüKoStPO/Kunz StrEG § 1 mn. 2.

accused person must be compensated for any pre-trial custody suffered, interim commitment to a psychiatric hospital, temporary detention, seizure, confiscation or temporary disqualification from driving.[69]

[69] MüKoStPO/Kunz StrEG § 2 mn. 2.

CHAPTER 4
§ 30 OWIG

Bibliography: Cordes/Reichling, Grenzen ordnungswidrigkeitenrechtlicher Sanktionierung bei Verbandsgeldbußen, NJW 2015, 1335; Gehring, Aus dem Entwurf des Verbandssanktionsgesetzes für eine Neuauflage lernen, NZWiSt 2022, 437; Groß/Reichling, Weshalb sich Korruption nicht mit den Mitteln des Ordnungswidrigkeitenrechts bekämpfen lässt, wistra 2013, 89; Laudien, Ein ordnungswidrigkeitsrechtliches Novum – Anmerkungen zum neuen Sanierungs- und Abwicklungsgesetz (SAG) aus strafrechtlicher Sicht, ZIS 2015, 244; Letzien, Internationale Korruption und Jurisdiktionskonflikte, 2018; Mansdörfer/Timmerbeil, Zurechnung und Haftungsdurchgriff im Konzern – Eine rechtsgebietsübergreifende Betrachtung, WM 2004, 362; Mühlhoff, Lieber der Spatz in der Hand … oder: Nach der Novelle ist vor der Novelle! Zu den wesentlichen Änderungen des allgemeinen Ordnungswidrigkeitenrechts und des Kartellordnungswidrigkeitenrechts durch die 8. GWB-Novelle, NZWiSt 2013, 321; Peukert/Sinn, Das Verbandssanktionengesetz – eine Historie des Scheiterns(?), Newsdienst Compliance 2021, 230005; Ransiek, Zur strafrechtlichen Verantwortung von Unternehmen, NZWiSt 2012, 45; Rogall, Die bußgeldrechtliche Verantwortlichkeit von juristischen Personen und Personenvereinigungen nach § 30 OWiG, AL 2017, 5; Tiedemann, Die „Bebußung" von Unternehmen nach dem 2. Gesetz zur Bekämpfung der Wirtschaftskriminalität, NJW 1988, 1169; Többens, Die Bekämpfung der Wirtschaftskriminalität durch die Troika der §§ 9, 130 und 30 des Gesetzes über Ordnungswidrigkeiten, NStZ 1999, 1.

Table of contents

A. Introduction 58
B. Regulatory fine imposed on legal persons and on partnerships (§ 30 OWiG) 59
I. General scope of § 30 OWiG 60
II. Addressee of administrative sanctions (§ 30 OWiG) 61
1. Legal entities 61
2. Partnerships with legal personality 61
3. Pre-incorporation enterprises and pre-enterprises 62
4. Foreign enterprises 62
5. Associations without legal personality 63
III. Representative of the legal entity 63
1. Executive bodies or officers of the legal person (§ 30 sub. 1 no. 1 OWiG) 64
a) Stock corporation (AG) 64
b) Partnership limited by shares (KGaA) 64
c) Limited liability enterprises (GmbH) 64
d) Associations with legal personality and foundations under private law 64
e) Societas Europaea (SE) 65
f) Cooperative 65
g) Legal entities under public law 65
2. Members of the executive board or management board of an association without legal personality (§ 30 sub. 1 no. 2 OWiG) 65
3. Partnership with legal personality (§ 30 sub. 1 no. 3 OWiG) 65
a) Civil law partnership (GbR) 66
b) General partnership (oHG) 66
c) Limited partnership (KG) 66

d) GmbH & Co. KG 66
e) European Economic Interest Grouping (EEIG) and partnership 67
4. Authorized representatives (§ 30 sub. 1 no. 4 OWiG) 67
a) Chief representative 67
b) General commercial power of representation (with procuration) 67
5. Other management personnel (§ 30 sub. 1 no. 5 OWiG) 67
6. Liability in a corporate group 68
IV. Infringement 68
V. Infringement is a breach of duty or results in enrichment 69
1. Breach of duty (§ 30 sub. 1 alt. 1 OWiG) 69
a) General duties 69
b) Criminal offence and administrative offence 70
c) Breaches of supervisory duty 70
2. Enrichment (§ 30 sub. 1 alt. 2 OWiG) 71
3. Attribution to the representative 71
C. Sanctions and confiscation of financial benefits 72
I. Administrative fine 72
1. Amount and assessment of the fine (§ 30 sub. 2 OWiG) 72
2. Addressee of the fine 74
a) Cumulative fine 74
b) Isolated fine 74
c) Anonymous fine 74
3. Unitary offence and multiple offences 75
II. Confiscation of profits (§ 30 sub. 5 OWiG) 75
III. Other consequences 75
D. Independent proceedings (§ 30 sub. 4 OWiG) 76
E. Seizure of assets (§ 30 sub. 6 OWiG) 77
F. Procedural obstacles 77
I. Statute of limitation 77
II. Double jeopardy (ne bis in idem) 78
G. Procedure in case of legal succession (§ 30 sub. 2a OWiG) 80
H. Jurisdiction and responsible authority 80
I. Infringement is an administrative offence 80
1. Responsible authority 80
2. Appeal against the regulatory fining notice 81
II. Infringement is a crime 81
1. Responsible authority 81
2. Appeal against administrative fining notice 82
I. Summary and outlook 82

A. Introduction

1 German criminal law does not sanction corporate entities with criminal sanctions.[1] The prevailing German perspective and legal situation maintains that corporate entities cannot be guilty – due to the lack of ability to reason just like an individual. Criminal punishment requires the intellectual capacity to act and thus individual imputability and personal responsibility.[2] In contrast to other countries, such as the United States of America, where corporate entities face criminal penalties, the German legal system

[1] BeckOK OWiG/Meyberg, 46. Ed. 1.4.2025, OWiG § 30 mn. 1.

[2] Cf. BGH 27.10.1953 – 5 StR 723/52, NJW 1953, 1838; BeckOK OWiG/Meyberg, 46. Ed. 1.4.2025, OWiG § 30 mn. 1. In this sense also WJS WirtschaftsStrafR-HdB/Raum, 5th edn 2020, Ch. 4 mn. 213.

is rather focused on the concept of imposing administrative fines and related measures against corporates.

However, there have already been (and still are) efforts in German politics to reform German criminal law.[3] One argument is, among others, that in the area of white-collar crime, enterprises profiting from employee misconduct should in principle also be subject to stronger sanctions.[4] Those efforts were followed by a draft[5] of a *Gesetz zur Stärkung der Integrität in der Wirtschaft* [i.e. Law to Strengthen Integrity in Business][6] to expand the scope of criminal law to companies. At the same time, corporate compliance measures were to be recognized and enterprises were to be encouraged to clarify criminal offences through internal investigations.[7] This was followed by an official government draft[8] and numerous critical debates on the planned regulations.[9] In the end, the bill failed because the coalition could not agree.[10] 2

In any case, this (failed) legislative bill shows that it will only be a matter of time before enterprises in Germany will also have to bear criminal liability. Until then, the Act on Regulatory Offences (OWiG) closes the gap to sanction corporate entities with its central (complex) provision: § 30 OWiG, which concentrates on the concept of attribution where the company may be held liable for the misconduct of its representatives. 3

B. Regulatory fine imposed on legal persons and on partnerships (§ 30 OWiG)

Generally, an administrative sanction under § 30 OWiG requires that an **individual acting on behalf of a legal person** – e.g. representative, senior management – **commits an infringement** and thus breaches business duties: 4

1. **legal persons** (→ mn. 9 et seqq.) – e.g.: AG, GmbH, SE
2. **representative of the legal person** (→ mn. 19 et seqq.) – e.g.: CEO, board member, director
3. **infringement by the representative** (→ mn. 60 et seqq.)

[3] Cf. coalition agreement (*Koalitionsvertrag*) of CDU, CSU and SPD, p. 16, 126, available in German at <https://archiv.cdu.de/system/tdf/media/dokumente/koalitionsvertrag_2018.pdf?file=1> (last accessed: 10.6.2025).

[4] Cf. the coalition agreement of CDU, CSU, SPD, p. 16, 126, available in German at <https://archiv.cdu.de/system/tdf/media/dokumente/koalitionsvertrag_2018.pdf?file=1> (last accessed: 10.6.2025).

[5] Prior to this, there was already a draft bill (*Referentenwurf, RefE*) from the Federal Ministry of Justice and Consumer Protection that was 'leaked'. At that time, it was still called the *Gesetz zur Bekämpfung der Unternehmenskriminalität* [i.e. Act to Combat Corporate Crime] and was harshly criticized for this name alone, cf. Peukert/Sinn Newsdienst Compliance 2021, 230005.

[6] Cf. draft bill *Entwurf eines Gesetzes zur Stärkung der Integrität in der Wirtschaft*, available in German at <https://www.bmj.de/SharedDocs/Downloads/DE/Gesetzgebung/RefE/RefE_Staerkung_Integritaet_Wirtschaft.pdf?__blob=publicationFile&v=3> (last accessed: 10.6.2025).

[7] Cf. draft bill, p. 1 (→ fn. 6).

[8] Cf. government draft (*Regierungsentwurf, RegE*) *Entwurf eines Gesetzes zur Stärkung der Integrität in der Wirtschaft*, available at <https://www.bmj.de/SharedDocs/Downloads/DE/Gesetzgebung/RegE/RegE_Staerkung_Integritaet_Wirtschaft.pdf?__blob=publicationFile&v=3> (last accessed: 10.6.2025).

[9] For a list of the various opinions (*Stellungnahmen*) on the *Regierungsentwurf*, cf. <https://www.bmj.de/SharedDocs/Gesetzgebungsverfahren/DE/2020_Staerkung_Integritaet_Wirtschaft.html> (last accessed: 10.6.2025).

[10] Gehring NZWiSt 2022, 437 (437).

4. **breach of business-duties** (→ mn. 67 et seqq.) or **enrichment of the legal person** (→ mn. 79 et seqq.)
5. **consequences**
   a) administrative fine (→ mn. 89 et seqq.)
   b) confiscation of profits (→ mn. 107 et seqq.)

I. General scope of § 30 OWiG

5 The wording of § 30 OWiG is rather technical and – even in the original German version– challenging when reading it for the first time. However, in the context of this chapter it seems important to refer to the wording of each paragraph for clarity reasons.

6 § 30 sub. 1 OWiG stipulates as follows:

(1) Where someone acting

1. as an **entity authorized to represent**[11] a legal person or as a member of such an entity,
2. as **chairman of the executive** committee of an association without legal capacity or as a member of such committee,
3. as a **partner authorized to** represent a partnership with legal capacity, or
4. as the **authorized representative with full power of attorney** or in a managerial position as procura-holder or the authorized representative with a commercial power of attorney of a legal person or of an association of persons referred to in numbers 2 or 3,
5. as **another person responsible on behalf of the management of the** operation or enterprise forming part of a legal person, or of an association of persons referred to in numbers 2 or 3, also covering supervision of the conduct of business or other exercise of controlling powers in a managerial position,

has committed a criminal offence or a regulatory offence as a result of which **duties** incumbent on the legal person or on the association of persons **have been violated**, or where the legal person or the association of persons has been enriched or was intended to be enriched, **a regulatory fine may be imposed on such person or association**.

7 § 30 OWiG connects the offence of an individual to a legal person. Therefore, the individual must have committed an offence and be the legal representative of the legal entity. Furthermore, the representative must have violated a business-related duty.

8 The application of § 30 OWiG therefore requires that:[12]

- a legal entity exists (sub. 1 no. 1–5),
- a specific criminal offence or misdemeanour has been committed,
- the individual who committed the criminal offence or misdemeanour (infringement) was a representative or in a leading position at the legal entity,
- duties incumbent on the legal person or on the association of persons have been violated, or that the legal person or the association of persons has been enriched or was intended to be enriched.

---

[11] The highlighting in the legal texts was done by the author and is not present in the original. The English version of § 30 OWiG is taken from <https://www.gesetze-im-internet.de/englisch_owig/englisch_owig.html>, translation provided by Neil Mussett (last accessed: 27.10.2025).

[12] See Krenberger/Krumm/Krenberger/Krumm OWiG § 30 mn. 6.

II. Addressee of administrative sanctions (§ 30 OWiG)

An administrative fine may be imposed on legal entities, associations without legal personality and partnerships with legal personality. Sole traders (*Einzelkaufmann*) are exempt from the imposition of such fines.[13] 9

Addressee	Examples
legal entities (→ mn. 10 et seqq.)	e.g. AG, KGaA, SE, GmbH
partnerships with legal personality (→ mn. 13)	e.g. oHG, KG, GbR
pre-incorporation enterprises and pre-enterprises (→ mn. 14 et seq.)	e.g. Vor-GmbH
foreign enterprises (→ mn. 16 et seq.)	e.g. Spanish Sociedad Limitada; British Limited
associations without legal personality (→ mn. 18)	e.g. trade unions

1. Legal entities

Legal entities are all organisations that are granted their own legal personality by the legal system. This includes stock corporations (*Aktiengesellschaft*, AG), partnerships limited by shares (*Kommanditgesellschaft auf Aktien*, KGaA), Societas Europaea (SE), which is considered a stock corporation, limited liability enterprises (*Gesellschaft mit beschränkter Haftung*, GmbH), cooperatives (*Genossenschaft*), registered associations (*eingetragener Verein*) and foundations (*Stiftungen*).[14] 10

There are enterprises with limited liability where one individual controls the enterprise and is its sole beneficial owner (*Ein-Mann-GmbH*). Those 'one-person enterprises' can also be the addressee of an administrative fine. In this case in particular, the responsible person cannot unburden himself by referring to assets of the enterprise that are separate from his own assets. If that person is burdened twice because of a sanction against him personally and his enterprise, this is supposed to be taken into account in the sentencing which is, however, at the discretion of the competent authority.[15] 11

In addition, a fine can also be imposed on legal entities under public law which operate under private law. Fines may also be imposed on a county[16] or a municipality[17]. 12

2. Partnerships with legal personality

A partnership with legal personality is a partnership that can acquire rights and incur liabilities (§ 14 sub. 2 BGB). This includes the general partnership (*offene Handelsgesellschaft*, oHG), the limited partnership (*Kommanditgesellschaft*, KG), the GmbH & Co. KG, the European Economic Interest Grouping (EEIG), the partnership, 13

---

13 BeckOK OWiG/Meyberg, 46. Ed. 1.4.2025, OWiG § 30 mn. 20.
14 KK-OWiG/Rogall OWiG § 30 mn. 34.
15 BeckOK OWiG/Meyberg, 46. Ed. 1.4.2025, OWiG § 30 mn. 23.
16 OLG Frankfurt 30.1.1976 – 2 Ws (B) 356/75, NJW 1976, 1276 et seq.
17 OLG Hamm 27.2.1979 – 1 Ss OWi 1/79, NJW 1979, 1312.

and the civil law partnership (*Gesellschaft bürgerlichen Rechts*, GbR) participating in legal transactions.[18]

3. Pre-incorporation enterprises and pre-enterprises

14 Pre-incorporation enterprises act prior to the formal conclusion of the partnership agreement and, therefore, in the pre-formation stage. It includes every action made by people or organizations in order to form a corporation, including planning, discussions and agreements. This involves tasks including conducting market research, creating business plans, obtaining finance and writing bylaws. These pre-incorporation enterprises are considered a GbR with regard to the legal personality[19] and can, therefore, be addressees of a fine, provided that they already participate in legal transactions.[20]

15 Pre-enterprises act in the period from their formation until their creation through entry in the commercial register. It is a temporary legal structure to carry out operations and enter into agreements on behalf of the future enterprise prior to its official registration. According to the prevailing opinion, administrative fines may also be imposed on pre-enterprises.[21] Pre-enterprises are subject to the founding provisions given in the statutes of association and to the law of the incorporated enterprise to be.[22]

4. Foreign enterprises

16 An administrative fine may be imposed on a foreign enterprise if the typology of the foreign enterprise is legally comparable to that of the legal person or partnership in Germany,[23] e.g. the Spanish Sociedad Limitada and the GmbH.[24] In addition, the infringement of the individual must be subject to German law.[25] For practical reasons, however, this will only come into question if the foreign enterprise has its registered office or assets in Germany.[26] Otherwise, investigative proceedings may end without a binding decision on the merits of the case due to a lack of knowledge about the perpetrator's place of residence or due to the absence of mutual legal assistance agreements with the relevant country.[27]

17 However, German administrative law (§ 30 OWiG) shall also apply to credit and banking institutions (Capital Requirements Regulation – CRR) under the German Banking Act (*Gesetz über das Kreditwesen* – KWG) if the CRR is domiciled in another state of the European Economic Area (EEA) and operates in Germany through a branch or provides cross-border services (§ 59 KWG).

---

[18] KK-OWiG/Rogall OWiG § 30 mn. 41; BeckOK OWiG/Meyberg, 46. Ed. 1.4.2025, OWiG § 30 mn. 26.

[19] MüKoGmbHG/Heinze GmbHG § 2 mn. 259.

[20] BeckOK OWiG/Meyberg, 46. Ed. 1.4.2025, OWiG § 30 mn. 33.

[21] KK-OWiG/Rogall OWiG § 30 mn. 44; BeckOK OWiG/Meyberg, 46. Ed. 1.4.2025, OWiG § 30 mn. 34 with reference to a different view Göhler/Gürtler/Thomas OWiG § 30 mn. 7.

[22] BGH 12.7.1956 – II ZR 218/54, NJW 1956, 1435; BGH 2.5.1966 – II ZR 219/63, NJW 1966, 1311 (1313).

[23] BeckOK OWiG/Meyberg, 46. Ed. 1.4.2025, OWiG § 30 mn. 28; KK-OWiG/Rogall OWiG § 30 mn. 33.

[24] BGH 2.11.2010 – 1 StR 544/09, NZWiSt 2012, 75 (79); cf. on the liability of the managing director for the legal obligations of a private limited company established in **England** with operational management in Germany BGH 14.3.2005 – II ZR 5/03, NJW 2005, 1648; cf. sanctions against a **Polish** company due to a violation of labour law, OLG Celle 30.11.2001 – 322 Ss 217/01 (OWiz), wistra 2002, 230; cf. sanctions against a **Swiss** bank because of assistance in German clients tax evasion LG Düsseldorf 21.11.2011 – 10 KLs 14/11, BeckRS 2012, 24554.

[25] BeckOK OWiG/Meyberg, 46. Ed. 1.4.2025, OWiG § 30 mn. 28; KK-OWiG/Rogall OWiG § 30 mn. 33.

[26] Cf. NK-WSS/von Galen/Schaefer OWiG § 30 mn 116; KK-OWiG/Rogall OWiG § 30 mn. 33.

[27] NK-WSS/von Galen/Schaefer OWiG § 30 mn 116.

5. Associations without legal personality

Associations without legal personality (*Vereine ohne Rechtspersönlichkeit*, § 54 BGB) **18**
serve to achieve a common, self-imposed purpose and their existence is independent of changes in membership. However, associations without legal personality have a constitution, association bodies and act as a cohesive entity under a specific association name. The main operation is not directed towards an economic business operation.[28] Common examples are trade unions and student fraternities.

III. Representative of the legal entity

Legal entities act through individuals that are entitled to act on behalf of the entity. **19**

According to § 30 OWiG, the offence or misdemeanour (infringement) must be **committed by a representative or person in charge of the entity**. This applies to bodies, **20**
executives or persons responsible for the enterprise in senior management positions, even if those individuals only perform supervisory or control activities. However, there must be a certain degree of independence and decision-making authority.[29]

According to the prevailing opinion, the act of appointment of the representative does **21**
not have to be effective. It is sufficient if the act is merely implemented on a factual basis.[30]

The extent of the power of representation within the respective enterprise is irrelevant **22**
for liability. It is also irrelevant whether restrictions of the power of representation are effective vis-à-vis third parties. Consequently, the entities have no possibility of limiting the circle of offenders under § 30 OWiG by imposing restrictions on their power of representation.[31]

Furthermore, it is not considered necessary to determine a specific individual who **23**
committed the infringement.[32] If several individuals are suspected, it is sufficient if the act was committed beyond reasonable doubt by any representative in accordance with § 30 sub. 1 no. 1–5 OWiG.[33] The responsible person does not have to be individualized.[34] It is only necessary to establish that a person in charge has acted culpably and reprehensibly.[35]

The applicable entities and their representatives under § 30 OWiG can be summarized **24**
as follows:

Entity	Representative
stock corporations (AG)	management board and individual members of the management board
partnerships limited by shares (KGaA)	general partners
limited liability enterprises (GmbH)	managing directors

---

28 KK-OWiG/Rogall OWiG § 30 mn. 38; BeckOK OWiG/Meyberg, 46. Ed. 1.4.2025, OWiG § 30 mn. 25.

29 WJS WirtschaftsStrafR-HdB/Raum, 5th edn 2020, Ch. 4 mn. 214.

30 Többens NStZ 1999, 1 (6); BGH 28.6.1966 – 1 StR 414/65, BGHSt 21, 101 = NJW 1966, 2225. For a different view, cf. KK-OWiG/Rogall OWiG § 30 mn. 86 with further references.

31 KK-OWiG/Rogall OWiG § 30 mn. 85 with further references.

32 Krenberger/Krumm/Krenberger/Krumm OWiG § 30 mn. 10.

33 WJS WirtschaftsStrafR-HdB/Raum, 5th edn 2020, Ch. 4 mn. 214; BeckOK OWiG/Meyberg, 46. Ed. 1.4.2025, OWiG § 30 mn. 57.

34 BeckOK OWiG/Meyberg, 46. Ed. 1.4.2025, OWiG § 30 mn. 57.

35 BGH 8.2.1994 – KRB 25/93, NStZ 1994, 346; BeckOK OWiG/Meyberg, 46. Ed. 1.4.2025, OWiG § 30 mn. 57.

Entity	Representative
associations with legal personality (e.g. GbR, oHG, KG) and foundations under private law (e.g. trade unions)	board of directors
Societas Europaea (SE)	members of the management board or administrative board
cooperative	members of the management board

1. Executive bodies or officers of the legal person (§ 30 sub. 1 no. 1 OWiG)

a) Stock corporation (AG)

25 The management board (*Vorstand*) is the governing body of the AG (§§ 78, 82 AktG). Therefore, the individual members of the management board are suitable perpetrators. The deputy members of the management board are also members of the management board (§ 94 AktG), as is the member of the management board appointed by the court (§ 85 AktG). The special representative appointed in accordance with § 30 BGB can also be a perpetrator of the infringement. In the event of a liquidation of the AG, the liquidators take the place of the executive board. These are usually the members of the management board, but the court may also appoint external liquidators (*Abwickler*, § 265 sub. 1, sub. 2 and sub. 3 AktG).[36]

b) Partnership limited by shares (KGaA)

26 In the case of a KGaA, the general partners are deemed to be members of the management board (§§ 282, 283 AktG).[37]

c) Limited liability enterprises (GmbH)

27 The GmbH is represented by the managing director(s) (*Geschäftsführer*, §§ 6, 35 GmbHG). The deputies of the managing directors are also representatives of the GmbH (§ 44 GmbHG). In the event of the dissolution of the GmbH, the liquidators take the place of the managing directors (§§ 66 et seqq., 70 GmbHG).[38]

d) Associations with legal personality and foundations under private law

28 The board of directors (*Vorstand*) is the legal body of a registered association (*eingetragener Verein*) in Germany and is responsible for representing it (§ 26 BGB). As a result, board members (*Vorstandsmitglieder*) may be regarded perpetrators of the infringement.

29 The same applies for foundations under private law, as the laws for associations are analogously implemented (§ 86 BGB). This means that foundation board members have the same rights and duties as association board members and can be held accountable for their acts in this capacity.

---

[36] KK-OWiG/Rogall OWiG § 30 mn. 63.

[37] BeckOK OWiG/Meyberg, 46. Ed. 1.4.2025, OWiG § 30 mn. 48.1.

[38] OLG Zweibrücken 14.12.1994 – 1 Ss 264/94, NStZ 1995, 293; KK-OWiG/Rogall OWiG § 30 mn. 66.

e) Societas Europaea (SE)

The SE is considered to be a stock corporation. It can be established either according to a dualistic system – management and supervisory body according to the German model (§§ 15 et seqq. SEAG (Act on the Implementation of Council Regulation (EC) No 2157/2001 of 8 October 2001 on the Statute for a European Company (SE)) – or a monistic system – management and supervisory function lie with the administrative board (*Verwaltungsrat*, §§ 20 et seqq. SEAG). The members of the respective management body, i.e. the management board or the administrative board, are, therefore, capable perpetrators of the infringement. 30

f) Cooperative

The cooperative (*Genossenschaft*) is represented by the ordinary and deputy members of the board of management (§§ 24, 35 GenG).[39] 31

g) Legal entities under public law

The representation of legal entities under public law shall be determined in accordance with the relevant law or from the statutes of association.[40] 32

2. Members of the executive board or management board of an association without legal personality (§ 30 sub. 1 no. 2 OWiG)

According to § 54 BGB, an association without legal personality (*Verein ohne Rechtspersönlichkeit*) is one that is not enrolled in the association registration and, hence, lacks legal identity. It cannot act on its own as a bearer of rights and obligations but is generally represented by board members (§§ 54, 26 BGB).[41] However, in addition to the board, special representatives can be appointed for particular transactions (§ 30 BGB). However, any infringements by special representatives are not covered by § 30 OWiG.[42] 33

3. Partnership with legal personality (§ 30 sub. 1 no. 3 OWiG)

The partnerships with legal personality and their representatives under § 30 OWiG can be summarized as follows: 34

Partnership	Representative
GbR	managing partners
oHG	managing partners
KG	managing partners (personally liable partners, *Komplementär*)
GmbH & Co. KG	managing partners

Furthermore, administrative proceedings can be executed if partners act on behalf of partnerships with legal personality. This relates to the following partnerships and their representatives (§ 30 sub. 1 no. 3 OWiG): 35

[39] KK-OWiG/Rogall OWiG § 30 mn. 67.
[40] BeckOK OWiG/Meyberg, 46. Ed. 1.4.2025, OWiG § 30 mn. 48.1.
[41] BeckOK OWiG/Meyberg, 46. Ed. 1.4.2025, OWiG § 30 mn. 48.2.
[42] KK-OWiG/Rogall OWiG § 30 mn. 71.

a) Civil law partnership (GbR)

36 A partnership under the BGB (*Gesellschaft bürgerlichen Rechts*, GbR) is a partnership under the German Civil Code formed by two or more parties (partners) with a joint objective. Generally, all partners are jointly entitled to represent the GbR (§ 709 sub. 1 BGB). However, a majority of votes between more than two partners can be determined in the partnership agreement (§ 709 sub. 2 BGB).

37 Furthermore, it is also possible to transfer the management to one or more partners to the exclusion of the others (§ 710 BGB) or to assign the management to all partners in such a way that each is entitled to act alone (see § 711 BGB).[43]

b) General partnership (oHG)

38 A general partnership under the German Commercial Code (HGB) (*offene Handelsgesellschaft* – oHG) is defined as an open trading enterprise where all partners have unlimited liability for the enterprise's obligations (§ 125 HGB).

39 Generally, all partners are authorized to represent the enterprise (§ 125 sub. 1 HGB). Therefore, the infringement of each partner is sufficient for the imposition of an administrative fine. The partnership agreement may provide that all or several partners are to have authority to represent the partnership only jointly (joint representation, § 125 sub. 2 HGB).

c) Limited partnership (KG)

40 A limited partnership (*Kommanditgesellschaft* – KG) is a partnership having at least one partner who bears unlimited liability (general partner – *Komplementär*) and another who bears limited liability up to their capital contribution (limited partner – *Kommanditist*).

41 The KG is represented only by the personally liable partners (general partners, §§ 161, 125 HGB). The partners with limited liability are excluded from representation (limited partners, § 170 HGB). However, sole representation of the KG can be transferred to an individual by contract. It is also possible to grant the limited partner commercial power of attorney which may constitute acting on behalf of the association.[44]

42 In the event of dissolution of the partnership, all partners, i.e. also the limited partners, are in principle appointed liquidators in accordance with §§ 161 sub. 2 and 146 HGB. Their actions can therefore also be relevant under § 30 OWiG.[45]

d) GmbH & Co. KG

43 The GmbH & Co. KG provides a hybrid structure between a KG and a GmbH: the general partner (*Komplementär*) is not an individual but a GmbH.

44 This structure offers limited liability protection (because no individual is exposed to liability) while still affording them operational flexibility as a partnership.

45 The management of the GmbH & Co. KG is executed by the GmbH which is a fully accountable partner. The limited partners (*Kommanditisten*) only contribute capital and have limited liability up to the assets invested.

46 The GmbH & Co. KG is represented by the GmbH (Komplementär). The managing partner of this GmbH is the responsible individual under § 30 OWiG.[46]

---

[43] KK-OWiG/Rogall OWiG § 30 mn. 78.
[44] See also BeckOK OWiG/Meyberg, 46. Ed. 1.4.2025, OWiG § 30 mn. 48.3.
[45] KK-OWiG/Rogall OWiG § 30 mn. 74.
[46] Cf. BGH 18.5.2017 – 3 StR 103/17, BeckRS 2017, 115055.

e) European Economic Interest Grouping (EEIG) and partnership

The European Economic Interest Grouping (EEIG) is a cooperative entity established **47** by European Union (EU) law, designed to facilitate cross-border cooperation among businesses within the EU.

The EEIG is a commercial enterprise also within the meaning of the HGB. The provi- **48** sions applicable to the oHG apply accordingly (§ 1 EWIVAG). It is, therefore, a partnership with legal personality (§ 30 sub. 1 no. 3 OWiG) to which the standards of the oHG apply.[47]

4. Authorized representatives (§ 30 sub. 1 no. 4 OWiG)

The scope of 'authorized representatives' covers, after the management level, also the **49** second level of authorized representatives.

Authorized representatives are chief representatives (*Generalbevollmächtigter*, **50** see §§ 164 et seqq. BGB), representatives with general commercial power of attorney (*Prokurist*, see §§ 48 et seqq. HGB) and trade representatives (*Handlungsbevollmächtigter*, see § 54 HGB).

a) Chief representative

Chief representatives perform wide management functions, so that their power of **51** representation is not limited.[48]

b) General commercial power of representation (with procuration)

The scope of the general commercial power of representation is determined by law **52** (§§ 49 and 54 HGB). The de facto status as a person with general commercial power of attorney is sufficient for § 30 OWiG to apply.

However, it is always necessary for the authorized signatory or trade representative to **53** hold a management position. In particular, a person is in a management position if he or she is responsible for the actual management of the enterprise at the highest level.[49] Detailed findings are necessary in this regard, which must be based on the organisational structure of the enterprise as well as the competences granted to the person concerned within the management and representation.[50]

5. Other management personnel (§ 30 sub. 1 no. 5 OWiG)

Besides authorized representatives in leading management positions of enterprises, **54** also other persons responsible on behalf of the management are covered (§ 30 sub. 1 no. 5 OWiG). This **very wide-ranging provision** is supposed to prevent circumvention of responsibilities.[51]

Management responsibility according to § 30 sub. 1 no. 5 OWiG also includes the **55** 'supervision of the conduct of business or other exercise of controlling powers in a managerial position'. Therefore, there are two groups of responsible persons, namely with **management authority** and with **supervisory and control authority**.[52]

---

47 KK-OWiG/Rogall OWiG § 30 mn. 76.

48 KK-OWiG/Rogall OWiG § 30 mn. 80 with reference to Göhler/Gürtler/Thomas OWiG § 30 mn. 12a.

49 BT-Drs. 12/192, 32.

50 KK-OWiG/Rogall OWiG § 30 mn. 81. So in the result also BeckOK OWiG/Meyberg, 46. Ed. 1.4.2025, OWiG § 30 mn. 48.4.

51 BT-Drs. 14/8998, 11.

52 KK-OWiG/Rogall OWiG § 30 mn. 82.

56 It has not yet been uniformly clarified which groups of persons or hierarchical levels in an enterprise have management authority.[53] In any case, the size of the enterprise is decisive. One indicator is whether the person has authority to represent the enterprise or authority to make decisions on behalf of the enterprise.

57 Persons with supervisory and control authority are – among others – responsible for a specific area of the enterprise, such as internal financial control or auditing. This also applies to the environmental officer with management powers and members of the supervisory board of an AG or GmbH.[54] Whether the specially appointed compliance officer or money laundering officer can be considered as a suitable perpetrator with 'monitoring and control powers' is disputed.[55]

58 However, besides formal responsibility which are determined by contracts with employees, it has to be noted that also the **factual management situation** is crucial. If a person does not have any formal management position in the company but in fact acts and is accepted as a manager, this person may be responsible under § 30 sub. 5 OWiG.[56]

6. Liability in a corporate group

59 According to the prevailing view, it is also possible for the parent company of a corporate group of companies to be held liable on the basis of the liability of the subsidiary if the parent company of the group is the corporate owner of the subsidiaries.[57] This is particularly possible in cases where one of the responsible representatives of the parent company named in § 30 sub. 1 no. 1–5 OWiG exercises a de facto controlling influence over the subsidiary with the aim of enriching the parent company.[58] As a result, liability of the parent company can only be ruled out in the rare cases in which offenders outside the group of persons specified in § 30 sub. 1 no. 1–5 OWiG commited infringements and a (supervisory) breach of duty by a person pursuant to § 30 sub. 1 no. 1–5 OWiG cannot be substantiated.[59]

IV. Infringement

60 A fine imposed in accordance with § 30 sub. 1 OWiG requires that a **criminal offence** or an **administrative offence** (infringement) has been committed by a representative of a legal entity.

61 With regard to the wide range of possible individual criminal offences and administrative offences in a corporate context, reference is made to the other chapters of this handbook.

---

[53] Cf. the comments in KK-OWiG/Rogall OWiG § 30 mn. 83.

[54] BT-Drs. 14/8998, 10.

[55] Cf. the comments in BeckOK OWiG/Meyberg, 46. Ed. 1.4.2025, OWiG § 30 mn. 53 with further references; KK-OWiG/Rogall OWiG § 30 mn. 84 with further references.

[56] Cf. BGH 13.12.2012 – 5 StR 407/12, NJW 2013, 624; BeckOK OWiG/Meyberg, 46. Ed. 1.4.2025, OWiG § 30 mn. 49.

[57] Mansdörfer/Timmerbeil WM 2004, 362 (368 et seq.); KK-OWiG/Rogall OWiG § 30 mn. 87; Reichling NJW 2012, 164 (166). Regarding a violation of obligatory supervision (§ 130 OWiG) in a multicorporate enterprise, see OLG München 23.9.2014 – 3 Ws 599/14 u. 3 Ws 600/14, CCZ 2016, 44 – Caracas.

[58] Mansdörfer/Timmerbeil WM 2004, 362 (368).

[59] Mansdörfer/Timmerbeil WM 2004, 362 (369).

Attempted offences are also relevant infringements leading to the imposition of fines.[60] The infringement must have been committed culpably by the relevant individual.[61] 62

Infringements committed abroad by an individual are also relevant under § 30 OWiG, if German criminal law or the German Act on Administrative Offences applies for the infringement.[62] 63

German criminal law applies in non-domestic cases, if particular crimes are committed, e.g. bribery, offences against physical integrity or the environment (see § 5 StGB). German criminal law also applies inter alia if the offence was committed abroad and the perpetrator is a German national (see § 7 StGB). 64

The Act on Regulatory Offences (OWiG) applies in non-domestic cases if the offence of the individual caused a damage or harmed any rights in Germany (see § 7 sub. 1 OWiG), which is intended to protect legal interests and rights in Germany irrespective of the place of the conduct.[63] 65

V. Infringement is a breach of duty or results in enrichment

The infringement of the individual must either have violated duties that affect the entity (alt. 1) or the enterprise must have been enriched by the act or an enrichment must at least have been intended (alt. 2). 66

1. Breach of duty (§ 30 sub. 1 alt. 1 OWiG)

Relevant are only infringements that violate business-related obligations,[64] which affect the legal entity or association of persons as the norm addressee, such as – among others – a taxpayer, an employer, an exporter of goods or a trader.[65] 67

There is no business-relation if the individual acts personally, i.e. like any other person and thus without specific reference to its position as a body of the legal entity.[66] 68

a) General duties

The duty to act lawful and with due care is a duty that applies to everyone according to the rule of law. However, general duties that apply to everyone can also become 'business-related' duties due to a factual connection with the legal person or association of persons.[67] For example, it is a general duty not to harm anybody. Besides, it is also a business-related duty to respect occupational safety according to labour law.[68] 69

Also, the person who operates a department store or a (technical) plant has to observe the obligations to protect third parties against any threats, and the person who supplies consumer goods has to avert possible hazards or damage to purchasers.[69] It is, therefore, 70

---

60 BeckOK OWiG/Meyberg, 46. Ed. 1.4.2025, OWiG § 30 mn. 61.
61 KK-OWiG/Rogall OWiG § 30 mn. 88.
62 KK-OWiG/Rogall OWiG § 30 mn. 88; BeckOK OWiG/Meyberg, 46. Ed. 1.4.2025, OWiG § 30 mn. 66.
63 BeckOK OWiG/Valerius OWiG § 7 mn. 8.
64 BT-Drs. V/1269, 60.
65 BeckOK OWiG/Meyberg, 46. Ed. 1.4.2025, OWiG § 30 mn. 80.
66 OLG Celle 26.11.2004 – 1 Ws 388/04, NStZ-RR 2005, 82.
67 BeckOK OWiG/Meyberg, 46. Ed. 1.4.2025, OWiG § 30 mn. 81; KK-OWiG/Rogall OWiG § 30 mn. 93.
68 KK-OWiG/Rogall OWiG § 30 mn. 93.
69 BeckOK OWiG/Meyberg, 46. Ed. 1.4.2025, OWiG § 30 mn. 81. Cf. also the examples in KK-OWiG/Rogall OWiG § 30 mn. 93.

conceivable, among other things, that negligent bodily injury can be the basis for an administrative fine against the enterprise according to § 30 OWiG.[70]

b) Criminal offence and administrative offence

71 Criminal offences under the StGB or administrative offences under the OWiG may also be business-related if those acts affect the business and sphere of activity of the legal entity or association of persons.

72 Examples are bribery (§§ 299, 331 et seqq. StGB),[71] environmental crimes (§§ 324 et seqq. StGB), violations of the Occupational Safety and Health Act (*Arbeitsschutzgesetz*, ArbSchG), the Act to Combat Undeclared Work and Unlawful Employment (*Schwarzarbeitsbekämpfungsgesetz*, SchwarzArbG) and tax obligations.[72]

c) Breaches of supervisory duty

73 Criminal offences and misdemeanours in companies are committed not only by representatives of an enterprise, but also at **lower hierarchical levels**. These levels are regularly not covered by § 30 OWiG.[73] However, an enterprise can still be held liable under § 30 OWiG if the owner of the enterprise or an affiliated company omits to provide the necessary supervision vis-à-vis the lower levels of the hierarchy.

74 In practice, the main case of violation of a business-related duty is the violation of the duty of supervision pursuant to § 130 sub. 1 OWiG:[74]

> (1) Whoever, as the owner of an operation or undertaking [enterprise], intentionally or negligently **omits to take the supervisory measures required to prevent contraventions**, within the operation or undertaking [enterprise], of duties incumbent on the owner **and the violation of which carries a criminal penalty or a regulatory fine**, shall be deemed to have committed a regulatory offence in a case where such contravention has been committed as would have been **prevented**, or **made much more difficult**, if there had been **proper supervision**. The required supervisory measures shall also comprise appointment, careful selection and surveillance of supervisory personnel.[75]

75 Besides the owner of the company, a violation of the duty of supervision may also be committed by assimilated company members (§ 9 OWiG) if they were instructed by the owner of the company.

76 The concrete duties of care are not defined in more detail in § 130 OWiG.[76] They may arise from special standards in different business fields, from court decisions and from the general principle that certain life circumstances give rise to responsibility for the conduct of other persons.[77]

---

[70] BT-Drs. V/1269, 60 et seq.

[71] BGH 27.4.2022 – 5 StR 278/21, BeckRS 2022, 13180; BGH 18.5.2017 – 3 StR 103/17, BeckRS 2017, 115055; BeckOK OWiG/Meyberg, 46. Ed. 1.4.2025, OWiG § 30 mn. 82 with reference to different view Groß/Reichling wistra 2013, 89 (89).

[72] BeckOK OWiG/Meyberg, 46. Ed. 1.4.2025, OWiG § 30 mn. 82.

[73] KK-OWiG/Rogall OWiG § 30 mn. 92.

[74] BeckOK OWiG/Meyberg, 46. Ed. 1.4.2025, OWiG § 30 mn. 78; KK-OWiG/Rogall OWiG § 30 mn. 92.

[75] The highlighting in the legal texts was done by the author and is not present in the original. The English version of § 130 OWiG is taken from <https://www.gesetze-im-internet.de/englisch_owig/englisch_owig.html>, translation provided by Neil Mussett (last accessed: 27.10.2025).

[76] Krenberger/Krumm/Krenberger/Krumm OWiG § 130 mn. 17; BeckOK OWiG/Beck OWiG § 30 mn. 39 et seqq.

[77] Krenberger/Krumm/Krenberger/Krumm OWiG § 130 mn. 17 with further references.

However, the principle of trust and of permitted risk must be recognized.[78] This means that the extent of the duty to supervise within one's own enterprise is to be determined by an overall assessment of the circumstances.[79] First and foremost, the type, size and organisation of the enterprise, the different monitoring possibilities, but also the experience gained in the past must be taken into account.[80] **77**

Any supervisory measure must be appropriate and objectively reasonable in order to prevent or significantly reduce the risk of a violation.[81] The necessary measures include, among others, the appointment, careful selection and monitoring of supervisors[82], the precise division of responsibilities and competences,[83] and the enforcement of measures such as admonishing, instructing or terminating unreliable employees.[84] **78**

2. Enrichment (§ 30 sub. 1 alt. 2 OWiG)

A fine may also be imposed if the infringement has either led to an actual enrichment of the legal person or association of persons or if an enrichment was at least intended. This also covers constellations of merely attempted infringements. It applies regardless of whether duties of the legal person or association of persons have been violated. Accordingly, the purpose of the provision is solely to sanction the (attempted) transfer of unlawful assets to the enterprise. **79**

Enrichment is defined as any improvement in assets, i.e. any increase in the asset's economic value.[85] This includes, for example, taxes wrongly received, expenses saved or profits from illegal transactions.[86] Indirect benefits, such as the attainment of a dominant market position, may also constitute enrichment.[87] Intangible benefits are, however, only included if they constitute an economically measurable advantage.[88] **80**

There must also be a *causal* connection between the infringement and the enrichment of the enterprise.[89] **81**

3. Attribution to the representative

A further requirement for the imposition of an administrative fine is that the individual that committed an infringement acted 'as' a body, representative, authorized representative or other management person at the time of the infringement. It is necessary that the act has a 'representative reference'.[90] This should distinguish business-related actions from private actions.[91] **82**

---

[78] KK-OWiG/Rogall OWiG § 130 mn. 42; Krenberger/Krumm/Krenberger/Krumm OWiG § 130 mn. 18.

[79] Krenberger/Krumm/Krenberger/Krumm OWiG § 130 mn. 18.

[80] OLG Zweibrücken 25.6.1998 – 1 Ss 100/98, NStZ-RR 1998, 311 et seq.; Krenberger/Krumm/Krenberger/Krumm OWiG § 130 mn. 18.

[81] Krenberger/Krumm/Krenberger/Krumm OWiG § 130 mn. 20.

[82] AG Köln 14.2.2019 – 902b OWi 163/19, BeckRS 2019, 6507 mn 13.

[83] OLG Düsseldorf 12.11.1998 – 2 Ss OWi 385–98 – (OWi) 112–98 III, NStZ-RR 1999, 151.

[84] Krenberger/Krumm/Krenberger/Krumm OWiG § 130 mn. 20; KK-OWiG/Rogall OWiG § 130 mn. 65.

[85] TK StGB/Perron StGB § 263 mn. 167.

[86] BeckOK OWiG/Meyberg, 46. Ed. 1.4.2025, OWiG § 30 mn. 86.

[87] KK-OWiG/Rogall OWiG § 30 mn. 99 with further references; BeckOK OWiG/Meyberg, 46. Ed. 1.4.2025, OWiG § 30 mn. 86.

[88] BeckOK OWiG/Meyberg, 46. Ed. 1.4.2025, OWiG § 30 mn. 86.

[89] KK-OWiG/Rogall OWiG § 30 mn. 101; BeckOK OWiG/Meyberg, 46. Ed. 1.4.2025, OWiG § 30 mn. 90.

[90] KK-OWiG/Rogall OWiG § 30 mn. 106.

[91] BeckOK OWiG/Meyberg, 346. Ed. 1.4.2025, OWiG § 30 mn. 68.

83 There must be a functional (objective) connection between the infringement, the scope of duties and the responsibilities of the representative.[92] It is not relevant whether the area of responsibility has been exceeded. The decisive factor is a 'mandated' and business-related action within the individual function in the association.[93] Therefore, the objective perspective of an outsider is important and not the subjective perspective of the acting person.[94]

84 There is, for example, a functional connection between the infringement and the duties of the representative if the representative bribes or deceives a contractual partner of the company in the course of business negotiations in exchange for closing a contract.[95] In contrast, there is no connection if the representative of a legal entity causes a traffic accident during a business trip.[96]

85 Any business-related infringements by a representative outside of what can be expected according to life experience can be considered an **excess**. Such acts of excess do not constitute a connecting act and cannot justify any liability of the enterprise under § 30 OWiG.

86 In addition, no fine may be imposed if the act of the body or representative is directed against the legal entity itself, such as in the case of falsely filing a tax return for the enterprise to conceal an embezzlement committed by the body member himself.[97]

C. Sanctions and confiscation of financial benefits

87

Sanctions		**Confiscation of profits**	**Other**
Intent: up to 10 million euros (higher sanctions possible in individual cases)	**Negligence:** up to 5 million euros (higher sanctions possible in individual cases)	Confiscation of profits gained through the infringement	e.g. registration in the competition register and central trade register

88 Infringements committed by representative, authorized representative or other management person may result in various sanctions for the enterprise. However, the principle of discretion (*Opportunitätsprinzip*) applies (§ 47 OWiG). This principle gives the prosecuting authorities discretion on whether to prosecute an administrative offence.

I. Administrative fine

1. Amount and assessment of the fine (§ 30 sub. 2 OWiG)

89 § 30 sub. 2 OWiG determines the statutory upper limit of the fine:[98]

(2) The regulatory fine shall amount

---

[92] KK-OWiG/Rogall OWiG § 30 mn. 106.
[93] HK-OWiG/Schmitt-Leonardy OWiG § 30 mn. 30.
[94] HK-OWiG/Schmitt-Leonardy OWiG § 30 mn. 30.
[95] Letzien Internationale Korruption, p. 166 with reference to Göhler/Gürtler/Thomas OWiG § 30 mn. 25.
[96] KK-OWiG/Rogall OWiG § 30 mn. 108.
[97] See KK-OWiG/Rogall OWiG § 30 mn. 122.
[98] BeckOK OWiG/Meyberg, 46. Ed. 1.4.2025, OWiG § 30 mn. 96.

1. in the case of a criminal offence committed with intent, to not more than **ten million euro**,
2. in the case of a criminal offence committed negligently, to not more than **five million euro**.

Where there has been commission of a regulatory offence, the maximum regulatory fine that can be imposed shall be determined by the maximum regulatory fine imposable for the regulatory offence concerned. If the Act refers to this provision, the maximum amount of the regulatory fine in accordance with the second sentence shall be multiplied by ten for the offences referred to in the Act. The second sentence shall also apply where there has been commission of an act simultaneously constituting a criminal offence and a regulatory offence, provided that the maximum regulatory fine imposable for the regulatory offence exceeds the maximum in accordance with the first sentence.

This means that the following fines can be determined: 90

- up to 10 million euros in case of an intentional criminal act, (§ 30 sub. 2 sent. 1 no. 1 OWiG);
- up to 5 million euros in case of a negligent criminal act, (§ 30 sub. 2 sent. 1 no. 2 OWiG); and
- in the case of an administrative offence, a fine in accordance with the maximum amount threatened for the administrative offence (§ 30 sub. 2 sent. 2 OWiG).

In the case of administrative offences directly referring to § 30 OWiG the responsible 91 authority can increase the fine up to a tenfold of the designated fine imposed for the underlying offence (§ 30 sub. 2 sent. 3 OWiG). Therefore, a violation of obligatory supervision in operations and enterprises (§ 130 OWiG) can lead to a fine of up to 10 million euros.[99] In individual cases, an even higher fine is possible.

In the case of violations of the German Act on the Recovery and Resolution of Credit 92 Institutions (*Sanierungs- und Abwicklungsgesetz* – SAG), a fine of up to 50 million euros is possible (§ 172 sub. 2 sent. 2 SAG).[100] Furthermore, individual violations of the German Banking Act (*Gesetz über das Kreditwesen* – KWG) may lead to a higher fine than 10 million euros (§ 56 sub. 6 no. 1 KWG). In the case of particularly serious violations of the Act Against Restraints of Competition (*Gesetz gegen Wettbewerbsbeschränkungen* – GWB), the fine may reach to up to 10 % of the annual turnover of the enterprise or corporate group generated in the business year preceding the authority's decision (§ 81c sub. 1 GWB).

The administrative fine shall consist of two parts: a **penalty** and the **confiscation of** 93 **financial benefits**.

According to the **punishment function**, the amount of the penalty considers the 94 necessity of punishing a legal violation. Therefore, the significance is crucial. The decisive factors are the unlawfulness of the act, the weight and extent of the breach of duty and its frequency. The severity of the damage and the further effects of the violation are also relevant.[101]

Furthermore, the administrative fine shall exceed the financial benefit that the per- 95 petrator has obtained from the commission of the administrative offence (§§ 30 sub. 3, 17 sub. 4 OWiG). Financial benefits essentially refer to the profit made, expenses saved, benefits of use and remuneration for the offence.[102] Therefore, the **confiscation function** of the fine is to confiscate unlawful profits.

When calculating the economic advantage, the '**net principle**' (*Nettoprinzip*) must 96 be applied. This means that expenses must be deducted from the profits obtained.[103]

---

[99] BeckOK OWiG/Meyberg, 46. Ed. 1.4.2025, OWiG § 30 mn. 96b.
[100] Cf. KK-OWiG/Rogall OWiG § 30 mn. 132; for criticism, cf.: Laudien ZIS 2015, 244; Rogall AL 2017, 5.
[101] KK-OWiG/Rogall OWiG § 30 mn. 136 with further references.
[102] KK-OWiG/Rogall OWiG § 30 mn. 141 with further references.
[103] BeckOK OWiG/Meyberg, 46. Ed. 1.4.2025, OWiG § 30 mn. 100.

Hypothetical profits and possible claims for compensation by third parties under civil law are also disregarded.[104]

97 By way of explanation: the '**gross principle**' (*Bruttoprinzip*) does not apply. It would cover all the revenue that has accrued to the person involved in the crime, without deduction of expenses or consideration.[105] The gross principle applies, however, in the context of confiscation law according to §§ 73 et seqq. StGB.[106]

98 Due to the possibility of confiscating financial benefits, the fines against enterprises can go far beyond the statutory maximum fine, up to a three-digit million amount.[107]

2. Addressee of the fine

99 There are different approaches to determine the addressee of an administrative fine.

a) Cumulative fine

100 A cumulative fine is imposed if the fine addresses the individual (who committed the infringement) together with the enterprise. A cumulative fine is the usual approach since § 30 sub. 4 sent. 1 OWiG only allows independent proceedings under certain conditions.[108]

b) Isolated fine

101 The isolated fine is imposed independently, i.e. independently of the prosecution of the person who committed the infringement. This applies, if criminal or administrative proceedings against the person who committed the infringement were not initiated at all, were terminated or the penalty was dispensed (§ 30 sub. 4 sent. 2 OWiG). In such cases an administrative fine against the enterprise may be imposed independently.[109]

c) Anonymous fine

102 An anonymous fine is imposed if the person who committed the infringement cannot be identified, but it is certain that the criminal or administrative offence was committed by a suitable perpetrator.[110] However, the fine addresses the enterprise while the relevant person who committed the infringement remains anonymous.

103 It is possible that several bodies, representatives, authorized representatives or other leading persons in an entity can be considered as perpetrators of the infringement, but it cannot be determined which person exactly committed the unlawful act. If the perpetration of the offence is not in doubt, an administrative fine may be imposed.[111] Besides, an anonymous administrative fine may be imposed if a breach of supervisory duty (§ 130 OWiG) has occurred, and it is also established that at least one perpetrator among the management bodies is responsible for this.[112]

---

[104] BeckOK OWiG/Meyberg, 46. Ed. 1.4.2025, OWiG § 30 mn. 100; KK-OWiG/Rogall OWiG § 30 mn. 117; BGH 18.5.2017 – 3 StR 103/17, BeckRS 2017, 115055 mn. 33.

[105] TK StGB/Eser/Schuster StGB § 73 mn. 9.

[106] BGH 27.4.2022 – 5 StR 278/21, NZWiSt 2022, 410 (414); → Ch. 5.

[107] See LG Düsseldorf 21.11.2011 – 10 KLs 14/11, BeckRS 2012, 24554.

[108] KK-OWiG/Rogall OWiG § 30 mn. 117.

[109] For the requirements in detail, cf. → mn. 114 et seqq.

[110] Cf. already → mn 23.

[111] Cf. already → mn 23.

[112] KK-OWiG/Rogall OWiG § 30 mn. 120; Tiedemann NJW 1988, 1169 (1173).

3. Unitary offence and multiple offences

104 Generally, one **unitary offence** (*Tateinheit*) leads to the violation of one criminal or administrative law. However, if the same procedural act violates more than one statute according to which it may be sanctioned as an administrative offence, or violates such a legal provision repeatedly, then only one administrative fine shall be assessed for the unitary offence (§ 19 OWiG).

105 Besides, if several managers are involved in **a connecting act**, their actions are only attributed once to the legal person or association of persons. However, the respective managers can be fined separately (§ 14 OWiG).[113]

106 If a manager has committed **multiple offences** (*Tatmehrheit*), a fine shall be imposed for each of these offences (§ 20 OWiG).[114]

II. Confiscation of profits (§ 30 sub. 5 OWiG)

107 The imposition of a fine on an enterprise shall preclude a confiscation of assets related to the same offence (§ 30 sub. 5 OWiG) to prevent double sanctioning:[115]

> (5) Assessment of a regulatory fine incurred by the legal person or association of persons shall, in respect of one and the same offence, preclude a confiscation order, in accordance with [§§] 73 or 73c StGB or in accordance with [§] 29a, against such person or association of persons.[116]

108 Consequently, even if no fine is imposed on the legal person, confiscation of the profits of the offence may be ordered (§§ 73, 73c StGB, 29a OWiG). The confiscation of profits against the enterprise requires that the enterprise obtained something due to an act which may be sanctioned by an administrative fine and the offender acted for the enterprise.[117]

III. Other consequences

109 Furthermore, the **confiscation of enterprise-owned property and rights** may be considered if they have been obtained through a criminal offence or a misdemeanour committed by representatives of the legal entity (§§ 74e StGB, 29 OWiG).[118]

110 In addition, in (rare) cases of **violations of the Economic Offences Act 1954 (WiStG)**, instead of confiscating the profits of an offence, the gain in profits of the underlying business resulting from the offence may be forfeited.[119] Possible offences include – among others – unreasonable rent increases.[120] It is required that the legal entity gained additional profits, i.e. the difference between the permissible price and the price obtained, from an unlawful act under the WiStG (§ 8 WiStG).

---

[113] BGH 9.5.2017 – 1 StR 265/16, BeckRS 2017, 114578 mn. 112; BeckOK OWiG/Meyberg, 46. Ed. 1.4.2025, OWiG § 30 mn. 108; KK-OWiG/Rogall OWiG § 30 mn. 154.

[114] BeckOK OWiG/Meyberg, 46. Ed. 1.4.2025, OWiG § 30 mn. 109. Concerns about this are expressed by KK-OWiG/Rogall OWiG § 30 mn. 152 and Cordes/Reichling NJW 2015, 1335 (1336 et seq.).

[115] BT-Drs. 7/550, 344.

[116] The English version of § 30 OWiG is taken from <https://www.gesetze-im-internet.de/englisch_owig/englisch_owig.html>, translated by Neil Mussett (last accessed: 27.10.2025).

[117] → Ch. 5.

[118] KK-OWiG/Rogall OWiG § 30 mn. 127 with further references.

[119] KK-OWiG/Rogall OWiG § 30 mn. 126.

[120] Cf. §§ 1–6 WiStG.

111 Furthermore, if fines according to § 30 OWiG are imposed against enterprises, those enterprises may be registered in the **competition register** (*Wettbewerbsregister*).[121] This may result in exclusion from public tender procedures:[122] public contracting authorities shall exclude an enterprise from participation at any point in the tender procedure when they are aware that a person whose conduct is imputable to the enterprise has been convicted by final judgement or a final administrative fine has been issued against the enterprise (§ 123 sub. 1 GWB) for a criminal offence such as – among other things – money laundering, bribery or fraud.[123]

112 In the event of a legally binding decision imposing a fine, e.g. in connection with the exercise of a trade, the enterprise will be registered in the **central trade register** (*Gewerbezentralregister*) if the fine exceeds 200 euros.

113 The German Act on Regulatory Offences and the German Criminal Code do not provide the dissolution of the enterprise.[124]

D. Independent proceedings (§ 30 sub. 4 OWiG)

114 Generally, as stated in → mn. 100, the administrative fine is imposed in a cumulative procedure against the perpetrator of the infringement and the enterprise. As a result, the fine against the enterprise shall in principle be ordered in the same decision as the decision regarding its representative.[125]

115 However, the fine may also be imposed independently if criminal or administrative proceedings against the person who committed the infringement were not initiated at all, were terminated or the penalty was dispensed (§ 30 sub. 4 sent. 1 OWiG):

> (4) If criminal proceedings or regulatory fining proceedings are not commenced on account of the criminal offence or of the regulatory offence, or if such proceedings are discontinued, or if imposition of a criminal penalty is dispensed with, the regulatory fine may be assessed independently.

116 Independent proceedings can also be carried out if it cannot be determined which of several management persons in question committed the offence. It is only necessary to establish that a responsible person (§ 30 OWiG) has committed the infringement in a reprehensible manner.[126]

117 If, however, the perpetrator remains unknown, this does not lead to the inadmissibility of the proceedings but compels their discontinuation, thus enabling independent proceedings.[127]

118 If both types of proceedings can be considered, the competent prosecuting authority has the option to choose at its discretion.[128]

---

[121] Cf. § 2 sub. 1 no. 3 WRegG.

[122] Cf. on this § 1 sub. 1 WRegG and KK-OWiG/Rogall OWiG § 30 mn. 122.

[123] → Ch. 24.

[124] KK-OWiG/Rogall OWiG § 30 mn. 128.

[125] Krenberger/Krumm/Krenberger/Krumm OWiG § 30 mn. 48.

[126] BGH 8.2.1994 – KRB 25/93, NStZ 1994, 346.

[127] BeckOK OWiG/Meyberg, 46. Ed. 1.4.2025, OWiG § 30 mn. 133 and KK-OWiG/Rogall OWiG § 30 mn. 166.

[128] BeckOK OWiG/Meyberg, 46. Ed. 1.4.2025, OWiG § 30 mn. 112 and KK-OWiG/Rogall OWiG § 30 mn. 176 et seqq. with further references.

In independent confiscation proceedings, the law generally stipulates a written procedure without a hearing.[129] However, the public prosecutor's office can apply for a hearing.[130] 119

E. Seizure of assets (§ 30 sub. 6 OWiG)

A seizure of assets to secure the enforcement of an administrative fine can be ordered if an administrative fining notice (*Bußgeldbescheid*) has been issued (§ 30 sub. 6 OWiG). This is supposed to prevent any displacement of assets that could prevent the setting and enforcement of the fine.[131] 120

It is required that the administrative fining notice has been issued. There must be indications that the enforcement of the fine is in danger. If, for example, the person concerned has sufficient assets, there is usually no reason to secure the fine.[132] 121

The requirements to prove a reason for a seizure of assets are high. There are many reasons for an enterprise to dispose or restructure assets.[133] According to case law, the decisive factors are, in particular, exceptional circumstances or if the purpose of the enterprise is solely manipulative and fraudulent.[134] 122

F. Procedural obstacles

I. Statute of limitation

The limitation period for the fine against the enterprise is based on the limitation period of the underlying offence.[135] Thus, if a criminal act or an administrative offence committed by a natural person leads to the liability of a legal person or association of persons under § 30 OWiG, the limitation period applicable to the act committed by the natural person shall apply in the proceedings against the legal person.[136] 123

If the infringement committed by the individual is time-barred, there is a legal obstacle to fine the enterprise.[137] 124

However, according to § 33 sub. 1 OWiG, the period of limitation shall be interrupted by 125

1. the initial examination of the person concerned, the notification that investigation proceedings have been initiated against him, or by the order requiring such examination or notification,
2. any judicial examination of the person concerned or of a witness, or by the order requiring such examination,

[129] See §§ 29a sub. 5, 87 sub. 3 OWiG; see also: BeckOK OWiG/Ganter OWiG § 87 mn. 62.
[130] See § 436 sub. 2 StPO in conjunction with § 434 sub. 3 StPO.
[131] BT-Drs. 17/11053, 23.
[132] BeckOK OWiG/Meyberg, 46. Ed. 1.4.2025, OWiG § 30 mn. 139c with reference to BT-Drs. 416/16, 85.
[133] Mühlhoff NZWiSt 2013, 321 (328).
[134] Mühlhoff NZWiSt 2013, 321 (328).
[135] BeckOK OWiG/Meyberg, 46. Ed. 1.4.2025, OWiG § 30 mn. 140.
[136] BGH 5.12.2000 – 1 StR 411/00, NJW 2001, 1436.
[137] BGH 5.7.1995 – KRB 10/95, NStZ-RR 1996, 147; BeckOK OWiG/Meyberg, 46. Ed. 1.4.2025, OWiG § 30 mn. 140.

3. any appointment of an expert by the prosecuting authority or the judge, if the person concerned has previously been examined or was informed of the initiation of the investigation proceedings,
4. any order by the prosecuting authority or by the judge for seizure or search, and by judicial decisions by which such order is upheld,
5. the temporary discontinuation of the proceedings by the prosecuting authority or the judge because of absence of the person concerned, as well as by any order of the prosecuting authority or the judge issued after such discontinuation of the proceedings to establish the whereabouts of the person concerned or to secure evidence,
6. any request by the prosecuting authority or the judge to undertake an investigatory act in a foreign country,
7. the statutory hearing of another authority by the prosecuting authority prior to conclusion of the investigations,
8. the transfer of the case to the administrative authority by the public prosecution office in accordance with [§] 43,
9. issuance of a regulatory fining notice, so far as such notice is served within two weeks, otherwise by service thereof,
10. receipt of the files at the local court in accordance with [§ 69 sub. 3 sent. 1] and [sub. 5 sent. 2] and referral of the case to the administrative authority in accordance with [§ 69 sub. 5 sent. 1],
11. any fixing of a date for a main hearing,
12. reference to the possibility of giving a decision without a main hearing [(§ 72 sub. 1 sent. 2)],
13. preferring public charges,
14. the opening of main proceedings,
15. a penal order or any other decision equivalent to a judgment.[138]

126 In independent proceedings involving an order imposing an incidental consequence or an administrative fine against a legal person or an association of persons, the period of limitation shall be interrupted by the same acts as referred to before for the purpose of carrying out independent proceedings (§ 33 sub. 1 sent. 2 OWiG).

127 In cumulative proceedings, the act interrupting the statute of limitations, for example ordering the interrogation or conducting it,[139] against the management person also have the effect of interrupting the statute of limitations against the association,[140] even if independent proceedings are conducted later.[141]

II. Double jeopardy (ne bis in idem)

128 In Germany the legal doctrine of *ne bis in idem* prohibits the duplication of trials or punishments for the same offence against an individual person or legal entity. This doctrine for both (individuals and legal entities) is set out in Art. 103 para. 3 GG (for criminal offences) and specified in § 84 OWiG (for administrative offences). In particular, the doctrine prohibits a duplication of trials and punishments, where a legally binding decision on the merits of the case exists. The only condition is that the facts and circumstances of both cases are identical.[142]

129 According to European law the right not to be tried or prosecuted twice is stated in Art. 50 CFR (Charter of Fundamental Rights of the European Union). According to the

---

[138] The English version of § 33 OWiG is taken from <https://www.gesetze-im-internet.de/englisch_owig/englisch_owig.html>, translated by Neil Mussett (last accessed: 27.10.2025).

[139] BayObLG 21.9.1995 – 1 ObOWi 460/95, NStZ-RR 1996, 46.

[140] BGH 28.6.2005 – KRB 2/05, NJW 2006, 163 (164); BeckOK OWiG/Meyberg, 46. Ed. 1.4.2025, OWiG § 30 mn. 141.

[141] BGH 5.12.2000 – 1 StR 411/00, NJW 2001, 1436 (1437).

[142] Cf. KK-OWiG/Lutz OWiG § 84 mn. 3 et seq.

European Court of Justice[143] ('ECJ'), ne bis in idem applies – contrary to its wording – not only to criminal offences, but also to proceedings and penalties which must be considered as 'criminal in nature'. The ECJ classifies proceedings and penalties as 'criminal in nature' by an assessment on account of the intrinsic nature of the offence or the degree of severity of the penalty in question.[144] Thus, administrative offences are also subject to Art. 50 CFR.

However, a recent ruling by the ECJ in the case *Volkswagen*[145] dated 14 September 2023 **130** shows that generally a duplication of proceedings might arise where a certain conduct is subject to prosecution in different jurisdictions. Therefore, companies which engage in cross border business activities or operate in different countries could be subject to a duplication of proceedings for the same conduct. Such a duplication of proceedings might be promoted due to a lack of international cooperation between countries and authorities. The ECJ set clear, that ne bis in idem applies as soon as a binding decision on the merits of the case takes place in one EU-Member State.[146] If a binding decision exists in one EU-Member State, authorities in another EU-Member State are bound to the decision and cannot prosecute or impose criminal or administrative penalties.[147] This also applies to proceedings or trials in one EU-Member State that took place before the binding decision in another EU-Member State became final or was initiated.[148] Therefore, the first legally binding decision of one EU-Member State counts.

However, according to the ECJ[149] – a violation of ne bis in idem can be justified in light **131** of Art. 52 CFR. The ECJ ruled on 30 January 2025 that a company may face multiple penalties – all potentially 'criminal in nature' – imposed by different authorities for identical facts, under separate national laws within the EU.[150] In the case, the Romanian natural gas provider 'Engie' reserved the right to adjust fixed prices in end-consumer contracts without properly demonstrating this right and subsequently adjusting prices due to rising supplementation costs. Engie faced two administrative fines by different authorities (both in Romania) for the same conduct. One authority charged Engie to have aggressively infringed a regulation concerning commercial practices (Directive 205/29). The second authority imposed an administrative fine for infringing transparency requirements as set out by European requirements (Directive 2009/73).[151]

The ECJ ruled that such a duplication of administrative fines (in the same EU-Member **132** State) may be justified under Art. 52 CFR, if there is a basis 'provided for by [national] law respecting the essence of Art. 50 of the Charter' and the concurrent penalties comply with the principle of proportionality.[152]

143 ECJ 30.1.2025 – C-205/23, ECLI:EU:C:2025:43 mn. 49 – ENGIE.
144 ECJ 30.1.2025 – C-205/23, ECLI:EU:C:2025:43 mn. 49 – ENGIE.
145 Cf. ECJ 14.9.2023 – C-27/22, ECLI:EU:C:2023:663 = EuZW 2023, 1045 – Volkswagen.
146 ECJ 14.9.2023 – C-27/22, ECLI:EU:C:2023:663 = EuZW 2023, 1045 mn. 58 et seq. – Volkswagen.
147 Cf. ECJ 14.9.2023 – C-27/22, ECLI:EU:C:2023:663 = EuZW 2023, 1045 mn. 77 – Volkswagen.
148 ECJ 14.9.2023 – C-27/22, ECLI:EU:C:2023:663 = EuZW 2023, 1045 mn. 77 – Volkswagen.
149 ECJ 30.1.2025 – C-205/23, ECLI:EU:C:2025:43 – ENGIE.
150 ECJ 30.1.2025 – C-205/23, ECLI:EU:C:2025:43 mn. 69 – ENGIE.
151 ECJ 30.1.2025 – C-205/23, ECLI:EU:C:2025:43 mn. 15 et seq. – ENGIE.
152 ECJ 30.1.2025 – C-205/23, ECLI:EU:C:2025:43 mn. 60 et seq. – ENGIE.

G. Procedure in case of legal succession (§ 30 sub. 2a OWiG)

133 In the event of partial or universal succession of the entity by means of splitting,[153] the fine may be imposed on the legal successors (§ 30 sub. 2a sent. 1 OWiG):

> (2a) In the event of a universal succession or of a partial universal succession by means of splitting [(§ 123 sub. 1 UmwG)], the regulatory fine in accordance with sub. 1 and 2 may be imposed on the legal successor(s). In such cases, the regulatory fine may not exceed the value of the assets which have been assumed, as well as the amount of the regulatory fine which is appropriate against the legal successor. The legal successor(s) shall take up the procedural position in the regulatory fine proceedings in which the legal predecessor was at the time when the legal succession became effective.[154]

134 When determining the fine against a legal successor, it should be noted that in such cases the fine may not exceed the value of the assets taken over and the amount of the fine appropriate to the legal successor. In particular, the valuations regularly required for corporate restructurings may provide necessary indications for determining the value of the assets taken over.[155] With regard to the limitation of the fine, it may be necessary to establish the circumstances that would have been relevant for the assessment of the hypothetical fine against the predecessor.[156]

H. Jurisdiction and responsible authority

135 Generally, the administrative authority shall have jurisdiction over the investigation of administrative offences, unless (in criminal law cases) the public prosecutor's office has such jurisdiction (§ 35 OWiG).

136 The responsibility for the investigations depends on the underlying connecting infringement.

I. Infringement is an administrative offence

1. Responsible authority

137 If the connecting infringement of an individual is a misdemeanour, the fine authority that is or would be responsible for punishing the misdemeanour shall decide in the combined and independent proceedings (§ 88 sub. 1, 2 OWiG).[157]

138 If there is a breach of the duty of supervision pursuant to § 130 OWiG that is linked to a criminal offence, the public prosecutor's office may assume jurisdiction. The prerequisite is that prosecution by the public prosecutor's office is appropriate (§ 42 sub. 1, 2 OWiG). There shall be a connection between a criminal offence and a regulatory offence if a

---

153 See § 123 sub. 1 UmwG (Transformation Act).

154 The English version of § 30 OWiG is taken from <https://www.gesetze-im-internet.de/englisch_owig/englisch_owig.html>, translation provided by Neil Mussett (last accessed: 27.10.2025).

155 BT-Drs. 17/11053, 22.

156 BT-Drs. 17/11053, 22.

157 BeckOK OWiG/Meyberg, 46. Ed. 1.4.2025, OWiG § 30 mn. 116.

person is accused of a criminal offence as well as of a regulatory offence, or if with regard to the same offence one person is accused of a criminal offence and another person of a regulatory offence.

If the underlying criminal proceedings, for example against the employee, are terminated, the public prosecutor's office may continue to impose an administrative fine under its own jurisdiction, unless it transfers the proceedings back to the administrative authority.[158] **139**

In the case of tax offences, the tax authority is responsible for the investigation of the administrative offence (§ 409 AO). **140**

2. Appeal against the regulatory fining notice

The person concerned has the right to appeal an administrative fining notice issued both in cumulative and independent proceedings (§ 67 OWiG). In this case, the administrative authority must consider whether to uphold or withdraw the decision (§ 69 sub. 2 sent. 1 OWiG).[159] **141**

If the administrative authority upholds the decision, the authority forwards the files to the public prosecutor's office (§ 69 sub. 3 OWiG). The public prosecutor's office submits the files to the judge at the district court if it neither discontinues the proceedings nor conducts further investigations (§ 69 sub. 4 sent. 2 OWiG); a court proceeding follows.[160] **142**

In this case, the criminal court orders the enterprises' participation as a secondary participant (*Nebenbeteiligte*) in the court proceedings (§ 444 sub. 1 StPO). **143**

The legal person or the association of persons is summoned to the main hearing; if its representative fails to appear with no sufficient excuse, the hearing may be conducted in its absence (§ 444 sub. 2 StPO). **144**

It is important to note that the rights of an accused individual also apply to the legal person.[161] This is because the legal person is in a procedural position that corresponds with an accused individual. This concerns primarily the right to remain silent, which is exercised by the representatives, who, consequently, cannot be heard as a witness in this scenario.[162] **145**

Furthermore, it should be noted that an enterprise can appeal the verdict.[163] The enterprise may only raise objections where it states that it was not heard in the main proceedings through no fault of its own.[164] For example, if the legal person was not properly summoned and, therefore, not legally heard. **146**

II. Infringement is a crime

1. Responsible authority

If the connecting infringement is a criminal offence, the responsibility to investigate lies with the public prosecutor's office. If the criminal proceedings have been terminated, **147**

[158] BeckOK OWiG/Meyberg, 46. Ed. 1.4.2025, OWiG § 30 mn. 116.
[159] Cf. in detail KK-OWiG/Rogall OWiG § 30 mn. 226 et seqq.
[160] See § 71 OWiG, § 411 sub. 1 sent. 2 StPO.
[161] Meyer-Goßner/Schmitt/Schmitt StPO § 444 mn 3a.
[162] KK-StPO/Schmidt/Scheuß StPO § 444 mn. 7, 8.
[163] See § 431 sub. 1–3, § 444 sub. 2 sent. 2 StPO.
[164] KK-StPO/Schmidt/Scheuß StPO § 444 mn. 12.

the administrative authority may start investigations regarding a misdemeanour (if any).[165]

2. Appeal against administrative fining notice

148 In **cumulative proceedings**, the administrative fine is assessed uniformly with the sanction against the individual by way of a verdict or penalty court order – and not by way of an administrative fining notice. The enterprise concerned may appeal the decision (§ 444 sub. 2 sent. 2 StPO; → mn. 141 et seqq.).[166]

149 In **independent proceedings**, the determination of the fine requires an application by the public prosecutor's office (§§ 444 sub. 3 sent. 1, 435 sub. 1 StPO). The court then decides by way of a court order, which may be appealed against immediately, i.e. within one week (§§ 434 sub. 2, 311 StPO). After an oral hearing, the court decides by way of a judgment (§ 434 sub. 3 StPO). The verdict of the criminal court is subject to appeal.[167]

I. Summary and outlook

150 Under German law, it is currently not possible to impose criminal sanctions on legal entities.[168] However, legal entities can be fined in accordance with § 30 OWiG if a person in a managerial position commits a criminal or administrative offence which, among other things, violates the enterprise's obligations.

151 The question of whether a criminal penalty or an administrative fine is imposed against legal entities is rather an academic discussion and ultimately a labelling issue. Legal persons will in any case – obviously – not have to fear a prison sentence. It is much more decisive, however, that a significant increase in the amount of fines – from the current maximum of 10 million euros – is to be expected. The forerunner of this development is the Data Protection Act – where fines of up to 4 % of the enterprise annual turnover apply. Also, according to the Act on Corporate Due Diligence Obligations in Supply Chains, fines of up to 2 % of the enterprise's annual turnover are possible. The (failed) draft of Corporate Criminal Law also provided a fine of up to 10 percent of the average annual turnover.

152 It is quite obvious that the German lawmakers are overall 'gearing up' to impose stricter and higher sanctions on enterprises.

---

165 BeckOK OWiG/Meyberg, 46. Ed. 1.4.2025, OWiG § 30 mn. 117.

166 KK-OWiG/Rogall OWiG § 30 mn. 214, 217; BeckOK OWiG/Meyberg, 46. Ed. 1.4.2025, OWiG § 30 mn. 122, 126.

167 Cf. BeckOK OWiG/Meyberg, 46. Ed. 1.4.2025, OWiG § 30 mn. 138; KK-OWiG/Rogall OWiG § 30 mn. 219.

168 Ransiek NZWiSt 2012, 45 (45).

CHAPTER 5
CONFISCATION

Bibliography: Bekritsky, Die Einziehung von Gesellschaftserträgen „für die Tat", NStZ 2022, 207; Bittmann, § 73b StGB: Die Einziehung beim Dritten in ihren feinen Verästelungen, wistra 2020, 265; Bittmann/Tschakert, Der Bereicherungszusammenhang beim Quasi-Durchgangserwerb gem. § 73b Abs. 1 S. 1 Nr. 2, ggf. i.V.m. § 73c StGB, und die Haftung des Täters oder Teilnehmers dabei als „anderer", wistra 2020, 217; Kämpfer/Schwerdtfeger, Unternehmen als Adressaten der Dritteinziehung von Taterträgen gem. § 73b StGB, StraFo 2020, 313; Köhler, Die Reform der strafrechtlichen Vermögensabschöpfung – Teil 1/2, NStZ 2017, 497; Köhler/Burkhard, Die Reform der strafrechtlichen Vermögensabschöpfung – Teil 2/2, NStZ 2017, 665; Köllner/Mück, Reform der strafrechtlichen Vermögensabschöpfung, NZI 2017, 593; Korte, Grundzüge der Reform der Vermögensabschöpfung, NZWiSt 2018, 231; Korte, Vermögensabschöpfung reloaded, wistra 2018, 1; Meyer, „Reformiert die Rückgewinnungshilfe!"–Denkanstöße für eine Generalüberholungder Vermögensabschöpfung, ZStW 2015 127, 241; Michalke, Vergleich und Einziehung – § 73e Abs. 1 StGB, wistra 2022, 492; Reh, Praxisprobleme im Umgang mit dem neuen Recht der Vermögensabschöpfung aus staatsanwaltschaftlicher Sicht, NZWiSt 2018, 20; Rettke, Die Bedeutung der Einziehung gemäß § 73 StGB – Die Aufwertung der strafrechtlichen Vermögensabschöpfung – Teil 1, NZWiSt 2019, 281; Sartorius/Henckel, Causa Cum/Ex finita? – Die steuerstrafrechtliche Bewertung von Cum/Ex-Transaktionen nach den Grundsatzurteilen von BGH und BFH, DStR 2022, 1029; Trüg, Die Reform der strafrechtlichen Vermögensabschöpfung, NJW 2017, 1913; Ullenboom, Die Einziehung von Taterträgen in Mehrpersonenverhältnissen, wistra 2020, 223.

Table of contents

A. Introduction: purpose and legal bases of confiscation 84
B. Overview on the systematics of the law on confiscation 85
  I. Legal bases for confiscation 86
  II. Procedural rules 87
  III. Mechanisms to provisionally secure assets 87
  IV. Schematic overview 88
C. The principle: confiscation from persons involved in the offence 88
  I. Requirements for confiscation 89
    1. Perpetrator or accessory 89
    2. Obtainment 89
    3. The asset 'obtained' 90
    4. 'By way of' or 'for' the offence 91
  II. Legal consequences 92
    1. Confiscation of an equivalent sum of money (§ 73c StGB) . 92
    2. Profits and surrogates 94
D. § 73b StGB: confiscation from third parties 94
  I. Requirements for representation cases 96
  II. Requirements of transfer and inheritance cases 97
  III. Legal consequences – more specifically: confiscation of equivalent sum of money 98
    1. Passing equivalent sum of money on to third party 99
    2. Realisation of the item obtained by the third party upon receipt 99
E. §§ 73d and 73e StGB, § 459g sub. 5 StPO: 'objections' against confiscation (deduction of expenditure, lapsing, proportionality) 100
  I. § 73d StGB: deduction of expenditure 100

II. § 73e sub. 1 StGB: lapsing ... 102
III. § 73e sub. 2 StGB and § 459g sub. 5 StPO: disenrichment and proportionality ... 103
F. Procedural principles ... 105
I. §§ 111b et seqq. StPO: provisional securing of assets ... 105
II. Procedure of criminal and/or confiscation proceedings ... 107
III. Enforcement proceedings ... 108

A. Introduction: purpose and legal bases of confiscation

1 Under the tenet 'crime must not pay', the German legislator is pursuing the goal of comprehensively disgorging assets derived from criminal or regulatory offences using the legal tool of 'confiscation', which was introduced in 2017.[1] The underlying legislative idea of this concept is that anyone who obtains an asset by means of an unlawful act should not be permitted to retain the asset. Instead, by definitively seizing any such assets, it is intended to 'restore', in economic terms, the asset situation that would have existed in the absence of the unlawful act.[2] Confiscation can only be ordered by the courts and only in favour of the judicial treasury.[3]

2 Evidently, the confiscated assets do not in all cases remain permanently with the judicial treasury. Where an individual or a company was deprived of their assets as a consequence of the criminal offence, the individual or the company ('injured party') can apply to the judicial treasury for the return of the confiscated assets (*Entschädigungsverfahren*, compensation procedure).

3 The rules on confiscation are primarily contained in the German Criminal Code (*Strafgesetzbuch*; §§ 73 et seq. StGB) and the German Code of Criminal Procedure (*Strafprozessordnung*; §§ 459 et seq. StPO). Confiscations based on a regulatory offence are governed by the provisions of the German Act on Regulatory Offences (*Gesetz über Ordnungswidrigkeiten*; § 29a OWiG). Even though legal entities are generally not subject to German criminal law, these provisions apply to companies and natural persons alike (cf. § 73b StGB, § 29a sub. 2 OWiG).

4 Confiscation must, in particular, be distinguished from the imposition of a fine (*Bußgeld*) against an individual or a company.[4] The imposition of a fine, which shall include an element of disgorgement (§ 17 sub. 4 OWiG), invariably implies a (derived) imputation of blame.[5] In contrast, according to the established case law of the Federal Constitutional Court (*Bundesverfassungsgericht*, 'BVerfG'), the law on confiscation does **not** (!) have a punitive character.[6] Accordingly, the confiscation order does not imply any blame or determination of guilt but is solely intended as a preventative and asset-adjusting measure under quasi-unjust enrichment rules. As a deterrent against the commission of

---

[1] Until 2017, the law on disgorgement in Germany was referred to as 'forfeiture' (*Verfall*). With effect from 1 June 2017, it was then fundamentally restructured by the Act on the Reform of Asset Recovery under Criminal Law (*Gesetz zur Reform der strafrechtlichen Vermögensabschöpfung*), Federal Law Gazette I (2017), pp. 872 et seq. For an overview, see Trüg NJW 2017, 1913; Köllner/Mück NZI 2017, 593; Köhler NStZ 2017, 497; Köhler/Burkhard NStZ 2017, 665; Korte NZWiSt 2018, 231; Korte wistra 2018, 1; BT-Drs. 18/9525, pp. 46 et seq.

[2] BT-Drs. 18/9525, pp. 45 et seq.

[3] See, for example, TK StGB/Eser/Schuster StGB § 73 mn. 28.

[4] Regarding companies: cf. → Ch. 4 on § 30 OWiG.

[5] WD 3-3000-118/22, p. 1 et seq; KK-OWiG/Rogall OWiG § 30 mn. 13, 15.

[6] BVerfG 10.2.2021 – 2 BvL 8/19, NJW 2021, 1222 (1223) et seq.

criminal offences, it serves to signal to potential perpetrators that they will not be able to retain any assets derived through criminal means.[7]

5 The confiscation of assets has significantly gained in relevance in German criminal proceedings, with assets in the billion euro range being confiscated every year.[8] Along with the defence against the actual allegation, it is therefore of vital importance for companies in particular to realise the potential financial risks that arise via the law on confiscation at an early stage in order to be able to have adequate regard to these risks in their defence.

6 Against this background, the following discussion serves to provide an introduction into the various types of confiscation and their requirements and to elucidate those key points that are of particular practical relevance, specifically regarding confiscation cases involving companies.

7 This discussion starts with an overview of the systematics of the law on confiscation (→ mn. 10 et seqq.), followed by an outline of the requirements according to which assets linked to a criminal offence can be confiscated from natural persons involved in the offence on the one hand (→ mn. 21 et seqq.) and third parties who were not involved on the other (natural persons and companies; → mn. 60 et seqq.). We will then address the objections that may be raised against impending confiscation (→ mn. 91 et seqq.). Finally, we will discuss provisional rights to take possession and the basic principles of confiscation proceedings (→ mn. 118 et seqq.).

8 However, this chapter does not contain an exhaustive discussion on all existing confiscation possibilities and situations. After all, even though the above-mentioned fundamental principle ('whoever derived any assets from a criminal offence must surrender these assets') sounds straightforward, the specific mechanisms and modes of operation of confiscation are extremely complex and controversial – overall, confiscation law is regarded as one of the most difficult fields of German criminal law.[9]

9 More specifically, this chapter does not address the option (also available under German law) of confiscating items used for or in the commission of a criminal offence or resulting from a criminal offence (means of crime, products of crime and objects of crime, cf. §§ 74 et seq. StGB), as this type of confiscation is less relevant in practice.

B. Overview on the systematics of the law on confiscation

10 The various types of confiscation differ in terms of their substantive statutory requirements (→ mn. 11 et seqq.) and the procedural structure of the confiscation proceedings (→ mn. 17 et seq.). Moreover, there are rules that govern the preliminary taking possession of assets that could potentially be subject to confiscation (→ mn. 19).

[7] Regarding the intended purpose, see BT-Drs. 18/9525, p. 1; Köhler NStZ 2017, 497 (498); BVerfG 14.1.2004 – 2 BvR 564/95, BeckRS 2004, 22094, mn. 103.

[8] Statistisches Bundesamt, Rechtspflege: Staatsanwaltschaften 2021, p. 14, available at (https://www.destatis.de/DE/Themen/Staat/Justiz-Rechtspflege/Publikationen/Downloads-Gerichte/staatsanwaltschaften-2100260217004.pdf?__blob=publicationFile, last accessed on 24.10.2024).

[9] Cf. e.g. regarding § 73b StGB: Bittmann wistra 2020, 265 ('Schwerpunkt dogmatischer Unklarheiten'); Matt/Renzikowski/Altenhain/Fleckenstein StGB § 73 mn. 9 (in respect of an equivalent sum of money or surrogates: 'unsuccessful' and 'inapplicable').

I. Legal bases for confiscation

11 Criminal law on confiscation provides four instruments for disgorging illegally obtained assets[10] and assisting victims of a criminal offence 'quickly and unbureaucratically' in asserting their claims under civil law[11]:

12 – simple confiscation (*Einziehung*, §§ 73 and 73b StGB),
– simple independent confiscation[12] (*selbstständige Einziehung*, § 76a sub. 1 to 3 StGB),
– extended confiscation (*erweiterte Einziehung*, § 73a StGB), and
– extended independent confiscation (§ 76a sub. 4 StGB)[13].

13 Simple confiscation under § 73 StGB is the default case of confiscation. Where a perpetrator or accessory derived an asset from or for an unlawful act and a court determines that this act constitutes a criminal offence, the court will order the confiscation of said asset.[14] If said asset no longer exists, an equivalent sum of money, or surrogates, may be confiscated. This does not mean, however, that confiscation from companies, which, under German law, can neither be perpetrator nor accessory to a criminal offence, is precluded. Any such companies would fall under the particularly relevant provision of § 73b StGB pursuant to which confiscation as per §§ 73 and 73e StGB may also be ordered against a party other than the perpetrator or the accessory if such third party has derived some benefit through the offence, provided that certain requirements have been met. In this case, the third party does not need to be a natural person – confiscation may be ordered against companies of any legal form.[15]

14 As a general rule, confiscation is ordered by the court during criminal proceedings against a person involved in the criminal offence (so-called subjective proceedings[16]). Furthermore, § 76a StGB also provides the option of independent confiscation proceedings. This means that in specific cases set out in § 76a StGB, confiscation is also possible by way of independent proceedings against a person who, by court order, becomes a party to the confiscation proceedings (*Einziehungsbeteiligter*)[17] if no criminal proceedings are conducted against any person involved in a specific criminal offence because, for example, the allegations are time-barred by the statute of limitation. In such cases (so-called objective proceedings[18]), it is therefore also possible to deprive an offending company from assets derived from a criminal offence, without any employee of that company being exposed to criminal proceedings.[19]

15 Under § 73a StGB, the court may also order the (extended) confiscation of assets during proceedings involving a specific criminal offence (e.g. fraud) if these assets were derived

---

[10] Regarding the objective of the confiscation provisions, see e.g. BT-Drs. 18/9525, p. 1; Köhler NStZ 2017, 497 (498); BVerfG 14.1.2004 – 2 BvR 564/95, BeckRS 2004, 22094, mn. 103.

[11] BT-Drs. 18/9525, p. 3.

[12] § 76a sub. 1 to 3 StGB specify – as per standard nomenclature – cases of independent confiscation (LK-StGB/Lohse § 76a mn. 11; Matt/Renzikowski/Altenhain/Fleckenstein StGB § 76a mn. 1; SSW StGB/Heine § 76a mn. 2; LTZ/Rübenstahl StGB § 76a mn. 4). The relevant provisions enable the non-conviction-based, and thus independent, confiscation of proceeds derived from criminal offences; the requirements for and the extent of disgorgement are, first of all, based on § 73 StGB.

[13] The (additional) instrument of non-conviction-based (independent) confiscation enshrined in § 76a sub. 4 StGB was first introduced into German law by the reform. It has its origin in Anglo-American law (see, for example, Marstaller/Zimmermann, Non-conviction-based confiscation in Deutschland?, 2018, p. 34). Regarding the term, see Meyer ZStW 127 (2015), 241, 259 et seq. with comment 70.

[14] See § 73 StGB.

[15] Cf. BGH 10.3.2021 – 1 StR 272/20, wistra 2022, 29 et seq. with comments by Borgel.

[16] Cf. Ullenboom ch. 12 mn. 254.

[17] Namely the person who is affected by the confiscation without having participated in the offence.

[18] Cf. Ullenboom ch. 12 mn. 254.

[19] Cf. BeckOK StGB/Heuchemer, 63. Ed. 1.11.2024, § 76a mn. 4.

from another offence that is **not** the subject matter of the proceedings (e.g. proceeds from drug dealing). It should be noted that the offence from which these assets are derived does not need to be established by the court; the determination that these are incriminated assets will suffice. This provision goes back to the Anglo-American system, which – under certain circumstances – permits confiscation even if the assets are derived from offences that cannot be determined.[20]

§ 76a sub. 4 StGB expands on the provision of § 73a StGB and provides the option of **16** confiscating assets of undetermined origin from persons presumably involved in the offending, as well as third parties, by way of objective proceedings, without the need for criminal proceedings against any specific person.[21] Again, the legislator based this approach on the Anglo-American system and adopted the idea of a 'non-conviction-based confiscation'.[22]

II. Procedural rules

These substantive-law provisions – i.e. the answer to the question of when confiscation **17** must, as a rule, be ordered – are supplemented by provisions regarding the question of which rights a party to the confiscation proceedings has in criminal proceedings and under which procedural rules the court may order confiscation (§§ 421 et seq. StPO). On principle, confiscation must be ordered during the criminal proceedings against the persons involved in the offending, with a public trial being the norm.[23] Parties to the confiscation proceedings, who were not involved in the offence, assume a position in these proceedings that is similar to that of an accused person.[24] They will have the right to inspect the files and to be represented by a lawyer.[25] Moreover, confiscation is also possible by way of objective proceedings (if the substantive requirements of § 76a StGB are met) solely against the party to the confiscation proceedings. In these cases, there is usually no trial; instead, such proceedings are conducted in writing.[26]

The rules governing the main proceedings are supplemented by procedural rules **18** regarding the execution of confiscation orders (§§ 459 et seq. StPO). This relates to the question of when and how the court-ordered confiscation can be executed. Since the reform of the law on disgorgement, these execution rules have increased considerably in relevance. For instance, the defence of disproportionality can essentially only be raised at the execution stage (cf. § 459g sub. 5 StPO).[27]

III. Mechanisms to provisionally secure assets

As proceedings in the area of economic criminal law often last for years and any pro- **19** ceeds derived from criminal offences can easily be spent or transferred over the duration of the criminal proceedings, the legislator has created instruments to provisionally secure

[20] Cf. TK StGB/Eser/Schuster StGB § 76a mn. 2.
[21] Matt/Renzikowski/Altenhain/Fleckenstein StGB § 76a mn. 7.
[22] See, for example, Marstaller/Zimmermann, Non-conviction-based confiscation in Deutschland?, 2018, p. 34; Meyer ZStW 127 (2015), 241 (259) et seq.
[23] TK StGB/Eser/Schuster StGB § 73 mn. 30. For instance, the issuance of an order imposing punishment (*Strafbefehl*) does not necessitate a public trial.
[24] LG Kiel 16.12.2019 – 3 KLs 8/17, BeckRS 2019, 62388 mn. 165.
[25] See §§ 424, 427 StPO.
[26] Cf. TK StGB/Eser/Schuster StGB § 76a mn. 17.
[27] Also → mn. 91 et seqq.

potential objects of confiscation. Where a criminal offence is suspected, §§ 111b et seq. StPO therefore provide the option of provisionally securing assets for the duration of the criminal proceedings. In practice, this is done by seizing the bank accounts of the accused person or third parties until completion of the criminal proceedings if it is suspected that the person concerned might 'salt away' the proceeds or assets (cf. § 111e StPO). These instruments to provisionally secure assets are of immense practical importance, as they can impair the relevant parties' commercial capacity to transact for years, without the commission of a criminal offence having actually been determined.[28]

IV. Schematic overview

20

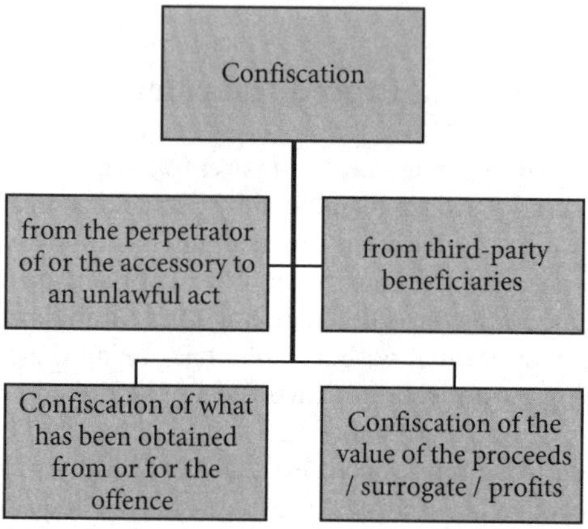

C. The principle: confiscation from persons involved in the offence

21 As a rule, all assets that were **obtained directly** from a criminal offence (**spoils**) or paid out as a **reward** (§ 73 StGB, together referred to as 'proceeds') may be confiscated from the persons involved in the offending, i.e. those natural persons who were either the perpetrator of or an accessory to a criminal offence. Provided that strict requirements have been met, assets which the party to the offence has **not obtained directly** but from a third party ('transferred spoils') may also be confiscated if it can nevertheless be assumed that the party to the offence would have obtained them 'by way of' the offence.[29] If the asset is not or no longer extant in its tangible form, the value of the proceeds or a surrogate may be confiscated.

[28] Cf. OLG Rostock 12.4.2018 – 20 Ws 42/18, BeckRS 2018, 45304 ('Pretrial detention for assets').

[29] BGH 6.6.2019 – 1 StR 75/19, NStZ-RR 2019, 279 with further citations. BGH 28.11.2019 – 3 StR 294/19, NJW 2020, 1309 mn. 31–33 goes even further. By contrast: BGH 15.1.2020 – 1 StR 529/19, BeckRS 2020, 6131 mn. 17 and 18; BGH 1.6.2021 – 1 StR 133/21, NZWiSt 2021, 392 et seq.

These basic principles can be visualised as follows: 22

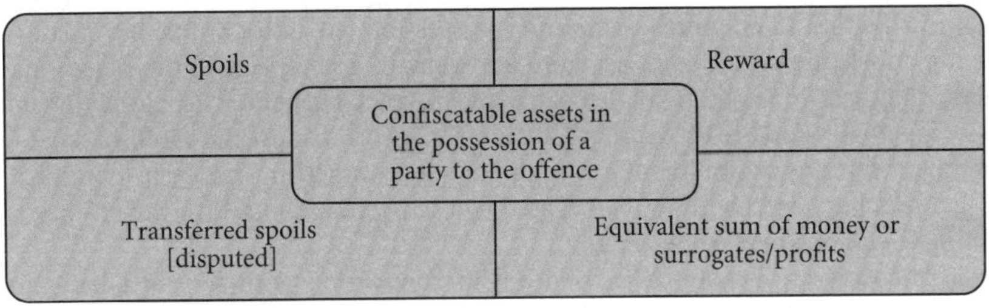

More specifically, the following rules apply: 23

I. Requirements for confiscation

§ 73 sub. 1 StGB is the fundamental provision of the law on confiscation. In accordance 24
with this provision, confiscation must be ordered if:

1. a perpetrator or an accessory 25
2. 'obtains'
3. 'something', namely an asset, and
4. this obtainment occurred 'by way of' or 'for' the offence.

The following discussion examines when these requirements are met. The resulting 26
legal consequences will be outlined under → mn. 44 et seqq.

27

Example 1: A and B assault C. While B is holding C, A takes 700 EUR and a watch from C. B does not receive a share in these items, but before the offence he received a football from A for his participation.

1. Perpetrator or accessory

Under German criminal law, anyone who commits a criminal offence, aids in its 28
commission (§ 27 StGB) or abets its commission (§ 26 StGB) is deemed to be either the perpetrator or the accessory (together: the **parties to the offence**). This does not apply to companies as, under German law, they are not capable of committing criminal offences.

Regarding example 1: both A and B are perpetrators in the assault on C. 29

2. Obtainment

'Obtainment' is in any case the core requirement for confiscation. A financial benefit 30
has been obtained once the party to the offence has gained actual control over the item in question.[30] Possession and ownership under civil law are irrelevant in this regard. Under the law on confiscation, it is solely the actual control that is decisive[31]: who has physical, and not just temporary, control over the item or legally profits from a benefit?

---

30 See, for example, BGH 13.12.2006 – 4 StR 421/06, NStZ-RR 2007, 121; MüKoStGB/Joecks/Meißner StGB § 73 mn. 24.

31 BGH 7.3.2019 – 5 StR 569/18, NStZ 2019, 272; Fischer, 69th edn 2022, StGB § 73 mn. 26.

In contrast, financial benefits that are merely offered or promised are not deemed to have been obtained.[32]

31 On this factual level, merely temporary possession (so-called transitory possession) does not constitute obtainment as, from an evaluating perspective, the person having temporary possession does not register an actual financial benefit.[33] People having merely temporary possession are those who, for example, just transport the spoils or store them for a time.[34] It is important to note, though, that once something has been 'obtained', the fact that this happened will not be negated by the person involved in the offence relinquishing their control at a later stage.[35]

32 Where confiscation may be carried out in connection with several parties to the offence, it must be assessed for each party separately (individually) which items they actually have obtained.[36] As confiscation always relates to a specific offence, multiple confiscation may be effected in cases where one and the same asset was obtained through independent criminal offences by several people.[37] However, where several parties to the offence obtain co-control or consecutive control over a confiscatable item or amount derived from one and the same criminal offence, these parties are jointly and severally liable.[38]

33 **Regarding example 1:** A has obtained 700 EUR and the watch. B, on the other hand, obtained the football. As B had no control over the watch or the money, he did not obtain them.

34 **Case variant 1b:** if, during the offence, A had given B 200 EUR from the 700 EUR instead of the football, B would have obtained the 200 EUR. In this case, the parties to the offence would be jointly and severally liable for the 200 EUR.

3. The asset 'obtained'

35 By 'obtained something' (*etwas erlangt*), the legislator refers to the entirety of the economically measurable profits the perpetrator or accessory has derived from or for the offence. Confiscatable assets therefore not only include chattels, real estate or rights *in rem* and *in personam* but also non-cash benefits, such as services, profits or an improved market position.[39]

36 Confiscation is governed by the so-called 'non-netting rule' (*Bruttoprinzip*)[40], meaning that the entire benefit derived is confiscated. § 73d StGB permits the deduction of any expenditure on the part of the perpetrator only if it was not 'spent or used in the commission or preparation of the unlawful act'.[41]

---

[32] LK-StGB/Lohse § 73 mn. 29.

[33] Cf. BGH 23.7.2020 – 1 StR 78/20, NZWiSt 2020, 436 mn. 10.

[34] BGH 24. Juli 2018 – 2 BvR 309/15, 2 BvR 502/16, NStZ 2019, 14 (headnote 2); BGH 7.6.2018 – 4 StR 63/18, BeckRS 2018, 13152 mn. 14.

[35] BGH 7.3.2019 – 5 StR 569/18, NStZ 2019, 272 (272); BGH 18.7.2018 – 5 StR 645/17, NStZ-RR 2018, 278 (279).

[36] BGH 23.1.2019 – 2 StR 525/18, BeckRS 2019, 1666; MüKoStGB/Joecks/Meißner § 73 mn. 24; NK-WSS/Lindemann/Bauerkamp StGB § 73 mn. 6; cf. prohibition of imputation BGH 21.8.2018 – 2 StR 311/18, NStZ 2019, 20; LK-StGB/Lohse § 73 mn. 33.

[37] Cf. Ullenboom ch. 5 mn. 98.

[38] BGH 15. 11. 2002 – 2 StR 302/02, NStZ 2003, 198; BGH 28.8.2018 – 1 StR 103/18, NStZ-RR 2018, 335; Fischer StGB § 73 mn. 29; Köhler/Burkhard NStZ 2017, 665 (669); expressing a critical view: MüKoStGB/Joecks/Meißner § 73 mn. 26 et seq.

[39] BT-Drs. 18/9525, p. 61 et. seq.

[40] Lackner/Kühl/Heger/Heger StGB § 73 mn. 4; TK StGB/Eser/Schuster StGB § 73 mn. 9.

[41] For deductions and defences, → mn. 91 et seqq.

In contrast, any intangible profit,[42] merely feasible potential capital appreciation,[43] **37**
entitlements to damages for pain and suffering or interest[44] cannot be confiscated under the terms of § 73 sub. 1 StGB.

Regarding example 1: assets linked to the criminal offence in example 1 are the watch, **38**
the 700 EUR and the football; these items can all potentially be confiscated.

4. 'By way of' or 'for' the offence

Once a benefit has been 'obtained' and the gateway to collection has thus been opened, **39**
it must be examined whether this transpired **'by way of'** or **'for'** the offence.

Assets are deemed to have been obtained **'by way of'** the offence if they accrue to the **40**
party to the offence through the realisation of the elements of the offence at some point over the course of its realisation, which typically refers to the spoils.[45] The causal link to what has been obtained 'by way of' the offence is determined solely on the basis of the principles of the law on unjust enrichment and constitutes, to this extent, quasi-unjust-enrichment.[46] More specifically, the point in time when an asset is deemed to have been obtained 'by way of' the offence is highly controversial, with the debate centring primarily on the question whether assets that were (directly) transferred to the perpetrator only after completion of the offence were in fact obtained 'by way of' the offence.[47] In certain cases, the courts are proceeding on the assumption that obtainment 'by way of' the offence also applies even if the relevant asset was transferred to the perpetrator at a later time.[48]

Assets have been obtained **'for'** the offence if they were afforded to the perpetrator **41**
as consideration for his unlawful act but are not based on the realisation of the offence itself – the typical scenario is the 'reward'.[49] In order to fulfil this criterion, it is vital that the reward is not obtained upon occasion of the offence but – with a view to the commission of the offence – explicitly as consideration.[50] This is generally not the case with regard to regular (salary) payments. It is only special bonuses or payments/benefits having a direct link to the offence that can be confiscated by virtue of being a reward 'for' the offence.[51] It is irrelevant whether the reward is given 'for' the offence in its entirety or only for specific aspects of the offence, such as preparatory measures or securing the spoils. Likewise, the point in time when the reward 'for' the offence is paid out is of no relevance for its qualification. It is also of no importance for the qualification of the offence whether the granting of a financial benefit in the form of the reward or the payment itself constitutes an unlawful act.[52]

---

[42] Matt/Renzikoswiki/Altenhain/Fleckenstein § 73 mn. 4.

[43] BGH 24. 10. 2000 – 5 StR 323/00, NStZ-RR 2001, 82; BGH 11.10.2005 – 1 StR 344/05, NStZ-RR 2006, 39, LK-StGB/Lohse § 73 mn. 24.

[44] TK StGB/Eser/Schuster StGB § 73 mn. 8.

[45] BGH 7.3.2019 – 5 StR 569/18, NStZ 2019, 272 (272); BGH 27.9.2018 – 4 StR 78/18, NStZ-RR 2019, 22; MüKoStGB/Joecks/Meißner § 73 mn. 36; BGH 8.2.2018 – 3 StR 560/17, NJW 2018, 2141 mn. 10; BGH 24.2.2021 – 1 StR 127/20, NStZ 2021, 668.

[46] BVerfG 10.2.2021 – 2 BvL 8/19, NJW 2021, 1222 (1223 et seq.).

[47] Bittmann/Tschakert wistra 2020, 217 et seq.

[48] BGH 21.5.2019 – 1 StR 92/19, NStZ-RR 2019, 279 with further citations. BGH 28.11.2019 – 3 StR 294/19, NJW 2020, 1309 mn. 31–33 goes even further. By contrast: BGH 15.01.2020 – 1 StR 529/19, BeckRS 2020, 6131 mn. 17 and 18; BGH 1.6. 2021 – 1 StR 133/21, NZWiSt 2021, 392 et seq.

[49] BeckOK StGB/Heuchemer, 63. Ed. 1.11.2024, StGB § 73 mn. 7; Bekritsky NStZ 2022, 207.

[50] TK StGB/Eser/Schuster StGB § 73 mn. 10.

[51] Cf. LG Bonn 18.3.2020 – 62 KLs – 213 Js 41/19, BeckRS 2020, 13619 mn. 1355 et seq., 1360, 1385; LG Bonn 01.06.2021 – 62 KLs – 213 Js 32/20 – 1/20, BeckRS 2021, 23346 mn. 900.

[52] LK-StGB/Lohse § 73 mn. 41.

42 **Regarding example 1:** A has obtained the 700 EUR and the watch 'by way of' the offence because he took them during the assault on C. B has obtained the football 'for' the offence because the football was consideration in return for his participation in the offence.

43 **Regarding case variant 1b:** to the extent that B took possession of the 200 EUR, this amount of money also constitutes monies obtained 'by way of' the offence. To the extent that A, after the completion of the offence, handed the money to B in return for his participation, the case is harder to assess, given that B – on closer examination – did not receive the money from A directly 'by way of' the offence but actually after the offence. In this scenario, however, the courts, in cases of doubt, tend to accept that the asset was obtained 'by way of' the offence and permit its confiscation.[53] That said, a different conclusion might be drawn if the proceeds were first received by a company, as intended, and then passed on to a party to the offence.[54]

II. Legal consequences

44 Where the aforementioned requirements have been met and no objections can be raised against the confiscation,[55] the court must order confiscation of what has been obtained, with the enriched party to the offence being the addressee of such order.

45 **Regarding example 1:** the 700 EUR and the watch would have to be confiscated from A. The football would have to be confiscated from B.

Regarding case variant 1b: the 700 EUR and the watch may be confiscated from A. The 200 EUR may be confiscated from B. Joint and several liability would be deemed to exist with regard to the 200 EUR. Accordingly, A and B together would have to pay a total of 700 EUR (and not 900 EUR), as only 700 EUR was taken from C.

46 However, oftentimes assets are obtained through criminal offences that cannot be delineated in this way or that have been subjected to further use before they could be confiscated. This is the case, for example, if money is transferred to the perpetrator and the legal independence of the claim is lost upon the money's receipt into a current account, as the individual claim cannot be delineated in the perpetrator's account (the money 'intermingles' with other – legal – funds[56] in the account), or if the perpetrator on-sells a stolen watch.

47 In these cases, the law provides that – given the impossibility of confiscating the actual assets obtained – the actual value of the item obtained may be confiscated, either in the form of an equivalent sum of money (→ mn. 50 et seqq.) or a surrogate (→ mn. 57 et seqq.), to enable the comprehensive disgorgement of the unjust enrichment.

48 **Case variant 1c:** A pays the sum of 700 EUR into his bank account. B swaps the football for a concert ticket.

49 In addition, any profits may also always be confiscated (→ mn. 57 et seqq.).

1. Confiscation of an equivalent sum of money (§ 73c StGB)

50 Where increases in assets in connection with criminal offences result from bank transfers or other payments, or where they consist in the saving of expenditure (which is arguably the standard case), confiscation of the specific item originating from the offence

---

[53] See e.g. BGH 19. 10. 2011 – 1 StR 336/11, NStZ-RR 2012, 81.
[54] See example 2 under → mn. 66.
[55] Further details under → mn. 91 et seqq.
[56] SSW StGB/Heine § 73c mn. 3.

is not possible. The same applies if the party to the offence utilises the original item, which would be the case, for example, if the money derived from the offence were spent. In all of these cases, the confiscatable original item simply no longer exists.[57]

For any such cases, § 73c StGB provides for the confiscation of an equivalent sum of **51** money. Consequently, if the confiscation of the original item is not possible due to the nature of the item obtained or for any other reason, the value of said item will be confiscated in the form of a monetary amount.

Confiscation of an equivalent sum of money also hinges on the core requirement for **52** confiscation: the party to the offence must have first obtained something in the sense of § 73 StGB, either by way of or for the offence.[58] However, confiscation of an equivalent sum of money does not necessarily require that the perpetrator (or third party within the meaning of § 73b StGB[59]) is still enriched.[60] As with the basic type of confiscation, if there are several parties to the offence, they are jointly and severally liable for the equivalent sum of money, provided they had joint control over the item (originally) obtained.[61]

The trial court must ascertain the value of the item obtained, which determines the **53** amount to be confiscated; an estimate is permissible.[62] If an equivalent sum of money is to be paid for items that no longer exist, the amount to be confiscated will be based on the market value of the item originally obtained. The market value corresponds to the sales value on the domestic market or the achievable realisation proceeds for goods of equal type and quality[63] at the time when the entitlement to this form of compensation arose.[64] Accordingly, if confiscation only retrospectively proves to be impossible, the point in time when the impossibility of physical confiscation occurred will be decisive.[65]

Regarding case variant 1c: A sum of money equivalent to 700 EUR may be confiscated **54** from A, as the original bank notes are no longer in his possession. The value of the football may be confiscated from B, unless the state opts to confiscate the concert tickets instead.[66]

In contrast, cases involving saved expenditure are more complicated, as no asset shift **55** that could be used as a point of reference has taken place.[67] This requires a case-by-case examination to ascertain whether the specific savings have, in fact, led to financial gain. In respect of tax fraud offences, the Federal Court of Justice found that, in these cases, confiscation draws on the actual measurable financial gain that the perpetrator derives from the offence and thus requires more than just meeting the constituent elements of the offence.[68] According to the Federal Court of Justice, this requires ascertaining a 'direct economic benefit' that must be reflected in the perpetrator's asset situation and that leads to an actual and measurable financial gain. In the view of the Federal Court of Justice, such a benefit does not automatically arise if a payment owed has not been made.[69]

---

[57] Cf. TK StGB/Eser/Schuster StGB § 73 mn. 7.

[58] BGH 11.10.2005 – 1 StR 344/05, NStZ-RR 2006, 39; LK-StGB/Lohse § 73c mn. 2.

[59] Also → mn. 60 et seqq.

[60] Matt/Renzikowski/Altenhain/Fleckenstein StGB § 73c mn. 1.

[61] Fischer StGB § 73c mn. 2a.

[62] BGH 24.8.2011 – 2 StR 109/11, wistra 2012, 107; MAH WirtschaftsStrafR/Corsten/Schilling § 13 mn. 71.

[63] TK StGB/Eser/Schuster StGB § 73c mn. 10; MAH WirtschaftsStrafR/Corsten/Schilling § 13 mn. 72.

[64] BT-Drs. 18/9525, p. 67; BeckOK BGB/Wendehorst, 72. Ed. 1.11.2024, BGB § 818 mn. 33; MAH WirtschaftsStrafR/Corsten/Schilling § 13 mn. 73.

[65] Matt/Renzikowski/Altenhain/Fleckenstein StGB § 73c mn. 4.

[66] → mn. 57 et seqq.

[67] Bittmann/Tschakert wistra 2019, 433.

[68] BGH 23.7.2020 – 1 StR 78/20, NZWiSt 2020, 436 mn. 10.

[69] Cf., e.g., BGH 23.7.2020 – 1 StR 78/20, NZWiSt 2020, 436 mn. 10; BGH 23.5.2019 – 1 StR 479/18, wistra 2019, 450 mn. 10 = BeckRS 2019, 17574.

56 **Case variant 1d:** A fails to declare his entire income in his tax return, resulting in a shortfall of 500 EUR in tax assessed. As A therefore 'saved' the expenditure of paying 500 EUR, this amount may be confiscated from him.

2. Profits and surrogates

57 Pursuant to § 73 sub. 2 StGB, any profits from what has been 'obtained' must also be confiscated, provided that these profits were in fact derived and not just expected or potentially derived.[70] As under civil law, profits under the law on confiscation constitute the usufruct of a right, both in the material and legal sense, such as benefits arising from use, including interest incurred on the proceeds from offences.[71]

58 In accordance with § 73 sub. 3 StGB, the trial court may also order confiscation of any objects which the party to the offence (no. 1) acquired by way of selling what has been obtained or as compensation for its destruction, damage or deprivation, or (no. 2) due to a right acquired. A surrogate in this sense is any kind of substitution of the previously obtained item among the assets of the party that is the addressee of the confiscation order, irrespective of whether said item is substituted by another item[72] or by a claim[73]. Confiscation of a surrogate relates solely to items that have directly replaced the item originally obtained.[74] It does not relate to any indirect gains.[75] The confiscation of a surrogate or the confiscation of an equivalent sum of money may only be ordered severally.[76]

59 **Regarding case variant 1c:** the concert ticket may be confiscated from B as a surrogate. However, the confiscation of a surrogate precludes the additional confiscation of the equivalent sum of money for the football. To the extent that A has actually received interest on the 700 EUR in his account, all such interest may also be confiscated as profits.

D. § 73b StGB: confiscation from third parties

60 One might think that the above-described rules are only of secondary importance for companies, since they are precluded as perpetrators or parties to the offence. This would, however, be a misguided assumption, as § 73b StGB also enables the issuance of a confiscation order against third parties, which also covers – along with natural persons – companies, provided that:

61 a) the third party has obtained something by way of the offence, and the perpetrator or accessory has acted on said third party's behalf; or
b) the item obtained has been transferred to the third party without consideration or without legal cause; or
c) the item obtained has been transferred to the third party and the third party recognised, or should have recognised, that said item originated from an unlawful act; or

---

[70] Fischer StGB § 73 mn. 31; MüKoStGB/Joecks/Meißner § 73 mn. 41.
[71] LK-StGB/Lohse § 73 mn. 45, NK-StGB/Lindemann/Bauerkamp StGB § 73 mn. 25.
[72] BGH 18.11.2015 – 2 StR 399/15, NStZ-RR 2016, 83.
[73] SSW StGB/Heine § 73 mn. 52.
[74] LK-StGB/Lohse § 73 mn. 46.
[75] Matt/Renzikowski/Altenhain/Fleckenstein StGB § 73 mn. 11; SSW StGB/Heine § 73 mn. 52; NK-WSS/Lindemann/Bauerkamp StGB § 73 mn. 26.
[76] BGH 8.2.2018 – 3 StR 560/17, NJW 2018, 2141 (2142).

d) the item obtained has devolved to an heir or has been transferred to a party entitled to the compulsory portion in an estate or as a beneficiary under a will.

If these requirements have been met, the actual asset obtained, including any profits 62
derived therefrom, may be confiscated from the third party (§ 73b sub. 1 StGB). Moreover, provided that the above requirements have been met, an object equivalent in value to the asset obtained may be confiscated. Moreover, the equivalent sum of money, or surrogates, may be confiscated as well should confiscation of the original item prove impossible. However, a number of specifics must be taken into account (§ 73b sub. 2 StGB[77]).

Accordingly, confiscation from a third party would be possible in the following cases:[78] 63

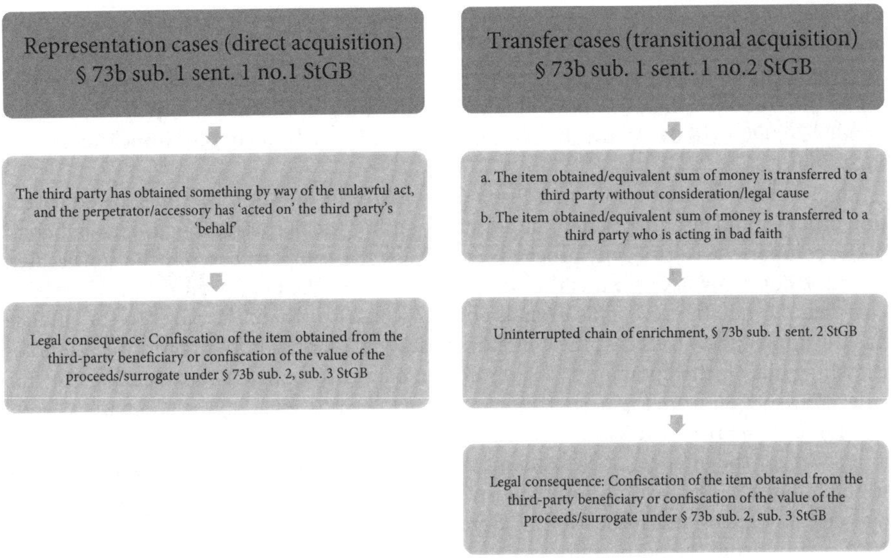

As this provision is the pivotal point of the confiscation ordered against a company, it 64
will be examined in greater detail below.

First of all, a distinction must be made between cases where the third party has received 65
the proceeds directly (representation cases, direct acquisition, sub. 1 sent. 1 no. 1) and cases where, after the offence, the proceeds were passed on to the third party by parties to the offence or others (transfer cases, transitional cases, sub. 1 sent. 1 no. 2 and 3).

Example 2: A is the managing director of Buchclub GmbH. Buchclub GmbH sells sec- 66
ond-hand books and operates a business that is, for all intents and purposes, legal. As A wishes to give the company's profits a bit of a boost, in his capacity as a representative of Buchclub GmbH, he pretends vis-à-vis B that he can sell him a particularly valuable first edition of the Gospel According to St. John. B then pays 20,000 EUR in cash to Buchclub GmbH. The book does not actually exist. A has power of control over Buchclub GmbH's cash register.

[77] Also → mn. 21 et seqq.

[78] Confiscation from an heir, beneficiary under a will and party entitled to the compulsory portion in an estate is not included in the chart as this case is not encountered often in practice.

I. Requirements for representation cases

67 Where the third party has received the proceeds directly 'by way of' the offence, these proceeds may be confiscated from the third party if a party to the offence acted 'on behalf of' the third party when committing the offence. The courts apply this last-mentioned requirement very broadly. It is considered sufficient that the party to the offence also acted in the best interest of the third party, even if only de facto and not discernible to an outsider.[79] According to the courts, a formal position, such as manager or employee, is not required. Instead, it is regarded as being sufficient if a representative of the third party and a party to the offence mutually cooperated while pursuing concurrent interests.[80] Only those consequences of the conduct of the party to the offence that are purely accidental or indirect should be disregarded.[81]

68 **Regarding example 2:** A has acted on behalf of Buchclub GmbH and is the perpetrator of the fraud. Buchclub GmbH obtained something by way of the offence because B handed 20,000 EUR over to Buchclub GmbH for the first edition of the Gospel According to St. John.

69 In practice, representation cases often give rise to the question whether the confiscation order should be addressed to the company and/or the perpetrator who acts on behalf of the company. As a rule, any proceeds derived by the company can only be confiscated from the company because it is the company – and not the perpetrator – who has been enriched by the offence.[82] This even applies in scenarios where the party to the offence has the opportunity to access the company's assets and/or holds an interest in, and takes drawings out of, the company.[83] However, the courts recognise two exceptions to this rule: confiscation from the perpetrator would **also** be possible if a) the company's assets are not separate from the assets of the party to the offence and the company only serves as a cover for the offence, or b) the asset inflow was immediately passed on to the party to the offence.[84] The assumption that any of these special situations apply requires special circumstances and indications.[85] Some sources are of the – erroneous – view that confiscation from the perpetrator is always possible, independent of the aforementioned case groups, if the company has passed the incriminated funds on to the perpetrator and this transfer was not based on a *bona fide* contract (*unbemakelter Vertrag*).[86] However, this view must be rejected, as it goes beyond the wording of § 73b StGB (*durch die Tat*, 'by way of the offence').

70 **Case variant 2a:** if Buchclub GmbH has passed the 20,000 EUR immediately on to A, confiscation from A is also possible. However, if A has only received his regular salary

---

[79] Cf. BT-Drs. 18/9525, p. 56; BGH 19.10.1999 – 5 StR 336/99, BGH 19.10.1999, 5 StR 336/99, BGHSt 45, 235 = BeckRS 1999, 30077650; BGH 19.10.1999 – 5 StR 336/99, NJW 2000, 297 mn. 39; BGH 23. 10. 2013 – 5 StR 505/12, NStZ 2014, 89 mn. 54; BGH 28.7.2021 – 1 StR 519/20NZWiSt 2021, 437 mn. 117.

[80] Cf. BGH 28.7.2021 – 1 StR 519/20, NZWiSt 2021, 437 mn. 119; also see Sartorius/Henckel DStR 2022, 1029.

[81] LG Bonn 02.01.2020 – 1 Vollz (Ws) 560/19, BeckRS 2020, 13618 mn. 1415.

[82] Established case law, see e.g.: BGH 15.1.2020 – 1 StR 529/19, NStZ 2020, 405 mn. 13 et seq. with further citations; BGH 14.11.2018 – 3 StR 447/18, wistra 2019, 188 mn. 11 with further citations; instructive: Bittmann/Tschakert wistra 2020, 217 et seq.; regarding partnerships: BGH 15.8.2018 – 5 StR 100/18, wistra 2019, 26 mn. 25 et seq.

[83] BGH 15.1.2020 – 1 StR 529/19, NStZ 2020, 405 mn. 15 with further citations; BGH 14.11.2018 – 3 StR 447/18, wistra 2019, 188 mn. 11 with further citations; BGH 21.5.2019 – 1 StR 92/19NStZ-RR 2019, 279 with further citations.

[84] Cf. Ullenboom wistra 2020, 225 et seq.

[85] BGH 21.5.2019 – 1 StR 92/19, NStZ-RR 2019, 279 with further citations.

[86] BGH 28.11.2019 – 3 StR 294/19, NJW 2020, 1309, by contrast however: BGH 15.1.2020 – 1 StR 529/19; BeckRS 2020, 6131 mn. 17, 18; BGH 1.6.2021 – 1 StR 133/21, NZWiSt 2021, 392 et seq.

from Buchclub GmbH, confiscation from A is not possible, even if his salary is paid from Buchclub GmbH's cash register and therefore partially originates from B's 20,000 EUR.

Moreover, only those scenarios where the third party obtains something 'by way of the **71** offence' fall under the representation cases covered by § 73b sub. 1 sent. 1 no. 1 StGB. On the other hand, the law does not mention the obtainment of a reward by the third party ('for the offence'). Some commentators contend that payment of a reward to the third party should also be subsumed under § 73b sub. 1 sent. 1 no. 1 StGB, as any reward – paid on behalf of the perpetrator to his company – should not remain with the third-party beneficiary.[87] However, given the unambiguous wording of the provision, this interpretation is not possible.[88] The correct view is that any reward paid to a third party on behalf of the perpetrator cannot be confiscated.

Case variant 2b: A promises B to help him to assault C. For this purpose, B then trans- **72** fers 100 EUR for A to Buchclub GmbH's bank account. In accordance with the correct legal view, confiscation from Buchclub GmbH pursuant to § 73b sub. 1 sent. 1 no. 1 StGB is not possible.

II. Requirements of transfer and inheritance cases

To the extent that proceeds are not directly passed on to the third party by way of the **73** offence, but incriminated amounts ('the item obtained') or an equivalent object have been passed on to the third party (transitional acquisition), § 73b sub. 1 sent. 1 no. 2 StGB applies (in the case of an object equivalent in value to the asset obtained being passed on: in conjunction with § 73b sub. 2 StGB).

Confiscation under § 73b sub. 1 sent. 1 no. 2 StGB is possible if the transfer of an **74** incriminated asset, i.e. originating from a criminal offence:

a) occurred without consideration or legal cause; or **75**
b) legal cause existed but the third party recognised, or should have recognised, that the item obtained originated from an unlawful act.

A transfer is deemed to exist if the third-party beneficiary has received the 'benefits **76** from the offence due to an uninterrupted chain of enrichment, starting with the party to the offence'.[89] It should be noted that § 73b sub. 1 sent. 1 no. 2 StGB applies to both the passing on of proceeds as well as the reward. The point in time when the item was transferred to the third party, or how many people gained control before that point in time, is irrelevant.[90] However, in order to somewhat limit this very wide purview of confiscation, potentially involving a large number of people, sentence 2 stipulates that confiscation along a 'chain of enrichment' is precluded if – somewhere along this chain – the item obtained was transferred to a third party for consideration and with legal cause.

If the transfer takes place without consideration or without legal cause, confiscation **77** is possible, irrespective of whether or not the recipient acted in bad faith. Arguably, the most relevant case group in this context is profit distributions from subsidiaries to their parent company. Some commentators opine that § 73b sub. 1 sent. 1 no. 2 StGB also enables confiscation at the parent company, without knowledge on the part of its employees or executive bodies being a decisive factor, as the profit distribution takes place without consideration.[91]

87 Bekritsky NStZ 2022, 209 et seq.
88 Of the same view: Sartorius/Henckel DStR 2022, 1028.
89 Fischer StGB § 73b mn. 9.
90 BT-Drs. 18/9525, p. 66; SSW StGB/Heine § 73b mn. 5.
91 Kämpfer/Schwerdtfeger StraFo 2020, 313 (315).

78 In contrast, cases where the transfer of incriminated assets takes place for consideration on the basis of a contract require a different assessment. In these cases, confiscation is only possible if the third party acted in bad faith, i.e. if the third party recognised, or should have recognised, that the item obtained originated from an unlawful act. It is, however, contentious at what point in time the third party should have recognised that the relevant item is an incriminated asset. The correct view is that – in concordance with § 73e sub. 2 StGB – recklessness is required.[92] Furthermore, with regard to companies it is not clear whose knowledge can be imputed to the company. The courts are of the opinion that, in any case, knowledge on the part of its executive bodies (executive board/management) must be attributed to the company.[93] It is also being debated whether the principles of knowledge imputation under general civil-law norms should be applied in analogy.[94]

79 **Case variant 2c:** apart from Buchclub GmbH, A is also the managing director of Papierhersteller GmbH. Buchclub GmbH orders paper costing 10,000 EUR from Papierhersteller GmbH. It pays this amount by passing on 10,000 EUR of the 20,000 EUR it received from B. Whether or not the money can be confiscated from Papierhersteller GmbH depends on whether Papierhersteller GmbH – namely A – acted in bad faith. As A had knowledge of the origin of the 10,000 EUR, confiscation at Papierhersteller GmbH is possible.

80 Lastly, § 73b sub. 1 sent. 1 no. 3 StGB also applies to cases where the item obtained is transferred as part of an inheritance. Under this provision, incriminated funds can also be confiscated from heirs.

81 **Case variant 2d:** A causes Buchclub GmbH to directly pay him the sum of 20,000 EUR from the fraud against B. The very next day, A dies. A's sole heir is his child K. Now the confiscation order can also be addressed to K in the amount of 20,000 EUR.

III. Legal consequences – more specifically: confiscation of equivalent sum of money

82 Provided that the above-mentioned requirements have been met, both the **actual asset obtained** (**Regarding example 2:** the 20,000 EUR that were handed over in cash (→ mn. 68)) or – if passed through – the **object equivalent in value to the asset obtained** may be confiscated. Further, (where it is impossible to confiscate the original item), an equivalent sum of money or a **surrogate** obtained, may be confiscated from the third-party beneficiary (§ 73b sub. 2 and sub. 3, 73c StGB). In addition, the actual profits derived may also be confiscated.[95]

83 Again, when confiscating from a third party, the confiscation of an equivalent sum of money is the usual scenario, given that – for non-cash transactions in particular – the original asset cannot be confiscated, as 'only' the value of the transfer exists in the bank account.[96] Despite its enormous relevance in practice, the provision that shall enable the confiscation of an equivalent sum of money from a third party (§ 73b sub. 2 StGB) is drafted in a less than illuminating manner, resulting in considerable application issues in practice as well as legal uncertainties.[97] As a rule, the following should be noted:

---

[92] Regarding this controversy: Kämpfer/Schwerdtfeger StraFo 2020, 313 (315).

[93] BGH 7.6.2018 – 4 StR 639/17, BeckRS 2018, 13999 mn. 3.

[94] In favour of applying §§ 31, 166, 278 BGB; Matt/Renzikowski/Altenhain/Fleckenstein StGB § 73b mn 5. Taking a – justified – critical view: Kämpfer/Schwerdtfeger StraFo 2020, 313 (315).

[95] For an overview, see TK StGB/Eser/Schuster StGB § 73b mn. 11.

[96] Also → mn. 21 et seqq.

[97] Matt/Renzikowski/Altenhain/Fleckenstein StGB § 73b mn. 9; Bittmann wistra 2020, 265 et seq.

1. Passing equivalent sum of money on to third party

§ 73b sub. 2 StGB relates, first of all, to transitional acquisition cases where the third party receives an 'item that corresponds to the value of the asset obtained' from a party to the offence or another third party. Although the wording does not necessarily support this, it is generally assumed that this relates also to all cases in which an equivalent sum of money is passed on to the third party **from the outset**,[98] only excluding saved expenditures.[99] § 73b sub. 2 StGB is said to also to apply if, for example, the perpetrator commingles the proceeds with lawful assets and only then passes them on to the third party. Furthermore, § 73b sub. 2 StGB is to apply both if **the perpetrator** *apriori* receives the original item and if the perpetrator himself receives only the equivalent sum of money to begin with.[100] 84

Case variant 2e: B doesn't hand over 20,000 EUR in cash to Buchclub GmbH but actually transfers this amount into Buchclub GmbH's bank account. Buchclub GmbH transfers 10,000 EUR of this sum to Papierhersteller GmbH for the purchase of paper. As a consequence of the transfer, it is only an equivalent sum of money that is passed on to Papierhersteller GmbH, as the original sum of 20,000 EUR paid to Buchclub GmbH cannot be delineated. In this case, the value of the proceeds is passed on, which also falls under § 73b sub. 2 StGB. 85

This broad scope of application is delimited by the requirement that the item must have been obtained through an 'uninterrupted chain of enrichment'.[101] This is intended to ensure that the assets transferred do in fact originate from the criminal offence.[102] Moreover, it is necessary that the transfer of the asset took place with the aim of depriving the creditor of any access to the equivalent sum of money or of concealing the offence.[103] Confiscation is therefore precluded if the link to the original benefits from the offence is no longer discernible and the transaction is not intended to deprive creditors of access to assets that include direct proceeds from the offence, nor to conceal the offence.[104] 86

Case variant 2f: the 20,000 EUR from the fraud against B is received into Buchclub GmbH's bank account, which has a balance of 3 million EUR from lawful transactions. A few days later, Buchclub GmbH purchases paper for 10,000 EUR from Papierhersteller GmbH; this paper is needed to print more books. In this case variant, there are strong indications that the sum of 10,000 EUR cannot be confiscated from Papierhersteller GmbH, despite A's bad faith. Given the commingling of the 10,000 EUR with the credit balance of 3 million EUR in Buchclub GmbH's bank account, it is hardly provable that the 10,000 EUR do, in fact, originate from the offence committed against B ('uninterrupted chain of enrichment'). It is, in any case, not evident that the money was passed on in order to deprive creditors of access to the funds or to conceal the offence. 87

2. Realisation of the item obtained by the third party upon receipt

The confiscation of an equivalent sum of money prescribed by § 73b sub. 2 StGB refers neither to § 73b sub. 1 sent. 1 no. 1 StGB nor to § 73c StGB. The rationale behind this is that § 73b sub. 1 sent. 1 no. 1 StGB relates solely to cases where no transitional acquisition 88

---

[98] Bittmann wistra 2020, 265 (266). Fischer StGB § 73b mn. 14; different opinion: Köhler/Burkhard NStZ 2017, 665 (667).
[99] BGH 3.3.2022 – 4 StR 156/20, wistra 2022, 77 mn.155 et seq.
[100] Matt/Renzikowski/Altenhain/Fleckenstein StGB § 73b mn. 9.
[101] Fischer StGB § 73b mn. 9.
[102] Cf. Matt/Renzikowski/Altenhain/Fleckenstein StGB § 73b mn. 9.
[103] BGH 3.3.2022 – 4 StR 156/20, wistra 2022, 293 et seq.
[104] BGH 3.3.2022 – 4 StR 156/20, wistra 2022, 293 et seq.

takes place but, instead, the third party 'directly' obtains an 'item', making any referral obsolete.[105]

89 However, this view is incorrect, as both the case group, where the third party receives an asset directly that can only be confiscated by way of confiscating an equivalent sum of money (for instance, bank transfer), and the case group, where the third party itself passes on the original item it had received, would remain unregulated without such referral. That said, even without any such referrals, the courts are assuming that in both of the aforementioned case groups an equivalent sum of money can be confiscated from the third party pursuant to § 73b sub. 1 sent. 1 no. 1 StGB and § 73c StGB.[106]

90 **Case variant 2g:** B transferred the money for the first-edition Gospel According to St. John directly to Buchclub GmbH's bank account. Any confiscation from Buchclub GmbH can only be effected as confiscation of an equivalent sum of money, since the transferred amount can no longer be clearly delineated.

E. §§ 73d and 73e StGB, § 459g sub. 5 StPO: 'objections' against confiscation (deduction of expenditure, lapsing, proportionality)

91 If confiscation is, in principle, permissible and the 'item obtained' has been determined, this does not yet mean that confiscation will be ordered for that very amount. §§ 73d and 73e StGB provide material restrictions that **reduce the amount that can be confiscated** or even **preclude confiscation altogether**. At the enforcement stage, these provisions are underpinned by § 459g sub. 5 StPO, which links the enforcement of a confiscation order to the **principle of proportionality**. If the enforcement is deemed to be disproportionate, this will also result in confiscation being **precluded**.

92 **Example 3:** A buys a table at the flea market that looks antique but is actually worthless. A pays 20 EUR for the table, which is what the table is really worth. A sells this table to B for 100,000 EUR as the supposed twin to the so-called Resolute Desk.

I. § 73d StGB: deduction of expenditure

93 Under § 73d sub. 1 sent. 1 StGB, the expenditure incurred by the addressee of the confiscation may be deducted from the specific item confiscated or its value – this is, in fact, supposed to be the standard scenario. At first glance, this sounds exceedingly 'generous'. However, the very next sentence of the provision significantly restricts its substance, which is of great relevance in practice. To wit, the provision stipulates that any expenditure 'spent or used in the commission of or preparation for the unlawful act' cannot be deducted. This does not apply (exception to an exception) only in cases where the expenditure was incurred to fulfil an obligation vis-à-vis the party injured by the

[105] Fischer StGB § 73b mn. 14.
[106] Cf. instructive: Bittmann wistra 2020, 265 (266).

offence. This exception to an exception applies, for instance, to expenditure incurred by the perpetrator to fulfil obligations under a contract that was fraudulently concluded.[107]

Regarding example 3: A has provided B with the table that's actually only worth 20 EUR. This sum of 20 EUR is therefore deductible; as a result, only 99,980 EUR can be confiscated from A. **94**

Case variant 3a: A gets his friend C, who is an expert valuer, to falsely certify the genuineness of the table and pays him 500 EUR for that. A presents this certificate to B prior to the purchase. As A has spent the sum of 500 EUR in the preparation for the offence, this amount cannot be deducted. **95**

'Expenditure' (*Aufwendungen*) under § 73d StGB generally encompasses any and all assets voluntarily used in the commission of the unlawful act at the time of 'obtainment' (*Erlangen*)[108] insofar as a factual connection to the illicit act exists.[109] The prohibition of deduction precludes any deduction if the party to the offence used the means 'deliberately and wilfully' for the commission of the offence[110]. However, this does not apply where expenditure is incurred for making 'payments that cannot be faulted', even if they originate from an 'act sanctioned under criminal law'.[111] The specific differentiation between the permissible and the impermissible deduction of expenditure is exceedingly difficult, so the courts have developed comprehensive case law on this issue, that distinguish between the individual offences. **96**

Expenditure negligently incurred in order to commit criminal offences or acts of negligence is not deemed to have been incurred 'deliberately' or 'voluntarily'[112] and therefore does not fall under the prohibition of deduction.[113] **97**

As per its wording, § 73d StGB also applies to expenditure incurred by a third party. However, it is highly unlikely that the third party would subjectively incur anything 'in the commission of the offence'. It is therefore doubtful whether the prohibition of deduction under § 73d sub. 1 sent. 2, first half of sentence, StGB would apply to any third party. According to the preferable view, this depends on whether the third party acted in bad faith with regard to the expenditure.[114] In respect of companies, this will undoubtedly give rise to the question of knowledge imputation, as is so often the case. **98**

Example 4: By paying a bribe of 10,000 EUR, managing director A of SauberBau GmbH obtains a construction contract for his company that will generate 100,000 EUR in remuneration. The contract is performed without any complaints; SauberBau GmbH incurs costs totalling 60,000 EUR for personnel and materials. The entire remuneration of 100,000 EUR must be confiscated from SauberBau GmbH. However, the 60,000 EUR in costs must be deducted from this amount, as they were incurred in return for fault-free work performance. The bribe of 10,000 EUR, on the other hand, is not deductible. **99**

---

[107] BT-Drs. 18/9525, p. 68; NK-WSS/Lindemann/Bauerkamp StGB § 73d mn. 15.
[108] Fischer StGB § 73d mn. 4 with further citations.
[109] Köhler NStZ 2017, 497 (505).
[110] Cf. BT-Drs. 18/9525, p. 68.
[111] Cf. BT-Drs. 18/9525, p. 68.
[112] Cf. BGH 30.5.2008 – 1 StR 166/07, NStZ 2009, 275 mn. 101.
[113] Cf. BT-Drs. 18/9525, p. 68.
[114] Matt/Renzikowski/Altenhain/Fleckenstein StGB § 73d mn. 4; different opinion: Köhler NStZ 2017, 497 (508); cf. BT-Drucks. 18/9525, p. 55.

II. § 73e sub. 1 StGB: lapsing

100 Pursuant to § 73e sub. 1 sent. 1 StGB, confiscation is precluded if the claim for restitution of the item obtained, or compensation for its value, that accrued to the injured party from the offence (hereinafter also: recourse or compensation claim) has lapsed. This is the most important exclusion under German law on confiscation.[115] This 'bar to confiscation' is also of great relevance in practice since it provides the opportunity of avoiding a confiscation order under criminal law (and its side effects, such as distraint, which is a particularly severe measure)[116] by entering into a settlement with the injured party.

101 In principle, the requirements for exclusion under § 73e sub. 1 sent. 1 StGB are straightforward: there must be a specific injured party who, by way of the offence, acquired a claim (of whatever kind) to the 'item obtained'. To the extent that this claim has lapsed, confiscation is precluded.

102 **Case variant 3b:** A repays B the sum of 100,000 EUR obtained for the table. Confiscation is therefore precluded.

103 The purpose of this provision is twofold: primarily, it aims to prevent the assertion of double claims against the addressee of the confiscation order. Secondly – but of no less relevance – the legislator intended to create a settlement-friendly provision that also brings claims that form the subject matter of confiscation under criminal law under the discretionary power of the injured holder of the claim.[117]

104 Accordingly, the essence of § 73e sub. 1 sent. 1 StGB can be summarised as follows: through satisfaction of the specific injured party (whether a natural person or a company), for example by entering into a settlement, the issuance of a confiscation order in criminal proceedings can be averted. This tenet applies to all types of confiscation, under §§ 73 to 73c StGB as well as, via the referral in § 76a sub. 1 StGB, to independent confiscation.

105 In the case of multiple injured parties, the respective claims must be differentiated, and confiscation is, of course, only precluded to the extent that the individual claims have lapsed. However, if no individual injured party exists but, instead, only the legal interests of the public are affected (e.g. in cases of facilitating the escape of a prisoner pursuant to § 120 StGB[118]), § 73e sub. 1 sent. 1 StGB does not apply.[119]

106 **Case variant 3c:** A sold the table to B and C who, having each paid 50,000 EUR, acquired ownership in equal parts. A now pays the sum of 50,000 EUR back to B. This amount of 50,000 EUR cannot be confiscated, whereas confiscation of the 50,000 EUR that C had paid is still possible.

107 The applicability of § 73e sub. 1 sent. 1 StGB in borderline cases, where the constituent elements of the provision protect both the legal interests of the public and individual legal interests, is problematic and largely unresolved. This issue arises, in particular, with regard to corruption offences (§§ 299 et seq. StGB)[120] that are particularly relevant for the corporate sector and intend to protect both market competition as well as the affected companies.[121] According to the view advocated here, § 73e sub. 1 sent. 1 StGB also applies to these cases.[122] After all, as elaborated above, under the case law of the BVerfG,

---

[115] Correct: Peters/Bröckers Vermögensabschöpfung mn. 190.
[116] → mn. 118 et seqq.
[117] BT-Drs. 18/9525, p. 69; cf. also BT-Drs. 18/11640, p. 79.
[118] Regarding the protected legal interest see e.g. BeckOK StGB/Dallmeyer, 63. Ed. 1.11.2024, StGB § 120 mn. 1.
[119] Of the same view: MüKoStGB/Joecks § 73 mn 11; Michalke wistra 2022, 492 (495).
[120] For details → Ch. 10.
[121] For greater details, see Michalke wistra 2022, 492 (495) et seq.
[122] With regard to § 299 StGB, also Michalke wistra 2022, 492 (495) et seq., different opinion: MüKoStGB/Joecks § 73e mn. 11, who relies, however, on the legislative rationale, which does not contain

confiscation is a purely preventative measure under quasi-unjust-enrichment rules that serves solely to disgorge any benefits derived from the offence.[123] However, to the extent that any restitution claims of the individual injured party have lapsed, the perpetrator is entitled to what he has obtained, which remains with him under civil law – the 'public' has no entitlements. Otherwise, the addressee of a confiscation order would be additionally penalised if the item obtained (of which the law no longer disapproves) would be 'taken away' from him by way of confiscation, since confiscation is specifically not intended as (further) punishment.

Moreover, it is doubtful – and contentious as to the details – whether payments made by one confiscation order addressee would also bring about a lapsing of the relevant claims against all other confiscation order addressees.[124] This question arises, for example, if both the company and the perpetrator acting on its behalf have obtained something, but only one of them enters into a settlement with the injured party. The correct view is that this question cannot be answered in the abstract but can only be assessed by reference to the actual agreement or the facts of the case. In similar situations, it is always advisable (to the extent desired) to include all potential confiscation order addressees in the settlement agreement to document that any claims against them have lapsed. **108**

In conclusion, the following should be noted: if payment by instalments is agreed as part of the settlement, the prevailing view is that the claim will only lapse for the amount in which payments were actually made to the injured party before confiscation was ordered.[125] **109**

Case variant 3d: A and B agree on the repayment of the sum of 100,000 EUR in monthly instalments of 1,000 EUR. Ten months later, A is convicted and confiscation is ordered. Since A has only paid 10,000 EUR to B by that time, B's claim has only lapsed in this amount. Accordingly, confiscation is ordered in the amount of 90,000 EUR. **110**

III. § 73e sub. 2 StGB and § 459g sub. 5 StPO: disenrichment and proportionality

To the extent that the injured party's claims have not lapsed in accordance with § 73e sub. 1 StGB, a third party acting in good faith – not a party to the offence! – can raise the objection of subsequent disenrichment as per § 73e sub. 2 StGB. Disenrichment means that the value of what has been obtained no longer forms part of the third party's assets and has not been replaced with any other asset either.[126] Furthermore, the relevant asset must not have been used to cover day-to-day living expenses, as this would mean that the third party saved himself expenses which he would have incurred 'anyway'.[127] Disenrichment will therefore usually be assumed if the third party has incurred expenditure on luxuries which he would not have done otherwise (e.g. holiday trips). **111**

Example 5: A and B pursue a criminal business model, whereby A favours B's companies when awarding contracts and B, in return, books 'free' luxury travel for A. A takes his mistress, the student C, with him on these trips; C acts in good faith. C would have never booked these luxury holidays for herself, as they are well beyond her financial means. Accordingly, under the **112**

---

any such statement.

[123] BVerfG 10.2.2021 – 2 BvL 8/19, NJW 2021, 1222 (1223) et seq.
[124] See Ullenboom ch. 8 mn. 174; Henckel jurisPR-StrafR 11/2022 Anm. 1.
[125] MüKoStGB/Joecks/Meißner § 73e mn. 11.
[126] Matt/Renzikowski/Altenhain/Fleckenstein StGB § 73e mn. 3 et seq.
[127] TK StGB/Eser/Schuster StGB § 73e mn. 4.

terms of § 73e sub. 2 StGB, the costs of the luxury trips cannot be confiscated from C as saved expenditure.

113 The required good faith is absent if the third party – at least recklessly – ignored the circumstances that give rise to confiscability at the time of his/her disenrichment.[128] Again, imputation within the company is problematic;[129] however, knowledge on the part of its executive bodies should be imputed in any case.[130]

114 **Case variant 5a:** A had told C about his 'special friend' B, who 'keeps him well plied with electronics' if A 'won't be a stickler for the rules' when it comes to awarding contracts. When C needs a new laptop, A 'procures' the laptop via B, so he proudly tells C. Only a few weeks later, C spills coffee over the laptop, rendering it unusable. In this case, § 73e sub. 2 StGB does not preclude the confiscation of the laptop's value from C, as she – at least recklessly – ignored its criminally relevant origin.

115 In the absence of good faith, the disenrichment of a *mala fide* third party can only be taken into account at the enforcement stage. After all, by operation of § 459g sub. 5 StPO, the order will not be enforced where this would be disproportionate, which can be assumed in the event of personal misfortune if this would impair social rehabilitation or even if there is no link whatsoever between the assets and the criminal offences.[131] *Mala fide* third parties as well as parties to the offence may invoke disproportionality.

116 Disenrichment, which used to be explicitly mentioned in the wording of the law as a sub-case of disproportionality, was one of the most important case groups of disproportionality until July 2021. Even after the amendment of the wording of the law, it would appear that parties affected by confiscation may still be able to invoke (partial) disenrichment in some situations, e.g. when they have paid taxes on the proceeds[132].[133] According to case law, it must probably be assumed that, in general, the objection of disenrichment may only be raised if the (entire) assets of the confiscation order addressee are less than the amount to be confiscated.[134] However, the correct view is that the only decisive factor is whether or not the very asset that the perpetrator derived is still part of his overall assets. Otherwise, the required link to the offence would be completely severed.[135] Under the amended law, the objection of disproportionality would arguably also be barred if the *mala fide* third party squandered the asset (in bad faith).[136]

117 The courts also place extremely high requirements on general disproportionality under § 459g sub. 5 StPO. This objection should nevertheless always be considered during enforcement proceedings and be raised where applicable.

---

[128] MüKoStGB/Joecks/Meißner § 73e mn. 15 et seq.

[129] → mn. 73 et seqq.

[130] MüKoStGB/Joecks/Meißner § 73e mn. 16.

[131] Cf., with numerous further citations and examples: KK-StPO/Appl StPO § 459 mn. 18. Taxes can only be taken into account if they can no longer be considered during taxation proceedings, see Korte wistra 2018, 1 (10).

[132] BeckOK StPO/Coen, 53. Ed. 1.10.2024, StPO§ 459g mn. 28; in this context, the fact that taxes have already been paid can presumably only be invoked if this can no longer be taken into account, or a correction is no longer possible, in the taxation proceedings, cf. KK-StPO/Appl StPO § 459 mn. 18.

[133] Instructive: Bittmann NStZ 2022, 8 (17); for an overview, see KK-StPO/Appl StPO § 459 mn. 17.

[134] Expressly with regard to the former wording of § 73c sub. 1 sent. 2 StGB repealed version: BGH 14.1.2016 – 1 StR 615/15, NStZ-RR 2016, 108, cf. also BGH 30. 5. 2008 – 1 StR 166/07, GRUR 2008, 818 mn. 113.

[135] Cf. regarding the repealed version: BGH 10. 10. 2002 – 4 StR 233/02, NJW 2003, 300 (headnote); BGH 20.7.2006 – 7 BJs 146/85-3 StB 8/06, NStZ-RR 2007, 11; regarding the debate see e.g.: MüKoStGB/Joecks/Meißner § 73e mn. 12 et seq.

[136] Cf. BT-Drs. 19/27654, p. 111. Regarding the correct interpretation of the legislative rationale: Bittmann NStZ 2022, 8 (17).

F. Procedural principles

Criminal proceedings in Germany can roughly be divided into three phases: the investigation by the prosecutor's office, the interlocutory and main proceedings before the court, and the enforcement proceedings. **118**

During the investigation, it is primarily the prosecutor's office that examines the question whether a criminal offence has been committed and whether confiscation from a party to the offence or a third party might be possible. Even at this stage, the state may provisionally seize assets that might potentially be subject to confiscation (cf. § 111b et seq. StPO). **119**

Where the prosecutor's office arrives at the conclusion that the requirements for confiscation have been met, it usually applies for confiscation in conjunction with the indictment. If the criminal court arrives at the same conclusion, it issues – usually when convicting the party to the offence – a confiscation order against the party to the offence or a third party (party to the confiscation proceedings). **120**

The subsequent enforcement of this confiscation order is conducted by the prosecutor's office once the confiscation order has become final and binding. Generally, the decision whether, following confiscation, the confiscated assets are paid out by the state to the party injured by the criminal offence is only made during this phase. This payment will only be made upon the injured party's application. **121**

Accordingly, as to the various stages of the proceedings and the pertinent rights, the following should be noted: **122**

I. §§ 111b et seqq. StPO: provisional securing of assets

§§ 111b et seq. StPO stipulate under which circumstances the state may provisionally secure assets subject to the final decision regarding confiscation. **123**

The purpose of these instruments is to prevent the potential confiscation order addressee from transferring the assets prior to the issuance of the confiscation order, which would leave the state unable to seize the relevant assets when attempting to enforce the confiscation order.[137] The provisional securing of assets can therefore be effected during the period from the commencement of the investigation until the confiscation order becomes legally binding.[138] **124**

Assets in physical form can be seized in accordance with § 111b StPO. Of much greater practical relevance is the distraint of assets governed by § 111e StPO, which permits the provisional securing of any assets (whatsoever) of the party concerned (e.g. garnishment of bank accounts) to ensure that an equivalent sum of money can be confiscated at a later stage. Distraint of assets can be ordered if the following four requirements are all met: **125**

The **first requirement** for the imposition of an asset distraint is the existence of an initial suspicion that criminal offences (§§ 73 and 73c StGB) have been committed.[139] Such a suspicion is deemed to exist if there is probable cause that the relevant set of facts **126**

---

[137] MAH WirtschaftsStrafR/Corsten/Schilling § 13 mn. 92.

[138] Schmitt/Köhler/Köhler StPO § 111e mn. 17.

[139] OLG Hamburg 26.10.2018 – 2 Ws 183/18, NZWiSt 2019, 106 (107) et seq.; Schmitt/Köhler/Köhler StPO § 111e mn. 4.

comprises a criminal offence.[140] Accordingly, the threshold to the assumption of initial suspicion is very low.

127 **In addition** to the initial suspicion, there must also be actual sufficient indications that the requirements for the confiscation of an equivalent sum of money have been met.[141] This means that the facts must bear out the assumption that the person against whom the distraint order is to be issued has received assets from a criminal offence.

128 **Thirdly**, a need for having the relevant assets secured must exist, meaning there must be specific indications which suggest that, without the order and enforcement of distraint, the later enforcement of the confiscation order would be **seriously jeopardised**. Specifically, there must be an impending risk that the asset situation will deteriorate or access to the affected party's assets will be significantly impeded.[142]

129 **Finally**, the distraint of assets must be proportionate. In order to assess proportionality, the state's interest in securing the assets and the ownership position of the affected party must be carefully weighed up, taking into consideration all pertinent factors. This assessment also takes into account the strength of the suspicion, the severity of the asset-securing measure, the duration of such measure and the volume of the assets secured.[143] Proportionality must be ensured at all times.[144] For instance, if an asset distraint is imposed at the beginning of an investigation and the investigation then potentially lasts for many years, this may result in a distraint that was initially permissible retrospectively becoming impermissible, which would require it to be lifted.[145]

130 The courts may order the distraint of assets at their reasonable discretion in accordance with § 111e sub. 1 sent. 1 StPO (cf. § 111j sub. 1 sent. 1 StPO).[146] However, where 'important reasons' give rise to the assumption that the requirements for the confiscation of an equivalent sum of money have been met, the statutory understanding is that distraint of assets should be ordered by default.[147]

131 **Example 6:** A has promised several customers delivery of the first edition of the Gospel According to St. John by Buchclub GmbH, but never made good on this promise (as he never intended to do so). In total, the defrauded customers paid 300,000 EUR to Buchclub GmbH for these books. When A learns of the investigation against him, he attempts to transfer 300,000 EUR from Buchclub GmbH's bank account to the bank account of his sister-in-law in Cyprus. The prosecutor's office realises this and applies for an order to distrain Buchclub GmbH's assets in the amount of 300,000 EUR.

132 **Case variant 6a:** as the requirements for asset distraint have been met in the above example, initially the requisite order was issued. However, the investigations have now been going on for four years, as the investigating authorities have difficulties locating and interviewing the injured parties. A therefore applies to have the distraint order lifted. The court grants the application, as a distraint has now become disproportionate due to the lapse of time.

---

[140] See e.g. BeckOK StPO/Huber, 53. Ed. 1.10.2024, StPO § 111b mn. 8; regarding the general requirements for initial suspicion, cf. BGH 1.6.1994 – 1 BJs 182/83 StB 10/94, NStZ 1994, 499 with further citations.

[141] GTZ/Gercke StPO § 111e mn. 4.

[142] BGH 3.6.2014 – KRB 2/14, NJW 2014, 3258; Schmitt/Köhler/Köhler StPO § 111e mn. 6.

[143] KK-StPO/Spillecke StPO § 111e mn. 9.

[144] BVerfG 17.4.2015 – 2 BvR 1986/14, wistra 2015, 348 (349).

[145] OLG Rostock 12.4.2018 – 20 Ws 42/18, StraFo 2018, 350 et seq = BeckRS 2018, 45304.

[146] In cases of imminent danger, the order can also be issued by the prosecutor's office, cf. § 111j sub. 1 sent. 2 StPO. Also see: MüKoStPO/Putzke/Scheinfeld § 426 mn. 6; Schmitt/Köhler/Köhler StPO § 426 mn. 3.

[147] HK-StPO/Gercke § 111e mn. 15; Schmitt/Köhler/Köhler StPO § 111e mn. 12.

In this context, it is important to note that § 111h sub. 2 sent. 1 StPO precludes the levying of execution against the distrained items and assets if a distraint of assets has been ordered. This should always be kept in mind whenever it is intended to underpin the pursuit of civil-law claims by filing a criminal complaint. **133**

II. Procedure of criminal and/or confiscation proceedings

The possibility of confiscation is first examined during the investigation by the prosecutor's office. Since the law assumes, as a general rule, that the person involved in the offence who is being investigated is also the potential addressee of the confiscation order, the legal position of a party affected by confiscation who is not identical to the person involved in the offence is only very rudimentarily outlined in §§ 426 and 428 StPO. **134**

It would appear, however, that the potential confiscation order addressee is given a **position that is similar to that of an accused person**.[148] Pursuant to § 426 StPO, he must be given the opportunity to be heard, and he has the right to remain silent as far as his participation in these proceedings is concerned. Under § 428 sub. 1 and sub. 2 StPO, he has the right to be represented by a lawyer, and under § 428 sub. 1 and sub. 2 in conjunction with § 147 StPO, he has the right to inspect the investigation file. **135**

If the prosecutor's office, at the completion of its investigation, arrives at the conclusion that the requirements for confiscation have, in principle, been met, it can nevertheless refrain from confiscation in certain cases (§ 421 sub. 1 and sub. 3 and § 435 sub. 1 sent. 2 StPO). This applies, in particular, to cases where the assets obtained are of negligible value or confiscation would require enormous effort. This may be the case, for instance, if the confiscation order addressee is insolvent[149] or if a confiscation order needs to be enforced abroad[150]. In all other cases, the prosecutor's office is required to apply for confiscation.[151] **136**

If the prosecutor's office intends to indict a person involved in the offence and confiscate assets in connection with the offence in question, the prosecutor's office will always apply for a confiscation order when submitting its indictment.[152] Any third parties to be subject to the confiscation order will be involved in this process as parties to the confiscation proceedings (cf. § 424 sub. 1 StPO). These joint proceedings (so-called subjective proceedings[153]) are the standard envisaged by the law.[154] In this case, a public trial would be conducted before a criminal court, and the court would issue a confiscation order at the end of the trial[155], unless the court, for its part, dispenses with confiscation under the terms of §§ 421 and 422 StPO. The position of the party to the confiscation proceedings in **137**

---

[148] Cf. e.g. the right to remain silent under § 426 sub. 2 StPO.

[149] Cf. LG Kiel 16.12.2019 – 3 KLs 8/17, BeckRS 2019, 62388 mn. 165.

[150] In this respect, the legislative rationale assumes a perpetrator without assets (BT-Drs. 18/9525, p. 87.), from which follows that the success potential of any enforcement measures must be taken into account when deciding to refrain from confiscation, cf. Rettke NZWiSt 2019, 281 (283). This would indicate that confiscation may also be dispensed with if enforcement abroad appears to be futile.

[151] BeckOK StPO/Temming, 53. Ed. 1.10.2024, RistBV 180 mn. 1; regarding the narrowing of the discretionary scope of the prosecutor's office, see Reh NZWiSt 2018, 20 (25).

[152] This already follows from the fact that independent confiscation under § 76a StGB can only be ordered in cases where subjective proceedings have been frustrated for legal or factual reasons, cf. MüKoStGB/Joecks/Meißner § 76a mn. 5.

[153] Regarding the term, cf. Ullenboom ch. 12 mn. 254.

[154] This follows, inter alia, from the fact that the independent proceedings under § 76a sub. 1 to 3 StGB are only permissible if the party to the relevant offence cannot (or can no longer) be prosecuted. Regarding § 76a sub. 4 StGB, cf. also SSW-StGB/Heine § 76a mn. 14.

[155] Pursuant to § 424 sub. 2 StPO, participation in the proceedings will not be ordered if the person concerned declares that he will not raise any objections to confiscation.

such a trial is set forth in greater detail in §§ 427 and 430 StPO. Upon commencement of the trial, the party to the confiscation proceedings, as a rule, has the position of a defendant in a criminal trial (§ 427 StPO). As per § 430 sub. 1 StPO, the hearing can proceed without him should he fail to appear before the court despite having been duly notified. If the party to the confiscation proceedings is present, he is entitled to exercise the same rights that the StPO provides for the defendant.

138 **Regarding example 6:** the prosecutor's office indicts A for fraud involving the first edition of the Gospel According to St. John. In addition, it also applies for the confiscation of the sum of 300,000 EUR from Buchclub GmbH. Buchclub GmbH is included in the proceedings as a party to the confiscation proceedings. At the end of the trial, the court sentences A to a suspended prison term of one year. In addition, it also orders the confiscation of a sum of money equivalent to 300,000 EUR from Buchclub GmbH.

139 **Case variant 6b:** Buchclub GmbH had transferred the sum of 300,000 EUR directly to A. In this case, the prosecutor's office, as part of its indictment, applies for the confiscation of 300,000 EUR from A and Buchclub GmbH. At the end of the trial, the court sentences A to a suspended prison term of one year. In addition, it also orders the confiscation of the equivalent of 300,000 EUR from Buchclub GmbH and A. Both are jointly and severally liable, so that this amount **only** needs to be paid **once**.

140 Not only can the issue of confiscation be heard in joint proceedings, confiscation is also possible in separate 'confiscation proceedings' (objective proceedings) that are conducted solely against the party to the confiscation proceedings.[156] These proceedings are governed by §§ 435 to 437 StPO. The legal position of parties to the confiscation proceedings corresponds to their position in subjective proceedings, cf. § 435 sub. 3 sent. 2 StPO. Simply put, such proceedings may be conducted whenever the parties to the offence – for whatever reason – cannot be prosecuted for a criminal offence, cf. § 76a StGB. It is possible, for instance, that the proceedings against the party to the offence are stayed against payment of a sum of money under § 153a StPO but the prosecutor's office still wishes to confiscate the assets obtained by the company where the party to the offence was employed. This confiscation would then be effected by way of independent confiscation proceedings (cf. § 76a sub. 3 StPO). The decision in these proceedings can be made by court order, so that the physical presence of the party to the confiscation proceedings is not mandatory (cf. § 436 sub. 2 in conjunction with § 434 sub. 2 to sub. 4 StPO).

141 **Case variant 6c:** A is now deceased and can therefore not be indicted. The prosecutor's office nevertheless wishes to confiscate the sum of 300,000 EUR from Buchclub GmbH. It therefore applies for independent confiscation proceedings against Buchclub GmbH. The criminal court issues an order for confiscation.

142 Lastly, confiscation may also be ordered against a party to the offence in connection with the issuance of an order imposing punishment (*Strafbefehl*, cf. § 407 sub. 2 StPO). Again, these proceedings are (initially) conducted solely in writing.

III. Enforcement proceedings

143 Where confiscation has been ordered, the prosecutor's office must enforce this order. § 459g StPO sets forth the provisions regarding enforcement. As the enforcement agency, the prosecutor's office is in charge of enforcement (cf. §§ 1, 3 and 4 StVollstrO), with a judicial officer having functional responsibility (§ 3 no. 4 lit. c) and § 31 sub. 2 sent. 1

[156] Cf. terminology and distinction from subjective proceedings: Ullenboom ch. 12 mn. 254.

RpflG. Confiscation is, first of all, effected in favour of the judicial treasury of the *Land* whose court decided in the first instance (cf. § 60 StVollstO).

During enforcement, the confiscation order addressee may, in particular, contend that confiscation is disproportionate (§ 459g sub. 5 StPO).[157] Similarly, confiscation is precluded in cases where the injured party's claim lapsed during the period between issuance of the confiscation order and enforcement, for example because the confiscation order addressee paid the relevant amount directly to the injured party (cf. § 459g sub. 4 StPO). When enforcing a confiscation order abroad, the additional requirements of mutual legal assistance must be complied with. **144**

The enforcement proceedings are of particular interest to persons who were adversely affected by the criminal offence.[158] They will be informed by the prosecutor's office that the confiscated sums can be paid to them up to an amount that corresponds to the loss they suffered from the criminal offence, cf. § 459i StPO. Thereafter, they can apply to the prosecutor's office to have the confiscated items/monies distributed to them (§ 459h sub. 1 in conjunction with § 459j StPO and/or § 459h sub. 2 in conjunction with § 459k StPO). This procedure serves to ensure that the injured parties receive the assets that they were deprived of via the criminal offence quickly and unbureaucratically (from the prosecutor's office), without having to bring a (costly) civil action themselves.[159] **145**

To have the prosecutor's office distribute the assets to them, injured parties must register their claims with the prosecutor's office within six months of being notified of the option of compensation (cf. §§ 459j sub. 1 and 459k sub. 1 StPO). Most prosecutor's offices provide forms for this purpose, which they send to the injured party together with information on the possibility of compensation. These forms look similar to this: **146**

Enforcement proceedings against: **147**
Criminal charge:

Reply to the notification from the prosecutor's office pursuant to § 459i StPO

Particulars:

First name, last name:
Date and place of birth:
Street address:
Town/city:
Account details:
Bank:
IBAN:

I have suffered a loss as a consequence of the following criminal offence:

Criminal offence:
Date/time of the offence:
Place of the offence:

As a result of the criminal offence, I have incurred the following loss:

(Note: For the purposes of these proceedings, only items that were relinquished to the perpetrator, or of which the perpetrator took possession, qualify as losses and are therefore limited in terms of their amount. Thus, damages for pain and suffering, property damage, etc. cannot be asserted in these proceedings. This does not affect your night to assert any further claims before the civil courts.)

---

157 → mn. 111 et seqq.
158 → mn. 128 et seqq.
159 BT-Drs. 18/9525, p. 3.

The loss must be quantified in terms of its exact amount.

Item
Value

I therefore claim the following total amount:

As evidence for the amount of the loss, I am eclosing the following documents:

(Note: Please submit the documents on which the determination of the value is based, such as proof of purchase, valuations.)

To be completed only for exchange agreements, e.g. purchase contract.

I will keep the item purchased, e.g. the defective car.

This item has the following value:

I have already rescinded the contract vis-à-vis the party concerned and will return the item purchased *(if available, please enclose anything that documents your declaration of recission).*

I affirm that my claims have not been passed to anyone else, such as an insurer under § 86 VVG, by way of assignment under § 398 BGB, or by way of release or performance, or have lapsed or are limited in any other way, such as settlement with the accused person/debtor.

If there are any changes regarding my claim, I will inform you.

or

My insurer has already indemnified me.
As proof, I am enclosing the following insurance documents:

and/or

My claims have been settled or passed on as follows:

148 If the injured party misses this deadline, they must apply for reinstatement to their former position or submit an executory title that shows their claim (cf. § 459j sub. 4 and 5 StPO and § 459k sub. 4 and 5 StPO).

149 Where the applicant's entitlement readily follows from the confiscation order, the prosecutor's office will surrender the item or the monetary amount directly to the injured party. Otherwise, a court would have to decide on the claim (§ 459j sub. 2 StPO and § 459k sub. 2 StPO).

150 **Example 6:** after the end of the trial against A, B receives notification that the confiscation of 300,000 EUR has been ordered against Buchclub GmbH. B then informs the prosecutor's office that he paid 20,000 EUR to Buchclub GmbH for the first edition of the Gospel According to St. John but never received the book. As no other injured parties register any claims and the judgment shows that B was one of the parties injured by A's offences, the sum of 20,000 EUR is paid to B.

151 Should the confiscated amount not suffice to satisfy all injured parties, the prosecutor's office will open insolvency proceedings upon application (§ 459h sub. 2 sent. 2 in conjunction with § 111i sub. 2 StPO), so that the injured parties can be compensated on a pro-rata basis during the insolvency proceedings. If insolvency proceedings are not instituted on the grounds of insufficiency of assets, the proceedings will be governed by § 459m StPO.

152 **Case variant 6d:** after the end of the trial against A, 15 people who each purchased a book for 20,000 EUR contact the prosecutor's office. However, only 150,000 EUR can be confiscated from Buchclub GmbH. The prosecutor's office therefore applies for the initiation of insolvency proceedings in respect of the assets of Buchclub GmbH, and the injured parties receive compensation on a pro-rata basis.

CHAPTER 6
COMPLIANCE MANAGEMENT SYSTEMS

Bibliography: Fleischer, Aktienrechtliche Compliance-Pflichten im Praxistest: Das Siemens/Neubürger-Urteil des LG München I, NZG 2014, 321; Goette/Barring, Compliance-Management-Systeme und Compliance Due Diligence, DStR 2021, 1238; Hauschka, Compliance, Compliance-Manager, Compliance-Programme: Eine geeignete Reaktion auf gestiegene Haftungsrisiken für Unternehmen und Management?, NJW 2004, 257; Pasewaldt/Karami, Unternehmensstrafrecht: Der Regierungsentwurf für ein Verbandssanktionengesetz (VerSanG) – wesentliche Inhalte und Auswirkungen auf die Compliance in der Medizinproduktebranche, MPR 2021, 6; Sonnenberg, Compliance-Systeme in Unternehmen – Einrichtung, Ausgestaltung und praktische Herausforderungen, JuS 2017, 917.

Table of contents

A. Introduction 112
B. Legal obligations to implement CMS in Germany 113
 I. Relevant provisions 113
 II. Obligation to obey CMS regulations against the background of German case law 114
C. Substantive design of CMS 116
 I. Prevention of illegal behaviour 117
  1. Risk assessment 117
   a) Identify the company's compliance risks 117
   b) Evaluate the likelihood and impact of compliance risks 117
   c) Develop preventive measures 117
  2. Codifying ethical principles (code of conduct) 118
   a) Ethical principles 118
   b) Compliance requirements 118
   c) Reporting channels and investigation procedures 118
   d) Best practices for developing and implementing a code of conduct 118
  3. Implementation of compliance guidelines 119
   a) Anti-bribery and corruption policy 119
   b) Gift policy 119
   c) Anti-money laundering policy 120
  4. Leadership's ethical stance 120
  5. Compliance trainings 121
 II. Controls to ensure compliance with legal requirements 122
  1. Reporting channels 122
  2. Procedural controls 123
  3. Investigation of compliance violations 124
   a) Internal investigations 124
   b) Audits 125
 III. Reasonable reactions to suspicious conduct 126
  1. Sanctioning employees 126
  2. Taking corrective measures 127
D. Common CMS pillars 127
E. Legal and regulatory challenges to CMS 129
F. Conclusion 129

A. Introduction

1 Compliance has become a paramount objective for businesses worldwide due to the increasing number of high-profile cases of corporate misconduct and non-compliance. The debate notably arrived in Germany following the major economic scandals involving Siemens, Bilfinger and MAN in the early 2000s. Compliance in a corporate context generally describes the obeyance of laws, rules, regulations, and ethical standards in business activities.[1] Companies that fail to comply with legal and regulatory requirements can face severe consequences; these include financial penalties, reputational damage and legal actions.[2]

2 In recent years, German companies witnessed high-profile cases of corporate misconduct and compliance violations that resulted in significant fines and penalties imposed by regulatory authorities. For example, the diesel emissions scandal that emerged in 2015 involving German Volkswagen that installed software to deceive emissions tests led to substantial fines and compensation payments. In 2021, the US reached a 1.5 billion USD settlement with Daimler AG over emission cheating in Mercedes-Benz diesel vehicles.[3] This case highlights the severe consequences of non-compliance, including financial penalties and reputational damage.

3 Another example of compliance failure in Germany is the lack of anti-money laundering controls in the financial sector. In 2020, Deutsche Bank was imposed with a corporate administrative fine amounting to 15 million EUR by the Federal Financial Supervisory Authority (*Bundesanstalt für Finanzdienstleistungsaufsicht*, BaFin) for insufficient anti-money laundering controls.[4] There have been numerous cases of companies being fined for violations of legal obligations, e.g., in the context of data protection, anti-trust law or consumer protection. Another case in 2019 concerned leading fashion retailer H&M being fined 35.3 EUR million for collecting excessive amounts of personal data from employees without their prior consent.[5]

4 These examples show the significance of implementing successful compliance management systems (CMS) helping to detect and prevent misconduct, within companies. To prevent and detect compliance violations, companies must establish and maintain an effective CMS, involving, among others, policies, procedures, trainings and controls that ensure business is carried out within legal and regulatory frameworks.[6] An effective CMS can not only protect a company from financial and reputation harm but also ensure that its employees are aware of their obligations and are encouraged to act in accordance with

---

[1] MAH WirtschaftsStrafR/Wessing/Dann § 4 mn. 4; Müller-Gugenberger WirtschaftsStrafR-HdB, 8th edn 2024, Ch. 31 mn. 31.4 et seqq.; Godzierz Compliance-Checklisten/Clodius § 4 mn. 1.

[2] Goette/Barring DStR 2021, 1238 (1239); Godzierz Compliance-Checklisten/Clodius § 4 mn. 6.

[3] https://www.justice. gov/opa/pr/us-reaches-15-billion-settlement-daimler-ag-over-emissions-cheating-mercedes-benz-diesel. (last accessed: 26.5.2025).

[4] J. Clarke, Deutsche Bank fined € 15m over money laundering failures, Financial Times, 6 December 2019 <https://www.ft.com/content/eeefa806-184b-11ea-9ee4-11f260415385> (last accessed 28.5.2025); J. Willmroth, Deutsche Bank zahlt 15 Millionen Euro Bußgeld, Süddeutsche Zeitung, 6 December 2019 <https://www.sueddeutsche.de/wirtschaft/deutsche-bank-razzia-2019-1.4713058> (last accessed 28.5.2025).

[5] Der Hamburgerische Beauftragte für Datenschutz und Informationsfreiheit [i.e. Hamburg Commissioner for Data Protection and Freedom of Information], Bußgeld wegen Datenschutzverstößen bei H&M <https://datenschutz-hamburg.de/fileadmin/user_upload/HmbBfDI/Pressemitteilungen/2020/2020-10-01-H_M.pdf> (last accessed: 26.5.2025).

[6] DICO Standard Arbeitskreis Compliance Management-Systeme 2021 p. 5 <https://www.dico-ev.de/wp-content/uploads/2021/03/STANDARD_CMS_2021.pdf> (last accessed: 28.5.2025); Eidam Unternehmen und Strafe Ch. 15 mn. 103; MAH WirtschaftsStrafR/Wessing/Dann § 4 mn. 5.

laws and ethical standards.[7] A well-designed and implemented CMS can help companies achieve their business objectives while mitigating legal risks and increasing trust at the same time.[8]

In Germany, companies are advised to have an effective CMS in place as failure to comply with legal obligations can result in severe penalties, including (costly) corporate administrative fines as well as criminal sanctions against individuals. Non-compliance can also result in reputational damage, loss of customer trust, and potential legal actions by affected parties[9] (as illustrated by the Volkswagen share price, which suffered severe losses after the misconduct was revealed). **5**

This chapter provides an overview of CMS and its legal framework in Germany, including the legal obligations and consequences of lacking an effective CMS. It also discusses the structure of an effective CMS, including its key components and benefits for companies and employees. The goal of this chapter is to provide an understanding of the importance of CMS in today's business environment and the steps that companies can take to establish and maintain effective compliance measures. **6**

B. Legal obligations to implement CMS in Germany

I. Relevant provisions

In Germany, the legal framework for CMS is extensive and complex. Excluding few specific regulated areas, there is no explicit provision on the implementation of a CMS. Nevertheless, the obligation to comply with applicable laws can be derived from regulations concerning diligent business management.[10] Therefore, legal literature assumes several provisions as basis for a compliance obligation, in particular, §§ 76, 91, 93 AktG, § 43 GmbHG, § 130 OWiG, § 831 BGB, amended by sector-specific provisions, such as § 25a KWG, § 23 VAG, § 80 WpHG, § 14 GwG, § 28 KAGB. **7**

According to § 93 AktG publicly traded companies must establish a CMS that is appropriate for their specific business activities and in accordance with the Business Judgement Rule.[11] The system must be designed to prevent legal violations and to detect any that may occur. The AktG also requires that the management board of the company regularly reviews and evaluates the effectiveness while exercising vast discretion. However, to meet the requirements, the board must establish a CMS that (generally) includes policies and procedures to identify and manage legal risks.[12] The system should include a clear code of conduct, as well as policies and procedures for areas such as anti-corruption, anti-money laundering, and data protection. The CMS should also include a risk assessment and management process, which should be regularly reviewed and updated.[13] **8**

---

[7] Godzierz Compliance-Checklisten/Clodius § 4 mn. 6.

[8] MAH WirtschaftsStrafR/Wessing/Dann § 4 mn. 9 et seq.; BHPR Antikorruptions-Compliance Ch. 33 mn. 2 et seqq.; PWC and Martin-Luther-Universität Wittenberg 2018, Wirtschaftskriminalität 2018 Mehrwert von Compliance – forensische Erfahrungen, p. 5 <https://www.ihk.de/blueprint/servlet/resource/blob/4163710/9e176ad20ab9bcdc4ef44e3e7ea60bef/pwc-wikri-2018-data.pdf> (last accessed 28.5.2025).

[9] Moosmayer/Lösler Corporate Compliance/Moosmayer/Lösler § 1 mn. 13, 19 et seq., 24 and 26.

[10] Sonnenberg JuS 2017, 917 (917 et seq.); Koch, 18th edn 2024, AktG § 76 mn. 19.

[11] Goette/Barring DStR 2021, 1238 (1239); MAH WirtschaftsStrafR/Wessing/Dann § 4 mn. 208.

[12] BHPR Antikorruptions-Compliance Ch. 33 mn. 7 et seqq.

[13] BHPR Antikorruptions-Compliance Ch. 33 mn. 49 et seqq.

9 In addition, implementation of a CMS is also required under the framework provided by the German Corporate Governance Codex (*Deutscher Corporate Governance Kodex*, DCGK). The obligation to comply with applicable laws and regulations under Principle 5 DCGK has already been formulated, while the establishment of an appropriate CMS tailored to the company's risk situation was only designed as a recommendation in section A.2 sentence 1 of the previous version of the DCGK.[14] During the 2022 revision of the DCGK, this recommendation has been strengthened in the light of § 91 sub. 3 AktG and is now included in the legally binding Principle 5 sentence 2 DCGK[15], which stipulates that the internal control and risk management systems also include a CMS tailored to the company's risk situation.

10 In addition to the aforementioned provisions and in the context of German case law (→ mn. 12), §§ 30, 130 OWiG state important provisions for legal persons (companies) to establish a functioning CMS. § 30 OWiG provides for the administrative liability of companies for the actions of their employees. This means that companies can be held liable for actions of their employees if they have not taken adequate measures to prevent legal violations. To avoid this, companies must establish a CMS that is appropriate for their specific business activities and designed to prevent legal violations.[16] Even though the requirements under which a CMS must be set up are at the discretion of the company's management, German case law provides minimum requirements for 'adequate measures' that need to be obeyed, in particular:[17]

- establishing policies and procedures to prevent illegal behaviour[18];
- controls to warrant compliance with legal requirements[19];
- investigation of (suspected) violations and reporting violations to the relevant authorities.[20]

11 In conclusion, the legal framework for CMS under German law is rather complex, and companies must comply with specific laws and regulations to establish an effective one. Therefore, it is essential for companies to understand the legal framework and to establish a CMS that is appropriate for their specific business activities.

II. Obligation to obey CMS regulations against the background of German case law

12 The importance of a functioning CMS is not only a theoretical concept based on a multitude of legal provisions but is also evident against the background of recent German case law.

13 The Regional Court Munich (*Landgericht München I*)[21] had to decide on a civil claim of Siemens AG against its former board member for damages amounting to 15 million EUR. According to Siemens AG a board member violated his duties by, in simplified

[14] Cf. KBFW/Kremer, 9th edn 2023, DCGK Abs. Grds 5 mn. 6.

[15] Cf. Regierungskommission, Rationale DCGK, Part 2, Ch. A.I., On principle 5, On A.4: <https://www.dcgk.de//files/dcgk/usercontent/en/download/code/220517_GCGC_Rationale.pdf> (last accessed 28.5.2025).

[16] BHPR Antikorruptions-Compliance Ch. 33 mn. 2; Müller-Gugenberger WirtschaftsStrafR-HdB, 8th edn 2024, Ch. 31 mn. 31.48.

[17] Moosmayer Compliance mn. 10 et seqq.

[18] Cf. OLG Hamm 16.7.2003 – 4 Ss OWi 373/03, BeckRS 2010, 7357 mn. 11 et seq.

[19] Cf. OLG Stuttgart 7.9.1976 – 3 Ss 526/76, BeckRS 1976, 108768.

[20] Cf. BGH 8.10.1984 – II ZR 175/83, BeckRS 1984, 31072035 mn. 12 et seq.

[21] LG München I 10.12.2013 – 5 HK O 1387/10, NZWiSt 2014, 183 (183 et seqq.).

terms, not taking sufficient measures to investigate and review the internal control systems despite his knowledge of existing 'black funds' and fake consulting contracts to disguise the payments of bribes. The Court ruled in favour of the claim and decided:[22]

1. a board member must ensure that the company is organised and supervised in such a way that no legal violations occur (such as bribes to officials of a foreign state or to foreign private individuals);
2. a board member fulfils their (legal) organisational duty only if they establish a compliance organisation focused on damage prevention and risk controls in the event of corresponding risk situations;
3. the scope of the compliance organisation is determined by the nature, size, and organisation of the company, the regulations to be observed, the geographic presence as well as suspected cases from the past;
4. compliance with the principle of legality and, accordingly, the establishment of a functioning CMS is part of the overall responsibility of the board.

The decision of the Regional Court Munich and the principles set therein are ground-breaking as far as compliance obligations and civil law consequences for responsible persons are concerned.[23] **14**

The German Federal Supreme Court (*Bundesgerichtshof*, BGH) had to decide in a criminal case[24] to what extent efforts to establish a functioning CMS would mitigate corporate administrative fines imposed on a company pursuant to § 30 OWiG for an underlying violation of criminal provisions by its employees. In this decision, the BGH sets out important principles for determining a corporate administrative fine pursuant to § 30 OWiG by stressing the following: **15**

> It is also relevant for determining the fine to what extent the party involved fulfilled its obligation to prevent legal violations from the sphere of the company and has installed an efficient compliance management system that is designed to avoid legal violations. It may also be relevant whether the party involved has optimised corresponding regulations and designed its internal processes in such a way that comparable violations of provisions will be significantly more difficult in the future because of this procedure.[25] **16**

Development of case law about considering compliance efforts during the imposition of corporate sanctions has also been incorporated in the latest draft of the German Corporate Sanctions Act (*Entwurf eines Verbandssanktionengesetzes*[26], VerbSanG), which states under § 15 sub. 3 No. 7 VerbSanG: **17**

> In determining the amount of the sanction, the court shall balance the circumstances that speak for and against the legal entity. In particular, consideration shall be given to (…) the legal entity's efforts to uncover and remedy the harm caused by the offence, as well as the measures taken by the legal entity after the offence to prevent and detect such offences in the future (…). **18**

Even though the VerbSanG was never passed, the proposal reflects the overall legal and political tendency and importance of compliance organisations under German law. **19**

---

[22] LG München I 10.12.2013 – 5 HK O 1387/10, NZWiSt 2014, 183 (188 et seqq.).

[23] Cf. Fleischer NZG 2014, 321 (328 et seq.).

[24] BGH 9.5.2017 – 1 StR 265/16, NZWiSt 2018, 379 with comments from Hugger/Pasewaldt and Adick/Linke.

[25] BGH 9.5.2017 – 1 StR 265/16, NZWiSt 2018, 379 mn. 118.

[26] Cf. Pasewaldt/Karami MPR 2021, 6 (6 et seqq.).

C. Substantive design of CMS

20 Although CMS is considered a highly important necessity under German law, there are no national regulations that specify its substantive design. Therefore, indications for the practical implementation are mostly found in manuals and specialised (legal) literature. In comparison, there are numerous sets of regulations in the private sector and on an international level that do specify requirements, such as:

- **ISO 37301**[27] containing guidelines for establishing, implementing, maintaining and improving a CMS,
- **OECD Guidelines for Multinational Enterprises**[28] containing recommendations for establishing CMS in multinational enterprises to promote ethical behaviour and compliance with laws,
- **Sapin II**[29] setting criteria that must be established for a functioning CMS, such as a code of conduct or ethics that defines and illustrates the expected conduct, risk assessment procedures, training programs for employees and managers and procedures for dealing with suspected violations of the CMS in France,
- **UK Bribery Act 2010**[30] setting requirements for companies to prevent bribery and corruption and containing recommendations for the establishment of a CMS,
- **US Foreign Corrupt Practices Act (FCPA)** setting requirements for companies to prevent bribery and corruption in connection with international business, containing recommendations for the establishment of a CMS,
- **US Sentencing Guidelines**[31] setting requirements for companies to prevent fraud and other criminal offences, containing recommendations for the establishment of a CMS,
- **Committee of Sponsoring Organisations of the Treadway Commission (COSO) framework** containing instructions for establishing an internal control system and implementing an effective risk management.

21 Despite these internationally recognised frameworks, a compliance organisation under German law can only be guided by German requirements, which have already been discussed above (→ mn. 7 et seqq.) and against the background of §§ 30, 130 OWiG and the principles developed by German case law and legal literature. Therefore, a functioning compliance management system must contain overriding principles to[32]:

i) prevent illegal behaviour;
ii) ensure compliance with legal requirements;
iii) ensure reasonable reactions to (suspicious) conduct.[33]

---

[27] Available at <https://www.iso.org/standard/75080.html> (last accessed 28.5.2025).

[28] Available at <https://web-archive.oecd.org/2023-06-27/95735-48004323.pdf> (last accessed: 1.7.2025).

[29] Available at <https://www.legifrance.gouv.fr/loda/id/JORFTEXT000033558528> (last accessed 28.5.2025); cf. Schumacher/Saby CCZ 2017, 68 (68 et seqq.); Querenet-Hahn/Kettenberger CB 2017, 8.

[30] Available at <https://assets.publishing.service.gov.uk/media/5d80cfc3ed915d51e9aff85a/bribery-act-2010-guidance.pdf> (last accessed 28.5.2025).

[31] Available at <https://www.ussc.gov/guidelines/2021-guidelines-manual-annotated> (last accessed 1.7.2025).

[32] Cf. BHPR Antikorruptions-Compliance Ch. 33 mn. 36 et seq.

[33] BHPR Antikorruptions-Compliance Ch. 33 mn. 36 et seqq; Moosmayer Compliance mn. 105.

I. Prevention of illegal behaviour

The prevention of illegal activities in a company can be a challenging task for management. The following is a summary of the basic elements for prevention that have become established within the framework of current regulations and in the everyday practice of companies. **22**

1. Risk assessment

A risk assessment is a critical part of any CMS and must be carried out regularly to ensure that the company's compliance risks are continuously monitored and managed. **23**

a) Identify the company's compliance risks

Firstly, a company must identify (inherent) compliance risks that are related to its business.[34] This involves recognising relevant laws and regulations that apply to the company's business sector as well as risks of compliance violations linked to such business activities. Therefore, the company's management, or in bigger organisations its compliance department, must review and highlight relevant legal and regulatory requirements, for example, by interviewing employees with the necessary expertise or liaising with outside counsel and supervisory authorities.[35] **24**

To ensure all relevant compliance risks are identified, companies should involve key employees from different departments, including legal, compliance, finance, data protection and employment, in the risk assessment process. **25**

b) Evaluate the likelihood and impact of compliance risks

Once compliance risks relevant to the specific company have been identified, the next step is to evaluate the likelihood and impact of each risk. For example, this must be established by analysing historical data, conducting scenario analysis, and assessing the organisation's risk appetite. **26**

When evaluating the likelihood and impact of compliance risks, organisations should use a risk matrix to help prioritise risks based on their likelihood and impact. This will help the organisation focus its resources on the most significant risks. **27**

c) Develop preventive measures

The company must also develop and implement preventive measures to mitigate the risks of compliance violations. This involves creating internal policies and procedures, implementing compliance controls, and providing training to employees. **28**

When developing preventive measures, organisations should involve employees from key departments to ensure that the tools are practical and effective. Companies should also conduct regular testing and monitoring of their preventive measures to ensure that they are working as intended. **29**

There are several frameworks that companies can use as a guideline to carry out a risk assessment. Some of the most commonly used frameworks include ISO 31000:2018, COSO Enterprise Risk Management Framework or the hallmarks under the ISO 37301. Companies should select a risk assessment framework that is appropriate for their specific needs and requirements related to their business operations. When selecting a framework, **30**

---

[34] Goette/Barring DStR 2021, 1238 (1239).

[35] BHPR Antikorruptions-Compliance Ch. 33 mn. 40 et seqq.; Müller-Gugenberger WirtschaftsStrafR-HdB, 8th edn 2024, Ch. 31 mn. 31.20.

companies must consider related factors such as the size and complexity of their operations, the regulatory environment of the business operation, and the risk appetite inherent to the company. Companies should also consider whether their selected framework is in line with their overall compliance strategy. Also, by carrying out risk assessments on a regular basis, companies can ensure that inherent risks are continuously monitored and addressed appropriately.

2. Codifying ethical principles (code of conduct)

31 Every CMS must have an underlying code of conduct which serves as a codified tone for ethical behaviour and compliance with laws and regulations within the company.[36]

a) Ethical principles

32 One main element of a code of conduct is setting out the ethical principles to which the company has committed itself. The principles set out therein reflect the company's values and culture and must therefore be clear, concise, and easy to understand for everyone.[37] Examples of ethical principles include integrity, honesty, fairness, and respect within the workplace.

33 When developing ethical principles for a code of conduct, companies should involve management and key staff of relevant departments to ensure that the principles are in line with the company's values and culture.

b) Compliance requirements

34 In addition to ethical principles, a code of conduct must outline laws, regulations, and ethical standards that apply to the company.[38] This includes providing general guidance on how to comply with those requirements, such as how to avoid conflicts of interest and how to handle confidential information. Ways of reporting suspected violations should also be included.

35 To ensure that the code of conduct is comprehensive and up to date, companies must review and update it regularly to reflect new legal developments.

c) Reporting channels and investigation procedures

36 The third key element of a code of conduct is establishing clear procedures for reporting and investigating any violations of the code or applicable laws and regulations. This includes providing guidance on who to report violations to, how this should be done, and the way reports will be investigated and addressed.

37 To encourage reporting and ensure that investigations are conducted in a fair and consistent manner, companies should provide employees with multiple reporting channels, such as a hotline, email, or in-person reporting. Additionally, companies should ensure that investigations are conducted by qualified personnel and that it is carried out transparently.

d) Best practices for developing and implementing a code of conduct

38 When developing and implementing a code of conduct, there are several key aspects that companies must consider:

---

[36] BHPR Antikorruptions-Compliance Ch. 33 mn. 53; MAH WirtschaftsStrafR/Wessing/Dann § 4 mn. 217 et seq.; Godzierz Compliance-Checklisten/Clodius § 4 mn. 29.

[37] Moosmayer Compliance mn. 155.

[38] Moosmayer Compliance mn. 155.

- involving relevant department staff in the development process will ensure that the code of conduct is in line with the company's values and culture and that it reflects its needs and concerns;
- providing regular training on the code of conduct and related policies and procedures shall develop the staff's understanding and improve compliance with legal and ethical requirements;[39]
- integrating the code of conduct into other compliance guidelines and policies will ensure consistency with other procedures.

Companies can use examples from other competitors in the same sector that are renowned for their high ethical standards as a starting point for developing their own code of conduct but should ensure that it is tailored to their specific needs. Additionally, companies should regularly review and update the code of conduct to keep it effective. **39**

3. Implementation of compliance guidelines

In addition to the general code of conduct, compliance guidelines are an integral part of an effective CMS. They are designed to provide guidance on how the company's staff should carry out their tasks. **40**

Compliance guidelines play a crucial role in ensuring that a company's business is carried out in an ethical and lawful manner. These guidelines provide a framework for employees to follow, helping to prevent compliance violations that could lead to legal, financial, or reputational harm. **41**

Since the concrete form of such policies depends on the size, the business field, and the sector of the respective company, it is not possible to summarise a conglomerate of generally applicable rules and guidelines. Nevertheless, compliance policies have been established in the practice of various sectors, considering industry-specific risks. Common policies can be, among others. **42**

a) Anti-bribery and corruption policy

An anti-bribery and corruption (ABC) policy is a compliance guideline that outlines a company's position against bribery, corruption, and similar unethical practices. This typically includes guidance on what constitutes as bribery and corruption, how to avoid conflicts of interest, and the procedures for reporting and investigating potential violations in that regard. The ABC policy is an essential component of an effective CMS, as it helps to ensure that the company carries out its business with integrity and avoid corrupt practices that could harm its reputation. **43**

b) Gift policy

A gift policy is a compliance guideline that outlines the company's approach to accepting and giving benefits and therefore amends or concretises the ABC policy. This policy typically includes guidance on what constitutes an acceptable benefit (e.g., gifts or other amenities), the value of gifts that may be accepted or given, and the procedures for reporting and investigating potential violations by employees and/or business partners in that regard. The gift policy should ensure that the company's employees do not engage in unethical or illegal behaviour due to benefits received or given in the sense of a commercial practice. **44**

---

[39] Godzierz Compliance-Checklisten/Clodius § 4 mn. 30.

c) Anti-money laundering policy

45 An anti-money laundering (AML) policy is a compliance guideline that outlines the company's efforts to prevent money laundering and terrorist financing during business operations. This typically includes guidance on customer due diligence, transaction monitoring as well as procedures for reporting and investigating potential violations. The AML policy shall help to prevent the company from being used as a channel for illegal funds.

46 Regardless of the size and resources of the company, developing and implementing compliance guidelines can be a complex, time-consuming and challenging task. However, there are several aspects that companies should bear in mind for their guidelines to be effective:

- **involve key staff.** Companies should involve employees, managers, and board members, in the development and implementation of compliance guidelines. This will help to ensure that the guidelines are practical, relevant and understandable.
- **regularly review and update the guidelines**. Compliance guidelines must react to changes in laws, regulations, and industry standards.
- **provide training**. Employees should receive regular training on the compliance guidelines to ensure that they understand the guidelines and know how to comply with them, especially, when the company's approach to the organisational procedure has changed.[40]

4. Leadership's ethical stance

47 The 'tone from the top' is a vital element in establishing an effective CMS.[41] It refers to the attitudes, behaviours, and commitment to ethical standards exhibited by the board, (mid-level) management, and other senior leaders. The leadership's ethical stance is a crucial determinant in shaping a company's values, culture, and ethical conduct and is therefore essential for a functioning CMS.[42]

48 When the company's leadership demonstrates a strong dedication to (self-imposed) ethical standards, it sends a clear message to employees that compliance within the firm is considered a top priority. This commitment can be demonstrated in various ways, such as through the development, communication, and actual practice of a code of conduct, and regular training.[43] Also, company leaders should regularly participate in compliance-related activities and openly discuss the importance of adhering to ethical standards whenever deemed appropriate.

49 A genuine commitment to ethical conduct from the company leaders is instrumental in fostering a culture of integrity throughout the organisation. Employees are more likely to adopt and internalise ethical values when they witness their leaders also actively promoting and adhering to these standards. Therefore, employees are encouraged to prioritise acting in line with ethical standards over personal gains and reducing the likelihood of compliance violations.

50 In addition to promoting a culture of integrity, the tone from the top also influences the company's approach to risk management. By actively engaging in risk assessments and mitigation strategies, company leaders can demonstrate their commitment to addressing

---

[40] Godzierz Compliance-Checklisten/Clodius § 4 mn. 34.

[41] BHPR Antikorruptions-Compliance Ch. 33 mn. 67; MAH WirtschaftsStrafR/Wessing/Dann Ch. 4 mn. 230 et seq.; Moosmayer Compliance mn. 144.

[42] Godzierz Compliance-Checklisten/Clodius § 4 mn. 9.

[43] BHPR Antikorruptions-Compliance Ch. 33 mn. 67.

potential compliance risks proactively. This approach helps create a culture of risk awareness, ensuring that employees at all levels understand and appreciate the importance of managing compliance risks.[44]

Further, the tone from the top plays an important role in promoting transparency and openness within the organisation.[45] When leaders encourage open communication and create an environment where employees feel comfortable reporting potential compliance concerns without fear of reprisals, it enables companies to identify and address issues before they escalate into more significant violations. **51**

In order to reinforce the leadership's ethical stance and enhance the effectiveness of the CMS, a company can implement ethics and compliance roundtables on a regular basis. These roundtables should involve top management, compliance officers, and leading employees from various departments, encouraging these individuals to have an open dialogue about compliance issues, ethical dilemmas, and best practices. By actively participating in and promoting these 'open mic' opportunities, management can demonstrate their commitment to ethical conduct, provide employees with necessary guidance, and support a culture of compliance within the company. **52**

5. Compliance trainings

Another essential element of a successful CMS is the implementation of comprehensive compliance training programs, which support adherence to the codified legal, ethical, and regulatory standards.[46] **53**

Compliance trainings play an indispensable role in equipping employees with the knowledge and skills required to understand and adhere to the organisation's ethical standards, legal requirements, and internal policies. Instructive compliance trainings not only help mitigate risks of misconduct but also promote a culture of integrity, accountability, and transparency within the company. **54**

Compliance trainings help employees understand the legal requirements of the company's business and the relevant laws and regulations that apply to their specific job roles, reducing the likelihood of (negligent) violations. Employees will gain enhanced decision-making skills which are needed to make lawful and/or ethically correct decisions in situations where a compliance breach is possible. Further, such trainings can strengthen the culture of accountability and integrity throughout the company and reduce risks of (costly) penalties and (possibly even more costly) reputational damages caused by misconduct. **55**

To maximise the effect of compliance trainings, companies should consider several aspects and adopt modern and attention-grabbing approaches, such as: **56**

- **right training for the right audience**. Customising training content to employees in different job roles and departments will help to ensure that the training is relevant and engaging for participants, increasing knowledge on relevant fields and application of their daily tasks.
- **use of diverse training methods**. Incorporating a mix of training formats (e.g., in-person workshops, online learning videos and webinars) will be attention-grabbing and maintain participants' interest.

---

44 MAH WirtschaftsStrafR/Wessing/Dann Ch. 4 mn. 230 et seq.

45 Bürkle Compliance/Schlierenkämper § 11 mn. 188 et seqq.; MAH WirtschaftsStrafR/Wessing/Dann Ch. 4 mn. 230 et seq.

46 Müller-Gugenberger WirtschaftsStrafR-HdB, 8th edn 2024, Ch. 31 mn. 31.25; BHPR Antikorruptions-Compliance Ch. 33 mn. 71; MAH WirtschaftsStrafR/Wessing/Dann § 4 mn. 236.

- **reinforce training with ongoing communication**. Support compliance training by regularly communicating the company's commitment to ethical conduct and compliance through various channels, such as newsletters, internal updates, team meetings or in the framework of personal appraisals to maintain employees' awareness of compliance requirements and the company's values.

57 Implementing tailored, engaging, and interactive training can promote a culture of compliance and integrity, reducing the risk of misconduct, costly fines, and reputational damage.

II. Controls to ensure compliance with legal requirements

58 Maintaining a functioning CMS is generally only possible by establishing effective and comprehensive controls. Such controls include both suitable channels to report potential misconduct and suspicious behaviour as well as procedures to investigate relevant reports.

1. Reporting channels

59 In practice, a reliable way to create functional reporting channels is to implement whistleblower systems to detect and prevent compliance violations. Whistleblower systems serve as a company's mechanism to detect misconduct of employees and/or the management.[47] By encouraging employees and key staff to report suspected violations, companies can proactively address issues in a timely manner to avoid severe legal and reputational consequences.[48]

60 For example, whistleblower systems enable companies to identify (potential) compliance violations or other issues at an early stage, allowing for prompt intervention and mitigation of risks due to alleged misconduct. Further, the presence of whistleblower systems promotes a culture of transparency and accountability within the company, as this may have a deterrent effect on employees who tend to violate compliance obligations.

61 However, to maximise the efficiency of whistleblower systems and ensure their successful integration into the CMS, companies must clearly communicate their existence and advertise the hotlines within the firm, providing guidance on how to access and use the reporting channels. This includes clear statements that callers will remain anonymous, if they choose to, and that any information provided will be treated confidentially. However, it must be clearly communicated to the anonymous information providers that deliberate false reports may have consequences and workplace-related aftermath.

62 Further, companies must commit to investigating all reports received through the reporting channel in a timely manner and thoroughly, taking appropriate actions based on the findings and providing feedback to the whistleblower when possible. This will build trust in the effectiveness of the system and its promotion within the firm. Therefore, it is essential to regularly evaluate the whistleblowing system and making adjustments when needed to ensure that it remains efficient and beneficial to the company.

---

[47] The importance of internal whistleblowing systems has also been recognized by the EU legislator through the adoption of the Whistleblower Directive (Directive EU 2019/1937) to protect whistleblowers.

[48] Müller-Gugenberger WirtschaftsStrafR-HdB, 8th edn 2024, Ch. 31 mn. 31.32 et seqq.; BHPR Antikorruptions-Compliance Ch. 33 mn. 78 et seqq.; MAH WirtschaftsStrafR/Wessing/Dann Ch. 4 mn. 256 et seqq.; Eidam Unternehmen und Strafe Ch. 15 mn. 107 et seqq.

As the infrastructure of smaller and mid-level organisations may not have the resources to implement sophisticated whistleblower systems, it may be considered to outsource this task to external service providers.[49] **63**

Involving external service providers or independent organisations in the management of the whistleblowing system can offer advantages. For example, it can contribute to a perception of increased impartiality when handling whistleblower reports, making employees more comfortable with reporting suspected violations. External partners can bring specialised knowledge and experience in handling whistleblower cases. Furthermore, by demonstrating a commitment to transparency and accountability through the involvement of external parties, companies can enhance their reputation among customers, investors, and regulators. **64**

Collaboration with external parties and regular internal promotions are essential aspects to consider when aiming to strengthen the efficiency of a whistleblowing system. By taking these measures, companies can create a more credible and unbiased reporting mechanism, fostering a culture of accountability and integrity. **65**

2. Procedural controls

Another key component of a CMS is the implementation of procedural controls, which are aimed at guaranteeing compliance with all prevention measures within the CMS and are designed to ensure the integrity and efficiency of business processes, identify and minimise risks, and maintain the reliability of financial and management reporting.[50] Such controls include various mechanisms, among others, process-accompanying controls, spot checks or automated control procedures. **66**

Process-accompanying controls are implemented within the company's routine and are designed to ensure that activities are carried out in line with relevant policies and procedures. They are generally conducted by way of ongoing checks during business tasks. The controls are carried out by the responsible personnel, particularly upper-level management or the compliance department. **67**

To guarantee the efficiency of such controls, however, it is crucial to clearly define roles and responsibilities within the company to ensure that duties are appropriately segregated, and no single individual has excessive control over any particular process. **68**

Periodic spot checks are random checks performed on a sample of transactions, documents, or activities to verify compliance with relevant rules and regulations. Spot checks can help identify potential issues or irregularities that may not be detected through process-accompanying controls and can serve as a deterrent for non-compliant behaviour. Also, in the case of periodic spot checks, a clear division of tasks is crucial and must be defined within the organisation. **69**

Therefore, the company must develop a risk-based approach for selecting the frequency and focus of spot checks, prioritising areas with higher risks for misconduct or where historical issues have been identified. **70**

In addition to manual process controls, organisations can also leverage technology and implement automated control mechanisms within their CMS to boost control procedures. Automated control mechanisms offer benefits, such as increased efficiency, reduced human error, and real-time monitoring of compliance risks.[51] **71**

---

[49] Müller-Gugenberger WirtschaftsStrafR-HdB, 8th edn 2024, Ch. 31 mn. 31.34; MAH WirtschaftsStrafR/Wessing/Dann Ch. 4 mn. 267.

[50] BHPR Antikorruptions-Compliance Ch. 33 mn. 83 et seqq.

[51] BHPR Antikorruptions-Compliance Ch. 33 mn. 87.

3. Investigation of compliance violations

72 Carrying out internal investigations and audits allows companies to locate the reasons for a breach of compliance provisions and rules committed by individuals,[52] and is a key factor for the development and improvement of the CMS.

a) Internal investigations

73 Internal investigations will help to identify and address potential violations of laws, regulations, or internal policies and help prevent negative consequences, such as legal and financial punishments as well as (costly) reputational damage. These investigations are vital for companies and help them to, in particular:

- identify and address potential violations;
- mitigate legal and financial risks by cooperating with authorities;
- improve corporate governance and accountability;
- protect their reputation;
- prevent future violations.

74 German law, however, does not provide a legal framework for how to carry out such investigations in a correct and diligent manner; fact-finding efforts are again at the sole discretion of the company's management and leaders. Hence, it is up to companies whether they have the investigation carried out by an internal department within the company or outsource this task to external service providers, such as a law firm or other forensics firms. Regardless of what management decides, the following steps should be considered in any internal investigation conducted:

75 Given the importance of internal investigations, it is recommended to establish internal 'compliance & integrity investigations' protocols as part of the compliance procedures. These protocols outline the procedures to be followed when initiating an internal investigation, including the roles and responsibilities of those involved in the investigation, regardless of whether the investigation is outsourced or not.

76 In general, internal investigations can involve the following steps, which can be carried out either fully or partly:

1. pointing out the potential violations that shall be investigated, determining the scope of the investigation, and identifying the resources needed to conduct the investigation;
2. reviewing relevant data, which includes documents such as emails, memos, contracts, and financial records, in order to identify any potential evidence of misconduct;
3. based on the outcome of the data and document review it should be considered whether interviews with relevant individuals shall be carried out. This generally includes questioning employees or other parties involved in the potential misconduct;
4. evaluating the evidence collected during the investigation, which involves reviewing the obtained information, identifying patterns, and determining whether there is sufficient information to support allegations of wrongdoing.
5. The outcome of the investigation should be documented in a final investigation report. The findings shall prompt the management to take appropriate remedial measures, if necessary (e.g., disciplinary actions, changes to policies, procedures, and guidelines, or corrective measures designed to prevent future misconduct).[53]

---

[52] BHPR Antikorruptions-Compliance Ch. 33 mn. 89; Müller-Gugenberger WirtschaftsStrafR-HdB, 8th edn 2024, Ch. 31 mn. 31.28; Moosmayer Compliance mn. 311.

[53] Moosmayer Compliance mn. 318 et seqq.

When conducting internal investigations, the following should be considered: 77

- **establish clear procedures**. These procedures should outline the roles and responsibilities of individuals involved in the investigation, the steps to be followed, and the resources needed to conduct the investigation.
- **maintaining confidentiality.** This will ensure the integrity of the investigation and help protect the privacy of those involved in the investigation while protecting whistleblowers or others who report potential compliance violations at the same time.
- **consider engaging outside counsel**. Engaging outside counsel can provide several benefits, among others, assessment from an objective perspective, ensuring that the investigation is conducted in compliance with applicable laws and regulations, and protection of the attorney-client privilege if applicable in the relevant jurisdiction.
- **involving key staff**. Involving senior management or the board of directors, can ensure that after the investigation in concluded appropriate remedial actions are taken.
- **sharing the outcome with investigation authorities**. The question whether to share the outcome of an internal investigation with authorities must be made on a case-by-case basis. While in some cases such cooperative approach might be beneficial to the company as it may reduce potential fines, there is a high risk of 'backfire' if (potentially) harmful conclusions are shared with competent authorities. The pros and cons should be discussed with the legal department or outside counsel.

b) Audits

Audits evaluate whether companies comply with regulations, internal policies, and 78
laws while ensuring compliance. They provide an independent and objective view of a business's controls, operations, and activities.[54]

Generally, audits are conducted either by company employees or an external auditing 79
firm, aimed at finding weaknesses and potential risks, evaluating the efficiency of internal controls, and identifying areas for improvement. Such audits can be carried out, inter alia, as risk-based audits to focus on high-risk areas of the business or by way of more general compliance audits focusing on ensuring compliance with laws and regulations (including currency of policies, guidelines and similar). Audits are also used as a tool to react to reported compliance violations within the firm, analysing specific misconduct as a result from company's CMS weaknesses and high-risk areas.

As in every well-working CMS the first step in executing audits is to establish the 80
objectives and scope, determining what areas of the business shall be audited, what the audit will focus on, and what the expected outcomes are. Once the audit objectives and scope have been determined, an audit plan and timeline must be developed. This includes the selection of an audit team, assigning roles and responsibilities, and documenting relevant information.[55]

The audit organisation can be outlined for example within a compliance policy in order 81
to simplify the most important points in advance in connection with the preparation of the audit. The general tasks within audits include the testing of controls, interviewing personnel, reviewing documents and analysing data. Any recognised weaknesses identified shall immediately be reported or summarised in an audit report for the attention of the management. After its completion (including the preparation of the relevant audit report) the outcome must be communicated to the competent departments within the company, ideally equipped with recommendations for improvement. Management must

[54] MLL Managerhaftung-HdB/v. Busekist/Federmann/Lochen § 13 mn. 446.
[55] MLL Managerhaftung-HdB/v. Busekist/Federmann/Lochen § 13 mn. 448.

also consider carrying out follow-up audits in periodic intervals to avoid similar compliance violations in the future.

82 The success of a conducted audit also depends on a strong tone from the top, engaging with business units and personnel to understand risks and controls, providing training and education on compliance and audit best practices in order to build a culture of continuous improvement.

83 Audits are critical for maintaining CMS and reducing risks in specific areas of the company. By understanding the different types of audits, planning and preparing them effectively, conducting thorough fieldwork, testing, reporting and following up appropriately, companies can ensure that they are operating within frame of compliance and mitigating potential risks.

III. Reasonable reactions to suspicious conduct

84 An effective CMS includes not only preventive measures, internal controls, and continuous review mechanisms but particularly the appropriate response measures in the event of identified compliance violations.[56] Consistent enforcement of sanctions, subsequent addressing of weaknesses, and further communication within and outside the company are particularly notable aspects of this area.

1. Sanctioning employees

85 By imposing penalties and consequences for non-compliant behaviour, sanctions serve not only as a powerful deterrent but also as a self-cleaning mechanism to maintain the function of the company's CMS.

86 Such sanctions should be imposed based on the severity of the misconduct and can occur in the form of:

- training that demonstrates the identified misconduct to avoid future violations;[57]
- warnings to make clear that future misconduct will not remain without consequences;[58]
- transfer of department/revocation of existing permits to relocate an employee from a specific risk area;[59]
- immediate termination of the employment if the relationship of trust has been irrevocably damaged.[60]

87 To implement effective sanctions, companies can establish an internal sanction policy and procedures. This policy should be communicated to all employees and members of the management to ensure that everyone is aware of the consequences in the event of misconduct. Potential violations and their associated sanctions should be identified, and responsibility should be allocated for sanction implementation and monitoring. Furthermore, it should be ensured that the works council or other employee representative are involved in the decision to impose sanctions.

88 Once sanctions are imposed it is also essential to assure the execution of necessary follow-up investigations and to make necessary adjustments. The sanctions policy and

[56] Moosmayer Compliance mn. 338.
[57] Moosmayer Compliance mn. 340.
[58] Moosmayer Compliance mn. 339.
[59] Moosmayer Compliance mn. 339.
[60] Moosmayer Compliance mn. 339.

procedures, in that regard, should be reviewed and revised as needed to improve their effectiveness. Also, the management must also maintain accurate records of all sanctions and their outcomes (including follow-up investigations).[61]

2. Taking corrective measures

Compliance violations require a systematic approach for developing and implementing a corrective action plan (CAP), including changes within the organisation, ongoing monitoring and reviews. **89**

Therefore, when developing a CAP, it is crucial to determine the root of the compliance violation, usually requiring a thorough investigation of the situation and the underlying reasons for the violation.[62] For example, if a company is found to be violating data privacy laws, the reason for this could be insufficient employee-training or a lack of controls. **90**

Once the origin of a misconduct has been identified, the CAP should be developed, aiming to fix and improve the relevant internal (insufficient) mechanisms. The plan should include, in particular, directives on the actions to be taken, who will be responsible for taking the actions, and a concrete timeline to complete this task.[63] **91**

For example, a CAP for a data privacy violation could include implementing new data handling procedures, additional employee training on obeying data privacy laws, and appointing a new data privacy officer. The plan should also include a timeline for completion and regular progress monitoring to ensure the objectives are met. **92**

Once the CAP has been developed, it is important to implement the changes in a timely manner. This can, in particular, include changes to policies, guidelines, and procedures, the use of new technology, or additional, more in-depth training for employees.[64] **93**

For example, a company that has been found to be violating anti-corruption laws may need to implement new ABC or gift policies and guidelines. The company may also need to use new technological solutions to monitor and track expenses related to these activities. Additionally, employees may need more training on the importance of compliance with anti-corruption laws. **94**

After the CAP has been implemented, it is important to regularly monitor and review the CMS. This includes monitoring compliance activities regularly, reviewing policies and procedures, and conducting periodic audits to assess the effectiveness of the system.[65] **95**

Referring to the afore-mentioned example, a company that has implemented new ABC or gift policies must conduct regular audits to ensure that employees are following the new procedures. The company should also review the policies on a regular basis and make sure that they are up-to-date and continue to address the risks identified. **96**

D. Common CMS pillars

The establishment of an adequate CMS requires consideration of the size and complexity of the company and its operations, as well as the potential risks and legal and **97**

---

[61] Moosmayer Compliance mn. 344 et seqq.

[62] Godzierz Compliance-Checklisten/Clodius § 4 mn. 47; Moosmayer Compliance mn. 311.

[63] BHPR Antikorruptions-Compliance Ch. 33 mn. 111; Ghassemi-Tabar/Ghassemi-Tabar DCGK G5 mn. 55.

[64] Cf. for cases of social responsibility violations Godzierz Compliance-Checklisten/Clodius § 5 mn. 60.

[65] Moosmayer Compliance mn. 286.

regulatory obligations inherent to the business carried out.[66] However, there are a few standardised mechanisms that have become established in the compliance practices of companies[67]

98 At first, the **size and complexity** of a company determines its CMS. In smaller companies, compliance tasks are usually integrated into the overall business operations under the responsibility of the management.[68] However, as companies grow and become more complex, a specialised compliance organisation usually becomes necessary. The compliance organisation in a large company typically includes several levels of responsibility, including a chief compliance officer, a compliance committee, as well as a team of compliance professionals.[69] Depending on the industry in which the company conducts its main business (e.g., finance, health care, capital markets, etc.) the compliance organisation can be even more challenging, as the responsible compliance department must also ensure that employees and management comply with industry-specific applicable laws and other regulations imposed by relevant supervisory authorities.[70]

99 A **reasonable staffing** of the compliance levels and the compliance department in particular is a critical component of a reliable CMS. The compliance department must have enough resources to meet the company's compliance obligations in order to implement effective measures. However, the personnel requirements still depend on the size and complexity of the company.[71] The compliance department's tasks include, among others:[72]

- developing and implementing compliance policies, guidelines, and procedures;
- carrying out risk assessments;
- monitoring and auditing of the implemented CMS;
- providing compliance training to employees and staff; and
- investigating and responding to compliance violations.

100 The **compliance officer** (CO) is a crucial part of any compliance organisation and is responsible for assuring that the company complies with relevant laws and regulations.[73]

101 Therefore, the CO is responsible for a wide range of duties within the CMS, including developing and implementing policies, guidelines, and procedures. To reach this goal, the CO must carry out a thorough analysis of the legal and regulatory environment in which the company carries out business, identify relevant risks associated with it and develop a framework that reflects best practices and the specific needs of the company.[74]

102 In addition, the CO is also responsible for monitoring the company's activities to identify potential compliance issues, including the supervision of staff at lower levels of the compliance department.[75] The CO's tasks involve conducting regular risk assessments, reviewing internal controls, and investigating any suspected compliance violations or, at the minimum, organising a structure by way of delegation that will guarantee the accomplishment of these tasks.[76]

103 In the event of compliance violations, the CO plays a major role in crisis management and works closely with management to investigate the issue, identify the root causes of the

---

[66] Moosmayer/Lösler Corporate Compliance/Klahold/Lochen § 13 mn. 4.
[67] Ghassemi-Tabar/Ghassemi-Tabar DCGK G5 mn. 26.
[68] Eidam Unternehmen und Strafe Ch. 15 mn. 75.
[69] Eidam Unternehmen und Strafe Ch. 15 mn. 80 et seq.
[70] Moosmayer/Lösler Corporate Compliance/Klahold/Lochen § 13 mn. 4.
[71] Moosmayer/Lösler Corporate Compliance/Klahold/Lochen § 13 mn. 48; Hauschka NJW 2004, 257 (259 et seq.).
[72] Moosmayer Compliance mn. 125.
[73] Eidam Unternehmen und Strafe Ch. 15 mn. 80 et seq.
[74] Cf. Moosmayer Compliance mn. 125.
[75] Eidam Unternehmen und Strafe Ch. 15 mn. 81.
[76] Cf. Moosmayer Compliance mn. 125.

misconduct and implement corrective measures to prevent similar incidents in the future. The CO also liaises with external parties such as regulators and auditors, to ensure that the company addresses the issue with the appropriate contact persons.[77] For efficiency, the CO must have the required knowledge of relevant laws and regulations that apply to the company's business area, which of course requires that the CO stays up to date with any changes to these laws and regulations to adjust the company's CMS accordingly.[78]

E. Legal and regulatory challenges to CMS

Despite the importance and advantages inherent in an efficient CMS, implementing it **104** can be challenging for each company, particularly when it comes to addressing the legal and regulatory complexities. Such challenges include labour law requirements, e.g., the lawful implementation of compliance regulations within employees' working contracts or data protection regulations when it comes to investigating and addressing compliance violations. In this context it is crucial for every compliance department to work closely with other company departments, such as HR, works council and employees responsible for data protection compliance.[79]

F. Conclusion

Compliance management systems have become increasingly important in modern **105** business practice, as companies are facing legal and regulatory challenges that potentially risk high fines and even more costly reputational damages. Therefore, an efficient CMS enables companies to address these risks by ensuring conformity with legal obligations and promoting ethical behaviour within the company.[80]

A very recent trend regarding CMS has been the increasing focus on environmental, **106** social, and governance (ESG) issues.[81] Companies are faced with growing demand from investors and consumers to demonstrate their commitment to ESG topics and therefore, an efficient CMS can also help to identify and mitigate risks related to ESG violations, such as environmental misconduct or supply chain labour abuses.

In conclusion, compliance management systems are a key risk management strategy **107** for companies, especially those operating in highly regulated environments. Therefore, as regulations continue to evolve and legal concerns become increasingly important, these systems, too, are likely to become even more essential for businesses in the future.

---

[77] Moosmayer/Lösler Corporate Compliance/Bürkle/Kinzl § 12 mn. 38.

[78] Moosmayer Compliance mn. 129 et seq.

[79] Moosmayer/Lösler Corporate Compliance/Bürkle/Kinzl § 12 mn. 63.

[80] Eidam Unternehmen und Strafe Ch. 15 mn. 71; Godzierz Compliance-Checklisten/Clodius § 4 mn. 1 et seq.; PWC and Martin-Luther-Universität Wittenberg 2018, Wirtschaftskriminalität 2018 Mehrwert von Compliance – forensische Erfahrungen <https://www.ihk.de/blueprint/servlet/resource/blob/4163710/9e176ad20ab9bcdc4ef44e3e7ea60bef/pwc-wikri-2018-data.pdf> (last accessed 28.5.2025).

[81] Moosmayer Compliance mn. 254; PWC and Martin-Luther-Universität Wittenberg 2018, Wirtschaftskriminalität 2018 Mehrwert von Compliance – forensische Erfahrungen <https://www.ihk.de/blueprint/servlet/resource/blob/4163710/9e176ad20ab9bcdc4ef44e3e7ea60bef/pwc-wikri-2018-data.pdf> (last accessed 28.5.2025).

CHAPTER 7
WHISTLEBLOWER SYSTEMS AS PART OF THE CMS

Bibliography: Gerdemann, EU-Kommission zur Zukunft des Hinweisgeberschutzgesetzes, ZRP 2024, 170; Lang, Datenschutzrechtliche Implikationen des Hinweisgeberschutzgesetzes – Einrichtung und Betrieb eines Hinweisgebersystems unter Beachtung datenschutzrechtlichere Vorgaben, ZD 2024, 17; Siemes, Die hinreichend begründete Annahme des Whistleblowers nach Art. 6 Abs. 1 lit. a Richtlinie (EU) 2019/1937 – Auslegung und Umsetzung, CCZ 2022, 293; Vogel, Praxistipps zum Hinweisgeberschutz, CB 2024, 158.

Table of contents

A. General introduction: whistleblowing and whistleblower protection in Germany 132
- I. Whistleblower protection before the introduction of the German Whistleblower Act (HinSchG) 132
- II. The transposition of Directive (EU) 2019/1937 of the European Parliament and the Council on whistleblower protection (WB Directive) 133
- III. The German Whistleblower Protection Act 134
- IV. The EU Commission's feedback on the national transposition laws 134

B. Requirements of the German HinSchG 135
- I. Scope of the law 135
  - 1. The personal scope: who can report? 135
  - 2. The material scope: what can be reported? 136
    - a) Violations covered according to § 2 HinSchG 136
    - b) Correlation to other provisions 139
    - c) Priority of security interests as well as confidentiality and secrecy obligations 139
- II. Internal or external reporting office 140
  - 1. Definition of a report 140
  - 2. Internal reporting office 140
  - 3. External reporting office 141
  - 4. The right of choice 142
- III. Requirements for the internal reporting office 142
  - 1. Organisational structure 142
    - a) General 142
    - b) Point of contention: group wide central internal reporting office versus decentralized reporting offices 143
    - c) Consequences for companies 144
  - 2. Reporting channels 145
  - 3. Internal communication with the whistleblower 146
  - 4. Procedure for receiving and following up on reports 146
    - a) Receiving and assessment of reports 146
    - b) Documentation of reports 147
    - c) Follow-up measures 148
- IV. Requirement of confidentiality 148
- V. The disclosure 149
- VI. Whistleblower protection and protection measures 150
  - 1. Protection requirements 150

2. Exclusion of responsibility ... 152
3. Prohibition of retaliation ... 152
4. Compensation for damages because of a retaliation ... 152
VII. Sanctions ... 153
C. Further legal frameworks ... 153
I. Co-determination right of the works council (BetrVG) ... 153
II. Data protection laws ... 154
D. Excursus: grievance mechanism according to the German Due Diligence Supply Chain Act (LkSG) ... 156
E. First steps for the set-up of a whistleblower system according to HinSchG ... 156
I. Gap analysis ... 156
II. Stakeholder management ... 156
III. Determination of responsibilities ... 156
IV. Review and adaption of internal policies ... 157
V. Communication measures ... 157

A. General introduction: whistleblowing and whistleblower protection in Germany

1 Germany's history contributes significantly to the fact that reports of possible misconduct in the form of violations of the law have negative connotations. During the Nazi regime as well as during the period of socialism in Germany, blowing the whistle on the authorities was a betrayal – an obvious conclusion in these times of oppression and tyranny. Shaped by history, it is not surprising that German companies maintain a divided relationship with the whistleblower and his or her protection. Whistleblowers are still often seen as 'disloyal' by superiors but also by colleagues.

2 At the same time, whistleblowing systems are well known to German companies. Generally, an effective compliance management system contains measures to prevent, detect and react. It aims to uncover any misconduct in the company at an early stage. A functioning whistleblowing system that is well frequented by employees serves as the primary source for reporting such reports and is therefore an important component of a compliance management system. At latest with the well-known Siemens/Neubürger decision[1] of the district court Munich on liability in the context of compliance violations, it has become clear that an effective compliance management system requires a functioning whistleblower system in order to be considered effective.

I. Whistleblower protection before the introduction of the German Whistleblower Act (HinSchG)

3 Nevertheless, the protection of whistleblowers (*hinweisgebende Person*) before the introduction of the HinSchG was seen as incomplete and inadequate.[2] This is mainly due

[1] LG München I 10.12.2013 – 5 HK O 1387/10, NZG 2014, 345.

[2] See draft bill of the Federal Ministry of Justice and Consumer Protection, Draft of a law for better protection of whistleblowers and on the implementation of the Directive on the protection of persons who report violations of Union law of 26.11.2020 ('RefE HinSchG'), p. 1, available at <https://www.bmjv.de/SharedDocs/Downloads/DE/Gesetzgebung/RefE/RefE_Hinweisgeberschutz.pdf?__blob=publicationFile&v=4> (last accessed: 27.5.2025).

to the fact that there was no legal obligation comprehensive for all sectors to introduce a whistleblower system before the HinSchG; only sector-specific obligations already included such an obligation before the HinSchG.[3] Therefore, the HinSchG also represents a 'paradigm shift'[4] in Germany.

II. The transposition of Directive (EU) 2019/1937 of the European Parliament and the Council on whistleblower protection (WB Directive)

4 In 2018, the EU-Commission emphasized the importance of internal whistleblowers and their protection. Without the courage of whistleblowers, internal organizational misconduct would remain uncovered. The clarification of these misconducts is in public interest; for the public interest, whistleblowers take great risks. Therefore, the protection of whistleblowers needed to be strengthened at EU level.[5]

5 The EU-Directive (Directive (EU) 2019/1937) on the 'protection of persons who report breaches of Union law' was published in the Official Journal of the EU on 26 November 2019 and entered into force on 16 December 2019. The aim of the Directive is to establish minimum standards for the protection of whistleblowers from discrimination resulting from reporting breaches of Union law.[6] The restriction of the material scope to EU law is due to the limited competence of the EU. The Directive provides for companies with at least 50 employees to set up a whistleblower system in order to be able to receive reports of possible violations of EU law. Reprisals against whistleblowers on the basis of the report are prohibited. In addition to the internal offices, external reporting offices are to be set up, to which whistleblowers can also turn. They have the right to choose which body they want to address. The protection of whistleblowers in the event of disclosure, i.e. going public, is also clearly regulated. The Directive supplements whistleblower protection with a provision on the procedural reversal of the burden of proof (*Beweislastumkehr*) in favour of whistleblowers. According to this, companies must prove in proceedings before a court or other authority that the object of the disadvantage of the whistleblower is that the measure is not disadvantageous and is based on sufficiently justified reasons. The Directive also provides for a claim for damages for the whistleblower in the event of retaliation. The implementation deadline for EU Member States ended on 17 December 2021.

6 Germany implemented the Directive after this deadline. The Federal Ministry of Justice and Consumer Protection presented a first draft in November 2020.[7] This draft failed and was not pursued until the end of the legislative period of the then government. Under the following SPD-led government a second draft bill made it into a government draft in 2022, and thus after the implementation deadline has expired. However, the first reading in the German Bundestag in September 2022 was once again leading to discussions and delay in the legislative process. Only after passing through the German *Vermittlungsausschuss*[8], the German Bundestag passed the long overdue HinSchG on 5 May 2023, which came then into force on 2 July 2023.

---

[3] Sector specific provisions are for example: § 25a sub. 1 sent. 6 no. 3 KWG; Art. 32 para. 3 MAR; § 23 sub. 1 sent. 3 VAG; § 4d sub. 1 FinDAG; §§ 12 sub. 5, 13 AGG; §§ 84, 85 BetrVG.

[4] Thüsing HinschG/Lüneborg HinSchG § 7 mn. 4.

[5] European Commission, COM(2018) 214 final, 1.

[6] Directive (EU) 2019/1937.

[7] See RefE HinSchG, available at <https://www.bmjv.de/SharedDocs/Downloads/DE/Gesetzgebung/RefE/RefE_Hinweisgeberschutz.pdf?__blob=publicationFile&v=4> (last accessed: 27.5.2025).

[8] Mediation committee to discuss critical points of a law and seek for solutions.

III. The German Whistleblower Protection Act

7 The aim of the HinSchG is, as well as the one of the WB Directive, to strengthen and ensure improved whistleblower protection so that whistleblowers are not at risk of being disadvantaged when reporting.[9] The law itself is divided into six sections: in the first section, the general provisions specify the scope of application, define the terms used and delimit the scope of application from other provisions. In the second section, the law specifies the report, the reporting options and how to deal with them. Section three regulates disclosure, section four individual protective measures and the protection requirements. Finally, section five regulates the sanctions in the event of a violation of the Whistleblowing Act, while section six concludes with final provisions on the authorisation to issue ordinances and transitional provisions.

8 The German Whistleblower Protection Act must be embedded in internal company processes if the scope of application of the HinSchG is met, i.e. for employers with at least 50 employees.

IV. The EU Commission's feedback on the national transposition laws

9 Not only Germany, but also other EU Member States have implemented the Directive belatedly. The Commission therefore initiated infringement proceedings against 24 states in February 2023, including Germany.[10] According to the ECJ's judgment from March 2025, which is based on Article 260 para. 3 TFEU, Germany was sanctioned to pay a lump sum of 34 million EUR for failure to transpose the Whistlblower Directive in time.[11]

10 Though all EU Member States have introduced a national whistleblower protection law based on the Directive at this point in time, the Commission is not satisfied with the implementation of the Directive in its entirety. The Commission makes this clear in its July 2024 report,[12] which is the summary of a number of expert opinions on national whistleblower protection laws. The report focuses on the implementation of the requirements on the scope of application, protective requirements and measures, the introduction of reporting offices (*Meldestelle*) within the Group, external reporting channels (*Meldekanäle*) and procedures, the processing for anonymous reports, the confidentiality requirement and sanctions. In summary, the Commission notes that all Member States have broadly transposed the Directive, but that improvements are needed. These are mainly in the establishment of internal reporting offices (*interne Meldestelle*) and the application of the group privilege or protective requirements and measures. According to the statement of the expert group, also the German legislator needs to adapt the law.

11 Particularly relevant for embedding in corporate processes is the Commission's understanding of the group privilege for reporting offices. A single reporting office at group level is, according to the Commission, not sufficient and contradicts the basic idea of

---

[9] BT-Drs. 20/3442, 2 (56).

[10] <https://germany.representation.ec.europa.eu/news/aktuelle-vertragsverletzungsverfahren-klage-gegen-deutschland-wegen-mangelnden-schutzes-von-2023-02-15_de> (last accessed: 27.5.2025); see also <eur-lex.europa.eu/legal-content/EN/TXT/PDF/?uri=CELEX:52024DC0269>, p. 2 (last accessed: 24.10.2025).

[11] Cf. <https://curia.europa.eu/jcms/upload/docs/application/pdf/2025-03/cp250029en.pdf> (last accessed: 24.10.2025)

[12] <https://eur-lex.europa.eu/legal-content/EN/TXT/PDF/?uri=CELEX:52024DC0269> (last accessed: 27.5.2025).

the Directive. The German HinSchG, on the other hand, assumes the application of the privilege as derived from the explanatory memorandum to the law. Both the Commission and the ECJ ascribe particular importance to the Whistleblower Protection Directive for the public interest, which is why poor implementation is not in the Commission's interest. If the ECJ will rule in favour of the Commission's statement, there is no question that the German legislature must remedy its shortcomings to make the HinSchG compliant with EU law. It remains to be seen whether and how the infringement proceedings will evolve.[13]

B. Requirements of the German HinSchG

Regardless of any legal obligations, the implementation of a whistleblowing system as part of a CMS is of upmost importance and offers major advantages for each company. It mainly functions as an early warning system to prevent manifesting misconduct in the company and protect the company against damages. In consequence, suitable remedial measures can be initiated at an early stage and further controls can be implemented, as most likely new risk areas are identified. **12**

This leads to a further valid aspect: a whistleblowing system needs an open speak-up-culture. Both in balance and interaction, demonstrates a prosperous ethics and compliance culture. The experience with whistleblowing cases followed by disclosure shows that a high standard of whistleblower protection is needed to demonstrate that such a speak-up culture is in place and lived up to. **13**

I. Scope of the law

1. The personal scope: who can report?

Pursuant to § 1 sub. 1 HinSchG, natural persons who have obtained information about violations in connection with their professional activity or in advance of a professional activity and who report or disclose it to the reporting offices provided for under HinSchG are to be protected from retaliation. This broad general clause is intended to meet the requirements of the WB Directive.[14] According to Art. 4 WB Directive, all persons who may have potentially become aware of an infringement in their professional environment are covered. In the light of the broad European concept of the definition 'employee', which goes beyond the classic German concept of employee,[15] can, for example, also be self-employed, interns, volunteers, board members of companies such as members of the supervisory board of a stock corporation. In addition, the scope of application extends to whistleblowers whose employment relationship has already ended or is in the process of being initiated. The scope of application is extended by the connection to professional activity. The law defines professional activity not only as the formal service or employment relationship, but also as the activities of employee representation. This term is also to be understood broadly and must be interpreted in the individual case, taking into account all circumstances. **14**

---

[13] For further details on the status quo of the current evaluation by the EU Commission, see Gerdemann ZRP 2024, 170 et seqq.

[14] BT-Drs. 20/3442, (33).

[15] Reufels/Soltysiak WhistleblowingR § 3 mn. 6.

15 Furthermore, according to § 1 sub. 2 HinSchG, the identity of the persons affected by the report or disclosure or who are the subject of the report, i.e. who are accused of misconduct, must be protected. Those affected can be, for example, witnesses named in the report; existing procedural rules should not be restricted for these groups of people.[16]

16 In addition to the persons designated in the personal scope of application in § 1 HinSchG, the HinSchG extends the protective measures under § 34 sub. 1 to other persons, namely those who confidentially support the whistleblower in submitting the report. The support itself must take place in a professional context; only mental and moral support in the private environment is not sufficient.[17] The substantive requirements of § 33 sub. 1 no. 2 and 3 HinSchG apply directly to the supporter himself; the bad faith of the whistleblower should therefore not be to the detriment of the supporter. It depends solely on the supporter whether he or she can invoke the prohibition of reprisals pursuant to § 36 HinSchG and damages from the perpetrator after reprisals pursuant to § 37 HinSchG.

17 Under § 34 sub. 2 no. 1 HinSchG, third parties can also invoke the protective measures mentioned in → mn. 111 if they have suffered reprisals based on the report or disclosure by the whistleblower. § 34 sub. 2 no. 2 HinSchG includes legal persons, partnerships with legal capacity and other associations of persons with legal capacity in the scope of protection, provided that a comparable risk situation exists. However, the legislature does not elaborate further on what is to be understood by a comparable risk situation. The meaning and purpose of the provision could be based on whether the business partner can receive reprisals.[18]

18 **Practical hint**: the personal scope of application of the HinSchG is to be understood broadly. Whistleblowers according to the personal scope could be employees, self-employed persons, trainees, employee-like persons, interns, board members, applicants, retired employees. If it is decided to open the whistleblower system to externals as well, the personal scope than also comprises business partners, suppliers and customers.

2. The material scope: what can be reported?

a) Violations covered according to § 2 HinSchG

19 The legislator has extended the material scope of application compared to the WB Directive.[19] Pursuant to § 2 HinSchG, the HinSchG initially applies to the reporting and disclosure of information on violations that are qualified as infringements under criminal law (sub. 1 no. 1), regardless of the protected interest of the violated criminal offence. This also includes ancillary criminal law which has a legal-political dimension. It is only appropriate to assume a significant violation in the case of unlawful conduct punishable by criminal law.[20]

20 Violations that are punishable by fines are also included, insofar as the violated provision serves to protect life, limb or health or to protect the rights of employees or their representative bodies (sub. 1 no. 2). § 2 sub. 1 no. 2 HinSchG is to be understood broadly in terms of its meaning and purpose, even if the scope of the administrative offences is limited by the addition. In practice, violations of requirements regarding occupational health and safety that are punishable by fines can be relevant as well.[21] The restriction is

---

[16] BT-Drs. 20/3442, (57).
[17] BT-Drs. 20/3442, (92).
[18] BT-Drs. 20/3442, (93).
[19] BT-Drs. 20/3442, (57).
[20] BT-Drs. 20/3442, (57).
[21] BT-Drs. 20/3442, (57); examples: violation of ArbZG, MiLoG, AÜG, or duties to provide information and information to representative bodies like § 121 BetrVG or § 36 SprAuG.

plausible in principle, as it excludes that violations of the law of only minor illegality do not fall within the scope of protection. However, the limitation entails a certain degree of uncertainty for the whistleblower and for the responsible reporting officers. It must be examined on a case-by-case basis whether the infringement is one that falls within the scope of application.

§ 2 sub. 1 no. 3 HinSchG lists other violations of federal and state legislation as well as directly applicable legal acts of the EU or Euratom, such as violations of product safety and conformity, money laundering, antitrust law or data protection law, the reporting of which also opens up the scope of the Act. In more detail: **21**

Lit. a) refers to laws on combating money laundering and terrorist financing, including in particular the Money Laundering Act and Regulation (EU) 2015/847 of the European Parliament and of the Council. This includes criminal offences under §§ 89c, 129a, 129b and 261 StGB, possibly in conjunction with §§ 25, 26 or 27 StGB, as well as violations of the GwG and KWG.[22] **22**

Lit. b) specifies requirements for product safety and conformity. The legislator is thus referring to requirements that are subject to Union harmonisation legislation and are set out in Annexes I and II to Regulation (EU) 2019/1020 of the European Parliament and of the Council of 20 June 2019 on market surveillance and compliance of products and amending Directive 2004/42/EU and Regulations (EU) No 765/2008 and (EU) No 305/2011. In addition, there are products within the scope of referring to the General Product Safety Directive (Directive 2001/95), the Directive on Simplifying Terms and Conditions of Transfers of Defence-related Products within the Community (2009/43/EC), the European Firearms Directive (91/477/EEC) and Regulation (EU) No 98/2013 on Marketing and Use of Explosives Precursors. Also, products which are in the scope of the Regulation (EU) 2018/858 on the Approval and Market Surveillance of Motor Vehicles.[23] **23**

Lit. c) refers to road safety requirements relating to road infrastructure safety management, safety requirements in road tunnels and authorisation to pursue the occupation of road haulier or road passenger transport operator (bus and coach operator). **24**

Lit. d) states requirements to ensure railway operational safety; lit. e) contains maritime safety requirements concerning European Union rules on the recognition of ship inspection and survey organisations, the liability and insurance of the carrier for the carriage of passengers by sea, the approval of marine equipment, maritime safety inspection, seafarer training, the registration of persons on passenger ships in maritime transport, and European Union rules and rules of procedure for the carriage of passengers by sea. It also refers to the Directive on safe loading and unloading of bulk carriers (2001/96/EC).[24] **25**

Lit. f) refers to requirements for civil aviation safety in the sense of averting dangers to operational and technical safety and in the sense of air traffic control. Lit. g) refers to legal requirements for the safe transport of dangerous goods by road, rail and rush ship. **26**

Lit. h) concerns the violation of environmental protection regulations, for example the Federal Nature Conservation Act (*Bundes-Naturschutzgesetz*, BNatSchG) or the Packaging Act (*Verpackungsgesetz*, VerpackG). Lit. h refers to requirements for radiation protection and nuclear safety and lit. j to laws to promote the use of energy from renewable sources and energy efficiency. **27**

Lit. k) concerns laws regarding food and feed safety, organic production and labelling of organic products, the protection of geographical indications for agricultural products and foodstuffs, including wine, aromatised wine products and spirits and traditional specialities guaranteed, the placing on the market and use of plant protection products **28**

[22] BT-Drs. 20/3442, (58).
[23] BT-Drs. 20/3442, (58).
[24] BT-Drs. 20/3442, (59).

and animal health and welfare, in so far as they support the protection of farm animals, the protection of agricultural animals, the protection of animals at the time of killing, the keeping of wild animals in zoos, the protection of animals used for scientific purposes, as well as the transport of animals and related processes.

29 According to let. l), general public health care provisions are also in the material scope. The passus refers to quality and safety standards for organs and substances of human origin, human and veterinary medicinal products, medical devices and cross-border patient care.

30 Lit. m) concerns laws regarding the manufacture, presentation and sale of tobacco and related products. Let. n) refers to regulations on consumer rights and consumer protection in relation to business-to-consumer contracts and protecting consumers in the field of payment accounts and financial services, price indication and unfair commercial dealings.

31 Lit. o) comprises laws referring to electronical communication. In concrete, it refers to regulations regarding the protection of privacy in electronic communications, the protection of the confidentiality of communications, the protection of personal data in the field of electronic communications, the protection of the privacy of users' terminal equipment and information stored in these terminals, protection against unreasonable nuisance caused by advertising by means of telephone calls, automatic calling machines, fax machines or electronic mail, as well as on caller number display and suppression and for inclusion in directories.

32 With lit. p), violations under the GDPR also fall within the material scope and with let q., measures for security in information technology.

33 Lit. r) comprises the regulation of the rights of shareholders of public limited companies, lit. s) requirements for auditing the financial statements of public-interest entities in accordance with § 316a sent. 2 HGB.

34 Lit. t) refers to violations of acts that regulate the accounting, including the accounting of companies that are capital market-oriented within the meaning of § 264d HGB, of credit institutions within the meaning of § 340 sub. 1 HGB, financial services institutions within the meaning of § 340 sub. 4 sent. 1 HGB, investment institutions within the meaning of § 340 sub. 4a sent. 1 HGB, institutions within the meaning of § 340 sub. 5 sent. 1 HGB, insurance undertakings within the meaning of § 341 sub. 1 HGB and pension funds within the meaning of § 341 sub. 4 sent. 1 HGB.

35 § 2 sub. 1 no. 4 to 8 HinSchG list specific individual laws that must be considered. These laws are in particular regulations for the award of public applications and concessions (§ 106 GWB), regulations in the field of financial services (§ 4d sub. 1 sent. 1 FinDAG), regulations in the field of taxation as well as laws to ensure fair competition (Art. 101, 102 TFEU, § 81 sub. 2 no. 1, 2 lit. a and no. 5, sub. 3 GWB).

36 **Practical hint**: to address the extensive material scope of § 2 HinSchG, it is advisable to conduct a comprehensive analysis of the business. This analysis should determine which specific provisions related to other violations of federal and state laws, as well as directly applicable legal acts of the EU or Euratom, are relevant.

37 Reports of ethical misconduct or violations of internal regulations, however, do not fall within the scope of protection.[25] Even though internal compliance rules are of great importance in the company, it is appropriate for the legislator not to include ethical conduct or internal regulations in the material scope of application. Firstly, the term 'ethical conduct' is too vague toe meet the principle of definiteness enshrined in the German Constitution. Secondly, internal regulations vary in their wording and design from one

[25] Vogel CB 2024, 158 (158).

company to another. If included in the material scope of application, the extent of protection varies depending on the company the whistleblower is employed by. This variation results in legal uncertainty, which is unlikely to be the legislature's intention.

Practical hint: the provisions of the German AGG do not fall within the material scope of the HinSchG, similar to breaches of internal regulations or the Code of Conduct. For companies, it might be beneficial to combine the reporting possibilities under HinSchG and AGG, or even extend the reporting system to include breaches of internal regulations. If this approach is taken, a clear communication strategy is essential. Whistleblowers must understand that the protection under HinSchG applies only in certain circumstances, specifically when reports fall in the material scope of the HinSchG. A company's voluntary expansion of the material scope by the company does not alter this. An expansion needs to be incorporated in a collective agreement at company level, if BetrVG is applicable.[26] 38

b) Correlation to other provisions

§ 4 HinSchG regulates the correlation of the HinSchG to other provisions. 39

According to § 4 sub. 1 HinSchG sector-specific regulations on the reporting of violations take precedence over the provisions of the HinSchG. In such cases, there are preferential rules of already existing sector-specific reporting channels. Since these reporting offices are considered to have special expertise and experience due to their many years of existence, it should be continued to be utilized. § 4 sub. 1 no. 1 to 12 HinSchG lists all relevant specific reporting offices. Special reporting offices with long standing experience are for example those according to §§ 6 sub. 4, 53 GwG, § 25a sub. 1 sent. 6 no. 3 KWG, § 58 WpHG or § 23 sub. 6 VAG.[27] 40

§ 4 sub. 2 sent. 1 HinSchG excludes the application of the Consumer Information Act (*Verbraucherinformationsgesetz*, VIG), the regulations of the German Freedom of Information Act (*Informationsfreiheitsgesetz*, IFG) as well as regulations of the state governments referring to the access of official information. According to sub. 3, §§ 81h to 81n GWB remain unaffected.[28] These regulate the requirements for dealing with leniency applicants in antitrust. At the request of a cartel participant as a leniency witness, the competition authority may refrain from imposing a fine or reduce it. § 4 sub. 4 HinSchG clarifies that German provisions of the Code of Criminal Procedure (StPO) remain unaffected as well. 41

c) Priority of security interests as well as confidentiality and secrecy obligations

§ 5 sub. 1 HinSchG regulates the priority of security interests, such as information from intelligence services or information relating to national security. Reports concerning these areas don't fall within the scope of the HinSchG. Accordingly, § 5 sub. 2 HinSchG stipulates that reports don't fall within the scope of the HinSchG if a duty of secrecy to protect classified information precludes it. This applies accordingly to judicial secrecy, lawyers' duty of confidentiality or medical confidentiality. 42

§ 6 HinSchG differentiates the law from the protection of trade secrets. Additionally, it helps to ensure that proportionality by restricting confidential information to a necessary level during disclosure.[29] 43

---

[26] Reufels/Soltysiak WhistleblowingR § 11 mn. 11.
[27] BT-Drs. 20/3442, (67).
[28] BT-Drs. 20/3442, (67) et seqq.
[29] BT-Drs. 20/3442, (71) et seqq.

44 **Practical hint**: it is recommended to revise any standard clauses in employment contracts on contractual confidentiality obligations. It should be made clear that, despite confidentiality obligations, the rights of employees under the HinSchG are not restricted.

II. Internal or external reporting office

1. Definition of a report

45 The term 'report' is legally defined in § 3 sub. 4 HinSchG. A report (*Meldung*) is the communication of information about violations to internal reporting offices or external reporting offices. According to § 3 sub. 2 sent. 1 HinSchG, violations are acts or omissions in the context of a professional, entrepreneurial or official activity that are unlawful and affect the provisions or areas of law that fall within the material scope of application according to § 2 HinSchG. The addition 'in the context of a professional, entrepreneurial or official activity' in turn serves to distinguish it from purely private misconduct. Pursuant to § 3 sub. 2 sent. 2 HinSchG, abusive acts or omissions that are contrary to the aim and purpose of the provision also fall within the scope of protection. In doing so, the legislator follows the opinion of the ECJ, which sees abusive practices as seriously damaging the public interest.[30]

46 Information on breaches are well-founded suspicions or knowledge of actual or possible violations that have already occurred or are very likely to occur at the employer where the whistleblower is or was employed, or at another body with which the whistleblower is or has been in contact due to his or her professional activity (§ 3 sub. 3 HinSchG). In doing so, contrary to the WB Directive, the legislature expanded the definition to include a subjective element.[31] Evidence of a violation is not required, because justified suspicions are sufficient, but it the term information does not include speculation or rumours. Whether a suspicion is justified is then based on subjective criteria that lie with the whistleblower himself. Pursuant to § 33 sub. 1 no. 2 HinSchG, he must have 'sufficient reason' to assume that the information he or she transmits is true. Thus, the subjective element only becomes relevant for the protection requirements.[32]

2. Internal reporting office

47 Pursuant to § 12 sub. 1 sent. 1 and 2 HinSchG, employers with at least 50 employees must set up at least one internal reporting office; the number of employees, on the other hand, is irrelevant if the employer is a company within the meaning of § 12 sub. 3 HinSchG.[33]

48 Pursuant to § 14 sub. 2 sent. 1 HinSchG, employers with up to 249 employees might share a reporting office.[34] In theory, an alternative that is highly unlikely to be chosen.

49 The term 'employer' (§ 3 sub. 8 HinSchG) includes natural persons as well as legal entities under public and private law, partnerships with legal capacity and other associations of persons with legal entities not mentioned in no. 1 and 2, § 3 sub. 10 HinSchG names legal entities under private law, such as public limited companies, limited partnerships

[30] BT-Drs. 20/3442, 65.

[31] Art. 5 no. 2 WB Directive is based exclusively on a purely objective suspicion, see in detail Siemes, CCZ 2022, 293 (296).

[32] BeckOK HinSchG/Colneric/Gerdemann, 5. Ed. 15.11.2024, HinSchG § 3 mn. 18.

[33] BT-Drs. 20/3442, (78).

[34] BT-Drs. 20/3442, (66).

or limited liability companies. The term 'employees' include employees, trainees, civil servants, judges, soldiers and persons who, due to their economic circumstances, occupy a position similar to that of an employee. This definition is also decisive for the calculation of the threshold value according to sub. 2.

Practical hint: to determine whether the threshold of 50 employees has been reached, it is necessary to evaluate the potential workforce to date and to assess future developments. A specific cut-off date is not decisive. The development of the workforce should be closely monitored. **50**

The employer is not only obliged to set up a reporting office, but also, according to § 12 sub. 4 HinSchG, to transfer the needed powers to the representative of the reporting office. In particular, individuals responsible for the reporting office must be put into position to examine reports and take follow-up actions. The task of the internal reporting office, in addition to processing the report and carrying out the validity check associated with it, is also 'to contribute to remedying any violations.'[35] This could also be done, in particular, through an internal investigation for the purpose of detailed fact-finding. Instead, purely 'administrative tasks'[36] within the framework of the procedural requirements under § 17 HinSchG are meant. The internal investigation in the true sense of the word, as well as decisions on further proceedings with the compliance-relevant facts, is not within the authority of the reporting office by law. This remains the core task of the employer within the framework of its duty to investigate.[37] **51**

Practical hint: this duty can be delegated.[38] Consequently, the unit or person responsible for the reporting office can assume the task of the reporting office manager as well as that of the investigating body. **52**

If a reporting office is not established, there is a risk of a fine for the employer in accordance with § 40 sub. 2 no. 2 HinSchG. **53**

3. External reporting office

According to § 19 sub. 1 HinSchG, the federal government must set up an external reporting office at the Federal Office of Justice. This office is to be addressed as an external reporting office except that federal states have set up their own reporting offices pursuant to § 20 HinSchG, the external reporting office of BaFin pursuant to § 21 HinSchG or the external reporting office of the Federal Cartel Office pursuant to § 22 HinSchG are responsible. In addition, the federal government can set up other external reporting offices according to § 23 HinSchG. All external reporting offices shall provide whistleblowers with information and advice on remedies and procedures to protect against retaliation. External reporting offices must also set up channels through which whistleblowers can submit reports. The offices must process the report in accordance with § 28 HinSchG. Anonymous reports should be accepted, but do not have to be processed according to the HinSchG. § 29 HinSchG then regulates a right of the external reporting office to information vis-à-vis natural persons and employers. As a follow-up measure, the external reporting office can contact the employer in accordance with § 29 sub. 2 HinSchG, refer the whistleblower to another competent authority, discontinue the proceedings due to lack of evidence or because of other reasons, or hand over the proceedings to a competent authority for further investigation.[39] **54**

---

[35] BT-Drs. 20/3442, (82).
[36] Thüsing HinSchG/Fischbach HinSchG § 13 mn. 14.
[37] Moosmayer Compliance mn. 13. For further details on the conduct of internal investigation → Ch. 8.
[38] Thüsing HinSchG/Fischbach HinSchG § 12 mn. 14.
[39] BT-Drs. 20/3442 (85) et seqq.

4. The right of choice

55 § 7 sub. 1 sent. 1 HinSchG establishes a free right of choice between the internal or the external reporting office for the whistleblower. The whistleblower can contact the external office directly or after contacting the internal reporting office. In any case, the whistleblower should be able to choose the reporting office 'that is most suitable in view of the case-specific circumstances.'[40] As a result, there is the possibility that the external reporting office will receive information about an internal company violation before the company does. § 7 sub. 2 HinSchG prohibits obstructing the report itself or the communication of the whistleblower with the reporting office.[41] The ban constitutes an administrative offence pursuant to § 40 sub. 1 no. 2 HinSchG.

56 **Practical hint:** this right of choice should be clearly communicated to all employees as potential whistleblowers. It is recommended to include this information in all company communications referring to whistleblowing and whistleblower protection.

57 § 7 sub. 3 sent. 1 HinSchG is particularly relevant for employers. It stipulates that incentives for the use of internal reporting offices should be set up. This is intended to implement the requirements of Art. 7 para. 2 WB Directive. The EU Member States must ensure that the internal reporting is preferred of the external. The legislator allows for discussion which specific incentives are appropriate.

58 § 7 sub. 3 sent. 2 HinSchG requires the employer to communicate clearly and easily accessible internally on the internal reporting process. It is crucial that both the communication and the incentives created do not hinder the reporting option, either to the external or the internal reporting office.[42]

59 **Practical hint:** as a general rule, an open speak-up culture is important to guarantee an effective whistleblower system. Therefore, transparent and supportive information in form of FAQ or flyer explaining the reporting process in a nutshell are essential.

Incentives for using the internal whistleblowing system could include, for example, leniency programs regarding employment law measures. However, it is doubtful whether such incentives are conducive to the desired ethics and integrity culture.

III. Requirements for the internal reporting office

1. Organisational structure

a) General

60 The legislator specifies minimum requirements for a reporting office in § 14 sub. 1 HinSchG. Otherwise, the obligated employer has organisational freedom. As long as the reporting office is equipped with the appropriate powers, staffed with independent, conflict-free, and trained personnel who have sole access to the reporting channels, the further design is up to the employer.[43]

61 Which organisational unit within the company or person is suitable, depends on the structure of the company.[44] Here, too, the legislator leaves room for interpretation and refers to integrity officers as suitable persons as examples.[45]

---

40 BT-Drs. 20/3442 (73).
41 BT-Drs. 20/3442 (73).
42 BT-Drs. 20/3442 (73).
43 BT-Drs. 20/3442 (79).
44 Recital 56 Directive (EU) 2019/1937.
45 BT-Drs. 20/3442 (80).

However, the organisational unit must be able to meet the minimum requirements under the HinSchG: it must be independent and be able to carry out the tasks specified under the HinSchG without conflicts of interest. The necessary expertise is a further decisive criterion for selecting the right unit. Those responsible for the reporting office must not only know the course of the procedure but also know how the requirements are to be implemented in concrete terms. 62

Practical hint: a suitable organisational unit might be the legal or compliance department as well as the department of internal auditing. The decision should be made in the long term so that the same department will operate the reporting office in the future. 63

As part of its organisational obligations, the employer must determine exactly which unit has the necessary expertise or is in a position to acquire it. In this respect, he also shall set aside a budget for training measures and for continuous further education, see § 15 sub. 2 HinSchG. 64

Practical hint: in order to provide the necessary expertise, a training concept on the basics of the HinSchG and an internal guideline for the reporting office on how to deal with reports should be offered. Soft skills such as the ability to rapport building or psychological aspects of the whistleblower must also be considered. 65

A third party may also hold the reporting office. This might be an external lawyer or other service provider such as business consultant in the function as ombudsperson. Hiring an ombudsperson is a practical solution, especially for smaller companies or those that do not have in-house expertise. 66

According to the German legislator, another group company can also assume responsibility for the reporting office as a third party in accordance with the principle of separation under group law. As a rule, this is likely to be the parent company. 67

b) Point of contention: group wide central internal reporting office versus decentralized reporting offices

In June 2021, the European Commission issued as answer to a request of the Nordic countries, how to interpret Art. 8 WB Directive. Art. 8 para. 1 WB Directive states that 68

Member States shall ensure that legal entities in the private and public sector establish channels and procedures for internal reporting and for follow-up, following consultation and in agreement with the social partners were provided for by national law.

According to Art. 8 para. 5 WB Directive also a 'third party' can be assigned as reporting channel. The investigation function cannot be outsourced.[46] According to Art. 8 para. 6 WB Directive mid-size companies with 50 to 249 employees 'may share resources as regards the receipt of reports and any investigation to be carried out'. 69

The European Commission reads this regulation including the respective Recital 54 in the way that within a group, only mid-sized companies can share resources, but companies with 250 or above employees must always establish own channels and own investigation resources, also if a group-wide reporting channel and investigation recourses are already established.[47] It is stated that a 'third party' is only 'a party external to the legal entity with which the reporting person has/had/is about to have a work-related relationship.'[48] This means in the understanding of the European Commission that 'a parent company (or any other company within the group, for what matter) would not be external to the subsidiary where the whistleblower has a work-based relation.'[49] The Commission furthermore added that nevertheless a group-wide internal reporting channel can be 70

[46] Recital 55 and 56 Directive (EU) 2019/1937.
[47] Letter of the European Commission of 2.6.2021 (JUST/C2/MM/rp (2021)393215), 2.
[48] Letter of the European Commission of 16.7.2021 (JUST/C2/MM/rp (2021)5129001), 2.
[49] Letter of the European Commission of 16.7.2021 (JUST/C2/MM/rp (2021)5129001), 2.

operated in parallel to decentralised local reporting systems, but cannot replace them. In 2024, the Commission reconfirmed this statement.[50]

71 According to this understanding, centrally operated group-wide reporting offices should be supported by decentralised reporting systems for group companies with 250 and above employees, wherever the transposed law follows this understanding.

72 Based on its interpretation of Art. 8 para. 5 WB Directive and the principle of separation under group law, the German legislator in contrast considers the establishment of a central reporting office as a group solution to be sufficient and appropriate, provided that this does not create any additional burden for the whistleblower. In this respect, the whistleblower must be able to submit the report, for example, in the predominant working language of the subsidiary. Group companies are independent third parties within the meaning of Art. 8 para. 5 WB Directive, which can be instructed to receive reports in the same way as external consultants or lawyers as ombudspersons. In any case, the legal entity commissioning the third party remains ultimately responsible for the follow-up and remedy of an established violation.[51] This understanding makes it easier for corporations to implement the HinSchG and ensures that reports are processed quickly and, above all, professionally, as the expertise is usually located at headquarters.[52]

c) Consequences for companies

73 It remains to be seen whether the German interpretation will persist, although many arguments speak for a central solution. Even if the European Court of Justice deems that the HinSchG is violating European Law, there is no risk for companies in Germany. A court judgement only has *inter partes effect* which would lead to the German Government being in charge for amending the law but not be binding for companies at the same time.

74 If there will be a change in the law, there are manageable possibilities to work with the understanding of the European Commission in the business practice, even if this complicates the established process. Especially an already implemented reporting system does not have to be replaced but should be supplemented by decentral, local channels (e.g., email addresses or phone numbers for the respective legal entity). The central reporting system should then be promoted as reports issued to the central reporting office can be handled centrally and do not have to be submitted to the affected legal entity for an internal investigation.[53]

75 At the present time, at least one central reporting office is sufficient for companies operating exclusively in Germany. This applies to employers with 50 to 249 employees as well as to those with 250 or more employees, even if they are combined into a group. If the company operates in other European countries as well, a through review of all implemented Whistleblowing Acts is necessary as other European countries followed the interpretation of the Commission stating that further decentralised reporting offices are obligatory.[54]

76 **Practical hint:** a combination of an internal reporting office and an external ombudsperson cannot be ruled out either; this option should be kept in mind in particular if the ECJ overturns the currently assumed group privilege and considers separate reporting offices for each legal entity in the group to be absolutely necessary. Also, in view of the differences in whistleblower protection legislation in other European countries, an ombudsperson can be a simple and quick solution to implement a decentralised reporting

---

[50] EU-Commission, COM(2024) 269 final, 6.

[51] BT-Drs. 20/3442, 79 and Ref-E HinSchG, 85.

[52] BT-Drs. 20/3442, 79.

[53] Letter of the European Commission of 2.6.2021 (JUST/C2/MM/rp (2021)393215), 5.

[54] Portugal, Poland, Romania or Sweden, just to name some examples.

office. If doing so, the company must appoint a unit or individual as contact person and in charge to decide upon the internal investigation and following remedial measures. Data protection laws as well as the co-determination right of the workers counsel need to be considered.

2. Reporting channels

Furthermore, the employer must set up reporting channels in accordance with § 16 sub. 1 sent. 1, 3 HinSchG, enabling the reporting office to be contacted and allowing whistleblowers to report violations. The specific design is up to the employer and can vary depending on the size of the company and business activities. The circumstances of the individual case should therefore be taken into account.[55] In any case, according to the wording of sent. 3, the reporting channels must be accessible to persons employed by employers as well as to temporary agency workers. The accessibility for external parties who are in contact with employers is not a must.[56] However, if employers decide to make it available to external parties as well, the information communicated within § 13 sub. 2 HinSchG must also be made available to externals.[57] **77**

Practical hint: a suitable reporting channel could be an IT-tool as reporting platform. This supports internally to process the reports but also guarantees the needed confidentiality. When deciding to use an IT-tool as reporting platform, provision regarding the works council as well as data protection laws need to be taken into consideration. **78**

The legislator also recommends ('should') the offer of anonymous reporting options (§ 16 sub. 1 sent. 5 HinSchG). Every company should consider this to ensure they also receive reports from whistleblowers who wish to benefit from the enhanced security of anonymity. **79**

Practical hint: whistleblowers often must overcome an inner barrier in order to approach the reporting office at all. This obstacle might be reduced if the whistleblower can initially remain anonymous. Drawing from practical experience, a frequently mentioned risk of denunciation when allowing anonymous reporting and the associated exploitation of the whistleblower system is very low. **80**

§ 16 sub. 2 HinSchG stipulates that only authorised personal are allowed to have access to the reporting channels. Authorised persons are the persons responsible for receiving and processing the report as well as auxiliary persons who provide support. As an example, the legislator cites IT specialists who provide technical support for reporting channels.[58] However, their access must be restricted to the extent necessary; this already follows from the confidentiality requirement (*Vertraulichkeitsgebot*) under §§ 8, 9 HinSchG. **81**

Reports can be submitted to the reporting office orally by telephone or other form of voice transmission as well as in text form, § 16 sub. 3 sent. 1 HinSchG. A personal meeting must be made possible at the request of the whistleblower within a reasonable time according to sent. 2 and 3. A digital meeting is also suitable, provided that the whistleblower consents.[59] **82**

Practical hint: if the whistleblower wishes to meet in person and travel expenses are incurred for this, the reporting office should be able to compensate for this accordingly, at least for employees of the employer. **83**

---

[55] BT-Drs. 20/3442, 80.
[56] See the wording of § 16 sub. 1 sent. 3 HinSchG: 'can be designed in this way'.
[57] Thüsing HinSchG/Fischbach HinSchG § 16 mn. 6.
[58] BT-Drs. 20/3442 (81).
[59] BT-Drs. 20/3442 (82).

3. Internal communication with the whistleblower

84 In principle, good and transparent communication with the whistleblower strengthens the trust in the whistleblower system. This also includes adequate information on the status of the report and the follow-up measures taken or why they were omitted. In this respect, information should be provided to the whistleblower as a matter of principle, and not only because of the legal requirement under § 17 sub. 2 HinSchG. In addition, repeated reports and disclosure through feedback could be avoided. In which extent it is communicated must be a case-by-case decision. The communication must not jeopardise the success of the investigation and must not impair the rights of the persons affected by the report.[60]

4. Procedure for receiving and following up on reports

a) Receiving and assessment of reports

85 For the processing of reports, § 17 HinSchG provides a described procedure that must be carried out in this way. In addition, § 11 HinSchG is relevant in the context of the proceedings. In all procedural steps, compliance with the confidentiality requirement pursuant to § 8 of the HinSchG (→ mn. 100 et seqq.) must also be observed.

86 The procedure stipulates that the reporting office acknowledges the receipt of the report after seven days at the latest, checks whether the reported violation falls within the material scope of application according to § 2 HinSchG, maintains contact with the whistleblower and conducts a plausibility check of the report. It asks the whistleblower for further information, if needed and takes follow-up measures in accordance with § 18 HinSchG. According to § 17 sub. 2 HinSchG the whistleblower needs to be informed about the status of processing its report three months after the acknowledgment of the receipt the latest. While communicating with the whistleblower, the above stated is to be considered.

87 In practice, it makes more sense to conduct the plausibility test before or at least in parallel with maintaining contact and asking questions according to No. 3 and 5. The plausibility check of the report is decisive for determining whether further questions need to be clarified with the whistleblower or whether further information needs to be obtained. The outcome of the plausibility check is also relevant for initiating follow-up measures according to § 18 HinSchG.

88 **Practical hint:** the above stated requirements must be embedded in an internal regulation for handling reports. At the very least, the internal regulation must clearly state responsibilities for the intake of the report as well as for follow-up measures including internal investigations of other departments, reflect the legally prescribed procedure under Art. 17 of the Whistleblowing Act and include regulations for handing over to the central investigation unit in compliance with the confidentiality requirement.

In addition to the question of actual responsibility and the examination of the opening of the scope of application of the HinSchG, the question of whether a potential conflict of interest exists must be asked. The regulation should include an escalation level so that alternative processors can be used if the conflict of interest is affirmed.

[60] BT-Drs. 20/3442 (82).

b) Documentation of reports

A further task of the reporting office includes the documentation of reports according to § 11 HinSchG.[61] The persons responsible for receiving the report must also document it in a permanently retrievable manner. Here, too, the confidentiality requirement pursuant to § 8 HinSchG must be observed. If the whistleblower reports by telephone, i.e. by telephone or via a digital meeting or in the course of a personal meeting, the conversation can also be recorded or a verbatim transcript can be drawn up with the consent of the whistleblower.[62] § 11 sub. 3 HinSchG speaks of 'consent' in the case of a personal meeting which is to be understood as 'consent' in the light of the GDPR.[63] Without consent, only a content log protocol may be issued. The consent must be recorded before the actual conversation begins by asking the whistleblower whether he or she consents to the recording. The consent should be documented accordingly when a transcription is issued. After the transcription, the recording must be deleted. In any case, the whistleblower must be openly informed of the possibilities of the forms of protocol to exercise a right of choice. **89**

Pursuant to § 11 sub. 4 HinSchG, the whistleblower must then be given the opportunity to check the issued minutes, to amend them if necessary and to confirm them by signature, including in electronic form. **90**

Practical hint: if the whistleblower changes the protocol, it is recommended that the originally created version be kept. **91**

The requirement in § 11 sub. 5 sent. 1 HinSchG to delete the documentation three years after the conclusion of the proceedings is viewed critically. Even the wording raises questions, as it is neither defined what the documentation refers to nor when it can be said that the proceedings have been concluded. The documentation of the report alone is to be taken into account and not the entire documentation in connection with the report. It is also not defined when a procedure is considered to have been concluded. It could be when the internal investigation itself or the implementation of measures, such as disciplinary measures, have been carried out. The HinSchG itself only stipulates information on the conclusion of the proceeding in § 18 no. 3 HinSchG, namely if the plausibility of the report is to be denied or the original initial suspicion has been dispelled. Hence, the conclusion is set when the reporting office finished its catalogue of duties and initiated follow-up measures according to § 18 HinSchG. **92**

For other documents related to the report, such as interim and final reports of the internal investigation by other responsible departments or interview transcripts of witness interviews, the general deletion periods pursuant to Art. 17 para. 1 lit. a GDPR applies. As soon as the purpose for storing the personal data is no longer necessary, it must be deleted. A possible alternative to deletion that companies should consider is the anonymization or pseudonymization of the documents. **93**

Practical hint: the entire concept of § 11 HinSchG involves a high level of complexity for companies, especially if the reporting office and the body responsible for the investigation are merged. Especially for companies operating EU wide, different deletion periods are to be considered. Therefore, a retention and deletion policy is recommended which guides all parties involved in the reporting process. **94**

---

[61] According to § 10 HinSchG, the reporting office is authorised to process personal data insofar as this falls within the scope of its task specified in § 13 HinSchG. Further personal data may also be collected and processed when follow-up measures are taken. The regulations of the GDPR or BDSG must be observed in principle. Details see Lang ZD 2024, 17 (17).

[62] Thüsing HinSchG/Fischer HinSchG § 11 mn. 10 et seq.

[63] Thüsing HinSchG/Fischer HinSchG § 11 mn. 16.

c) Follow-up measures

95 § 18 HinSchG provides the reporting office with a non-exhaustive catalogue of measures, depending on the result of the validity test pursuant to § 17 sub. 1 no. 4 HinSchG. The measures are limited to the function that the reporting office performs. This does not involve conducting an extensive internal investigation to clarify the facts of the report.

96 If the reporting office requires additional information to complete the plausibility check, it may conduct a preliminary investigation and interview the mentioned witnesses. In doing so, it must adhere to generally accepted guidelines for conducting interviews, even if these are not legally mandated.[64] According to § 18 no. 2 HinSchG, the reporting office may refer the whistleblower to another competent department within the company; this also presupposes that the reporting office has established the plausibility of the report but sees no indication of further action. This is particularly the case if minor allegations are the subject of the report. Based on practical experience, however, the reporting office will not reject a whistleblower who has submitted a valid report but will make use of the follow-up measure in § 18 no. 4 lit. a HinSchG and submit the report to the competent department responsible for conducting internal investigations. This department then takes further measures to clarify and remedy the infringement.

97 In accordance with § 18 no. 4 lit. b HinSchG, the reporting office may also forward the report to an authority.

98 **Practical hint:** the management responsible should provide the reporting office with clear organisational instructions regarding which personnel shall be involved before the report is handed over to the authority.

99 If the report cannot be conclusively assessed or no initial suspicion of a violation of the law has been established, the reporting office can conclude the procedure, § 18 no. 3 HinSchG.

IV. Requirement of confidentiality

100 The requirement of confidentiality (*Vertraulichkeitsgebot*) according to § 8 HinSchG with the exception regulated in § 9 HinSchG is an important part of the protection regime of the HinSchG.[65] It helps to protect whistleblowers from discrimination and thus to a functioning whistleblower system.

101 In addition to protecting the identity of the whistleblower (no. 1), the scope of protection of § 8 sub. 1 sent. 1 HinSchG encompasses individuals affected by the report (no. 2) as well as others named in the report (no. 3). The latter group particularly includes witnesses, while those affected are individuals accused of wrongdoing. The concept of identity should be interpreted broadly; any information that could lead to conclusions about the whistleblower's identity is also included in the scope of protection. The requirement of protecting the identity applies at all stages of the procedure, even after the proceedings have been concluded.[66]

102 The group of persons permitted to access the identities is strictly limited. Only those directly responsible for handling the report are authorized to access this information. Within the reporting office, access to the identity should be restricted exclusively to those individuals processing the report. Others only may learn of the identities if it is neces-

---

[64] BeckOK HinSchG/Dilling, 5. Ed. 15.11.2024, HinSchG § 18 mn. 33.

[65] Thüsing HinSchG/Stille HinSchG § 9 mn. 1; see also Recital 82 Directive (EU) 2019/1937: 'essential ex ante measure to prevent retaliation'.

[66] BT-Drs. 3442/20, 74.

sary for supporting tasks. According to § 8 sub. 2 HinSchG, the obligation to maintain confidentiality also applies in cases where the whistleblower submits their report to a non-designated reporting office.

However, the confidentiality requirement is not absolute. § 9 HinSchG outlines excep- **103** tions that are more limited concerning the identity of the whistleblower compared to that of the group of persons mentioned in → mn. 16 et seq. According to sub. 1, the identity of a person who intentionally or through gross negligence reports false information about violations is not protected. In such cases, the identity of whistleblowers might be disclosed in order to pursue claims for damages under § 38 HinSchG.

§ 9 sub. 3 HinSchG is particularly relevant for corporate practice. Information regard- **104** ing the identity of the whistleblower, or any other details that could lead to conclusions about their identity, may only be disclosed if this is necessary and the whistleblower has previously provided consent in text form in accordance with § 126b sub. 1 BGB. These conditions must be fulfilled cumulatively.[67] Therefore, if the reporting office wants to pass on the report including the identity to the internally responsible investigation body or to an external law firm for the purpose of conducting an internal investigation, prior consent from the whistleblower is required.

§ 9 sub. 4 no. 2 to 8 HinSchG provides for a facilitated disclosure of the identity of the **105** other individuals, while remaining within the boundaries set by Art. 14 GDPR.[68] According to § 9 sub. 4 no. 2 HinSchG, the identity of the person concerned may be disclosed to the investigation unit without their consent. According to no. 3, disclosure for the purpose of implementing follow-up measures is also permissible without consent.

Practical hint: the requirement of confidentiality offers a significant advantage in civil **106** proceedings. If the reporting office maintains the whistleblower's identity confidential, it is highly likely that the absence of causality between a retaliatory measure and the submission of the report can be proven. Responsibilities regarding access to the identities must be clearly defined. Expanding the reporting office to include additional groups of persons, for example to facilitate reporting obligations, is not advisable. Such an expansion would complicate the burden of proof in civil proceedings. The structure of the reporting office must strictly adhere to the principle of necessity, tailored to the size of the company and the volume of reports.

V. The disclosure

The disclosure (*Offenlegung*) legally defined in § 3 sub. 5 HinSchG refers to the making **107** available of information about violations to the public. Disclosure is not to be understood as another form of reporting, but downstream of internal or external reporting. It is to be understood as an exception that is subject to strict conditions.[69] The law provides for two alternatives, according to which disclosure is legally permissible. If these are not present, the protective provisions of the HinSchG do not apply.

Pursuant to § 32 sub. 1 no. 1 HinSchG, the whistleblower may contact the public if **108** he or she has submitted an external report and this has not been remedied within the prescribed period or no feedback has been given on the follow-up measures taken. This burdens the company with a failure of the authority, which does not seem appropriate. Reputational damage, often accompanied by economic losses, is thus in the hands of the

[67] Authentic text of § 9 sub. 2 no. HinschG: 'and'.
[68] Handel Meldestellenbeauftragte Ch. 66.
[69] BT-Drs. 20/3442, 90.

authority. Disclosure requires external reporting beforehand. The preceding internal report alone is not sufficient.[70]

109 Pursuant to § 32 sub. 1 no. 2 HinSchG, the whistleblower may choose to go public if he or she had sufficient reason to believe that, according to lit. a, the violation constitutes a threat to the public interest due to imminent danger, that reprisals are to be feared under lit. b in the event of the report, or that evidence could be suppressed or destroyed in accordance with lit. c, agreements could be made or that other circumstances make it unlikely that the external reporting office will take effective follow-up action. According to the legislator it must be examined on a case-by-case basis, whether such circumstances exist.[71] This formulation is so broad that it cannot comply with the requirement of certainty, especially with regard to the negative consequences for companies.

110 Sub. 2 prohibits the disclosure of incorrect information and punishes a violation thereof with a fine under § 40 sub. 1 HinSchG. The passage of § 32 sub. 2 HinSchG is one of the few passages in the HinSchG that also focuses on the protection of companies and, above all, the persons concerned.

VI. Whistleblower protection and protection measures

111 The key for a well-functioning reporting system is to protect the whistleblower against any negative consequences due to reporting a possible violation. Companies should therefore ensure comprehensive whistleblower protection even without a legal obligation.

112 **Practical hint:** if the scope of possible violations that can be reported comprises breaches of internal regulations such as the Code of Conduct, an internal whistleblower protection standard needs to be guaranteed. This should be explained in an internal whistleblowing policy. It is especially important to clarify the distinction between the legally mandated whistleblowing protection according to HinSchG and the on-top offered internal whistleblowing protection.

1. Protection requirements

113 Only if the requirements of § 33 sub. 1 HinSchG are cumulatively fulfilled, the protective measures under §§ 35 to 37 HinSchG are triggered. § 33 sub. 1 HinSchG lays down procedural and content-related requirements.

114 First, the whistleblower must have submitted a report to an internal or external reporting office in accordance with sub. 1 no. 1 or have disclosed information in accordance with the requirements of § 32 HinSchG. The requirement of subsection (no. 1) is not fulfilled if the whistleblower reports to a body other than the reporting office set up for the receipt of reports under the HinSchG. The employer complies with the requirements of the HinSchG only by setting up an internal reporting office. In this way, he ensures that reports are processed in accordance with the requirements of the HinSchG. In consequence, only reports submitted to the specific reporting office can trigger the scope. In particular, he can thus comply with the confidentiality requirement under §§ 8, 9 HinSchG. If reports to entities other than the designated reporting office were to also trigger the protection requirement, it would be detrimental to the employer.

115 § 33 sub. 1 no. 2 and 3 HinSchG require that the whistleblower had sufficient reason to believe at the time of the report that the information reported or disclosed was correct and

---

[70] Thüsing HinSchG/Lüneborg HinSchG § 32 mn. 11.
[71] BT-Drs. 3442/20 (91).

fell within the scope of the HinSchG. The decisive point in time is therefore an ex-ante assessment by the whistleblower. The combination of 'sufficient reason' and 'assumption' means that there is a subjective-objective requirement for the protection of good faith on the part of the whistleblowers.[72] The assumption of the whistleblower must therefore be based on a sufficient reason; thus, the subjective characteristic of the assumption is objectified by that of the sufficient reason. The subject matter of both characteristics is the truth about the reported or disclosed information about violations pursuant to § 3 sub. 3 HinSchG. This is the case if the actual event corresponds to the reported event; the correctness of the legal classification by the whistleblower is irrelevant. Untrue, misleading or inaccurate information, on the other hand, is generally not protected. The whistleblower, on the other hand, is protected if he or she provides such information 'in good faith'; however, he or she must be convinced of the accuracy of the information. If a whistleblower acts despite residual doubts, this must be interpreted in his or her favour as a report 'in good faith'. The whistleblower cannot invoke protection if the information he or she reports is already fully public knowledge.[73]

Whistleblowers who intentionally, knowingly or through gross negligence report or even disclose false information do not enjoy protection. As a principle, the assumption of the whistleblower must refer to factual evidence. It is sufficient if the information is obvious and plausible and is feasible with a certain degree of probability according to general life experience. The verification of the information by the whistleblower by means of his or her own evidence may not be required. This could hold back potential whistleblowers from reporting; furthermore, it would in turn run counter to the basic idea of whistleblower protection. The legislator states that 'the submission of information may not be made lightly without an effort to verify, provided that the effort is reasonable.'[74] The principle of reasonableness must therefore always be assumed.[75] As a rule, verification on the basis of access rights to the evidence already existing in the course of the work activity is reasonable; if these are not used, no protection can be granted. Anyone who fails to provide obvious opportunities to obtain evidence does not act with sufficient reason to believe that the information is true.[76] The verification effort is not reasonable if the whistleblower runs the risk of being discovered or acts in a criminally relevant manner himself.[77] **116**

Subjective motives of the whistleblower for the report do not play a role in good faith. If the whistleblower had sufficient reason to believe that the information was true, he or she is protected, even if the motive for the report is guided by other reasons. **117**

Whether the reported information is then also a violation that falls within the scope of application of the HinSchG cannot be burdened with the whistleblower for assessment, see § 33 sub. 1 no. 3 HinSchG. The understanding of the legal layman must be taken into account. If available, job-specific knowledge and understanding must be taken into account.[78] **118**

72 For details, see Siemes CCZ 2022, 293 (298).
73 BT-Drs. 20/3442, (92).
74 BT-Drs. 20/3442, (92).
75 Thüsing HinSchG/Lüneborg HinSchG § 33 mn. 27.
76 Thüsing HinSchG/Lüneborg HinSchG § 33 mn. 27.
77 BT-Drs. 20/3442 (92)
78 BT-Drs. 20/3442 (92).

2. Exclusion of responsibility

119 According to § 35 sub. 1 HinSchG, the whistleblower cannot be held responsible (*Ausschluss der Verantwortlichkeit*) for obtaining or accessing information. The limit lies in the criminally relevant conduct of the whistleblower. Sub. 2 concerns disclosure; according to this, the whistleblower must have sufficient reason to believe that the disclosure is necessary. In this respect, the obligation for the whistleblower to check is increased by the element of necessity.[79]

3. Prohibition of retaliation

120 The prohibition of retaliation (*Verbot von Repressalien*) under § 36 sub. 1 HinSchG is of particular importance. After all, the fear of retaliation is the ultimate burden for whistleblowers to report possible violations of laws. Retaliation as a result of the report as well as the attempt of it are prohibited. This also applies to whistleblowers involved in the violation.

121 The term 'retaliation' (*Repressalien*) is legally defined in § 3 sub. 6 HinSchG; it has a broad scope. In principle, any act with a negative impact on the whistleblower is to be regarded as reprisal that is not objectively justified. In addition, withholding benefits can also be detrimental.[80] The permissible conduct of the whistleblower must be causal for the disadvantageous reaction of the employer.

122 § 36 sub. 2 HinSchG lays down the rule on the burden of proof (*Beweislast*). According to this, it is presumed that disadvantages suffered by a whistleblower are retaliations that are related to the previous report of the whistleblower. The whistleblower must assert this accordingly. Next, the employer, as the retaliator, must prove that the disadvantage was based on sufficiently justified reasons or that these were not based on the notification or disclosure. As a rule, this rebuttal should succeed if the employer can give objectively justified reasons for the measure.[81] Documentation of measures taken in the HR department and by managers as well as compliance with the confidentiality requirement are therefore elementary for a refutation to succeed.

4. Compensation for damages because of a retaliation

123 If the whistleblower has suffered material damage because of retaliation, this must be compensated according to § 37 sub. 1 HinSchG. Compensation for non-material damage is excluded. The respondent to the compensation is the perpetrator of the retaliation; typically, this is the employer.[82] A claim to the establishment of an employment relationship or to career advancement is excluded under § 37 sub. 2 HinSchG.

124 The whistleblower may also be liable for damages pursuant to § 38 HinSchG if he or she reports or discloses false information through gross negligence or intentionally. The costs incurred for the internal investigation, for example, could be claimed.

[79] BT-Drs. 20/3442 (94).
[80] EuArbRK/Fest RL (EU) 2019/1937 Art. 19 mn. 18.
[81] BT-Drs. 20/3442, (96).
[82] BT-Drs. 20/3442, (96).

VII. Sanctions

The fine provisions of § 40 HinSchG specify sanctions that apply in the event of a violation of the obligations specified in the HinSchG and comprehensively lists the possible administrative offences. 125

§ 40 sub. 1 HinSchG sanctions the deliberate disclosure of incorrect information. The purpose of the provision is to deter whistleblowers from abusing the disclosure option.[83] 126

§ 40 sub. 2 HinSchG stipulates three cases of administrative offences in the context of whistleblowing to an internal or external reporting office. According to no. 1, an administrative offence is committed by anyone who obstructs a report or communication contrary to § 7 sub. 2 HinSchG. This includes not only the complete prevention, but also the restriction of reporting or communication by the employer itself or other persons who are in contact with the employer.[84] Even the attempt to obstruct constitutes an administrative offence. According to no. 2, the failure to set up and operate a reporting office pursuant to § 12 sub. 1 sent. 1 HinSchG is also sanctioned, as well as according to no. 3 the violation of the prohibition of retaliation as well as the attempt to take retaliation, see § 40 sub. 5 in conjunction with no. 3. The violation of the confidentiality requirement is comprehensively protected by § 40 sub. 3 and sub. 4 HinSchG; negligent action also constitutes an administrative offence. 127

The amount of the fine varies from 10,000 EUR to 50,000 EUR, pursuant to § 40 sub. 6 sent. 1 HinSchG. § 40 sub. 6 sent. 2 HinSchG orders the applicability of § 30 sub. 2 sent. 3 OWiG. Consequently, the fine can be increased tenfold in the event of obstruction of reporting or communication, a violation of the prohibition of retaliation and a violation of the confidentiality requirement. 128

C. Further legal frameworks

When implementing a reporting system there are further legal frameworks to be considered. 129

I. Co-determination right of the works council (BetrVG)[85]

In a company in which a works council (*Betriebsrat*) is existent, the co-determination rights (*Mitbestimmungsrecht*) of the works council must be taken into consideration. The rights of the works council are also applicable for companies which have their company seat outside of Germany. Co-determination rights cannot be overruled by foreign laws if the company is operating in Germany.[86] 130

Hence, before setting up a system, the works council needs to be informed in due course, § 80 sub. 2 BetrVG. An open communication regarding the purpose of a whistleblowing system with the works council is recommended. 131

The relevant paragraph for co-determination rights is § 87 BetrVG. According to § 87 sub. 1 no. 1 BetrVG the works council co-determine in questions concerning the organi- 132

[83] BT-Drs. 20/3442, (97).
[84] BT-Drs. 20/3442, (98).
[85] See Reufels/Soltysiak WhistleblowingR § 10 mn. 6; Handel Meldestellenbeauftragte Ch. 10.
[86] BAG 22.7.2008 – 1 ABR 40/07, NZA 2008, 1248 (1254).

zation of the company and the conduct of the employees in the company, insofar as there are no statutory or collectively agreed regulation.

133 As the setup per se is required by HinSchG at least for companies with 50 employees, there is no co-determination right of the works council whether a whistleblower system is setup at all. Nevertheless, the law provides leeway for certain questions of how the system is implemented. In these cases, the co-determination rights need to be adhered to.

134 With the introduction of the reporting channels, the employer specifies the reporting path for employees that they must follow to fall within the scope of protection of the HinSchG. This presents a conduct that goes beyond the legal obligation to merely introduce a reporting system or the obligation under employment contract. The purpose in doing so is to create a regulated process for reporting. Hence, this is to be qualified as regulation of the organization of the company.

135 The employer can decide to extend the responsibility of the internal reporting office regarding breaches of the employer's Code of Conduct, the AGG or other internal regulations. This goes in parallel beyond of the material scope of the law. In consequence, if an internal process foresees a process for reporting possible breaches which are not in the original scope of the law, this is to be qualified as a measure to control the employees' conduct.[87]

136 Most companies might decide to use an IT tool as one of the reporting channels. § 87 sub. 1 no. 6 BetrVG stipulates a co-determination right with regard to technical equipment which is designed to monitor the behaviour or performance of employees. An IT tool is regularly used to collect information and data on the report and the persons named in the report. It cannot be ruled out that this will interfere with the employees' personal areas. This, in turn, is not perceptible to employees; as a rule, the processes to clarify the reported circumstances report run in the background. The purpose of the clarification is to determine whether an employee conducted a breach of laws. Hence, its conduct will be reviewed and monitored. In this respect, the works council should be involved accordingly to.

137 If additional staff is needed to maintain or operate the reporting office, the works council is to be addressed according to § 99 sub. 1 no. 1 BetrVG.

138 Often discussed is the obligation for employees to report possible breaches of laws. A duty to report would intervene in the employees' behaviour. The co-determination right of the works council According to § 87 sub. 1 no. 1 BetrVG is triggered. Generally, setting up a duty to report has no further effect on an effective whistleblower system. On the contrary, an obligation might lead to resentment and coercion that makes employees shy away from reporting.

II. Data protection laws[88]

139 Data protection laws are a constant companion in processing reports and further internal investigations following the report.

140 Before setting up an internal reporting office including reporting channels and procedures, a data protection impact assessment according to Art. 35 sub. 1 GDPR needs to be completed. This must assess the consequences of the processing operations for the protection of personal data.

---

[87] HML Corporate Compliance/Mengel § 39 mn. 71 et seq.

[88] See Handel Meldestellenbeauftragte Ch. 4; Lang ZC 2024, 17 et seq.

Data protection law is also integral to the HinSchG from its inception: a breach of the GDPR requirements triggers the material scope according to § 2 sub. 1 no. 3 lit. p HinSchG. 141

The requirement of confidentiality then stipulates in more detail the dealing with the identity of all involved persons which is, of course, a personal data according to GDPR. As reports regularly contain several information about personal data, the processing of the report must be in alignment with data protection laws. § 10 HinSchG gives guidance on how to process the personal data adequately. Furthermore, the requirements of the German data protection law as well as the ones of the GDPR are also applicable.[89] 142

The relevant provisions for processing of personal data during the reporting process are Art. 6 para. 1. sent. 1 lit. c, para. 3 sent. 1 GDPR with § 10 HinSchG. It stipulates that the reporting office shall process the submitted personal data insofar as necessary to fulfil their responsibilities according to §§ 13 and 24 HinSchG. The reporting office is allowed to review the data and furthermore, collect further personal data and process data further to operate reporting channels, to carry out the procedure for receiving and following up on reports and to take follow-up measures.[90] It is legally necessary if there is no other equally effective remedy at hand. In other words, the processing of the data is needed to fully execute the task according to § 13 HinSchG. 143

According to § 10 sent. 2, 3 HinSchG in conjunction with Art. 9 para. 2 lit. g GDPR, sensitive personal data shall be also processed if necessary. 144

The tension between the GDPR and the HinSchG is unavoidable when it comes to the information and clarification obligations under Art. 14 GDPR and Art. 15 GDPR. The personal data contained in the report is usually processed without the knowledge of the data holder. According to Art. 14 GDPR, the data subject must be informed of all circumstances of the processing. If Art. 14 para. 3 GDPR is interpreted narrowly, data subjects must be informed of the processing within one month. The obligation to inform could have a negative impact on the processing of the report and a subsequent internal investigation. Information must be provided, but only in exceptional cases under Art. 14 para. 5 lit. b GDPR, when all evidence has been secured. 145

The right to information pursuant to Art. 15 para. 1 GDPR is limited within the framework of the reporting procedure. Not all data has to be released; limiting the content of the request for information protects all participants in the internal investigation, in particular to protect the whistleblower. 146

Art. 17 para. 1 GDPR stipulates the right to erasure of processed personal data. This is also incorporated in § 11 sub. 5 HinSchG. The documentation shall be deleted three years after the closure of the procedure. It can be assumed that the purpose of the retention, the preservation of evidence for possible court proceedings, is fulfilled at the end of the three years.[91] A longer retention period is possible if it is necessary and proportionate. 147

Practical hint: as the responsible reporting office has to consider data protection laws in each step, data protections laws should be reflected in the respective internal policy. Furthermore, it is crucial to have retention and deletion policy for the reporting office. 148

---

89 BT-Drs. 20/3442 (76).
90 BT-Drs. 20/3442 (76).
91 BT-Drs. 20/4909 (54).

D. Excursus: grievance mechanism according to the German Due Diligence Supply Chain Act (LkSG)

149 The complaints procedure (*Beschwerdeverfahren*) according to § 8 LkSG (→ Ch. 18 mn. 107 et seqq.) is in parallel to the whistleblower procedure according to HinSchG. Both proceedings are of equal rank.

150 If a reporting system has been set up and is already available to external parties, generally in form of an IT system as reporting channel, this can be also used as intake for grievances according to § 8 LkSG. However, if deciding to include the grievance mechanism, it must be ensured that the requirements of the LkSG and HinSchG are fulfilled in parallel. It must especially be clearly defined who takes over the processing of a complaint under the LkSG, especially if the complaints under the LkSG do not affect the company's own area of responsibility. A thorough interface management especially with the purchasing department is important.

E. First steps for the set-up of a whistleblower system according to HinSchG

I. Gap analysis

151 Evaluate the current status quo of the whistleblower system. Take the setup into consideration regarding the scope of applicability and the internal policies such as the Code of Conduct, the internal regulation for the compliance management system and internal policies on handling reports. Evaluate the scope of the reporting system (internal versus external). Also ensure to have covered the entire EU and the respective nation whistleblower acts when conducting a gap analysis.

II. Stakeholder management

152 Evaluate who is necessary for the process and which role is fulfilled by each stakeholder (e.g., reporting office, department responsible for conducting internal investigations, HR, whistleblowers). Implement specific internal policies that describe the collaboration of each department if there are interfaces.

III. Determination of responsibilities

153 If there is a current organisation in charge for the intake of whistleblower reports, keep the process and just adapt it. It might be needed due to the requirement of confidentiality, to minimize the group of people having access to the reporting office. If there is no reporting office at all, analyse which internal department has the necessary competence to fulfil the duties of the HinSchG. HR is in general not the suitable position as to assure the clear differentiation between the department issuing possible disciplinary measure which can be seen as retaliation due to a report.

IV. Review and adaption of internal policies

It is recommended to have an internal policy on dealing with reports and the internal investigation process following a report. If you already have one, adapt the policies adequately to the HinSchG and assess especially whether the criteria are fulfilled as stipulated in § 17 HinSchG. Also, ensure that all stakeholders are trained in dealing with the principle of confidentiality. An internal policy on handling reports should be reflected in an internal policy on whistleblowing. Adapt the Code of Conduct adequately and include at least the prohibition of retaliation, whistleblower protection measures and the existence of a designated reporting office. **154**

V. Communication measures

Inform all employees about the internal reporting office according to HinSchG. Use general communication channels which are well known in the company. **155**

CHAPTER 8
INTERNAL INVESTIGATIONS

Bibliography: Fuhrmann, Internal Investigations: Was dürfen und müssen die Organe beim Verdacht von Compliance Verstößen tun?, NZG 2016, 881; Greco/Caracas, Internal investigations und Selbstbelastungsfreiheit, NStZ 2015, 7; Herrmann/Zeidler, Arbeitnehmer und interne Untersuchungen – ein Balanceakt, NZA 2017, 1499; Jüttner, Muster von Unternehmenskriminalität als vernachlässigter, aber notwendiger Teil einer Compliance-Risiko-Analyse, CCZ 2022, 276; Klaas, Die datenschutzkonforme Weitergabe von Ermittlungsergebnissen aus internen Untersuchungen – Teil 1: Nationale Behörden, CCZ 2020, 256; Kölbel, Wirtschaftskriminalität und unternehmensinterne Strafrechtsdurchsetzung, MSchrKrim 2008, 22; Krug/Skoupil, Befragungen im Rahmen von internen Untersuchungen – Vorbereitung, Durchführung und Umgang mit den Ergebnissen, NJW 2017, 2374; Kuhlmann, Interne Untersuchungen – Langer Atem zahlt sich aus, CCZ 2019, 310; Miege, „Wie machen es eigentlich andere Unternehmen?" – „Interne Untersuchungen in Deutschland – 2022" – eine DICO-Studie, CCZ 2023, 1; Müller, Internal Investigations – Zulässigkeit von strafrechtlichen Ermittlungen durch den Arbeitgeber, öAT 2023, 1; Naber/Ahrens, Befragung von Mitarbeitern im Rahmen von Internal Investigations – Vorgehensweise und aktuelle Herausforderungen, CCZ 2020, 36; Ott/Lüneborg, Internal Investigations in der Praxis – Umfang und Grenzen der Aufklärungspflicht, Mindestaufgriffsschwelle und Verdachtsmanagement, CCZ 2019, 71; Pelz, Die Beschlagnahmefähigkeit von Unterlagen aus Internal Investigations – zugleich eine Besprechung von BVerfG, Beschluss vom 27.6.2018, Az. 2 BvR 1405/17, 2 BvR 1780/17, CCZ 2018, 211; Rainhardt/Kaindl, Mitarbeiterinterviews im Rahmen von Internal Investigations – ein schmaler Grat zwischen Befragung und Verhör, CB 2017, 210; Schmidt, Steuerliche Handlungspflichten der Unternehmensleitung im Rahmen einer Internal Investigation, CCZ 2012, 121; Stück, Unternehmensinterne Untersuchungen im Fokus von Rechtsprechung und Gesetzgebung, ArbRAktuell 2020, 408; Süße/Eckstein, Aktuelle Entwicklungen im Bereich „Interne Untersuchung", Newsdienst Compliance 2014, 71009; Taschke, Zur Entwicklung der Verfolgung von Wirtschaftsstrafsachen in der Bundesrepublik Deutschland – Bemerkungen aus der Praxis, NZWiSt 2012, 9; ders., Zur Entwicklung der Verfolgung von Wirtschaftsstrafsachen in der Bundesrepublik Deutschland – Teil 3: Auf dem Weg zur Privatisierung der Strafverfolgung, NZWiSt 2012, 89; Weiß, Compliance der Compliance – Strafbarkeitsrisiken bei Internal Investigations, CCZ 2014, 136; Zimmermann/Lingscheid, Internal Investigations – Best Practice bei Interviews mit Mitarbeitern, CB 2013, 23.

Table of contents

A. Introduction 160
B. Legal and factual obligations to conduct internal investigations 161
C. Basic principles governing the internal investigation process 163
    I. Impartialness and independence 163
    II. Fairness, professionalism, consistency 164
    III. Timeliness 164
    IV. Protection of anonymity, confidentiality, need-to-know-principle 164
    V. Non-retaliation 165
    VI. Adequate documentation 165
D. Cooperating with authorities 166
E. Investigation steps 167
    I. Plausibility assessment: case or no-case decision 168
    II. Initiation of an investigation (investigation mandate) 169
    III. Scope of the investigation (investigation plan) 169

IV. Investigation measures 170
1. Collection of data 171
2. Interviews 172
a) Order of interviews 172
b) Time and place 173
c) Introduction 174
d) Purpose/background of the interview 174
e) Duty to self-incriminate? 174
f) Information on data processing and handling of interview notes 175
g) Confidentiality 175
h) Right to bring an attorney/member of the works council 175
i) Structuring the interview 176
3. Other measures 177
V. Investigation report 178
VI. Briefing of relevant stakeholders 179
VII. Remediation process 180
1. Disciplinary measures 180
a) Decision body 180
b) Typical sanctions 181
c) Determination of appropriate disciplinary measures 181
2. Other remedial measures 182
3. Interim measures 182
VIII. Data retention and deletion cycle 183

A. Introduction

1 Within the past years, internal investigations have been as much a focus point in media coverage as in the daily practice of legal experts.[1] But what do we really mean when we use this term? Internal investigations are about clearing up suspicions of violations of the law, internal policies, and self-obligations in connection with activities of a legal entity (i.e. its employees and management) by either a dedicated function within an entity, usually the compliance department, and/or external (legal) advisors.[2]

2 This is of course not a new development – legal experts have always been clarifying fact scenarios to properly defend clients, state claims etc.; this is nothing less than the core of the legal craft. However, the term internal investigation signifies something more than these more or less basic legal skills: it implies an establishment and application of procedural constructs for conducting this work on clarifying allegations of wrongdoing within an organisation, the specialization and growing of specific departments within

[1] Fuhrmann NZG 2016, 881.

[2] Cf. Klaas CCZ 2020, 256; Müller öAT 2023, 1; Kuhlmann CCZ 2019, 310 (311); Godzierz Compliance-Checklisten/Shahhosseini/Ahrens § 11 mn. 15 et seq.

legal entities and external counsels and the arrival of this instrument in the reality of legislators[3] and authorities which reward this form of privatisation of criminal proceedings[4].

The unwanted public attention and the severe penalties imposed in grave cases like the Siemens, MAN and Ferrostaal corruption scandals, Volkswagen's Diesel incident or the finance industry's cum-ex cases, incentivized managers to implement structures that allow an increasingly thorough approach to internal investigations.[5] Ultimately, the term is a symbol for the significance of such private investigation efforts and their growing relevance in the landscape of corporate practices and criminal defence strategies.[6] **3**

Another reason why the discussion on internal investigations has broadened in the past years is their complexity. Most cases touch on various areas of law, the most common being labour law, data protection law, corporate law, criminal law, civil law, tax law, accounting, insider law and environmental law.[7] In addition, the subject matters to be investigated are more often than not intricate (e.g. technologically and/or factually) and require expert knowledge outside the legal field. **4**

B. Legal and factual obligations to conduct internal investigations

The legal obligation to promptly conduct internal investigations after allegations of misconduct committed by employees have become known results from the supervisory duties applying to the management of a legal entity under German law.[8] Ignoring this **5**

---

[3] Cf. Ott/Lüneborg CCZ 2019, 71; Momsen/Grützner WirtschaftsSteuerStrafR-HdB/Grützner/Klaas/Wybitul § 16 mn. 2. Two recent legal developments are once again changing how internal investigations are conducted. These are, on the one hand, the latest developments in the area of whistleblower protection rights (Whistleblower Protection Directive (EU) 2019/1937 and the corresponding national implementation laws such as the German Whistleblower Protection Act (*Hinweisgeberschutzgesetz*, HinSchG)). These provisions are primarily directed at providing appropriate reporting channels. However, the strict provisions governing the protection of whistleblowers and the data of accused persons and third parties also impact the handling of information during an internal investigation. This is especially true for cases in which other company functions need to be consulted as subject matter experts or when – within a group of companies – a report is made to another group company than the one actually concerned and the latter needs to be informed about said report. In these cases, the sharing of information is made especially difficult under the new legislation. On the other hand, there is the Act on Corporate Due Diligence Obligations in Supply Chains (*Lieferkettensorgfaltspflichtengesetz*, LkSG) that – at least indirectly – puts more emphasis on internal investigations. This Act obliges companies to follow up on any reports on potential human rights violations and risks to the environment. In most companies this leads to an extension of the scope of when internal investigations are being conducted since some allegations in the sphere of human rights and environmental issues might not be considered violations of laws, internal policies or self-obligations but lie on a lower threshold. Since compliance departments are usually staffed with investigation experts, conducting investigations within the scope of the Act on Corporate Due Diligence Obligations in Supply Chains this naturally falls within their competencies. The coming years will show how much of an increase of cases to be investigated will result from this Act. However, it is another example of how the complexity of internal investigations is constantly increasing.

[4] Cf. Taschke NZWiSt 2012, 9 (89); Kölbel MschrKrim 2008, 22 (33); HML Corporate Compliance/Wessing § 46 mn. 3; Müller öAT 2023, 1.

[5] Rainhardt/Kaindl CB 2017, 210; Schmidt CCZ 2012, 121; Fuhrmann NZG 2016, 881; Süße/Eckstein Newsdienst Compliance 2014, 71009.

[6] Herrmann/Zeidler NZA 2017, 1499 (1500).

[7] Momsen/Grützner WirtschaftsSteuerStrafR-HdB/Grützner/Klaas/Wybitul § 16 mn. 2.

[8] Irrespective of the legal base for such supervisory duties – i.e. §§ 130, 30 OWiG; 91 sub. 2, 93 sub. 1, 76 sub. 1 AktG; 80 WpHG; 25a KWG – it is generally acknowledged that the management of a company must conduct internal investigations whenever suspicions of a compliance violation are identified; LG

duty to follow up on allegations of misconduct and to put an end to identified wrongdoing can result in a direct liability of the responsible management of a company and/or other persons such duties have been delegated to, e.g. compliance officers (§§ 130, 9, 14 OWiG).[9] Furthermore, the responsible management of a company and/or other persons whom supervisory duties have been delegated to may be held liable for violations of employees below management level if such violations could have been prevented or substantially hindered by appropriate supervision (§§ 130 sub. 1, 9 OWiG). The fines imposed in such cases can reach up to 1 million EUR (§ 130 sub. 3 sent. 1 OWiG).

6 The liability of the respective legal entities for violations of criminal or administrative law is twofold: on the one hand, legal entities are liable for infringements committed by their management if these are simultaneously violations of the entity's duties or if the infringements led to or were meant to lead to an enrichment of the legal entity (§ 30 sub. 1 OWiG). On the other hand, legal entities can also be held responsible for infringements of entity-related duties committed by employees below management level if such violations could have been prevented or substantially hindered by appropriate supervision (§§ 130 sub. 1, 30, 9 OWiG). It should be noted that authorities are increasingly moving their approach from prosecuting individual wrongdoing to sanctioning companies for violations committed by their employees or management. This is true for the prosecution of extensive national cases but can especially be observed in international circumstances since this is a way for authorities to subtract complexity from the case at hand which is due to § 30 sub. 4 OWiG.[10] This provision stipulates that entities may be fined even if no individual has been subject to criminal or administrative proceedings because of an otherwise identified violation of criminal or administrative law. Thus, violations committed by employees can be attributed to the management of an entity without authorities having to establish individual contributions in a detailed manner.[11]

7 All in all, the consequences of identified misconduct can result in fines, a listing in a commercial central register (§ 149 sub. 2 no. 3 GewO, which can lead to blacklisting/ineligibility for competing for public contracts), reputational damages, decrease of share prices, and other administrative measures such as the withdrawal of permits.[12] Fines can reach up to 10 million EUR in cases in which managers acted with intent and up to 5 million EUR if violations were committed negligently (§ 30 sub. 2 sent. 1 OWiG). The severity of sanctions following a violation of an administrative offence depends on the financial penalty stipulated in the respective regulation but can reach up to ten times the amount of the regulated maximum fine (§ 30 sub. 2 sent. 2 et seq. OWiG). Even higher fines may be determined in cases in which these frameworks for penalties do not exceed the economic advantages gained from a violation.[13] Respective administrative fines may be accompanied by further amounts to be paid due to confiscation of proceeds.[14]

8 In addition to the legal obligations forcing the management of a company to install internal investigations as a tool to mitigate liability risks, conducting such investigative measures is essential when it comes to generally assessing wrongdoing within the company and preventing greater future losses which can result both from the incident itself

München I 10.12.2013 – 5 HK O 1387/10, BeckRS 2014, 01998, NZWiSt 2014, 183 (187); Pelz CCZ 2018, 211 (217); MüKoAktG/Spindler AktG § 91 mn. 63; Krug/Skoupil NJW 2017, 2374.

[9] Moosmayer Compliance mn. 311; Süße/Eckstein Newsdienst Compliance 2014, 71009.

[10] NK-WSS/Gräfin von Galen/Schaefer OWiG § 30 mn. 43; BeckOK OWiG/Meyberg, 44. Ed. 1.1.2024, OWiG § 30 mn. 57.

[11] KK-OWiG/Rogall OWiG § 30 mn. 120.

[12] Rotsch Criminal Compliance/Momsen § 34 B mn. 11; Momsen/Grützner WirtschaftsSteuerStrafR-HdB/Grützner/Klaas/Wybitul § 16 mn. 18, 38.

[13] Cf. §§ 30 sub. 3, 17, sub. 4 OWiG; cf. → Ch. 5.

[14] Cf. §§ 73 et seqq. StGB, 29a OWiG.

but also from potential reputational damages.[15] By shedding light on the facts of a case throughout the course of an internal investigation, the management will be able to have a clearer picture of the severity of possible violations and to control and/or mitigate any risks.[16] Internal investigations are therefore an essential part of an adequate compliance management system. The sooner a company is able to act on potential compliance violations, the more effective the mitigation of damages for the company and third parties will be.

Furthermore, following up on reports of potential violations via internal investigations sets a clear tone from the top and the middle[17] that signals employees that misconduct will be neither encouraged nor tolerated by the company's management.[18] Such investigations are thus an adequate way of preventing employees from engaging in misconduct and a basis for sanctions if violations are identified.[19] **9**

All in all, the aforementioned legal and factual obligations led to a drastic increase of the efforts put into preventing respective criminal and administrative violations on the one hand and following up on any indications of wrongdoing from a repressive point of view on the other hand, thus making internal investigations an essential part of every effective compliance management system. **10**

The following paragraphs will outline important aspects of the internal investigation process which should be taken into consideration when conducting such fact-finding exercises. Depending on the size of the legal entity or a group of companies respectively and the amount of reports/cases (to be expected), it might be advisable to summarize them in a procedural guideline which reliably governs future internal investigations, creates objectivity and comparability in handling different cases and – last but not least – builds a strong foundation that can be revised and improved as required. **11**

C. Basic principles governing the internal investigation process

Although the German Code of Criminal Procedure (*Strafprozessordnung*, StPO) does not apply to internal investigations, it is common ground that basic procedural principles apply.[20] **12**

I. Impartialness and independence

For one, all investigation measures conducted must be objective, free from any personal concerns, interests, views, or preferences of the personnel involved.[21] Persons tasked with clarifying allegations of misconduct must at all times be neutral, objective, and free **13**

---

[15] Grigoleit/Grigoleit/Rachlit AktG § 142 mn. 30.

[16] IBP Compliance Ch. 6 mn. 2; Momsen/Grützner WirtschaftsSteuerStrafR-HdB/Grützner/Klaas/Wybitul 4 § 16 mn. 11.

[17] The importance of the tone from the middle – meaning the communication and examples coming from middle management – can hardly be overemphasized due to the proximity to the larger group of employees. The management board needs to set the general tone, but it is the middle management that carries it to the rest of the employees and serves as role models; cf. Kuhlmann CCZ 2019, 310 (311).

[18] MüKoGmbHG/Fleischer GmbHG § 43 mn. 190 et seqq.

[19] Dieners Gesundheitswesen-Compliance-HdB/Zedtwitz von Armin/Cahnbley Ch. 9 mn. 1.

[20] Rotsch Criminal Compliance/Moosmayer § 34 B mn. 76.

[21] HML Corporate Compliance/Wessing § 46 mn. 1.

from any conflicts of interest, presumption or prejudice as to whether an alleged misconduct has occurred. Potential conflicts of interest must be disclosed to the responsible compliance organisation within a legal entity or, if such does not exist, the responsible management. This includes the management itself that must be neutral with respect to the investigation. If this is not the case, it must be assured that the compliance organisation can report to a different management representative that might be part of a management body on a higher level. It must be ensured that all matters are investigated independently.[22] Specific determinations and ultimate conclusions must not be drawn before the fact-finding stage of an internal investigation is completed.

II. Fairness, professionalism, consistency

14 It must be ensured, that every person that might be the subject of a report may in another way become part of an internal investigation – be it as a reporter or witness – must be treated equally, with respect and dignity. Under no circumstances should the responsible organisation permit or tolerate the usage or authorization of any illegal or unethical investigation tactics or techniques. To ensure this, the responsible compliance organisation must make sure that only appropriately qualified and trained personnel, which has been instructed on its role-specific obligations, is employed.[23] Such approach will support a consistent application of investigation and – ultimately – remediation measures. This is most important with regard to disciplinary measures, which should be imposed in a transparent and comparable manner safeguarding a fair process.

III. Timeliness

15 All steps that might be necessary during an internal investigation and potential follow-up remedial actions should be performed as efficiently as possible while ensuring a holistic fact-finding which permits a thorough root cause analysis. While certain activities may need to be carried out immediately due to certain time-critical aspects, it should be noted that potential time pressure should not lead to rushed decisions or premature conclusions.

IV. Protection of anonymity, confidentiality, need-to-know-principle

16 The latest German legislation on whistleblower protection encourages (but does not oblige) all legal entities bound by the German Whistleblower Protection Act (*Hinweisgeberschutzgesetz*, HinSchG) to enable anonymous reporting (§ 16 sub. 1 sent. 4, 5 HinSchG).[24] This reflects the common corporate practice, which treats anonymous reports just as seriously as reports made by individuals who reveal their identity. Most established compliance departments consider evaluating all kinds of reports – often enough *especially* anonymous ones since severe cases often involve a considerable personal risk for the reporter who self-protects by not revealing his identity – to be in the best interest of the entity they represent. This is the only way to holistically address compliance

[22] Ott/Lüneborg CCZ 2019, 71 (80).
[23] Godzierz Compliance-Checklisten/Shahhosseini/Ahrens § 11 mn. 27 et seq.
[24] The German Whistleblower Protection Act was issued on 31 May 2023.

issues and other risks, and the only chance to prevent whistleblowers from going public with their allegations.[25]

Persons involved in the process of clarifying allegations of wrongdoing must be obliged to handle all information received, created, and retained during the fulfilment of their roles or tasks confidentially and in accordance with applicable laws and regulations. Case-related (personal) information may be shared on a strict need-to-know basis only. In case of whistleblowers deciding to report anonymously, appropriate safeguards must be in place to avoid identities from being identified and/or disclosed. 17

V. Non-retaliation

It should go without saying that no type of retaliation or threats of retaliation against whistleblowers, who filed reports in good faith or are otherwise involved in an investigation (e.g., as witnesses or investigating resources), should be tolerated or encouraged.[26] Furthermore, the German Whistleblower Protection Act stipulates that any violation of this principle may be fined with up to 50.000 EUR for individuals[27] and 500.000 EUR for legal entities[28] in addition to granting affected whistleblowers a claim for damages.[29] 18

Legal entities should take any allegations with respect to retaliatory measures seriously and follow up on them as compliance cases. The functioning of a compliance management system depends to the outmost extent on a (corporate) culture in which whistleblowers feel comfortable and safe enough to report misconduct. On the other side of the spectrum are reporters that make intentionally false allegations which should also be regarded as a compliance violation and be followed-up accordingly. 19

VI. Adequate documentation

It should be ensured that all relevant steps and decisions taken during the stages of an internal investigation (such as the decision on the plausibility of a report, the investigation itself, remedial steps and the closure of any report/case) are accurately recorded and reported to the appropriate stakeholders (i.e. the responsible compliance organisation, management, possibly other relevant functions).[30] It should be a standard process that the investigation team composes a report at the end of every investigation. The report should include an accurate summary of the fact scenario presented, the evidence collected, conclusions on potential root causes, and recommendations on remedial actions (see for more details → mn. 70 et seqq.). 20

[25] Godzierz Compliance-Checklisten/Shahhosseini/Ahrens § 11 mn. 26.

[26] Godzierz Compliance-Checklisten/Shahhosseini/Ahrens § 11 mn. 26.

[27] §§ 40 sub. 2 no. 3, sub. 6 sent. 1, 36 sub. 1 sent. 1 HinSchG; cf. also BeckOK HinSchG/Herold, 4. Ed. 15.8.2024, HinSchG § 40 mn. 128 et seq.

[28] §§ 40 sub. 2 no. 3, sub. 6 sent. 2, 36 sub. 1 sent. 1 HinSchG, 30 sub. 2 sent. 2 OWiG; cf. also BeckOK HinSchG/Herold, 4. Ed. 15.8.2024, HinSchG § 40 mn. 131 et seq.

[29] § 37 HinSchG. It is noteworthy that § 36 sub. 2 HinSchG includes a reversion of the burden of proof, meaning the defendant would have to prove that allegations of an act of retaliation are not valid.

[30] Ott/Lüneborg CCZ 2019, 71 (79).

D. Cooperating with authorities

21 The responsible management and compliance organisation should, however, also lay down ground rules on whether or not potential findings on misconduct should be communicated towards relevant authorities. The appropriate approach should be defined anew for every case since the circumstances are always unique.

22 Generally, it can be differentiated between internal investigations taking place simultaneously to or as a consequence of preliminary proceedings initiated by a public authority and informing public authorities on the results of an internal investigation without any prior knowledge of public authorities.[31]

23 Legal entities will generally have a strong interest to conduct internal investigations upon the notification of preliminary proceedings by public authorities. It is the only way to gain a timely understanding of the fact scenario, potential risks as well as a basis to act i.a. with respect to (interim) remedial measures such as personnel changes, reporting lines, changes in the chain of management, representation letters, etc. In case of the involvement of public authorities, it is generally advisable to act very transparently towards them and support the proceedings, even though the targeted legal entity might not agree with the allegations and/or have a differing legal opinion. This includes handing over investigation reports, interview notes, collected evidence, etc.[32] Cooperative behaviour like this is usually rewarded with the omission of – potentially publicity-provoking[33] – searches, confiscations (which may lead to chance discoveries) and/or a predetermination of the direction of proceedings. It is legitimate for legal entities to support employees that might be interviewed by authorities with their own legal support and thus building their overall defence.[34] Supporting the authorities' preliminary proceedings is also likely to speed up the process and to have a strongly mitigating effect on potential fines.[35] It is highly advisable to coordinate any measures to be taken in an internal investigation with the involved authorities to prevent any allegations of collusion, obstruction of proceedings, etc.[36]

24 It should be noted that the client-attorney-privilege does not apply when the defendant is a legal entity; this is irrespective of whether work products created in the course of an internal investigation which would be seized by an authority are in the custody of external counsels or any involved company lawyers.[37] Therefore, public authorities could seize any sort of internal investigation-related documents anyway, which is why it is usually advisable to present them to signal a willingness to cooperate with public proceedings.

---

[31] Momsen/Grützner WirtschaftsSteuerStrafR-HdB/Grützner/Klaas/Wybitul § 16 mn. 70 et seqq.

[32] Please refer to Klaas CCZ 2020, 256 (260) regarding a comprehensive account of the data protection aspects to be considered when handing over data to public authorities based on different legal bases.

[33] Cf. Godzierz Compliance-Checklisten/Shahhosseini/Ahrens § 11 mn. 33 et seqq. regarding strategies on internal and external communication.

[34] Herrmann/Zeidler NZA 2017, 1499 (1505); Moosmayer Compliance mn. 351; Momsen/Grützner WirtschaftsSteuerStrafR-HdB/Grützner/Klaas/Wybitul § 16 mn. 58. Please note that fees paid for the employee's attorney are subject to income tax – omitting (forgetting) to pay these can lead to committing a tax offence, cf. MAH Strafverteidigung/Scharf § 43 mn. 95.

[35] BGH 09.05.2017 – 1 StR 265/16 = NZWiSt 2018, 379; Süße/Eckstein Newsdienst Compliance 2014, 71009; Ott/Lüneborg CCZ 2019, 71.

[36] Rotsch Criminal Compliance/Bittmann § 35 B. mn. 9 et seqq.; Moosmayer Compliance mn. 351; Krug/Skoupil NJW 2017, 2374 (2375).

[37] Cf. regarding external counsel LG Hamburg 15.10.2010 – 608 Qs 18/18 = NJW 2011, 942 – HSH Nordbank – opposing this legal opinion: LG Mannheim 3.7.2012 – 24 Qs 1/12, 24 Qs 2/12, BeckRS 2012, 15309 Moosmayer Compliance mn. 351; Momsen/Grützner WirtschaftsSteuerStrafR-HdB/Grützner/Klaas/Wybitul § 16 mn. 58.

Even in situations where there are no (preliminary) proceedings by public authorities (yet), compliance organisations and the responsible management will have to decide whether the (intermediary) results of an internal investigation, which clearly indicate/prove punishable misconduct, should be brought to the attention of the responsible authorities or not and if so, when[38]. In order to find sensible answers to these questions, it should first be assessed whether omitting to make a report to the responsible authority would itself be considered a violation. This is usually not the case since there is no general duty to self-report[39] – however, there are exceptions such as e.g. in cases of infringements of the German Fiscal Code.[40] Another aspect that can be taken into consideration is the likelihood of authorities identifying the misconduct at hand,[41] i.a. during periodic audits. In other cases, it might be in the best interest of a legal entity to report on identified misconduct, typically when the legal entity suffered damages as in cases of embezzlement, theft, etc.,[42] or when the investigation team's measures do not suffice to dig deeper, i.e. when there is a need for searches or other coercive instruments only authorities would be able to exercise.[43] The decision will be more difficult with regard to cases in which employees possibly acted to the detriment of third parties, i.e. via fraudulent or corruptive practices. If it is decided that a case should be reported to the authorities, extra scrutiny should be placed on the timing. It should be thoroughly assessed when potential self-reports are handed in to prevent premature determinations. 25

It should also not be disregarded that German authorities typically grant lower fines when entities self-report, a typical example being leniency programmes for crown witnesses but also the general leeway public prosecutors have when deciding on fines.[44] Thus, the authorities could – instead of imposing a fine following § 30 sub. 4 OWiG which could lead to the exclusion of the fined entity from public procurement – decide to only declare a forfeiture of the proceeds of the violation (§ 29a OWiG). In addition to this, authorities would be able to base any number on a mere estimation (§ 29a sub. 4 OWiG) which is why the concerned entity's representatives should show a high level of cooperation to influence this margin of discretion in their favour. 26

All in all, every case is coloured by individual factors which is why the assessment on whether or not – and if yes, when – to report a case to the responsible authorities must be done on a case-by-case-basis. 27

E. Investigation steps

It is widely recognized[45] that the following aspects are the main pillars of every investigation: 28

---

[38] Cf. Müller öAT 2023, 1 (4), who advocates for an early involvement of authorities due to their far-reaching compulsory powers to i.a. conduct searches etc. that investigation teams do not have.

[39] Stück ArbRAktuell 2020, 408.

[40] Cf. § 153 AO which obliges any taxpayer to correct tax statements once inaccuracies are identified; Schmidt CCZ 2012, 121 (122, 127 et seqq.).

[41] Momsen/Grützner WirtschaftsSteuerStrafR-HdB/Grützner/Klaas/Wybitul § 16 mn. 78.

[42] Moosmayer Compliance mn. 352.

[43] Cf. Müller öAT 2923, 1 (3).

[44] Herrmann/Zeidler NZA 2017, 1499 (1500); Moosmeyer Compliance mn. 355.

[45] Momsen/Grützner WirtschaftsSteuerStrafR-HdB/Grützner/Klaas/Wybitul § 16 mn. 84; Moosmeyer Compliance mn. 320.

- initial validation of a report regarding its plausibility; closing of implausible reports ('no case decision') (→ mn. 30 et seq.);
- initiation of an investigation if the report is plausible (→ mn. 32);
- scoping: legal assessment of proposed investigation steps and, in more complex investigations, outline of the necessary investigation steps in an investigation plan (→ mn. 33 et seqq.);
- conducting investigation measures, i.e. document review, interviews, e-discovery, etc. (→ mn. 37 et seqq.);
- assembling the investigation report (fact scenario, legal assessment, remediation steps) (→ mn. 70 et seqq.);
- briefing of relevant management and reporter (if applicable) (→ mn. 76 et seq.);
- follow-up on implementation of remediation measures (→ mn. 78 et seqq.).

29 These steps shall be specified in the following paragraphs.

I. Plausibility assessment: case or no-case decision

30 As outlined above, the management of a legal entity must conduct an internal investigation as soon as they gain knowledge of alleged misconduct by employees.[46] Such allegations may be raised via reporters using electronic tools that typically allow for written and verbal reports,[47] ombudsmen, external counsel, internal audit reports, emails, phone calls, letters – which usually stem from employees, customers, suppliers, competitors or other third parties –, or the media. It is advisable to open any existent reporting channels for grievances of human rights violations, too, since the latest European and German supply chain legislation obliges larger companies to provide a grievance mechanism.[48] Including reports on potential human rights violations in the general reporting mechanisms is also sensible from an investigation's point of view. For one, the majority of human rights cases involve some sort of misconduct that would fall within the responsibility of an investigation function anyway. Furthermore, the work (i.e. analysing documents, conducting interviews, writing reports, etc.) that needs to be done in such cases is focussed on clarifying a fact scenario, which is, in the end, what the investigation function is well trained to do.

31 But when are allegations of misconduct substantiated enough to initiate an internal investigation? There are no legal provisions that would provide guidance on this question. However, the principles stipulated by the German Code of Criminal Procedure for the initiation of preliminary proceedings by the public prosecutor's office (§ 152 sub. 2 StPO) can be reverted to.[49] Following this, there must be sufficient factual indications of a compliance violation, meaning that such indications must be plausible.[50] This is the case when the reporter states specific facts that make a violation in the sphere of the legal entity seem probable and the allegations are relevant[51] from a compliance point of view.[52]

---

[46] Rotsch Criminal Compliance/Momsen § 34 B mn. 17.

[47] Most tools allow anonymized reporting – which is frequently used – while also providing a secure channel for communicating with the reporters if they are open to it.

[48] This obligation targets all companies with at least 3,000 employees from 1 January 2023 and all entities with at least 1,000 employees from 1 January 2024 on (§ 1 sub. 1 LkSG).

[49] Moosmayer Compliance mn. 312, 214; Ott/Lüneborg CCZ 2019, 71 (76).

[50] Ott/Lüneborg CCZ 2019, 71; Rotsch Criminal Compliance/Momsen § 34 B mn. 20 et seqq.

[51] The principle of proportionality applies, meaning that not all minor allegations necessarily have to be investigated – the management has a certain margin of discretion in this regard.

[52] Ott/Lüneborg CCZ 2019, 71 (73, 76).

It should be noted that as much as mere rumours are not sufficient to initiate an internal investigation, the benchmark should not be too strict either.[53]

II. Initiation of an investigation (investigation mandate)

Whenever allegations of misconduct are plausible according to the principles stated above, a formal investigation mandate should be issued either by the responsible management or – if applicable – the head of or a specialised delegate in the compliance organisation, ideally in adherence to the four-eyes-principle.[54] Such investigation mandate legitimises any subsequent investigation measures.[55] The investigation mandate should specify the allegations in question, the scope of the investigation and designate an adequate investigation team and an investigation lead. Should a case require the consultation of other functions (e.g. HR, ax, security, audit, IP, legal, etc.) or external resources (e.g. advisors such as law firms, auditors, etc.),[56] a corresponding note should be made in the investigation mandate. As a general principle, the staffing of an investigation team should be well balanced and offer specific business knowledge and in-depth investigation expertise. It is also essential that the investigation team is equipped with an independent standing towards local management and/or the business. While assembling the investigation team, it should be checked whether special circumstances require a specific setup of the team due to e.g. cultural aspects or peculiarities of the allegations. For instance, it will usually make sense to compose a team of female investigators if the report is directed at harassment and the witnesses/alleged victims are all female. 32

III. Scope of the investigation (investigation plan)

The principle of proportionality applies to the decision to conduct an internal investigation as well as to the scope of such investigation.[57] It should be ensured that the scope covers all allegations at present and foresees investigation measures that are suited to work through all aspects of the report while simultaneously addressing all related risks. The management's obligation to investigate misconduct is limited to clarifying responsibilities and reinstating compliance of operations for the future.[58] The principle of proportionality thus restricts the extent of measures that would be considered appropriate to clarify a fact scenario, which may be due to unimportance of a fact scenario compared to the cost of an investigation measure, low chance of successful litigation, no potential to sanction former employees, etc. It should also be clarified whether the investigation should be conducted in an open or covert manner, the latter making sense especially when it is likely that accused persons could destroy evidence. 33

Naturally, as more information comes to light, the scope of an investigation might change throughout its course leading to constant adjustments.[59] In larger cases it is advisable to lay down an investigation plan at the beginning to create an overview of 34

[53] Rotsch Criminal Compliance/Momsen § 34 B. mn. 16; Momsen/Grützner WirtschaftsSteuerStrafR-HdB/Grützner/Klaas/Wybitul § 16 mn. 53.

[54] Cf. Godzierz Compliance-Checklisten/Shahhosseini/Ahrens § 11 mn. 30.

[55] Moosmayer Compliance mn. 312, 214; Ott/Lüneborg CCZ 2019, 71 (76).

[56] Godzierz Compliance-Checklisten/Shahhosseini/Ahrens § 11 mn. 17.

[57] Momsen/Grützner WirtschaftsSteuerStrafR-HdB/Grützner/Klaas/Wybitul § 16 mn. 58.

[58] Ott/Lüneborg CCZ 2019, 71 (78).

[59] Ott/Lüneborg CCZ 2019, 71 (78); IBP Compliance Ch. 6 mn. 36.

measures that need to be conducted, and measures already taken to be ready to report promptly to relevant stakeholders.[60] The aims of the investigation should also be noted at the beginning. The most basic aim that will be pursued in every case is the clarification of the allegations i.e. certain relevant events in the past and the assessment of responsibilities which is a prerequisite for the evaluation of potential liability risks and remediation measures.[61] An investigation plan should also outline potentially implicated policies and/or procedures, employed resources, relevant reporting lines and potential approval requirements involved as well as an estimate of timelines.

35 Irrespective of the complexity of an internal investigation, all investigation steps must be legally assessed before they are conducted.[62] The importance of this cannot be stressed enough. For one, investigations serve the aim to reinstate compliance with applicable laws and/or internal rules. It is thus essential that the investigation team acts in compliance with the law to prevent further violations which would make the investigation and its results at least questionable.[63] Depending on the severity of non-compliance of the investigation team with applicable rules and regulations, the consequences of such violations might result in detrimental legal consequences such as liabilities for themselves and their management, and an inability to use results of an investigation as evidence in a legal dispute and thus make it impossible to enforce (damage) claims.[64]

36 The most relevant obstacles to consider are found in German criminal law, data protection law, labour and civil law.[65] A few typical examples shall be pointed out here, however, this list is of course far from exhaustive: it is, for example, necessary to obtain a data protection clearing in the context of securing and assessing data in the course of an e-discovery.[66] In international contexts, it might also be necessary to consider whether the data in question may be accessed from and transferred to another country. Another aspect that may be of relevance is the question whether the works council must be informed with regard to employee interviews and whether there are any entity-specific regulations in place – as a general rule, the works council must be put in a position to assess whether or not such situation might result in a duty to act for the employees represented.[67] It could also be necessary to assess whether certain evidence may be used, meaning to check whether it was obtained in a legal way or not. This might be especially relevant regarding video material, voice recordings or other evidence that is considered especially sensitive from a data protection point of view.

IV. Investigation measures

37 Once the decision to initiate an internal investigation is taken, the phase of collecting information starts. There is surely no one-size-fits-all approach, however, the most common data sources are documentations such as emails, files, project documentation etc.,

---

[60] Cf. Godzierz Compliance-Checklisten/Shahhosseini/Ahrens § 11 mn. 30.

[61] Klaas CCZ 2020, 256 (257); IBP Compliance Ch. 6 mn. 34 et seqq.

[62] Süße/Eckstein Newsdienst Compliance 2014, 71009.

[63] Cf. Weiß CCZ 2014, 136 regarding a comprehensive account of relevant provisions of German Criminal Law investigation teams have a risk of violating during an internal investigation.

[64] Müller öAT 2023, 1 (2); Godzierz Compliance-Checklisten/Shahhosseini/Ahrens § 11 mn. 17, 86 et seqq.; IBP Compliance Ch. 6 mn. 31.

[65] IBP Compliance Ch. 6 mn. 33.

[66] Süße/Eckstein Newsdienst Compliance 2014, 71009; Cf. Momsen/Grützner WirtschaftsSteuerStrafR-HdB/Grützner/Klaas/Wybitul § 16 mn. 199 et seqq. and Herrmann/Zeidler NZA 2017, 1499 (1500) for a comprehensive discussion of the role data protection law plays in the context of investigation measures.

[67] Naber/Ahrens CCZ 2020, 36 (38).

and interviews. It is common practice to first work through any data that can be accessed to collect as much information as possible in order to then ask relevant questions in the interview stage and maybe even be able to reproach interviewed persons with evidence.[68]

1. Collection of data

The first step in the data collection phase is usually the assessment of what kind of data could likely hold relevant information, which department has control over it and which persons would be useful points of contact.[69] It can make sense to conduct so-called informatory interviews before collecting any data to find out about internal processes relevant to the allegations. This will usually enable the investigation team to decide on a useful data collection approach and also identify persons that are able to provide relevant data. All in all, it should be decided on a well-balanced, systematic approach that moves between collecting enough documentation that makes it likely to identify relevant evidence and collecting too much that makes a review inefficient and lengthy. The evaluation of samples can be a helpful approach when the investigation team is faced with large amounts of data. **38**

It is necessary to differentiate between general business data and personal data.[70] Based on labour and civil law, the employer is entitled to review any business data, irrespective of who is responsible for their creation and filing.[71] If an internal investigation, however, requires a review of data in personnel files, the potentially colliding personal rights of the employee and the interest of the employer to investigate allegations must be weighed prior to any investigative measures.[72] The same principles apply to a review of email accounts which are typically especially sensitive with respect to personal data that is not purely business-related and thus needs to be protected.[73] **39**

In many cases it is necessary to conduct an e-discovery, meaning securing email and other virtually saved data (so-called 'litigation hold') which will subsequently be filtered and reviewed according to certain search terms.[74] Before securing any data, it must be reflected who might be relevant custodians and where useful data might be found, e.g. emails, chat data such as Microsoft Teams or WhatsApp etc. Due to the sensitivity of accessing potentially massive amounts of sensitive data, this is a task that should either be fulfilled by internal resources that are especially trained in the field of IT forensics or external experts that should be called in to support such measures.[75] Securing data at an early stage in the internal investigation will have the benefit of protecting it from being manipulated or deleted (this of course applies to all kinds of data, whether it is electronic or hard copies). The decision to actually access the data can be made at a later stage in the investigation. Because of the importance of this process step, it is emphasised again that the review of secured data requires a prior data protection assessment.[76] **40**

[68] Krug/Skoupil NJW 2017, 2374 (2375).

[69] Momsen/Grützner WirtschaftsSteuerStrafR-HdB/Grützner/Klaas/Wybitul § 16 mn. 167.

[70] Cf. Dieners Gesundheitswesen-Compliance-HdB/Zedtwitz von Armin/Cahnbley Ch. 9 mn. 49.

[71] IBP Compliance Ch. 6 mn. 39.

[72] IBP Compliance Ch. 6 mn. 44.

[73] IBP Compliance Ch. 6 mn. 46 et seq.

[74] Cf. Dieners Gesundheitswesen-Compliance-HdB/Zedtwitz von Armin/Cahnbley Ch. 9 mn. 31 et seqq.; Godzierz Compliance-Checklisten/Shahhosseini/Ahrens § 11 mn. 37.

[75] Godzierz Compliance-Checklisten/Shahhosseini/Ahrens § 11 mn. 37.

[76] Godzierz Compliance-Checklisten/Shahhosseini/Ahrens § 11 mn. 17; please see IBP Compliance Ch. 6 mn. 47 et seqq. for details on the differences that apply when the private usage of company email is allowed versus when it is not.

41 All collected documents and other data should be reviewed by the investigation team and put – as much as possible at this stage – into context. In highly technical, scientific, or, for other reasons, highly specific cases it might be necessary to consult subject matter experts for an explanation of documentation and/or certain processes. This will likely lay a valuable foundation for the following interviews.

2. Interviews

42 It is safe to say that interviews are an essential part of (almost) every internal investigation. They provide the description of first-hand experiences, allow an assessment of the credibility of a witness, and may even help the investigation team to fill blanks in the fact scenario presented by other data.[77] In order to make the most of an interview, the investigation team should prepare an as much as possible comprehensive guideline with all relevant questions while approaching interviewees on rather short notice to make use of potential surprising effects.[78] It can also make sense to keep the topic of the interview rather vague or unknown altogether should there be any potential of interviewees destroying evidence.[79]

43 There is no set of legal provisions governing interviews conducted during an internal investigation under German law,[80] however, there are some best practices that shall be outlined here:

a) Order of interviews

44 The most appropriate order of interviews must be assessed on a case-by-case basis. Usually, so-called informatory interviews with persons such as subject matter experts who are able to give an overview on processes and/or describe/explain specific specialised topics should be prioritised so that the investigation team can establish a deeper understanding of the wider circumstances the alleged misconduct might have played out in.[81] The information collected in these interviews gives the investigation team a good understanding of events which will help them dive deeper into the issues at hand with the witnesses, which would usually be interviewed in the second phase. At the end of this phase, the investigation team will ideally have collected important information on the event the whistleblower reported on and be knowledgeable about the alleged concerned person(s) who should be confronted at last if the investigation strategy and/or other timing factors allow.[82] It may be necessary to approach certain interviewees several times, however, confronting a person with allegations for the first time – especially the alleged person(s) – has a momentum that cannot be upheld during repeated conversations.[83]

45 The investigation team might, especially if some time has passed since the alleged violation took place, come across the obstacle that persons that could have given valuable insights have left the company. It must be decided on a case-by-case basis whether such persons can and should be approached nevertheless. This can make sense especially if the person was a trusted colleague that will likely respect the confidentiality of the investigation, has essential knowledge relevant for the case, and left the company on good terms.

---

[77] Herrmann/Zeidler NZA 2017, 1499 (1505); Krug/Skoupil NJW 2017, 2374.

[78] Zimmermann/Lingscheid CB 2013, 23 (24).

[79] Reinhardt/Kaindl CB 2017, 210 (212).

[80] Krug/Skoupil NJW 2017, 2374; however, please note that provisions may be set within a works agreement.

[81] Momsen/Grützner WirtschaftsSteuerStrafR-HdB/Grützner/Klaas/Wybitul § 16 mn. 368.

[82] Momsen/Grützner WirtschaftsSteuerStrafR-HdB/Grützner/Klaas/Wybitul § 16 mn. 368.

[83] Krug/Skoupil NJW 2017, 2374 (2375).

However, there is always a risk of external persons leaking confidential information presented to them during the interview to the public, which is why in many cases it is not advisable to ask former employees to participate in the interview process. The sensitivity of a case should at all times be matched with an equally cautious approach.

Another deciding factor when considering the order of interviews is whether there is a likelihood that some persons might destroy evidence.[84] To prevent this, as described above, data collection activities should be performed beforehand but where this is not possible, the timing of the interview can be essential. **46**

b) Time and place

The success of an interview can depend on the time and location in which it is taking place. Interviews can be done on the premises of the entity or, especially when witnesses are worried about being seen by colleagues, other appropriate venues.[85] If the conversation is held on the premises, a neutral meeting room should be chosen. Generally, interviews should be held in a calm and neutral environment and a comfortable time frame should be assigned so that all participants have enough energy to focus on a potentially lengthy and difficult conversation. This is especially relevant for interviews that are being held across different time zones as seen on many occasions during the Covid-19 pandemic when investigation teams were often not able to travel to meet interviewees in person and had to switch to remote interviews, i.e. conducting video calls. **47**

The ongoing debate among investigation professionals of whether there should be a return to the pre-pandemic way of doing interviews in person since all travel restrictions have been lifted by now, should, in the author's opinion, be decided in accordance with the needs of each case.[86] It has been proven that investigations can be done entirely remotely when circumstances require it. Naturally, there were severe downsides to this, such as investigators not being able to make sure that conversations were held in a confidential space since they would not be able to check for third parties listening or recordings being done, interviewees not switching on their cameras and thus not allowing for a personal impression which is an essential part of any credibility assessment, or simply an increase of the already difficult task to read people's facial expressions and body language and trying to figure out whether they are under distress, likely lying etc. – this is in many cases close to impossible through a screen. It is most certainly also harder to create a comfortable atmosphere and bond with interviewees over camera. **48**

With all these downsides in mind, there are very significant upsides to conducting remote interviews that have shown great value with regard to efficiency.[87] For one, practicing remote interviews emphasised that not all interviews are that sensitive that they would have to be done in person necessarily. Informatory interviews especially can very well be done remotely since the interviewees themselves are usually not affected by the allegations. The same is usually true for less central witnesses and in cases where the investigation team would have additional, rather short queries after having already conducted an interview. Furthermore, for less severe allegations it might suffice to conduct completely remote investigation since there is little pressure on the participants on the one hand and less importance/risk on the other hand for the entity. All in all, remote interviews are likely to save a lot of time on the side of the investigation team and thus will make them much more efficient as before the pandemic. A well-balanced general **49**

---

[84] Zimmermann/Lingscheid CB 2013, 23 (24).

[85] Zimmermann/Lingscheid CB 2013, 23 (24); Naber/Ahrens CCZ 2020, 36 (39).

[86] Cf. Miege CCZ 2023, 1 (4) for the results of a survey during which representatives of 103 (mostly) German companies were asked to rate the influence of the pandemic on internal investigations.

[87] Godzierz Compliance-Checklisten/Shahhosseini/Ahrens § 11 mn. 71.

approach that includes both in-person and remote interviews will lead to an increase of productivity while still ensuring high quality outcomes.

c) Introduction

50 The interview should always start with an introduction of the interviewing investigation team and a little small talk to create a positive and constructive atmosphere which is likely to calm the nerves of potentially anxious interviewees.[88] However, it should be made clear, that the investigation team is representing the employer and thus do not serve the interests of the interviewee.[89] The team should always comprise at least two persons so that one person can focus on asking questions and following up on unclear aspects of the interviewee's report while the other one takes proper and extensive notes.[90] This is also sensible with respect to purposes of proof. While it is not advisable to have investigators conduct interviews on their own, they should be sensitised that a large number of persons may very likely intimidate an interviewee and thus be detrimental to a good atmosphere.

51 Taking notes is the standard way to document interviewee statements. Although permissible under German law, it is rather uncommon to film or take a voice recording of the conversation. All participants must agree if the latter approach is chosen.

d) Purpose/background of the interview

52 Following the introduction, a short account of the purpose of the interview is given, which will usually be the assessment of a fact scenario as presented by a reporter.[91] Depending on the strategy chosen for the interview, the investigation team either describes the alleged misconduct in detail or remains rather vague at this point and lets the interviewees talk more or less freely before approaching them with allegations. The latter approach is usually used in the context of interviewing the alleged subject.

e) Duty to self-incriminate?

53 Next, it should be clarified that the interview is not a labour law hearing and that the ultimate goal of the investigation team is to establish facts. Although the extent of the duty of employees to (truthfully) testify towards their employers is disputed,[92] the author deems that – in most cases – the right approach is to inform interviewees that any information collected during the interview can become part of an investigation report which will be kept strictly confidential but could become part of a civil litigation case, criminal charges, or could be confiscated by the public prosecutor and thus become the subject of official proceedings.[93] The author considers it part of a fair process to inform interviewees that they might incriminate themselves through their statements.[94] Investigation teams may also consider adding that interviewees do not have to burden themselves but are allowed to skip certain questions or end the interview altogether and consult with an attorney.[95] There may be, however, situations in which such explanations may foreseeably

[88] Momsen/Grützner WirtschaftsSteuerStrafR-HdB/Grützner/Klaas/Wybitul § 16 mn. 396 et seq.

[89] Zimmermann/Lingscheid CB 2013, 23 (24).

[90] Cf. Krug/Skoupil NJW 2017, 2374 (2378).

[91] IBP Compliance Ch. 6 mn. 75.

[92] IBP Compliance Ch. 6 mn. 71 et seqq.; Naber/Ahrens CCZ 2020, 36 (38); Momsen/Grützner WirtschaftsSteuerStrafR-HdB/Grützner/Klaas/Wybitul § 16 mn. 364, 432 et seqq., Süße/Eckstein Newsdienst Compliance 2014, 71009.

[93] Süße/Eckstein Newsdienst Compliance 2014, 71009; IBP Compliance Ch. 6 mn. 76.

[94] Müller öAT 2023, 1 (2 et seq.); cf. Greco/Caracas NStZ 2015, 7 with a comprehensive discussion of this topic.

[95] Krug/Skoupil NJW 2017, 2374 (2375).

lead to witnesses not cooperating with the investigation team and making incomplete, incorrect or no statement at all. The preferable approach has to be assessed separately for every situation.

f) Information on data processing and handling of interview notes

The interviewees must – since this is considered data processing – be informed that 54 their personal data and the information reported will be saved in the form of interview notes.[96] Some practitioners in the field ask interviewees to review and sign these notes after completion of the interview.[97] It should be noted that this practice is not a necessity and can easily lead to complex discussions and potential detrimental substantial changes to the notes.[98] It is only natural that interviewees might at a later point after the interview, especially when given time to go through the notes and reflect on their statements, have a more collected and guarded way of framing events.[99] If such approach is chosen nevertheless, the investigation team should mark any changes made by the interviewee so that any differing accounts can be distinguished.

g) Confidentiality

Additionally, interviewees should be informed of their duty to keep the investigation 55 and the interview itself strictly confidential and that any violation of this may lead to claims for damages and other disciplinary measures.[100] Another note should be made that any retaliatory acts towards a whistleblower or other persons providing information on a case are forbidden and will be strictly followed-up on as compliance violations. If existent, reference should be made to any internal framework governing the internal investigation process.

h) Right to bring an attorney/member of the works council

It is common practice to allow an interviewee to bring support to an interview, i.e. 56 usually an attorney or a member of the works council.[101]

It is a strategic question whether or not the employer covers the costs of an attorney. 57 There are good arguments for employers to cover such costs if the employee is (also) subject to proceedings by the public prosecutor's office or other authorities.[102] It is usually in the best interest of an entity to support the engagement of a defence attorney in such cases since legal support is likely to secure the procedural correctness of any measures towards the employee. Furthermore, a defence attorney can support the employee in pursuing and staying true to a particular defence strategy (especially relevant regarding accused persons) and may also facilitate the alignment of a potential joint defence strategy. Please note that most defence attorneys will not agree to the rates stipulated in the German Act on the Remuneration of Lawyers (*Rechtsanwaltsvergütungsgesetz*, RVG) but will charge higher fees.[103]

---

[96] Cf. Art. 13, 14 GDPR that stipulate the relevant informatory duties, Momsen/Grützner WirtschaftsSteuerStrafR-HdB/Grützner/Klaas/Wybitul § 16 mn. 363; Herrmann/Zeidler NZA 2017, 1499 (1500).

[97] IBP Compliance Ch. 6 mn. 80; cf. Krug/Skoupil NJW 2017, 2374 (2378).

[98] Naber/Ahrens CCZ 2020, 36 (42).

[99] Cf. Krug/Skoupil NJW 2017, 2374 (2378).

[100] Momsen/Grützner WirtschaftsSteuerStrafR-HdB/Grützner/Klaas/Wybitul § 16 mn. 459 et seqq.

[101] Cf. Reinhardt/Kaindl CB 2017, 210 (212); Rotsch Criminal Compliance/Momsen § 34 B mn. 14; Momsen/Grützner WirtschaftsSteuerStrafR-HdB/Grützner/Klaas/Wybitul § 16 mn. 450 et seqq. for more details.

[102] Please cf. → fn. 34 regarding the requirement to pay income tax when the employer covers attorney fees for employees; Naber/Ahrens CCZ 2020, 36 (39).

[103] Naber/Ahrens CCZ 2020, 36 (39).

58 An employee may bring a member of the works council to an interview if internal works agreements provide such a right. If not, it must be assessed on a case-by-case basis whether the prerequisites of a legal participation right of the works council are fulfilled.[104] If both is not the case, it will be a mere strategic question whether the interviewee will be allowed to bring the works council member of his choice for support.

i) Structuring the interview

59 It is highly advisable to give a structure to the interview by preparing a guideline with all the aspects outlined above that the interviewee should be informed on, which are then followed by a list of questions.[105] These are based on the fact scenario identified so far and clustered by topic.[106] Bundling related questions can make a lot of sense when larger ground needs to be covered, and will prevent the interviewers to get lost in the details – this will also enable them to act more flexibly in the course of the interview. In many cases, witnesses will answer a question more broadly to give the interviewers a good understanding of contexts which leads to sub-questions often being answered without the interviewer having to explicitly ask. Furthermore, the natural course of an interview might lead to the discussion of aspects that the investigation team had planned to address at a later point in the interview. A thorough outline is thus a crucial basis for the investigation team to review during the interview whether any relevant aspects have not yet been discussed due to the flow of the conversation.

60 Investigation teams should adhere to a friendly, open, and non-judgemental way of communicating with interviewees.[107] Most importantly, they should remind themselves that the way certain fact scenarios present themselves at first can completely change throughout an investigation. This is especially true with respect to interviews. The perception of one witness may completely or in parts differ from the account of another. A proper investigation team does not only have an open and neutral mindset towards interviewees and their reports at the beginning of a case; they maintain this stance throughout the course of the investigation. This is especially true with regard to conducting interviews which can be influenced by prejudice towards certain interviewees that might have resulted from prior interviews or other data. It is essential that investigators are willing to constantly rethink their understanding of the course of events based on the latest picture the evidence accumulated so far may draw.

61 The interviewee should, as a warm-up, first be asked about his current position, responsibilities, and – if relevant – about his prior career.[108] This allows the interviewee to present himself and helps setting a comfortable tone for the conversation. This will usually be followed by more general questions regarding the fact scenario the investigation team is trying to establish while becoming more and more specific as the interview progresses. It is essential that the investigation team leaves a lot of space for interviewees to present their account of the events in a – as much as possible – freely and uninterrupted manner.[109] This aim can best be met by formulating open questions (wh-questions: what? who? when? where? why?).[110] This is the only way to capture a description of the course of events that

---

[104] Cf. §§ 81 sub. 4 sent. 3, 82 sub. 2 sent. 2, 83 sub. 1 sent. 2, 84 sub. 1 sent. 2 BetrVG, cf. Krug/Skoupil NJW 2017, 2374 (2376); Naber/Ahrens CCZ 2020, 36 (39).

[105] Momsen/Grützner WirtschaftsSteuerStrafR-HdB/Grützner/Klaas/Wybitul § 16 mn. 392 et seqq.

[106] Cf. Krug/Skoupil NJW 2017, 2374 (2375).

[107] Zimmermann/Lingscheid CB 2013, 23 (24).

[108] Zimmermann/Lingscheid CB 2013, 23 (24).

[109] Momsen/Grützner WirtschaftsSteuerStrafR-HdB/Grützner/Klaas/Wybitul § 16 mn. 389; Krug/Skoupil NJW 2017, 2374 (2376).

[110] Zimmermann/Lingscheid CB 2013, 23 (24).

is not (extensively) altered by interpretations of the interviewers.[111] Additional questions should be asked when descriptions are either fragmented or frankly too succinct.[112] The right place to ask more confrontative and narrow questions, which is usually a part where the interviewers take up more speaking time, is at the end of the interview. These serve to validate former accounts or to discuss potential inconsistencies between the data and explanations presented by interviewees themselves or in contrast with other information collected. It goes without saying that any attempts to threaten or pressure interviewees into answering questions are not acceptable.[113]

Any evidence that an interviewee could sensibly be confronted with should be prepared 62 in alignment with the questions. There is also the (rather rarely used) option to provide relevant documents to interviewees prior to an interview so that they can prepare.[114] While this might make sense in complex scenarios that occurred a long time ago, this approach should usually not be used with implicated persons or when there is a risk that sensitive company data might be leaked.[115]

Finally, interviews should be ended with asking interviewees whether there is anything 63 else they would like to report and by emphasizing again that the interview itself and all the topics spoken about are highly confidential and may not be shared with third parties.

3. Other measures

Other measures that can be considered, although rather rarely conducted, are searches 64 and video surveillance.

Especially searches are admissible in order to clarify and prevent criminal violations.[116] 65 This can include searching lockers, closets and other shelves and compartments used by employees as long as they are owned by the employer.[117] Searching personal belongings, bags, clothes and other private containers, however, can only be done with the consent of the respective employee, since these spaces are protected by the general right of privacy under German law.[118]

Hidden video surveillance is justifiable only in very limited cases with concrete indi- 66 cations of criminal misconduct that must be detrimental to the employer.[119] In addition, there must be no milder measures that could lead to the same success in clarifying the allegations and the principle of proportionality must be respected. The same requirements apply to the surveillance of computer programmes via keyloggers, automatic screenshots, etc.[120]

Other than securing and reviewing emails without knowledge of the employees con- 67 cerned, secretly wiretapping and recording (telephone) conversations is illegal since such measures violate data protection laws and also the general right to privacy.[121]

111 Cf. Krug/Skoupil NJW 2017, 2374 (2376).
112 Zimmermann/Lingscheid CB 2013, 23 (24).
113 Süße/Eckstein Newsdienst Compliance 2014, 71009.
114 Krug/Skoupil NJW 2017, 2374 (2375); Naber/Ahrens CCZ 2020, 36 (40).
115 Cf. Krug/Skoupil NJW 2017, 2374 (2375).
116 BAG 13.12.2007 – 2 AZR 537/06 = NJW 2008, 2732; BAG 15.04.2014 – 1 ABR 2/13 = NZW 2014, 551; Stück ArbRAktuell 2020, 408 (409).
117 Cf. BAG 20.06.2013 – 2 AZR 546/12 = NZA 2014, 143.
118 BAG 15.04.2014 – 1 ABR 2/13 = NZW 2014, 551.
119 BAG 21.06.2012 – 2 AZR 153/11 = NJW 2012, 3594; Stück ArbRAktuell 2020, 408 (410).
120 BAG 27.07.2017 – 2 AZR 681/16 = NZA 2017, 1327.
121 BAG 23.04.2009 – 6 AZR 189/08 = NJW 2010, 104.

68 More exotic measures such as DNA analysis are also strictly forbidden if conducted without consent by the respective employee.[122] Such measures obviously have a grave impact on the right of privacy and should thus, if considered at all, never be done in disagreement.

69 Any other measures such as open-source research, detective work, observations, etc. must always be assessed with respect to data protection and personality rights of the persons concerned and/or applicable specific regulations and, finally, must be appropriate and proportionate.[123]

V. Investigation report

70 The point at which the investigation team deems that they have either clarified the allegations presented by the whistleblower and/or exhausted all (legal) means of investigation accessible to them, marks the end of the investigation. If the internal investigation, based on the available and reviewed facts and evidence, confirms the allegations and/or[124] identifies a compliance violation, the respective facts, evidence, and conclusions shall be summarised in an investigation report.[125]

71 Key to an investigation report is that the investigation team structures all information presented to them in a comprehensible manner that allows third parties not involved in the investigation to understand the key facts and conclusions.[126] The investigation team shall thus independently assess and weigh evidence and describe why some data or information given by interviewees is credible or less credible. The report should be condensed, yet, for the sake of objectivity and transparency give enough information that enables third parties to comprehend the reasoning behind the report.

72 Every investigation report shall contain recommendations on remedial actions. This includes disciplinary measures regarding any subjects found responsible for having conducted or aided and abetted a compliance violation based on the respective severity of their wrongdoing, and/or their impact, and/or their level of personal responsibility, while also taking all potential mitigating and aggravating factors into account.

73 In most cases it is also necessary to propose other remedial actions that address identified process weaknesses, control failures or system shortcomings. Depending on the case, the investigation team's competencies allow for more or less detailed recommendations. Irrespective of this, the part on recommendations for remedial actions should always make clear who is responsible to take action, otherwise it will be hard to hold specific functions responsible in the follow-up process.

74 The structure of an investigation report is typically similar to the following:

- reference to the investigation mandate (when and by whom was it issued?);
- scope of the investigation (case number; source of the report; date; name of the reporter if known; attachments if provided by reporter);
- investigation team;

[122] Müller öAT 2023, 1 (3).

[123] Müller öAT 2023, 1 (4); Stück ArbRAktuell 2020, 408 (409).

[124] An investigation report should also be drafted when the original allegations were not found to be substantiated but another compliance violation surfaced throughout the investigation. The investigation team is of course obliged to clarify such chance discoveries as well and should lay down all relevant facts in the report.

[125] Thüsing Beschäftigtendatenschutz/Granetzny § 20 mn. 86; Dieners Gesundheitswesen-Compliance-HdB/Zedtwitz von Armin/Cahnbley Ch. 9 mn. 48.

[126] Dieners Gesundheitswesen-Compliance-HdB/Zedtwitz von Armin/Cahnbley Ch. 9 mn. 49.

- description of investigation steps (actions taken; description of the appropriateness of the measures according to applicable law; strategy/logic of the approach and timing of measures);
- management summary regarding allegations, findings, and key remediation actions;
- fact finding and evaluation (separated by allegation if there are more than one): (i) account of the fact scenario, its background and involved persons; (ii) outline of the applicable law and internal regulations; (iii) description of identified misconduct;
- conclusions ('lessons learned') including description of lack of controls and process weaknesses;
- recommendations for remediation measures (disciplinary actions and/or procedural improvements);
- outline of reporting requirements and/or further action items and/or risk exposure (if applicable);
- note on feedback to reporter (if reporter can be reached).

If the allegations were not found to be substantiated, a shorter notice (clearance report) **75** should be drawn up that outlines the investigation measures taken and why the identified fact scenario did not support the whistleblower's report.

VI. Briefing of relevant stakeholders

Once the investigation report is concluded, the investigation team informs the respon- **76** sible management by presenting its findings. To protect a whistleblower or other implicated persons from retaliation, it might be necessary to amend an investigation report before handing it over to third parties.[127] The investigation team should be aware of its advisory function to the management, meaning, they should outline the identified facts, explain legal implications, and propose appropriate remedial actions which often includes involving other specialist functions. Although the management is responsible to take on the task of following through with all necessary remedial actions, the investigation team plays an important role in overseeing the remediation process and supports the management in making sure to nudge all involved functions to actually execute all agreed upon measures.

Part of the remedial actions may also be to inform relevant stakeholders outside of the **77** respective entity. These can include, as the case may be, other companies of a group, business partners, authorities etc. Especially with larger company groups located in different countries, forwarding information containing personal data between the different group companies should always be assessed with respect to data protection law. While forwarding information within the European Economic Area (EEA) is subject to the general rules of the GDPR, it must be evaluated whether there is an appropriate data protection level when personal data is provided to a recipient outside the EEA.[128]

---

[127] The report can either be rephrased or the respective names and information that would point to the respective person can be blackened.

[128] Rotsch Criminal Compliance/Moosmeyer § 34 B mn. 78; Cf. Momsen/Grützner WirtschaftsSteuerStrafR-HdB/Grützner/Klaas/Wybitul § 16 mn. 587 et seqq. for a comprehensive description of data protection requirements for the different scenarios.

VII. Remediation process

78 Remediation is an essential response to any (partially) substantiated compliance violation or other shortcomings identified during an internal investigation. It is the management's obligation to carefully follow up on identified personal misconduct and procedural weaknesses; omissions to implement appropriate remediation measures can lead to the management's personal liability.[129] It is thus essential to consider whether similar misconduct is likely to play out in another part of the company or other group company, why there were no controls in place to stop the misconduct from happening or why implemented controls were not sufficient to prevent the violation, responsibilities for remediation measures, and how and by whom future improvements to the compliance management system should be controlled.[130] Identifying and thoroughly addressing individual misconduct as well as process and/or controlling failures serves the continuous improvement of the compliance management system of the concerned entity and fosters organisational development.[131] An analysis of potential patterns that might show systematic issues throughout different cases is an essential part of an efficient remediation process.[132]

79 The overall accountability for the decision on and implementation of disciplinary measures and other remedial actions lies with the responsible management. It is advisable that the management consults with the right experts regarding specific measures. This is essential especially with regard to misconduct violating laws since it is the management's legal obligation to put a stop to such actions. This can only be ensured when the respective specialists are asked to take on or oversee remediation measures concerning their field of expertise, and when they assess what would be necessary to establish processes that ensure compliance in the future.

1. Disciplinary measures

a) Decision body

80 Disciplinary measures should, due to their sensitivity and the rather complex and employee-friendly German labour law, not be imposed by the management alone. It is sensible to at least include a human resources function and maybe – depending on the severity and complexity of the case – also a labour law specialist. In larger groups of companies, it can make sense to establish a disciplinary process that calls for a specific group-wide setup of a committee deciding on disciplinary actions.[133] A unified approach will foster comparability and objectivity throughout the group and thus promote a fair treatment of employees.

81 Such disciplinary committees would usually comprise the above-mentioned human resources and labour law expertise, but also a representative of the compliance department entrusted with the internal investigation serving as rapporteur and objective observer, and – if appropriate – any other subject matter experts involved in the investigation. In more complex cases, all these functions should convene in a more formal setting, either in person or at least via video call, while in simpler cases a circular or emails should suffice.

---

[129] Süße/Eckstein Newsdienst Compliance 2014, 71009; Momsen/Grützner WirtschaftsSteuerStrafR-HdB/Grützner/Klaas/Wybitul § 16 mn. 629.

[130] Momsen/Grützner WirtschaftsSteuerStrafR-HdB/Grützner/Klaas/Wybitul § 16 mn. 631.

[131] Godzierz Compliance-Checklisten/Shahhosseini/Ahrens § 11 mn. 88.

[132] Jüttner CCZ 2022, 276 et seqq.

[133] Cf. Rotsch Criminal Compliance/Moosmeyer § 34 B mn. 77.

b) Typical sanctions

The responsible management, supported by the respective human resources department is accountable for the implementation of any disciplinary measures. Local laws and co-determination requirements (involvement of works council or similar) must be taken into account when deciding on such measures. Under § 36 HinSchG, the German Whistleblower Protection Act foresees a revision of the burden of proof for whistleblowers claiming to having been subjected to retaliation; the human resources function should therefore make sure to document all disciplinary measures adopted and their underlying rationale in accordance with its regular documentation processes (i.e., in personnel files). Such documentation may turn out to be valuable in potential future labour law litigation cases when the former employer must proof that a disciplinary measure was founded on misconduct of the employee and thus is no act of retaliation. **82**

Typical examples[134] for disciplinary measures are: **83**

- admonition, (formal) warning, verbal or written;
- reduction or forfeiture of variable compensation;
- withholding or dismissal of promotion, demotion or transfer to another position;
- suspension;
- notice of termination or summary dismissal.

c) Determination of appropriate disciplinary measures

The decision-making process for determining disciplinary measures consists of four stages: (i) assessing the severity of the identified misconduct, (ii) identifying the level of personal responsibility, (iii) consideration of any mitigating and aggravating factors, and (iv) the conclusion. **84**

Indicators for severe misconduct are for example the seriousness of an offence (e.g., violations of antitrust law, corruption, tax evasion, serious cases of (sexual) harassment, accounting-related fraud), repeated, systematic or organised conduct, physical danger to employees or third parties, involvement of members of management or even senior management, relevance for more than one group company or the entire group, public attention of misconduct due to significant financial implications or damage to reputation. **85**

Determining the level of personal responsibility can be categorised by the level of intent, the gravest being wilful and malicious intent marked by personal gain, resulting in a criminal offence. In these cases, the respective individual acted knowingly or with wilful disregard which resulted in financial, organisational, and/or reputational damage and led to personal enrichment. The conduct of individuals on the next less severe level is marked by committing a compliance violation wilfully and maliciously. The individuals in these cases also disregarded applicable norms knowingly or wilfully, however, without their actions leading to personal enrichment. This stage is followed by individuals who acted recklessly and without a harmful intent. Here, individuals should have known about their non-compliant actions but tried to serve the interests of the organisation without any personal gains in mind. The least severe level of personal responsibility is negligence, which marks misconduct that is caused by carelessness, lack of knowledge and/or training or other errors. **86**

Typical aggravating factors that can be taken into consideration are large losses, reputational damages or other substantial harm caused by the identified misconduct, dishonest and systematic behaviour, frequency, repetition, prolonged duration, personal enrichment, criminal nature of the violation, a senior position of the employee, acts of **87**

[134] Cf. Godzierz Compliance-Checklisten/Shahhosseini/Ahrens § 11 mn. 81 et seqq.

concealment, high costs of the investigation, fines, settlements/disputes, establishing a toxic culture, physical and/or mental harm to others, obstruction of the investigation, etc. Mitigating factors on the other hand can be seen in any behaviour displayed that is supportive of the investigation (truthfulness, transparency, etc.) and remedial actions, acts committed in the best interest of the organisation, inabilities to follow processes due to misunderstanding/lack of training or knowledge, faulty/lacking processes, rules or guidelines, individual hardships, efforts to repair any damages incurred, etc.

88 All these factors should be carefully weighed to finally identify appropriate disciplinary measures on a case-by-case-basis.

2. Other remedial measures

89 The approach to other remedial actions concerning processes or controls should be more flexible since there is a seemingly unlimited variety of measures suitable to address different cases. Remedial measures shall be specified and tailored to address the identified shortcomings, avoid recurrence of misconduct, and foster organisational learning. Taking up the facts and general recommendations from the investigation report, specific remedial actions should be defined and implemented by the responsible management with the support of the respective affected functions.

90 Each remediation measure should be assigned to competent specialist functions or dedicated central functions responsible for governing a certain area of expertise (e.g. quality department, tax department, data protection department, etc.) first. The management and designated specialist functions will form a working group which will exchange information on the progress of remediation measures on an appropriate basis. In cases with a larger extent of remediation measures, it can be recommendable to conduct regular meetings (typically either in person or via video call) to keep potentially intertwined working streams up to date on the overall progress, while in less severe cases, again, updating the working group via email etc. should be sufficient.

3. Interim measures

91 At each stage of the investigation, the investigation team must consider whether credible evidence indicates imminent risk of harm and thus requires suitable interim measures or whether it is reasonable to immediately stop any ongoing misconduct, prevent (further) breaches, or the increase of a risk for damages of the relevant entity or any third party. If this is the case, the investigation team together with the responsible management and any other potentially involved functions should initiate an interim decision-making process.[135]

92 If any interim disciplinary measures must be taken, the decision body outlined above should discuss on short notice. If urgent, this can be done in a simplified manner, e.g. via email. If the nature of the interim measure is more procedural, the investigation team should approach the most competent function while ensuring that all necessary approvals, especially those of the responsible management, are obtained. All decisions should be documented for a potential later review and reported to all relevant stakeholders on a need-to-know basis.

93 Examples for interim measures are:

- personal coaching of affected employees to make them stop relevant misconduct;

---

[135] Cf. Momsen/Grützner WirtschaftsSteuerStrafR-HdB/Grützner/Klaas/Wybitul § 16 mn. 471 et seqq.

- restriction/withdrawal of access to specific tools, data bases, IT systems, properties, etc.;
- deprivation of powers of attorney, internal/external authority, enforcement of blocking periods;
- withholding of variable compensation components and/or promotions;
- suspension to limit the risk of obstruction of the investigation, misuse of assets, and/ or damage to the respective entities' reputation;
- negotiation with or blacklisting of business partners, or termination and replacement of business relationships;
- 'ringfencing': replacement of certifiers when preliminary findings give reason to doubt the integrity of an individual, thus limiting the risk of false (financial) reporting;
- measures to protect individuals from harassment, extortion, etc. through the engagement of personal security, implementation of mandatory home office, etc.

VIII. Data retention and deletion cycle

Any data collected during an internal investigation must be documented, retained, **94** and deleted in accordance with the applicable internal rules and policies as well as data protection regulations. A retention schedule should be established which determines that personal data is not kept longer than necessary, meaning, if there is no legal reason to retain and store the respective data, it should be deleted accordingly.

CHAPTER 9
INTERNATIONAL COOPERATION IN CRIMINAL MATTERS

Bibliography: Burchard, Europäische E-Evidence-Verordnung, ZRP 2019, 164; Costa/Cardoso/Ramos, The second life of the European arrest warrant: an analysis of the protective potential of mutual recognition against extradition to third states, TCLR 3, 2024, 18; Hüttemann, Die E-Evidence-Verordnung: Pioniermodell für das digitale Zeitalter oder Preisgabe der Staatlichkeit?, NZWiSt 2024, 81; Schomburg/Heimrich, Mutual Recognition of Extradition Decisions – A Critical Analsysis on the ECJ's Judgment in Kamekris: A Missed Opportunity? preprint eucrim 2025, Vol. 20(3); Schomburg/Müller, INTERPOL – Eine Fallanalyse, WiJ 2022, 25; Schomburg/Reitner, Die Bestimmung des 'idem factum' nach Art. 50 GrCh, Art. 54 SDÜ bei wirtschaftsstrafrechtlichen Vorwürfen, ZWH 2021, 189; Sunde, Auslieferung durch die Schweiz bei Steuerdelikten, NStZ 2022, 527.

Table of contents

A. Introduction: legal bases of international cooperation in criminal matters ... 186
B. Extradition ... 188
I. Introduction ... 188
II. Procedure ... 189
III. Interpol/SIS ... 192
IV. Extradition to third countries ... 193
1. Requirements for extradition under the IRG ... 193
a) Double criminality ... 193
b) Reciprocity ... 194
c) Statute of limitation ... 194
2. Bars to extradition ... 195
a) Non-extradition of German nationals and procedure on extradition of EU citizens ... 195
b) Other bars to extradition including specialty ... 196
c) § 73 IRG: threat of 'violation of core principles of German legal system' ... 196
d) Absentia ... 197
e) Ne bis in idem ... 197
f) Fiscal offences ... 198
3. Aut dedere aut judicare ... 199
V. Extradition between EU Member States: EAW ... 199
1. Introduction ... 199
2. Formal aspects ... 199
3. Deadlines and procedure ... 200
4. Requirements of surrender ... 200
a) Double criminality ... 200
b) Reciprocity ... 201
c) Statute of limitation ... 201
5. Bars to extradition ... 201
a) Mandatory reasons for refusal of surrender ... 201
b) Optional reasons for refusal of surrender ... 202
c) European ordre public (§ 73 sent. 2 IRG) ... 202

C. Mutual legal assistance ... 202
I. Introduction ... 202
II. Procedure ... 203
1. Incoming requests ... 204
2. Outgoing requests ... 205
III. Interpol ... 205
IV. Mutual legal assistance with third countries ... 206
V. Mutual legal assistance within the European Union ... 207
1. European Investigation Order (EIO) ... 208
2. Joint Investigation Teams (JITs) ... 211
3. European Preservation and Production Order (e-Evidence) 211
4. European Public Prosecutor's Office (EPPO) ... 213
D. Transfer of sentenced persons ... 214
I. Enforcement of foreign judgments in Germany ... 214
II. Enforcement of German judgments abroad ... 215
E. Execution of fines ... 216

A. Introduction: legal bases of international cooperation in criminal matters

1 While international cooperation in criminal matters is a very formalised procedure under German law, German authorities generally take a very cooperative approach vis-à-vis requests from other countries. In doing so, they rely on the commitment of the German Constitution (*Grundgesetz*, GG) to international law (Art. 25, 59 para. 2 GG) which requires German courts to give effect to international law and the principle of mutual trust[1] to allow as far as possible for mutual legal assistance (*Rechtshilfefreundlichkeit*).[2] Due to the complexity of the matters, specialist knowledge is often required to adequately deal with the relevant proceedings. The complexity arises in light of the various factors that may impact the legal requirements of individual requests for mutual legal assistance in a broad sense (encompassing extradition, enforcement assistance and other requests) and the complex structure of the key statute, the Act on International Cooperation in Criminal Matters (*Gesetz über die internationale Rechtshilfe in Strafsachen*, IRG).[3] These factors include amongst others:

2 – Is the request aimed at the extradition/surrender of a wanted person (such request being referred to as an 'extradition request') or other forms of cooperation, for example the provision of information, the questioning of witnesses or suspects, search and seizure of evidence etc. (such request being referred to as an 'MLA request', → mn. 61 et seqq.)?
– Is Germany requesting cooperation (such request being referred to as an 'outgoing request') or requested to cooperate by another country (such request being referred to as an 'incoming request')?

[1] BVerfG 17.5.2017 – 2 BvR 893/17, NStZ-RR 2017, 226 (228).
[2] Federal Ministry of Justice and Consumer Protection (*Bundesministerium der Justiz und für Verbraucherschutz*, BMJV), Referentenentwurf: Entwurf eines Gesetzes zur Neuregelung des Rechts der Internationalen Rechtshilfe in Strafsachen, p. 267, 283 <https://www.bmjv.de/SharedDocs/Downloads/DE/Gesetzgebung/RefE/RefE_IRG-Reform.pdf?__blob=publicationFile&v=2> (last accessed: 21.10.2025);
[3] The IRG is currently being revised; a draft law was recently published (cf. fn. 2) but has not been adopted yet.

- Is there an existing international treaty (including declarations and reservations) in force between Germany and the other country? In case of multiple 'layers' of international law, one has to distinguish: Is the particular request governed by a specific bilateral treaty, if not, is there a multilateral treaty applicable? Such a treaty may create an obligation to cooperate with the requesting state under international law.

Germany requests extradition from Switzerland in a case of tax evasion. Whether or not Switzerland is obliged to extradite is generally governed by the 1957 European Convention. Art. 5 of the 1957 European Convention refers to separate agreements with regard to fiscal offences. The Second Additional Protocol to this agreement is such a separate agreement and includes an obligation to extradite for fiscal offences such as tax evasion in Art. 2 of the 1957 European Convention. However, Switzerland has declared it will not apply Art. 2 with the result that there would be no obligation to extradite. Still, the Convention Implementing the Schengen Agreement (CISA) applies between Switzerland and Germany, which in Art. 63 provides an obligation to extradite for certain taxes.[4] As a result, Switzerland is under an obligation to extradite if the case concerns certain taxes. 3

Once the legal basis for a request has been established, the legality of this request can 4 be assessed. The procedure, too, varies depending on the above factors.

According to the principle of trust in 'the adherence to the rules of mutual legal assis- 5 tance in criminal matters and of international law'[5], German authorities and courts will generally trust and rely on the description of facts as provided by the requesting state. Consequently, a defence on the merits of the case is practically impossible.[6]

A common feature in the non-EU context is the distinction between the legal and the 6 political decision. The legal aspects of mutual legal assistance (admissibility/*Zulässigkeit*) are closely regulated in the IRG and generally determined by prosecutors and courts. The Federal Foreign Office (*Auswärtiges Amt*) together with the Federal Ministry of Justice and Consumer Protection (*Bundesministerium der Justiz und für Verbraucherschutz*, BMJV), Referentenentwurf: Entwurf eines Gesetzes zur Neuregelung des Rechts der Internationalen Rechtshilfe in Strafsachen, p. 267, 283 <https://www.bmjv.de/SharedDocs/Downloads/DE/Gesetzgebung/RefE/RefE_IRG-Reform.pdf?__blob=publicationFile&v=2> (last accessed: 21.10.2025);are vested with the authority to make the political decision on cooperation (granting/*Bewilligung*) as cooperation is in every case considered a matter of international policy. However, these Federal Ministries have delegated their authority to make such decisions to the regional authorities of the sixteen German States (*Bundesländer*), the consequence of this being the involvement of multiple players on several legal and political levels adding to the already existing legal complexity of the cases.

Collaboration with EU Members States is widely transposed from EU law. These 7 mechanisms are based on the principle of mutual trust and mutual recognition (see Art. 82 TFEU) and provide for a framework for speedy proceedings and an enhanced cooperation. Germany has – in particular through the Federal Constitutional Court (*Bundesverfassungsgericht*, BVerfG) – established exceptions from these principles, in

[4] Note that Art. 63 CISA is no longer valid but remains in force between Germany and Switzerland, see Sunde NStZ 2022, 527 and WJS WirtschaftsStrafR-HdB/Hackner Ch. 27 mn. 52; see Council Decision of 27 November 2008 (2008/903/EG).

[5] BVerfG 22.11.2019 – 2 BvR 517/19, NStZ-RR 2020, 59.

[6] See § 10 sub. 2 IRG but also Art. 14 para. 3 Treaty between the United States of America and the Federal Republic of Germany concerning Extradition ('US-Germany Extradition Treaty'). German courts generally take the more extradition-friendly approach of the IRG over Art. 14 para. 3 of the US-Germany Extradition Treaty, cf. OLG Dresden 2.12.2008 – OLG Ausl 117/08, BeckRS 2009, 3648 but also OLG Karlsruhe 20.11.1990 – 1 AK 34/90, NJW 1991, 2225.

particular with regard to the threat of a violation of the fundamental principles of German law (§ 73 sent. 1 IRG), which can result from – amongst others – violations of the right to a fair trial or threats of torture and inhumane and degrading treatment.[7] The Court of Justice of the European Union (CJEU) adopted and further developed these exceptions from the principles of mutual trust and mutual recognition opening opportunities to defend against surrender and against other forms of cooperation even under the strict regime of the European Arrest Warrant (EAW)[8] and European Investigation Order (EIO → mn. 77 et seqq.)[9].[10]

8 Cooperation between defence counsel in the requesting and the requested country is crucial to a successful defence in such matters, since any form of cooperation is based on proceedings in the requesting state. Should these local proceedings be terminated, the request to Germany will become void. If this aim cannot be achieved, cooperation with defence counsel in the requesting state can allow the defence to establish procedural deficiencies or other human rights violations in that state, thereby strengthening the case against the request for cooperation. Even if such engagement does not terminate the legal assistance, it may help to assess the benefits of accepting or not challenging the request (e.g. through a waiver to extradition) which in turn can improve a suspect's position in the national proceedings in the requesting state.

B. Extradition

I. Introduction

9 With the implementation of the Council Framework Decision of 13 June 2002 on the European Arrest Warrant and the Surrender Procedures between Member States – 2002/584 JHA (EAW Framework Decision), German extradition law entered a new phase.[11] While ordinarily extradition was a burdensome and slow process both for the authorities and for the individual concerned even under the 1957 European Convention, this changed significantly with the EAW (→ mn. 48 et seqq.). Designed as a mechanism of surrender with strict deadlines for the final decision on the execution of the EAW (60 days)[12] and the surrender itself (10 days)[13], it has also in practice sped up the process. As a counterpart to the general notion of mutual trust and mutual recognition, which are based on a common understanding of fundamental rights, the ability of an individual to fight surrender to another jurisdiction has decreased. Further, German citizens no longer have a 'safe haven' in Germany; they can be surrendered to another EU Member State under an EAW

[7] BVerfG 9.3.1983 – 2 BvR 315/83, BVerfGE 63, 332 (337) = NJW 1983, 1726 (1727); BVerfG 31.5.1994 – 2 BvR 1193/93, NJW 1994, 2883.

[8] Council Framework Decision 2002/584/JHA of 13.6.2002 on the European Arrest Warrant and the surrender procedures between Member States (OJ L 190, 18.7.2002, p. 1–20) ('EAW Framework Decision').

[9] Directive 2014/41/EU of the European Parliament and of the Council of 3 April 2014 regarding the European Investigation Order in criminal matters (OJ L 130, 1.5.2014, p. 1–36) ('EIO Directive').

[10] CJEU 5.4.2016 – C-404/15, C-659/15 PPU, ECLI:EU:C:2016:198 NJW 2016, 1709 – Aranyosi and Căldăraru; CJEU 25.7.2018 – C-216/18 PPU, ECLI:EU:C:2018:586 = EuGRZ 2018, 396 – LM; CJEU 29.7.2024 – C-318/24 PPU, ECLI:EU:C:2024:658 = BeckRS 2024, 18334 mn. 76 – P.P.R.

[11] For details on the EAW in relation to German law see for instance Schomburg/Lagodny/Hackner IRG Vor § 78 mn. 3 et seqq.; EnzEuR XI/Burchard § 14 mn. 1 et seqq.; HdB-EuStrafR/Heintschel-Heinegg § 37 mn. 14 et seqq.

[12] Art. 17 para. 3 EAW Framework Decision; § 83c sub. 1 IRG.

[13] Art. 23 para. 2 EAW Framework Decision; § 83c sub. 4 IRG.

(→ mn. 48 et seqq.), following a change of the GG. In relation to countries outside of the EU, Art. 16 para. 2 sent. 1 GG applies, whereby Germany does not extradite its own nationals.

In contrast to the EAW (→ mn. 48 et seqq.), extradition to other (non-EU) countries remains subject to strict formal requirements, providing a greater scope for defence activity. Most of these cases concern European non-EU countries (Turkey, Serbia, Switzerland, Bosnia and Herzegovina, North Macedonia).[14] In the past, Russian and American requests played a significant role, with Russian requests effectively not being served in light of the ongoing war in Ukraine. In most of these cases, extradition is governed by a bilateral or multilateral treaty, such as the 1978 Treaty between the United States of America and the Federal Republic of Germany concerning Extradition ('US-Germany Extradition Treaty') or, alternatively, the 1957 European Convention. **10**

II. Procedure

Incoming EAW (→ mn. 48 et seqq.) and third country extradition requests share a common procedure. Often enough, this procedure is being triggered by an entry in the Interpol systems and based on a Red Notice or Diffusion.[15] Within the EU, the Schengen Information System (SIS) takes a similar role. **11**

The German Federal Criminal Police Office (*Bundeskriminalamt*, BKA) serves as National Central Bureau (NCB)/SIRENE Office and as such operates the relevant police systems that trigger an arrest. Once arrested, the wanted person must be appointed legal counsel (§ 40 sub. 2, sub. 5 no. 1 IRG) and presented to a local court (*Amtsgericht*, AG) without undue delay and at least on the day following apprehension (§ 22 sub. 1 IRG). There, the person may respond to the allegations and be informed about his/her right to retain counsel, a potential (irrevocable) consent to extradition (§ 41 sub. 1 IRG) and speciality. Often enough, local judges are not familiar with extradition proceedings and have only a very narrow ability to assess the case.[16] As a result, individuals are remanded in custody in the vast majority of cases. The competence of the local court judge generally ends with this decision; he only discloses/announces the following decisions to the individuals, but has no material role after the initial decision. Rather, the case is handed over to the General Public Prosecutor's Office (*Generalstaatsanwaltschaft*, GenStA) which frequently requests additional information from the requesting state as the description of facts in the Interpol/SIS notice is often limited. **12**

Unfortunately, German law does not currently provide for a deadline for the provision of such additional information but only requires the decision by the Higher Regional Court (*Oberlandesgericht*, OLG) to be requested 'without undue delay' (§ 22 sub. 3 sent. 2 in conjunction with § 21 sub. 4 sent. 2 IRG). This is highly problematic from a constitutional law perspective as until a decision by the competent court is rendered, the individual may remain in custody for days if not weeks without a proper basis of information.[17] **13**

---

[14] For the latest extradition statistics (from 2022) see Federal Office of Justice (*Bundesamt für Justiz*, BfJ), Bekanntmachung der Auslieferungsstatistik für das Jahr 2022 (26.2.2024) <https://www.bundesjustizamt.de/SharedDocs/Downloads/DE/Justizstatistiken/Auslieferungsstatistik_2022.pdf?__blob=publicationFile&v=2> (last accessed: 31.1.2025).

[15] BeckFormB Strafverteidiger/Köberer XIII. E. 1., p. 1165.

[16] Per BVerfG 16.9.2010 – 2 BvR 1608/07, StV 2011, 170 (171 et seq.) = BeckRS 2010, 54123 mn. 27 et seqq. the constitution requires that the local court judge must have at least a minimal duty to assess, whether limits to extradition are obviously applicable in the case.

[17] The commentators, referring to OLG Karlsruhe 31.8.2006 – 1 AK 39/06, NJW 2006, 3510, consider the GenStA to be obliged to refer the case files to the OLG within 7 days, see Schomburg/Lagodny/Hackner IRG § 21 mn. 9; GPKGB Int. Rechtshilfeverkehr/Böhm, 136. EL Juni 2024, IRG § 21 mn. 44.

If and when the information arrives, the GenStA determines whether an arrest warrant shall be issued and makes the respective application to the OLG. For the remaining proceedings, the GenStA and the OLG remain in charge of the proceedings.

14 German courts take a strict stance on risk of flight and individuals will often be remanded in custody with no statutory deadline for the duration of this detention.[18] Depending on the timing of the arrival of the extradition documents and the requirement of diplomatic assurances and clarifications of the facts and circumstances of extradition, the case and the detention can last up to a year or, as approved by the BVerfG,[19] even longer in cases of particularly serious offences.

15 Once the OLG has decided about the arrest warrant, proceedings usually continue with the requesting state providing the extradition documents. The deadlines under the IRG are set out in § 16 sub. 2 IRG (three months for non-European states). Some of the most relevant extradition treaties provide for a deadline of 40 to 60 days (see Art. 16 para. 4 sent. 1 of the 1957 European Convention; Art. 16 para. 4 of the US-Germany Extradition Treaty). To meet this deadline, the requesting state must provide the documents in a timely manner and in German to allow the OLG to review and decide on the continuation of the detention based on these documents. If the requesting state fails to provide the information on time, release must be ordered.[20]

16 Once the extradition documents have arrived, the court will decide on the continuation of the detention. Either upon instruction by the court or of its own right, the prosecutor will request additional information on the requirements or bars to extradition such as statute of limitation, double criminality or procedural aspects such as prison conditions, medical treatment or aspects regarding the rule of law in the requesting state. The latter aspects fall within the scope of § 73 IRG, which is broadly used as a defence in extradition (→ mn. 36 et seqq.). The OLG and the GenStA must decide, whether, in case of extradition, there is a risk of violation of the fundamental principles of German law in the requesting state. To mitigate this risk, the requested state can provide diplomatic assurances. The BVerfG takes the view that, in accordance with the principle of trust in public international law, assurances that meet certain criteria can generally be trusted.[21] It is for the defence to raise sufficient doubts as to whether the assurances may be trusted.[22] Most importantly though, this trust in an assurance cannot be questioned by reference to the general circumstances/human rights situation in the requesting state; the risk must pertain specifically to the particular case at hand.[23] For example, a general reference to prison conditions in a requesting state will be insufficient. Rather, deficiencies must be shown in respect of the specific prison where the wanted person would be detained in case of his/her extradition.[24]

17 If this – often long-lasting – exchange of information and assurances and the entailing arrest exceeds two months starting on the day of the apprehension, the OLG must decide

---

[18] Positively though, the BVerfG most recently reiterated the requirements on the reasoning of the continuation of arrest BVerfG 23.1.2025 – 2 BvR 5/25, BeckRS 2025, 447 mn. 31 et seq.

[19] BVerfG 6.7.1982 – 2 BvR 856/81, BVerfGE 61, 28 = BeckRS 2011, 55927.

[20] OLG Düsseldorf 4.2.2003 – III-4 Ausl (A) 1/03 – 49/03 III, NStZ-RR 2003, 151 (152); cf. also OLG Karlsruhe 9.7.1996 – 1 AK 21/96, NJW 1996, 3426; OLG Hamm 12.4.2002 – 4 Ausl 67/02 (39/02), NStZ 2002, 665.

[21] BVerfG 22.10.2019 – 2 BvR 1661/19, NStZ-RR 2020, 62 (64); BVerfG 4.12.2019 – 2 BvR 1832/19, NVwZ 2020, 144 (146); BVerfG 2.2.2016 – 2 BvR 2486/15, BeckRS 2016, 41837 mn. 22; more generally BVerfG 24.7.2017 – 2 BvR 1487/17, NVwZ 2017, 1526 (1529 et seq.). On the criteria set out by the European Court of Human Rights (ECtHR), see ECtHR NVwZ 2013, 487 mn. 187 et. seqq. – Othman (Abu Qatada)/UK.

[22] Cf. for instance BVerfG 9.3.2016 – 2 BvR 348/16, BeckRS 2016, 43820 mn. 11; Schomburg/Lagodny/Gleß/Wahl/Zimmermann IRG § 73 mn. 42c.

[23] BVerfG 28.7.2016 – 2 BvR 1468/16, BeckRS 2016, 49757 mn. 52.

[24] Cf. OLG Bremen 28.12.2022 – 1 AuslA 50/22, BeckRS 2022, 45190 mn. 18.

on the continuation of the detention (§ 26 sub. 1 IRG). With ongoing proceedings, the likelihood that the individual will be extradited (§ 15 sub. 2 IRG) and proportionality become increasingly important for this decision.[25] At the same time, the defence will be able to understand the court's considerations on the legality of extradition from these decisions. Once the GenStA has received all requested information, it requests a decision on the admissibility of extradition from the OLG (§ 29 sub. 1 IRG). If the GenStA considers extradition illegal, it must request the court to refuse the extradition.[26] At least in case of an EAW the GenStA is required to make an application to rule on the inadmissibility of the surrender.[27] The court is technically not bound by the application[28] but will in practice release the individual.

If the court declares extradition admissible, the individual has no formal right of **18** appeal and will be surrendered unless they can present new material facts (§ 33 IRG) or file a constitutional complaint with the BVerfG (Art. 94 para. 1 no. 4a GG). Therefore, and as most recent cases show, in addition to such a constitutional complaint, defence counsel should immediately file an application for interim measures with the BVerfG under § 32 BVerfGG[29] and notify both the GenStA and the OLG of his/her intention to file such application in order to avoid surrender which would create irreversible facts. The BVerfG will regularly decide on such an application within a few hours[30] or days, depending on the urgency of the matter. Due to this procedure, requests for interim measures from the European Court of Human Rights (ECtHR) are relatively rare in extradition. The (separate) decision on the granting of extradition can be challenged in court[31] but the criteria remain vague.[32]

Recent efforts to modernise the IRG have come to an abrupt halt due to a change **19** in the government, with necessary reforms on crucial procedural aspects (such as the introduction of an appeal) pending.[33] Further issues, such as the lack of an oral hearing, deadlines for provision of documents after the initial apprehension etc. remain unsolved.

On a European procedural level, defence counsel will have to consider that even a **20** successful refusal of extradition does not, in the most cases, bar extradition proceedings (including arrest) in another EU Member State.[34] This principle was confirmed in a recent CJEU judgement.[35] However, some decisions in national proceedings do create binding

---

[25] BVerfG 27.7.1999 – 2 BvR 898/99, NJW 2000, 1252.

[26] OLG Celle 6.1.2025 – 2 OAus 68/24, BeckRS 2025, 78 mn. 9; GPKGB Int. Rechtshilfeverkehr/Böhm, 136. EL Juni 2024, IRG § 29 mn. 9; against this practice OLG Rostock 15.2.2016 – 20 OLGAusl 21/15, BeckRS 2016, 3710 mn. 5; Schomburg/Lagodny/Riegel IRG § 29 mn. 5; for a mitigating view Schomburg/Lagodny/Schierholt IRG § 12 mn. 3.

[27] BGH 18.8.2022 – 4 ARs 13/21, BeckRS 2022, 35141; Hackner/Schierholt Int. Rechtshilfe mn. 307.

[28] Cf. OLG Brandenburg 15.1.2024 – 1 OAus 2/24, BeckRS 2024, 609.

[29] Schomburg/Lagodny/Riegel IRG § 32 mn. 35 et seq.

[30] BVerfG 28.6.2024 – 2 BvQ 49/24, BeckRS 2024, 14932.

[31] BVerwG 18.05.2010 – 1 B 1/10, BeckRS 2010, 49810; OLG München 4.4.2017 – 1 AR 328/16, BeckRS 2017, 136317 mn. 25 et seqq.

[32] Schomburg/Lagodny/Schierholt IRG § 12 mn. 22 et seqq.; NK-RechtshilfeR/König/Voigt 2. Hauptteil IRG § 12 mn. 152.

[33] For the Draft Law (*Referentenentwurf*) see BMJV, Referentenentwurf: Entwurf eines Gesetzes zur Neuregelung des Rechts der Internationalen Rechtshilfe in Strafsachen <https://www.bmjv.de/SharedDocs/Downloads/DE/Gesetzgebung/RefE/RefE_IRG-Reform.pdf?__blob=publicationFile&v=2> (last accessed: 21.10.2025).

[34] See OLG Braunschweig 16.9.2022 – 1 AR (Ausl.) 17/22, BeckRS 2022, 25122.

[35] Regarding the extradition to Island and Norway: CJEU 14.9.2023 – C-71/21, ECLI:EU:C:2023:668 = BeckRS 2023, 24046 mn. 52, 55, 61 – Sofiyska gradska prokuratura; regarding an EAW: CJEU 29.7.2024 – C-318/24 PPU, ECLI:EU:C:2024:658 = BeckRS 2024, 18334 mn. 43 – P.P.R.; CJEU 19.6.2025 – C-219/25 PPU, ECLI:EU:C:2025:456 = BeckRS 2025, 13494; see for a critical analysis: Schomburg/Heimrich preprint eucrim, Vol. 20(3).

effect such as *ne bis in idem*.[36] After a final judicial decision by one Schengen State or EU Member State establishing that the *ne bis in idem* principle applies with regard to acts covered by the Red Notice or extradition request of a third (Schengen or third party) state, both the mutual trust and the right to freedom of movement (Art. 21 para. 1 TFEU) read in the light of Art. 50 CFR preclude authorities of other Schengen or EU Member States from making a provisional arrest or keeping that person in custody.[37] The CJEU later clarified that these principles also bar extradition and also apply to third-country nationals on whom a sentence has been imposed in an EU Member State and whose extradition is sought by a third country.[38] The restriction of the principle of mutual recognition of national decisions to *ne bis in idem* and most recently also the refugee status[39] is, in the view of the author, insufficient. Contrary to the aforementioned CJEU judgment, if extradition has been successfully challenged in one Member State on the basis of a violation of human rights or political persecution – i.e. based on principles that apply equally throughout Europe – this decision should also have binding effect in other Member States.[40]

III. Interpol/SIS

21 Interpol Red Notices and Diffusions as well as entries in the SIS remain a key source for law enforcement authorities and often lead to an arrest upon entering or leaving Germany. Notably, red notices, diffusions and SIS entries (jointly referred to as notices) are sufficient bases for an arrest under § 19 IRG.

22 For all notices, the BKA serves as NCB/SIRENE Office. The BKA serves as the point of contact for individuals seeking to determine whether a notice has been issued against them.[41] The process is usually lengthy but nevertheless quicker than requests made to the Commission for the Control of Interpol's Files (CCF). On SIS, there is no other source of information except the SIRENE Office of other Member States.[42]

23 Requests for deletion of a Red Notice or Diffusion can be made with the CCF (Art. 29 Statute of the Commission for the Control of Interpol's Files (SCCF)). Responses are regularly received only after several months and the threshold for deletion is very high. At the same time, decisions taken by CCF suffer from a severe lack of transparency, both regarding the procedure and the interpretation of the rules in the decisions.[43] For SIS entries, there is no procedure to delete in the requested state but rather, such a request has to be directed at competent authorities in the requesting state.[44]

---

[36] CJEU 12.5.2021 – C-505/19, ECLI:EU:C:2021:376 = NJW 2021, 2348 – WS; CJEU 28.10.2022 – C-435/22 PPU, ECLI:EU:C:2022:852 = NJW 2023, 349 – HF.

[37] CJEU 12.5.2021 – C-505/19, ECLI:EU:C:2021:376 = NJW 2021, 2348 – WS.

[38] CJEU 28.10.2022 – C-435/22 PPU, ECLI:EU:C:2022:852 = NJW 2023, 349 – HF.

[39] CJEU 18.6.2024 – C-352/22, ECLI:EU:C:2024:521 = NStZ-RR 2024, 321 – Generalstaatsanwaltschaft Hamm.

[40] See European Criminal Bar Association (ECBA), Statement on Mutual Recognition of Extradition Decisions (21.6.2022) <https://ecba.org/extdocserv/publ/ECBA_STATEMENT_Mutualrecognitionextraditiondecisions_21June2022.pdf> (last accessed: 31.1.2025).

[41] Schomburg/Lagodny/Riegel/S. Schomburg/Trautmann IRG Vor § 19 mn. 59 et seq.

[42] Art. 58 Council Decision 2007/533/JHA (SIS-II-Decision).

[43] For details cf. Schomburg/Lagodny/Riegel/S. Schomburg/Trautmann IRG Vor § 19 mn. 71 et seqq.; Schomburg/Müller WiJ 2022, 25.

[44] Schomburg/Lagodny/Riegel/S. Schomburg/Trautmann IRG Vor § 19 mn. 27, 30.

Note that even the deletion of Red Notice does not exclude bilateral requests outside Interpol's channels and that such deletion decision is not binding on the judicial authorities of other EU Member States.[45] 24

IV. Extradition to third countries

Extradition to non-EU Member States from Germany is generally governed by the IRG. The most relevant scenarios in practice are incoming extradition requests. These are governed purely by the IRG unless the requesting state has entered into a treaty with Germany governing extradition. If and to the extent that such a treaty exists, it takes precedence over the IRG, § 1 sub. 3 IRG. The most prominent example of this is the EAW creating its own system of surrender in accordance with §§ 80 et seq. IRG. In addition to the EAW cases, multilateral and bilateral treaties provide for such sets of rules. 25

The complexity of the search for the relevant legal basis can be illustrated in the following example: an incoming request on what is believed to concern a political offence would be governed by § 6 sub. 1 IRG in case of a third country request. If the request comes from an EU Member State, political offence is no longer a bar to extradition. However, if the request comes from a third country such as the United States of America having a bilateral extradition treaty with Germany, the political offence exception may be invoked in accordance not with the general rule in § 6 para 1 IRG but under Art. 4 of the US-Germany Extradition Treaty as amended by the Supplementary Treaties of 21 October 1986 and 18 April 2006. In interpreting this treaty, German courts will need to take into account multilateral treaties where applicable, such as the Agreement on extradition between the European Union and the United States of America from 19 July 2003. If this contains additional rules on the specific question (political offence), it will take primacy over the national law including bilateral treaties.[46] 26

1. Requirements for extradition under the IRG

If and to the extent that no other rules apply, the IRG sets – amongst others – the following requirements for extradition for incoming requests for prosecution – as compared to requests for transfer of sentenced persons (→ mn. 94 et seqq.). 27

a) Double criminality

A fundamental principle under German law is the requirement of double criminality under § 3 sub. 1 IRG which reads: 'Extradition is only permissible if the offence is also an unlawful act under German law which fulfils the elements of a criminal provision or if it would also constitute such an act under German law in the case of analogous conversion of the facts.' This principle does not require that the criminal offence in the extradition request is a criminal offence under German law or that a comparable offence exists. Rather, the underlying facts are central for this assessment. If those facts constitute a criminal offence, the criterion is fulfilled. To establish this, courts and prosecutors regularly request additional information from the requesting state. 28

Under § 3 sub. 2 IRG, a request for extradition is only admissible if the offence is punishable under German law with a maximum sentence of imprisonment of at least one 29

[45] CJEU 29.7.2024 – C-318/24 PPU, ECLI:EU:C:2024:658 = BeckRS 2024, 18334 mn. 56 et seqq. – P.P.R.
[46] Cf. CJEU 28.10.2022 – C-435/22 PPU, ECLI:EU:C:2022:852 = NJW 2023, 349 mn. 110 et seqq. – HF.

year. The same applies if the facts described in the request constitute such offence. This sentencing threshold is designed to exclude minor offences from extradition.

b) Reciprocity

30 Outside the details of the individual case and on a more interstate basis, § 5 IRG requires reciprocity (*Gegenseitigkeit*). If, for example, the requesting state does not extradite to Germany at all, Germany must refuse extradition likewise for lack of reciprocity. However, in modern extradition practice governed by treaties, this concept has a rather limited scope of application. Nevertheless, a detailed assessment of the criterion may show that the requesting state does not extradite for fiscal offences – see for example Art. 5 of the 1957 European Convention and Art. 2 of the Second Additional Protocol to the 1957 European Convention. In such a case, an argument of reciprocity may succeed, even though reciprocity is generally excluded as a necessary requirement under the 1957 European Convention (Art. 2 para. 7).[47]

c) Statute of limitation

31 As provided for in § 9 no. 2 IRG, a statute of limitation is a requirement for extradition. This criterion plays a double role as requirement and bar to extradition at the same time. First, extradition is barred for lack of a punishable offence in the requesting state, if the information provided by that state already shows that the limitation period has passed (cf. Art. 10 of the 1957 European Convention).[48] Generally, however, German courts will not rule on the statutes of limitation in the requesting state. Only in exceptional circumstances – depending for example on the alleged offence and the reasons for the delay – will passage of time as such be a bar to extradition under § 73 IRG.[49] Furthermore, if Germany could claim jurisdiction for the offence which is subject to the extradition request, extradition is inadmissible if the offence would be time-barred under German law. When assessing the statute of limitation, German law on this aspect has to be taken into account in its entirety. This includes not only the original periods provided in § 78 StGB ranging from 3 years to 30 years (being unlimited for murder). Rather, when determining statute of limitation, one must assess the provisions on stay and interruption of the limitation period. For example, a search warrant or an arrest warrant can interrupt the limitation period (§ 78c sub. 1 no. 4, 5 StGB). Difficulties can arise regarding the existence or the legal validity of such interruption measures in the requesting state. The traditional stance of the Federal Court of Justice (*Bundesgerichtshof*, BGH) is that such measures are relevant under Art. 10 of the 1957 European Convention (though not under the regime of the EAW → mn. 48 et seqq.) insofar as that measure would be relevant if it were taken by a German authority and as long as the measures are 'functionally equivalent'.[50] Typically, it is for the defence to raise questions if the statute of limitations can be an issue in the case at hand and the GenStA will often need to enquire with the requesting state.

---

[47] Cf. BGH 11.3.1981 – 4 ARs 18/80, BGHSt 30, 55 (60 et seqq.) = NJW 1981, 1166.

[48] GPKGB Int. Rechtshilfeverkehr/Vogel/Burchard, 136. EL Juni 2024, IRG § 9 mn. 54.

[49] Cf. OLG Hamm 16.6.1998 – (2) 4 Ausl. 563/96 (75/97), NStZ-RR 1998, 351 (352); OLG Hamm 17.5.2001 – (2) 4 Ausl. 629/97 (33/01), BeckRS 2001, 30181425; both citing the unpublished decision BVerfG 31.8.1986 – 2 BvR 661/81.

[50] BGH 26.7.1984 – 4 ARs 8/84, BGHSt 33, 26 = NJW 1985, 570; OLG München 7.3.2013 – OLG Ausl. 14 Ausl. A 1033/12, NStZ-RR 2013, 179. For criticism see NK-RechtshilfeR/Kubiciel 2. Hauptteil IRG § 9 mn. 97; Schomburg/Lagodny/Zimmermann IRG § 9 mn. 30.

2. Bars to extradition

a) Non-extradition of German nationals and procedure on extradition of EU citizens

A first bar to extradition to non-EU countries is provided by the GG, which forbids the extradition of German nationals to other (non-EU) countries (Art. 16 GG). The CJEU has decided that the principle of non-discrimination in EU law (Art. 18, 21 TFEU) does not require this prohibition to be extended to EU citizens as the restriction on equal treatment is justified by the objective of preventing the risk of impunity for persons who have committed an offence.[51] However, in order to comply with the principle of non-discrimination the national authorities will have to notify the Member State of which the citizen in question is a national and, should that Member State so request, surrender that citizen to it in accordance with the EAW Framework Decision, provided that that Member State has jurisdiction, pursuant to its national law, to prosecute that person for offences committed outside its national territory.[52] On the other hand, the CJEU has refused an obligation of the host Member State to refuse extradition and to conduct its own criminal prosecution for offences committed in a third State and applying its own jurisdiction should it have such.[53] Likewise the home Member State is not obliged to exert its jurisdiction and issue an EAW (→ mn. 48 et seqq.) to prevent extradition to the third country.[54] The requested Member State must set a reasonable time for the home Member State to issue an EAW (→ mn. 48 et seqq.) and after passage of such time may continue the extradition to the third country. This leaves open the possibility of such a duty to arise under national law, an issue that has not been tested in Germany.[55] 32

Case: 33
A citizen of EU-Country A and subject to an extradition warrant from Non-EU-Country B is arrested in Germany. Germany has to enquire with Country A whether Country A intends to issue an EAW which in turn would take precedence over the extradition warrant from Country B.

In cases of extradition for the purpose of enforcing a custodial sentence, equal considerations apply. In those cases, however, impunity is avoided by executing a sentence instead of extraditing. This option can easily be extended to all EU citizens. Thus, a Member State, whose national law prohibits the extradition of its own nationals out of the European Union for the purpose of enforcing a sentence and makes provision for the possibility that such a sentence pronounced abroad may be served on its territory, is required to ensure that an EU citizen residing permanently in its territory receives the same treatment as that accorded to its own nationals in relation to extradition.[56] Even when there is an obligation under an extradition treaty to extradite and the transfer of the sentence is only possible with consent of the requesting state, the requested Member 34

---

[51] CJEU 6.9.2016 – C-182/15, ECLI:EU:C:2016:630 = NJW 2017, 378 mn. 37 – Petruhhin; CJEU 10.4.2018 – C-191/16, ECLI:EU:C:2018:222 = NJW 2018, 1529 mn. 47 – Pisciotti.

[52] CJEU 6.9.2016 – C-182/15, ECLI:EU:C:2016:630 = NJW 2017, 378 mn. 50 – Petruhhin; CJEU 10.4.2018 – C-191/16, ECLI:EU:C:2018:222 = NJW 2018, 1529 mn. 50 et seqq. – Pisciotti.

[53] CJEU 17.12.2020 – C-398/19, ECLI:EU:C:2020:1032 = BeckRS 2020, 35417 mn. 64 et seqq. – Generalstaatsanwaltschaft Berlin (Extradition vers l'Ukraine). Dissenting opinion Costa/Cardoso/Ramos TCLR 3 (2024), 18 (24 et seq.).

[54] CJEU 17.12.2020 – C-398/19, ECLI:EU:C:2020:1032 = BeckRS 2020, 35417 mn. 49 et seqq. – Extradition vers l'Ukraine.

[55] For Portugal see Costa/Cardoso/Ramos TCLR 3 (2024), 18 (26 et seqq.).

[56] CJEU 13.11.2018 – C-247/17, ECLI:EU:C:2018:898 = BeckRS 2018, 2816 mn. 31 et seqq. – Raugevicius.

State must use all mechanisms available to seek the consent of that third state and may only extradite, if it nevertheless cannot receive that consent and if the extradition does not infringe the rights of the individual concerned under the CFR.[57]

b) Other bars to extradition including specialty

35 In addition to the bars derived from EU law, the IRG provides certain individual bars to extradition. Such specific rules are set out in §§ 6, 7, 8 and 11 IRG stipulating that extradition is inadmissible for political offences (§ 6 sub. 1 IRG), political prosecution (§ 6 sub. 2 IRG), military offences (§ 7 IRG), offences carrying the death penalty – the real risk of execution being sufficient – (§ 8 IRG)[58] or where there is a risk that if extradited, the person sought will be subject to prosecution or sentencing regarding offences outside the extradition request (rule of specialty, § 11 IRG). Of these bars to extradition, specialty (*Spezialität*) is probably the most common factor to consider when defending against extradition. According to the rule of specialty, the individual sought may only be prosecuted, sentenced and deprived of their liberty with regard to the offence sought under the extradition request. The person must also not be re-extradited to another country without Germany's prior consent. From a formal perspective, the extradition request itself may give rise to a challenge on specialty if it fails to specify the underlying facts accurately (for example failing to describe the alleged victim, the relevant time frame or co-perpetrators). From a legal perspective, the rules of procedure of the requesting state may be relevant for such challenge, in particular, if they allow for broader prosecution of offences outside the ones described in the request and if they do not allow the defendant to raise specialty as a defence in his own right.[59]

c) § 73 IRG: threat of 'violation of core principles of German legal system'

36 In addition, § 73 IRG provides for a general clause whereby all acts of legal assistance must be in line with 'basic principles of the German legal system'. However, the 'German legal system' must be interpreted in the broader sense, including its incorporation of international law obligations in accordance with the Art. 23 et seqq. GG. This also includes the fundamental rights incorporated from the EU and the protection under the ECHR. The latter is of fundamental relevance with a view to long-standing principles set out by the ECtHR in its decisions, in particular on the right to a fair trial (Art. 6 ECHR) and the protection from inhuman and degrading treatment (Art. 3 ECHR) to name only few. With regard to Art. 3 ECHR German courts have taken a strict approach on prison conditions both regarding extradition to EU and non-EU Member States. The 'burden of proof' remains high in such cases. It is the obligation of the person sought to show not only general deficits in the requesting state but rather a specific threat for the requested person in case of its extradition. However, if such a risk is established, courts will even refuse requests to rule of law countries. In this context, the OLG Karlsruhe recently refused extradition to the UK, considering the prison conditions in Wandsworth prison a risk of inhuman and degrading treatment under Art. 3 ECHR.[60]

---

[57] CJEU 22.12.2022 – C-237/21, ECLI:EU:C:2022:1017 = NJW 2023, 589 mn. 49 et seqq. – S.M.

[58] Note that not only the risk of death penalty will be sufficient but that ECtHR 7.7.1989 – no. 14038/88, BeckRS 1989, 113923 mn. 92 et seqq. – Soering/UK also considered an Art. 3-risk from the 'death row phenomenon' alone.

[59] BVerfG 17.5.2017 – 2 BvR 893/17, NStZ-RR 2017, 226 (229); OLG Hamburg 17.8.2023 – Ausl 63/22, NJW 2024, 159 (161 et seq.).

[60] OLG Karlsruhe 10.3.2023 – 301 OAus 1/23, BeckRS 2023, 20285. English version available at <https://eucrim.eu/documents/31/OLG_Karlsruhe_Beschl._10.3.2023_-_Translation_ROn4Hnw.pdf> (last accessed: 31.1.2025).

In terms of sentencing, the BVerfG,[61] similar to the ECtHR,[62] has established a high threshold for disproportionate sentencing, arguing that the German sentencing perspective cannot be applied to other States and therefore, even significant differences in sentencing do not suffice as a bar to extradition. According to a recent decision by the ECtHR, the existence of a legal framework allowing for a pardon may be sufficient to exclude a violation of Art. 3 ECHR.[63] The BVerfG considers extradition to be barred only if life-sentences are regularly enforced up to the inmate's death and a pardon will only be granted if it has been preceded by an irreversible process of physical decay.[64] 37

d) Absentia

Extradition requests following a trial and sentencing *in absentia* have given rise to a considerable number of decisions by both German and European courts.[65] In very simple terms, a trial *in absentia* can constitute a bar to extradition under § 73 IRG, Art. 6 ECHR. This does however not apply if the person sought was informed to attend the proceedings,[66] was defended in trial in an effective manner[67] and absconded[68]. In the latter case, extradition can even be admissible if there is no possibility of a full re-trial including a hearing on the facts of the case. In all other cases, such re-trial must be assured by the requesting state and must be in accordance with the guarantees under Art. 6 ECHR. 38

e) Ne bis in idem

Under § 9 no. 1 IRG, extradition is inadmissible if a German court has rendered a judgment regarding the acts of the person sought. Of the extradition treaties, namely Art. 9 of the 1957 European Convention and Art. 8 of the US-Germany Extradition Treaty contain similar provision. This bar to extradition applies independent of the nationality of the person sought – a foreign national sentenced in Germany is protected from extradition, just as a German citizen against extradition for the same acts. 39

Case: 40
A citizen of Country A and subject to an extradition warrant from Country B must not be extradited from Germany if he has been sentenced in Germany for the same facts.

---

[61] BVerfG 6.7.2005 – 2 BvR 2259/04, BVerfGE 113, 154 = NJW 2005, 3483; BVerfG 16.1.2010 – 2 BvR 2299/09, BeckRS 2010, 45668 mn. 19 et seq.; cf. also BGH 19.6.2012 – 4 ARs 5/12, NJW 2012, 2980 (2984).

[62] ECtHR 9.7.2013 – 66069/09, 130/10, 3896/10, NJOZ 2014, 1582 – Vinter/UK; ECtHR 4.9.2014 – 140/10, NJOZ 2016, 389 – Trabelsi/Belgium; ECtHR 3.11.2022 – no. 22854/20 – Sanchez-Sanchez/UK.

[63] ECtHR 13.2.2024 – no. 34392/21, BeckRS 2024, 3690 mn. 57 – Horne/UK; similarly, BVerfG 6.7.2005 – 2 BvR 2259/04, NJW 2005, 3483 (3484 et seq.).

[64] BVerfG 16.1.2010 – 2 BvR 2299/09, BeckRS 2010, 45668 mn. 28.

[65] CJEU 10.8.2017 – C-270/17 PPU, ECLI:EU:C:2017:628 = BeckRS 2017, 121028 – Tupikas; CJEU 10.8.2017 – C-271/17 PPU, ECLI:EU:C:2017:629 = BeckRS 2017, 121046 – Zdziaszek; CJEU 22.12.2017 – C-571/17 PPU, ECLI:EU:C:2017:1026 = NJW 2018, 924 – Ardic; CJEU 21.12.2023 – C-398/22, ECLI:EU:C:2023:1031 = BeckRS 2023, 36820 – RQ; BVerfG 15.12.2015 – 2 BvR 2735/14, NJW 2016, 1149.

[66] ECtHR 28.8.2018 – no. 12307/16, BeckRS 2018, 62446 mn. 64 et seq. – Vyacheslav Korchagin/Russia; ECtHR 1.3.2006 – no. 56581/00, BeckRS 2006, 143932 mn. 99 – Sejdovic/Italy; OLG Düsseldorf 26.1.1987 – 4 Ausl. (A) 5/80-47/87 III, NStZ 1987, 466; OLG Karlsruhe 21.12.1982 – 1 AK 25/82, NStZ 1983, 225 (226).

[67] ECtHR 21.1.1999 – no. 26103/95, BeckRS 1999, 4189 mn. 34 – Van Geyseghem/Belgium; cf. also BVerfG 17.11.1986 – 2 BvR 1255/86, NJW 1987, 830.

[68] ECtHR 7.6.2022 – no. 4099/12 mn. 32 et seqq. – Yeğer/Turkey.

41 The term 'offence' is interpreted in the sense of a procedural act (*Tat im prozessualen Sinn*) in the sense of § 264 StPO rather than referring to the same type of criminal offence. This term broadly corresponds with the EU approach.[69]

42 The decisions triggering the *ne is in idem* effect are listed in § 9 no. 1 IRG exhaustively. Judgments include convictions and acquittals. Notably, the list in § 9 no. 1 IRG appears to be broader than the current interpretation of the *bis* element under Art. 50 CFR and Art. 54 CISA, including decisions refusing the opening of trial under § 204 StPO and neither requiring a final disposition of the case nor containing an enforcement provision.

43 While § 9 no. 1 IRG generally only refers to judgments by German courts, it has to be interpreted in a way that is compatible with EU law.[70] As such, not only German judicial decisions but also decision of judicial authorities of other Member States can trigger a bar to extradition if they relate to the same set of facts and if the sentence has been served or the acquittal is final and binding.

44 **Case:**
A citizen of Country A and subject to an extradition warrant from Country B must not be extradited from Germany if he has been sentenced in France for the same facts.

45 Unless provided for differently in an extradition treaty, judgments by judicial authorities of non-German states do not trigger § 9 no. 1 IRG or the general prohibition of *ne bis in idem* in Art. 103 para. 3 GG (an Indian national sentenced in India for the same facts can nevertheless be extradited from Germany to the United States of America).[71] However, Art. 50 CFR and Art. 54 CISA provide for an EU-wide and Schengen-wide application of *ne bis in idem*. This not only precludes double jeopardy within the Schengen area (and a corresponding extradition), but also forbids extradition to third countries of any person whose trial has been finally disposed of in any Contracting State to the CISA for the same acts, provided that, if a penalty has been imposed, it has been enforced, is actually in the process of being enforced or can no longer be enforced under the laws of the sentencing Contracting Party.[72]

f) Fiscal offences

46 In extradition law, fiscal offences play a special role since historically, they were included in extradition treaties only if explicitly provided for (see for example Art. 5 of the 1957 European Convention). The Second Additional Protocol to the 1957 European Convention changed this situation and created an obligation to extradite for the countries party to it, with several notable declarations and reservations[73] to it, excluding certain types of taxes.

---

[69] On the autonomous European meaning cf. CJEU 16.11.2010 – C-261/09, ECLI:EU:C:2010:683 = NStZ 2011, 466 mn. 38 et seqq. – Mantello; CJEU 29.4.2021 – C-665/20 PPU, ECLI:EU:C:2021:339 = BeckRS 2021, 8925 mn. 72 et seqq. – X; on the application to various forms of economic crime cf. Schomburg/Reitner ZWH 2021, 189.

[70] Cf. CJEU 12.5.2021 – C-505/19, ECLI:EU:C:2021:376 = NJW 2021, 2348 – WS; Schomburg/Lagodny/Zimmermann IRG § 9 mn. 23.

[71] BVerfG 31.3.1987 – 2 BvM 2/86, NJW 1987, 2155 (2158).

[72] CJEU 12.5.2021 – C-505/19, ECLI:EU:C:2021:376 = NJW 2021, 2348 – WS; CJEU 28.10.2022 – C-435/22 PPU, ECLI:EU:C:2022:852 = NJW 2023, 349 – HF.

[73] See Council of Europe, Reservations and Declarations for Treaty No. 098 – Second Additional Protocol to the 1957 European Convention (ETS No. 098) <https://www.coe.int/en/web/conventions/full-list?module=declarations-by-treaty&numSte=098&codeNature=0> (last accessed: 31.1.2025).

3. Aut dedere aut judicare

If an individual successfully fights extradition, he or she may nevertheless face prosecution in Germany under the principle of *aut dedere aut judicare* enshrined in § 7 sub. 2 no. 2 StGB.[74] According to this section, German law applies to offences committed abroad, inter alia, if 'the act is a criminal offence at the place of its commission' and if the offender was 'a foreign national at the time of the offence, was found to be staying in Germany and, although extradition legislation would permit extradition for such an offence, is not extradited because no request for extradition is made within a reasonable period, is rejected or the extradition is not feasible.' These local German investigations following an unsuccessful extradition request often enough suffer from a certain unwillingness of the requesting state and – in particular if extradition was refused on grounds of Art. 6 ECHR – requesting evidence from this state may prove problematic for German law enforcement authorities. 47

V. Extradition between EU Member States: EAW

1. Introduction

Since its introduction in 2004, the EAW has simplified surrender between the EU Members States and states applying similar mechanisms, i.e. Iceland and Norway (Surrender Agreement EU/IS-NO[75]) and most recently the United Kingdom (Part Three, Title VII of the EU-UK Trade and Cooperation Agreement (TCA)[76]). Being a framework decision, the EAW Framework Decision had to be transposed into national law and as a consequence, the national rules may differ from Member State to Member State. Germany incorporated the EAW into the IRG (§§ 80 et seqq.). 48

While 'traditional extradition' consisted of the decision on admissibility and granting of extradition, the surrender under the EAW Framework Decision is a purely legal mechanism. Surrender is generally mandatory and the CJEU is generally cautious in guarding this principle against attempts by national authorities to restrict the execution of EAWs.[77] 49

2. Formal aspects

The EAW must be based on a national arrest warrant and is a separate instrument from this national warrant.[78] This follows from the general objective of the EAW Framework Decision that the person concerned should be provided procedural safeguards and fundamental rights already at the first stage of the surrender proceedings. Consequently, the validity of an EAW stands and falls with the underlying national warrant.[79] As a further consequence, the EAW must be issued by a judicial authority (Art. 1 para. 1, 2 50

[74] For details cf. MAH WirtschaftsStrafR/Schomburg § 15 mn. 22.

[75] Agreement between the European Union and the Republic of Iceland and the Kingdom of Norway on the surrender procedure between the Member States of the European Union and Iceland and Norway (OJ L 292, 21.10.2006, pp. 2–19).

[76] Trade and Cooperation Agreement between the European Union and the European Atomic Energy Community, of the one part, and the United Kingdom of Great Britain and Northern Ireland, of the other part (OJ L 149, 30.4.2021, pp. 10–2539).

[77] See e.g. CJEU 31.1.2023 – C-158/21, ECLI:EU:C:2023:57 = NJW 2023, 1267 – Puig Gordi.

[78] CJEU 1.6.2016 – C-241/15, ECLI:EU:C:2016:385 = NJW 2017, 49 mn. 30 et seqq., 58 – Bob-Dogi; CJEU 13.1.2021 – C-414/20 PPU, ECLI:EU:C:2021:4 = BeckRS 2021, 66 – MM; CJEU 10.11.2016 – C-453/16 PPU, ECLI:EU:C:2016:860 = BeckRS 2016, 82663 mn. 27 – Özçelik.

[79] Cf. OLG Nürnberg 10.1.2024 – Ws 1141/23 and Ws 1176/23, NStZ-RR 2024, 87.

and Art. 6 para. EAW Framework Decision). The German Public Prosecutor's Office (*Staatsanwaltschaft*, StA) is for lack of independence not considered to be such a judicial authority, requiring German EAWs to be issued by a court upon application by the StA.[80] However, this question is one for the issuing authority only. The executing authority may not deny enforcement of the EAW because it considers the issuing authority not to be a 'judicial authority' within the meaning of EAW Framework Decision.[81] EAW templates simplify the procedure of their issuance. To simplify the procedure even further, judicial authorities may communicate directly between each other instead of communicating via diplomatic channels, as remains common in traditional extradition proceedings with non-EU countries. Nevertheless, the completed EAW form must contain the requested information including a description of the relevant information on the requested person and the details of the judicial authority and the national arrest warrant or judgment as well as the facts allowing the court of the executing state to understand the allegations and the maximum applicable sentence, § 83a IRG.

3. Deadlines and procedure

51 The EAW generally creates an obligation to surrender and sets out procedures including strict timeframes requiring a decision within 60 days on admissibility of extradition following the initial apprehension and a deadline of 10 days for the surrender following the final decision.

52 The extradition procedure largely remains the same as in cases of requests from third countries with the deadlines applying. Since the EAW is a surrender mechanism and does not differentiate between the admissibility and the granting of extradition, the granting decision is limited to § 83b IRG and is generally exercised by the GenStA and – due to the lack of independence – with full judicial review by the OLG on this aspect.[82]

4. Requirements of surrender

a) Double criminality

53 Within the simplified procedure, double criminality shall not be assessed if the facts fall within a certain category of 32 types of offences in Art. 2 para. 2 EAW Framework Decision (§ 81 no. 4 IRG), provided they are punishable in the issuing Member State by a custodial sentence or a detention order of at least three years in the version applicable to the facts giving rise to the case.[83] These offences include corruption, fraud, including that affecting the financial interests of the EU, laundering of the proceeds of crime, counterfeiting currency, computer-related crime and environmental crime and swindling, thereby broadly excluding the double criminality test in economic crime. Nevertheless, in the absence of a harmonised categorisation of offences within the EU Member States, there remains room for argument on which particular national offence may be categorised within Art. 2 para. 2 EAW Framework Decision. Outside this catalogue of offences, double criminality still applies. The difficulty in practice is that many offences will be considered fraud or similar offences under the catalogue. While in many cases, this categorisation is correct, because the material law in the EU has not been harmonised, it remains difficult to challenge the categorisation by the issuing judicial authority which has significant

---

[80] CJEU 27.5.2019 – C-508/18, C-82/19 PPU, ECLI:EU:C:2019:456 = NJW 2019, 2145 – OG and PI; see further CJEU 9.10.2019 – C-489/19 PPU, ECLI:EU:C:2019:849 = NJW 2020, 203 – NJ.

[81] CJEU 31.1.2023 – C-158/21, ECLI:EU:C:2023:57 = NJW 2023, 1267 mn. 81 et seqq. – Puig Gordi.

[82] OLG Brandenburg 15.1.2024 – 1 OAus 2/24, BeckRS 2024, 609 mn. 30 et seq.

[83] CJEU 3.3.2020 – C-717/18, ECLI:EU:C:2020:142 = EuGRZ 2020, 226 – X.

impact on the further procedure. According to the Higher Regional Courts of Karlsruhe and Munich, the categorisation can only be challenged successfully if it was arbitrary.[84] However, the EAW must allow a plausibility-check as to whether the alleged facts can substantiate the alleged offence.[85]

b) Reciprocity

In the EAW context, reciprocity is no requirement for surrender, § 82 IRG. 54

c) Statute of limitation

In accordance with Art. 4 no. 4 EAW Framework Decision, § 9 no. 2 IRG also applies 55 in the EAW context if German courts have jurisdiction.[86]

5. Bars to extradition

The reasons to refuse extradition are limited. Within the EU, the prohibition on extra- 56 diting German nationals is lifted (Art. 16 para. 2 sent. 2 GG, § 80 IRG). Likewise, there is no bar on extradition for criminal acts of a military or political nature (§ 6 sub. 1 and 7 IRG do not apply, § 82 IRG).[87] The fact that there is also no explicit bar to surrender in cases of imminent political prosecution or capital punishment is not to be interpreted as widening the scope of extradition. Rather, the EAW Framework Decision is not to be interpreted in a way as to require surrender in cases of a suspected political or otherwise discriminatory prosecution (Recital 12 sent. 2 EAW Framework Decision). This means that political prosecution (§ 6 no. 2 IRG) can be invoked as a defence to extradition. The rule of specialty (§ 11 IRG) does not play a role in surrender under the EAW, § 82 IRG.

a) Mandatory reasons for refusal of surrender

Mandatory reasons for refusal of surrender include *ne bis in idem* (§ 83 sub. 1 no. 1 IRG), 57 the lack of criminal responsibility (§ 83 sub. 1 no. 2 IRG) and judgments *in absentia* (§ 83 sub. 1 no. 3; sub. 2–4 IRG). For the latter, the requirements are similar to those outlined in → mn. 38): if the person was summoned or informed in due time and was informed that a judgment could be rendered *in absentia*, has waived or failed to exercise its right to an appeal or if the person can request for a (full) retrial, extradition may be admissible.

German citizens enjoy a specific level of protection and may, as a principle, trust in 58 being sentenced in their home country.[88] Extradition of a German is only admissible if the requesting state has guaranteed that the person, if sentenced, may return to Germany to serve the sentence and if the offence has a substantial link to the requesting Member State. Whether such link exists needs to be assessed in each individual case and may depend on the place of commission of the offence, the nationality of the victim and where the impact of the offence occurred. If the offence – or an accessory act to it – took place in Germany, courts will need to thoroughly balance the facts, taking into account the individual's trust in being tried in its home country but also the effectiveness of the prosecution, § 80

[84] OLG Karlsruhe 10.8.2006 – 1 AK 30/06, NJW 2006, 3509; cf. also OLG München 9.10.2012 – OLG Ausl 14 Ausl A 1025/12, BeckRS 2012, 222772 mn. 13.

[85] OLG Karlsruhe 10.8.2006 – 1 AK 30/06, NJW 2006, 3509; OLG Karlsruhe 15.8.2013 – 1 AK 45/13 BeckRS 2014, 22317.

[86] On the interruption of the limitation period by foreign prosecutorial acts in that context see BVerfG 3.9.2009 –2 BvR 1826/09, NJOZ 2010, 1436 – Christoforakos I; OLG Karlsruhe 25.3.2013 – 1 AK 102/11, BeckRS 2013, 6052 mn. 9.

[87] BeckFormB Strafverteidiger/Köberer XIII. E. 1., p. 1171.

[88] BVerfG 3.9.2009 –2 BvR 1826/09, NJOZ 2010, 1436 mn. 14.

sub. 2 IRG.[89] The latter may also include an assessment of the availability of evidence and in particular the effect on witnesses. With additional effective cross-border investigative measures such as the EIO (→ mn. 77 et seqq.) or orders under the E-Evidence Regulation (→ mn. 85 et seqq.), the relevance of this criterion has yet to be tested. The necessary assessment may prove particularly difficult with offences such as forming criminal or terrorist organisations acting across borders.

b) Optional reasons for refusal of surrender

59 Optional grounds of refusal include prosecution and termination of proceedings in the executing state for the same offence (§ 83b sub. 1 no. 1, 2 IRG) and preference given to another request for extradition (§ 83b sub. 1 no. 3 IRG). An EAW for the purposes of execution of a custodial sentence or detention order may be refused where the requested person is a national or a resident of Germany with a legitimate interest to have his sentence executed in Germany (Art. 4 no. 6 EAW Framework Decision; § 83b sub. 2 no. 2 IRG). This ground for refusal must in principle also be applicable to non-EU nationals.[90]

c) European ordre public (§ 73 sent. 2 IRG)

60 With numbers of EAWs rising and showing the positive impact of the EAW on the surrender between Member States, so has scrutiny on surrender both by the CJEU and national courts, such as the BVerfG. Starting with *Aranyosi and Căldăraru*, the CJEU has begun to accept that mutual trust and mutual recognition end where obvious violations of human rights are threatened by other EU Member States. Since Art. 1 para. 3 EAW Framework Decision requires Member State to respect fundamental rights and fundamental legal principles as enshrined in Art. 6 TEU. The enforcement of an EAW must therefore not lead to inhuman or degrading treatment[91] or a violation of the right to a fair trial.[92] The principle of proportionality is itself not adequately considered by the EAW Framework Decision. The imminent risk of such treatment must be assessed by the executing judicial authority in a two-step process: the first question is whether the shortcomings in the issuing Member State are systemic or generalized and – if so – the second question becomes whether the individual in the specific case will therefore be exposed to a real risk of a violation of his fundamental rights.[93]

C. Mutual legal assistance

I. Introduction

61 When it comes to mutual legal assistance (MLA) in a broader sense, a distinction is drawn between surrender proceedings (→ mn. 48) and other legal assistance instruments. The latter are understood as assistance between States during the phase of an ongoing

---

[89] BVerfG 15.1.2016 – 2 BvR 1860/15, NJW 2016, 1714 (1715 et seq.).

[90] CJEU 6.6.2023 – C-700/21, ECLI:EU:C:2023:444 = StV 2023, 690 = BeckRS 2023, 12454 (O.G.).

[91] CJEU 5.4.2016 – C-404/15, C-659/15 PPU, ECLI:EU:C:2016:198 = NJW 2016, 1709 – Aranyosi and Căldăraru.

[92] CJEU 25.7.2018 – C-216/18 PPU, ECLI:EU:C:2018:586 = EuGRZ 2018, 396 – LM.

[93] CJEU 5.4.2016 – C-404/15, C-659/15 PPU, ECLI:EU:C:2016:198 = NJW 2016, 1709 mn. 91 et seqq. – Aranyosi and Căldăraru; CJEU 25.7.2018 – C-216/18 PPU, ECLI:EU:C:2018:586 = EuGRZ 2018, 396 mn. 73 et seqq. – LM.

criminal investigation or an ongoing trial (§ 59 sub. 2 IRG; for legal assistance concerning the execution of a final (judicial) decision → mn. 94 et seq.).[94] Unfortunately, in this field, an almost incomprehensible legal framework has evolved over the years, which renders it very difficult for practitioners to identify the applicable legal instrument.[95] In the more narrow sense MLA measures may cover, amongst others, requests for information from another State or the transfer of evidence such as interrogation of witnesses or suspects abroad.[96] Legal assistance mechanisms are often employed in white-collar crime cases, as they frequently contain a cross-border element. However, until recently MLA requests have been considered long and slow processes as such requests are often based on old and sometimes outdated bi- or multilateral treaties between States (essentially, treaties under international law) such as the 1959 European Convention on Mutual Assistance in Criminal Matters ('1959 CoE Mutual Assistance Convention') and its additional protocols. Especially with view to electronic data and evidence, which are increasingly important during investigations, law enforcement authorities often fear that MLA requests may not be 'efficient' enough to prevent loss or destruction of evidence. In this regard, over the past few years, especially within the European Union, efforts have been intensified to create quicker and more efficient mechanisms between Member States based on the principles of mutual trust and mutual recognition. In the following chapter, we will first outline common procedural elements of legal assistance (→ mn. 62 et seqq.), before addressing in detail MLA measures with third countries (→ mn. 70 et seqq.) and between EU Member States (→ mn. 73 et seqq.).

II. Procedure

In Germany, the procedure for MLA is in principle regulated by the IRG. Part 5 of the IRG sets out general provisions with regards to MLA (applicable also to third countries) whereas Part 10 of the IRG regulates MLA within the EU. Part 7 of the IRG contains general provisions applicable to both MLA with third countries as well as within the EU. In cases of bi- or multilateral international MLA agreements (i.e. treaties, conventions), such instruments take precedence over the provisions of the IRG (§ 1 sub. 3 IRG). When there is no international agreement, Germany may however provide MLA at its own discretion following the provisions set out in Part 5 and 7 of the IRG. This constitutes a particularity of German law, as other States will only provide MLA on the basis of a formal agreement.[97] 62

As a general rule, MLA requires a 'request of a competent authority of a foreign state' and may only be rendered 'in those cases in which German courts and executive authorities could render mutual legal assistance to each other' (§ 59 sub. 3 IRG). In other words, Germany may only grant MLA if and when a similar measure would be legally allowed under German law.[98] This also means that evidence which is not admissible in German courts (e.g. statements obtained through prohibited examination methods) must not be subjected to MLA measures.[99] As we have seen above with regards to extradition requests, 63

---

[94] For details cf. WJS WirtschaftsStrafR-HdB/Hackner Ch. 27 mn. 2 et seqq.

[95] For an instructive overview see Schomburg/Lagodny/Trautmann/Zimmermann IRG Vor § 59 mn. 35 et seqq.

[96] WJS WirtschaftsStrafR-HdB/Hackner Ch. 27 mn. 10 et seqq.

[97] Schomburg/Lagodny/Trautmann/Zimmermann IRG Vor § 59 mn. 37.

[98] According to WJS WirtschaftsStrafR-HdB/Hackner Ch. 27 mn. 16 also national provisions limiting requests for information such as tax secrets shall be respected.

[99] Schomburg/Lagodny/Trautmann/Zimmermann IRG § 59 mn. 50, but referencing the older (unpublished) decision OLG München 19.12.1984 – OLG Ausl. 113/82, in which the court took a different approach.

German courts will exceptionally refuse requests for MLA when this would harm undeniable principles of constitutional law or minimum standards under international law.[100] As such, MLA is inadmissible if, for example, in the requesting state fundamental conditions according to Art. 6 ECHR (right to a fair trial) are not respected[101] or where MLA may lead to the death penalty to be imposed or enforced.[102] The risk of trade secrets becoming known can only exceptionally exclude MLA as being contrary to the principle of proportionality.[103]

64 The procedure of MLA requests depends on whether it concerns 'incoming requests' or 'outgoing requests':

1. Incoming requests

65 The procedure set out in the IRG is, generally speaking, twofold: one authority is responsible for authorising MLA (granting authority) and another authority is responsible for rendering MLA (rendering authority). If the granting authority holds that the conditions for rendering the requested MLA are met, the rendering authority is bound by that decision and must then perform the MLA measure (§ 60 IRG). The granting authority is assessing in particular whether the request was issued by a competent authority in the requesting state (§ 59 sub. 1 IRG) and whether the requested measure would be admissible in a purely domestic case (§ 59 sub. 3 IRG). In cases of a bi- or multilateral agreement, the authority evidently also assesses whether both the material and procedural requirements set out in the agreement are met. As a general rule, the authority further assesses whether any limits to MLA such as violations of fundamental rights or of the fair-trial principle apply (§ 73 IRG).[104] Unlike in extradition cases (→ mn. 9 et seqq.), MLA (unless provided otherwise in applicable agreements) does not necessarily require reciprocity (cf. § 5 IRG) or an extraditable offence (cf. § 3 sub. 2 IRG) and is not generally excluded in cases of political or fiscal offences.[105] It is also not excluded if a conviction in Germany for the same acts exists or prosecution of the offence would be statute-barred under German law.[106] The requirement of double-criminality also does not generally apply (with the exception of § 66 IRG concerning handing over of objects). Different rules may apply in the case of MLA within the EU, as for instance Art. 11 para. 1 lit. d Directive 2014/41/EU ('EIO Directive') contains a provision that allows for refusals of requests when the principle of *ne bis in idem* applies. In the case of EU MLA instruments such as the EIO (→ mn. 77 et seqq.), granting and rendering authority usually coincide.

66 If the rendering authority is a court and it considers the conditions for MLA as not met, it may request the OLG to rule on the matter. Also, the GenStA may request the court to issue such a decision (§ 61 sub. 1 sent. 2 alt. 1 IRG). The legal remedies for the person concerned are limited to cases concerning the handing over of objects (§ 61 sub. 1 sent. 2

---

[100] BGH 7.7.1999 – 1 StR 311–99, NStZ 1999, 634 (*obiter*; threat of death penalty); OLG Hamburg 1.10.1984 – Ausl. 11/84, StV 1984, 521 (mass court martials in violation of the fair trial principle); Schomburg/Lagodny/Trautmann/Zimmermann IRG § 59 mn. 44.

[101] Schomburg/Lagodny/Trautmann/Zimmermann IRG § 59 mn. 51.

[102] BGH 7.7.1999 – 1 StR 311/99, NStZ 1999, 634; Schomburg/Lagodny/Trautmann/Zimmermann IRG § 59 mn. 45. Cf. to the contrary, however, OLG Karlsruhe 26.6.1990 – 1 AK 22/90, NStZ 1991, 138 (139 et seq.) and the critical annotation by Lagodny on the admissibility of mutual legal assistance where the death penalty could be imposed.

[103] BGH 23.6.1977 – 4 ARs 7/77, BGHSt 27, 222 (227) = BeckRS 1977, 108831.

[104] Schomburg/Lagodny/Trautmann/Zimmermann/Schierholt § 60 mn. 8.

[105] Cf. however Art. 2 lit. a of the 1959 CoE Mutual Assistance Convention, which still applies to those states, to whom Art. 2 of the Additional Protocol to that Convention does not apply.

[106] OLG Stuttgart 30.7.2015 – 1 Ausl. 218/15, NStZ-RR 2015, 387; OLG Karlsruhe 4.1.2016 – 1 AK 64/15, BeckRS 2016, 1185 mn. 12; Schomburg/Lagodny/Trautmann/Zimmermann IRG § 59 mn. 39.

alt. 2, § 66 IRG).[107] In addition, the German jurisprudence takes the view that the right to request a court decision is held not by the person concerned, that is the person accused in the requesting state, but only by a third person who claims his or her rights to be infringed by the measure (§ 66 sub. 2 no. 3 IRG).[108] Such a restriction to legal remedies seems incompatible with Art. 19 para. 4 GG (right to an effective remedy) and is not required by the wording of § 61 IRG.[109] Nevertheless, the question is yet to be resolved by the courts.[110] According to the German courts, the person concerned shall raise arguments against the authorisation of MLA when challenging the concrete investigatory measure under national law (*Integrationslösung*).[111] In any event, the rights of the defence regarding incoming requests are the same as they would be in purely German cases, including i.e. access to the case files and rights to be present at hearings.[112]

2. Outgoing requests

Outgoing requests are not regulated comprehensively by Part 5 of the IRG but rather are fragmented throughout the IRG. The admissibility of such requests must be examined according to the general procedural rules under German law, in particular, provisions in the German Code of Criminal Procedure (*Strafprozessordnung*, StPO), the Youth Courts Act (*Jugendgerichtsgesetz*, JGG) and the Courts Constitution Act (*Gerichtsverfassungsgesetz*, GVG) (§ 77 sub. 1 IRG). Investigatory measures which require a judicial decision according to German law (e.g. search warrants) also require a prior judicial decision in outgoing requests for MLA.[113] In some jurisdictions, the national law of the requested states may provide for further procedural requirements to be followed before MLA may be rendered.[114] As with incoming requests the rights of the defence in Germany are determined by German law.[115] **67**

Part 10 of the IRG dealing with MLA within the EU contains a few provisions dealing explicitly with outgoing requests (e.g. § 91j IRG). **68**

III. Interpol

Interpol plays a role in facilitating MLA through the issuance of Blue Notices, concerning the collection of additional information about a person's identity, location or activities in relation to a criminal investigation, and – more rarely – Black Notices, when an Interpol member seeks information on an unidentified body, and Purple Notices, issued to seek or provide information on *modus operandi*, objects, devices and concealment methods **69**

[107] OLG Stuttgart 9.11.2015 – 1 ARs 116/15, ZWH 2016, 126 (127) and the critical annotation by Lagodny.

[108] OLG Stuttgart 9.11.2015 – 1 ARs 116/15, ZWH 2016, 126 et seq.; OLG Nürnberg 4.9.2012 – 1 OLG Ausl 166/11, BeckRS 2012, 20158; OLG Köln 27.7.2004 – Ausl 92/04, BeckRS 2004, 18654; OLG Frankfurt 17.9.2003 – 2 Ausl. II 11/96, NStZ 2005, 349; GPKGB Int. Rechtshilfeverkehr/Johnson, 136. EL Juni 2024, IRG § 61 mn. 12.

[109] Schomburg/Lagodny/Lagodny/Zimmermann IRG § 61 mn. 16.

[110] Cf. BGH 18.8.2022 – 4 ARs 2/21, BeckRS 2022, 25302 mn. 19.

[111] BVerfG 24.6.1997 – 2 BvR 1581/95, BeckRS 1997, 126335; OLG Frankfurt 17.9.2003 – 2 Ausl. II 11/96, NStZ 2005, 349; Schomburg/Lagodny/Trautmann/Zimmermann Vor § 59 mn. 55 et seqq.; GPKGB Int. Rechtshilfeverkehr/Johnson, 136. EL Juni 2024, IRG § 61 mn. 12, 15.

[112] WJS WirtschaftsStrafR-HdB/Hackner Ch. 27 mn. 17.

[113] WJS WirtschaftsStrafR-HdB/Hackner Ch. 27 mn. 16a.

[114] WJS WirtschaftsStrafR-HdB/Hackner Ch. 27 mn. 16a.

[115] WJS WirtschaftsStrafR-HdB/Hackner Ch. 27 mn. 17.

used by criminals. Recently, Interpol has instituted Silver Notices to identify and trace criminal assets.

IV. Mutual legal assistance with third countries

70 MLA with third countries is possible in two different ways: either on the basis of bi- or multilateral MLA treaties regulating rights and obligations of Contracting States or, if no such treaty exist, on the basis of a purely political/diplomatic decision to assist another State without any legal obligation to do so (principle of sovereignty of States). In the latter case, provisions of the IRG (in particular, Part 5) are applicable. In practice, it is much more common for States to request – and even more so, to provide – MLA on the basis of bi- or multilateral treaties. Germany has concluded numerous MLA treaties over the years, with some of the earliest treaties dating back to the 1870s.[116] The BMUV provides a regularly updated list of countries indicating whether or not an MLA treaty exists with the respective country – this is also a very useful tool for defence lawyers when facing cases with a cross-border element and MLA issues as an examination of the applicable treaty is an indispensable requirement to advise clients in this regard.

71 As most MLA treaties vary as regards the scope of the measures they apply to (some treaties may apply only for specific investigation measures) or the necessity of particular procedural requirements, a detailed description of each treaty or each contractual clause would go beyond the scope and the aim of this chapter. In the daily practice, the 1959 CoE Mutual Assistance Convention will play a significant role, in particular since it also forms the basis of post-Brexit assistance between EU Member States and the UK (cf. Art. 633 TCA).

72 As an example for a bilateral treaty, we will therefore focus on the – in practical terms highly relevant – 2003 Treaty on MLA in criminal matters between Germany and the United States ('US-Germany-MLA-Treaty). The treaty was signed in October 2003 following nearly 30 years of negotiations and is accompanied by a Supplementary Treaty dated 18 April 2006. This became necessary as parallel to the signing of the US-Germany-MLA-Treaty, the EU had also concluded an MLA treaty with the United States (2003 Agreement on mutual legal assistance between the European Union and the United States of America ('EU-US-MLA-Treaty').[117] Art. 1 para. 1 US-Germany-MLA-Treaty sets out, that Contracting Parties 'undertake to afford each other, through their competent authorities, the widest measure of mutual assistance in criminal investigations and proceedings', covering MLA measures such as locating or identifying persons or items, serving documents, taking the testimony or statements of persons, transferring persons in custody for testimony or other purposes, providing documents, records, and other items, executing searches and seizures, special investigative techniques such as telecommunications surveillance, undercover investigations, and controlled deliveries, assisting in proceedings related to immobilisation and forfeiture of assets, restitution, collection of fines and any other form of assistance not prohibited by the laws of the Requested State (Art. 1 para. 2 US-Germany-MLA-Treaty). It becomes clear from the treaty that as a general rule MLA shall be granted and only in exceptional circumstances MLA may

---

[116] The earliest legal assistance treaties of Germany date back to the 1870s. For example, the collection E 30/1 Bü 199 in the Main State Archive Stuttgart contains documents on the extradition of prosecuted individuals between Germany and foreign countries from 1868 to 1927, see <https://www2.landesarchiv-bw.de/ofs21/olf/struktur.php?anzeigeKlassi=028&bestand=4167&> (last accessed: 31.1.2025).

[117] Agreement on mutual legal assistance between the European Union and the United States of America (OJ L 181, 19.7.2003, p. 34–42).

be denied (Art. 3 US-Germany-MLA-Treaty: 'Assistance may be denied if execution of the request would prejudice the sovereignty, security, or other essential interests of the Requested State.'). This is common in MLA treaties as both Contracting Parties want to express their willingness and determination to further judicial (and to some extent police) cooperation in the interest of effective law enforcement. As in the past years, requests for preserving and producing/transmitting electronic data have become increasingly frequent and important, the EU and the US have intensified their efforts to cooperate in such matters as well, especially after the US had adopted the Clarifying Lawful Overseas Use of Data Act (CLOUD Act), which obliges American service providers to produce data even if stored overseas. Negotiations for an EU-US Agreement on the exchange of electronic evidence are currently ongoing.[118]

V. Mutual legal assistance within the European Union

MLA has a long tradition between today's EU Member States but was often characterised as being inefficient and slow. Already in 1959 Member States of the Council of Europe had adopted the 1959 CoE Mutual Assistance Convention, which was supplemented by its 1978 and 2001 Additional Protocols,[119] and which, up until today, remains in force and applicable if no other legal instrument applies. In 2000, the EU Member States concluded the Convention on Mutual Assistance in Criminal Matters between EU Member States ('2000 EU Mutual Assistance Convention'),[120] which was one of the key legal instruments in the field of MLA within the EU. Both conventions have been widely superseded by the EIO Directive (Art. 34 para. 1 lit. a EIO Directive) and other EU law instruments. The legal framework was previously characterised by numerous, almost countless legal instruments.[121] As a legal practitioner it is therefore indispensable to differentiate between those instruments as they may differ in terms of subject, scope and Member States that are bound by these instruments. 73

Over the years, as the European Union – with the exceptions of Denmark and Ireland, who have opted out of the 'Area of Freedom, Security and Justice' (AFSJ) – has obtained more competences in criminal matters, new instruments have been adopted to create swifter and more efficient mechanisms. Since the entrance into force of the Lisbon Treaty in 2009, the EU has an explicit competence to adopt legal instruments within the field of judicial cooperation in criminal matters. Art. 82 para. 1 TFEU states that '[j]udicial cooperation in criminal matters in the Union shall be based on the principle of mutual recognition of judgments and judicial decisions' and allows the EU legislator to adopt measures to 'lay down rules and procedures for ensuring recognition throughout the 74

[118] Council Decision authorising the opening of negotiations with a view to concluding an agreement between the European Union and the United States of America on cross-border access to electronic evidence for judicial cooperation in criminal matters, Council Document 9114/19.

[119] WJS WirtschaftsStrafR-HdB/Hackner Ch. 27 mn. 66; Germany ratified the 1959 CoE Mutual Assistance Convention on 30.11.1977, the 1978 Additional Protocol on 14.9.1981 and the 2001 Second Additional Protocol on 25.9.2007.

[120] Denmark and Ireland have opted out of the European Investigation Order (EIO) under their respective arrangements with the EU. Consequently, the 2000 EU Mutual Assistance Convention remains the primary legal framework for mutual legal assistance between these states and other EU Member States, see Bundesministerium der Finanzen, Merkblatt zur Internationalen Rechtshilfe in Steuerstrafsachen, 15.6.2022. In addition, the EU Convention retains its importance for certain investigative measures that are not fully covered by the EIO. A prominent example of this is the formation of Joint Investigation Teams (JITs).

[121] Examples for other legal assistance instruments: Seizure and Confiscation – Regulation (EU) 2018/1805, Combating Money Laundering and Terrorist Financing – Directive (EU) 2018/1673.

Union of all forms of judgments and judicial decisions' (Art. 82 para. 1 lit. a TFEU) or to 'facilitate cooperation between judicial or equivalent authorities of the Member States in relation to proceedings in criminal matters and the enforcement of decisions' (Art. 82 para. 1 lit. d TFEU). The EU has, therefore, the competence to adopt both Directives and Regulations within the field of MLA.

75 In contrast to MLA with third countries (→ mn. 70 et seqq.), within the EU, MLA is based on the principle of mutual recognition. It is often referred to as a 'cornerstone' of cooperation in the EU and was first applied in the EAW Framework Decision (→ mn. 48 et seqq.). Mutual recognition is founded on the idea that the EU Member States shall mutually trust that fundamental rights and the rule of law are respected in other Member States. Hence, judicial decisions of one Member State are in principle to be recognised in another Member State, therefore do not have to be assessed in detail with regards to the legal requirements of the executing Member State. In essence, judicial decisions in one Member State are treated like 'domestic' judicial decisions. Evidently, as some Member States such as Poland or Hungary are (still) currently facing rule of law issues, the principle of mutual recognition is put to the test, however, it continues to be the basis for MLA in the EU.

76 The most common and most frequently used instruments are EIOs (→ mn. 77 et seqq.) and JITs (→ mn. 84 et seqq.). The EU has also adopted the E-Evidence Regulation (→ mn. 85 et seqq.),[122] which will enter into force in 2026 and will mark a 'new era' of MLA as it shifts the traditional MLA regime (between judicial authorities of two Member States) towards the possibility of judicial authorities requesting preservation and production by electronic evidence directly from (private) service providers in other Member States (→ mn. 86 et seqq.). Since June 2021, the European Public Prosecutor's Office (EPPO) (→ mn. 93 et seqq.) has become operational. Even though this is, strictly speaking, not a measure of MLA, but a measure of enhanced cooperation (Art. 86 TFEU), the European Delegated Prosecutors (EDPs) may conduct 'cross-border investigations' and may assign the enforcement of investigatory measures (such as searches or premises) to EDPs in another Member State (→ mn. 93) and therefore, shall also be addressed in this chapter.

1. European Investigation Order (EIO)

77 The EIO was introduced with Directive 2014/41/EU in April 2014 and was transposed into national law in 2017 by including the §§ 91a et seqq. IRG.[123] According to those provisions, judicial authorities of Member States (issuing authority) may request from another judicial authority (executing authority) to perform a wide range of investigatory measures. In recent years, the EIO has become one of the most frequently used mutual recognition instruments.[124]

78 The scope of the EIO Directive covers any measure with the exception of JITs (Art. 3 EIO Directive; § 91a sub. 2 IRG) and therefore widely replaces previous MLA instruments such as the CoE Mutual Assistance Convention and the 2000 EU Mutual Assistance Con-

[122] Regulation (EU) 2023/1543 of the European Parliament and of the Council of 12 July 2023 on European Production Orders and European Preservation Orders for electronic evidence in criminal proceedings and for the execution of custodial sentences following criminal proceedings.

[123] BT-Drs. 18/9757, 26.9.2016, <https://dserver.bundestag.de/btd/18/097/1809757.pdf> (last accessed: 31.1.2025).

[124] See for instance Eurojust, Annual Report 2023, <https://www.eurojust.europa.eu/sites/default/files/assets/eurojust-annual-report-2023-en.pdf> (last accessed: 31.1.2025).

vention.[125] Additionally, § 91a sub. 2 IRG states that EIOs do not apply to cross-border surveillance and hearings of a suspect by telephone conference. As a prerequisite, EIOs must be 'necessary and proportionate for the purpose of the proceedings referred to in Art. 4 taking into account the rights of the suspected or accused person' (Art. 6 para. 1 lit. a EIO Directive) and (as for any MLA measure, § 59 sub. 3 IRG) 'the investigative measure(s) indicated in the EIO could have been ordered under the same conditions in a similar domestic case' (Art. 6 para. 1 lit. b EIO Directive).

In case of incoming requests, in particular the following conditions as set out in § 91b **79**
IRG must be met:

- if national criminal procedure law requires for some measures either a designated criminal offence (e.g. § 100a sub. 2 StPO) or a minimum punishment threshold, an EIO may only be executed if the offence which gave rise to the EIO meets those requirements (§ 91b sub. 1 no. 1 IRG);
- rights to refuse to give evidence or information (§§ 52, 53, 55 StPO) must be respected;
- pursuant to § 73 sent. 2 IRG, rendering mutual assistance must be compatible 'with the obligations which the Federal Republic of Germany is under pursuant to Art. 6 of the Treaty on European Union and the Charter of Fundamental Rights of the European Union'.

In cases where one of those conditions is not met, the executing authority shall notify the issuing authority without undue delay (§ 91b sub. 5 IRG). § 91c IRG provides for specific admissibility conditions for special types of mutual assistance such as audio-visual hearings, information requests concerning bank accounts or monitoring of financial transactions.

When an EIO is issued by another Member State, the German authorities are obliged **80**
to recognise the EIO 'without any further formality being required, and ensure its execution in the same way and under same modalities as if the investigative measure concerned had been ordered by an authority of the executing State' (Art. 9 para. 1 EIO Directive). The grounds for refusal to execute an EIO are limited in order to ensure that the procedure is as swift as intended by the European legislator. Grounds for refusal include for instance a violation of the *ne bis in idem* principle (Art. 11 para. 1 lit. d EIO Directive; § 91e sub. 1 no. 2 IRG) or potential harm to national security interests (Art. 11 para. 1 lit. b EIO Directive; § 91e sub. 1 no. 1 IRG). When an EIO may interfere with an ongoing criminal investigation in Germany or the evidence requested are already being used in other proceedings in Germany, the German (executing) authorities may defer its authorisation of the EIO (§ 91e sub. 2 IRG). In cases where an EIO was issued unlawfully, the CJEU takes the view that the question of admissibility of evidence remains, in principle, a question of the respective national law of the issuing state – however, in its recent decision regarding EncroChat the CJEU held that 'national criminal courts are required to disregard information and evidence if the person concerned is not in a position to comment effectively on the evidence and the evidence are likely to have a preponderant influence on the findings of fact'[126].

[125] CJEU 9.1.2025 – C-583/23, ECLI:EU:C:2025:6 = BeckRS 2025, 35 – Delda, the CJEU clarified the notion of 'investigative measure' (Art. 1 and 3 EIO Directive) in the sense that (1) an order by which a judicial authority of one Member State requests a judicial authority of another Member State to serve on a person an indictment relating to him or her, (2) an order by which a judicial authority of a Member State requests a judicial authority of another Member State to remand a person in custody pending trial for purposes other than those referred to in Articles 22 and 23 of that directive, or to require him or her to make a bail payment does not constitute an EIO.

[126] CJEU 30.4.2024 – C-670/22, ECLI:EU:C:2024:372 = NJW 2024, 1723.

81 The EIO Directive provides for very short deadlines to execute an EIO: § 91g IRG sets out that authorisation of the EIO shall be given 'without delay' but no later than 30 days after receipt of the request. In cases where the issuing authority requests the securing of evidence, authorisation shall be given, if possible, within 24 hours after receipt of the request. Following authorisation, the executing authority shall perform the investigatory measure within 90 days, otherwise the executing authority must notify the issuing authority of the delay and the reasons thereof (§ 91g IRG).

82 As regards outgoing requests, that is Germany requesting the authorities of another Member State to perform investigatory measures, the CJEU has specified in two decisions the requirement of 'issuing authority' within the meaning of Art. 2 lit. c EIO Directive. On the one hand, unlike the issuance of EAWs, the Court considers the German public prosecutor's office to be sufficiently independent to issue EIOs.[127] On the other hand, German tax authorities may not issue EIOs without validation by a judicial authority.[128]

83 Art. 14 para. 1 EIO Directive states that Member States shall ensure that legal remedies equivalent to those available in a similar domestic case are applicable to the investigative measures indicated in the EIO. Also, Art. 14 para. 2 EIO Directive clarifies that substantive reasons for issuing the EIO may be challenged only in an action brought in the issuing state – this shall however be without prejudice to the guarantees of fundamental rights in the executing state. It becomes clear that the European legislator considers the issuing state to be primarily competent to handle remedies against EIOs.[129] When transposing Art. 14 EIO Directive into national law, the German legislator did not see the need to create new legal remedies. Instead, it considered existing remedies against the investigative measure in question, such as a request for judicial confirmation pursuant to § 98 sub. 2 sent. 2 StPO (analogously) or a complaint pursuant to § 304 StPO to be sufficient.[130] Following the jurisprudence of the BVerfG, applicants may also address grounds for inadmissibility of MLA within those remedies (*Integrationslösung*).[131] In addition, § 91j sub. 1 IRG refers to the remedies foreseen in § 61 sub. 1 IRG when it concerns requests for the handing over of objects. Until recently, it was contested in the legal literature whether – based on Art. 14 para. 2 second part of the phrase EIO Directive – it is admissible to argue against the issuing of the EIO (e.g. lack of suspicion etc.) in the executing state. The legislator did not clarify this when transposing the Directive into national law.[132]

---

[127] CJEU 8.12.2020 – C-584/19, ECLI:EU:C:2020:1002 = NJW 2021, 1373.

[128] CJEU 2.3.2023 – C 16/22, ECLI:EU:C:2023:148 = BeckRS 2023, 2909. The direct use of judicial mutual legal assistance by a customs or tax authority that conducts an investigation into a tax offence under § 386 of the German Fiscal Code (AO) is now possible under the revised German declaration on Art. 24 of the 1959 CoE Mutual Assistance Convention, which entered into force on 19.3.2021. As a result, it is no longer necessary to transfer the case pursuant to § 386 sub. 4 AO or for the tax authority to request the public prosecutor's office to submit a corresponding mutual legal assistance request on its behalf via domestic administrative assistance, see WJS WirtschaftsStrafR-HdB/Hackner Ch. 27 mn. 113.

[129] CJEU 24.10.2019 – C-324/17, ECLI:EU:C:2019:892 = BeckRS 2019, 25316 – Gavanozov I; CJEU 11.11.2021 – C-852/19, ECLI:EU:C:2021:902 = BeckRS 2021, 33900 – Gavanozov II.

[130] BT-Drs. 18/9757, 26.9.2016, p. 30 et seqq., <https://dserver.bundestag.de/btd/18/097/1809757.pdf> (last accessed: 31.1.2025).

[131] BT-Drs. 18/9757, 26.9.2016, p. 30, <https://dserver.bundestag.de/btd/18/097/1809757.pdf> (last accessed: 31.1.2025); BVerfG 24.6.1997 – 2 BvR 1581/95, BeckRS 1997, 126335; OLG Dresden 30.11.2010 – OLG Ausl 74/10, NStZ-RR 2011, 146; Brahms/Gut NStZ 2017, 388 (394).

[132] BT-Drs. 18/9757, 26.9.2016, p. 31, <https://dserver.bundestag.de/btd/18/097/1809757.pdf> (last accessed: 31.1.2025).

2. Joint Investigation Teams (JITs)

84 As mentioned above, JITs do not explicitly fall within the scope of the EIO Directive and therefore continue to be regulated by Art. 13 2000 EU Mutual Assistance Convention in connection with the 2002 Council Framework Decision 2002/465/JHA on joint investigation teams (JIT-FD). As such, JITs may be set up by mutual agreement of the authorities of two or more Member States; a JIT requires a specific purpose and a limited period of time during which investigations shall be carried out in one or more Member States (Art. 13 2000 EU Mutual Assistance Convention). It is their purpose to provide a more direct and efficient channel for authorities to communicate and cooperate than traditional means of MLA. JITs allow authorities to directly exchange information and evidence as well as set up and carry out investigation operations together, including allowing operatives of one Member State to participate and be present during investigatory measures on the territory of another Member State. JITs are often both financially and logistically supported by Eurojust.[133]

Some legal instruments such as the Second Protocol to the 1959 CoE Mutual Assistance Convention allow for the establishment of JITs between EU Member States and Non-Member States. Such provisions also exist on UN level in the field of organized crime.[134]

3. European Preservation and Production Order (e-Evidence)

85 In 2023, the EU has adopted a new legal instrument intended to facilitate the preservation and transmission of electronic evidence between Member States: the E-Evidence Regulation.[135] As electronic evidence have become one of the most frequently used evidence in criminal investigations, the EU has identified a need to set up a system that functions in a swift and efficient manner – even the already tight deadlines set out in the EIO Directive were considered insufficient to avoid destruction or loss of potential evidence.[136] Already in 2018, the EU Commission had published a first Commission proposal for a Regulation, but due to severe concerns and disputes between the EU Parliament and the Council, it was only in late 2022/early 2023 that a consensus was found to adopt the E-Evidence Regulation. It is not surprising that the Regulation has caused such disputes as it, essentially, creates a new MLA paradigm, and some might say, a new era of MLA.

86 The E-Evidence Regulation shifts the traditional MLA regime (between judicial authorities of two Member States) towards the possibility of judicial authorities (issuing authority) requesting preservation and production of electronic evidence directly from (private) service providers in other Member States (executing authority).

87 A distinction is drawn between European Preservation Orders and European Production Orders:

- 88 **European Preservation Orders** oblige service providers to secure electronic evidence if it is 'necessary for and proportionate to the purpose of preventing the removal, deletion or alternation of data' (Art. 6 para. 2 E-Evidence Regulation). Other than a European Production Order, preservation orders may be issued for all criminal offences if

---

133 See for instance Eurojust, Annual Report 2023, p. 83, <https://www.eurojust.europa.eu/sites/default/files/assets/eurojust-annual-report-2023-en.pdf> (last accessed: 31.1.2025).

134 UN Convention against Transnational Organized Crime adopted on 15 November 2000.

135 Regulation (EU) 2023/1543 of the European Parliament and of the Council of 12 July 2023 on European Production Orders and European Preservation Orders for electronic evidence in criminal proceedings and for the execution of custodial sentences following criminal proceedings (OJ L 191, 28.7.2023, p. 118–180).

136 Recital 8 E-Evidence Regulation.

they could have been issued under the same conditions in a similar domestic case and for the execution of a custodial sentence or a detention order of at least four months (Art. 6 para. 3 E-Evidence Regulation). Also, no distinction is drawn between the types of data that should be preserved: traffic data, subscriber data, data requested for the sole purpose of identifying the user and content data.

- **European Production Orders** will usually be combined with preservation orders, as the issuing state usually has an interest in obtaining the data preserved in the executing state to be used in criminal proceedings. The conditions for the issuance of a European Production Order are stricter than for preservation orders as the impact upon the fundamental rights of the data subject is significantly higher when those data are transmitted to the issuing state. Therefore, production orders may only be issued if the following conditions are met:
  - the order shall be 'necessary for and proportionate to the purpose of the proceedings' (Art. 5 para. 2 E-Evidence Regulation);
  - orders concerning subscriber data and data requested for the sole purpose of identifying the user may be issued for all criminal offences and for the execution of a custodial sentence or a detention order of at least four months (Art. 5 para. 3 E-Evidence Regulation);
  - orders concerning traffic data or content data, as such data are more sensitive, may only be issued for criminal offences punishable in the issuing state by a custodial sentence of a maximum of at least three years (Art. 5 para. 4 lit. a. E-Evidence Regulation) or for certain offences listed in Art. 5 para. 4 lit. b. and c. E-Evidence Regulation) or for the execution of a custodial sentence or a detention order of at least four months for criminal offences referred to in Art. 5 para. 4 lit. a, b and c E-Evidence Regulation.

89 The European Parliament has argued during the legislative debate that (private) service providers will not be able to properly assess whether an order fulfils the legal requirements as set out in the Regulation and therefore, there is a significant risk of abuse and unlawful orders.[137] Therefore, following lengthy debates with the Council, it was agreed that in the case of production orders concerning the more sensitive traffic and content data, the executing authority shall be notified of the order at the same time that the order is addressed to the service provider (Art. 8 para. 1 E-Evidence Regulation). This however shall not apply if the issuing authority has reasonable grounds to believe that the offence has been committed, is being committed or is likely to be committed in the issuing state and the person whose data are requested resides in the issuing state (Art. 8 para. 1 E-Evidence Regulation). Hence, a close relation between the issuing state and the person concerned justified for the European legislator to foresee a lower level of protection even though highly sensitive data are at stake for the person concerned.[138]

90 Similarly to the EIO Directive, the E-Evidence Regulation provides for fairly short deadlines for service providers to comply with the orders: data shall be preserved without undue delay and shall in principle be preserved for 60 days, with an option to be preserved for another 30 days (Art. 11 E-Evidence Regulation). The data shall then be transmitted to the issuing state within 10 days, and in emergency cases within 96 hours (Art. 10 para. 2, 3, 4 E-Evidence Regulation). In cases where a notification to the executing authority is required, this authority may raise (the limited) grounds for refusals within the short

---

[137] European Parliamentary Research Service (EPRS), Cross-border access to electronic evidence, <https://www.europarl.europa.eu/RegData/etudes/ATAG/2023/747924/EPRS_ATA(2023)747924_EN.pdf> (last accessed: 31.1.2025).

[138] Such concerns were also raised in the legal literature, see for instance Burchard ZRP 2019, 164; Hüttemann NZWiSt 2024, 81.

time frame of 10 days after receipt of the order (Art. 10 para. 3 in connection with Art. 12 E-Evidence Regulation). It is expected that Member States hosting a high number of service providers will be unable to properly assess the orders as regards their legality and therefore the risk of unlawful orders being executed by service providers is increased. This also poses a risk for the person concerned in the issuing state as the Regulation does not provide for a clear rule on admissibility of evidence if obtained unlawfully.[139]

The Regulation foresees that every person whose data were sought shall have the right **91** to an effective remedy, in principle, in the issuing state (Art. 18 para. 2 E-Evidence Regulation). It will be up to the national legislator to define the scope of and the conditions for such a remedy.

Despite its legal character as Regulation, some of the provisions of the Regulation **92** (such as provisions on remedies) shall be transposed into national law to ensure that the provisions accord with the national legal framework. The Regulation will be applicable law in all Member States from August 2026 onwards (Art. 34 E-Evidence Regulation).

4. European Public Prosecutor's Office (EPPO)

Already in the 1990s, the idea was developed to particularly protect the 'financial **93** interests of the EU', in other words the EU budget, by means of criminal law and through a designated European Public Prosecution's Office.[140] It took however almost 20 years for the EU to (finally) adopt Regulation 2017/1939/EU implementing enhanced cooperation on the establishment of the European Public Prosecutor's Office ('EPPO Regulation').[141] The EPPO became operational in June 2021.[142] As the name suggests, the EPPO is a measure of enhanced cooperation and therefore not an MLA instrument *strictu sensu*. Nonetheless, the Regulation contains elements that result in law enforcement authorities assisting each other closely when it comes to the prosecution of criminal offences affecting the financial interests of the Union which are provided for in Directive 2017/1371/EU (PIF Directive) (Art. 4 EPPO Regulation). The key element of the EPPO Regulation is that the EPPO is 'an indivisible Union body operating as one single Office with a decentralised structure' (Art. 8 para. 1 EPPO Regulation). It can thus act in different Member States without requiring MLA. Most importantly, Art. 30, 31 EPPO Regulation allow for investigatory measures being executed in another Member State than the one handling the case (e.g. searches of premises in another Member State). This competence was understood quite broadly as not only the investigatory measures listed in Art. 30 EPPO Regulation but also 'any measures which are available to prosecutors under national law in similar national cases' may be requested from the EDP in another Member State (Art. 31 EPPO Regulation; Recital 71 EPPO Regulation). It is expected that EPPO will use these means extensively in the future, as they will allow for even closer cooperation between law enforcement authorities than with means of MLA. Hence, it is also not surprising that these provisions have led to the first decision of the CJEU on the EPPO.[143]

---

[139] The European Parliament had advocated to include a provision concerning the admissibility of evidence which reads as follows: 'Electronic information that has been obtained in breach of this Regulation, including where the criteria laid down in this Regulation are not fulfilled, shall not be admissible before a court. Where electronic information has been obtained before a ground for non-recognition listed in Art. 10a (new) has been invoked, it neither shall be admissible before a court.' This provision was not adopted in the final text.

[140] Delmas-Marty.

[141] Pechstein/Nowak/Häde/Hinterhofer AEUV Art. 86 mn. 1 et seqq.

[142] Annual Report, European Public Prosecutor's Office, <https://www.eppo.europa.eu/sites/default/files/2024-03/EPPO_Annual_Report_2023.pdf> (last accessed: 31.1.2025).

[143] CJEU 21.12.2023 – C-281/22, ECLI:EU:C:2023:1018 = NJW 2024, 487.

D. Transfer of sentenced persons

I. Enforcement of foreign judgments in Germany

94 German citizens (Art. 3 para. 1 lit. a of the Council of Europe Convention on the Transfer of Sentenced Persons) sentenced abroad may wish to serve their sentence in a German prison to allow visits from relatives and ensure re-integration without language and culture barriers. The same is true for foreign nationals residing in Germany. Enforcement in Germany may also be preferred to avoid harsh prison conditions abroad or long sentences. While initially, the transfer of a sentenced person was introduced for such humanitarian reasons and was based on the concept of consent, the consent not only of the states involved but also of the sentenced person, the latter has become increasingly irrelevant over the time.

95 The legal mechanism for non-EU and non-treaty-based cases is provided for in § 48 IRG. However, the majority of non-EU cases falls under the Council of Europe Convention on the Transfer of Sentenced Persons. This, amongst others, grants the individual's right to request the transfer, Art. 2 para. 2 sent. 2 Council of Europe Convention on the Transfer of Sentenced Persons. If the sentenced person is abroad, the transfer of the sentenced person and the enforcement of the sentence in Germany will only take place with its consent (§ 49 sub. 2 IRG; cf. also Art. 3 para. 1 lit. d Council of Europe Convention on the Transfer of Sentenced Persons). However, under Art. 2 of the Additional Protocol to the Council of Europe Convention on the Transfer of Sentenced Persons and Art. 68, 69 CISA a transfer is possible without consent in cases of flight. This covers any case in which the sentenced person willingly – by active flight or by not returning for enforcement – procured his unavailability for enforcement of the sentence in the sentencing state.[144]

96 Other than in extradition cases, cases of transfer of sentenced persons to Germany are dealt with by the regional courts (*Landgericht,* LG) and the respective prosecutor, not the OLG or the GenStA, § 50 IRG. According to § 51 IRG, the prosecutor and LG of the individual's last place of residence are competent. The question of local competence alone may pose challenges or conflicts where an individual moved within Germany or had changing/non-permanent residence in Germany in the past. Berlin is competent if no place of residence can be established, § 51 sub. 3 IRG. This aspect, in combination with the fact that such matters are rather rare and unusual for Regional Courts and Prosecutors, can cause severe delay in the proceedings.

97 Following preparations by the prosecutor (§ 52 IRG), which includes the gathering of the relevant information, in particular the foreign sentence, the LG will decide on the admissibility of the transfer of sentence (*exequatur* decision, § 54 IRG), in particular whether the proceedings meet the minimum requirements as set out in § 49 IRG, such as a trial in line with the ECHR in the convicting state and if the offence would have been punishable as criminal or administrative offence under German law.

98 If the sentenced person has an interest in the transfer, it is advisable for German and local/foreign counsel (see § 53 IRG) to speed up the process by providing the prosecutor with the relevant documents and information on the trial abroad.

99 If the requirements are met, the court will determine the sentence enforceable in Germany. When converting the sentence into a German sentence, the court is generally bound by the foreign decision. Consequently, even sentences not foreseen under German

[144] KG 16.7.2007 – 1 AR 105/06-2/5 Ws 53/06, NJW 2008, 673 with a critical annotation by Böhm; OLG Dresden 9.6.2011 – Ausl 184/10, NStZ 2012, 102 (103); Schomburg/Lagodny/Hackner IRG Vor § 48 mn. 11.

law may have to be served. On the lower end, this can cause the enforcement of particularly short sentences (below six months, § 47 StGB). Such sentences – had it been initially rendered by a German court – could only be enforced under special circumstances. On the higher end, even particularly long sentences can be enforced in Germany, § 54a IRG. The latter is particularly concerning in the author's view, since the individual facing a sentence that otherwise may be considered a violation of human dignity (Art. 1 para. 1 GG) must give its irrevocable consent to serving such a sentence in Germany while being abroad and while facing such sentence – it appears obvious that the decision is not based on a voluntary decision. At the same time, § 54a IRG allows a sentenced person to avoid the additional burden of serving such quasi-indefinite sentence abroad.

When converting the sentence, a German court will consider not only the time served **100** for the specific conviction until the transfer of the sentenced person but also other reductions applicable to the sentence under the respective national law. These considerations and reductions can play a vital role when determining the timing of a potential early release under German law after half or two-thirds of the sentence have been served (§ 57 StGB).

The incoming request for a transfer of sentence from other EU countries falls under **101** § 84 IRG and is admissible only under the conditions set out in §§ 84a and b IRG, in particular regarding judgments *in absentia* and *ne bis in idem*. These provisions transfer the rules of the Framework Decision 2008/909/JHA ('Framework Decision on the Mutual Recognition to Judgments in Criminal Matters')[145] into German law.

II. Enforcement of German judgments abroad

A convicted individual may seek to serve the sentence imposed in Germany in their **102** home country. To that end, a foreign national may request to be transferred to serve a sentence imposed by a German court in another country, § 71 IRG.

Often, requests from **non-EU countries** will be governed by the Council of Europe **103** Convention on the Transfer of Sentenced Persons. The requirements for a transfer of a sentenced persons are set out in Art. 3 Council of Europe Convention on the Transfer of Sentenced Persons. Generally, a transfer under this agreement is possible only with the sentenced person's consent (Art. 3 para. 1 lit. d. Council of Europe Convention on the Transfer of Sentenced Persons).

Under IRG, i.e. in the non-treaty context, a person may be transferred without its **104** prior request if the 'enforcement in the foreign state is in the sentenced person's or in the public interest', § 71 sub. 1 no. 2 IRG. This applies even to German nationals, under the stricter requirements of § 71 sub. 2 IRG. In particular, § 71 sub. 2 IRG applies only to non-custodial sentences.

Procedurally, similar to extradition decisions, the OLG is competent to decide about **105** incoming requests, i.e. the transfer of a sentenced person from Germany to another state (§ 71 sub. 4 IRG). As an alternative to the transfer of sentence used in practice, an individual may be released from prison under § 456a StPO and expelled with a re-entry ban.

The transfer of the sentenced person to another EU country is governed by § 85 IRG. **106** Different from the case of enforcement in non-EU countries, the enforcement authority, i.e. the Public Prosecutor's Office (§ 451 StPO), may be competent to take the decision to

[145] Council Framework Decision 2008/909/JHA of 27 November 2008 on the application of the principle of mutual recognition to judgments in criminal matters imposing custodial sentences or measures involving deprivation of liberty for the purpose of their enforcement in the European Union (OJ L 327, 5.12.2008, p. 27–46).

transfer enforcement to another EU Member State if the individual consents. The transfer does not require the consent of the sentenced person, but its interests will have to play a major role in the decision, even though the general interests of justice have to be considered as well.[146] If the Public Prosecutor's Office declines the transfer, it has to give reasons and the sentenced person can appeal the decision (§ 85 sub. 5 IRG).

E. Execution of fines

107 The execution of foreign sentences in Germany does not only concern the execution of custodial sentences but also fines. Such fines may either be issued by a criminal court as punishment for criminal offences (*Geldstrafe*) or by an administrative authority for administrative offences, (*Ordnungswidrigkeiten*; *Bußgeld*). The latter, in practice, concern most frequently traffic violations abroad, but may also become of relevance when issuing administrative fines against companies. As Germany does not recognise corporate criminal liability *strictu sensu*, companies may not be punished with a *Geldstrafe* but may only be issued an (administrative) fine notice (→ mn. 108).

108 The execution of fines is regulated by Part 4 and Part 9 (sub-chapter 2) of the IRG whereas Part 4 provides for general provisions on execution of fines (and sentences overall) and Part 9 covers the execution of fines within the EU. In 2005, the EU has adopted Framework Decision 2005/214/JHA on the application of the principle of mutual recognition to financial penalties ('Framework Decision on Mutual Recognition of Financial Penalties'). Pursuant to Art. 4 Framework Decision on Mutual Recognition of Financial Penalties, the executing states 'shall recognise a decision (…) without any further formality being required and shall forthwith take all the necessary measures for its execution'. Hence, whenever the conditions set out in the Framework Decision on Mutual Recognition of Financial Penalties are met (and the executing state did not invoke one of the very limited grounds for refusal, cf Art. 7 Framework Decision on Mutual Recognition of Financial Penalties), the executing state shall automatically execute the financial penalty in accordance with its national law (Art. 9 para. 1 Framework Decision on Mutual Recognition of Financial Penalties). The European legislator was aware that not all EU Member States recognise corporate criminal liability in their respective national law and therefore, to ensure the broadest possible scope of application, stated in Art. 9 para. 3 Framework Decision on Mutual Recognition of Financial Penalties that 'a financial penalty imposed on a legal person shall be enforced even if the executing State does not recognise the principle of criminal liability of legal persons.' In essence, this means that for instance a fine issued against a (German) company by a French or a Dutch authority (where corporate criminal liability exists) must be executed by Germany as executing state even though Germany does not recognise corporate criminal liability *strictu sensu*. In such cases, the foreign punishment is 'transposed' into a German fine notice issued to the company concerned (§ 30 OWiG).

109 The Framework Decision on Mutual Recognition of Financial Penalties was transposed into national law by Germany in 2010 by adding §§ 86–87q IRG.[147] According to those provisions, it was necessary to obtain a court order in case of fines against companies (§ 87i

---

[146] KG 26.10.2015 – (4) 151 AR 38/15 (197/15), BeckRS 2015, 19929 mn. 12 et seqq.; Schomburg/Lagodny/Hackner IRG § 85 mn. 10 et seq.

[147] BGBl. 2010 I Nr. 52, 18.10.2010, <https://www.bundesjustizamt.de/SharedDocs/Downloads/DE/EUGeld/Gesetz_2005_214_JI.pdf?__blob=publicationFile&v=3>.

sub. 1 no. 2 IRG). However, in 2020, the legislator decided to eliminate the requirement of a court order as this was seen as a pure formality and led to a burden on the justice system.[148] This was justified in the view of the legislator as the BfJ as competent authority has to assess all procedural requirements and its decision may be challenged with legal remedies. Hence, a 'second' court involvement was considered unnecessary. Interestingly, the legislator referred to punishments for traffic violations in the Netherlands as main practical example for the execution of fines against companies. It therefore remains to be seen how punishments against companies will be dealt with in white-collar situations, for example violations against supply chain regulations.

[148] BGBl. 2020, p. 2474 et seqq., 26.11.2020, <https://www.bgbl.de/xaver/bgbl/start.xav#__bgbl %2F%2F*%5B%40attr_id%3D%27bgbl120s2474.pdf%27%5D__1738249384017> (last accessed: 31.1.2025).

CHAPTER 10
CORRUPTION OFFENCES

Bibliography: Heuking/von Coelln, Die Neuregelung des § 299 StGB – Das Geschäftsherrenmodell als Mittel zur Bekämpfung der Korruption?, BB 2016, 323; Littwin, Aktuelle Entwicklungen bei der steuerlichen Behandlung von Schmier- und Bestechungsgeldern, BB 1998, 2398; Wolf, Modernization of the German Anti-Corruption Criminal Law: The Next Steps, 8 German Law Journal 295 (2007).

Table of contents

A. General remarks 220
I. The term of corruption 220
II. The economic significance of corruption 220
B. The legal framework 221
C. Types of corruption offences 223
I. Offences committed in public office 223
1. Circle of perpetrators 223
2. Accepting and granting benefits 224
a) Discharge of a duty 225
b) The definition of 'benefit' 225
c) The unlawful agreement 226
d) Limitations 227
3. Taking and giving bribes 227
4. Subjective elements of crime and mistakes 228
5. Especially serious cases 229
6. Foreign bribery 230
7. Perpetration and participation 231
8. Place of commission of offence 232
9. Sanctions 232
10. Attempt, completion and termination 233
11. Statute of limitations 233
12. Asset recovery 234
II. Offences against competition 234
1. Taking and giving bribes in commercial practice 234
2. The requirements in detail 235
a) Circle of perpetrators 235
aa) Employees or agents 235
bb) The definition of 'business' 236
b) The criminal actions 236
aa) In the course of a business activity 236
bb) The notion of benefit 236
cc) Taking and giving bribes 237
dd) The unlawful agreement 237
3. Especially serious cases 238
4. Applicability of German criminal law in cases involving foreign countries 238
5. Attempt 239
6. Request to prosecute 240
7. Statute of limitations 240
8. Asset recovery 240

III. Procedural law 241
1. Special investigative powers........................... 241
2. Jurisdiction 241
3. Registration of final convictions in the competition register 241
D. Compliance: how to prevent corruption 242

A. General remarks

I. The term of corruption

1 The meaning and scope of the term corruption is subject to different approaches of the respective disciplines. There is no single definition. In essence, corruption describes the exchange of benefits in breach of rules. The main causes of corrupt behaviour are rooted in human nature, namely in the pursuit of money and power. In an ethical and moral sense, corruption can refer to all forms of behaviour in which persons with specific functions obtain advantages judged to be inappropriate at the expense of the general public.[1] Corruption can furthermore be defined as the abuse of power, namely the abuse of a public mandate, by violating legal norms. However, from a criminal law point of view, corruption is not limited to traditional settings involving public officials. There is a growing public awareness that not only public officials are corruptible, but that corruptive behaviour is also relevant in the private sector. This concerns, on the one hand, the fact that large parts of traditional public tasks have been privatised and are carried out by private individuals who do not act as public officials. On the other hand, the phenomenon of corruption in the private sector is by no means limited to privatisation of public tasks, but can be identified in any business sector, mainly in departments that are particularly susceptible to corruption such as purchasing and procurement.[2]

2 The German Criminal Code (*Strafgesetzbuch*) does not refer to the term corruption. In the field of criminal law, corruption is used as a generic term for certain criminal offences. The most relevant provisions of the German Criminal Code refer to more specific definitions such as 'giving, offering or promising' as well as 'taking, demanding or accepting the promise' of benefits or bribes.

II. The economic significance of corruption

3 The actual number of corruption crimes committed and their economic impact are difficult to estimate due to the clandestine nature of their commission. The crimes uncovered represent only a small fraction of the crimes actually committed.

4 The most recent crime statistics of the German Federal Criminal Police Office (*Bundeskriminalamt*) show 3,841 corruption crimes and 1,507 suspects registered by the

---

[1] Momsen/Grützner WirtschaftsSteuerStrafR-HdB/Grützner/Behr § 30 mn. 8 et seq.
[2] ARR WirtschaftsStrafR-HdB Part 5 Ch. 2 mn. 1.

police authorities for the year 2023.[3] In comparison, with regard to economic offences the German Federal Criminal Police Office recorded 38,925 cases.[4]

The majority of the registered crimes concern public administration. 55 % of the bribed persons were public officials. Among the industries associated with giving bribes, the construction industry accounted for the vast majority. In its report, the German Federal Criminal Police Office quantifies the damage caused by corruption offences in 2021 at 61 million EUR. However, it is extremely difficult to determine a precise and valid amount, since the obtaining of approvals for instance or other competitive advantages caused by corruption cannot be measured in detail.[5] On the supplier side, compliant competitors suffer substantial material damages if they are not awarded contracts due to corruption. Corruption causes inefficiency and injustice in the distribution of profits and costs, since on the one hand competition is eliminated or restricted and on the other hand businesses include the costs of bribes in their price calculations. In addition, hardly quantifiable intangible damages resulting from corruption should not be neglected. In the public sector, corruption can undermine the basic trust of the society in the rule of law, the independence of public institutions and the incorruptibility of its representatives. It affects the integrity of the economic system and creates a business environment that is not conductive to fair competition, which can discourage foreign investment and stifle economic growth. In the private sector, allegations of corruption damage the reputation and, as a result, the economic value of the company. Corruption leads to misguided business decisions affecting innovation and development and reduces the productivity of businesses. Corrupt business practices have therefore long since ceased to pay off for businesses. Criminal proceedings with regard to corruption offences not only lead to loss of reputation and risks for the suspected employees but can also jeopardise the existence of the company due to the imposition of significant fines. **5**

B. The legal framework

The combat against corruption is primarily governed by criminal law. The German Criminal Code addresses solely natural persons. Currently, there is no corporate criminal liability under German law. Legal persons can only be held liable for corruption offences under the regime of regulatory fines which can be imposed according to the Act on Regulatory Offences (*Ordnungswidrigkeitengesetz*, OWiG). **6**

The criminal offences of the German Criminal Code address both corruption in the public sector and in the private sector. Corruption in the private sector has been a criminal offence under German law for more than a century. In 1909, a provision was added to the German Act against Unfair Competition (*Gesetz gegen den unlauteren* **7**

---

[3] Bundeskriminalamt, Korruption, Bundeslagebild 2023, p. 4, https://www.bka.de/SharedDocs/Downloads/DE/Publikationen/JahresberichteUndLagebilder/Korruption/korruptionBundeslagebild2023.html?nn=28078 (last accessed: 26 March 2025); cf. WJS WirtschaftsStrafR-HdB/Bannenberg, 5th edn 2020, Ch. 13 mn. 16 et seqq. with regard to the limitations of the statistics.

[4] Bundeskriminalamt, Wirtschaftskriminalität, Bundeslagebild 2023, p. 5, https://www.bka.de/SharedDocs/Downloads/DE/Publikationen/JahresberichteUndLagebilder/Wirtschaftskriminalitaet/wirtschaftskriminalitaetBundeslagebild2023.html?nn=28030 (last accessed: 26 March 2025).

[5] Bundeskriminalamt, Korruption, Bundeslagebild 2023, p. 18, https://www.bka.de/SharedDocs/Downloads/DE/Publikationen/JahresberichteUndLagebilder/Korruption/korruptionBundeslagebild2023.html?nn=28078 (last accessed: 26 March 2025).

Wettbewerb, UWG) that criminalised bribe payments among actors of the private sector.[6] It took almost another hundred years until the provision was transferred to the German Criminal Code by the German Anti-Corruption Act of 1997.[7] The aim of the legislator in transferring this provision to the core criminal law was to raise the public's awareness of the social harmfulness of corrupt behaviour.[8] Nevertheless, corruption in business used to be a well-known phenomenon often perceived as inevitable. An illustrative example is provided by the fact that it was not until 1996 that the German legislature suppressed the tax deductibility of bribes.[9]

8 In the last decades, various legal measures have been implemented at international level which have driven the development of anti-corruption legislation in Germany, such as the 1997 OECD Convention on Combating Bribery of Foreign Public Officials in International Business Transactions, the 1999 Council of Europe Criminal Law Convention on Corruption and the 2003 United Nations Convention against Corruption. The German legislator lagged behind international and social developments.[10] Some of the obligations arising from the conventions were only fulfilled in the recent past by adapting German criminal law.[11]

9 In detail, German criminal law on corruption is structured as follows:

10 The offences governing bribery involving public officials provide four categories of bribery:[12]

- acceptance of advantages in fulfilling one's public duty (§ 331 StGB);
- acceptance of advantages as incentive for violating one's duties (§ 332 StGB);
- giving advantages for actions in fulfilling of one's public duties (§ 333 StGB);
- giving advantages as incentive for actions in violation of one's public duties (§ 334 StGB).

11 § 335a StGB expands the scope of the aforementioned provisions to foreign and international officials and judges. It provides a legal basis to prosecute both the active and passive side of corruption in specific international settings under German criminal law.

12 Corruption in the private sector is governed by § 299 StGB. The provision prohibits the acceptance and giving of bribes in a commercial business context. §§ 299a, 299b StGB provide special provisions sanctioning corruption in the healthcare sector.[13]

13 Moreover, the German Criminal Code governs acts of bribing voters (§ 108b StGB) as well as taking of bribes by and giving of bribes to elected officials (§ 108e StGB), such as members of parliaments (including Bundestag, *Länder* parliaments and the European Parliament) and equivalent bodies on local level.

14 In addition to criminal law, corruption involving public officials is subject to civil service law. The civil service law itself contains a number of behavioural commands and prohibitions that are intended to prevent corruption or, in the event of violations, may have disciplinary consequences. Particularly relevant are violations on the ban on accepting rewards and gifts.[14] Violations of official duties can have different disciplinary consequences. The most severe disciplinary consequences occur when the offender has been sentenced to at least one year's imprisonment or to at least a six months' imprison-

---

[6] LK-StGB/Lindemann StGB § 299 Ch. 'Entstehungsgeschichte' [i.e. 'Origin'].
[7] BGBl. 1997 I 2038.
[8] BT-Drucksache 13/5584, 15.
[9] BGBl. 1995 I 1250 (1253); see also Littwin BB 1998, 2398.
[10] Momsen/Grützner WirtschaftsSteuerStrafR-HdB/Grützner/Behr § 30 mn. 3.
[11] Anti-Corruption Act of 20 November 2015, BGBl. 2015 I 2025.
[12] Cf. the figure of Wolf 8 German Law Journal 297 (2007).
[13] → Ch. 21 mn. 133 on medical criminal law for more details on corruption offences in the healthcare sector.
[14] § 42 sub. 1 BeamtStG, § 71 sub. 1 BBG.

ment for corruption. In this case, the status as a civil servant ends when the judgement is final[15] which includes the entitlement to salary and pension lapses.[16] In other cases, consequences such as reprimands, fines, reduction of remuneration, transfer, demotion, removal from civil service or reduction or withdrawal of pension under disciplinary law may be considered in disciplinary proceedings.

C. Types of corruption offences

As mentioned above, German criminal law distinguishes between corruption offences in public office and corruption offences against competition (→ mn. 6). **15**

I. Offences committed in public office

The corruption offences committed in public office are regulated in §§ 331 et seq. StGB. The protected legal interests are the fairness of the public service (*öffentlicher Dienst*) and the public's trust in this fairness.[17] It should be noted that the pecuniary interest of the employing body is not protected.[18] **16**

1. Circle of perpetrators

The offences of accepting benefits (§ 331 StGB) and taking bribes (§ 332 StGB) are genuine official offences (*echte Amtsdelikte*). That means that only the designated group of persons can be perpetrators of these offences. In contrast, §§ 333, 334 StGB (granting benefits and giving bribes) are everyone's offences (*Jedermannsdelikte*). **17**

The designated offenders in §§ 331 sub. 1, 332 sub. 1 StGB are public officials, European officials or persons entrusted with special public service functions. This special position must exist at the time of the offence.[19] The terms 'public official', 'European official' and 'person entrusted with special public service functions' are further defined in § 11 sub. 1 no. 2, 2a, 3 and 4 StGB: **18**

A **public official** (*Amtsträger*) is any person who, under German law, **19**

a) is a civil servant or judge,
b) carries out other public official functions or
c) has otherwise been appointed to serve with an authority or other agency or has been commissioned to perform public administrative services, regardless of the organisational form chosen to perform such duties.

It can be difficult to determine if the counterpart is a public official.[20] Especially § 11 sub. 1 no. 2 lit. c) StGB can be problematic. The decisive factor is whether it is a longer-term activity that goes beyond a single assignment and whether it is integrated into the structure of the authority.[21] In this context, employees of a legal entity under private law may **20**

---

[15] § 24 sub. 1 BeamtStG, § 41 sub. 1 BBG.
[16] § 41 sub. 2 BBG.
[17] Fischer/Lutz StGB § 331 mn. 2.
[18] Fischer/Lutz StGB § 331 mn. 2.
[19] Fischer/Lutz StGB § 331 mn. 4.
[20] Rotsch Criminal Compliance/Beckemper § 12 mn. 15.
[21] Fischer/Lutz StGB § 331 mn. 4a.

also be public officials in this sense if this legal entity under private law is entrusted with the performance of public duties by contract or by its articles of association and is subject to state control to an extent that makes it appear to be an extended arm of the state.[22]

21 A **European official** (*Europäischer Amtsträger*) is any person who

a) is a member of the European Commission, the European Central Bank, the European Court of Auditors or any court of the European Union,
b) is a civil servant or other member of staff of the European Union or of an institution established by European Union law, or
c) is tasked with carrying out the tasks of the European Union or the tasks of an institution established by European Union law.

22 Only European officials and not any foreign officials can be perpetrators of the §§ 331, 332 StGB. For more on foreign officials → mn. 62 et seqq.

23 A **person entrusted with special public service functions** (*für den öffentlichen Dienst besonders Verpflichteter*) is any person who, without being a public official, is employed by or acts for

a) an authority or other agency which performs public administrative services, or
b) an association or other alliance, business or enterprise which carries out public administrative services for an authority or other agency

and who is formally required by law to perform the duties of those functions in a conscientious manner.

24 §§ 331 sub. 2 and 332 sub. 2 StGB relate to **judges, members of a court of the European Union** or **arbitrators** who demand, allow themselves to be promised or accept a benefit for themselves or a third party in return for the fact that they performed or will in the future perform a judicial act. The term 'judge' (*Richter*) is defined in § 11 sub. 1 no. 3 StGB as any person who, under German law, is either a professional judge (*Berufsrichter*) or an honorary judge (*ehrenamtlicher Richter*).

2. Accepting and granting benefits

25 Accepting and granting benefits according to §§ 331, 333 StGB is given if the benefit is granted without a reference to a specific official act.

26 Accepting benefits (*Vorteilsannahme*) means that a public official, a European official or a person entrusted with special public service functions demands, allows him- or herself to be promised or accepts a benefit for him- or herself or for a third party in return for the discharge of a duty (§ 331 sub. 1 StGB) or that a judge, a member of a court of the European Union or an arbitrator demands, allows him- or herself to be promised or accepts a benefit for him- or herself or for a third party in return for the fact that he or she performed or will in the future perform a judicial act (§ 331 sub. 2 sent. 1 StGB).

27 Granting benefits means mirror-like that someone offers, promises or grants a public official, a European official, a person entrusted with special public service functions or a soldier in the Federal Armed Forces (*Bundeswehr*) a benefit for that person or a third party in return for the discharge of a duty (§ 333 sub. 1 StGB) or that someone offers, promises or grants a judge, a member of a court of the European Union or an arbitrator a benefit for that person or a third party in return for the fact that they performed or will in the future perform a judicial act (§ 333 sub. 2 StGB).

[22] Fischer/Lutz StGB § 331 mn. 4b, with practical examples in mn. 4c.

a) Discharge of a duty

28 Concerning the contribution of the official, the discharge of a duty (*Dienstausübung*) includes all acts which form part of the official's official duties and which are performed by the official in an official capacity.[23] § 336 StGB states that the omission to act is equivalent to the performance of an official act or of a judicial act within the meaning of §§ 331 to 335a StGB.

29 The prevailing view is that this includes activities in which the officeholder deliberately abuses his or her position.[24]

30 Private acts are not covered, even if the office offers the opportunity to do so, or if they are carried out using expertise acquired in the office or using official influence or prestige.[25]

31 § 331 StGB applies to both the performance of services in breach of official duties and in accordance with official duties.[26] In the case of sufficiently specific official acts, the qualification of § 332 applies.[27]

32 Judicial acts (§ 331 sub. 2 StGB) are those protected by the independence of the judiciary, i.e. in particular the conduct of legal proceedings, but not mere judicial administrative activities.[28] Unlike § 331 sub. 1 StGB, it has to be a specific judicial act.

b) The definition of 'benefit'

33 The term of 'benefit' (*Vorteil*) is one of the central ones in §§ 331 et seq. StGB. The only statutory provision on the concept of advantage is found in § 337 StGB. This provision deals with the special case of the remuneration of arbitrators. The latter is only deemed a benefit within the meaning of §§ 331 to 335 StGB if arbitrators demand it, allow it to be promised to them or accept it from a party unbeknown to the other, or if one party offers, promises or grants it to them unbeknown to the other.

34 In general, 'benefit' means any benefit provided by the donor that objectively improves the economic, legal or personal position of the public official or a third party, whether materially or immaterially,[29] and to which the public official is not entitled.[30]

35 Unlike the concept of pecuniary benefit in the context of the offence of fraud (§ 263 StGB), the characteristic of advantage does not presuppose that the assets of the person giving the advantage are diminished and that the recipient is enriched.[31] Rather, it can only be determined from an overall perspective whether such an advantage exists.

36 Firstly and foremost, the term 'benefit' covers all types of non-monetary benefit, including discounts, invitations to events, etc.[32] There is no value limit: Any benefit, even if of low value, is included.[33]

37 Furthermore, intangible benefits such as honours and improved career opportunities are also covered.[34] However, this presupposes that an improvement in the official's posi-

---

23 BGHSt 31, 264 (280) = NJW 1983, 2509 (2513); MüKoStGB/Korte StGB § 331 mn. 107; Fischer/Lutz StGB § 331 mn. 6 et seq.

24 BeckOK StGB/Trüg, 64. Ed. 1.2.2025, StGB § 331 mn. 16 et seq. with further references.

25 TK StGB/Eisele StGB § 331 mn. 33.

26 Fischer/Lutz StGB § 331 mn. 9.

27 Fischer/Lutz StGB § 331 mn. 9.

28 BeckOK StGB/Trüg, 64. Ed. 1.2.2025, StGB § 331 mn. 18.

29 BGHSt 31, 279 = NJW 1983, 2.509 (2.512).

30 BGHSt 47, 295 = NJW 2002, 2.801 (2.804).

31 Fischer/Lutz StGB § 331 mn. 11a; cf. the chapter on fraud for more details (→ Ch. 11 mn. 57 et seqq.).

32 BeckOK StGB/Trüg, 64. Ed. 1.2.2025, StGB § 331 mn. 19 et seqq. with further references.

33 Fischer/Lutz StGB § 331 mn. 11c.

34 Fischer/Lutz StGB § 331 mn. 11e et seq.

tion can be established, which is difficult to do in individual cases and on which there is only isolated case law.[35]

38 In cases where there is a contract between the official and the person giving the advantage and the consideration is adequate, it is disputed whether the conclusion of the contract cannot constitute a benefit or whether there is no unlawful agreement (→ mn. 40 et seqq.).[36]

39 Since an amendment to the law in 1997, benefits for a third party are also explicitly covered. The third party can be not only a private person, but also the employing body of the public official or a legal person or a partnership under private law.[37] For the subjective elements of crime, it is necessary that the official is aware of and consents to the granting of the benefit to the third party.[38] If the public official only learns of the donation to the third party after the fact, it is sufficient if he or she consents to its receipt and use by the third party.[39]

c) The unlawful agreement

40 There must be a special relationship between the acceptance of the benefit and the performance of an official act. The acceptance of the benefit must be an equivalent for the provision of the service, which is expressed by the word 'for' (German: *für*).[40] The agreement between the accepting public official and his or her counterpart on this relationship of equivalence is referred to as an 'unlawful agreement' (*Unrechtsvereinbarung*), which forms the core of the offence of bribery.[41]

41 There must be an at least tacit understanding between the public official and the person offering, promising or granting the benefit that the benefit is in exchange for the performance of a duty or the unlawful performance of an official act.[42]

42 In contrast to § 299 StGB, the unlawful agreement may relate to a future as well as to a past performance of duty, as is clear from the wording of §§ 331 sub. 2 sent. 1, 332 sub. 2 sent. 1, 333 sub. 2 StGB: 'in return for the fact that they performed or will in the future perform a judicial act' (similar: § 334 sub. 2 sent. 1 no. 1, 2 StGB).

43 To avoid even the appearance of corruption, within the scope of § 331 StGB a general link between the benefit and the provision of the service in the sense of a reciprocal relationship is sufficient and a link to a specific service is not required.[43] This has been the case since the wording in § 331 sub. 1 StGB has been changed in 1997. Before, it stated as in § 332 sub. 1 StGB that the benefit has to be in context with the performance of an official act. The current legal situation means that initiation payments ('grooming', German: *Anfüttern*) and the so-called 'sweetening' (*Klimapflege*) for the creation of general goodwill (e.g. invitations to cultural, sporting, culinary or other events of monetary value) also fall within the scope of the offence.[44] This makes it difficult to distinguish between legal and illegal actions in specific situations.[45]

---

[35] BeckOK StGB/Trüg, 64. Ed. 1.2.2025, StGB § 331 mn. 21 et seqq. with further references.
[36] BeckOK StGB/Trüg, 64. Ed. 1.2.2025, StGB § 331 mn. 22 et seqq.
[37] Fischer/Lutz StGB § 331 mn. 14a.
[38] BeckOK StGB/Trüg, 64. Ed. 1.2.2025, StGB § 331 mn. 23.2.
[39] TK StGB/Eisele StGB § 331 mn. 29.
[40] MüKoStGB/Korte StGB § 331 mn. 116.
[41] Fischer/Lutz StGB § 331 mn. 21.
[42] BeckOK StGB/Trüg, 64. Ed. 1.2.2025, StGB § 331 mn. 27.
[43] Fischer/Lutz StGB § 331 mn. 23.
[44] BeckOK StGB/Trüg, 64. Ed. 1.2.2025, StGB § 331 mn. 29.
[45] Fischer/Lutz StGB § 331 mn. 24.

d) Limitations

44 As the requirements for an unlawful agreement are rather low, it is generally agreed that there is a need to limit what is considered illegal. In order to ensure that constellations that are not generally condemned do not fall within the scope of §§ 331, 333 StGB, the unwritten criteria of social adequacy (*Sozialadäquanz*) has been established. This should include benefits that are out of politeness or courtesy and are both socially acceptable and generally approved from a legal perspective, such as gifts of low value at the turn of the year or on anniversaries.[46] A reliable value limit has not been established. Rather, it depends on the specific position of the official and the particular customs.[47] With regard to promotional gifts, which are more common in the private sector, stricter standards apply to public officials.[48]

45 In addition to this limitation at the level of the elements of the offence, §§ 331 sub. 1 and 333 sub. 3 StGB determine that the offence does not entail criminal liability if the competent authority, within the scope of its powers, either previously authorised the acceptance of the benefit or the official promptly makes a report to the competent authority and it authorises the acceptance. This only applies to §§ 331 sub. 1 and 333 sub. 1 StGB, that means the offender has to be a public official, European official or person entrusted with special public service function and not a judge, member of a court of the European Union or arbitrator (§§ 331 sub. 2, 333 sub. 2 StGB). Furthermore, the offender may not have demanded the benefit. An authorisation is not possible regarding the acceptance of benefits for official or judicial acts in breach of official or judicial duties (§ 332 StGB).

46 The approval of the acceptance of benefits by civil servants is governed by § 71 BBG (*Bundesbeamtengesetz*, Federal Civil Service Act) for federal civil servants and corresponding provisions in state laws for state civil servants. Accordingly, there is a general ban on the acceptance of rewards, gifts and other benefits, but exceptions are possible with the approval of the highest authority (this responsibility can be delegated). According to § 46 DRiG (*Deutsches Richtergesetz*, German Judiciary Act), the civil service regulations apply to judges accordingly. However, permission can only be granted for non-judicial acts as judicial acts fall under the scope of §§ 331 sub. 2, 332 sub. 2 StGB.[49]

47 The authorisation can exist in advance or can be obtained retroactively for the specific case. If it existed in advance, that is a ground for justification (*Rechtfertigungsgrund*).[50] A retroactive authorisation requires that the official promptly makes a report to the competent authority. If the acceptance of the benefit was admissible, this also constitutes a ground for justification.[51] If the acceptance was not admissible, but the competent authority authorises it anyway, this is a ground for annulment of the sanction (*Strafaufhebungsgrund*).[52]

3. Taking and giving bribes

48 The corruption offences are even more severe when they concern a specific official act and the performance of this act breaches official duties or if the performance of a judicial act breaches judicial duties. These offences are named 'taking bribes' (*Bestechlichkeit*) and 'giving bribes' (*Bestechung*) and are regulated in §§ 332, 334 StGB.

---

46 Fischer/Lutz StGB § 331 mn. 25.
47 BeckOK StGB/Trüg, 64. Ed. 1.2.2025, StGB § 331 mn. 36.
48 Fischer/Lutz StGB § 331 mn. 26a.
49 TK StGB/Eisele StGB § 331 mn. 56.
50 Prevailing opinion, see BeckOK StGB/Trüg, 64. Ed. 1.2.2025, StGB § 331 mn. 45.1 for further details.
51 Fischer/Lutz StGB § 331 mn. 36.
52 TK StGB/Eisele StGB § 331 mn. 62.

49 Taking bribes means that a public official, a European official or a person entrusted with special public service functions demands, allows him- or herself to be promised or accepts a benefit for him- or herself or for a third party in return for the fact that he or she performed or will in the future perform an official act, and thereby breached or would breach his or her official duties (§ 332 sub. 1 sent. 1 StGB) or a judge, a member of a court of the European Union or an arbitrator demands, allows him- or herself to be promised or accepts a benefit for him- or herself or for a third party in return for the fact that he or she performed or will in the future perform a judicial act, and thereby breached or would breach his or her judicial duties (§ 332 sub. 2 sent. 1 StGB).

50 Giving bribes means mirror-like that someone offers, promises or grants a public official, a European official, a person entrusted with special public service functions or a soldier in the Federal Armed Forces a benefit for that person or a third party in return for the fact that they have performed or would in future perform an official act, and thereby breached or would breach their official duties (§ 334 sub. 1 sent. 1 StGB) or that someone offers, promises or grants a judge, a member of a court of the European Union or an arbitrator a benefit for that person or a third party in return for the fact that they (1) performed a judicial act and thereby breached their judicial duties or (2) would perform a judicial act and would thereby breach their judicial duties (§ 334 sub. 2 sent. 1 StGB).

51 In contrast to §§ 331 sub. 1, 333 sub. 1 StGB, only specific or determinable actions meet the requirements of §§ 332 sub. 1, 334 sub. 1 StGB.[53]

52 The performance of the official or judicial act must breach official or judicial duties. The breach of duty does not arise merely from the connection with the benefit, as in the case of §§ 331, 333 StGB, but the official or judicial act itself must be a breach of duty.[54] On the one hand, this is the case when the perpetrator deviates from existing requirements for the performance or omission of an official act (bound decision, German: *gebundene Entscheidung*).[55] If the decision about the performance is discretionary for the official (discretionary decision, German: *Ermessensentscheidung*), there is a breach of duty if the discretion is abused or exceeded, but also if the offender allows him- or herself to be influenced by the benefit in exercising his or her discretion and otherwise remains within the scope of the discretion.[56] This presupposes that the offender has or had at least two alternative courses of action.[57]

53 If the unlawful agreement concerns a future act, this already falls under the scope of §§ 332, 334 StGB when the public official has indicated to the other person that he or she is willing (1) to breach his or her duties by doing the act or (2) to the extent that the act is within his or her discretion, to allow him- or herself to be influenced by the benefit when exercising his or her discretion and if the person who offers, promises or grants the benefit attempts to induce the public official to do so (§§ 332 sub. 3, 334 sub. 3 StGB). In this respect, only the unlawful agreement is relevant. It is therefore irrelevant if the official secretly reserves the right not to act in breach of duty.[58]

4. Subjective elements of crime and mistakes

54 The subjective elements of crime require intent, at least in the form of conditional intent (*bedingter Vorsatz*). In particular, with regard to § 11 sub. 1 no. 2 lit. c) StGB it may

---

53 BeckOK StGB/Trüg, 64. Ed. 1.2.2025, StGB § 332 mn. 2.
54 BeckOK StGB/Trüg, 64. Ed. 1.2.2025, StGB § 332 mn. 4.
55 Fischer/Lutz StGB § 332 mn. 8.
56 Fischer/Lutz StGB § 332 mn. 9a.
57 BeckOK StGB/Trüg, 64. Ed. 1.2.2025, StGB § 332 mn. 8.
58 Fischer/Lutz StGB § 332 mn. 12.

be problematic in individual cases to determine whether the person acting was aware of his or her position as a public official, even though it is sufficient that the person concerned is aware of the circumstances and facts relating to his or her position as a public official, but not of the legal or contractual basis in detail.[59]

If the official mistakenly assumes that there is an authorisation (§ 331 sub. 3 StGB), this 55 is a justification error (*Erlaubnistatbestandsirrtum*).[60] If, on the other hand, the official errs concerning the limits of an authorisation, this is an error in law (*Rechtsfehler*) that can exclude guilt if the mistake was unavoidable (*Verbotsirrtum*, § 17 StGB).[61] With regard to social adequacy, also a distinction must be made: If the official mistakenly assumes circumstances that would justify social adequacy, this is a mistake of fact that excludes intent (*Tatbestandsirrtum*, § 16 sub. 1 StGB).[62] In contrast, if the perpetrator is mistaken about the range of social adequacy, this is a mistake of law.[63] For the counterpart of the official, it is also a justification error if he or she mistakenly assumes that there is an authorisation.[64] If he or she mistakenly assumes that an authorisation is possible, this is a mistake of law.[65]

In the context of taking bribes, the breach of duty is a normative objective element of 56 crime (*normatives Tatbestandsmerkmal*). The intent must also refer to this element.[66] If the official mistakenly assumes that he or she is not acting in breach of his or her duties, there is a mistake of fact and criminal liability can only be considered according to § 331 StGB.[67] If, on the other hand, the official mistakenly assumes that he or she is acting in breach of duty, the offence is an attempt to commit a criminal offence according to § 332 sub. 1 sent. 3 or sub. 2 StGB and by the same act (§ 52 StGB, German: *Tateinheit*) a criminal offence according to § 331 StGB.[68] The same applies to the counterpart of the official.[69]

5. Especially serious cases

§ 335 sub. 2 StGB specifies when an especially serious case of taking and giving bribes 57 (§§ 332 and 334 StGB) and with that a higher penalty range (→ mn. 69 et seqq.) typically occurs:

1. the act relates to a major benefit,
2. the offender accepts continued benefits which are demanded in return for the fact that the offender would perform an official act in the future, or
3. the offender acts on a commercial basis or as a member of a gang whose purpose is the continued commission of such offences.

Whether a benefit is major depends on whether the magnitude of the benefit is clearly 58 out of the ordinary.[70] This is to be determined independently of the standards for other offences, also independently of § 300 sent. 2 no. 1 StGB.[71] The importance of the official

---

59 BGH 18.10.2012 – 3 StR 208/12 = BeckRS 2013, 503, mn. 22.
60 MüKoStGB/Korte StGB § 331 mn. 210.
61 MüKoStGB/Korte StGB § 331 mn. 210.
62 BeckOK StGB/Trüg, 64. Ed. 1.2.2025, StGB § 331 mn. 52.
63 Fischer/Lutz StGB § 331 mn. 31.
64 TK StGB/Eisele StGB § 333 mn. 12.
65 TK StGB/Eisele StGB § 333 mn. 12.
66 Fischer/Lutz StGB § 332 mn. 16.
67 Fischer/Lutz StGB § 332 mn. 16.
68 BeckOK StGB/Trüg, 64. Ed. 1.2.2025, StGB § 332 mn. 13.
69 Fischer/Lutz StGB § 334 mn. 7.
70 Fischer/Lutz StGB § 335 mn. 5.
71 TK StGB/Eisele StGB § 335 mn. 3.

act is irrelevant.[72] The circumstances of the official's life are to be taken into account only to a limited extent.[73] Otherwise, there would be an individualisation that would be difficult to predict in order to determine the internal discipline of the official.[74] In any case, with assets of less than 10,000 EUR, one cannot assume a large scale.[75]

59 § 335 sub. 2 no. 2 StGB constitutes an increased penalty for repeat offenders. At least three offences are required.[76] The continued acceptance of unsolicited benefits is not sufficient, the offender has to have demanded the benefits.[77] Furthermore, he or she has to have demanded the benefits for future performances of official acts. Rewards for already performed official acts are not covered.[78] The official also has to have accepted and not only demanded the benefits.

60 Acting on a commercial basis (§ 335 sub. 2 no. 3 alt. 1 StGB) means the intention to obtain a permanent source of income of some size by repeatedly committing the offence.[79] Given that subjective element, the first offence can already be on a commercial basis.[80] It is not only the recipient of the benefit who may be acting on a commercial basis by seeking a source of income from the benefit, but also the counterpart, for whom the offence may only provide an indirect source of income as a result of the official act in breach of official duties.[81]

61 A gang (§ 335 sub. 2 no. 3 alt. 2 StGB) has to consist of at least three members.[82] The members can be only officials, only non-officials or of both groups.[83]

6. Foreign bribery

62 In the event that the recipient of the benefit is a foreign or international official, § 335a StGB provides for criminal liability under German law. The provision was newly inserted by the Law on the Fight against Corruption of 20 November 2015[84] and replaced various previously existing provisions in other laws. The scope of application of the corruption offences has been gradually extended since 1998.[85]

63 § 335a StGB states that:[86]

> (1) For the purposes of applying [§] 331 [sub. 2], [§] 333 [sub. 2] and [§§] 332 and 334, in each case also in conjunction with [§] 335, to an offence relating to a future judicial act or a future official act, the following are equal to
>
> 1. a judge:
>   a member of a foreign or an international court;

---

[72] Fischer/Lutz StGB § 335 mn. 5.
[73] TK StGB/Eisele StGB § 335 mn. 3.
[74] Fischer/Lutz StGB § 335 mn. 5.
[75] For further details see MüKoStGB/Korte StGB § 335 mn. 9.
[76] Fischer/Lutz StGB § 335 mn. 9.
[77] Fischer/Lutz StGB § 335 mn. 8.
[78] MüKoStGB/Korte StGB § 335 mn. 15.
[79] BeckOK StGB/Trüg, 64. Ed. 1.2.2025, StGB § 335 mn. 6.
[80] BeckOK StGB/Trüg, 64. Ed. 1.2.2025, StGB § 335 mn. 6.
[81] MüKoStGB/Korte StGB § 335 mn. 16.
[82] Fischer/Lutz StGB § 335 mn. 11.
[83] MüKoStGB/Korte StGB § 335 mn. 17.
[84] *Gesetz zur Bekämpfung der Korruption*, BGBl. 2015 I 2025.
[85] For further details see Fischer/Lutz StGB § 335a mn. 2 et seq.
[86] The English version of § 335a StGB is taken from <https://www.gesetze-im-internet.de/englisch_stgb/englisch_stgb.html>, translated by Prof Dr Michael Bohlander, completely and regularly updated by Ute Reusch (last accessed: 27.10.2025).

2. any other public official:
   a) an official of a foreign state and a person entrusted with performing public functions for a foreign state,
   b) an official of an international organisation and a person entrusted with performing functions for an international organisation,
   c) a soldier of a foreign state and a soldier entrusted with performing functions for an international organisation.

(2) For the purposes of applying [§] 331 [sub. 1] and [§] 333 [sub. 1] and [3] to an offence relating to a future judicial act or a future official act, the following are equal to

1. a judge:
   a member of the International Criminal Court;
2. any other public official:
   a member of staff of the International Criminal Court.

(3) For the purposes of applying [§] 333 [sub. 1] and [3] to an offence relating to a future official act, the following are equal to

1. a soldier in the Federal Armed Forces:
   a soldier in the non-German troops of one of the member states of the North Atlantic Treaty Organization deployed in Germany and who are residing in Germany at the time of the unlawful act;
2. any other public official:
   a member of staff of these troops;
3. a person entrusted with special public service functions:
   a person who is employed by the troops or acts for them and has been formally obliged by general or specific instructions issued by a higher service unit of the troops to conscientiously discharge his or her duties.

An important difference to §§ 331 et seq. StGB is that the offence must relate to a future judicial act or a future official act. In this respect, the wording of the law is based on the texts of the international treaties, which served as a model and do not provide for the punishment of subsequent bribes.[87] **64**

The law of the state whose official was bribed governs the question of whether the performance of the official act breached the official duties of the recipient of the benefit.[88] So-called facilitation payments, which are intended to speed up or facilitate the process, are covered if they influenced a decision that was at the discretion of the official.[89] **65**

7. Perpetration and participation

The genuine official offences cannot be committed by anyone. Therefore, another participant who is not a public official can neither commit the offence as a joint offender (§ 25 sub. 2 StGB) nor through the public official as an indirect offender (§ 25 sub. 1 alt. 2 StGB). **66**

If someone induces a public official to commit a corruption offence ('abetting', German: *Anstiftung*, § 26 StGB) or assists the act of a public official ('aiding', German: *Beihilfe*, § 27 StGB), a mitigated penalty applies in accordance with §§ 28 sub. 1, 49 sub. 1 StGB. It must be borne in mind that the criminal liability of the beneficiaries and the donors of the benefits is conclusive and that they cannot therefore be considered as participants in the acts of their respective counterparts in the legal sense.[90] **67**

---

[87] NK-WSS/Gaede § 335a StGB mn. 16.
[88] BGH 13.2.2014 – 1 StR 336/13, BeckRS 2014, 9500.
[89] Fischer/Lutz StGB § 335a mn. 5b.
[90] Fischer/Lutz StGB § 331 mn. 38.

8. Place of commission of offence

68 According to § 9 sub. 1 StGB, in general 'an offence is deemed to have been committed at every place where the offender acted or, in the case of an omission, was required to act or in which the result, if it is an element of the offence, occurs or was to have occurred as envisaged by the offender'. When determining the place of commission of a corruption offence, it must be taken into account that the offences of bribery and corruption – whether towards or by public officials or equivalent persons or in business transactions – are abstract endangering offences (*abstrakte Gefährdungsdelikte*).[91] Accordingly, the place of the offence cannot be determined by a success that is part of the offence within the meaning of § 9 sub. 1 var. 3 or 4 StGB, so that the seat of a bribing company alone does not establish a place of the offence, nor does causing an anti-competitive improvement or its occurrence. Corruption offences do not have a result within the meaning of § 9 sub. 1 StGB.[92] The place of the offence can therefore only be the place where the statement leading to the unlawful agreement is made or accepted, or where the advantage is demanded, offered, promised, granted or accepted.[93]

9. Sanctions

69 The sanctions for officials demanding, allowing to be promised or accepting benefits and for natural persons offering, promising or granting benefits to officials are imprisonment for a term not exceeding three years or a fine (§ 331 sub. 1 and § 333 sub. 1 StGB). If the official is a judge, the imprisonment for demanding, allowing to be promised or accepting benefits and for offering, promising or granting benefits can be up to five years or a fine (§ 331 sub. 2 sent. 1 and § 333 sub. 2 StGB).

70 For the more severe offence of taking bribes, the sanction is always imprisonment. The sanction for the official is imprisonment for a term of between six months and five years, § 332 sub. 1 sent. 1 StGB. In less serious cases, the penalty is imprisonment for a term not exceeding three years or a fine, § 332 sub. 1 sent. 2 StGB. If the official is a judge, the sanction is imprisonment for a term of between one year and 10 years, § 332 sub. 2 sent. 1 StGB. With a minimum penalty of imprisonment of one year this corruption offence is a serious criminal offence (*Verbrechen*) according to § 12 sub. 1 StGB. In less serious cases, the penalty is imprisonment for a term of between six months and five years, § 332 sub. 2 sent. 2 StGB.

71 The penalty for giving bribes is imprisonment for a term of between three months and five years, § 334 sub. 1 sent. 1 StGB. In less serious cases, the penalty is imprisonment for a term not exceeding two years or a fine pursuant § 334 sub. 1 sent. 2 StGB. If the official is a judge, the sanction is imprisonment for a term of between three months and five years if the judge performed a judicial act and thereby breached his or her judicial duties, and imprisonment for a term of between six months and five years if the judge would perform a judicial act and would thereby breach their judicial duties.

72 For especially serious cases (→ mn. 57 et seqq.) of taking and giving bribes according to § 332 sub. 1 sent. 1, also in conjunction with § 332 sub. 3 StGB, and § 334 sub. 1 sent. 1 and sub. 2, also in conjunction with § 334 sub. 3 StGB, the penalty is imprisonment for a term of between one year and ten years, § 335 sub. 1 no. 1 StGB. For the especially serious cases of taking and giving bribes according to § 332 sub. 2, also in conjunction with § 332 sub. 3 StGB, the penalty is imprisonment for a term of at least two years, § 335 sub. 1 no. 2

[91] MüKoStGB/Krick StGB § 299 mn. 420; MüKoStGB/Korte StGB § 331 mn. 12.
[92] Fischer StGB § 9 mn. 9.
[93] BGH 26.7.2018 – 3 StR 626/17, BeckRS 2018, 38747.

StGB. Although the minimum penalty is one or even two years this does not lead to a classification as a serious criminal offence according to § 12 sub. 1 StGB as especially serious cases never change the classification of an offence.[94]

10. Attempt, completion and termination

The attempt of a corruption offence is punishable in the form of taking bribes, § 332 sub. 1 sent. 3 StGB. If the official is a judge, also the attempt of accepting benefits is punishable, § 331 sub. 2 sent. 2 StGB; and the attempt of taking bribes according to § 332 sub. 2 sent. 1 StGB is punishable as per § 23 sub. 1 alt. 1 StGB as it is a serious criminal offence (cf. → mn. 73). For the person who is giving the benefit, the attempt of a corruption offence is only punishable in the form of giving bribes to a judge, § 334 sub. 2 sent. 2 StGB. **73**

In the case of a demand, the immediate step towards the realisation of the offence (§ 22 StGB) is the making of a statement directed to it; in the case of a promise, it is an at least conclusive act of acceptance of the benefit; and in the case of an acceptance, it is actions that are intended to lead directly to the receipt of the benefit.[95] **74**

The offence is completed (*Vollendung*) when, in the case of a demand, the other party becomes aware of the official's demand; when, in the case of a promise, the official behaves in a way that shows agreement with the unlawful agreement; and when, in the case of an acceptance, the official accepts the benefit.[96] **75**

The offence is terminated (*Beendigung*) with the last partial act of the official act and the acceptance of the benefit.[97] It is terminated at the latest when the recipient of the benefit leaves office: benefits received at a later date do not even constitute an offence.[98] If the official act is carried out only after the benefit has been received, according to the case law in the cases of §§ 332, 334 StGB, the termination occurs only with the completion of this act, although this act itself is not part of the offence.[99] **76**

11. Statute of limitations

The limitation period varies and is based on the respective maximum sentence. It is five years for the offences which are punishable by a maximum sentence of imprisonment of more than one year but no more than five years (§ 78 sub. 3 no. 4 StGB), which are most of the corruption offences, namely §§ 331 sub. 1, sub. 2, 332 sub. 1, 333 sub. 1, sub. 2, 334 sub. 1, sub. 2 StGB. **77**

The limitation period is 10 years in the case of offences which are punishable by a maximum sentence of imprisonment of more than five years but no more than 10 years (§ 78 sub. 3 no. 3 StGB), which is only § 332 sub. 2 StGB. **78**

The higher maximum penalty for the especially serious cases (§ 335 StGB) and the lower maximum penalty for less serious cases (§ 332 sub. 1 sent. 2, sub. 2 sent. 2, 334 sub. 1 sent. 2 StGB) do not have an influence on the limitation period according to § 78 sub. 4 StGB. **79**

According to § 78a StGB, the limitation period begins to run as soon as the offence is terminated (→ mn. 76). **80**

---

94 BeckOK StGB/Trüg, 64. Ed. 1.2.2025, StGB § 335 mn. 1.
95 Fischer/Lutz StGB § 331 mn. 30c.
96 BeckOK StGB/Trüg, 64. Ed. 1.2.2025, StGB § 331 mn. 53.
97 Fischer/Lutz StGB § 331 mn. 30a.
98 BeckOK StGB/Trüg, 64. Ed. 1.2.2025, StGB § 331 mn. 55.
99 BGH 19.06.2008 – 3 StR 90/08 = BeckRS 2008, 14732 mn. 7 et seqq.

12. Asset recovery

81 According to §§ 73 et seq. StGB, the proceeds of the corruption can be confiscated.[100] If the public official receives a benefit for an official act which harms his or her employer, he or she has in principle not received this benefit 'by the act', but 'for the act' within the meaning of § 73 sub. 1 StGB.[101] The benefit is obtained by the act only in those cases in which it accrues to the perpetrator from the assets of the employer, i.e. it is the mirror image of the disadvantage of the employer.[102] On the other hand, the public official's counterpart, or in most cases the company for which he or she works, has benefited from the illegal act in terms of the total consideration, not just the profit ('gross principle', German: *Bruttoprinzip*).[103] These proceeds can be confiscated from the company under the conditions set out in § 73b StGB. In cases of corruption, usually § 73b sub. 1 sent. 1 no. 1 StGB will be fulfilled if the offender acted on the company's behalf. In most cases the proceeds will not consist in particular objects so that the confiscation will be ordered with respect to a sum of money equal to the value of what was obtained, § 73c StGB. The value of the obtained object is calculated according to § 73d sub. 1 StGB: any expenditure of the offender is to be deducted, but only if the expenditure was not spent or used in the commission or preparation of the unlawful act. For example, if a contract for work or services is obtained by means of bribery, the expenses incurred for the performance of the work (in particular the costs of personnel and materials) must be taken into account as a reduction of the value of the obtained.[104] The retroactive exception in § 73d sub. 1 sent. 2 at the end StGB, 'unless it was used to comply with an obligation against the injured party', is not applicable to cases of corruption since corruption offences are not offences serving the protection of individual rights.[105] Accordingly, the preclusion in § 73e sub. 1 StGB, when the injured party's claim to compensation has expired, is also not applicable. The amounts collected will accrue to the treasury upon completion of the relevant confiscation proceedings.

II. Offences against competition

82 The legislator grouped offences related to taking and giving bribes in commercial practice and in the health care sector in a common division of the German Criminal Code under the title 'Offences against competition' (*Straftaten gegen den Wettbewerb*). The title highlights, on the one hand, the affiliation with offences of economic criminal law and, on the other hand, that the primary purpose of the offences is to protect fair competition, whether in the private sector in general or in the health sector in particular.

1. Taking and giving bribes in commercial practice

83 § 299 StGB regulates bribery in commercial transactions in the private sector. It governs both active and passive bribery addressing employees of a company as possible recipients of an undue benefit. The provision provides two different models that serve different legal interests. § 299 sub. 1 no. 1 StGB and § 299 sub. 2 no. 1 StGB aim at protecting fair

[100] → Ch. 5 for a general overview of confiscation proceedings.
[101] Fischer/Lutz StGB § 331 mn. 37a.
[102] Fischer/Lutz StGB § 331 mn. 37a.
[103] MüKoStGB/Korte StGB § 332 mn. 58; Fischer/Lutz StGB § 73 mn. 21, 23.
[104] BT-Drucksache 18/9525, 68.
[105] BGH 31.07.2018 – 3 StR 620/17 = BeckRS 2018, 21037 mn. 30; also → mn. 16.

competition whereas § 299 sub. 1 no. 2 StGB and § 299 sub. 2 no. 2 StGB serve to protect the economic integrity of the principal.

According to § 299 sub. 1 no. 1 StGB, anyone who, in commercial practice in the capacity as an employee or agent of a business demands, allows themselves to be promised or accepts a benefit for themselves or a third party in return for giving an unfair preference to another in the competitive purchase of goods or services in Germany or abroad incurs a penalty of imprisonment for a term not exceeding three years or a fine. Inversely, § 299 sub. 2 no. 1 StGB prohibits active bribery in commercial transactions, which involves offering, promising or granting a benefit to an employee or agent of a business or a third party in return for giving that person or another an unfair preference in the competitive purchase of goods or services. **84**

According to § 299 sub. 1 no. 2 StGB, anyone who, in commercial practice in the capacity as an employee or agent of a business, without the permission of the business demands, allows themselves to be promised or accepts a benefit for themselves or a third party in return for performing or refraining from performing an act in the competitive purchase of goods or services, thereby breaching the duty incumbent on them towards the business, incurs the same penalty as provided under sub. 1. The criminal liability of active acts of bribery (offering, promising or granting a benefit) in this constellation results from § 299 sub. 2 no. 2 StGB. **85**

2. The requirements in detail

a) Circle of perpetrators

Active bribery according to § 299 sub. 2 StGB can be committed by any natural person. The circle of perpetrators is not limited to individuals who are necessarily engaged in business as entrepreneurs or employees of a company. **86**

With regard to passive bribery (§ 299 sub. 1 StGB), however, only employees or agents of a business can be bribed. **87**

aa) Employees or agents. An **employee** is anyone who, on the basis of a contract or at least de facto, is in an employment relationship with the owner of the company and is subject to instructions.[106] The classification of the contract under labour law is just as irrelevant as its validity under civil law, provided that the person actually acts on behalf of the employer.[107] It is even irrelevant whether remuneration for work is owed or paid.[108] The essential criteria applied for defining an employment relationship is a subordination relationship.[109] The term 'employees' also includes managing directors and board members of corporations.[110] **88**

Agents are individuals who are legally or factually entitled to act on behalf of the company and who are able to influence the business interests of the company.[111] Subordinate auxiliaries are not covered by the provision.[112] Business owners are neither employees nor agents and therefore cannot be bribed. If the company is a limited liability company or a stock corporation, the entirety of all shareholders is considered to be the owner.[113] Therefore, the bribery of all shareholders of a company is not punishable under § 299 StGB, even **89**

[106] NK-StGB/Dannecker/Schröder StGB § 299 mn. 38.
[107] ARR Wirtschaftsstrafrecht/Rönnau Part 5 Ch. 2 mn. 19.
[108] MüKoStGB/Krick StGB § 299 mn. 45.
[109] BGH 28.7.2021 – 1 StR 506/20, NJW 2021, 3606.
[110] BGH 9.8.2006 – 1 StR 50/06, NJW 2006, 3290; NK-StGB/Dannecker/Schröder StGB § 299 mn. 40.
[111] BGH 13.05.1952 – 1 StR 670/51, BeckRS 1952, 30394133.
[112] BayObLG 20.7.1995 – 4 St RR 4/95, NJW 1996, 268.
[113] BGH 28.7.2021 – 1 StR 506/20, NJW 2021, 3606.

if some of them perform management tasks as employees. Furthermore, criminal liability does not apply if all shareholders agree to the bribery of an employee of the company.[114]

90 **bb) The definition of 'business'.** The term 'business' is according to established case-law subject to broad interpretation.[115] The concept encompasses every entity engaged in an economic activity, regardless of the legal status of the entity or the way in which it is financed.[116] Economic activity shall cover the exchange of goods and services on a given market.[117] The business does not have to operate for profit. The provision also covers social and charitable enterprises, as long as they participate in the market.[118]

b) The criminal actions

91 Unlike the offences governing bribery involving public officials, § 299 StGB covers both passive (sub. 1) and active bribery (sub. 2) in a single provision.

92 **aa) In the course of a business activity.** Any criminal action prohibited under § 299 StGB has to be committed in the course of a business activity (*im geschäftlichen Verkehr*). Again, the term is broadly interpreted covering all measures serving to promote any business objective, i.e., any activity pursuing an economic purpose in which participation in competition is expressed.[119] In other words, any connection with a business operation and any contact with the business operation are sufficient.

93 **bb) The notion of benefit.** The key element and subject of any act of bribery is the notion of benefit. **Benefit** (*Vorteil*) within the meaning of § 299 StGB can be anything that somehow improves the situation of the recipient and to which he or she is not entitled.[120] In principle, the term can be interpreted in the same way as the identical notion in § 331 StGB (→ mn. 33 et seqq.). Hence, it covers monetary benefits, such as the granting of additional income, the granting of loans, discounts or invitations to holiday trips but also intangible benefits[121] such as honours, career advancement or sexual favours[122].

94 Acts of hospitality, which involves exchanging gifts or invitations to foster a positive relationship with business partners, can provide an advantage to the recipient with the immanent risk of being prosecuted by the investigation authorities. There are no specific provisions addressing this matter under German criminal law. In particular, there is no *de minimis* limitation, defining a strict threshold under which gifts are excludes from the scope of the provision. However, it is recognised by case law that habitually acknowledged, relatively low-value attentions on given occasions may be excluded from the offence.[123] In this respect, the decisive factor is whether the specific benefit is objectively capable of influencing a business decision in an improper manner or in a manner that jeopardises free and fair competition.[124] Various public authorities issued internal guidelines that establish a threshold of 25 EUR. It is generally agreed that the threshold in the private sector should be higher.[125] Depending on the industry and the position of the recipient, a gift with a value of 50 EUR can have a different significance. It therefore remains a question of

---

[114] BGH 28.7.2021 – 1 StR 506/20, NJW 2021, 3606.
[115] HK-StrafR/Bannenberg StGB § 299 mn. 6.
[116] BGH 10.7.1957 – 4 StR 5/57, NJW 1957, 1604.
[117] BGH 13.5.1952 – 1 StR 670/51, BeckRS 1952, 30394133.
[118] BGH 9.10.1990 – 1 StR 538/89, NJW 1991, 367.
[119] Momsen/Grützner WirtschaftsSteuerStrafR-HdB/Grützner/Behr § 30 mn. 66.
[120] BGH 18.6.2003 – 5 StR 489/02, NJW 2003, 2996.
[121] BGH 3.12.1987 – 4 StR 554/87, NJW 1988, 2547.
[122] BGH 29.3.1994 – 1 StR 12/94, BeckRS 1994, 7928.
[123] BGH 23.10.2002 – 1 StR 541/01, NJW 2003, 763.
[124] BeckOK StGB/Momsen/Laudien, 64. Ed. 1.2.2025, StGB § 299 mn. 37.
[125] Momsen/Grützner WirtschaftsSteuerStrafR-HdB/Grützner/Behr § 30 mn. 237.

the individual case. According to the case law, the following aspects are to be taken into account: the plausibility of the purpose of the alleged granting of benefits, position of the recipient of the benefit, relationship between the persons involved, clandestine approach of the granting of benefits and the nature and value of the benefit.[126]

cc) Taking and giving bribes. § 299 sub. 1 StGB prohibits to demand, allow oneself to be promised or accept a benefit. The described acts correspond to those criminalising bribery of public officials (see § 331 sub. 1 StGB and § 332 sub. 1 StGB). § 299 sub. 2 StGB prohibits active bribery which is defined as offering, promising or granting a benefit. Again, the terms are identical with those of the corresponding offences involving public officials (see § 333 sub. 1 and § 334 sub. 2 StGB). 95

dd) The unlawful agreement. Both active and passive bribery under § 299 StGB have to be linked to a concrete consideration. According to the so-called competition model, a person is criminally liable for the offence of taking and giving bribes in commercial practice if the offender demands, allows him- or herself to be promised or accepts a benefit or if he or she offers, promises or grants a benefit in return for giving an unfair preference in the competitive purchase of goods or services. Preference in this context means a decision on irrelevant grounds between at least two applicants, i.e. it presupposes competition and disadvantage of a competitor.[127] Both are determined according to the subjective imagination of the offender.[128] Thus, competition and disadvantage of a competitor does not have to exist objectively at the time of the offence. It is sufficient if, in the perpetrator's mind, a competitive relationship is supposed to exist at the time of the preferential treatment.[129] 96

A preferential treatment is any intended improvement of the economic position of the offender or a third party, to which the offender or the third party is not entitled.[130] Again, it is not necessary that the preferential treatment had the intended effect[131], since § 299 StGB aims at protecting against the abstract danger of acts restricting competition.[132] The preferential treatment is unfair if it violates the principles of fair business dealings. This is the case, if the intended competitive advantage is not based exclusively on factual considerations, but on the advantage offered, promised or granted.[133] 97

The preference does not necessarily have to consist in the conclusion of a contract itself or in the ordering of goods and services.[134] It covers, for example, measures aiming at reducing the potential group of bidders in favour of a certain competitor. It also includes the disclosure of information about the offer or a trade secret of a co-bidder.[135] 98

The intended preference has to be future-oriented. Grants to induce the general goodwill of the beneficiary without any reference to a specific unfair preference or grants to reward past preferences are not covered.[136] Therefore, it is essential to determine precisely if a specific grant refers to a targeted preferential treatment. The provision typically encompasses case constellation in which, for example, an employee working in the procurement department commissions a company which did not submit the best offer 99

---

[126] BGH 14.10.2008 – 1 StR 260/08, NJW 2008, 3580, 2008, 3580.
[127] BGH 18.6.2003 – 5 StR 489/02, NStZ 2004, 41.
[128] BGH 18.6.2003 – 5 StR 489/02, NJW 2003, 2996.
[129] TK StGB/Eisele StGB § 299 mn. 28.
[130] TK StGB/Eisele StGB § 299 mn. 32.
[131] BGH 29.4.2015 – 1 StR 235/14, NStZ-RR 2015, 278.
[132] BGH 9.8.2006 – 1 StR 50/06, NJW 2006, 3290.
[133] BGH 16.7.2004 – 2 StR 486/03, NJW 2004, 3129.
[134] MüKoStGB/Krick StGB § 299 mn. 234.
[135] BGH 9.8.2006 – 1 StR 50/06, NJW 2006, 3290.
[136] BGH 27.3.1968 – I ZR 163/65, NJW 1968, 1572.

compared to its competitors because the employee had been promised a benefit in return for its favourable selection decision.

100 In 2015 the criminal offence of taking and giving bribes in commercial practice was extended to covering the case in which an employee or agent of a company, without the consent of his or her company, performs or refrains from performing an act in violations of his or her duties with regard to the purchase of goods or services.[137] The provision covers acts regardless of whether they affect competition. Neither the occurrence of a risk of distortion of competition nor a pecuniary loss on the part of the company are decisive, but only the violation of the employee's or agent's duties towards the principal. The extension of the criminal offence aims at the protection of the employer's interest in the loyal and unbiased performance of duties by its employees and agents.[138] The willingness to violate the latter must be the subject of the so-called unlawful agreement with the perpetrator. The duties can arise from the law, from contractual rules, internal guidelines or in-house regulations for individual departments or also from an individual instruction of a direct superior.[139] It is necessary that the regulations relate to the purchase of goods or services.

101 Acts with the consent of the affected company are not punishable. Such consent presupposes that the principle has the power to dispose of the matter. Apart from cases involving a sole proprietorship, consent must be given by a natural person on behalf of the company, which involves mainly persons who are legally or contractually authorised to represent the company.[140]

102 The extension applies to cases, for example, in which an employee places an order without obtaining comparative bids in breach of internal guidelines in return for a personal benefit.

3. Especially serious cases

103 § 300 StGB defines especially serious cases of taking and giving bribes in commercial practice and in the healthcare sector. A case is considered especially serious if the offence relates to a major benefit or the offender acts on a commercial basis or as a member of a group whose purpose is the continued commission of such offences. A major benefit is assumed starting from amounts of 25,000 EUR[141] or 50,000 EUR[142]. The provision does not establish an additional offence but it increases the possible penalty for taking and giving bribes in commercial practice. In such especially serious cases, an offence under § 299 StGB incurs a penalty of imprisonment for a term of between three months and five years.

4. Applicability of German criminal law in cases involving foreign countries

104 In the context of international business relations, the question regularly arises in companies as to whether and, if so, when German criminal law is applied to facts with an international connection. In order to answer the question, a distinction must be made as to whether the scope of application of § 299 StGB covers the foreign facts and whether German criminal law applies in principle.

---

[137] BGBl. 2015 I 2025.
[138] BT-Drucksache 18/4350, 21.
[139] Heuking/von Coelln BB 2016, 323.
[140] Momsen/Grützner WirtschaftsSteuerStrafR-HdB/Grützner/Behr § 30 mn. 88 et seq.
[141] NK-StGB/Dannecker/Schröder StGB § 300 mn. 11.
[142] LK-StGB/Lindemann StGB § 300 mn. 4.

Pursuant to § 299 sub. 1 no. 1 and sub. 2 no. 1 StGB, acts committed in foreign competition are covered by the scope of application of the provision. In this respect, the application of § 299 StGB is neither limited to German employees and agents nor to German companies. Therefore, § 299 sub. 1 no. 1 and sub. 2 no. 1 StGB are, in principle, applicable to acts committed by foreign employees and agents of foreign companies. 105

If the facts fall within the scope of § 299 StGB, the application of German criminal law is governed by the general rules of international criminal law (§§ 3–9 StGB), which define the scope of domestic criminal jurisdiction. Pursuant to § 3 StGB, German criminal law applies to acts committed on German territory. If the act was committed at least partially on German territory, German criminal law applies. According to § 9 sub. 1 StGB an offence is deemed to have been committed at every place where the offender acted. If a perpetrator of an offence under § 299 StGB has (also) acted domestically, a domestic act has been committed and German criminal law is applicable, e.g. by sending an offer, by demanding the benefit, by transferring money from Germany or handing over cash in Germany. Both the place of sending and the place of receiving in Germany are sufficient to qualify the act as a domestic act. 106

For acts committed exclusively abroad, German criminal law is applicable pursuant to § 7 sub. 1 or sub. 2 no. 1 StGB, if they are committed by a German national or against a German national, provided that the act is a criminal offence at the place of its commission or if that place is not subject to any criminal law jurisdiction. German nationals can only be natural persons. Offences against companies registered in Germany are not covered by the provision.[143] 107

The double criminality criteria does not require congruence between the foreign and German elements of the crime. It is sufficient that the specific act is punishable from any legal point of view under the foreign criminal law.[144] Further, it is not necessary that the threats of punishment are identical. However, the specific act has to be punishable with a criminal penalty and not only with a fine.[145] In order to determine whether the act is punishable at the place of its commission, grounds for justification and excuse under the foreign criminal law are to be taken into account.[146] In various countries, bribery in the private sector – in contrast to bribery of public officials – is not (yet) punishable.[147] This current status may therefore limit criminal liability under German law. Furthermore, the application of German criminal law is excluded if the foreign legal system determines the granting of certain benefits as socially adequate and thus not punishable.[148] It will often be necessary to obtain an expert opinion on the foreign legal situation in criminal proceedings. However, grounds for justification and excuse will not be taken into account if the relevant provisions are manifestly contrary to internationally recognized legal principles.[149] 108

5. Attempt

§ 299 StGB does not provide that the attempt is punishable (cf. § 23 sub. 1 StGB). However, with the variants of 'demanding' and 'offering', the provision criminalises a 109

---

143 NK-StGB/Dannecker/Schröder StGB § 299 mn. 148.
144 BGH 21.4.2021 – 1 StR 447/20, NStZ-RR 2021, 292.
145 BGH 30.9.1976 – 4 StR 683/75, NJW 1976, 2354.
146 BGH 23.10.1996 – 5 StR 183/95, NJW 1977, 951.
147 LK-StGB/Lindemann StGB § 299 mn. 69.
148 ARR WirtschaftsStrafR-HdB Part 3 Ch. 2 mn. 109.
149 BGH 23.10.1996 – 5 StR 183/95, NJW 1997, 951.

unilateral act that does not depend on the occurrence of a certain result as a completed offence.[150]

6. Request to prosecute

110 In the public sector, corruption offences are categorised as so-called official offences (*Offizialdelikte*) which can be prosecuted without a request for prosecution. In the private sector, corruption offences are prosecuted only upon request (§ 301 sub. 1 StGB). Entitled to file the request is the 'victim' of the offence, according to § 77 sub. 1 StGB. In cases under § 299 sub. 1 no. 1 and sub. 2 no. 1 StGB the victim can not only be the principal of the employee or agent acting in breach of duty but also a competitor. In contrast, under § 299 sub. 1 no. 2 and sub. 2 no. 2 StGB only the business is entitled to file a request. In addition, the chambers of industry and commerce as well as associations with legal capacity for the promotion of commercial and professional interests are also entitled to file a request for offences under § 299 sub. 1 no. 1 and sub. 2 no. 1 StGB according to § 301 sub. 2 StGB.

111 If none of the entitled persons or entities files a request, the criminal prosecution authority may also choose to pursue the case if it deems there to be a special public interest which calls for *ex officio* intervention (§ 301 sub. 2 StGB). According to no. 242a sub. 1 RiStBV (*Richtlinien für das Straf- und Bußgeldverfahren*, Instructions on Criminal Procedure and Administrative Fines Procedure), such an interest is to be assumed, in particular, if the offender has a relevant criminal record, if he or she has acted in cooperation with public officials, if several businesses are affected, if the majority of the enterprise is owned by the public sector and performs public duties, considerable damage is imminent or has occurred or if there are sufficient indications that a person entitled to file a request refrains from filing the request due to fear of economic or professional disadvantages.

7. Statute of limitations

112 The limitation period of offences under § 299 StGB is five years pursuant to § 78 sub. 3 no. 4 StGB. The limitation period begins to run as soon as the offence is terminated (§ 78a StGB). The termination of the offence includes not only the realisation of the elements as defined by the criminal offence but also such circumstances that deepen the substantive unlawfulness of the offence because they perpetuate or intensify the attack on the protected legal interest.[151] This definition has the effect that the limitation period begins relatively late.[152] Offences under § 299 StGB are terminated only when the unfairly preferential treatment is terminated and the benefit is received in full.[153] If the bribe is paid in instalments, for example, the termination does not occur until the last instalment is paid.

8. Asset recovery

113 In the case of offences under § 299 StGB, according to the reformed law, all flows of assets are to be considered under confiscation aspects, which are causally connected with the exchange of benefits in violation of rules because they are obtained by the act of bribery (§§ 73 sub. 1, 73c StGB).[154]

---

[150] BGH 10.7.1957 – 4 StR 5/57, NJW 1957, 1604.
[151] BGH 19.6.2008 – 3 StR 90/08, NJW 2008, 3076.
[152] Momsen/Grützner WirtschaftsSteuerStrafR-HdB/Grützner/Behr § 30 mn. 345.
[153] BGH 12.12.2017 – 2 StR 308/16, NStZ 2018, 178.
[154] → Ch. 5 for a general overview of confiscation proceedings.

On the one hand, the bribe paid (or its value) is subject to confiscation from the person who received it. **114**

On the other hand, with regard to the offender actively bribing, it is to be determined what has been obtained from the unfair preferential treatment in competition, for example in the case of a manipulated contract award. As a first step, according to §§ 73 sub. 1, 73c StGB, the entire remuneration for the order is subject to confiscation in principle. As a second step, specific expenditures can be deducted, if the amount spent was not used in the commission or preparation of the unlawful act (§ 73d sub. 1 StGB). Consequently, costs for execution of the order such as material and personnel costs may be deducted, but obviously not the bribe payment. **115**

III. Procedural law

1. Special investigative powers

Offences pursuant to § 299 StGB under the further conditions of an especially serious case according to § 300 sent. 2 StGB and offences pursuant to §§ 332, 334 StGB are listed as serious crimes under § 100a sub. 1, 2 no. 1 lit. t) and lit. v) StPO (*Strafprozessordnung*, Code of Criminal Procedure) which allows the investigating authorities to obtain a court order to intercept and record the telecommunication of accused persons. **116**

In the cases specified in § 300 sent. 2 no. 2 StGB the use of undercover investigators is admissible if there are sufficient factual indications that an offence of substantial significance has been committed (§ 110a sub. 1 sent. 1 no. 3 and 4 StPO).[155] Their use is admissible only if other means of investigating the offence would offer no prospect of success or would be much more difficult (§ 110a sub. 1 sent. 3 StPO). **117**

2. Jurisdiction

Investigative proceedings relating to complex fraud and corruption schemes shall, in principle, be conducted at the place of business of the principal perpetrator or the organisation for which he or she acts, or at that of other parties involved.[156] If the regional court (*Landgericht*) has jurisdiction as court of first instance or in the case of appeals against judgements of courts with lay judges, according to § 74c sub. 1 sent. 1 no. 5a, 6 lit. a) GVG (*Gerichtsverfassungsgesetz*, Courts Constitution Act) jurisdiction shall be vested in a criminal division as an economic offences division. **118**

3. Registration of final convictions in the competition register

Convictions of natural persons under §§ 299, 299a, 299b, 333, 334 StGB can have far-reaching consequences for the companies that employed the offenders. In the so-called competition register (*Wettbewerbsregister*), legally binding convictions for taking and giving bribes in commercial practice and in the healthcare sector as well as granting benefits and giving bribes are entered under the name of the company concerned if the conduct of the natural person can be attributed to the company (§ 2 sub. 1 no. 1 lit. a) WRegG, **119**

---

155 MüKoStGB/Krick StGB § 299 mn. 708.

156 No. 16 of the 'Agreements on Jurisdiction and Related Agreements of the General Prosecutors' (*Zuständigkeitsvereinbarungen und damit im Zusammenhang stehende Absprachen der Generalstaatsanwältinnen und Gerenalstaatsanwälte*), see BeckOK StPO/Gertler, 54. Ed. 1.1.2025, RiStBV 2 mn. 3.1 et seqq.

§ 123 sub. 1 no. 6, 8 GWB). This is the case if the natural person was responsible for the management of the enterprise, which also includes the supervision of the management or other exercise of controlling powers in a senior position (§ 2 sub. 3 WRegG). The registration leads to the exclusion of the company from the award of public contracts. Before awarding a contract, public contracting authorities are obliged to obtain information on the respective bidder if the contract value exceeds 30,000 EUR (§ 6 sub. 1 sent. 1 WRegG). If the register contains a relevant entry, the public contracting authority shall exclude the bidder from the procurement procedure (§ 123 sub. 1 GWB).

D. Compliance: how to prevent corruption

120 Preventing corruption is an important topic for both the public sector and private companies. Therefore, it is not surprising that anti-corruption is one of the traditional and well-developed fields in classical compliance.[157] As usual with compliance measures, the risk factors for the specific company must be determined. Important characteristics are the respective industry, if the company operates nationally or internationally (and in which countries) and if there have been cases of corruption in the past. Based on this, the respective adequate measures are to be determined. In addition to usual measures of compliance management systems such as conducting audits, training and unfailingly pursuing violations, the rotation of employees within the purchasing organisation is an effective measure to prevent corruption.[158] Moreover, the implementation of a four-eye principle can effectively prevent unlawful agreements. In general, procurement processes should always be documented comprehensively and transparently.[159] The implementation of binding behavioural guidelines for procurement processes can be an effective support for employees.[160]

121 It can be observed that the compliance rules are even stricter than the law would require.[161] To avoid even the appearance of bad faith, it is often generally forbidden for public officials to accept gifts and most companies prohibit any granting of advantages to public officials that can no longer be considered socially customary.

---

[157] Godzierz Compliance-Checklisten/Pyrcek § 15 mn. 1; for a general overview of Compliance Management Systems → Ch. 6.

[158] HML Corporate Compliance/Herb, 3rd edn 2016, § 19 mn. 42.

[159] HML Corporate Compliance/Herb, 3rd edn 2016, § 19 mn. 41.

[160] HML Corporate Compliance/Herb, 3rd edn 2016, § 19 mn. 41.

[161] Rotsch Criminal Compliance/Beckemper § 12 mn. 23.

CHAPTER 11
FRAUD AND SUBSIDY FRAUD

Bibliography: Bockelmann, Anmerkung zu BGH, Urteil vom 20.06.1961 – 5 StR 184/61, NJW 1961, 1936; Brand/Hotz, Der „VW-Skandal“ unter wirtschaftsstrafrechtlichen Vorzeichen, NZG 2017, 976; Hefendehl, Abgasmanipulationen und Thermofenster, wistra 2023, 177; Isfen, Mehr Schein als Sein – die VW-Abgasaffäre aus strafrechtlicher Sicht, JA 2016, 1; Magnus/Heß, „Der Abgasskandal“, JA 2022, 471; Mischke, Der Subventionsbetrug – eine strafrechtliche Haftungsfalle, KommJur 2011, 281; Mosbacher, Steuerhinterziehung bei „Cum-ex“ als gewerbsmäßiger Bandenbetrug?, NZWiSt 2021, 1916; Puppe, Das Cum/Ex-Model und die Lehre von der Konkurrenz, NStZ 2021, 596; Saliger/Rüsse, Wider einen subjektiven Schadensbegriff im Strafrecht, NStZ 2021, 513; Sartorius, Der Zweck heiligt die Mittel nicht, DStR 2021, 1597; Sunde, Auslieferung durch die Schweiz bei Steuerdelikten, NStZ 2022, 527; Tolksdorf/Schellhaas, Einzelfragen des Subventionsbetrugs im Zusammenhang mit falschen Angaben im Antrag auf Corona-Soforthilfe, NZWiSt 2021, 344; Venn, Die prozessuale Feststellung des Irrtums beim (Massen-)Betrug, NStZ 2023, 257; Wolf, Der Betrugsschaden beim Erwerb von Dieselfahrzeugen mit illegalen Abschalteinrichtungen, NStZ 2023, 263.

Table of contents

A. Introduction ... 244
B. Practical relevance ... 245
I. Fraud (§ 263 StGB) ... 245
II. Subsidy fraud (§ 264 StGB) ... 246
C. The offence of fraud under § 263 StGB ... 247
I. § 263 sub. 1 StGB: foundational prerequisites of fraud ... 247
1. Objective elements of the offence (*actus reus*) ... 247
a) Deception about facts ... 247
aa) Deception ... 247
bb) Deception has to relate to facts ... 249
b) Error in thought/misconception ... 250
c) Disposal of assets ... 251
d) Pecuniary loss ... 251
aa) Legal definition ... 252
bb) Special constellations ... 252
cc) Triangular fraud ... 253
2. Subjective elements of the offence (*mens rea*) ... 253
II. § 263 sub. 3 and 5 StGB: severe cases with special need for sanctioning ... 254
1. § 263 sub. 3 StGB: standard examples where increased penalty range usually is applied ... 254
2. § 263 sub. 5 StGB: qualification offence where increased penalty range has to be applied ... 255
III. Other provisions of § 263 StGB at a glance ... 256
1. § 263 sub. 2 StGB ... 256
2. § 263 sub. 4 StGB ... 256
3. § 263 sub. 6 StGB ... 257
IV. Diesel scandal ... 257
1. Case study to illustrate the criminal law dimension of the diesel scandal ... 258
2. Criminal liability from the perspective of the end customer 259

a) Deception about facts within the meaning of § 263 StGB 259
b) Error in thought within the meaning of § 263 StGB 260
c) Disposal of assets within the meaning of § 263 StGB ... 261
d) Pecuniary loss within the meaning of § 263 StGB 261
e) Indirect perpetration? 262
3. Interim result 263
D. The offence of subsidy fraud under § 264 StGB 264
I. Definition of subsidy (§ 264 sub. 8 StGB) 265
1. Subsidies under federal or state law 265
2. Subsidies under the law of the European Union 266
II. Facts relevant to the subsidy (§ 264 sub. 9 StGB) 266
III. The criminal acts (§ 264 sub. 1 StGB) 266
1. Subsidy fraud through incorrect or incomplete information (§ 264 sub. 1 no. 1 StGB) 267
2. Subsidy fraud by using the benefit contrary to restrictions on use (§ 264 sub. 1 no. 2 StGB) 267
3. Subsidy fraud through non-disclosure of subsidy-relevant circumstances (§ 264 sub. 1 no. 3 StGB) 267
4. Subsidy fraud through the use of a certificate obtained by providing incorrect or incomplete information (§ 264 sub. 1 no. 4 StGB) 268
IV. Active repentance (§ 264 sub. 6 StGB) 268
V. Secondary penalty and secondary consequence (§ 264 sub. 7 StGB) 268

A. Introduction

1 The statutory offence of fraud (*Betrug*) governed by § 263 StGB is one of the central provisions of German 'white-collar' criminal law. The statute sanctions – in simplified terms – the infliction of pecuniary damages on another person or entity by means of deception with the intention of self-enrichment or the enrichment of others.

2 While § 263 StGB governs the fundamental concept of 'fraudulent behaviour', specific instances of fraud in German criminal law are often regulated in other special provisions, that can enjoy priority of application over § 263 StGB in their respective fields. There are many cases to which colloquially speaking the term fraud might be applied but where, in fact, § 263 StGB is not applicable.[1]

3 One example for this is the offence of 'tax fraud' which is not governed by § 263 StGB, but instead falls under the purview of a specific provision within the German tax code, namely § 370 AO. The structure of § 370 AO significantly differs from § 263 StGB and where 'tax fraud' is concerned, § 370 AO is exclusively applied, superseding § 263 StGB (although this doctrine has recently been challenged, → mn. 11 et seq.).[2]

4 In the same vein, the offence of subsidy fraud (*Subventionsbetrug*) under § 264 StGB specifically governs 'fraud-related' offences where state subsidies have been unlawfully 'obtained' through the provision of false or incomplete information. In such instances, § 264 StGB also supersedes § 263 StGB.[3]

---

[1] Cf. Fischer StGB § 263 mn. 235 et seqq.
[2] Cf. Fischer StGB § 263 mn. 237 (although exceptions may arise regarding church taxes).
[3] Fischer StGB § 263 mn. 236.

This chapter commences by explaining § 263 StGB, thereby elaborating on the core concept of fraud within German criminal law. Subsequently, it delves into the statutory offence of subsidy fraud as defined in § 264 StGB, using it as an example of a statute that, in part, builds upon, in part deviates from the principles established in § 263 StGB. 5

B. Practical relevance

The practical relevance of both provisions can hardly be overstated. This holds especially true today. 6

I. Fraud (§ 263 StGB)

There are two 'mammoth' investigative proceedings being conducted in Germany today (although it would be more accurate to say that each of these proceedings in fact consists of numerous investigative proceedings that are, in turn, conducted by many different public prosecutor's offices in Germany). 7

Namely, the so called 'diesel' proceedings on the one hand and the so called 'cum/ex' proceedings on the other. 8

Within the 'diesel complex' various car manufacturers and their (former) employees are being investigated on the suspicion of having defrauded countless customers through the sale of vehicles with manipulated exhaust systems (for more details → mn. 92 et seqq.). The central legal provision in these investigations is § 263 StGB.[4] 9

Within the 'cum/ex complex' countless suspects are being investigated on the suspicion of (aiding and abetting) tax fraud. Even after reading nothing more than the introduction to this chapter, the attentive reader might now conclude (and rightfully so) that at least these proceedings would not touch upon § 263 StGB. After all, § 370 AO supersedes § 263 StGB where 'tax fraud' is concerned (→ mn. 3).[5] 10

Nevertheless, § 263 StGB also became a surprise visitor in the 'cum/ex' proceedings, when one of the main suspects in the cum/ex investigative proceedings remained at large and out of reach of the German authorities, residing in Switzerland. In principle (meaning: with few but relevant exceptions), Switzerland does not extradite on the suspicion of 'tax fraud' or rather on the suspicion of 'fiscal tax evasion'.[6] The German state, however, wanted to have said main suspect extradited because of such suspicions. In a sort of legal sleight of hand,[7] the Frankfurt Higher Regional Court in a much-criticised decision found a 'practical' legal solution to this dilemma: breaking with decades of legal doctrine, it ruled that the main suspect in question was not only a suspect with regard to the offence of 'tax fraud' pursuant to § 370 AO but also with regard to defrauding the German state in general, thereby applying § 263 StGB to a tax matter.[8] This strategy succeeded and the decision of the Frankfurt Higher Regional Court was soon followed by the extradition 11

---

[4] Cf. Hefendehl wistra 2023, 177 (178); Wolf NStZ 2023, 263; Venn NStZ 2023, 257; Brand/Hotz NZG 2017, 976 (977 et seqq.).

[5] → mn. 3; cf. Fischer StGB § 263 mn. 237 (also regarding exceptions where church taxes are concerned).

[6] Regarding the legal background in Swiss law as well the Swiss court proceedings regarding cum/ex, cf. Sunde NStZ 2022, 527 (529 et seqq.).

[7] Fischer StGB § 263 mn. 237a (freely translated): 'The decision was obviously motivated by the goal of enabling extradition by Switzerland in a specific individual case (cf. point VII of the decision).'

[8] OLG Frankfurt 9.3.2021 – 2 Ws 132/20, NZWiSt 2021, 229 (236 et seqq.).

of the main suspect in question,[9] who has in the meantime been convicted not once but twice by two different courts for cum/ex offences.[10]

12 The ruling of the Frankfurt Higher Regional Court did, in the end, not revolutionise German legal doctrine but was promptly rejected by overwhelming parts of the German legal community.[11] Nevertheless, this episode highlights: wherever you look in German white-collar criminal law, often you will come across § 263 StGB – even where it, strictly speaking, does not belong.

II. Subsidy fraud (§ 264 StGB)

13 In comparison to § 263 StGB, the special provision governing subsidy fraud (*Subventionsbetrug*), § 264 StGB, has long led a shadowy existence until the COVID-19 pandemic catapulted the provision to the centre of German criminal law practice: during the pandemic, the German government made significant state subsidies available to businesses grappling with pandemic-related (financial) challenges. Especially in early stages of the pandemic, the administrative process for the application to such subsidies was in disarray which was promptly exploited by bad players in the market. Various organizations 'plundered' state coffers by fraudulently applying for subsidies.[12] Now, only a few years later, the German authorities are cracking down on such illicit applications for state aid. This was notably illustrated on 1 June 2023, when a member of a group that had joined together with the goal of committing such subsidy fraud was sentenced to 10 years in prison.[13] A punishment commonly reserved for manslaughter cases rather than cases of white-collar criminal law in Germany.

---

[9] Cf. Redaktion beck-aktuell, Cum-Ex-Schlüsselfigur Berger an Deutschland ausgeliefert, 24.2.2022, becklink 2022355.

[10] Cf. editorial FD-StrafR 2023, 457675; LG Bonn 13.12.2022 – 62 KLs – 213 Js 116/20 – 2/20, BeckRS 2022, 44306; LG Wiesbaden 30.5.2023 – 6 KLs – 1111 Js 18753/21, BeckRS 2023, 11574.

[11] Fischer StGB § 263 mn. 237a; MüKoStGB/Schmitz/Wulf AO § 370 mn. 617; LG Wiesbaden 1.9.2021 – 6 KLs – 1111 Js 18753/21, wistra 2021, 409; Sartorius DStR 2021, 1597; especially remarkable is the following quote of a German Federal Court Judge (freely translated), Mosbacher NZWiSt 2021, 1916 (1919): 'A legal opinion that no one else holds, because it contradicts established case law and the legal system, cannot simply be established without any further justification only for the purpose of an otherwise impossible extradition. This seems as if it is not the law that is speaking here, but only power'; for a dissenting view from this prevailing legal opinion cf. Puppe NStZ 2021, 596.

[12] Cf. https://www.sueddeutsche.de/panorama/kriminalitaet-duesseldorf-corona-subventionsbetrug-rund-53-millionen-euro-schaden-dpa.urn-newsml-dpa-com-20090101-230103-99-91264 (last accessed: 13.1.2025) (freely translated): 'Many white-collar criminals have abused unbureaucratic state Corona aid for subsidy fraud. In the first two pandemic years of 2020 and 2021 alone, the damage caused by such offences in North Rhine-Westphalia totalled around 53 million euro'.

[13] Cf. Redaktion beck-aktuell, Lange Haftstrafen nach millionenschwerem Corona-Subventionsbetrug, 2.6.2023, becklink 2027261, also available at <https://rsw.beck.de/aktuell/daily/meldung/detail/lg-hamburg-bis-zu-zehn-jahre-haft-fuer-millionenschweren-corona-subventionsbetrug>, (last accessed: 18.6.2025); LG Hamburg 1.6.2023 – 618 KLs 2/22, BeckRS 2023, 12358.

C. The offence of fraud under § 263 StGB

14 § 263 StGB has a total of 6 substantive paragraphs,[14] establishing a comprehensive system on the foundational prerequisites of 'fraud' as well as corresponding sentencing rules and guidelines.

I. § 263 sub. 1 StGB: foundational prerequisites of fraud

15 The individual prerequisites of the offence of fraud are laid out in § 263 sub. 1 StGB:

> (1) Whoever, with the intention of obtaining an unlawful pecuniary benefit for themselves or a third party, damages the assets of another by causing or maintaining an error under false pretences or distorting or suppressing true facts incurs a penalty of imprisonment for a term not exceeding five years or a fine.[15]

16 The provision includes both requirements on the 'external side of the offence', i.e. what the perpetrator must have done (*actus reus*: '(1) Whoever […] damages the assets of another by causing or maintaining an error under false pretences or distorting or suppressing true facts […]'), as well as on 'internal or subjective side of the offence', i.e. necessary intent of the perpetrator (*mens rea*: '(1) Whoever, with the intention of obtaining an unlawful pecuniary benefit for themselves or a third party, […]'). Finally, § 263 sub. 1 StGB puts forward a penalty frame ranging from a fine to five years of imprisonment: '(1) Whoever, […], incurs a penalty of imprisonment for a term not exceeding five years or a fine.'

1. Objective elements of the offence (*actus reus*)

17 On an objective level, criminal liability for fraud pursuant to § 263 sub. 1 StGB presupposes that the perpetrator:

a) deceives another person about facts (→ mn. 18 et seqq.),
b) thereby causing this person to suffer an **error in thought** (→ mn. 37 et seqq.),
c) bringing about an erroneous **disposition of wealth** by this person (→ mn. 45 et seqq.),
d) leading to pecuniary loss (→ mn. 51 et seqq.).

a) Deception about facts

18 The primary prerequisite for criminal liability pursuant to § 263 sub. 1 StGB is the perpetrator's **deception** about **facts**.

19 **aa) Deception.** Deception (*Täuschung*) in the context of § 263 sub. 1 StGB is an overall behaviour intended to cause or to perpetuate an error/misconception (*causing or*

---

[14] § 263 sub. 7 StGB has been deleted and, insofar as it still appears in legal texts, only serves as a placeholder.

[15] The English versions of § 263 StGB used in this Chapter are taken from <https://www.gesetze-im-internet.de/englisch_stgb/englisch_stgb.html>, translated by Prof Dr Michael Bohlander, completely and regularly updated by Ute Reusch (last accessed: 27.10.2025).

maintaining an error, → mn. 15).[16] Deception can occur by express statements, by conclusive conduct, as well as by omission in breach of a duty to disclose.[17]

20 Express statements are the most easily accessible example. They are present when someone explicitly states false facts.

21 **Example for explicitly stating false facts**
A orders 100,000 surgical masks from B and informs B, before concluding the contract, that he is solvent and can pay the purchase price by quick money transfer within 24 hours of receiving the goods. In fact, A is insolvent. He plans to pass the masks on to a third party and never pay B the money owed. The masks are delivered. A does not transfer the purchase price to B.

22 Deception by conclusive conduct is more difficult to spot but occurs very frequently in practice.

23 **Example for deception by conclusive conduct**
A orders 100,000 surgical masks from B. B firmly assumes that A can and wants to pay for the masks although A has never said so. The masks are delivered. A does not transfer the purchase price to B.

24 In this example, it would have to be interpreted whether A, according to the general view of the market following the view of an objective bystander,[18] by ordering the masks, impliedly declared that he was able and willing to pay the purchase price incurred. Deception through conclusive conduct is assumed if, from the aforementioned point of view, a falsehood is not expressly declared but is implied by certain conduct.[19]

25 Deceptions by omission (*Unterlassung*) are relatively rare and can be difficult to distinguish from deceptions by conclusive behaviour. Varying propositions for making this distinction are discussed in German legal literature.[20] Using the previous example, it can be argued, for example, that A conclusively declared that he was able and willing to pay the purchase price when placing his order. Conversely, it could be argued that A omitted to inform B about his inability or unwillingness to pay when placing the order. Conclusive declarations of false facts and the omission of telling the truth regarding the same facts are always two sides of the same coin. Each case needs individual examination to determine the legal focus of a specific conduct and needs to be assessed accordingly. The focus may either be on the conclusive content of the declaration or on the failure to inform in breach of duty.

26 The distinction between the two alternatives (however arbitrary it might appear in some cases) is important. Increased legal requirements exist for assuming criminal liability on the basis of omission (see § 13 StGB). Deception by omission is only a punishable offence under § 263 sub. 1 StGB if the omission violates the perpetrator's duty to inform (§ 13 StGB). Such a duty can result, among other things, from express statutory obligations to notify or report, from explicit agreements, from special relationships of trust, from a duty to monitor sources of danger, as well as from previous misbehaviour of the perpetrator.

[16] LKH/Heger StGB § 263 mn. 6; also cf. Fischer StGB § 263 mn. 14.
[17] Cf. Fischer StGB § 263 mn. 15a et seqq.
[18] Cf. Fischer StGB § 263 mn. 21.
[19] Cf. Fischer StGB § 263 mn. 21.
[20] Cf. Fischer StGB § 263 mn. 38a; LKH/Heger StGB § 263 mn. 12 each with further references.

For instance, pursuant to § 28a SGB IV employers who are obliged to report to the social security authorities have to provide certain information about their employees. An omission of this duty to disclose can lead to certain contributions not being levied for social security purposes, thereby causing damages and fulfilling the offence of fraud.[21] 27

However, the threshold for assuming the existence of such a duty to inform is high as with its assumption criminal liability with all its severe consequences is established. 28

bb) Deception has to relate to facts. Any deception – be it by express statement, conclusive behaviour or omission in breach of duty – can only be relevant under § 263 StGB if it relates to **facts**. This legal requirement intends to exclude deceptions about one's own value judgements as well as future circumstances from the offence. Deceptions concerning value judgements or mere opinions are not punishable pursuant to § 263 StGB. According to the prevalent definition recognised in German criminal law, facts – in contrast to value judgements or opinions – are events of the past or present that are amenable to proof.[22] Events of the future cannot be amenable to proof and can, therefore, not be facts in the sense of § 263 sub. 1 StGB because they have not yet occurred.[23] 29

In contrast to deceptions regarding value judgements or opinions, deceptions regarding internal facts fall under § 263 sub. 1 StGB. 30

Example 31

Internal facts comprise a person's knowledge and intentions. A person who sits down in a bar and orders a drink, knowing full well that he does not want to pay for it, deceives the waiter about his willingness to pay. The person's willingness to pay (or rather the lack thereof) constitutes an internal fact within the meaning of § 263 StGB.[24]

The demarcations 'express versus implied deception or deception by omission' as well as the examination of whether there is deception about an external or internal fact are difficult and have to be approached on a case-by-case basis. The legal problems that can arise in this context can be illustrated particularly clearly by the example of sports betting fraud: 32

Example 33

A football match between Team X and Team Y takes place in the second national football league. A, a sports betting enthusiast, manages to bribe the referee of the match so that the referee agrees to influence the match in favour of Team Y. One day before the match A goes to a betting office and bets 10,000 EUR on a victory for Team Y by purchasing a betting slip from an employee of the betting office and submitting it. The next day, Team Y wins and the betting office pays A a substantial profit.

Criminal liability for fraud in sports betting cases was and is disputed in German literature.[25] In the aforementioned example, A expressly did not give any information at all to the betting office. He merely submitted a betting slip and left the betting office. However, following German jurisprudence the submission of a betting slip in the betting office always includes a conclusive declaration that the respective match has not been 34

---

21 Brettel/Schneider WirtschaftsStrafR § 3 mn. 21.

22 Cf. Brettel/Schneider WirtschaftsStrafR § 3 mn. 7 et seq.; Fischer StGB § 263 mn. 6.

23 Cf. Brettel/Schneider WirtschaftsStrafR § 3 mn. 8; Fischer StGB § 263 mn. 7a.

24 Cf. Bockelmann NJW 1961, 1936 in a note on a ruling of the German Federal Court of Justice, BGH 20.6.1961 – 5 StR 184/61, NJW 1961, 1934.

25 Cf. Fischer StGB § 263 mn. 1a with a compilation of literature on the subject.

manipulated in advance according to the bettor's own knowledge – or in the words of the German Federal Court of Justice:

35 The defendant [...] impliedly declared when handing in the betting slips that he was not involved in the manipulation of the betting object and thereby deceived the employee of the betting office so that the latter concluded the respective betting contracts by mistake, which caused damage to the betting providers due to deception.[26]

36 This exemplifies the case-by-case approach courts will take when construing the meaning of a certain overall behaviour.

b) Error in thought/misconception

37 The deceived person must have suffered an error in thought caused by the perpetrator's deception. Such an error exists if the deceived person has formed a misconception regarding a fact (meaning a conception which is contrary to reality) due to the deception.[27]

38 An examination to this effect leads to problems where the deceived person may not have formed a concrete (mis-)conception about a partial aspect addressed by the deception (for example, because the deceived person did not recognise the deception's specific relevance), but rather generally thought 'everything was in order'.[28]

39 The broad misconception 'that everything is in order' can be sufficient for the assumption of an 'error in thought' in the sense of § 263 sub. 1 StGB, as long as this general awareness relates to concrete (factual) circumstances and conditions that are affected by the deception.[29]

40 This is to be distinguished from cases in which the addressee of a deception does not think at all about the facts relevant to the deception or does not know them (so-called *ignorantia facti*). In such cases, there is also no error in thought or misconception within the meaning of § 263 StGB.

41

Example

An entrepreneur submits an invoice to his customer's accounting department and asks for the invoice amount to be transferred. The customer's accountant is instructed to check the invoice only for mathematical correctness. He does not check whether the invoice is also materially correct, i.e. whether the service invoiced therein was actually performed. As a rule, he will not think about this at all and will – in this context – thus not even be subject to a general misconception that 'everything is in order' – instead, he has no idea at all of and no view on the aforementioned facts (material correctness of the invoice).[30]

42 The examination of the existence of an error in thought pursuant to § 263 sub. 1 StGB then rarely causes problems in practice. Proving that said error specifically derived from the deception in question is where difficulties arise.

43 Generally speaking, where the deceived person was already under a misapprehension before the 'deception' occurred, but the misapprehension was deliberately maintained or reinforced by the perpetrator a sufficient link between deception and error in thought is assumed.[31]

---

[26] Cf. BGH 15.12.2006 – 5 StR 181/06, NJW 2007, 782 (783) (freely translated).

[27] LKH/Heger StGB § 263 mn. 18a.

[28] Cf. LKH/Heger StGB § 263 mn. 18a.

[29] Cf. BGH 25.1.2012 – 1 StR 45/11, NJW 2012, 1377 (1382); LKH/Heger StGB § 263 mn. 18a.

[30] Example derived from Brettel/Schneider WirtschaftsStrafR § 3 mn. 31, who in turn based their example on BGH 11.10.2004 – 5 StR 389/04, NStZ 2005, 157.

[31] Cf. LKH/Heger StGB § 263 mn. 20.

If, on the other hand, the pre-existing error in thought is neither caused, reinforced nor maintained but merely exploited by the 'perpetrator', no sufficient connection between deception and error in thought is assumed and the prerequisites for fraud pursuant to § 263 sub. 1 StGB are not met.[32] **44**

c) Disposal of assets

Furthermore, pursuant to § 263 sub. 1 StGB, the deceived person must bring about a disposal of assets. **45**

Any action, acquiescence or omission that has the direct effect of reducing wealth constitutes a disposal of assets relevant under § 263 sub. 1 StGB.[33] Whether the reduction in wealth/disposal of assets is met by equivalent compensation is – at this point of the examination of the prerequisites laid out in § 263 sub. 1 StGB – irrelevant.[34] However, it is imperative that the deceived person personally (!) brings about the disposal of assets.[35] **46**

Notably, in this context an additional unwritten causality requirement must be met in that the disposition of wealth must have been brought about because of the erroneous misconception (that in turn was caused through deception). Although not explicitly stated in § 263 sub. 1 StGB this is a generally recognised prerequisite of the offence.[36] **47**

This causality-requirement becomes uncertain, if the deceived person acted entirely independently from their own misconception, i.e. if it becomes apparent that the 'deceived person' was completely indifferent to the facts infected by his error in thought when making his decision. **48**

Another point of contention regarding the prerequisite of a disposal of assets pursuant to § 263 sub. 1 StGB is determining, what assets are protected under German criminal law. According to the (still) prevailing opinion in German jurisprudence and legal literature – any details are highly disputed –[37], only such assets are protected under § 263 sub. 1 StGB and can thus be subject to a disposal of assets relevant under § 263 sub. 1 StGB that are part of the sum of all economic goods of value of a natural or legal person (so-called economic property doctrine).[38] **49**

However, this definition is of limited practical use as it leads to the follow-up question of what then constitutes an 'economic' good. In practice, in the absence of clear legal statutory rules on this issue, fragmented case law has emerged that acts as guidance (in Germany *stare decisis* does not apply) for practitioners.[39] **50**

d) Pecuniary loss

Three essential points then remain with regard to the subsequent and final 'objective' prerequisite of § 263 sub. 1 StGB namely that the examined disposal of assets must have caused a pecuniary loss: **51**

---

32 Cf. LKH/Heger StGB § 263 mn. 20.

33 Prevailing opinion in German legal literature and jurisprudence, cf. LKH/Heger StGB § 263 mn. 22; BGH 11.3.1960 – 4 StR 588/59, NJW 1960, 1068 (1069); BGH 29.6.2005 – 4 StR 559/04, NJW 2005, 2789 (2790); BGH 10.8.2016 – 2 StR 579/15, NStZ 2017, 351 (352).

34 LKH/Heger StGB § 263 mn. 22; BGH 21.12.1982 – 1 StR 662/82, NJW 1983, 1130 (1130).

35 LKH/Heger StGB § 263 mn. 22.

36 LKH/Heger StGB § 263 mn. 21 with further references.

37 Cf. Fischer StGB § 263 mn. 1a with an extensive compilation of literature on the subject.

38 LKH/Heger StGB § 263 mn. 33 with further references; BGH 18.7.1961 – 1 StR 606/60, NJW 1961, 1876; BGH 22.11.2012 – 1 StR 537/12, NJW 2013, 1750 (1751): 'Fraud (§ 263 StGB) and embezzlement (§ 266 StGB) protect wealth understood as the sum of all monetary goods assigned to a person according to the overall legal order' (freely translated).

39 Cf. LKH/Heger StGB § 263 mn. 34 et seqq. with further references.

52 **aa) Legal definition.** Firstly, we turn to the definition of the element of the offence of pecuniary loss itself: a pecuniary loss within the meaning of § 263 sub. 1 StGB is assumed if the total economic value of someone's wealth is reduced by the disposal of assets by the deceived person when taking into account the disposal's immediate compensation;[40] the determination of which is carried out by so-called overall balancing.[41] In the context of the overall balancing, the (legally protected) overall assets before the disposal of assets are compared with the legally protected assets after the disposal of assets.

53 If the overall assets are worth less after the disposal of assets than before when also taking into account any received consideration, there is a pecuniary loss in the sense of § 263 sub. 1 StGB.

54 In court proceedings, in a first step it is mandatory to determine *whether* a pecuniary loss exists. In a second step, the exact amount of the pecuniary loss can be estimated – beyond certain individual cases –[42] in compliance with the *in dubio pro reo* principle.[43]

55 **bb) Special constellations.** There are, however, a few special constellations in which, at first glance, a comparison of the assets of the injured party before and after the disposal of assets does not mathematically show a 'loss', but in which nevertheless the existence of a pecuniary loss in the sense of § 263 sub. 1 StGB and thus criminal liability for fraud is affirmed in German jurisprudence and large parts of German legal literature. In this respect, three legal doctrines are recognised:

56 – the first legal doctrine to be mentioned in this context takes into account sufficiently **concrete threats to assets** (also called **damage-equivalent threats to assets**).[44] The existence of a pecuniary loss pursuant to § 263 sub. 1 StGB is assumed, if said loss has not yet manifested itself after the relevant disposal of assets but the risk for such a loss has heightened significantly in such a way that the probability of a definitive loss of an asset component at the time of the disposal of assets (by the deceived) is so great that this already results in an objective reduction in the total asset value.[45] For instance, jurisprudence has affirmed a concrete threat to assets (as a factual pecuniary loss), in cases of fraudulent risk transactions, which in reality involved a much higher risk of loss than contractually disclosed and agreed upon.[46]

57 – The legal doctrine of **individual damage impact**,[47] in turn, focuses on the concrete purpose of the object of a disposition of assets for the buyer or purchaser. The case law takes into account that not every object has the same value for every target group. According to the legal concept of individual damage impact, a pecuniary loss in the sense of § 263 sub. 1 StGB is assumed,
   – if a service is counterbalanced by a consideration of equal value in the abstract,

[40] LKH/Heger StGB § 263 mn. 36 with further references.

[41] Cf. LKH/Heger StGB § 263 mn. 36 with further references.

[42] LKH/Heger StGB § 263 mn. 36 with further references.

[43] In German criminal law, already the conclusion of a contract itself can cause a pecuniary loss within the meaning of § 263 StGB when contractually promised services/goods and consideration do not correspond in value. However, even in such cases the pecuniary loss must also be precisely quantified, LKH/Heger StGB § 263 mn. 36; BVerfG 7.12.2011 – 2 BvR 2500/09 i.a., NJW 2012, 907 (916).

[44] Cf. Fischer StGB § 263 mn. 156 et seqq.

[45] Cf. Fischer StGB § 263 mn. 159.

[46] Cf. BGH 18.2.2009 – 1 StR 731/08, NJW 2009, 2390, arguing at the same time that the term 'damage-equivalent threat to assets' is redundant as in such cases following established legal principles a pecuniary loss within the meaning § 263 StGB can established without the necessity of employing supplemental nomenclature; LKH/Heger StGB § 263 mn. 40.

[47] Cf. Brettel/Schneider WirtschaftsStrafR § 3 mn. 51 et seqq.

  - but is not, or not fully, usable by the party concerned for the contractually stipulated purpose and cannot be used by this party in any other reasonable way, namely by reselling it without particular difficulty.[48]
- The last 'case law' to be highlighted was, until recently, only rarely discussed in relation to white-collar criminal law but became more relevant in the course of the 'diesel scandal' (→ mn. 92 et seqq.).[49] The case group of the so-called **misappropriation of purpose doctrine** concerns cases in which the deceived person without legal obligation[50] deliberately gives away assets without (equivalent) remuneration but is deceived with regard to a non-economic element of this disposition in assets. For example, if someone pretends to collect donations for a 'charitable' purpose, but in reality keeps the money for himself instead of using it for the purported purpose.[51] In such case, the assumption of pecuniary loss shall depend on whether the purpose pursued with the expenditure was missed, even if the financial loss itself would have occurred either way.[52] 58

cc) **Triangular fraud.** Finally, the question arises if a pecuniary loss pursuant to § 263 sub. 1 StGB exists if the person committing the disposal of wealth is not at the same time the owner of the assets in question and thus not the 'injured party'. 59

This can indeed be the case. The person who makes the disposal of assets and the person or entity who suffers the pecuniary loss can differ as long as there is a sufficiently close relationship between both (so-called **triangular fraud** (*Dreiecksbetrug*)).[53] Following prevailing jurisprudence, for this criterion to be met it has to be examined whether the person making the disposal of assets can be assigned to the 'camp' of the injured party. The prerequisite for this association is an especially close relationship of the disposer to the damaged property or wealth.[54] 60

It is important to note that the relationship between disposal of assets and pecuniary loss differs from that between error in thought and disposal of assets. A criminal offence of fraud necessarily presupposes that the person who makes the disposal of assets is also the person who is subject to a deception-related error in thought (which in turn must be causal for the disposition of wealth). However, the person making the disposal of assets and the injured party suffering the pecuniary loss because of it do not have to be identical. 61

2. Subjective elements of the offence (*mens rea*)

With regard to the internal side of the offence, the perpetrator must know about and accept all characteristics of the objective elements of the offence as well as the causal connections linking them.[55] Furthermore, he must intend the enrichment of himself or a third party as the goal or necessary intermediate goal of his actions.[56] The pursued (self-)enrichment must be of the same substance as the pecuniary loss caused and must be unlawful (e.g. the enrichment would not be unlawful if the deceiver had an enforceable legal claim to it).[57] 62

---

[48] LKH/Heger StGB § 263 mn. 48a with further references.
[49] Cf. Isfen JA 2016, 1 (4 fn. 44).
[50] LKH/Heger StGB § 263 mn. 56.
[51] Cf. LKH/Heger StGB § 263 mn. 56; BGH 30.4.1987 – 4 StR 79/87, wistra 1987, 255 (256).
[52] LKH/Heger StGB § 263 mn. 56.
[53] Cf. LKH/Heger StGB § 263 mn. 28 et seqq.
[54] Cf. BGH 7.3.2017 – 1 StR 41/17, BeckRS 2017, 113897 mn. 12 et seqq.; BGH 16.1.1963 – 2 StR 591/62, BGHSt 18, 221 (223 et seq.) = BeckRS 1963, 105143; Brettel/Schneider WirtschaftsStrafR § 3 mn. 161 with further references; Fischer StGB § 263 mn. 82 with further references.
[55] LKH/Heger StGB § 263 mn. 57.
[56] LKH/Heger StGB § 263 mn. 58.
[57] LKH/Heger StGB § 263 mn. 59; 61.

63 If the aforementioned criteria are met, the offence of fraud in its basic form (within the meaning of § 263 sub. 1 StGB) is fulfilled.

64 § 263 sub. 2 et seqq. StGB then expand on the base offence by determining special provisions such as – among other things – sentencing guidelines for particularly severe cases of fraud.

II. § 263 sub. 3 and 5 StGB: severe cases with special need for sanctioning

65 Under German law there are usually two types of sentencing guidelines that can expand on the penalty range put forward by a base offence such as fraud in its basic form (meaning fraud pursuant to § 263 sub. 1 StGB):

1. § 263 sub. 3 StGB: standard examples where increased penalty range usually is applied

66 In German criminal law, so called **standard examples** define situations of either particular severity or triviality in which 'as a rule' certain aggravations or mitigations of punishment have to be considered.[58] These standard examples only concern the assessment of appropriate sentencing.[59] They serve as a strong indicator that – when compared to the base offence – a certain higher or lower penalty range must be applied. Standard examples, however, do not constitute an obligation on the part of the court to apply the indicated penalty range.[60]

67 Even in relevant factual constellations, it remains the task of the court to examine whether the individual case really is a particularly serious or trivial case. The court must, therefore, examine whether the circumstantial effect of a standard example can be refuted in the individual case.[61]

68 With this in mind, § 263 sub. 3 StGB contains so-called standard examples for particularly **serious** cases of fraud:

69 (3) In especially serious cases, the penalty is imprisonment for a term of between six months and 10 years. An especially serious case typically occurs where the offender

1. acts on a commercial basis or as a member of a gang whose purpose is the continued commission of forgery of documents or fraud,
2. causes a major financial loss or acts with the intention of placing a large number of persons in danger of financial loss by the continued commission of fraud,
3. places another person in financial hardship,
4. abuses his or her powers or position as a public official or European official or
5. pretends that an insured event has happened after they or another person have set fire to an object of significant value or destroyed it, in whole or in part, by setting fire to it or caused the sinking or grounding of a ship.

---

[58] Cf. Roxin/Greco StrafR AT I § 10 mn. 134.
[59] Cf. Roxin/Greco StrafR AT I § 10 mn. 134.
[60] Cf. Roxin/Greco StrafR AT I § 10 mn. 134.
[61] Cf. Roxin/Greco StrafR AT I § 10 mn. 134.

In practice, courts will only rarely assume that despite a standard example within the meaning of § 263 sub. 3 StGB being met there is no particularly serious case of fraud.[62] In general, standard examples, even if the application of their penalty range is not strictly speaking mandatory, serve as very strong indicators that the increased penalty range (e.g. of § 263 sub. 3 StGB) should be applied ('imprisonment for a term of between six months and 10 years') and courts only rarely deviate from this indication. **70**

In concrete terms, with respect to § 263 StGB, the standard examples of § 263 sub. 3 sent. 2 no. 1 alt. 1 and 2 StGB are of particular practical relevance: **71**

- in the case of § 263 sub. 3 sent. 2 no. 1 alt. 1 StGB ('[...] where the offender [1.] acts on a commercial basis [...]'), a person acts on a **commercial basis** if he intends to obtain a not only temporary source of income of some extent and duration by repeatedly committing the offence of fraud. **72**
  This definition will likely apply to most fraud cases in white-collar criminal law as most fraudulent endeavours serve the aim of generating an (illicit) source of income. **73**
  When examining this standard example it is important to check, whether the perpetrators actually acted in order to obtain a source of income of some extent and duration for **themselves** (!). § 263 sub. 3 no. 1 alt. 1 StGB is not applicable, where a perpetrator acted solely for the benefit of his company.[63] However, the boundaries between acting in self-interest and for the benefit of a third party often are fleeting. For example, if a person working in sales defrauds customers primarily in the financial interest of his employer (third party), but receives a sales-target-related bonus, § 263 sub. 3 sent. 2 no. 1 alt. 1 StGB can also be applied, even if this person's personal gains (e.g. through his personal bonus) are minute compared to his employer's earnings from the fraudulent sales. **74**
- Regarding § 263 sub. 3 sent. 2 no. 1 alt. 2 StGB ('[...] where the offender acts [...] as a member of a gang whose purpose is the continued commission of forgery of documents or fraud, [...]') a **gang** under German law is assumed where a group of at least three people has agreed to commit fraud offences over a certain period of time.[64] **75**
  Since fraud offences in white-collar criminal law are often committed in corporate settings with many persons involved, a gang-like commission is regularly assumed by the investigative authorities. **76**

2. § 263 sub. 5 StGB: qualification offence where increased penalty range has to be applied

Apart from the aforementioned 'standard examples' in German criminal law, there are also so-called qualification offences where – if the prerequisites are met – an increased penalty range has to be (!) applied. **77**

§ 263 sub. 5 StGB contains such a qualification offence expanding on § 263 sub. 1 StGB: **78**

> (5) Whoever commits fraud on a commercial basis as a member of a gang whose purpose is the continued commission of offences under §§ 263 to 264 or §§ 267 to 269 incurs a penalty of imprisonment for a term of between one year and 10 years, in less serious cases imprisonment for a term of between six months and five years. **79**

---

62 For a well-known exception from this 'rule of thumb' see OLG Dresden 25.4.2014 – 2 OLG 24 Ss 778/13, BeckRS 2014, 10082 regarding welfare fraud constellations.

63 Cf. Fischer StGB § 263 mn. 210; LKH/Heger StGB § 263 mn. 66.

64 Cf. Fischer StGB § 263 mn. 211, § 244 mn. 34, 36.

80 The qualification offence provides for an (compared to § 263 sub. 1 StGB) increased penalty range (minimum sentence of one year; maximum sentence of ten years of imprisonment) for such fraud offences that have been committed in a gang-like manner **and** on a commercial basis (→ mn. 71 et seqq.).

81 Notably, the qualification offence is also applicable to other special offences of fraud (such as subsidy fraud pursuant to § 264 StGB, → mn. 126 et seqq.).

III. Other provisions of § 263 StGB at a glance

82 In addition, § 263 StGB contains the following provisions:

1. § 263 sub. 2 StGB

83 § 263 sub. 2 StGB also makes the mere **attempt** to defraud a criminal offence:

84 (2) The attempt is punishable.

85 In German criminal law, criminal acts that are not completed but merely 'attempted' are not generally sanctioned but rather only where the legislator sees a specific need for such additional deterrence. In principle, criminal liability for attempted offences exists in such cases where the relevant criminal provisions provide for a minimum term of imprisonment of one year (§§ 23 sub. 1; 12 sub. 1 StGB) or where a statute expressly states that the attempt of an offence is also punishable by law. The latter is the case here (§ 263 sub. 2 StGB).

2. § 263 sub. 4 StGB

86 § 263 sub. 4 StGB declares certain provisions of the statute on theft to be applicable also to the offence of fraud:

87 (4) § 243 sub. 2 and §§ 247 and 248a apply accordingly.

88 This 'reference provision' is often overlooked in practice, which can lead to serious consequences. Read in context, it puts forwards the following rules:

- the assumption of a standard example pursuant to § 263 sub. 3 StGB (→ mn. 65 et seqq.) is barred if only **minor damages** are caused by the fraud in question (§ 263 sub. 4 alt. 1 in conjunction with § 243 sub. 2 StGB);
- **fraud with regard to low-value items** is only prosecuted upon application by the person entitled to make the application (usually the person injured by the fraud), unless the prosecuting authorities see a special public interest for prosecuting the case (§ 263 sub. 4 alt. 3 in conjunction with § 248a StGB; so-called relative application offence);
- fraud is prosecuted exclusively on the application of the person entitled to make the application if the offender's guardian or custodian was injured by the offence or if the injured person lived in a domestic relationship with the offender (§ 263 sub. 4 alt. 2 in conjunction with § 247 StGB; so-called absolute application offence).

89 Particularly in **family businesses**, there may regularly be cases in which the requirement to file a criminal complaint applies. Since the law sets strict deadlines for filing a criminal complaint (three months from the person entitled to file a criminal complaint becoming aware of the offence and the offender), an unfiled criminal complaint can sometimes mean the end of the proceedings – even where damages are substantial. This

provision should be observed in fraud constellations, especially when filing or preparing a criminal complaint.

3. § 263 sub. 6 StGB

§ 263 sub. 6 StGB in turn, provides for the possibility, for serious fraud offences, to place the offender, after forfeiting a six-month prison sentence, under so-called supervision of conduct, meaning under the supervision of social workers who help the offender reintegrate into life in freedom: **90**

(6) The court may make an order for the supervision of conduct (§ 68 sub. 1). **91**

IV. Diesel scandal

The most prominent fraud case occupying the German investigating authorities and courts today is the diesel scandal, in the context of which various car companies are being investigated for using manipulated software in series-produced vehicles through which during test situations (e.g. when undergoing tests of German authorities or the technical control board) exhaust emissions were kept in compliance with regulations even though in reality – meaning in real-life situations on the road – the software (supposedly) did not keep exhaust behaviour in line with emissions regulations. **92**

In 2023, former Audi-executive Stadler received a suspended prison sentence of 1 year and 9 months for his involvement in the diesel scandal.[65] In the same trial, two other former Audi-employees also received similar prison sentences of 1 year and 9 months as well as 2 years respectively that were also suspended on parole.[66] All three individuals have appealed the verdict.[67] Furthermore, in May 2025, four Volkswagen executives were sentenced by the Braunschweig Regional Court.[68] A former head of diesel engine development was sentenced to four and a half years in prison.[69] The former head of drive electronics was sentenced to two years and seven months in prison.[70] A former chief **93**

[65] Cf. Redaktion beck aktuell, Dieselskandal: Ex-Audi-Chef Stadler wegen Betrugs verurteilt, 27.6.2024, becklink 2027523, also available at <https://rsw.beck.de/aktuell/daily/meldung/detail/lg-muenchen-dieselskandal-ex-audi-chef-stadler-wegen-betrugs-verurteilt> (last accessed: 18.6.2025); LG München II 27.6.2023 – W5 KLs 64 Js 22724/19, juris.

[66] Cf. Redaktion beck-aktuell, Dieselskandal: Ex-Audi-Chef Stadler wegen Betrugs verurteilt, 27.6.2024, available at <https://rsw.beck.de/aktuell/daily/meldung/detail/lg-muenchen-dieselskandal-ex-audi-chef-stadler-wegen-betrugs-verurteilt> (last accessed: 18.6.2025).

[67] Cf. Redaktion beck-aktuell, Ex-Audi-Chef Stadler legt Revision ein, 4.3.2023, becklink 2027602, also available at <https://rsw.beck.de/aktuell/daily/meldung/detail/ex-audi-chef-stadler-legt-revision-ein#:~:text=Die%20Verteidiger%20des%20ehemaligen%20Audi,teilte%20das%20Gericht%20heute%20mit.> (last accessed: 18.6.2025).

[68] Cf. Redaktion beck-aktuell, Dieselskandal: Frühere VW-Manager zu Haftstrafen verurteilt, 26.5.2025, becklink 2034400, also available at <https://rsw.beck.de/aktuell/daily/meldung/detail/lg-braunschweig-6kls411js4903215-vw-manager-dieselskandal-haft-betrug> (last accessed: 18.6.2025).

[69] Cf. Redaktion beck-aktuell, Dieselskandal: Frühere VW-Manager zu Haftstrafen verurteilt, 26.5.2025, becklink 2034400, also available at <https://rsw.beck.de/aktuell/daily/meldung/detail/lg-braunschweig-6kls411js4903215-vw-manager-dieselskandal-haft-betrug> (last accessed: 18.6.2025).

[70] Cf. Redaktion beck-aktuell, Dieselskandal: Frühere VW-Manager zu Haftstrafen verurteilt, 26.5.2025, becklink 2034400, also available at <https://rsw.beck.de/aktuell/daily/meldung/detail/lg-braunschweig-6kls411js4903215-vw-manager-dieselskandal-haft-betrug> (last accessed: 18.6.2025).

development officer and a department head each received suspended sentences.[71] This verdict also is not yet final and the defence lawyers intend to appeal.[72]

94 Even without the above-mentioned rulings, which aren't final yet, there's no end in sight for the criminal investigations into the diesel scandal. In Braunschweig alone, there's still a case against former VW boss Martin Winterkorn pending at the regional court, and indictments against 31 other people are still open. All this goes to say: both from an economic and legal point of view, the diesel scandal is of a special dimension.

95 In economic terms, the dimensions of the diesel scandal have been discussed at length in the national and international press.[73] However, the economic damage calculations circulated in connection with various press reports are far removed from the damages in question under German criminal (fraud) law. This is because the press reports regularly take an economic view of the consequences of the diesel scandal. In German criminal law, however, criminal liability must be established with regard to specific cases, meaning for each and every car sale specifically. For every such sale all the prerequisites have to be proven in order to establish criminal liability pursuant to § 263 StGB.

96 Any calculation of fraudulent damages must refer to a (!) concrete disposition of assets, which in turn must be based on a concrete deception by a natural person as well as a related misconception of the deceived person. The (German) criminal law perspective thus always represents a microscopic view into an otherwise almost limitless complex. The fact that investigative authorities then take many such 'looks through the microscope' and sometimes also assign criminal liability for several observed cases to one perpetrator, does not change this.

97 With this in mind, from a legal point of view, proceedings surrounding the diesel scandal face two difficulties:

98 Firstly, even where there is clear evidence of vehicle manipulation, almost every element/prerequisite of the basic offence of fraud is problematic when establishing criminal liability for fraud in diesel cases (→ mn. 100 et seqq.).

99 Secondly, however, the aforementioned 'clear evidence' is, in practice, a mythical creature and proving the constituent elements of the offence encounters, in practice, considerable difficulties. Legal complexity and evidentiary difficulties thus intertwine here and make the cases resulting from the diesel scandal highly complicated.

1. Case study to illustrate the criminal law dimension of the diesel scandal

100 This can be well illustrated by a simple example, which – in a slightly modified form – was published by Dorothea Magnus and Julia Heß as a 'mock exam' in a German legal training magazine:[74]

101

Facts of the case

In 2019, the Germany-based company 'X-AG' launched a model series with diesel engines of a new design. During the development phase, the research and development department

[71] Cf. Redaktion beck-aktuell, Dieselskandal: Frühere VW-Manager zu Haftstrafen verurteilt, 26.5.2025, becklink 2034400, also available at <https://rsw.beck.de/aktuell/daily/meldung/detail/lg-braunschweig-6kls411js4903215-vw-manager-dieselskandal-haft-betrug> (last accessed: 18.6.2025).

[72] Cf. Redaktion beck-aktuell, Dieselskandal: Frühere VW-Manager zu Haftstrafen verurteilt, 26.5.2025, becklink 2034400, also available at <https://rsw.beck.de/aktuell/daily/meldung/detail/lg-braunschweig-6kls411js4903215-vw-manager-dieselskandal-haft-betrug> (last accessed: 18.6.2025).

[73] Cf. e.g. Reuters, The state of legal cases in VW's diesel scandal, 27.6.2023, available at <https://www.reuters.com/sustainability/state-legal-cases-vws-diesel-scandal-2023-06-27/> (last accessed: 13.1.2025).

[74] Facts according to Magnus/Heß JA 2022, 471 et seq.

determined that the engine designed would probably not comply with the legally prescribed exhaust emission limits in regular driving operation. Finally, hidden software was installed in the vehicle model, by means of which the defeat device in the engine control unit was manipulated. As a result, the vehicle model untruthfully indicated that it complied with the exhaust emission values.

The manipulation remained undetected in the official inspection procedure. After type approval was granted, the model went into series production with manipulated software. Typical for the business model of X-AG, sales were to be made only through partner car dealerships. The partner car dealerships, such as that of the sole trader H, each acquired the manipulated vehicles at a purchase price of 40,000 EUR and sold them independently to the end customer. H's contact person was the employee M who worked in the sales department of X-AG. M had expressly assured H that the model was free of defects in accordance with previous practice at X-AG.

In 2020, K visited H's car dealership and purchased a vehicle of the manipulated model series at a purchase price of 40,000 EUR. Neither H nor M were aware of the 'cheating software' in the vehicle sold to K. The vehicle was also free of defects. H also declared to K that the vehicle was free of defects.

In line with this example the German investigative authorities are confronted with numerous proceedings, which are directed either **102**

- against car sellers on the suspicion of having defrauded the end customer, or
- against employees of intermediaries or car dealerships (in this case X-AG).

The mock examination case was, of course, even more detailed. Among other things, the exam case further provided:[75] **103**

- which employee of X-AG was responsible for the implementation of the manipulated software;
- the information that the board of directors had been comprehensively informed about the manipulation and – after consultation with the legal department – voted by majority for the mass production of the vehicle model with manipulation software;
- that neither the middleman (H) nor the end customer (K) would have bought the vehicle, had they known about the software manipulations.

In this respect, it is important to look at which parts of the exam's facts were *not* incorporated in the example used above (in order to ensure practical relevance). **104**

In practice precisely these points – that are handed out as additional facts in exams – are difficult to prove 'in the real world', which in turn has an effect on the examination of the prerequisites of fraud. **105**

2. Criminal liability from the perspective of the end customer

Let us approach the 'exam case' taking the **perspective of the end customer**: K goes to H's car dealership and buys a manipulated vehicle from him. Neither K nor H know about the software manipulation and the fact that exhaust emission limits were not complied with. **106**

With this in mind let us examine the prerequisites of § 263 StGB one by one: **107**

a) Deception about facts within the meaning of § 263 StGB

We would first need a factual **deception about facts** of H vis-à-vis K: **108**

- the German Federal Court of Justice has ruled in a civil law matter that the inclusion of illegal defeat devices in cars manipulating a car's nitrogen oxide emission constitutes

[75] Magnus/Heß JA 2022, 471 et seq.

a defect in the legal sense within affected vehicles.[76] Applying this line of reasoning, it could be examined if the (implied) declaration that a vehicle is free of such a defect would have to be construed as deception within the meaning of § 263 StGB (the fact that H himself did not even know that his declaration of fact was false has an effect elsewhere; keyword: subjective element of the offence/*mens rea*). However, the premise for this approach, namely that a salesperson in selling a car makes the implied statement that the car is free of defects, has been strongly refuted in German legal literature,[77] mainly and rightfully so because the examination of the quality of the goods to determine whether they correspond to the buyer's own quality expectations is fundamentally the responsibility of the buyer and the seller, therefore, does not implicitly declare that the goods are free of defects upon sale.[78]

- Another perspective revolves around whether a vehicle's characteristics align with certain advertising promises. It is then contended that when selling the vehicle, the seller makes the implied statement that the cars include the advertised features.[79]
- Yet another approach is based on the idea that when a vehicle is sold, the salesperson either has a duty to disclose if the vehicle does not comply with the legal requirements[80] or even implies that the vehicle is in compliance with its legal requirements.[81]
- All in all to this day it remains obscure, where – if at all –, in a vehicle sale in which exhaust values and exhaust devices are not explicitly discussed at all, the deception (by implication or omission) is actually to be seen.[82]

109 For the sake of the example, let us assume that there has been deception within the meaning of § 263 StGB and continue with the examination.

b) Error in thought within the meaning of § 263 StGB

110 The question then arises as to whether K, at the very least, suffered from the general **misconception/error in thought** that 'everything was in order' and thus formed a relevant error in thought in the sense of § 263 StGB.[83] Here the distinction from the so-called *ignorantia facti* becomes essential (→ mn. 40). An extension of the general idea that 'everything is fine' must not go so far as to impute to the addressee of the deception that he has formed ideas about facts about which he in fact had no – not even abstract ('everything is fine') – ideas.[84] Legal practice and jurisprudence make use of certain facilitations when dealing with the examination of the prerequisite of misconception within the meaning of § 263 StGB regarding mass fraud proceedings such as the diesel complex.[85] For example, the use of questionnaires in preliminary proceedings as well as the recourse to general principles of experience in the judicial assessment of evidence.[86] Nevertheless, a proper judicial clarification of the facts requires the examination of a representative number of witnesses, so that any such clarification in cases like the present one represents a Herculean task for the courts. This is particularly true since, due to the numerous complications

---

[76] BGH 8.1.2019 – VIII ZR 225/17, BeckRS 2019, 2206.

[77] Cf. Hefendehl wistra 2023, 177 (180) with further references.

[78] Matt/Renzikowski/Saliger StGB § 263 mn. 46b; Hefendehl wistra 2023, 177 (180); regarding the general evaluation of this legal question in other areas of application, TK StGB/Perron StGB § 263 mn. 51, each with further references.

[79] Cf. LG Hildesheim 17.1.2017 – 3 O 139/16, VuR 2017, 111 (115).

[80] LG Mönchengladbach 1.6.2017 – 10 O 84/16, BeckRS 2017, 132861 mn. 42.

[81] Seemingly supportive of this notion, Brand/Hotz NZG 2017, 976 (977).

[82] Cf. On the issue as a whole, Matt/Renzikowski/Saliger StGB § 263 mn. 46a et seq.

[83] Cf. LKH/Heger StGB § 263 mn. 18a.

[84] Cf. Brand/Hotz NZG 2017, 976 (978).

[85] Cf. Venn NStZ 2023, 257.

[86] Cf. Venn NStZ 2023, 257 (258 et seqq.).

in the legal adjudication of diesel cases, it is disputed whether the 'facilitation of evidence' otherwise used in mass fraud proceedings may be applied at all in the diesel complex.[87]

c) Disposal of assets within the meaning of § 263 StGB

A **disposal of assets** pursuant to § 263 StGB is evident here: K paid 40,000 EUR for a vehicle of the manipulated model series. **111**

Note on evidence **112**

The first prerequisite of § 263 StGB that in practice meets great obstacles regarding its burden of proof then is the element of **causality between misconception and disposal of assets** in the sense of § 263 StGB (e.g. proving K paid the (full) purchase price for the car **because** he thought the car did not employ manipulated and non-compliant exhaust software and mechanisms).[88] It is, to put it bluntly, difficult to say how many end customers in Germany, the country of 'no speed limits', might still have bought the vehicles for the same price if they had known that the vehicle did not comply with certain exhaust emission limits, but could nevertheless be used without restrictions on German roads.

The question cannot be answered categorically which means that in practice each individual case, i.e. each vehicle sale, has to be considered on its own merits. The danger that, from today's perspective, vehicle buyers 'in hindsight' and after years of the media's attention to the diesel scandal might provide at the very least impaired or distorted testimony is high. **113**

d) Pecuniary loss within the meaning of § 263 StGB

However, even if the existence of an erroneous disposition of assets is affirmed, the question arises as to whether K in consequence, as the end customer, suffered an actual **pecuniary loss**. **114**

The response to this question is not straightforward because K has indeed received a vehicle from X-AG for the money he paid and the extent to which the software-manipulated emission control system might justify a diminished market value of the vehicle is disputed in the literature and case law to this day. The mere existence of a material defect in the vehicle does not automatically mean that it is worth less and that there is a pecuniary loss within the meaning of § 263 StGB.[89] **115**

Different proposals for establishing a 'pecuniary loss' in the sense of § 263 StGB are discussed in German legal literature ranging from **116**

- economic approaches (attributing a certain arithmetical value to the emission control system for the 'functioning and compliant version' of which the buyer has supposedly paid but not received anything in return [delta = pecuniary loss]);[90] to
- more subjective approaches that want to take into account a possible decommissioning order that exists in parts of Germany and assume an individual damage impact as a result of the associated unusability of the vehicle for the buyer (→ mn. 57).[91]

---

87 Cf. Hefendehl wistra 2023, 177 (183).

88 Cf. Brand/Hotz NZG 2017, 976 (978).

89 Cf. Wolf NStZ 2023, 263 (266); Brand/Hotz NZG 2017, 976 (979); Hefendehl wistra 2023, 177 (184) with further references regarding authors and civil court jurisprudence holding opposing views.

90 Cf. Wolf NStZ 2023, 263 (267).

91 Cf. e.g. MüKoStGB/Hefendehl StGB § 263 mn. 1005, regarding cases where the buyer cannot use a car with a manipulative defeat device because the car was supposed to serve another contractually recognized purpose beyond its existing function as a means of transportation, which in light of the defeat

- Still others want to establish a pecuniary loss according to the misappropriation of purpose doctrine (→ mn. 58). It is argued that the buyer (e.g. K) also pursues an idealistic purpose with his car purchase (e.g. environmental protection) for which he pays but does not receive anything or at least nothing equivalent in return.[92]
- Last but not least Frank Saliger argues (convincingly) that in most diesel related cases the existence of a pecuniary loss within the meaning of § 263 StGB has to be rejected as a whole if held to the legal standards established in criminal law.[93]

117 The trend in case law seems to point a different way although contradictory court decisions exist: when assessing civil claims, some civil courts have had to examine incidentally whether § 263 StGB was fulfilled and have affirmed this – i.e. also the existence of a pecuniary loss within the meaning of the provision.[94] The transferability of the evaluations made in the aforementioned civil law decisions to criminal law is disputed in German legal literature.[95] However, the Munich Regional Court (II) recently issued a criminal law ruling in the diesel case[96] that also affirmed the existence of a pecuniary loss within the meaning of § 263 StGB (regarding the ruling in detail → mn. 120 et seqq.).

e) Indirect perpetration?

118 However, even if one now affirms a pecuniary loss following one legal argument or the other, one inevitably encounters the problem that the car salesman (e.g. H) did not know about the vehicle manipulations and cannot have **made** himself **liable to criminal prosecution for fraud for lack of criminal intent**.

119 In principle, this does not necessarily mark the conclusion of a criminal investigation under German criminal law. If a person (e.g. someone working at X-AG) indirectly prompted an intermediary (e.g. H) by virtue of superior knowledge to commit criminal offences in good faith, that person according to German law can also be held liable (so-called **indirect perpetration**, *mittelbare Täterschaft*). However, once again, this is where the burden of proof comes back into play: almost every economic complex in white-collar crime law deals with multiple events involving many different persons within turn just as many different responsibilities who have often collaborated in a division of labour. The question of who knew what and who – to what extent – participated in the decision-making process (here: regarding the decision to put the manipulated vehicles on the market) is just as elementary as it is hard to prove. This is where real difficulties in addressing the diesel scandal from the perspective of German criminal law arise.

---

device cannot be fulfilled, for example, if an organization is committed to the immediate elimination of vehicles with fossil fuel technology and consequently cannot include just such a vehicle in its vehicle fleet.

[92] Cf. Isfen JA 2016, 1 (4 Fn. 44).

[93] Cf. Matt/Renzikowski/Saliger StGB § 263 mn. 46c.

[94] Cf. e.g. LG Hildesheim 17.1.2017 – 3 O 139/16, VuR 2017, 111 (115); LG Mönchengladbach 1.6.2017 – 10 O 84/16, BeckRS 2017, 132861 mn. 49; LG Krefeld 19.7.2017 – 7 O 147/16, BeckRS 2017, 117776 mn. 48; Matt/Renzikowski/Saliger StGB § 263 mn. 46a.

[95] Against such a transferability, cf. Saliger/Rüsse NStZ 2021, 513 (516 et seqq.); emphasising the autonomy of criminal law vis-à-vis civil as well as the limits of the subjectivisation of the prerequisite of a 'pecuniary loss' within the meaning of § 263 StGB under German criminal law, cf. Hefendehl wistra 2023, 177 (178 et seq.); in favour of a – in large parts – joint treatment of the legal prerequisite of 'pecuniary loss' in criminal and civil law, cf. Wolf NStZ 2023, 263.

[96] Cf. Redaktion beck-aktuell, Ex-Audi-Chef Stadler legt Revision ein, 4.3.2023, becklink 2027602, also available at <https://rsw.beck.de/aktuell/daily/meldung/detail/ex-audi-chef-stadler-legt-revision-ein#:~:text=Die%20Verteidiger%20des%20ehemaligen%20Audi,teilte%20das%20Gericht%20heute%20mit.> (last accessed: 18.6.2025).

3. Interim result

The legal difficulties that diesel fraud proceedings bring to the fore explain why only a few criminal court proceedings on the diesel complex have seen the light of day to date (on the status quo → mn. 93 et seq.). How many convictions there will be at the end of the processing of the diesel complex remains to be seen. Considering the factual and legal uncertainties that cannot be dismissed, however, it is to be expected that these could be fewer than the press coverage and public interest in the matter might initially suggest. The Stadler ruling, which in the meantime has been published[97] but is not yet final, provides initial insight into how the criminal courts might proceed, but the criminal investigation into the diesel scandal is far from over. **120**

The Stadler ruling was based on the following facts: senior employees of Audi AG, including the defendants P. and H., were involved in the development of diesel vehicles in which illegal defeat devices were deliberately installed so that the vehicles emitted higher levels of nitrogen oxide than permitted during operation.[98] The vehicles were sold nationwide through a network of authorized dealers with sales staff acting in good faith.[99] The management, specifically P. and H., accepted that customers would be misled by misleading sales documents about the non-compliant nature of the vehicles and would make purchase decisions that would damage their financial interests, even though the vehicles were not actually roadworthy or eligible for registration.[100] The defendant Stadler, as CEO of Audi-AG and member of the executive board of VW-AG, was involved in relevant decision-making processes and recognized the possibility of legal violations, but failed to take any steps to clarify the situation or stop sales.[101] **121**

The court found that the necessary deception had been committed by the sales documents and registration certificates implicitly suggesting compliance with the registration requirements and the roadworthiness of the vehicles. The court considered this to be a significant (implicit) statement (deception) vis-a-vis the initial purchasers regarding the suitability for use and compliance with emission standards, as this was of central importance for market access and the traffic law status of the vehicles.[102] The purchasers were in a relevant error, as they assumed that all regulations had been complied with.[103] The disposal of assets consisted in the conclusion of the purchase agreements;[104] the pecuniary loss lay in the purchase at the regular new car price, although the market value was reduced by approximately 5 % due to the illegal defeat devices or rather in the negative balance derived therefrom.[105] **122**

P. and H. were convicted as indirect (co-)perpetrators under criminal law, as the actual sales employees acted without intent, while the court assumed that P. and H. had control over the act and a personal interest.[106] The court convicted the defendant Stadler of fraud by omission as an indirect perpetrator: despite being aware of the facts, he had culpa- **123**

---

[97] Cf. LG München II 27.6.2023 – W5 KLs 64 Js 22724/19, juris.
[98] Cf. LG München II 27.6.2023 – W5 KLs 64 Js 22724/19, juris mn. 3.
[99] Cf. LG München II 27.6.2023 – W5 KLs 64 Js 22724/19, juris mn. 3, 74.
[100] Cf. LG München II 27.6.2023 – W5 KLs 64 Js 22724/19, juris mn. 3, 6306.
[101] Cf. LG München II 27.6.2023 – W5 KLs 64 Js 22724/19, juris mn. 15 et seqq.
[102] Cf. LG München II 27.6.2023 – W5 KLs 64 Js 22724/19, juris mn. 6296, 6301 et seqq.
[103] Cf. LG München II 27.6.2023 – W5 KLs 64 Js 22724/19, juris mn. 6353, 6358.
[104] Cf. LG München II 27.6.2023 – W5 KLs 64 Js 22724/19, juris mn. 6364.
[105] Under German law, in cases where the conclusion of the contract already results in a negative balance of assets, but the agreed services are actually exchanged, as in this case, the obligation and the dispositive transaction are to be treated as a single unit and the values of the services actually rendered are to be offset in order to determine the damage, cf. LG München II 27.6.2023 – W5 KLs 64 Js 22724/19, juris mn. 6370 et seqq.
[106] Cf. LG München II 27.6.2023 – W5 KLs 64 Js 22724/19, juris mn. 6384, 6387 et seqq., 6432 et seqq.

bly failed to disclose the true nature of the vehicles or to initiate a sales stop. The court affirmed the defendant's duty to act as a guarantor arising from a special relationship of trust in business, interference (through earlier communications initiated by him), and his position as an executive with a corresponding duty to monitor and ensure the legality of the company's actions.[107]

124 The examination of § 263 StGB with regard to the diesel complex highlights the vagueness of the German criminal provision on fraud and explains why – as indicated at the beginning – § 263 StGB appears in so many places in German white-collar criminal law.

125 The elements of the offence are broad and indeterminate. This allows the provision to be applied initially to many circumstances. On the other hand, this range of application leaves the requirements of § 263 StGB open to interpretation, which means that in complex economic cases almost all of the elements of the offence have to be closely examined and their understanding is often disputed in literature and case law.

D. The offence of subsidy fraud under § 264 StGB

126 § 264 StGB is – as explained above – a specific form of the fraud offence regulated in § 263 StGB (*lex specialis*[108]). Only acts of fraud in the context of the granting or use of 'subsidies' (*Subventionen*) are covered.[109] The granting and use of subsidies apparently appeared to the – German and European – legislator to be particularly susceptible to fraud. For this reason, § 264 StGB criminalizes acts that are not yet punishable under § 263 StGB. Specifically, § 264 StGB is therefore dogmatically an independent attempt offence prior to fraud.[110]

127 The offence is not free of constitutional criticism;[111] this concerns the breadth of the definition of subsidy and, in particular, criminal liability for recklessness. However, the prevailing legal opinion does not share these concerns and assumes § 264 StGB to be constitutional.[112]

128 § 264 StGB is divided into nine subsections. § 264 sub. 1 StGB regulates the elements of the basic offence of subsidy fraud in four variants. The provision includes both requirements on the 'external side of the offence' (what must the perpetrator have done, *actus reus*) as well as on the internal or subjective side of the offence (necessary intent of the perpetrator, *mens rea*). The penalty for the basic offence of subsidy fraud ranges from a fine to five years of imprisonment. This penalty range is increased for particularly serious cases of subsidy fraud in accordance with § 264 sub. 2 StGB (from six months to ten years of imprisonment). The penalty range is increased again in accordance with § 264 sub. 3 StGB by reference to § 263 sub. 5 StGB for a qualification offence (→ mn. 77 et seqq.).

129 § 264 sub. 4 and 5 StGB regulate – albeit only for individual variants of subsidy fraud – the criminal liability for attempted subsidy fraud (§ 264 sub. 4 StGB) and the criminal liability for reckless conduct (§ 264 sub. 5 StGB), → mn. 85, → mn. 147.

130 § 264 sub. 6 StGB regulates – in the case of active repentance – a ground for annulment of the sentence. § 264 sub. 7 StGB, on the other hand, regulates an optional secondary

[107] Cf. LG München II 27.6.2023 – W5 KLs 64 Js 22724/19, juris mn. 6472, 6481 et seqq., 6509, 6514.
[108] Cf. Fischer StGB § 264 mn. 5.
[109] Fischer StGB § 264 mn. 6.
[110] Fischer StGB § 264 mn. 4.
[111] Cf. Fischer StGB § 264 mn. 3 et seq.
[112] Cf. Fischer StGB § 264 mn. 3.

penalty and an optional secondary consequence in the event that an offender is sentenced to more than one year of imprisonment for subsidy fraud.

Finally, § 264 sub. 8 StGB provides a very technical definition of what constitutes a subsidy and § 264 sub. 9 StGB defines what constitutes subsidy-relevant facts within the meaning of the provision. **131**

I. Definition of subsidy (§ 264 sub. 8 StGB)

The scope of application of subsidy fraud pursuant to § 264 StGB is limited to clearly defined 'subsidies'. **132**

1. Subsidies under federal or state law

On the one hand, this concerns subsidies under federal or state law (§ 264 sub. 8 sent. 1 no. 1 StGB). Specifically, these are benefits from public funds (from the federal government, federal states or municipalities[113]) that are granted as special support directly to businesses or companies to promote the economy (in whole or in part) without market consideration.[114] **133**

There is no market consideration if there is a difference between the price and the market value.[115] This may also be the case if a property is sold at a favourable price.[116] **134**

The subsidy must serve the purpose of promoting the economy (at least in part).[117] The term 'economy' is to be understood broadly; this includes all commercially operated facilities.[118] However, it does not include the promotion of education, culture, research and healthcare or – in general – the social sector.[119] For example, the promotion of theatres, research institutes,[120] hospitals and youth facilities is, therefore, not covered.[121] It is disputed to what extent the promotion of sport – insofar as the sporting activity is integrated into a commercial enterprise – falls within the scope of the offence.[122] **135**

The recipient must be a business or company. However, public enterprises and companies are not covered under § 264 sub. 8 sent. 2 StGB. The legal form of the business and the intention to make a profit are irrelevant; associations can, therefore, also be covered by the offence.[123] **136**

A current example of subsidies within the meaning of § 264 sub. 8 sent. 1 no. 1 StGB are the so-called 'Corona emergency aid' subsidies granted by the federal government during the COVID-19 pandemic.[124] **137**

---

[113] Fischer StGB § 264 mn. 7.
[114] Cf. Fischer StGB § 264 mn. 7 et seqq.
[115] Cf. Fischer StGB § 264 mn. 9.
[116] OLG Rostock 17.1.2012 – 1 Ws 404/11, ZWH 2012, 239.
[117] Fischer StGB § 264 mn. 10.
[118] Fischer StGB § 264 mn. 10.
[119] Fischer StGB § 264 mn. 10; TK StGB/Perron StGB § 264 mn. 15.
[120] The situation is different, however, if the institute serves the ultimate purpose of promoting the economy, cf. TK StGB/Perron StGB § 264 mn. 15.
[121] Cf. TK StGB/Perron StGB § 264 mn. 15.
[122] Cf. Fischer StGB § 264 mn. 10.
[123] Fischer StGB § 264 mn. 11.
[124] Fischer StGB § 264 mn. 8; Tolksdorf/Schellhaas NZWiSt 2021, 344 et seq.

2. Subsidies under the law of the European Union

138 On the other hand, benefits from public funds under European Union law that are provided at least in part without market consideration are covered, § 264 sub. 8 sent. 1 no. 2 StGB. This variant has a wider scope of application than the benefits provided by the federal government, federal states and municipalities under § 264 sub. 8 sent. 1 no. 1 StGB. This is because it is not necessary for the benefit to serve to promote the economy. Therefore, benefits in the social and cultural sector, for example, are covered by the offence.[125] It is irrelevant whether the grant is awarded directly by the European Union or by an intermediary national authority.[126]

139 The so-called *de minimis* European Union subsidies, for example, are of practical relevance here.[127]

II. Facts relevant to the subsidy (§ 264 sub. 9 StGB)

140 The offences in § 264 sub. 1 no. 1, 3 and 4 refer to 'subsidy-relevant facts' in respect of which – in abbreviated form – incorrect information was provided (→ mn. 145 et seqq.) or necessary information was omitted (→ mn. 151 et seqq.). What constitutes subsidy-relevant facts is defined in § 264 sub. 9 StGB.

141 § 264 sub. 9 no. 1 StGB covers facts that have been designated as relevant to a subsidy by or on the basis of a law. 'Law' means laws in the substantive sense, i.e. also legal ordinances, statutes and legal acts of the European Union, but not ministerial decrees.[128] It must be clearly recognizable that the fact referred to is relevant to the subsidy.[129] If the labelling is unambiguous, the term 'subsidy-relevant' does not have to be used for clarification.[130]

142 § 264 sub. 9 no. 2 StGB covers facts on which the approval, granting, reclaiming, continuation or retention of a subsidy or a subsidy benefit is dependent by law or under the subsidy agreement.

143 As with § 263 StGB, only facts fall under the purview of the provision, not value judgements and opinions (→ mn. 29).

III. The criminal acts (§ 264 sub. 1 StGB)

144 The offences described in § 264 sub. 1 StGB must be committed within or in the context of a subsidy procedure.[131] The subsidy procedure itself is not defined in § 264 StGB but is derived from the German Subsidies Act (SubVG, *Subventionsgesetz*). § 2 sub. 1 SubVG states that the subsidy procedure begins with the application for approval and ends – in principle – with the granting of the subsidy or with the final rejection of the application.[132]

---

[125] Fischer StGB § 264 mn. 12.
[126] Fischer StGB § 264 mn. 12; BeckOK StGB/Momsen/Laudien, 64. Ed. 1.2.2025, § 264 mn. 22.
[127] Cf. Mischke KommJur 2011, 281 (285).
[128] Fischer StGB § 264 mn. 13; BeckOK StGB/Momsen/Laudien, 64. Ed. 1.2.2025, § 264 mn. 24.
[129] Cf. Fischer StGB § 264 mn. 14; BeckOK StGB/Momsen/Laudien, 64. Ed. 1.2.2025, § 264 mn. 25.
[130] Fischer StGB § 264 mn. 14; BeckOK StGB/Momsen/Laudien, 64. Ed. 1.2.2025, § 264 mn. 25.
[131] Cf. Fischer StGB § 264 mn. 18 et seq.
[132] Cf. Fischer StGB § 264 mn. 19.

1. Subsidy fraud through incorrect or incomplete information (§ 264 sub. 1 no. 1 StGB)

The first type of illicit conduct sanctioned under § 264 sub. 1 StGB relates to the provision of incorrect or incomplete information to a subsidy provider about facts relevant to the subsidy that are advantageous to the declarant or another party. The subsidy provider is the authority responsible for approving a subsidy or another body involved in the subsidy procedure (see § 264 sub. 1 no. 1 StGB). 145

Incorrect information is information that does not correspond to reality.[133] The incorrect – or incomplete – declaration must give the subsidy provider an incomplete overall picture. The incorrectness or incompleteness of the information must be advantageous for the perpetrator or the other party, i.e. it must improve the prospect of the grant in the abstract.[134] 146

The act is punishable if committed intentionally, but according to § 264 sub. 5 StGB it is also punishable if committed recklessly. This requires particular indifference or gross carelessness.[135] The perpetrator must have been able to recognize the relevance of the subsidy and the action required of him without further ado according to his individual abilities.[136] As a rule, anyone who does not take care of the award requirements at all or only very superficially, does not give any thought to the question of completeness or accepts the preliminary work of an unreliable or untested employee without checking it, will be considered as acting recklessly.[137] 147

2. Subsidy fraud by using the benefit contrary to restrictions on use (§ 264 sub. 1 no. 2 StGB)

The second type of illicit conduct sanctioned under § 264 sub. 1 StGB relates to the unlawful use of benefits received. Restrictions on use can, for example, arise directly from the regulations on which the granting of the subsidy is based.[138] However, they can also result from a contract or administrative act.[139] 148

The actual improper use is sanctioned, not the breach of an obligation to provide information about the intended improper use at the time of application.[140] 149

The act is punishable if committed intentionally, but according to § 264 sub. 5 StGB, it is also punishable if committed recklessly. Furthermore, this type of act is also punishable if attempted. 150

3. Subsidy fraud through non-disclosure of subsidy-relevant circumstances (§ 264 sub. 1 no. 3 StGB)

The third type of illicit conduct sanctioned under § 264 sub. 1 StGB is the non-disclosure of subsidy-relevant circumstances. The offence covers the failure to comply with disclosure obligations. These duties of disclosure can arise in particular from statutory law, e.g. § 3 sub. 2 SubVG. 151

133 BGH 9.11.2009 – 5 StR 136/09, NStZ 2010, 327; Fischer StGB § 264 mn. 23.
134 Fischer StGB § 264 mn. 24.
135 BGH 20.5.2010 – 5 StR 138/10, NStZ-RR 2010, 311; Fischer StGB § 264 mn. 37.
136 BGH 13.12.2012 – 5 StR 542/12, ZWH 2013, 228; Fischer StGB § 264 mn. 37.
137 OLG Hamburg 3.1.1984 – 2 Ws 459/83, NStZ 1984, 219; Fischer StGB § 264 mn. 37.
138 Fischer StGB § 264 mn. 25.
139 Fischer StGB § 264 mn. 25.
140 Fischer StGB § 264 mn. 26.

152 The act is punishable if committed intentionally, but also if committed recklessly in accordance with § 264 sub. 5 StGB.

4. Subsidy fraud through the use of a certificate obtained by providing incorrect or incomplete information (§ 264 sub. 1 no. 4 StGB)

153 Finally, the fourth type of illicit conduct sanctioned under § 264 sub. 1 StGB is the use of false certificates. Here there is a partial overlap with the first type of action, § 264 sub. 1 no. 1 StGB, as well as with the third type of action, § 264 sub. 1 no. 3 StGB, if the false certificate has already been obtained through criminal acts.[141]

IV. Active repentance (§ 264 sub. 6 StGB)

154 By way of so-called 'active repentance' (*tätige Reue*), § 264 sub. 6 StGB provides a ground for setting aside the penalty for anyone who voluntarily prevents the subsidy from being granted as a result of the offence (§ 264 sub. 6 sent. 1 StGB) or – if the subsidy is not granted without any action on their part – makes a voluntary and serious effort to prevent the subsidy from being granted.

155 The grounds for annulment apply to all criminal acts and to both intentional and reckless acts. As the particularly serious cases in subsection 2 are merely sentencing rules, the ground for setting aside the sentence also applies in these cases.[142] It is disputed whether the reason for setting aside the sentence – although this is not explicitly mentioned in § 264 sub. 6 StGB – also applies to the offence of § 264 sub. 3 StGB in conjunction with § 263 sub. 5 StGB.[143]

V. Secondary penalty and secondary consequence (§ 264 sub. 7 StGB)

156 In the case of subsidy fraud, the ability to hold public office and the ability to obtain rights from public elections can be revoked as a so-called secondary penalty if the perpetrator or participant is sentenced to more than one year of imprisonment (§ 264 sub. 7 sent. 1 StGB). As a so-called secondary consequence, objects to which the offence relates (so-called objects of the offence) can be confiscated (§ 264 sub. 7 sent. 2 StGB).

---

[141] Cf. Fischer StGB § 264 mn. 29 et seqq.

[142] Fischer StGB § 264 mn. 40.

[143] In favour Fischer StGB § 264 mn. 40, on the other hand NK-StGB/Hellmann § 264 mn. 160.

CHAPTER 12
BREACH OF TRUST

Bibliography: Dierlamm, Untreue – ein Auffangtatbestand?, NStZ 1997, 534; Fischer, Der Gefährdungsschaden bei § 266 StGB in der Rechtsprechung des BGH, StraFo 2008, 269; Fischer, Die Niederlassung von EU-Kapitalgesellschaften in Deutschland nach dem Brexit – ein Überblick, NZG 2021, 483; Jahn, Untreue bei Sonderzahlung für die Vorstandsmitglieder einer Aktiengesellschaft (Fall Mannesmann), JuS 2006, 379; Jahn/Ziemann, „Untreuestrafrecht 2.0", ZIS 2016, 552; Ransiek, Risiko, Pflichtwidrigkeit und Vermögensnachteil bei der Untreue, ZStW 2004, 634; Schünemann, Die „gravierende Pflichtverletzung" bei der Untreue: dogmatischer Zauberhut oder taube Nuss?, NStZ 2005, 473.

Table of contents

A. Introduction 270
B. Elements of the crime 270
I. Abuse alternative and breach of fidelity alternative 271
1. Abuse alternative 271
2. Breach of fidelity alternative 272
3. Conclusion regarding the two alternatives 273
II. Assets of another person 273
III. Safeguarding duty 274
1. Stock corporations 275
a) Board of directors 275
b) Supervisory board 275
c) Shareholders 276
2. Limited liability companies 276
a) Director 276
b) Supervisory board 276
c) Advisory board 277
d) Shareholders 277
3. Partnerships 277
4. Public institutions 277
5. Employees 277
6. Compliance officers 277
7. Auditors and tax consultants 278
8. Lawyers 278
IV. Breach of safeguarding duty 278
1. Discretionary decisions 278
a) Business Judgment Rule 278
b) Grave breach of duty 279
2. Consent 279
3. Foreign entities 281
a) Other EU Member States 281
b) Non-EU Member States 282
V. Pecuniary damage 282
VI. Subjective elements of the crime 284
C. Commission of and complicity in a breach of trust 284
D. Legal consequences 285
E. Most relevant cases 285
I. Risky transactions 286

II. Slush funds 287
III. Bribes/kick-back 288
IV. Compliance 288
V. Criminal offences 289
VI. Assumption of fines and defence costs 289
VII. Remuneration and bonus payments 290
VIII. Sponsorship 290
IX. De facto managing director 290
X. Group of companies (cash pooling) 291
F. Conclusion 291

A. Introduction

1 §266 StGB (*Untreue*) is a central norm of white-collar criminal law. While §263 StGB (*Betrug*, fraud) protects a victim's assets against attacks 'from the outside',[1] §266 StGB aims to protect the assets against attacks 'from within': breach of trust, therefore, presupposes a certain relationship of trust between the victim and the perpetrator. The perpetrator betrays this trust placed in them by intentionally damaging the victim's assets.

2 Breach of trust has become significant in modern business because ownership and management are often separated. Therefore, it is mainly relevant in a corporate context. This explains the relatively low number of convictions – compared to fraud cases – which are, nevertheless, often accompanied by an immense volume of damage.[2] The close relationship between victim and perpetrator means that reported cases are comparatively often solved successfully. On the other hand, substantial underreporting is likely since corporate victims might shy away from reporting internal violations with minor damages in order not to create bad publicity.

3 Despite the relatively low number of convictions, §266 StGB is frequently included in charges brought by public prosecutor offices in preliminary investigations. This may be attributed to the fact that §266 StGB can cover a wide range of factual scenarios and, therefore, can be interpreted as a catch-all clause (*Auffangtatbestand*) in the context of corporate criminal law. As the renowned Professor Ransiek pointedly put it: '§266 passt immer.'[3] – '§266 StGB always fits.' This finding is remarkable as the provision of §266 StGB does not read like a typical catch-all provision but rather like a highly technical and specialised one, as the following section demonstrates by portraying the specific elements of the crime in detail.

B. Elements of the crime

4 §266 StGB criminalises anyone who abuses the power conferred to them by law, by commission of an authority or legal transaction to dispose of the assets of another person or to make binding agreements for another person,[4] or whoever breaches their duty to

---

[1] → Ch. 11.

[2] Fischer StGB §266 mn. 3.

[3] Ransiek ZStW 2004, 634.

[4] German law distinguishes between a binding agreement and a disposal of assets. This distinction is also reflected in the wording of §266 StGB. However, in this Chapter, this will not be given further consideration since both types of transaction can equally lead to criminal liability under §266 StGB.

safeguard the pecuniary interests of another person which are incumbent upon them by law, by commission of an authority, legal transaction or fiduciary relationship, and thereby adversely affects the person whose pecuniary interests they were responsible for.

I. Abuse alternative and breach of fidelity alternative

The foregoing paragraph, which closely reflects the wording of the actual provision, reveals that § 266 StGB comprises two alternatives (*Tatbestandsalternativen*): the so-called **abuse alternative** (→ mn. 7 et seqq.) and the so-called **breach of fidelity alternative** (→ mn. 10 et seqq.). While there have been extensive legal disputes about the **relation** between these two alternatives, it is most helpful to know that, over several decades, settled case law has emerged[5] that is supported by the prevailing academia.[6] According to this view, the abuse alternative is simply a special subcategory of the breach of fidelity alternative or, in other words, the breach of fidelity alternative serves as a catch-all clause. Initial point of the dispute is the question whether only the breach of fidelity alternative presupposes a **safeguarding duty**, or whether this requirement is likewise to be read into the abuse alternative. As the German Federal Court of Justice does the latter, the criminal liability under the abuse alternative does, in practice, not reach further than the breach of fidelity alternative. Consequently, courts are frequently leaving the question open whether the specific characteristics of the abuse alternative are met. However, with regard to the judicial duty to concretise the offence, it is preferable to draw a line between the two alternatives. 5

To differentiate the alternatives from one another, the following distinctions apply: 6

1. Abuse alternative

The abuse alternative (*Missbrauchsalternative*) requires the perpetrator to act in the form of a **valid legal transaction** towards a third party. For this, the perpetrator must generally be authorised to dispose of the assets of another person (the trustor). This alternative is fulfilled if the disposition in the external relationship (between the perpetrator and the third party) exceeds the limits of the perpetrator's legal capacity in the internal relationship (between the perpetrator and their trustor).[7] 7

The **power** to dispose of the assets of the trustor or to make binding agreements for the trustor can be conferred on the trustee/perpetrator by law, by commission of an authority or legal transaction. The power may also result from the interaction of several overlapping legal grounds, so that the types of conferrals will often be mixed. Typical forms of conferral **by law** would be marriage (§§ 1353, 1357 BGB) and parental care (§§ 1626, 1631 BGB). The conferral by **commission of an authority** can be given by appointment to public office (e.g. tax officer, mayor) or by appointment for a particular case (e.g. insolvency administrator). Conferrals by **legal transaction** are achieved by granting power of agency under § 164 BGB or by giving consent under § 185 BGB. In the first case, the trustee is acting as a legitimised representative in the name of the trustor. In the second case, they 8

[5] BGH 26.7.1972 – 2 StR 62/72, BGHSt 24, 386 = NJW 1972, 1904; BGH 13.6.1985 – 4 StR 213/85, BGHSt 33, 244 = NJW 1985, 2280; BGH 6.12.2001 – 1 StR 215/01, BGHSt 47, 187 = NJW 2002, 1585 – SSV Reutlingen; BGH 21.12.2005 – 3 StR 470/04, BGHSt 50, 331 = NJW 2006, 522 – Mannesmann.

[6] MüKoStGB/Dierlamm/Becker, 4th edn 2022, StGB § 266 mn. 25 et seqq. with further references.

[7] This strict differentiation between the internal and the external relationship is characteristic of the German law of representation. Typically, the extent of the legal ability in the external relationship is greater than the powers granted in the internal relationship.

act in their own name but with the (prior or subsequent) consent of the trustor (e.g. as a commission agent, § 383 HGB). Regularly, power of agency is granted in the context of a mandate (§ 662 BGB), a service contract (§ 611 BGB) or a contract over the non-gratuitous management of the affairs of another person (§ 675 BGB).

9 In any case, the power needs to be **validly conferred**. If the act of appointment or the granting of power of agency were invalid, criminal liability under the abuse alternative is out of the question. The merely factual possibility of disposing of another person's property on the basis of rules of good faith (e.g. §§ 932 et seqq., 407 BGB; §§ 366, 56 HGB) or of obligating another person by *prima facie* entitlement is not sufficient.[8] This is different, however, if the perpetrator abuses a power of agency that expired in the internal relationship but was, originally, validly granted and continues to have an external effect under §§ 170 et seqq. BGB or according to §§ 168, 674 BGB.[9] Although this could also be a case of *prima facie* entitlement, this constellation is considered to fall under the abuse alternative as it is just a consequence of the legal granting of power of agency itself, not of any other factual circumstances.

2. Breach of fidelity alternative

10 On the other hand, the breach of fidelity alternative (*Treubruchsalternative*) does not require the perpetrator to act in the form of a valid legal transaction. In this alternative, the criminal act consists of **any act relevant to the pecuniary interests** that breaches a duty in the internal relationship. Therefore, it also comprises **purely factual or invalid legal actions** such as theft (*Diebstahl*, § 242 StGB)[10] or misappropriation (*Unterschlagung*, § 246 StGB), the unauthorised use of property of another person, the thwarting of an expectable deal, the granting of certain bonus payments that cannot bring any future-related benefit to the company,[11] or the creation of slush funds.[12]

11 Compared to the abuse alternative, lower requirements are also placed on the establishment of the internal relationship, as not only the three possibilities mentioned for the abuse alternative apply (by reason of law, by commission of an authority, by legal transaction) but also a mere **fiduciary relationship**. This term covers cases in which the parties wish to establish or maintain a legal relationship but in doing so, civil law complications arise. The legislator has thus made it possible to disregard 'subtleties' of civil law in the question of criminal liability. This becomes relevant in constellations of **invalid legal relationships** as well as **expired legal relationships**. Especially the case of the so-called **de facto managing director** is of great practical relevance. This term describes a person who actually exercises the management with the consent of the shareholders and has a de facto preponderance over the formally appointed managing director. While the de facto managing director can be liable under the breach of fidelity alternative, the formally appointed (but de facto powerless) managing director will still be contractually obliged to safeguard the pecuniary interests of the company.[13]

12 Disagreement exists about constellations in which the **invalidity of the legal relationship is due to a violation of a statutory prohibition or public policy** (§§ 134, 138 BGB). On the one hand, it is agreed that anyone who omits to carry out an unlawful order does

[8] Cf. BGH 16.6.1953 – 1 StR 67/53, BGHSt 5, 61 = NJW 1954, 202.

[9] OLG Stuttgart 14.3.1985 – 3 Ss (14) 823/84, NStZ 1985, 365 (366); OLG Koblenz 14.7.2011 – 2 Ss 80/11, NStZ 2012, 330.

[10] BGH 12.7.1962 – 1 StR 282/62, BGHSt 17, 360 = NJW 1962, 1685.

[11] BGH 21.12.2005 – 3 StR 470/04, BGHSt 50, 331 = NJW 2006, 522 – Mannesmann; also → mn. 92 et seq.

[12] → mn. 78.

[13] → mn. 96 et seq.

not commit a breach of trust.[14] On the other hand, cases remain in which the perpetrator uses the assets in breach of an illegal agreement. While the German Federal Court of Justice formerly refused to see a fiduciary relationship in these cases,[15] it now assumes the possibility of a breach of fidelity.[16] This follows its premise that there should be no legal vacuums. However, it must be further examined whether the assets that have been disposed of are worthy of legal protection.[17]

3. Conclusion regarding the two alternatives

In conclusion, it should be emphasised that both the so-called abuse alternative and 13
the so-called breach of fidelity alternative rest on the existence of a safeguarding duty.[18] Under the broader scope of the breach of fidelity alternative, any act that affects the assets of another person[19] by violating this duty[20] and, thereby, causes a pecuniary damage[21] falls within the scope of § 266 StGB – and constitutes criminal liability if all of these elements are encompassed by intent.[22]

II. Assets of another person

§ 266 StGB protects the **assets of another person** (*fremdes Vermögen*). According 14
to established case law, the term 'assets' includes the sum of the monetary goods that a person can actually dispose of.[23] This means that, in principle, any asset with a market value can be subject to a breach of trust, regardless of its legal classification and whether it has been legally obtained. Thus, the provision of § 266 StGB also protects **illegally acquired assets**. Furthermore, the provision protects pecuniary prospects that relate to a realisable inflow of assets and, therefore, have a measurable economic value according to the perception of the market at the time of an offence.

Whether assets belong to **another person** must be determined under civil law – eco- 15
nomic considerations do not matter. For example, the assets of an incorporated company (such as a limited liability company) are not the assets of its shareholders or representatives. Their assets are strictly separated (cf. § 1 sub. 1 AktG, § 6 GmbHG). This is even the case where there is only one shareholder of an entity. However, it is different for partnerships (e.g. a partnership according to § 705 BGB or § 1 PartGG), since it is assumed that the partnership's assets are the joint assets of the partners themselves. Thus, in the common case of a partly limited partnership that is using a limited liability company as the general partner (GmbH & Co. KG), a breach of trust by the managing director of the general partner to the detriment of the partly limited partnership is not possible, since the partly limited partnership does not represent third-party assets from the perspective of the general partner. However, a breach of trust to the detriment of the co-partners can be considered.

---

[14] BGH 19.1.1965 – 1 StR 497/64, BGHSt 20, 143 = NJW 1965, 770.
[15] BGH 27.3.1953 – 2 StR 146/52, NJW 1954, 889.
[16] BGH 17.11.1955 – 3 StR 234/55, BGHSt 8, 254 = NJW 1956, 151; BGH 19.1.1965 – 1 StR 497/64, BGHSt 20, 143 = NJW 1965, 770; BGH 26.10.1998 – 5 StR 746-97, NStZ-RR 99, 184.
[17] → mn. 57.
[18] → mn. 16 et seqq.
[19] → mn. 14 et seq.
[20] → mn. 37 et seqq.
[21] → mn. 55 et seqq.
[22] → mn. 63 et seqq.
[23] BGH 18.7.1961 – 1 StR 606/60, BGHSt 16, 220 = NJW 1961, 1876.

III. Safeguarding duty

16 A breach of trust requires, in both above-mentioned alternatives,[24] that the perpetrator is obliged to safeguard the pecuniary interests of another person. Since this element is very broad, it must be interpretated restrictively so that only circumstances worthy of criminal liability are covered. A **safeguarding duty** can, therefore, not be assumed in cases of mere association with another person's pecuniary interests or if the pecuniary interests are only taken into consideration through general collateral duties (*Nebenpflichten*). For example, the compliance guidelines of a company do not establish safeguarding duties relevant under criminal law but only substantiate the content of already existing safeguarding duties.[25] Also, the duty to fulfil a contract is as such not protected by § 266 StGB.[26] It is rather required that the perpetrator has a particularly **elevated duty**. Whether this is the case is decided by taking a view of the **overall picture**. In this respect, it is primarily important whether the asset management constitutes the main object of the (legal) relationship, whether the matter is of a certain economic importance and whether the obligated party has a certain freedom and autonomy to act; in other words: the possibility to make a responsible decision within a certain scope of discretion.[27] It lies in the nature of such an overall consideration that, in the individual case, a safeguarding duty can be assumed, although one of the characteristics mentioned (e.g. scope of discretion) is very reduced or even missing, provided that another characteristic (e.g. economic importance) is of elevated significance.

17 The contractual relationship between potential perpetrator and victim must also be taken into account: a safeguarding duty can usually be assumed with a **mandate** (§ 662 BGB) or a transaction on a **commission** basis (§ 383 HGB).[28] In the case of an **employment contract** (*Arbeitsvertrag*, § 611a BGB), the duty to look after the employer's pecuniary interests must be the essential object of the contractual relationship. It does not simply follow from the fact that an employee has to perform acts which in the course of their employment affect the employer's assets.[29] It must also be considered that a safeguarding duty cannot be assumed if the employee's activity is predefined in all conceivable details and leaves no room for autonomous decisions. Simple contracts for the **exchange of goods** regularly give priority to one's own interests over the interests of the other. Therefore, the general duty to fulfil such contracts cannot be equated with a safeguarding duty. This particularly includes **purchase agreements** (*Kaufvertrag*, § 433 BGB). Not even an agreement on a retention of title (*Eigentumsvorbehalt*, § 449 BGB) establishes a safeguarding duty of the buyer, even if the parties have agreed on a specific storage of the purchased object.[30] A safeguarding duty can come into consideration if the seller still has to purchase the goods and the parties agree to use the payment only for that purchase.[31] The same applies for **contracts to produce a work** (*Werkvertrag*, § 631 BGB).[32] Likewise, a **loan contract** (*Darlehensvertrag*, § 488 BGB) will only come with a safeguarding duty if a

---

[24] → mn. 5 et seq.

[25] → mn. 86 et seq.

[26] BGH 8.5.1951 – 1 StR 171/51, BGHSt 1, 186 (188) = BeckRS 2010, 16716; BGH 5.7.1968 – 5 StR 262/68, BGHSt 22, 190 = NJW 1968, 1938; BGH 3.5.2012 – 2 StR 446/11, NStZ 2013, 40.

[27] BGH 4.11.1952 – 1 StR 441/52, BGHSt 3, 289 (294) = BeckRS 1952, 31195087; BGH 3.3.1953 – 1 StR 5/53, BGHSt 4, 170 (172) = NJW 1953, 1272; BGH 3.5.2012 – 2 StR 446/11, NStZ 2013, 40.

[28] BGH 8.5.1951 – 1 StR 171/51, BGHSt 1, 186 (188) = BeckRS 2010, 16716.

[29] BGH 3.3.1953 – 1 StR 5/53, BGHSt 4, 170 (172) = NJW 1953, 1272.

[30] Cf. BGH 5.7.1968 – 5 StR 262/68, BGHSt 22, 190 = NJW 1968, 1938.

[31] BGH 8.5.1951 – 1 StR 171/51, BGHSt 1, 186 (190) = BeckRS 2010, 16716.

[32] BGH 3.5.1978 – 3 StR 30/78, NJW 1978, 2105 (2106).

specific appropriation of the loan has been agreed. A **leasing agreement** will not establish a safeguarding duty.[33]

The safeguarding duty must exist at the time of the criminal act. The duty will usually expire with the termination of the underlying legal relationship. For example, an omission by a managing director of an insolvent company may be irrelevant under § 266 StGB if the powers of administration and disposal had already been transferred to the insolvency administrator.[34] **18**

The following groups of persons have safeguarding duties as indicated: **19**

1. Stock corporations

a) Board of directors

The members of the board of directors have a safeguarding duty towards the stock corporation. Under corporate law, the board of directors is subject to the duties described in §§ 76 et seqq. AktG. In accordance with these duties, the board of directors must manage the company in its own responsibility pursuant to § 76 sub. 1 AktG. In doing so, the board of directors has the comprehensive duty to safeguard the assets of the company entrusted to it and to act in the best interests of the company in all its decisions, in particular to ensure the company's advantage and to prevent it from incurring losses. However, the board of directors is granted a wide scope of choice in all entrepreneurial decisions, since entrepreneurial activity would be inconceivable without such discretion.[35] The safeguarding duty can also include the establishment of a monitoring system and a compliance organisation pursuant to § 91 sub. 2, 3 AktG.[36] **20**

A safeguarding duty does not apply to decisions concerning the remuneration of the members of the board of directors. Under the AktG, these decisions are excluded from the board's powers and assigned exclusively to the supervisory board (§§ 87, 112 AktG). This arrangement recognises that, when it comes to their own remuneration, the financial interests of board members typically diverge from those of the company and it ensures that another body represents the company to avoid a conflict of interests. However, if this area of decision-making is legally excluded from the powers of the members of the board of directors, they cannot be obliged to safeguard the financial interests of the company in this regard. Their practical ability to influence decisions of the supervisory board does not change this legal situation.[37] **21**

b) Supervisory board

The supervisory board has a safeguarding duty towards the stock corporation, as it is obliged to supervise management decisions of the board of directors (§ 111 AktG).[38] This includes the duty to intervene against resolutions of the board of directors that are harmful to the corporation as well as the duty to assert claims for damages of the corporation against the board of directors.[39] **22**

---

[33] OLG Köln 6.10.1987 – Ss 292/87, NJW 1988, 3219.

[34] BGH 3.2.1993 – 3 StR 606/92, NJW 1993, 1278; → Ch. 15 for questions relating to insolvency law.

[35] BGH 21.4.1997 – II ZR 175/95, BGHZ 135, 244 = NJW 1997, 1926 – ARAG/Garmenbeck; BGH 12.10.2016 – 5 StR 134/15, NJW 2017, 578 mn. 26 – HSH Nordbank.

[36] → Ch. 6 for details on compliance management systems.

[37] BGH 21.12.2005 – 3 StR 470/04, BGHSt 50, 331 = NJW 2006, 522 mn. 80 – Mannesmann.

[38] BGH 6.12.2001 – 1 StR 215/01, BGHSt 47, 187 (201) = NJW 2002, 1585 (1588) – SSV Reutlingen; for further details regarding the so-called Business Judgment Rule → mn. 40 et seqq.

[39] BGH 21.4.1997 – II ZR 175/95, BGHZ 135, 244 = NJW 1997, 1926 – ARAG/Garmenbeck; BGH 6.12.2001 – 1 StR 215/01, BGHSt 47, 187 (201) = NJW 2002, 1585 – SSV Reutlingen.

23 Even though the supervisory board has only limited powers to intervene (e.g. dismissal of members of the board of directors, refusal to approve the annual financial statements, calling of the general meeting), it must make use of them. In contrast to this, there is no duty to supervise shareholders' resolutions.

24 In addition, the supervisory board is obliged to safeguard the assets of the stock corporation when determining the executive remuneration. An arbitrarily high remuneration is not permitted (§§ 116, 93 AktG). Furthermore, the criteria of § 87 AktG can be applied, as it specifies the company's interest. As in the case of the board of directors, there is no safeguarding duty for members of the supervisory board regarding the **negotiation** of remuneration for their own activities because of the conflict of interests entailed. However, a safeguarding duty can be assumed if it is not a matter of the negotiation but of the **settlement** and **payment** of a remuneration in deliberate violation of a statute within the meaning of § 113 AktG.[40]

25 The scope of the supervisory duties is regulated by § 116 AktG, which refers to the corresponding application of the standards of care for board members according to § 93 AktG.

c) Shareholders

26 The shareholders do not have a safeguarding duty towards their stock corporation or towards other shareholders, as they do not have sufficient authority to issue instructions to the board of directors (cf. § 76 sub. 1 AktG).

2. Limited liability companies

a) Director

27 The director of a limited liability company has a safeguarding duty only towards the company pursuant to § 43 GmbHG. However, there is no safeguarding duty towards the shareholders[41] (on the contrary, the duty to safeguard the interests of the company may compel the managing director to take measures directed against the shareholders). To determine the scope of the duties of care, the articles of association and the management agreement, the object, structure, sector, size and purpose of the company must be taken into account. In the event of a conflict of interests, the interests of the company must be given priority. This also applies to the deputy managing director (cf. § 44 GmbHG) and to the de facto managing director.[42]

b) Supervisory board

28 The safeguarding duties of the supervisory board of a limited liability company are comparable to those of the supervisory board of a stock corporation (§ 52 GmbHG in connection with § 111 AktG),[43] irrespective of whether it is a statutory or a facultative supervisory board.

---

[40] OLG Braunschweig 14.6.2012 – Ws 44/12, Ws 45/12, NJW 2012, 3798 (3799 et seq.): if the chairperson of the supervisory board becomes aware of imminent payments to members of the supervisory board in violation of the articles of association, they must convene the supervisory board pursuant to § 110 sub. 1 AktG in order to obtain a resolution urging the executive board to change the unlawful course of action.

[41] BGH 25.4.2006 – 1 StR 519/05, NStZ 2006, 401 (402).

[42] → mn. 96 et seq.

[43] → mn. 22 et seqq.

c) Advisory board

An advisory board is subject to the same obligations as the supervisory board if it is entrusted with advising and supervising the management, i.e. if it performs the tasks of a supervisory board. In case the advisory board has only advisory and representative functions, it is not obliged to a safeguarding duty. 29

d) Shareholders

The prevailing legal opinion does not attribute a safeguarding duty to the shareholders of a limited liability company (as in the case of the shareholders of a stock corporation).[44] However, an emerging legal opinion in academia opposes this and assumes a duty to protect the company against breaches of the capital maintenance principles (§ 30 et seqq. GmbHG) and interventions that could destroy its existence.[45] 30

3. Partnerships

The **managing partner** of a partnership has a safeguarding duty towards the co-partners.[46] 31

4. Public institutions

Officials in management positions who independently have significant budgetary resources at their disposal have a safeguarding duty (e.g. mayor; district administrator; head teacher; etc.). 32

5. Employees

Employees in management positions who independently have significant budgetary resources at their disposal have a safeguarding duty (e.g. branch manager or subsidiary manager;[47] head of department, e.g. legal department and internal audit,[48] human resources[49]). 33

6. Compliance officers

Compliance officers will usually have a safeguarding duty towards the company insofar as they are not only responsible for the optimisation of internal processes and the detection and prevention of breaches of duty directed against the company but also for the prevention of legal violations, in particular criminal offences committed by company employees in connection with the company's activities.[50] 34

---

44 TK-StGB/Perron StGB § 266 mn. 26 with further references.
45 ARR WirtschaftsStrafR-HdB/Seier/Lindemann Pt. 7 Ch. 2 mn. 328 et seqq. with further references.
46 For the relation to the partnership itself→ mn. 15, 50.
47 BGH 21.10.2003 – 1 StR 544/02, BeckRS 2003, 9868 mn. 25.
48 BGH 17.7.2009 – 5 StR 394/08, BGHSt 54, 44 = NJW 2009, 3173.
49 BGH 17.9.2009 – 5 StR 521/08, BGHSt 54, 148 = NJW 2010, 92 (96) – Gebauer/Volkert.
50 BGH 17.7.2009 – 5 StR 394/08, BGHSt 54, 44 = NJW 2009, 3173 (3175).

7. Auditors and tax consultants

35 Auditors and tax consultants have a safeguarding duty towards their clients.[51]

8. Lawyers

36 The same applies for lawyers, pursuant to the legal services agreement (i.e. a contract over the non-gratuitous management of the affairs of another person, § 675 BGB). A safeguarding duty exists in particular with regard to the proper assertion of claims and with regard to funds received from a third-party which are to be stored or forwarded in a trust account (cf. § 4 BORA, § 43a sub. 7 BRAO). However, lawyers do not have a safeguarding duty for their clients' assets when charging them fees. The violation of a contractual duty not to demand and collect higher fees than the fees actually owed is not subject to liability under § 266 StGB.[52]

IV. Breach of safeguarding duty

37 The perpetrator must act in breach of their safeguarding duty. A breach of other duties is not relevant in the context of the criminal offence of breach of trust. Since the scope and limits of the safeguarding duties are determined by the underlying legal relationship, the details depend on legal provisions, guidelines and specific instructions by the trustor. This means that civil and/or administrative law assessments have to be carefully considered in the evaluation of the criminal liability under § 266 StGB.

38 In this respect, it is important to keep in mind that actions that are permissible under civil law will not be considered to be a breach of duty under § 266 StGB. The other way around, however, not just any conduct that breaches civil law obligations will result in criminal liability for breach of trust.

1. Discretionary decisions

39 While it is rather easy to determine whether a duty has been violated in the case of non-discretionary decisions, decisions that leave a scope for discretion can pose difficulties. The loss of assets resulting from such a decision does not necessarily indicate that a duty has been breached. However, due to the well-known psychological phenomenon of **hindsight bias** (*Rückschaufehler*), there is a risk that investigating authorities could prematurely reach such a conclusion. Therefore, to assess a breach of duty under § 266 StGB, certain restrictive standards must be observed and the assessment must take a clear ***ex ante* perspective**.

a) Business Judgment Rule

40 § 93 sub. 1 sent. 2 AktG defines the scope of duties for discretionary decisions taken by the board of directors of a stock corporation. It stipulates that there is no breach of duty if a board member, when taking an entrepreneurial decision, could reasonably assume that they were acting in the **best interests** of the company on the basis of **appropriate information**. Accordingly, entrepreneurial decisions allow for **considerable discretion**. The legislator has recognised that entrepreneurial decisions are often based on experience,

[51] BGH 3.8.2005 – 2 StR 202/05, NStZ 2006, 38 (39).
[52] OLG Karlsruhe 20.12.1990 – 2 Ws 265/89, NStZ 1991, 239 (240).

imagination, and instinct as well as a sense for future developments, market dynamics and possible reactions of customers and competitors. This can never be completely replaced by objective information. § 93 AktG is, therefore, not intended to diminish the courage to take entrepreneurial risks.[53] Thus, a violation of the duty of care under § 93 sub. 1 sent. 1 AktG can only be affirmed if there is a clearly unjustifiable act. In other words, as the German Federal Court of Justice describes it, a management error must be apparent to a neutral observer.[54]

The **concept** of the 'Business Judgment Rule' is not limited to § 93 AktG and stock corporations but can be found **in all forms of entrepreneurial activity** even without express statutory regulation.[55] Therefore, in the absence of a statutory provision, § 93 AktG and the related case law can serve as a point of reference. **41**

Furthermore, the wide scope of discretion also covers decisions regarding **sponsorships** and **donations**.[56] Such decisions can be business-driven as long as they aim to increase the social standing of a company and thereby – directly or indirectly – promote its economic development. **42**

b) Grave breach of duty

As criminal law is the most invasive form of state intervention, it should – according to the so-called *ultima ratio* principle – only serve as the last resort. This raises the question whether any breach of a civil law obligation is sufficient to establish criminal liability for a breach of trust, or whether a **higher standard** – a 'grave breach of duty' – is required. This question is widely discussed, including between the different senates of the German Federal Court of Justice.[57] The German Constitutional Court also did not provide clarity.[58] All decisions in this context have in common that they concern **discretionary decisions** by a potential perpetrator. The necessarily broad scope of action that is being granted to a decision-maker should be taken into account. The offence of breach of trust is, therefore, not to be limited by the characteristic of a grave breach of duty if the decision to be taken does not allow for any scope of action.[59] Justifiably, many recognise a concurrence with the 'Business Judgment Rule' in these situations. The additional criterion of a 'grave breach of duty' only reflects the broad scope of entrepreneurial decisions. As far as cases are conceivable in which there is no concurrence with the 'Business Judgment Rule', the criterion of a grave breach of duty can be applied. **43**

2. Consent

An obliged person is not in breach of their safeguarding duty if the action is taken with the consent of the owner of the assets. Consent may be declared explicitly or impliedly. In any case, it must be declared **validly**. Thus, a declaration of consent that is invalid cannot exclude criminal liability under § 266 StGB. If the declaration of consent violates legal **44**

---

[53] BT-Drs. 15/5092, 11 et seq.

[54] BGH 12.10.2016 – 5 StR 134/15, NJW 2017, 578 (579 et seq.) – HSH Nordbank.

[55] BT-Drs. 15/5092, 12.

[56] Although the first senate of the German Federal Court of Justice addressed this as a question of a 'grave breach of duty': BGH 6.12.2001 – 1 StR 215/01, BGHSt 47, 187 = NJW 2002, 1585 – SSV Reutlingen.

[57] Assuming this: BGH 6.4.2000 – 1 StR 280/99, BGHSt 46, 30 = NJW 2000, 2364; BGH 6.12.2001 – 1 StR 215/01, BGHSt 47, 187 = NJW 2002, 1585 – SSV Reutlingen; rejecting this assumption: BGH 21.12.2005 – 3 StR 470/04, BGHSt 50, 331 = NJW 2006, 522 – Mannesmann; BGH 26.11.2015 – 3 StR 17/15, BGHSt 61, 48 = NJW 2016, 2585 – Nürburgring; BGH 12.10.2016 – 5 StR 134/15, NJW 2017, 578 – HSH Nordbank.

[58] BVerfG 23.6.2010 – 2 BvR 2559/08, BVerfGE 126, 170 = NJW 2010, 3209.

[59] BGH 21.12.2005 – 3 StR 470/04, BGHSt 50, 331 (346) = NJW 2006, 522 (527) – Mannesmann; OLG Braunschweig 14.6.2012 – Ws 44/12, Ws 45/12, NJW 2012, 3798 (3800).

requirements, it is invalid as well. On the other hand, where consent is given, it is not void merely because the trustor made a disadvantageous decision due to their economic inexperience. However, this does not apply if the perpetrator has deliberately exploited this inexperience.

45 The consent must be given **prior to an offence**. Thus, for example, the consent of a future sole shareholder is irrelevant to the question of criminal liability but may – depending on the circumstances – influence the sentencing as a significant mitigating factor.[60] If no consent was given prior to an act in breach of the safeguarding duty, criminal liability may, however, be excluded under the doctrine of **presumed consent**. This requires that it was not possible to obtain the trustor's consent in due time. The act needs to be in the interest of the trustor (e.g. expenses for the protection of the trustor's good reputation) or indifferent to the trustor's interests (e.g. the short-term withdrawal of small sums of money).

46 Special problems arise if the trustor is a **legal person**. A legal person can declare its consent through a valid resolution of its decision-making body, thereby excluding criminal liability under § 266 StGB. Consent can also be declared by the legal person's **organs and representatives** as long as they remain within the scope of their competences. Any consent declared outside of these competences is invalid and cannot exclude criminal liability. This is particularly relevant when the representative commits a breach of trust by consenting to another person's breach of duty. It is evident that a board of directors cannot exclude liability by 'consenting' to its own actions in breach of duty. This results from the distribution of competences in corporations.

47 As mentioned, criminal liability can be excluded by the valid consent of the **decision-making body** of a legal person that is in charge of the regulation of the internal affairs. The specific requirements and limitations for such consent vary depending on the type of legal entity.

48 The supreme decision-making body of **limited liability companies** is the shareholders' meeting (§ 48 GmbHG). This entails the shareholders' authority to issue instructions to the managing directors pursuant to § 37 GmbHG and to amend the articles of association pursuant to § 53 GmbHG. One might assume that the consent of the majority shareholder alone would exclude the offence, regardless of whether all shareholders have participated in the decision. This could be concluded from the rules on the decision-making process of limited liability companies, which follow the majority principle (§ 47 GmbHG). According to recent decisions of the German Federal Court of Justice, however, only the consent of all shareholders or a majority resolution of the corporate body representing **all shareholders** has the effect of excluding the offence. Thus, in any case, minority shareholders must be meaningfully involved.[61] Consequently, if such a consent to the action of the obliged person is given, there is in principle no breach of duty. However, it is recognised that criminal liability for breach of trust may, nevertheless, be considered if the consent of the shareholders to a legal transaction breaches the loyalty towards the limited liability company and is thus **invalid**. The German Federal Court of Justice previously assumed this in cases in which the consent violates the principles of a prudent businessman.[62] However, since the shareholders are in principle free to dispose of the company's assets, the German Federal Court of Justice has meanwhile limited the scope of invalid consents to acts of the obligated person which endanger the economic existence of the limited lia-

[60] BGH 21.12.2005 – 3 StR 470/04, BGHSt 50, 331 = NJW 2006, 522 (525 et seq.) – Mannesmann.
[61] BGH 27.8.2010 – 2 StR 111/09, BGHSt 55, 266 = NJW 2010, 3458 (3461) – Trienekens.
[62] BGH 29.5.1987 – 3 StR 242/86, BGHSt 34, 379 (386) = NJW 1988, 1397 (1399).

bility company,[63] which is certainly the case in the event of an attack on the share capital protected by § 30 GmbHG.[64]

Whether the same principles apply to **stock corporations** is highly controversial. Discrepancies arise from the special features of stock corporations regarding the distribution of competences and the much stricter principles of capital maintenance (§§ 57 et seqq. AktG). The German Federal Court of Justice affirmed the shareholders' power to exclude criminal liability by consenting, following the above-mentioned principles applicable to limited liability companies.[65] However, according to the prevailing opinion, this power is restricted significantly. Shareholders of a stock corporation may only consent to asset transfers as far as they concern the appropriation of distributable profits (§§ 57 sub. 3, 58 sub. 4 AktG). Such a resolution must not violate any legal provisions or be invalid for any other reasons. If there is an invalid resolution of the general meeting, the board of directors must disregard it, as it must manage the company independently (§ 76 sub. 1 AktG). **49**

For **partnerships** there are no special restrictions, as only the assets of the partners, not of the partnership itself are affected. The consent of all partners, therefore, excludes a breach of trust. If only certain partners give their consent, these partners cannot be victims of a breach of trust.[66] **50**

3. Foreign entities

a) Other EU Member States

Complicated questions arise with regard to legal persons that have been established in another Member State of the EU but have their administrative centre in Germany. These constellations are governed by Art. 49, 54 TFEU (**freedom of establishment**). Pursuant to the concept of freedom of establishment, legal persons who are legally operating in one Member State of the EU may carry out economic activities in a stable and continuous way in another Member State. To eliminate all forms of discrimination it is required that the relationship between a legal person and its legal representatives and organs is determined according to the law governing the formation of the legal person.[67] In most European legal systems (e.g. Germany, France, Luxemburg) the domicile theory applies, according to which the legal person needs to follow the law of the state in which it has its administrative centre. In contrast, the common law countries follow the foundation theory which applies the law of the state in which the legal entity was established. Following the concept of freedom of establishment, Member States that follow the domicile theory can still prohibit a domestic entity from retaining its legal form when moving to a different state.[68] On the other hand, foreign entities cannot be prohibited from relocating their administrative centre while retaining their foreign legal form.[69] This implies that **51**

---

63 BGH 24.8.1988 – 3 StR 232/88, BGHSt 35, 333 (336) = NJW 1989, 112 (113).

64 BGH 24.8.1988 – 3 StR 232/88, BGHSt 35, 333 (336) = NJW 1989, 112 in accordance with BGH 21.6.1999 – II ZR 47–98, BGHZ 142, 92 = NJW 1999, 2817.

65 BGH 21.12.2005 – 3 StR 470/04, BGHSt 50, 331 = NJW 2006, 522 – Mannesmann: the consent must be granted either by the sole shareholder or by a resolution of the general meeting. Dissenting: Fischer StGB § 266 mn. 102.

66 BGH 10.7.2013 – 1 StR 532/12, NJW 2013, 3590 (3593) mn. 44 et seq.

67 ECJ 30.9.2003 – C-167/01, ECLI:EU:C:2003:512 = NJW 2003, 3331 (3333 et seq.).

68 ECJ 16.12.2008 – C-210/06, ECLI:EU:C:2008:723 = NZG 2009, 61 – Cartesio. It should be mentioned that a lot of these countries do not prohibit this anymore, cf. Fischer NZG 2021, 483 (486 et seqq.).

69 ECJ 9.3.1999 – C-212/97, ECLI:EU:C:1999:126 = NZG 1999, 298 – Centros; ECJ 5.11.2002 – C-208/00, ECLI:EU:C:2002:632 = NZG 2002, 1164 – Überseering; ECJ 30.9.2003 – C-167/01, ECLI:EU:C:2003:512 = NZG 2003, 1064 – Inspire Act.

national law must recognise the foreign entity's statute that follows the law applicable in their home country.

52 Therefore, the general applicability of § 266 StGB to foreign companies operating in Germany (§§ 3, 9 StGB) is not affected, as the granting of protection under criminal law does not constitute a disproportionate restriction of the freedom of establishment. However, if criminal liability of a representative is to be considered, the breach of duty must be determined according to the entity's statute, i.e. according to the rules of the applicable foreign law.[70] Therefore, it is irrelevant whether the breach of duty determined under foreign law has an equivalent in German law or vice versa. For example, the fact that the director of a foreign entity operating in Germany has acted in a manner detrimental to the company's assets cannot be assessed according to §§ 30, 31 GmbHG.

b) Non-EU Member States

53 The same applies where treaties provide for rules comparable to EU law. This applies to entities that are established in **EFTA** countries that are members of the **EEA** (Iceland, Liechtenstein, Norway), as Art. 31, 34 of the EEA Agreement contain very similar rules on freedom of establishment. It also applies to the **US**, which has such a bilateral treaty with Germany.[71] For the **UK**, as a result of Brexit, Art. 49, 54 TFEU no longer apply.[72] It is now questionable whether the EU-UK Trade and Cooperation Agreement contains comparable provisions (particularly in Art. 128–130). Recent case law rejects this.[73]

54 Where there is no freedom of establishment, the domicile theory applies the law of the country where the entity actually has its administrative centre.

V. Pecuniary damage

55 The breach of a safeguarding duty must lead to a pecuniary damage to the trustor. The courts must quantify the amount of the pecuniary damage they assume and explain how it was determined in an economically comprehensible manner. The pecuniary damage comprises any loss of assets caused by the wrongful act. A potential reduction in assets is to be determined according to the principle of **overall balancing**: a comparison of all assets immediately before and after the conduct in breach of a duty to the detriment of the trustor. A disadvantage must be measurable in monetary terms from an economic point of view. Therefore, mere damage to the reputation or the credit rating of the trustor is not covered by criminal liability under § 266 StGB.

56 According to the principle of overall balancing, there is no damage if a loss is **compensated** by economic advantages occurring at the same time. On the other hand, sufficient compensation is obviously not provided if assets are stolen or given away for free. More specifically, compensation cannot be assumed, if goods or services are sold below market price, acquired at excessive prices or if work resources of the trustor are used for the sole benefit of the perpetrator.

57 A compensation cannot only come from advantages that can be legally enforced. Rather, an **economic approach** has to be applied. However, this economic approach is, in some cases, to be **modified through normative considerations**.[74] Although such

---

[70] BGH 13.4.2010 – 5 StR 428/09, NStZ 2010, 632 (634).

[71] Art. XXV para. 5 sent. 2 of the Treaty of Friendship, Commerce and Navigation, signed on 29.10.1954.

[72] BGH 16.2.2021 – II ZB 25/17, NZG 2021, 702.

[73] OLG München 5.8.2021 – 29 U 2411/21, NZG 2021, 1518.

[74] BGH 23.10.2018 – 1 StR 234/17, BeckRS 2018, 37760 mn. 42; BVerfG 1.11.2012 – 2 BvR 1235/11, NJW 2013, 365 (366).

normative aspects can certainly play a role in the determination of a pecuniary damage, they must not supersede economic considerations. Therefore, even in case of the use of entrusted assets for illicit purposes, it must be examined whether the illicit transaction was disadvantageous from an overall economic point of view. Accordingly, the question of whether a loss of assets is immediately compensated by a pecuniary advantage depends not only on the legal existence of the claims on which payment is to be made but also on the economic value of the return which the trustor has received. Such claims will often be worthless as they can be legally reclaimed. However, cases exist in which there is no risk of reclaim of the payments, although the underlying legal transactions are void. A pecuniary damage is rejected in these cases.[75] This applies in particular to cases in which both contracting parties behaved illegally when concluding a contract, so that an incentive for clandestine behaviour is to be expected on both sides.

A pecuniary damage is assumed in cases in which concrete and secure **profit expectations** are not realised due to the perpetrator's actions. For example, the German Federal Court of Justice affirms a breach of trust when the perpetrator thwarts the possibility of a particularly advantageous deal between the trustor and a third party by having the third party promise them a benefit for the conclusion of the contract, which the third party then recovers from the – correspondingly increased – remuneration (so-called kick-back payments)[76]. The same applies if the perpetrator breaches their duty by omitting to increase the trustor's assets. Again, a relevant loss of profit is only to be assumed in the case of a concrete acquisition opportunity, not in the case of merely uncertain prospects or expectations. 58

When acknowledging the relevance of profit expectations, it is only consequential that expected losses must also be taken into account. This is done via the figure of the **concrete endangerment of assets**. However, especially with this concept of a pecuniary damage it must be ensured that it is not confused or blended with the separate requirement of a breach of a safeguarding duty.[77] Furthermore, § 266 StGB does not provide for liability for a merely attempted act. This must not be undermined by excessively lowering the standards of the requirement of a pecuniary damage. Accordingly, like all other damages, the damage caused by a concrete endangerment of assets must be quantified by the courts. Economically, the asset value must already be reduced due to the concrete danger of their final loss. The amount of this loss of the assets value is to be determined on the basis of the probability of a final loss. 59

Examples of concrete endangerment of assets that may be assumed to constitute pecuniary damage to the trustor are: 60

- granting loans without sufficient security;
- issuing an excessive land charge (especially in connection with fake invoices);
- assuming a suretyship with a very high probability of being claimed;
- waiving liens;
- diverting revenue to a hidden account.

Where the objective determination of the damage does not result in a negative overall balance, it can be examined in a second step whether there are indications that a pecuniary damage can nevertheless be assumed under the concept of a **personal impact**.[78] This aspect is supposed to protect the trustor's economic freedom. However, according to the courts, any consideration of a personal impact must have an exceptional character, as the 61

---

[75] Cf. BGH 23.10.2018 – 1 StR 234/17, BeckRS 2018, 37760.
[76] For more details regarding kick-back payments → mn. 82 et seqq.
[77] As described in → mn. 37 et seqq.
[78] BVerfG 1.11.2012 – 2 BvR 1235/11, NJW 2013, 365 (367); BGH 8.1.2020 – 5 StR 366/19, BGHSt 64, 246 = NJW 2020, 628 (630).

objective value of the consideration is regularly decisive. Under the concept of personal impact, a pecuniary damage can be assumed in the following situations, despite an objectively existing compensation:

- the service is of no subjective value for the trustor. This can, for example, be the case if a property is acquired that is completely unusable for the company's purposes.
- a service is imposed on the trustor which they would not reasonably have wanted in this way or at this time. This may include, for example, an excessively luxurious trip for the members of the supervisory board, granted by the board of directors of an indebted stock corporation.
- the costs incurred make the timely fulfilment of other more urgent tasks impossible or lead to a difficult financial situation. This is, for example, the case with investments that drain the company of all its liquidity.[79]

62 Finally, a pecuniary damage can be rejected if the perpetrator consistently has financial means available to compensate for the loss of assets caused by them.

VI. Subjective elements of the crime

63 The perpetrator must act with at least conditional intent (*dolus eventualis*). Such intent must encompass all elements of the offence as described above: the existence of a safeguarding duty, its breach, and the resulting pecuniary damage. If, for example, the perpetrator genuinely but mistakenly believes that their conduct complies with their safeguarding duties or that the trustor has consented, they lack awareness of a breach of duty, and therefore act without intent (§ 16 sub. 1 sent. 1 StGB).

64 A general good intention to ultimately serve the trustor's interests (e.g. generating illicit funds to secure a lucrative contract through bribery) does not negate intent with respect to any of the elements of the crime.

65 Negligence alone is insufficient to ground liability for breach of trust; the perpetrator must have acted with intent.

C. Commission of and complicity in a breach of trust

66 German criminal law differentiates between committing an offence (*Täterschaft*, § 25 StGB) and complicity in an offence by aiding and abetting (§§ 26 et seq. StGB). In the case of breach of trust, this distinction depends on whether a safeguarding duty exists, as this is a 'special personal characteristic'. This special personal characteristic establishes the perpetrator's criminal liability (§ 28 StGB).[80] Only a person who has a safeguarding duty can be held liable for the actual commission of a breach of trust. Others may, nevertheless, be held liable as aiders (*Gehilfe*) or abettors (*Anstifter*), in which case their sentence must be mitigated (§§ 28 sub. 1, 49 sub. 1 StGB).[81]

67 Where **several persons** share the special personal characteristic of a safeguarding duty, they may be regarded as joint offenders (§ 25 sub. 2 StGB). For example, this can apply to

[79] BGH 14.5.2020 – 1 StR 147/20, BeckRS 2020, 13656.

[80] BGH 12.9.1996 – 1 StR 509/96, NStZ 1997, 281.

[81] This mitigation could be combined with a potential mitigation under § 27 sub. 2 sent. 2 StGB insofar as the position as an aider does not result exclusively from the absence of a safeguarding duty, cf. BGH 8.1.1975 – 2 StR 567/74, BGHSt 26, 53 = NJW 1975, 837.

the members of the board of directors: each individual member is obliged to safeguard the company's pecuniary interests. To this end, they must use every legally permissible means to prevent resolutions that would damage those interests. Even if a member **abstains** or is **outvoted**, their safeguarding duty requires them to initiate further countermeasures (such as informing the supervisory board or the shareholders).

Whenever the power of disposal or to make binding agreements is conferred on a **legal entity**, it is necessary to consider § 14 sub. 1 StGB. Without this provision, the **organs and representatives** of the entity could not be held liable under § 266 sub. 1 alt. 1 StGB[82] as they themselves have no personal safeguarding duty. Accordingly, they lack the 'special personal characteristic'. To avoid impunity, § 14 sub. 1 StGB extends the scope of commission of an offence: any provision that demands a 'special personal characteristic' for criminal liability also applies to the representative if these characteristics do not exist in the person of that representative but in the entity they represent. **68**

To give an example: a limited liability company – such as a financial institution – maintains a business relation with a customer through which the company is entitled to dispose of that customer's assets. Pursuant to § 14 sub. 1 StGB, the managing director of the company can be held liable for a breach of trust concerning the assets of the customer. The same can apply in corporate groups when board members of a controlling company invest the assets of a subsidiary into the group to such an extent that the subsidiary's existence would be endangered in the event of the loss of the assets.[83] **69**

On the other hand, if the managing director acts against the interest of the very company they represent, there is no need to invoke § 14 StGB: in this relationship the managing director is already subject to a safeguarding duty towards the limited liability company as their trustor. **70**

D. Legal consequences

In regular cases (§ 266 sub. 1 StGB), the penalty is imprisonment for a term not exceeding five years or a fine. In particularly serious cases (§ 266 sub. 2 in connection with § 263 sub. 3 StGB), the range of punishment is increased to imprisonment from 6 months to 10 years. The cases listed in § 263 sub. 3 StGB are merely indicative. **71**

In practice, the case of causing a substantial financial loss is of particular importance (§ 263 sub. 3 sent. 2 no. 2 StGB), although it has not been conclusively clarified where the threshold for such a substantial loss lies. **72**

E. Most relevant cases

'Unless dealing with one of the classic cases of breach of trust, neither the courts nor the prosecution know whether § 266 StGB applies or not.'[84] This remark dates back to 1954 and stems from the preparatory materials for the criminal law reform of the newly **73**

---

[82] In some cases, they might be held liable under § 266 sub. 1 alt. 2 StGB (breach of fidelity alternative), assuming that there is a fiduciary relationship between the representative and the third party.

[83] Cf. BGH 13.5.2004 – 5 StR 73/03, BGHSt 49, 147 = NJW 2004, 2248 – Bremer Vulkan.

[84] Translated from Mayer Untreue 333 (337).

founded Federal Republic of Germany. It has been frequently cited and endorsed ever since.[85] It is still relevant today since it reveals two key insights: first, criminal liability under § 266 StGB is generally difficult to assess; the details outlined above underscore this difficulty but are intended to assist in its evaluation.[86] Second, there are, indeed, 'classic cases' of breach of trust in which the assessment is more straightforward. Below, ten rather common constellations of possible breach of trust will be examined in greater detail:

I. Risky transactions

74 Risky transactions inherently involve the possibility of loss. Forecasting whether a transaction will result in a profit or a loss carries significant uncertainty. However, risk-taking is by no means exceptional but rather central to economic life: every commercial decision entails the chance that expectations will not be met and losses will occur. Risky transactions occur across all sectors of the economy, not only in banking and capital markets (although credit transactions remain the prototypical example). As noted above,[87] § 266 StGB is not intended to prohibit legitimate entrepreneurial risk-taking. Whether a risky transaction amounts to a breach of trust depends, in the final analysis, particularly on the questions of a breach of duty and a resulting pecuniary damage.

75 Whether a risky transaction breaches a **safeguarding duty** depends on the internal relationship between the trustor and the decision-maker. Legal regulations, contractual agreements and the trustor's (actual or presumed) will establish the permissible **risk framework**. Where valid consent has been given, no breach of duty arises for transactions within that framework. Determining criminal liability, therefore, requires thorough analysis of the trustor's specific risk policy. Particularly relevant are the trustor's own guidelines, which may – explicitly or implicitly – permit or prohibit certain risks (for example requiring investments to be made 'conservatively' or allowing them to be 'aggressive'; in other words: the trustor's 'risk appetite'). Such guidelines govern the scope of permissible action, regardless of general standards of commercial due diligence. Therefore, a trustor may narrowly limit the powers and prohibit any daring action. A breach of duty then also exists if taking a risk not covered by the guidelines appears extremely worthwhile from the point of view of a prudent businessperson. On the other hand, the trustor may also permit extremely reckless undertakings that go far beyond the general rules of proper care. Otherwise, if there are no guidelines by the trustor or if these guidelines are not sufficiently specific, the risk policy is based on the standard market practice (from the point of view of a prudent businessperson). In this case, it will generally be assumed that risky transactions are permissible as they are common in business life. The resulting scope for decision-making is exceeded if the transaction in question is clearly and evidently economically unjustifiable. A safeguarding duty may be breached if the perpetrator makes a decision without carefully weighing the opportunities and risks. The same applies – unless permitted by guidelines or customary rules – if the perpetrator takes extreme risks of loss, only to obtain a highly doubtful prospect of profit ('as a gambler would do').[88]

76 Where a risky transaction breaches a duty, one must then carefully assess whether it also **resulted in pecuniary damage** to the trustor. In particular, a damage in the form

[85] Cf. only Dierlamm NStZ 1997, 534 (536); Jahn JuS 2006, 379 (379); Fischer StraFo 2008, 269 fn. 10; Jahn/Ziemann ZIS 2016, 552 (552); with reservations: Schünemann NStZ 2005, 473 (473).

[86] → mn. 4.

[87] → mn. 40 et seqq.

[88] BGH 12.6.1990 – 5 StR 268/89, NJW 1990, 3219 (3220).

of a **concrete endangerment of assets** comes into consideration.[89] According to older case law, such damage already occurred if the risky transaction involved an unjustifiable risk of loss. According to a decision of the German Constitutional Court, this approach was inadmissible, as it confused or blended the conduct (breach of duty) and the result (pecuniary damage).[90] Therefore, the more recent case law applies the principle of overall balancing to risky transactions. Under this principle, there is no pecuniary damage in a risky transaction if the investment is economically compensated by the combination of the **possible profit** and the **probability of occurrence**. To quantify the damage in the case of capital investments, the investment sum is usually compared to the market value of the investment (although such market value may be difficult to determine). Where interest rate swaps are concluded in breach of duty, damage occurs in the amount of the market value of the derivative (the amount of a provision for contingent liabilities (§ 249 HGB) may be referred to).

The concept of **personal impact** must also be considered.[91] The trustor may not want 77 to allow any risky transactions and such transactions are merely imposed on them. Therefore, it must be asked whether the trustor has any use for them. For example, a trustor seeking to invest conservatively in their retirement savings would not want to be invested in highly speculative funds – even if they are purchased at market prices. Nevertheless, any resale value must be offset against the unfavourable costs.

II. Slush funds

A slush fund (in German often referred to as *Schwarze Kasse*) is set up by withdraw- 78 ing the trustor's funds from the regular financial channels and transferring them into accounts, funds or trusts outside of those systems. Such diversion may be intended to place the assets beyond the reach of authorities (e.g. the tax office[92]) or to enable the perpetrator to use them for their own purposes – although possibly in the trustor's interest. As always, no breach of duty occurs if the slush fund is established with the trustor's (valid) consent.

Not only does someone who establishes or maintains a slush fund breach their safe- 79 guarding duty; an obliged person who becomes aware of the existence of such a fund but fails to inform the trustor likewise acts in breach of duty. One might initially question the causal link between that omission and any ensuing damage – particularly if no further payments into the already established fund are made. However, the safeguarding duty not only commands preserving the trustor's assets but also optimising them. Therefore, a failure to disclose the slush fund and to assert claims to recover those assets may also constitute a breach of trust.

To constitute pecuniary damage to the trustor, the resources of the slush funds do not 80 have to be irretrievably lost through investment. A definitive loss already occurs upon the creation, maintenance and non-disclosure of a slush fund, since the trustor permanently loses control of the assets. Once the slush fund is in place, the trustor cannot access these assets because they are held under other names. Unlike cases where the perpetrator can compensate losses from their personal resources, retaining funds in a slush account is not considered to be sufficient to compensate the damage. Accordingly, pecuniary damage also arises if assets are diverted into a slush fund in order to use them in the trustor's interest, even when this saves the trustor expenses in the same amount.

---

89 → mn. 59.

90 BVerfG 23.6.2010 – 2 BvR 2559/08, BVerfGE 126, 170 = NJW 2010, 3209.

91 → mn. 61.

92 For questions relating to tax evasion → Ch. 13.

81 It makes no difference whether the slush fund is established domestically or abroad.

III. Bribes/kick-back

82 There are distinct offences regarding the giving and taking of bribes (§§ 299 et seqq., 331 et seqq. StGB).[93] However, such conduct may also amount to a breach of trust under § 266 StGB. For example, bribes may be given through (hidden) commissions.

83 The **taking** of commissions gives rise to liability for a breach of trust only if the trustor has not (implicitly) consented to such behaviour. This general limitation is especially important in the context of bribery because such conduct is still commonplace in certain sectors of the economy. However, if taking commissions is expressly prohibited (either by internal policy or by law), a breach of duty has to be presumed. In addition, the conduct must cause pecuniary damage to the trustor, which is not automatic with every commission payment. Each case requires careful consideration: pecuniary damage arises where the granting of a bribe induced the perpetrator to enter into an economically disadvantageous transaction for the trustor. Likewise, damage occurs if the trustee accepts an inferior offer from the bribing party over a better one from another party.

84 A transaction is likely to be economically disadvantageous when the perpetrator and the briber agree on a **kick-back** payment. In such schemes, the briber obtains compensation by adding the amount spent on the bribe to the amount charged to the trustor. Pecuniary damage to the trustor arises only if the briber would also have concluded the contract at a price reduced by the amount of the bribe. In other words, the trustor must have had a realistic prospect of concluding the transaction in question at a price reduced by the kick-back; the German Federal Court of Justice presumes this.[94]

85 The **giving** of bribes will regularly be in the trustor's apparent interests, as they secure a lucrative contract in return. However, any consent to such payments is typically invalid due to the breach of legal prohibitions. The key question then becomes whether the outflow of assets through the bribe payments is offset by a corresponding inflow. No offset occurs where the bribe serves not to secure a specific mandate but rather to establish or foster a 'good relationship' between the parties. If, however, the bribe directly results in a contract, the inflow will regularly compensate for the bribe payment – up to the point where the risk of detection becomes so high that accounting provisions must be recognised.

IV. Compliance

86 As noted above,[95] the safeguarding duty may require **management** to establish a compliance management system.[96] However, criminal liability under § 266 StGB arises only if the company itself directly suffers pecuniary damage as a result of a failure to set up such a system – a loss that will often be difficult to quantify. **Compliance officers** may have a safeguarding duty as well.[97]

87 Typically, safeguarding duties relevant under § 266 StGB are not created by the compliance guidelines of a company. Nevertheless, those compliance guidelines often specify

---

[93] For details on this → Ch. 10 on corruption.

[94] BGH 2.12.2005 – 5 StR 119/05, BGHSt 50, 299 = NJW 2006, 925 – Kölner Müllskandal.

[95] → mn. 20.

[96] For details regarding compliance management systems → Ch. 6.

[97] → mn. 34.

the content and scope of already existing safeguarding duties. It is, therefore, important to carefully calibrate how strict compliance guidelines should be: overly stringent directives could lead to an unnecessary criminal liability risk of the company's employees for breach of trust – and possibly even the risk of a sanction for the company itself.

V. Criminal offences

A non-pecuniary criminal offence by an entity's organ or a representative does not, by itself, give rise to criminal liability for breach of trust under § 266 StGB. While one might assume such liability – since the entity can be sanctioned for an administrative offence following a criminal offence of one of its organs or representatives (§ 30 OWiG)[98] – only the breach of a duty that directly and specifically protects the trustor's assets is relevant to § 266 StGB. Liability under § 30 OWiG does not constitute such a duty. However, many organisations maintain internal financial protection policies that expressly prohibit the (intentional) commission of any criminal offence in the course of employment. **88**

VI. Assumption of fines and defence costs

Employers may in principle cover **fines** (§ 40 StGB; § 17 OWiG), payments to a non-profit organisation or to the treasury (*Staatskasse*) to terminate proceedings (§ 153a StPO), or **defence costs** for an employee. However, such payments can constitute breach of trust under § 266 StGB in individual cases. To avoid criminal liability, the employer's assumption of costs must demonstrably serve their interests. As this will usually be difficult to predict, the person making such a decision will have a broad scope of discretion. **89**

An employer's decision to assume **fines** may well be in the company's interest – for example, by convincing an employee to forego appeals and, thereby, avoiding negative publicity. The same rationale applies even more to payments made under § 153a StPO to a non-profit organisation or to the treasury, since these will result in a termination of the proceedings. Avoiding a public trial will generally benefit the company by preventing extensive media coverage and the resulting reputational risks. Furthermore, if employees must participate in court hearings as defendants or witnesses, they will be unavailable to work for the company during this time. One must also consider the psychological stress on employees involved in a trial and the risk of business secrets being disclosed in the course of public court hearings. Additionally, covering an employee's fine can foster loyalty among valued staff. Where a fine is imposed on a board member whose conduct breached their duty to the company, the decision to assume the fine and the related costs must be taken by the supervisory board. **90**

A company may be obliged to cover an employee's **defence costs** under its duty of care towards its employees. However, this obligation may cease if the alleged criminal offences are directed against the company or give rise to justified damage claims against it. Absent a legal duty to assume the defence costs, the company must then assess whether assuming defence costs remains, nevertheless, in its interest – for example, if a competent defence of the employee could also help to avert a corresponding sanction against the company under § 30 OWiG or to avoid the negative press of a public trial. **91**

[98] For details on sanctions according to § 30 OWiG → Ch. 4.

VII. Remuneration and bonus payments

92 The supervisory board must observe its safeguarding duty when determining executive **remuneration** (though not when negotiating its own).[99] Remuneration must not be arbitrarily high (§§ 116, 93 AktG) but should be appropriate in relation to each board member's duties, performance responsibilities, and the company's economic situation. Where remuneration exceeds customary levels, special justification is required (§ 87 sub. 1 AktG).

93 An employment contract may include one-off or annual **bonus payments** tied to business performance as a variable remuneration component. Determining such bonuses typically allows broad discretion. Even where no contractual basis for bonuses exists, voluntary bonus payments may be made. In that case, it is essential to distinguish between bonuses that are offset by a corresponding benefit to the company – such as incentivising exceptional performance among current or future executives – and purely gratuitous payments. The key question is whether the bonus payment is accompanied by compensation that is appropriate in relation to the reduction of the company's assets. Such compensation may consist in signalling to current or prospective executives that exceptional performance is rewarded. In this respect, even a voluntary bonus for an outgoing executive may serve a legitimate purpose if it encourages future engagement. However, a voluntary bonus that serves solely as a reward without offering any prospective benefit to the company may constitute misappropriation of company assets and lead to liability for breach of trust.[100]

VIII. Sponsorship

94 Sponsoring of social institutions and projects (sporting, cultural, etc.) is generally permissible and falls within entrepreneurial discretion in the form of the business judgment rule. A sponsorship decision will have to consider all of the following criteria[101]:

- alignment with business objectives. The sponsorship advances or supports activities closely connected to the company's core mission or market presence.
- proportionality to financial capacity. The commitment is in reasonable proportion to the company's assets and budgetary constraints.
- transparency in decision-making. The rationale, selection process and financial terms are clearly documented and communicated internally.
- appropriate, business-related motives. The primary purpose is to benefit the company – such as building brand recognition or strengthening community goodwill – and not to serve private interests.

95 Where all these criteria are carefully considered and can be affirmed, the sponsorship decision should be deemed a proper exercise of discretion and not a breach of safeguarding duty.

IX. De facto managing director

96 A 'de facto managing director' is treated like a formally appointed managing director for the purposes of criminal liability for breach of trust, since both will owe identical safeguarding duties to the company. Such a director is someone who, with the consent

---

[99] → mn. 24.
[100] BGH 21.12.2005 – 3 StR 470/04, BGHSt 50, 331 = NJW 2006, 522 (524) – Mannesmann.
[101] Cf. BGH 6.12.2001 – 1 StR 215/01, BGHSt 47, 187 = NJW 2002, 1585 (1587).

of the shareholders, effectively assumes the company's management without formal appointment – either because a formal appointment is invalid or because they take on the role informally. They must perform core management functions in practice, and where a nominal director remains in office (in German commonly called a *Strohman*), must nonetheless predominate by exercising management powers to a significant extent, determined on the basis of the overall impression. The absence of typical organ powers – such as bank signatory authority or external representation – weighs against recognising a de facto role, whereas the ability to issue binding instructions to the nominal director – and thereby steer corporate policy – is strongly indicative of a de facto role. Shareholder approval, even if informal, is essential to legitimise the de facto managing director.

A formally appointed yet effectively powerless managing director remains contractually obliged to safeguard the company's pecuniary interests and may, therefore, still be liable for breach of trust under § 266 StGB. In practice, however, the powerless director will typically no longer act on the company's behalf. While such inaction could, theoretically, amount to breach of trust by harmful passivity, their passivity is usually permitted by the shareholders and thus covered by their consent. **97**

X. Group of companies (cash pooling)

In a group of companies, the managing directors of a **parent company** may be liable for breach of trust if they deal with a subsidiary's assets in a way that threatens the subsidiary's solvency. Their safeguarding duties may arise from a formal control agreement or from acting as a de facto managing director of the subsidiary. Even where the subsidiary consents, such consent will be invalid for transactions that endanger its continued existence. At the same time, the managing directors of the **subsidiary** have a duty to examine whether the parent company requires an intervention that threatens the existence of the subsidiary and may in this regard be liable under § 266 StGB themselves. **98**

These principles are particularly relevant in the context of **cash pooling** arrangements, which play a central role in the cash management of a (de facto) group of companies. In such schemes, group entities lend to and borrow from one another in order to offset individual surpluses and deficits, often through the involvement of a bank, which provides an account that consolidates daily balances. 'Upstream' loans (i.e. payments from a subsidiary to a parent company) can be especially problematic: both the management of the parent company and the management of the subsidiary may be liable under § 266 StGB if they fail to ensure that an upstream loan does not threaten the subsidiary's solvency. The key considerations include whether the resulting intercompany debt is of value, whether it can be immediately recovered in an insolvency scenario, and whether any hedging arrangements exist. A timely flow of information between the parent company and the subsidiary is essential to maintain a continuous assessment of default risk, thereby allowing the management on both levels to fulfil their safeguarding duties. **99**

F. Conclusion

In conclusion, the offence of breach of trust under § 266 StGB plays a considerable practical role in the context of corporate criminal liability. A proper assessment of liability for breach of trust requires not only knowledge of general civil law and specific corporate **100** law but, where relevant, also familiarity with administrative law. Recurring patterns and settled case law can provide guidance in navigating these legal complexities. As with any complex legal matter, obtaining qualified legal advice remains essential in practice.

CHAPTER 13
TAX

Bibliography: Groß, Steuerstrafrechtliche Beratung von Kreditinstituten im Zusammenhang mit Cum-ex-Trades, PStR 2013, 296.

Table of contents

A. Introduction: criminal tax law in the judiciary's focus 294
B. Substantive criminal tax law 295
I. Tax evasion (§ 370 AO) 295
1. Acts constituting the offence 296
a) By committing an action (§ 370 sub. 1 no. 1 AO) 296
b) Omission (§ 370 sub. 1 no. 2 AO) 297
c) Failure to use revenue stamps or revenue stamping machines (§ 370 sub. 1 no. 3 AO) 298
2. Results of the offence 298
a) Understatement of tax (§ 370 sub. 4 sent. 1 AO) 298
b) Other unwarranted tax advantages (§ 370 sub. 4 sent. 2 AO) 299
c) Prohibition of set-off (§ 370 sub. 4 sent. 3 AO) 299
3. Causality 300
4. Intent 300
5. Unlawfulness and culpability 302
6. Attempted tax evasion (§ 370 sub. 2 AO) 302
7. Especially serious cases of tax evasion (§ 370 sub. 3 AO) ... 303
8. Voluntary disclosure under § 371 AO 304
a) Requirements of § 371 sub. 1 AO 304
aa) Personal submission and agency 304
bb) Declaration of correction 305
cc) Extent of corrections 306
b) Obligation to pay tax arrears (§ 371 sub. 3 AO) 306
c) Reasons for exclusion (§ 371 sub. 2 AO) 307
aa) Issue-related reasons for exclusion 307
bb) Offence related reasons for exclusion 307
cc) Personal reason for exclusion 308
9. Voluntary disclosure under § 389a AO 309
10. Statute of limitations 309
11. Scale of penalties and determination of penalty 310
12. Participation in tax offences 311
II. Other tax offences 311
1. Customs violation (§ 372 AO) 311
2. Customs fraud (smuggling) committed on a serial basis or as part of a gang and involving the use of violence (§ 373 AO) 311
3. Purchasing and handling tax-evaded goods (§ 374 AO) 312
4. Forging of revenue stamps (§§ 148, 149 StGB in conjunction with § 369 sub. 1 no. 3 AO) 312
5. Aiding after the fact (§ 257 StGB in conjunction with § 369 sub. 1 no. 4 AO) 312

6. Impairment of VAT revenues committed on a serial basis as part of a gang (§ 26c UStG) 313
III. Confiscation (§§ 73 et seq. StGB) 313
C. Procedural law relating to criminal tax law 313
I. Investigating authorities 313
1. Revenue authorities 314
a) Unit that imposes regulatory fines or prosecutes 314
b) Tax investigation unit 314
2. Prosecutor's office 315
II. Investigation measures 315
III. Defence 315
1. Defence counsel 315
2. Mandatory defence 316
3. Possibilities for discontinuance of the proceedings 316
IV. Relationship between criminal tax law proceedings and taxation proceedings 316
D. Law on regulatory tax offences 317
I. Reckless understatement of tax (§ 378 AO) 317
1. Potential perpetrators 317
2. Acts constituting the offence, result of the offence and causality 318
3. Recklessness 318
4. Voluntary disclosure exempting from regulatory fines (§ 378 sub. 3 AO) 319
a) Requirements 319
b) Reason for exclusion 320
5. Legal consequences and statute of limitations 320
II. Other tax-related regulatory offences 320
1. General minor tax fraud (§ 379 AO) 320
2. Compromising withholding taxes (§ 380 AO) 321
3. Compromising VAT revenues (§ 26a UStG) 321
III. Procedural law 321

A. Introduction: criminal tax law in the judiciary's focus

1 Criminal tax law is one of the main focus areas of the advisory services provided to individuals and companies in Germany in the field of economic criminal law. At present, law enforcement authorities are displaying a high degree of willingness to prosecute and bring charges on allegations of tax offences. In fact, fiscal interests are often enforced by way of criminal tax law. Over recent years, the legislator has tightened numerous criminal tax law rules (e.g., restricted options for voluntary disclosure, extended limitation periods), thereby continually increasing sanctionary pressure.

2 Investigations of tax-driven share transactions over the dividend record date (so-called cum/ex transactions and similar trading strategies), involving a large number of banks as well as law firms and corporate consultancy firms, still attract intense media coverage.[1] According to media reports, the respective prosecutor's offices in charge are currently conducting more than 100 separate investigations involving some 1,700 accused persons. Many banks have already made tax repayments in the triple-digit million euro order, several accused bank managers, stock traders and tax lawyers have been sentenced to (multi-year) prison terms.

[1] Cf. Groß PStR 2013, 296 et seqq.

3 Although, Germany was the first to initiate cum/ex proceedings, other European countries seem to follow up. Besides others, France, Belgium, Netherlands, and Austria commenced criminal and regulatory proceedings into tax driven trades. This also led to new ways of mutual legal assistance (so-called: joint investigation teams), allowing authorities to conduct investigative measures cross-border and sharing information without time consuming requests for mutual legal assistance. For instance, in March 2023 newspapers reported, that several French banks had been searched in Paris regarding their alleged involvement in cum/cum structures with German prosecutors present as well.

4 The reappraisal of these cases will occupy both the judiciary and the defence for years to come. The State of North-Rhine Westphalia already finished the construction of a new courthouse in view of the upcoming cum/ex indictments.

5 Aside from cum/ex cases, companies and their executive bodies and employees are also increasingly faced with criminal tax law allegations in other areas: Tax investigators are setting their sights, more and more, on private equity funds and their managers. M&A deals are increasingly subject to critical reviews and occasionally result in the initiation of criminal tax law proceedings. Also, when tax audits identify additional income, these cases are now, with greater frequency, passed on to those authorities that impose regulatory fines or prosecute. As a consequence, punishable acts and legal tax avoidance strategies are often intermingled.

B. Substantive criminal tax law

6 Germany's substantive criminal tax law is governed by §§ 369 to 376 AO (*Abgabenordnung*, Fiscal Code). In addition, individual taxation laws and the Criminal Code (*Strafgesetzbuch*, StGB) also contain penal provisions (cf. § 369 sub. 1 AO). Criminal tax law is accessory to substantive tax law. It is only substantive tax law that gives rise to declaration and cooperation obligations, whose breach would be punishable, and that defines the extent of the state's tax claims.[2] Pursuant to § 369 sub. 2 AO, the general criminal law provisions apply to criminal tax law on a supplementary basis, unless a more specialised provision takes precedence.

I. Tax evasion (§ 370 AO)

7 The criminal offence of tax evasion (*Steuerhinterziehung*) under § 370 AO is the central criminal tax law provision. It protects the state's interest in complete and timely tax revenues.[3] § 370 sub. 1 AO provides that anyone who furnishes the revenue authorities or other authorities with incorrect or incomplete facts concerning matters that are relevant for tax purposes (no. 1), or fails to inform the revenue authorities of facts that are relevant for tax purposes when obliged to do so (no. 2), or fails to use revenue stamps or revenue stamping machines when obliged to do so (no. 3) and, as a result, understates taxes or derives unwarranted tax advantages for themselves or for another person, is liable to prosecution.

8 This basic set of facts is complemented by the provisions in § 370 sub. 2 to 7 AO, which prescribe the punishability of attempted offences (sub. 2), provide for stricter penalties in

[2] Klein/Jäger AO § 370 mn. 5.
[3] MüKoStGB/Schmitz/Wulf AO § 370 mn. 2.

especially serious cases (sub. 3) and define the point in time when the offence of understating tax has been realised (sub. 4). Furthermore, § 370 sub. 5 AO clarifies that tax evasion may also be committed in relation to goods whose importation, exportation or transit is prohibited. By operation of § 370 sub. 6 AO, certain levies administered by another country may also be subject to German criminal law while § 370 sub. 7 AO expands the scope of application to offences committed outside the AO's territory of application.[4]

1. Acts constituting the offence

9 Pursuant to § 370 sub. 1 no. 1 to 3 AO, tax evasion may be committed in three different ways.

a) By committing an action (§ 370 sub. 1 no. 1 AO)

10 § 370 sub. 1 no. 1 AO is a declaration offence. The criminal act is the stating of incorrect or incomplete information regarding tax-relevant facts vis-à-vis the revenue authorities or other authorities. The perpetrator may be anyone who is in a position to have an effect on the assessment, imposition or enforcement of tax owed.[5] Accordingly, even a person who is not subject to any tax obligations under the law may be deemed an accomplice, as long as the requirements of joint perpetration under § 25 sub. 2 StGB (in conjunction with § 369 sub. 2 AO) have been met.[6]

11 Facts within the meaning of § 370 AO are specific past or current circumstances that can be taken in evidence.[7] Future events are not facts. However, internal facts, such as intentions or assumptions, may also come under this constituent element of the offence.[8] Facts must be distinguished from mere value judgements, such as conclusions, forecasts or legal views, as these cannot be taken in evidence.[9] Accordingly, if taxpayers base their tax return on an erroneous legal view but disclose all relevant facts, this does not constitute a declaration relating to facts.

12 Secondly, the fact must be of relevance for tax purposes – not every statement made vis-à-vis the revenue authorities is relevant under criminal tax law. Tax relevance is deemed to exist if the facts must be included in order to complete a taxable event and thus influence both the grounds for and the amount of the tax claim or tax advantage, or if they could otherwise cause the revenue authorities to act upon the tax claim.[10]

13 The tax-relevant statements of fact must be incorrect or incomplete. § 150 sub. 2 AO requires all information contained in a tax return to be truthful. Information is deemed to be incorrect if all relevant taxation bases have been accurately declared as far as their existence is concerned, but the amount involved was incorrectly declared.[11] Where reference is made to false declarations by third parties, this also constitutes incorrect information. When making declarations vis-à-vis the revenue authorities, the accuracy of third-party declarations is inferred.[12] On the other hand, information is incomplete if all taxation bases have been correctly recorded in terms of their amount, but the taxpayer failed to disclose individual taxation bases.[13]

---

[4] Klein/Jäger § 370 mn. 1.
[5] Hüls/Reichling/Schott AO § 370 mn. 20.
[6] BGH 9.4.2013 – 1 StR 586/12, NJW 2013, 2449 (2451).
[7] Hüls/Reichling/Schott AO § 370 mn. 53.
[8] Kohlmann/Ransiek, 84th edn August 2024, AO § 370 mn. 228.
[9] Kohlmann/Ransiek, 84th edn August 2024, AO § 370 mn. 228.
[10] BGH 27.9.2002 – 5 StR 97/02, NStZ-RR 2003, 20 (21).
[11] WJS WirtschaftsStrafR-HdB/Pflaum Ch. 22 mn. 46.
[12] Kohlmann/Ransiek, 84th edn August 2024, AO § 370 mn. 246.
[13] WJS WirtschaftsStrafR-HdB/Pflaum Ch. 22 mn. 46.

According to the case law on § 370 sub. 1 no. 1 AO, a disclosure obligation exists with regard to all elements of the factual situation, whose legal relevance is – objectively – doubtful. This is the case, in particular, if the taxpayer's views regarding the interpretation of legal terms or the subsumption of certain facts deviates from case law, revenue administration guidelines or standard assessment practice.[14] **14**

Moreover, the information needs to have been stated vis-à-vis a revenue authority or another authority. § 6 sub. 1 and sub. 2 AO contains a legal definition of authorities and revenue authorities; tax offices fall under § 6 sub. 2 no. 5 AO. In accordance with the case law of the First Criminal Senate of the Federal Court of Justice (*Bundesgerichtshof*, BGH), which has jurisdiction over appeals on points of law in criminal tax law cases, error (*Irrtum*) on the part of a tax officer is not a prerequisite for the offence under § 370 sub. 1 no. 1 AO.[15] Tax evasion can, in fact, be committed in relation to an assessment officer, who is aware of the incorrectness of the information and thus acts in bad faith. **15**

b) Omission (§ 370 sub. 1 no. 2 AO)

§ 370 sub. 1 no. 2 AO is a genuine offence by omission. Anyone failing to inform the revenue authorities of facts that are relevant for tax purposes when obliged to do so is liable to prosecution. This variant of the offence also constitutes a special offence. According to BGH case law, only those who are under a special obligation to clarify tax-relevant facts can be perpetrators – or accomplices – of tax evasion by omission.[16] **16**

Pursuant to § 149 sub. 1 sent. 1 AO, tax-related declaration obligations arise, first and foremost, from individual tax laws. For legal entities, their legal representatives (e.g., managing director, executive board) are required to meet their declaration obligations (§ 33 sub. 1 and 34 sub. 1 sent. 1 AO).[17] Tax declaration obligations that are of relevance in practice are: **17**

- the obligation to file a personal income tax return, § 25 sub. 3 sent. 1 EStG (*Einkommensteuergesetz*, Income Tax Act) in conjunction with §§ 56 and 60 EStDV (*Einkommensteuer-Durchführungsverordnung*, Income Tax Implementation Ordinance);
- the obligation to file a corporate income tax return, § 31 sub. 1 KStG (*Körperschaftsteuergesetz*, Corporate Income Tax Act) in conjunction with §§ 56 and 60 EStDV;
- the obligation to file a preliminary value-added tax (VAT) return, § 18 sub. 1 sent. 1 UStG (*Umsatzsteuergesetz*, Value Added Tax Act); and
- the obligation to correct declarations, § 153 sub. 1 sent. 1 no. 1 AO.

§ 153 sub. 1 sent. 1 no. 1 AO is of great relevance in practice. This provision stipulates an obligation to report and correct if taxpayers realise in hindsight – but before expiry of the assessment period – that a declaration made by them, or on their behalf, is incorrect or incomplete and that this could lead, or has already led, to an understatement of tax. The obligation to correct extends to all inaccuracies and omissions that the taxpayers themselves have caused. There is, however, no obligation to correct errors made by the tax office.[18] **18**

As per the wording of the law, the correction must be effected without undue delay. What exactly constitutes 'without undue delay' depends on the specific situation, as **19**

---

[14] BFH 22.11.2018 – V R 65/17, DStR 2019, 265 (270).
[15] BGH 14.12.2010 – 1 StR 275/10, NStZ 2011, 283 (283).
[16] BGH 9.4.2013 – 1 StR 586/12, NJW 2013, 2449 (2451).
[17] Klein/Rüsken AO § 34 mn. 1.
[18] BFH 4.12.2012 – VIII R 50/10, DStR 2013, 703 (705).

there is no general rule. However, with regard to complex company-related sets of circumstances, two weeks would presumably still be deemed appropriate.[19] It is, in any case, advisable to duly document the internal review in order to be able to objectively substantiate the actual time required vis-à-vis the revenue authorities in cases of doubt.

20 In the view of the BGH, a reporting and correction obligation under § 153 sub. 1 sent. 1 no. 1 AO also exists if the taxpayer previously committed tax evasion, with *dolus eventualis* (*bedingter Vorsatz*), through an active deed in accordance with § 370 sub. 1 no. 1 AO and only subsequently becomes fully aware of the incorrectness or incompleteness of the information he provided.[20] For the taxpayer, this view is disadvantageous in that the limitation period under criminal law will thus commence and expire at a later time.[21]

21 A further constituent element of § 370 sub. 1 no. 2 AO is failure to act (omission). An omission contrary to duty within the meaning of the criminal provision requires failure to comply with the duty to declare within the period set for this purpose.[22] However, in individual cases, the obligation to declare may be suspended if compliant behaviour cannot reasonably be expected in the given situation. This applies to situations where taxpayers would incriminate themselves if they were to disclose facts of tax relevance, for example if they are already the subject of criminal tax law proceedings.[23]

22 Lastly, tax evasion by omission requires that the revenue authorities be unaware of the tax-relevant facts.[24] As opposed to the offence under § 370 sub. 1 no. 1 AO, this offence cannot be committed in relation to an assessment officer who acts in bad faith. However, in individual cases, this may constitute attempted tax evasion pursuant to § 370 sub. 1 no. 2, sub. 2 AO and §§ 22, 23 sub. 1 StGB (in conjunction with § 369 sub. 2 AO).[25]

c) Failure to use revenue stamps or revenue stamping machines (§ 370 sub. 1 no. 3 AO)

23 § 370 sub. 1 no. 3 AO punishes the failure, contrary to duty, to use revenue stamps (*Steuerzeichen*) or revenue stamping machines (*Steuerstempler*). As with the offence under § 370 sub. 1 no. 2 AO, this constitutes a genuine offence by omission. In practice, this variant hardly plays any role, its only application results from § 17 TabStG (*Tabaksteuergesetz*, Tobacco Tax Act).

2. Results of the offence

24 § 370 sub. 1 AO specifies two results which the offence aims at: the unlawful reduction of the tax assessment through understatement and the achievement of an unwarranted tax advantage.

a) Understatement of tax (§ 370 sub. 4 sent. 1 AO)

25 In accordance with § 370 sub. 4 sent. 1 AO, taxes are deemed to have been understated (*verkürzt*) in particular if they are not assessed at all, in full or in time; this also applies if the tax has been assessed on a preliminary basis or subject to the proviso of a review or if

---

[19] Klein/Rätke AO § 153 mn. 20.

[20] BGH 17.3.2009 – 1 StR 479/08, NJW 2009, 1984 (1986); different opinion: JJR/Joecks AO § 370 mn. 263; Kohlmann/Ransiek, 84th edn August 2024, AO § 370 mn. 337.

[21] JJR/Joecks AO § 370 mn. 263.

[22] Klein/Jäger AO § 370 mn. 72.

[23] Klein/Jäger AO § 370 mn. 73.

[24] BGH 14.12.2010 – 1 StR 275/10, NStZ 2011, 283 (284); OLG Köln 31.1.2017 – III-1 RVs 253/16, wistra 2017, 363 (365).

[25] OLG Köln 31.1.2017 – III-1 RVs 253/16, wistra 2017, 363 (366).

a tax declaration is equivalent to a tax assessment subject to the proviso of a review. A tax assessment is too low if the tax assessed falls short of the amount of tax the public purse is entitled to.[26] It is solely the improper tax assessment that is of criminal relevance under this provision – the non-payment of tax is not punishable under § 370 AO.

With regard to offences under § 370 sub. 1 no. 1 AO, the intended result of understating tax is achieved, in relation to taxes that are subject to an assessment (e.g., personal or corporate income tax) when the taxpayer is notified of the incorrect tax assessment (§ 155 sub. 1 sent. 1 and sent. 2, § 157 AO). Under the terms of § 122 sub. 2 no. 1 AO, a tax assessment notice is deemed to have been given on the third day after posting. By operation of § 168 sent. 1 AO, which equates self-assessed tax returns to tax assessments that are subject to review, the result of understating self-assessment taxes (such as payroll tax) is achieved at the time when the self-assessed return is lodged. 26

For self-assessment taxes, the offence of tax evasion by omission (§ 370 sub. 1 no. 2 AO) is completed when the deadline for filing has expired.[27] For taxes that are subject to an assessment, the result being sought by the offence is achieved once a tax estimate notice that is too low is issued.[28] If no tax estimate notice is issued, the result being sought by the offence is achieved at the time when the assessment would have taken place if a compliant return had been filed. This is the case, at the latest, once the competent tax office has largely finalised its assessment processes for the relevant tax types and the relevant period.[29] These processes are deemed to have been largely completed when 90–95 % of the target has been achieved.[30] 27

b) Other unwarranted tax advantages (§ 370 sub. 4 sent. 2 AO)

The second result of the offence is the achievement of other unwarranted tax advantages. § 370 sub. 4 sent. 2 AO states that tax advantages also include tax rebates and that unwarranted tax advantages are deemed derived to the extent that these are wrongfully granted or retained. As the understating of tax is, in itself, a tax advantage, this constituent element is given a broad interpretation.[31] As per the BGH's definition, these advantages are intrinsically of a tax type, based on the revenue authority taking action.[32] 28

Said tax advantages may be: 29

- imputation or refund of a tax credit that does not actually exist,[33]
- granting of a deadline extension under § 109 AO,
- deferment of tax liabilities under § 222 AO,
- remission of tax under § 227 AO, and
- suspension of enforcement of a tax assessment notice under § 361 sub. 2 AO, § 69 sub. 2 FGO (*Finanzgerichtsordnung*, Code of Procedure for Fiscal Courts).

c) Prohibition of set-off (§ 370 sub. 4 sent. 3 AO)

§ 370 sub. 4 sent. 3 AO contains a special provision in the form of a prohibition of set-off. As per this provision, it is irrelevant for the commission of tax evasion, or the amount 30

---

[26] MüKoStGB/Schmitz/Wulf AO § 370 mn. 94.
[27] BGH 19.1.2011 – 1 StR 640/10, BeckRS 2011, 4341 mn. 6.
[28] BGH 22.8.2012 – 1 StR 317/12, wistra 2013, 65 (66).
[29] BGH 19.1.2011 – 1 StR 640/10, BeckRS 2011, 4341 mn. 8.
[30] Klein/Jäger AO § 370 mn. 92a; Kohlmann/Ransiek, 84th edn August 2024, AO § 370 mn. 413; in the case of simple matters, a maximum processing period of one year may apply, BGH 19.1.2011 – 1 StR 640/10, BeckRS 2011, 4341 mn. 9.
[31] Kohlmann/Ransiek, 84th edn August 2024, AO § 370 mn. 425.
[32] BGH 10.12.2008 – 1 StR 322/08, NJW 2009, 381 (383).
[33] BGH 28.7.2021 – 1 StR 519/20, NStZ 2022, 176 (181).

of tax evaded, whether said tax could have been reduced for other reasons or whether the tax advantage could have been claimed 'for other reasons' (*aus anderen Gründen*).[34] 'Other reasons' refers to facts invoked by the perpetrator during criminal proceedings in order to justify his conduct, even though he did not cite them during the taxation proceedings.[35] Accordingly, only those tax advantages must be attributed to the perpetrator that are derived from the incorrect return itself or, in the case of omission, that the perpetrator would have been entitled to had he provided correct information.[36]

31 However, the BGH is of the view that the prohibition of set-off does not apply if there is a direct economic link between non-disclosed circumstances that give rise to higher taxation and likewise non-disclosed circumstances that reduce the level of taxation.[37] Whether or not a direct economic link exists, depends largely on a value judgement and is currently decided on a case-by-case basis.[38] Grounds for a reduction, as well as tax advantages that cannot be taken into account due to the prohibition of set-off, may have a mitigating effect during sentencing, as it is only the (tax-related) consequences of the offence attributable to the perpetrator of tax evasion that can be held against the perpetrator.[39]

3. Causality

32 A causal link must exist between the acts constituting the offence under § 370 sub. 1 no. 1 to 3 AO and the result achieved by way of the offence ('causality', German: *Kausalität*). In the event of tax evasion through an active deed, this is the case if without the incorrect information, the result of the offence would not have been achieved (*conditio sine qua non*). For tax evasion through omission, this is the case if compliance with the obligation to declare would have necessarily resulted in the result of the offence being negated.[40] In the absence of a causal link, for example because the tax office disregards the incorrect information in arriving at its decision, this can still amount to attempted tax evasion.

4. Intent

33 Furthermore, criminal liability for tax evasion also requires intent (*Vorsatz*), § 15 StGB (in conjunction with § 369 sub. 2 AO). Contingent intent (*dolus eventualis*), i.e. acting wilfully and knowingly with the aim of realising all the constituent elements of an illegal act, is sufficient.[41] According to the BGH's established case law, the intent to evade taxes necessarily implies that the perpetrator is aware of the existence and the amount of the tax claim, or at least considers these to be likely, and wants to reduce such tax claim or tacitly accepts such reduction.[42] It is not necessary, however, that the taxpayer is certain of the existence and amount of the tax claim, or has knowledge of the specific type of levy or the legal basis of the tax claim.[43]

34 Contingent intent must always be distinguished from (deliberate) negligence. Contingent intent and deliberate negligence differ in that the person acting with deliberate

---

[34] Klein/Jäger AO § 370 mn. 129.

[35] BGH 28.1.1987 – 3 StR 373/86, NJW 1987, 1273 (1276).

[36] BGH 13.9.2018 – 1 StR 642/17, NStZ 2019, 150 (150).

[37] BGH 11.3.2021 – 1 StR 470/20, NStZ 2021, 745 (746).

[38] JJR/Joecks AO § 370 mn. 96 et seq.

[39] BGH 11.3.2021 – 1 StR 470/20, NStZ 2021, 745 (746).

[40] Kohlmann/Ransiek 84th edn August 2024, AO § 370 mn. 570 et seq.

[41] MüKoStGB/Schmitz/Wulf AO § 370 mn. 387.

[42] BGH 10.2.2022 – 1 StR 484/21, NStZ 2022, 418 (so called 'tax claim theory').

[43] BGH 8.9.2011 – 1 StR 38/11, NStZ 2012, 160 (161); KG Berlin 14.12.2016 – (4) 121 Ss 175/16 (205/16), NZWiSt 2017, 355 (358).

negligence does not approve of the consequences recognised as possible and therefore trusts that these will not occur, whereas a person acting with conditional intent approves of their occurrence in such a way that he acts with reckless disregard for the consequences or, at the least, accepts the realisation of the offence.[44] The presumption of intent is precluded if the taxpayer did not recognise the possibility that an offence could have been realised; the fact that the taxpayer 'could have' or 'should have' recognised this possibility constitutes, at the most, extremely careless or negligent conduct.[45]

In practice, the determination of intent is therefore a question of fact that needs to be answered on a case-by-case basis.[46] In the absence of a confession, intent to evade tax, being an internal fact that eludes cognition by the prosecutor's offices and the courts, can only be proven by way of circumstantial evidence. The mere fact that a taxpayer signed an incorrect tax return is, by itself, not sufficient to determine intent: it does not permit any conclusions as to the taxpayer's understanding and perception.[47] As part of its evaluation, the court must also consider in its assessment the way in which business people deal with the duties of enquiry that exist in their respective industry.[48] 35

According to case law, the following indications of intentional conduct on the part of the taxpayer may be referred to: 36

- tax-related and business experience;
- prior investigations or convictions under criminal tax law;
- notes on the revenue administration's standard forms and fact sheets;
- discussion of a particular tax topic by the public at large;
- deliberate concealment of business structures (e.g., offshore arrangements, the use of nominees);
- the use of tax circumvention structures by a layperson; and
- failure to obtain legal advice in cases of doubt.

However, if the taxpayer erroneously assumes that no tax claim exists, case law considers this an error with regard to the circumstances of the offence, which precludes intent, § 16 sub. 1 sent. 1 StGB (in conjunction with § 369 sub. 2 AO).[49] As per the guidelines set by the BGH, the determination of any such error requires that all circumstances that formed the taxpayer's understanding and perception be assessed. In its determination, the court is under no obligation to indiscriminately accept any exculpatory statements of the taxpayer.[50] In the view of the revenue authorities, the existence of a tax compliance management system may be an indication that the taxpayer did not act with intent. 37

The courts rejected the presumption of intentional tax evasion in the following situations, for example: 38

- the defendant failed to declare the private use of a company vehicle in his income tax return; however, in view of the advice received from his tax adviser, he assumed that such use was tax-neutral;[51]
- after the revenue authorities had advised him of shortcomings, the defendant took measures to ensure proper payroll tax accounting in his business, and there was nothing to suggest that these measures had not been implemented;[52]

---

[44] BGH 11.2.2020 – 1 StR 119/19, NStZ 2020, 487 (488).

[45] KG Berlin 14.12.2016 – (4) 121 Ss 175/16 (205/16), NZWiSt 2017, 355 (359); FG Hamburg 6.12.2001 – VI 103/99, BeckRS 2001, 21009794.

[46] LK-StGB/Bülte § 15 mn. 63.

[47] Cf. OLG München 15.2.2011 – 4 StRR 167/10, BeckRS 2011, 5051.

[48] BGH 8.9.2011 – 1 StR 38/11, NStZ 2012, 160 (162).

[49] BGH 18.8.2020 – 1 StR 296/19, NStZ 2021, 297 (298).

[50] BGH 8.9.2011 – 1 StR 38, NStZ 2012, 160 (161).

[51] OLG Köln 30.9.2014 – 1 RVs 91/14, BeckRS 2014, 18661 mn. 133.

[52] OLG Karlsruhe 8.2.1996 – 2 Ss 107/95, BeckRS 1996, 2072.

- the court considered the inconsistent evaluation of the particular tax issue by courts and revenue authorities as an indication against intentional trade tax evasion by the defendant.[53]

5. Unlawfulness and culpability

39 Furthermore, punishability under § 370 AO requires unlawful and culpable conduct. The justifications available under the StGB are of no relevance for criminal tax law.[54] In individual cases, the possibility of a mistake in law pursuant to § 17 sent. 1 StGB (in conjunction with § 369 sub. 2 AO) may have to be considered. As per this provision, culpability (*Schuld*) may not be extant if a taxpayer is unaware of the unlawfulness of his conduct. If the taxpayer was able to avoid this error, his sentence may be mitigated, § 49 sub. 1 StGB (in conjunction with § 17 sent. 2 StGB). According to case law, § 17 StGB may apply to misconceptions regarding tax reporting obligations.[55]

6. Attempted tax evasion (§ 370 sub. 2 AO)

40 Pursuant to § 370 sub. 2 AO, attempted tax evasion is also liable to prosecution. An attempt at tax evasion is deemed to have been made if the taxpayer, according to his own perception, has taken a direct and immediate step towards the realisation of the offence (§ 22 StGB), but not all objective elements of § 370 AO have been realised.[56] In cases of tax evasion committed through an active deed in accordance with § 370 sub. 1 no. 1 AO, the taxpayer is deemed to have taken a direct and immediate step when submitting the incorrect tax return. In cases of failure to file a tax return under the terms of § 370 sub. 1 no. 2 AO, the attempt is deemed to commence when the statutory deadline for filing has expired.[57]

41 Under § 24 sub. 1 sent. 1, second alternative StGB (in conjunction with § 369 sub. 2 AO), the taxpayer can abandon the attempt, in which case no penalty will be incurred. In accordance with this provision, anyone who voluntarily prevents the completion of the offence will be exempt from punishment. The provisions regarding voluntary disclosure (exempting the taxpayer from punishment) do not preclude the application of the provisions concerning the abandonment of an attempt as set out in the general part of the StGB.[58] If the perpetrator has already made incorrect or incomplete statements, he must correct them. In cases of omission to file, the perpetrator must rectify any such omission and comply with his tax obligations.[59]

42 In addition, the act of abandoning the attempt must be voluntary. This is the case if the perpetrator has remained 'master of his decisions' and he still considers the execution of his criminal plan feasible, that is to say: he is neither hindered by external constraints nor rendered incapable by virtue of mental pressure from completing the offence. Whether an external circumstance triggered his rethink or whether the perpetrator was moved

[53] OLG Hamm 2.8.2001 – 2 Ws 156/01, DStRE 2002, 1095 (1096).
[54] Hüls/Reichling/Schott § 370 mn. 291.
[55] Cf. FG Hessen 7.5.2018 – 10 K 477/17, NZWiSt 2019, 137 (139); BayObLG 17.10.1975 – 4 St 81/75, NJW 1976, 635 (635).
[56] Kohlmann/Ransiek, 84th edn August 2024, AO § 370 mn. 692.
[57] Cf. BGH 12.6.2013 – 1 StR 6/13, wistra 2013, 430 (431).
[58] BGH 19.3.1991 – 5 StR 516/90, NJW 1991, 2844 (2846).
[59] Kohlmann/Ransiek, 84th edn August 2024, AO § 370 mn. 735.

by a third party to abandon the offence, does not, in and of itself, affect the autonomy of his decision.[60]

Once the result being sought by the offence is achieved, the offence has been completed and its perpetration can no longer be abandoned. For taxes that are subject to an assessment, the attempt to evade taxes through an active deed can therefore be abandoned up until the point in time when the incorrect tax assessment notice is issued; with regard to the failure to file a tax return for these types of taxes, this failure may be rectified up until the fictitious point in time when the assessment would take place. On the basis of § 168 sent. 1 AO (in conjunction with § 370 sub. 4 sent. 1 AO), the only option with regard to self-assessment taxes would be for the taxpayer to make a voluntary disclosure, as the offence would have been completed upon the expiry of the tax return deadline. **43**

7. Especially serious cases of tax evasion (§ 370 sub. 3 AO)

§ 370 sub. 3 AO lists presumptive examples of especially serious cases of tax evasion. **44** First of all, the existence of a presumptive example serves as an indication. The trial judge must then decide, taking into consideration all the circumstances of the specific case, whether or not the presumptive effect can be rebutted.[61] However, even without the existence of any presumptive example, an unspecified especially serious case may be in evidence if the offence, in the light of an overall assessment of all factors influencing the measure of penalty, with due regard to fault and culpability, differs to such a degree from the average empirical cases that a penalty outside the ordinary scale would be warranted.[62]

In this context, § 370 sub. 3 sent. 2 no. 1 AO is of great relevance in practice. Under this **45** provision, an especially serious case is generally deemed to exist if taxes are understated, or tax advantages are obtained, on a large scale. According to the BGH's case law, tax evasion in excess of 50,000 EUR is always deemed to be on a large scale.[63] Whether or not this threshold has been exceeded must be determined for each individual offence on a substantive basis. Where several acts of tax evasion have been committed concurrently in one act, these will be combined.[64] Particularly in business contexts, the above threshold may be easily exceeded in individual cases.

Moreover, the especially serious case of tax evasion as a member of a gang (*Bande*) **46** under § 370 sub. 3 sent. 2 no. 5 AO should also be kept in mind. This offence requires the formation of a gang of at least three people who band together for the purpose of repeatedly committing acts to evade value-added tax or excise duties. In the view of the BGH, such a gang may also exist within a commercial enterprise.[65] One legal author is of the opinion that the commission of tax offences as part of a gang may, in individual cases, also occur as an unspecified especially serious case, even without any connection to excise duties or value-added tax.[66]

---

[60] BGH 7.10.2021 – 1 StR 315/21, NStZ 2022, 94 (95).
[61] BGH 21.5.2019 – 1 StR 159/19, wistra 2019, 466 (467).
[62] BGH 21.8.2012 – 1 StR 257/12, NZWiSt 2013, 224 (226 et seq).
[63] BGH 27.10.2015 – 1 StR 373/15, NJW 2016, 965 (966).
[64] BGH 15.12.2011 – 1 StR 579/11, NJW 2012, 1015 (1016).
[65] Cf. BGH 15.5.2018 – 1 StR 159/17, BeckRS 2018, 24407 mn. 156 et seq.
[66] Kohlmann/Ransiek, 84th edn August 2024, AO § 370 mn. 1126.1.

8. Voluntary disclosure under § 371 AO

47 Other than general criminal law, criminal tax law provides for the possibility of achieving an exemption from punishment by correcting tax-related misdemeanours.[67] § 371 sub. 1 sent. 1 AO stipulates that whoever, in relation to all tax offences for a given type of tax, fully rectifies the incorrect particulars submitted to the revenue authority, supplements the incomplete particulars submitted to the revenue authority or furnishes the revenue authority with the previously omitted particulars shall not be punished for tax evasion. Voluntary disclosure (*Selbstanzeige*) under § 371 AO is a personal ground for exemption from punishment.[68] Although the submission of a voluntary disclosure will, first of all, trigger the instigation of criminal tax law proceedings, these proceedings will be discontinued if the requisite requirements have been met.

48 The privileged status conferred upon tax offenders by offering them the possibility of voluntary disclosure is highly controversial from a legal-policy perspective – this provision has been tightened multiple times over recent years. The BGH is of the opinion that this provision has two objectives: on the one hand, it aims to provide an incentive for tax evaders to take the initiative and open up revenue sources previously concealed from the revenue authorities by providing the correct information. On the other hand, it aims to reward the return to tax compliance.[69] Although great emphasis is generally placed on the state's fiscal interest, the opportunity to return to tax lawfulness is of equally vital importance.

49 After all, the taxpayer has a 'life-long continuing obligation' vis-à-vis the state. Consecutive tax returns are checked for plausibility and consistency. If a taxpayer wishes to disclose previously concealed tax sources, this will undoubtedly give rise to the question of why he or she did not do so in previous returns. For fear of incriminating themselves, taxpayers might therefore continue to remain non-compliant. The opportunity to make a voluntary disclosure solves this dilemma, as the taxpayer can 'come clean' across the board without fear of punishment.

a) Requirements of § 371 sub. 1 AO

50 Pursuant to § 371 sub. 1 sent. 1 AO, voluntary disclosure requires a declaration of correction to be made vis-à-vis the revenue authorities. As per § 371 sub. 1 sent. 2 AO, the declaration of correction must cover all tax offences for a given type of tax that have not yet become time-barred, but in any case at least all tax offences for a given type of tax within the last ten calendar years. The taxpayer's motivation in this regard is of no relevance, it is solely the objective return to tax compliance that is decisive.[70]

51 **aa) Personal submission and agency.** As the voluntary disclosure is a personal ground for exemption from punishment, this exemption is only granted to those perpetrators or accessories who personally make such voluntary disclosure. This does not, however, preclude the submission of a voluntary disclosure via a representative. What is decisive is that the taxpayer has caused the disclosure to be made, which is therefore attributable to him. However, the fact that voluntary disclosure made by another person may be in the best interest of the taxpayer does not suffice.[71] It is therefore advisable that this agency be adequately documented between the parties.

---

[67] Adick/Bülte FiskalStrafR/Groß Ch. 19 mn. 1.
[68] Adick/Bülte FiskalStrafR/Groß Ch. 19 mn. 3.
[69] BGH 20.5.2010 – 1 StR 577/09, NJW 2010, 2146 (2147).
[70] Adick/Bülte FiskalStrafR/Groß Ch. 19 mn. 12.
[71] KG Berlin 24.11.2016 – (4) 121 Ss 169/16 (195/16), NStZ-RR 2017, 215 (216).

Furthermore, it is always necessary that the person represented is known to the revenue authorities (so-called 'disclosed agency' (*offene Stellvertretung*)).[72] Undisclosed agency (*verdeckte Stellvertretung*) is permissible only in certain cases. Undisclosed agency is deemed to exist if the reporting person has caused the voluntary disclosure, but his identity is not disclosed to the revenue authority; on the one hand, it hinders the initiation of an investigation and can, on the other hand, also be used to protect any third parties from prosecution that may be involved in the offending. **52**

However, in the opinion of the BGH, undisclosed agency is not possible if the perpetrator or accessory would need to be set a deadline for the repayment of evaded taxes under the terms of § 371 sub. 3 AO. That said, if it is already clear at the time of making voluntary disclosure that no tax repayment claim exists, disclosed agency is possible.[73] Moreover, undisclosed agency is not possible in situations where any voluntary disclosure would be invalid by operation of § 371 sub. 2 no. 3 or no. 4 AO, and refraining from prosecution would only be possible under § 398a sub. 1 AO, as this would require the setting of a deadline for the payment of a penalty surcharge.[74] **53**

bb) Declaration of correction. Voluntary disclosures are not subject to any specific formal requirements, they do not even have to be designated as such.[75] Voluntary disclosures may also be made by inference by way of filing a tax return.[76] However, for evidentiary reasons, the submission of a voluntary disclosure and its receipt by the revenue authorities should be adequately documented.[77] It is advisable to avoid the term 'voluntary disclosure' and instead refer to a 'supplementary tax return' so as not to imply, from the outset, that this is a case of intentional tax evasion. In this way, the voluntary disclosure could later on still be interpreted as a declaration of correction under § 153 sub. 1 sent. 1 AO or a 'minor voluntary disclosure' under § 378 sub. 3 AO. **54**

Its content must comply with the requirements which the taxpayer should have already met when he or she initially performed his or her tax declaration obligations.[78] Any incorrect or incomplete information must be corrected or supplemented, any omitted information must be subsequently submitted.[79] The revenue authority must be brought into a position to assess the taxes owed, without having to enter into any further (lengthy) investigation of the facts.[80] The sole disclosure of the origin of undeclared income, without stating the specific amounts, is not sufficient.[81] Accordingly, tiered voluntary disclosure is not permitted.[82] Voluntary disclosure would be tiered if the taxpayer, as a first step, discloses the existence of non-declared income and then, only as a second step, submits precise figures.[83] **55**

In contrast, valid voluntary disclosure may be deemed to exist if the amount of the income to be declared retroactively has been estimated.[84] Minor differences between such **56**

---

[72] BGH 5.5.2004 – 5 StR 548/03, NJW 2005, 2720 (2721); KG Berlin 24.11.2016 – (4) 121 Ss 169/16 (195/16), NStZ-RR 2017, 215 (216).

[73] BGH 5.5.2004 – 5 StR 548/03, NJW 2005, 2720 (2721).

[74] Kohlmann/Schauf, 84th edn August 2024, AO § 371 mn. 89.

[75] Adick/Bülte FiskalStrafR/Groß Ch. 19 mn. 13; cf. BGH 5.5.2004 – 5 StR 548/03, NJW 2005, 2720 (2721).

[76] Kohlmann/Schauf, 84th edn August 2024, AO § 371 mn. 147.

[77] Adick/Bülte FiskalStrafR/Groß Ch. 19 mn. 13.

[78] Hüls/Reichling/Schott § 371 mn. 50.

[79] BGH 20.5.2010 – 1 StR 577/09, NJW 2010, 2146 (2147).

[80] BGH 20.5.2010 – 1 StR 577/09, NJW 2010, 2146 (2149).

[81] Klein/Jäger AO § 371 mn. 50.

[82] BGH 20.5.2010 – 1 StR 577/09, NJW 2010, 2146 (2149).

[83] Adick/Bülte FiskalStrafR/Groß Ch. 19 mn. 17.

[84] Adick/Bülte FiskalStrafR/Groß Ch. 19 mn. 19; Kohlmann/Schauf, 84th edn August 2024, AO § 371 mn. 254.

an estimate and the required content do not have a detrimental effect. However, where the amount evaded is exceeded by more than five per cent, this will not be considered minor. Where the difference is less than five per cent, an overall assessment must be carried out as a second step to see whether the content-related deviations from the legally required content of a complete voluntary disclosure can still be considered minor.[85] The assessment must also examine whether any such deviations are deliberate or whether the voluntary disclosure can still be regarded as a return to tax compliance, despite the existing deviations.[86]

57 cc) **Extent of corrections.** As per § 371 sub. 1 sent. 2 AO, the declaration of correction must cover all tax offences for a given type of tax in their entirety. The general assumption is that each individual tax law (such as EStG, UStG) constitutes a discrete tax type.[87] It is also being debated whether special forms of levying under a given tax law can also constitute separate tax types.[88] In view of the exceptional character of the provision, it is likely that the courts would opt for a more restrictive interpretation. Where several tax evasion offences have been committed concurrently in one act (*Tateinheit*, § 52 StGB), thereby affecting several tax types, voluntary disclosures will only be deemed valid if they have been made for all the relevant tax types.[89]

58 In terms of timing, voluntary disclosure must cover all tax offences for a given type of tax that have not yet become time-barred, but in any case at least all tax offences for a given type of tax within the last ten calendar years. The standard limitation period for tax evasion is five years, § 78 sub. 3 no. 4 StGB (in conjunction with § 369 sub. 2 AO). Accordingly, a minimum correction period of ten calendar years applies to these offences. For especially serious cases of tax evasion under § 370 sub. 3 sent. 2 no. 1 to 6 AO, § 376 sub. 1 AO prescribes a 15-year limitation period, so that any supplementary tax returns would have to cover 15 calendar years.

59 As the law does not mention years but rather calendar years, all of the calendar years that precede the voluntary disclosure would have to be included.[90] Pursuant to no. 11 sub. 3 AStBV (St.) 2025 (*Anweisungen für das Straf- und Bußgeldverfahren – AStBV (St) 2025*, Guidelines for criminal proceedings and proceedings on regulatory offences (tax) 2025), issued by the highest revenue authorities of the *Länder*, all tax offences committed during the calendar year in which the voluntary disclosure is made must also be included in such disclosure. Based on a 10-calendar-year period, if submitting a voluntary disclosure in 2023, corrections would be required for the calendar years 2012 to 2022 as well as any offences committed during 2023.[91] As a consequence, the submission of an abundance of documents would be required in complex situations.

b) Obligation to pay tax arrears (§ 371 sub. 3 AO)

60 Where taxes have already been understated or unwarranted tax advantages have already been derived, the parties to the offence can only attain exemption from punishment if they pay the tax that was evaded to their benefit, plus penalty interest for tax evasion. As per the wording of § 371 sub. 3 sent. 1 AO, the obligation to pay tax arrears only applies to the person who benefited from the tax evasion. When ascertaining whether something has been derived to the benefit of the perpetrator, this is not assessed solely on

---

[85] BGH 25.7.2011 – 1 StR 631/10, NJW 2011, 3249 (3255).
[86] BGH 25.7.2011 – 1 StR 631/10, NJW 2011, 3249 (3255).
[87] MüKoStGB/Kohler AO § 371 mn. 56.
[88] Hüls/Reichling/Schott § 371 mn. 60.
[89] Klein/Jäger AO § 371 mn. 42.
[90] Klein/Jäger AO § 371 mn. 57.
[91] Cf. Kohlmann/Schauf, 84th edn August 2024, AO § 371 mn. 122.

the basis of purely tax-law-related aspects but also from an economic perspective.[92] For instance, when business taxes are evaded, the party who participates in the profits may be the beneficiary.[93] Perpetrators or accessories who do not derive any benefit from the tax evasion will be exempt from prosecution, even without any additional tax payment.[94]

c) Reasons for exclusion (§ 371 sub. 2 AO)

§ 371 sub. 2 AO lists reasons for exclusion that would negate any voluntary disclosure, with the effect that the perpetrator will not be exempt from punishment. These reasons can be categorised as follows: § 371 sub. 2 sent. 1 no. 1 letters a), c), d) and e) AO specify issue-related reasons for exclusion. § 371 sub. 2 sent. 1 no. 1 letter b), no. 3 and 4 AO specify offence-related reasons for exclusion, and § 371 sub. 2 sent. 1 no. 2 AO specifies a personal reason for exclusion.[95] 61

aa) Issue-related reasons for exclusion. § 370 sub. 2 sent. 1 no. letter a) AO precludes exemption from punishment if anyone involved in the offending or his representative, or the beneficiary within the meaning of § 370 sub. 1 AO or his representative, has been notified of an audit in accordance with § 196 AO. The reason for exclusion hinges on the notification of an audit order – the mere announcement or arranging an appointment does not trigger the exclusionary effect. A valid audit order – which does not necessarily have to be lawful – is sufficient.[96] What is decisive, however, is that the exclusionary effect is limited to the material and temporal scope of the field audit advised. 62

In the absence of an audit order, or if the revenue administration is unable to prove that it has been received, the exclusionary effect materialises, in any case, upon the arrival of an official from the revenue authority to conduct the audit, § 371 sub. 2 sent. 1 no. 1 letter c) AO. Officials within the meaning of this provision include assessment tax officers, field and special auditors, tax and customs investigators as well as officers in charge of fiscal supervision or tax inspections.[97] An official is deemed to have arrived once he or she enters the audit location with the intention of conducting an audit (so-called 'doormat theory').[98] The exclusionary effect ends upon the completion of the tax audit; the taxpayer can then make a voluntary disclosure for any offences that were not discovered in the course of the audit.[99] 63

Furthermore, the arrival of an official from the revenue authority also has an exclusionary effect if said official has come to investigate a criminal or a regulatory tax offence (§ 371 sub. 2 sent. 1 no. 1 letter d) AO) or to conduct a VAT inspection, payroll tax inspection or an inspection under any other tax provisions and has identified himself (§ 371 sub. 2 sent. 1 no. 1 letter e) AO). 64

bb) Offence-related reasons for exclusion. Voluntary disclosure is precluded pursuant to § 371 sub. 2 sent. 1 no. 1 letter b) AO if anyone involved in the offending or his representative has been notified of the initiation of criminal proceedings or regulatory fine proceedings. Notification is premised on two elements: it must become unambiguously clear to the taxpayer that criminal or regulatory fine proceedings have been instituted against him, and he must have been informed about the specific allegations and there- 65

92 BGH 4.7.1979 – 3 StR 130/79, NJW 1980, 248 (248).
93 MüKoStGB/Kohler AO § 371 mn. 151.
94 WJS WirtschaftsStrafR-HdB/Pflaum Ch. 22 mn. 128.
95 Hüls/Reichling/Hüls/Reichling § 371 mn. 103.
96 Kohlmann/Schauf, Steuerstrafrecht, 84th edn August 2024, AO § 371 mn. 423, 427.
97 Adick/Bülte FiskalStrafR/Groß Ch. 19 mn. 36.
98 Hüls/Reichling/Hüls/Reichling § 371 mn. 122, 124.
99 Adick/Bülte FiskalStrafR/Groß Ch. 19 mn. 37.

fore the tax types involved.[100] This notification is not subject to any formal requirements and may also be inferred; however, in general it will be made by way of formal service in accordance with § 3 et seq. VwZG (*Verwaltungszustellungsgesetz*, Act on Service in Administrative Procedures).[101] Voluntary disclosure can be revived if the investigations under § 170 sub. 2 StPO, § 153 StPO or § 398 AO are discontinued and the *nolle prosequi* is taken on file.[102]

66 § 371 sub. 2 sent. 1 no. 3 AO precludes exemption from punishment if the tax understated or the unwarranted tax advantage derived by the taxpayer for himself or for another person exceeds the amount of 25,000 EUR per offence. This is determined on the basis of the nominal amount; where several tax evasion offences have been committed concurrently in one act, the relevant amounts must be totalled.[103] Voluntary disclosure is also precluded by operation of § 371 sub. 2 sent. 1 no. 4 AO in especially serious cases specified in § 370 sub. 3 sent. 2 no. 2 to 6 AO. However, it is possible to refrain from prosecution even if the 25,000 EUR threshold is exceeded, or in especially serious cases, provided that the requirements of § 398a AO have been met.[104]

67 cc) **Personal reason for exclusion.** A further reason for exclusion is if the tax offence has already been discovered (§ 371 sub. 2 sent. 1 no. 2 AO). According to case law, an offence has been discovered if a preliminary assessment of the offence arrives at the conclusion that a conviction is probable. However, the requirements for the probability prognosis must not be exaggerated. Discovery within the meaning of § 371 sub. 2 sent. 1 no. 2 AO cannot be equated with the usual degrees of suspicion. Accordingly, discovery does not require probable cause under §§ 170 sub. 1, 203 StPO nor the identification of the perpetrator of the tax evasion.[105]

68 The definition of discovery in § 371 sub. 2 sent. 1 no. 2 AO implies a double, two-tiered prognosis. First of all, suspicion must be assessed on an interim basis, taking into consideration all information available, which is usually still incomplete. Based on this merely provisional assessment, the set of circumstances to which the suspicion relates must also be capable, in law, to warrant a conviction for a criminal or regulatory tax offence. If it is probable that a set of circumstances exists that would warrant the conviction for a criminal or regulatory tax offence, the offence is deemed to have been discovered.[106]

69 Tax evasion may not only be discovered by the revenue or law enforcement authorities but also by private individuals. In such cases, however, discovery is premised on the assumption that the findings will be passed on to the competent authority. Similarly, the discovery may also be made by foreign authorities if the relevant country provides mutual legal assistance under international treaties.[107]

70 Further requirements are that the taxpayer was aware of the discovery of the offence or expected it, in due consideration of all relevant circumstances. Given the more sophisticated investigative possibilities and also the closer international cooperation, the requirements for the assumption of 'constructive notice', i.e., that the taxpayer knew of the discovery, are not high. At present, this reason for exclusion is primarily based on the objective requirement of discovery and only to a lesser degree on the subjective element.[108]

---

[100] MüKoStGB/Kohler AO § 371 mn. 208.
[101] Hüls/Reichling/Hüls/Reichling § 371 mn. 143.
[102] Klein/Jäger AO § 371 mn. 154.
[103] Klein/Jäger AO § 371 mn. 186; cf. BGH 15.12.2011 – 1 StR 579/11, NJW 2012, 1015 (1016).
[104] Adick/Bülte FiskalStrafR/Groß Ch. 19 mn. 46 et seqq.
[105] BGH 9.5.2017 – 1 StR 265/16, NZWiSt 2018, 379 (382).
[106] BGH 9.5.2017 – 1 StR 265/16, NZWiSt 2018, 379 (382).
[107] BGH 9.5.2017 – 1 StR 265/16, NZWiSt 2018, 379 (382).
[108] BGH 20.5.2010 – 1 StR 577/09, DStR 2010, 1133 (1136).

It therefore suffices that the taxpayer considers discovery to be possible in the light of circumstances known to the taxpayer, even if some uncertainty remains.[109]

9. Voluntary disclosure under § 389a AO

Where voluntary disclosure (exempting the taxpayer from punishment) is negated solely as a consequence of the reasons for exclusion under § 371 sub. 2 sent. 1 no. 3 or no. 4 AO, the authorities can abstain from prosecution on the basis of § 398a sub. 1 AO if the party to the offence pays the taxes evaded to their benefit plus penalty interest thereon (no. 1), and an additional 'penalty surcharge' to the state treasury (no. 2), within an appropriate period of time set for this purpose. 71

This penalty surcharge amounts to: 72

- 10 % of the evaded tax where the amount evaded does not exceed 100,000 EUR;
- 15 % of the evaded tax where the amount evaded exceeds 100,000 EUR but does not exceed 1,000,000 EUR; and
- 20 % of the evaded tax where the amount evaded exceeds 1,000,000 EUR.

Where the requirements of § 398a AO have been met, it is mandatory that the proceedings be dropped. This constitutes an impediment to prosecution.[110] No entry will be made into the German Federal Criminal Records Register (*Bundeszentralregister*).[111] However, § 389a sub. 3 AO provides for the possibility of resuming the proceedings, should the revenue authority come to the realisation that the information provided as part of the voluntary disclosure was incomplete or incorrect. 73

10. Statute of limitations

The standard limitation period for tax evasion is five years, § 78 sub. 3 no. 4 StGB (in conjunction with § 369 sub. 2 AO). For especially serious cases of tax evasion under § 370 sub. 3 sent. 2 no. 1 to 6 AO, § 376 sub. 1 AO prescribes a 15-year limitation period. By operation of § 78a sent. 1 StGB, the limitation period commences upon completion of the offence. The offence of tax evasion is generally completed upon the incorrect tax assessment. In cases of tax evasion by omission (taxes that are subject to an assessment) the decisive factor is the point in time when the perpetrator, who failed to lodge a tax return, would have been assessed at the latest (unless a tax estimate notice was issued).[112] 74

Pursuant to § 78c sub. no. 1 to 12 StGB and § 376 sub. 2 AO, the limitation period can be interrupted by certain events and resumes thereafter as per § 78c sub. 3 StGB. Under § 376 sub. 2 AO, the limitation period for a tax offence can be interrupted by the initiation of regulatory fine proceedings against the accused person. In cases of 'simple' tax evasion, prosecution would in any case be precluded if ten years have passed since completion of the offence. In especially serious cases of tax evasion, the absolute limitation period prescribed by § 376 sub. 3 AO is 37.5 years. 75

The German legislator extended the limitation period for serious cases of tax evasion in 2020 to give the authorities more time to solve the complex cum/ex cases. Nevertheless, one gets the impression here that the legislator has lost the standards. The statute of limitations (*Verjährung*) for serious tax evasion now is on a par with the statute of limitations for voluntary manslaughter. For other typical white-collar offences like fraud, however, 76

[109] OLG Schleswig-Holstein 30.10.2015 – 2 Ss 63/15 (71/15), wistra 2016, 119 (120).
[110] Hüls/Reichling/Schott AO § 398a mn. 30.
[111] MüKoStGB/Kohler AO § 371 mn. 21.
[112] Klein/Jäger AO § 370 mn. 201.

a maximum statutory limitation of 10 years applies. It is an example of how bad cases make bad law.

11. Scale of penalties and determination of penalty

77 Where someone is convicted for tax evasion, the penalty is determined over three steps: as a first step, the scale of penalties must be determined in accordance with § 370 AO. Tax evasion may be punished by imprisonment of up to five years or a fine (§ 370 sub. 1 AO). In especially serious cases under § 370 sub. 3 AO, a prison sentence ranging from six months to ten years may be imposed; the imposition of a fine is no longer an option.[113] In the event of a conviction for multiple cases of tax evasion, a penalty of up to 15 years imprisonment in total may be imposed (§ 54 sub. 2 StGB (in conjunction with § 369 sub. 2 AO)).

78 As a second step, the measure of culpability must be ascertained using the criteria listed in § 46 StGB (in conjunction with § 369 sub. 2 AO). In respect of § 370 AO, the amount evaded is the decisive criterion in the determination of the penalty.[114] As per its established case law, the BGH therefore usually imposes an unconditional term of imprisonment of no less than two years if the amount evaded is at least 1 million EUR, unless particularly weighty mitigating factors exist.[115] In any case, mitigating and aggravating factors must be weighed up against one another.

79 Factors having a mitigating effect are, in particular, when the perpetrator pays the evaded taxes and makes an early confession. In contrast, a factor with an aggravating effect exists if the perpetrator conducts his or her offending in a way that was, from the outset, designed to impair public tax revenues on a large scale, for example because the perpetrator used the 'tax office as a bank' under false pretences or because the perpetrator conducted tax evasion in other regards on a serial basis or even 'as a business'.[116]

80 As a third step, the actual sentence will be determined: most cases of petty tax crimes or tax crimes of medium gravity (amount evaded up to 50,000 EUR) are punished by a fine. In these cases, a determination of the penalty in the strictest sense usually does not occur. Instead, sentencing is based on 'regional tariffs'. The imposition of eight to twelve daily penalty units per each evaded 1,000 EUR is quite common.

81 No generalised statements can be made regarding the penalties to be expected in cases of serious or organised tax crime, as these are, ultimately, decided on a case-by-case basis. The most prominent example here are the cum/ex proceedings, in which one of the main players received a suspended sentence for hundreds of millions in – largely self-serving – tax evasion due to his full cooperation. Others involved who only had limited involvement and knowledge and therefore have been less helpful for the investigation received up to five years and six months for significantly less (not self-serving) evaded taxes.

82 Equally incomprehensible are the convictions of the so-called *spiritus rector* of the cum/ex system before the Bonn Regional Court and the Wiesbaden Regional Court. While the Bonn Regional Court decided on a sentence of eight years for tax damages in the amount of 270 million EUR, the Wiesbaden Regional Court sentenced the defendant to eight years and three months for tax damages in the amount of 113 million EUR (involving less criminal contribution). The fact that the 70-year-old defendant had to face both trials, in two states, at the same time, due to the lack of agreement between the public prosecutor's offices, seems to have been given little consideration in the sentencing.

---

[113] MüKoStGB/Schmitz/Wulf AO § 370 mn. 503.

[114] BGH 2.12.2008 – 1 StR 416/08, NJW 2009 528 (531).

[115] BGH 2.12.2008 – 1 StR 416/08, NJW 2009, 528 (532).

[116] BGH 2.12.2008 – 1 StR 416/08, NJW 2009, 528 (533).

12. Participation in tax offences

First of all, the general principles apply to participation in a tax offence (abetting, § 26 StGB, and aiding, § 27 StGB). In respect to aiding and abetting under criminal tax law, special requirements apply regarding intent on the part of the accomplice concerning actions that are not related to any particular occupation or profession (such as bank transfers overseas). Where the main perpetrator's actions are solely aimed at committing a punishable act and if the accomplice is aware of this, the accomplice is committing an act of aiding and abetting. However, if this person only considers it possible that his actions may be used to commit a criminal offence, this usually does not yet qualify as a punishable act of aiding and abetting, unless he recognises the risk that the other person will commit a punishable act to such a degree that he must be deemed to have acquiesced to providing aid resulting in the furtherance of a perpetrator who is discernibly intent on committing an illegal act.[117] **83**

II. Other tax offences

1. Customs violation (§ 372 AO)

Anyone who imports, exports or transports goods in violation of a prohibition is deemed to have committed a customs violation under § 372 AO. Bans on movement (*Bannbruch*) primarily serve public health, safety and economic policy purposes, rather than tax purposes.[118] Bans on movement are stipulated in individual laws, such as the Weapons Act (*Waffengesetz*, WaffG) and the Explosives Act (*Sprengstoffgesetz*, SprengG). Import, export or transit requires a movement of goods, driven by human will, that crosses a customs border.[119] As far as the mental element is concerned, intent is required. If the perpetrator is unaware of the ban on movement, he does not act with intent (§ 16 sub. 1 sent. 1 StGB).[120] **84**

2. Customs fraud (smuggling) committed on a serial basis or as part of a gang and involving the use of violence (§ 373 AO)

§ 373 AO is a criminal offence based on § 370 AO (in respect of evasion of import or export duties) and § 372 AO (in respect of customs violation) that includes further qualifying constituents. The basic elements of the crime are superseded.[121] Import and export duties are legally defined by Art. 5 no. 20, no. 21 Union Customs Code. These duties comprise the levies to be paid when importing or exporting goods, such as taxes on energy products, tobacco, beer and sparkling wine.[122] The qualifying elements of § 373 AO are: acting on a serial basis (sub. 1), carrying a firearm (sub. 2 no. 1), carrying any other weapon, tool or means to overcome or prevent resistance (sub. 2 no. 2) as well as perpetration as part of a gang (sub. 2 no. 3). **85**

---

117 Klein/Jäger AO § 370 mn. 224.
118 Klein/Jäger AO § 372 mn. 1.
119 MüKoStGB/Ebner AO § 372 mn. 30.
120 Klein/Jäger AO § 372 mn. 13.
121 BGH 9.11.2017 – 1 StR 204/17, wistra 2018, 133 (133).
122 Klein/Jäger AO § 373 mn. 25.

3. Purchasing and handling tax-evaded goods (§ 374 AO)

86 Anyone who purchases or otherwise acquires for himself or for a third party, sells or helps to sell products or goods in connection with which (a) excise duties, or import and export duties, have been evaded or (b) the illegal import, export or transit of goods pursuant to § 372 sub. 2 and § 373 AO has been committed, with the aim of enriching himself or a third party, is punishable under § 374 sub. 1 AO. § 374 AO is intended to combat a condition contrary to tax law that has been brought about by the predicate offence of another, which condition is perpetuated by the perpetrator for their own benefit.[123] The law enforcement authorities consider this provision a catch-all provision in cases where they are able to prove the handling of untaxed goods but not the act of tax evasion.

87 Punishability requires the existence of an item derived from an intentional and unlawful predicate offence under §§ 370, 372 sub. 2 and 373 AO; culpable conduct on the part of the predicate offender, however, is not required.[124] The procurement of such an item necessitates the bringing about of one's own actual control (or that of a third party) in accord with the predicate offender.[125] From a subjective perspective, it is necessary that the perpetrator must realise, or expect the possibility, that said item was obtained by way of an unlawful act under §§ 370, 372 sub. 2 and 373 AO. The perpetrator does not need to know exactly what kind of predicate offence has been committed, but he must envisage that it was tax evasion or customs violation.[126]

4. Forging of revenue stamps (§§ 148, 149 StGB in conjunction with § 369 sub. 1 no. 3 AO)

88 The forging of value stamps under §§ 148 and 149 StGB is a tax offence under the terms of § 369 sub. 1 no. 3 AO when it relates to revenue stamps. The legal interest protected is the security and reliability of transactions using revenue stamps.[127] Its practical relevance is currently limited to tobacco tax.

5. Aiding after the fact (§ 257 StGB in conjunction with § 369 sub. 1 no. 4 AO)

89 Aiding after the fact under § 257 StGB also falls under the tax offences under § 369 sub. 1 no. 4 AO if it relates to the tax offence of another person. The predicate offence under criminal tax law must have been committed intentionally and unlawfully; culpability is not necessary.[128] Any act that is objectively capable and, subjectively, performed with the intention of securing the benefits procured through, or resulting from the predicate offence, against their privation is deemed to be an offence as defined in § 257 sub. 1 StGB.[129] The person aiding after the fact must be acting with intent with regard to the predicate offence, detailed knowledge is not a prerequisite.

---

[123] BGH 15.4.1980 – 5 StR 135/80, NJW 1980, 2204 (2204); cf. BGH 7.11.2007 – 5 StR 371/07, NStZ 2008, 409 (411).
[124] JJR/Jäger AO § 374 mn. 17.
[125] JJR/Jäger AO § 374 mn. 30.
[126] OLG Hamm 26.2.2003 – 2 Ss 144/03, BeckRS 2003, 30308996.
[127] Kohlmann/Ransiek, 84th edn August 2024, AO § 369 mn. 36.
[128] Kohlmann/Ransiek, 84th edn August 2024, AO § 369 mn. 53.
[129] Fischer/Fischer/Lutz StGB § 257 mn. 7.

6. Impairment of VAT revenues committed on a serial basis as part of a gang (§ 26c UStG)

Anyone who fails to make an advance payment, or to pay any shortfall or an assessed tax with regard to VAT on time, either on a serial basis or as a member of a gang, may be liable to prosecution under § 26c UStG (in conjunction with § 26a sub. 1 UStG). Even if the due date is exceeded by just one day, this may be punishable.[130] This offence is thus a *genuine offence by omission*. Where this offence is committed as part of a gang, intent must also extend to the participation of another gang member; in the case of serial commission, this must match the perpetrator's *mens rea*.[131] **90**

III. Confiscation (§§ 73 et seq. StGB)

Proceeds from tax offences may be confiscated (*Einziehung*) in accordance with §§ 73 et seq. StGB. Under § 73 sub. 1 alt. 1 StGB, any asset that an accomplice receives as a result of the offence committed is deemed to have been derived from a tax offence. In cases of tax evasion, the reduced tax may constitute an asset obtained within the meaning of § 73 sub. 1 StGB, as the perpetrator saves the expenditure for these taxes.[132] Under recent case law, the time-barring of a tax claim through limitation no longer precludes confiscation (§ 73e sub. 1 sent. 2 StGB). **91**

Inter alia, confiscation (from a third party) of the gains from the tax offence, or an equivalent sum of money, may be ordered against a company (§§ 73 sub. 1, 73b sub. 1 no. 1, 73c sent. 1 StGB) if the perpetrator or accessory has acted on behalf of the company concerned. Acting 'on behalf of' must be deemed to have occurred when the person acting, during the unlawful act or, at any rate, in connection with the unlawful act, also acted in the interest of the third party, if only de facto.[133] **92**

C. Procedural law relating to criminal tax law

The procedural law relating to criminal tax law is governed by §§ 385 to 408 AO. Pursuant to § 385 sub. 1 AO, the general principles for criminal proceedings – first and foremost the StPO and the Courts Constitution Act (*Gerichtsverfassungsgesetz*, GVG) – also apply to criminal tax law proceedings, subject to any special rules that may exist. The criminal proceedings and the taxation procedure run in parallel (§ 393 AO). **93**

I. Investigating authorities

In some cases, the revenue authority itself may conduct the criminal tax law proceedings, as this authority possesses specialised expertise and is already familiar with the facts of the case by virtue of the taxation proceedings. The criminal tax law proceedings themselves are conducted by the prosecutor's office. **94**

---

130 JJR/Webel UStG § 26b mn. 11.
131 NK-WSS/Pelz UStG § 26c mn. 27.
132 BGH 5.6.2019 – 1 StR 208/19, NJW 2020, 79 (80).
133 LG Bonn 18.3.2020 – 62 KLs – 213 Js 41/19 – 1/19, BeckRS 2020, 13619 mn. 1408.

1. Revenue authorities

95 Pursuant to § 386 sub. 1 sent. 1 AO, the competent revenue authority investigates the facts of the case if it suspects the commission of a tax offence. Under the terms of § 386 sub. 2 AO, the revenue authority independently conducts the proceedings within the parameters of §§ 399 sub. 1, 400 and 401 AO, provided that the offence is solely a tax offence or an offence that is deemed equivalent to a tax offence (§ 386 sub. 2 no. 2 AO). Where an arrest warrant has already been issued against the accused person, these proceedings are precluded (§ 386 sub. 3 AO).

a) Unit that imposes regulatory fines or prosecutes

96 Within the competent revenue authority, the unit that imposes regulatory fines or prosecutes (*Bußgeld- und Strafsachenstelle*) is in charge of the criminal tax law proceedings. This unit acts as the 'tax crime prosecutor' within the revenue authority. In accordance with § 399 sub. 1 AO (in conjunction with § 386 sub. 2 AO), this unit exercises the rights and obligations of the prosecutor's office during investigations.[134] In independent proceedings, the unit is not bound by any instructions issued by the prosecutor's office.

97 After completion of the investigation, this unit decides whether to discontinue the proceedings or to apply for the issuance of an order imposing punishment if the criminal matter appears to be appropriate to be dealt with in summary proceedings (§ 400 half-sent. 1 AO). Criminal tax law proceedings involving an amount evaded in the million-euro range[135] are generally not suitable for summary proceedings; this also applies to especially serious cases under § 370 sub. 3 AO.[136] If the laying of charges is necessary, all relevant files must be passed on to the prosecutor's office.

98 However, the revenue authority may choose to refer the criminal matter to the prosecutor's office at any time (§ 386 sub. 4 sent. 1 AO). Under no. 22 sub. 1 sent. 2 AStBV (St) 2025, immediate referral is an option should special circumstances require that the investigations be continued under the responsibility of the prosecutor's office. This may be the case, for example, if telecommunication surveillance is sought (no. 1), the order of a remand in custody appears to be necessary (no. 2) or the imposition of a term of imprisonment is to be expected that cannot be ordered by way of summary proceedings.

99 In turn, the prosecutor's office may take charge of the proceedings in accordance with § 386 sub. 4 sent. 2 AO (so-called 'right of evocation'). In the opinion of the BGH, the revenue authorities must inform the prosecutor's offices about all pending tax investigations that could be subject to evocation at an early stage, at regular meetings for example.[137] This obligation to involve the prosecutor's office also – or even specifically – applies to those cases where a decision needs to be made regarding whether valid voluntary disclosure within the meaning of § 371 AO has occurred.[138]

b) Tax investigation unit

100 The tax investigation unit is another agency that forms part of the revenue authority. The activities of the tax investigation unit are set out in § 404 AO, under which it acts as the 'tax police', possessing the same powers as the police does under the StPO.[139] Pursuant to § 208 sub. 1 no. 2 AO, its purview also extends to the taxation procedure. However, in

---

[134] WJS WirtschaftsStrafR-HdB/Pflaum Ch. 22 mn. 198.
[135] Klein/Jäger AO § 400 mn. 5.
[136] No. 84 sub. 3 AStBV (St) 2025.
[137] BGH 30.4.2009 – 1 StR 90/09, NJW 2009, 2319 (2319).
[138] BGH 20.5.2010 – 1 StR 577/09, DStR 2010, 1133 (1136).
[139] WJS WirtschaftsStrafR-HdB/Pflaum Ch. 22 mn. 210.

both types of proceedings, the tax investigation unit acts solely as an investigative body, with the decision-making authority for taxation proceedings still lying with the competent tax office and, for criminal tax proceedings, remaining with the fines and criminal investigations office or the prosecutor's office.[140]

2. Prosecutor's office

The prosecutor's offices in charge of criminal tax matters are special prosecutor's **101**
offices (§ 143 sub. 4 GVG) for economic and criminal tax law matters and possess specialised expertise. As with other criminal matters, the prosecutor's office is the 'master of the investigations' in criminal tax law proceedings.[141] Where the prosecutor's office conducts the investigation, the revenue authority that would otherwise have had jurisdiction has the same rights and obligations as the agencies of the police force (§ 402 sub. 1 AO). In addition, § 403 AO grants this revenue authority the right to participate in the proceedings conducted by the prosecutor's office.

II. Investigation measures

In criminal tax law proceedings, the investigating authorities have all the usual enforce- **102**
ment measures under the StPO at their disposal (e.g., search and seizure). Requests for surrender of documents addressed to banks with regard to the accused person's business and bank account are of particular importance (§ 95 sub. 1 StPO). Banking secrecy does not exist in Germany. If the addressee of such a request refuses to comply, coercive measures may be imposed (§ 95 sub. 2 StPO). In cases where the relevant documents are located outside Germany, they may be obtained by way of mutual legal assistance. International cooperation in fiscal matters has continually intensified over recent years.

In the investigation of tax offences, the state is moreover resorting to unconventional **103**
means, such as purchasing so-called tax CDs. These CDs contain the data of taxpayers and are usually (illegally) obtained abroad and then offered to the German authorities for purchase. The German Federal Constitutional Court (*Bundesverfassungsgericht*, BVerfG) does not share concerns voiced that any data obtained in this manner are not inadmissible as they were unlawfully obtained. According to the BVerfG, the criminal offences committed by an informer must not be taken into consideration when assessing whether or not unlawfully obtained evidence is admissible, as the provisions of the StPO are only directed at the state.[142]

III. Defence

1. Defence counsel

A lawyer acting as counsel of the defence in criminal tax law proceedings has the **104**
same role as in other proceedings. Pursuant to § 392 sub. 1 half-sent. 1 AO, tax advisers, tax agents, auditors and chartered accountants may also be appointed as defence counsel insofar as the revenue administration itself conducts the criminal tax law proceedings.

---

140 WJS WirtschaftsStrafR-HdB/Pflaum Ch. 22 mn. 211.
141 WJS WirtschaftsStrafR-HdB/Pflaum Ch. 22 mn. 225.
142 BVerfG 9.11.2010 – 2 BvR 2101/09, NStZ 2011, 103 (105 et seq).

Defence by a tax adviser alone is subject to certain risks, as the tax adviser, given his or her role as an adviser, is often already involved in the case, which may result in a conflict of interests. Moreover, a successful defence also requires sufficient knowledge of criminal procedural law.

105 In any case, members of tax-advisory professions can conduct the defence in conjunction with a lawyer or a law professor (§ 392 sub. 1 half-sent. 2 AO). Particularly in complex criminal tax law proceedings that require a great degree of investigation, a joint defence would be advisable. The mutual supplementation of criminal law and tax law offers a solid foundation for developing the objectives of the defence and the defence strategy.

2. Mandatory defence

106 Some commentators argue that charges on allegations of tax offences always constitute cases of mandatory defence under § 140 sub. 2 StPO (in conjunction with § 385 sub. 1 AO)[143], as the assessment of both punishability and the tax loss incurred depends on (complex) substantive tax law. Ultimately, this is a question that must be decided on a case-by-case basis. After all, even allegations of tax offences may be based on a straightforward set of circumstances. However, the absence of mandatory defence counsel at the trial would constitute an absolute ground for appeal under § 338 no. 5 StPO (in conjunction with § 140 StPO).

3. Possibilities for discontinuance of the proceedings

107 The defence in criminal tax law proceedings takes place predominantly during the investigation and can often result in the discontinuance of the proceedings. A number of provisions allow the consensual termination of criminal tax law proceedings, without guilty verdict. Where the amount of tax evaded does not exceed 1,500 EUR the proceedings may be discontinued under the terms of § 398 sent. 1 AO[144] or § 153 StPO (in conjunction with § 385 sub. 1 AO) on the grounds of insignificance.

108 Even for higher amounts, the proceedings can still be discontinued pursuant to § 153a StPO (in conjunction with § 385 sub. 1 AO). In this case, the discontinuance would be dependent on the payment of a fine, which would be assessed on the basis of the offender's financial circumstances and the tax loss incurred. No particular upper thresholds for such losses exist, so that even in cases, where the amounts evaded run into the six digits, discontinuance may be possible in individual cases, provided that special circumstances apply.

IV. Relationship between criminal tax law proceedings and taxation proceedings

109 As per § 393 sub. 1 sent. 1 AO, the rights and obligations of taxpayers and the revenue authority during taxation proceedings and criminal proceedings are governed by the provisions applicable to the relevant proceedings. Both proceedings are run in parallel, but the position of the taxpayer is quite different: whereas the taxpayer has a duty of cooperation in connection with taxation proceedings, in criminal tax law proceedings the

143 BeckOK StPO/Krawcyk, 53. Ed. 2024, § 140 mn. 34.
144 Cf. Klein/Jäger AO § 398 mn. 4.

taxpayer can exercise their right to remain silent in accordance with § 136 sub. 1 sent. 2 StPO (in conjunction with § 385 sub. 1 AO).

Pursuant to § 393 sub. 1 sent. 2 AO, coercive measures are impermissible during criminal tax law proceedings. Should a tax audit discover sufficient indications of a tax offence by the taxpayer, § 10 BpO (*Betriebsprüfungsordnung*, Tax Audit Code) requires that the field audit only be continued once the taxpayer has been informed of the initiation of criminal proceedings. The taxpayer must also be informed that he can no longer be forced to cooperate in the taxation procedure. A breach of the prohibition to use coercive measures will result in any evidence obtained being inadmissible. **110**

D. Law on regulatory tax offences

Regulatory tax offences are governed by §§ 377 to 384a AO; further regulatory offences are set forth in the individual taxation laws. Pursuant to § 377 sub. 2 AO, the provisions of Part 1 of the Act on Regulatory Offences (*Gesetz über Ordnungswidrigkeiten*, OWiG) apply to tax-related regulatory offences insofar as the AO or other tax laws do not stipulate otherwise. Based on § 1 sub. 1 OWiG, any unlawful and censurable act which meets all the constituent elements of a tax law provision that permits sanctioning in the form of a regulatory fine constitutes a regulatory offence.[145] **111**

I. Reckless understatement of tax (§ 378 AO)

The counterpart to § 370 AO with regard to regulatory tax offences is § 378 AO (*leichtfertige Steuerverkürzung*). This provision also serves for the protection of the state's interest in complete and timely tax income.[146] Anyone who, as a taxpayer or when looking after the affairs of a taxpayer, recklessly commits any of the acts specified in § 370 sub. 1 AO, commits a regulatory offence under § 378 sub. 1 sent. 1 AO. The practical relevance of this provision is enormous, as it serves as a catch-all provision whenever intentional tax evasion cannot be proven.[147] **112**

1. Potential perpetrators

In contrast to tax evasion through an active deed in accordance with § 370 sub. 1 no. 1 AO, § 378 AO restricts the group of potential perpetrators to the taxpayer and persons looking after the affairs of the taxpayer. However, under § 33 sub. 1 AO, it is not only the tax debtor (*Steuerpflichtiger*) or the party liable for the taxes who is deemed to be the taxpayer but also anyone who is required to fulfil obligations imposed on him by tax laws.[148] In addition, this provision also includes anyone who is treated as being equivalent to the taxpayer under §§ 34, 35 AO, such as the legal representative of a legal or natural person (§ 34 sub. 1 AO). **113**

---

145 Hüls/Reichling/Groß § 377 mn. 3.
146 Hüls/Reichling/Groß § 378 mn. 2.
147 BGH 8.9.2011 – 1 StR 38/11, NStZ 2012, 160 (161).
148 Kohlmann/Heuel, 84th edn August 2024, AO § 378 mn. 11.1.

114 The constituent element 'looking after the affairs of a taxpayer' must be given a broad interpretation and includes anyone who acts on behalf of the taxpayer.[149] This is generally the case for tax advisers, tax agents, lawyers, auditors and chartered accountants.[150] On a second tier, employees or other vicarious agents (such as holders of a general commercial power of attorney, accountants and personal assistants) may also be perpetrators, provided they undertake their work with a certain degree of autonomy.[151] However, if the tax adviser only prepares the tax return for the taxpayer, who then lodges the return, the tax adviser has not autonomously entered any information within the meaning of § 378 AO.[152]

2. Acts constituting the offence, result of the offence and causality

115 The acts constituting the offence as per § 378 sub. 1 sent. 1 AO correspond to those listed in § 370 sub. 1 no. 1 to 3 AO. As a result of the offence, taxes must have been understated (§ 378 sub. 1 sent. 2 in conjunction with § 370 sub. 4 sent. 1 AO) or an unwarranted tax advantage must have been obtained.[153] A causal connection only exists if the understatement of tax is the very result of the breach of the duty of care, i.e., if it represents the realisation of the risk that is inherent in such a breach.[154]

3. Recklessness

116 The commission of a regulatory offence under § 378 sub. 1 sent. 1 AO requires recklessness (*Leichtfertigkeit*). According to the BGH's case law, anyone who disregards the degree of care which he would have been obligated, and capable, to exercise in light of the special circumstances of the individual case as well as his personal abilities and knowledge, even though it should have been obvious to him that this would result in an understatement of tax acts recklessly. Taxpayers are required to inform themselves about all tax obligations applicable to them in their sphere of life. This applies, in particular, with regard to those tax-law obligations that arise from operating a business or pursuing a professional activity.[155]

117 As a rule, no taxpayer is obligated to review every single detail of a tax return prepared by his tax adviser. Instead, he is usually entitled to rely on the tax adviser preparing the tax return correctly and completely if he has provided the tax adviser with all the information necessary to prepare the tax return.[156] However, the continued engagement of an adviser may be deemed reckless if discernible doubts as to the adviser's reliability exist.[157]

118 Whether or not an offence has been committed recklessly is essentially a question of fact which the trial judge must answer in consideration of the circumstances of the individual case as well as the knowledge of, and the sources of information available to, the perpetrator.[158] Proof of an objective breach of the duty of care alone does not suffice, the subjective elements of the offence must also be proven in their entirety.[159] It is always

---

[149] Klein/Jäger AO § 378 mn. 8.
[150] Hüls/Reichling/Groß § 378 mn. 8.
[151] Kohlmann/Heuel, Steuerstrafrecht, 84th edn August 2024, AO § 378 mn. 18.
[152] Cf. BFH 29.10.2013 – VIII R 27/10, DStR 2013, 2694 (2695).
[153] Hüls/Reichling/Groß § 378 mn. 19.
[154] FG Köln 12.9.2012 – 5 K 1348/11, DStRE 2014, 937 (939).
[155] BGH 17.12.2014 – 1 StR 324/14, wistra 2015, 191 (194).
[156] BFH 17.11.2015 – X R 35/14, BeckRS 2016, 94458 mn. 28.
[157] Kohlmann/Heuel, Steuerstrafrecht, 84th edn August 2024, AO § 378 mn. 85.
[158] BGH 13.1.1988 – 3 StR 450/87, NStZ 1988, 276 (277); cf. BFH 24.7.2014 – V R 44/13, DStR 2014, 1827 (1828).
[159] Hüls/Reichling/Groß § 378 mn. 20.

necessary to prove the existence of circumstances that should have raised doubts on the part of the perpetrator.[160]

The courts have deemed recklessness to be present in the following situations, for example: 119

- the taxpayer provides the tax adviser with a signed blank tax return form and then lodges the return which was completed by the tax adviser without checking it first;[161]
- the taxpayer, who held legal qualifications, was explicitly advised of his potential tax obligation as well as the audit powers of the tax office having local jurisdiction;[162]
- a traveller arriving at an airport with goods that must be declared uses the green exit without informing himself of the meaning of the green and red exits;[163]
- the managing director of a limited liability company acted recklessly, because he failed to comply with his control obligations in respect of VAT returns, even though he should have been aware of them.[164]

In contrast, the courts rejected recklessness in the following situations: 120

- the taxpayer, who has no tax-specific knowledge, incorrectly completes a rather abstract standard form of the revenue administration that only makes reference to the headers of statutes;[165]
- the taxpayer is mistaken about a tax issue that even professional judges are not readily aware of;[166]
- the notary retained by the taxpayer mistakenly reported a share transfer to an authority that had no jurisdiction.[167]

4. Voluntary disclosure exempting from regulatory fines (§ 378 sub. 3 AO)

In cases of reckless understatement of tax, § 378 sub. 3 AO offers the possibility of avoiding the imposition of a fine by making a voluntary disclosure (so-called 'minor voluntary disclosure'). This constitutes a personal ground for setting aside the regulatory fine.[168] Compared to the requirements under § 371 AO, the prerequisites for validity under § 378 sub. 3 AO are much less stringent. 121

a) Requirements

Pursuant to § 378 sub. 3 sent. 1 AO, no fine will be imposed if the perpetrator corrects the incorrect information submitted to the revenue authority, supplements any incomplete information submitted to the revenue authority or furnishes the revenue authority with the previously omitted information, before the perpetrator or their representative has been notified of the initiation of criminal or regulatory fine proceedings for the offence. Where tax has already been understated or tax advantages have already been obtained, a fine will not be imposed if the perpetrator pays, within a reasonable period of time allowed, the taxes that were understated to their benefit as a result of the offence. 122

Given its purpose of opening up revenue sources for the state, minor voluntary disclosure always requires that the taxpayer contributes, independently of the authority's 123

160 Kohlmann/Heuel, Steuerstrafrecht, 84th edn August 2024, AO § 378 mn. 60.
161 BayObLG 1.3.2002 – 4 St RR 2/2002, NStZ-RR 2002, 274 (275).
162 FG Baden-Württemberg 12.10.2010 – I B 176/09, BeckRS 2011, 95420.
163 BFH 16.3.2007 – VII B 21/06, DStRE 2007, 789 (790).
164 LG Berlin 8.7.2020 – (559) 246 Js 873/15 Ls Ns (17/20), BeckRS 2020, 49583 mn. 37.
165 FG Sachsen-Anhalt 9.9.1999 – 2 K 120/99, BeckRS 1999, 30813705.
166 FG Mecklenburg-Vorpommern 26.2.2003 – 3 K 639/00, BeckRS 2003, 16792.
167 FG Köln 12.9.2012 – 5 K 1348/11, DStRE 2014, 937 (938).
168 Adick/Bülte FiskalStrafR/Groß Ch. 19 mn. 61.

investigations, to the correction of previously incorrect information.[169] The declaration of correction does not have to relate to all not yet time-barred tax offences, and there is no minimum level of correction that must be met. In contrast to § 371 AO, partial disclosure is possible.[170]

124 However, as the distinction between reckless and intentional tax evasion is fluid, minor voluntary disclosure may well prove to be a boomerang. In individual cases, the law enforcement authorities could act on the presumption that the offence was committed with intent and therefore assess the validity of disclosure solely under the terms of § 371 AO. It should therefore always be carefully examined whether the documents submitted could possibly serve to prove intent.

b) Reason for exclusion

125 It is solely the notification that criminal or regulatory fine proceedings have been initiated that precludes valid voluntary disclosure. All other reasons for exclusion specified in § 371 sub. 2 AO do not apply.[171]

5. Legal consequences and statute of limitations

126 Violations of § 378 AO may be punished by a fine ranging from 5 EUR (§ 17 sub. 1 OWiG (in conjunction with § 377 sub. 2 AO)) to 50,000 EUR (§ 378 sub. 2 AO). Pursuant to § 17 sub. 4 OWiG in conjunction with § 377 sub. 2 AO, the amount of the fine may exceed the statutory maximum in order to exceed the financial benefit that the perpetrator has derived from the commission of the regulatory offence. If more than one regulatory offence has been committed, each one must be assessed separately (no aggregated penalty), § 20 OWiG (in conjunction with § 377 sub. 2 AO).[172] The reckless understatement of tax is subject to a limitation period of five years, § 384 AO.

II. Other tax-related regulatory offences

1. General minor tax fraud (§ 379 AO)

127 This provision penalises certain acts that are apt to prepare an understatement of tax or to obtain unwarranted tax advantages.[173] § 379 sub. 1 no. 1 to 6 AO sanctions general minor tax fraud by issuing incorrect documents and recording incorrect information. This provision does not require the tax claim to be compromised – it suffices that the relevant act is able to do so.[174] § 379 sub. 2, 3 AO sanctions violations of tax-related documentary and cooperation obligations. However, these variants do not require any aptitude to compromise, mere administrative disobedience is sufficient.[175] This provision applies on a subsidiary basis in relation to §§ 370 and 378 AO. Depending on the violation committed, the maximum fine may be 25,000 EUR, 10,000 EUR or 5,000 EUR.

---

[169] OLG Oldenburg 18.9.1997 – Ss 335/97 (I/102), DStRE 1998, 650 (650); different opinion: OLG Karlsruhe 30.11.1995 – 2 Ss 158/95, NStZ 1996, 197 (197), according to which the recognition of an audit result can also be sufficient.

[170] Hüls/Reichling/Groß § 378 mn. 44.

[171] Hüls/Reichling/Groß § 378 mn. 43.

[172] Kohlmann/Heuel, 84th edn August 2024, AO § 378 mn. 123.

[173] Klein/Jäger AO § 379 mn. 1.

[174] Hüls/Reichling/Reichling § 379 mn. 51.

[175] Hüls/Reichling/Reichling § 379 mn. 9.

2. Compromising withholding taxes (§ 380 AO)

Under § 380 sub. 1 AO, anyone who intentionally or recklessly fails to comply either completely, in full or on time with his or her obligation to withhold or remit to revenue authorities tax amounts that are due commits a regulatory offence. This provision is accessory to substantive tax law, with the obligations whose non-fulfilment is subject to a sanction set forth in individual tax laws (such as the obligation to withhold payroll tax, § 38b EStG). The perpetrator can only be the person who is obligated under the relevant tax law; this is a special offence.[176] This provision applies on a subsidiary basis in relation to the understatement offences of §§ 370 and 378 AO. A fine of up to 50,000 EUR may be imposed for this regulatory offence, § 380 sub. 2 AO. 128

3. Compromising VAT revenues (§ 26a UStG)

By imposing a regulatory fine, § 26a sub. 1 UStG penalises the non-payment or incomplete payment of VAT by the relevant due date.[177] Moreover, § 26a sub. 2 no. 1 to 7 UStG applies to regulatory offences that are primarily related to the issuance, retention or submission of invoices or other documents and the submission of the recapitulative statement.[178] Depending on the specific violation, the law provides for a maximum fine of either 30,000 EUR, 5,000 EUR or 1,000 EUR (§ 26a sub. 3 UStG). 129

III. Procedural law

Tax-related regulatory fine proceedings are governed by §§ 409 to 412 AO. Pursuant to § 410 sub. 1 AO, the provisions for criminal tax law proceedings apply analogously. In addition, the general procedural provisions of the OWiG also apply. However, by virtue of § 47 sub. 1 sent. 2 OWiG (in conjunction with § 410 AO), the opportunity principle (*Opportunitätsprinzip*) applies, meaning that the authority will prosecute at its reasonable discretion.[179] In accordance with no. 104 sub. 3 AStBV (St) 2025 the authority may abstain from prosecution, in particular if the understated amounts do not exceed 5,000 EUR. 130

---

176 Klein/Jäger AO § 379 mn. 6.
177 Sölch/Ringleb/Schüler-Täsch, 102. EL Oktober 2024, § 26a mn. 17.
178 BeckOK UStG/Hannisch, 42. Ed. 15.9.2024, § 26a mn. 1.
179 Hüls/Reichling/Groß § 377 mn. 4.

CHAPTER 14
MONEY LAUNDERING

Bibliography: Bülte, Zu den Gefahren der Geldwäschebekämpfung für Unternehmen, die Rechtsstaatlichkeit und die Effektivität der Strafverfolgung, NZWiSt, 2017, 276; Fels, Der Geldwäsche-Straftatbestand des § 261 StGB und die Anwaltspraxis, AnwBl Online, 2022, 621; Krauß, EU-Geldwäschepaket: Ein neues effizienteres Rahmenwerk, AnwBl Online, 2022, 602; Teichmann/Schnell, Geldwäsche im Immobiliensektor, Compliance Berater, 2022, 429; Teichmann/Wittmann, Money laundering in the United Arab Emirates: the risks and the reality, Journal of Money Laundering Control 2022, vol. 26 no. 4, 709.

Table of contents

A. Introduction: the fight against money laundering 324
B. Repressive approach: § 261 StGB 326
I. Systematic overview 326
II. Objective element 327
1. Object of the crime 327
2. Required action of an individual 328
a) Catalogue (§ 261 sub. 1 and 2 StGB) 328
b) Actions abroad (§ 261 sub. 9 StGB) 328
c) Omission 329
3. Qualification (§ 261 sub. 4 StGB); serious cases of money laundering (§ 261 sub. 5 StGB) 329
4. Restrictions and active repentance 329
a) Self-laundering (§ 261 sub. 7 StGB) 329
b) Active repentance (§ 261 sub. 8 StGB) 329
III. Subjective element 330
IV. Punishable attempt 330
V. Sanctions and measurements 330
1. Threat of criminal punishment 330
2. Confiscation (§ 73 et seqq. StGB) 330
VI. Practical questions regarding defence attorneys 331
1. Risk of culpability by accepting remuneration 331
2. Active repentance of professional secrecy bearers 332
C. The German Money Laundering Act 332
I. Background and relevance 333
II. Obliged entities (§ 2 sub. 1 GwG) 333
1. Financial sector 333
2. Traders in goods 333
3. High-risk professions 333
4. Legal professionals 334
5. Other service providers 334
III. Obligations imposed by the Money Laundering Act 335
1. Risk management (§ 4 GwG) 335
a) Components of risk management 335
b) Scope of risk management in the light of the 'risk-based approach' 336
2. Risk analysis (§ 5 GwG) 336
a) Content of the risk analysis 336
b) Obligation to document and review 336

3. Internal control and safeguard measures (§ 6 GwG) 337
4. Money Laundering Officer (§ 7 GwG) 338
a) Area of responsibility 338
b) Position within the company 338
c) Obliged entities 338
d) Duty of disclosure 338
5. Due diligence obligations (§ 10 GwG) 338
a) General due diligence obligations (§ 10 sub. 1 GwG) ... 338
b) Different forms of due diligence obligations 339
aa) Risk-oriented scope of measures 339
bb) Events triggering due diligence **339**
cc) Enhanced due diligence (§ 15 GwG) 340
6. Restrictions for in-house lawyers 340
7. Identification obligation (§ 11 et seqq. GwG) 341
a) Obligation under § 11 sub. 1 GwG 341
b) Real estate agents 341
c) Exemption clause (§ 11 sub. 3 GwG) 341
d) Cooperation duty (§ 11 sub. 6 GwG) 341
8. Transparency register (§§ 18 et seqq. GwG) 342
9. Reporting obligation of obliged entities (§§ 43 et seqq. GwG) 343
a) General information on the reporting duty 343
b) Reporting obligation for supervisory authorities (§ 44 GwG) 344
c) Specifics regarding the report 344
aa) Relation to the criminal complaint (§ 158 StPO) 344
bb) Form of reporting 344
cc) Reporting obligation for lawyers 344
dd) Reporting obligation (§ 43 GwG) versus self-incrimination (§ 261 sub. 9 sent. 1 StGB) 345
d) Recommended procedure after filing the report 346
aa) Hold of transactions 346
bb) 'Tipping-off ban' 346
IV. Supervision by authorities: BaFin 346
V. Recent developments: EU Money Laundering Package 347
1. AMLA 347
2. EU Money Laundering Regulation 347
3. Sixth Money Laundering Directive 348
4. Regulation on transfer of funds 348
D. Conclusion 349

A. Introduction: the fight against money laundering

1 Money laundering is a problem on the national as well as on the international level, and both policymakers and lawmakers are presented with a hydra-like challenge – for every head chopped off, it regrows two more. The fight against money laundering is complex. Both in Europe and in Germany, the measures and attempts aiming at keeping this highly volatile phenomenon under control have been, are being and will continue to be updated on a frequent basis.

2 On the national level, Germany targets money laundering from two angles. While the German Criminal Code (*Strafgesetzbuch*, StGB) establishes a criminal offence in § 261 StGB, the Money Laundering Act (*Geldwäschegesetz*, GwG) is a pre-emptive regulation

for certain persons and business areas and obliges them to diligent and transparent course of action.

The application of the relevant statutes in practice faces several difficulties. Fre- 3
quent changes and updates of the law, complicated wording of § 261 StGB over time, its wide scope of application and the variety of obligations under the Money Laundering Act (GwG) are complicating the fight against money laundering. Notwithstanding, the phenomenon has gained more and more attention and continues to be a challenge. The number of money laundering reports keeps skyrocketing. The Financial Intelligence Unit (FIU), a special force established within the German customs authorities in order to combat money laundering, registered more than 300,000 reports in 2023, almost twice as many as in 2020.[1] Not least, the negative public perception was shaped by Germany's international reputation as a 'paradise for money launderers'[2], a problem which is particularly evident on the real estate market – money laundering is facilitated since Germany still allows cash payments for properties, and property owners are not subject to a reporting obligation (in contrast to the financial sector).[3]

Although the legislative intention to fight money laundering is persistent, the German 4
legislator is continuously facing problems with the implementation of its own agenda. The development of the legal fight against money laundering began with the Act to Combat Illicit Drug Trafficking and other forms of Organized Crime in 1992,[4] which introduced the provision of § 261 StGB to the German Criminal Code. In the following year, the German Money Laundering Act became effective.[5] Both Acts are the result of international and European developments that made it mandatory to criminalize money laundering.

Until this day, international and European developments have a significant impact 5
on the German legislative course. On the international level, the Financial Action Task Force (FATF) develops legal guidelines and measures to fight money laundering, provides recommendations on an effective implementation of such measures and monitors the corresponding processes. On the European level, the German law on money laundering is mainly based on EU Directives, which aim to achieve unification and harmonization amongst the Member States, hereby also taking the FATF recommendations into account. The interpretation of the German law must therefore always be carried out as guided by European requirements. Within these requirements, the German concept of the fight against money laundering consists of a repressive and a preventive angle. The repressive approach (as laid down in § 261 StGB) serves the criminal prosecution of money laundering offences. The preventive approach on the other hand aims to prevent the occurrence of money laundering at its outset. For this purpose, the German Money Laundering Act (GwG) establishes legal obligations for certain economic actors. The following will provide an overview of both approaches. While it is necessary to be aware of potential criminal liability, and particularly with regard to a trend towards a limitless expansion of § 261 StGB (all-crimes approach), it may well be even more important for businesses to deal with the preventive angle of the GwG. Its requirements for risk management and the extent of the obligations imposed by the law enable businesses to effectively prevent criminal liability.

---

[1] Annual Report 2023, Financial Intelligence Unit, p. 12, <https://www.zoll.de/SharedDocs/Downloads/DE/Links-fuer-Inhaltseiten/Fachthemen/FIU/fiu_jahresbericht_2023_en.pdf?__blob=publicationFile&v=2> (last accessed: 7.4.2025).

[2] MAH WirtschaftsStrafR/Berndt/Müller/Hümmrich-Welt § 21 mn. 1.

[3] Teichmann/Schnell CB 2022, 429; Teichmann/Wittmann Journal of Money Laundering Control 2022, Vol. 26 no. 4, 709 et seqq.

[4] BGBl. 1992 I 1302.

[5] BGBl. 1993 I 1770.

6 Despite this two-pronged approach, the fight against money laundering remains a great challenge for German authorities. The German law enforcement authorities are increasingly focusing on the investigation of the predicate offence associated with money laundering. Since the burden of proof for offences under § 261 StGB remains as high as general criminal law standards demand, the actual prosecution of money laundering in practice tends to fade into the background. Statistical surveys show that although a growing number of investigation proceedings are initiated by the authorities, only few cases are concluded. In 2020, 36.371 investigation proceedings for money laundering opened by German investigation authorities were subsequently discontinued. Only 629 proceedings resulted in indictments, and a further 773 in penal orders.[6]

7 In addition to the difficulties encountered in practice, international developments frequently make it necessary to adjust the existing legal framework on money laundering. On 11 February 2021, and in fulfilment of the obligation to implement the European Union Directive 2017/1673, the German legislator passed a law to improve the fight against money laundering with criminal legal measures (*Gesetz zur Verbesserung der strafrechtlichen Bekämpfung der Geldwäsche*). A reform of the criminal offence (§ 261 StGB) was at the core of the reform which not only implemented the provisions of the EU Directive but exceeded its requirements with an encompassing expansion (all-crimes approach). Hence, the new version of § 261 StGB significantly expanded criminal liability for money laundering. According to the explanatory remarks of the legislator, the revised version intends to provide an improvement to the practicability and puts a stronger focus on law enforcement by enabling an even more intensive prosecution.[7] At the same time, the reform aimed at facilitating the provisions on the standard of proof. The fight against money laundering has seen yet another reform, aiming at facilitating the work for investigation authorities and courts. While there are doubts about its actual practicability and the attempt to cover everything aroused quite some criticism, the all-crimes approach could launch a new era for the fight against money laundering.

B. Repressive approach: § 261 StGB

I. Systematic overview

8 § 261 StGB is part of division 21 of the German Criminal Code ('Aiding after the fact and handling stolen goods'). Just like the other provisions of this division, money laundering classifies as an affiliated crime which presupposes a preceded unlawful act (within the meaning of § 11 sub. 1 no. 5 StGB) from which the objects of money laundering originate. While the Criminal Code generally words and defines its offences in a simple form to capture criminal actions, the wording of § 261 StGB is quite long and complicated.

9 For a basic understanding, the offence is structured as follows:

10 The acts required to fulfil the offence of money laundering are written down in sub. 1 and 2 of the provision. Sub. 3 determines the criminal liability of the attempt.

11 The range of penalties has been adjusted insofar as the former minimum penalty of three months' imprisonment has been dropped for the basic offence. The lower end of

[6] Financial Action Task Force, Anti-money Laundering and Counter-terrorist Financing Measures – Mutual Evaluation Report – Germany, 2022, p. 78, <https://www.fatf-gafi.org/content/dam/fatf-gafi/mer/Mutual-Evaluation-Report-Germany-2022.pdf> (last accessed: 7.4.2025).

[7] BT-Drs. 19/24180, 20.

the range of sentences was extended, and it is now possible to impose a penalty payment instead (cf. § 261 sub.1 sent. 1 StGB).

Sub. 4 provides for an increased range of sentences, with three months up to five years imprisonment in case the perpetrator acted as a person entrusted with public service functions pursuant to the German Money Laundering Act (cf. § 2 GwG). Sub. 5 establishes a sentencing rule (from six months to ten years) in serious cases. Sub. 6 now establishes criminal liability for recklessness. This causes a massive increase in criminal liability, especially considering the deletion of the former catalogue of predicate offences (all-crimes approach, see → mn. 19 et seqq.). **12**

Following a ruling by the German Federal Constitutional Court based on Art. 12 GG and the constitutional right of professional freedom, § 261 sub. 1 sent. 3 and sub. 6 sent. 2 StGB target the special constellation where a defence counsel is involved in a transaction. The clauses establish the 'criminal defence counsel privilege' in order to protect the client lawyer relationship as well as the professional practice of criminal lawyers. Pursuant to this rule, a criminal defence lawyer can only be held liable for money laundering by accepting a fee for his work if he had reliable knowledge of its illegal origin at the time of the receipt. **13**

Sub. 7 regulates the special case of 'self-laundering' (*Selbstgeldwäsche*): anyone who is liable for the participation in the predicate offence is only punishable under sub. 1–6 if he or she places the object on the market and thereby conceals its unlawful origin. **14**

Sub. 8 offers the possibility of active repentance; anyone who voluntarily reports his offence to the competent authority or who voluntarily initiates such a report is free of punishment if the following conditions are met: the offence must have gone undetected, and the perpetrator must be aware of this fact. Furthermore, impunity can be achieved under the same conditions if the perpetrator causes the seizure of the object. **15**

Acts committed abroad can also be suitable predicate offences for money laundering. § 261 sub. 9 no. 2 letter a to h StGB lay down the conditions for such criminal liability. **16**

Sub. 10 contains a reference to the provisions on confiscation under § 74a StGB. § 261 sub. 10 sent. 3 StGB now stipulates that §§ 73 to 73e StGB are expressly applicable in addition to §§ 74 and 74a StGB. **17**

The following paragraphs illustrate the necessary fact pattern for criminal liability under § 261 StGB. As any criminal offence, both the objective and the subjective fact pattern must be met to establish criminal liability. **18**

II. Objective element

1. Object of the crime

§ 261 StGB requires an object that originates from an unlawful predicate offence. All objects that contain an asset are suitable objects for money laundering. This includes not only movable and immovable property, but also rights. After the 2021 reform, this object can originate from *any sort* of illegal act. In the former version of § 261 StGB, the object had to originate from an offence listed in the catalogue of the old version of § 261 sub. 1 sent. 2 StGB. **19**

As mentioned above, the extensive all-crimes approach is one of the most significant innovations of the recent legal adjustments, and the lawmakers have completed a paradigm shift by abolishing the previous catalogue of predicate offences. Any criminal offence can be considered as a suitable predicate offence for money laundering now. In **20** general, the predicate offence must have been committed, but even a punishable attempt (as defined by the StGB for certain offences) of the predicate offence is sufficient.

21 When it comes to the origin of the incriminated object, the revised version of § 261 StGB still demands that it 'derived' from an unlawful act. The term has a very broad scope of application and includes surrogate objects (after exchange and conversion).[8] The causal connection between the object and the predicate offence is sufficient, which is the case whenever the object has its cause in the unlawful act[9] – as cash received from drug deals, for instance. The object is further considered to be 'derived' from an unlawful act in the case of *intermixture*. The deposit of incriminated money into a bank account which already holds a credit balance, for example, causes the whole account balance to be tainted and therefore suitable as an object of crime for money laundering.[10]

22 Overall, the new all-crimes approach in combination with the broad understanding of the term 'derived' and the criminal liability for recklessness (now established in sub. 6) cause a massive increase of criminal liability.

2. Required action of an individual

a) Catalogue (§ 261 sub. 1 and 2 StGB)

23 Another adjustment that was brought upon by the reform and implementation of the latest EU Directive[11] (see → mn. 7) was the restructuring of the acts required by § 261 StGB. § 261 StGB now penalizes anyone who *conceals* an object resulting from an illegal act (§ 261 sub. 1 sent. 1 no. 1 StGB; e.g. ransom money; fraudulently obtained funds; counterfeit money; bribes) with the intention of thwarting the discovery, confiscation or determination of the origin, *exchanges*, *transfers* or *spends* it (§ 261 sub. 1 sent. 1 no. 2 StGB), *procures* it for himself or a third party (§ 261 sub. 1 sent. 1 no. 3 StGB) or *keeps* or *uses* it for himself or a third party if he knew the origin of the object at the time at which he obtained it (§ 261 sub. 1 sent. 1 no. 4 StGB). Moreover, pursuant to § 261 sub. 2 StGB, anyone who conceals facts that may be of importance for finding, confiscating, or determining the origin of an object under sub. 1 shall be punished. Despite the recent restructuring of § 261 StGB, various questions regarding the interpretation of the codified actions remain unclarified.

24 Lawyers are particularly at risk of criminal liability if, as a result of an invoice issued by them, money is booked to their account which originates from an account containing incriminated funds. In this case, the variants of obtaining, keeping or using an incriminated object within the meaning of § 261 sub. 1 sent. 1 no. 3 and 4 StGB may apply.[12]

b) Actions abroad (§ 261 sub. 9 StGB)

25 Acts committed abroad have already been considered suitable predicate criminal offences in the former version of § 261 StGB. The previous version assumed that such acts abroad could only lead to criminal liability if they were also punishable at the foreign location (*lex loci*). This principle is now defused by the introduction of a catalogue consisting of eight criminal offences that were determined by an EU Convention. An action abroad is therefore now covered by the money laundering offence if threatened with punishment in the country of action *or* if it falls under the catalogue.

---

[8] Fischer StGB § 261 mn. 11.
[9] BGH 18.2.2009 – 1 StR 4/09, BeckRS 2009, 8881.
[10] Fels AnwBl Online 2022, 621; Glaser p. 12 et seqq.
[11] Directive (EU) 2018/843.
[12] Fels AnwBl Online 2022, 621.

c) Omission

It is possible to commit money laundering by omission. In this context, the German Money Laundering Act (GwG) becomes particularly relevant, as the omission is usually met if the obliged entity (such as financial institutions, insurance companies, investment businesses or real estate agents) does not fulfil its obligations under the Money Laundering Act. 26

For any concerned business, it is therefore essential to be adequately informed about the existing obligations regarding the reporting obligation and the required risk management. The second part of this article goes into detail, and its perusal provides a corresponding insight. 27

3. Qualification (§ 261 sub. 4 StGB); serious cases of money laundering (§ 261 sub. 5 StGB)

§ 261 StGB also contains increased criminal liability qualifications. Pursuant to § 261 sub. 4 StGB, whoever commits an act according to sub. 1 or sub. 2 as an obliged party according to § 2 GwG will be punished with imprisonment from three months to five years. This reference illustrates the accessoriness of the provision to the Money Laundering Act. 28

Above that, § 261 sub. 5 StGB regulates particularly serious cases, which are threatened with a penalty of six months up to ten years. § 261 sub. 5 sent. 2 StGB determines that a particularly serious case is given if the perpetrator acts commercially or as a member of a gang that has been created to continually commit money laundering. 29

4. Restrictions and active repentance

a) Self-laundering (§ 261 sub. 7 StGB)

§ 261 StGB contains certain restrictions. Pursuant to § 261 sub. 7 StGB, anyone who is already liable to prosecution for participating in the predicate criminal offence can only be punished if he or she introduces the object to the market and thereby conceals its unlawful origin, so-called 'self-laundering'. According to German case law, it does not matter whether the perpetrator has completed or even terminated the predicate offence. Even a conviction according to the principles of alternative findings is sufficient. 30

Conversely, the mere self-interested exploitation of the object obtained without disguising circumvention of mechanisms to protect the integrity of the economic and financial circuit (such as the use of cash to carry out everyday transactions) can be expected from the previous offender and therefore does not constitute an independent injustice e compared to the predicate offence. 31

b) Active repentance (§ 261 sub. 8 StGB)

Furthermore, § 261 sub. 8 StGB contains the possibility of active repentance, a personal reason for impunity. Anyone who voluntarily reports his or her offence to the competent authority or voluntarily arranges for such a report to be given, will not be penalized if the offence had not already been discovered (completely or partially) at that time. It is required that the perpetrator has knowledge about the fact that the offence has not been discovered yet or, based on a reasonable assessment of the situation, could have expected that it has not been discovered yet. Finally, the perpetrator must cause the seizure of the object in the cases of § 261 sub. 1 or 2 StGB in order to receive the privilege of active repentance. 32

III. Subjective element

33 As any other criminal offence, § 261 StGB demands that the perpetrator acts with intent. This includes any form of intent; conditional intent (*dolus eventualis*) is therefore sufficient. The subjective requirements are fulfilled if the perpetrator at least approvingly accepts that the object originates from an unlawful predicate offence, and it is not necessary that the money launderer possesses knowledge of either the specific previous perpetrator or the exact details of the unlawful predicate offence.

34 Even recklessness may be punishable regarding the criminal origin of the object (§ 261 sub. 6 StGB). According to existing case law, an action is considered to be reckless if the criminal origin of the object is almost inevitable and the perpetrator acts nevertheless, ignoring this fact due to gross negligence or indifference.[13]

35 § 261 sub. 1 sent. 3 and sub. 6 sent. 2 StGB increase the subjective requirements regarding the special case of the **attorney privilege**: anyone who accepts a fee for his work as a criminal defence lawyer is only acting with intent in the cases of sentence 1 number 3 and 4 if he had reliable knowledge of its origin at the time of accepting the fee. Regarding the cases of § 261 sub. 1 no. 3 and 4 StGB, the increased criminal liability for recklessness (§ 261 sub. 6 sent. 1 StGB) does not apply to the criminal defence lawyer accepting a fee. With the inclusion of these regulations, the legislator has implemented rulings of the Federal Constitutional Court.[14] Reversely, this means that the privilege does not apply to other professional groups (particularly to lawyers and tax consultants working under civil law).

IV. Punishable attempt

36 Pursuant to § 261 sub. 3 StGB, the attempt of money laundering is punishable.

V. Sanctions and measurements

1. Threat of criminal punishment

37 If the act is committed with intent, money laundering is punished with imprisonment of up to five years or a monetary fine, cf. § 261 sub. 1 sent. 1 StGB. Pursuant to sub. 6, cases of recklessness are punished with a prison sentence of up to two years or a fine. Sentences for fulfilling the qualification (§ 261 sub. 4 StGB) or a particularly serious case (§ 261 sub. 5 StGB) range between three months up to five years and, in case of the latter, six months to ten years.

2. Confiscation (§ 73 et seqq. StGB)

38 An important scheme when it comes to prosecuting money laundering offences is the confiscation of objects. According to § 261 sub. 10 sent. 1 StGB, objects related to the offence may be confiscated. The following outlines the relevant regulations on confisca-

[13] Representative of many: BGH 17.07.1997 - 1 StR 791/96, NStZ 1998, 42 (44) = BGHSt 43, 158 (168); BGH 24.1.2006 - 1 StR 357/05 NStZ 2006, 343 = NJW 2006, 1297 (1298 et seq.) = BGHSt 50, 347 (351); 24.6.2008 - 5 StR 89/08NJW 2008, 2516 (2517 et seq.).

[14] Fischer StGB § 261 mn. 44 et seqq.

tion and provides an overview of the specifics when it comes to confiscation and money laundering:

Primarily the addressee of a confiscation measure must be determined. In the usual scenario, confiscation is directed against the owner or the person who has a right to the object, cf. § 74 sub. 3 StGB, according to which confiscation is only admissible if the perpetrator is the owner of the affected object or is an entitled person. § 261 sub. 10 sent. 2 StGB orders the application of § 74a StGB though, which derogates the principle established above. The exemption made in § 74a StGB demands that the owner or entitled person contributed at least recklessly to the fact that the object was being used as a crime instrument or that it became an object of the crime. Alternatively, it is sufficient that the owner/entitled person has acquired the object in question in a reprehensible manner and in knowledge of the circumstances that would have permitted the confiscation. In both cases, the requirements must be fulfilled at the time of the confiscation decision. **39**

Furthermore, the object must be suitable for confiscation. § 261 sub. 10 sent. 3 StGB points out that the confiscation of **criminal proceeds** (pursuant to §§ 73 to 73e StGB) not only remains applicable but has priority over confiscating the *objects of crime* (cf. § 74 sub. 2 StGB, optionally in conjunction with §§ 74a and 74c StGB). **40**

Pursuant to § 73 sub. 1 StGB, the confiscation of the **proceeds of a crime** presupposes that the perpetrator or accomplice has obtained something through or for an unlawful act. The key condition is therefore the unlawful act (in the sense of § 11 sub. 1 no. 11 StGB) itself. Assets or objects are obtained through an unlawful act if the perpetrator or participant received them in any phase during the realization of the constituent elements of the offence, with the prey as the most obvious example. Benefits are obtained *for* an unlawful act if they are granted in return for an illegal action (rather than being based on the realization of the facts). **41**

The area of independent confiscation has also witnessed some significant changes in the context of the recent legal adjustments which are particularly relevant for the offence of money laundering: the court may now independently order that an object will be confiscated or rendered unusable, if it is impossible to prosecute or convict a specific person for a criminal offence, (provided that the conditions of the measurements are met in all other respects), cf. § 76a sub. 1 sent. 1 StGB. This adjustment allows to confiscate profits generated from the use of incriminated objects or even their subsequent surrogates (for example rental income). Since the catalogue of § 76a sub. 4 sent. 3 StGB also refers to money laundering (cf. § 76a sub. 4 sent. 3 no. 1f StGB) which – above that – has a very large area of application due to the new all-crimes approach, the area of application for an independent confiscation has been considerably expanded. **42**

VI. Practical questions regarding defence attorneys

1. Risk of culpability by accepting remuneration

A defence lawyer's remuneration still poses a risk for him in practice. Even though the German legislator recently included the attorney privilege in § 261 sub. 1 sent. 3 and sub. 6 sent. 2 StGB (see → mn. 35) and tried to create a degree of legal certainty when it comes to the threat of committing money laundering by accepting a fee, defence lawyers need to apply a risk assessment. The external circumstances of the payment are important indicators when it comes to determining whether the attorney had a certain level of knowledge about the origin of the money that was used to pay the fees. It is advisable to precisely document the process, regardless of the type of payment. In view of the increased **43** standard of care for cash payments, it is advisable to give preference to cashless payment transactions.

2. Active repentance of professional secrecy bearers

44 § 261 sub. 8 StGB contains the possibility of active repentance (→ mn. 32). Anyone who voluntarily reports the offence to the competent authority or voluntarily arranges for such a report to be given will not be penalized if the offence had not already been discovered (completely or partially) at that time. § 261 sub. 8 StGB seems to collide with § 203 StGB, the criminal offence of violation of private secrets. Therefore, the question arises as to how § 261 sub. 8 StGB must be viewed in connection with persons that are subject to professional secrecy (for example physicians, pharmacists, lawyers etc.). According to § 203 sub. 1 StGB, a bearer of professional secrecy is subject to punishment if he or she unlawfully discloses another's secret, in particular a secret relating to that person's personal sphere of life or to a business or trade secret which was revealed or otherwise made known to them in their capacity, and it depends on the interpretation of the term 'unlawfully' in § 203 StGB. There is a controversy whether § 48 GwG ('Exemption from liability') can be used as a justification for the disclosure of the information[15] or if this constellation must be treated according to the principles established for conflict of duties[16]. The latter would mean that a criminal defence attorney, who makes use of the personal benefits of sub. 8 regularly commits the offence of betrayal of secrets (§ 203 sub. 1 no. 3 StGB).[17] More detailed information on this conflict can be found under 'reporting obligation for lawyers' (see → mn. 122 et seqq.).

C. The German Money Laundering Act

45 Anti-money laundering measures are based on two general approaches. Complementary to the repressive approach against individuals (§ 261 StGB), legislative measures also aim on the prevention of money laundering. In Germany, this goal is mainly manifested in the Money Laundering Act (*Geldwäschegesetz*, GwG), which came into force on 26 June 2017 and stipulates extensive due diligence obligations. These obligations entail a direct relation of this preventive measures to the combating of money laundering under criminal law. Violations of the GwG's obligations can lead to criminal prosecution as reckless or even intentional money laundering. The GwG indirectly extends beyond its directly scope of application. It is mandatory for large, but also medium-sized companies to implement an appropriate compliance system to prevent money laundering that meets the requirements of the GwG. The respective functionaries in a company must have in-depth knowledge of its regulations.

---

[15] cf. e.g. BeckOK StGB/Ruhmannseder, 64. Ed. 1.11.2024, § 261 mn. 74.

[16] cf. Winkler Strafbarkeit des Strafverteidigers p. 221 et seqq.; cf. also BVerfG 30.3.2004 - 2 BvR 1520, 1521/01, NStZ 2004, 259; Schrader p. 91 et seqq.

[17] BeckOK StGB/Ruhmannseder, 64. Ed. 1.11.2024, § 261 mn. 74.

I. Background and relevance

The Money Laundering Act is based on the Fourth EU Money Laundering Directive (EU 2015/849). This legislation significantly expands the circle of obliged persons as well as the obligations affecting them. The most relevant innovations were the introduction of risk management, the establishment of an electronic transparency register, the introduction of a new central office at customs (FIU) and the obligation to submit suspicious transaction reports electronically only. **46**

On 1 January 2020, the revised Money Laundering Act came into force, which was amended due to the Fifth EU Money Laundering Directive (EU 2018/843). The revised Act added important regulations to further strengthen the framework for the prevention of money laundering and terrorist financing. **47**

II. Obliged entities (§ 2 sub. 1 GwG)

§ 2 sub. 1 GwG determines the addressees of the Money Laundering Act by defining the obliged entities (*Verpflichtete*). **48**

The GwG is not only aimed at companies and financial institutions, but also at a broader group of natural persons. However, the persons listed in § 2 GwG are only subject to the obligations laid down by the Money Laundering Act to the extent that they act in the exercise of their trade or profession. Knowledge of an unlawful asset transfer, for example, does not trigger any obligations under the Money Laundering Act if it is exclusively obtained in a private way.[18] **49**

The group of obliged entities can be classified into five categories: **50**

1. Financial sector

Companies in the financial sector are initially the 'natural addressees' of the GwG. This group includes credit institutions (no. 1), financial services institutions (no. 2), payment institutions and electronic money institutions (no. 3), certain payment and e-money institutions based in another contracting state of the Agreement on the European Economic Area, independent businesspersons who distribute or redeem the electronic money of a credit institution (no. 5), financial companies (no. 6), insurance undertakings (no. 7), insurance intermediaries (no. 8) and asset management companies (no. 9). **51**

2. Traders in goods

The second category includes dealers of goods, art brokers and art storekeepers (insofar as warehousing takes place in duty-free zones) (no. 16). **52**

3. High-risk professions

There are certain professions that carry an increased risk of money laundering. Therefore, the legislator considers them as obliged under the Money Laundering Act. This includes estate agents (no. 14), auditors, chartered accountants, tax advisors, authorised tax agents (no. 12) as well as agents for payment services and e-money agents in the sense of § 1 sub. 9 and 10 ZAG. **53**

---

[18] Diergarten/Fraulob GwG § 2 p. 135.

4. Legal professionals

54 Lawyers and legal advisors who are member of a bar association as well as patent attorneys and notaries may also be obliged as far as they are involved in planning or carrying out certain activities for their clients (no. 10 lit. a). Furthermore, § 2 sub. 1 no. 11 GwG stipulates that even not bar admitted legal advisors as well as persons registered under § 10 RDG are also obliged, insofar as they carry out activities mentioned in § 2 sub. 1 no. 10 GwG. There has been controversy in the past as to whether an in-house lawyer is considered an obliged entity within the meaning § 2 sub. 1 no. 10 GwG. However, since the revised version of the Money Laundering Act came into force on 1 January 2020, there is no longer any doubt that in-house lawyers are also subject to money laundering obligations. § 10 sub. 8a GwG now explicitly mentions in-house lawyers for the first time. Although § 10 sub. 8a GwG does not expressly establish the position of an in-house lawyer as an obliged entity, it presupposes such position. The provision serves as a clarification of the legislator's intention to include in-house lawyers in the circle of those obliged under § 2 sub. 1 no. 10 GwG.

55 Lawyers and other professionals mentioned in § 2 sub. 1 no. 10 lit. a) aa) to ee) GwG are considered as obliged entities if they provide services to their clients in relation to buying and selling real estate or commercial companies, asset management (esp. money and securitites), opening or managing bank, savings or securities accounts, organizing funds for the purpose of establishing, operating or managing companies or partnerships as well as establishing, operating or managing (trust) companies, partnerships or similar arrangements.

56 The same obligations arise for this group of people if they carry out financial or real estate transactions in the name and for the account of their clients (no. 10 lit. b), advise the client on their capital structure, industrial strategy, or related issues (no. 10 lit. c), provide advice or services in connection with any merger or acquisition (no. 10 lit. d) or participate in the establishment, operation or administration of trust companies, corporations or similar structures (no. 10 lit. e).

57 It is sufficient that the lawyer (legal attorney/patent attorney/notary) engages in the mere planning and implementation of one of the transactions mentioned above; a representation of interests is not necessary. The provisions of the Money Laundering Act are already applicable if independent and impartial advice is provided.[19]

58 Apart from the activities just listed, lawyers do not fall within the scope of the Money Laundering Act. Criminal defence or the mere conduction of civil proceedings thus do not trigger any obligation under the Money Laundering Act. Hence the following rule applies:

1. lawyers generally do not have to identify their clients when initiating a business relationship that relates exclusively to legal advice;[20]
2. criminal defence attorneys (who exclusively operate as such) are not obliged under the GwG.[21]

5. Other service providers

59 No. 13 includes service providers for companies and trust assets or trustees who do not belong to the professions already mentioned under no. 10 to 12.

---

19 MAH WirtschaftsStrafR/Berndt/Müller/Hümmrich-Welt § 21 mn. 184.
20 Diergarten/Fraulob GwG § 2 p. 148.
21 Herzog/Figura GwG § 2 mn. 151.

III. Obligations imposed by the Money Laundering Act

1. Risk management (§ 4 GwG)

According to § 4 sub. 1 GwG, the obliged entities must have money laundering risk management in place. These risk management measures must be appropriate with regard to nature and scope of the business activities, cf. § 4 sub. 1 GwG. The GwG thus ties in with the risk-based approach of the FATF Recommendations and obliges to implement an adequate and effective risk management system.[22] Contrary to the previous wording of the Anti-Money Laundering Act, the revised law no longer explicitly provides the obligation for risk management only for specific institutions/companies, but is now generally directed at all obliged entities equally. The distinction between obliged entities within the financial sector and those outside was abandoned with the new version of the law (just as intended by the FATF Recommendations and implementation of the Fourth EU Money Laundering Directive).[23] 60

This equal treatment of different groups, however, meets with criticism as it does not sufficiently take into account the individual and different susceptibility to money laundering of different economic branches and industries.[24] 61

a) Components of risk management

Pursuant to § 4 sub. 2 GwG risk management includes risk analysis (§ 5 GwG) and internal security measures (§ 6 GwG). Risk management is considered to be effective if it easily allows the obliged entity to identify a suspicious transaction, analyse its risk factors and, based on the previous analysis, initiate the required process to prevent money laundering.[25] 62

The Money Laundering Act stipulates that responsibility for risk management lies with the management level. Pursuant to § 4 sub. 3 GwG, a member of the management is to be appointed to bear responsibility for risk management and compliance with the relevant provisions. The assignment to management level shows the importance of risk management and stipulates that management level cannot transfer responsibility when it comes to such important preventive measures. In accordance with this legislative assessment, a member of the management must approve the risk analysis and the internal security measures, cf. § 4 sub. 3 sent. 2 GwG. 63

The responsibility to ensure compliance with the money laundering regulations can only be transferred to a 'Money Laundering Officer' (*Geldwäschebeauftragter*) if he or she is responsible for the implementation as a member of the management level. Although the name of the individual member of the management does not have to be transmitted to BaFin, it must be clearly documented in the interests of proper and appropriate risk management.[26] The assignment of risk management to a member of the management level is mandatory. The assignment of risk management to a member of the management level is mandatory. Violations of this duty can be sanctioned by administrative fines (§ 56 sub. 1 no. 1 GwG). 64

---

[22] cf. BT-Drs. 18/11555, 109.

[23] The FATF Recommendations, 2012–2025, International Standards on Combating Money Laundering and the Financing of Terrorism & Proliferation, Interpretive Note to Recommendation 1 no. 1 p. 29 <https://www.fatf-gafi.org/content/dam/fatfgafi/recommendations/FATF%20Recommendations%202012.pdf.coredownload.inline.pdf> (last accessed: 7.4.2025); obligated parties outside the financial sector are referred to by the FATF as 'designated non-financial bodies and professions' (DNFBPS).

[24] Herzog/Herzog GwG § 4 mn. 2.

[25] Herzog/Herzog GwG § 4 mn. 4.

[26] Diergarten/Fraulob GwG § 2 p. 172.

b) Scope of risk management in the light of the 'risk-based approach'

65 According to § 4 sub. 1 GwG, type and scope of risk management are generally based on the appropriateness in relation to the business activity. Nevertheless, variations may result from the indefinite legal term 'appropriate' (cf. § 4 sub. 1 GwG) or certain limitations made for real estate agents or dealers of goods (cf. § 4 sub. 4 and 5 GwG). Reasons can be found in the risk-based approach, which is based on the idea that not every customer, every transaction or every financial product poses the same risk of money laundering. The opposite of the 'risk-based approach' is the 'rule-based approach', where monitoring measures are applied homogenously. The risk-based approach has the advantage of economic and effective use of resources by introducing a process based on experience and individual risk assessment.[27] The individual risk factors to be considered may, for instance, be related to the respective institution, the customer, or the type of transaction.

66 Although the obliged entities have discretionary powers about the necessary measures, these must be individually adapted to the type and scope of the business activity. The adequacy of the risk management must be assessed based on a previous risk analysis or, if necessary, in accordance with the results of the national risk analysis[28].

2. Risk analysis (§ 5 GwG)

a) Content of the risk analysis

67 § 5 GwG contains regulations concerning the required risk analysis. The obliged entities are required to determine and evaluate the risks of money laundering and terrorist financing associated with the business activities they engage in. In cases where the obliged entity is the parent company of a group, the requirement applies to the whole group. Generally, the extent of the risk analysis depends on the nature and size of the business, § 5 sub. 1 sent. 3 GwG. The obliged entities must pay particular attention to certain risk factors specified in annexes 1 and 2 of the GwG (specifying costumer risk factors, product, service, transaction, or delivery channel risk factors as well as geographical risk factors). Additionally, the information made available based on the national risk assessment must be considered within the risk analysis.

b) Obligation to document and review

68 The obligation to conduct risk analysis includes the duty to:

1. document the risk analysis (§ 5 sub. 2 no. 1 GwG),
2. regularly review and, as appropriate, update the risk analysis (§ 5 sub. 2 no. 2 GwG) and,
3. upon request, make the most recent version of the risk analysis available to the supervisory authority (§ 5 sub. 2 no. 3 GwG).

69 According to the German legislator, a 'regularly' review in the sense of § 5 sub. 2 no. 2 GwG means at least once a year.[29]

70 § 5 sub. 4 GwG establishes an exception from the documentation requirement. The supervisory authority may exempt the obliged entity from documenting the risk analysis

---

[27] MAH WirtschaftsStrafR/Berndt/Müller/Hümmrich-Welt § 21 mn. 192.

[28] Erste Nationale Risikoanalyse – Bekämpfung von Geldwäsche und Terrorismusfinanzierung 2018/2019: <https://www.bundesfinanzministerium.de/Content/DE/Downloads/Broschueren_Bestellservice/2019-10-19-erste-nationale-risikoanalyse_2018-2019.pdf?__blob=publicationFile&v=7> (last accessed: 7.4.2025).

[29] BR-Drs. 182/17, 125.

if this entity demonstrates that specific risks of the respective industry are clear and understood.

3. Internal control and safeguard measures (§ 6 GwG)

§ 6 GwG is intended to prevent (or at least impede) the misuse of obliged entities to transfer profits from criminal offences into the legal money circuit. Since this criminal policy objective cannot be achieved by state surveillance only, obliged entities must actively protect themselves against such abuse. In order to manage and mitigate the risks of money laundering and terrorist financing, obliged entities must implement appropriate business and customer-oriented internal safeguard measures by means of policies, procedures and control measures in accordance with § 6 sub. 1 GwG. Furthermore, obliged entities must monitor the functionality of the internal safeguard measures and update them where necessary. The measures are only appropriate if they correspond to the individual risk situation of the obliged entity and counteract in a sufficient way. 71

§ 6 sub. 2 GwG lists a non-conclusive catalogue of possible security measures. According to the provision, internal safeguards particularly include the development of internal principles, procedures, and controls in relation to dealing with 72

- the risk of money laundering and terrorist financing,
- customer due diligence requirements,
- compliance with the reporting obligation,
- the recording of information, and
- the retention of and compliance with other provisions under the Money Laundering Act.

Further internal safeguard measures to be considered are: 73

- the appointment of a Money Laundering Officer,
- the establishment of group-wide procedures (in cases of obliged entities that are parent companies of a group),
- the development and updating of appropriate measures to prevent the abuse of new products and technologies,
- (appropriate) reliability screening of employees, and
- an initial and ongoing training of employees with regard to the typologies and current methods of money laundering and terrorist financing including the relevant provisions and obligations.

Review of the above policies and procedures as part of an independent inspection may serve as an internal safeguard where such a review is appropriate given the nature and size of the business. The exemplary catalogue demonstrates how extensive internal safeguard measures can be and what extensive resources must be raised consequently. This may cause a significant burden for the obliged entity.[30] § 6 sub. 3 GwG transfers the obligation to conduct internal controls and safeguards to the company, when the natural person is only obliged under the Money Laundering Act due to their professional activities as an employee. This restriction is especially relevant for in-house lawyers (cf. → mn. 89 et seqq.). 74

[30] MAH WirtschaftsStrafR/Berndt/Müller/Hümmrich-Welt § 21 mn. 206.

4. Money Laundering Officer (§ 7 GwG)

75 § 7 GwG substantiates the obligation established in § 6 sub. 2 no. 2 GwG to appoint a Money Laundering Officer and his deputy. This obligation is supposed to secure and increase the effectiveness of the measurements taken.

a) Area of responsibility

76 According to § 7 sub. 1 sent. 2 GwG, the Money Laundering Officer is responsible for ensuring compliance with money laundering regulations. His scope of responsibility covers all company related money laundering matters and is thus exceedingly wideranging.

b) Position within the company

77 The Money Laundering Officer necessarily needs to occupy a prominent position in the company in order to ensure independence and effective performance of his/her duties. Consequently, the money laundering officer therefore has to belong to the management level as defined in § 1 sub. 15 GwG. He or she must be a senior manager with sufficient knowledge about the risks posed to the obliged entity and necessary decision-making powers to counteract them (§ 7 sub. 1 sent. 1 GwG).

c) Obliged entities

78 Only obliged entities listed in § 2 sub. 1 no. 1 to 3, 6, 7, 9 and 15 GwG must appoint a Money Laundering Officer. The requirement exists for credit institutions, financial services institutions as well as payment and e-money institutions, § 2 sub. 1 no. 1 to 3 GwG. Furthermore, it applies to financial companies (no. 6), insurance companies (no. 7), capital management companies etc. (no. 9) and to the organizers and brokers of gambling (no. 15). The supervisory authority (§ 50 GwG) may determine on a case by case basis that obliged entities may refrain from appointing a Money Laundering Officer. However, the supervisory authority may also order companies to appoint a Money Laundering Officer even though they are not obliged to do so under sub. 1.

d) Duty of disclosure

79 The obliged entity is required to inform the supervisory authority in advance about the appointment and removal of the Money Laundering Officer and his deputy (§ 7 sub. 4 sent. 1 GwG). The supervisory authority should thus be given the opportunity to verify the required professional qualification and reliability of the appointed Money Laundering Officer and/or his deputy. The supervisory authority is entitled to demand the obliged entity to withdraw the appointment if, based on their opinion, the appointed person or his/her deputy does not possess the necessary qualification or reliability (§ 7 sub. 4 GwG).

5. Due diligence obligations (§ 10 GwG)

a) General due diligence obligations (§ 10 sub. 1 GwG)

80 The general due diligence obligations are regulated in § 10 sub. 1 GwG and form the core of the preventive framework of combating money laundering and terrorist financing. These obligations contain:

1. identifying the contracting party and (where applicable) the person acting on their behalf and checking whether the person acting on behalf of the contracting party is entitled to do so,

2. clarifying whether the contracting party is acting on behalf of a beneficial owner and, if so, identifying the beneficial owner,
3. in certain cases obtaining and evaluating information on the purpose and intended nature of the business relationship,
4. assessing with appropriate risk-oriented procedures whether the contracting party or the beneficial owner is a politically exposed person, a family member or a person known to be a close associate, and
5. continuously monitoring the business relationship, including the transactions carried out during the business relationship, to ensure that they are consistent with
   - the documents and information available to the obliged entities about the contracting party and, where applicable, the beneficial owner, about their business activity and customer profile, and
   - (where necessary) the information available to the obliged entity about the source of wealth.

Furthermore, as part of their continuous monitoring activities, obliged entities must ensure that the relevant documents, data or information are updated regularly on an risk-based approach. This catalogue of due diligence obligations reflects what is known as the 'know your customer' principle.[31] 81

b) Different forms of due diligence obligations

The Money Laundering Act distinguishes between general, consolidated, and aggravated due diligence obligations. The obliged entities are always obliged to comply with the general due diligence obligations listed under § 10 sub. 1 GwG. However, these duties are extended within certain prerequisites by the GwG. 82

aa) Risk-oriented scope of measures. The identification obligation is the core element of the so-called 'know your costumer' principle and follows the same standard. Nevertheless, the specific scope of the other measures depends on the respective risk of money laundering and terrorist financing, § 10 sub. 2 sent. 1 GwG. This provision is an example of the application of the 'risk-based approach'. This represents the most significant principle of the Money Laundering Act, which gives obliged entities a certain degree of discretion in deciding on the appropriate measures. 83

In this context, the obliged entities must pay particular attention to the risk factors specified in annexes 1 and 2 of the Money Laundering Act as well as the following aspects: 84

1. the purpose of the account or the business relationship,
2. the level of assets deposited by the customer, or the size of the transactions carried out, and
3. the regularity or the duration of the business relationship.

Obliged entities must be able to prove to the supervisory authorities (upon request) that the extent of the measures they have adopted is adequate based on their individual risk profile, § 10 sub. 2 GwG. 85

bb) Events triggering due diligence.

There are certain events triggering the application of general due diligence obligations (§ 10 sub. 3 GwG): First and foremost, the general due diligence obligations must be performed upon establishing a business relationship. Although such a business relationship does not exist, the general obligations apply in specific cases when transferring money (as described in § 10 sub. 3 no. 2 lit. a GwG) or in other transactions with a value 86

[31] Bülte NZWiSt 2017, 276 (279).

of 15,000.00 EUR or more (§ 10 sub. 3 no. 2 lit. b GwG). The general due diligence obligations must also be met whenever facts indicate that assets associated with a transaction or business relationship are subject of money laundering (§ 10 sub. 3 no. 3 lit. a GwG) or associated with terrorist financing (§ 10 sub. 3 no. 3 lit. b GwG). Lastly, the general due diligence obligations are to be performed under § 10 sub. 3 no. 4 GwG also if doubts arise as to the accuracy of the information gathered in accordance with the Money Laundering Act concerning the identity of the contracting party, a person acting on behalf of the contracting party or the beneficial owner.

87 Furthermore, obliged parties must comply with the general due diligence obligations for all new customers. In existing business relationships, the general due diligence obligations have to be carried out on a risk-oriented basis, especially if relevant circumstances of the business relationship changed.

88 **cc) Enhanced due diligence (§ 15 GwG).** Obliged entities are required to perform increased due diligence according to § 15 sub. 1 sent. 1 GwG, if they determine that there may be an increased risk of money laundering or terrorist financing. These enhanced obligations must be met in addition to the general due diligence obligations arsing from § 10 sub. 1 GwG. This provision illustrates again the risk-based approach taken by the Money Laundering Act. Possible circumstances of enhanced due diligence obligations are listed in a non-exhaustive catalogue in § 15 sub. 3 GwG. According to the law, an increased risk of money laundering exists, for example, if a contractual partner of the obliged party or a beneficial owner is a politically exposed person. Enhanced due diligence obligations may also result from the specific structure of the transaction if it deviates to a particular extent from market standards.

6. Restrictions for in-house lawyers

89 In-house lawyers do not have to perform all of the obligations. According to § 10 sub. 8a GwG, in-house lawyers are explicitly exempted from the general due diligence obligations established by § 10 sub. 1 GwG, if the company itself is an obliged entity according to § 2 sub. 1 GwG.

90 In addition, the obligation to maintain risk management pursuant to § 4 GwG is also transferred to the company as an employer. In-house lawyers are hence released from their obligations which, according to § 4 sub. 2 GwG, includes the execution of risk analysis (§ 5 GwG) and internal safeguard measures (§ 6 GwG).

91 The execution of internal measures is explicitly transferred to the employing company by the provision in § 6 sub. 3 GwG. Unfortunately, there is no regulation comparable to § 6 sub. 3 GwG for the catalogue of obligations in § 5 GwG. Nevertheless, the obligation to conduct internal security measures is also transfered since the privileging of the in-house lawyer is intended to relate to risk management overall. Risk analysis is one of the two elements of risk management (cf. § 4 sub. 2 GwG). This assumption is also in line with the legislation: the explanatory memorandum to § 10 sub. 8a GwG refers to the fact that the transfer of obligations was intended to create a regulation comparable to the regulations applicable to 'risk management'.[32] This reference shows that § 6 sub. 3 GwG is meant to include both elements of risk management (internal safeguard measures and risk analysis). Unfortunately, experience with regional bar associations has shown that some of them adhere very strictly to the wording of § 6 sub. 3 GwG and reject a complete transfer of obligations to the employing company. However, this assumption is not compatible with the legislative intention and must be rejected.

---

[32] BT-Drs. 19/15196, 7.

7. Identification obligation (§ 11 et seqq. GwG)

a) Obligation under § 11 sub. 1 GwG

According to § 11 sub. 1 GwG, obliged entities must identify contracting parties, persons acting on their behalf and beneficial owners, before establishing a business relationship or executing a transaction. Non-compliance with the identification obligations constitutes an administrative offence under § 56 sub. 1 sent. 1 no. 26 to 30 GwG. § 11 sub. 4 clarifies which information must be collected. The identification must take place before the start of the business relationship. However, § 11 sub. 1 sent. 2 GwG allows a deviation from this principle: the identification may also be completed while the business relationship is being established if this is necessary to avoid interrupting the normal course of business and (cumulatively) if there is only a low risk of money laundering or terrorist financing. Nevertheless, the exemption established in sentence 2 does not apply to transactions. According to the legislator, the identification must always take place before a transaction is carried out. 92

There is a special regulation for institutions under the German Banking Act (*Kreditwesengesetz*, KWG). According to § 25j KWG and in deviation from § 11 sub. 1 GwG, the identity check can also be completed immediately during the establishment of the business relationship, for example during the opening of an account or securities account. It should be noted that this special regulation only relates to the verification of the information on identity (cf. § 12 GwG), but not to the assessment of the information determined in § 11 sub. 4 and 5 GwG. Another deviation can be found in § 54 sub. 1 VAG which contains a special regulation for insurance companies. 93

b) Real estate agents

§ 11 sub. 2 GwG contains a simplification for real estate agents (§ 2 sub. 1 no. 14 GwG). The real estate agent must identify the contracting parties as soon as a 'serious interest' in the execution of the real estate purchase contract is expressed. According to the explanatory memorandum to the law, such 'serious interest' is given when a draft purchase contract is available, a reservation agreement or a preliminary contract has been concluded or when, for example, a notary appointment has been agreed. In the case of a rental or lease agreement, identification is required at the latest before conclusion of the contract. 94

c) Exemption clause (§ 11 sub. 3 GwG)

§ 11 sub. 3 GwG contains exceptions from the identification obligation to avoid unnecessary administrative work. According to the provision, identification may be omitted if the obliged entity has already identified the person on an earlier occasion (in the performance of its due diligence requirements) and recorded the information. Nevertheless, the obliged entity must carry out a new identification if there is doubt whether the obtained information is still correct. 95

d) Cooperation duty (§ 11 sub. 6 GwG)

The contracting party is obliged to cooperate in the identification process (§ 11 sub. 6 GwG). However, compliance with this obligation is not subject to an administrative offence. However, the obliged entity should refuse to enter into a business relationship if the contracting party refuses to provide cooperation. If the lack of cooperation means that the obliged party cannot comply with its due diligence obligations, the business relationship must be discontinued and the intended transactions cannot be carried out 96

(§ 10 sub. 9 GwG). The same applies if the obliged entity is unable to perform the general due diligence obligations by other reasons either.

8. Transparency register (§§ 18 et seqq. GwG)

97 The transparency register, which is regulated in §§ 18 et seqq. GwG contains a record of beneficial owners from all legal entities under private law, registered partnerships, and other legal structures in the sense of § 21 GwG. The register-keeping office does not check whether the data is correct and complete.[33] Therefore, there is no public belief in the transparency register. The transparency register only offers support for the obliged entities, but no reliable and binding basis for determining the beneficial owner.[34] For further verification it might be useful to conduct further research in registries such as the commercial register, or the register of associations, which can also be reviewed on the website of the transparency register.

98 With the latest amendments to the Money Laundering Act (Transparency Register (*Transparenzregister*) and Financial Information Act), which came into force on 1 August 2021, the previous notification fictions pursuant to § 20 sub. 2 GwG have ceased without replacement. Thus, all legal entities under private law and registered partnerships are obliged to report to the transparency register now.

99 According to § 19 sub. 1 GwG, the following information on the beneficial owner is accessible via the transparency register:

1. first name and surname,
2. date of birth,
3. place of residence, and
4. nature and extent of the beneficial interest.

100 The access to the information of the transparency register has been public since the implementation of the Fifth EU Money Laundering Directive.[35]

101 The only exceptions were the date of birth and place of residence, which were not publicly available. § 23 sub. 1 sent. 2 GwG stipulated that only the month and year of birth of the beneficial owner, their country of residence and nationality were publicly accessible for inspection.

102 The European Court of Justice recently ruled that the provision of the Money Laundering Directive (according to which unrestricted inspection of the transparency register must be guaranteed) is invalid, because it would constitute a serious violation of the fundamental rights of Art. 7 CFR (respect for private life) and Art. 8 CFR (the protection of personal data).[36] In Germany, the administrative practice reacted to the ruling of the European Court of Justice. The register-keeping body (*Bundesanzeiger Verlag*) announced that requests for inspection of the transparency register can no longer be granted unconditionally. Instead, the legal situation according to the previous Fourth Money Laundering Directive is applicable again. Accordingly, the inspection of the transparency register by members of the public is linked to a legitimate interest (§ 23 sub. 1 sent. 1 no. 3 GwG old version). Members of the public must now justify their requests for inspection of the transparency register and demonstrate a legitimate interest in inspection.

---

[33] BT-Dr. 18/115555, 126.

[34] Diergarten/Fraulob GwG § 2 p. 351.

[35] Information is accessible under www.transparenzregister.de.

[36] ECJ 22.11.2022 – C-37/20, C-601/20, ECLI:EU:C:2022:912 = BeckRS 2022, 32382.

9. Reporting obligation of obliged entities (§§ 43 et seqq. GwG)

a) General information on the reporting duty

The comprehensive reporting obligations regulated in §§ 43 et seqq. GwG aim to convey the cases identified by the obliged entities to the federal authorities. The Money Laundering Act relies heavily on the concept of whistleblowing by protecting individual sources and thereby motivating them to pass on suspicions. However, this circumstance must also be viewed critically since it gives rise to fears of a development towards a system of denunciation and a bureaucratic apparatus.[37] **103**

The core piece of the reporting obligations is established in § 43 sub. 1 GwG. Obliged entities are required to file a report to the German Financial Intelligence Unit (FIU). A report is required if facts indicate: **104**

- that assets related to a business relationship, brokerage or transaction are derived from a criminal offence which could constitute a predicate offence for money laundering (§ 43 sub. 1 no. 1 GwG),
- that a business transaction, a transaction, or property is related to terrorist financing (§ 43 sub. 1 no. 2 GwG), or
- that the contracting party has not met its obligation under § 11 sub. 6 sent. 3 GwG to disclose whether it intends to establish, continue or conduct the business relationship or transaction on behalf of a beneficial owner, (§ 43 sub. 1 no. 3 GwG).

The reporting obligation exists irrespective of the value of the asset concerned or the amount of the transaction. It is not necessary that the illegal source of the asset is established (cf. § 261 sub. 1 StGB). Rather, it is sufficient that facts point to the circumstances described in § 43 GwG. Suspicion in the sense of criminal procedural law is not required, since it cannot be the task of the obliged entities to carry out criminal law assessments.[38] **105**

Furthermore, it must be noted that a report in the sense of § 43 GwG does not qualify as a criminal complaint in the sense of § 158 sub. 1 StPO.[39] The required degree of suspicion for the report is lower in comparison to the criminal complaint. The German Financial Intelligence Unit provides reference points for the assessment of suspicious facts (so-called *Typologiepapiere*). These reference points are accessible for obliged entities via the internal area of the German Financial Intelligence Unit website[40]. Because of the involvement of legal laymen, the requirements for a sufficient suspicion in the sense of § 43 GwG are generally not overstated. However, this does not include reports that are shot in the dark without any sufficient basis for the claim. It is advisable to thoroughly document the assessment process, especially when refraining from filing a report, so that the supervisory authorities may be able to retrace the assessment process. **106**

If the assessment of the indications has given rise to suspicion, the obliged parties must submit the reports to the German Financial Intelligence Unit 'without delay' § 43 sub. 1 GwG. This requirement has turned out to be rather problematic: in order to be able to act within this timeframe, obliged parties submit their reports without first pursuing the suspicion in more detail. This may cause an enormous number of reports. Since the German Financial Intelligence Unit is already overtasked, there is a risk that relevant cases may not be processed. This raises the question of whether the obliged entities are allowed to conduct their own investigations (through their Money Laundering Officer) before **107**

---

37 MAH WirtschaftsStrafR/Berndt/Müller/Hümmrich-Welt § 21 mn. 270, mn. 266.

38 RAK München, Auslegungs- und Anwendungshinweise GwG, 6th edn 2021, p. 50 <https://www.rak-muenchen.de/fileadmin/user_upload/Auslegungs-_und_Anwendungshinweise_der_RAK_Muenchen_-_6._Aufl.pdf> (last accessed: 7.4.2025).

39 cf. BT-Drs. 17/6804, 35.

40 www.zoll.de/fiu-intern.

they report a suspected case of money laundering or terrorist financing. According to the current legal status, such authority must be negated. Pursuant to German jurisprudence[41] a Money Laundering Officer is not able to avoid an unnecessary report by conducting own investigations prior to the report. The obligation of the Money Laundering Officer to investigate only relates to facts that arise from the environment of the business relationship and that he is entitled to have at his disposal based on this relationship. Such information must then be obtainable and able to be evaluated in the shortness of the examination period provided by § 43 sub. 1 GwG. The Money Laundering Officer has neither the right nor the obligation to carry out investigations on behalf of the obliged entity. On the contrary: if investigations are carried out, there is a risk that a suspected case will be reported too late which may cause a fine. The German Federal Financial Supervisory Authority (BaFin, see → mn. 124 et seqq.) has explicitly taken up this judicial assessment and has incorporated it in its interpretation and application guidelines.

b) Reporting obligation for supervisory authorities (§ 44 GwG)

108 Complementary to this provision addressing the obliged entities, § 44 GwG regulates a reporting obligation for supervisory authorities. The supervisory authority is required to file a report to the German Financial Intelligence Unit without delay if facts indicate that assets are related to money laundering or terrorist financing.

c) Specifics regarding the report

109 **aa) Relation to the criminal complaint (§ 158 StPO).** Regarding the notification itself, some specific questions arise. For example, the question as to whether the obliged person has the choice of reporting to the German Financial Intelligence Unit under the Money Laundering Act or whether the obliged entity must immediately file a criminal complaint with the local police or prosecutors office.

110 Generally, there is no obligation to file a criminal complaint (except in the cases of § 138 StGB). From the perspective of an obliged entity, a report under the Money Laundering Act has the advantage that it bears the possibility to stop the transaction or refrain from further carrying out the business.[42] According to § 48 sub. 1 GwG, in both cases, when filing a report under § 43 sub. 1 GwG or making criminal complaint under § 158 StPO, the obliged entity must not be held liable for the report or complaint unless a false report or criminal complaint has been filed with wilful intent or gross negligence.

111 **bb) Form of reporting.** Pursuant to § 45 GwG, the report under § 43 sub. 1 or § 44 GwG must be filed electronically. If electronic data transmission is disrupted, transmission by post is permissible. Due to the special need for a uniform data transmission procedure, reports under § 44 GwG are also obligatory for the supervisory authorities of the federal states. Incorrect, incomplete, and untimely reports lead to fines according to § 56 sub. 1 no. 59 GwG. If the obliged party has filed a criminal complaint without delay and has waived a report pursuant to § 43 GwG, there should no longer be any scope for the application of sanctions pursuant to § 56 sub. 1 no. 59 GwG.

112 **cc) Reporting obligation for lawyers.** Due to the legal duty of confidentiality, the reporting obligation laid down in § 43 sub. 1 GwG does not apply to lawyers (precisely to the obliged entities under § 2 sub. 1 no. 10 and 12 GwG) if the reportable matter relates to information they received in the course of providing legal advice or legal representation (§ 43 sub. 2 sent. 1 GwG). However, the reporting obligation continues to exist according

[41] OLG Frankfurt a.M. 10.4.2018 – 2 Ss-OWi 1059/17, NZWiSt 2019, 219.
[42] MAH WirtschaftsStrafR/Berndt/Müller/Hümmrich-Welt § 21 mn. 273.

to § 43 sub. 2 sent. 2 GwG if the lawyer knows that the contracting party has used or is using the legal representation for the purpose of money laundering, terrorist financing or another criminal offence.

Whenever the client asks his lawyer to profitably invest the money obtained from a previous crime (all-crimes approach), the lawyer must not only resign or terminate the mandate, but also file a complaint of suspected money laundering. In this context, a particular problem arises when the lawyer learns secrets concerning third parties that are not subject to his duty of confidentiality, but whose information at least affects the interests of his own client.[43] **113**

The decision between the duty to report and the duty of confidentiality can thus often be critical. If a lawyer files a report that he was not obliged to file, there is a risk that he will be prosecuted for violating his duty of confidentiality under § 203 sub. 1 no. 3 StGB. Although it is true that the obligation to report suspicious cases of money laundering is partly seen as a justification in the context of § 203 StGB, this restriction can only apply if the report was justified. Conversely, if a lawyer (for clarification: this does not include criminal defence attorneys) does not file a report although he suspects a case of money laundering and the suspicion later proves to be justified, he risks making himself liable to prosecution under § 261 sub. 6 sent. 1 StGB for reckless money laundering. In other cases, one could argue that § 48 sub. 1 GwG applies. According to the provision, whoever files a report under § 43 sub. 1 GwG or a criminal complaint under section 158 StPO must not be held liable for this report or criminal complaint unless a false report or criminal complaint has been filed with wilful intent or gross negligence. However, it is unclear whether § 48 GwG also includes criminal liability under § 203 sub. 1 no. 3 StGB. Due to this uncertainty, caution is required when dealing with hasty suspicious activity reports.[44] **114**

dd) Reporting obligation (§ 43 GwG) versus self-incrimination (§ 261 sub. 9 sent. 1 StGB). § 43 sub. 4 GwG makes a statement about the relationship between the reporting obligation established by the Money Laundering Act and the possibility of self-incrimination within the meaning of § 261 sub. 1 sent. 1 StGB. The necessity for this clarification is based on the following background: **115**

§ 261 sub. 1 StGB demands that the previous act has not already been discovered in whole or in part. In the past, this has led to the controversial question, if the filing of a report according to the GwG (explicitly or impliedly) also contains self-disclosure in the sense of § 261 sub. 8 StGB. If not so, the consequence would have been that the previous report may have caused the inapplicability of the privilege established in § 261 sub. 8 StGB. In the past it was recommendable (in accordance with the precautionary principle) to cumulatively file the report and incriminate oneself.[45] **116**

This conflict is now resolved by § 43 sub. 4 sent. 1 GwG: if a matter reported to the German Financial Intelligence Unit also contains the information necessary for a criminal complaint in accordance with § 261 sub. 9 sent. 1 StGB, the report is deemed to be a voluntary self-incrimination within the meaning of § 261 sub. 8 sent. 1 StGB. The duty to file a report therefore does not deprive the obliged entities from the possibility to obtain impunity by self-incrimination. **117**

---

43 RAK München, Auslegungs- und Anwendungshinweise GwG, 2nd edn 2019, p. 32, <https://www.rak-muenchen.de/fileadmin/downloads/06-Mitgliederservice/03-Geldwaesche/AHH_GwG.pdf> (last accessed: 7.4.2025).

44 RAK München, Auslegungs- und Anwendungshinweise GwG, 2nd edn 2019, p. 32, <https://www.rak-muenchen.de/fileadmin/downloads/06-Mitgliederservice/03-Geldwaesche/AHH_GwG.pdf> (last accessed: 7.4.2025).

45 MAH WirtschaftsStrafR/Berndt/Müller/Hümmrich-Welt § 21 mn. 278.

d) Recommended procedure after filing the report

118 **aa) Hold of transactions.** After filing the report, the obliged entities are often confronted with the question on how to resume forward. § 46 sub. 1 GwG contains the obligation to withhold a transaction about which a report has been filed. Such transactions may be carried out at the earliest if:

1. the German Financial Intelligence Unit or the public prosecution office has informed the obliged entity that it consents to the execution (§ 46 sub. 2 no. 1 GwG), or
2. the third working day has elapsed after the day on which the report was sent without the execution of the transaction having been prohibited by the German Financial Intelligence Unit or the public prosecution office. (§ 46 sub. 2 no. 2 GwG).

119 This principle is partially mitigated by sub. 2 of the regulation. According to that the execution of the transaction is permitted if it is impossible to postpone the transaction or if postponement could frustrate proceedings in relation to a suspected criminal offence. In this case, the report under § 43 sub. 1 GwG must be filed subsequently by the obliged entity without delay.

120 **bb) 'Tipping-off ban'.** Furthermore, the obliged entity must consider how to deal with a contractual partner after filing the report. In this respect it is important to know that § 47 GwG stipulates a prohibition regarding the disclosure of information ('tipping-off ban').

121 An obliged entity is not allowed to inform the contracting party, the instructing party of the transaction or other third parties of the (intended) filing of a report under § 43 sub. 1 GwG, an investigation launched on a report under § 43 sub. 1 GwG, or a demand for information under § 30 sub. 3 sent. 1 GwG.

122 This ban is intended to prevent those affected from gaining knowledge of reports and ongoing investigations and subsequently using this knowledge to secure unlawfully obtained assets or putting criminal investigations at risk.[46]

123 Violating the tipping-off ban may cause a regulatory offence pursuant to § 56 sub. 2 no. 7 GwG or even criminal offences (esp. obstruction of prosecution or punishment in the sense of § 258 sub. 1 StGB).

IV. Supervision by authorities: BaFin

124 The Federal Financial Supervisory Authority (*Bundesanstalt für Finanzdienstleistungsaufsicht*, BaFin) ensures that companies and natural persons under its supervision implement any statutory obligations adopted for this purpose. This includes the compliance with the Money Laundering Act, the Insurance Supervision Act, the Payment Services Supervision Act and the Investment Code. In 2003, BaFin established the Department for the Prevention of Money Laundering, which carries out money laundering supervision of all institutions, companies and persons specified under § 50 GwG. The department is also responsible for the supervision of the implementation of statutory regulations to prevent the commission of other criminal offences within the meaning of § 25h KWG. On an international level, the Department for the Prevention of Money Laundering also represents BaFin in various international and European bodies, such as the Financial Action Task Force on Money Laundering (FATF) or the Committee on Anti Money Laun-

[46] Herzog/Barreto de Rosa § 47 mn. 3.

dering (AMLC), a sub-committee of the Joint Committee of the European Supervisory Authorities.[47]

V. Recent developments: EU Money Laundering Package

The former legal framework for combating money laundering in the EU was defined by directives. However, EU directives do not have direct effect in the Member States but must be transposed by them into national law. In the past, this has led to differences between the regulations of individual Member States. In addition, the lack of a central coordinating body at EU level makes cooperation between the national authorities of the Member States difficult.[48] Money laundering remains a cross-border and international problem. **125**

On 9 July 2024, the new legislative package to combat money laundering came into force. The EU package is based on the Action Plan for a Comprehensive EU Policy on the Prevention of Money Laundering and Terrorist Financing, which the Commission presented on 7 May 2020. The legislative package was adopted by the European Parliament on 24 April 2024 and published in the Official Journal of the EU on 19 June 2024. The package consists of the Directive (EU) 2024/1640 ('Sixth Money Laundering Directive') and the Regulation (EU) 2024/1624 ('EU Money Laundering Regulation'). Member States and obliged entities now have three years to comply with the new requirements. The Sixth Anti-Money Laundering Directive must be transposed into national law by 10 July 2027. From the same date, the Money Laundering Ordinance will be directly applicable and, where relevant, will take precedence over the Money Laundering Act (GwG). The following is an overview of some of the most important changes: **126**

1. AMLA[49]

The EU-wide supervision introduces a common methodological standard for combating money laundering. The role of the Anti-Money Laundring Authority (AMLA) varies depending on the sectors, Art. 5 Regulation (EU) 2024/1620. In non-financial sectors the authority fulfills a coordination role. In the financial sector, however, it also directly supervises financial institutions that are exposed to the highest risk of money laundering and terrorism financing. Concerning the national FIUs, the Authority facilitates the cooperation by establishing standards for reporting and exchanging information, supporting joint operational analyses, and by hosting a central online system. **127**

2. EU Money Laundering Regulation[50]

The provisions on obliged entities were adopted from the previous Fifth Money Laundering Directive into the EU Money Laundering Regulation. In addition, the circle of obliged parties was expanded, Art. 3 et seqq. Regulation (EU) 2024/1624. Providers of crypto services, crowdfunding services and actors under residence schemes are now also covered. This expansion is to be seen as a reaction to international requirements and the risks of modern technologies. Furthermore, trustees are now obliged to obtain certain information about the trustor, the nature of the trust relationship and the beneficial **128**

---

47 Cf. <https://www.bafin.de/ref/19579174> (last accessed: 7.4.2025).
48 Krauß AnwBl 2022, 602 et seq.
49 Regulation (EU) 2024/1620.
50 Regulation (EU) 2024/1624.

owner, to keep it available and to keep it up to date, just like an obliged entity. The EU Regulation also specifies the requirements for the obliged entities and sets out detailed and risk-based rules for the application of due diligence obligations to customers, Art. 19 et. Seqq. Regulation (EU) 2024/1624. In addition, the requirements regarding non-EU countries are revised and unified.

129 Furthermore, the EU Money Laundering Regulation contains a uniformly valid definition of the beneficial owner on EU level. In this course, the requirements for beneficial ownership are significantly lowered compared to the former legal situation. According to the new regulation, it is sufficient if more than 25 % of the capital shares or voting rights are held at each level of participation. In addition, the regulation defines other means of control that can lead to beneficial ownership, including veto rights, certain managerial rights and close family ties to owners or controlling persons. As a result, the number of beneficial owners to be reported to the transparency register is likely to increase in almost all German companies. Companies based outside the EU must also report their beneficial owners to a transparency register in an EU Member State under certain conditions. This is especially the case when entering a business relationship with a contractual partner in the EU who is obliged to carry out a customer check under the AMLA (e.g. banks, insurance companies, lawyers or tax consultants). The EU thus aims on global standards in combating money laundering, as it did with the GDPR regarding data protection.

3. Sixth Money Laundering Directive[51]

130 The Sixth Money Laundering Directive replaces the former Directive and contains provisions that are not appropriate for the EU Money Laundering Regulation. A key element of this Directive is the obligation for Member States to set up centralised automated mechanisms, such as central registers or electronic data retrieval systems. These should enable the rapid identification of all natural or legal persons who hold or control payment accounts, bank accounts, custody accounts, crypto-asset accounts or safe-deposit boxes in their territory.

4. Regulation on transfer of funds[52]

131 The fourth element of the Commission's legislative package concerns the amendment of the 2015 Money Laundering Directive[53]. The amendment extends the scope of the existing regulation to include transfers of crypto assets, since crypto assets are increasingly used for money laundering and other criminal purposes. According to the new Regulation, full information about the sender and beneficiary of such transfers will have to be included by crypto-asset service providers with all transfers of virtual assets, just as payment service providers currently do for wire transfers, Art. 14 et seqq. Regulation (EU) 2023/1113. This aims to ensure financial transparency on exchanges in crypto-assets, making it more difficult for them to be misused for criminal purposes.

---

[51] Directive (EU) 2024/1640.
[52] Regulation (EU) 2023/1113.
[53] Directive (EU) 2015/847.

D. Conclusion

In summary, combating money laundering is a complex issue that is subject to constant change due to international influences. It remains to be seen whether the efforts of the German legislator and the recent legislative changes at the European level will help succeed with the combat against money laundering. Because the issue is ubiquitous for economic stakeholders, it is essential to be aware of the relevant regulations and constantly monitor legislative developments. Only those who are familiar with and understand the legal requirements can set up effective risk management to prevent (criminal) liability for money laundering. 132

CHAPTER 15
INSOLVENCY

Bibliography: Hoffmann, Grenzen der Einflussnahme auf Unternehmensleitungsentscheidungen durch Kreditgläubiger, WM 2012, 10; IDW Verlautbarungen editing status 10.1.2022, IDW Life 9/2022, IDW S 11; IDW Verlautbarungen editing status 10.1.2022, IDW Life 9/2022, IDW PS 340; Prütting, Der Vermögensschutz von Gesellschaften gegenüber externer Einflussnahme – geprüft am Beispiel der GmbH, ZGR 2015, 849.

Table of contents

A. Management's duties during the crisis of the company 353
I. Crisis detection and monitoring 353
1. General duties of management to manage the company's business properly and carefully 353
2. Duty for early crisis detection 353
3. Definition of crisis and of developments that jeopardise the company 353
4. Measures for early crisis detection 354
II. Crisis management, duty to restructure the company 355
1. General crisis management 355
2. Measures for crisis management 355
III. Specifically: monitoring of the company's financial situation . 356
IV. General duties 357
1. Employee social security contributions and tax liabilities .. 357
2. Payments to shareholders 357
3. Destructive intervention 358
4. Influence as shareholder 358
5. Reporting duties, supervisory bodies 358
B. Management's duties after insolvency has occurred 359
I. Filing for insolvency 359
1. Duty to file for insolvency 359
2. Reasons to file for insolvency 360
a) Illiquidity (§ 17 InsO) 360
b) Over-indebtedness (§ 19 InsO) 362
c) Imminent illiquidity (§ 18 InsO) 362
II. Payment restrictions 362
III. Behaviour towards contractual partners 363
IV. Management of company assets 363
V. Duties within insolvency proceedings 364
1. Shift of duties to creditors 364
2. Obligation to cooperate and provide information 364
VI. Duties in self-administration proceedings 365
C. Management's criminal liability in the context of insolvency 365
I. Overview of 'Insolvency Offences' (§§ 283 et seqq. StGB) 366
1. Period/state of the company 366
2. Perpetrators 366
3. Intent and negligence 367
4. Extra-criminal consequences 367
II. Bankruptcy (§ 283 StGB) 367
III. Breach of duty to keep commercial records (§ 283b StGB) 368

IV. Preferential treatment of creditors (§ 283c StGB) 368
V. Preferential treatment of debtors (§ 283d StGB).............. 368
D. Characteristics of German insolvency proceedings 368
I. Purpose and overview 368
II. Insolvency application 369
III. Preliminary insolvency proceedings 369
IV. Main insolvency proceedings 370
1. Court order opening insolvency proceedings 370
2. Creditors' meeting.................................... 370
3. Lodging of claims (insolvency creditors), verification meeting 370
4. Pending contracts 371
5. Insolvency claw back.................................. 371
6. Distribution of quota payment 371
V. Creditor ranking and qualification of creditor claims 371
VI. Creditors' involvement in insolvency proceedings 372
VII. Shareholder rights in insolvency proceedings 372
VIII. Self-administration 373
E. Pre-insolvency reorganisation proceedings (StaRUG) 373
I. Overview of course of proceedings 373
1. Notice of StaRUG proceedings to court.................. 373
2. Restructuring plan 374
3. Voting mechanism..................................... 374
4. Effects of court approval 374
5. Moratorium 374
II. Alternative approach and comparison to insolvency proceedings... 375
III. Management duties during the proceedings 376
1. Notification in case of insolvency...................... 376
2. Conduct proceedings with diligence of prudent businessman 376
3. Notification in case of changes in proposed restructuring . 376
4. Duties for company's auditors and advisors 377
F. Applicable law, jurisdiction and recognition of StaRUG and insolvency proceedings 377

1 In a crisis or even insolvency scenario of a company, German law imposes specific duties on its managing directors. These duties mainly aim at safeguarding the interests of creditors. Key duties include the duty for early crisis detection and crisis management and the duty to file for insolvency after the company has become over-indebted or illiquid.

2 This chapter discusses these duties in depth and highlights potential civil and criminal liability. This discussion also includes a detailed explanation of the reasons to file for insolvency under German law, characteristics of German insolvency proceedings and pre-insolvency reorganization proceedings (StaRUG) as well as matters around the applicable law, jurisdiction and recognition of proceedings in an international context.

A. Management's duties during the crisis of the company

I. Crisis detection and monitoring

1. General duties of management to manage the company's business properly and carefully

The management of a limited liability entity (such as a limited liability company (*GmbH*) or corporation (*AG*)) is obliged to manage the company with the diligence of a prudent businessman (*sorgfältige Geschäftsleitung*, § 43 sub. 1 GmbHG, § 93 sub. 1 AktG). This duty of diligent corporate management leads to a multitude of individual duties. In particular, management has an obligation to control and monitor the business (*Steuerungs- und Überwachungsaufgabe*). In doing so, management must critically observe the course of the business, the development of yearly results and the overall economic situation of the company. This duty exists in general and irrespective of an emerging crisis. 3

2. Duty for early crisis detection

The general duty to manage the company's business properly and carefully also includes the obligation to continuously monitor any developments that may jeopardise the continued existence of the company (duty of early crisis detection, *Krisenfrüherkennungspflicht*). On 1 January 2021, § 1 StaRUG, that specifically stipulates this duty, was introduced into law.[1] Before that, the duty of early crisis detection and management had been derived from the general duties of a company's management (§ 43 sub. 1 GmbHG, § 91 sub. 2 AktG). § 1 StaRUG now only stipulates minimum requirements in the interest of legal clarity as well as more special and advanced duties than under the general rules. This is particularly relevant for companies that are not organised in the legal form of a corporation or a limited liability company. 4

3. Definition of crisis and of developments that jeopardise the company

The law does not define 'developments that may jeopardise the continued existence of the company'. Typically, this is understood to mean developments that (i) could have a material adverse effect on the company's net assets, financial position and operational results and (ii) individually or in combination with other risks counteract the goal of the company to operate as a going concern. It is assumed that these effects pose a risk for the company becoming illiquid or over-indebted if they continue to occur unimpeded. 5

The duty of early crisis detection exists for the entire period of the company's existence and irrespective of whether certain signs of crisis have already occurred. The point at which developments within a company pose a threat to its existence depends on the specific company and cannot be determined in general. Depending on the stage of the crisis, conclusions can be drawn as to whether it is (barely) an economic crisis or a crisis that jeopardises the existence of the company. At an advanced stage of the crisis (especially 6

[1] For StaRUG proceedings in general → mn. 125 et seqq.

a profit and/or liquidity crisis), it is more likely that negative developments threaten the existence of the company.[2]

7 The following stages of a crisis are commonly recognised:[3]

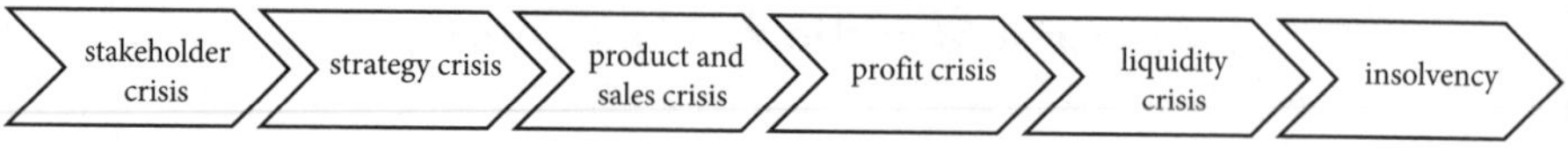

- first stage: stakeholder crisis (*Stakeholderkrise*);
- second stage: strategy crisis (*Strategiekrise*);
- third stage: product and sales crisis (*Produkt- und Absatzkrise*);
- fourth stage: profit crisis (*Erfolgskrise*);
- fifth stage: liquidity crisis (*Liquiditätskrise*);
- sixth or final stage: insolvency (*Insolvenzreife*).

8 The aim of management must be to identify the crisis as early as possible. As the crisis progresses, the demands on management also increase and the scope for action decreases. The intensity and depth of crisis detection and management outlined in → mn. 10 et seqq. increases with the development of a crisis.

9 It is not possible to define for all companies in general when a profit and/or liquidity crisis exists. However, there are certain warning signals that point to such a crisis. For a profit crisis, these signals include a drop in returns, a decline in demand and an increase in costs. A liquidity crisis is especially indicated by payment difficulties and the necessity to ask for payment deferrals or longer payment terms.

4. Measures for early crisis detection

10 In order to fulfil the duty for crisis detection, managers are required to establish an organisational system that ensures continuous monitoring of relevant developments (*Überwachungssystem*, see also § 91 sub. 2 AktG[4]). The form and the scope of the duty (i.e. the *how*, not the *if*) depends on the size, sector and structure of the business of the company as well as its legal form. The larger the company, the higher the requirements and necessity for organisational systems for risk monitoring and crisis detection. Since the goal of monitoring is to successfully counteract developments in a timely manner, it must be ensured that developments can be detected sufficiently early. A deteriorating crisis leads to an increased monitoring duty.

11 Management must take appropriate countermeasures and report to its supervisory bodies (supervisory board or shareholders' meeting) if it identifies such developments.[5] The following measures are especially recommended, although specifics may apply depending on the size, sector and concrete situation of the company and its business:

- monitoring of the financial situation of the company, i.e. by liquidity planning with a planning horizon of 18 to 24 months;

---

[2] IDW Verlautbarungen editing status 10.1.2022, IDW Life 9/2022, IDS S 11 mn. 2. The Institute of Public Auditors in Germany (*Institut der Wirtschaftsprüfer in Deutschland e.V., IdW*) is a privately run organization established to serve the interests of its members who comprise both individual German public auditors (*Wirtschaftsprüfer*) and German public audit firms (*Wirtschaftsprüfungsgesellschaften*).

[3] IDW Verlautbarungen editing status 10.1.2022, IDW Life 9/2022, IDW PS 340 mn. 8. IDW: Illustration: Kubis/Tödtmann Vorstand-HdB/Steffan/Poppe Ch. 9 mn. 9.

[4] For additional information see The Institute of Public Auditors in Germany (*Institut der Wirtschaftsprüfer in Deutschland e.V., IdW*) ES 16, dated 3 February 2025 (https://www.idw.de/idw/idw-verlautbarungen/idw-ers-fab-15.html).

[5] For additional information → mn. 37 et seqq.

- setting up an integrated financial planning, which is also updated during the year (especially after risks have been identified);
- monitoring and evaluating economic and legal developments with a focus on risk identification and assessment for the specific company and its business model;
- establishing an appropriate reporting system and reporting lines, communicating adequate risk awareness within the company with the objective of detecting and identifying risks;
- analysing the development of the order book as well as the behaviour of customers and suppliers; and
- implementing an early warning system.

It is advisable to carefully document the measures used for early crisis detection as well as its implementation so that evidence is available if need be. **12**

Implications from intra-group relationships must always be taken into account if there is a possibility that risks arising at the level of a group company could have an impact on other companies of the group. It is advisable to establish a clear definition of responsibilities and roles. Sufficient resources must be made available and staff must be appropriately trained. **13**

II. Crisis management, duty to restructure the company

1. General crisis management

The general duty to manage the company's business properly and carefully (→ mn. 3) also results in the obligation to manage the crisis. If management has identified developments that may jeopardise the continued existence of the company, it is obligated to analyse the extent of the crisis and the reasons for it. It must also examine all possible countermeasures with the diligence of a prudent businessman. It must implement appropriate and promising measures in consultation with the shareholders and, if applicable, significant creditors. **14**

This duty is usually referred to as the duty to implement crisis management and to take countermeasures if necessary (*Krisenmanagement*) and the obligation to restructure the company (*Sanierungspflicht*). It exists for every type of limited liability company (§ 93 sub. 1 sent. 1 AktG, § 1 sub. 2 StaRUG). **15**

2. Measures for crisis management

Management must take action against (an impending) crisis when it detects signs of crisis. The scope of the crisis management depends on the company's business activities and risk situation. The specific measures depend on how the identified crisis situation of the company can best be solved. **16**

The following actions can in principle be considered: **17**

- taking performance/operational or financial restructuring measures;
- negotiating a financial restructuring with financing parties, e.g. deferrals or waivers;
- taking efforts to obtain equity measures or shareholder loans;
- seeking to take advantage of state aid or other legal relief;
- negotiating possible adjustments to existing contractual agreements (where possible and appropriate); and

- preparing and implementing a StaRUG procedure[6].

18 Management has a discretionary power of judgement that is not subject to judicial review when it comes to selecting the appropriate measures. However, management must make its decision taking into account what is in the best interests of the company based on adequate information (*Business Judgement Rule*[7]). It must adhere to shareholder resolutions (unless the resolutions are contrary to binding law). In view of the wide scope for discretion in the appropriate measures, management should carefully document their reasoning and the underlying forecasts.

19 Acting against this duty may cause management's liability (§ 93 sub. 2 sent. 1 AktG, § 43 sub. 2 GmbHG).

III. Specifically: monitoring of the company's financial situation

20 Part of management's duties is the obligation to monitor the company's financial situation. Management is obligated to analyse whether the company (on individual, not group level) can meet its obligations when due. It must continuously monitor whether any conditions exist that would trigger compulsory initiation of insolvency proceedings.[8] While this duty exists irrespective of a crisis, it becomes especially important during a late profit and early liquidity crisis. It is also in management's own interest to comply with this duty since management has the duty to file for insolvency when a company is insolvent.

21 Management monitors the company's financial situation with a liquidity forecast/ liquidity planning (*Liquiditätsplanung*) as the most important economic instrument in liquidity management. Liquidity forecasts show expected cash inflows and outflows in future periods (pre set-off).

22 On the one side, they show a prognosis of cash and cash equivalents (*liquide Mittel*) available during the prognosis period. All liquid funds to which the company (presumably) has access must be included in the liquidity forecast, irrespective of from where these funds originate. However, funds from (indirect) shareholders can normally only be included in the liquidity forecast (*Liquiditätsplanung*) if the shareholder has with legally binding effect committed to providing the funds.[9]

23 On the other side, liquidity forecasts include all liabilities that (presumably, probability of more than 50 %) become due within the same time frame. For the respective periods, the payment obligations falling due must be covered by the corresponding payment funds available at the time.

24 If the company operates or takes part in a cash pool, the liquidity that flows from it to the company and back must be included in the analysis if it is more likely than not that the payments can be expected. If the entity operating the cash pool is in a crisis, an entity that pays into the cash pool is only permitted to continue to do so (and funds can be included in the analysis) as long as it can expect to be repaid. The liquidity that is essential for the survival of the paying entity must be available to it at all times and not be paid into the cash pool.

25 Free of subjective influences, the forecast is prepared taking into account all information on future developments available at the time when the forecast is drawn up. This

[6] For StaRUG → mn. 125 et seqq.

[7] This principle is regulated for corporations in § 93 sub. 1 sent. 2 AktG. It is also applied to limited liability companies (*GmbH*).

[8] → mn. 46 et seqq. for details on these conditions.

[9] BGH 13.7.2021 – II ZR 84/20, NZI 2021, 872.

information includes all transactional data, but also patterns and correlations that may have proven stable in the past.

26 The results of this liquidity analysis should be documented in order to be able to prove to an insolvency administrator in potential insolvency proceedings that management's duties have been fulfilled. The intervals at which the analysis is to be conducted depend on the intensity of the crisis. The more severe the crisis has become, the more often the company's liquidity situation must be analysed. In an imminent crisis, liquidity planning should be made on a daily basis.

IV. General duties

27 In a late profit or early financial crisis, management should especially ensure that the following duties are met[10]:

1. Employee social security contributions and tax liabilities

28 Failing to pay employee social security contributions exposes management to a risk of criminal liability according to § 266a sub. 1 StGB and a risk of civil liability (§ 823 sub. 2 BGB). Under § 34 sub. 1 AO, management must also fulfil the company's tax liabilities. If the management breaches these obligations with intent or gross negligence it is personally liable according to § 69 AO and/or has committed an administrative offence.[11]

2. Payments to shareholders

29 Payments to the company's shareholders should be placed under special scrutiny. Under German capital maintenance rules, the registered share capital of the company may not be paid out to the shareholders (§ 30 sub. 1 sent. 1 GmbHG, § 57 sub. 1 sent. 1 AktG). Certain exceptions apply. For instance, payments are not prohibited should a profit and loss transfer agreement exist or if the payment gives rises to a (valid and enforceable) claim for consideration or restitution against the shareholder of the same value as the payment (§ 30 sub. 1 sent. 2 GmbHG and § 57 sub. 1 sent. 3 AktG). The term payment is interpreted very broadly. It also includes assigning claims or transferring shareholdings or real estate as well as rendering services or licensing. Such capital outflow to shareholders needs to be compensated (claim for restitution of the same value).

30 The receiving shareholders are liable to the company for the repayment of any payments made to the contrary (§ 31 sub. 1 GmbHG, § 62 sub. 1 AktG). If the repayment cannot be obtained from the recipient, the remaining shareholders are liable insofar as it is necessary to satisfy the creditors of the company.

31 Even if the registered share capital would not be impaired, payments to shareholders that lead to the company's illiquidity[12], are prohibited under § 15b sub. 5 sent. 1 InsO. Management is liable to the company for any payments to the contrary and is obligated to repay the paid amounts (§ 15b sub. 4 InsO).

---

[10] Special duties for managing directors of listed companies may apply additionally during a crisis and within insolvency proceedings.

[11] For more details → Ch. 19 (Criminal labour law) and → Ch. 13 (Tax).

[12] For details on illiquidity → mn. 46 et seqq.

3. Destructive intervention

32 In a group of companies, it is especially important to ensure that there is no intervention by the parent company with respect to a subsidiary that jeopardises the subsidiary's existence (*existenzvernichtender Eingriff*, § 826 BGB).

33 Under this concept, shareholders are prohibited from interfering with the subsidiary assets in a way that jeopardises its existence.[13] This prohibition includes a withdrawal of funds (without appropriate compensation) that are essential to maintaining the subsidiary's business operations.[14] If the withdrawal would trigger or deepen the subsidiary's insolvency, it could also cause liability.

34 If the subsidiary's management assists shareholders in taking such action, they can be liable for damages.

4. Influence as shareholder

35 It is not unusual for shareholders to have a strong influence over the company. Using that influence to intentionally cause another representative of a corporation to act to the detriment of the corporation may lead to personal liability for any resulting damage (§ 117 sub. 1 AktG). This other representative may be a member of the executive or supervisory board, a holder of a general power of attorney (*Prokurist*) or an authorised representative (*Handlungsbevollmächtigter*). Members of the supervisory board assisting the shareholders in taking such action can be liable for damages.

36 It has not yet been decided by the German Federal Court of Justice (*Bundesgerichtshof*, BGH) if this statutory liability extends to members of a limited liability company.[15] In contrast to the management of a corporation, the management of a limited liability company is bound by shareholders' instructions. This follows from §§ 6 sub. 3, 37 sub. 1, 38 sub. 1, 46 no. 5 and 6 GmbHG and stands in fundamental contrast to the situation in corporations where such influence cannot exist (§ 76 AktG).[16] The German legislator granted the shareholders of a limited liability company the right to issue instructions without attaching liability (unless contrary to the law).[17] They are allowed to damage the company since this would only be to their own detriment. However, against the backdrop of the concept of destructive intervention[18] (that penalises actions that are ultimately to the detriment of the creditors not the shareholders), shareholders should carefully evaluate whether they give instructions that are simply to the detriment of themselves or whether these instructions fall under the definition of destructive intervention.

5. Reporting duties, supervisory bodies

37 Shareholders and board members must be continually informed of the company's financial situation. Management must immediately report to any existing supervisory

---

[13] BGH 16.7.2007 – II ZR 3/04, BeckRS 2007, 12790.

[14] BGH 16.7.2007 – II ZR 3/04, BeckRS 2007, 12790.

[15] Controversially discussed in legal literature; against the extension: BeckOGK/Schall, 1.10.2024, AktG § 117 mn. 35, regarding the conventional GmbH but not so clear for the other types of a GmbH, especially for the co-determined GmbH with mandatory supervisory board, which is closest to a corporation in its structure; in favour of the extension: Hoffmann WM 2012, 10 (13); Prütting ZGR 2015, 849 (in each case without detailed justification).

[16] BGH 8.1.2019 – II ZR 364/18, BeckRS 2019, 4455; Altmeppen GmbHG § 37 mn. 3.

[17] BeckOGK/Schall, 1.10.2024, AktG § 117 mn. 35; dissenting view Prütting ZGR 2015, 849; Hoffmann WM 2012, 10 (13).

[18] For more information → mn. 32–34.

bodies of the company (supervisory board or shareholders' meeting) and inform them of (i) risks identified that could jeopardise the company's existence and (ii) the countermeasures to be taken and the respective implementation status. If necessary, they must involve the bodies in the crisis management and bring about the necessary resolutions without delay. Whether a supervisory body must be consulted before certain measures are taken depends on the general provisions of company law. Typically, the articles of association, bylaws and rules of procedure of the management contain corresponding provisions.

If annual financial statements or an interim balance sheet reveal that half of the **38** registered share capital has been lost (i.e. is no longer covered by assets), directors must immediately call a shareholders' meeting (§ 49 sub. 3 GmbHG, § 92 AktG). A breach of this duty can result in civil and criminal liability.

For corporations, the supervisory board's duty to monitor management (§ 111 AktG) **39** intensifies the further the company's crisis has progressed. In contrast, the shareholders' meeting of a limited liability company has no general obligation but the right to monitor and control the management of a limited liability company (§ 46 no. 6 GmbHG). The intensity of monitoring duty is a shareholders' decision and depends on the company's structure.

B. Management's duties after insolvency has occurred

A company's insolvency triggers special duties for its management.[19] Here and in **40** the following, 'insolvency' or 'insolvent' is meant to be illiquidity (*Zahlungsunfähigkeit*, § 17 InsO) or over-indebtedness (*Überschuldung*, § 19 InsO). Mere imminent illiquidity (*drohende Zahlungsunfähigkeit*, § 18 InsO) usually does not give rise to these duties (unless explicitly mentioned otherwise)[20].

I. Filing for insolvency

1. Duty to file for insolvency

Under German law, the management of a company with (ultimate) limited liability is **41** obligated to file for insolvency after the company became insolvent. Filing is to be made without undue delay but at the latest within three weeks after the company became illiquid and six weeks after the company became over-indebted (§ 15a sub. 1 InsO).

The full period can only be used if there is a realistic prospect that the insolvency can **42** be remedied within this time.[21] If the company is only imminently illiquid, management is not obligated to file for insolvency but remains entitled (in agreement with the company's shareholders).

The duty to file lies with the individual member of the company's management. If a **43** limited liability company is without management, the duty to file for insolvency lies with each shareholder, unless he or she is not aware of the insolvency or of the lack of manage-

[19] Special duties for managing directors of listed companies may apply additionally during a crisis and within insolvency proceedings.

[20] The duties mentioned under → mn. 3 et seqq. still apply.

[21] BGH 24.1.2012 – II ZR 119/10, NZI 2012, 413 (414).

ment (§ 15a sub. 3 InsO). The same is true for a corporation's advisory board members if the corporation does not have active managers.

44 Intentional or negligent late filing can lead to personal civil (in particular under § 823 sub. 2 BGB i.c.w. § 15a sub. 1 InsO) and criminal liability for the company's management (§ 15a sub. 4, sub. 5 InsO). Intentional late filing is punishable with imprisonment of up to three years or with a fine. Negligent late filing can lead to imprisonment of up to three years or to a fine.

45 The duty and any potentially arising liability are personal and cannot be passed on to the company. It concerns the individual members irrespective of their responsibilities within the (management or advisory) board. The duty is fulfilled by submitting a true and complete application.[22]

2. Reasons to file for insolvency

a) Illiquidity (§ 17 InsO)

46 A company is illiquid if it cannot meet its due liabilities (§ 17 sub. 1 InsO). The German Federal Court of Justice has issued several rulings on the specifics of this definition[23]: a company is illiquid if (i) its available liquid funds and (ii) those liquid funds that presumably become available within the following three weeks are insufficient to meet at least 90 % of (a) its due liabilities and (b) those liabilities that presumably become due within the following three weeks. Presumably means that the liquid funds or the liabilities are more likely than not (more than 50 % likelihood[24]).

47 The following steps have to be carried out to determine whether the company is illiquid:

1. liquidity status at a certain date: the available liquid funds on the verification date are to be compared with the liabilities due on this date. If the company can meet all due liabilities with the available liquid funds, the company is not illiquid.
2. liquidity forecast: in case of a liquidity gap in the liquidity status, the liquid funds that are currently available and that will presumably become available within three weeks are to be compared with the existing liabilities and those becoming due within three weeks.
   - If the liquidity gap is less than 10 %, the company is not illiquid. However, if the gap will foreseeably enlarge within the near future (approx. six months) to more than 10 % and it cannot be predicted with certainty that the liquidity gap can then be closed, illiquidity exists.
   - If the liquidity gap is 10 % or more, the company can be considered illiquid. Only in exceptional cases can the situation be considered a mere "payment delay" (e.g. seasonal businesses).

48 Against the background of management's personal (and also criminal) liability, the exceptions to the 10 % rule should be applied very cautiously.

49 Available liquid funds include cash, cheques and bank deposits or credit lines. They are available if the company has immediate access (cf. → mn. 46 (lit. (i)). They become available if access is granted within the following three weeks (cf. → mn. 46 (lit. (ii)). If the company is able to sell non-cash assets leading to cash inflow within three weeks, this inflow is also relevant for future cash.

---

[22] For details and the necessary content of the application → mn. 97–99.

[23] BGH 24.5.2005 – IX ZR 123/04, NZI 2005, 547; BGH 12.10.2006 – IX ZR 228/03, NZI 2007, 36; BGH 19.7.2007 – IX ZB 36/07, NZI 2007, 579; BGH 19.12.2017 – II ZR 88/16, NZI 2018, 204.

[24] For more details on liquidity planning → mn. 21 et seqq.

Liabilities include all liabilities that are due (or become due within the three week period) and that are directed at a payment of the company. Liabilities that are directed at an activity, such as the construction of a building, are not included. A liability is due if it must be paid (under contractual or statutory rules) and if the creditor sincerely demands payment of the liability (*ernsthaftes Einfordern*). The latter is presumed unless there is reason to believe otherwise (factual deferral of payment, tolerated overdraft of payment targets). 50

51

Example 1: the company has available liquid funds of 100 EUR and will receive liquid funds in the next three weeks of 250 EUR. Due liabilities on the verification date amount to 110 EUR. During the next three weeks, additional liabilities of 270 EUR will become due.

1. Liquidity status: as of the verification date, the company can only meet (100 / 110) x 100 = 90.91 % of its liabilities. The liquidity gap is 9.09 %.
2. Liquidity forecast: taking into account the upcoming three weeks, the company can meet (100+250) / (110+270) x 100 = 92.10 % of its liabilities. The liquidity gap is 7.9 %. Unless the gap will foreseeably enlarge within the near future (approx. six months) to more than 10 % and it cannot be predicted with certainty that the liquidity gap can then be closed, the company is not illiquid.

52

Example 2: the company has available liquid funds of 100 EUR and will receive liquid funds in the next three weeks of 50 EUR. Due liabilities on the verification date amount to 210 EUR. During the next three weeks, additional liabilities of 270 EUR will become due.

1. Liquidity status: as of the verification date, the company can only meet (100 / 210) x 100 = 47.62 % of its liabilities. The liquidity gap is 52.38 %.
2. Liquidity forecast: taking into account the upcoming three weeks, the company can meet (100+50) / (210+270) x 100 = 31.25 % of its liabilities. The liquidity gap is 68.75 %. The company can be considered illiquid (unless in exceptional rare cases, see → mn. 47).

53

Example 3: the company has available liquid funds of 200 EUR and will receive liquid funds in the next three weeks of 50 EUR. Due liabilities on the verification date amount to 10 EUR. During the next three weeks, additional liabilities of 70 EUR will become due.

1. Liquidity status: as of the verification date, the company can meet all of its liabilities. It is not illiquid.
2. Liquidity status not necessary (but advisable to continuously check liquidity status).

Illiquidity is presumed if the company has stopped making payments (§ 17 sub. 2 InsO). 54
The German Federal Court of Justice understands this payment stop to be a behaviour of the company which is noticeable for third parties, and which would typically allow for the conclusion that a debtor is unable to meet his or her due liabilities (at least the circles of people involved around the debtor must be able to come to that conclusion).[25] Circumstantial evidence is evaluated as indicative signs. A strong sign would be non-payment of substantial debt, especially employee wages, taxes or social security[26]. But also, the failure to comply with payment promises[27] or accumulating seizures, attachments or fruitless seizures by the bailiff[28] could be seen as an indication for a payment stop.

[25] BGH 21.6.2007 – IX ZR 231/04, NJW-RR 2007, 1419.
[26] BGH 17.12.2015 – IX ZR 61/14, NZI 2016, 134 (135).
[27] BGH 24.3.2016 – IX ZR 242/13, NZI 2016, 454.
[28] BGH 18.7.2013 – IX ZR 143/12, NZI 2013, 932.

b) Over-indebtedness (§ 19 InsO)

55 A company is over-indebted pursuant to § 19 sub. 2 InsO if (i) its assets no longer cover its existing liabilities (balance sheet over-indebtedness) and (ii) it is not more likely than not that the business can be continued because it does not have sufficient liquidity to meet its financial obligations (when they become due) in the following twelve months (going-concern prognosis).

56 To verify balance sheet over-indebtedness, an over-indebtedness balance sheet is to be drawn up. On the asset side, the company's actual assets are to be realistically reported as of the verification date, disclosing hidden reserves and using liquidation values. On the liability side, all liabilities and provisions are to be reported (provisions are classified as liabilities if it is more likely than not that they will be incurred). They are recognized with the amount for which there is a realistic probability of a claim. Equity or share capital is not taken into account. Balance sheet over-indebtedness requires that the liabilities exceed the assets.

57 A positive going concern prognosis only exists if there is an intention to continue as a going concern.[29] Additionally, it has to be more likely than not that during the next twelve months, the company will have sufficient liquidity to repay liabilities when they become due.

c) Imminent illiquidity (§ 18 InsO)

58 A company is imminently illiquid pursuant to § 18 InsO if it is more likely than not that it will not be able to meet its liabilities at the time they become due within the upcoming 24 months. Management has to draw up a liquidity forecast for the upcoming 24 months[30] to check if this is the case. Unlike in the case of illiquidity, the company must be able to meet all of its liabilities (not 90 % or more) and when they are due (not within three weeks).

59 Imminent illiquidity does not give rise to the obligation to file for insolvency (see § 15a sub. 1 InsO). The company may opt to do so to increase the possibility of a successful restructuring or to use special rights within insolvency proceedings (see § 270d InsO). Since there is no obligation to file for insolvency when the company is only imminently illiquid, managing directors of a limited liability company should consult with the company's shareholder prior to filing. Failure to do so may lead to civil liability.[31] It is recommended to request a formal shareholders' resolution for evidentiary purposes. It is disputed if the same applies for corporations.

II. Payment restrictions

60 After the occurrence of insolvency, no payments shall be made for the company with company funds (§ 15b sub. 1 InsO). This provision serves to protect the company's creditors from a reduction of the later insolvency estate. The term 'payment' is to be understood broadly. It includes the typical payment in cash or by bank transfer but also the assignment of claims and the transfer of assets.

61 As an exception to this rule, payments that are compatible with the diligence of a prudent businessman are permissible. During the time period in which management actively works on remedying insolvency or prepares all necessary documentation to file for insolvency, payments are considered 'compatible with the diligence of a prudent busi-

[29] BGH 9.10.2006 – II ZR 303/05, NZI 2007, 44.
[30] For details → mn. 21 et. seqq.
[31] OLG München 21.3.2013 – 23 U 3344/12, NZG 2013, 742.

nessman' if they are necessary to keep the business as a going concern (§ 15b sub. 2 sent. 1 InsO). An objective standard must be applied for this purpose. Payments are admissible if an objectively thinking creditor would have agreed to the payment in the interest of maintaining value-preserving business operations. This includes, for example, payments for goods for the company's business operations, rent for business premises or salary payments to employees (without taxes and employer social security contributions[32]). However, payments are not permissible if no compensation will be received after the payment (i.e. the goods to be paid have already been delivered).

Management is not allowed to pay due taxes. In the interim period from the occurrence of insolvency until the opening of preliminary proceedings the delayed or omitted tax payment has no effect on the management's personal liability (§ 15b sub. 8 sent. 1 InsO). However, this exemption only applies if management fulfils its insolvency filing obligations in a timely manner pursuant to § 15a InsO.[33] 62

After the time period in which management actively works on remedying insolvency or prepares all necessary documentation to file for insolvency has lapsed, payments are usually no longer considered 'compatible with the diligence of a prudent businessman' and are therefore not permissible. Payments may even lead to criminal liability under § 266 StGB for embezzlement and misappropriation of funds. 63

As mentioned in → mn. 31, payments to shareholders leading to illiquidity are not permitted (§ 15b sub. 4 InsO). 64

Management of the insolvent company is personally liable in the event of improper payments and is obligated to reimburse the company for the amount paid (§ 15b sub. 4 InsO). This obligation extends not only to the individual director who initiated the payment, but to all directors of the company. 65

III. Behaviour towards contractual partners

Duties towards contractual counterparties include not entering into new contracts and not placing orders if their fulfilment is not assured. If new contracts or orders are made or if the company receives (unpaid) deliveries, the counterparty must be informed (in documented form) about the crisis and possible consequences. Otherwise, a director might be exposed to personal criminal and civil liability risks due to fraudulent representation (§ 263 StGB). 66

IV. Management of company assets

Directors may be exposed to civil or criminal liability, (i) if they fail to comply with their legal duty to prepare the company's annual accounts and/or to keep the company's accounts properly, (ii) if they act contrary to proper management and this decreases the company's assets, or (iii) if, despite the company's illiquidity, they favour the company's creditors to the detriment of the company's assets.[34] 67

---

[32] For details on payments of employee social security contributions → Ch. 19 (Criminal labour law).
[33] → mn. 41 et seqq.
[34] Further on criminal liability → mn. 77 et seqq.

V. Duties within insolvency proceedings

1. Shift of duties to creditors

68 The main goal of insolvency proceedings is to satisfy creditors in the best possible way (§ 1 InsO).[35] Therefore, the best possible realisation of the debtor's assets is a fundamental task of insolvency proceedings and always the benchmark for decisions to be taken within the proceedings.

2. Obligation to cooperate and provide information

69 After filing for insolvency, management and members of the supervisory board are obligated to provide the insolvency court, the insolvency administrator, the creditors' committee (*Gläubigerausschuss*) and, on the order of the court, the creditors' meeting[36] (*Gläubigerversammlung*) with information on all circumstances relating to the proceedings (*allgemeine Auskunftspflicht*, §§ 101 sub. 1 sent. 1, 97 sub. 1 sent. 1 InsO). Management and the members of the supervisory board must support the (preliminary) insolvency administrator in performing all responsibilities and duties (*Mitwirkungspflicht*, §§ 101 sub. 1 sent. 1, 97 sub. 2 InsO). The members of the management and supervisory board are obligated to make themselves available at any time in order to fulfil their duties to provide information and to cooperate and must refrain from all acts that conflict with the fulfilment of these duties (*Präsenzpflicht*, §§ 101 sub. 1 sent. 1, 97 sub. 3 InsO). There is no right of appeal against any court orders in this context (§ 6 sub. 1 InsO).

70 In terms of content, management and supervisory board must provide information on all factual, economic and legal circumstances which may be connected with the insolvency proceedings. These may, for example, relate to transactions entered into by the company, questions of the validity or contestability of such transactions or facts needed for raising possible objections or defences for the benefit of the company. They must provide information on the whereabouts of individual assets, in particular foreign assets, possible rights to separation or rights to separate satisfaction. Questions relating to the company's accounting, questions of tax information or questions relating to the company structure and possible claims against shareholders may also have to be answered. Under §§ 101 sub. 1 sent. 1, 97 sub. 1 sent. 1, sent. 2 InsO, the management and supervisory board shall also even disclose facts which are likely to lead to prosecution for a criminal or an administrative offence. However, such information may be used in criminal proceedings only with the debtor's consent (§ 97 sub. 1 sent. 1, sent. 3 InsO).

71 It is advisable to always provide correct information. This is because the court has the right to have the members of the management and supervisory board affirm on oath that he or she has provided the information requested from him or her correctly and completely to the best of his or her knowledge and belief (§§ 101 sub. 1 sent. 1, 98 sub. 1 InsO). False sworn statements may lead to criminal liability. If management refuses to provide information, the court can have the members detained (after a hearing, §§ 101 sub. 1 sent. 1, 98 sub. 2 InsO). With regard to such information that could have criminal consequences, a prohibition on exploitation in criminal proceedings applies (§ 97 sub. 1 sent. 3 InsO).

---

[35] For more details on the proceedings → mn. 94 et seqq.

[36] → mn. 107.

VI. Duties in self-administration proceedings

If the court orders self-administration (*Eigenverwaltung*[37]), management has additional obligations. This is because in self-administration, the debtor (and not the insolvency administrator) continues to manage the company's business. The intention is to protect creditors and ensure that the goals of insolvency proceedings are achieved. The court may only order self-administration upon application by the company via its management. 72

All of management's actions must be carried out in the best interest of the creditors. Management is no longer exclusively responsible only to shareholders and the company. They must, if necessary, revise earlier decisions. 73

The company's management has the duty to prepare the balance sheet and list of creditors referred to in §§ 151 et seqq. InsO (§ 281 sub. 1 InsO) and to give a detailed report in the creditors' meeting on the causes of insolvency and the current status of the insolvency proceedings (§ 281 sub. 2 InsO). Standard accounting duties also lie with management (§§ 281 sub. 3, 66, 155 InsO). The supervisory board of a company is not subject to this obligation, since it has no influence on the management of the insolvent company (§ 276a sub. 1 InsO). 74

Furthermore, management has to realise collateral that constitutes rights to separate satisfaction (*Gegenstände, an denen ein Absonderunsgrecht besteht*) for the benefit of these creditors (§ 282 sub. 1 sent. 1 InsO). Management has the obligation to review and potentially dispute claims filed by the creditors (§ 283 sub. 1 InsO). It needs to realise the insolvency estate and honour rights to separate satisfaction (*Absonderungsrechte*) in accordance with § 166 InsO. It is also management's obligation to distribute the insolvency estate to the insolvency creditors at the end of the proceedings (§§ 281, 283 sub. 2 InsO). 75

Management may be subject to further duties, since §§ 270 et seqq. InsO are not exhaustive in this respect. In the absence of a statutory allocation of responsibility, responsibility is to be determined on the basis of general principles. 76

C. Management's criminal liability in the context of insolvency

A number of criminal offences are possible in the context of insolvency. The offence of § 15a sub. 4 InsO (failure to file a request for the opening of proceedings in due time) has already been addressed in → mn. 41 et seqq. This provision is also applicable to the members of the representative body of a Societas Europaea (SE) with a dualistic system. The looming loophole in criminal liability in the case of an SE with a monistic system is closed by § 53 sub. 4 SEAG. 77

Credit institutions and insurance undertakings are not authorised to file a request for the opening of proceedings. However, they are obliged to notify the respective supervisory authorities (§ 46b KWG, § 311 VAG). A violation of these obligations is punishable under § 55 KWG and § 331 sub. 2 no. 3 VAG. 78

§ 2 BauFordSiG is also to be mentioned, as it defines criminal liability for recipients of loans for construction if they stop the payments to the creditors or become insolvent after using the money contrary to its purpose. 79

Finally, the German criminal code itself enlists a number of so-called insolvency offences in §§ 283 et seqq. StGB: 80

---

[37] For more details on this type of proceeding → mn. 123, 124.

I. Overview of 'Insolvency Offences' (§§ 283 et seqq. StGB)

1. Period/state of the company

81 The 24th division of the StGB, which contains §§ 283 et seqq. StGB, is titled 'Insolvency Offences' (*Insolvenzstraftaten*). However, the offences cannot only be committed in the state of insolvency (as defined in → mn. 40: illiquidity under § 17 InsO or over-indebtedness under § 19 InsO), but already before if these actions lead to an insolvency (see §§ 283 sub. 1, 4, 283c, 283d StGB) or even regardless of the financial situation of the company (§ 283b StGB). In principle, the criminal law terms are derived from insolvency law.[38] However, special characteristics of criminal law must be taken into account (such as the principles of certainty or *in dubio pro reo*).

82 That being said, all the offences under §§ 283 et seqq. StGB only entail criminal liability if the perpetrator (i) has suspended payments or (ii) if insolvency proceedings have been opened over the company's assets or the opening has been refused on the grounds of insufficiency of assets. This limitation of liability follows from § 283 sub. 6 StGB. The other offences of the division refer to this paragraph. The limitation of liability serves to not additionally impose an existence-threatening criminal procedure on crisis-stricken companies. The German Federal Court of Justice understands a payment stop to be a behaviour of the company which is noticeable for third parties, and which would typically allow for the conclusion that a debtor is unable to meet his or her due liabilities (at least the circles of people involved around the debtor must be able to come to that conclusion).[39] The criterion of opened insolvency proceedings or its refusal on the grounds of insufficiency of assets depends on the legal force of the formal legal act (§§ 26, 27 InsO).

2. Perpetrators

83 Only certain persons can be perpetrators of the insolvency offences of §§ 283 to 283c StGB, with the exception § 283d StGB, where anyone can be a perpetrator since the norm serves precisely to cover the actions of an external party. The other offences can only be committed by the debtor itself. Liability for another person's debt can also lead to liability as a perpetrator. In the case of §§ 283 sub. 1, sub. 4 no. 1, sub. 5 no. 1, 283c StGB, the debtor additionally needs to be in a state of illiquidity, over-indebtedness or imminent illiquidity. The accounting offences (§ 283 sub. 1 no. 5 to 7 (also i.c.w. § 283 sub. 2); § 283b StGB) can, moreover, only be committed by merchants (§§ 1, 2, 3 sub. 2 HGB).

84 As always, if special personal characteristics give rise to criminal liability, they also apply to the representative if these characteristics do not exist in the person of that representative but in the entity, partnership or person represented (§ 14 StGB). According to § 14 sub. 1 no. 1 StGB, the representative of a legal person who acts as its organ is liable. This primarily covers managing directors and board members of legal entities, but also includes de facto managing directors. § 14 sub. 1 no. 2, 3 StGB includes persons that act as a representing partner of a partnership with legal capacity or as a statutory representative (e.g. the insolvency administrator).

---

38 For a definition of illiquidity and over-indebtedness → mn. 46 et seqq.

39 BGH 21.6.2007 – IX ZR 231/04, NJW-RR 2007, 1419.

3. Intent and negligence

The various offences under §§ 283 et seqq. StGB mostly require intent; only for certain offences, as specified in § 283 sub. 4, 5 StGB, negligence is sufficient. **85**

4. Extra-criminal consequences

Within the first five years after a binding conviction for an intentionally committed insolvency offence, the convicted person is barred from acting as a managing director of a limited liability company (§ 6 sub. 2 no. 3 lit. b GmbHG) or as a member of the executive board of a corporation (§ 76 sub. 3 no. 3 lit. b AktG). In addition, in the event of a binding conviction for an insolvency offence, the licence to exercise certain trade businesses (§§ 34c sub. 2 no. 1, 34d sub. 5 sent. 2, 34f sub. 2 no. 1, 34i sub. 2 no. 1 GewO) and the license for an itinerant business (§ 57 sub. 2 GewO) must be refused by the trade control authority. **86**

II. Bankruptcy (§ 283 StGB)

The debtor must already be (imminently) illiquid or over-indebted at the time of the act constituting the offence in order for § 283 sub. 1 StGB (*Bankrott*) to apply. Under § 283 sub. 2 StGB an illiquidity or over-indebtedness must be caused by the act. Unlike sub. 1, sub. 2 does not cover imminent illiquidity. The acts constituting the offence covered by § 283 StGB are: **87**

- setting aside/concealing/destroying/damaging of assets forming part of the (later) insolvency estate in a manner contrary to the requirements of proper business conduct (sub. 1 no. 1);
- engaging in loss-making or speculative transactions in a manner contrary to the requirements of proper business conduct; gambling and betting (sub. 1 no. 2);
- procuring goods or securities on credit and selling/otherwise disposing of them for considerably less than their value in a manner contrary to the requirements of proper business conduct (sub. 1 no. 3);
- feigning the rights of others or recognising fictitious rights (sub. 1 no. 4);
- omitted or defective keeping of commercial records (sub. 1 no. 5);
- setting aside/concealing/destroying/damaging of commercial records before the expiry of the retention period (sub. 1 no. 6);
- omitted or defective preparation of balance sheets (sub. 1 no. 7);
- reducing assets in a manner grossly contrary to the requirements of proper business conduct (sub. 1 no. 8).

It is disputed whether foreign accounting obligations are covered by no. 5 to 7. In any case, the general clause in no. 8 serves to close the potential gap in criminal liability. **88**

The phrase 'in a manner contrary to the requirements of proper business conduct' is a requirement for several offences (no. 1, 2, 3 and 8). Unlike in consumer insolvency (*Verbraucherinsolvenz*), in the entrepreneurial context the principles of diligence of a prudent businessman can be used to determine proper business conduct. According to some, the standard of § 15b InsO is to be applied, provided that its requirements are met. **89**

§ 283a StGB stipulates a more severe penalty for especially serious offences. **90**

III. Breach of duty to keep commercial records (§ 283b StGB)

91 § 283b StGB mainly corresponds to the bankruptcy offences of § 283 sub. 1 no. 5 to 7 StGB. However, it does not require the debtor to be in a state of over-indebtedness or (imminent) illiquidity at the time of the offence or to become insolvent as a result of the act. The obligation to keep commercial records can result from §§ 238 sub. 1, 240, 242 HGB, §§ 150, 152 AktG and §§ 41 et seqq. GmbHG.

IV. Preferential treatment of creditors (§ 283c StGB)

92 § 283c StGB assumes criminal liability for debtors who, in the knowledge of their own illiquidity, grant a creditor a security or satisfaction to which that creditor is not entitled in general or not in such a manner or not at that time. However, § 283c StGB privileges such a debtor (with a lower penalty) compared to the offence under § 283 sub. 1 no. 1 StGB.

V. Preferential treatment of debtors (§ 283d StGB)

93 § 283d StGB complements § 283 sub. 1 no. 1 StGB for the scenario that a third-party acts with the consent or on behalf of the person in crisis.

D. Characteristics of German insolvency proceedings

I. Purpose and overview

94 Insolvency proceedings under German law serve to satisfy the creditors of a debtor (here: the company) collectively (§ 1 InsO). This aim is achieved by implementing one of the following three options: (i) sale of the business as a going concern (asset deal) and liquidation of the remaining legal entity, (ii) insolvency plan proceedings, preserving the legal entity or (iii) piece by piece sale of the business and liquidation of the legal entity. German law also recognises self-administration in which the debtor's management keeps the legal authority to run the business acting for and on behalf of the company[40]. Regardless of the means to satisfy the debtor's creditors or whether or not the court orders self-administration, the procedural rules that generally apply to the insolvency proceedings are the same (with certain exceptions to insolvency plan proceedings[41]).

95 Insolvency proceedings can only be initiated if the company is either over-indebted, illiquid or imminently illiquid[42]. They are collective proceedings affecting the company's stakeholders as a whole. Insolvency proceedings and reasons to file for insolvency always refer to the individual company and not to groups of companies. However, for groups in insolvency, certain procedural peculiarities apply to align the different proceedings (§§ 269a et seqq. InsO).

---

[40] For management's duties in self-administration proceedings, → mn. 72. For more details on self-administration proceedings → mn. 123.

[41] Consumer insolvency proceedings are excluded in the following analysis.

[42] → mn. 58.

German insolvency proceedings are characterised by a chronological division into preliminary insolvency proceedings and main insolvency proceedings. 96

II. Insolvency application

Insolvency proceedings are not commenced *ex officio* but only upon application. An insolvency application can be filed by a creditor or by the debtor's management with the competent insolvency court. It must be in German (or at least bilingual) and include the information necessary to identify the debtor company (name, address, company registration number in the commercial register), to check the court's jurisdiction and the applicant's authority to file the application. The applicant must express its intent to request the opening of insolvency proceedings over the company's assets as a whole. 97

The requirements for a management application are wider than if a creditor applies for insolvency over the company's assets. Management must provide facts that support the company's insolvency (over-indebtedness or (imminent) illiquidity). Usually, the application also explains the reasons for the current crisis and mentions the turning point that ultimately led to the insolvency. The application has to include a list of the company's creditors (identifying certain creditor groups) and state whether the business has already been shut down or is ongoing. In the latter case, management is obligated to include information on the balance sheet total, turnover and number of employees for the previous fiscal year. Usually, applications also contain a list of the company's assets, especially if the application is based on over-indebtedness. For the company's management it is important to note that the application is the first document that the court and the future insolvency administrator receive. While, of course, many things can be clarified or explained again during the course of the proceedings, the application can and should be used to make one's case and especially to explain why the filing was made during the statutory time period. 98

If a creditor files for insolvency, they have to convince the court that they have an undisputed due and enforceable claim against the debtor and that there is a mandatory reason to open insolvency proceedings (illiquidity or over-indebtedness). Creditors' applications cannot be based on imminent illiquidity alone. 99

III. Preliminary insolvency proceedings

After an insolvency application is filed, preliminary proceedings commence and normally take two to three months. During this time, the court determines whether the requirements for opening the insolvency proceedings are met. This is the case if reasons to open insolvency proceedings exist (over-indebtedness or (imminent) illiquidity) and the company's assets are sufficient to cover the costs of the insolvency proceedings (court fees and fees for insolvency administrator or custodian). The court usually appoints an expert to evaluate these prerequisites. 100

During the preliminary proceedings, the court has to take all measures that are necessary to safeguard the insolvency estate (§ 21 InsO). This usually includes the appointment of a preliminary insolvency administrator whose consent is needed for certain business decisions of the management[43]. 101

---

[43] For appointment of (preliminary) custodian in self-administration proceedings → mn. 123.

102 Other safeguarding measures may include a preliminary creditors' committee[44], stay of enforcement actions or the order that (certain) receivables of the company can only be paid on a special account of the preliminary insolvency administrator.

103 While main decisions concerning the company's assets can only be made in the main insolvency proceedings (after the court has decided that the prerequisites to open the proceedings are satisfied), in practice, it is during the preliminary insolvency proceedings that the general course and chances of success of the proceedings are set. This includes the decision to start an M&A process, (temporary) shut down of the business for lack of sufficient funds to uphold business operations or the successful communication to internal and external stakeholders of the company ensuring their ongoing support.

104 Most court decisions (in the preliminary and main insolvency proceedings) are made public on an official website of all insolvency courts in Germany: https://www.insolvenzbekanntmachungen.de.

IV. Main insolvency proceedings

1. Court order opening insolvency proceedings

105 If the prerequisites are met (reason for insolvency and sufficient funds), the court orders the opening of insolvency proceedings and appoints an insolvency administrator (§ 27 InsO). The right to dispose of and manage the company's assets, is transferred to the insolvency administrator (§ 80 InsO). He or she is the leading figure of the proceedings and is subject to the supervision of the insolvency court (§ 58 InsO).

106 The insolvency administrator and not management must fulfil the company's bookkeeping and accounting obligations under commercial and tax law with regard to the insolvency estate.

2. Creditors' meeting

107 When the court orders the opening of the proceedings, the court also sets a date for the creditors' meeting which usually takes place no later than six weeks after the opening. At the meeting, the creditors decide on the further progress of the proceedings on the basis of a report of the insolvency administrator. This includes the decision to sell or shut down the business or to pursue insolvency plan proceedings.

3. Lodging of claims (insolvency creditors), verification meeting

108 Regular insolvency creditors no longer have the option to initiate or pursue enforcement actions against the debtor concerning the insolvency estate (§ 89 InsO). Instead, they have to lodge their claims with the insolvency administrator and get their claims entered into the insolvency table kept by the insolvency administrator within a certain period (§ 174 InsO). However, a delayed filing generally does not exclude the claim (subject to the general periods of limitation/prescription), but merely triggers a small court fee (approximately 20 EUR).

109 The merits of the claims are reviewed in the verification meeting that is set by the court in the opening decision. Once the claim is verified and accepted, the creditor is entitled

[44] → mn. 120.

to receive the insolvency quota which is distributed at the end of the proceedings. The proceeds from the proceedings are only distributed to the creditors with accepted claims.

4. Pending contracts

Upon commencement of insolvency proceedings, mutual obligations deriving from bilateral, not or not completely performed contracts become unenforceable until and unless the insolvency administrator chooses to perform the contractual obligations (§ 103 InsO, *pending contracts*). 110

If the insolvency administrator chooses not to perform pending contracts, the rights and receivables arising from such contracts will finally remain unenforceable. The contractual partner can seek compensation for any damages deriving from the non-performance as a non-privileged insolvency creditor by lodging their claim. If the insolvency administrator chooses to perform a pending contract, the contractual obligations of the debtor become enforceable and are regarded as preferential claims. 111

5. Insolvency claw back

If certain requirements are met, actions made prior to the application to open insolvency proceedings can later be voided under insolvency claw back rules by the insolvency administrator (or the custodian in self-administration proceedings). The hardening periods vary depending on the statute and range from one month to ten years. As a generalization, the company must be illiquid or at least imminently illiquid at the time of the action to be voided and the receiving party must have knowledge of the (imminent) illiquidity (whereby knowledge of circumstances which necessarily indicate (imminent) illiquidity is equivalent). This does not apply, however, for a repayment of shareholder loans made within one year of the application or for securities granted within ten years of the application. These actions can be clawed back without any further subjective requirements. 112

6. Distribution of quota payment

After the realisation of the debtor's assets[45], the final distribution takes place (§ 196 InsO). The insolvency administrator first satisfies the creditors with preferential claims. Proceeds from encumbered assets are paid to the security holders. The remaining insolvency estate is divided equally among the unsecured creditors by paying out the insolvency quota. In Germany, insolvency quotas usually rank in the lower 1 digit range. 113

Once the insolvency estate is completely distributed, the insolvency proceedings are terminated by the insolvency court (§ 200 InsO). At the same time, the legal entity of the company is fully terminated and shortly after deleted from the commercial register. 114

V. Creditor ranking and qualification of creditor claims

German law recognises the following types of creditors: preferential creditors (§ 53 InsO, *Massegläubiger*), regular insolvency creditors (§ 38 InsO, *Insolvenzgläubiger*), creditors with the right to separation (§ 47 InsO, *Aussonderungsberechtigte*), creditors with the 115

[45] Via (i) sale of the business as a going concern (asset deal), (ii) insolvency plan proceedings, or (iii) piece by piece sale of the business and liquidation of the debtor company, also → mn. 94.

right to separate satisfaction (§§ 49 et seqq. InsO, *Absonderungsberechtigte*) and subordinated creditors (§ 39 InsO, *nachrangige Insolvenzgläubiger*).

116 Unless a claim is subordinated by law (i.e. claims for repayment of shareholder loans, § 39 InsO) or contractually, any claim against the debtor originating before the opening of the proceedings is a regular (unsecured) insolvency claim and will be settled by the insolvency quota (§ 38 InsO). Only if regular insolvency creditors are satisfied in full will subordinated creditors receive any payments.

117 Preferential creditors only include court fees, fees of the (preliminary) insolvency administrator/custodian and (preliminary) creditors' committee (§ 54 InsO) as well as any new claims that are entered into or originate during the preliminary proceedings with the court's consent or during the main proceedings (§ 55 sub. 1, sub. 2 InsO). VAT liabilities that were established with the consent of the preliminary insolvency administrator are also considered preferential claims (§ 55 sub. 4 InsO). Preferential claims are settled before regular insolvency creditors receive the insolvency quota.

118 Creditors with a right to separation can claim that the item is in fact not part of the insolvency estate. These rights must be considered a right in rem (i.e. simple retention of title right). These creditors can request to surrender the object to them.

119 If a creditor holds securities, it is considered a creditor with the right to separate satisfaction. Such securities may be one of the following: mortgage or land charge, transfer of title in movables, assignment of claims, pledge over movables or rights or extended retention of title rights. This means that the item is sold (details vary based on the type of security) and the proceeds of the security are paid to said creditor only (up to the amount of the secured claim and less a lump sum for the estate of usually 9 %). The remainder of the claim (claim less realization proceeds) becomes a regular unsecured insolvency claim.

VI. Creditors' involvement in insolvency proceedings

120 As insolvency proceedings serve to satisfy the company's creditors, their vote is decisive for the most relevant decisions concerning the insolvency proceedings. They form their vote in the creditors' assembly (*Gläubigerversammlung*, §§ 74 et seqq. InsO). In larger proceedings, the court usually establishes a (preliminary) creditors' committee of three to nine creditors (§ 67 InsO). If certain thresholds are met, a preliminary creditors' committee is obligatory (§ 22a sub. 1 InsO)[46]. It is the responsibility of the creditors' committee to support and monitor the activities of the (preliminary) insolvency administrator (§ 69 InsO). For certain actions of particular importance, the administrator requires the creditors' committee's consent (§ 160 InsO).

121 The creditors' committee can make a binding proposal for the preliminary insolvency administrator by a unanimous vote. If in urgent cases the court did not hear the creditors' committee prior to appointing a preliminary administrator, the committee may subsequently replace the preliminary insolvency administrator by a unanimous vote.

VII. Shareholder rights in insolvency proceedings

122 Upon the opening of insolvency proceedings, shareholders lose their influence over management of the company as well as (in the vast majority of cases) their potential finan-

---

[46] For the preceding business year, two out of the three have to be met: (i) at least 50 employees, (ii) total balance sheet assets of at least 6,000,000 EUR, revenues of at least 12,000,000 EUR.

cial gain from their shares. As early as when the preliminary insolvency administrator is appointed, shareholder instructions become fruitless as management cannot execute the instructions without the consent of the preliminary administrator (at least where this does not simply involve strategic, non-legal acts)[47]. Shareholders only receive parts of the proceeds from the proceedings if all creditors (even subordinated creditors) have been paid in full. Shareholder loans or any actions that are to be considered economically equivalent to a shareholder loan are subordinated by law (§ 39 sub. 1 sent. 1 no. 5 InsO).

VIII. Self-administration

Under German insolvency law, a company can undergo insolvency proceedings in self-administration. Self-administration may be ordered by the court not only for the preliminary, but also for the (main) insolvency proceedings. If self-administration is granted, the company's management will keep the power to run the business under the supervision of a court-appointed custodian. The management must do so for the benefit and in the best interest of the creditors and not the company's shareholders. Shareholders lose their power to influence management (§ 276a sub. 1 InsO). Usually, self-administration will serve the goal to implement an insolvency plan or sell the business as a going concern. **123**

Self-administration is only ordered upon the company's request. Together with the application, management must submit detailed documentation including liquidity planning and a concept for the successful implementation of the insolvency proceedings (§ 270a InsO). **124**

E. Pre-insolvency reorganisation proceedings (StaRUG)

Following the Directive (EU) 2019/1023 on preventive restructuring frameworks,[48] the German legislator issued the Act on the Stabilisation and Restructuring Framework for Businesses (StaRUG), thereby introducing pre-insolvency restructuring proceedings. The Act entered into force on 1 January 2021. By using StaRUG proceedings, a company can restructure its financial balance sheet when it is imminently illiquid (§ 18 InsO) but not yet illiquid or over-indebted.[49] Affected creditors vote on a restructuring plan in groups. If the necessary majorities are met, the court approves the plan that becomes binding on all affected parties, including dissenting creditors. The company's management remains in power during StaRUG proceedings. In some cases, the court can appoint a custodian to supervise management's actions (§ 73 StaRUG). **125**

I. Overview of course of proceedings

1. Notice of StaRUG proceedings to court

StaRUG proceedings are initiated by a notice of the company's management to the competent court (§ 31 sub. 1 StaRUG). The jurisdiction of the court is determined by **126**

[47] For shareholder influence in self-administration proceedings → mn. 123.
[48] OJ L 172/18 26.6.2019.
[49] For details on reasons for insolvency → mn. 46 et. seqq.

§§ 35 et seqq. StaRUG. In Germany, the competent restructuring courts are local courts (*Amtsgerichte*, § 34 sub. 1 StaRUG).[50] The local jurisdiction (*örtliche Zuständigkeit*) follows the company's centre of main interest. Under § 35 StaRUG, the restructuring court in whose district the debtor has his centre of main interest has exclusive local jurisdiction.[51]

127 Together with the notice, management needs to submit a draft of the restructuring plan, explain the current state of the negotiations with affected creditors and the precautions that have been taken to ensure that the company can fulfil its duties during the proceedings.

2. Restructuring plan

128 During the proceedings, the company (its management) completes the restructuring plan. The plan does not have to affect all stakeholders of the company. Instead, it is the company's choice what creditors it intends to include in the proceedings, as long as the selection follows appropriate selection criteria (§ 8 StaRUG). Employees cannot be included in the proceedings (§ 4 no. 1 StaRUG). The affected creditors are divided into groups based on their existing rights (§ 9 StaRUG).

3. Voting mechanism

129 The creditors vote on the plan in groups. The plan is approved if each group consents with a majority of 75 % (based on their claim value, § 25 StaRUG). If a group does not consent, it can be crammed down if (i) the group members are presumably not worse off under the plan than under a realistic alternative approach without a restructuring plan, (ii) the group members participate appropriately in the economic value to be distributed to the affected parties and (iii) the majority of the groups have approved the plan (if only two groups have been formed, the approval of the other group is sufficient if not exclusively formed by shareholders or subordinated creditors).

4. Effects of court approval

130 The court approves the restructuring plan upon the company's application (§ 60 StaRUG). With the approval, the actions listed in the plan come into effect (§ 67 StaRUG). It is important for the company that this effect applies in relation to all affected parties irrespective of whether they voted against the plan or did not vote at all.

5. Moratorium

131 During the course of the proceedings, the company can make use of a moratorium. To the extent necessary to preserve the prospects of a successful restructuring, the court may order that (i) measures of compulsory enforcement against the company are prohibited or temporarily suspended (stay of enforcement, *Vollstreckungssperre*), and (ii) certain rights to movable assets may not be enforced by the creditor and that such assets may be used for the continuation of the business insofar as they are of considerable importance for this purpose (realisation freeze, *Verwertungssperre*, § 49 StaRUG).

---

[50] Some state legislators have decided that only one or some of their local courts can serve as restructuring courts.

[51] See § 37 StaRUG for proceedings involving groups of companies.

§ 44 sub. 1 StaRUG stipulates that StaRUG proceedings as such cannot negatively influence a contract of the company (*Verbot von Lösungsklauseln*): specifically, it cannot be agreed that upon initiation of StaRUG proceedings or use of instruments of the proceedings (i) contracts are automatically terminated, (ii) contractual services become due or (iii) the contractual party may refuse its services. Clauses to the contrary are invalid (§ 44 sub. 2 StaRUG).[52] 132

II. Alternative approach and comparison to insolvency proceedings

In some circumstances, management of the company has the choice what restructuring tool – insolvency or StaRUG proceedings – they use for their company. This is namely the case if the company is not yet insolvent. It is important to note that upon insolvency, management is obligated to file for the opening of insolvency proceedings within certain deadlines irrespective of any existing shareholder instructions to the contrary.[53] StaRUG proceedings can no longer be used. Generally, insolvency proceedings and StaRUG proceedings can be compared as follows: 133

Insolvency proceedings	StaRUG proceedings
Insolvency proceedings necessarily involve all creditors and stakeholders of the company.	The company can select creditors that are affected by the restructuring plan (appropriate selection criteria must be applied).
The court may appoint insolvency administrator who takes over the business, self-administration possible.	Always self-administration proceedings (appointment of custodian possible to supervise management).
Proceedings are public, potential negative implications for company's business, insolvency stigma.	The company can opt for non-public proceedings (however, effects of non-public proceedings are not recognized under EU law outside of Germany).
The company benefits from insolvency money paid by the Federal Employment Agency for three months for employees' wages (§ 165 SGB III).	No insolvency money, wages must be paid as usual.
Termination of employment contracts is possible, easier and less costly.	Employees cannot be affected by the proceedings, their rights cannot be impaired.
Under specific circumstances, the company can terminate long-term continuing obligations (i.e. rental/leasing agreements) (§§ 109 et seqq. InsO).	Contracts cannot be terminated.

Absent an insolvency, management is well advised to carefully evaluate both options and to document its decision. In a limited liability company, management should include the company's shareholders in the decision making process and request formal instructions by shareholder resolution on how to proceed to prevent any personal liability. 134

[52] This does not apply to contracts falling under § 104 InsO, which are commodity futures and financial performance contracts (*Warentermin- und Finanzleistungsverträge*) and agreements on liquidation netting (*Liquiditionsnetting*), financial collateral within the meaning of § 1 sub. 17 KWG and transactions that are subject to the netting of claims and benefits within the framework of a system within the meaning of § 1 sub. 16 KWG, § 44 sub. 3 StaRUG.

[53] → mn. 41.

Pending any case law to the contrary, management of a corporation should proceed in the same way, if possible.

III. Management duties during the proceedings

1. Notification in case of insolvency

135 After the proceedings have been initiated[54], management's duty to file for insolvency[55] is suspended. However, as the StaRUG-proceedings are intended to be pre-insolvency proceedings, management remains obligated to inform the court if the company becomes insolvent without undue delay (§ 42 sub. 1 StaRUG[56]) or file an application to open insolvency proceedings with the insolvency court (§§ 32 sub. 3, 42 sub. 2 StaRUG). Failure to inform the court or file for insolvency is punishable with up to three years of prison or with a fine (§ 42 sub. 3 StaRUG) and may cause civil liability (§ 42 sub. 1 sent. 2 StaRUG i.c.w. § 823 sub. 2 BGB).

2. Conduct proceedings with diligence of prudent businessman

136 The management of a company has the duty to conduct the proceedings with the diligence of a prudent businessman (*ordentlicher und gewissenhafter Geschäftsleiter*) and to protect the interests of the creditors as a whole (§§ 32 sub. 1, 43 sub. 1 sent. 1 StaRUG). In the interest of the creditors, the management is obligated to refrain from measures which are incompatible with the objective of the restructuring concept or which jeopardise its prospects of success (§ 32 sub. 1 sent. 2 StaRUG).

137 In the event of a breach of this duty, management is liable to the company in the amount of the loss incurred by the creditors (§ 43 sub. 1 sent. 2 StaRUG). If management does not have the knowledge that is necessary to comply with these duties, it is advisable to engage appropriate advisors to avoid any liability. Due to the extensive liability, it might also be advisable to take out D&O insurance for the management prior to initiating StaRUG proceedings or to amend existing policies. It is important to note that the general duties of management under § 93 sub. 1 AktG or § 43 sub. 1 GmbHG as well as § 1 StaRUG continue to apply and are not superseded by §§ 32, 43 StaRUG.

3. Notification in case of changes in proposed restructuring

138 The restructuring court and the custodian (*Restrukturierungsbeauftragter*), if appointed, must be notified without delay of any substantial amendments regarding the restructuring and the current state of negotiations (§ 32 sub. 2 StaRUG). In the case of an existing stabilisation order pursuant to § 49 StaRUG, the company must also inform the restructuring court of any material change regarding the restructuring plan (§ 32 sub. 2 StaRUG). In addition, the management is obligated to immediately notify the restructuring court if they come to the conclusion that the restructuring does no longer have any prospects of successful implementation (§ 32 sub. 4 StaRUG).

---

[54] → mn. 126.
[55] → mn. 41.
[56] For illiquidity also see § 32 sub. 2 StaRUG.

4. Duties for company's auditors and advisors

StaRUG also includes obligations for the company's consultants, namely tax advisors, tax agents, auditors, certified accountants and lawyers. § 102 StaRUG establishes comprehensive information and warning duties for advisors who participate in the preparation of annual financial statements (*Erstellung des Jahresabschlusses*). There are no corresponding obligations when preparing other financial statements such as the tax balance sheet, consolidated financial statements or interim reports. Auditors are subject to special duties under § 321 HGB. **139**

Under § 102 StaRUG, the listed consultants need to inform the company's management if the company might be insolvent or imminently illiquid and what implications follow from it. This duty exists if indications for an existing insolvency are obvious and if the consultants must assume that the company's management is not aware of the possible insolvency. **140**

It is important for the management to note that the consultants' obligations do not affect existing duties for the management. **141**

F. Applicable law, jurisdiction and recognition of StaRUG and insolvency proceedings

The Insolvency Regulation (Regulation (EU) 2015/848 on Insolvency Proceedings) regulates international jurisdiction to open (pre-)insolvency proceedings, mutual recognition of judgments in the context of these proceedings, the powers of the insolvency administrator in other Member States and the relationship between the various proceedings in the different Member States.[57] **142**

The central prerequisite for the applicability of the Insolvency Regulation is that insolvency proceedings (already opened or to be opened) are listed in Annexes A and B for the respective Member State.[58] **143**

German (preliminary) insolvency proceedings and public StaRUG proceedings (*öffentliche Restrukturierungssachen*) are part of Annex A of the Insolvency Regulation. Public StaRUG proceedings must be made public pursuant to §§ 84 to 88 StaRUG. As a direct consequence, the Insolvency Regulation applies to these proceedings. There is no comparable statute applying to confidential restructuring proceedings (*vertrauliche Restrukturierungssachen*). Only with public announcement will the restructuring case qualify as insolvency proceedings within the meaning of the Insolvency Regulation. **144**

Applying the Insolvency Regulation means the following in a member state[59]: **145**

- International jurisdiction, Art. 3 Insolvency Regulation: the courts of the Member State within the territory of which the centre of the company's main interests is situated, shall have jurisdiction to open the proceedings. The centre of main interests is the place where the company conducts the administration of its interests on a regular basis and which is ascertainable by third parties. This is presumed to be the place of the regis-

[57] Jurisdiction, applicable law and recognition of foreign non-EU insolvency or restructuring proceeding are regulated by §§ 343 et seqq. InsO.

[58] This does not apply to insolvency proceedings concerning the assets of insurance undertakings or credit institutions, investment firms providing services involving the holding of funds or securities of third parties, and collective investment undertakings.

[59] With the exception of Denmark.

tered office (rebuttable presumption). Art. 3 Insolvency Regulation is also applicable if this centre of main interests lies outside of the European Union.

- Applicable law, Art. 7 Insolvency Regulation: the law applicable to proceedings and their effects, their conduct and closure are that of the Member State whose courts opened the proceedings. Art. 7 para. 2 Insolvency Regulation lists specific topics falling under this clause. Art. 8 to 18 Insolvency Regulation contain exceptions to this rule and stipulate peculiarities for certain areas (i.e. employment contracts or third parties' rights in rem).
- Recognition, Art. 19, 32 Insolvency Regulation: the proceedings and any other judgments handed down concerning the course and closure of the proceedings and compositions approved by the court are automatically recognised in other Member States with no further formalities. They can be enforced in all Member States.

CHAPTER 16
DATA PROTECTION (CRIMINAL) LAW[1]

Bibliography: Basar, Nemo-Tenetur im Datenschutzbußgeldverfahren nach „Deutsche Wohnen SE"; Anerkennung der Selbstbelastungsfreiheit jur. Personen als zwingende Folge der Definition eines Datenschutzvergehens als „genuine Verbandstat", PinG 1/2025, 16; Dietrich, Modelle eines Unternehmensstrafrechts und ihre Effektivität Österreich – Verbandsverantwortlichkeit, NZWiSt 2016, 186; Düwell/Brink, Beschäftigtendatenschutz nach der Umsetzung der Datenschutz-Grundverordnung: Viele Änderungen und wenig Neues, NZA 2017, 1081; Ihwas, Datenschutzstrafrecht: Eine Übersicht ergangener Bußgelder und gerichtlicher Entscheidungen (2021-2022), CCZ 2023, 23; Ihwas, Das neue Datenschutzstrafrecht – Bußgeldrisiken für Unternehmen nach der DSGVO und Strafbarkeitsrisiken für Individualpersonen nach dem BDSG, NZWiSt 2021, 289; Ihwas, Anmerkung zu EuGH Urt. 5.12.2023 – C-807/21 („Deutsche Wohnen"), NZWiSt 2024, 313; Klaas/Schäfer, EuGH zu Geldbußen gegen Unternehmen im Datenschutzrecht – Anforderungen an das Verschulden und Verantwortlichkeit in (Rechts-)Nachfolgefällen (Teil 1), NZWiSt 2024, 293; Küpper, Ungarn: Strafbarkeit und Bestrafung juristischer Personen, WiRO 2022, 266; Piltz/Pradel, Wie lange dauern 72 Stunden? Umgang mit der EU-weiten Fristenverordnung am Beispiel der DS-GVO, ZD 2019, 152; Roßnagel/Rost, Eine Geldbuße kommt selten allein: Geldbußen im Kontext aufsichtsbehördlichen Handelns, ZD 2023, 502; Scholz ZRP, Strafbarkeit juristischer Personen?, 2000, 435; Süße/Püschel, UK Bribery Act 2010 aktuell – Die Strafverfolgung von Unternehmen unter Sec. 7 UKBA gewinnt an Fahrt, CCZ 2016, 131; Uecker, Die Einwilligung im Datenschutzrecht und ihre Alternativen – Mögliche Lösungen für Unternehmen und Vereine, ZD 2019, 248; Wybitul/Basar/Hager, Die anwaltliche Tätigkeit in Verfahren wegen Geldbußen nach Art. 83 DS-GVO, ZD 2023, 488; Wybitul/Sürup/Pötters, Betriebsvereinbarungen und § 32 BDSG: Wie geht es nach der DS-GVO weiter? – Handlungsempfehlungen für Unternehmen und Betriebsräte, ZD 2015, 559.

Table of contents

A. Introduction 380
B. European data protection law and German criminal law 381
I. Compatibility of national rules with European law 381
II. Differences between data protection law and criminal law 381
1. Differences in accountability 382
2. Differences in obligation to cooperate 383
C. Liabilities within the GDPR 385
I. Roles and responsibilities 385
1. Data controller (Art. 24 GDPR) 385
2. Data processor (Art. 28 GDPR) 386
3. Data protection officer (Art. 37–39 GDPR; § 38 BDSG) 388
II. Art. 83 para. 4 GDPR 390
1. Security of processing (Art. 32 GDPR) 390
2. Notification of a personal data breach (Art. 33 GDPR) 392
3. Internal or external data protection officer (Art. 37 GDPR) 392
III. Art. 83 para. 5 GDPR 393
1. Basic principles of processing (Art. 5, 6 GDPR) 393
2. Data subjects' rights (Art. 12 et seq. GDPR) 394

[1] The authors are lawyers that work in the white-collar crime boutique Lilie • Ihwas based in Frankfurt am Main. Both specialise in data protection criminal law and are also certified external data protection officers. The authors thank Ass. iur. Paulina Hanß for her support in creating this chapter.

D. Liabilities within the BDSG 395
I. Relationship between GDPR and BDSG 395
II. Scope of application of the BDSG 396
1. Responsibility 396
2. Penal provisions (§ 42 sub. 1 and 2 BDSG) 397
3. Suitable addressees of the penal provision 398
4. Definition of 'personal data that is not publicly accessible' . 399
5. Special conditions in § 42 sub. 1 BDSG 400
a) No. 1: 'transferring the data to a third party' 400
b) No. 2: 'otherwise making them accessible' 400
c) 'for commercial purposes' 400
6. Special conditions in § 42 sub. 2 BDSG 400
a) No. 1: 'processing without authorization' 400
b) No. 2: 'fraudulently acquiring' 400
c) 'in return for payment or with intention of enriching oneself or someone else or harming someone' 401
III. Special provisions for employee data protection (§ 26 BDSG) .. 401
1. Personal scope of application 401
2. Effects of applicability and relationship to general rules ... 403
3. The provision of § 26 sub. 1 sent. 1 BDSG 403
4. The provision of § 26 sub. 1 sent. 2 BDSG 404
5. Increased requirements for consent pursuant to § 26 sub. 2 BDSG 405
6. Effects of collective agreements 406
7. Latest decisions by the Court of Justice of the European Union 407
IV. § 43 BDSG 407
E. Conclusion 408

A. Introduction

1 The Roman statesman Lucius Seneca once said, 'If one does not know to which port one is sailing, no wind is favourable.' This is how most companies feel at the moment when they have to implement a data protection management system. Data protection law has undergone a huge change in the last years. With the implementation of the General Data Protection Regulation ('GDPR') on 25 May 2018 data protection law has left its status of 'nobody-care's-law' to being one of the most significant changes in the recent history of law and has been getting a high amount of (legal) attention. There have been several multi-million EUR fines against companies in the whole European Union ('EU'). In 2023 the world's largest social network service received a fine of 1.2 billion EUR.[2]

2 Overall, there are still many unknowns and legal uncertainties which is quite astonishing if one takes into account how much personal data are being processed every day. Every company must navigate those uncertainties to the best of its abilities. One of the best examples is the data transfer to the United States. The biggest and most relevant IT companies are US companies. There are some IT services only those IT companies can provide, especially if it comes to scaling cloud services on a level that a DAX company would need – or just think about the usage of video conference systems. However, there have been several attempts to achieve the transfer of data to the United States with no legal risk but those attempts have not succeeded so far. The last legal instrument to justify

[2] European Data Protection Board, Press Report of 22 May 2023, <https://edpb.europa.eu/news/news/2023/12-billion-euro-fine-facebook-result-edpb-binding-decision_en> (last accessed: 12.2.2025).

transatlantic data transfer – which is still in place – is the 'EU-US Data Privacy Framework'[3] which has been established during the presidency of Joe Biden. But with the change in US government and the government's agenda one might think that the EU-US Data Privacy Framework might not hold.[4]

So it seems to be only a matter of time until the Court of Justice of the European Union (CJEU) will have to decide on the legality of data transfer on the basis of this agreement. So again, one does not know where this 'wind' will take us. And this is just one of the current legal uncertainties companies are facing. 3

Coming to the nature and the background of this publication, there are even more legal uncertainties if one takes into account the interaction and interdependency of (European) data protection law and (German) criminal law. There are many legal specialties when it comes to data protection law in the context of criminal law in Germany. In this chapter, we will try to navigate those uncertain waters. 4

B. European data protection law and German criminal law

I. Compatibility of national rules with European law

Questions regarding the compatibility of European and German law in terms of data protection are in fact questions regarding the interaction between different fields of law. Problems appear where data protection law and criminal regulations overlap and contradict each other. While the first and foremost part of current data protection rules has its seeds in European law, criminal law in general is genuinely subject of every European Union (EU) member state's legislative power.[5] The development of common European standards in terms of criminal law under the leadership of the EU has not yet resulted in an assignment of legislative power to the EU in this area.[6] 5

Data protection law in its European context is based on the GDPR, introduced in 2018; therefore, in its present form it still does not exist for a long period of time. The GDPR is directly applicable in all Member States and provides a coherent framework regarding data protection law. Nevertheless, due to an opening clause in the GDPR Member States are allowed to enact laws regarding data protection as well. In response to this, the German legislator renewed the Federal Data Protection Act (*Bundesdatenschutzgesetz* – 'BDSG') and used its competence to complement the application of European data rules and adjust it to the German legal system. 6

II. Differences between data protection law and criminal law

Differences between European data protection law and German criminal law occur and come with far-reaching consequences. 7

[3] Commission Implementing Decision EU 2023/1795 of 10 July 2023 pursuant to Regulation (EU) 2016/679 of the European Parliament and of the Council on the adequate level of protection of personal data under the EU-US Data Privacy Framework.

[4] noyb, US-Cloud bald illegal? Trump schlägt erstes Loch in EU-US-Datenabkommen, https://noyb.eu/de/us-cloud-soon-illegal-trump-punches-first-hole-eu-us-data-deal (last accessed: 3.5.2025).

[5] Paal/Pauly/Frenzel BDSG § 42 mn. 2.

[6] See the term 'Strafrecht, Europäisches' in HdLexEU.

1. Differences in accountability

8 The main difference is the accountability. In data protection law, the controller is the one that is accountable for data processing – and therefore any infringements that might happen during the processing. According to Art. 4 no. 7 GDPR, an individual person as well as a legal person – e.g. a company – can be the controller. The controller is liable under Art. 83 GDPR: Art. 83 GDPR states that in case of a data protection infringement a fine can be imposed on the controller. In German law, this fine is deemed as a regulatory offence according to § 41 sub. 1 BDSG and the rules of proceedings are laid out in the Act on Regulatory Offences, the *Ordnungswidrigkeitengesetz* (OWiG). A company can, in the capacity as a controller, be subject of such a regulatory proceeding. These are led by the data protection authorities.[7] According to § 1 sub. 1 OWiG, regulatory offences do – in case of an infringement – result in an administrative fine. Therefore, in most regulatory proceedings the company itself will be subject of the investigation because the company is the controller and therefore the primarily liable subject.[8]

9 However, there can also be formal criminal proceedings by a public prosecutor – instead of a data protection authority – which can also be initiated through an infringement of data protection rules. This is where data protection law and criminal law collide: until now formal criminal proceedings led by a public prosecutor can only target individuals and not legal institution such as companies. Other efforts of the German legislator have not been successful so far[9]. This is based on the rule of German law, which prescribes that punishment only follows *personal* and *individual* guilt. In other countries, corporate criminal liability is already possible. For example, the French Code Pénal (Art. 121-2) contains the possibility of imposing a penalty on legal persons or associations of persons.[10] More European examples are The Netherlands,[11] Hungary,[12] and Austria[13] – and also the UK as a non-EU-member.[14] Consequently, penalties based on German criminal law can only be imposed against individuals.[15] Penalties result from formal *criminal proceedings* led by a public prosecutor.[16]

10 Not all penal provisions can be found in the German Criminal Code (*Strafgesetzbuch*, StGB); the term *Nebenstrafrecht* is used when speaking of these 'supplementary penal

[7] According to § 35 OWiG, the administrative authority is responsible for prosecuting administrative offences. In this sense, administrative authority means any state agency that is authorised by law or legal ordinance to prosecute administrative offences, according to BeckOK OWiG/Inhofer, 45. Ed. 1.1.2025, OWiG § 35 mn. 1.

[8] There may be exceptions in the case of so-called excess acts by employees. If an employee commits an administrative offence from his or her workplace, but not in the exercise of his or her professional duties but for private reasons, he himself becomes the data controller pursuant to Art. 4 para. 7 GDPR. The fine is then imposed on the employee, not on the company, for examples see Ihwas CCZ 2023, 23 mn. 27. Nonetheless, § 130 OWiG also states that the management of the company can be subject to regulatory proceedings as well if they refrain from proper supervisory measures.

[9] The introduction of corporate criminal law has been discussed in Germany for several years. On the basis of current law, the exclusion of corporate liability is undisputed. Only natural persons can 'act' within the meaning of § 14 StGB (Acting as agent). However, due to the ongoing reform efforts, especially in comparison to other countries, the introduction of corporate criminal law seems likely in the future; LKH/Heger StGB § 14 mn. 1a.

[10] LKH/Heger StGB § 14 mn. 14.

[11] Scholz ZRP 2000, 435.

[12] Küpper WiRO 2022, 266.

[13] Dietrich NZWiSt 2016, 186.

[14] Süße/Püschel CCZ 2016, 131.

[15] LKH/Heger StGB § 14 mn. 1a.

[16] Pursuant to § 152 StPO, the public prosecutor's office brings the charges. If the individual is convicted, a penalty is imposed in accordance with the Criminal Code, which results from the respective criminal offence.

provisions outside the StGB'. Concerning criminal data protection law, such a provision can be found in § 42 BDSG.[17] Proceedings regarding this provision are the main liability in terms of management liability since companies cannot be subject to such proceedings but their management can be. Even though data protection authorities do not lead such criminal proceedings they can initiate them by way of a formal criminal complaint (§ 42 sub. 3 sent. 2 BDSG). Nonetheless, even if the data protection authority files such a complain the public prosecutor stays in charge of the proceedings and makes his own assessment. For the public prosecutor – and especially for a court – the legal opinion of another public authority is just that: another legal opinion and there can be many.[18]

In regulatory fine proceedings, the competent supervisory authority is able to impose administrative fines on its own in accordance with § Art. 58 para. 2 lit. i) GDPR. The supervisory authority could be seen as an equivalent to the public prosecutor's office in those proceedings because it determines all circumstances and decides if sanctions should be imposed or not. § 41 sub. 1 BDSG determines the applicability of the rules of the OWiG regarding violations in terms of Art. 83 GDPR. According to § 46 sub. 2 OWiG, the supervisory authorities' powers are similar to those of the prosecution in criminal matters, which some data protection authorities already use on a regular basis.[19] 11

2. Differences in obligation to cooperate

Beyond data protection rules, the BDSG – in contrast to the GDPR – also contains criminal rules. This does not mean that the GDPR contains no sanction regulations, but it just allows the imposition of administrative fines not criminal sanctions. The German legislator used the opening clause of Art. 84 GDPR and enacted § 42 BDSG, the main criminal regulation in the context of data protection law which is currently becoming increasingly important. The past few years were characterised by the implementation of the new data protection rules. Public prosecutors were lenient against the background of the massive amount of work addressees of the new regulations had to deal with and supervisory authorities primary considered themselves to be in an advisory role.[20] 12

In some constellations data protection law and criminal law both claim validity but the general principles do not fit together. This becomes clear when European data law is seen as public law but sometimes there is a smooth transition from administrative procedures into administrative fine proceedings or a criminal law context. According to Art. 57 para. 1 GDPR supervisory authorities essentially fulfil three tasks: (1) they monitor compliance with data protection rules, (2) sanction violations, and (3) advise the public on the risks, regulations, guarantees and rights associated with data processing. As a characteristic part of administrative procedures all involved parties can be affected by the obligation to cooperate with the authority which also includes the person concerned.[21] In 13

[17] Data Protection Acts of the German federal states – each one has its own Data Protection Act – do contain such penal provisions as well. But they are only admissible if the perpetrator is a civil servant.

[18] KG 17.02.2023 – 10 U 146/22, BeckRS 2023, 2618: the legal opinion of the data protection authority is not binding for the court.

[19] Cf. 26. Tätigkeitsbericht Datenschutz Niedersachsen 2020 [i.e. 'Activity Report for Lower Saxony'], p. 91 <https://datenschutzarchiv.org/fileadmin/Dokumente/2020/26_TB_LfD_Niedersachen_2020_oDR-Nr_27052021.pdf> (last accessed: 17.4.2025). The activity reports are published annually by the data protection supervisory authorities of the federal states. In particular, they report on current developments, processed cases and fines imposed in their area of responsibility; Koreng/Lachenmann DatenschutzR-FormHdB/Nolde/Stürzl Form. O. I. 1.

[20] 17. Tätigkeitsbericht zum Datenschutz Mecklenburg-Vorpommern 2021 [i.e. 'Activity Report for Mecklenburg-Western Pomerania'], p. 7 <https://datenschutzarchiv.org/fileadmin/Dokumente/2021/17_TB_LfD_Meck-Vorpom_2021_oDsNr_3105.2022.pdf> (last accessed: 17.4.2025).

[21] BeckOK VwGO/Breunig, 72. Ed. 1.7.2024, § 86 mn. 44.

contrast to that, German criminal law does not know any obligation for an accused person to take part in criminal proceedings against him. This equally applies to regulatory fine proceedings as they result in sanctions as well. The so-called *nemo tenetur* principle[22] demonstrates that self-incrimination cannot be expected of anybody. Regarding to Art. 83 para. 8 GDPR, which determines that the exercise by the supervisory authorities shall be subject to procedural safeguards, the German legislator introduced § 42 sub. 4 and § 43 sub. 4 BDSG[23]. Both regulations are specifically meant to prevent self-incrimination through restrictions on the use of notifications pursuant to Art. 33 GDPR in criminal proceedings and regulatory fine proceedings.[24] Even though, the difference between summary procedures and criminal proceedings respectively regulatory fine proceedings ends up in an area of conflict where the portrayed principles can hardly be brought in line. Art. 83 para. 8 GDPR does not extend national procedural safeguards on GDPR's regulations.[25] Procedural safeguards according to Art. 83 para. 8 GDPR have to be interpreted in the context of European law and are geared towards the realisation of European data protection rules not German criminal law.[26] This means on the one hand companies and their employees have to support the supervisory authority extensively with their investigations and proceedings by European data protection law. That for example includes the notification of personal data breaches to the supervisory authority (Art. 33 GDPR) or the obligation to provide records of processing activities (Art. 30 para. 4 GDPR). Violations in this context can result in substantial fines.[27] On the other hand, the same persons who have to report a data breach are exposed to the danger of becoming a subject of a criminal investigation afterwards.[28] It is not unusual that future accused persons collaborate with data protection authorities in earlier phases of the proceedings to fulfil their obligations and give information to them from which criminal suspicion arises.

14 To differentiate between various stages of the proceedings is difficult with regard to time and contents. The question arises whether criminal suspicion on its own leads to the point that someone has the right to refuse to give evidence or if it depends on the initiation of formal criminal or regulatory fine proceedings. It is necessary for data protection authorities as well as persons concerned to keep an eye on it and make sure the *nemo tenetur* principle is not undermined.[29] It should always receive attention to predict future developments at an early point of the proceedings and ensure the protection of individual rights. In fact, exposed persons should primarily take care of it by their own. The consultation of a specialised lawyer who represents the individual not the company can be helpful at this point.

15 Due to this fact, it can be helpful for companies to seek legal advice in data protection law early on in proceedings. On the one hand, they can participate in the process to avoid possible, substantial fines and on the other hand, this can ensure that the *nemo tenetur* principle is not undermined. The interests of all parties have to be reconciled, which is sometimes difficult, especially in the absence of legal advice.

---

[22] BVerfG 27.04.2010 – 2 BvL 13/07, BeckRS 2010, 50089.

[23] BT-Drs. 18/11325, 109 (cf. Zu § 42 (Strafvorschriften) [i.e. Regarding § 42 (Penal provisions)], Zu § 43 (Bußgeldvorschriften) [i.e. Regarding § 43 (Provisions on administrative fines)]); Koreng/Lachenmann DatenschutzR-FormHdB/Koglin Form. A. III. 6.

[24] WJS WirtschaftsStrafR-HdB/Knierim, 5th edn 2020, Ch. 5 mn. 162.

[25] Kühling/Buchner/Bergt DS-GVO Art. 83 mn. 112.

[26] BeckOK DatenschutzR/Holländer DS-GVO Art. 83 mn. 4.

[27] 'Fine of up to 10,000,000 EUR or up to 2 percent of the total annual worldwide turnover generated by the company in the previous year', according to Spindler/Schuster/Laue DS-GVO Art. 33 mn. 23.

[28] There are German States that do not use the information from a data breach report in administrative fine proceedings (→ mn. 45).

[29] See Basar PinG, 1/2025, 16 et seqq.

C. Liabilities within the GDPR

Most relevant liabilities for a company lie within the GDPR itself. Art. 83 GDPR codifies the imposing of administrative fines on a controller if there is an infringement against the rules of the GDPR. The fine can be up to 10 million EUR or two percent of the company's revenue – whichever is the highest – (Art. 83 para. 4 GDPR) or 20 million EUR or four percent of the company's revenue (Art. 83 para. 5 GDPR). The applicability of respective regulation – Art. 83 para. 4 or Art. 83 para. 5 GDPR – depends on the infringement. However, to fully understand how administrative fines work within the GDPR it is necessary to understand the legal framework and therefore certain terms and definitions which will be described hereafter. 16

I. Roles and responsibilities

1. Data controller (Art. 24 GDPR)

Art. 4 para. 7 GDPR says that 17

> **'Controller'** means the natural or legal person, public authority, agency or other body which, alone or jointly with others, determines the purposes and means of the processing of personal data; where the purposes and means of such processing are determined by Union or Member State law, the controller or the specific criteria for its nomination may be provided for by Union or Member State law.

The data controller is the entity the data subjects entrust with their personal data. They carry responsibility and decide the purpose and means of processing personal data. This includes what type of data gets processed for what reason and in which way[30], measured by the principle of proportionality.[31] The measures taken by the data controller must consider possible risks to the subject's data and severity of a possible breach.[32] The data controller is accountable for adhering to the principles related to processing of personal data according to Art. 5 GDPR.[33] Codes of conduct, which may be provided by the supervisory authorities and approved certification mechanisms such as a seal mark provided under GDPR, can be used to demonstrate the compliance with the regulations.[34] 18

Their general responsibilities are outlined within Art. 24 GDPR. 19

Art. 24 para. 1 GDPR states general responsibilities for a controller. It states that the data controller must implement and maintain technical and organizational measures (TOMs) to protect the data of its users during processing.[35] Implementing and upholding those technical and organizational measures is a very important aspect of the GDPR. Technical measures are understood as all measures that entail the data process- 20

---

[30] BeckOK DatenschutzR/Schmidt/Brink DS-GVO Art. 24 mn. 19; Paal/Pauly/Martini DS-GVO Art. 24 mn. 31 to 35.

[31] BeckOK DatenschutzR/Schmidt/Brink DS-GVO Art. 24 mn. 20–21; Paal/Pauly/Martini DS-GVO Art. 24 mn. 28–30; Sharma p. 63.

[32] BeckOK DatenschutzR/Schmidt/Brink DS-GVO Art. 24 mn. 19; Ehmann/Selmayr/Bertermann DS-GVO Art. 24 mn. 6; Paal/Pauly/Martini DS-GVO Art. 24 mn. 21.

[33] Paal/Pauly/Martini DS-GVO Art. 24 mn. 25.

[34] Paal/Pauly/Martini DS-GVO Art. 24 mn. 44–46; Sharma p. 64; NK-DatenschutzR/Petri/Stief DS-GVO Art. 24 mn. 26–27; Spindler/Schuster/Nink DS-GVO Art. 24 mn. 16.

[35] Ehmann/Selmayr/Bertermann DS-GVO Art. 24 mn. 12; Paal/Pauly/Martini DS-GVO Art. 24 mn. 20; Koreng/Lachenmann DatenschutzR-FormHdB/Lachenmann Form. A. I.

ing operation itself. Examples would be access controls, encryption, pseudonymization, anonymization of data and transmission controls to ensure the ongoing security of the processing.[36] Organizational measures are there to manage and control the data processing, they include record keeping, implementing effective and compliant policies and procedures to ensure data protection, a dual control principle as well as training courses and instructions for employees.[37]

21 If the data controller fails to maintain these measures, it can result in substantial fines. Insufficient TOMs are one of the major possible liability issues.

22 The implementation of those measures must be regularly reviewed and updated (Art. 24 para. 1 sent. 2 GDPR). The regulation does not state a specific period of time for those updates and reviews. While a former draft still included a period of two years, Art. 24 para. 1 GDPR states now, the measures shall be reviewed and updated 'where necessary'.[38] This means that a review and update is only necessary where circumstances or changes give rise for such an audit.[39]

23 The general responsibility and accountability of the data controller includes maintaining a record of processing activities, Art. 30 GDPR.[40] The effective documentation of processing activities is essential to ensure that the data controller can provide the necessary information to the local supervisory authority according to Art. 58 para. 1 lit. a) GDPR in case of administrative proceedings or an investigation.[41]

24 The very high level of responsibility is reflected as well in the fact, that the data controller must provide the data subject with all information where their personal data are collected (Art. 13 et seqq. GDPR) and is liable for compensation (Art. 82 GDPR) and administrative fines (Art. 83 GDPR) in case of non-compliance.[42]

25 The GDPR even applies in cases in which personal data should be processed in places outside of the EU while being overseen within the EU. In this case it is mandatory for the data controller to designate a representative who shall be based in the EU (Art. 27 para. 1, 3 GDPR). The representative shall be addressed in addition to the data controller in all matters of compliance (Art. 27 para. 4 GDPR). This ensures that European authorities can contact the representative, even if the controller is based outside of the EU, where the EU has no jurisdiction. Also, being based outside the EU does not exempt the data controller from legal responsibility. It is the data subject's right to bring legal actions against the data controller or data processor (Art. 27 para. 5 GDPR).

2. Data processor (Art. 28 GDPR)

26 Art. 4 para. 8 GDPR states:

> **'Processor'** means a natural or legal person, public authority, agency, or other body which processes personal data on behalf of the controller.

---

[36] BeckOK DatenschutzR/Schmidt/Brink, 51. Ed. 1.8.2024, DS-GVO Art. 24 mn. 15; Paal/Pauly/Martini DS-GVO Art. 24 mn. 21.

[37] BeckOK DatenschutzR/Schmidt/Brink, 51. Ed. 1.8.2024, DS-GVO Art. 24 mn. 15; Paal/Pauly/Martini DS-GVO Art. 24 mn. 22.

[38] BeckOK DatenschutzR/Schmidt/Brink, 51. Ed. 1.8.2024, DS-GVO Art. 24 mn. 23; Ehmann/Selmayr/Bertermann DS-GVO Art. 24 mn. 13.

[39] Paal/Pauly/Martini DS-GVO Art. 24 Art. 24 mn. 38.

[40] Ehmann/Selmayr/Bertermann DS-GVO Art. 30 mn. 4; BeckOK DatenschutzR/Schmidt/Brink, 51. Ed. 1.8.2024, DS-GVO Art. 24 mn. 13; Koreng/Lachenmann DatenschutzR-FormHdB/Kremer/Sander Form. C. II.

[41] BeckOK DatenschutzR/Schmidt/Brink, 51. Ed. 1.8.2024, DS-GVO Art. 24 mn. 13; Wybitul/Basar/Hager ZD 2023, 488 (489).

[42] BeckOK DatenschutzR/Schmidt/Brink, 51. Ed. 1.8.2024, DS-GVO Art. 24 mn. 18; Paal/Pauly/Martini DS-GVO Art. 12 mn. 10.

The collection and processing of data can be an operation not conducted exclusively by the data controller. A data processor can be involved in the processing. They act on behalf of the data controller by contract. Two criteria[43] must be met for these persons to be considered a data processor: 27

1. the data processor must be an **independent legal or natural entity** from the data controller;[44]
2. the data processor is **instruction-dependent and does not specify the purpose of the data processing**; the controller remains the one to determine the purposes and means of processing.[45]

Examples for data processors are cloud computing services or data centres.[46] 28

The moment a data processor acts independent of the objectives of the data controller, e.g., by merging the data received upon delegation with their own database or uses the data for their own purposes and therefore can make independent decisions on the purpose and means of processing, they become joint controllers (Art. 26 GDPR) with the original data controller.[47] In that case, according to Art. 28 para. 10 GDPR, the data processor gets treated like a data controller and has the same responsibility as well as being liable under Art. 82–84 GDPR.[48] 29

The data controller has a certain set of responsibilities in selecting a data processor. A processor may only be chosen to carry out the processing on behalf of the controller if they can provide a sufficient guarantee that they have implemented the necessary TOMs to ensure compliance with the GDPR as well as the protection of data subjects' rights.[49] This guarantee can be sufficiently given by presenting the controller with approved codes of conduct according to Art. 40 GDPR or a certification according to Art. 42 GDPR.[50] The data controller, as the responsible party, has the obligation to monitor the continued compliance of the data processor.[51] In the event of a violation of the data processor's obligations, the data processor must be expressly notified. In serious cases or in the event of repeated violations of Art. 29 GDPR, the contractual relationship should be terminated.[52] 30

Further, it is mandatory that the data controller maintains a written processing contract with the data processor. This contract must adhere to certain clauses mandated by the GDPR, which should therefore be incorporated into the contract or agreement. The following information is mandatory to be placed within the processing contract[53]: 31

1. subject matter;
2. duration;
3. nature and purpose;
4. the types of personal data;

[43] BeckOK DatenschutzR/Spoerr, 51. Ed. 1.8.2024, DS-GVO Art. 28 mn. 17.

[44] BeckOK DatenschutzR/Spoerr, 51. Ed. 1.8.2024, DS-GVO Art. 28 mn. 17.

[45] BeckOK DatenschutzR/Spoerr, 51. Ed. 1.8.2024, DS-GVO Art. 28 mn. 18–21.

[46] Gola/Schomerus BDSG/Gola/Klug/Körffer, 12th edn 2015, BDSG § 11 mn. 7–8.

[47] Sharma p. 113.

[48] BeckOK DatenschutzR/Spoerr, 51. Ed. 1.8.2024, DS-GVO Art. 28 mn. 104–105; Paal/Pauly/Martini DS-GVO Art. 28 mn. 76.

[49] BeckOK DatenschutzR/Spoerr, 51. Ed. 1.8.2024, DS-GVO Art. 28 mn. 33–36; Paal/Pauly/Martini DS-GVO Art. 28 mn. 19.

[50] BeckOK DatenschutzR/Spoerr, 51. Ed. 1.8.2024, DS-GVO Art. 28 mn. 90; Ehmann/Selmayr/Bertermann DS-GVO Art. 28 mn. 31; Paal/Pauly/Martini DS-GVO Art. 28 mn. 19, 67–69.

[51] Paal/Pauly/Martini DS-GVO Art. 28 mn. 20.

[52] Paal/Pauly/Martini DS-GVO Art. 29 mn. 24; NK-DatenschutzR/Petri DS-GVO Art. 28 mn. 94; BeckOK DatenschutzR/Spoerr, 51. Ed. 1.8.2024, DS-GVO Art. 29 mn. 24.

[53] BeckOK DatenschutzR/Spoerr, 51. Ed. 1.8.2024, DS-GVO Art. 28 mn. 50–84; Paal/Pauly/Martini DS-GVO Art. 28 mn. 23–58.

5. categories of data subjects;
6. the obligations and rights of the controller.

32 To make this process easier for the data controller, the contract may include so called 'standard contractual clauses' (Art. 28 para. 6 to 8 GDPR).[54]

33 According to Art. 28 para. 2, 4 GDPR, it is prohibited for the data processor to subcontract or subprocess the work assigned to them.[55] It is only permitted to assign a 'sub-processor' with the explicit approval of the data controller (Art. 28 para. 2 GDPR). In that case, the sub-processor must adhere to the same mandatory contractual terms and legal requirements. The processor remains liable to the data controller in case the sub-processor does not ensure the appropriate technical and organizational measures (Art. 28 para. 4 GDPR).

34 The duties of the data processor include only conducting activities under the documented instructions of the controller and following all security measures under GDPR as well as ensuring compliance with it. The processor must be bound by a confidentiality clause[56] and make sure only individuals who are responsible for the processing have received instructions from the controller. After the termination of processing, the data processor must delete or return all personal data.[57] Finally, the data processor shall assist the data controller in demonstrating compliance with the regulations of the GDPR.[58]

35 Data processing outside the EU is permitted in accordance with the regulations of Art. 44 et seqq. GDPR, which ensure an extra level of protection.[59] Especially problematic is the transfer of data to the United States. There have been several attempts to guarantee the same Level of data protection in the United States as in the EU. Currently, the adequacy decision issued by the European Commission on 10 July 2023 referred to as the 'EU-US Data Privacy Framework', applies to data transfers between the United States and Germany.[60] As already said above, a review of this agreement by the Court of Justice of the European Union is expected to take place soon,[61] especially in reference to the change in US Government, which has been mentioned in the introduction.

3. Data protection officer (Art. 37–39 GDPR; § 38 BDSG)

36 The data protection officer, in short DPO, is appointed by the controller. An organization is required to appoint a DPO under one of the following circumstances (Art. 37 para. 1 GDPR, § 38 sub. 1 BDSG):

1. if the data is processed by a public authority or body, except for courts acting in their judicial capacity (Art. 37 para. 1 GDPR);
2. if the activities conducted consist of processing operations that require regular and systematic monitoring of users on a large scale (Art. 37 para. 1 GDPR);

---

[54] BeckOK DatenschutzR/Spoerr, 51. Ed. 1.8.2025, DS-GVO Art. 28 mn. 95; Paal/Pauly/Martini DS-GVO Art. 28 mn. 70–74.

[55] BeckOK DatenschutzR/Spoerr, 51. Ed. 1.8.2025, DS-GVO Art. 28 mn. 72; Paal/Pauly/Martini DS-GVO Art. 28 mn. 59.

[56] BeckOK DatenschutzR/Spoerr, 51. Ed. 1.8.2025, DS-GVO Art. 28 mn. 63.

[57] Ehmann/Selmayr/Bertermann DS-GVO Art. 28 mn. 31.

[58] Ehmann/Selmayr/Bertermann DS-GVO Art. 28 mn. 30.

[59] Ehmann/Selmayr/Bertermann DS-GVO Art. 28 mn. 9.

[60] Com(2023) 4745 final; 'Angemessenheitsbeschluss zum EU-US Data Privacy Framework in Kraft getreten', Press Report, BfDI, 10.7.2023, <https://www.bfdi.bund.de/SharedDocs/Kurzmeldungen/DE/2023/17_Angemessenheitsbeschluss-EU-US-DPF.html> (last accessed: 12.2.2025).

[61] 'European Commission gives EU-US data transfers third round at CJEU', noyb, 10.7.2023, <https://noyb.eu/en/european-commission-gives-eu-us-data-transfers-third-round-cjeu> (last accessed: 12.2.2025).

3. if the activities involve processing large quantities of special categories of data and personal data relating to criminal convictions and offences (Art. 37 para. 1 GDPR); the 'special category of data' is defined under Art. 9 GDPR, which states 'personal data revealing racial or ethnic origin, political opinions, religious or philosophical beliefs, or trade union membership, and the processing of genetic data, biometric data for the purpose of uniquely identifying a natural person, data concerning health or data concerning a natural person's sex life or sexual orientation shall be prohibited.' Personal data relating to criminal convictions and offences are per se sensible and therefore separately regulated in Art. 10 GDPR;
4. if the controller constantly employs as a rule at least 20 persons dealing with the automated processing of personal data (§ 38 sub. 1 BDSG);
5. if the controller undertakes processing subject to a data protection impact assessment pursuant to Article 35 of Regulation (EU) 2016/679 (§ 38 sub. 1 BDSG);
6. if the controller commercially processes personal data for the purpose of transfer, of anonymized transfer or for purposes of market or opinion research (§ 38 sub. 1 BDSG).

A single DPO can be appointed by a group of undertakings, provided that the DPO is easily accessible from each establishment (Art. 37 para 2. GDPR). To be qualified for the position, the DPO must have expert knowledge of data protection law and practices. It is possible for organisations to either appoint an internal DPO for their own purposes or an external DPO can be employed under a service contract (Art. 9 para. 6 GDPR).

The DPO's main task is the protection of the personal data of the users in accordance **37**
with the GDPR. Art. 39 GDPR outlines the tasks of the DPO. They include:

- informing and advising the controller or the processor and the employees who conduct processing of their obligations to the GDPR and the compliance with national provisions, meaning for private companies in Germany, the German Federal Data Protection Act (BDSG);[62]
- monitoring the compliance with the GDPR and BDSG, including assignment of responsibilities, awareness-raising and training of staff involved in processing operations, and the related audits;[63]
- providing advice where it is requested in regard to the data protection impact assessment and monitor its performance;[64]
- cooperating with the supervisory authority (the independent public authority established by a Member State according to Art. 51 GDPR);[65]
- acting as the contact point for the supervisory authority on issues relating to processing.[66]

It is mandatory to involve the DPO into data processing operations in a timely man- **38**
ner. Timely means that the DPO must have enough time and opportunity to become acquainted with the details of the data processing operation and to issue an opinion. This also includes having the opportunity to change or add aspects of the processing at an early stage.[67] Proper involvement according to the GDPR requires the organization or the department in charge of the data processing operation to inform the DPO proactive-

---

62 Ehmann/Selmayr/Heberlein DS-GVO Art. 39 mn. 9–11.

63 BeckOK DatenschutzR/Moos, 51. Ed. 1.11.2021, DS-GVO Art. 39 mn. 8–16; Ehmann/Selmayr/Heberlein DS-GVO Art. 39 mn. 12–15.

64 Ehmann/Selmayr/Heberlein DS-GVO Art. 39 mn. 16–18.

65 BeckOK DatenschutzR/Moos, 51. Ed. 1.11.2021, DS-GVO Art. 39 mn. 20–22.

66 Paal/Pauly/Martini DS-GVO Art. 39 mn. 9.

67 Ehmann/Selmayr/Heberlein DS-GVO Art. 38 mn. 8.

ly.[68] In their role, the DPO is independent (Art. 38 para. 3 GDPR) and reports directly to top management, which shall help to ensure that data protection remains a high priority.

39 The DPO's contact details shall be included in relevant reports and published by the data controller or data processor, e.g., on the website within the privacy policies section.

II. Art. 83 para. 4 GDPR

40 This provision regulates the imposition of fines of up to 20,000,000 EUR or up to 2 % of a company's annual turnover in the event of breaches of obligations by controllers and processors in certain cases, certification bodies or supervisory bodies. It should be noted that in a case against Deutsche Wohnen SE, the CJEU has recently issued a decision which sets out the standards that apply to the imposition of fines under the GDPR[69]. The court ruled that the imposition of fines pursuant to Art. 83 para. 4 to 6 GDPR against a legal entity as the controller, unlike German administrative offences law in §§ 30, 130, 9 OWiG[70], does not require any attributable conduct of an identifiable natural person. At the same time, according to the court, Art. 83 GDPR is to be interpreted in such a way that it stipulates intentional or negligent violation of the GDPR on the part of the responsible company as a prerequisite for the imposition of a fine. As a result, the infringement just does not have to be attributed to an identifiable natural person within the company or take place with the knowledge of the corporate's bodies[71]. Ultimately, neither the proceedings against Deutsche Wohnen SE are likely to have been brought to a final solution, nor should the interpretation and principles established by the CJEU be regarded as conclusive – for example, the requirements for determining the specific infringement remain open.

There have already been many administrative fine proceedings so far. The following shall give a categorized overview on the most relevant administrative fines for companies:

1. Security of processing (Art. 32 GDPR)

41 According to Art. 32 GDPR, an example of a breach of duty by a controller shows when it does not take sufficient technical and organizational measures to protect personal data.

42 According to the Brandenburg State Commissioner for Data Protection, it violates Art. 32 of the GDPR if requests for information are answered by e-mail and the required password for a transmitted file is sent directly in a second e-mail in plain text. The rapid transmission of the password does not ensure that the required protection of the data is in place. This also results from the fact that the time interval between the two e-mails was very short. Accordingly, a six-figure fine was imposed on this company.[72] Therefore, the password should always be sent on a separate way of communication, e.g. via SMS.

43 Another example is the imposition of a fine of 1.2 million EUR on a health insurance company. The health insurance company had operated sweepstakes in recent years and collected personal data from participants, including information about their health insurance affiliation. Without a legal basis for processing, this information was used to attract

---

[68] Ehmann/Selmayr/Heberlein DS-GVO Art. 38 mn. 7.

[69] CJEU 05.12.2023 – C-807/21, ECLI:EU:C:2023:950 = BeckRS 2023, 34616.

[70] MAH Strafverteidigung/Grözinger § 50 mn. 125.

[71] Klaas/Schäfer NZWiSt 2024, 293; Koreng/Lachenmann DatenschutzR-FormHdB/Koglin Form. A. II. 2; a detailed discussion can be found at: Ihwas NZWiSt 2024, 313 (319 et seq.).

[72] Cf. Tätigkeitsbericht Datenschutz Brandenburg 2020 [i.e. 'Activity Report for Brandenburg], p. 53 <https://datenschutzarchiv.org/fileadmin/Dokumente/2020/22_TB_LfD_Brandenburg_2020_oDrsNr_03052021.pdf> (last accessed: 17.4.2025).

new customers to the health insurance company. Up to this point, such a large fine had never been imposed in the state of Baden-Württemberg.[73] This shows that the unlawful processing of data for marketing purposes can result in heavy fines.

In Lower Saxony, a company was fined 65,500 EUR for operating its website with software that had not been updated by the software manufacturer with security updates since 2014. The software was no longer adequate by current technical standards to sufficiently protect personal data. The software was outdated and had significant security gaps. As a result, there was a risk that users' passwords could have been determined, which constituted a violation of Art. 32 GDPR.[74] This fine shows that automatic updates can be a simple and efficient technical and organizational measure to protect personal data. Furthermore, it shows that outdated software has to be replaced to fulfil GDPR requirements and safe processing of personal data. In this case, the fine was imposed on the basis of a notification pursuant to Art. 33 GDPR by the company.[75] This shows how difficult it is when a controller has to report a data breach and does not want to bring himself into sanctioning proceedings. The risk of initialize such proceedings by themselves can make companies negate their obligation to report and take the risk of getting caught – which is not in the spirit of the GDPR. 44

Therefore, in the German state of Hesse, this is handled differently. If a company reports a data breach pursuant to Art. 33 GDPR because a data protection obligation pursuant to Art. 32 GDPR or the principles of processing pursuant to Art. 5 GDPR have been violated, the content of the report may not lead to any sanction for the company. This is because the company is obliged to report a data breach and could refrain from reporting if it has to expect a fine. The company may not be sanctioned for the notification of the data breach.[76] 45

In Hamburg, a company operating in the healthcare sector was fined a six-figure sum in 2021 as well. The company was unable to guarantee data protection when sending out doctors' letters because no suitable technical and organizational measures were in place. As a result, doctors' letters were sent to the wrong recipient. The company was even told several times by the recipient that the doctor's letters were not addressed to her. During the proceedings, further violations were also uncovered.[77] In this case, sensible data was sent to the wrong person – more than once. If an error occurs – e.g. a wrong person receives an email – it should be analysed and measures shall be taken to prevent repetition, especially in the case of sensible data as it was the case in Hamburg. 46

It is also deemed a violation if a social media service provider stores user passwords without encryption. In Baden-Württemberg, due to such a breach of obligations during a hacker attack, 330,000 user passwords were published on the internet, which constitutes a massive infringement of these individuals' rights.[78] As a result, a fine of 20,000 EUR was 47

---

[73] Cf. Tätigkeitsbericht Baden-Württemberg 2020 [i.e. 'Activity Report for Baden-Württemberg], p. 61, <https://datenschutzarchiv.org/fileadmin/Dokumente/2020/36_TB_LfD_Ba-W%C3%BC_2020_16-9850_08022021.pdf> (last accessed: 17.4.2025).

[74] Cf. 26. Tätigkeitsbericht Niedersachsen 2020 [i.e. 'Activity Report for Lower Saxony'], p. 97 <https://datenschutzarchiv.org/fileadmin/Dokumente/2020/26_TB_LfD_Niedersachen_2020_oDR-Nr_27052021.pdf> (last accessed: 22.4.2025).

[75] Cf. 26. Tätigkeitsbericht Niedersachsen 2020, p. 97 <https://datenschutzarchiv.org/fileadmin/Dokumente/2020/26_TB_LfD_Niedersachen_2020_oDR-Nr_27052021.pdf>> (last accessed: 22.4.2025).

[76] Roßnagel/Rost ZD 2023, 502 (506).

[77] Tätigkeitsbericht Datenschutz Hamburg 2021 [i.e. 'Activity Report for Hamburg'], p. 67 <https://datenschutz-hamburg.de/fileadmin/user_upload/HmbBfDI/Datenschutz/Taetigkeitsberichte_Datenschutz/Taetigkeitsberichte_PDF/30._taetigkeitsbericht_datenschutz_2021.pdf> (last accessed: 22.4.2025).

[78] Cf. Tätigkeitsbericht Baden-Württemberg 2018, p. 73 <https://www.baden-wuerttemberg.datenschutz.de/wp-content/uploads/2019/02/LfDI-34.-Datenschutz-T%C3%A4tigkeitsbericht-Internet.pdf> (last accessed: 29.4.2025).

imposed on the social media service – not the hacker –, which constituted a very high fine in the state Baden-Württemberg in 2019. Due to the fact that it was just at the beginning of GDPR – it was only in place roundabout one year – and data protection authorities were not giving many fines so that companies could adapt to GDPR. But unprotected passwords should never be an 'organizational measure'. This will also apply to passwords being taped under the keyboard of the respective computer or password lists being stored in the desk drawer.

2. Notification of a personal data breach (Art. 33 GDPR)

48 According to Art. 33 GDPR, the controller must report to the data protection authorities about a violation of the protection of personal data within 72 hours after he found out about the violation. An exception of the reporting obligation only applies if there is no risk for the rights and freedom of the person concerned by the violation.

49 A fine can be imposed in case of a delay. A clinic had to pay a fine of 6,800 EUR because the clinic reported a data breach a few days late – it was seven instead of three days after the incident. It did not matter to the data protection authority that it was a weekend during this time.[79] When calculating the due date companies must be aware that deadlines measured by hours according to the GDPR do not exclude weekends or holidays. In the 'European way' of calculating a due date must be done according to the legal provisions of Council Regulation (EEC, EURATOM) No 1182/71, published on 3 June 1971. Often, national rules, such as in the GDPR, conflict with the rules on time limits in Regulation No 1182/71.[80] However, due to the primacy of application of EU law, the time limits in the regulation take precedence. If a data breach is detected, it must be reported within 72 hours, as already explained. However, the time limit does not begin until knowledge is gained. In addition, there must be at least two working days to the end of the deadline because it is a 3-day deadline within the meaning of Art. 3 para. 5 of the regulation, so that the deadline can exceed 72 hours in exceptional cases.[81]

3. Internal or external data protection officer (Art. 37 GDPR)

50 A fine may also be imposed if there is a breach of Art. 37 GDPR, i.e. if a data controller does not appoint a data protection officer, although the requirements of Art. 37 GDPR are fulfilled and the appointment is therefore mandatory. A fine can also be imposed if the appointed person is unsuitable and does not have the required data protection knowledge. Companies must assure themselves that their data protection officer has the respective knowledge. In most cases it is best suitable to allocate this task to an outside counsel.

51 Such a violation was seen when the shareholder of a specialised clinic was appointed as data protection officer.[82] The data protection officer was considered unsuitable. Because, at the same time as a shareholder, he had an economic interest in the success of the clinic and still had to fulfil his duties as data protection officer – which usually do not align with economic interest, at least in the short run. In this position, he would also have had

---

[79] Cf. 48. Tätigkeitsbericht Datenschutz Hessen 2019 [i.e. 'Activity Report for Hesse], p. 136 et seq. <https://datenschutzarchiv.org/fileadmin/Dokumente/2019/48_TB_LfD_Hessen_2019_oDrsNR_13052020.pdf> (last accessed: 17.4.2025).

[80] Piltz/Pradel ZD 2019, 152 (153).

[81] Piltz/Pradel ZD 2019, 152 (156).

[82] Cf. Jahresbericht Datenschutz und Informationsfreiheit Berlin 2021 [i.e. 'Activity Report for Berlin'], p. 142 <https://datenschutzarchiv.org/fileadmin/Dokumente/2021/TB_LfD_Berlin_2021_oDrsNr_24052022.pdf> (last accessed: 17.4.2025).

to strictly control the clinic. In the opinion of the Berlin Data Protection Commissioner, this was not possible due to a conflict of interest, which is why a fine was imposed.[83]

A fine may also result from a pure formal violation of Art. 37 GDPR if the change of a data protection officer is not reported to the competent data protection authority. In case of a worldwide operating social media service a subsidiary firm forgot to formerly inform the data protection authority of the change of the data protection officer. For this reason – not because the data protection officer was not competent or a data protection officer was not in place, just because someone forgot to inform the data protection authority, the company had to pay a fine of 51,000 EUR.[84] Accordingly, it is not sufficient to have a data protection officer. This must also be reported to the data protection authority. 52

III. Art. 83 para. 5 GDPR

Compared to Art. 83 para. 4 GDPR, Art. 83 para. 5 GDPR can impose fines of up to 20,000,000 EUR or up to 4% of a company's annual income in the event of a breach of obligations mentioned therein. Accordingly, the breaches mentioned there are to be considered even more serious. The following shall be another categorized overview on administrative fine proceedings in Germany: 53

1. Basic principles of processing (Art. 5, 6 GDPR)

Art. 5 of the GDPR describes minimum requirements and contains important principles for the processing of personal data. For example, the principle of purpose limitation, the principle of integrity and confidentiality.[85] If a responsible person violates Art. 5 GDPR, a fine can be imposed. 54

As a result of such a violation, a fine of 50,000 EUR was imposed on an online bank. An infringement of Art. 5 and 6 GDPR was seen by the data protection commissioner because the bank blacklisted the names of former customers to prevent money laundering. As a result, it was not possible for these customers to open additional accounts with this bank. In doing so, it was not checked whether these customers were actually suspects on the basis of such a criminal offence.[86] Although companies must comply with the legal requirements for data processing in order to prevent money laundering, this may only be done to a certain level. The data protection rights of customers must still be adequately protected.[87] 55

Art. 6 GDPR indicates the legal basis on which data processing by a controller may take place. If data processing takes place without a basis, a fine will be imposed. 56

For example, a fine may be imposed due to all-day video surveillance if there is no legal basis for it. In the German State of Saarland, such data processing was carried out by a company with a total of 14 cameras.[88] The provisions of Art. 30 and Art. 13 of the 57

[83] Jahresbericht Datenschutz und Informationsfreiheit Berlin 2021, p. 142, <https://datenschutzarchiv.org/fileadmin/Dokumente/2021/TB_LfD_Berlin_2021_oDrsNr_24052022.pdf> (last accessed: 17.4.2025).

[84] Tätigkeitsbericht Datenschutz Hamburg 2019, p. 105 et seqq, <https://datenschutzarchiv.org/fileadmin/Dokumente/2019/28_TB_LfD_Hamburg_2019_oDrsNr_13022020.pdf> (last accessed: 17.4.2025).

[85] BeckOK DatenschutzR/Schantz, 51. Ed. 1.11.2021, DS-GVO Art. 5 mn. 12, 35.

[86] Jahresbericht Datenschutz und Informationsfreiheit Berlin 2019, p. 161 <https://datenschutzarchiv.org/fileadmin/Dokumente/2019/TB_LfD_Berlin_2019_oDrsNr_03042020.pdf> (last accessed: 17.4.2025).

[87] Jahresbericht Datenschutz und Informationsfreiheit Berlin 2019, p. 162 <https://datenschutzarchiv.org/fileadmin/Dokumente/2019/TB_LfD_Berlin_2019_oDrsNr_03042020.pdf> (last accessed: 17.4.2025).

[88] 30. Tätigkeitsbericht Datenschutz Saarland 2021 [i.e. 'Activity Report for Saarland'], p. 135 <https://datenschutzarchiv.org/fileadmin/Dokumente/2021/30_TB_LfD_Saarland_2021_17-09_22062022.pdf>

GDPR were violated because no processing activity was documented and there was no information sign. This constituted a major infringement on the rights of the persons affected by the video surveillance.[89]

58 In general, video surveillance is a hot topic in data protection law. Very easily, a company can violate data protection rules by surveilling their employees. Recently the Administrative Court of Hannover issued a decision on the topic. And the decision shows how video surveillance can be within the rule of law. The facts of the case were as follows[90]:

59 The company technically monitored and evaluated the work processes of its employees using data scanners. The employee objected to this and instituted a data protection monitoring procedure. As a result, the company was prohibited from collecting data, as it violated data protection regulations.

60 The company defended itself against this in court. In their view, they had a legitimate interest in evaluating the data. This allowed them to see when employees worked faster or slower and where their weaknesses and strengths lay. This allowed them to give performance-reviews and objective feedback to employees.

61 The court ruled in the right of the company, as the monitoring was based on § 26 BDSG. According to this provision, personal data of employees may be processed for purposes of the employment relationship if this was necessary for the performance of the employment relationship or the termination. The court was not of the opinion that the interference with the employees' right of informational self-determination was out of proportion to the interests of the company. However, the judgement is not yet final, as an appeal has been filed by the employee.

2. Data subjects' rights (Art. 12 et seq. GDPR)

62 Art. 12 et seq. of the GDPR clarifies the rights of individuals whose data are processed. These include the right of access (Art. 15 GDPR), the right to rectification (Art. 16 GDPR), the right to erasure (Art. 17 GDPR) or the right to data portability (Art. 20 GDPR). All these rights must not be violated by the person responsible. If such a violation does occur, a fine will be imposed.

63 In the German state of Hesse, a fine was imposed on a corporation following complaints made by citizens to the Hessian Data Protection Commissioner.[91] One individual requested information and deletion of the personal data but was informed that providing the information was not possible. The reason given was that only data entered by the person themselves had been stored, and therefore, any other data had already been deleted. In another case, the same company ignored a data subject's request for information until the government authority intervened. For both instances, a combined fine in the mid-five-digit range was imposed based on violations of Art. 83 para. 5 lit. b) in conjunction with Art. 15 and Art. 12 para. 3 sent. 1 of the GDPR.[92]

64 Another case of violation of the principle of comprehensibility contained in Art. 12 GDPR occurred in the German state of Brandenburg. There, requests for data information in German were not answered by the asked companies themselves but by an external ser-

(last accessed: 17.4.2025).

[89] 30. Tätigkeitsbericht Datenschutz Saarland 2021, p. 137 <https://datenschutzarchiv.org/fileadmin/Dokumente/2021/30_TB_LfD_Saarland_2021_17-09_22062022.pdf> (last accessed: 17.4.2025).

[90] VG Hannover 9.2.2023 – 10 A 6199/20, NZA-RR 2023, 264.

[91] 49. Tätigkeitsbericht Hessen 2020 [i.e. 'Activity Report for Hesse], p. 159 <https://datenschutzarchiv.org/fileadmin/Dokumente/2020/49_TB_LfD_Hessen_2020_oDrsNR_01062021.pdf> (last accessed: 17.4.2025).

[92] 49. Tätigkeitsbericht Hessen 2020, p. 159 <https://datenschutzarchiv.org/fileadmin/Dokumente/2020/49_TB_LfD_Hessen_2020_oDrsNR_01062021.pdf> (last accessed: 17.4.2025).

vice provider, who responded in English. This was also deemed a violation of the principle of transparency because the external service provider used its own logo to answer the request – but it was the company which has been asked to fulfil the request and the one who collected the data. A fine of 50,000 EUR was imposed as a result of the violations.[93]

D. Liabilities within the BDSG

I. Relationship between GDPR and BDSG

65 European secondary law mainly comes in two different shapes: as directives and as regulations. Directives are aimed at the EU's Member States. They generally have to be implemented by every country itself, so they are not immediately binding to public authorities, companies or individual persons.[94] An exception is only made for directives if their deadline for transposing expired and if the directive is sufficiently clear and precise.[95]

66 Regulations are applicable in all EU Member States from the moment they get enacted, so public authorities, companies and individuals must observe them. Regulations finally rule all matters that fall within their scope. Member states are not allowed to enact further national rules in this area, as it is only subject of the EU's legislative power. Nevertheless, regulations can include opening clauses or specification clauses which transpose legislative procedures into national competence. They often appear in contexts where national legislative competences would be undermined, or where Member States are in a more appropriate position to create reasonable solutions.

67 Before the GDPR was introduced, European data protection law was only embodied through EU Data Protection Directive 95/46 EC. After what has been said, the legal design of those EU data protection rules was not suitable to bind all involved players. Instead, it merely provided the basis for transposing legal acts by the Member States. In this respect, the Member States had a certain amount of leeway, which led to inconsistent data protection rules throughout Europe.[96]

68 EU Data Protection Directive 95/46 EC expired with the entry into force of the GDPR. The GDPR is directly applicable and constitutes an EU-wide standard for all data protection matters.

69 In addition, all Member States are partially obligated by the GDPR[97] or have the option to create accompanying laws. As a result, Germany enacted the new BDSG, which was introduced on the same day as the GDPR: 25 May 2018[98]. It is an important aspect that

[93] Tätigkeitsbericht Brandenburg 2019 [i.e. 'Activity Report for Brandenburg], p. 31, <https://datenschutzarchiv.org/fileadmin/Dokumente/2019/21_TB_LfD_Brandenburg_2019_oDrsNr_240320209.pdf> (last accessed: 17.4.2025).

[94] Calliess/Ruffert/Ruffert EUV/AEUV Art. 288 mn. 24; 'Die unmittelbare Wirkung des Rechts der Europäischen Union' (The direct effect of the European Union law), < https://eur-lex.europa.eu/DE/legal-content/summary/the-direct-effect-of-european-union-law.html> (last accessed: 20.2.2025).

[95] ECJ 4.12.1974 – C-41-74, ECLI:EU:C:1974:133 = BeckRS 2004, 71134: In this case, just public authorities can be obligated to consider directives even if the act of transposition has not yet happened. This ensures that Member States cannot determine if directives take effect or not and that the rights of individuals are not ignored or violated because the Member State has not complied with the transposition deadline.

[96] Laue/Kremer Neues DatenschutzR/Laue § 1 mn. 1, 2.

[97] Kühling/Buchner/Bergt BDSG § 42 mn. 1.

[98] BGBl. 2017 I 44, Art. 8 sub. 1, p. 2132.

the BDSG just complements the GDPR; so according to § 1 sub. 5 BDSG, the regulations of BDSG shall not be applicable where GDPR's rules apply. This means, the GDPR takes precedence over the BDSG. In addition, further German data protection rules alongside the BDSG take priority over those of BDSG (§ 1 sub. 2 sent. 1 BDSG). An example is §§ 284 et seqq. SGB V[99], which regulates the transmission of patient data for invoicing purposes and therefore is the exclusive legal basis for processing such data.

II. Scope of application of the BDSG

1. Responsibility

70 In addition to corporate responsibility, the legal liability of individual persons is the subject of data protection law as well. The media primarily reports about huge fines that companies received in the past, as this is of big interest for the public. For example, the fines imposed by data protection authorities of 14.5 million EUR on the real estate group 'Deutsche Wohnen SE'[100] and 10.4 million EUR on the internet group 'notebooksbilliger.de' were reported publicly.[101]

71 However, reports of individual sanctions will follow as the criminal provision of § 42 BDSG[102] gains in importance.[103] Supervisory authorities have the possibility of using the power of criminal law to promote data protection matters by making a demand for penalty[104], if they deem a data protection matter as an infringement of § 42 BDSG. This can possibly be the beginning of criminal proceedings against individual persons. Another indication for the growing importance of § 42 BDSG is that there have been attempts in the past to bring the penal provisions of the BDSG into the German Criminal Code (*Strafgesetzbuch* – 'StGB'), the central set of criminal law regulations in Germany. Most recently, the former governing party FDP introduced a bill to integrate the regulation into the German Criminal Code in 2021.[105]

72 Former versions of the BDSG included penal provisions as well.[106] However, these were much less significant. This is demonstrated by the fact that there have only been a few convictions in this context over the years.[107] Furthermore, the corresponding regulations contained significantly lower threats of punishment. It developed from up to one year imprisonment[108] over two years[109] to three years nowadays. It once more has to be mentioned that those former regulations have not been dependent on binding European law

---

99 *Sozialgesetzbuch V* (Social Security Code V).

100 Berliner Beauftragte für Datenschutz und Informationsfreiheit, 'Berliner Datenschutzbeauftragte verhängt Bußgeld gegen Immobiliengesellschaft', 5.11.2019 <https://www.datenschutz-berlin.de/fileadmin/user_upload/pdf/pressemitteilungen/2019/20191105-PM-Bussgeld_DW.pdf> (last accessed: 28.4.2025).

101 Landesdatenschutzbeauftragter Niedersachsen, 'LfD Niedersachsen verhängt Bußgeld über 10,4 Millionen Euro gegen notebooksbilliger.de', 8.1.2021 <https://lfd.niedersachsen.de/startseite/infothek/presseinformationen/lfd-niedersachsen-verhangt-bussgeld-uber-10-4-millionen-euro-gegen-notebooks-billiger-de-196019.html> (last accessed: 12.2.2025).

102 It must be noted here that § 42 BDSG is a criminal provision. Therefore, in cases of § 42 BDSG, the public prosecutor's office is leading the proceedings and not the data protection authority.

103 Paal/Pauly/Frenzel BDSG § 42 mn. 11.

104 Paal/Pauly/Frenzel BDSG § 42 mn. 9; Kühling/Buchner/Bergt BDSG § 42 mn. 58.

105 BT-Drs. 19/28777.

106 § 32 BDSG (former version), BT-Drs. 7/1027, 12; § 44 BDSG (former version), BGBl. 2001 I no. 23, p. 904.

107 Gola/Heckmann/Ehmann BDSG § 42 mn. 2.

108 § 32 BDSG (former version), BT-Drs. 7/1027.

109 § 44 BDSG (former version), BGBl. 2001 I no. 23, p. 904.

because the GDPR is the first act to bindingly rule data protection law throughout Europe. For that reason, previous assumptions on BDSG's former penal provisions should not simply be taken over.[110] They must be interpreted in the context of the current European data protection rules that outshine all national regulations.

2. Penal provisions (§ 42 sub. 1 and 2 BDSG)

§ 42 BDSG has been enacted by the German legislator based on the opening clause of Art. 84 GDPR.[111] It has the following wording:[112] 73

> (1) The following actions done deliberately and without authorization with regard to the personal data of a large number of people which are not publicly accessible shall be punishable with imprisonment of up to three years or a fine:
> 1. transferring the data to a third party or
> 2. otherwise making them accessible
>
> for commercial purposes.
> (2) The following actions done with regard to personal data which are not publicly accessible shall be punishable with imprisonment of up to two years or a fine:
> 1. processing without authorization, or
> 2. fraudulently acquiring
>
> and doing so in return for payment or with the intention of enriching oneself or someone else or harming someone.
> (3) Such offences shall be prosecuted only if a complaint is filed. The data subject, the controller, the Federal Commissioner and the supervisory authority shall be entitled to file complaints.
> (4) A notification pursuant to Art. 33 GDPR or a communication pursuant to Art. 34 para. 1 GDPR may be used in criminal proceedings against the person required to provide a notification or a communication or relatives as referred to in § 52 sub. 1 StPO only with the consent of the person required to provide a notification or a communication.

§ 42 sub. 1 and § 42 sub. 2 BDSG represent two different penal provisions, § 42 sub. 3 and 4 BDSG contain procedural rules.[113] As § 42 sub. 1 and 2 BDSG are part of German criminal law, the general regulations of the German Criminal Code apply.[114] 74

§ 42 sub. 1 BDSG has a wide range of applications, which will let it importance grow. The provision captures constellations in which perpetrators transmit a large number of individuals' personal data that is not publicly accessible to a third party without being authorized to do so (§ 42 sub. 1 no. 1 BDSG). The same applies for any other provision of the data (§ 42 sub. 1 no. 2 BDSG). In both constellations, perpetrators must act commercially. 75

§ 42 sub. 2 BDSG concerns cases in which the perpetrator processes personal data that is not generally accessible without authorization (§ 42 sub. 2 no. 1 BDSG) or obtains such data by providing false information (§ 42 sub. 2 no. 2 BDSG). In both cases, the perpetrator has to act in return for payment or with the intention of enriching himself or anybody else or of causing harm to another. 76

---

[110] Gola/Heckmann/Ehmann BDSG § 42 mn. 7.

[111] Paal/Pauly/Frenzel BDSG § 42 mn. 1; BeckOK DatenschutzR/Brodowski, 51. Ed. 1.2.2025, BDSG § 42 mn. 5; MAH Strafverteidigung/Grözinger § 50 mn. 143.

[112] The English version of § 42 BDSG is taken from <https://www.gesetze-im-internet.de/englisch_bdsg/index.html>, translation provided by the Language Service of the Federal Ministry of the Intererior (last accessed: 27.10.2025).

[113] Gola/Heckmann/Ehmann BDSG § 42 mn.1; Kühling/Buchner/Bergt BDSG § 42 mn. 1.

[114] Kühling/Buchner/Bergt BDSG § 42 mn. 1, BeckOK DatenschutzR/Brodowski, 51. Ed. 1.2.2025, BDSG § 42 mn. 5.

3. Suitable addressees of the penal provision

77 Although the provision by its nature has been in place for several decades, the personal scope of application is still much discussed.[115] This originates from the wording of the penal provisions.[116] The English translation already indicates the lack of specifically designated addressees because it just describes the illegal action and says nothing about the actor. For the original German wording, it was decided to address the regulation to 'anybody' who acts as described.[117]

78 This seems problematic because all other regulations of the BDSG do only apply to a limited group of persons as it is said in § 1 BDSG. They refer on particular groups such as 'controllers' and do not target everybody.[118] This results in the discussion if the penal provisions of § 42 sub. 1 and 2 BDSG must be interpreted restrictively – so they were mainly applicable on controllers – or should really include every individual person, even if they are not an addressee of the BDSG.[119]

79 Legislative materials regarding the former version of BDSG[120] from the 1970s allow the conclusion that the penal provisions are aimed at third parties, which basically means everybody. Furthermore, § 1 sent. 2 BDSG addresses 'private bodies' and does not exclude any individual person. This provision defines the BDSG's general scope of application.[121] Some representatives of the jurisprudence and literature have drawn the conclusion from it that the BDSG's penal provisions are addressed at everyone[122], which would lead to a wide range of applications.

80 On the other hand, there are several arguments in favour of ensuring that the penal provisions of the BDSG – like the other regulations of the BDSG – focus on data controllers and processors, but not on private individuals. Otherwise, there is a contradiction because private individuals were allowed to disregard most data protection regulations but were covered by the corresponding criminal provisions.[123] Problematic in particular is the fact that the right to process data is determined by standards of the BDSG that do not address private individuals.[124] Furthermore, it seems hardly compatible with the fundamental principle of legal certainty if criminal provisions in a special law – in this case § 42 BDSG – have wider scopes of application than the special law's other rules. Criminal regulations have a particularly strong impact on the rights of individuals (*ultima ratio*[125]), which is the reason why they must be particularly concrete and narrowly designed.[126] Furthermore, the existence of § 84 BDSG, which extends the effect of § 42 BDSG to public

[115] BeckOK DatenschutzR/Brodowski, 51. Ed. 1.2.2025, BDSG § 42 mn. 15; Kühling/Buchner/Bergt BDSG § 42 mn. 3; KMW DatenschutzsanktionenR-HdB/Klaas § 8 mn. 13; Koreng/Lachenmann DatenschutzR-FormHdB/Nolde/Stürzl Form. O. I. 2.

[116] Kühling/Buchner/Bergt BDSG § 42 mn. 3, Gola/Heckmann/Ehmann BDSG § 42 mn. 8.

[117] Gola/Heckmann/Ehmann BDSG § 42 mn. 8; KMW DatenschutzsanktionenR-HdB/Klaas § 8 mn. 14.

[118] BeckOK DatenschutzR/Brodowski, 51. Ed. 1.2.2025, BDSG § 42 mn. 15; KMW DatenschutzsanktionenR-HdB/Klaas § 8 mn. 16, 17.

[119] HK-DS-GVO/BDSG/Heghmanns BDSG § 42 mn. 7; Kühling/Buchner/Bergt BDSG § 42 mn. 3; BeckOK DatenschutzR/Brodowski, 51. Ed. 1.2.2025, BDSG § 42 mn. 15.

[120] BT-Drs. 7/1027, 31.

[121] Gola/Heckmann/Gola/Reif BDSG § 1 mn. 1.

[122] cf. HK-DS-GVO/BDSG/Heghmanns BDSG § 42 mn. 7; Gola/Heckmann/Ehmann BDSG § 42 mn. 8; LG Aachen 18.2.2011 – 71 Ns-504 Js 506/09/129/10, BeckRS 2011, 20917 regarding the former version of § 42 BDSG.

[123] BeckOK DatenschutzR/Brodowski, 51. Ed. 1.2.2025, BDSG § 42 mn. 15.

[124] BeckOK DatenschutzR/Brodowski, 51. Ed. 1.2.2025, BDSG § 42 mn. 15.

[125] According to the ultima ratio principle, criminal law is always to be used as a last option, as it interferes particularly severely with a person's legal interests. Accordingly, the application of criminal law can only be considered if no other options exist or if they are insufficient.

[126] MüKoStGB/Schmitz StGB § 1 mn. 53; LKH/Heger StGB § 1 mn. 2.

bodies, only makes sense if § 42 BDSG is not in itself directed at everyone.[127] Otherwise the referral would be useless.

81 So far, there has been no decision by the Higher Courts on this issue. There is only a decision of the Regional Court of Aachen from the year 2011 regarding the former § 44 BDSG – which was basically the same regulation – which concluded that private individuals should be liable to the BDSG.[128] It currently cannot be anticipated which opinion the competent prosecution or court would follow in a specific case at the present time.

4. Definition of 'personal data that is not publicly accessible'

82 By their very nature, data protection matters are subject to a fundamental tension. The individual's right to his or her personal data from Art. 2 para. 1, Art. 1 para. 1 GG[129] must be brought into balance with the right of third parties from Art. 5 GG to obtain information from public sources. Both rights are fundamental components of democratic systems based on the rule of law.

83 In the context of the criminal provisions, the question of which of the rights prevails therefore depends on the characteristic of the free accessibility of the data. If publicly accessible data has been handled, the criminal provisions of § 42 BDSG do not apply.[130] Consequently, the characteristic serves to limit criminal liability and to distinguish the prohibited conduct from the conduct approved by fundamental rights.

84 The BDSG in its current version does not contain a definition of when personal data is to be classified as publicly accessible. Moreover, this also applies to the GDPR, which is why any definition could not be adopted. However, in addition to the BDSG, the term is also used in the German Criminal Code and the German Basic Law, which makes it quite common.

85 Former versions of the BDSG contained a definition in § 10 sub. 5 sent. 2 BDSG (former version) that was also applied in criminal law contexts.[131] According to this definition, personal data is generally accessible if anyone can use it without or after prior registration, admission or payment of a fee. This definition is still used to some extent in the commentary literature when the term has to be interpreted.[132] Notable in this context are two decisions from higher German courts: the Federal Court of Justice ruled in 2013 that data is generally accessible if it can be accesses without legal barriers of any kind; this shall also apply even if the legal barriers are not particularly high and can be easily circumvented by means of false statements.[133] In a current decision from 2021 the *Bayerisches Oberstes Landesgericht* (BayObLG) adapted this ruling,[134] so that one can say that a legal barrier is sufficient to exclude data from being generally accessible.

[127] BeckOK DatenschutzR/Brodowski, 51. Ed. 1.2.2025, BDSG § 84 mn. 4, 5.

[128] LG Aachen 18.02.2011 – 71 Ns-504 Js 506/09-129/10, BeckRS 2011, 20917.

[129] *Grundgesetz* (Basic Law).

[130] Kühling/Buchner/Bergt BDSG § 42 mn. 8; HK-DS-GVO/BDSG/Heghmanns BDSG § 42 mn. 8.

[131] BT-Drs. 18/5088, 45.

[132] For an in-depth overview see: Ihwas NZWiSt 2021, 289 (294 et seq.).

[133] BGH 4.6.2013 – 1 StR 32/13, NJW 2013, 2530 (2533).

[134] BayObLG 26.10.2021 – 202 StRR 126/21, BeckRS 2021, 36406: object of the decision is the regulation Art. 23 para. 1 Bayerisches Datenschutzgesetz ('Bavarian Data Protection Act'), which is very similar to § 42 BDSG.

5. Special conditions in § 42 sub. 1 BDSG

a) No. 1: 'transferring the data to a third party'

86 The regulation of § 42 sub. 1 no. 1 BDSG focuses on the transmission of data. This includes any disclosure to third parties. The offence is structured in such a way that the data must actually enter the third party's sphere of perception.

b) No. 2: 'otherwise making them accessible'

87 Making data accessible in another way means giving third parties the possibility to take note of the data. It is not necessary that a third party actually obtains knowledge of the data.

c) 'for commercial purposes'

88 Both alternatives require that the perpetrator makes the data available to a large number of people while acting without authorization and on a commercial basis. The greatest problems of interpretation arise with regard to the characteristic 'large number', as this is defined differently in the German Criminal Code in various respective regulatory contexts. Since the characteristic is therefore imprecise and is also interpreted differently in various provisions, doubts arise as to the specificity of criminal provisions which is a fundamental principal of law.[135] Considering the special features of data protection law, it seems appropriate to require at least ten or more persons.

89 The situation is clearer with regard to the other characteristics of this regulation: whether an authorization exists or not is determined by the provisions of the GDPR or the BDSG.[136] Furthermore, a person acts commercially – in accordance with the German Criminal Code – if he intends to open up a permanent source of income by repeatedly committing the same kind of offence.[137]

6. Special conditions in § 42 sub. 2 BDSG

a) No. 1: 'processing without authorization'

90 According to Art. 4 para. 2 GDPR 'processing means any operation or set of operations which is performed on personal data or on sets of personal data, whether or not by automated means, such as collection, recording, organisation, structuring, storage, adaptation or alteration, retrieval, consultation, use, disclosure by transmission, dissemination or otherwise making available, alignment or combination, restriction, erasure or destruction'.

91 The wording basically covers any type of processing and is therefore kept open. For this reason, doubts could arise in principle as to whether the definition is specific enough. For example, there is some criticism that the 'use' of data has not been included in the standard. While the application of the definition of § 4 sub. 2 BDSG in this context is partly considered unlawful, it is partly argued that the definition should only be applied to data processing that causes or deepens damage to the confidentiality of the data at issue.

b) No. 2: 'fraudulently acquiring'

92 The last variant concerns the obtaining of personal data by means of incorrect information. At this point, the unpunished exploitation of security vulnerabilities must be

---

[135] Auernhammer § 42 BDSG mn. 8; Paal/Pauly/Frenzel DS-GVO BDSG § 42 mn. 6.
[136] Kühling/Buchner/Bergt DS-GVO BDSG § 42 mn. 23.
[137] BGH 8.11.1951 – 4 StR 563/51, NJW 1952, 113; Kühling/Buchner/Bergt DS-GVO BDSG § 42 mn. 27.

distinguished from the punishable deceptive act. This is the only variant in which a legitimization – e.g. according to Art. 6 GDPR – is irrelevant when assessing the criminal liability. Therefore, this variant contains a high risk for criminal liability because the threshold is very low.

c) 'in return for payment or with intention of enriching oneself or someone else or harming someone'

Both variants finally require regarding the motivation of the crime that the perpe- 93
trator acts against payment, with the intention of enrichment or with the intention of causing damage. Following the legal definition of § 11 sub. 1 no. 9 StGB, 'a consideration means any pecuniary benefit given in exchange for someone's acts'. This characteristic is subjective in nature, which is why it is only the existence of an agreement that matters, regardless of whether it is also legally effective or not.[138] In other respects, the pecuniary advantages sought are assigned to the variant of the intention to enrich oneself or others. The still sufficient existence of an intent to harm concerns cases in which the perpetrator seeks to cause some kind of material or immaterial damage to third parties.

III. Special provisions for employee data protection (§ 26 BDSG)

1. Personal scope of application

§ 26 BDSG contains specific provisions for the relationship between employers and 94
employees that take precedence over the general rules of GDPR.[139] Its wording is as follows:[140]

> (1) Personal data of employees may be processed for employment-related purposes where necessary for hiring decisions or, after hiring, for carrying out or terminating the employment contract or to exercise or satisfy rights and obligations of employees' representation laid down by law or by collective agreements or other agreements between the employer and staff council. Employees' personal data may be processed to detect crimes only if there is a documented reason to believe the data subject has committed a crime while employed, the processing of such data is necessary to investigate the crime and is not outweighed by the data subject's legitimate interest in not processing the data, and in particular the type and extent are not disproportionate to the reason.
> (2) If personal data of employees are processed on the basis of consent, then the employee's level of dependence in the employment relationship and the circumstances under which consent was given shall be taken into account in assessing whether such consent was freely given. Consent may be freely given in particular if it is associated with a legal or economic advantage for the employee, or if the employer and employee are pursuing the same interests. Consent shall be given in written or electronic form, unless a different form is appropriate because of special circumstances. The employer shall inform the employee in text form of the purpose of data processing and of the employee's right to withdraw consent pursuant to Art. 7 para. 3 GDPR.
> (3) By derogation from Art. 9 para. 1 GDPR, the processing of special categories of personal data as referred to in Art. 9 para. 1 GDPR for employment-related purposes shall be permitted if it is necessary to exercise rights or comply with legal obligations derived from labour law, social security and social protection law, and there is no reason to believe that the data subject has an overriding legitimate interest in not processing the data. Sub. 2 shall also apply to consent to the

---

[138] BGH 18.7.1995 – 1 StR 320/95, NStZ 1995, 540.
[139] Gola/Heckmann/Gola/Pötters BDSG § 26 mn. 4.
[140] The English version of § 26 BDSG is taken from <https://www.gesetze-im-internet.de/englisch_bdsg/index.html>, translation provided by the Language Service of the Federal Ministry of the Interérior (last accessed: 27.10.2025).

processing of special categories of personal data; consent must explicitly refer to these data. § 22 sub. 2 shall apply accordingly.
(4) The processing of personal data, including special categories of personal data of employees for employment-related purposes, shall be permitted on the basis of collective agreements. The negotiating partners shall comply with Art. 88 para. 2 GDPR.
(5) The controller must take appropriate measures to ensure compliance in particular with the principles for processing personal data described in Art. 5 GDPR.
(6) The rights of participation of staff councils shall remain unaffected.
(7) Sub. 1 to 6 shall also apply when personal data, including special categories of personal data, of employees are processed without forming or being intended to form part of a filing system.
(8) For the purposes of this Act, employees are

1. dependently employed workers, including temporary workers contracted to the borrowing employer;
2. persons employed for occupational training purposes;
3. participants in benefits to take part in working life, in assessments of occupational aptitude or work trials (persons undergoing rehabilitation);
4. persons employed in accredited workshops for persons with disabilities;
5. volunteers working pursuant to the *Jugendfreiwilligendienstegesetz* [i.e.Youth Volunteer Service Act] or the *Bundesfreiwilligendienstgesetz* [i.e. Federal Volunteer Service Act];
6. persons who should be regarded as equivalent to dependently employed workers because of their economic dependence; these include persons working at home and their equivalents;
7. federal civil servants, federal judges, military personnel and persons in the alternative civilian service.

Applicants for employment and persons whose employment has been terminated shall be regarded as employees.

95 § 28 sub. 8 BDSG determines who is an 'employee' in this context.[141] According to § 28 sub. 8 no. 1 BDSG, the main group of persons protected by the provision is represented by dependently employed workers. This group's rights are obviously in danger of being disregarded against the background of corporate interests. Furthermore, such workers are in an inappropriate position to defend themselves against their employer.

96 If one assumes this regulatory purpose, it becomes apparent why it is much discussed if leading employees of companies should be subject of the provision as well.[142] First of all, a distinction must be made between the corporate bodies of a company and its other executive employees. Most leading employees must base their decisions on the instructions of higher-level bodies, so they are without any doubt subject to the definition of § 26 sub. 8 no. 1 BDSG.[143] In contrast to that, corporate bodies and their members (CEO, executive board, supervisory board) are partly not assigned to the scope of the provision at all because they are seen as a part of the employer not employees.[144] On the other hand, it is also argued that it again depends on whether the person in question is bound by instructions.[145]

---

[141] BeckOK DatenschutzR/Riesenhuber, 51. Ed. 1.2.2025, BDSG § 26 mn. 21.

[142] Taeger/Gabel/Zöll BDSG § 26 mn. 107, BeckOK DatenschutzR/Riesenhuber, 51. Ed. 1.2.2025, BDSG § 26 mn. 22.

[143] BeckOK DatenschutzR/Riesenhuber, 51. Ed. 1.2.2025, BDSG § 26 mn. 22.

[144] Kühling/Buchner/Maschmann BDSG § 26 mn. 7; BeckOK DatenschutzR/Riesenhuber, 51. Ed. 1.2.2025, BDSG § 26 mn. 22.

[145] BeckOK DatenschutzR/Riesenhuber, 51. Ed. 1.2.2025, BDSG § 26 mn. 22.

2. Effects of applicability and relationship to general rules

§ 26 BDSG can take precedence over the general rules of Art. 6 GDPR. It constitutes a more specific legal provision and has been introduced on the basis of the opening clause of Art. 88 para. 1 GDPR.[146] **97**

Art. 88 para. 1 GDPR determines that **98**

> Member States may, by law or by collective agreements, provide for more specific rules to ensure the protection of the rights and freedoms in respect of the processing of employees' personal data in the employment context, in particular for the purposes of the recruitment, the performance of the contract of employment, including discharge of obligations laid down by law or by collective agreements, management, planning and organisation of work, equality and diversity in the workplace, health and safety at work, protection of employer's or customer's property and for the purposes of the exercise and enjoyment, on an individual or collective basis, of rights and benefits related to employment, and for the purpose of the termination of the employment relationship.

Art. 88 para. 2 GDPR concretizes that **99**

> those rules shall include suitable and specific measures to safeguard the data subject's human dignity, legitimate interests and fundamental rights, with particular regard to the transparency of processing, the transfer of personal data within a group of undertakings, or a group of enterprises engaged in a joint economic activity and monitoring systems at the work place.

Overall, § 26 BDSG specifically addresses the processing of personal data by employers in the context of the employment relationship. Data processing on the basis of a consent of the employee is only allowed in compliance with the increased requirements for the voluntary nature of consent pursuant to § 26 sub. 2 BDSG. Following the purpose of more specific regulations, § 26 BDSG takes precedence over general rules in case of its applicability. If, on the other hand, § 26 BDSG is not applicable, for example because it concerns the processing of personal data of a company's CEO, Art. 6 GDPR is applicable.[147] **100**

3. The provision of § 26 sub. 1 sent. 1 BDSG

Firstly, § 26 sub. 1 sent. 1 BDSG provides a specific legal basis for the processing of personal data by the employer in the context of the employment relationship. Accordingly, data may be processed if this is necessary for the decision on the establishment of an employment relationship, its implementation or termination. The provision is to be interpreted extensively and includes every processing that affects the employment contract's purposes.[148] **101**

Secondly, this applies not only to data processing by the employer, but also to some situations where employees' representatives process personal data. This depends on the specific purpose. It must be about the exercise or satisfaction of rights and obligations resulting from law, collective agreements or other agreements between the employer and staff council. The provision covers two main cases: the transmission of personal data from the employer to the employees' representation and data processing by employees' representations.[149] **102**

---

[146] BeckOK DatenschutzR/Riesenhuber, 51. Ed. 1.2.2025, BDSG § 26 mn. 1.
[147] Gola/Heckmann/Gola/Pötters BDSG § 26 mn. 96; Kühling/Buchner/Maschmann BDSG § 26 mn. 7.
[148] Taeger/Gabel/Zöll BDSG § 26 mn. 38.
[149] HK-DS-GVO/BDSG/Tiedemann BDSG § 26 mn. 31; Gola/Heckmann/Gola/Pötters BDSG § 26 mn. 39.

103 Both alternatives are subject to the condition that the data processing is required to realize one of the presented purposes. This leads to a proportionality test.[150] It is to be carried out in three steps. At step one it must be checked if the processing is the appropriate tool, to fulfil the aimed purpose.[151] Only such purposes are permitted that belong to the data processor's legit tasks.[152] At step two it must be determined if there is any less intrusive, equally appropriate means against the background of the employee's right to the protection of his or her personal data from Art. 8 of the Charter of Fundamental Rights of the EU.[153] Furthermore, the general principle of data economy must be observed in this context.[154] At step three the different matters must be brought into balance. These are the rights of the employee and the rights and the employers' interests. The procedure must be held in a way that considers the different interests as far as possible.[155] Employers' actions could only be legit if employees' rights do not prevail.[156]

4. The provision of § 26 sub. 1 sent. 2 BDSG

104 Data processing for the purpose of detecting criminal acts committed by an employee is only permitted under strict conditions.

105 It has to be mentioned that this provision only applies to the processing of personal data of the suspect himself.[157] Of course, it must be crimes – not contractual breaches or misdemeanours[158] – that were committed in the context of the employment relationship.[159] In contrast to that, suspicion of serious contract violation or committed misdemeanours against a specific employee leads to the applicability of § 26 sub. 1 sent. 1 BDSG.[160] From this it can be deduced that the processing of third parties' personal data for investigations criminal offences, misdemeanours or breaches of contract on the part of another employee must take place in accordance with Art. 6 para. 1 sent. 1 lit. f) GDPR.

106 § 26 sub. 1 sent. 2 BDSG does not only extend to actions during the working hours, but also to those that stand in contrast to the employment contract's regulations[161]. In any case, there must be facts that allow the conclusion that the employee concerned has committed a criminal offence. Only the data of the employee himself may be processed, not that of the employee's clients or relatives. The processing authorization is also limited to the suspected employee himself.[162]

107 An exception applies if the suspicion extends to several or if the data of the suspected person cannot be collected without evaluating the data of other employees. So-called 'accidental findings' concerning other employees may still be used in the case of covert video surveillance.[163] The degree of suspicion corresponds to the 'initial suspicion'

---

[150] BT-Drs. 18/11325, 96; BeckOK DatenschutzR/Riesenhuber, 51. Ed. 1.2.2025, BDSG § 26 mn. 63 et seqq.
[151] Kühling/Buchner/Maschmann BDSG § 26 mn. 18.
[152] BeckOK DatenschutzR/Riesenhuber, 51. Ed. 1.2.2025, BDSG § 26 mn. 197.
[153] Gola/Heckmann/Gola/Pötters BDSG § 26 mn. 29; BAG 20.6.2013 – 2 AZR 546/12, NZA 2014, 143.
[154] Taeger/Gabel/Voigt BDSG DS-GVO Art. 5 mn. 27.
[155] Gola/Heckmann/Gola/Pötters BDSG § 26 mn. 31.
[156] ErfK/Franzen BDSG § 26 mn. 11.
[157] Taeger/Gabel/Zöll BDSG § 26 mn. 66, Kühling/Buchner/Maschmann BDSG § 26 mn. 58.
[158] Düwell/Brink NZA 2017, 1081 (1084).
[159] ErfK/Franzen, 23rd edn 2023, BDSG § 26 mn. 36.
[160] Gola/Heckmann/Gola/Pötters BDSG § 26 mn. 65.
[161] BeckOk DatenschutzR/Riesenhuber, 51. Ed. 1.2.2025, BDSG § 26 mn. 133.
[162] BeckOK DatenschutzR/Riesenhuber, 51. Ed. 1.2.2025, BDSG § 26 mn. 132.
[163] BAG 22.9.2016 – 2 AZR 848/15, NJW 2017, 843.

known in German criminal law.[164] The referenced facts must be documented to allow retrospective reviews.[165]

108 As in § 26 sub. 1 sent. 1 BDSG, the implementation of a proportionality test is mandatory and the previously presented standards apply.[166]

5. Increased requirements for consent pursuant to § 26 sub. 2 BDSG

109 As known from GDPR's general rules (Art. 4 no. 11, Art. 6 para. 1 sent 1 lit. a), Art. 7), personal data processing can be based on consent. It is not surprising that universal requirements on consent apply. This for example includes the reference to a concrete processing case[167].

110 The consent given by employees justifies the processing of their personal data by employers, § 26 para. 2 GDPR[168]. It represents a particular problem that most employees are generally willing to follow their employers' instructions which could be explained by their economic dependence on their jobs[169]. This results in an imbalance of power which brings with it the danger that the data protection consent may be given due to the fear of disadvantages.

111 For that reason, the consent's voluntary nature is stipulated as the provision's key characteristic and increased requirements are placed on it. To ensure its compliance, the circumstances in which the consent is given and the employee's extend of dependence towards the employer must be evaluated.[170] This depends very much on the individual case, whereby aspects such as the specific type of data referred to, the time of consent or the interests of both parties can be significant.[171] However, it also becomes apparent that there can be various sources of error. Besides that, § 26 sub. 2 BDSG requires the written or electronic form. In addition, the employee must be informed in writing about the purpose of the data processing and his or her right to revoke the consent before it is given[172].

112 The specific situation and dependence towards the employer must be considered and evaluated on a case-by-case basis to determine whether or not the decision is voluntary.[173] In this context, positive indicators are defined as the attainment of legal or economic advantage through the granting of consent or similar interests between employer and employee.

113 The case-by-case consideration and the typical dependency in the context of employment relationships lead to legal imponderables and make consent appear unsuitable as a legal basis for data processing in this context.[174]

114 Data processing by employers based on consent is not advisable overall, since consent can be revoked by the employee at any time of his choosing[175] – even shortly after he has given it. This has the effect of placing the lawfulness of the processing in the hands of the consenting person. That leads to difficulties on the part of the employer, especially

[164] Gola/Heckmann/Gola/Pötters BDSG § 26 mn. 58.
[165] BAG 27.7.2017 – 2 AZR 681/16, NZA 2017, 1327.
[166] Gola/Heckmann/Gola/Pötters BDSG § 26 mn. 61.
[167] BeckOK DatenschutzR/Riesenhuber, 51. Ed. 1.2.2025, BDSG § 26 mn. 46a.
[168] HK-DS-GVO/BDSG/Tiedemann BDSG § 26 mn. 37.
[169] Gola/Heckmann/Gola/Pötters BDSG § 26 mn. 67.
[170] Kühling/Buchner/Maschmann BDSG § 26 mn. 63.
[171] Kühling/Buchner/Maschmann BDSG § 26 mn. 63.
[172] BeckOK DatenschutzR/Riesenhuber, 51. Ed. 1.2.2025, BDSG § 26 mn. 50.
[173] Kühling/Buchner/Maschmann BDSG § 26 mn. 63; Gola/Heckmann/Gola/Pötters BDSG § 26 mn. 68.
[174] Gola/Heckmann/Gola/Pötters BDSG § 26 mn. 68.
[175] Taeger/Gabel/Zöll BDSG § 26 mn. 84.

in the case of internal investigations.[176] In this context, it is almost typical that affected employees revoke their consent, but companies are obligated to conduct internal investigations by law. This is particularly unfortunate because it is sometimes assumed that from the moment consent is obtained for the first time, it is no longer possible to fall back on alternative relevant legal permissions (Art. 6 GDPR). This is justified with the thesis that the employer would have expressed that it is precisely the consent that should be decisive.[177] Consequently, the employee alone decides whether to prevent data processing by revoking the consent. It can be argued against this that employers who attach importance to the inclusion of the will of their employees are in fact penalized, while those who resort to parallel applicable legal permissions are privileged. In the end, however, it all comes down to the opinion of the relevant data protection authorities or the competent court.[178]

6. Effects of collective agreements

115 According to § 26 sub. 4 BDSG, the creation of collective agreements between employers and work councils offers another possibility to enact legal processing bases.[179] It provides the advantage of being able to concretize general legal provisions and find data processing solutions that fit a whole company.[180] In contrast to the provision of § 26 sub. 1 sent. 1 BDSG, this paragraph does not provide a data processing basis on itself but clarifies that employers and employees' representations are allowed to create new processing bases together.[181] Such agreements must provide a level of protection that complies with the provisions of § 75 sub. 2 BetrVG and Art. 88 para. 2 GDPR. This includes the protection of employees' fundamental rights, privacy rights and interests[182] due to the implementation of tools that guarantee transparency in data processing according to Art. 5 para. 1 lit. a) GDPR.[183] Of course, the other fundamental principles of Art. 5 GDPR must be complied as well.[184] The provision even allows the processing of special categories of personal data where required which once more leads into a proportionality test.[185] Agreements that do not reach the demonstrated standards are inapplicable.[186] To avoid breaches of transparency principles, collective agreements should include the information that data processing may continue to be carried out on the basis of Art. 6 GDPR and § 26 BDSG.[187] This avoids upcoming complications if the collective agreement turns out ineffective. If, on the other hand, created regulations are effective, they take precedence over the more general statutory regulations which they concretize, because of their special nature.

---

[176] Gola/Heckmann/Nolte/Werkmeister DS-GVO Art. 17 mn. 16.

[177] DSK Kurzpapier Nr. 20 – Consent under the GDPR, 3: no 'arbitrary switching between consent and other legal bases'; EDPB, Guidelines 05/2020 on consent under Regulation 2016/679, Version 1.1, 4 May 2020; Uecker ZD 2019, 248 (249), Kühling/Buchner/Buchner/Kühling DS-GVO Art. 7 mn. 18.

[178] As example see an decision from the Austrian Federal Administrative Court (BVwG 31.8.2021 – W256 2227693-1/10E) that says there is no general restriction in switching from an unlawful consent to another legal basis.

[179] Kühling/Buchner/Maschmann BDSG § 26 mn. 63; Gola/Heckmann/Gola/Pötters BDSG § 26 mn. 52.

[180] HK-DS-GVO/BDSG/Tiedemann BDSG § 26 mn. 55; Gola/Heckmann/Gola/Pötters BDSG § 26 mn. 52; Kühling/Buchner/Maschmann BDSG § 26 mn. 65.

[181] BeckOK DatenschutzR/Riesenhuber, 51. Ed. 1.2.2025, BDSG § 26 mn. 52; HK-DS-GVO/BDSG/Tiedemann BDSG § 26 mn. 31.

[182] Taeger/Gabel/Zöll BDSG § 26 mn. 92.

[183] Taeger/Gabel/Zöll BDSG § 26 mn. 94.

[184] Kühling/Buchner/Maschmann BDSG § 26 mn. 68; Taeger/Gabel/Zöll BDSG § 26 mn. 95.

[185] Taeger/Gabel/Zöll BDSG § 26 mn. 90; Kühling/Buchner/Maschmann BDSG § 26 mn. 66.

[186] Ratgeber zum Beschäftigtendatenschutz des LfDI BW, 4th edn 2020, p. 16 <https://www.baden-wuerttemberg.datenschutz.de/wp-content/uploads/2020/04/Ratgeber-Besch%C3%A4ftigtendatenschutz.pdf> (last accessed: 19.2.2025).

[187] Wybitul/Sürup/Pötters ZD 2015, 559 (562); Kühling/Buchner/Maschmann BDSG § 26 mn. 69.

7. Latest decisions by the Court of Justice of the European Union

The Court of Justice of the European Union issued a verdict in which the court found that Art. 23 para. 1 sent. 1 Hessian Data Protection Act probably does not fulfil the requirements of Art. 88 para. 1 and 2 GDPR.[188] Usually, that might not concern private companies since the Hessian Data Protection Act only applies to public entities. But Art. 23 Hessian Data Protection Act has almost the same wording as § 26 BDSG, which all companies have to take as legitimisation to justify processing of their employees' data. With this legitimisation gone, companies must justify the processing of employee data by another legitimisation – and document that in the records of processing activities (Art. 30 GDPR). The Hessian Data Protection Commissioner has issued a handout on what currently to do with this verdict.[189] It states that the respective court – Administrative Court of Wiesbaden[190] – that made the admission to the CJEU has to rule whether the Hessian Data Protection Act is still admissible. But the CJEU also said that, in its opinion, Art. 23 Hessian Data Protection Act might not be a 'more specific rule' as Art. 88 para. 1 GDPR demands – and therefore inadmissible. So far, there is no due date of the decision of the Administrative Court. 116

But the handout from the Hessian Data Protection Commissioner clearly states that the decision from the CJEU will also have an effect on the usage of § 26 BDSG due to its same wording in reference to Art. 23 Hessian Data Protection Act.[191] It also states that controller should think of another legal basis to process employee data then § 26 BDSG.[192] 117

IV. § 43 BDSG

Last but not least, there is § 43 BDSG. The regulation supplements Art. 83 GDPR in several aspects.[193] The first paragraph refers to consumer credits. It determines that a person commits a regulatory offence if, pursuant to no. 1, he fails to handle a request for information correctly in violation of § 30 sub. 1 BDSG[194], or if, contrary to § 30 sub. 2 sent. 1 BDSG, he generally fails to provide a consumer with information or does not provide information correctly, completely or in time pursuant to no. 2.[195] Both alternatives require intentional or negligent action. § 43 sub. 2 BDSG states a regulatory fine of up to 50,000 EUR as legal consequence.[196] 118

With § 43 sub. 3 BDSG the German legislator used its permission from Art. 83 para. 7 GDPR and excluded authorities and public institutions according to § 2 sub. 1 BDSG from 119

---

[188] CJEU 30.03.2023 – C-34/21, ECLI:EU:C:2023:270 = BeckRS 2023, 5635.

[189] The handout 'Handreichung zur Verarbeitung personenbezogener Daten von Beschäftigten im Lichte des EuGH-Urteils vom 30.3.2023 Rs. C-34/21', which is only available in German, can be downloaded here: <https://datenschutz.hessen.de/sites/datenschutz.hessen.de/files/2023-04/handreichung_beschaeftigtendatenschutz_eugh-urteil.pdf> (last accessed: 12.2.2025).

[190] VG Wiesbaden 21.12.2020 – AZ 23 K 360/20.WI.PV, BeckRS 2020, 40028.

[191] Handout 'Handreichung zur Verarbeitung personenbezogener Daten von Beschäftigten im Lichte des EuGH-Urteils vom 30.3.2023 Rs. C-34/21', p. 5 <https://datenschutz.hessen.de/sites/datenschutz.hessen.de/files/2023-04/handreichung_beschaeftigtendatenschutz_eugh-urteil.pdf> (last accessed: 19.2.2025).

[192] Handout 'Handreichung zur Verarbeitung personenbezogener Daten von Beschäftigten im Lichte des EuGH-Urteils vom 30.3.2023 Rs. C-34/21', p. 6 <https://datenschutz.hessen.de/sites/datenschutz.hessen.de/files/2023-04/handreichung_beschaeftigtendatenschutz_eugh-urteil.pdf> (last accessed: 19.2.2025).

[193] Gola/Heckmann/Ehmann BDSG § 43 mn. 1.

[194] Gola/Heckmann/Ehmann BDSG § 43 mn. 4.

[195] Gola/Heckmann/Ehmann BDSG § 43 mn. 5.

[196] Gola/Heckmann/Ehmann BDSG § 43 mn. 6.

the imposition of regulatory fines.[197] This privilege, which remained unfounded in the legislative process, faces some criticism because authorities and other public institutions must also ensure the protection of personal data.[198]

120 According to § 43 sub. 4 BDSG, law enforcement authorities and courts may not use such information for regulatory fine proceedings that have been taken from notifications of personal data breaches in accordance with Art. 33 GDPR or Art. 34 para. 1 GDPR. The prohibition only applies with respect to the declarant or notifier and the relatives referred to in § 52 sub. 1 StPO.[199] If the person concerned consents to the utilization, however, it is permissible.[200] In this way, the provision takes into account the tensions between data protection law and criminal law described above and gives effect to the *nemo tenetur* principle.[201] It should be noted that only those notifications have the blocking effect that are objectively necessary and meet the legal requirements.[202]

E. Conclusion

121 This chapter can only give an overview regarding the complex legal challenges of data protection law these days. When it comes to the combination of data protection law and criminal law, even more legal challenges await. Since every company processes a huge amount of personal data, the risk of an infringement is inherent. If this risk collides with an employee whose contract gets terminated the risk will realise itself. It is common in German arbitration cases to file a request according to Art. 15 GDPR and threaten to file a complaint to the competent data protection authority (Art. 77 GDPR). If the former employee knows about data protection weaknesses of the company, he will use those in his arbitration case. In Germany, this has been a very common approach to get a better severance package. More often than not, a complaint – sometimes from a former employee – is the reason for administrative fine proceedings. The best way of evading such proceedings is to comply with the rules of the GDPR – or at least to try to comply. If basic rules of the GDPR are negated, the data protection authorities will most likely fine the respective company. But if the data protection authorities can see that the company has a data protection compliance system – even if it does not fulfil every last condition – there must not necessarily be a fine at the end since the data protection authority can also issue a reprimand (Art. 58 para. 2 lit. b) GDPR). Companies should, therefore, take it seriously that data protection is a top-management issue and cannot be ignored. As shown in this chapter, there are numerous possibilities how data protection law can be a liability issue which, therefore, must be addressed properly.

122 So even after more than seven years of GDPR – not counting the two years of preparation time – data protection law has still many unknowns and one cannot know the further course for sure. But the fog is lifting and slowly but surely data protection law is setting its course – not into unknown lands as Christopher Columbus did but to more legal certainty. There will be many interesting decisions by the CJEU in the near future which will bring clarity to current legal uncertainties.

---

[197] Kühling/Buchner/Bergt BDSG § 43 mn. 3.
[198] Gola/Heckmann/Ehmann BDSG § 43 mn. 9.
[199] Kühling/Buchner/Bergt BDSG § 43 mn. 6; KMW DatenschutzsanktionenR-HdB/Basar § 5 mn. 22.
[200] Kühling/Buchner/Bergt BDSG § 43 mn. 6.
[201] Gola/Heckmann/Ehmann BDSG § 43 mn. 10; Kühling/Buchner/Bergt BDSG § 43 mn. 9; see Basar PinG 1/2025, 16 et seqq.
[202] Kühling/Buchner/Bergt BDSG § 43 mn. 7.

CHAPTER 17
IT CRIMINAL LAW

Bibliography: Brodowski/Hartmann/Sorge, Automatisierung in der Strafrechtspflege, NJW 2023, 583; Ceffinato, Einführung in das Internetstrafrecht, JuS 2019, 337; Eckel/Rottmeier, „Liken als Haten": Strafverfolgung von Hatespeech in Sozialen Netzwerken, NStZ 2021, 1; Fährmann, Digitale Beweismittel und Datenmengen im Strafprozess, MMR 2020, 228; Kipker/Dittrich, Rolle der Kritischen Infrastrukturen nach dem neuen NIS-2-Umsetzungs- und Cybersicherheitsstärkungsgesetz, MMR 2023, 481; Krause, Rechtsprechungsübersicht zum Internetstrafrecht, NStZ 2021, 599; Kruse/Grzesiek, Die Online-Durchsuchung als „digitale Allzweckwaffe" – Zur Kritik an überbordenden Ermittlungsmethoden, KritV, 2017, 331; Kumkar, Deepfakes – Risiken und Regulierung im europäischen Verordnungsentwurf für künstliche Intelligenz, K&R 2023, 32; Schönknecht, Beweisbeschaffung in den USA zur Verwendung in deutschen Verfahren, GRURInt 2011, 1000 Schumann, Das 41. StrÄndG zur Bekämpfung der Computerkriminalität, NStZ 2007, 675; Singelnstein, Möglichkeiten und Grenzen neuerer strafprozessualer Ermittlungsmaßnahmen – Telekommunikation, Web 2.0, Datenbeschlagnahme, polizeiliche Datenverarbeitung & Co, NStZ 2012, 593.

Table of contents

A. The phenomenon of cybercrime and its significance for IT criminal law ... 410
B. Fundamentals of IT criminal law ... 412
I. Technological aspects ... 412
II. Legal aspects ... 413
1. Relevant legislation at national and European Union level . 413
2. Applicability of German criminal law ... 414
3. Special features of IT criminal law ... 415
C. Typical offences in IT criminal law ... 416
I. Notions and procedural foundations ... 416
II. Protection of the digital sphere of personal life and privacy ... 416
1. Spying on data (§ 202a StGB) ... 417
2. Phishing (§ 202b StGB) ... 418
3. Acts preparatory to data espionage and phishing (§ 202c StGB) ... 418
4. Handling stolen data (§ 202d StGB) ... 419
III. Cyber-specific offences causing damage ... 419
1. Data manipulation (§ 303a StGB) ... 419
2. Computer sabotage (§ 303b StGB) ... 420
IV. Computer fraud (§ 263a StGB) ... 421
V. Electronic forgery offences (§§ 269 and 270 StGB) ... 422
VI. Copyright offences ... 422
VII. Data protection violations ... 423
VIII. Offences relating to statements ... 424
IX. Special cybercrime offences ... 424
1. 'Cyberstalking' (§ 238 sub. 1 no. 5–7 StGB) ... 424
2. 'Skimming' (§§ 152b sub. 5, 149 sub. 1 no. 1 StGB) ... 425
3. Pornographic illustrations ... 425
4. CEO fraud (§ 263 sub. 1 StGB) ... 426
D. Practice of IT criminal law ... 426
I. Investigation procedure and preservation of evidence in IT criminal cases ... 427

II. Challenges and special characteristics in IT criminal proceedings ... 428
III. International cooperation regarding IT offences ... 429
IV. Case studies from the field of IT criminal law ... 430
1. Case study 1: data manipulation and its consequences ... 430
2. Case study 2: criminal proceedings in cases of cyberbullying ... 431
3. Case study 3: international cooperation in cases of data theft ... 431
V. Outlook and future developments in IT criminal law ... 432

A. The phenomenon of cybercrime and its significance for IT criminal law

1 #GermanyRIP – in January 2023, the hacker group 'Killnet' launched a campaign of retaliation against German authorities and companies under this hashtag. Using a distributed denial of service (DDoS) attack, websites of airports, companies belonging to the energy and financial sectors, and federal authorities were attacked. They were offline for several hours. In recent times, this was just one of numerous cyberattacks on German stakeholders and institutions. At the end of September 2023, a German hotel chain fell victim of a hacker attack. The hacker group 'ALPHV' published millions of names, addresses, and travel data of guests on the darknet, including credit card information – a total of six terabytes of data was published. This was primarily data from termed emergency lists, which are created daily to ensure that in the event of a fire, for example, everyone is evacuated. One of the most serious attacks in 2023 occurred in October. The hacker group 'Akira' carried out a ransomware attack on a municipal IT service provider. They encrypted all data and placed a blackmail letter. As a result, 72 German municipalities and public administrations were barely able to operate.[1] The same group also attacked a German hotel group in May 2025. The company claimed, that after 'Akira' stole its data, it tried to blackmail the hotel group – however without any success.[2] In October 2024, a large confessional health and social services provider in Berlin and North-East Germany experienced a major cyberattack that encrypted their central servers and disrupted their IT systems. It caused significant disruptions, including temporarily halting ambulance traffic to their hospitals.[3]

2 According to the Federal Criminal Police Office's (*Bundeskriminalamt*, 'BKA') **Cybercrime Federal Situation Report**, the threat situation for companies posed by cyberattacks remained persistently high in 2024, primarily shaped by ransomware attacks and hacktivist DDoS campaigns.[4] Both, the quantity and quality of attacks have increased, which is particularly due to the international nature of cybercrimes. Foreign-based cybercrimes

[1] Cf. <https://kommunalwiki.boell.de/index.php/Cyberangriff_auf_die_S%C3%BCdwestfalen-IT_2023> (last accessed: 25.2.2025).

[2] Cf. <https://www.tagesschau.de/inland/regional/mecklenburgvorpommern/ndr-cyberattacke-auf-arcona-gruppe-russlandnahe-hacker-identifiziert-100.html> (last accessed: 11.6.2025).

[3] Cf. <https://www.johannesstift-diakonie.de/cyberangriff> (last accessed: 10.6.2025); cf. <https://www.tagesspiegel.de/berlin/nach-dem-cyber-angriff-in-berlin-hacker-erbeuten-womoglich-daten-von-200000-patienten-12578750.html> (last accessed: 10.6.2025).

[4] BKA: Cybercrime, Bundeslagebild 2024 (ie, Federal Situation Report 2024), p. 32, available at <https://www.bsi.bund.de/DE/Service-Navi/Publikationen/Lagebericht/lagebericht_node.html> (last accessed: 25.2.2025).

(includes crimes from unknown bases) increased by approximately 6 % to 201,877 cases, significantly exceeding domestic incidents. The Bitkom e.V. estimated the financial damage caused explicitly by cyberattacks to companies in Germany in 2024 at 178.6 billion EUR, marking a significant increase of 30.4 billion EUR compared to 2023 and representing the highest recorded sum to date. This damage accounts for three-quarters of the total recorded damages, which stands at 266.6 billion EUR and includes analogue and digital theft, industrial espionage, and sabotage. **Initial access brokers** are a central element of the threat situation. These specialised actors provide access to company networks for cyber criminals, which in turn enables a large number of attacks. The BKA reported 950 ransomware attacks nationwide in 2024. **Ransomware** remains a central threat, continuously evolving, and causing significant damage to companies and private individuals. While zero-day vulnerabilities and specific malware variants remain particularly dangerous, 186 **IT vulnerabilities** were exploited for cybercriminal activities in 2024, with Zero-Day vulnerabilities being particularly significant. Furthermore, attacks on **IT supply chains** increase the attack potential for cyber criminals. The increasing interconnectedness of companies through IT service providers implies that an attack on a single entity in the supply chain can affect numerous companies and authorities simultaneously. As a result, liability issues arise within the supply chain. **Artificial intelligence (AI)** is increasingly being used for cybercriminal activities, augmenting the capabilities of cybercriminals, with a further intensification of AI-supported criminal offences expected. AI-supported phishing campaigns are also seeing a qualitative and quantitative increase. Despite investigative successes against perpetrator infrastructure, the danger persists, as perpetrators are often globally dispersed and difficult to apprehend.[5]

It is not surprising that criminals focus on cyber-attacks. Compared to other types of offences, the detection risk is rather low. However, the chances of success and profit prospects are relatively high because the modern world of data is so closely interconnected in our information and communication society.[6] Since the BKA began compiling statistics on the phenomenon of cybercrime in 2007, the number of cases has risen rapidly. This development has also created new legal challenges, particularly in the field of criminal law. As a result, a sub-discipline of criminal law has emerged among lawyers – i.e., IT criminal law. 3

The term 'IT criminal law' encompasses criminal offences that play a particularly frequent role as a result of Internet and computer use and criminal offences that were even created in this context.[7] Yet, **computer criminal law** and **internet criminal law** may be distinguished. While computer criminal law concerns offences committed using a computer, internet criminal law focuses on communication between computer networks.[8] However, this distinction is irrelevant for criminal proceedings linked to the respective offence under the German Criminal Code; rather, it serves to systematise the offences. 4

In addition, IT criminal law pertains to criminal offences committed by misusing computer systems, i.e., where the information technology system is used as a means to commit criminal offences. Criminal offences directed against **information technology systems** and **data** are also covered. This means that data, which is described as the gold of the 21st century, itself becomes the object of the offence.[9] The fact that these offences under IT criminal law are not covered by the traditional offences under the German 5

[5] Cf. <https://www.bsi.bund.de/DE/Service-Navi/Publikationen/Lagebericht/lagebericht_node.html> (last accessed: 10.6.2025).
[6] Kochheim Cybercrime mn. 1.
[7] Auer-Reinsdorff/Conrad IT- und DatenschutzR-HdB/Hassemer § 43 mn. 21.
[8] HKV Computer- und InternetStrafR § 1 mn. 7.
[9] Ceffinato JuS 2019, 337 (337).

Criminal Code of 1872, such as 'movable property belonging to another person', poses a challenge. This has already raised countless legal questions and called for amendments to existing laws.

6 Cybercrime is also characterised by its cross-border nature and technical complexity. Consequently, trained specialised law enforcement personnel is essential to ensure effective prosecution. To this end, centralised units within the investigating authorities, both nationally and internationally, have been installed that specialise in combating cybercrime. An important player at EU level is the **European Cybercrime Centre**. Within Germany, the **Cybercrime Division** (*Abteilung Cybercrime*, 'CC'), the **National Cybercrime Cooperation Centre** (*Nationale Kooperationsstelle Cybercrime*, 'NKC') of the BKA, as well as the **Central Cybercrime Contact Points** (*Zentrale Ansprechstellen Cybercrime*, 'ZAC') within the State Criminal Police Offices (*Landeskriminalämter*, 'LKA') are the relevant points of contact for this specialised field.

7 Given the shift of criminal offences to the digital world, it is not surprising that – in recent years – the investigating authorities' activities have also become increasingly 'digital'. Furthermore, the legislator has introduced corresponding investigative powers.[10] For lawyers who provide legal advice in the areas of IT compliance, IT security, or in the defence of accusations of cybercrime, it is essential to understand not only the changing legal situation but also the technical background.

B. Fundamentals of IT criminal law

8 To categorise the relevant criminal norms both technological and legal aspects will be examined first.

I. Technological aspects

9 All information technology systems are considered objects of cybercrime. This term is based on the German fundamental IT right (Art. 2 para. 1 in conjunction with Art. 1 para. 1 GG), which protects the **confidentiality** and **integrity** of information technology systems. This includes all digital devices that are used to store personal data. In addition to computers and smartphones, this also includes other **IT systems** such as **clouds**.[11]

10 The digital devices, which initially process information unconnectedly, become a **telecommunication system** when connected to the Internet.[12] This classification is relevant for any investigation measure by the law enforcement authorities, because the law imposes different requirements on the respective legal bases.

11 Cybercrime includes all acts and operating procedures that are committed against or by means of information technology systems.[13] **Malware** and **ransomware** are methods of cybercrime alongside the classic case of **hacking**, which is used to penetrate a third-party IT system.[14] Malware is a collective term for all malicious programmes; ransom-

---

[10] For more details, → mn. 125.

[11] BVerfG 20.4.2016 – 1 BvR 966/09, NJW 2016, 1781 (1794); MAH Strafverteidigung/Grözinger § 50 mn. 295.

[12] Kochheim Cybercrime mn. 48.

[13] Kochheim Cybercrime mn. 45.

[14] Schumann NStZ 2007, 675.

ware enables the perpetrator to encrypt an IT system to prevent access by the authorised person.[15]

Another tool of cyber criminals that is often underestimated is known as 'social engineering'. Social engineering involves collecting and analysing freely available, often personal, information about a natural or legal person to deduce further conclusions. The intention for the data analysis can be manifold and ranges from obtaining private access rights to creating a deceptively genuine website of a well-known brand for fraudulent purposes. Essentially, social engineering is used for manipulation and suggestion.[16] **12**

Consequently, cybercrime is primarily about the abuse of technical devices and their information and communication technology. The use of information and communication technology to coordinate criminal offences must be distinguished from this and is not covered by the technological scope of cybercrime.[17] **13**

II. Legal aspects

Legal researchers have already identified an enormous need for action when it comes to criminal offences in the field of IT criminal law due to the diverse technological aspects of cybercrime. **14**

1. Relevant legislation at national and European Union level

This has already led to legislative acts at both national and EU level. **15**

At German national level, a new cybersecurity strategy was adopted in 2021 which was then substantiated by the National Cybersecurity Agenda (*Nationale Cybersicherheitsagenda*) of 2022. With this approach, Germany aims to achieve the highest possible level of security and to ensure efficient cybersecurity by means of clarifying the distribution of tasks and better interconnecting the individual players.[18] The **Act to Combat Right-Wing Extremism and Hate Crime** (*Gesetz zur Bekämpfung von Rechtsextremismus und Hasskriminalität*) of 30 March 2021 also broke new ground in terms of countering IT criminal offences.[19] The German Federal Ministry of Justice and Consumer Protection ('BMJV') launched a legislative project in April 2023 by publishing a 'key points paper' for a law against digital violence. The BMJV initiated this project to strengthen the victims' rights to obtain offender data and allow court-ordered account suspensions, with an initial draft law expected by autumn 2023. However, the project was delayed as the BMJV is still developing the draft, needing to incorporate recent rulings from the European Court of Justice and the Federal Court of Justice that affect cross-border data disclosure and jurisdiction. **16**

However, it is precisely because of the often-transnational nature of criminal offences in the field of cybercrime that EU regulations are of particular importance. Primarily, the EU does not regulate criminal law, but the internal market. Therefore, it uses directives and regulations to establish rules that affect economic matters. In this context, a focus is placed on the control of communication services. However, to effectively combat criminal offences, including IT offences, **harmonisation** of **national criminal law systems** **17**

[15] MAH Strafverteidigung/Grözinger Ch 50 mn. 7.
[16] Kochheim Cybercrime mn. 333.
[17] Kochheim Cybercrime mn. 49.
[18] Kipker Cybersecurity-HdB/Kipker Ch. 1 mn. 16d.
[19] BGBl. 2021, part I, no. 13, p. 441.

and intensive **cooperation** between **law enforcement authorities** is increasingly being demanded and implemented.[20]

18 The **Council of Europe's Convention on Cybercrime** ('CCC'), signed on 23 November 2001, is one of the most important EU legal acts to combat cybercrime.[21] In addition, new developments are worth mentioning.

19 These include the **NIS2 Directive**, which was adopted at EU level in 2023 and aims to ensure a high common level of cybersecurity throughout the EU.[22] One of the most important regulations is Art. 21 NIS2 Directive. It stipulates that companies must be obliged to take appropriate risk management measures to reduce the security risks to network and information systems. In addition, the Directive holds the companies' management bodies responsible for the establishment and implementation of such risk management measures in accordance with Art. 20 and 32 para. 6 NIS2 Directive, if these measures are not implemented in the company in compliance with the requirements. The deadline for transposing the directive into national law ended on 17 October 2024. A draft bill (**NIS2UmsuCG**) for the transposition of the directive is currently pending in Germany. § 38 sub. 2 NIS2UmsuCG (ie, the German draft bill to transpose the NIS2 Directive) establishes **management liability**. According to this provision, the managing director is personally liable for damages resulting from the breach of his supervisory duties.[23] Furthermore, § 38 sub. 4 NIS2UmsuCG stipulates that directors of particularly important entities must regularly attend training courses in order to acquire sufficient knowledge and skills to fulfil their obligations under § 38 sub. 1 NIS2UmsuCG.[24]

20 In addition, the **Regulation on Digital Operational Resilience for the Financial Sector** (*Verordnung über die Betriebsstabilität digitaler Systeme des Finanzsektors*; abbreviated as '**DORA**') was adopted in November 2022. This regulation is intended to improve the EU financial sector's resilience to serious operational disruptions and cyberattacks. Another EU regulation on cybersecurity is the **Cyber Resilience Act**. It is intended to increase the resilience of products containing digital components against cyberattacks through introducing binding cybersecurity requirements.

21 Moreover, the **Digital Services Act** ('DSA') is applicable since 17 February 2024. This is a law on digital services that establishes standardised regulations for the entire European Union. It is intended to facilitate the removal of illegal content on the internet by imposing comprehensive due diligence obligations on online platforms. With this new act, the EU legislator aims to combat hate speech (*Hassrede*) on the internet, for example, but also the sale of counterfeit products.[25]

2. Applicability of German criminal law

22 In IT criminal law, we face the particular problem of the borderless nature of the internet, which often calls into question the competence of national criminal prosecution authorities.[26] German criminal law applies in accordance with §§ 3 and 9 StGB primarily if the place of the offence lies in Germany.[27]

---

[20] HKV Computer- und InternetStrafR § 1 mn. 98.
[21] HKV Computer- und InternetStrafR § 1 mn. 125.
[22] Art. 1 para. 1 Directive (EU) 2022/2555.
[23] Kipker/Dittrich MMR 2023, 481 (485).
[24] Kipker/Dittrich MMR 2023, 481 (486).
[25] Cf. <https://www.bundesregierung.de/breg-de/themen/digitalisierung/gesetz-ueber-digitale-dienste-2140944> (last accessed: 25.2.2025).
[26] MAH Strafverteidigung/Grözinger Ch. 50 mn. 8.
[27] Kipker Cybersecurity-HdB/Keber Ch. 17 mn. 35.

In this context, it is not necessary for the effect, such as damages, to have occurred in Germany. The only decisive factor is that the criminal act, which can ultimately lead to the criminal effect abroad, was carried out in Germany (**place of action**). It is therefore decisive for the applicability of German criminal law pursuant to § 9 sub. 1 var. 1 StGB that the cybercriminal is physically located in Germany when the offence is committed.[28] 23

At the same time, however, it is sufficient if only the effect of the offence materialises in Germany, although the perpetrator acted from abroad (**place of effect**). In this case, too, German criminal law is applicable pursuant to § 9 sub. 1 var. 3 and 4 StGB. 24

Generally speaking, it is not easy to determine in which country the offence is committed. For example, a particular problem arises when an offence is committed on the internet and the internet is used as a means of communication. According to the traditional understanding, the place of the offence in this constellation is the place where the data transmission is initiated, i.e., the place from which the Internet is accessed.[29] Others consider it sufficient for German criminal law to apply when the perpetrator stores data from abroad on a computer located in Germany.[30] 25

In certain cases, German criminal law may also apply to offences committed abroad pursuant to §§ 5, 6, and 7 StGB. 26

3. Special features of IT criminal law

Only human behaviour conducted by a natural person can be punishable under German criminal law. To be punishable under German criminal law, the specific behaviour must be punishable as an offence under StGB.[31] 27

A special feature of criminal liability in IT criminal law applies to the **providers of information technology systems** or other communication platforms, particularly social media platforms. According to the German understanding of criminal acts or omissions, they are only subject to a risk of criminal liability if they facilitate criminal offences or participate themselves in the dissemination of criminal content.[32] The criminal liability of such a service provider is generally only incurred if it fails to delete the criminal content and is therefore subject to the special requirements of criminal liability for aiding by omission.[33] This requires a **guarantor position**. Such a position is established if the perpetrator of the omission is legally responsible for averting the outcome pursuant to § 13 sub. 1 StGB, i.e. she or she must be obliged to avert the outcome. For example, such an obligation may follow from the perpetrator creating a source of danger or bearing responsibility for it.[34] Platform operators, who operate a platform whose predominant purpose is dedicated to committing criminal offences usually have a **guarantor position** because they create a source of danger. By contrast, it is controversial whether a platform provider of a social network, whose purpose is to open a communication space, may bear a guarantor status (based on omission) and thus criminal liability.[35] 28

However, the platforms' liability as legal entities under the law on administrative offences remains unaffected by the criminal liability of the platform operator. 29

[28] Cf. <https://www.strafrecht-digital.com/tatortbestimmung-im-internet/> (last accessed: 25.2.2025).
[29] HKV Computer- und InternetStrafR § 2 mn. 18.
[30] HKV Computer- und InternetStrafR § 2 mn. 23.
[31] Kipker Cybersecurity-HdB/Brodowski Ch. 17 mn. 34.
[32] Eckel/Rottmeier NStZ 2021, 1 (5).
[33] Eckel/Rottmeier NStZ 2021, 1.
[34] TK-StGB/Bosch StGB § 13 mn. 11.
[35] Eckel/Rottmeier NStZ 2021, 1 (6).

C. Typical offences in IT criminal law

30 Typical offences in the field of cybercrime include offences relating to personal life and privacy (*Lebens- und Geheimnisbereich* → mn. 36 et seqq.), offences causing damage (*Beschädigungsdelikte* → mn. 57 et seqq.), computer fraud (→ mn. 73 et seqq.), electronic forgery offences (*elektronische Urkundsdelikte* → mn. 82 et seqq.), copyright offences (→ mn. 85 et seqq.), data protection violations (→ mn. 89 et seqq.), and offences relating to statements (*Äußerungsdelikte* → mn. 97 et seqq.). Furthermore, there are some cyber-specific means to commit certain offences (→ mn. 102 et seqq.). Besides the typical offences of IT criminal law, however, it is also conceivable that offences within the meaning of the StGB are committed indirectly by using information technology systems, which at first glance would not be classified as cybercrime. In the case of attacks on the IT systems of hospitals, for example, this may even involve the killing of a person through the misuse of IT systems.[36]

I. Notions and procedural foundations

31 Whenever IT criminal law refers to 'data', it refers to information that is not directly perceptibly stored or transmitted (cf. § 202a sub. 2 StGB).

32 In addition, the **authorisation to dispose of data** depends on the act of scripting, i.e., it depends on the person who first caused the data to be stored.[37]

33 If **negligence** is not expressly criminalised under German criminal law, the respective offence must have been committed **intentionally**.

34 It may also be that several punishable offences have been committed (*Tatmehrheit*), for which a **total penalty** is then fixed. In such cases, an aggregated penalty (*Gesamtstrafe*) must be imposed; this is referred to as **joinder of offences**. By contrast, only one penalty is imposed for several punishable offences that are **committed by one act** (*Tateinheit*).[38]

35 If the offence is only prosecuted on request, a **request to prosecute** pursuant to § 77b sub. 1 StGB must be filed within a period of three months. Otherwise, the offence will not be prosecuted. Pursuant to § 77b sub. 2 StGB, the period commences upon the expiry of the day on which the person entitled to file the request gains knowledge of the offence and the identity of the perpetrator.

II. Protection of the digital sphere of personal life and privacy

36 §§ 202a et seqq StGB protect the sphere of personal life and privacy (*Lebens- und Geheimnisbereich*) by criminalising unauthorised access to other people's data. Pursuant to § 205 sub. 1 StGB, the offences under §§ 202a, 202b, and 202d StGB are only prosecuted upon request, unless the prosecuting authorities deem it necessary to intervene *ex officio* due to a special public interest.

---

[36] Kipker Cybersecurity-HdB/Brodowski Ch. 17 mn. 32.

[37] HKV Computer- und InternetStrafR § 3 mn. 402; TK-StGB/Eisele StGB § 202a mn. 9; OLG Nürnberg 23.1.2013 – 1 Ws 445/12, ZD 2013, 282.

[38] Fischer StGB Vor § 52 mn. 1, 39.

Filing a request to prosecute is a prerequisite for trial and provides the victim with a choice as to whether he or she wishes to accept the disclosure of his or her personal life and privacy as a result of the criminal proceedings.[39] 37

1. Spying on data (§ 202a StGB)

§ 202a StGB is one of the central provisions of IT criminal law and protects the **data owner's right of disposal.**[40] Pursuant to § 202a StGB, whoever, without being authorised to do so, obtains access for themselves or another to data which were not intended for them incurs a penalty of imprisonment for a term not exceeding three years. The data must be specially protected against unauthorised access. 38

In addition to **computer espionage**, which involves penetrating other people's IT systems in order to copy data or programmes, cases of **data theft** and **data disclosure** are also considered criminal acts.[41] 39

A perpetrator gains unauthorised access to data if he or she acts against the will of the person authorised to dispose of the data.[42] 40

In addition, the data must be specially protected against unauthorised access. This is the case if the special **interest in confidentiality** becomes apparent through the precautions taken, without data access having to be completely prevented. It is sufficient if access is impeded.[43] It must be assessed on a case-by-case basis whether the access – in a specific case – was protected. An exception applies to the mass use of malicious software. In such a case, a pragmatic estimate can be used to assess the circumventing of special security measures. In a 2018 decision, for example, the German Federal Court of Justice (*Bundesgerichtshof*, 'BGH') estimated that approximately 75 % of computer systems are protected by means of a **firewall.**[44] 41

Typical cases of data espionage can include the use of **Trojans**, **keyloggers**, or **hacking.**[45] In addition, the intrusion into the access authorisation systems of pay TV providers can generally be regarded as spying on data within the meaning of § 202a sub. 1 StGB.[46] In such constellations, the decisive factor is whether the operator of the **card-sharing server** is itself a customer of the pay TV provider and merely misuses the data. Then, only aiding the spying of data by unauthorised third parties can be assumed.[47] 42

For the individual hacking techniques, it is essential to always check whether an access protection has been bypassed. There is only a criminal offence if this is the case. Therefore, **skimming**, a technique by which the magnetic strip of a payment card is read, does not constitute an offence pursuant to § 202a StGB. In these cases, the data is copied in encrypted form and the card is only unlocked at the ATM by entering the corresponding PIN. Therefore, skimming does not involve circumventing access security. By contrast, indirectly obtaining access is also an offence if, for example, the perpetrator induces by deception the authorised person to install malware.[48] Crypto theft can also constitute an offence pursuant to § 202a StGB. However, **phishing** does not constitute an offence pur- 43

39 WJS WirtschaftsStrafR-HdB/Bär Ch. 15 mn. 101.
40 TK-StGB/Eisele § 202a mn. 1a; HKV Computer- und InternetStrafR § 3 mn. 344.
41 MAH Strafverteidigung/Grözinger § 50 mn. 9.
42 MAH Strafverteidigung/Grözinger § 50 mn. 33.
43 BGH 13.5.2020 – 5 StR 614/19, NStZ-RR 2020, 278.
44 BGH 27.7.2017 – 1 StR 412/16, NStZ 2018, 401.
45 MAH Strafverteidigung/Grözinger § 50 mn. 34.
46 Krause NStZ 2021, 599.
47 OLG Celle 31.8.2016 – 2 Ss 93/16, MMR 2017, 342.
48 MAH WirtschaftsStrafR/Beukelmann § 30 mn. 22 et seq; MAH Strafverteidigung/Grözinger § 50 mn. 34 seqq.

suant to § 202a StGB, because the authorised person discloses the data to the perpetrator voluntarily although by deception.[49]

44 The possibility of gaining knowledge of data is sufficient for committing the result of the offence of **obtaining.** Storage is not required.[50]

2. Phishing (§ 202b StGB)

45 In contrast to data espionage, § 202b StGB criminalises the interception of data that is not specially protected with a penalty of imprisonment for a term not exceeding two years.[51]

46 Unauthorised intercepting of data from a non-public data transmission or from an electromagnetic broadcast from a data processing facility using technical means is punishable under § 202b StGB. Particularly, the criminal offence alternative of § 202b alt. 1 StGB is of high practical relevance; it requires external access to an ongoing data transmission.[52]

47 Data is only protected during the transmission process. Stored data that was transmitted prior to the offence is not covered by the scope of protection of the provision.[53]

48 In contrast to § 202a StGB, obtaining the power of disposal over the data is required for constituting 'obtaining' under § 202b StGB; merely gaining access is not sufficient.[54] **Encrypted data** is only deemed to have been obtained once it has been decrypted. Nevertheless, it is sufficient if the perpetrator has obtained the necessary key.[55]

49 Typical cases that fall under § 202b alt. 1 StGB are purported **man-in-the-middle attacks** and the disclosure of access data.[56] When intercepting data within a Wi-Fi network, a distinction must be made: if the router requires authorisation in order to connect, § 202a sub. 1 StGB applies, because this constitutes an access barrier.[57] If access is possible without an authorisation requirement, at least criminal liability pursuant to § 202b StGB is possible.[58] If **spyware** is installed as well, criminal liability for **data manipulation** under § 303a StGB and §§ 269 and 270 StGB may be possible.[59]

50 By contrast, the use of peripheral devices or purported side channel attacks constitute data interception from electromagnetic broadcasts pursuant to § 202b alt. 2 StGB.[60]

3. Acts preparatory to data espionage and phishing (§ 202c StGB)

51 Under § 202c StGB, certain preparatory acts for **espionage and interception of data** are also punishable with a penalty of imprisonment not exceeding two years. Criminal acts considered preparatory to a criminal offence under §§ 202a and 202b StGB are the **acquisition**, **sale**, **supplying** to another party, **dissemination**, or **making available in another way** of passwords or other security codes that enable access to data or computer programmes for the purpose to committing such an offence.

---

[49] HKV Computer- und InternetStrafR § 3 mn. 351.
[50] MAH Strafverteidigung/Grözinger § 50 mn. 34.
[51] TK-StGB/Eisele StGB § 202b mn. 1.
[52] MAH Strafverteidigung/Grözinger § 50 mn. 42.
[53] BT-Drs. 16/3656, 11.
[54] HKV Computer- und InternetStrafR § 3 mn. 381.
[55] MAH Strafverteidigung/Grözinger § 50 mn. 43.
[56] MAH Strafverteidigung/Grözinger § 50 mn. 9, 44.
[57] Kochheim Cybercrime mn. 643.
[58] MAH Strafverteidigung/Grözinger § 50 mn. 40.
[59] Kochheim Cybercrime mn. 643.
[60] HKV Computer- und InternetStrafR § 3 mn. 380.

In addition to passwords and security codes, all hacker tools such as **password generators** (known as **KeyGen**), **keyloggers**, **Trojan Horses**, and other **viruses** that either spy on the computer or install a 'backdoor' are the object of an offence under § 202c StGB.[61] **52**

The objects of the offence need not be data within the meaning of § 202a sub. 2 StGB. Rather, passwords that are, for instance, written down are also covered by the scope of § 202c sub. 1 no. 1 StGB.[62] **53**

4. Handling stolen data (§ 202d StGB)

Pursuant to § 202d StGB, anyone who provides access to data that another person has procured by an unlawful act for the purpose of **enriching** themselves or a third party or **harming** another person is criminally liable. § 202d StGB provides for various alternative criminal offences. In addition to **providing access**, the **procurement**, **supply**, and **dissemination** of unlawfully obtained data is punishable by a penalty of imprisonment for a term not exceeding three years. **54**

Anyone who obtains the data exclusively for the fulfilment of lawful official or professional duties is not liable to prosecution under § 202d sub. 3 StGB, despite having committed an act that violates § 202d sub. 1 StGB. This exemption from the criminal offence is particularly relevant for tax investigators and journalists.[63] **55**

In addition to intent, the intention to enrich or harm is required. The perpetrator acts with the **intention to enrich** him or herself if he or she intended to gain a pecuniary advantage for him or herself or a third party as a result of the offence. **Intent to cause harm** occurs when the perpetrator's intention is to cause harm to the victim. This is assumed, for example, for immaterial damage caused by exposing the victim on the internet.[64] **56**

III. Cyber-specific offences causing damage

Another group of offences in the field of cybercrime are cyber-specific offences causing damage pursuant to §§ 303a et seqq StGB. Although these offences are included in the section on criminal damage, they do not protect the right of ownership, but rather rights of use similar to ownership, since data is not considered property.[65] Just like criminal damage pursuant to § 303 StGB, § 303a sub. 1 and sub. 2 StGB and § 303b sub. 1–3 StGB are offences that can only be **prosecuted upon request** (*relatives Antragsdelikt*) unless there is a **special public interest**, § 303c StGB. **57**

Pursuant to §§ 303a sub. 3 and 303b sub. 5 in conjunction with § 202c StGB, the preparatory acts mentioned in → mn. 49 et seqq. may also be punishable as data manipulation or computer sabotage offences. **58**

1. Data manipulation (§ 303a StGB)

Under § 303a StGB, anyone who **deletes**, **suppresses**, renders **unusable**, or **alters** data without authorisation incurs a penalty of imprisonment for a term not exceeding two years. **59**

---

[61] MüKoStGB/Graf StGB § 202c mn. 12.
[62] Fischer StGB § 202c mn. 3; HKV Computer- und InternetStrafR § 3 mn. 384.
[63] Kipker Cybersecurity-HdB/Brodowski Ch. 17 mn. 49.
[64] BeckOK StGB/Weidemann, 65 Ed. 1.5.2025, StGB § 202d mn. 22 et seq.
[65] MüKoStGB/Wieck-Noodt StGB Vor § 303 mn. 1 et seq.

60 Protected is the usability of data in which a third party has a directly legally protected interest and with regard to which that person is entitled to an **owner-like authorisation to dispose of the data**. It is possible that the owner of the data carrier is different from the person who holds the **right to use** the data. In this constellation, the legal relationship between the parties determines who is **authorised to dispose of the data**.[66]

61 Data is **deleted** when it is rendered unrecognisable. Data must be irretrievably lost rendering reconstruction impossible.[67]

62 Data is **suppressed** if the authorised party is deprived of the possibility of access or disposal. Besides storing data in different directories and changing suffixes, also the labelling of the directory as 'hidden' and its encryption are covered.[68] It is not required that the authorised person wishes to access the data during the suppression period. The possible interference with the intention to access the data is sufficient.[69]

63 The term 'rendering unusable' refers to removing the intended usability of data.[70] This can occur, for example, by altering control characters or data record separators, or by any change that impedes the executability of a file or alters the meaning of the information value.[71]

64 **Alteration of data** encompasses any form of content-related reorganisation that leads to impaired function or a change in the information content or value.[72]

65 Any unlawful **impairment of the usability** of data can, therefore, be considered an offence under § 303a StGB. Infringements of the right of disposal of the person authorised to dispose of the data and infringements of the interests of the person affected by the data content (cf. § 41 BDSG) can lead to illegality.[73]

2. Computer sabotage (§ 303b StGB)

66 Computer sabotage is an offence punishable by a penalty of imprisonment for a term not exceeding three years if a person interferes with the proper functioning of data processing operations. Data processing encompasses not only the individual data processing operation but also any further handling and utilisation of data.[74]

67 It is necessary that the data processing is significant for another person. For private individuals, this is the case if the data processing has a central function in the way they organise their lives. Consequently, this includes data processing operations connected to employment, literary, scientific, or artistic activities. So-called trivial cases are excluded.[75]

68 Moreover, the impairment shall not be insignificant. A **significant impairment** of uninterrupted operations includes, for example, the impairment of technical functions, interruptions, or disruptions to the data flow, programme changes resulting in a system crash, or causing inaccurate content results.[76]

---

[66] TK-StGB/Hecker StGB § 303a mn. 3; BeckOK StGB/Weidemann, 65 Ed. 1.5.2025, StGB § 202d mn. 2, 4 et seq.
[67] BT-Drs. 10/5058, p. 34.
[68] Kochheim Cybercrime mn. 664.
[69] HKV Computer- und InternetStrafR § 3 mn. 413.
[70] Fischer StGB § 303a mn. 11.
[71] Kochheim Cybercrime mn. 664.
[72] BT-Drs. 10/5058, p. 35.
[73] BT-Drs. 10/5058, p. 34.
[74] BT-Drs. 10/5058, p. 35.
[75] BT-Drs. 16/3656, p. 13.
[76] Fischer StGB § 303b mn. 9.

Computer sabotage can be committed through various acts of sabotage. This includes an illegal manipulation of data within the meaning of § 303a sub. 1 StGB. For further details, please refer to the explanations in → mn. 23 et seqq. 69

Furthermore, entering data into and transmitting data to a data processing system is punishable pursuant to § 303b sub. 1 no. 2 StGB. Data is entered if a direct influence on data processing operations is possible and the perpetrator – metaphorically speaking – implements the malicious code in the target system. Data is transmitted if it travels a physical distance during the transmission process. This requires a completed technical process that requires a network connection. This alternative of the offence particularly encompasses denial-of-service (DoS) attacks. In such cases, a coordinated attack by an attack system using a large quantity of simultaneous requests loads the system in such a way that communication proves at least considerably more impeded.[77] In contrast to a DDoS attack, in which several different attack systems attack a system from several locations, a DoS attack is carried out from one location targeting one system.[78] 70

The act of sabotage under § 303b sub. 1 no. 2 StGB also requires the subjective element of **intent to cause harm**. The intent to cause harm covers any detrimental consequence or impairment of legitimate interests, without the perpetrator necessarily seeking financial loss. A decisive factor is the perpetrator's awareness that the detriment is the necessary consequence of the offence.[79] 71

Destroying, damaging, rendering unusable, removing, or altering a data processing system may also be considered acts of sabotage. This includes any interference with the hardware to achieve the damaging effect specified by the offence.[80] 72

IV. Computer fraud (§ 263a StGB)

Computer fraud is an act of deception related to data processing in which data processing is initiated contrary to the motives of its operator, causing a disposition of assets and resulting in a pecuniary benefit for the perpetrator.[81] Computer fraud is punishable by a penalty of imprisonment for a term not exceeding five years. 73

In contrast to **computer sabotage**, which focuses on destruction, computer fraud punishes the traffic-related manipulation of data processing operations.[82] 74

Such manipulation can be caused by the incorrect configuration of a program (known as programme manipulation), the use of incorrect or incomplete data (known as input manipulation), the unauthorised use of data, or any other unauthorised influence on the processing operation. 75

Every data processing operation involves programmes. Programmes constitute fixed operating instructions for the data processing system. Perpetrators manipulate these instructions during programme manipulation.[83] 76

Computer fraud can also be committed by influencing the result of a data processing operation through the introduction of incorrect or incomplete data. 77

---

[77] WJS WirtschaftsStrafR-HdB/Bär Ch. 15 mn. 130.

[78] Cf. <https://www.bsi.bund.de/DE/Themen/Verbraucherinnen-und-Verbraucher/Cyber-Sicherheitslage/Methoden-der-Cyber-Kriminalitaet/DoS-Denial-of-Service/dos-denial-of-service_node.html> (last accessed: 25.2.2025).

[79] BT-Drs. 16/3656, p. 13.

[80] Fischer StGB § 303b mn. 13.

[81] Kochheim Cybercrime mn. 712.

[82] Kochheim Cybercrime mn. 663.

[83] BeckOK StGB/Schmidt, 65 Ed. 1.5.2025, StGB § 263a mn. 23.

78 The unauthorised use of data sanctions the unauthorised influence on an automated data processing operation. This requires a missing authorisation to use the corresponding data. According to the prevailing interpretation, unauthorised use of data is established if the use of the data is of a deceptive nature, i.e., if such a use would at least impliedly deceive a natural person.[84]

79 As a catch-all element, the 'other unauthorised interference' comprises cases of purported output manipulation – i.e., manipulation relating to the output of data –, hardware manipulation, and other influences on the ongoing data processing operation using command input devices (termed console manipulation).[85]

80 The criminal result of computer fraud lies in influencing the outcome of a data processing operation where the result deviates from the result that would have been achieved if the programme had been running as programmed.[86] Such a deviation must have caused a pecuniary disposition by the computer that resulted in a pecuniary loss. In addition to an actual pecuniary reduction, a concrete threat to assets is also sufficient.[87]

81 Moreover, also this offence requires that the offender acted with the intention of enrichment.

V. Electronic forgery offences (§§ 269 and 270 StGB)

82 According to § 269 sub. 1 StGB, the storage, modification, and use of probative data is punishable by a penalty of imprisonment for a term not exceeding five years if the perpetrator intended to deceive legal transactions. § 270 StGB equates the deception of legal transactions with cases of falsely influencing data processing. It particularly covers cases in which falsified data or documents are entered directly in the computer.[88]

83 Phishing emails, for example, constitute an offence within the meaning of § 269 StGB if the bank or company under whose name the email is sent actually exists. In all other cases, the comparability with a document is disputed.[89]

84 The **suppression of data of probative value** is punishable pursuant to § 274 sub. 1 no. 2 StGB and is also punishable by a penalty of imprisonment for a term not exceeding five years. This includes any act that prevents the authorised parties from using the data.[90]

VI. Copyright offences

85 All forms of unauthorised use of third-party programmes and data are sanctioned under §§ 106 et seqq. UrhG (ie, Act on Copyright and Related Rights). Under these provisions, the authors' rights of disposing of their rights of use and exploitation of their works are particularly protected.[91]

86 Pursuant to § 7 UrhG, the author is the creator of a work.

---

[84] WJS WirtschaftsStrafR-HdB/Bär Ch. 15 mn. 20.
[85] MüKoStGB/Hefendehl/Noll StGB § 263a mn. 141.
[86] BGH 30.8.2016 – 4 StR 153/16, NStZ-RR 2016, 371.
[87] TK-StGB/Perron StGB § 263a mn. 30.
[88] WJS WirtschaftsStrafR-HdB/Bär Ch. 15 mn. 47.
[89] Fischer StGB § 269 mn. 8.
[90] MüKoStGB/Erb StGB § 274 mn. 14.
[91] Erbs/Kohlhaas/Kaiser, 255. EL Januar 2025, UrhG § 106 mn. 5.

A work also displays the following characteristics: it is the intellectual creation of its author and must reflect a creation. In other words, works must presuppose an identifiable object with sufficient accuracy and objectivity.[92] **87**

Under § 106 UrhG, anyone who reproduces, distributes, or communicates to the public a work without the consent of the right holder is liable to prosecution and a penalty of imprisonment for a term not exceeding three years. Additionally, § 107 UrhG penalises the unauthorised affixing of a designation of authorship with a penalty of imprisonment for a term not exceeding three years, thereby specifically protecting the author's personality rights.[93] **88**

VII. Data protection violations

The criminal liability for data protection violations protects personal data that is not generally accessible, i.e., data for which access to the data is legally restricted.[94] **89**

Furthermore, criminal liability pursuant to § 42 sub. 1 and sub. 2 BDSG is linked to the lack of authorisation. The authorisation provisions of the GDPR and the BDSG are of particular importance in this context.[95] **90**

Under § 42 sub. 1 BDSG, anyone who **transfers** such data to **a large number of people** to a third party (no. 1) or makes them otherwise **accessible** (no. 2) while acting **commercially** is liable to imprisonment of up to three years. **91**

It has not yet been decided what constitutes a large number of persons. Various viewpoints spread from a number of 20 persons to over 100 persons.[96] **92**

Data is **transferred** if it enters the sphere of influence of a third party in such a way that the third party can easily access it.[97] Additionally, data is made otherwise **accessible** if at least one third party can access this data and thus gain knowledge of its information content. The content does not need to be individualised or concretised.[98] **93**

Under § 42 sub. 2 BDSG, anyone who **processes** such data (no. 1) or **acquires** data fraudulently (no. 2) and does so **in return for payment** or with the **intention** of **enriching** oneself or someone else or **harming** someone else, is punishable with imprisonment of up to two years. **94**

According to Art. 4 para. 2 GDPR, data processing includes any collection, recording, organisation, structuring, storage, adaptation or alteration, retrieval, consultation, use, disclosure by transmission, dissemination, or otherwise making available, alignment or combination, restriction, erasure or destruction of personal data. **95**

According to § 42 sub. 3 sent. 1 BDSG, the criminal provision constitutes an offence upon request (*Antragsdelikt*). Consequently, offences are only prosecuted at the request of the person entitled to make the request pursuant to § 42 sub. 3 sent. 2 BDSG. **96**

---

92 CJEU 12.9.2019 – C-683/17, EU:C:2019:721 = GRUR 2019, 1185 et seq.
93 WJS WirtschaftsStrafR-HdB/Bär Ch. 15 mn. 144.
94 BGH 4.6.2013 – 1 StR 32/13, NJW 2013, 2530.
95 MAH Strafverteidigung/Grözinger § 50 mn. 146 et seq.
96 KMW DatenschutzsanktionenR-HdB/Klaas § 8 mn. 26.
97 MAH Strafverteidigung/Grözinger § 50 mn. 151.
98 BeckOK DatenschutzR/Brodowski, 51. Ed. 1.2.2025, BDSG § 42 mn. 33.

VIII. Offences relating to statements

97 Offences relating to statements (*Äußerungsdelikte*) constitute a category of cybercrime when committed via IT-systems. **Insult** is punishable under § 185 StGB and is punishable by imprisonment for a term not exceeding one year. Whether an insult within the meaning of the provision has occurred must be examined in different steps. Firstly, the meaning of the statement must be determined. Secondly, a balance must be struck between freedom of expression and personal rights, provided that no exceptions to the balancing requirement apply. Priority must always be given to the personality rights if the statement is an **abusive criticism**, **formal insult**, or **violation of human dignity**.[99]

98 As part of the balancing process, the specific means by which the defamatory statement was disseminated must also be considered. In this respect, dissemination via the internet intensifies the defamatory effect, because the statement is permanently accessible to the general public.[100]

99 The dangerous dissemination of personal data pursuant to § 126a StGB also falls within the category of offences relating to statements. Accordingly, anyone who publicly disseminates personal data of another person in a meeting or by disseminating content pursuant to § 11 sub. 3 StGB is liable to a penalty of imprisonment for a term not exceeding two years.

100 Dissemination in accordance with § 126a StGB no. 1 is deemed to be dangerous if it is suitable and intended to expose the person concerned, or a person close to them, to the risk of serious criminal offences being directed against them. A further case of dangerous dissemination arises if the dissemination is suitable and intended to expose the protected person to the risk of another unlawful act against their sexual self-determination, physical integrity, personal liberty, or against an object of significant value (§ 126a StGB no. 2).

101 Pursuant to § 126a sub. 3 in conjunction with § 86 sub. 3 StGB, criminal liability is excluded if the act serves civic information, to prevent unconstitutional activities, to promote the arts or science, research or teaching, to report about current or historical events, or for similar purposes.

IX. Special cybercrime offences

102 In addition, some offences have cyber-specific characteristics.

1. 'Cyberstalking' (§ 238 sub. 1 no. 5–7 StGB)

103 Cyberstalking is covered under the criminal offence provision pursuant to § 238 sub. 1 no. 5–7 StGB. Under this provision, anyone who stalks another person, without being authorised to do so, in a manner suited to not insignificantly restricting that person's lifestyle is criminally liable to a penalty of imprisonment for a term not exceeding three years.

104 Stalking can be carried out in the manners listed in § 238 StGB. All these alternatives have in common that the perpetrator approaches the victim, interferes with the victim's personal sphere of life, and thereby impairs the victim's freedoms of action and decision.[101]

105 The criminal act of cyberstalking may be that the perpetrator repeatedly commits an offence under § 202a StGB, § 202b StGB, or § 202c StGB to the detriment of that person,

[99] BVerfG 19.12.2021 – 1 BvR 1073/20, NJW 2022, 680.
[100] BVerfG 19.5.2020 – 1 BvR 2397/19, NJW 2020, 2622.
[101] HKV Computer- und InternetStrafR § 3 mn. 247 et seq.

one of his or her relatives, or another person close to him or her (§ 238 sub. 1 no 5 StGB). Although the circumstances must be determined on a case-by-case basis, even a low single-digit number of repetitions may be sufficient to warrant criminal liability.[102]

Furthermore, disseminating or making available to the public an image of the person, one of his or her relatives, or another person close to him or her (§ 238 sub. 1 no. 6) also constitutes a criminal offence. **106**

Disseminating or making available content referred to in § 11 sub. 3 StGB is also punishable as an offence if the content is suited to disparaging or negatively affecting public opinion about that person by feigning that person's authorship (§ 238 sub. 1 no. 7). **107**

Cyberstalking encompasses cases in which the perpetrator gains unauthorised access to the victim's data. Although these cases are usually punishable under § 202a StGB, § 238 sub. 1 StGB is more specific when the provision's additional requirements are met.[103] **108**

2. 'Skimming' (§§ 152b sub. 5, 149 sub. 1 no. 1 StGB)

The clandestine scanning of a magnetic stripe (known as skimming) is punishable under §§ 152b sub. 5 and 149 sub. 1 no. 1 StGB.[104] For payment cards with a guarantee function, such an act is punishable pursuant to § 152b sub. 5 in conjunction with § 149 sub. 1 no. 2 StGB incurring a penalty of imprisonment for a term not exceeding five years or a fine. **109**

The counterfeiting of payment cards with a guarantee function subsequent to skimming is punishable under § 152b sub. 1 StGB with a penalty of imprisonment for a term of between one year and ten years. Sub. 2 of that provision contains a qualification for cases that are committed commercially or by a gang (*Bande*). In these cases, the penalty is imprisonment for a term of at least two years. **110**

3. Pornographic illustrations

Cyber-grooming is punishable under § 176a StGB. Under this provision, a person who causes a child to perform sexual acts is liable to prosecution. Physical proximity between the perpetrator and the victim is not required. It is sufficient if the perpetrator is aroused by the idea that the child is performing sexual acts on him or herself.[105] **111**

The clandestine recording of children, but also of other persons, using malware to activate a victim's webcam is covered by § 201a StGB in addition to data manipulation pursuant to § 303a StGB. Should the child also be coerced to record him or herself by means of threats, this constitutes an offence under § 176a sub. 1 no. 2 StGB. A juvenile perpetrator between the ages of 14 and 18 may be punished for coercion pursuant to § 240 StGB or for the production and distribution of juvenile pornographic material pursuant to § 184c StGB.[106] **112**

A perpetrator is also liable to prosecution if the victim follows the perpetrator's sexual acts over the internet via webcam.[107] Already the acoustic perception of such acts by a child, for example via the telephone, is sufficient.[108] Exhibitionist acts, i.e., exposing a man's penis to another person without his or her consent, is covered by § 183 StGB, but **113**

[102] BT-Drs. 19/28679, p. 12.
[103] BT-Drs. 19/28679, p. 12.
[104] MAH Strafverteidigung/Grözinger § 50 mn. 34.
[105] BeckOK StGB/Ziegler, 65. Ed. 1.5.2025, StGB § 176a mn. 5 et seq.
[106] Kochheim Cybercrime mn. 1731.
[107] BGH 21.4.2009 – 1 StR 105/09, NStZ 2009, 500.
[108] BGH 21.10.2014 – 1 StR 79/14, NStZ 2015, 27.

requires the simultaneous physical presence of both persons.[109] Consequently, the unsolicited sending of so-called 'dick pics' appears not to be punishable under § 183 StGB and is only in exceptional cases punishable under § 184 StGB. Conversely, exhibitionist acts in front of a child that are transmitted via the internet, for example via a webcam, are subject to the offence of the aforementioned § 176a StGB.[110]

114 §§ 184 et seqq. StGB penalise the procurement, possession, and dissemination of child and youth pornographic writings and content. The term 'content' is legally defined in § 11 sub. 3 StGB and covers all possible types of technical communication, in particular, via the Internet but also via the telephone.[111] The background to its criminal liability is that there must have been real abuse prior to any child pornography; thus, its distribution at least indirectly facilitates the sexual abuse of children.[112]

4. CEO fraud (§ 263 sub. 1 StGB)

115 In what is known as 'CEO fraud', cyber criminals pretend to be the managing director of a company and trick employees into transferring money abroad. For example, social engineering or the use of malicious software is used to gain comprehensive information about the company. With the help of artificial intelligence, 'deep fakes' are created that deceptively imitate the managing director and can issue corresponding instructions.[113]

116 The deception of the CEO's identity and the pretence of a corresponding order by the CEO causes the employees' misconception, which regularly results in a payment order by the employee and thus results in the erroneous disposition of funds. Regularly, this will be a constellation of a triangular fraud (*Dreiecksbetrug*) in terms of § 263 sub. 1 StGB.[114]

117 A particularly worrying case recently unfolded in Switzerland. Cyber criminals used a video image of the managing director created using artificial intelligence and simulated a video conference with the deceived victim.[115]

D. Practice of IT criminal law

118 Apart from the legal framework, law enforcement authorities face a number of deficiencies in the prosecution of IT offences.

---

[109] Fischer StGB § 183 mn. 5.

[110] BGH 21.4.2009 – 1 StR 105/09, NStZ 2009, 500.

[111] MüKoStGB/Renzikowski StGB § 176 StGB mn. 46.

[112] BGH 9.10.2012 – 4 StR 381/12, NStZ-RR 2014, 8; BGH 31.7.2013 – 2 StR 220/13, NStZ-RR 2013, 339.

[113] Cf. <https://www.ncsc.admin.ch/ncsc/en/home/aktuell/im-fokus/2024/wochenrueckblick_14.html> (last accessed: 25.2.2025).

[114] Cf. <https://www.strafrecht-digital.com/ceo-fraud-phaenomen-und-strafrechtliche-bewertung/#_ftn1> (last accessed: 25.2.2025).

[115] Cf. <https://www.ncsc.admin.ch/ncsc/en/home/aktuell/im-fokus/2024/wochenrueckblick_14.html> (last accessed: 25.2.2025).

I. Investigation procedure and preservation of evidence in IT criminal cases

In principle, digital evidence is secured just like physical evidence. The rules on searches pursuant to §§ 102 et seqq. StPO and seizure pursuant to §§ 94 et seqq. StPO also apply when securing digital evidence.[116] 119

For example, the investigating authorities are entitled under § 81b sub. 1 StPO to take fingerprints when seizing a mobile phone to unlock the device. However, accessing the data stored on the mobile phone is not justified under § 81b sub. 1 StPO. The authorisation to access the stored data is rather found in § 110 sub. 3 StPO.[117] However, the argument can be made that the taking of fingerprints within the meaning of § 81b StPO now serves two purposes, i.e., to identify the accused and access data. This blurs the clear distinction made in the StPO between identification measures and evidence securing measures. Moreover, the originally encrypted data is subsequently treated as unencrypted data during the review and preservation of evidence by the investigating authorities.[118] 120

Against this background, it is also questioned whether the accused is obliged to provide the smartphone PIN code during an investigation. Considering the principle of freedom from self-incrimination (known as the '*nemo tenetur* principle'), this is denied. Although a decision has not yet been made by the supreme court as to whether biometric unlocking may be enforced against the will of the accused to access the data stored on a smartphone, on the grounds of the *nemo tenetur* principle, this should also be denied. From an evaluative perspective, treating fingerprints, PINs, and biometric unlocking different is not plausible.[119] Unlocking the smartphone without the assistance of the accused is not only very time-consuming, but also costly. 121

Besides emails and chat histories, which are understood as classic digital evidence, other data on a technical device may also be considered. Such traces are mainly analysed and secured by IT forensic experts using various methods to guarantee the probative value of data.[120] The IT forensic expert's investigative findings can then either be introduced into the trial as an expert opinion and thus as an object of inspection or the forensic expert can be heard in the trial as an expert witness. 122

In addition, specific IT investigation measures include, in particular, (source) telecommunications surveillance pursuant to § 100a StPO, covert remote search of information technology systems pursuant to § 100b StPO, traffic data information pursuant to § 100g StPO, subscriber data requests pursuant to § 100j StPO, the capture of usage data with telemedia services pursuant to § 100k StPO, the examination of electronic storage media pursuant to § 110 sub. 3 StPO, and the use of observing investigators in public data networks pursuant to §§ 161 and 163 StPO[121] or undercover investigators on the darknet as per § 110a StPO. 123

The **examination of electronic storage media** according to § 110 sub. 3 StPO is not limited to the object of the search, but extends to external storage media such as **clouds**, provided that access to the external storage space is possible from a device located in the area of control affected by the search.[122] It is disputed whether the external storage 124

---

116 HSH MMR-HdB/Sieber/Brodowski part 19.3 mn. 165.

117 LG Ravensburg 14.2.2023 – 2 Qs 9/23, NStZ 2023, 446.

118 Cf. <https://www.strafrecht-digital.com/landgericht-ravensburg-nutzung-von-fingerabdruecken-zur-entsperrung-beschlagnahmter-mobiltelefone-ist-rechtmaessig/> (last accessed: 25.2.2025).

119 Cf. <https://www.strafrecht-digital.com/category/it-strafrecht/page/2/> (last accessed: 25.2.2025).

120 HSH MMR-HdB/Sieber/Brodowski part 19.3 mn. 165.

121 Kipker Cybersecurity-HdB/Brodowski Ch. 17 mn. 58.

122 Singelnstein NStZ 2012, 593 (598).

medium must be located in Germany and whether a distinction must be made between publicly accessible and access-protected data when the external storage media is located abroad.[123] Some experts demand that the physical storage must be located in Germany to prevent any interference with the sovereign rights of foreign states.[124] Opponents argue that the mere possibility of accessing data from within Germany is sufficient to prevent an infringement of the **principle of sovereignty.**[125]

125 In the case of **remote searches of information technology systems**, the investigating authorities infiltrate IT systems using technical means such as surveillance software; they can read and record stored content.[126] Such an investigation extends over a longer period of time and, therefore, not only allows isolated access to the information technology system, but also enables the collection of data during the entire period of the investigation, i.e., a **total system surveillance.**[127] In addition, these systems often provide the possibility to perceive the environment audiovisually due to their technical features. Compared to 'open searches' pursuant to § 102 StPO, telecommunications surveillance pursuant to 100a StPO, and **acoustic surveillance of private premises** pursuant to § 100c StPO, remote searches of information technology systems thus offer much more far-reaching possibilities. However, the core area of the private way of living is not sufficiently protected by limiting the use of remote searches of information technology systems to the catalogue offences listed in § 100b StPO.[128] Together with the covert remote search of information technology systems, the source telecommunications surveillance is one of the most relevant investigative measures in practice. **Source telecommunications surveillance** pursuant to § 100a sub. 1, sub. 2 and sub. 3 StPO enables surveillance of an IT system as regards ongoing telecommunications. In some cases, even encrypted communications may be intercepted with the help of software.[129]

126 Increasing digitalisation of personal information, in particular, intensifies interference with fundamental rights in connection with the available investigative measures. It is easy to obtain highly personal information, for example by creating movement or personality profiles of suspects.[130]

II. Challenges and special characteristics in IT criminal proceedings

127 Cybercrime prosecution is characterised by the special attribute that it usually involves secret investigative measures which interfere more intensively with the fundamental rights of the accused.[131] As a rule, these investigative measures require the **prior judicial decision** (*Richtervorbehalt*). Accordingly, the permissibility of some such measures depends on the prior authorisation by a judge.

128 When collecting evidence, regardless of whether the offence is committed as a cybercrime offence, the investigating authorities must provide the court with a sound basis on which the decision can be made. The rights of the accused, particularly, the protection

[123] KK-StPO/Heinrichs/Weingast § 110 mn. 8a.
[124] MüKoStPO/Hauschild StPO § 110 mn. 18.
[125] KK-StPO/Heinrichs/Weingast § 110 mn. 8a.
[126] MüKoStPO/Rückert StPO § 100b mn. 35.
[127] MüKoStPO/Rückert StPO § 100b mn. 43.
[128] Kruse/Grzesiek KritV, 2017, 331 (349 et seq).
[129] BeckOK StPO/Graf, 55. Ed. 1.1.2025, StPO § 100a mn. 77 et seq.
[130] HKV Computer- und InternetStrafR § 4 mn. 9.
[131] HKV Computer- und InternetStrafR § 4 mn. 8.

of the delinquent's privacy must be respected. A special consideration in IT criminal law requires to minimise the additive effects of using technology.[132]

Due to the lack of physicality of the data, digital evidence in cybercrime often harbours a considerable uncertainty factor, since data is particularly **susceptible to forgery, loss,** and **error.**[133] 129

Moreover, digital evidence is often only available for a short period of time, which means that law enforcement authorities must act particularly quickly. However, a rapid response is often hampered because the rights of the accused across different legal systems must be aligned when perpetrators operate internationally.[134] 130

Another practically relevant aspect relates to the **confiscation** of unlawfully obtained pecuniary advantages held as cryptocurrencies. §§ 73 et seqq. StGB allow for the confiscation of illegally obtained assets. These can either be confiscated in their original form or a sum of money equal to the value of what was obtained (i.e., § 73c StGB) can be confiscated. Cryptocurrencies represent economic benefits that can also be confiscated in their original form pursuant to § 73 sub. 1 StGB. However, determining the realisable value of cryptocurrencies depends on the market value, which is at times subject to strong fluctuations.[135] 131

III. International cooperation regarding IT offences

International cooperation is essential when prosecuting IT offences. Such cooperation includes but is not limited to the following measures. 132

Firstly, states can request the assistance of another state in criminal prosecution by way of **international mutual legal assistance in criminal matters.**[136] At EU level, the central regulatory framework for criminal law cooperation between EU Member States is Directive 2014/41/EU on the European Investigation Order in criminal matters (**EIO Directive**).[137] In Germany, the provisions were transposed by the Act on International Mutual Assistance in Criminal Matters (*Gesetz über die internationale Rechtshilfe in Strafsachen*, 'IRG'). 133

Pursuant to rulings by higher courts, the **utilisability** and **usability** of foreign investigation results, such as data originating from foreign telecommunications surveillance, are governed by the law of the state conducting the criminal proceedings and which intends to use the information originating from abroad as evidence.[138] 134

An important tool for the preservation of evidence in the European judicial area is the European Production Order pursuant to Art. 5 and the European Preservation Order pursuant to Art. 6 of EU Regulation 2023/1543, which can be used to order the **production** and **preservation** of **digital evidence**. Such orders are directed at service providers of another EU Member State that store data that may be used as digital evidence in criminal proceedings. 135

---

[132] Kochheim Cybercrime mn. 1973.

[133] Fährmann MMR 2020, 228 (229).

[134] Kipker Cybersecurity-HdB/Brodowski Ch. 17 mn. 55.

[135] Cf. <https://www.strafrecht-digital.com/rechtliche-voraussetzungen-und-praktische-umsetzung-der-einziehung-von-kryptowaehrungen-im-strafverfahren/> (last accessed: 25.2.2025).

[136] Cf. the Act on International Mutual Assistance in Criminal Matters. For more on international mutual legal assistance in criminal matters → Ch. 9.

[137] Handbuch Wirtschafts- und Steuerstrafrecht/Hackner Ch. 27 mn. 68c.

[138] OLG Hamburg 29.1.2021 – 1 Ws 2/21, BeckRS 2021, 2226; BGH 21.11.2012 – 1 StR 310/12, NStZ 2013, 596.

136 Another option is to obtain a European Investigation Order under §§ 91a et seqq. IRG. Based on a court decision, the investigating authorities can be authorised to carry out specific investigative measures in another Member State.[139]

137 Other orders that can be issued include the **preservation and disclosure** of stored **computer and traffic data** ('quick freeze') (Art. 16 and 17 CCC), the **production of data** (Art. 18 CCC), the **search and seizure** of stored **computer data** (Art. 19 CCC), and the **real-time collection of traffic** and content **data** (Art. 20 and 21 CCC), regarding foreign data, on the basis of the CCC. This convention applies not only to almost all EU Member States, but also to the USA, Canada, Australia, and Israel.[140]

IV. Case studies from the field of IT criminal law

138 In this section, we present three case studies from the field of IT criminal law to illustrate selected problems and possible courses of action from practical experience.

1. Case study 1: data manipulation and its consequences

139 During a commercial transaction amounting to 2 million EUR between A-GmbH (ie, Limited Liability Company under German Law) and B-GmbH, T, the managing director of B-GmbH, was asked to provide a bank guarantee to cover the risk of non-payment.

140 T then forged an email by X-Bank in which the issuing of a bank guarantee for B-GmbH was confirmed. T forwarded the forged email to A-GmbH to pretend that the required bank guarantee had been issued. When B-GmbH failed to honour its payment obligations towards A-GmbH, A-GmbH turned to X-Bank. At this point, it became apparent that the email submitted by T was forged. X-Bank had never issued a bank guarantee for B-GmbH. A-GmbH then filed a criminal report against T.

141 Under German criminal law, an email is not considered a document; consequently, it does not constitute **forgery of documents** pursuant to § 267 StGB.[141] Nevertheless, the **forgery of data of probative value** is punishable pursuant to § 269 StGB. Also, emails are considered data and are therefore covered by § 269 StGB.[142]

142 Investigation proceedings were initiated against T on suspicion of **forgery of data of probative value** pursuant to § 269 StGB. In the course of the investigation, the police searched the headquarters of B-GmbH following a court order, questioned employees as witnesses, and also examined T's business relationships with other companies for possible forged emails.

143 T is entitled to inspect the files, provided that no legitimate interests by third parties conflict with this. He is also entitled to defence by a lawyer, who is also entitled to inspect the files. Furthermore, the email in question can be used as evidence in criminal proceedings.

---

[139] MAH Strafverteidigung/Grözinger § 50 mn. 333.
[140] MAH Strafverteidigung/Grözinger § 50 mn. 335.
[141] BeckOK StGB/Weidemann, 65. Ed. 1.5.2025, StGB § 267 mn. 7.
[142] Fischer StGB § 269 mn. 4.

2. Case study 2: criminal proceedings in cases of cyberbullying

Politician K was, among others, publicly called a 'bitch' and 'scumbag' by T on a social media platform. In addition, various memes of her were created and distributed on social media. 144

K applied to the competent court under § 21 sub. 2 and sub. 3 TDDDG for information and disclosure against the social media platform to receive personal data about the authors of the hate comments. The competent court granted the application only with regards to some of the comments and disclosed T's personal data to K. The decision was based on the argument that only some of the criticised comments were to be considered **formal insults**. 145

K appealed against this decision by lodging a constitutional complaint with the BVerfG. The BVerfG ruled that even politicians do not have to tolerate all forms of public criticism. The judiciary's fundamental task is to protect all citizens' **personal rights**. Courts must therefore scrutinise the meaning of every single statement and weigh it against the personal rights of the statement's addressee. A balancing is only dispensable in exceptional cases, this is if the statement in dispute is characterised as **abusive criticism** (*Schmähkritik*). Abusive criticism in the constitutional sense is assumed if the statement no longer bears any comprehensible connection to a factual dispute and is basically only about the baseless disparagement of the affected person. Therefore, in the case of **formal insults** or direct attacks on **human dignity**, a balancing of rights is dispensable by way of exception and the offence under § 185 StGB is always fulfilled.[143] 146

After K had obtained the personal data of the authors of the hate comments, she reported, among others, the hate comments written by T to the authorities. 147

Although there is no specific paragraph on cyberbullying in German criminal law, defamatory behaviour on the internet does not go unpunished. 148

The public prosecutor's office in Frankfurt am Main initiated preliminary proceedings on the grounds of insult pursuant to § 185 StGB. 149

In addition, K can have the postings deleted pursuant to §§ 823, 1004 sub. 1 sent. 1, sent. 2 BGB, Art. 2 para. 1, Art. 1 para. 1 GG, Art. 8 ECHR.[144] According to this law, social media platforms are obliged to consistently remove illegal posts. Although a service provider is not obliged to review all posts searching for an infringement without cause before they are published. As soon as a service provider becomes aware of specific illegal content, it must not only block the information in question or the access to said information, but must also take suitable measures to prevent further similar infringements.[145] 150

3. Case study 3: international cooperation in cases of data theft

US citizen O invested in Bitcoin and stored them in a wallet with an American e-wallet provider, which stores the private keys that enable access to the cryptocurrencies. Hacker T used a phishing attack to obtain the login details of O's account and stole Bitcoin from him worth 1 million EUR. 151

O initiated a private investigation and used a **blockchain analysis** to reveal that the Bitcoins illegally stolen from his wallet had been split up, transferred through a series of wallets, and were ultimately transferred to a wallet operated by the same American e-wallet provider as his own. 152

---

143 BVerfG 19.12.2021 – 1 BvR 1073/20, NJW 2022, 680.
144 OLG Frankfurt a.M. 25.1.2024 – 16 U 65/22, MMR 2024, 334.
145 LG Frankfurt 8.4.2022 – 2-03 O 188/21, MMR 2022, 494.

153 O initiated discovery proceedings against the e-wallet provider in the USA. In the course of these proceedings, the parties are obliged to disclose all information relevant to the proceedings.[146] As a result of this disclosure obligation, the e-wallet provider informed O that T was the owner of the e-wallet containing some of O's Bitcoin. This also allowed O to learn that T was a German citizen and resident in Cologne.

154 He filed a criminal report in Germany with the ZAC in North Rhine-Westphalia. O presented the ZAC with the data from the blockchain analysis and the results of the discovery procedure, which included T's personal data.

155 The ZAC then initiated preliminary proceedings against T for money laundering pursuant to §§ 261 sub. 1 no. 2, 3, 4 and 261 sub. 2 StGB in conjunction with § 263a sub. 1 StGB, data manipulation pursuant to § 303a StGB, and data espionage pursuant to § 202a StGB.

156 T was subsequently kept under surveillance for several weeks. Furthermore, telecommunication surveillance for his mobile phone was ordered. As part of the further investigation, a search warrant was issued for T's home and the warrant was executed. In addition, an asset seizure was ordered at the request of the ZAC. Consequently, T's bank accounts were frozen and cash found during the search was attached. In the subsequent court proceedings, the assets were first confiscated and then paid to O.

V. Outlook and future developments in IT criminal law

157 The current legislative developments already illustrate the enormous significance of cybercrime and the dimension that IT criminal law will continue to assume in the future.

158 On the one hand, we can observe a change in the motives for offences. Committing criminal offences is no longer purely financially motivated. Rather, attacks on information technology systems are increasingly also motivated by political and ideological motives.[147] According to § 46 sub. 2 StGB, the motives for the offence play a special role when the penalty is fixed. If such motives are racist, xenophobic, anti-Semitic, or otherwise inhumane, they can have an aggravating effect.

159 On the other hand, we can observe a trend towards AI tools being used for criminal purposes. AI tools also enable less technically skilled criminals to carry out complex attacks. However, they also harbour potential for improving cyber security, for example by detecting phishing or closing security gaps. AI systems may also assist the chronically overburdened law enforcement authorities in managing their day-to-day tasks.

160 **AI models** have already been developed to filter image content that infringes criminal law; in this example, the content was child and youth pornography. The system demonstrated a high hit rate. At the same time and due to the particular sensitivity of criminal law, technical programmes cannot replace the judicial apparatus, at least not at present. These programmes are merely tools that can facilitate the work of the investigating authorities.[148]

161 Another field of application for AI in criminal law concerns lawyers. For example, **legal chatbot models** can be used to perform automated legal checks independently. Analogous to the use of AI models to support the criminal prosecution authorities, the application of artificial intelligence by lawyers also requires extensive training material from which the automated system can learn independently. In order to be able to replace legal advice

---

[146] Schönknecht GRUR-Int 2011, 1000 (1000).

[147] Cybercrime, Bundeslagebild 2024, p. 24, available in German at <https://www.bsi.bund.de/DE/Service-Navi/Publikationen/Lagebericht/lagebericht_node.html> (last accessed: 25.2.2025).

[148] Brodowski/Hartmann/Sorge NJW 2023, 583 (588).

provided by a human being, this training material must be of high quality and quantity. So far, both are lacking.[149]

162 By contrast, the use of artificial intelligence not only enables criminal offences to be carried out more quickly and on a larger scale, but also with a higher quality of means. Phishing emails, for example, may be made more realistic. Moreover, the creation of deceptively real-looking photos or audio recordings with the help of artificial intelligence (known as 'deepfakes') can also constitute criminal behaviour,[150] for example, in the form of CEO fraud (→ mn. 115 et seqq.).

163 Additionally and with the help of AI tools, it is no longer necessary to be a technical genius to commit IT offences. For example, large-scale phishing campaigns can be carried out using artificial intelligence even if the victim lacks extensive technical knowledge.[151]

164 Owing to the fact that AI systems learn autonomously, the follow-up question is whether and who can be held criminally liable for work products that are considered criminally relevant. In particular, the opacity of the decision-making process (known as 'black box' algorithms) creates problems in attributing criminal liability to the developer of the AI system, because in such cases the developer him or herself cannot explain the decision-making process.[152]

---

149 Cf. <https://www.lto.de/persistent/a_id/53983/> (last accessed: 25.2.2025).

150 Kumkar K&R 2023, 32 (32 et seq).

151 Cybercrime, Bundeslagebild 2024, p. 11 <https://www.bsi.bund.de/DE/Service-Navi/Publikationen/Lagebericht/lagebericht_node.html> (last accessed: 25.2.2025).

152 HKV Computer- und InternetStrafR § 5 mn. 21.

CHAPTER 18
SUPPLY CHAIN DUE DILIGENCE

Bibliography: Baade, Lieferkettensorgfaltspflichtengesetz – Arbeitsrechtliche Compliance-Maßnahmen, DStR 2022, 1617; Fleischer, Grundstrukturen der lieferkettenrechtlichen Sorgfaltspflichten, CCZ 2022, 205; Gehling/Ott/Lüneborg, Das neue Lieferkettensorgfaltspflichtengesetz – Umsetzung in der Unternehmenspraxis, CCZ 2021, 230; Giesberts, Sorgfaltspflichten für die Lieferkette – Das deutsche Gesetz und der EU-Richtlinienentwurf, NVwZ 2022, 1497; Junge/Kapoor/Keller, Die zivilrechtliche Haftung nach der europäischen Lieferkettenrichtlinie (CSDDD), ZIP 2025, 1; Gurlit, Grundrechtsbindung von Unternehmen, NZG 2012, 249; Lutz-Bachmann/Vorbeck/Wengenroth, Menschenrechte und Umweltschutz in Lieferketten – der Regierungsentwurf eines Sorgfaltspflichtengesetzes, BB 2021, 906; Nietsch/Wiedmann, Adressatenkreis und sachlicher Anwendungsbereich des neuen Lieferkettensorgfaltspflichtengesetz, NJW 2022, 1; Ruttloff/Wagner/Reischl/Skoupil, Auf dem Weg zum Chief Sustainability Officer (CSO) – Teil 1, CB 2021, 364; Sagan/Schmidt, Das Lieferkettensorgfaltspflichtengesetz, NZA-RR 2022, 281; Stemberg, Die drei "Schlüsselkriterien" des Beschwerdeverfahrens nach § 8 Lieferkettensorgfaltspflichtengesetz, CCZ 2022, 92; Stöbener de Mora/Noll, Grenzenlose Sorgfalt? – Das Lieferkettensorgfaltspflichtengesetz, NZG 2021, 1237; Wagner/Ruttloff, Das Lieferkettensorgfaltspflichtengesetz – Eine erste Einordnung, NJW 2021, 2145.

Table of contents

A. Disclaimer: legal status as of October 2025 ... 436
B. Introduction ... 437
C. The developement of business and human rights ... 439
I. United Nations ... 439
II. OECD ... 439
III. National Action Plan on Business and Human Rights ... 440
IV. European Union ... 440
V. Climate litigation and court proceedings ... 441
VI. NGOs and case studies ... 441
1. NGOs ... 441
2. Human Rights and Business Dilemmas Forum ... 442
VII. Media coverage ... 442
D. Regulatory content of the LkSG ... 442
I. Introduction ... 442
II. BAFA handouts ... 443
III. Scope of application (§ 1 LkSG) ... 444
1. Legal form ... 444
2. Number of employees ... 444
3. Foreign enterprises ... 445
4. Affiliated enterprises ... 445
IV. Definitions (§ 2 LkSG) ... 446
1. Human rights-related risks and responsibilities ... 446
2. Environmental risks and responsibilities ... 447
3. Supply chain ... 448
a) End customer ... 449
b) Own business area ... 449
c) Direct and indirect suppliers ... 449
V. Due diligence obligations (§ 3 LkSG) ... 450
1. Content ... 450
2. Appropriate manner ... 451

3. Cooperation within the supply chain 452
4. Standards, audits and certifications..................... 452
VI. Risk management (§ 4 LkSG)............................ 453
1. Appropriate and effective............................. 453
2. Responsibilities 454
VII. Risk analysis (§ 5 LkSG) 454
VIII. Preventive measures (§ 6 LkSG) 455
1. Statement on human rights (§ 6 sub. 2 LkSG)............ 455
2. Preventive measures in own business area (§ 6 sub. 3 LkSG) 455
3. Preventive measures vis-à-vis direct suppliers (§ 6 sub. 4 LkSG)... 456
IX. Remedial action (§ 7 LkSG) 456
X. Complaints procedure (§ 8 LkSG).......................... 457
XI. Indirect suppliers (§ 9 LkSG) 458
1. Definition and identification of indirect suppliers 458
2. Procedures 458
XII. Documentation and reporting obligations (§ 10 LkSG) 459
XIII. Monitoring and enforcement by BAFA 460
1. Competent authority................................. 460
2. Orders and measures (§ 15 LkSG)....................... 460
3. Access rights (§ 16 LkSG) 460
4. Obligation to provide information and surrender documents (§ 17 LkSG)............................... 460
5. Obligation to tolerate and cooperate (§ 18 LkSG). 461
6. Repressive investigations 461
XIV. Sanctions.. 461
1. Overview of sanctions................................. 461
2. Exclusion from the award of public contracts (§ 22 LkSG) . 462
3. Provisions on administrative fines (§ 24 LkSG) 462
a) Violation of due diligence obligations 462
b) Addressee 463
c) Administrative fines 463
d) Sentencing....................................... 464
E. Conclusion 465

A. Disclaimer: legal status as of October 2025

1 The legal framework governing supply chains in Germany and the European Union is currently marked by complexity and fragmentation. Different timelines and shifting political compromises created a confusing atmosphere for companies.

2 This chapter reflects the legal framework of Germany's Supply Chain Due Diligence Act (*Lieferkettensorgfaltspflichtengesetz,* LkSG) as in force since 1 January 2023. As of June 2025, the LkSG continues to be in force as binding German law.

3 The new coalition agreement between German political parties CDU, CSU and SPD for the 21st legislative period (starting from April 2025) introduces the government's intention to abolish the LkSG, likely replacing it with an 'International Corporate Responsibility Act' designed to transpose the EU Corporate Sustainability Due Diligence Directive (CSDDD) in a less bureaucratic manner.[1] As a first step in this direction, the German government has passed a draft law on 3 September 2025 that provides for the removal of

[1] See coalition agreement between CDU, CSU and SPD for the 21st legislative period mn. 1909 et seqq.

reporting obligations and most administrative offences from the LkSG.[2] For this reason, on 1 October 2025, the Federal Office for Economic Affairs and Export Control (BAFA) announced that it is already ceasing the review of reports and will only impose administrative fines in cases of severe human rights violations.[3] However, even if the LkSG is formally repealed, its core obligations cannot be wholly discarded – because the implementation of the CSDDD remains mandatory under European law. Member States are bound by its transposition deadline of 26 July 2027.[4] Furthermore, it must be noted that while the non-regression clause in Art. 1 para. 2 CSDDD does not constitute an outright prohibition on any legislative adjustments, there are considerable legal concerns that a substantial reduction of existing LkSG standards – such as narrowing its scope of application or lowering due diligence requirements – could violate the directive's requirements.

In conclusion, this chapter describes the legislative situation as of mid-2025. Although 4
the LkSG continues to apply today, its eventual fate hinges on how Germany reconciles the coalition's deregulatory ambitions with the binding requirements of CSDDD implementation. Practitioners should monitor any legislative activity on this matter closely.

B. Introduction

The attention for human rights and the environment has grown steadily in the last 5
decades through consistent efforts by international communities, NGOs (non-governmental organisations) and media coverage. As with other international and cross-border matters, however, there was a significant lack of enforceable corporate responsibility and sanctions on the national level in Germany.

On 1 January 2023 the Act on Corporate Due Diligence Obligations for the Preven- 6
tion of Human Rights Violations in Supply Chains (*Lieferkettensorgfaltspflichtengesetz*, LkSG) came into legal force. German lawmakers responded to a long-standing debate about corporate responsibility for global supply chains and set a milestone in Germany. The LkSG implemented the UN Guiding Principles on Business and Human Rights from 2011[5] and the German government's National Action Plan on Business and Human Rights (NAP) from 2016[6].[7]

---

[2] Draft Law to Amend the Supply Chain Due Diligence Act – Relieving Companies through an Implementation- and Enforcement-Friendly Approach, <https://www.bmas.de/SharedDocs/Downloads/DE/Gesetze/Regierungsentwuerfe/reg-gesetz-zur-aenderung-des-lieferkettensorgfaltspflichtengesetzes.pdf?__blob=publicationFile&v=2> (last accessed: 27.10.2025).

[3] See BAFA Notification <https://www.bafa.de/SharedDocs/Kurzmeldungen/DE/Lieferketten/20251001_Vereinfachung_LksG.html> (last accessed: 27.10.2025).

[4] This deadline was postponed: As part of the EU Commission's proposed 'Omnibus' simplification package (February 2025), the transposition period for the CSDDD was extended by one year, moving the deadline from 26 July 2026 to 26 July 2027.

[5] UN, Guiding Principles on Business and Human Rights, <https://www.auswaertiges-amt.de/blob/266624/b51c16faf1b3424d7efa060e8aaa8130/un-leitprinzipien-de-data.pdf (German); <https://www.ohchr.org/sites/default/files/documents/publications/guidingprinciplesbusinesshr_en.pdf> (last accessed 22.6.2025) (English).

[6] German Federal Government, National Action Plan on Implementation of the UN Guiding Principles on Business and Human Rights (NAP), <https://www.auswaertiges-amt.de/blob/297434/8d6ab29982767d5a31d2e85464461565/nap-wirtschaft-menschenrechte-data.pdf> (German); <https://www.auswaertiges-amt.de/resource/blob/610714/fb740510e8c2fa83dc507afad0b2d7ad/nap-wirtschaft-menschenrechte-engl-data.pdf> (last accessed 22.6.2025) (English).

[7] Stöbener de Mora/Noll NZG 2021, 1237.

7 The LkSG establishes for the first time in Germany legally binding requirements, backed by sanctions, for enterprises in Germany to comply with human rights-related and environment-related legal positions.[8] Violations of the LkSG may be punished with an administrative fine of up to 2 % of the companies' average annual turnover.

8 Not only German companies with their registered office in Germany are affected. The LkSG also covers foreign companies with a branch office in Germany.

9 The LkSG sets out requirements for enterprises' compliance management systems and states multiple due diligence obligations (*Sorgfaltspflichten*). Among other things, these include establishing risk management and taking preventive and remedial measures.

10 While the LkSG establishes a regulatory framework to counteract human rights violations, the LkSG leads to legal uncertainty because some legal terms are undefined. One example is the principle of appropriateness/adequacy[9], which sets the general framework for the implementation of due diligence obligations. Enterprises are required to establish, monitor and further develop appropriate and effective processes to implement their due diligence obligations.

11 However, the concretisation and definition of a 'reasonable' adherence is within the responsibility of the BAFA and depends on the further development of the law, such as jurisprudence.

12 It is important to note that the requirements of the LkSG are complex and still evolving due to the latest handouts and FAQ's of the BAFA. As with compliance in general, enterprises must carefully observe these developments and adapt their own prevention processes regularly.

13 This chapter provides a general overview of the LkSG requirements:

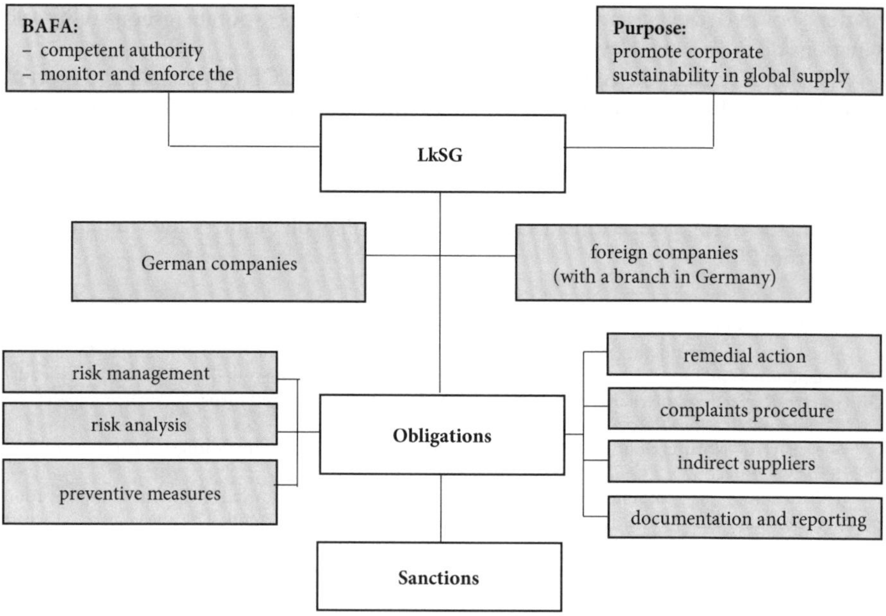

[8] Wagner/Ruttloff NJW 2021, 2145; Sagan/Schmidt NZA-RR 2022, 281.

[9] The German term *angemessen* is translated differently in several legal sources. For consistency reasons this chapter uses the translation 'appropriate' respectively 'appropriateness'.

C. The developement of business and human rights

It is internationally recognised that human rights are primarily a direct obligation of states and not of private individuals.[10] Nevertheless, the importance of corporate responsibility in transnational activities has grown steadily in recent decades. Thus – in addition to environmental protection – the role of enterprises and in particular multinational corporations have increasingly been discussed in politics with regard to human rights.[11] This is shown by regulatory works, governmental procedures as well as the work of NGOs and case studies. 14

The LkSG is the result of a long and tough legislative process in Germany.[12] In fact, the idea of a legal act to ensure compliance with human rights and environmental obligations in global supply chains is not a novelty.[13] The LkSG fits into a legal development within the European Union and the United Nations that pursues the goal of responsible and sustainable global businesses. Media coverage also highlights the emerging international attention to human rights and environmental protection in recent years. 15

I. United Nations

The attempt to establish a global standard for enterprises to comply with human rights in supply chains began with the introduction of the UN Guiding Principles on Business and Human Rights[14] in 2011.[15] The initiator of these principles was at that time the UN Special Representative for Business and Human Rights, John Ruggie. The aim was to avoid violations of human rights by enterprises and to implement appropriate mechanisms. In addition, all countries – especially those with challenging human rights situations – should introduce and enforce human rights standards.[16] As in general, UN standards of conduct were not subject to any sanctions. 16

II. OECD

The OECD Guidelines for Multinational Enterprises[17] are also important for promoting responsible corporate governance.[18] They were first published in 1976 and last comprehensively revised in 2011 following an international consultation process.[19] These guidelines are legally non-binding recommendations made by governments to multi- 17

---

[10] Gurlit NZG 2012, 249 (250).
[11] Stöbener de Mora/Noll NZG 2021, 1237.
[12] Wagner/Ruttloff NJW 2021, 2145.
[13] Wagner/Ruttloff NJW 2021, 2145.
[14] UN, Guiding Principles on Business and Human Rights, <https://www.ohchr.org/sites/default/files/documents/publications/guidingprinciplesbusinesshr_en.pdf> (last accessed 22.6.2025).
[15] BT-Drs. 19/28649, 23.
[16] Stöbener de Mora/Noll NZG 2021, 1237.
[17] OECD, Guidelines for Multinational Enterprises, <https://www.oecd.org/content/dam/oecd/de/publications/reports/2023/06/oecd-guidelines-for-multinational-enterprises-on-responsible-business-conduct_a0b49990/abd4d37b-de.pdf (German); <https://www.oecd.org/content/dam/oecd/en/publications/reports/2023/06/oecd-guidelines-for-multinational-enterprises-on-responsible-business-conduct_a0b49990/81f92357-en.pdf> (last accessed 22.6.2025) (English).
[18] WRW LkSG/Ruttloff/Kappler mn. 327.
[19] HML Corporate Compliance/Spießhofer § 11 mn. 24; WRW LkSG/Ruttloff/Kappler mn. 327.

national enterprises.[20] However, participating states committed to implementing the guidelines in accordance with the OECD Council Decision on the OECD Guidelines for Multinational Enterprises.[21]

III. National Action Plan on Business and Human Rights

18 To implement the UN Guiding Principles on Business and Human Rights (→ mn. 16) and the OECD Guidelines for Multinational Enterprises (→ mn. 17), the German government enacted a National Action Plan on Business and Human Rights (NAP) at the end of 2016.[22] In terms of content, this plan describes five core elements of human rights due diligence: A policy statement on respect for human rights, a procedure for identifying adverse human rights impacts, measures to avert such impacts, reporting and a grievance mechanism.[23]

19 In doing so, it initially relied on voluntarism by expressing its 'expectations' of enterprises: The goal was for at least 50 % of enterprises based in Germany with more than 500 employees to have integrated the elements of human rights due diligence defined in the NAP into their corporate processes by 2020.[24] This target was missed. For example, a 2020 survey – conducted as part of the NAP – showed that still too few enterprises met the NAP requirements set out for them herein.[25] This meant that the concept of voluntary self-commitment on the part of enterprises had failed and the foundation stone for a law had been laid.[26]

IV. European Union

20 On 23 February 2022, the European Commission presented a proposal for a directive on corporate due diligence with regard to sustainability, the Corporate Sustainability Due Diligence Directive (CSDDD).[27] Following a controversial legislative process, the CSDDD was officially adopted by the European Parliament on 24 April 2024[28] and by

---

20 Cf. OECD Guidelines for Multinational Enterprises, p. 15, <https://www.oecd.org/content/dam/oecd/en/publications/reports/2023/06/oecd-guidelines-for-multinational-enterprises-on-responsible-business-conduct_a0b49990/81f92357-en.pdf> (last accessed 22.6.2025).

21 Cf. OECD Guidelines for Multinational Enterprises, p. 15, <https://www.oecd.org/content/dam/oecd/en/publications/reports/2023/06/oecd-guidelines-for-multinational-enterprises-on-responsible-business-conduct_a0b49990/81f92357-en.pdf> (last accessed 22.6.2025).

22 The Federal Government, NAP, <https://www.auswaertiges-amt.de/resource/blob/610714/fb740510e8c2fa83dc507afad0b2d7ad/nap-wirtschaft-menschenrechte-engl-data.pdf> (last accessed 22.6.2025).

23 Cf. The Federal Government, NAP, p. 8 et seqq, <https://www.auswaertiges-amt.de/resource/blob/610714/fb740510e8c2fa83dc507afad0b2d7ad/nap-wirtschaft-menschenrechte-engl-data.pdf> (last accessed 22.6.2025).

24 The Federal Government, NAP, p. 7 et seqq, <https://www.auswaertiges-amt.de/resource/blob/610714/fb740510e8c2fa83dc507afad0b2d7ad/nap-wirtschaft-menschenrechte-engl-data.pdf> (last accessed 22.6.2025).

25 Only 13–17 % of German enterprises with more than 500 employees integrated the measures set out in NAP into their business processes, see NAP Monitoring, p. 2, <https://www.auswaertiges-amt.de/blob/2375460/543e6de4d80a95b8e26186ca4da44f27/nap-monitoring-ergebnisindikation-data.pdf> (last accessed 22.6.2025).

26 BT-Drs. 19/28649, 23.

27 <https://eur-lex.europa.eu/legal-content/EN/TXT/HTML/?uri=CELEX:52022PC0071&from=EN> (last accessed 22.6.2025).

28 <https://www.europarl.europa.eu/doceo/document/TA-9-2024-0329_EN.pdf> (last accessed 22.6.2025).

the Council on 24 May 2024[29]. The CSDDD was then published on 5 July 2024.[30] It must be implemented by the Member States by 26 July 2027.

21 The CSDDD and the LkSG essentially pursue the same basic idea that enterprises have to fulfil human rights and environmental due diligence obligations themselves and within their supply chain. In its current version, the CSDDD contains significantly more far-reaching regulations in some cases than the LkSG. This applies for example to civil liability, which until now does not exist in the LkSG.[31]

22 However, it is to be expected that many of these far-reaching obligations – like civil liability – will be simplified again. This simplification is part of the so-called 'omnibus package', which was proposed by the European Commission in February 2025 and is currently in the legislative process[32].

V. Climate litigation and court proceedings

23 Various state proceedings show that corporate entities are increasingly confronted with disputes related to human rights and environmental protection. For example, a court in The Hague ruled that 'Shell' must reduce its greenhouse gas emissions by a net 45 % until 2030 compared to 2019 levels. This was preceded by a lawsuit filed by the Dutch environmental organisation 'Milieudefensie' together with 17,000 citizens. The plaintiffs were supported through donations in the amount of half a million euro to cover the legal costs.[33]

24 Generally, the UN Global Climate Litigation Report of 2020 shows that cases nearly doubled in 38 countries since 2017.[34]

25 Human rights and environmental topics also have an impact on German Constitutional Law. In 2021 the German Federal Constitutional Court (*Bundesverfassungsgericht,* BVerfG) obliged the German government to regulate gas emissions for the period after 2030 in more detail by the end of 2022.[35] Thus, the German Federal Constitutional Court concluded, among other things, that the provisions of the German Climate Protection Act (*Bundes-Klimaschutzgesetz,* KSG) contain a lack of sufficient requirements for further emission reductions.

VI. NGOs and case studies

1. NGOs

26 In addition to Amnesty International and Greenpeace, which have been advocating for human rights and environmental standards in the supply chain for years[36], the initiative 'Stop Ecocide International' (SEI) was founded in 2017. The SEI advocates for the

---

[29] <https://www.consilium.europa.eu/en/press/press-releases/2024/05/24/corporate-sustainability-due-diligence-council-gives-its-final-approval/pdf/> (last accessed 22.6.2025).

[30] EU, Corporate Sustainability Due Diligence Directive (CSDDD), <https://eur-lex.europa.eu/legal-content/EN/TXT/?uri=CELEX:32024L1760> (last accessed 22.6.2025).

[31] Junge/Kapoor/Keller ZIP 2025, 1.

[32] See <https://finance.ec.europa.eu/news/omnibus-package-2025-04-01_en> (last accessed 22.6.2025).

[33] Cf. <https://www.deutschlandfunk.de/shell-verliert-klima-prozess-das-urteil-von-den-haag-und-100.html> (last accessed 22.6.2025).

[34] Cf. <https://www.unep.org/resources/report/global-climate-litigation-report-2020-status-review> (last accessed 22.6.2025).

[35] BVerfG 24.3.2021 – 1 BvR 2656/18, 1 BvR 78/20, 1 BvR 96/20, 1 BvR 288/20, NJW 2021, 1723.

[36] See, e.g., <https://www.greenpeace.de/publikationen/s03111-greenpeace-lieferkettengesetz-stellungnahme-20200818a.pdf> (last accessed 22.6.2025).

criminalization of 'ecocide' under international criminal law. It describes itself as the 'driving force and communications hub' for the 'growing global movement' and makes it its mission to 'activate and develop global cross-sector support for this goal'.[37]

2. Human Rights and Business Dilemmas Forum

27 The Human Rights and Business Dilemmas Forum is co-hosted by United Nations Global Compact and Verisk Maplecroft and is funded by the GE Foundation. The forum aims to support global enterprises in their efforts to better understand and address human rights impacts in their operations and supply chains. Users can access in-depth analysis on human rights issues as well as case studies that illustrate how other enterprises have addressed the human rights dilemmas they face in a responsible and sustainable manner.[38]

VII. Media coverage

28 Media reports also regularly draw international attention to human rights and environmental protection. Examples include working conditions in textile factories in Bangladesh[39], child labour in mineral extraction in India[40], groundwater depletion in India due to sugar plantations[41], the leak of 16 million litres of crude oil from a pipeline in Nigeria[42], a toxic waste dump in Chile[43], suppliers accused of union busting in Cambodia[44] and wineries involved in an alleged slave labour scandal[45].

D. Regulatory content of the LkSG

I. Introduction

29 The LkSG intends to improve the international human rights situation, to ensure legal certainty and a fair competition.[46] Besides, the German legislator anticipates highlighting

[37] Cf. <https://www.stopecocide.de/wer-wir-sind> (last accessed 22.6.2025).

[38] <https://hrbdf.org/about/> (last accessed 22.6.2025).

[39] Cf. <https://www.bpb.de/kurz-knapp/hintergrund-aktuell/268127/vor-fuenf-jahren-textilfabrik-rana-plaza-in-bangladesch-eingestuerzt/; <https://www.sueddeutsche.de/panorama/bangladesch-feuer-in-textilfabrik-toetet-sieben-frauen-1.1584455> (both links last accessed: 22.6.2025).

[40] Cf. <https://www.tdh.de/fileadmin/user_upload/inhalte/04_Was_wir_tun/Themen/Kinderarbeit/Mica/Dossier_Ausbeutung_Mica_2021.pdf>; <https://www.tagesschau.de/wirtschaft/weltwirtschaft/kinderarbeit-micaminen-indien-101.html> (last accessed: 22.6.2025).

[41] <https://www.spiegel.de/wirtschaft/wut-auf-brause-multi-umweltschuetzer-geisseln-coca-colas-wasserverbrauch-a-472470.html> (last accessed 22.6.2025); see also <https://www.stern.de/wirtschaft/news/cola-streit–warum-die-inder-coca-cola-und-pepsi-boykottieren-7355944.html and <https://taz.de/Boykott-von-Coca-Cola-und-Pepsi-in-Indien/!5385578/> (last accessed 22.6.2025).

[42] <https://taz.de/Oelkatastrophe-in-Nigeria/!5055401/> (last accessed 22.6.2025).

[43] <https://www.business-humanrights.org/en/latest-news/lawsuit-against-boliden-over-export-of-toxic-waste-to-chile-its-health-impact-on-arica-residents-starts-in-sweden/> (last accessed 22.6.2025).

[44] <https://www.business-humanrights.org/en/from-us/updates-from-bhrrc/weekly-update-15-march-cambodia-puma-and-vf-corporation-suppliers-accused-of-union-busting/> (last accessed 22.6.2025).

[45] <https://www.business-humanrights.org/en/latest-news/brazil-well-known-wineries-involved-in-slave-labor-scandal/> (last accessed 22.6.2025).

[46] BT-Drs. 19/28649, 2, 23.

Germany's responsibility as a major economic power with international ties. Germany benefits from its global procurement and sales markets. However, this also entails the responsibility to counter the risk of intransparency and often inadequate enforcement of internationally recognized human rights in supply chains.

The LkSG represents a historic paradigm shift in German law for foreign trade entre- 30
preneurial engagement:[47] For the first time, business partner and supply chain due diligence obligations are required. The LkSG also establishes general legal requirements for enterprises to set up a compliance management system.[48]

II. BAFA handouts

The regulatory content of certain individual legal terms in the LkSG is unclear.[49] This 31
applies, for example, to the requirement of the LkSG that enterprises should exercise due diligence obligations in an 'appropriate' manner.

It is important to note that the federal authority BAFA provides handouts which 32
include guidelines for an interpretation of the LkSG and its undefined legal terms and ambiguities.[50]

Furthermore, an updated overview of 'Questions and Answers on the Supply Chain 33
Act' is published continuously by the Federal Ministry for Economic Affairs and Energy (BMWE), the Federal Ministry of Labour and Social Affairs (BMAS) and the BAFA.[51]

In addition, the Corporate Social Responsibility (CSR) initiative of the BMAS offers 34
enterprises various support services for the practical implementation of due diligence. On the website of the CSR initiative, the general guide 'SME Compass of the Helpdesk Business & Human Rights' offers small and medium-sized enterprises (SMEs) specific options on how a supply chain management can be designed in an environmentally and socially responsible manner.[52] Moreover, practical examples are explained to illustrate how enterprises of different sectors and sizes meet the requirements of human rights due diligence, what approaches they develop and how they can implement them in practice.[53]

It is to be expected that further administrative practice and decisions of the adminis- 35
trative and civil courts will shape the LkSG standard in the coming years.[54] Enterprises (will) need to monitor these developments closely.

---

47 Stöbener de Mora/Noll NZG 2021, 1237.

48 Gehling/Ott/Lüneborg CCZ 2021, 230 (231).

49 WRW LkSG/Ruttloff/Wagner/Wagner, Preface, X; Gehling/Ott/Lüneborg CCZ 2021, 230 (233).

50 WRW LkSG/Ruttloff/Wagner/Wagner, Preface, X; Gehling/Ott/Lüneborg CCZ 2021, 230 (233); Giesberts NVwZ 2022, 1497.

51 BMAS, FAQ on the Supply Chain Act, <https://www.csr-in-deutschland.de/EN/Business-Human-Rights/Supply-Chain-Act/FAQ/faq.html> (last accessed 22.6.2025).

52 Cf. SME Compass of the Helpdesk Business & Human Rights], available at <https://kompass.wirtschaft-entwicklung.de/en/due-diligence-compass/downloads> (last accessed 22.6.2025).

53 Cf. <https://www.csr-in-deutschland.de/DE/Wirtschaft-Menschenrechte/Umsetzungshilfen/Praxisbeispiele/praxisbeispiele.html> (last accessed 22.6.2025).

54 WRW LkSG/Ruttloff/Wagner/Wagner, Preface, XII.

III. Scope of application (§ 1 LkSG)

36

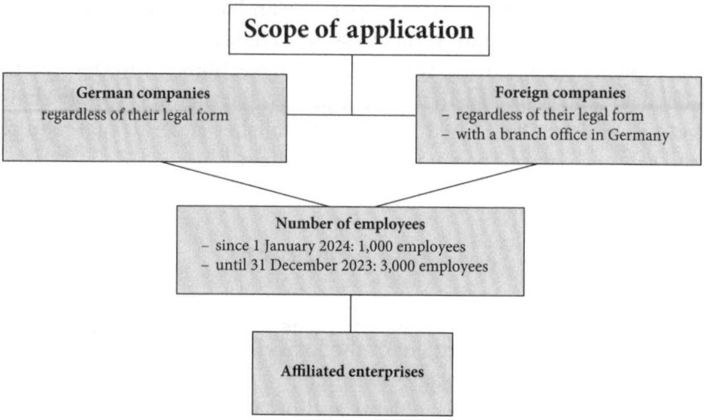

1. Legal form

37 The LkSG applies to individuals and enterprises regardless of their legal form (§ 1 sub. 1 sent. 1 LkSG) such as stock corporations (AG) or limited liability enterprises (GmbH). Also, partnerships with legal capacity, such as civil law partnerships (GbR), general partnerships (oHG) and limited partnerships (KG) are subject to the LkSG.[55]

38 In addition, the LkSG applies to legal entities under public law operating in the private market, i.e. foundations (*Stiftungen*) and non-profit cooperations (*gemeinnützige Gesellschaften*).[56]

2. Number of employees

39 To be directly subject to the LkSG, an enterprise must have at least a certain number of employees.

40 As of 1 January 2023, the LkSG did apply to enterprises with their head office, principal place of business or registered office in Germany and that normally employ at least 3,000 employees in Germany and abroad (§ 1 sub. 1 sent. 1 LkSG).

41 The number of 'normally' employed personnel should be calculated retrospectively. Furthermore, the forecast of future personnel development must be considered prospectively.[57] The time period considered both retrospectively and prospectively is to be sufficiently long so that short-term fluctuations in occupancy rates do not affect the

[55] As the LkSG applies across all industries, the banking and insurance industry is also generally within the scope of application. When applying the Act to enterprises in the banking and insurance industry, however, particularities that are specific to this sector and its products must be taken into account. The BAFA Guidance 'Banking and Insurance Industry' provides assistance and advice on practical significance, see <https://www.bafa.de/SharedDocs/Downloads/DE/Lieferketten/handreichung_kredit_versicherung.html> (German); <https://www.bafa.de/SharedDocs/Downloads/EN/Supply_Chain_Act/guidance_banking_and_insurance_industry.html> (English), (both links last accessed 22.6.2025).

[56] Gehling/Ott/Lüneborg CCZ 2021, 230 (231); cf. BMAS, FAQ on the Supply Chain Act, 3.1, available at <https://www.csr-in-deutschland.de/EN/Business-Human-Rights/Supply-Chain-Act/FAQ/faq.html> (last accessed: 22.6.2025).

[57] See The Federal Government, LkSG-Draft, p. 13, <https://www.bmas.de/SharedDocs/Downloads/DE/Gesetze/Regierungsentwuerfe/reg-sorgfaltspflichtengesetz.pdf?__blob=publicationFile&v=2> (last accessed 22.6.2025); see also BMAS, FAQ on the Supply Chain Act, 3.5, available at <https://www.csr-in-deutschland.de/EN/Business-Human-Rights/Supply-Chain-Act/FAQ/faq.html> (last accessed: 22.6.2025).

applicability or non-applicability of the law. This is intended to achieve stability, planning certainty and ultimately legal certainty for enterprises.[58]

The circumstances defining the unique development of the enterprise must be identified for the forecast. This includes, in particular, the employer's actual decisions on change, such as if ongoing labour reductions to a specific level are anticipated in the future. These decisions must have been made by the accountable corporate body, and nothing impeding their execution must be significant. Hence, it is insufficient to just anticipate a worsening of the order situation or the possibility of a factory closure.[59] **42**

From 1 January 2024 the threshold was reduced to enterprises with more than 1,000 employees (§ 1 sub. 1 sent. 3 LkSG). This means that a significant proportion of large enterprises is covered by the scope of the LkSG since 2024.[60] **43**

Yet, because larger organisations can contractually transfer regulatory compliance to smaller enterprises, even businesses with fewer than 1,000 employees are impacted.[61] **44**

The employee threshold is established in accordance with the general employee definition of German labour legislation. According to this, senior executives and employees who are on probation are taken into account in addition to part-time and full-time workers, as long as they have worked for at least six months. The list excludes civil servants, apprentices, independent contractors and freelancers.[62] **45**

3. Foreign enterprises

Foreign enterprises are also subject to the LkSG if they have a branch office in Germany pursuant to § 13d HGB and if they meet the employee threshold 1,000 (since 1 January 2024) in Germany (§ 1 sub. 1 sent. 2 LkSG). **46**

A branch office (*Zweigniederlassung*) is considered to exist if there is a location for business that is distinct from the primary location and conducts its own legal transactions externally, rather than only temporarily for the purposes of the business, with a certain level of organisational and factual independence.[63] **47**

4. Affiliated enterprises

Multicorporate enterprises or groups are usually organized through affiliated enterprises. **48**

According to § 15 AktG affiliated enterprises are legally independent enterprises that, in their relationship inter se, are enterprises in which a majority ownership interest is held. **49**

Within affiliated enterprises, employees of all enterprises belonging to the group who are employed in Germany must be taken into account when calculating the number of employees of the parent enterprise; employees posted abroad are also included (§ 1 sub. 3 LkSG). **50**

---

[58] See German Federal Government, LkSG-Draft, p. 13, <https://www.bmas.de/SharedDocs/Downloads/DE/Gesetze/Regierungsentwuerfe/reg-sorgfaltspflichtengesetz.pdf?__blob=publicationFile&v=2> (last accessed 22.6.2025).

[59] See German Federal Government, LkSG-Draft, p. 13, <https://www.bmas.de/SharedDocs/Downloads/DE/Gesetze/Regierungsentwuerfe/reg-sorgfaltspflichtengesetz.pdf?__blob=publicationFile&v=2> (last accessed 22.6.2025).

[60] Wagner/Ruttloff NJW 2021, 2145.

[61] So-called trickle-down effect, cf. Wagner/Ruttloff NJW 2021, 2145; also Baade DStR 2022, 1617.

[62] Detailed listing can be found at BMAS, FAQ on the Supply Chain Act, 3.4, available at <https://www.csr-in-deutschland.de/EN/Business-Human-Rights/Supply-Chain-Act/FAQ/faq.html> (last accessed: 22.6.2025).

[63] BeckOK HGB/Müther, 46. Ed. 1.4.2025, HGB § 13d mn. 16.

51 In the relationship between the parent enterprise and the subsidiary, the employees are allocated 'upwards', i.e. the employees of all subsidiaries are counted towards the parent enterprise. Conversely, however, neither the employees of the parent enterprise nor those of the subsidiary are attributed to the subsidiary.[64]

IV. Definitions (§ 2 LkSG)

52 The LkSG applies in case of human rights-related or environment-related risks. A risk within the meaning of the LkSG is a condition in which, on the basis of factual circumstances, there is a sufficient probability that a violation of one of the following prohibitions is imminent:

1. Human rights-related risks and responsibilities

53 The violation of a duty related to human rights occurs in the case of a violation of the following prohibitions (§ 2 sub. 2 no. 1–12 LkSG)[65]:

1. the prohibition of the employment of a child under the age at which compulsory schooling ends according to the law of the place of employment, provided that the age of employment is not less than 15 years, except where the law of the place of employment provides this in accordance with Article 2 para. 4 and Articles 4 to 8 of Convention No. 138 of the International Labour Organization of 26 June 1973 concerning Minimum Age for Admission to Employment (Federal Law Gazette 1976 II pp. 201, 202);
2. the prohibition of the worst forms of child labour for children under 18 years of age; in accordance with Article 3 of Convention No. 182 of the International Labour Organization of 17 June 1999 concerning the Prohibition and Immediate Action for the Elimination of the Worst Forms of Child Labour (Federal Law Gazette 200111 pp. 1290, 1291) this includes:
   a) all forms of slavery or practices similar to slavery, such as the sale and trafficking of children, debt bondage and serfdom, as well as forced or compulsory labour, including the forced or compulsory recruitment of children for use in armed conflicts,
   b) the use, procuring or offering of a child for prostitution, for the production of pornography or for pornographic performances,
   c) the use, procuring or offering of a child for illicit activities, in particular for the production of or trafficking in drugs,
   d) work which, by its nature or the circumstances in which it is carried out, is likely to harm the health, safety or morals of children;
3. the prohibition of the employment of persons in forced labour; this includes any work or service that is required of a person under threat of punishment and for which he or she has not made himself or herself available voluntarily, for example as a result of debt bondage or trafficking in human beings; excluded from forced labour are any work or services that comply with Article 2 para. 2 of Convention No. 29 of the International Labour Organization of 28 June 1930 concerning Forced or Compulsory Labour (Federal Law Gazette 1956 II p. 640, 641) or with Article 8 para. 3 lit. b and c of the International Covenant of 19 December 1966 on Civil and Political Rights (Federal Law Gazette 1973 II pp. 1533, 1534);
4. the prohibition of all forms of slavery, practices akin to slavery, serfdom or other forms of domination or oppression in the workplace, such as extreme economic or sexual exploitation and humiliation;

---

[64] See BMAS, FAQ on the Supply Chain Act, 4.6, available at <https://www.csr-in-deutschland.de/EN/Business-Human-Rights/Supply-Chain-Act/FAQ/faq.html> (last accessed: 22.6.2025).

[65] Translation taken from the CSR initiative's website, slightly adapted <https://www.csr-in-deutschland.de/SharedDocs/Downloads/EN/act-corporate-due-diligence-obligations-supply-chains.pdf?__blob=publicationFile> (last accessed: 14.7.2025).

5. the prohibition of disregarding the occupational safety and health obligations applicable under the law of the place of employment if this gives rise to the risk of accidents at work or work-related health hazards, in particular due to:
   a) obviously insufficient safety standards in the provision and maintenance of the workplace, workstation and work equipment;
   b) the absence of appropriate protective measures to avoid exposure to chemical, physical or biological substances;
   c) the lack of measures to prevent excessive physical and mental fatigue, in particular through inappropriate work organization in terms of working hours and rest breaks; or
   d) the inadequate training and instruction of employees;
6. the prohibition of disregarding the freedom of association, according to which
   a) employees are free to form or join trade unions,
   b) the formation, joining and membership of a trade union must not be used as a reason for unjustified discrimination or retaliation,
   c) trade unions are free to operate in accordance with applicable law of the place of employment, which includes the right to strike and the right to collective bargaining;
7. the prohibition of unequal treatment in employment, for example on the grounds of national and ethnic origin, social origin, health status, disability, sexual orientation, age, gender, political opinion, religion or belief, unless this is justified by the requirements of the employment; unequal treatment includes, in particular, the payment of unequal remuneration for work of equal value;
8. the prohibition of withholding an adequate living wage; the adequate living wage amounts to at least the minimum wage as laid down by the applicable law and, apart from that, is determined in accordance with the regulations of the place of employment;
9. the prohibition of causing any harmful soil change, water pollution, air pollution, harmful noise emission or excessive water consumption that
   a) significantly impairs the natural bases for the preservation and production of food,
   b) denies a person access to safe and clean drinking water,
   c) makes it difficult for a person to access sanitary facilities or destroys them or
   d) harms the health of a person;
10. the prohibition of unlawful eviction and the prohibition of unlawful taking of land, forests and waters in the acquisition, development or other use of land, forests and waters, the use of which secures the livelihood of a person;
11. the prohibition of the hiring or use of private or public security forces for the protection of the enterprise's project if, due to a lack of instruction or control on the part of the enterprise, the use of security forces
    a) is in violation of the prohibition of torture and cruel, inhumane or degrading treatment,
    b) damages life or limb or
    c) impairs the right to organize and the freedom of association;
12. the prohibition of an act or omission in breach of a duty to act that goes beyond no. 1 to 11, which is directly capable of impairing a protected legal position in a particularly serious manner, and the unlawfulness of which is obvious upon reasonable assessment of all the circumstances in question.

2. Environmental risks and responsibilities

The following environmental prohibitions are listed (§ 2 sub. 3 no. 1-8 LkSG[66]): **54**

1. the prohibition of the manufacture of mercury-added products pursuant to Article 4 para. 1 and Annex A Part I of the Minamata Convention on Mercury of 10 October 2013 (Federal Law Gazette 2017 II pp. 610, 611) (Minamata Convention);

[66] Translation taken from the CSR initiative's website, slightly adapted <https://www.csr-in-deutschland.de/SharedDocs/Downloads/EN/act-corporate-due-diligence-obligations-supply-chains.pdf?__blob=publicationFile> (last accessed: 14.7.2025).

2. the prohibition of the use of mercury and mercury compounds in manufacturing processes within the meaning of Article 5 para. 2 and Annex B Part I of the Minamata Convention from the phase-out date specified in the Convention for the respective products and processes;
3. the prohibition of the treatment of mercury waste contrary to the provisions of Article 11 para. 3 of the Minamata Convention;
4. the prohibition of the production and use of chemicals pursuant to Article 3 para. 1 lit. a and Annex A of the Stockholm Convention of 23 May 2001 on Persistent Organic Pollutants (Federal Law Gazette 2002 II pp. 803, 804) (POPs Convention), last amended by decision of 6 May 2005 (Federal Law Gazette 2009 II pp. 1060, 1061), in the version of Regulation (EU) 2019/1021 of the European Parliament and of the Council of 20 June 2019 an persistent organic pollutants (OJ L 169 of 26 May 2019 pp. 45-77), as last amended by Commission Delegated Regulation (EU) 2021/277 of 16 December 2020 (OJ L 62 of 23 February p. 1-3);
5. the prohibition of the handling, collection, storage and disposal of waste in a manner that is not environmentally sound in accordance with the regulations in force in the applicable jurisdiction under the provisions of Article 6 para. 1 lit. d (i) and (ii) of the POPs Convention.
6. the prohibition of exports of hazardous waste within the meaning of Article 1 para. 1 and other wastes within the meaning of Article 1 para. 2 of the Basel Convention on the Control of Transboundary Movements of Hazardous Wastes and their Disposal of 22 March 1989 (Federal Law Gazette 199411 pp. 2703, 2704) (Basel Convention), as last amended by the Third Ordinance amending Annexes to the Basel Convention of 22 March 1989 of 6 May 2014 (Federal Law Gazette II pp. 306, 307), and within the meaning of Regulation (EC) No 1013/2006 of the European Parliament and of the Council of 14 June 2006 on shipments of waste (OJ L 190 of 12 July 2006 pp. 1-98) (Regulation (EC) No 1013/2006), as last amended by Commission Delegated Regulation (EU) 2020/2174 of 19 October 2020 (OJ L 433 of 22 December 2020 pp. 11-19)
   a) to a party that has prohibited the import of such hazardous and other wastes (Article 4 para. 1 lit. b of the Basel Convention),
   b) to a state of import as defined in Article 2 No. 11 of the Basel Convention that does not consent in writing to the specific import, in the case where that state of import has not prohibited the import of such hazardous wastes (Article 4 para. 1 lit. c of the Basel Convention),
   c) to a non-party to the Basel Convention (Article 4 para. 5 of the Basel Convention),
   d) to a state of import if such hazardous wastes or other wastes are not managed in an environmentally sound manner in that state or elsewhere (Article 4 para. 8 sent. 1 of the Basel Convention);
7. the prohibition of the export of hazardous wastes from countries listed in Annex VII to the Basel Convention to countries not listed in Annex VII (Article 4 A of the Basel Convention, Article 36 of Regulation (EC) No 1013/2006) and
8. the prohibition of the import of hazardous wastes and other wastes from a non-party to the Basel Convention (Article 4 para. 5 of the Basel Convention).

55 There is no catch-all provision in the area of environmental obligations.[67]

3. Supply chain

56 The definition of the supply chain (*Lieferkette*) is very broad and concerns all steps in Germany and abroad that are necessary for the manufacture of products of a company and the provision of its services. This covers both the extraction of raw materials and the delivery to the end customer (*Endkunde*, § 2 sub. 5 LkSG). The term 'necessary steps in the supply chain' covers, for example, the office supplies of an industrial enterprise, building cleaning or canteen operations.[68]

---

[67] Wagner/Ruttloff NJW 2021, 2145 (2146).

[68] Cf. BMAS, FAQ on the Supply Chain Act, 2.4, available at <https://www.csr-in-deutschland.de/EN/Business-Human-Rights/Supply-Chain-Act/FAQ/faq.html> (last accessed: 22.6.2025).

The supply chain covers an enterprise's actions in its own business when supplying end customers, direct suppliers and indirect suppliers. 57

a) End customer

The end customer of a product is (a) the person for whom the product is intended and who actually uses it, or (b) the entity that processes the product so that it becomes part of a new product according to the perception of the market. Thus, the determination of end customers depends on the perspective or role of the company in the supply chain. The end customers are not necessarily direct contractual partners. In simplified terms, this means that producers supply intermediate products to manufacturers, who assemble them into end products.[69] 58

The end customer of a service is the person for whom the service is intended and who uses the service. They are also usually direct contractual partners.[70] 59

b) Own business area

The company's own business area (*eigener Geschäftsbereich,* §2 sub. 6 LkSG) covers every enterprise activity that helps it to accomplish its business objective inside the definition of its own business area. Any action for the development and commercialization of goods and services falls under this, whether it takes place domestically or internationally. In affiliated enterprises, the parent company's own business area includes a group company if the parent company exercises a decisive influence (*bestimmender Einfluss*) on the group company. 60

According to the BAFA, the BMWE and the BMAS, the question of whether a decisive influence exists is based on the overall view of the economic, personnel, organisational and legal ties between the subsidiary and the parent company. Indications are, for example, a high majority shareholding in the subsidiary, a group-wide compliance system, responsibility for the control of core processes in the subsidiary, similar business areas or overlapping personnel.[71] 61

c) Direct and indirect suppliers

Two requirements are placed on the company's direct supplier (*unmittelbarer Zulieferer,* §2 sub. 7 LkSG): First, it must be a contractual partner of the company. Secondly, the supplier must provide goods or services that are necessary for the manufacture of the company's products or services. In other words, it is a question of products or services that the company exploits economically as part of its own value chain. Supply relationships in which the company is the end customer are therefore excluded.[72] 62

If there is no contractual relationship with the company, it fulfils the characteristic of an indirect supplier (*mittelbarer Zulieferer*) in accordance with §2 sub. 8 LkSG.[73] Accordingly, the supply chain also includes companies that supply products and services to the company's direct contractual partners. 63

---

[69] See BMAS, FAQ on the Supply Chain Act, 6.10, available at <https://www.csr-in-deutschland.de/EN/Business-Human-Rights/Supply-Chain-Act/FAQ/faq.html> (last accessed: 22.6.2025).

[70] See BMAS, FAQ on the Supply Chain Act, 6.11, available at <https://www.csr-in-deutschland.de/EN/Business-Human-Rights/Supply-Chain-Act/FAQ/faq.html> (last accessed: 22.6.2025).

[71] See BMAS, FAQ on the Supply Chain Act, 4.11, available at <https://www.csr-in-deutschland.de/EN/Business-Human-Rights/Supply-Chain-Act/FAQ/faq.html> (last accessed: 22.6.2025).

[72] Sagan/Schmidt NZA-RR 2022, 281 (284).

[73] Sagan/Schmidt NZA-RR 2022, 281 (284) with reference to Grabosch LkSG/Grabosch §2 mn. 39.

V. Due diligence obligations (§ 3 LkSG)

1. Content

64 In order to prevent or minimize risks to human rights, environmental risks, or to stop the violation of human rights-related or environment-related obligations, enterprises are required to exercise due regard for the human rights-related and environment-related due diligence obligations in their supply chains (§ 3 sub. 1 LkSG).

65 The due diligence obligations (*Sorgfaltspflichten*) include:

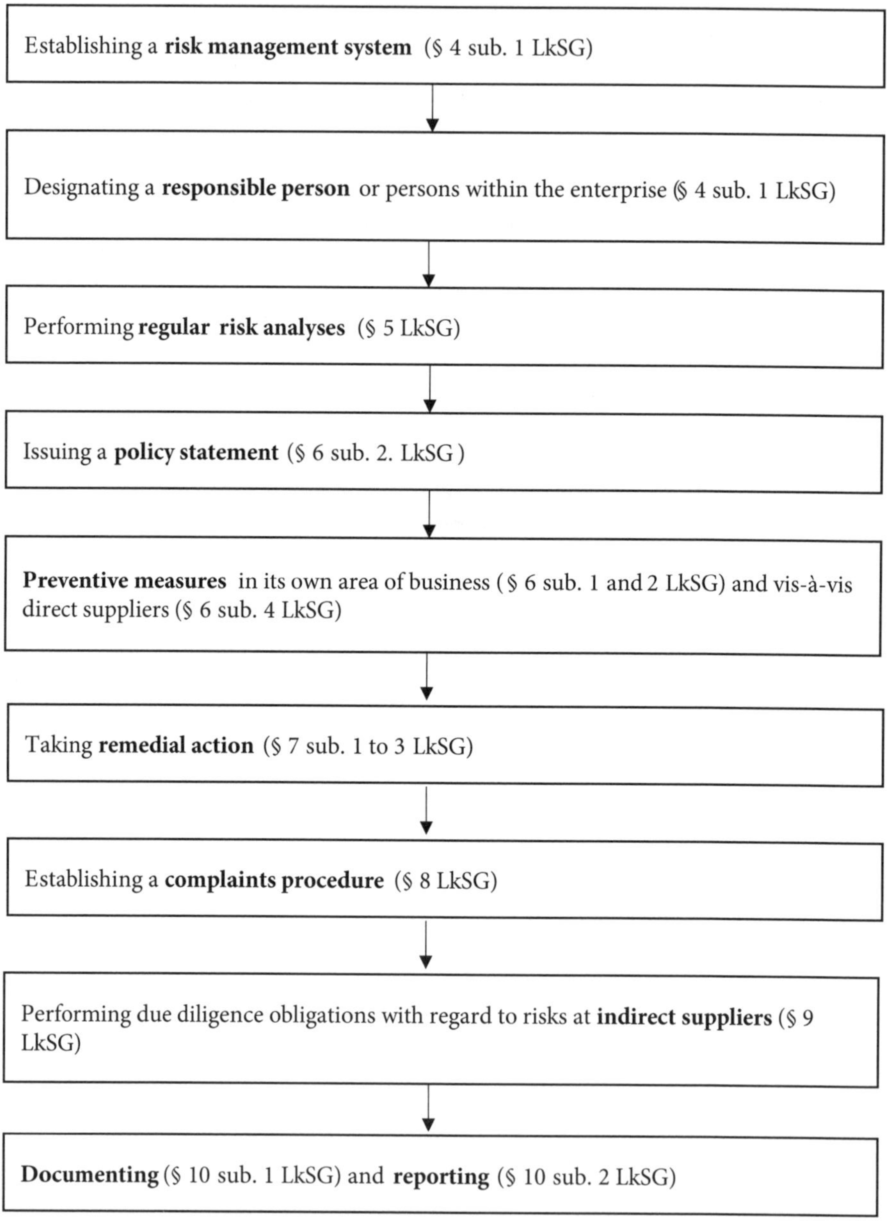

2. Appropriate manner

The due diligence obligations under the LkSG have to be appropriate. As a result, enterprises are not required to take all conceivable measures, but only those that are necessary and reasonable considering the specific risk disposition.[74] This opens some discretion under the business judgement rule in deciding which risks to address first and which measures are reasonable in this context.[75] **66**

The LkSG does not establish an obligation to prevent damage to human rights or the environment, but an obligation to make efforts to prevent it. This means that enterprises may not guarantee that no human rights or environmental obligations are violated in their supply chains. Rather, they must be able to prove that they have complied with due diligence obligations.[76] **67**

The appropriate manner (*angemessene Weise*) of acting in accordance with the due diligence obligations is determined according to (§ 3 sub. 2 LkSG) **68**

- the nature and extent of the business activities of the enterprise,
- the ability of the enterprise to influence the party directly responsible for a human rights-related or environment-related risk or the violation of a human rights-related or environment-related obligation,
- the severity of the violation that can typically be expected, the reversibility of the violation, and the probability of the occurrence of a violation of a human rights-related or an environment-related obligation as well as
- the nature of the causal contribution of the enterprise to the risk to human rights-related or environment-related risk or to the violation of a human rights-related or environment-related obligation.

Even with these interpretations, the term 'appropriate manner' remains an undefined legal term. Concrete requirements for the standard of due diligence remain unclear. This leads to legal uncertainties which, particularly in view of the massive risk of fines, raises concerns regarding the constitutional principle of certainty (*Bestimmtheitsgrundsatz*) under Article 103 para. 2 GG.[77] **69**

On 23 December 2022, BAFA published a handout on the principle of appropriateness (*Prinzip der Angemessenheit*) according to the requirements of the Act on Corporate Due Diligence Obligations in Supply Chains.[78] **70**

The handout provides, among other things, guidance on the practical implementation of an appropriate standard of reasonableness regarding the individual due diligence obligations, such as the establishment of risk management and the selection and implementation of preventive and remedial measures. **71**

Among other things, BAFA suggests several factors to determine risks for human rights-related and environment-related obligations:[79] **72**

---

[74] Fleischer CCZ 2022, 205 (211); Wagner/Ruttloff NJW 2021, 2145 (2146).

[75] Cf. BMAS, FAQ on the Supply Chain Act, 6.4, available at <https://www.csr-in-deutschland.de/EN/Business-Human-Rights/Supply-Chain-Act/FAQ/faq.html> (last accessed: 22.6.2025).

[76] Cf. German Federal Government, LkSG-Draft, p. 23, <https://www.bmas.de/SharedDocs/Downloads/DE/Gesetze/Regierungsentwuerfe/reg-sorgfaltspflichtengesetz.pdf?__blob=publicationFile&v=2> (last accessed 22.6.2025).

[77] WRW LkSG/Ruttloff/Kappler mn. 473; Wagner/Ruttloff NJW 2021, 2146.

[78] See BAFA, Handout on the principle of appropriateness according to the requirements of the Act on Corporate Due Diligence Obligations for the Prevention of Human Rights Violations, <https://www.bafa.de/SharedDocs/Downloads/DE/Lieferketten/handreichung_angemessenheit.pdf?__blob=publicationFile&v=3> (last accessed 22.6.2025) (German); <https://www.bafa.de/SharedDocs/Downloads/EN/Supply_Chain_Act/guidance_appropriateness.html?nn=1469788> (last accessed 22.6.2025) (English).

[79] See BAFA, Handout on the principle of appropriateness according to the requirements of the Act on Corporate Due Diligence Obligations for the Prevention of Human Rights Violations, p. 11, <https://www.

- operating in or sourcing from countries where there are high risks to human rights and the environment (risk country)[80];
- operating in or belonging to a sector in which there are typically high risks to human rights and the environment (risk sector);
- raw materials that are demonstrably extracted in conflict or high-risk regions, or that are usually accompanied by violations of human rights or environmental damage.

73 To implement an appropriate risk management BAFA advocates to determine resources, establish internal responsibilities and to create internal structures.

74 The handout helps to build and to shape the risk management within compliance management systems. However, the reader of the handout is left with the impression that concrete statements by the German government are rare to find.

3. Cooperation within the supply chain

75 The successful fulfilment of due diligence obligations will in many cases require close cooperation between enterprises and their suppliers. According to the BAFA, this cooperation is also laid down in the LkSG and is already required when setting up a risk management system. Enterprises will also need the support of their suppliers when it comes to risk analysis, preventive and remedial measures and the complaints procedure. In the context of cooperation with suppliers that do not fall within the scope of the LkSG themselves, however, enterprises need to ensure that they do not transfer their own obligations to the supplier. This is because such a transfer is not permitted. Each obligated enterprise remains responsible for fulfilling the due diligence obligations imposed on it.[81]

76 As enterprises sometimes made too far-reaching demands towards their suppliers, the BAFA published a handout on 'Collaboration in the supply chain between obliged enterprises and their supplier' in August 2023.[82] The handout shows in particular the limits of the use of suppliers by obligated enterprises based on the principles of appropriateness and effectiveness and gives concrete recommendations for cooperation within the supply chain.

4. Standards, audits and certifications

77 In order to fulfil their due diligence obligations, enterprises can make use of instruments such as third-party standards, audits and certifications. In December 2024, the BAFA therefore published a handout on 'standards, audits and certifications as instruments in the due diligence process'. The handout shall provide companies with concrete

bafa.de/SharedDocs/Downloads/EN/Supply_Chain_Act/guidance_appropriateness.html?nn=1469788> (last accessed 22.6.2025).

[80] BAFA is also referring to UN Working Group on Business and Human Rights, 'Heightened Human Rights Due Diligence for Business in Conflict-Affected Contexts: A Guide', <https://www.undp.org/publications/heightened-human-rights-due-diligence-business-conflict-affected-contexts-guide> (last accessed 22.6.2025).

[81] Cf. BAFA, Handout on collaboration in the supply chain between obliged enterprises and their supplier, p. 1, <https://www.bafa.de/SharedDocs/Downloads/EN/Supply_Chain_Act/guidance_cooperation_supply_chain.pdf?__blob=publicationFile&v=6> (last accessed 22.6.2025).

[82] Cf. BAFA, Handout on collaboration in the supply chain between obliged enterprises and their supplier, <https://www.bafa.de/SharedDocs/Downloads/EN/Supply_Chain_Act/guidance_cooperation_supply_chain.pdf?__blob=publicationFile&v=6> (last accessed 22.6.2025).

guidance on the selection and use of standards, audits and certifications as an instrument for fulfilling due diligence obligations.[83]

It should be noted, however, that enterprises cannot avoid their own responsibility to fulfil due diligence obligations under the LkSG by engaging external third parties.[84] 78

There is no obligation for enterprises to use instruments like standards, audits and certifications. BAFA also does not provide any assessments, recommendations or rankings of specific providers.[85] 79

VI. Risk management (§ 4 LkSG)

1. Appropriate and effective

Enterprises must establish an appropriate and effective risk management system to comply with due diligence obligations. The risk management (*Risikomanagement*) must be implemented in all relevant business processes through appropriate measures (§ 4 sub. 1 LkSG).[86] 80

Enterprises must also examine areas with particularly high risks for human rights and the environment in their own business areas as well as those of their direct suppliers.[87] 81

Effective are those measures that make it possible to identify and minimize human rights and environment-related risks and to prevent, end or minimize the extent of human rights-related or environment-related obligations if the enterprise has caused or contributed to these risks or violations within the supply chain (§ 4 sub. 2 LkSG). 82

In BAFA's view, a measure is effective 83

> if it can in fact improve or help to improve the situation of people or protection of the environment. This must be considered from an ex ante perspective when planning and implementing measures. The Act also explicitly demands a review of effectiveness in the individual due diligence obligations. This means that companies are required to regularly check whether their own measures and processes have in fact achieved the desired effect and to make adjustments if necessary.[88]

Enterprises are responsible for preventing, stopping or minimising violations of human rights-related or environmental risks if they have caused or contributed to them. 84

Risks are deemed to have been caused if an enterprise alone has directly caused them or has causally contributed to the creation or intensification of the risk through its actions. The enterprise has contributed to a risk if it has not acted alone, for example if several enterprises order from the same factory, then each enterprise makes a contribution. 85

---

[83] Cf. BAFA, Guidance on standards, audits and certifications as instruments in the due diligence process, <https://www.bafa.de/SharedDocs/Downloads/DE/Lieferketten/handreichung_standards_audits_und_zertifizierungen.pdf?__blob=publicationFile&v=5> (last accessed: 22.6.2025).

[84] Cf. BAFA, Guidance on standards, audits and certifications as instruments in the due diligence process, p. 6, <https://www.bafa.de/SharedDocs/Downloads/DE/Lieferketten/handreichung_standards_audits_und_zertifizierungen.pdf?__blob=publicationFile&v=5> (last accessed: 22.6.2025).

[85] Cf. BAFA, Guidance on standards, audits and certifications as instruments in the due diligence process, p. 1, <https://www.bafa.de/SharedDocs/Downloads/DE/Lieferketten/handreichung_standards_audits_und_zertifizierungen.pdf?__blob=publicationFile&v=5> (last accessed: 22.6.2025).

[86] Baade DStR 2022, 1617 (1618).

[87] Cf. BMAS, FAQ on the Supply Chain Act, 6.1, available at <https://www.csr-in-deutschland.de/EN/Business-Human-Rights/Supply-Chain-Act/FAQ/faq.html> (last accessed: 22.6.2025).

[88] See BAFA, Handout on the principle of appropriateness according to the requirements of the Act on Corporate Due Diligence Obligations for the Prevention of Human Rights Violations, p. 6 (English), <https://www.bafa.de/SharedDocs/Downloads/EN/Supply_Chain_Act/guidance_appropriateness.html?nn=1469788> (last accessed 22.6.2025).

2. Responsibilities

86 The enterprise must ensure that it is determined who within the enterprise is responsible for monitoring risk management, for example by appointing a human rights officer. Senior management must seek information on a regular basis, at least once a year, about the work of the responsible person or persons (§ 4 sub. 3 LkSG).

VII. Risk analysis (§ 5 LkSG)

87 Enterprises must conduct an appropriate risk analysis (*Risikoanalyse*) to identify the human rights-related and environment-related risks in its own business area and at its direct suppliers[89] (§ 5 sub. 1 sent. 1 LkSG).

88 With regard to the individual implementation of the risk analysis, the German legislator recommends that a two-step procedure be undertaken: First, an overview of the enterprise's own procurement processes, the structure and actors at the immediate supplier, and the most important groups of people who may be affected by the enterprise's business activities should be determined by means of a risk mapping.[90] The identified risks should then be assessed and – if necessary – prioritised in a second step. Decisive criteria for prioritisation include the severity and likelihood of the violation as well as the influence an enterprise can exert on mitigating the risk.[91]

89 In the opinion of the BAFA, the BMWE and the BMAS, the companies have a wide scope for action. Accordingly, it is crucial that the company can justify the appropriateness of the measures (§ 3 sub. 2 LkSG) and why a particular risk is being addressed as a priority.[92] One criterion, for example, is the severity of the identified risk in conjunction with a relevant causal contribution (e.g. large purchasing volume of a certain raw material).[93]

90 The human rights situation is often dynamic.[94] Therefore, the risk analysis should be updated regularly. In addition, the risk analysis must react to any – sometimes unexpected – events in the own business area or in the supply chain. This may be the case if new products, projects or business areas are introduced or the business activity or business principles are changed (§ 5 sub. 4 sent. 1 LkSG).[95]

91 The results of the risk analysis must be communicated to the relevant departments within the company, e.g. the board of management or the purchasing department (§ 5 sub. 3 LkSG).

92 On 17 August 2022, BAFA published a handout 'Guidance on conducting a risk analysis as required by the German Supply Chain Due Diligence Act'.[96] It describes the requirements for a risk analysis as well as the role of the risk analysis in the due diligence

---

[89] BT-Drs. 19/28649, 44; Wagner/Ruttloff NJW 2021, 2145 (2148); Baade DStR 2022, 1617 (1618).

[90] BT-Drs. 19/28649, 44.

[91] BT-Drs. 19/28649, 45.

[92] Cf. BMAS, FAQ on the Supply Chain Act, 8.3, available at <https://www.csr-in-deutschland.de/EN/Business-Human-Rights/Supply-Chain-Act/FAQ/faq.html> (last accessed: 22.6.2025).

[93] Cf. BMAS, FAQ on the Supply Chain Act, 8.3, available at <https://www.csr-in-deutschland.de/EN/Business-Human-Rights/Supply-Chain-Act/FAQ/faq.html> (last accessed: 22.6.2025).

[94] BT-Drs. 19/28649, 45.

[95] BT-Drs. 19/28649, 45.

[96] Cf. BAFA, Guidance on conducting a risk analysis as required by the GermanSupply Chain Due Diligence Act, <https://www.bafa.de/SharedDocs/Downloads/DE/Lieferketten/handreichung_risikoanalyse.pdf;jsessionid=87B9584A1B2104B1ABD43FE2327566CF.1_cid381?__blob=publicationFile&v=6> (last accessed 22.6.2025) (German); <https://www.bafa.de/SharedDocs/Downloads/EN/Supply_Chain_Act/guidance_risk_analysis.html?nn=1469788> (last accessed 22.6.2025) (English).

process and offers assistance as well as practical guidance for its implementation.[97] In particular, BAFA provides guidance on the implementation steps of the risk analysis, from its preparation and execution to the evaluation of the results.

Besides, BAFA's handout on the principle of 'appropriateness' also addresses the internal risk analysis by providing guiding questions for preparing and conducting risk analyses.[98] For example, BAFA recommends that when carrying out the risk analysis, it should be checked whether the information gathered via existing sources is sufficient to identify the specific risks and to weigh and prioritize them, taking into account the 'appropriateness' criteria.[99] **93**

VIII. Preventive measures (§ 6 LkSG)

If an enterprise identifies a risk in the course of a risk analysis, it must take appropriate preventive measures (*Präventionsmaßnahmen*) without undue delay (§ 6 sub. 1 LkSG): **94**

- statement on human rights (§ 6 sub. 2 LkSG, → mn. 95 et seq.);
- preventive measures in own business area (§ 6 sub. 3 LkSG, → mn. 97);
- preventive measures vis-à-vis direct supplieres (§ 6 sub. 4 LkSG → mn. 98 et seq.)

1. Statement on human rights (§ 6 sub. 2 LkSG)

The management must issue a policy statement on its human rights strategy (*Menschenrechtsstrategie,* § 6 sub. 2 sent. 1 and 2 LkSG) which must be communicated to employees, direct suppliers, the public and, if necessary, the works council.[100] The declaration must include, among other things, a description of the process how to comply with the due diligence obligations (§ 6 sub. 2 sent. 3 LkSG). **95**

The declaration of principles (*Grundsatzerklärung*) is not issued until it has been made publicly available by the company's management, e.g. on the company's homepage. It is not sufficient if the declaration is only available through the intranet. However, vis-à-vis direct suppliers, it is sufficient if the general terms and conditions of delivery or a purchase order contain a link to the company's website on which the policy statement is published.[101] **96**

2. Preventive measures in own business area (§ 6 sub. 3 LkSG)

The enterprise must lay down appropriate preventive measures in its own area of business, in particular: **97**

---

[97] Cf. BAFA, Guidance on conducting a risk analysis as required by the GermanSupply Chain Due Diligence Act, p. 3, <https://www.bafa.de/SharedDocs/Downloads/EN/Supply_Chain_Act/guidance_risk_analysis.html?nn=1469788> (last accessed 22.6.2025).

[98] See BAFA, Handout on the principle of appropriateness according to the requirements of the Act on Corporate Due Diligence Obligations for the Prevention of Human Rights Violations, <https://www.bafa.de/SharedDocs/Downloads/EN/Supply_Chain_Act/guidance_appropriateness.html?nn=1469788> (last accessed 22.6.2025).

[99] See BAFA, Handout on the principle of appropriateness according to the requirements of the Act on Corporate Due Diligence Obligations for the Prevention of Human Rights Violations, p. 16 et seq., <https://www.bafa.de/SharedDocs/Downloads/EN/Supply_Chain_Act/guidance_appropriateness.html?nn=1469788> (last accessed 22.6.2025).

[100] BT-Drs. 19/28649, 46.

[101] Cf. BMAS, FAQ on the Supply Chain Act, 9.1, available at <https://www.csr-in-deutschland.de/EN/Business-Human-Rights/Supply-Chain-Act/FAQ/faq.html> (last accessed: 22.6.2025).

- the implementation of the human rights strategy in the relevant business processes set out in the policy statement,
- the development and implementation of appropriate procurement strategies (*Beschaffungsstrategien*) and purchasing practices that prevent or minimize identified risks,
- the delivery of training in the relevant business areas,
- the implementation of risk-based control measures to verify compliance with the human rights strategy contained in the policy statement in its own business area.

3. Preventive measures vis-à-vis direct suppliers (§ 6 sub. 4 LkSG)

98 The enterprise must lay down appropriate preventive measures vis-à-vis a direct supplier, in particular:

- the consideration of human rights-related and environment-related expectations when selecting a direct supplier,
- contractual assurances from a direct supplier that it will comply with the human rights-related and environment-related expectations required by the enterprise's senior management and appropriately address them along the supply chain,
- the implementation of initial and further training measures to implement the contractual assurances made by the direct supplier,
- agreeing on appropriate contractual control mechanisms and their risk-based implementation to verify compliance with the human rights strategy at the direct supplier.

99 The effectiveness of the preventive measures must be reviewed once a year. An ad hoc review is required if the enterprise must expect a significantly changed or significantly expanded risk situation in its own business area or at its direct supplier for example due to the introduction of new products, projects or a new business field (§ 6 sub. 5 LkSG).

IX. Remedial action (§ 7 LkSG)

100 If the enterprise discovers that a violation of a human rights-related or environment-related obligation has already occurred or is imminent in its own business area or at a direct supplier, it must take appropriate remedial action without any delay to prevent or end the violation or to minimize the extent of the violation (§ 7 sub. 1 LkSG).

101 In the enterprise's own business area, the remedial action (*Abhilfemaßnahme*) must be carried out in such a way that it ends the violation (§ 7 sub. 1 sent. 3 LkSG). The aim is to prevent the violation of human and environmental rights in the future and not merely to eliminate consequences that have already occurred.[102] In the enterprise's own business area abroad, as well as in the business area of group subsidiaries attributed under § 2 sub. 6 sent. 3 LkSG, the remedial action must 'as a rule' lead to the cessation of the violation (§ 7 sub. 1 sent. 4 LkSG).

102 If the violation of a human rights-related or an environment-related obligation at a direct supplier is one that the enterprise cannot end in the foreseeable future, it must draw up and implement a concept for ending or minimizing the violation without undue delay (§ 7 sub. 2 LkSG). The concept must contain a concrete timetable. When drawing up and implementing the concept, the following measures in particular must be taken into consideration:

[102] Sagan/Schmidt NZA-RR 2022, 281 (288).

- the joint development and implementation of a plan to end or minimize the violation with the enterprise causing the violation,
- joining forces with other enterprises in sector initiatives and sector standards to increase the ability of influencing the entity that causes or may cause a harm,
- a temporary suspension of the business relationship while efforts are made to minimize the risk.

As ultima ratio, the business relationship shall be terminated permanently (§ 7 sub. 3 **103** LkSG).

The termination of a business relationship is only required if **104**

- the violation of a protected legal position or an environment-related obligation is assessed as very serious,
- the implementation of the measures developed in the concept does not remedy the situation after the time specified in the concept has elapsed,
- the enterprise has no other less severe means at its disposal and increasing the ability to exert influence has no prospect of success.

The principle of 'enablement before withdrawal' applies. This should encourage enter- **105** prises not to withdraw from regions with weak standards, but to work locally with their suppliers or within the industry to minimise risks.[103]

The effectiveness of the measures taken must be reviewed once a year and on an ad **106** hoc basis if the risk situation changes (§ 7 sub. 4 sent. 1 LkSG). If the measures prove to be ineffective, they must be updated (§ 7 sub. 4 sent. 3 LkSG).

X. Complaints procedure (§ 8 LkSG)

The enterprise must ensure that an appropriate internal complaints procedure **107** (*Beschwerdeverfahren*) is in place to establish an effective risk management.[104] The complaints procedure enables persons to report human rights-related and environment-related risks as well as violations of human rights-related or environment related obligations that have arisen as a result of the economic actions of an enterprise in its own business area or of a direct supplier (§ 8 sub. 1 LkSG).

The design of the complaints procedure is measured by a number of 'key criteria' **108** that must be implemented:[105] For example, enterprises must establish rules of procedure and make them publicly available, along with clear and comprehensible information on how to reach the enterprise, who is responsible, and how the complaints procedure is conducted.[106] In addition, it must be ensured that complaints are not associated with any disadvantages for the whistleblower.[107]

As an alternative to the internal procedure, enterprises can also participate in cor- **109** responding external complaints procedures that provide the aforementioned requirements.[108]

---

[103] Cf. German Federal Government, LkSG-Draft, p. 32 et seq, <https://www.bmas.de/SharedDocs/Downloads/DE/Gesetze/Regierungsentwuerfe/reg-sorgfaltspflichtengesetz.pdf?__blob=publicationFile&v=2> (last accessed 22.6.2025).

[104] Thus, the complaints procedure serves as an 'early warning system' within the supply chain, cf. in detail Stemberg CCZ 2022, 92 (93).

[105] WRW LkSG/E. Wagner/S. Wagner mn. 658.

[106] See § 8 sub. 2 LkSG and § 8 sub. 4 sent. 1 LkSG.

[107] See § 8 sub. 4 sent. 2 alt. 3 LkSG. Further criteria in WRW LkSG/E. Wagner/S. Wagner mn. 659.

[108] See § 8 sub. 1 sent. 6 LkSG and BT-Drs. 19/28649, 49.

110 BAFA published the handout 'Guidance on the complaints procedure under the German Supply Chain Due Diligence Act'.[109] Among other things, it sets out criteria for reviewing the effectiveness of an existing complaints procedure and provides checklists and recommendations for action.[110]

111 Besides any internal complaint procedures, it must be noted that BAFA has set up an online complaint form.[111] Complaints due to any violations within the meaning of the LkSG can be submitted directly to BAFA.

XI. Indirect suppliers (§ 9 LkSG)

112 Due diligence obligations generally apply to the enterprises' own business area and with regards to their direct suppliers. However, § 9 LkSG highlights certain due diligence obligations for enterprises' indirect suppliers.

1. Definition and identification of indirect suppliers

113 An indirect supplier is any enterprise which is not a direct supplier and whose supplies are necessary for the production of the enterprises' product or for the provision and use of the relevant service (§ 2 sub. 8 LkSG).

114 However, in cases where an enterprise has structured a direct supplier relationship in an improper manner or has engaged in a transaction in order to circumvent the due diligence obligations with regard to the direct supplier, an indirect supplier is deemed to be a direct supplier (§ 5 sub. 1 sent. 2 LkSG).

115 Due diligence obligations regarding indirect suppliers lead to challenges for internal compliance management systems.

116 Enterprises must determine which indirect suppliers are part of their supply chains. For this purpose, the direct suppliers must obviously also be consulted in order to clarify the – partly unknown – supply chains of the direct suppliers.

2. Procedures

117 If the indirect suppliers have been identified, the following procedure must be executed (§ 9 LkSG).

118 The enterprise must set up the complaints procedure in such a way that it also enables persons to report human rights-related or environment-related risks as well as violations of human rights-related or environment-related obligations that have arisen due to the economic actions of an indirect supplier (§ 9 sub. 1 LkSG).

119 If an enterprise has actual indications that suggest that a violation of a human rights-related or an environment-related obligation at indirect suppliers may be possible

[109] See BAFA, Guidance on the complaints procedure under the German Supply Chain Due Diligence Act, <https://www.bafa.de/SharedDocs/Downloads/DE/Lieferketten/handreichung_beschwerdeverfahren.html?nn=1469750> (last accessed 22.6.2025) (German); <https://www.bafa.de/SharedDocs/Downloads/EN/Supply_Chain_Act/guidance_complaints_procedure.html?nn=1469788> (last accessed 22.6.2025) (English).

[110] Cf. BAFA, Guidance on the complaints procedure under the German Supply Chain Due Diligence Act, p. 16 et seq, available at <https://www.bafa.de/SharedDocs/Downloads/EN/Supply_Chain_Act/guidance_complaints_procedure.html?nn=1469788> (last accessed: 22.6.2025).

[111] See <https://www.bafa.de/DE/Lieferketten/Beschwerde_einreichen/beschwerde_einreichen_node.html> (last accessed 22.6.2025).

(substantiated knowledge, *substantiierte Kenntnis*), it must without undue delay and as warranted (§ 9 sub. 3 LkSG)
- carry out a risk analysis,
- lay down appropriate preventive measures vis-à-vis the party responsible, such as the implementation of control measures, support in the prevention and avoidance of a risk or the implementation of sector-specific or cross-sector initiatives to which the enterprise is a party,
- draw up and implement a prevention, cessation or minimization concept and
- update its policy statement, if necessary.

For substantiated knowledge it is sufficient if there are indications within the enter- **120**
prise's sphere of control. This includes, for example, reports through the internal complaint's system.[112] With regard to the organisational duty the management must regularly inform itself about the work of the responsible risk manager.

Indications may include reports on human rights situations in the enterprise's produc- **121**
tion region, the fact that a supplier belongs to an industry with particular human rights or environmental risks, or indications from responsible authorities.

XII. Documentation and reporting obligations (§ 10 LkSG)

The compliance with due diligence obligations must be continuously documented. The **122**
documentation must be kept for at least seven years from its creation (§ 10 sub. 1 LkSG).

Additionally, businesses must create an annual report on how well they performed **123**
their due diligence duties in the preceding fiscal year and publish it free of charge on their website no later than four months after the end of the fiscal year for a term of seven years (§ 10 sub. 2 sent. 1 LkSG).

The report must at least state in a comprehensible manner (§ 10 sub. 2 sent. 2 LkSG), **124**
- whether the enterprise has identified any human rights-related and environment-related risks or violations of a human rights-related or environment-related obligation, and if so, which ones,
- what the enterprise has done to fulfil its due diligence obligations with reference to the measures; this also includes the elements of the policy statement as well as the measures taken by the enterprise as a result of complaints,
- how the enterprise assesses the impact and effectiveness of the measures and
- what conclusions it draws from the assessment for future measures.

However, it has to be noted that, according to the draft law of the German Government **125**
of 3 September 2025, the reporting obligation (§ 10 sub. 2 LkSG) is to be abolished without replacement.[113] For this reason, BAFA is already no longer enforcing the reporting obligation (as of October 2025).[114]

---

[112] See BMAS, FAQ on the Supply Chain Act, 6.14, available at <https://www.csr-in-deutschland.de/EN/Business-Human-Rights/Supply-Chain-Act/FAQ/faq.html> (last accessed: 22.6.2025).

[113] Draft Law to Amend the Supply Chain Due Diligence Act – Relieving Companies through an Implementation- and Enforcement-Friendly Approach, <https://www.bmas.de/SharedDocs/Downloads/DE/Gesetze/Regierungsentwuerfe/reg-gesetz-zur-aenderung-des-lieferkettensorgfaltspflichtengesetzes.pdf?__blob=publicationFile&v=2>.

[114] See BAFA Notification <https://www.bafa.de/SharedDocs/Kurzmeldungen/DE/Lieferketten/20251001_Vereinfachung_LksG.html>.

XIII. Monitoring and enforcement by BAFA

1. Competent authority

126 The BAFA is responsible for the official monitoring and enforcement of the LkSG (§ 19 sub. 1 LkSG).

127 The BAFA examines ex officio the compliance with the due diligence obligations (§ 14 sub. 1 no. 1 LkSG). In addition, BAFA will take action at the request of a person who substantiates a violation or its imminent occurrence (§ 14 sub. 1 no. 2 LkSG).

128 Persons who, for example, report violations of human rights in the supply chain will often find it impossible or very difficult to demonstrate that enterprises have violated their due diligence obligations. Therefore, it must be at least possible or cannot be ruled out from the outset that a violation of a legal position as a result of a breach of due diligence obligations has occurred or that such a violation is imminent.[115]

129 BAFA follows a risk-based approach in its official inspections (§ 19 sub. 2 LkSG). BAFA checks the compliance with corporate due diligence obligations for possible violations of protected legal positions or environmental obligations and takes appropriate measures.[116] This means that BAFA will focus on the enterprises with the greatest risks and, in cases of doubt, is likely to refrain from in-depth checks without specific cause in the case of enterprises with a lower risk profile.[117]

2. Orders and measures (§ 15 LkSG)

130 The competent authority makes the appropriate and necessary orders (*Anordnungen*) and takes the appropriate and necessary measures (*Maßnahmen*) to detect, end and prevent violations of the obligations.

131 This includes

- summoning people;
- ordering the enterprise to submit, within three months of the notification of the order, a corrective action plan, including clear timelines for its implementation and
- requiring the enterprise to take specific action to fulfil its obligations.

3. Access rights (§ 16 LkSG)

132 If it is necessary for the performance of its duties, the competent authority and its representatives are authorised

- to enter and inspect the enterprise's premises, offices and commercial buildings during normal business or operating hours and
- to inspect and examine, within normal business or operating hours, the enterprise's business documents and records from which it is possible to deduce whether the due diligence obligations have been complied with.

4. Obligation to provide information and surrender documents (§ 17 LkSG)

133 Enterprises and persons summoned are obliged to provide the competent authority, upon request, with the information and to surrender the documents required by the authority. The obligation also extends to information on affiliated enterprises, direct

115 BT-Drs. 19/28649, 54.
116 WRW LkSG/Ruttloff/Hahn mn. 1406.
117 WRW LkSG/Ruttloff/Hahn mn. 1407.

and indirect suppliers and the surrender of documents of these enterprises insofar as the enterprise or person obliged to provide information or surrender documents has the information at its disposal or is in a position to obtain the requested information due to existing contractual relationships (§ 17 sub. 1 LkSG).

This includes, among other things, information and evidence to determine whether an enterprise is subject to the LkSG or fulfils its due diligence obligations (§ 17 sub. 2 LkSG). 134

5. Obligation to tolerate and cooperate (§ 18 LkSG).

Enterprises must tolerate the measures of the competent authority and its representatives and support them in the implementation of the measures. This also applies to the enterprise owners and its representatives, and in the case of legal persons, to the persons appointed to represent them by law or under the legal person's statutes. 135

6. Repressive investigations

In case of proceedings to investigate violations of the LkSG, the responsible authority can carry out searches and seizure of documents and data with the involvement of the public prosecutor's offices and competent courts.[118] 136

XIV. Sanctions

1. Overview of sanctions

137

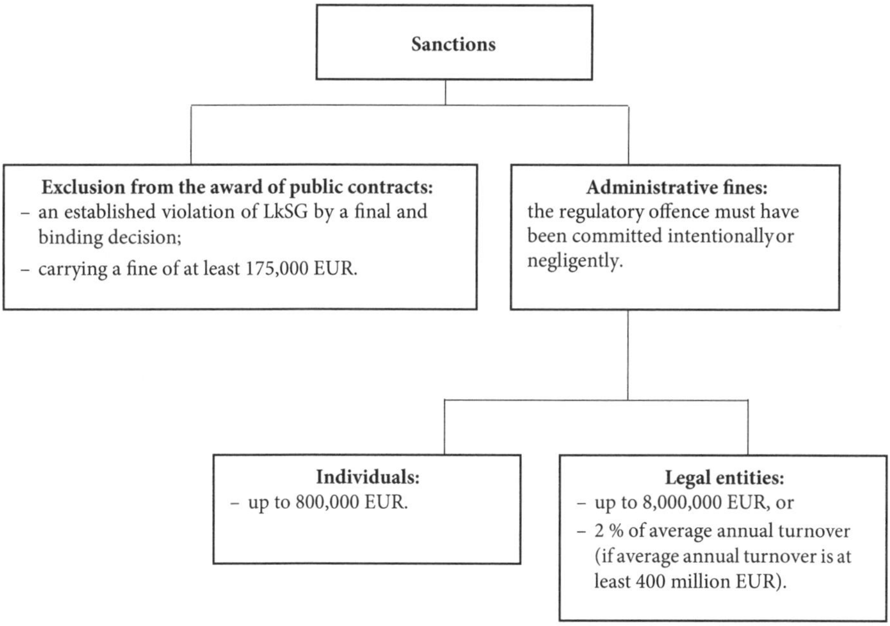

[118] Cf. in detail WRW LkSG/Ruttloff/Hahn mn. 1616 et seqq.

2. Exclusion from the award of public contracts (§ 22 LkSG)

138 If a violation of the LkSG has been established by final and binding decision, enterprises shall, as a rule, be excluded from participation in a procedure for the award of a supply, works or service contract by the contracting authorities referred to in §§ 99 and 100 GWB.

139 An exclusion requires a violation of the LkSG that has been established by final and binding decision carrying a fine of at least 175,000 EUR, depending on the violation of the LkSG.

140 However, enterprises may execute a proceeding of 'self-cleaning' (*Selbstreinigung*, § 125 GWB):

141 Public contracting authorities shall not exclude an enterprise, where a reason for exclusion from participation in the procurement procedure does not exist, when the enterprise has proven that it

- has paid or undertaken to pay compensation for any damage caused by the criminal offence or misconduct;
- has comprehensively clarified the facts and circumstances associated with the criminal offence or misconduct and the damage caused thereby by actively collaborating with the investigating authorities and the public contracting authority; and
- has taken concrete technical, organisational and personnel measures that are appropriate to prevent further criminal offences or misconduct.

3. Provisions on administrative fines (§ 24 LkSG)

142 In case of a violation, the LkSG determines administrative fines against individuals and enterprises. The LkSG and German Law in general do not provide provisions for criminal charges against corporate entities at all. However, the LkSG charges corporate entities with administrative fines.

143 The LkSG sanctions not only a direct violation of human rights or any direct harm to the environment. It is sufficient by the LkSG that the violation is considered an abstract endangerment offence (*abstraktes Gefährdungsdelikt*). This means that the act endangers the protected legal interests in the abstract. Accordingly, no actual violation of legal interests must be imminent. However, it has to be noted that, according to the draft law of the German government dated 3 September 2025, the number of administrative offences is to be reduced, with fines being imposed only in cases of severe human rights violations.[119] Consequently, BAFA is no longer initiating new administrative offence proceedings, except in cases involving serious human rights violations.[120]

a) Violation of due diligence obligations

144 Among other things, the LkSG sanctions the violation of the following due diligence obligations (§ 24 sub. 1 in conjunction with §§ 4–10, 12 LkSG):

- the enterprise fails to determine who within the enterprise is responsible for monitoring risk management (§ 24 sub. 1 no. 1 LkSG)

---

[119] Draft Law to Amend the Supply Chain Due Diligence Act – Relieving Companies through an Implementation- and Enforcement-Friendly Approach, <https://www.bmas.de/SharedDocs/Downloads/DE/Gesetze/Regierungsentwuerfe/reg-gesetz-zur-aenderung-des-lieferkettensorgfaltspflichtengesetzes.pdf?__blob=publicationFile&v=2>.

[120] See BAFA Notification <https://www.bafa.de/SharedDocs/Kurzmeldungen/DE/Lieferketten/20251001_Vereinfachung_LksG.html>.

- the enterprise does not carry out a risk analysis, does not carry it out correctly, completely or in time (§ 24 sub. 1 no. 2 LkSG)
- the enterprise fails to ensure that a complaints procedure is implemented (§ 24 sub. 1 no. 8 LkSG)
- fails to keep documentation or does not keep it for at least seven years (§ 24 sub. 1 no. 9 LkSG)

A violation of due diligence obligation requires that a person committed a regulatory offence intentionally or by negligence. However, as stated above, most administrative offences related to violations of due diligence obligations are to be abolished. **145**

b) Addressee

Violations of the LkSG can be penalised with administrative fines. **146**

If a person violates obligations under the LkSG, sanctions apply to individuals, such as the management of the relevant enterprise. In addition to board members and managing directors, this applies, for example, to human rights officers[121], environmental protection officers[122], compliance officers[123] or chief sustainability officers[124]. **147**

In addition, all management personnel of an enterprise can be considered liable for an administrative offence under § 9 OWiG. In particular, the executive bodies of the respective enterprises, e.g. the managing director or the board members, can be fined.[125] As per this, a law according to which special personal characteristics, relationships or conditions (special personal characteristics) justify the possibility of punishment is also to be applied to the representative if these characteristics are not present in the representative but are present in the person represented. **148**

Personal relationships concern, for example, the relationships of a person to his environment, whether to other persons, things or institutions. Examples of this are status designations such as organizer, trader, entrepreneur, owner of a sales outlet, operator of a restaurant, employer, participant in foreign trade, construction manager, operator of a plant, owner of a vehicle or acquirer of an object.[126] **149**

Fines can be imposed on legal persons exclusively under the conditions of § 30 OWiG.[127] Therefore, a fine can be imposed on a legal person, for example, if an authorized representative body of a legal entity has committed a criminal offence or administrative offence by which duties affecting the legal entity or association of persons have been violated or the enterprise has been or was to be enriched.[128] **150**

c) Administrative fines

The LkSG distinguishes between administrative fines against individuals and legal entities. **151**

Administrative fines against individuals can range, depending on the violation of the LkSG, up to 800,000 EUR. The maximum amount of the fine is halved in the case of negligent conduct § 17 sub. 2 OWiG.[129] **152**

---

[121] Cf. § 4 sub. 3 LkSG.
[122] BT-Drs. 14/8998, 10.
[123] WRW LkSG/Skoupil mn. 1569 with reference to BGH 29.8.2008 – 2 StR 587/07, NJW 2009, 89.
[124] WRW LkSG/Skoupil mn. 1569 with reference Ruttloff/Wagner/Reischl/Skoupil CB 2021, 364.
[125] WRW LkSG/Skoupil mn. 1569.
[126] BeckOK OWiG/Valerius, 46. Ed 1.4.2025, § 9 mn. 8 with further evidence.
[127] WRW LkSG/Skoupil mn. 1570.
[128] WRW LkSG/Skoupil mn. 1571.
[129] WRW LkSG/Skoupil mn. 1573.

153 Generally, enterprises can be fined with the same amount as individuals. However, the fine can be increased for certain violations: For example, if preventive measures were not taken or not taken in time the maximum fine is increased tenfold. Accordingly, an administrative fine up to 8 million EUR is possible (§ 24 sub. 2 sent. 2 LkSG, § 30 sub. 2 sent. 3 OWiG).

154 In addition, the LkSG provides for a much further increase of fines in certain cases: For example, a legal entity with an average annual turnover of more than 400 million EUR can be fined up to 2 % of its average annual turnover. This applies if remedial measures (§ 7 LkSG) were not taken or not taken in time in the case of a violation of human rights or environmental obligations.

155 The calculation of the average annual turnover of the legal person or association of persons is based on the worldwide turnover of all natural and legal persons as well as all associations of persons in the last three financial years preceding the decision by the authority insofar as these persons and associations of persons operate as an economic unit (§ 24 sub. 3 sent. 2 LkSG).

156 The relation of administrative fines to annual turnovers follows a legislative trend[130], which allows increasingly higher fines to be imposed on corporate entities in Germany.[131]

d) Sentencing

157 The sentencing is at the discretion of the responsible authority, which must be exercised proportionately.[132]

158 The basis for the sentencing of the administrative fine for legal persons and associations of persons is the significance of the administrative offence. Besides, the economic circumstances of the legal person or association of persons have to be taken into account in the assessment (§ 24 sub. 4 LkSG).

159 The LkSG states that, among other things, the following aspects have to be taken into consideration:

- the charge against the perpetrator of the administrative offence,
- the motives and objectives of the perpetrator of the administrative offence,
- significance, extent and duration of the administrative offence,
- the type of execution of the administrative offence, in particular the number of perpetrators and their position in the legal person or association of persons,
- the effects of the administrative offence,
- previous administrative offences for which the legal person or association of persons is responsible.

160 In addition, the enterprise's compliance management system may also be relevant for the assessment of the sanction: For example, the assessment of the fine may consider, among other things, whether and to what extent the enterprise has taken precautions to avoid and detect administrative offences.[133]

161 Thus, the legislator is complying with today's practice of investigating authorities, which regularly takes into account an enterprise's compliance measures in a mitigating manner.[134] This also corresponds with the jurisprudence of the German Federal Court of

---

[130] Even before the implementation of the LkSG, the annual turnover of a company could be decisive for the maximum amount of a fine (including the confiscation of financial benefits) in antitrust, data protection, money laundering and capital market law, among others.

[131] WRW LkSG/Skoupil mn. 1530 with reference to Lutz-Bachmann/Vorbeck/Wengenroth BB 2021, 906 (913).

[132] BT-Drs. 19/28649, 57.

[133] WRW LkSG/Skoupil mn. 1593.

[134] WRW LkSG/Skoupil mn. 1593.

Justice (*Bundesgerichtshof*, BGH). Accordingly, it has to be recognised in the sentencing to which extent enterprises have fulfilled their duty to prevent violations of the law and if an effective compliance management has been implemented.[135]

The assessment of the administrative fine against individuals considers the regular scope (§ 17 sub. 3 OWiG):[136] The significance of the administrative offence and the charge faced by the individual shall form the basis for the assessment of the administrative fine. The perpetrator's financial circumstances shall also be taken into account; however, they shall, as a rule, be disregarded in cases involving negligible regulatory offences. **162**

E. Conclusion

The LkSG introduces a fundamental paradigm shift in Germany. German and international enterprises with a branch office in Germany have multiple due diligence obligations to comply with human rights-related and environment-related risks in their supply chains.[137] **163**

Therefore, compliance management systems must also focus on the enterprises supply chains.[138] The extension of risk analysis to direct and indirect suppliers leads to significant challenges. Thereby, some legal terms of the LkSG are undefined. Although these legal terms should be specified by BAFA's handouts, the exact legal framework of the LkSG remains unclear. Best practice will probably be established only gradually.[139] **164**

In light of the coalition agreement and the corresponding plan to first abolish reporting obligations and most administrative offences, and later to repeal the entire LkSG in order to replace it with an 'International Corporate Responsibility Act', it remains to be seen how German law in the area of supply chain due diligence will develop. **165**

135 BGH 9.5.2017 – 1 StR 265/16, BeckRS 2017, 114578 mn. 118.

136 WRW LkSG/Skoupil mn. 1584.

137 Nietsch/Wiedmann NJW 2022, 1; Wagner/Ruttloff NJW 2021, 2145; Giesberts NVwZ 2022, 1497 (1505).

138 Baade DStR 2022, 1617 (1624).

139 Baade DStR 2022, 1617 (1624).

CHAPTER 19
CRIMINAL LABOUR LAW

Bibliography: Bitter, Reform des Insolvenz- und Restrukturierungsrechts zum 1.1.2021 in Kraft getreten, GmbHR 2021, R16; Friedrich, Straf- und ordnungswidrigkeitenrechtliche Haftungsrisiken bei Verstößen gegen das Mindestlohngesetz, CB 2022, 8; Herrlinger/Ahlenstiel, Durch Selbstreinigung aus dem Wettbewerbsregister, WuW 2022, 396; Ignor/Rixen, Grundprobleme und gegenwärtige Tendenzen des Arbeitsstrafrechts, NStZ 2002, 510; Johnson, Die rechtskonforme Vergütung von Betriebsratsmitgliedern: Das Begünstigungsverbot als unterschätzte Compliance-Falle?, CCZ 2021, 75; Loose, Die neue Rechtsprechung des Bundesgerichtshofs zur Beendigung von Taten gemäß § 266 a Abs. 1 StGB und § 266 a Abs. 2 Nr. 2 StGB, NStZ 2021, 709; Mosbacher, Aktuelle Rechtsprechung des BGH mit Compliance-Bezug, CCZ 2023, 45; Pasewaldt, Straftaten gegen Betriebsverfassungsorgane und ihre Mitglieder gem. § 119 BetrVG, ZIS 2007, 75; Rettenmaier/Reichling, Das leichtfertige Nichtabführen von Sozialversicherungsbeiträgen, NJW 2020, 2147; Rieble, Gewerkschaftsbestechung?, CCZ 2008, 121; Rieble/Klebeck, Strafrechtliche Risiken der Betriebsratsarbeit, NZA 2006, 758; Rönnau/Wegner, (Weitere) Reform des Insolvenzrechts durch das SanInsFoG – Was bleibt von der Vorrangrechtsprechung?, ZInsO 2021, 1137; Schröder, Quo vadis Arbeitsrecht?, ArbRAktuell 2016, 177; Theile, Arbeitgebervorsatz (§ 266 a StGB) und der Fiktionstatbestand des § 10 AÜG, NZWiSt 2022, 311.

Table of contents

A. Introduction 468
B. Withholding of social security contributions 469
I. Objective elements of the crime 469
1. Employer 469
2. Contribution duty to social security 470
3. Lawful conduct possible and reasonable 471
II. Subjective element of the crime 472
III. Justification 473
IV. Legal consequences and statute of limitation 473
1. Very serious case 473
2. Self-disclosure 474
3. Back payment and late payment surcharges 474
4. Statute of limitation 475
C. Work safety 476
I. Act on work safety 476
1. § 25 ArbSchG 476
2. § 26 ArbSchG 477
a) Persistent repeating 478
b) Endangering life or health 478
3. § 209 SGB VII 478
II. Act on Working Hours 478
III. Employees requiring special protection 479
1. Protection of working pregnant women and mothers 479
2. Protection of working adolescents and children 480
3. Protection of employees with severe handicaps 480
D. Illegal employment 481
I. Combating undeclared work and unlawful employment 481
1. § 8 SchwarzArbG 482
a) § 8 sub. 1 SchwarzArbG 482

b) § 8 sub. 2 SchwarzArbG 482
c) § 8 sub. 3 SchwarzArbG 483
d) § 8 sub. 4 and 5 SchwarzArbG 483
2. § 10 SchwarzArbG 483
3. § 10a SchwarzArbG 484
4. § 11 SchwarzArbG 484
II. Securing a general minimum wage 485
1. Non-payment of general minimum wage 485
2. Further regulatory offences 485
3. Risk of wage usury 486
III. Protecting hired-out employees 486
1. § 15 sub. 1 AÜG 486
2. § 15a AÜG and § 16 sub. 1 no. 2, sub. 2 AÜG 487
3. Further regulatory offences 487
IV. Employees posted across borders 488
E. Collective labour law 488
I. Protection of works councils 489
1. § 119 sub. 1 no. 1 BetrVG 489
2. § 119 sub. 1 no. 2 BetrVG 489
3. § 119 sub. 1 no. 3 BetrVG 490
4. Criminal complaint 491
II. Protection of committee of spokespersons 491
F. Procedural peculiarities 491
I. Authorities involved 491
1. Finanzkontrolle Schwarzarbeit 492
2. Work safety authorities 493
3. Deutsche Rentenversicherung 494
4. Tax authorities 494
II. Extra-criminal consequences 494
1. Exclusion from leading positions in GmbH and AG 494
2. Unreliability pursuant to § 35 sub. 1 GewO 494
3. Entry in Gewerbezentralregister and Wettbewerbsregister 495
4. Exclusion from public tenders 495

A. Introduction

1 Criminal labour law is a sub-area of economic criminal law,[1] which companies have to deal with relatively often – mostly as part of general compliance measures to avoid potential misconduct. However, even criminal proceedings focussing on criminal labour law are not uncommon – especially concerning the withholding of social security contributions (§ 266a StGB).

2 For the purposes of the following analysis, the term criminal labour law shall refer to criminal as well as regulatory offences[2] sanctioning violations against labour law provisions.[3] In principle, only employers can commit these offences.[4]

3 To begin with, the most relevant offence in practice, the withholding of social security contributions (§ 266a StGB), will be described (→ mn. 4 et seqq.). Further, offences

[1] Ignor/Rixen NStZ 2002, 510 (510); GKR ArbStrafR-HdB/Gercke Ch. 1 mn. 1; Petri ArbStrafR A mn. 6.

[2] For the difference between criminal law provisions and regulatory offences see → Ch. 4.

[3] Similar GKR ArbStrafR-HdB/Gercke Ch. 1 mn. 12.

[4] BeckOK StGB/v. Heintschel-Heinegg, 64 Ed. 1.2.2025, StGB § 266a mn. 1; GKR ArbStrafR-HdB/Gercke Ch. 1 mn. 14; Petri ArbStrafR A mn. 6. The few offences, which only employees can violate, will not be part of the following analysis.

relating to work safety (→ mn. 44 et seqq.), and the prevention of illegal employment (→ mn. 77 et seqq.) will be explained as well as the provisions to protect the collective labour law (→ mn. 127 et seqq.). Finally, the procedural peculiarities in the context of proceedings relating to criminal labour law will be presented (→ mn. 144 et seqq.).

B. Withholding of social security contributions

The withholding of social security contributions, as stipulated in § 266a StGB, is the most relevant offence of criminal labour law in practice.[5] This provision is supposed to protect the interests of the social community by ensuring that all social security contributions are paid.[6] 4

In the following, the objective as well as the subjective elements of the crime will be described (→ mn. 6 et seqq. and → mn. 21 et seqq.). Furthermore, it is explained when the perpetrator's behaviour may be justified (→ mn. 25 et seqq.). Lastly, the legal consequences will be set out (→ mn. 29 et seqq.). 5

I. Objective elements of the crime

According to § 266a StGB, an employer, who fails to pay the employee's contributions required under social security laws when due (§ 266a sub. 1 StGB) or provides false information to the competent authorities or fails to inform them of facts relevant under social security laws and thereby withholds the employer's social security contributions (§ 266a sub. 2 StGB), is liable to prosecution. Social security contributions are contributions to health, nursing care, pension, accident, and unemployment insurance. Whether the employer in fact pays the loan to the respective employee is irrelevant in case of § 266 sub. 1 as well as sub. 2 StGB. 6

According to § 266a sub. 3 StGB, the employer is also subject to prosecution if they do not pay other due parts of the employee's remuneration, which they are obliged to transfer to another person, without informing the employee. This applies, for example, to garnishments or contributions to pension funds. In practice, criminal prosecution based on § 266a sub. 3 StGB is fairly uncommon.[7] 7

1. Employer

Social security laws, in conjunction with labour laws, determine whether someone is an employer in the meaning of § 266a StGB (and not just a customer of a contractor).[8] 8

The actual circumstances are decisive for this determination, not what the parties agreed contractually.[9] Employment is the opposite of self-employed work (§ 7 sub. 1 sent. 1 9

[5] GKR ArbStrafR-HdB/Gercke Ch. 2 mn. 11.

[6] BVerfG 18.12.2002 – 1 BvR 244/98, NJW 2003, 961 (961) with further references; BGH 14.1.2014 – II ZR 192/13, NJW 2014, 1244 mn. 23; BT-Drs. 18/11272, 19 et seq.

[7] GKR ArbStrafR-HdB/Gercke Ch. 2 mn. 71.

[8] BGH 24.6.2015 – 1 StR 76/15, NStZ 2015, 648 (649); cf. also BGH 13.12.2018 – 5 StR 275/18, NStZ-RR 2019, 151 (151 et seq.).

[9] BGH 24.6.2015 – 1 StR 76/15, NStZ 2015, 648 (649); BSG 25.1.2006 – B 12 KR 30/04 R, BeckRS 2006, 41119; BSG 24.1.2007 – B 12 KR 31/06 R, NZS 2007, 648 (650).

SGB IV). If a person is integrated into another person's work organisation and must follow their instruction, the relationship is likely to be considered an employment pursuant to social security laws (§ 7 sub. 1 sent. 2 SGB IV).

10 The Federal Social Court (*Bundessozialgericht*) has tried to clarify this further by case law. According to its precedents, employment is characterised by the employee being personally dependent on the employer. This is the case if the employee is part of the enterprise and subject to the employer's right to decide when, where, how long, and how they have to work. In contrast to this, a self-employed person bears their own entrepreneurial risk, has their own place of business, may dispose of their own labour and is essentially free to arrange their activity and working time. Whether someone is employed or self-employed depends on which characteristics predominate. The overall picture of the work performance is decisive for the assessment of the matter.[10]

11 In practice, the employer is often a legal entity. For such constellations, criminal law provides that the relevant management personnel, in particular managing directors or board members, shall be considered as employers within the meaning of the relevant criminal provisions (cf. § 14 StGB).[11] Moreover, a so-called de facto managing director, i.e. someone who is not officially appointed as managing director but acts as such in practice, can also be an employer.[12]

12 Regarding the hiring-out of employees (*Arbeitnehmerüberlassung*) the following applies:[13] if the hiring-out of employees complies with the relevant laws, the lender (the person lending an employee to another company, *Verleiher*) remains the employer and the hirer (the person receiving the hired-out employee, *Entleiher*) does not become the employer.[14] However, if the hiring-out of employees is unlawful, the hirer is considered to be the employer and thus a potential perpetrator under § 266a StGB (§ 9, § 10 sub. 1 AÜG).[15] If the lender continues to pay the employee's salary, that person is also considered to be an employer and potentially criminally liable under § 266a StGB (§ 10 sub. 3 AÜG).[16]

2. Contribution duty to social security

13 The applicability of § 266a StGB is dependent on social security laws. This means that the withholding of social security contributions is only punishable if there is an obligation to pay social security contributions pursuant to the respective social security laws.[17]

14 If an A1 certificate (formerly: E-101 certificate) of a Member State of the EU was issued, German social security laws do not apply and there is no criminal liability under

---

[10] BSG 25.1.2006 – B 12 KR 30/04 R, BeckRS 2006, 41119; BSG 24.1.2007 – B 12 KR 31/06 R, NZS 2007, 648 (650); BSG 29.07.2015 – B 12 KR 23/13 R, BSGE 119, 216 = BeckRS 2015, 73497 mn. 16; cf. BGH 13.12.2018 – 5 StR 275/18, NStZ-RR 2019, 151 (151 et seq.).

[11] For § 14 StGB please see → Ch. 2.

[12] Fischer StGB § 266a mn. 5 with further references.

[13] Please see → mn. 112 et seq. for details regarding hired-out employees.

[14] BGH 31.3.1982 – 2 StR 744/81, BGH 31.3.1982 – 2 StR 744/81, BGH 19.10.1999 – 5 StR 336/99, BGHSt 31, 32 = BeckRS 9998, 102916; BGH 05.05.1983 – 4 StR 133/83, NStZ 1984, 26 (26 et seq.); GKR ArbStrafR-HdB/Gercke Ch. 2 mn. 24; Erbs/Kohlhaas/Häberle, 255. EL Januar 2025, AÜG Vor § 1 mn. 3.

[15] BGH 31.3.1982 – 2 StR 744/81, BGH 19.10.1999 – 5 StR 336/99, BGHSt 31, 32 = BeckRS 9998, 102916; BGH 05.05.1983 – 4 StR 133/83, NStZ 1984, 26 (26 et seq.); GKR ArbStrafR-HdB/Gercke Ch. 2 mn. 24; Theile NZWiSt 2022, 311 (312).

[16] BGH 13.6.2001 – 3 StR 126/01, NStZ 2001, 599 (600); LG Oldenburg 8.7.2004 – 2 KLs 65/04, BeckRS 9998, 20791; GKR ArbStrafR-HdB/Kraft Ch. 2 mn. 661.

[17] Cf. BGH 24.10.2006 – 1 StR 44/06, BGH 24. 10. 2006 – 1 StR 44/06, BGHSt 51, 124 mn. 9 et seqq. = BeckRS 2006, 13846; cf. BGH 28.05.2002 – 5 StR 16/02, BGHSt 47, 318 = NJW 2002, 2480 (2480 et seq.); cf. BGH 24.10.2007 – 1 StR 160/07, NJW 2008, 595 (595); cf. BGH 2.12.2008 – 1 StR 416/08, BGHSt 53, 71 = NJW 2009, 528 (539); Fischer StGB § 266a mn. 9a et seqq. with further references.

§ 266a StGB,[18] even if this A1 certificate was fraudulently acquired.[19] This is not the case for non-EU-states, even if there is a bilateral agreement between the foreign state and Germany, since such an agreement is not comparable with the legal character of the European Union.[20]

In a judgment, the judge must – in principle – explain in detail which social security contributions were not paid.[21] However, this requirement is significantly lowered in the case of mere non-payment of duly declared contributions.[22] Moreover, should it not be possible to describe the specific social security contributions owed, the contributions may – under certain circumstances – be estimated.[23] 15

3. Lawful conduct possible and reasonable

Since § 266a sub. 1 StGB punishes the omission of a legal duty,[24] one can only be criminally liable if lawful conduct (i.e. the payment of the employee's social security contributions) was possible and reasonable for them.[25] 16

Therefore, in principle, an employer is not liable to prosecution if they were insolvent at the time when they should have paid the social security contributions.[26] However, if the employer has failed to take precautionary measures for securing the payment of the employee's social security contributions when there were signs of liquidity problems, they may still be liable to prosecution pursuant to the Federal Court of Justice.[27] 17

Moreover, an employer is not liable to prosecution if and to the extent that the insolvency court has ordered a general prohibition of disposal (§ 21 sub. 2 no. 2 InsO), since that forbids the employer to pay the employee's social security contributions when due, or if the insolvency proceedings have already been opened.[28] 18

Lastly, the employer is not criminally liable, should it not be reasonable to pay the social security contributions. This is the case, for example, if the employer had needed to take out a loan to pay the social security contributions and obtaining such a loan would 19

---

[18] BGH 24.10.2006 – 1 StR 44/06, BGH 24.10.2006 – 1 StR 44/06, BGHSt 51, 124 mn. 16 et seqq. = BeckRS 2006, 13846; BGH 30.4.2024 – 1 StR 426/23, NStZ 2024, 681 (682); cf. CJEU 27.4.2017, C-620/15, ECLI:EU:C:2017:309 = ZAR 2017, 384 – A-Rosa Flussschiff GmbH; MüKoStGB/Radtke StGB § 266a mn. 24 et seqq.

[19] BGH 30.4.2024 – 1 StR 426/23, NStZ 2024, 681 (682); BGH 11.9.2024 – 5 StR 325/24, BeckRS 2024, 25575 mn. 17. However, charges based on fraud (§ 263 StGB) regarding the application for such certificate are still possible.

[20] BGH 24.10.2007 – 1 StR 160/07, BeckRS 2007, 18920, BGHSt 52, 67 = NJW 2008, 595 (596); discussed but not answered in: BGH 24.10.2006 – 1 StR 44/06, BGHSt 51, 124 = BeckRS 2006, 13846.

[21] BGH 11.8.2010 – 1 StR 199/10, NStZ-RR 2010, 376 (376); Fischer StGB § 266a mn. 9d with further references.

[22] BGH 7.10.2010 – 1 StR 424/10, NStZ 2011, 161 (161 et seqq.); Fischer StGB § 266a mn. 9d.

[23] BGH 10.11.2009 – 1 StR 283/09, NStZ 2010, 635 (636) referring to BVerfG 20.3.2007 – 2 BvR 162/07 mn. 11; BGH 13.6.2001 – 3 StR 126/01, NStZ 2001, 599 (600) referring to BGH 08.01.1992 – 2 StR 102/91, NStZ 1993, 40 (41); Fischer StGB § 266a mn. 9d with further references.

[24] BGH 28.5.2002 – 5 StR 16/02, BGHSt 47, 318 = NJW 2002, 2480 (2481); with regard to § 266a sub. 2 StGB this is different: BGH 08.01.1992 – 2 StR 102/91, NJW 2011, 3047 (3047).

[25] BGH 28.5.2002 – 5 StR 16/02, BGHSt 47, 318 = NJW 2002, 2480 (2481); BGH 18.11.1997 – VI ZR 11-97, NJW 1998, 1306 (1306).

[26] BGH 28.5.2002 – 5 StR 16/02, BGHSt 47, 318 = NJW 2002, 2480 (2481) with further references; GKR ArbStrafR-HdB/Gercke Ch. 2 mn. 50 with further references; Fischer StGB § 266a mn. 15.

[27] BGH 28.5.2002 – 5 StR 16/02, BGHSt 47, 318 = NJW 2002, 2480 (2481); BGH 11.10.2018 – 1 StR 257/18, BeckRS 2018, 33540; KG Berlin 4.12.2009 – (1) 1 Ss 427/09 (22/09), BeckRS 2010, 362; criticised by Rönnau/Wegner ZInsO 2021, 1137 (1139) as well as Fischer StGB § 266a mn. 17a with very good arguments.

[28] MüKoStGB/Radtke StGB § 266a mn. 72 with further references; OLG Dresden 18.1.2010 – 3 Ss 603/09, NStZ 2011, 163 (163); OLG Braunschweig 27.5.2015 – 1 Ss 14/15, BeckRS 2015, 132134 mn. 9.

constitute a criminal offence – e.g. fraud.[29] The payment of social security contributions is also not reasonable if such payment endangered the basic needs (food supply and similar) of the employer.[30]

20 Please also see → mn. 25 et seqq. outlining a potential temporary justification for employers who do not pay social security contributions in an economic crisis of the company (despite still having sufficient financial means to do so).

II. Subjective element of the crime

21 Only if the employer acts intentionally, they can be punishable pursuant to § 266a StGB. According to the recent jurisdiction of the Federal Court of Justice, an employer does not act intentionally if they err about whether they are considered an employer in the legal meaning.[31] Therefore, an employer acts intentionally only if they were aware of the relevant factual circumstances and understood the implications of labour and social security laws – at least from a layperson's perspective. The employer must at least have considered their position as an employer and the consequent obligation to pay social security contributions as a probability. Moreover, they must have accepted that they may violate this obligation.

22 Before this recent change of jurisdiction, criminal courts ruled that an employer could only be excused if they could not have avoided the assumption that they are not an employer in the legal meaning.[32] As there is a status determination procedure pursuant to § 7a SGB IV at the German pension insurance (*Deutsche Rentenversicherung*) to determine whether the respective employment is subject to social security contributions, the employer was in practice rarely excused if they did not undergo this procedure.[33] It is still possible for potential employers to initiate such a status determination procedure. However, the fact that the accused employer could have initiated such a status determination procedure may no longer be relevant for the question whether the defendant is excused or not – although this has not yet been explicitly stated by the Federal Court of Justice.

23 The new jurisdiction offers more potential to defend an accused employer. Particularly in complex legal constellations, e.g. hiring-out employees (*Arbeitnehmerüberlassung*), the question whether an alleged offender has erred should always be considered.

24 However, if the employer has not acted intentionally, they may be subject to the regulatory offence pursuant to § 8 sub. 3 SchwarzArbG should they have acted recklessly (grossly negligent).[34]

---

[29] MüKoStGB/Radtke StGB § 266a mn. 66.

[30] TK StGB/Perron StGB § 266a mn. 10.

[31] BGH 24.9.2019 – 1 StR 346/18, BGHSt 64, 195 = NJW 2019, 3532; cf. BGH 24.1.2018 – 1 StR 331/17, NStZ-RR 2018, 180; BGH 17.9.2020 – 1 StR 576/18, NStZ 2021, 304.

[32] BGHZ 133, 370 = NJW 1997, 130 (133); BGH 7.10.2009 – 1 StR 478/09, NStZ 2010, 337; BGH 24.1.2018 – 1 StR 331/17, NStZ-RR 2018, 180.

[33] BGH 7.10.2009 – 1 StR 478/09, NStZ 2010, 337 (337) with further references.

[34] Please also see → mn. 90 et seqq. for this regulatory offence.

III. Justification

Even if the employee agreed to the employer not paying their social security contributions, this does not exculpate the employer of their criminal liability, as the duty to pay these contributions is not at the employee's disposal.[35] 25

In general, the duty to pay the social security contributions overrides any other payment duty.[36] However, the Federal Court of Justice accepted that the employer is not liable to prosecution if they failed to pay the social security contributions in the event of a financial crisis, as long as the deadline to file for insolvency is still running.[37] 26

Pursuant to the law reform at the beginning of 2021,[38] the payment prohibitions under company law concerning legal persons were summarised in § 15b sub. 1 sent. 1 InsO. As long as the representative body of the legal entity fulfils their obligations under insolvency law in accordance with § 15a InsO, i.e. files an insolvency application for the legal entity in due time, they do not violate any tax obligations even if the taxes are not paid (§ 15b sub. 8 InsO). Although this provision (§ 15b sub. 8 InsO) does not explicitly cover the duty to pay social security contributions, the idea and the official justification of the law calls for the provision to be applied to social security contributions as well.[39] 27

Therefore, even after this recent change of the law, an employer does not violate the law if they do not pay the social security contributions during the period where the insolvency application is still feasible, i.e. during the time when they examine the possibilities of segregation. 28

IV. Legal consequences and statute of limitation

In principle, a prison sentence of up to five years or a fine may be imposed for a violation of § 266a StGB. 29

1. Very serious case

In a so-called very serious case, there is even the threat of a prison sentence of six months to ten years (§ 266a sub. 4 StGB). 30

A very serious case is one in which the offender withholds contributions on a large scale out of gross self-interest. An offender acts out of gross self-interest if they mainly and condemnably focus on their own advantage exceeding any normal commercial drive.[40] However, this is not the case if they act out of a financial emergency trying to 31

---

[35] GKR ArbStrafR-HdB/Gercke Ch. 2 mn. 103; LG Nürnberg-Fürth 25.06.1987 – 6 O 1233/87, NJW 1988, 1856 (1857).

[36] BGH 28.5.2002 – 5 StR 16/02, BGHSt 47, 318 = NJW 2002, 2480 (2481); BGH 30.07.2003 – 5 StR 221/03, BGHSt 48, 307 = NJW 2003, 3787; Fischer StGB § 266a mn. 16 with further references.

[37] BGH 30.7.2003 – 5 StR 221/03, NJW 2003, 3787; BGH 9.8.2005 – 5 StR 67/05, NJW 2005, 3650 (3652); BGH 28.5.2002 – 5 StR 16/02, BGHSt 47, 318 = NJW 2002, 2480.

[38] *Gesetz zur Fortentwicklung des Sanierungs- und Insolvenzrechts* [i.e. Act on the further development of reorganisation and insolvency law of 20.12.2020, BGBl. 2020 I 3256 et seqq].

[39] BR-Drucks. 619/20, 226; MüKoStGB/Radtke StGB § 266a mn. 68a, 76; Bitter GmbHR 2021, R16 (R18); cf. also Rönnau/Wegner ZInsO 2021, 1137 (1147).

[40] BGH 7.3.2019 – 3 StR 192/18, NStZ-RR 2019, 216 (217) with further references; BGH 13.6.2013 – 1 StR 226/13, NStZ 2014, 105.

save their business and the employees' jobs.[41] Large scale means a total damage of at least 50,000 EUR.[42]

32 § 266a StGB establishes further very serious cases as such where, inter alia, the crime was committed as a member of a criminal gang or by having used falsified receipts to cover up the criminal act.

2. Self-disclosure

33 There is the possibility to avoid a sentence if the employer discloses their misbehaviour towards the competent authority. According to § 266a sub. 6 sent. 1 StGB, the court may refrain from imposing a penalty if the employer informs the authority collecting the social security contributions in writing what amount of contributions are withheld at due date or immediately thereafter and explains why it was impossible to pay the contributions on time, despite the employer's serious efforts to do so. However, it is at the court's discretion whether it refrains from punishing the employer.

34 If the employer not only discloses their wrongdoing but also pays the social security contributions within the reasonable period determined by the competent authority, the law orders the offender to not be punished (§ 266a sub. 6 sent. 2 StGB). This is a mandatory exemption from punishment and not at the court's discretion.[43]

35 In practice, this regulation usually leads to the defence counsel and the public prosecutor's office discussing the discontinuation of the criminal proceedings without any consequences pursuant to § 153b StPO in conjunction with § 266a sub. 6 StGB or § 153 StPO based on the guilt being minimal. Yet, it is also possible that the proceeding is discontinued only if the employer fulfils certain conditions, for example having to pay a contribution to a non-profit organisation (§ 153a StPO).

3. Back payment and late payment surcharges

36 If the employer has not paid the due social security contributions, they must pay them in arrears. The competent authority – the health insurance collecting the social security contributions (§ 28h sub. 1, 2 SGB IV) or the German pension insurance (*Deutsche Rentenversicherung*, § 28p sub. 1 sent. 4 SGB IV) – issues a corresponding contribution notice (being an administrative act) towards the employer.

37 Should the social security contribution not have been paid, it is – in general – considered that the amount paid to the employee is a net wage (§ 14 sub. 2 sent. 2 SGB IV). This means the salary that the employer had agreed with the employee does not include any social security contribution or applicable taxes. The employer then has to pay social security contributions calculated on this net wage amount. In consequence, the employer has to pay higher social security contributions. However, the Federal Social Court has clarified that this calculation based on the net wage is only feasible if the employer has intentionally not paid the social security contributions.[44]

38 In addition, the employer has to cover late payment surcharges. Pursuant to § 24 sub. 1 sent. 1 SGB IV, the employer must pay a late payment surcharge of 1 % of the amount not paid on time for each month. However, pursuant to § 24 sub. 2 SGB IV, late payment

[41] TK StGB/Perron StGB § 266a mn. 29b.

[42] BeckOK StGB/Wittig, 64. Ed. 1.2.2025, StGB § 266a mn. 58 with further references; cf. BGH 27.10.2015 – 1 StR 373/15, NJW 2016, 965 referring to § 370 sub. 3 no. 1 AO; BGH 29.4.2015 – 1 StR 235/14, NStZ-RR 2015, 278 (280) referring to §§ 299, 300 sub. 1 no. 1 StGB.

[43] GKR ArbStrafR-HdB/Gercke Ch. 2 mn. 110.

[44] BSG 9.11.2011 – B 12 R 18/09 R, NJOZ 2012, 1860 (1863).

surcharges are not owed if the employer was unaware of their obligation to pay through no fault of their own. Therefore, a surcharge for late payment can only be imposed if the employer considered it possible that they must pay social security contributions and accepted this risk when not paying these contributions.[45]

It should also be noted that non-payment of social security contributions may lead to the employer having to pay the employee's contribution in addition to the employer's social security contribution. This is because the employer can only claim the employee's social security contributions by deducting these from the employee's wage (§ 28g sent. 2 SGB IV). An employer can only make up for omitted deductions by the following three salary payments (§ 28g sent. 3 SGB IV).[46] If they fail to do so, the employer has to cover the employee's social security contributions. **39**

If the employer considers the contribution notice of the competent authority to be unlawful, they can file an objection against it and, if the objection is rejected, file a lawsuit with the social court. The legal procedure at the social courts usually takes a long time and it is not uncommon for a final social court ruling to be issued only after the conclusion of the criminal proceedings. This means that a criminal court may decide the social law question of whether there was an obligation to pay the social security contribution without knowing the subsequent decision of the specialised social court. **40**

In addition, the competent authority (the health insurance collecting the social security contributions or the *Deutsche Rentenversicherung*) will often, especially if the company that employed the workers is insolvent, take civil action against the responsible persons, relying on a tort norm that links to the breach of this criminal norm (§ 823 sub. 2 BGB in conjunction with § 266a StGB).[47] **41**

4. Statute of limitation

The five-year statute of limitations (§ 78 sub. 3 no. 4 StGB) for § 266a sub. 1, 2 no. 1 and no. 2 StGB uniformly begins with the last due date of the duty to pay the social security contributions pursuant to the recent Federal Court of Justice's jurisdiction. **42**

The Federal Court of Justice has abandoned its previous rulings on § 266 sub. 1 StGB and § 266 sub. 2 no. 2 StGB, according to which the statute of limitations only began to run when the obligation to pay social security contributions had expired, which led to considerably longer limitation periods (more than 30 years!).[48] Hence, in ongoing criminal proceedings under § 266a StGB, it should be examined whether the offences may be time-barred by now.[49] **43**

---

[45] BSG 12.12.2018 – B 12 R 15/18 R, DStR 2019, 1165 (1167); BSG 4.9.2018 – B 12 KR 11/17 R, BeckRS 2018, 33290 mn. 26.

[46] Kreikebohm/Dünn SGB IV/Nieder SGB IV § 28g mn. 2 et seq.; KassKomm/Wehrhahn, 77. EL März 2013, SGB IV § 28g mn. 7.

[47] BGHZ 133, 370 = NJW 1997, 130; BGHZ 187, 337 = NZI 2011, 111.

[48] BGH 13.11.2019 – 1 StR 58/19, NStZ 2020, 159; BGH 15.7.2020 – 2 ARs 9/20, BeckRS 2020, 19829; BGH 2.7.2020 – 4 ARs 1/20, BeckRS 2020, 17188; BGH 6.2.2020 – 5 ARs 1/20, BeckRS 2020, 2837; BGH 4.2.2020 – 3 ARs 1/20, BeckRS 2020, 3029; BGH 1.9.2020 – 1 StR 58/19 = NJW 2020, 3469; Schelzke jurisPR-StrafR 23/2020 Comment 3 with further references.

[49] Schelzke jurisPR-StrafR 23/2020 Comment 3 with further references; cf. also Loose NStZ 2021, 709 (709 et seqq.).

C. Work safety

44 This section deals with violations of work safety regulations that are subject to criminal or regulatory fine proceedings. Such provisions are usually to be found at the end of each act on work safety.

45 The respective criminal and regulatory offences are characterised by the so-called blanket regulation technique.[50] This means that the criminal and regulatory offence simply states that a violation of a certain work safety regulation is subject to criminal prosecution or regulatory fine proceedings. Therefore, to understand what exactly is prohibited, it is necessary to read the criminal and regulatory offence together with the work safety regulation that it refers to. As a rule, a normal violation of work safety laws can lead to a regulatory offence. If the violation has, however, been committed under aggravating circumstances, the violation may constitute a criminal offence.

46 Violations of legal provisions on work safety may trigger critical media coverage. Moreover, in recent years, the public, but also the legislator – as shown by the recently passed *Lieferkettensorgfaltspflichtgesetz* (LkSG, Act on Corporate Due Diligence Obligations in Supply Chains)[51] – have increasingly demanded companies to focus on their corporate social responsibility. Therefore, law enforcement authorities will probably pursue violations of work safety regulations with more dedication in the future.

47 The following explanations intend to provide an overview of the most important criminal and regulatory offences regarding work safety: the *Arbeitsschutzgesetz* (ArbSchG, Occupational Safety and Health Act, → mn. 48 et seqq.), the *Arbeitszeitgesetz* (ArbZG, Act on Working Hours, → mn. 60 et seqq.), and the laws directed at employees needing special protection (→ mn. 65 et seqq.). However, to avoid overstretching the scope of this chapter, the explanations cannot claim to be exhaustive.

I. Act on work safety

48 The *Arbeitsschutzgesetz* (ArbSchG, Occupational Safety and Health Act) is intended to protect the life and health of employees and thus preserve their working capacity.[52] Accordingly, the ArbSchG contains provisions on what measures the employer must take to secure work safety. The ArbSchG is supplemented by different ordinances further specifying the requirements for the employer.

1. § 25 ArbSchG

49 § 25 ArbSchG constitutes regulatory offences: whoever intentionally or negligently violates an ordinance enacted pursuant to § 18 sub. 1 or § 19 ArbSchG (§ 25 sub. 1 no. 1 ArbSchG) referring to this regulatory offence, or as employer or responsible person contravenes against an enforceable administrative act pursuant to § 22 sub. 3 ArbSchG (§ 25 sub. 1 no. 2 lit. a ArbSchG),[53] commits a regulatory offence. The regulatory fine is either

---

[50] For blanket regulations see: Fischer StGB § 1 mn. 9 et seqq.; MüKoStGB/Schmitz, 5th edn 2024, StGB § 1 mn. 44 et seq., 70 et seqq.

[51] BGBl. 2021 I 2959 et seqq.; please see → Ch. 18.

[52] BeckOK StGB/Nicolai, 64. Ed. 1.2.2025, ArbSchG § 26 mn. 1.

[53] § 25 sub. 1 no. 2 lit. b ArbSchG is directed at employees only. Therefore, this provision is not explained here.

up to 5,000 EUR (§ 25 sub. 1 no. 1 ArbSchG) or even up to 30,000 EUR (§ 25 sub. 1 no. 2 lit. a ArbSchG).

With regard to § 25 sub. 1 no. 1 ArbSchG, the *Baustellenverordnung* (BaustellV, i.e. Ordinance regarding construction sites), intended to improve the safety and health protection of workers on construction sites (§ 1 sub. 1, § 7 BaustellV), is most relevant in practice.[54] However, violations of rather unknown ordinances, such as the *Biostoffverordnung* (BioStoffV, i.e. Ordinance on Biological Agents), which prescribes protective measures for activities involving biological substances (§ 1, § 25 BioStoffV), can also establish a regulatory offence.[55] **50**

Legal ordinances that were issued pursuant to § 18 sub. 3 ArbSchG on the basis of an epidemic situation of national significance, in particular ordinances for the protection against Covid-19, which were applied (at least) in the years 2020 to 2022, are not covered by this regulatory offence as § 25 ArbSchG does not refer to ordinances pursuant to § 18 sub. 3 ArbSchG. **51**

§ 25 sub. 1 no. 2 ArbSchG is violated if the employer or a responsible person does not comply with an enforceable administrative act issued by the supervisory authority (§ 22 sub. 3 no. 1 ArbSchG). Moreover, this is the case if they do not comply with an enforceable administrative act ordering which measures are required to avert a particular danger to the life and health of the employees (§ 22 sub. 3 no. 2 ArbSchG). Here it is sufficient for such an administrative act to be enforceable. Whether the administrative act is also lawful is irrelevant as long as it is not so unlawful that it must be considered void.[56] **52**

In theory, any person can commit the regulatory offence pursuant to § 25 sub. 1 no. 1 ArbSchG. However, the respective ordinances, to which this regulatory offence refers, usually establish that only the employer can breach the law. Only an employer or responsible person can violate § 25 sub. 1 no. 2 ArbSchG. **53**

If the employer is a legal person, the relevant management personnel, in particular managing directors or board members, are regularly considered employers within the meaning of this provision pursuant to § 9 OWiG.[57] **54**

§ 13 ArbSchG establishes a responsible person as, inter alia, the employer's legal representative, the partner of a commercial partnership authorised to represent that partnership or other persons who were ordered to care for work safety by the employer.[58] **55**

2. § 26 ArbSchG

§ 26 ArbSchG defines criminal offences. A term of imprisonment of up to one year or a fine shall be imposed on anyone who intentionally and persistently repeats an act described in § 25 sub. 1 no. 2 ArbSchG (§ 26 no. 1 ArbSchG, → mn. 57) or who endangers the life or health of a worker by an intentional act described in § 25 sub. 1 no. 1 or no. 2 lit. a ArbSchG (§ 26 no. 2 ArbSchG, → mn. 58). **56**

---

[54] Cf. OLG Hamm 9.8.2006 – 1 Ss OWi 417/06, BeckRS 2008, 5501; cf. OLG Zweibrücken 12.6.2001 – 1 Ss 117/01, NStZ-RR 2002, 91; cf. OLG Celle 18.9.2013 – 322 SsRs 203/13, BeckRS 2013, 18896.

[55] BayObLG 24.1.2001 – 3 ObOWi 119/00, BeckRS 2001, 30157159.

[56] Erbs/Kohlhaas/Ambs/Häberle, 255. EL Januar 2025, ArbSchG § 25 mn. 7 et seqq.

[57] For § 9 OWiG please see → Ch. 4 mn. 75.

[58] Erbs/Kohlhaas/Ambs/Häberle, 255. EL Januar 2025, ArbSchG § 13 mn. 8 explaining that this applies besides § 9 OWiG.

a) Persistent repeating

57 Someone persistently repeats an act if they violate the regulation several times out of misconduct or indifference. At least one previous violation is required to establish a persistent repeating.[59]

b) Endangering life or health

58 The offence stipulated in § 26 no. 2 ArbSchG is a so-called concrete endangering offence.[60] This means that no damage must have occurred.[61] The risk that someone could have suffered a condition deviating adversely from the normal state of bodily functions by the unlawful behaviour is sufficient for prosecution.[62] However, if there was an actual damage to health or life, prosecution for bodily injury or even homicide cannot be ruled out.[63]

3. § 209 SGB VII

59 Regarding work safety, § 209 SGB VII must also be taken into account. This regulation establishes that the violation of accident prevention regulations issued by the *Berufsgenossenschaften* (employers' liability insurance association) – being the social security institutions responsible to prevent occupational accidents and diseases and work-related health hazards – is also a regulatory offence (§ 209 sub. 1 no. 1 SGB VII).

II. Act on Working Hours

60 The *Arbeitszeitgesetz* (ArbZG, Act on Working Hours) was passed, in particular, to protect the safety and health of employees as well as to secure work-free Sundays and public holidays (§ 1 ArbZG).[64] Accordingly, the ArbZG contains provisions on when and for how long an employee may work.

61 § 22 ArbZG sanctions certain intentional or negligent violations against the ArbZG by employers as regulatory offences. In particular, this concerns the unlawful exceeding of the legal working hours and the failure to grant breaks from work.[65] Apart from one exception,[66] the respective regulatory offences can be punished with a regulatory fine of up to 30,000 EUR.

62 Pursuant to § 23 ArbZG, some intentional violations of § 22 ArbZG are subject to criminal prosecution in case the employer intentionally endangers the health or working capacity of an employee by breaking the law (§ 23 sub. 1 no. 1 ArbZG) or persistently

---

[59] BGH 5.7.2011 – 3 StR 87/11, BGHSt 56, 271 = NJW 2011, 3174 with further references.

[60] GKR ArbStrafR-HdB/Kraft Ch. 2 mn. 979 with further references.

[61] Erbs/Kohlhaas/Ambs/Häberle, 255. EL Januar 2025, ArbSchG § 26 mn. 6; GKR ArbStrafR-HdB/Kraft Ch. 2 mn. 979 with further references.

[62] Erbs/Kohlhaas/Ambs/Häberle, 255. EL Januar 2025, ArbSchG § 26 mn. 5.

[63] GKR ArbStrafR-HdB/Kraft Ch. 2 mn. 979 and 1061 et seqq. See for example: LG Osnabrück 20.9.2013 – 10 KLs 16/13, BeckRS 2013, 198487 (negligent homicide due to disregard of safety and occupational health regulations); OLG Zweibrücken 1.2.2016 – 1 OLG 1 Ss 76/15, BeckRS 2016, 2644 (negligent bodily injury due to breach of safety regulations on construction sites).

[64] BDW ArbZeitG § 1 mn. 2 et seq.; BeckOK StGB/Nicolai, 64. Ed. 1.2.2025, ArbZG § 23 mn. 1.

[65] So also Schröder ArbRAktuell 2016, 177 (177 et seqq.).

[66] This exception only applies if the employer fails to display a copy of ArbZeitG (§ 16 sub. 1 ArbZG). For this breach of law a regulatory fine of only up to 5,000 EUR may be imposed (§ 22 sub. 1 no. 8, sub. 2 ArbZG).

repeats the violation (§ 23 sub. 1 no. 2 ArbZG).[67] Such violation can be punished with imprisonment of up to one year or a fine.

63 If the employer intentionally violates the ArbZG and, thereby, (only) negligently endangers the health or working capacity of an employee, the potential penalty is lower (up to six months imprisonment or a fine).

64 In the few published judgments regarding § 22 and § 23 ArbZG, the issue at hand was whether the permissible working hours were exceeded, which was prosecuted as a regulatory offence.[68] In such cases, it must be taken into account that the consent of the employee does not justify a violation against the ArbZG, unless the law explicitly offers the possibility to extent the working hours.[69]

III. Employees requiring special protection

65 The legislator has passed different acts protecting employees requiring special protection, inter alia, mothers (→ mn. 66 et seqq.), children and adolescents (→ mn. 70 et seqq.), as well as people with handicaps (→ mn. 76).

1. Protection of working pregnant women and mothers

66 The *Mutterschutzgesetz* (MuSchG, Maternity Protection Act) is primarily supposed to protect mothers and children (§ 1 sub. 1 MuSchG).[70] It seeks to do so – in addition to a prohibition of dismissal (§ 17 MuSchG) – in particular through regulations intended to protect the health of the mother and the child.

67 § 32 MuSchG defines which violations by the employer against this act constitute a regulatory offence. Inter alia, intentionally or negligently employing a mother before and after childbirth (in general six weeks before estimated date of birth and eight weeks after birth), letting her work overtime or not allowing her to attend doctor's appointments is punishable with a regulatory fine. In principle, this fine can be up to 30,000 EUR. Although it is illegal to lay-off a woman during her pregnancy and within four months after her giving birth (§ 17 MuSchG), violating this regulation is no regulatory offence.

68 Some intentional violations of these regulatory offences can be prosecuted as criminal offence if the employer intentionally endangers the health of the woman or her child (§ 33 MuSchG).[71] In such cases, the employer is liable to imprisonment of up to one year or a fine.

69 There are no decisions on the prosecution of regulatory or criminal offences of the MuSchG published in the well-known databases.

---

[67] The ArbZG uses the same definitions as the ArbSchG. Therefore, please see for the definitions → mn. 56 et seqq.

[68] KG Berlin 8.7.1998 – 2 Ss 109/98 – 3 Ws (B) 342/98, BeckRS 1998, 157166; OLG Thüringen 2.9.2010 – 1 Ss Bs 57/10, BeckRS 2010, 23535; cf. OLG Saarbrücken 8.10.2020 – Ss Bs 57/2020 (20/20 OWi) mn. 10, BeckRS 2020, 51412.

[69] Cf. OLG Thüringen 2.9.2010 – 1 Ss Bs 57/10, BeckRS 2010, 23535.

[70] BeckOK StGB/Nicolai, 64. Ed. 1.2.2025, MuSchG § 33 mn. 1 et seqq.

[71] The MuSchG uses the same definition as the ArbSchG. Therefore, please see for the respective definition → mn. 56 et seqq.

2. Protection of working adolescents and children

70 The *Jugendarbeitschutzgesetz* (JArbSchG, Youth Employment Protection Act) is intended to protect adolescents and children from overwork, overstress and dangers at the workplace.

71 The employment of children is generally prohibited, but the JArbSchG also provides exceptions to this principle. In addition, the JArbSchG establishes stricter provisions for the employment of adolescents compared to adults. A child within the meaning of the JArbSchG is anyone under the age of 15 years (§ 2 sub. 1 JArbSchG); an adolescent is anyone from 15 to 18 years old (§ 2 sub. 2 JArbSchG).

72 § 58 sub. 1 to 4 JArbSchG and § 59 JArbSchG declare certain violations of the JArbSchG to be regulatory offences. § 58 sub. 1 to 4 JArbSchG refers to violations of material provisions of the JArbSchG; § 59 JArbSchG to violations of formal provisions.[72]

73 For example, § 58 sub. 1 no. 1 and no. 12 JArbSchG impose the risk of a regulatory fine should someone unlawfully employ a child or let an adolescent work for more than five days a week (violation of a material provision).[73] A regulatory fine up to 15,000 EUR may be imposed for such a violation of a material provision.

74 According to § 59 sub. 1 no. 9 JArbSchG, for example, an employer may be fined if they do not keep a register recording which adolescents worked for them (violation of a formal provision). In principle, such a violation of a formal provision is punishable by a regulatory fine of 2,500 EUR.

75 Violations of the material provisions (§ 59 sub. 1 to 4 JArbSchG), which establish a regulatory offence, can be prosecuted as a criminal offence if the employer acts intentionally and, thereby, intentionally endangers the health or working capacity of the child or adolescents or persistently repeats the violation (§ 58 sub. 5 JArbSchG).[74] The employer is then liable to a sentence of up to one year imprisonment or a fine. If the employer only causes the danger to the child or adolescent negligently, they are liable to a (lower) sentence of up to six months of imprisonment or a fine (§ 58 sub. 6 JArbSchG).

3. Protection of employees with severe handicaps

76 The SGB IX contains regulations intended to enable severely disabled people to participate in the working life. § 238 SGB IX stipulates that specific violations against such regulations may constitute regulatory offences punishable with a regulatory fine of up to 10,000 EUR. There are no decisions by criminal courts concerning § 238 SGB IX published in the well-known databases. Still, it is likely that public prosecutor's offices may have prosecuted employers because of violations against the SGB IX but discontinued such prosecution against the employer agreeing to pay a contribution to a non-profit organisation (§ 153a StPO).

---

[72] GKR ArbStrafR-HdB/Gercke Ch. 2 mn. 1008.

[73] Cf. OLG Schleswig-Holstein 6.9.1982 – 2 Ss OWi 692/81, BeckRS 1982, 6097 for employing an adolescent more than five days a week; cf. OLG Hamm 14.8.1987 – 6 Ss OWi 445/86, BeckRS 1987, 31363915 for employing adolescents overtime; cf. OLG Schleswig-Holstein 7.1.1970 – 1 Ss 499/69, FHArbSozR 17 Nr. 3111 for employing children.

[74] The JArbSchG uses the same definitions as the ArbSchG. Therefore, please see → mn. 56 for the definitions.

D. Illegal employment

77 This section deals with criminal or regulatory offences punishing violations of laws directed against illegal employment. According to the legislator, such regulations are necessary since illegal employment causes considerable economic damages.[75]

78 The subsequent explanations focus on the essential criminal and regulatory provisions concerning illegal employment established by the *Schwarzarbeitsbekämpfungsgesetz* (SchwarzArbG, Act to Combat Undeclared Work and Unlawful Employment, → mn. 82 et seqq.), the *Mindestlohngesetz* (Act Regulating a General Minimum Wage, MiLoG, → mn. 105 et seqq.), the *Arbeitnehmerüberlassungsgesetz* (Act on Temporary Agency Work, AÜG, → mn. 112 et seqq.), and the *Arbeitnehmerentsendegesetz* (AEntG, Posted Workers Act, → mn. 121 et seqq.). However, to avoid overstretching this section, the explanations cannot claim to be exhaustive.

79 In this section, the confiscation (§§ 73 et seqq. StGB and § 29a OWiG) is of specific importance.[76] The confiscation is meant to ensure that crime does not pay. Therefore, the convicted – and under certain circumstances any third person having received money from a criminal or regulatory offence – will be ordered to pay back the money they received from the crime. There are two aspects, which should be kept in mind regarding confiscation and illegal employment.

80 Firstly, should an employer not have paid the minimum wage, the criminal courts will likely order a confiscation of the complete minimum wage without deducting the wage the employer actually paid to the employees.[77]

81 Secondly, it should be noted, that § 17 sub. 4 OWiG provides that the regulatory fine should exceed the economic advantage the offender has derived from the regulatory offence; if the statutory regulatory fine framework is not sufficient for this, it may be exceeded.[78] This means that in such cases significantly higher regulatory fines are possible.

I. Combating undeclared work and unlawful employment

82 The *Schwarzarbeitsbekämpfungsgesetz* (SchwarzArbG, Act to Combat Undeclared Work and Unlawful Employment) is supposed to prevent undeclared work and unlawful employment (§ 1 sub. 1 SchwarzArbG). To secure these targets, the SchwarzArbG establishes various regulatory and criminal offences. The most important ones are described and explained in the following.

83 The respective criminal and regulatory offences are characterised by the so-called blanket regulation technique, meaning the criminal and regulatory offences simply state that a violation of a certain regulation is subject to criminal prosecution or regulatory fine

[75] BT-Drs. 15/2573, 1, 17; cf. also Schneider/Bookmann, Die Größe der Schattenwirtschaft – Methodik und Berechnungen für das Jahr 2020, p. 22 <https://www.iaw.edu/pressemitteilungen-detail/pressemitteilung-vom-4-februar-2020-trotz-verlangsamten-wirtschaftswachstums-im-jahr-2020-weiterer-rueckgang-der-schattenwirtschaft-in-deutschland.html?file=files/dokumente/Schattenwirtschaft%20Studie%202020_Methodik_und_Berechnungen.pdf> (last accessed: 3.3.2025).

[76] Please see → Ch. 5 for more details regarding the confiscation.

[77] OLG Düsseldorf 30.8.2013 – IV-1 Ws 13/13 OWi, BeckRS 2013, 19117, referring to the old laws on confiscation; OLG München 07.06.2018 – 2 Ws 115/18 B, NZWiSt 2019, 275 referring to the new laws on confiscation.

[78] Please see → Ch. 5 for more details regarding the confiscation.

proceedings. This means that it is necessary to read the criminal and regulatory offence together with the respective regulation to which it refers in order to understand what is actually forbidden. Due to legislative mistakes, there have been false references within the regulatory as well as criminal offences of the SchwarzArbG in the past.[79] Therefore, criminal defence lawyers should always assess carefully the respective references.

1. § 8 SchwarzArbG

84 § 8 SchwarzArbG establishes different regulatory offences. For the lighter offences, the potential regulatory fine is up to 50,000 EUR. For more severe regulatory offences there is the threat of a regulatory fine of up to 500,000 EUR.

a) § 8 sub. 1 SchwarzArbG

85 Regulatory offences are deemed to have been committed if someone intentionally violates the obligation to register or obtain a permit for their company (§ 8 sub. 1 no. 1 SchwarzArbG). Furthermore, it is a regulatory offence if someone has services or work carried out although they know or negligently do not know that the person undertaking these has violated their duty to register or obtain a permit for their company (§ 8 sub. 1 no. 2 SchwarzArbG).

86 However, in both cases, a regulatory fine can only be imposed if a substantial volume of work or services was carried out. Therefore, search warrants and regulatory orders imposing a regulatory fine must clearly argue why works or services of a substantial volume were undertaken.[80]

87 The SchwarzArbG does not define what a substantial volume is. Pursuant to precedent cases, substantial volume is determined based on objective standards. The decisive questions to define whether works or services of substantial volume were carried out are: was the manpower used fully, predominantly or continuously? Were the works and services undertaken for a longer time, often or intensively? Is prior training and education required for such services and works? Does someone need materials or assistants to undertake these? The more questions are answered in the affirmative the more likely it is that a substantial volume of work or services was carried out. Whether the person concerned has received economic benefits of a substantial volume, is not important. They may even have made a loss.[81]

88 If no substantial volume of works or services was carried out or if the potential perpetrator merely acted negligently, other laws establish corresponding regulatory offences with lower fines.[82]

b) § 8 sub. 2 SchwarzArbG

89 § 8 sub. 2 SchwarzArbG establishes regulatory offences for violations of very different provisions of the SchwarzArbG. Among other things, this provision applies to breaching the obligation to carry and present identity papers, to tolerate inspections by the compe-

[79] For details see GKR ArbStrafR-HdB/Gercke Ch. 2 mn. 364 explaining that § 11 sub. 1 no. 1 and no. 3 SchwarzArbG were referring to a non-existing § 4 sub. 3 sent. 2 AufenthG. This should be kept in mind for all cases before 1.3.2020 as this could exclude the criminal liability (cf. § 2 sub. 3 StGB).

[80] BVerfG 21.4.2008 – 2 BvR 1910/05, BeckRS 2008, 35234; cf. also BVerfG 05.03.2012 – 2 BvR 1345/08, NJW 2012, 2097; AG Tübingen 5.7.2011 – 11 OWi 13 Js 20928/10, BeckRS 2011, 19912.

[81] OLG Hamm 18.2.2008 – 3 Ss OWi 51/08 = GewArch 2008, 215 (216); OLG Hamm 1.4.2008 – 3 Ss OWi 167/08 = BeckRS 2008, 8266 mn. 13.

[82] § 146 sub. 2 no. 2 und § 145 sub. 1 no. 1 lit. b GewO as well as § 117 sub. 1 no. 1 HwO [i.e. *Handwerksordnung*, Law on the Organisation of Skilled Trades].

tent authorities, but also to disregard the prohibition to employ day labourers. Penalties are imposed for intentional but also negligent violations of these regulations.

c) § 8 sub. 3 SchwarzArbG

Pursuant to § 8 sub. 3 of the SchwarzArbG, withholding social security contributions is a regulatory offence if the employer acted recklessly but not intentionally. Someone acts recklessly when breaching the law with increased (gross) negligence.[83] **90**

The intentional withholding of social security contributions is a criminal offence under § 266a StGB. Therefore, § 8 sub. 3 SchwarzArbG works – to put it simply – like a catch-all clause.[84] Since pursuant to recent court decisions, an employer does not violate § 266a StGB intentionally if they mistakenly think they are not an employer,[85] § 8 sub. 3 SchwarzArbG might be applied more often in the future.[86] **91**

Comparable to § 266a sub. 6 StGB, § 8 sub. 9 SchwarzArbG offers the possibility of self-disclosure to avoid punishment. According to this provision, no fine is imposed if the employer informs the authority collecting the social security contributions in writing what amount of contributions is withheld at due date or immediately thereafter, explains why it is impossible to pay the contributions on time despite the employer having made serious efforts to do so, and pays the withheld contributions subsequently within the reasonable period determined by the authority. **92**

d) § 8 sub. 4 and 5 SchwarzArbG

§ 8 sub. 4 and 5 SchwarzArbG establish the most significant regulatory offences in terms of the legal consequences. According to these provisions, it is a regulatory offence to intentionally issue or circulate an incorrect receipt for the execution of services or works facilitating undeclared work or illegal employment. A regulatory fine of up to 100,000 EUR may be imposed for such misbehaviour. The fine is even to up to 500,000 EUR if a perpetrator obtains financial advantages on a large scale out of gross self-interest[87] or acts as a member of a criminal gang having joined forces to committing such crimes continuously. The legislator introduced this regulatory offence claiming there are companies only founded to put such false receipts into the economic cycle.[88] **93**

2. § 10 SchwarzArbG

The purpose of § 10 SchwarzArbG is to criminalise the illegal employment of foreigners. In addition to protecting the German labour market, this provision shall protect foreign employees who cannot turn to the competent authorities safeguarding their social rights because of the illegal employment.[89] **94**

---

[83] OLG Köln 23.01.2015 – III-1 RBs 340/14, GewArch 2015, 188 referring to § 28a sub. 4 SGB IV; KK-OWiG/Rengier, 5th edn 2018, StPO § 10 mn. 49 with further references.

[84] Rettenmaier/Reichling NJW 2020, 2147 (2148); BT-Drs. 19/8691, 54.

[85] For details on the subjective element of § 266a StGB, please see → mn. 21 et seqq.

[86] Cf. BT-Drs. 19/8691, 54; cf. Jansen jurisPR-StrafR 25/2020 Comment 2; cf. von der Meden juris-PR-StrafR 23/2019 Comment 3.

[87] For the definition of financial advantages on a large scale out of gross self-interest, see → mn. 30 et seqq.

[88] BT-Drs. 19/8691, 54 et seq.; GKR ArbStrafR-HdB/Gercke Ch. 2 mn. 285 et seq.

[89] OLG Frankfurt 25.2.2005 – 1 Ss 9/04 mn. 12, BeckRS 2005, 3526, referring to a former version of this provision.

95 Pursuant to § 10 SchwarzArbG, a person is criminally liable if they employ a non-EU-foreigner[90] without the respective work permit under working conditions that are clearly less favourable than those of German employees.

96 The penalty in general is imprisonment up to three years or a fine. In very serious cases, the punishment is imprisonment of between six months and five years. Acting out of gross self-interest[91] may establish a very serious case. This may also be the case if the perpetrator acts on a commercial basis. An employer acts on a commercial basis if they plan to commit the crime repeatedly to create a permanent and significant source of income for themselves.[92]

97 Assessing whether working conditions for foreigners are clearly less favourable compared to those of German employees requires an overall comparative view of the working conditions of the foreign and a similar German employee.[93] The mere fact that a foreign employee has not been registered for social security alone does usually not constitute such disproportion.[94] However, a wage difference of one-third or even one-half is most likely an indication of disproportion.[95]

98 If the employer is not criminally liable under § 10 SchwarzArbG, they may nevertheless have violated § 404 sub. 1, sub. 2 no. 3 SGB III or § 98 sub. 2a no. 1 AufenthG. These regulations provide for regulatory fines if one intentionally or negligently employs foreigners without the appropriate work permit. In that case, the question whether the foreigner was employed under working conditions that are clearly less favourable than those of German employees is irrelevant. A regulatory fine of up to 500,000 EUR may be imposed for the violation of § 404 sub. 1, sub. 2 no. 3 SGB III or § 98 sub. 2a no. 1 AufenthG.

3. § 10a SchwarzArbG

99 In regular business life, a violation of § 10a SchwarzArbG is quite uncommon. Pursuant to § 10a SchwarzArbG, a person who employs a non-EU-foreigner without the required work permit while exploiting the circumstance that a third party commits the crime of forced labour (§ 232b StGB) or forced prostitution (§ 232a sub. 1 to 5 StGB) against the non-EU-foreigner. This is punishable with imprisonment of up to three years or with a fine.

4. § 11 SchwarzArbG

100 According to § 11 sub. 1 no. 1 SchwarzArbG the larger-scale employment of foreign nationals from non-EU-states[96] lacking the required work permits is a criminal offence. § 11 sub. 1 no. 1 SchwarzArbG is violated if at least six foreigners without the required work permit are simultaneously employed or commissioned with services.[97]

---

[90] At the moment there are no specific rules on new EU states which must be observed: GKR ArbStrafR-HdB/Gercke Ch. 2 mn. 174 et seqq.

[91] For the definition of gross self-interest, see → mn. 96.

[92] BGH 14.04.1981 – 1 StR 676/80, NStZ 1981, 303 (304); BGH 11.10.1994 – 1 StR 522/94, NStZ 1995, 85.

[93] BGH 25.10.2017 – 2 StR 50/17, NStZ 2018, 546 (547); OLG Frankfurt 25.2.2005 – 1 Ss 9/04, NStZ-RR 2005, 184 referring to a former version of this criminal provision.

[94] BGH 25.10.2017 – 2 StR 50/17, NStZ 2018, 546 (547).

[95] GKR ArbStrafR-HdB/Gercke Ch. 2 mn. 322 referring to BGH 22.04.1997 – 1 StR 701/96, BGHSt 43, 53 = NJW 1997, 2689 and BT-Drs. 18/9095, 28.

[96] At the moment there are no specific rules on new EU states which must be observed: GKR ArbStrafR-HdB/Gercke Ch. 2 mn. 174 et seqq.

[97] Cf. BGH 25.10.2017 – 1 StR 310/16, NStZ 2018, 221.

§ 11 sub. 1 no. 2 SchwarzArbG penalises an employer who persistently repeats to intentionally employ foreign nationals from non-EU-states[98] lacking the appropriate work permits. In that case, the total number of foreigners working simultaneously is irrelevant. The definition of persistently repeating is most likely to be defined in the same manner as in § 26 ArbSchG.[99] **101**

§ 11 sub. 1 no. 3 SchwarzArbG makes it a criminal offence to employ underage foreign nationals from non-EU-states. **102**

If § 11 SchwarzArbG is violated, a prison sentence of up to one year or a fine may be imposed; in very serious cases – especially if the perpetrator acted out of gross self-interest[100] – a prison sentence of up to three years or a fine can be imposed. **103**

If someone is not criminally liable under § 11 SchwarzArbG, they may nevertheless have violated § 404 sub. 1, sub. 2 no. 3 SGB III or § 98 sub. 2a no. 1 AufenthG.[101] **104**

II. Securing a general minimum wage

The *Mindestlohngesetz* (MiLoG, Act Regulating a General Minimum Wage) establishes a general minimum wage that applies across all sectors to all employees working in Germany (§§ 1, 20 MiLoG). § 21 MiLoG contains regulatory offences primarily directed at the employer. **105**

1. Non-payment of general minimum wage

A regulatory fine of up to 500,000 EUR may be imposed if the employer intentionally or negligently fails to pay the minimum wage on time (§ 21 sub. 1 no. 9, § 20 MiLoG). The same applies, if an entrepreneur has work or services carried out to a considerable extent by another enterprise that they know or negligently do not know does not pay the minimum wage on time (§ 21 sub. 2 MiLoG). **106**

Two aspects, already clarified by the criminal courts, should be kept in mind in investigations with regard to § 21 sub. 1 no. 9, sub. 2 MiLoG. Firstly, benefits of any kind – such as the provision of a vehicle or the payment of a company pension – do not count as wage.[102] Secondly, the regulatory order imposing a regulatory fine must clearly indicate who has not received the minimum wage and for how long. It is not sufficient to give this information in an annex to a regulatory order.[103] **107**

It is obvious that § 21 sub. 2 MiLoG requires that compliance measures are undertaken. Before commissioning an external contractor, but also during the term of the contract, an entrepreneur should critically check whether the minimum wage is actually paid.[104] **108**

2. Further regulatory offences

In addition to these regulatory provisions directed at the non-payment of the minimum wage, § 21 MiLoG contains provisions which can (only) result in a fine of up to **109**

---

98 At the moment there are no specific rules on new EU states which must be observed: GKR ArbStrafR-HdB/Gercke Ch. 2 mn. 174 et seqq.

99 For the respective definition, see → mn. 57.

100 For the definition gross self-interest, see → mn. 96.

101 For these regulatory offences, please see → mn. 94 et seqq.

102 BayObLG 26.11.2020 – 201 ObOWi 1381/20, NJW 2021, 2667 (2268).

103 AG Dortmund 18.2.2019 – 729 OWi – 257 Js 149/19 – 34/19, BeckRS 2019, 6840 mn. 3.

104 Friedrich CB 2022, 8 (11 et seqq.).

30,000 EUR. These regulatory offences refer to violations of formal requirements under the MiLoG, such as the obligations to cooperate, the transmission of data, the registration of employees or record-keeping obligations.

3. Risk of wage usury

110 Cases in which the wage paid to the employee is strikingly lower than the minimum wage, might also constitute the criminal offence of wage usury pursuant to § 291 sub. 1 no. 3 StGB, if an emergency, lack of experience, lack of judgment or substantial will weakness of the employee is exploited. The potential penalty for such wage usury is imprisonment up to three years or a fine.

111 A strikingly lower wage in terms of criminal law is considered a wage of only two-third or one-half of the minimum wage or even less.[105]

III. Protecting hired-out employees

112 In general, it is possible to hire one company's employee to work in another. However, an employer who wishes to hire-out an employee (*Leiharbeitnehmer*) to work in another company must obtain a specific permission from the local employment agency (*Agentur für Arbeit*, § 1 sub. 1 sent. 1 AÜG). To avoid any misunderstanding, an A1 certificate (formerly E-101 certificate) does not include this permit.[106]

113 The regulations of the *Arbeitnehmerüberlassungsgesetz* (AÜG, Act on Temporary Agency Work) serve to, in particular, protect the hired-out worker.[107] Hence, § 8 sub. 1 AÜG stipulates the hirer's obligation to pay the hired-out workers the same salary as their own employees and ensure the same work conditions (principle of equality).

114 In practice, it is often necessary to differentiate between the hiring-out of an employee (with the consequence of the AÜG being applicable) and a service contract between two companies with the employee working as an auxiliary for their employer at another company (with the consequence of the AÜG not being applicable). In order to differentiate between these two constellations, § 1 sub. 1 sent. 2 AÜG considers it a hiring-out of an employee (and not just a service contract) if the employee is integrated into the work organisation of the hirer and subject to their instructions.

115 The AÜG contains criminal provisions in § 15 as well as § 15a and regulatory offences in § 16.

1. § 15 sub. 1 AÜG

116 § 15 sub. 1 AÜG addresses the lender of employees (the person lending employees to another company). The lender is subject to prosecution if they hire-out a non-EU employee[108] to a third party without the appropriate work permit and without a permit to hire-out employees. The potential penalty is up to three years of imprisonment or a fine.

---

[105] OLG Köln 28.3.2003 – 1 Zs 120/03 – 19/03, NStZ-RR 2003, 212 (213) with further references (two-third of minimum wage); cf. Friedrich CB 2022, 8 (9) (two-third of minimum wage); cf. also BT-Drs. 18/9095, 28 (one-half of minimum wage).

[106] OLG Bamberg 9.8.2016 – 3 Ss OWi 494/16, DStR 2016, 2349 (2350).

[107] Erbs/Kohlhaas/Häberle, 255. EL Januar 2025, AÜG Vor. § 1 mn. 3; OLG Hamm 18.10.2016 – III-3 RBs 277/16, BeckRS 2016, 19209 mn. 14; BT-Drs. 6/2303, 9; GKR ArbStrafR-HdB/Kraft Ch. 2 mn. 367.

[108] At the moment there are no specific rules on new EU states which must be observed: GKR ArbStrafR-HdB/Gercke Ch. 2 mn. 174 et seqq.

In a very serious case, the penalty is even six months to five years of imprisonment (§ 15 sub. 2 AÜG). A very serious case is assumed, if the offender acts on a commercial basis[109] or out of gross self-interest[110] (§ 15 sub. 2 AÜG).

2. § 15a AÜG and § 16 sub. 1 no. 2, sub. 2 AÜG

§ 15a AÜG is directed at the hirer (the person receiving the hired-out employees, *Entleiher*). Pursuant to § 15a sub. 1 AÜG, it is a punishable offence if the hirer intentionally allows a non-EU foreigner[111] to work without the required work permit under working conditions that are clearly less favourable than the working conditions of German hired-out workers who perform the same or comparable work.[112] The penalty is imprisonment of up to three years or a fine. In very serious cases (committing the crime on a commercial basis or out of gross self-interest)[113] the penalty is imprisonment of six months to five years. **117**

According to § 15a sub. 2 AÜG, a hirer who allows more than five non-EU foreigners[114] to work at the same time without the required work permit or who persistently repeats employing a non-EU foreigner without such work permit exposes themselves to prosecution. The hirer may face imprisonment of up to one year or a fine. If the offender acts out of gross self-interest,[115] the penalty is even imprisonment of up to three years or a fine. **118**

If the hirer only allows up to four foreign employees from non-EU states[116] to work for him without the respective work permit at the same time and without persistent repetition, they only violate a regulatory offence, which can be committed intentionally or negligently (§ 16 sub. 1 no. 2 AÜG). The potential regulatory fine is up to 500,000 EUR (§ 16 sub. 2 AÜG). **119**

3. Further regulatory offences

Moreover, the AÜG stipulates further regulatory offences affecting the hirer as well as the lender. These relate, in particular, to intentional or negligent violations of the provisions on whether and under what conditions the hiring-out of employees is considered legal (§ 16 sub. 1 no. 1 to 1f, 2a to 6, 7a to 10, 14 to 18 AÜG).[117] A regulatory fine can also be imposed on anyone who fails to comply with their obligations to cooperate with the authorities (§ 16 sub. 1 no. 6a, 11 to 13 AÜG). Depending on what provision was violated, regulatory fines of up to 1,000 EUR or up to 500,000 EUR may be imposed. **120**

---

[109] Please see → mn. 96 for the definition of commercial basis.

[110] For the definition gross self-interest, see → mn. 96.

[111] At the moment there are no specific rules on new EU states which must be observed: GKR ArbStrafR-HdB/Gercke Ch. 2 mn. 174 et seqq.

[112] To assess what clearly less favourable working conditions are, please see → mn. 97 et seqq.

[113] Please see → mn. 96 for the definition of commercial basis and → mn. 31 for the definition of gross self-interest.

[114] At the moment there are no specific rules on new EU states which must be observed: GKR ArbStrafR-HdB/Gercke Ch. 2 mn. 174 et seqq.

[115] For the definition of gross self-interest, see → mn. 31.

[116] At the moment there are no specific rules on new EU states which must be observed: GKR ArbStrafR-HdB/Gercke Ch. 2 mn. 174 et seqq.

[117] Cf. BayObLG 22.1.2020 – 201 ObOWi 2474/19, NJW 2020, 1597 (engaging hired-out employees for more than 18 months).

IV. Employees posted across borders

121 When the *Arbeitnehmerentsendegesetz* (AEntG, Posted Workers Act) was passed, its main purpose was to secure appropriate minimum working conditions for employees posted cross-border and employees regularly working in Germany. However, after legislative reforms, the AEntG now does not only cover cross-border cases but also purely domestic ones.[118] Therefore, the purpose of the AEntG is, inter alia, to secure fair working conditions for all employees working in Germany (§ 1 sent. 1 AEntG). In practice, there are more domestic than cross-border cases under review.[119]

122 On the one hand, the AEntG orders that the fundamental German rules of employment, such as the minimum wage, maximum working hours, minimum holidays, minimum rest periods, and work safety regulations, are applicable to employment relationships between an employer abroad and its workers employed in Germany (§ 2 sub. 1 AEntG). In the case of long-term postings of employees, which generally occur from twelve months onwards (§ 13b sub. 1 sent. 1 AEntG), almost all German rules of employment apply.

123 On the other hand, pursuant to § 8 AEntG German employers and employers from abroad must comply with collective agreements of which they are a party or which have been declared binding for the entire industry.

124 In § 23 AEntG two different groups of regulatory offences are established. According to § 23 sub. 1 no. 2 to 9 AEntG, certain intentional or negligent violations of obligations to report to or to cooperate with the authorities may be punishable with a regulatory fine of up to 30,000 EUR.

125 However, the regulatory offences established by § 23 sub. 1 no. 1 and sub. 2 AEntG, which can result in a fine of up to 500,000 EUR, are much more significant and relevant in practice. Pursuant to § 23 sub. 1 no. 1 AEntG, an employer is in breach of the law if they intentionally or negligently fail to grant their employees at least the working conditions stipulated in a collective agreement binding for the respective industry.

126 According to § 23 sub. 2 AEntG, it is a regulatory offence to engage a contractor who does not comply with the applicable working conditions if the perpetrator is aware of this non-compliance or negligently not aware. Here it is, again, obvious that compliance measures must be undertaken. Before commissioning an external contractor, but also during the term of the contract, an entrepreneur should critically check whether the contractor complies with the applicable working conditions.

E. Collective labour law

127 The collective labour law, regulating the relationships between employers and the representative bodies of employees, is firmly rooted in the German tradition. The freedom of association, which guarantees that unions and employers' associations can be founded, is even guaranteed by the constitution (Art. 9 para. 3 GG). In addition to this freedom of association, there is the right to negotiate collective agreements including the right to strike and the right of co-determination for employees in companies.

---

[118] Cf. GKR ArbStrafR-HdB/Kraft Ch. 2 mn. 681.
[119] WJS WirtschaftsStrafR-HdB/Riediger/Schilling, 5th edn 2020, Ch. 20 mn. 253.

The collective labour law establishes criminal offences in § 119 BetrVG (*Betriebsverfassungsgesetz*, Works Constitution Act, → mn. 129 et seqq.) and in § 34 SprAuG (*Sprecherausschussgesetz*, Executives' Committee Act, → mn. 141 et seqq.). 128

I. Protection of works councils

The criminal provision of § 119 BetrVG is intended to protect the activities of works 129 councils and their members to create a balance between the entrepreneurial freedom of choice on the one hand and the employees' right of self-determinate working.[120]

This criminal provision has been known to a wider public since the criminal pro- 130 ceedings in the Siemens[121] and Volkswagen[122] cases and became increasingly important afterwards – at least in the context of companies' compliance measures.[123] Not only can the employer be a potential perpetrator of the criminal provisions of § 119 sub. 1 BetrVG, but in principle anyone.[124] A violation of this criminal provision can result in a prison sentence of up to one year or a fine.

1. § 119 sub. 1 no. 1 BetrVG

§ 119 sub. 1 no. 1 BetrVG makes it a criminal offence to obstruct and influence works 131 councils' elections – in particular by threatening with disadvantages or promising advantages. Obstruction is any measure that impedes or delays the election, its preparation or its conclusion.[125] Influencing the electorate directly (e.g. by buying votes) as well as granting advantages affecting the election indirectly is prohibited.[126] The employer is subject to strict neutrality and in particular may not campaign for certain candidates.[127] However, such conduct is only punishable if the election is actually obstructed or influenced; the mere activity aimed at such obstruction or influence does not constitute a crime.[128]

2. § 119 sub. 1 no. 2 BetrVG

Pursuant to § 119 sub. 1 no. 2 BetrVG, anyone who obstructs or disturbs the activities 132 of a works council is liable to prosecution. For example, an employer may be prosecuted

---

[120] Cf. BGH 17.9.2009 – 5 StR 521/08, BGHSt 54, 148 = NJW 2010, 92 (97); BGH 13.9.2010 – 1 StR 220/09, BGHSt 55, 288 = NJW 2011, 88 (91); cf. also BGH 10.1.2023 – 6 StR 133/22, BeckRS 2023, 143 with LG Braunschweig 28.9.2021 – 16 KLs 406 Js 59398/16 (85/19), BeckRS 2021, 47174, as the preliminary instance, where the defendants were not charged with § 119 sub. 1 BetrVG as there was no criminal complaint filed but with embezzlement (§ 266 StGB) of company's money.

[121] BGH 13.9.2010 – 1 StR 220/09, BGHSt 55, 288 = NJW 2011, 88.

[122] BGH 17.9.2009 – 5 StR 521/08, BGHSt 54, 148 = NJW 2010, 92.

[123] Rotsch Criminal Compliance/Eisele § 22 mn. 65; cf. also LAG Köln 21.1.2008 – 14 TaBV 44/07, BeckRS 2008, 52737.

[124] GKR ArbStrafR-HdB/Richter Ch. 2 mn. 1131.

[125] BayObLG 29.7.1980 – RReg 4 St 173/80, BayObLGSt 1980, 64; LG Braunschweig 28.4.1999 – 37 Ns 703 Js 15338/98, NStZ-RR 2000, 93 (93 et seq.); MüKoStGB/Mosbacher BetrVG § 119 mn. 7 et seqq.; BeckOK ArbR/Werner, 75. Ed. 1.3.2025, BetrVG § 119 mn. 2 with further references.

[126] BGH 13.9.2010 – 1 StR 220/09, BGHSt 55, 299 = NJW 2011, 88 mn. 51 et seq.

[127] BGH 13.9.2010 – 1 StR 220/09, BGHSt 55, 299 = NJW 2011, 88 (94).

[128] ErfK/Kania, 22nd edn 2022, BetrVG § 119 mn. 2; BeckOK ArbR/Werner, 75. Ed. 1.3.2023, BetrVG § 119 mn. 1 with further references; Rieble/Klebeck NZA 2006, 758 (767).

if they ban members of the works council from the company's premises[129] or advise employees to skip an employees' meeting organised by a works council.[130]

133 However, disregarding the works council's rights of co-determination – for example by failing to consult the works council before dismissing an employee – does, by itself, not constitute a criminal offence,[131] unless the employer repeatedly and persistently disregards these rights or deliberately pushes the works council aside.[132] Yet, if this threshold to criminal liability is not crossed, a violation of the duty to inform or give statement to the works council may be prosecuted as a regulatory offence according to § 121 BetrVG.

3. § 119 sub. 1 no. 3 BetrVG

134 Pursuant to § 119 sub. 1 no. 3 BetrVG, anyone who favours or discriminates against a works council's member because of their activities on the works council may also be liable to prosecution. This provision is meant to ensure the independence of works council members.[133]

135 A works council's member is disadvantaged, for example, if they are assigned to a worse job by their employer.

136 Unlike the punishable commercial bribery (§ 299 StGB)[134], favouritism in case of § 119 sub. 1 no. 3 BetrVG does not require an agreement between the person providing the bribe and the recipient; it is sufficient that the recipient is put in a better position for the sake of their activity for the works council.[135] Pursuant to § 37 sub. 1 BetrVG, members of the works council exercise their office on an honorary basis only, without remuneration, and, in principle, only receive their former salary while being released from their employee's duties. Therefore, the threshold to a criminal offence can quickly be exceeded, if the employer grants (hidden) benefits to works council's members.[136]

137 If a works council's member receives an excessive salary from the employing company, representatives of the company may also face criminal charges of embezzling company's funds (§ 266 StGB).[137] Should the excessive salary have been deducted from the company's tax, criminal charges based on tax evasion (§ 370 AO) are also likely.[138]

138 Should it only be noticed retrospectively that a works council's member received an excessive salary, there is the risk that, if the representatives of the company do not reclaim the excessive salary and do not correct the company's tax declaration, they may face criminal charges of embezzlement (§ 266 StGB) and tax evasion (§ 370 AO).[139]

---

[129] LG Siegen 13.11.1986 – 6 Ls 25 Js 354/84 S 2/85.

[130] OLG Stuttgart 09.09.1988 – 1 Ws 237/88, NStZ 1989, 31 (31).

[131] BAGE 4, 306 = NJW 1958, 37 (39) referring to an older version of the criminal provision; Richardi BetrVG/Annuß BetrVG § 119 mn. 21; BeckOK ArbR/Werner, 63. Ed. 1.6.2022, BetrVG § 119 mn. 6.

[132] BAGE 4, 306 = NJW 1958, 37 (39); Richardi BetrVG/Annuß BetrVG § 119 mn. 20; cf. Pasewaldt ZIS 2007, 75 (79).

[133] MüKoStGB/Mosbacher BetrVG § 119 mn. 21.

[134] Please see → Ch. 10 on corruption for details.

[135] Rieble CCZ 2008, 121 (125).

[136] GKR ArbStrafR-HdB/Richter Ch. 2 mn. 1152 et seq. with further references.

[137] BGH 17.9.2009 – 5 StR 521/08, BGHSt 54, 148 = NJW 2010, 92 (95 et seq.); BGH 10.1.2023 – 6 StR 133/22, BeckRS 2023, 143 with LG Braunschweig 28.9.2021 – 16 KLs 406 Js 59398/16 (85/19), BeckRS 2021, 47174 as the preliminary instance; BGH 20.6.2018 – 4 StR 561/17, NStZ-RR 2018, 349 (350); different *obiter dictum* in BGH 13.9.2010 – 1 StR 220/09, BGHSt 55, 288 = NJW 2011, 88 (90 et seq.); Mosbacher CCZ 2023, 45 (46); Johnson CCZ 2021, 75 (80).

[138] Mosbacher CCZ 2023, 45 (46); Johnson CCZ 2021, 75 (80).

[139] Mosbacher CCZ 2023, 45 (46).

4. Criminal complaint

The criminal offences of § 119 BetrVG can only be prosecuted if either the works council, the electoral board, the employer or a union (active in the company) has filed a criminal complaint (§ 119 sub. 2 BetrVG).[140] Procurators of the company are not entitled to file such a complaint.[141] **139**

If a works council requires legal assistance to exercise its right to file a criminal complaint, the employer has to bear the costs thereof.[142] **140**

II. Protection of committee of spokespersons

The BetrVG does not cover managerial employees, i.e. employees working in senior positions for their employer (§ 5 sub. 3 BetrVG). Therefore, in companies with at least ten senior employees, a committee of spokespersons can be elected based on the SprAuG. **141**

Founding a committee of the spokespersons as well as its activity is – similar to the provisions of § 119 sub. 1 BetrVG[143] – protected by the criminal provision of § 34 sub. 1 SprAuG which stipulates up to one year's imprisonment or a fine. This criminal offence can also only be prosecuted if a criminal complaint by the committee of the spokespersons, the electoral board or the employer is filed (§ 34 sub. 2 SprAuG). **142**

Disregarding the committee of the spokespersons' right of co-determination alone does not constitute a criminal offence unless the employer repeatedly and persistently disregards these rights or deliberately pushes the committee of the spokespersons aside. In case this threshold is not exceeded, the violation of the right of co-determination may constitute a regulatory offence pursuant to § 36 SprAuG. **143**

F. Procedural peculiarities

In this section, some procedural peculiarities of criminal and regulatory fine proceedings related to criminal labour law will be highlighted, namely which authorities can be involved in such proceedings (→ mn. 145 et seqq.) and which consequences outside the criminal proceedings may occur (→ mn. 164 et seqq.). **144**

I. Authorities involved

Besides the public prosecutor's office, other authorities may be involved in criminal and regulatory fine proceedings concerning criminal labour law. The most important authorities are described in the following. **145**

---

[140] In the case BGH 10.1.2023 – 6 StR 133/22, BeckRS 2023, 143 with LG Braunschweig 28.9.2021 – 16 KLs 406 Js 59398/16 (85/19), BeckRS 2021, 47174, mn. 387 as the preliminary instance, no criminal complaint was filed. Therefore, the defendants were not also charged with § 119 sub. 1 no. 3 BetrVG.

[141] BGH 17.9.2009 – 5 StR 521/08, BGHSt 54, 148 = NJW 2010, 92 (97 et seq.).

[142] LAG Düsseldorf 12.8.1993 – 14 TaBV 54/93 = NZA 1994, 1052.

[143] For details on the criminal provision, please see → mn. 129 et seqq.

1. Finanzkontrolle Schwarzarbeit

146 The authorities of the customs administration are of particular importance when prosecuting the withholding of social security contributions (§ 266a StGB) or any other criminal and regulatory offence directed at combating illegal employment.[144] The so-called *Finanzkontrolle Schwarzarbeit* (Financial Control for Undeclared Work), based at the respective *Hauptzollamt* (main customs offices), is the responsible department of the customs administration and a subordinate to the *Generaldirektion VII* (general customs directorate VII).[145]

147 §§ 2 et seqq. SchwarzArbG stipulate that the *Finanzkontrolle Schwarzarbeit* has the right to conduct inspections and that the employer has to tolerate these and cooperate with the *Finanzkontrolle Schwarzarbeit*. These regulations are so-called preventive police measures, which do not require any particular suspicion that a criminal or regulatory offence was committed.[146]

148 The *Finanzkontrolle Schwarzarbeit* checks whether the company is compliant with the various laws on illegal employment, in particular the *Mindestlohngesetz* (MiLoG), the *Arbeitnehmerüberlassungsgesetz* (AÜG) and the *Arbeitnehmerentsendegesetz* (AEntG). Often, these pre-emptive checks are the starting point for criminal or regulatory fine proceedings.

149 Should the *Finanzkontrolle Schwarzarbeit* exercise its right to enter the company's premises, it may be necessary to point out that this right applies to exceptional cases only.[147] Moreover, the *Finanzkontrolle Schwarzarbeit* is not authorised to carry out dawn raid at a company.[148] According to constitutional law, in principle only a judge can order a dawn raid (and not the *Finanzkontrolle Schwarzarbeit*).[149]

150 Furthermore, it should be kept in mind that according to § 5 sub. 1 sent. 2 SchwarzArbG, there is a right to withhold information, if providing the information would expose one (or their close relatives) to the risk of being prosecuted for a criminal or regulatory offence. The SchwarzArbG does not require the *Finanzkontrolle Schwarzarbeit* to inform the person concerned about this right. However, because of the right to freedom from self-incrimination and the principle of fair trial, it is reasonable to argue for an obligation to inform the respective persons based on their constitutional rights (and an exclusion of evidence improperly obtained) at least if there is a reasonable possibility that a criminal or regulatory offence has been committed.[150]

151 If an inspection within the scope of §§ 2 et seqq. SchwarzArbG reveals that a criminal or regulatory offence has been committed, the *Finanzkontrolle Schwarzarbeit* must discontinue its pre-emptive inspection and open preliminary criminal or regulatory fine proceedings establishing specific rights for the accused persons and witnesses.[151] If

---

[144] Please see → mn. 77 et seqq. for the respective criminal and regulatory offences.

[145] Höchstetter p. 446 et seqq. referring to the legal situation since 2016; GKR ArbStrafR-HdB/Gercke Ch. 1 mn. 198 et seqq.; WJS WirtschaftsStrafR-HdB/Riediger/Schilling, 5th edn 2020, Ch. 20 mn. 3 et seq.

[146] FG Hamburg 20.10.2010 – 4 K 34/10, BeckRS 2011, 94442; Erbs/Kohlhaas/Ambs/Lutz, 255. EL Januar 2025, SchwarzArbG § 2a mn. 1a; GKR ArbStrafR-HdB/Gercke Ch. 1 mn. 209.

[147] Höchstetter p. 161.

[148] Petri ArbStrafR D mn. 389.

[149] GKR ArbStrafR-HdB/Gercke Ch. 1 mn. 207; cf. Erbs/Kohlhaas/Ambs/Lutz, 255. EL Januar 2025, SchwarzArbG § 3 mn. 5 et seqq.

[150] In detail: Höchstetter p. 238 et seqq., 271; Petri ArbStrafR D mn. 404 et seqq. However, OLG Bamberg 15.1.2013 – 2 Ss OWi 897/12 = GewArch 2013, 212 does not see such obligation.

[151] GKR ArbStrafR-HdB/Gercke Ch. 1 mn. 213 with further references; OVG Magdeburg 14.10.2019 – 1 M 92/19 = BeckRS 2019, 25853 mn. 16.

the *Finanzkontrolle Schwarzarbeit* fails to do so, any evidence found may not be used in criminal or regulatory fine proceedings.[152]

152 The *Finanzkontrolle Schwarzarbeit* is not only responsible for the pre-emptive inspections pursuant to §§2 et seqq. SchwarzArbG, but also investigates criminal and regulatory offences related to illegal employment for the public prosecutor's office (§ 14 SchwarzArbG).

153 § 14a sub. 1 SchwarzArbG even allows the *Finanzkontrolle Schwarzarbeit* to independently conduct preliminary proceedings in cases where social security contributions pursuant to § 266a StGB are withheld if the public prosecutor's office handed over the respective criminal case to the *Finanzkontrolle Schwarzarbeit*. However, such handover is impossible, among other circumstances, if the case is particularly complex (§ 14a sub. 2 no. 4 SchwarzArbG). In any case, the public prosecutor's office can take the matter back from the *Finanzkontrolle Schwarzarbeit* at any time (§ 14a sub. 4 SchwarzArbG).

154 If the *Finanzkontrolle Schwarzarbeit* conducts the investigation on its own, it may apply for an order imposing punishment (*Strafbefehl*) to the competent criminal court via the public prosecutor's office if the investigation provides sufficient grounds for a charge of withholding of social security contributions (§ 266a StGB); otherwise, it must submit the files to the public prosecutor's office (§ 14b sub. 3 SchwarzArbG).

155 Finally, the *Finanzkontrolle Schwarzarbeit* is also responsible for the prosecution of some of the regulatory offences regarding illegal employment (for further details see: § 12 sub. 1 no. 4 SchwarzArbG, § 21 sub. 4 in conjunction with § 14 MiLoG and § 23 sub. 4 in conjunction with § 16 AEntG, § 16 sub. 3 AÜG).

2. Work safety authorities

156 Each of the 16 states (*Bundesländer*) of the Federal Republic of Germany determines which authority is responsible for monitoring whether work safety regulations are met and for prosecuting potential regulatory offences regarding work safety.[153]

157 To pre-emptively monitor whether a company complies with the work safety regulations, these authorities have the right to access and inspect the company (§§ 21 et. seq. ArbSchG).[154] In such pre-emptive audits, the person obliged to provide information may refuse to answer questions or submit documents, which would expose themselves (or close relatives) to the risk of prosecution (§ 22 sub. 1 sent 3 ArbSchG). By law, the authorities have to inform the person under obligation to provide the information that they have this right to remain silent (§ 22 sub. 1 sent. 4 ArbSchG). In case of a violation of this obligation, the evidence improperly obtained may be excluded.[155]

158 For regulatory fine proceedings due to the violation of the law on severely disabled persons, the *Bundesagentur für Arbeit* (Federal Employment Agency) is the competent authority (§ 238 sub. 3 SGB IX).

159 Should there be a suspicion that not only a regulatory offence, but a criminal provision regarding work safety was violated, the local public prosecutor's office is responsible for the respective criminal proceedings.

---

152 OVG Magdeburg 14.10.2019 – 1 M 92/19 = BeckRS 2019, 25853 mn. 16; Petri ArbStrafR D mn. 406 et seq.; Höchstetter p. 268 et seq.

153 KKS/Schucht ArbSchG § 21 mn. 65 et seqq.; GKR ArbStrafR-HdB/Gercke Ch. 1 mn. 238 et seq.; § 36 OWiG in conjunction with the respective regulations by the sixteen states.

154 In detail: MAH ArbR/Bücker, 6th edn 2024, § 174 mn. 87.

155 Petri ArbStrafR D mn. 42.

3. Deutsche Rentenversicherung

160 The authorities responsible for the pension funds, in practice usually the *Deutsche Rentenversicherung* (German pension insurance), review whether the employer fully complies with their social security obligations at least every four years (§ 28p sub. 1 sent. 1 SGB IV). Such audits are often the reason for criminal proceedings related to the withholding of social security contributions (§ 266a StGB) being initiated.

161 In practice, in preliminary proceedings regarding the withholding of social security contributions (§ 266a StGB), the public prosecutor's office often asks the *Deutsche Rentenversicherung* to determine whether and to what extent social security contributions have not been paid. In consequence, the *Deutsche Rentenversicherung* is treated like an expert witness in the preliminary proceedings, despite being the authority potentially disadvantaged and, therefore, potentially being biased.

4. Tax authorities

162 In many criminal proceedings regarding criminal labour law, the public prosecutor's office also investigates whether the income taxes for the employees have been paid. This is the case because the employer must deduct these taxes from the employee's wage and wire it to the competent tax authority (§ 38, § 41a EStG). If an employer has violated this obligation, the employer may have committed tax evasion should the employee not have paid their income taxes.

163 In such cases, the public prosecutor's office will often ask the tax authority to give their expertise in the preliminary proceedings.

II. Extra-criminal consequences

164 In any proceedings concerning criminal labour law, criminal defence lawyers need to keep an eye on potential extra-criminal consequences. The following explanations shall help with that but cannot exhaustively describe all possible extra-criminal consequences.

1. Exclusion from leading positions in GmbH and AG

165 A person who has been sentenced to a term of imprisonment of at least one year for withholding social security contributions (§ 266a StGB) cannot be managing director of a *Gesellschaft mit beschränkter Haftung* (GmbH) or a member of the executive board of an *Aktiengesellschaft* (AG) for a period of five years from the date of the final sentence (§ 6 sub. 2 sent. 2 no. 3 lit. e GmbHG, § 76 sub. 3 no. 3 lit. e AktG).

2. Unreliability pursuant to § 35 sub. 1 GewO

166 Pursuant to § 35 sub. 1 GewO, a person may be prohibited from carrying on a business if there are facts which show their unreliability and such prohibition is necessary to protect the general public or their employees. The GewO does not define what constitutes unreliability. Most assume a person to be unreliable within the meaning of § 35 sub. 1 GewO if they do not offer any guarantee that they will carry out their business properly

in the future.[156] If an employer persistently breaches their obligation under social security laws – being criminally liable pursuant to § 266a StGB – they may generally be considered unreliable.[157]

3. Entry in Gewerbezentralregister and Wettbewerbsregister

The *Bundesamt für Justiz* (Federal Ministry of Justice) maintains the *Gewerbezentralregister* (Central Trade and Industry Register, § 149 sub. 1 GewO). Final decisions imposing regulatory fines connected to the business are entered in this register if the fine was more than 200 EUR (§ 149 sub. 2 no. 3 GewO). **167**

Moreover, any business-related final convictions for a criminal offence pursuant to § 10, § 11 SchwarzArbG, § 15 und § 15a AÜG and § 266a sub. 1, 2 und 4 StGB are registered if the sentence was more than three months of imprisonment or if a fine of more than 90 daily rates was imposed (§ 149 sub. 2 no. 4 GewO). **168**

The competent criminal courts and regulatory fine authorities have to inform the *Bundesamt für Justiz* about the respective decisions so that these can be entered in the register (§ 149 sub. 3 sent. 1 GewO). An entry is in general deleted after five years (cf. § 153 GewO). **169**

Moreover there is a *Wettbewerbsregister* (Competition Register) hold by the *Bundeskartellamt* (Federal Cartel Office) in which certain business-related convictions and fines are registered (§ 2 WRegG [*Wettbewerbsregistergesetz*, Competition Register Act]). **170**

Entries in this register are generally deleted three or five years (depending on the severity of the non-compliance) after the final decision (§ 7 sub. 1 WRegG). However, a company may seek early deregistration by showing that it has undertaken a so-called 'self-cleaning' (*Selbstreinigung*) within the meaning of § 123 sub. 4 sent. 2 or § 125 GWB (§ 8 WRegG). In the case of violations of § 266a StGB, § 123 sub. 4 sent. 2 GWB applies. For self-cleaning, this provision requires that the company has paid the social security contributions or has committed to paying them including interest, late payment and penalty surcharges. For any other criminal and regulatory offence in connection with criminal labour law, § 125 GWB applies. Pursuant to this provision, a company cleaned itself if it compensated any damage, cooperated with the competent authorities and introduced compliance measures.[158] **171**

4. Exclusion from public tenders

Pursuant to § 123 sub. 4 GWB, a company must be excluded from public tenders if it has not fulfilled its obligation to pay taxes or social security contributions in cases where this has been established by a final judicial or administrative decision or where the contracting authority can prove the breach of such obligation in another suitable manner. **172**

In addition, pursuant to § 21 SchwarzArbG, § 21 AEntG, § 19 MiLoG and § 98c AufenthG, a company can be excluded from a public tender in case of violations of specific criminal and regulatory offences directed at combating illegal employment. **173**

---

[156] BVerwGE 65, 1 = NVwZ 1982, 503 (503 et seq.); VGH München 20.7.2016 – 22 ZB 16.284, BeckRS 2016, 50123 mn. 9; Petri ArbStrafR J mn. 45.

[157] BayVGH 5.10.2018 – 22 ZB 18.841, BeckRS 2018, 25015 mn. 17.

[158] In detail: Herrlinger/Ahlenstiel WuW 2022, 396 (398 et seqq.).

CHAPTER 20
ENVIRONMENTAL CRIMINAL LAW, PRODUCT CRIMINAL LAW, AND FOOD CRIMINAL LAW[1]

Bibliography: Horn, Bindung des Strafrechts an Entscheidungen der Atombehörde? – Lehren aus dem Alkem-Urteil, NJW 1988, 2335; Kühne, Strafrechtliche Produkthaftung in Deutschland, NJW 1997, 1951; Schmidt-Salzer, Konkretisierungen der strafrechtlichen Produkt- und Umweltverantwortung, NJW 1996, 1.

Table of contents

A. Environmental criminal law 498
I. Introduction 498
II. Environmental criminal offences 499
1. Unauthorised waste management (§ 326 StGB) 500
2. Unauthorised operation of facilities (§ 327 StGB) 502
3. Unauthorised shipment of waste 503
a) Unauthorised shipment of hazardous waste (§ 326 sub. 2 StGB) 503
b) Illegal shipment of hazardous waste (§ 18a AbfVerbrG). 504
c) Illegal shipment of non-hazardous waste (§ 18b AbfVerbrG) 505
4. Water pollution (§ 324 StGB) 505
5. Soil pollution (§ 324a StGB) 506
6. Air pollution (§ 325 StGB) 507
7. Causing noise, vibrations and non-ionising radiation (§ 325a StGB) 507
8. Unauthorised handling of radioactive substances and other hazardous substances and goods (§ 328 StGB) 508
9. Endangering protected areas (§ 329 StGB) 509
10. Causing severe danger by releasing poisons (§ 330a StGB) . 509
11. Protection of wildlife and biodiversity 510
a) § 17 TierSchG 510
b) § 71 BNatSchG 510
c) § 71a BNatSchG 511
B. Product criminal law 512
I. Introduction 512
II. Legal sources and offences 512
1. Core criminal law 512
2. Secondary criminal law 513
III. Duties of the entrepreneur 513
1. Product development 513
2. Sale 514
3. Recall of the defective product 514
4. Case law 515
a) Leather spray case 515
b) Lipobay scandal 516
c) Wood preservative proceeding 517

[1] I would like to thank my two assistants, Katharina Sachen and Hannah Clüsserath, for their excellent support with the articles on environmental criminal law, product criminal law and food criminal law.

d) Monza Steel case ... 517
e) Eschede ICE accident case ... 518
f) Thalidomide proceedings ... 518
g) Ice-rink in Reichenhall case ... 519
h) Bienenstich case ... 520
C. Food criminal law ... 520
I. Introduction ... 520
II. Legal sources and offences ... 521
1. Core criminal law ... 521
2. Secondary criminal law ... 521
III. Criminal offences ... 521
1. Production ... 522
2. Treatment ... 522
3. Placing on the market ... 522
4. Transfer ... 523
5. Export ... 523
IV. Obligations of the entrepreneur ... 523
1. Duty of investigation ... 523
2. Auditing duty ... 524
3. Obligation of representation and delegation ... 524
4. Information duty ... 524
5. Traceability ... 525

A. Environmental criminal law

I. Introduction

1 Environmental criminal law is considered to be expert criminal law due to its complex and convoluted requirements that refer to non-criminal provisions (so-called *Blankettnorm*). Its main objective is to sanction environmental offences committed by business enterprises.[2] Particular relevance is given to environmental criminal law in the case of conduct in the business world involving the handling of hazardous waste. Since nearly every commercial or industrial sector requires environmentally relevant permits,[3] violating them can have criminal consequences. In addition to repressive sanctioning efforts, environmental criminal law also pursues a general preventive goal. The threat of legal sanctions is thus also intended to have a deterrent effect. Environmental criminal law as part of commercial criminal law[4] serves as *ultima ratio* for the protection of the environment.

2 German law does not have a uniform environmental code. Each area of law is regulated in separate legislation. Until the amendment of the Criminal Code by the 18th Criminal Law Amendment Act, there was also no uniform environmental criminal code. It was not until 1 July 1980, with the broad approval of all political parties, that a new 29th division was created in the Criminal Code (StGB), which henceforth bundled offences against the environment. In addition to the StGB, further criminal provisions can be found in special laws such as §§ 27 et seqq. ChemG (Chemicals Act) and §§ 71, 71a BNatSchG (Federal Nature Conservation Act). A distinction is made between environmental criminal law in the narrower sense (core criminal law of the StGB) and in the broader sense (secondary

[2] Börner UmweltStrafR mn. 58; Saliger UmweltStrafR mn. 15.
[3] Börner UmweltStrafR mn. 58.
[4] Börner UmweltStrafR mn. 58.

criminal law). Important areas of environmental criminal law involve the protection of water, soil, nature, immission and radiation, as well as protection against the improper handling of waste and sewage.

In environmental criminal law, the principle of accessoriness of administrative law applies. This is an integral part of environmental criminal law and illustrates a strict interdependence between criminal and administrative law. Thus, criminal law cannot prohibit what administrative law allows. 3

According to the norms of environmental criminal law, it is therefore not a criminal offence to act in accordance with the relevant administrative regulations and decisions of the administration.[5] The interdependence between criminal and administrative law can be clearly seen in the wording of most environmental offences. These require either an action without a corresponding permit (e.g. § 326 sub. 1 StGB: 'Whoever, without being authorised to do so […] discharges […] waste […]'), an action against administrative acts issued by authorities (e.g. § 327 sub. 1 StGB: 'Whoever […] contrary to an enforceable prohibition') or an action contrary to a statutory instrument (e.g. § 329 sub. 1 StGB: 'Whoever, contrary to a statutory instrument […]').[6] The authorities that grant or deny administrative permits and licences are therefore of decisive importance. If no permit is granted, if such a permit is exceeded or if an action is carried out after the expiry of the time limit of the permit, the action is not legitimised under administrative law and criminal liability is possible. The performance of an act prior to the granting of a permit is also relevant under criminal law, irrespective of the fact that a possibility to obtain a permit existed at the time of the act. Also significant with regard to possible criminal liability are tolerations by public authorities, whose legal consequences are still controversial and depend on the individual case.[7] 4

II. Environmental criminal offences

The offences under environmental criminal law protect the environment in its various media (air, water, soil) and other manifestations (flora and fauna) as the elementary natural basis of human life.[8] Thus, in addition to the protection of environmental goods, environmental offences also serve to protect human life and health.[9] Environmental protection under criminal law should not be limited to the protection of human life and health against environmental hazards; it must also include the protection of elementary bases of life such as water, air and soil as part of the human living environment and recognise such ecological protected goods as legal goods.[10] 5

The most important criminal offences are §§ 326 et seqq. StGB, as well as § 17 TierSchG and §§ 71, 71a BNatSchG. 6

[5] TK-StGB/Schittenhelm StGB Vor § 324 et seqq. mn. 12.

[6] Translations of §§ 326 sub. 1, 327 sub. 1 and 329 sub. 1 StGB are taken from <https://www.gesetze-im-internet.de/englisch_stgb/englisch_stgb.html>, translated by Prof Dr Michael Bohlander, completely and regularly updated by Ute Reusch (last accessed: 27.10.2025).

[7] TK-StGB/Schittenhelm StGB Vor § 324 et seqq. mn. 20; MüKoStGB/Schmitz StGB Vor § 324 mn. 42.

[8] MüKoStGB/Schmitz StGB Vor § 324 mn. 19.

[9] Saliger UmweltStrafR mn. 44.

[10] BT-Drs. 8/2382, 9 et seq.

1. Unauthorised waste management (§ 326 StGB)

7 § 326 sub. 1 StGB captures any handling of hazardous waste that takes place either outside an authorised facility (alt. 1) or in substantial deviation from a prescribed or authorised procedure (alt. 2). § 326 StGB is a so-called endangerment offence (*Gefährdungsdelikt*). It is to be distinguished from a so-called offence of success (*Erfolgsdelikt*), which requires an actual success in the form of a violation of a legal interest. For the existence of an endangerment offence, a mere endangering of legal interests is sufficient. Within the endangerment offences, a distinction is made between concrete and abstract endangerment offences. Concrete endangerment offences require a form of conduct that does not actually impair the legal interest but does concretely endanger it. Abstract endangerment offences generally cover dangerous acts that do not necessarily have to lead to a concrete endangerment of the legal interest. The offences covered by § 326 StGB constitute abstract endangerment offences, as it is neither important that the environmental goods mentioned have actually been harmed nor that they have been concretely endangered.

8 The Criminal Code does not contain an autonomous definition of the term 'waste' under criminal law. When introducing the provisions of environmental criminal law into the 29th section of the StGB in the wake of the reform of environmental criminal law in 1980, the legislator deliberately chose not to define a criminal definition of waste. Instead, reference was made to the definitions of waste management law when determining the term for the Criminal Code.[11] The Federal Court of Justice (BGH) thus often had to deal with the question of what is considered waste under criminal law, so that a constant case law[12] on the concept of waste under criminal law has been developed: the concept of waste under criminal law is to be defined autonomously on the basis of the definitions under waste administrative law, but without its restrictions of application (e.g. § 2 sub. 2 KrWG). In this respect, the definition of waste under criminal law is broader than the definition under waste management law, because the concept of waste under criminal law also covers waste that is not subject to the scope of the currently applicable *Kreislaufwirtschaftsgesetz* (KrWG, Closed Substance Cycle Waste Management Act). In accordance with waste administrative law, the concept of waste under criminal law therefore also includes a subjective concept of waste, which is linked to the owner's will to dispose of it, and an objective concept of waste, so-called compulsory waste, which the owner must dispose of due to a high potential danger or no reasonable economic use. In addition, the exclusion of the restrictions on use ensures that the concept of waste under criminal law also covers waste that is not subject to the scope of the currently applicable KrWG. This understanding of the concept of waste under criminal law is also supported by the prevailing literature.[13] In the literature, however, the transferability of the concept of waste under administrative law is justifiably restricted at one point: a reference to the concept of waste in the KrWG is ruled out insofar as the regulations there are not compatible with the applicable principles of criminal procedure, such as the presumption of innocence. Thus, among other things, the application of the fictions under waste law of

---

[11] BT-Drs. 8/2382, 17.

[12] BGH 26.4.1990 – 4 StR 24/90, BGHSt 37, 21 (24) = BeckRS 1990, 957; BGH 26.2.1991 – 5 StR 444/90, BGHSt 37, 333 (335) = BeckRS 1991, 2873; BGH 6.6.1997 – 2 StR 339/96, BGHSt 43, 219 (220) = BeckRS 1997, 5953; BGH 23.10.2013 – 5 StR 505/12, BGHSt 59, 45 (47) = BeckRS 2013, 19624; BGH 5.8.2021 – 2 StR 307/20, BGHSt 66, 219 (220) = BeckRS 2021, 33668.

[13] Matt/Renzikowski/Rettenmaier/Gehrmann StGB § 326 mn 6 et seqq.; MüKoStGB/Alt StGB § 326 mn. 20 et seq.; TK-StGB/Schittenhelm StGB § 326 mn. 2 et seqq.

§ 3 sub. 2 and 3 KrWG cannot be considered, as they contain assumptions to the disadvantage of the accused person.[14]

9 The criminal liability of unlawful handling of waste requires that the waste is dangerous under criminal law, since the provision of § 326 StGB, at least in its current version, only covers hazardous waste. Solely criminal law is decisive for the definition of 'hazardous waste'. The hazardousness of the waste that is decisive for unlawful handling is described in § 326 sub. 1 StGB itself. According to this, the waste must contain or be capable of producing poisons or disease agents dangerous to the public and transmissible to humans or animals (no. 1), be carcinogenic, toxic to reproduction or mutagenic to humans (no. 2), prone to explode, spontaneously combustible or of more than merely minor radioactive quality (no. 3) or, by their nature, composition or quantity, capable of permanently contaminating or otherwise adversely affecting water, air or soil (no. 4a) or endangering a population of animals or plants (no. 4b). Nevertheless, the hazardousness according to the *Abfallverzeichnisordnung* (List of Wastes Ordinance), which is decisive in terms of waste law, is of indicative importance.

10 The handling of hazardous waste must have been carried out in violation of administrative law. The offence is punishable by imprisonment for up to five years or a fine.

11 Sub. 2 covers the unauthorised shipment of hazardous waste as so-called waste tourism. Accordingly, anyone who ships hazardous waste into, out of or through the area of application of the StGB in contravention of a prohibition or without the necessary authorisation shall be punished. This is intended to combat a significant part of European and international commercial crime.[15] Also for cases under sub. 2, the range of punishment is imprisonment for up to five years or a fine.

12 Sub. 3 standardises the criminal liability of non-delivery of radioactive waste in violation of administrative obligations. This paragraph provides for a reduced threat of punishment of up to three years imprisonment or a fine.

13 The offence under sub. 6 does not entail criminal liability if harmful effects on the named environmental goods can be obviously excluded due to a merely small amount of waste.

14 The especially serious offence of deliberate handling of hazardous waste is regulated in § 330 StGB. Generally, such a case occurs if there is a particularly significant impairment of water, soil or a protected area as defined in § 329 sub. 3 StGB, if the public water supply is endangered, if the population of animals or plants of a strictly protected species is permanently damaged or if the perpetrator acts out of profit motive. Since § 330 StGB is a so-called *Regelbeispiel* (presumptive example), the existence of the listed conditions is on the one hand only indicative and on the other hand the list is not exhaustive. The presumption of the existence of an especially serious offence can therefore be rebutted.[16] For the especially serious offences under § 326 StGB, § 330 sub. 1 StGB provides for an increased range of sentences of imprisonment from six months up to ten years. In cases of § 330 sub. 2 StGB, the law provides for an imprisonment of one year up to ten years, in less serious cases of sub. 2 no. 1 six months up to five years, in less serious cases of sub. 2 no. 2 imprisonment of one year up to ten years.

15 In the case of § 326 sub. 1 StGB, the court may, at its discretion, mitigate the penalty in accordance with the provisions of § 49 sub. 2 StGB or refrain from imposing a penalty entirely if the perpetrator voluntarily averts the danger or remedies the condition he has

---

[14] Krell UmweltStrafR mn. 146; Saliger UmweltStrafR mn. 279 et seq.; TK-StGB/Schittenhelm StGB § 326 mn. 2g; Matt/Renzikowski/Rettenmaier/Gehrmann StGB § 326 mn. 6, 10; MüKoStGB/Alt StGB § 326 mn. 20.

[15] For unauthorised shipments of waste to § 326 sub. 2 StGB → mn. 25 et seqq.

[16] MüKoStGB/Alt StGB § 330b mn. 4.

caused before it results in substantial damage (§ 330b sub. 1 sent. 1 StGB). It is not necessary to avert the development of the danger; it is sufficient to contain it before it can turn into considerable damage.[17] The significant damage is conceived as a serious damage to health or a significant material value.[18] If the danger is averted without the perpetrator's intervention or if the unlawfully caused condition is eliminated, it is sufficient for the perpetrator to make a voluntary and serious effort to achieve the goal (§ 330b sub. 2 StGB). Necessarily, according to the perpetrator's conception, his effort must at least be suitable to avert the occurrence of the danger.[19]

2. Unauthorised operation of facilities (§ 327 StGB)

16 § 327 StGB constitutes another important core offence of environmental criminal law and sanctions the unauthorised operation of environmentally hazardous installations.

17 It protects the authority's competence to review and make decisions on the licensing and monitoring of potentially environmentally hazardous installations. The primary concern is the administrative control and monitoring activities in the interest of hazard prevention.[20]

18 Sub. 1, 2 sent. 1 and sent. 3 constitute abstract endangerment offences.[21] Accordingly, a success that can be separated from the abstract endangerment or a concrete endangerment of environmental goods or other persons is not required for the realisation of the offence. Sub. 2 sent. 2, on the other hand, is classified as a potential endangerment offence. The prerequisite is that the type of operating is generally capable of harming the life or body of another person, animal, plant, water, air or soil.

19 Furthermore, it is a so-called *Sonderdelikt* (special offence), which can only be perpetrated by entrepreneur of waste facilities. Since these are usually legal entities, the criminal liability of the natural persons acting on behalf of this legal entity requires the application of the rule of attribution in § 14 StGB.

20 Sub. 1 sanctions the operation of a nuclear facility (no. 1 alt. 1), the holding or partial dismantling of an operable or inoperative nuclear installation (no. 1 alt. 2) and the substantial modification of such an installation or its operation. Also punishable is the substantial modification of a plant (in which nuclear fuel is used) or its location (no. 2). All acts must have been carried out without the required permit or in contravention of an enforceable prohibition. The term 'facility which requires a permit' includes those that serve the processing, utilisation or storage of nuclear fuel.[22] Also of importance is the criminal liability of operating pipeline facilities requiring a permit (sub. 2 sent. 1 no. 2) and waste disposal facilities (sub. 2 sent. 1 no. 3) without the permit or approval of plan required under the respective law or in contravention of an enforceable prohibition. An offence under sub. 1 is punishable by imprisonment of up to five years or a fine.

21 Sub. 2 regulates the criminal liability of the illegal operation of other facilities that do not fall under the definition of facilities in sub. 1. § 327 sub. 2 no. 1 StGB criminalises the unauthorised operation of facilities that fall under the Federal Immission Control Act (*Bundes-Immissionsschutzgesetz*, BImSchG). Alt. 1 covers facilities requiring a permit (exhaustive list of facilities in the annex to the Fourth Federal Immission Control Regu-

---

[17] BeckOK StGB/Witteck, 65. Ed. 1.5.2025, StGB § 330b mn. 3; LKH StGB § 330b mn. 2; LK-StGB/Möhrenschlager, 12th edn 2019, StGB § 330b mn. 2.

[18] BeckOK StGB/Witteck, 65. Ed. 1.5.2025, StGB § 330b mn. 3; TK-StGB/Schittenhelm StGB § 330b mn. 3.

[19] BeckOK StGB/Witteck, 65. Ed. 1.5.2025, StGB § 330b mn. 4; MüKoStGB/Alt StGB § 330b mn. 6.

[20] Horn NJW 1988, 2335 (2337).

[21] BeckOK StGB/Witteck, 65. Ed. 1.5.2025, StGB § 330b mn. 6; MüKoStGB/Alt StGB § 330b mn. 2.

[22] TK-StGB/Schittenhelm StGB § 327 mn. 3.

lation (*Bundes-Immissionsschutzverordnung*, BImSchV)) and their unauthorised operation. Alt. 2, on the other hand, covers facilities that do not require a permit and punishes their operation in contravention of an enforceable prohibition order. The operation must thereby have been prohibited to protect against hazards (prohibitions pursuant to § 25 sub. 2 BImSchG). § 327 sub. 2 no. 3 StGB sanctions anyone who operates a waste disposal facility within the meaning of the KrWG either without the permit or planning approval required by the respective law or in contravention of an enforceable prohibition based on the respective law. This means that only facilities requiring authorisation under the KrWG are covered, since the authorisation of waste disposal facilities since 1993 has largely been governed by the BImSchG.[23] These facilities, which require planning approval or authorisation, are only dumps, i.e. disposal facilities for depositing waste above or below ground level, including internal waste disposal facilities (§ 3 sub. 27 KrWG).)[24] A dump can be described as a functional unit which, from the point of view of an average observer, is intended for the indefinite deposit of a not inconsiderable quantity of waste.[25] Decisive is the final disposal. This is missing in the case of disposal for waste recovery.[26] Accordingly, waste disposal facilities that serve the recovery of waste and facilities in which waste disposal is carried out are not covered (§ 35 sub. 1 KrWG).

The penalty in cases of sub. 2 is imprisonment for up to three years or a fine. 22

§ 327 StGB sub. 3 also provides for penalties for negligence with different penalties for 23
the cases of sub. 1 and 2. Cases of sub. 1 are sanctioned with imprisonment for up to three years or a fine, cases of sub. 2 with imprisonment for up to two years or a fine.

The especially serious offence of § 327 StGB is regulated in § 330 StGB. The explana- 24
tions under → mn. 7 et seqq. apply accordingly.

3. Unauthorised shipment of waste

a) Unauthorised shipment of hazardous waste (§ 326 sub. 2 StGB)

§ 326 sub. 2 StGB criminalises the illegal shipment of hazardous waste into, out of 25
or through the area of application of the German StGB. It is a potential endangerment offence in which the transboundary shipment act – the unauthorised transport of hazardous waste – must be potentially capable of creating a danger to the protected legal interests.[27] However, the shipment of waste is only punishable if it takes place in contravention of a prohibition or without an administrative authorisation. Here, again, the principle of the accessoriness of administrative law plays a decisive role. This is made clear by the term 'unauthorised'.

The offence of shipment is to be understood as any transport in the sense of a change of 26
location of the hazardous waste that has a cross-border connection. This includes import ('into the area of application'), transit ('through the area of application') and export ('from the area of application').[28]

The provision is subsidiary to the more specific § 18a AbfVerbrG (Waste Shipment 27
Act), so that it only has a very limited scope of application.[29] Only § 326 sub. 2 StGB covers the unauthorised transfer of environmentally hazardous waste according to § 326

---

[23] BGH 23.10.2013 – 5 StR 505/12, BGHSt 59, 45 (50) = BeckRS 2013, 19624.
[24] TK-StGB/Schittenhelm StGB § 327 mn. 17.
[25] MüKoStGB/Alt StGB § 327 mn. 32; TK-StGB/Schittenhelm StGB § 327 mn. 17.
[26] BGH 23.10.2013 – 5 StR 505/12, BGHSt 59, 45 (50) = BeckRS 2013, 19624.
[27] MüKoStGB/Alt StGB § 326 mn. 5; TK-StGB/Schittenhelm StGB § 326 mn. 12a.
[28] BeckOK StGB/Witteck, 65. Ed. 1.5.2025, StGB § 326 mn. 33; MüKoStGB/Alt StGB § 326 mn. 83.
[29] BeckOK StGB/Witteck, 65. Ed. 1.5.2025, StGB § 326 mn. 32.

sub. 1 StGB.[30] The scope of application of § 326 sub. 2 StGB therefore does not extend to hazardous waste as defined in § 18a AbfVerbrG. § 326 sub. 2 StGB does not cover waste that is classified as hazardous according to Directive 2008/98/EC.[31] The existing scope of application is limited to wastes that are excluded from the scope of application of the AbfVerbrG and consequently from the provisions of §§ 18a, 18b AbfVerbrG pursuant to Art. 1 para. 3 Waste Shipment Regulation.[32] These in turn must fall under a hazardous characteristic of § 326 sub. 1 no. 1–4 StGB.[33]

28 The penalty is imprisonment for up to five years or a fine.

29 § 330 StGB also provides for a particularly serious offence for § 326 sub. 2 StGB. The statements under → mn. 7 et seqq. apply accordingly.

30 In cases of § 326 sub. 2 StGB, active repentance according to § 330b StGB and an associated mitigation of the sentence or a waiver of punishment is also conceivable. The statements under → mn. 7 et seqq. apply accordingly.

b) Illegal shipment of hazardous waste (§ 18a AbfVerbrG)

31 Of great importance for the punishability of illegal waste shipments is § 18a AbfVerbrG, which sanctions the illegal shipment of hazardous waste. § 18a sub. 3 AbfVerbrG indirectly mentions life, health of other persons, animals, plants, water, air, soil and foreign bodies as objects of protection.

32 The penal provision in sub. 1 is a so-called *Blankettnorm*, that refers to two European legislative acts. Art. 3 no. 1 of Directive 2008/98/EC[34] defines waste as any substance or object which the holder intends or is required to dispose of. According to Art. 3 no. 2 of the Directive, waste is hazardous if it has one or more of the hazardous properties listed in Annex III. Thus, in contrast to § 326 sub. 2 StGB, the hazardousness of the waste does not result from § 326 sub. 1 StGB. In order to determine when an illegal shipment of this hazardous waste exists, the provision refers to Art. 2 no. 35 lit. a, b, c, g, f and Art. 34, 39, 40, 41, 43 (in sub. 1 no. 2 lit. a) and Art. 36, 40 (in sub. 1 no. 2 lit. b) Regulation (EC) No. 1013/2006.[35] The German penal provision must therefore be read in conjunction with European Regulation (EC) No. 1013/2006 and Directive (EC) 2008/98. The threat of punishment in cases of sub. 1 is imprisonment for up to five years or a fine.

33 Sub. 2 provides for criminal liability in the event that an intentional act under sub. 1 leads to a risk to the life or health of another person, to animals or plants, to waters, to the air or to the soil or to third-party property of significant value. The offence is also punishable by imprisonment of up to five years or a fine.

34 Sub. 3 provides for an increased range of punishment of imprisonment from six months to five years for an act under sub. 1 that is persistently repeated (no. 1) or is committed for profit (no. 2). Sub. 6 also provides for an increased range of punishment for cases in which the act under sub. 1 leads to the death of another person.

35 § 18a sub. 9 AbfVerbrG provides for the possibility of active repentance in cases of sub. 1, 2 and 8. If the perpetrator voluntarily averts the danger or remedies the condition he has caused before significant damage occurs, the penalty may be reduced in accordance with § 49 sub. 2 StGB or the penalty may be waived completely. If the danger is averted

---

[30] TK-StGB/Schittenhelm StGB § 326 mn. 12a.

[31] TK-StGB/Schittenhelm StGB § 326 mn. 12a.

[32] MüKoStGB/Alt StGB § 326 mn. 81.

[33] MüKoStGB/Alt StGB § 326 mn. 137.

[34] Directive 2008/98/EC of the European Parliament and of the Council of 19 November 2008 on waste and repealing certain Directives, OJ L 312 22.11.2008, 3.

[35] Regulation (EC) No 1013/2006 of the European Parliament and of the Council of 14 June 2006 on shipments of waste, OJ L 190 12.7.2006, 1.

or the unlawfully caused condition is removed without the offender's intervention, a voluntary and serious effort is sufficient.

c) Illegal shipment of non-hazardous waste (§ 18b AbfVerbrG)

In contrast to § 18a AbfVerbrG, § 18b AbfVerbrG also punishes the illegal shipment 36
of waste that is not hazardous. Apart from the object of the crime, the penal provision is structured in the same way as § 18a AbfVerbrG.

Sub. 1 and 2 provide for a range of punishment of imprisonment for up to two years 37
or a fine. If the perpetrator of the act referred to in sub. 3 acts for profit or persistently repeats the act referred to in sub. 1, the penalty shall be increased to imprisonment for a term of up to five years or a fine. An act under sub. 4 shall be punishable by imprisonment for a term of one to ten years. In less serious cases under sub. 4, sub. 5 provides for a lesser penalty of imprisonment from six months to five years. If an act under sub. 1 causes the death of another person, sub. 6 provides for a penalty of imprisonment of not less than three years, and in less serious cases under sub. 6 a penalty of imprisonment of one year to ten years. In the case of negligent conduct in the cases referred to in sub. 1 or 2, the penalty shall be imprisonment for a term of up to one year or a fine.

§ 18b sub. 9 AbfVerbrG stipulates the possibility of active repentance for cases under 38
sub. 1, 2 and 8. The explanations under → mn. 31 et seqq. apply accordingly.

4. Water pollution (§ 324 StGB)

§ 324 StGB (*Gewässerverunreinigung*) criminalises the unlawful pollution of waters. Its 39
main purpose is the protection of water bodies.[36] The term 'water body' includes groundwater, all surface waters and also the sea (§ 330d sub. 1 no. 1 StGB). Along with air and soil, water is the most important basis of life and is therefore considered an environmental good with all its functionalities that deserves special protection by humans.

Unlike §§ 326, 327 StGB, § 324 StGB is an offence of success.[37] The offence therefore 40
requires a result of the offence – the unauthorised pollution or lasting alteration of the characteristics of water bodies. However, a concrete endangerment or actual damage to humans, animals or plants is not required.[38]

Pollution requires a deterioration of the physical, chemical or biological properties due 41
to the introduction of substances. This is the case if the external appearance of the water body is less pure after the offender's intervention than before, i.e. in particular in the case of turbidity, foam formation and traces of oil.[39] However, not every minor pollution is subject to § 324 StGB, since pollution is to be equated with the adverse alteration of the water's characteristics.[40] For example, heavy pollution of only a small part of the water body may fail to meet the threshold of materiality, whereas partial pollution is also sufficient.[41] Pollution of a water body is to be determined on the basis of the concrete circumstances of the individual case, such as size and depth of the water body, water flow, speed of the flowing water on the one hand, and quantity and hazardousness of the introduced substance on the other.[42] The variant of the offence of other adverse modification of the

36 MüKoStGB/Alt StGB § 324 mn. 1; TK-StGB/Heine/Schittenhelm StGB § 324 mn. 3.
37 TK-StGB/Heine/Schittenhelm StGB § 324 mn. 1.
38 MüKoStGB/Alt StGB § 324 mn. 23.
39 TK-StGB/Heine/Schittenhelm StGB § 324 mn. 8.
40 OLG Frankfurt 22.5.1987 – 1 Ss 401/86, NJW 1987, 2754.
41 BGH 26.2.1991 – 5 StR 444/90, NStZ 1991, 282; TK-StGB/Heine/Schittenhelm StGB § 324 mn. 8.
42 OLG Karlsruhe 21.1.1982 – 3 Ss 238/81, BeckRS 1982, 3550; TK-StGB/Heine/Schittenhelm StGB § 324 mn. 8; BT-Drs. 8/2382, 14.

water body's characteristics forms the generic term and includes such impairments that cannot be covered by the variant of pollution.[43] The prevailing opinion in jurisprudence and literature, however, requires the determination of a minus in water quality.[44]

42 In addition to intentional water pollution, negligent pollution is also possible. Pursuant to sub. 2, an attempt to pollute waters pursuant to sub. 1 is also punishable.

43 Intentional acts under sub. 1 are punishable by imprisonment for up to five years or a fine, negligent acts under sub. 3 by imprisonment for up to three years or a fine.

44 § 330 StGB also provides for especially serious cases for § 324 StGB. The explanations under → mn. 7 et seqq. apply accordingly.

5. Soil pollution (§ 324a StGB)

45 Unauthorised soil pollution (*Bodenverunreinigung*) is regulated in § 324a StGB. Soil is also protected under criminal law as an essential habitat and basis of life for plants, animals and humans. The aim of the legislator is to protect the soil and its ecologically important functions for humans and the environment.[45]

46 The offence under sub. 1 requires a violation of obligations under administrative law, which may result from a legal provision or an administrative act. Penalties are imposed for the input, allowance of substances to penetrate and release of substances. This can occur indirectly, for example through exhaust gases, or directly, for example through the excessive use of plant protection products.[46]

47 In the context of § 324a StGB, a significant soil change must have occurred. The materiality can result on the one hand from the potentially dangerous quality of the contamination or other adverse change (no. 1) and on the other hand from its significant extent (no. 2).[47] For the definition of adverse change, the definition of § 324 StGB can be used in a slightly modified form. According to this definition, it includes any change in the physical, chemical or biological condition of the soil that impairs the ecologically significant soil functions.[48] As with § 324 StGB, contamination is a sub-case of general alteration.[49] This includes all visible and ecologically detrimental changes to the condition of the soil.[50] These are significant if they are capable of harming the health of another person, animals, plants or other objects. A general dangerousness is sufficient for this purpose.[51] No. 1 is therefore an offence of success. If the soil alteration is not significant, the offence can still be committed under no. 2, provided that a certain quantity (economically and commercially significant) is present.[52]

48 As with § 324 StGB, the offence can be committed intentionally or negligently. Sub. 2 provides for the criminal liability of the attempt.

49 The intentional commission of the offence in sub. 1 is punishable by imprisonment of up to five years or a fine. In the case of the negligent commission of an offence under sub. 3, the penalty is imprisonment for up to three years or a fine.

---

[43] OLG Karlsruhe 21.1.1982 – 3 Ss 238/81, BeckRS 1982, 3550.

[44] OLG Celle 11.2.1986 – 1 Ss 435/85, NJW 1986, 2326 (2327); OLG Frankfurt 12.10.1995 – 1 Ss 382/93, BeckRS 1995, 6466; TK-StGB/Heine/Schittenhelm StGB § 324 mn. 9.

[45] BT-Drs. 12/192, 15.

[46] MüKoStGB/Alt StGB § 324a mn. 16 et seqq.

[47] Matt/Renzikowski/Rettenmaier/Gehrmann StGB § 324a mn. 6.

[48] TK-StGB/Heine/Schittenhelm StGB § 324a mn. 9.

[49] Matt/Renzikowski/Rettenmaier/Gehrmann StGB § 324a mn. 7.

[50] MüKoStGB/Alt StGB § 324a mn. 19; Matt/Renzikowski/Rettenmaier/Gehrmann StGB § 324a mn. 7.

[51] Matt/Renzikowski/Rettenmaier/Gehrmann StGB § 324a mn. 8.

[52] MüKoStGB/Alt StGB § 324a mn. 19; Matt/Renzikowski/Rettenmaier/Gehrmann StGB § 324a mn. 9.

For § 324a StGB, especially serious cases are provided for in § 330 StGB. The statements under → mn. 7 et seqq. apply accordingly. 50

6. Air pollution (§ 325 StGB)

§ 325 StGB provides for the criminalisation of air pollution (*Lufverunreinigung*). The protected legal good of § 325 StGB is the air, which, along with water and soil, is the most important environmental medium, as well as the health of humans, animals, plants and other objects of significant value.[53] 51

Pursuant to sub. 1, anyone who causes changes in the air during the operation of an installation in breach of administrative duties shall be considered to have committed a criminal offence. These changes must be capable of harming the health of another person, animals, plants or other property of significant value outside the area of the installation belonging to the installation. However, a concrete damage does not have to have occurred.[54] 52

Sub. 2 provides for punishability for the release of pollutants in significant quantities into the air during the operation of an installation. This must be done in violation of administrative duties. Sub. 3 covers the release of pollutants to a significant extent in breach of administrative obligations, irrespective of the operation of an installation. If the offence is already covered by sub. 2, sub. 3 is subsidiary.[55] 53

§ 325 StGB can be committed intentionally (sub. 1, 2, 3), negligently (sub. 4) as well as recklessly (sub. 5). According to § 325 sub. 1 sent. 2 StGB, only the attempt of an act according to sub. 1 sent. 1 is punishable. 54

According to sub. 7, the operation of motor vehicles, rail vehicles, aircraft and watercraft, which may cause a change in the air, is explicitly excluded from criminal liability. 55

Cases under sub. 1 are punishable by imprisonment of up to five years or a fine, as are cases under sub. 2. For a negligent commission of sub. 1 or 2, sub. 4 provides for imprisonment of up to three years or a fine. In cases of sub. 3, a prison sentence of up to three years or a fine shall likewise be imposed. In the case of reckless commission of subsection 3, subsection 5 provides for a penalty of imprisonment of up to one year or a fine. 56

§ 330 StGB also provides for especially serious cases for § 325 StGB. The explanations under → mn. 7 et seqq. apply accordingly. 57

7. Causing noise, vibrations and non-ionising radiation (§ 325a StGB)

Also relevant under criminal law may be the causing of noise, vibrations and non-ionising radiation (*Verursachen von Lärm, Erschütterungen und nichtionisierenden Strahlen*). 58

§ 325a StGB protects human health against hazards caused by noise in sub. 1, and in sub. 2 it also protects property and financial interests in other people's animals or property.[56] 59

Only noise originating from an installation is protected. The action must also violate an obligation under administrative law and the noise must be capable of harming the health of another person outside the area belonging to the installation.[57] 60

---

[53] BeckOK StGB/Witteck, 65. Ed. 1.5.2025, StGB § 325 mn. 4; MüKoStGB/Alt StGB § 325 mn. 1.

[54] MüKoStGB/Alt StGB § 325 mn. 38 et seqq.

[55] BeckOK StGB/Witteck, 65. Ed. 1.5.2025, StGB § 325 mn. 43; MüKoStGB/Alt StGB § 325 mn. 57.

[56] LK-StGB/Heghmanns, 12th edn 2019, StGB § 325a mn. 2; TK-StGB/Heine/Schittenhelm StGB § 325a mn. 1.

[57] BeckOK StGB/Witteck, 65. Ed. 1.5.2025, StGB § 325a mn. 6.

61 The term 'noise' includes all effects spread by sound waves which, due to their nature, extent or duration, can be irritating, disturbing, unpleasant or detrimental to a normally noise-sensitive person.[58] Insignificant impairments, on the other hand, are not covered.[59]

62 The penalty in cases under sub. 1 is imprisonment for up to three years or a fine, in cases under sub. 2 imprisonment for up to five years or a fine. If the perpetrator acts negligently, the law imposes imprisonment of up to two years or a fine in cases of sub. 1 and imprisonment of up to three years or a fine in cases of sub. 2.

63 For cases of § 325a StGB, § 330 StGB provides for an especially serious offence. The statements under → mn. 7 et seqq. apply accordingly.

64 In cases of § 325a sub. 2 StGB, active repentance according to § 330b StGB and an associated mitigation of the sentence or a waiver of punishment is possible. The explanations under → mn. 7 et seqq. also apply here accordingly.

8. Unauthorised handling of radioactive substances and other hazardous substances and goods (§ 328 StGB)

65 § 328 StGB aims to protect the environmental goods of human life and health, to protect property against hazards resulting from the handling of radioactive or otherwise hazardous substances, and to protect the administrative bodies' authority to control the handling of such substances.[60]

66 The offence under sub. 1 punishes both the production, storage, transport, processing, treatment or other use and the import or export of nuclear fuels and other radioactive substances in violation of administrative law.

67 Sub. 2 sanctions both the violation of the obligation to deliver radioactive substances under the Atomic Energy Act (AtG) (no. 1), the uncontrolled distribution of radioactive substances (no. 2), and the causing or promoting of a nuclear explosion (no. 3, 4).

68 The offence of sub. 3 sanctions on the one hand the storage, processing, treatment or other use of radioactive and dangerous substances and mixtures (no. 1), and on the other hand the transport, dispatch, packing or unpacking, loading or unloading, receipt or transfer of dangerous goods (no. 2).

69 Sub. 1 and 2 are abstract endangerment offences. A success that can be delimited from the offence is not a precondition. Sub. 3, on the other hand, is a concrete endangerment offence, the offence is only fulfilled with the occurrence of the danger to the protected interests mentioned.[61]

70 If sub. 1, 2 or 3 are committed intentionally, the penalty is imprisonment for up to five years or a fine. If the offence is committed negligently, the penalty is imprisonment for up to three years or a fine.

71 § 330 StGB also provides for an especially serious offence for § 328 StGB. The explanations under → mn. 7 et seqq. apply accordingly.

72 In cases of § 328 sub. 1–3 StGB, active repentance according to § 330b StGB and an associated mitigation of the sentence or a waiver of punishment is also conceivable. The explanations under → mn. 7 et seqq. apply accordingly.

---

[58] Franzheim/Pfohl UmweltStrafR mn. 236; Michalke Umweltstrafsachen mn. 224; Sack Umweltschutz-Strafrecht, 48th edn 2022, StGB § 325a mn. 24; LK-StGB/Möhrenschlager, 12th edn 2019, StGB § 325a mn. 4.

[59] TK-StGB/Heine/Schittenhelm StGB § 325a mn. 5.

[60] MüKoStGB/Alt StGB § 328 mn. 1.

[61] BeckOK StGB/Witteck, 65. Ed. 1.5.2025, StGB § 328 mn. 3.

9. Endangering protected areas (§ 329 StGB)

§ 329 StGB criminalises the endangerment of areas in need of protection (*Gefährdung schutzbedürftiger Gebiete*). The norm aims to preserve areas worthy of protection and thus the individual environmental media such as water, soil and air, as well as particularly valuable components of the flora and fauna.[62] These shall be protected from noise and air pollutionf. **73**

Sub. 1 to 4 each protect different areas and types of areas. Sub. 1 includes areas requiring special protection from harmful environmental effects caused by air pollution or noise, or areas that are already highly polluted and where even a slight increase in emissions causes unacceptable environmental damage (so-called smog areas). Sub. 2 includes water and medicinal spring protection areas, which are defined according to § 51 et seq., 53 Federal Water Act (WHG), as well by federal state law. Sub. 3 includes nature conservation areas within the meaning of § 23 BNatSchG, national parks within the meaning of § 24 BNatSchG, as well as areas temporarily secured as nature conservation areas within the meaning of § 22 sub. 3 BNatSchG. The objects of protection under sub. 4 are areas under 'Natura 2000'. **74**

Sub. 1 and 2 provide for a threat of punishment of imprisonment of up to three years or a fine, sub. 3 and 4 for imprisonment of up to five years or a fine. If the offender acts negligently, sub. 5 provides for imprisonment of up to two years or a fine for cases under sub. 1 and 2, and imprisonment of up to three years or a fine for cases under sub. 3. If the offender recklessly commits sub. 4, he or she is liable to a custodial sentence not exceeding three years or to a monetary penalty. **75**

§ 330 StGB also provides for an especially serious offence for § 329 StGB. The explanations under → mn. 7 et seqq. apply accordingly. **76**

10. Causing severe danger by releasing poisons (§ 330a StGB)

§ 330a StGB, which sanctions serious endangerment through the release of poisons, aims to protect human life and health.[63] Sub. 1 of the provision constitutes a concrete endangerment offence, whereas sub. 2 can be classified as an injury offence.[64] In this respect, sub. 2 represents a qualification of success based on sub. 1. Also covered by sub. 3 are unnamed less serious cases of sub. 1 and 2. A less serious case of sub. 1 may be cases in which the danger is less serious or in the case of toxic substances that are less dangerous.[65] A less serious case as defined in sub. 2 may be considered if the death of another person was unknowingly caused by negligence. However, if there is a serious breach of the due diligence obligation, a less serious case is not possible.[66] Sub. 4 and 5 define the range of punishment for acts that are not purely intentional. Sub. 4 covers cases in which the offender intentionally commits the act – i.e. the release or distribution of poisons – but only negligently causes the danger because he or she mistakenly or through carelessness trusted that it would not occur.[67] In cases under sub. 5, the offender commits the offence recklessly and causes the danger negligently.[68] **77**

---

62 BeckOK StGB/Witteck, 65. Ed. 1.5.2025, StGB § 328 mn. 3; Matt/Renzikowski/Rettenmaier/Gehrmann StGB § 329 mn. 3.
63 BeckOK StGB/Witteck, 65. Ed. 1.5.2025, StGB § 330a mn. 3; MüKoStGB/Alt StGB § 330a mn. 1.
64 MüKoStGB/Alt StGB § 330a mn. 2; Fischer StGB, § 330a mn. 1.
65 BeckOK StGB/Witteck, 65. Ed. 1.5.2025, StGB § 330a mn. 11.
66 BeckOK StGB/Witteck, 65. Ed. 1.5.2025, StGB § 330a mn. 11.
67 BeckOK StGB/Witteck, 65. Ed. 1.5.2025, StGB § 330a mn. 14.
68 BeckOK StGB/Witteck, 65. Ed. 1.5.2025, StGB § 330a mn. 15.

78 Sub. 1 criminalises the release or distribution of substances containing or capable of producing poisons. In this context, a poison is any inorganic or organic substance which, under certain conditions, is generally capable of destroying the health or life of a human being due to its chemical or chemical-physical effect or quantity.[69] At the very least, it must be capable of considerably impairing essential body abilities and functions.[70] The release or distribution of the poison must result in a concrete risk of death or serious harm to the health of a human being or harm to the health of a large number of people.[71]

79 Sub. 2 is a qualification of success (in the case of a qualification of success, the basic offence is linked to a serious result, which the offender must only be held liable for due to negligence or, in some cases, recklessness in accordance with § 18 StGB) in relation to sub. 1 and always applies if the act under sub. 1 has negligently or intentionally caused the death of another person.

80 Cases under sub. 1 are punishable by imprisonment of one to ten years, cases under sub. 2 by imprisonment of not less than three years. In less serious cases of sub. 1, sub. 3 provides for a reduction of the range of punishment to imprisonment from six months to five years, and in less serious cases of sub. 2, imprisonment from one year to ten years. If the perpetrator acts negligently in the cases of sub. 1, he or she is liable to imprisonment of up to five years or a fine, and in the case of a reckless act and negligent causation of danger, to imprisonment of up to three years or a fine.

81 In the cases of § 330a sub. 1, 3 and 4 StGB, an active repentance according to § 330b StGB and an associated mitigation of the sentence or a waiver of punishment is possible. The explanations under → mn. 7 et seqq. apply accordingly.

11. Protection of wildlife and biodiversity

82 Wildlife and biodiversity are also protected by environmental criminal law. The most important criminal law norms are § 17 TierSchG and §§ 71, 71a BNatSchG.

a) § 17 TierSchG

83 § 17 TierSchG protects the moral order in the relationship between humans and animals.[72] The protection of animals has become a fundamental state objective through its enshrinement in Art. 20a GG. The killing of a vertebrate without good cause, as well as crude or cruel mistreatment of animals, is punishable. Vertebrates are subject to protection under criminal law because they – like humans – have a pronounced ability to feel pain.[73] The offence under § 17 TierSchG can be committed by anyone, provided, however, that the offence is successful.[74] However, the indicated unlawfulness of the act can be omitted for various reasons. Reasons for justification can be, for example, self-defence, various states of emergency, as well as legal authorisations or official tolerations or approvals. Acts of welfare in the interest of the animal or those that serve to avert danger are also exempt.[75]

b) § 71 BNatSchG

84 §§ 71 and 71a BNatSchG protect biodiversity and the diversity of species.

---

[69] MüKoStGB/Alt StGB § 330a mn. 7.
[70] BeckOK StGB/Witteck, 65. Ed. 1.5.2025, StGB § 330a mn. 6.
[71] BeckOK StGB/Witteck, 65. Ed. 1.5.2025, StGB § 330a mn. 9; MüKoStGB/Alt StGB § 330a mn. 10.
[72] MüKoStGB/Pfohl TierSchG § 17 mn. 1.
[73] BeckOK GG/Rux, 61. Ed. 15.3.2025, GG Art. 20a mn. 26.
[74] MüKoStGB/Pfohl TierSchG § 17 mn. 6.
[75] MüKoStGB/Pfohl TierSchG § 17 mn. 100 et seqq.

§ 71 BNatSchG prohibits the killing, destruction or removal of animal and plant species listed in the Habitats Directive[76] and to be regarded as particularly strictly protected species. A violation of EU species protection law is also punishable. This includes the EU Species Protection Regulation[77], which contains provisions on the criminalisation of trade in strictly protected wild animal and plant species listed in Appendix A. The Regulation implements provisions of the two relevant Directives (Habitats Directive and Birds Directive[78]), as well as the Washington Convention on International Trade in Endangered Species[79]. It is directly applicable in every Member State. The Regulation was implemented in German law by the *Bundesnaturschutzgesetz* (Federal Nature Conservation Act) and the *Bundesartenschutzverordnung* (Federal Species Protection Ordinance). The EU Species Protection Regulation specifies which species are considered strictly protected. These include whales, some monkey species, sea turtles and some land turtles, as well as some cacti and orchids. Acting in a professional or customary manner as well as a planned extermination increase the penalty. If the offence is merely negligent or reckless, which provides for a lower penalty, a certain threshold of seriousness must have been exceeded.[80] **85**

c) § 71a BNatSchG

§ 71a BNatSchG generally deals with violations in the handling of especially as well as **86**
strictly protected species.

Sub. 1 no. 1 criminalises the killing of an animal of a wild European bird species as **87**
well as the removal or destruction of its developmental forms, if it is a specially protected species. This includes species listed in Art. 4 para. 2 or Annex I of Directive 2009/147/EC. These European bird species are especially protected species. A corresponding definition can be found in § 7 sub. 2 no. 13 lit. b, bb BNatSchG in conjunction with § 7 sub. 2 no. 12 BNatSchG. Accordingly, species listed in Annex A or B of Regulation (EC) No. 338/97 are considered to be specially protected species. Examples include various subspecies of ducks, hummingbirds, falcons, herons, storks, flamingos and many other species.

Also punishable under sub. 1 no. 2 lit. a and b are the possession or custody as well as **88**
the processing of certain specimens of strictly (a) or especially protected (b) wild animal and plant species. Also in this case, the prohibition of direct interventions in nature and in the plant household as well as the prohibition of marketing serve the preservation of biodiversity.[81] The strictly protected species are listed in Annex IV of Directive 92/43/EEC (§ 7 sub. 2 no. 14 BNatSchG), the specially protected species in Art. 4 para. 2 or in Annex I of Directive 2009/142/EC. Again, § 7 sub. 2 no. 13 lit. b, bb in conjunction with § 7 sub. 2 no. 12 BNatSchG must be consulted for a more detailed definition of the specially protected European bird species.

Sub. 2. sanctions the sale, purchase, offering for sale or purchase and holding or trans- **89**
porting for sale (no. 1) and the acquisition, display or use for commercial purposes (no. 2) of an example of a species listed in Annex B.

---

[76] Council Directive 92/43/EEC of 21 May 1992 on the conservation of natural habitats and of wild fauna and flora.

[77] Council Regulation (EC) No 338/97 of 9 December 1996 on the protection of species of wild fauna and flora by regulating trade therein.

[78] Directive 2009/147/EC of the European Parliament and of the Council of 30 November 2009 on the conservation of wild birds.

[79] Convention on International Trade in Endangered Species of Wild Fauna and Flora of 03 March 1973.

[80] BeckOK UmweltR/Schrader, 64. Ed 1.4.2022, BNatSchG § 71 mn. 18c.

[81] MüKoStGB/Pfohl BNatSchG § 71a mn. 1.

B. Product criminal law

I. Introduction

90 Product criminal law is also considered to be product liability under criminal law. If a company places products on the market that are hazardous to health or have adverse effects on health, this can result in considerable criminal law risks for the company's members. This becomes relevant if instruction errors or observation errors during production or distribution or violations of recall obligations can be proven. Both actions and omissions in connection with the product that are necessary and feasible can be prosecuted under criminal law.

91 On the one hand, criminal product liability is based on the general criminal offences of the StGB for the protection of physical health and life, and on the other hand on a large number of criminal provisions contained in subsidiary laws. In addition, there is the so-called case law, which has a decisive influence on criminal product liability in Germany.

92 At present, criminal law does not recognise any independent criminal liability of a company. Criminal investigations can only be conducted against individual persons within the company.[82] In this case, the corporate (mis)conduct is usually attributed to the decision-makers and subordinate employees (§ 14 StGB). Accordingly, all persons named in § 14 StGB can be held liable: in addition to the shareholder authorised to represent the company, legal representatives and agents may also be liable to prosecution. In addition to considerable damage to its image, the company may also suffer economic consequences. § 30 OWiG provides for the possibility of imposing a fine on the company itself. Likewise, according to § 130 OWiG, the owner of the enterprise can be fined for violating a supervisory duty. §§ 73 et seqq. StGB also provide for the possibility of confiscation.[83]

II. Legal sources and offences

1. Core criminal law

93 The StGB as the core criminal law does not know any special criminal offences that exclusively cover health impairment caused by defective products. Rather, criminal liability is determined according to the general provisions of the StGB. Since criminal product liability cases mostly involve health impairment, the relevant legal interests are the life and health of the end consumer of the product. The general provisions of the StGB on the protection of life (§§ 212, 222 StGB) apply here, provided that a homicide offence comes into consideration. If the consumer suffers bodily harm as a result of the defective product and if this was caused negligently or intentionally, criminal liability is conceivable according to §§ 223 et seqq. StGB.[84] § 314 sub. 1 no. 2 StGB also covers the selling, offering for sale or placing on the market of objects mixed with substances that are harmful to health and intended for public sale or consumption.

---

[82] BeckOK StGB/Momsen/Laudien, 65. Ed. 1.2.2025, StGB § 14 mn. 31 et seqq.
[83] TK-StGB/Perron/Eisele StGB § 14 mn. 47.
[84] Cf. BeckRA-HdB/Lenz § 27 mn. 180; Kühne NJW 1997, 1951 (1952).

2. Secondary criminal law

In the area of criminal product liability, there are also special criminal provisions in secondary criminal law. In particular, the German Food, Commodities and Feed Code (§§ 58, 59 LFGB), the German Medicines Act (§§ 95, 96 AMG), the German Medical Devices Act (§§ 40, 41 MPG), the German Equipment and Product Safety Act (§ 20 GPSG), the Product Safety Act (§ 29 ProdSG), the Construction Products Act (§ 9 BauPG) and the Chemicals Act (§ 27 ChemG) provide for criminal liability, for example, in the event that defective or health-endangering products are placed on the market or are not recalled in breach of duty.[85] **94**

III. Duties of the entrepreneur

Criminal liability of the entrepreneur responsible for the product can result both from an active act and from an omission. However, the latter is only punishable if the entrepreneur is legally responsible for the fact that the success does not materialise. A corresponding guarantor obligation is required for criminal liability for omission.[86] The entrepreneur has such an obligation in the sense that he must ensure both the production and the distribution of the product. This responsibility results in obligations which the entrepreneur must fulfil in a due and proper manner. If he fails to do so, he runs the risk of criminal liability in the event of a violation of legal interests that occurs due to the defective product. The person responsible for the product is then held criminally liable for producing and placing the product on the market (action) if he or she violates a corresponding duty of care (omission).[87] **95**

There are different obligations attached to the different stages starting with product development up to the recall of a defective product which is already on the market. **96**

1. Product development

In the initial stage of product development or production, the entrepreneur has not only safety and monitoring obligations but also instruction obligations. The latter should serve in particular to avoid design and manufacturing defects. **97**

If the entrepreneur fails in designing his products, he may be liable to prosecution if the subsequent use of the products results in damage to third parties. Likewise, the entrepreneur may be liable to prosecution if, although there was no design defect, he intentionally or negligently produces defective products that lead to damage. In this case, §§ 222, 223 et seqq. StGB come into consideration. **98**

When designing the product, the entrepreneur must ensure that the operational safety of his products is guaranteed. They must be suitable for the intended use. An average user is to be taken as a reference. However, liability is limited to the core area, i.e. only to the actual area of use of the product. Any operating errors or the use by a user who is not familiar with the product must be considered. On the other hand, he is not criminally liable in the case of atypical conditions or consequences that may arise from his product. Before putting his product into production, he must test it sufficiently.[88] **99**

---

[85] Kühne NJW 1997, 1951 (1954).
[86] BeckOK StGB/Heuchemer, 65. Ed. 1.5.2025, StGB § 13 mn. 33; BeckRA-HdB/Lenz § 27 mn. 180.
[87] NK-WSS/Burchard StGB § 13 mn. 9.
[88] BeckOGK/T. Voigt, 1.5.2025, BGB § 823 mn. 651; Schmidt-Salzer Entscheidungssammlung Produkthaftung p. 17 et seq.

100 During the manufacture of his products, the entrepreneur is obliged to carry out quality controls. If his product is manufactured by human labour, the requirements for the inspection obligations are higher than in the case of automatic production. He has to be informed about which manufacturing defects can occur and whether they could be relevant for the average consumer. He has the duty to control potential sources of defects through manufacturing means and to devise a suitable quality control system that detects manufacturing defects. This can take the form of a special inspection procedure. The entrepreneur is free to decide how to ensure the quality of his products. If he does not fulfil these obligations, or only insufficiently, he is liable for potential damages.[89]

2. Sale

101 Generally, only products that do not pose a risk to the consumer may be distributed and placed on the market. It is the duty of the entrepreneur to ensure that the product is safe. The entrepreneur has a guarantor's duty insofar as he ensures and supervises the production and distribution of the product. He is therefore subject to both safeguarding and monitoring obligations.[90]

102 If, after a thorough examination, it turns out that the product is defective and poses a risk to the consumer, it may not be marketed. If, despite the defectiveness, the product is placed on the market and a consumer is harmed as a result, both intentional and negligent bodily injury or homicide offences come into consideration.[91]

103 Before the entrepreneur markets his product, he has a duty to instruct. He must therefore inform the consumer about the specific dangers associated with the use of the product and how such dangers can be avoided. If it can be assumed that the user is aware of the dangers, an exception to the reference requirement is permissible. However, the average consumer must be used as the reference point. The instruction must be complete, clear and unambiguous. Here, too, criminal liability is conceivable if the user violates such a duty and a third party suffers damage as a result.[92]

3. Recall of the defective product

104 Even after a product has been placed on the market, the entrepreneur is obliged to supervise it on the market. He must ensure that the relevant information is collected and passed on and must evaluate claims and warranty cases.[93]

105 If the product subsequently turns out to be dangerous, he has a duty to protect (e.g. production stop, labelling or media warning duties), and in extreme cases he even has a duty to recall the product.[94] This even applies if the defects were not initially identifiable or it cannot be determined with certainty what their cause was.[95] The same applies in the event that the actual production or placing on the market of a defective product was done unintentionally or with due care. The entrepreneur then has a guarantor's duty to avert damage, which results from his position as a guarantor from previous dangerous

[89] Schmidt-Salzer Entscheidungssammlung Produkthaftung p. 17 et seq.

[90] BeckOGK/T. Voigt, 1.5.2025, BGB § 823 mn. 660.

[91] BeckOGK/T. Voigt, 1.5.2025, BGB § 823 mn. 666 et seqq.

[92] Schmidt-Salzer Entscheidungssammlung Produkthaftung p. 16 et seq.; NK-ProdR/Ackermann BGB § 823 mn. 104 et seqq.

[93] BeckOGK/T. Voigt, 1.5.2025, BGB § 823 mn. 676; Schmidt-Salzer Entscheidungssammlung Produkthaftung p. 19 et seq.; NK-ProdR/Ackermann BGB § 823 mn. 122 et seqq.

[94] BGH 16.12.2008 – VI ZR 170/07, BGHZ 179, 157 mn. 10 = BeckRS 2009, 4229; NK-ProdR/Ackermann BGB § 823 mn. 668 et seqq., 670 et seqq.; Rengier StrafR AT, 14th edn 2022, § 50 mn. 59.

[95] BGH 6.7.1990 – 2 StR 549/89, BGHSt 37, 106 mn. 27 = BeckRS 1990, 1008.

behaviour. If he does not comply with this obligation, intentional omissions are conceivable, even if they are based on a positive action such as a management decision. In these cases, the focus of the blame[96], which is important in distinguishing between actions and omissions, lies in the omission of consumer protection or the recall.

If a corresponding defect is discovered during production, the entrepreneur is obliged to re-inspect the products remaining in the warehouse. In order to prevent proven defects in the future, he must revise construction plans if the cause of the defect has been clarified, and carry out inspections and type tests if the cause of the defect has not been clarified. If he fails to do so and damage occurs as a result, criminal liability is conceivable.[97] **106**

4. Case law

In the past, there were several landmark decisions that substantially dealt with the criminal liability of those responsible for products and thus significantly shaped criminal product law as a whole.[98] **107**

a) Leather spray case[99]

The so-called *Lederspray Fall* (leather spray case), which has received the most attention, was about the criminal liability of a leather spray manufacturer who offered his products for leather care on various markets. Despite numerous reports of damage, in which complaints about serious health problems such as breathing difficulties, coughing, fever, pulmonary oedema, etc. accumulated, only one active ingredient in the formula was changed. A short-term production and distribution stop was cancelled after further damage reports due to inconclusive internal investigations. At a special meeting of the management it was decided to put warnings on the cans, but to resume distribution due to lack of evidence of toxic properties. The management relied on the objection that a recall and warning action was only appropriate in cases of a 'real' product defect. After there were repeated reports of damage, the Federal Health Office and the Federal Ministry of Youth, Family and Health intervened, imposed a sales stop and ordered a recall. **108**

After the Regional Court of Mainz convicted the defendants of negligent bodily harm because of the events before and up to the special meeting, and of intentional bodily harm because of the events after the meeting, the Federal Supreme Court, as the court of appeal, ruled on their criminal liability. In addition to a conviction for negligent bodily harm by active action (§ 229 StGB), the BGH also convicted the defendants of intentional dangerous bodily harm by omission (§§ 223 sub. 1, 224 sub. 1 no. 5, 13 sub. 1 StGB). **109**

Among other things, the court was confronted with the problem of proving causality between the nature of the product and the health damage that occurred. Since it could not be proven beyond doubt in the case whether and, if so, which (toxic) substance in the leather spray was responsible for the damage to health, the BGH established the concept of general causality in the decision. Accordingly, in order to assume causality, courts would have to exclude all possible causes of the damage to health in a procedure of exclusion. If no other cause of damage could be considered, a causal connection would exist.[100] **110**

Also of fundamental importance was the question regarding the duties of a managing director and the distribution of tasks within the management of a company. According **111**

---

[96] BGH 17.2.1954 – GSSt 3/53, BGHSt 6, 46 (59) = BeckRS 1954, 20.

[97] Schmidt-Salzer Entscheidungssammlung Produkthaftung p. 19 et seq.

[98] ARR WirtschaftsStrafR-HdB/Kuhlen, 5th edn 2019, Ch. 1 B. mn. 5 et seqq.

[99] BGH 6.7.1990 – 2 StR 549/89, BGHSt 37, 106 = BeckRS 1990, 1008; Michalke Umweltstrafsachen mn. 500–502; Müller-Gugenberg WirtschaftsStrafR-HdB mn. 56.16.

[100] BGH 6.7.1990 – 2 StR 549/89, BGHSt 37, 106 mn. 27 = NJW 1990, 2560.

to the principle of trust, the members of the management may rely on the fact that other members also behave lawfully within their assigned area of responsibility. Overall responsibility for all areas of responsibility is therefore the exception. Such a responsibility is only conceivable in the case of an inter-departmental problem and describes the principle of general responsibility and universal responsibility of the management. One guiding principle of the decision was that the manufacturer (distributor) who brought defective products onto the market has a duty to avert the damage. This could be done by a recall. Furthermore, the court ruled that in the case of a multi-member entity, each managing director is obliged to do everything possible to achieve a positive recall decision.[101]

112 The Federal Court of Justice also stated that any dangerous prior conduct constitutes a guarantor's liability for reasons of inherent negligence and thus a duty to recall or warn the consumer exists. According to the court, it is the responsibility of the entrepreneur to ensure that the danger arising from the defective product does not result in damage. Accordingly, not only 'the person who causes the damage by positive action is liable, but also the person who fails to avert the impending damage'.[102]

113 This landmark decision was essential for the development of product liability under criminal law.

b) Lipobay scandal[103]

114 In the Bayer drama about the cholesterol-lowering drug Cerivastatin (Lipobay), more than 50 deaths were linked to the use of the drug. The drug was said to have caused muscle weakness (rhabdomyolysis) as a side effect, which can lead to organ failure, muscle tissue breakdown and death. The public prosecutor's office in Cologne accused company employees of not having immediately stopped the distribution of Lipobay after the side effects had been discovered. In addition to a criminal offence according to § 95 sub. 1 no. 1, sub. 4 AMG, there was also an accusation of negligent bodily injury (*fahrlässige Körperverletzung*, § 229 StGB). A sentence was never imposed because the employees never ignored the risks of the medicinal product when it was approved or marketed. Every intolerance was reported immediately. In Spain, Bayer was sentenced to pay a fine because the instruction leaflet had not adequately warned of the risks, such as muscle breakdown.[104]

115 Another legal problem of the case was the proof of causality (*Kausalitätsnachweis*). The Higher Regional Court of Cologne[105] ruled in an individual case in which the plaintiff suffered from rhabdomyolysis that the proof of causality between the previous intake of Lipobay and the damage that occurred could not be established despite detailed diagnostics. This should be the case because other possible causes, such as an autoimmune process or an infection, might also become a serious possibility.[106]

116 In addition to the determination of a general causality (*generelle Kausalität*), which exists if the medicine is generally capable of causing damage of the supposed kind, it is however always necessary to prove a specific causality (*konkrete Kausalität*) in the individual case. If this cannot be established, there is no criminal liability.

---

[101] BGH 6.7.1990 – 2 StR 549/89, BGHSt 37, 106 mn. 64 = NJW 1990, 2560 (2565).
[102] BGH 6.7.1990 – 2 StR 549/89, BGHSt 37, 106 mn. 34 = NJW 1990, 2560 (2563).
[103] Lenz Produkthaftung § 2 mn. 25; Müller-Gugenberg WirtschaftsStrafR-HdB mn. 56.11.
[104] Müller-Gugenberg WirtschaftsStrafR-HdB mn. 56.11.
[105] OLG Köln 24.1.2007 – 5 U 6/04, BeckRS 2007, 4503.
[106] OLG Köln 24.1.2007 – 5 U 6/04, BeckRS 2007, 4503.

c) Wood preservative proceeding[107]

The Regional Court of Frankfurt/Main[108] had to decide on a case in which the commercial and technical manager of a wood preservative company was accused of negligent and intentional bodily harm, and in several cases also of releasing poison with the risk of death or serious bodily harm. Users suffered physical injuries which were associated with the production and distribution of the wood preservative. 117

Even though the causal relationship between the biocidal ingredients of the wood preservatives and the health damage had not been scientifically clarified beyond doubt, it assumed causality, based on the argumentation of the BGH in the 'leather spray case'. As in that case, there was no uniform clinical picture among the consumers of the wood preservative. In order to assume a general causality with regard to the question of whether the substance can cause such damages at all, the Regional Court of Frankfurt/Main relied on a scientific expert opinion which was not undisputed. The Regional Court of Frankfurt/Main based the individual causality on the technique of circumstantial evidence by means of an overall assessment of the facts speaking for and against individual causality.[109] 118

The BGH[110] overruled this decision in 1995, claiming a violation of material law. The Regional Court had based its decision on the findings of recent medical research without, however, presenting the criticism in the scientific community against these findings and without dealing with this criticism in a factual manner. The BGH made it clear which requirements must instead be met in order to prove causality between possible product defects and the consequences of damage. It ruled that absolute certainty is not required and that instead it is sufficient that the court of fact adequately presents the state of scientific dispute and deals with it adequately.[111] 119

Furthermore, the BGH made a distinction between unconscious negligence and intent. It denied intentional commission because the defendants, encouraged by scientists, considered the wood preservatives to be harmless according to their state of information. According to the court, they did not recognise the measures that were legally required.[112] 120

The Regional Court of Frankfurt/Main[113], the court to which the case was referred back after annulling the first-instance judgement, ceased the proceedings pursuant to § 153a StPO. 121

d) Monza Steel case[114]

In 1972, after the tyre manufacturer Monza Steel had started producing and selling high-speed tyres a year earlier, defects occurred in the steel belted tyres. These led to major accidents in which seven people died and 22 were seriously injured. The company's management was accused of not having tested the tyres sufficiently, of having released them into production too early and of having reacted too late to reports of damage.[115] 122

---

107 LG Frankfurt/Main 27.7.1990 – 5/26 Kls 65 Js 8793/84, ZUR 1994, 33; BGH 2.8.1995 – 2 StR 221/94, BGHSt 41, 206 = BeckRS 1995, 5057; LG Frankfurt 6.11.1996 – 5/29 KLs 65 Js 8793/84, NJW 1997, 1994; Michalke Umweltstrafsachen mn. 503–507; Müller-Gugenberg WirtschaftsStrafR-HdB mn. 56.17.

108 LG Frankfurt/Main 27.7.1990 – 5/26 Kls 65 Js 8793/84, ZUR 1994, 33.

109 LG Frankfurt/Main 27.7.1990 – 5/26 Kls 65 Js 8793/84, ZUR 1994, 33 (35); Schmidt-Salzer NJW 1996, 1 (6).

110 BGH 2.8.1995 – 2 StR 221/94, BGHSt 41, 206 = BeckRS 1995, 5057.

111 BGH 2.8.1995 – 2 StR 221/94, BGHSt 41, 206 mn. 42 = BeckRS 1995, 5057.

112 BGH 2.8.1995 – 2 StR 221/94, BGHSt 41, 206 mn. 55 = BeckRS 1995, 5057.

113 LG Frankfurt 6.11.1996 – 5/29 KLs 65 Js 8793/84, NJW 1997, 1994.

114 LG München II 21.4.1978 – IV KLs 58 Js 5534/76; Schmidt-Salzer Entscheidungssammlung Produkthaftung p. 300; Michalke Umweltstrafsachen mn. 499; Müller-Gugenberg WirtschaftsStrafR-HdB mn. 56.31.

115 Müller-Gugenberg WirtschaftsStrafR-HdB mn. 56.31.

123 In a subsequent trial before the Regional Court of Munich II, the head of development, an employee of the company, was accused of negligently causing the death of a car driver. The Regional Court of Munich II sentenced him to one year's imprisonment on probation for involuntary manslaughter.

124 Also in this case, the decisive and disputed technical problem lay in the determination of the causal connection. The Regional Court of Munich II had to discuss to what extent the tyre defects that occurred were a single outlier or an attributable serial defect or whether the defect was due to a driving error. After hearing numerous experts, the court came to the conclusion that there had been a serial defect. These were attributable to the defendant because he had not carried out the necessary tests and inspections or had only carried them out insufficiently.[116]

e) Eschede ICE accident case[117]

125 The railway accident in Eschede on 3 June 1998 resulted in the derailment of an ICE train. The cause of the accident was the breakage of a wheel tyre, which led to consequential damage. The Regional Court of Lüneburg[118] ruled on the charges of a department president of Deutsche Bahn, a senior technical advisor of the Federal Railway and an operating engineer of the wheel tyre manufacturing plant. They were charged with bodily harm to 105 people and involuntary manslaughter of 101 people. The accusation was based on the inadequate testing of the wheels as well as on serious failures on the part of the Deutsche Bahn with regard to approval and maintenance. As it could not be established whether the defendants could have recognised the danger of the tyre breaking, the court ceased the proceedings.

f) Thalidomide proceedings[119]

126 In the 1960s, there was a trial in which the drug 'thalidomide' was suspected of causing nerve damage and malformations in newborn babies. In 1958 and 1959 there were isolated reports of side effects (especially nerve damage) of the product, in 1960 and 1961 the reports became more frequent. In 1961, Chemie Grünenthal GmbH changed the instructions for use and added a note about the side effects. The product was not taken off the market until the end of 1961.[120]

127 The executives and scientific staff of the chemical company were charged with bodily harm and involuntary manslaughter. The prosecution accused them of not having warned sufficiently about the side effects of the drug. For example, a declaration of non-hazardousness had been included in the instructions for use, although clinical and other tests had only justified a declaration of 'there are no known indications of danger'.[121]

128 The Regional Court of Aachen[122] ceased the proceedings against the defendants. It first stated that even if thalidomide had not been sufficiently pharmacologically and clinically tested before it was put on the market, the manufacturer would not have been at fault. Even a proper and conscientious pharmacological examination would not necessarily have revealed the occurrence of the side effects. However, the Regional Court of Aachen saw the blame of the defendants in the failure to inform the public about the side effects

---

[116] Michalke Umweltstrafsachen mn. 499.

[117] LG Lüneburg 8.5.2003 – 17 KLs 15/01; LG Lüneburg 19.5.2003 – 17 KLs 15/05; OLG Celle 5.6.2003 – 2 Ws 185/03, BeckRS 2003, 163258; Lenz Produkthaftung § 2 mn. 30.

[118] LG Lüneburg 8.5.2003 – 17 KLs 15/01.

[119] LG Aachen 18.12.1970 – 4 KMs 1/68, 15–115/67, JZ 1971, 507.

[120] BT-Drs. WD 7-3000-150/17, 4.

[121] Schmidt-Salzer NJW 1996, 1 (2).

[122] LG Aachen 18.12.1970 – 4 KMs 1/68, 15–115/67, JZ 1971, 507.

of thalidomide in a timely and proper manner. Thus, the drug had continued to be distributed despite knowledge of the side effects.[123]

The court came to the conclusion that the thalidomide contained in the medication was the cause of the physical deformities, but that this had not been foreseeable for the supervisors and colleagues. In this initial phase, they had been justified in trusting that the highly qualified colleague would fulfil his task properly, in particular that he would not commit such an instructional error.[124] It was remarkable how the Regional Court of Aachen substantiated the causality. Different expert opinions were available, which, however, came to two different conclusions. While some ruled out causality between thalidomide and the damage, others came to the opposite conclusion.[125] The existing research dispute was not decided by the scientific community itself, but by the Regional Court of Aachen in the exercise of its judicial conviction. 129

g) Ice-rink in Reichenhall case[126]

In the case involving the collapse of the roof of the ice rink in Reichenhall, a civil engineer was accused of negligent homicide and bodily injury at the Traunstein Regional Court.[127] Due to heavy snowfall, which had led to a high layer of snow on the roof, the roof collapsed. The collapsing roof buried several people. The civil engineer was accused by the public prosecutor's office of having failed to carry out a dutiful manual inspection of the roof structure and of having made positive statements about the structural condition of the roof.[128] 130

The Regional Court of Traunstein acquitted the defendant on factual grounds. However, the judgement was overturned by the BGH and referred back to the Regional Court of Traunstein. The focus of the BGH's judgement was based on the omission. The court came to the conclusion that the acceptance of a contract for the inspection of structural defects of an ice rink for the purpose of determining the need for renovation and the measures necessary for the elimination of the dangers posed by these defects to the general public triggered a guarantor status of the commissioned civil engineer. The contractual assumption also created a protective function towards the general public.[129] 131

The BGH also made it clear that in order to prove the causal connection between the omitted act and the success, it had to be determined whether the addition of the required act ('manual examination' of the supports of the roof of the hall) would have led to the omission of the success (death/physical injury) with a probability bordering on certainty. The requirement for establishing the missing causality of the breach of duty was whether the city would have acted if it had been notified of the defects.[130] While the Regional Court of Traunstein expressed doubts in this respect and denied a quasi-causality, the BGH stated that the Regional Court of Traunstein had not shown without legal error that the responsible persons of the city had failed to take measures to eliminate the source of danger despite the required warnings.[131] 132

---

123 LG Aachen 18.12.1970 – 4 KMs 1/68, 15–115/67, JZ 1971, 507 (514).
124 Schmidt-Salzer NJW 1996, 1 (2).
125 LG Aachen 18.12.1970 – 4 KMs 1/68, 15–115/67, JZ 1971, 507 (514).
126 BGH 13.11.2008 – 4 StR 252/08, BGHSt 53, 38 = NJW 2010, 1087.
127 LG Traunstein 27.10.2011 – 6 KLs 200 JS 865/06 (3), BeckRS 2009, 86563.
128 LG Traunstein 27.10.2011 – 6 KLs 200 JS 865/06 (3) mn. 2, BeckRS 2009, 86563.
129 BGH 13.11.2008 – 4 StR 252/08, BGHSt 53, 38 mn. 17 et seq = BeckRS 2008, 25406.
130 BGH 13.11.2008 – 4 StR 252/08, BGHSt 53, 38 = BeckRS 2008, 25406.
131 BGH 13.11.2008 – 4 StR 252/08, BGHSt 53, 38 = BeckRS 2008, 25406.

h) Bienenstich case[132]

133 After eating almond *Bienenstich* (a traditional German cake), a large number of consumers suffered from nausea, abdominal pain, vomiting and diarrhoea. The cake was infested with staphylococci. The BGH ruled on criminal liability under § 223 StGB for failing to recall the contaminated food.

134 The BGH denied the employee's criminal liability. The employee had fulfilled his duties by informing the managing director responsible for sales and distribution about the state of affairs and by advocating a comprehensive recall campaign in the meeting of the managing directors – although the managing directors decided not to carry out such a warning campaign. The BGH came to the conclusion that he could not be expected to do more, as he was subject to the instructions of the management. In particular, he was not obliged to carry out a warning or recall campaign himself against the declared will of the management.[133]

135 On the other hand, the BGH convicted the managing director of the food wholesaler as an accessory to bodily harm by omission, since he had at least tacitly agreed to the decision not to carry out a recall. He had been aware of the 'very obvious probability' of further illnesses and had nevertheless failed to take the necessary precautions. In this respect, the BGH determined that the managing director had at least acted with conditional intent.[134]

C. Food criminal law

I. Introduction

136 Food criminal law includes all criminal law regulations that concern the handling of food and also those that extend to animal feed, cosmetic products and consumer goods (§ 2 LFGB). Of particular relevance to criminal law are, for example, wrongly labelled, contaminated or spoiled food that have entered the market.[135] One example is the 'rotten meat' scandal, which attracted a large amount of media attention.[136] In numerous cases, spoiled meat and sausage products were relabelled and thus put on the market. Goods whose best-before date had been expired for some time were given a new, more recent date. In addition, sausage and meat products were found on the market that were no longer suitable for consumption and were a health hazard for the consumer. In this case, criminal liability according to the LFGB came into consideration.[137]

137 Food criminal law was established in order to protect consumers in the consumption of foodstuffs and thus to protect them from considerable health risks and damage. In addition to the protection of human life and health, it also serves to protect justified consumer interests. The consumer should also be protected from threats or disinformation (§ 1 sub. 1 LFGB).[138]

---

[132] BGH 4.5.1988 – 2 StR 89/88, LMRR 1988, 29; Müller-Gugenberg WirtschaftsStrafR-HdB mn. 56.15.

[133] BGH 4.5.1988 – 2 StR 89/88, LMRR 1988, 29.

[134] BGH 4.5.1988 – 2 StR 89/88, LMRR 1988, 29.

[135] BGH 27.3.2008 – 3 StR 526/07, BeckRS 2008, 6867; BGH 22.4.2020 – 1 StR 261/19, BeckRS 2020, 8564; LG Berlin 22.1.2006 – 505 Qs 1-4/06; LG Stuttgart 1.2.2019 – 11 KLs 176 Js 42172/15, BeckRS 2019, 47480; LG Hechingen 28.9.2020 – 11 Ns 27 Js 11792/17, BeckRS 2020, 48050; MAH AgrarR/Sandkuhl/Bellinghausen § 24 mn. 134.

[136] BGH 27.3.2008 – 3 StR 526/07, BeckRS 2008, 6867.

[137] MAH AgrarR/Sandkuhl/Bellinghausen § 24 mn. 135.

[138] Streinz/Meisterernst/Sackreuther LFGB Vor § 58 et seqq. mn. 1 et seq.

National criminal food law is shaped by European law, in particular by regulations that have led to a far-reaching harmonisation of both legal systems. German criminal food law thus represents the implementation of EU law at the national level. General regulations as well as the definition of basic concepts in food criminal law were made by the European Basic Regulation, whose specifications were largely implemented by the LFGB.[139] 138

Criminal food law refers to non-criminal provisions in its requirements.[140] 139

II. Legal sources and offences

1. Core criminal law

The StGB does not provide for a separate offence under food criminal law. However, in connection with the handling of food, criminal liability under the general provisions of the StGB is conceivable. In case of bodily injury or death of the consumer due to contaminated or spoiled food, criminal liability for bodily injury according to §§ 223 et seqq. StGB or ('involuntary') manslaughter according to §§ 212 et seqq., 222 StGB are conceivable. Likewise, in cases of food crime, a criminal offence of fraud according to § 263 StGB or a criminal offence of bribery or corruptibility in commercial transactions according to § 299 StGB can be considered. Also conceivable is a dangerous poisoning according to § 314 StGB, as well as a falsification of documents according to § 267 StGB in the case of a falsification of certificates, delivery notes or bills. 140

Furthermore, criminal liability under the Organic Farming Act (§§ 12, 13 ÖLG), the Wine Act (§§ 48, 49 WeinG) and the Trademark Act (§§ 143 et seq. MarkenG) may be considered. The latter is particularly relevant in the case of trademark infringement, infringement of Community trademarks or use of geographical indications. Equally conceivable is criminal liability under the Act Against Unfair Competition (§§ 16 et seqq. UWG) in the case of punishable advertising or betrayal of business and trade secrets. 141

2. Secondary criminal law

Of particular importance in secondary criminal law are §§ 58 and 59 LFGB. The entrepreneur is obliged to comply with the legal requirements mentioned there. If he violates them, he is liable to prosecution. For example, he must ensure that he observes the provisions of § 5 LFGB when producing, treating or placing a foodstuff on the market. This includes prohibitions for the protection of health. Likewise, according to § 10 LFGB, he may not place substances with pharmacological effects on the market. 142

Other norms that also serve the above-mentioned protected goods are, for example, § 7 LSpG (Food Specialities Act), § 10 RiFlEtikettG (Beef Labelling Act) and § 8 MilchMargG (Milk and Margarine Act). 143

III. Criminal offences

Prohibitions under food criminal law and the sanction regulations referring to them are not limited to the last step in the trade and production chain. Dangerous acts can already be sanctioned in advance. In any event, active commission of the act is not 144

139 Sosnitza/Meisterernst/Roffael/Wallau, 191. EL November 2024, LFGB Vor § 58 mn. 26.
140 Streinz/Meisterernst/Sackreuther LFGB Vor § 58 et seqq. mn. 4.

required. The offences under criminal food law can in principle be committed by omission even if the requirements of § 13 StGB are met.[141] According to §§ 58, 59 LFGB, it is a criminal offence to violate these regulations during production, treatment, marketing or export.

1. Production

145 When manufacturing products, the manufacturer is obliged to ensure that these products are safe. In order to do so, he has to monitor the production and take samples.

146 The term 'production' (*Herstellen*) is legally defined in § 3 sub. 1 no. 2 LFGB and means 'the obtaining, including the slaughter or killing, of live animals whose meat is intended to be used as food, the manufacturing, the preparation, the processing and the mixing'.

147 This includes all development, manufacturing and processing steps, from primary production, processing, mixing and packaging to acceptance of the finished product.[142]

148 Production is understood to be any primary production of plant and animal products, including fishing.[143]

149 The production presupposes an effect on the material substance of the product through treatment or processing with the aid of human or mechanical activity.[144]

150 The preparation as a subcategory of the production means any craft, factory or kitchen processing which makes the food suitable for consumption or preservable.[145] The term 'production' also includes the treatment and processing of a good.[146]

2. Treatment

151 § 3 sub. 1 no. 3 LFGB defines treatment (*Behandeln*) as 'weighing, measuring, filling, stamping, printing, packaging, cooling, freezing, deep-freezing, thawing, storing, transporting and any other activity that is not to be regarded as manufacturing or placing on the market'. The treatment serves as a catch-all term for such acts that fall neither under production nor under placing on the market.[147]

3. Placing on the market

152 The placing on the market as an offence is legally defined as 'the holding of food or feed for the purpose of sale, including offering for sale or any other form of transfer, whether free of charge or not, and the sale, distribution or other forms of transfer themselves'. This is derived directly from Art. 3 no. 8 Regulation (EC) No. 178/2002, to which § 3 no. 1 LFGB refers. This legal definition applies generally and is not limited to food and feed.

[141] Sosnitza/Meisterernst/Roffael/Wallau, 191. EL November 2024, LFGB Vor § 58 mn. 183.

[142] Erbs/Kohlhaas/Rohnfelder/Freytag, 255. EL Januar 2025, LFGB § 3 mn. 8 et seqq.; Streinz/Meisterernst/Meisterernst/Boch LFGB § 3 mn. 3 et seq.

[143] Erbs/Kohlhaas/Rohnfelder/Freytag, 255. EL Januar 2025, LFGB § 3 mn. 9; Sosnitza/Meisterernst/Rathke, 191. EL November 2024, LFGB § 3 mn. 10; Streinz/Meisterernst/Meisterernst/Boch LFGB § 3 mn. 3.

[144] Erbs/Kohlhaas/Rohnfelder/Freytag, 255. EL Januar 2025, LFGB § 3 mn. 10; Sosnitza/Meisterernst/Rathke, 191. EL November 2024, LFGB § 3 mn. 11.

[145] Erbs/Kohlhaas/Rohnfelder/Freytag, 255. EL Januar 2025, LFGB § 3 mn. 11; Sosnitza/Meisterernst/Rathke, 191. EL November 2024, LFGB § 3 mn. 13; Streinz/Meisterernst/Meisterernst/Boch LFGB § 3 mn. 5.

[146] Erbs/Kohlhaas/Rohnfelder/Freytag, 255. EL Januar 2025, LFGB § 3 mn. 12 et seq.; Sosnitza/Meisterernst/Rathke, 191. EL November 2024, LFGB § 3 mn. 14 et seq.; Streinz/Meisterernst/Meisterernst/Boch LFGB § 3 mn. 5.

[147] Sosnitza/Meisterernst/Rathke, 191. EL November 2024, LFGB § 3 mn. 16.

4. Transfer

153 The transfer includes the transport of products as well as products that can be confused with food. This is prohibited if they do not comply with the European and national requirements of food law. This is regulated by § 53 sub. 1 sent. 1 LFGB, which, however, allows exceptions according to § 54 LFGB for foodstuffs, cosmetic products and consumer goods that have been lawfully produced and lawfully marketed within the EU, the EEC, the EEA or another contracting state. In addition to the transport of the goods across the internal border of the EU, offences that are directly related to the transport are also covered. The transfer is accomplished when the goods cross the border and ends when the goods arrive at their destination.[148]

5. Export

154 Export requires the transfer of goods across the external border of the European Union. As in the case of introduction, export is accomplished when the border is crossed and ends as soon as the goods are at rest.

IV. Obligations of the entrepreneur

155 In German food criminal law, the fundamental principle of chain responsibility applies. From the producer to the retailer, each participant in the chain is responsible for the proper condition of the goods in his or her area of responsibility. Each participant has to check for him/herself whether the goods comply with the provisions of food law. The due diligence is limited to the entrepreneur's own area of responsibility and, as a rule, does not extend to the entire chain. However, the content and scope of the duty of care may vary.[149]

156 The designated food entrepreneur has obligations which he must fulfil in order to avoid potential criminal liability. He must comply with all provisions of food law. He has a due diligence to ensure that he produces and/or distributes food that is safe for the consumer and complies with the legal requirements. General requirements and principles are laid down in the Basic Regulation for European Food Law (Regulation (EC) No. 178/2002).[150] It states that the primary responsibility for the safety of food lies with the food entrepreneur. The food entrepreneur must ensure that additives and innovative foods are authorised, that harmful remains of pesticides do not get into the products and that allergens, for example, are properly labelled.

157 In addition to these primary duties, he also has general obligations such as ensuring general hygiene within the company.

1. Duty of investigation

158 The principle that the food entrepreneur must ensure the safety of the food also implies the obligation to inform himself about the food law regulations applicable to

[148] Sosnitza/Meisterernst/Rathke, 191. EL November 2024, LFGB § 3 mn. 8.

[149] Sosnitza/Meisterernst/Roffael/Wallau, 191. EL November 2024, LFGB Vor §§ 58 et seqq mn. 140 et seq.; Streinz/Meisterernst/Sackreuther LFGB Vor § 58 et seqq. mn. 91.

[150] Regulation (EC) No 178/2002 of the European Parliament and of the Council of 28 January 2002 laying down the general principles and requirements of food law, establishing the European Food Safety Authority and laying down procedures in matters of food safety.

him, both at national and European level. The food entrepreneur has a so-called duty of investigation.[151] The results of the investigation shall be critically examined by the food entrepreneur. He must not interpret them in his favour. The entrepreneur must obtain comprehensive information in time from independent and competent bodies, such as interest groups. In addition, the entrepreneur is required to continue his education on a regular basis or by attending specialist conferences, meetings and seminars or by reading the relevant specialised press and thus to be informed about the latest state of food law problems.[152]

2. Auditing duty

159 Of particular importance for the entrepreneur is also the duty to audit. In addition to the obligation to train employees, Art. 5 Regulation (EC) No. 852/2004 provides for an obligation to establish, implement and maintain one or more independent procedures based on the HACCP (Hazard Analysis and Critical Control Points) principles. These should include explanations on hazard analyses, critical control points, the setting of threshold levels, the monitoring of critical control points, corrective measures, verification measures and documentation.[153]

160 Furthermore, incoming goods and quality inspections must be carried out.[154] Products must be checked for impurities and vermin, hygiene, temperature and packaging material. An analysis of value-determining components should also be carried out.[155]

161 During storage, it must be ensured that the products are not adversely affected. Tests during storage may be necessary. The processor is obliged to take random samples. Final products must be checked.[156]

3. Obligation of representation and delegation

162 Since the duties of enquiry and examination cannot always be fulfilled by one employee alone, a delegation of tasks is necessary. In doing so, the delegator must ensure that the delegate has the necessary knowledge and review the delegate. Furthermore, the delegate is responsible for the proper organisation of the company.[157]

4. Information duty

163 In certain cases mentioned in Art. 19 Regulation (EC) No. 178/2002, information or notification to the competent authority is mandatory.[158]

[151] BayObLG 24.2.1972 – RReg. 8 St 1/72, BayObLGSt 1972, 52; BayObLG 6.10.1992 – 4 St RR 134/92, LMRR 1992, 33.
[152] Streinz/Kraus LebensmittelR-HdB/Bertling, 48. EL Juni 2024, III mn. 63.
[153] Streinz/Kraus LebensmittelR-HdB/Bertling, 48. EL Juni 2024, III mn. 64.
[154] Streinz/Meisterernst/Sackreuther LFGB Vor § 58 et seqq. mn. 95.
[155] Streinz/Kraus LebensmittelR-HdB/Bertling, 48. EL Juni 2024, III mn. 64.
[156] Streinz/Kraus LebensmittelR-HdB/Bertling, 48. EL Juni 2024, III mn. 64.
[157] Streinz/Kraus LebensmittelR-HdB/Bertling, 48. EL Juni 2024, III mn. 72–74; Streinz/Meisterernst/Sackreuther LFGB Vor § 58 et seqq. mn. 98 et seqq.
[158] Streinz/Kraus LebensmittelR-HdB/Bertling, 48. EL Juni 2024, III mn. 74a.

5. Traceability

Finally, the entrepreneur must also ensure traceability of the products placed on the market. Thus, there must be the possibility that all raw materials and ingredients can be traced through the entire food chain. This requirement applies to all entrepreneurs at all stages of production, processing and distribution to protect consumers.[159] **164**

In addition, a system and procedure must be established to disclose the above information to the competent authority upon its request. **165**

In order to facilitate the traceability of products, sufficient labelling of foodstuffs is also required.[160] **166**

---

[159] Sosnitza/Meisterernst/Rathke, 191. EL November 2024, EG-Lebensmittel-Basisverordnung Art. 18 mn. 1 et seqq.

[160] Streinz/Kraus LebensmittelR-HdB/Bertling, 48. EL Juni 2024, III mn. 75.

CHAPTER 21
CRIMINAL LIABILITY IN MEDICAL PRACTICE UNDER GERMAN LAW

Table of contents

A. Introduction ... 528
B. Criminal law risks in connection with medical treatment ... 529
I. Medical treatments as bodily harm ... 529
1. Prerequisites for consent ... 530
2. A closer look: information ... 530
3. Presumed consent ... 530
II. Negligent bodily injury and negligent killing ... 531
1. Breach of duty of care as a basis ... 531
2. Causality between breach of duty of care and bodily injury or death ... 532
3. Protective purpose connection ... 533
4. Objective and subjective foreseeability ... 533
III. Failure to render assistance ... 533
IV. Killing upon request, facilitating suicide as recurring pursuit ... 533
1. Killing upon request ... 534
2. Facilitating suicide as a recurring pursuit ... 535
V. Abortion ... 535
VI. Breaches of the duty of confidentiality ... 536
1. Another's secret ... 536
2. Physician as offenders ... 536
3. Disclose ... 537
4. Unauthorised ... 537
5. Commitment errors ... 538
VII. Issuance of incorrect health certificates ... 538
C. Economic criminal law in medicine ... 539
I. Billing fraud ... 539
1. Billing systems in the healthcare sector ... 540
a) Liquidation according to the German Medical Fee Index (GOÄ) ... 540
b) Billing by the panel physician ... 541
c) Billing by the hospitals vis-à-vis the health insurance funds ... 542
2. Billing fraud in the healthcare sector ... 543
a) Deception about facts ... 543
b) Error of a human counterpart ... 544
c) Error-based disposition of assets ... 544
d) Pecuniary detriment ... 545
e) Intent and intention to obtain an unlawful pecuniary benefit for oneself or a third party ... 546
f) Possible situations in practice ... 546
II. Embezzlement, especially embezzlement by panel physicians ... 547
1. Obligation to safeguard pecuniary interests of another person ... 547
2. Violation of the obligation to safeguard pecuniary interests ... 548
3. Pecuniary disadvantage ... 549
4. Intent ... 549

III. Corruption offences 549
1. Taking and giving bribes in healthcare sector (§§ 299a, 299b StGB) 549
2. Taking and giving bribes in commercial practice (§ 299 StGB) 551
3. Accepting and granting benefits, taking and giving bribes (§§ 331 et seqq. StGB) 552
D. Offences concerning medicinal products and pharmaceuticals 553
I. AMG 553
II. MPDG 555

A. Introduction

1 For the most part, the German medical criminal law does not include any statutory provisions specifically for the medical sector. Rather, many criminal offences laid down in the German Criminal Code (*Strafgesetzbuch*, StGB) are also applicable in the medical sector and the respective active parties. In particular, the risks of criminal liability in connection with medical treatments are not subject to any specific laws, but physicians and other medical personnel may also be liable to prosecution for bodily harm, homicides and failure to render assistance. If their actions are performed for a company, a liability of the company management must be considered. The economic criminal law in the field of medicine also includes offences that are known from general economic criminal law. Thus, billing fraud and embezzlement by panel physicians are versions of the general offences of fraud and embezzlement. While the general provisions apply in all of these areas, they are adapted through the specific legal and factual requirements of the medical sector. An increasingly specialized body of case law (and literature) is developing in this field. Partly, this leads to criminal offences only applicable to the medical sector. In the area of corruption, for example, new specific rules for giving and taking bribes in the healthcare sector have been created in §§ 299a, 299b StGB in 2016. Other offences, such as killing upon request or abortions pose criminal risks not only, but especially for physicians and other medical personnel. Wherever they are subject to special legal obligations – such as confidentiality obligations – there is a risk of criminal liability in case the obligations are violated.

2 But why is this relevant for companies? The healthcare sector is one of the industries with the highest turnover in Germany. Physicians as well as other medical and nursing staff work in big hospitals or even hospital groups, *Medizinische Versorgungszentren* (MVZ, i.e. medical care centres (MCC)) and different healthcare facilities. Some of these healthcare companies are run by physicians, but often the non-medical management, which is trained in business administration, is the focus of criminal investigations. Pharmacies are also dynamic businesses. Due to different organizational structures, criminal conduct of physicians and other medical and nursing staff or pharmacists in management positions may have the same effect on the company as criminal conduct of employed medical personnel, which was favoured, enabled, promoted or at least not prevented by the organizational structure created by the management. As in many other industries, compliance plays a major role in the healthcare sector.

3 The high turnover of the industry is based on a large number of invoices for treatment and other services. These must meet the strict requirements of the German Social Code (SGB) or the German Medical Fee Index (*Gebührenordnung für Ärzte*, GOÄ). In many cases, however, the details of billing for a specific treatment are not adequately regulated.

The payers have an interest in saving costs and sometimes exert considerable pressure on the service providers. Often, this pressure results in investigative proceedings, i.e., due to an allegation of a billing fraud, although there is an open dispute about the correct billing method.

This is one reason for the increase of investigative proceedings in the healthcare sector. Moreover, the inhibition threshold of patients and relatives to raise allegations of negligence during or after treatment is also noticeably reduced, which in many cases is accelerated by the chronic understaffing of nursing staff and the lack of time for proper communication (both potential organizational deficiencies). At the same time, numerous new regulations, such as the Medical Device Law Implementation Act (*Medizinprodukte-Durchführungsgesetz*, MPDG) and the Infection Protection Act (*Infektionsschutzgesetz*, IfSG), place very differentiated demands on the organization of medical facilities. Their managers must weave a dense web of compliance requirements to ensure that all specifications are (and can be) met and to provide a safety net in case of any misconduct. **4**

The following provides an overview of the most relevant offences of medical criminal law aiming to give a first impression of possible problems without any claim to completeness. **5**

B. Criminal law risks in connection with medical treatment

Numerous criminal law risks arise from treatment by physicians or other medical personnel. This already includes the question of the extent to which the impact on the patient inherent in the treatment is justified, whether the treatment was carried out in accordance with the relevant standards, or whether it was permissible to carry it out at all. In order to keep the presentation clear, the following will focus on physicians as treatment providers. **6**

I. Medical treatments as bodily harm

According to German criminal law, medical treatments constitute bodily harm and are therefore potentially punishable, even if they are carried out *lege artis*.[1] The significance of a treatment does not play a decisive role. Any form of physical impact on the patient's body is included, even non-invasive measures. This interpretation does not ignore the fact that the curative treatment as a whole is intended to improve the patient's physical status and health. However, it takes into account that the encroachment of the patient's physical integrity does fulfil the offence of bodily harm. Therefore, it is incumbent upon him to permit this encroachment. If the treatment is carried out without the patient's consent, it constitutes bodily harm. **7**

If this is done intentionally – i.e. with the knowledge and will of the physician – according to § 223 sub. 1 StGB and if certain additional circumstances are fulfilled, the bodily harm may qualify as dangerous bodily harm according to § 224 sub. 1 StGB or as grievous bodily harm according to § 226 sub. 1 StGB. **8**

In principle, the treatment does not lead to a criminal liability for bodily harm of the physician if the patient has effectively declared consent to the treatment or if there is **9**

[1] Cf. only BGH 30.1.2019 – 2 StR 325/17, BeckRS 2019, 21605.

presumed consent. In the structure of the offence, these lead to the justification of the conduct constituting the offence and thus to impunity.

1. Prerequisites for consent

10 Effective consent must be expressly or impliedly declared by the patient and requires the patient's capacity to consent. The patient must be sufficiently insightful and his decision must not have been induced by threat or coercion. Likewise, the consent must not be based on deception.[2]

11 The patient must be authorised to dispose of the legal interests concerned. This is generally the case with individual legal interests. In the case of bodily harm, the provision of § 228 StGB and the immorality standardised therein define the limit. According to this provision, bodily harm is unlawful despite consent if the act offends common decency. Common decency is defined as the sense of decency of all those who think fairly and justly, so that both the values of individual social groups and the subjective judgement of the person called upon to decide on bodily harm must be considered. Specific cases discussed in this respect include doping in sport or non-indicated surgery.

2. A closer look: information

12 In the case of medical treatments, effective consent requires sufficient information. The purpose of this is to enable the patient to make an informed and self-determined decision (informed consent) and must therefore be carried out properly, completely and conscientiously.

13 The requirements for informed consent in medical law are regulated in § 630e BGB. According to this, the treating party is obliged to inform the patient of all and any circumstances which are relevant to consent. This includes in particular the nature, extent, implementation, anticipated consequences and risks involved in the measure, as well as its necessity, urgency, suitability and prospects for success with regard to the diagnosis or the therapy. Possible alternative treatments must be pointed out, if they exist.

14 In practice, criminal and economic risks often result from inadequate documentation of the information being provided. In this context, for company management, it is not only of considerable importance to insist on the proper implementation of informed consent, but also to ensure that – in addition to the treatment documentation – the proper information and subsequent consent are also duly documented.

3. Presumed consent

15 It is not always possible to plan medical treatment and obtain informed consent from the patient in advance. Often, there are emergencies in which it is not possible to obtain consent for various reasons. In these cases, the physician may still be justified if there is presumed consent. In addition to the impossibility of obtaining consent, this presupposes that no opposing will of the patient is evident and that the treatment is within the presumed will of the patient.[3] This will must be determined on the basis of personal circumstances and individual interests as they are discernible prior to the treatment. It is not decisive what would be objectively reasonable. If it turns out after the treatment that

[2] Cf. on the previous points: Prütting/Gierok StGB § 228 mn. 10.
[3] Cf. Prütting/Gierok StGB § 228 mn. 23 et seq.

the patient would not have wanted the treatment had he been asked, this has no effect on the previously assumed presumed consent.

Conversely, if there is an expressly declared will, for example in the form of a living will, treatment contrary to this declared will can lead to criminal liability for (intentional) bodily harm. 16

II. Negligent bodily injury and negligent killing

Apart from cases in which there is a lack of effective consent on the part of the patient, the focus of criminal liability risks in medical treatment is on crimes of negligence. Even if a violation of the professional duty of care of the physician is established, as a rule, his intent – i.e. knowledge and intention of the factual result – cannot be affirmed. Even in the case of obvious breaches of a duty of care, it is regularly assumed – also by the investigating authorities – that a physician aligns his actions with the welfare of the patient and does not intentionally seek to harm him. Nevertheless, in individual cases, tangible reasons may lead to the assumption of intent. 17

1. Breach of duty of care as a basis

The accusation of criminal liability for negligent bodily injury under § 229 StGB or negligent killing under § 222 StGB always presupposes a violation of the required standard of care. This standard of care must be determined in each individual case. Medical treatments must be rendered *lege artis*. This requires compliance with the specialist standard, i.e. the professional standard of an experienced specialist in the respective field, and thus the respective state of medical science.[4] If a treatment rendered is not tenable when measured against this standard, this constitutes medical malpractice. The practitioner does not have to formally fulfil the qualifications of a specialist, but the treatment must be of a corresponding quality. 18

In many cases, such standards for treatment are laid down in guidelines of professional societies. These are not generally binding, but can often provide criminal law with a considerable reference point for the respective state of the art. The individually different requirements for physicians depending on their specialisation (general practitioner or specialist) and place of work (general practitioner's practice or specialised clinic) must also be considered. 19

Malpractice can occur during the assessment, diagnosis or the choice of therapy. It should be noted that physicians are generally granted the freedom to choose methods and in individual cases may even be obliged to deviate from a guideline or other recommendations in order to achieve the best possible treatment for the patient.[5] 20

In addition, especially in larger entities of the healthcare sector, further risks for malpractice arise from the organizational structure, such as the insufficient composition, selection, allocation and control of the persons deployed and their cooperation. When physicians from different disciplines and different hierarchical levels cooperate with each other and with other medical and nursing staff, it is necessary to delineate clear responsibilities. In particular, a distinction must be made between the horizontal and vertical division of labour:[6] 21

4 BGH 19.11.1997 – 3 StR 271/97, BeckRS 1997, 30003083.
5 Cf. MAH MedR/Terbille/Feifel, 3rd edn 2020, § 1 mn. 577.
6 Cf. for the following Prütting/Kessler StGB § 222 mn. 12 et seq.

22 In inpatient hospital treatment, physicians from different departments regularly collaborate. Within the framework of this horizontal division of labour, the principle of individual and personal responsibility applies, according to which each specialist is responsible for the tasks and activities assumed in his specialist area. At the same time, the principle of trust applies. This stipulates that each person involved in hospital treatment may rely on the other person fulfilling their share of the tasks with the necessary knowledge and due care.

23 Furthermore, there is a vertical division of labour among physicians as well as between physicians and other staff. A head physician, for example, cannot himself carry out all the tasks that belong to his specialist department. Rather, it is imperative for a functioning hospital operation that he delegates tasks to qualified and reliable staff, who in turn take them over according to the principle of personal responsibility. In each case, it must also be considered whether a task may be delegated to non-medical staff or must be delegated to subordinate physicians.

24 In investigative proceedings, an expert opinion is usually obtained to clarify the question of whether a malpractice in the sense of a breach of the duty of care has occurred. Since the public prosecutors themselves do not know the requirements of due care required in an individual case in detail and are not in a position to compare these with the treatment carried out, this task is performed by experts from the respective field.

25 When defending or representing a company in investigative proceedings, such expert opinions must also be critically examined in the interest of the company. Often, the expert opinions are open to attack because they themselves do not comply with the required methodology and standards. Regularly, the patient's documents and factual information provided to the expert are also incomplete.

2. Causality between breach of duty of care and bodily injury or death

26 If the factual outcome of a breach of the duty of care by the practitioner is the patient's death or bodily injury, the decisive factor is whether the breach of the duty of care caused the outcome. This is generally the case if the acts of the practitioner cannot be disregarded without the success being lost. In case law, and thus also in the practice of the investigating authorities, the relevant standard developed is whether the result of the offence, death or bodily harm, would have been eliminated with virtual certainty if the practitioner had acted in accordance with the duty of care.[7]

27 This question is to be answered primarily from a medical point of view and must therefore, usually, be answered by the expert who has already been commissioned with the question of the breach of the duty of care. In this context, especially in the area of negligent killing, it is not sufficient for the expert to establish the possibility of survival. Rather, on the basis of comprehensibly presented arguments, he must come to the conclusion that the patient would, with virtual certainty, have lived at least several hours longer.

28 If the public prosecutor or the judge cannot be convinced of the causality on the basis of the expert's statements, which are to be critically questioned, in case of doubt it must be assumed in favour of the accused that there is no causality.

3. Protective purpose connection

29 Another important prerequisite for criminal liability for negligent killing or negligent bodily injury is the connection between the breached duty of care and the result that

---

[7] Prütting/Kessler StGB § 222 mn. 21.

occurred. This is only the case if the duty breached was intended to prevent this specific outcome.[8]

4. Objective and subjective foreseeability

Moreover, the outcome must be objectively foreseeable and subjectively foreseeable for the practitioner. Considering the expectable course of events, the outcome must be able to be regarded as expectable in the ex-ante perspective. This is not the case if the course of events is entirely unusual and only thus brings about the respective outcome. **30**

III. Failure to render assistance

The German Criminal Code also stipulates in § 323c sub. 1 StGB that anyone is liable to prosecution for failure to render assistance, who does not render assistance in the case of an accident or a common danger or emergency although it is necessary and can reasonably be expected under the circumstances, in particular if it is possible without substantial danger to that person and without breaching other important duties. **31**

This is a criminal offence that can be committed by anyone. However, physicians and other medical practitioners are particularly affected, as their training gives them special capabilities to provide assistance. If they do not apply these or if a patient requests treatment and this is refused, the offence may become relevant. For this to be the case, however, one of the three situations defined in the offence must be fulfilled, which cannot be affirmed every time a patient presents himself at a physician's practice. For example, an accident is a sudden event that entails the immediate danger of (further) considerable damage to a protected legal asset.[9] This is not necessarily the case, for example, with a patient who comes to the hospital after falling down three days ago and, after a waiting time that he perceives as unreasonable, claims that it would be a failure to render assistance because it was not provided immediately. Such cases, offer neither a sudden event nor is it recognisable what the immediate danger of further injury should be. **32**

The assistance must be necessary and reasonable in the cases defined by law, in particular without substantial danger to oneself and without breaching other important duties. During the Covid pandemic with the obligation to wear masks in healthcare facilities, the treatment of persons who refused to wear masks was considered unreasonable by investigating authorities, partly also because of the considerable danger to the practitioner. **33**

Criminal liability for failure to render assistance requires intent. **34**

IV. Killing upon request, facilitating suicide as recurring pursuit

The field of 'assisted suicide' is extraordinarily complex. Debates in society cause the legal situation to waver, while at the same time healthcare institutions and their staff must remain capable of acting in this critical field. The problem was further highlighted by the recent ruling of the Federal Constitutional Court[10] on facilitating suicide as a recurring **35**

---

[8] Prütting/Kessler StGB § 222 mn. 21.

[9] Prütting/Gierok StGB § 323c mn. 1 et seqq.

[10] BVerfG 26.2.2020 – 2 BvR 2347/15, 2 BvR 651/16, 2 BvR 1261/16, 2 BvR 1593/16, 2 BvR 2354/16, 2 BvR 2527/16, BeckRS 2020, 2216.

pursuit, which abolished the offence of § 217 StGB. Problems are caused by the sometimes diametrically opposed aspects of the physician's obligation to treat on the one hand and the patient's self-responsible, self-endangering behaviour on the other. For example, the further development of medical devices entails the possibility to prolong life even where it is no longer considered worth living and impossible to live with dignity, at least for the patient.

1. Killing upon request

36 § 216 StGB charges whoever kills another person on the basis of that person's express and earnest request with imprisonment of six months to five years. The killing must be intentional. The offence illustrates the dichotomy between the patient's right to self-determination and the law's restriction to consent. Although suicide is exempt from punishment in the German legal system, the patient cannot effectively consent to an act of killing by another person.

37 In detail, a differentiation must be made between various measures that lead to a shortening of life:

38 A targeted, painless killing or acceleration of death, which corresponds to the express wish of the dying person (so-called 'direct' assisted suicide), fulfils the elements of the offence of § 216 StGB and is thus prohibited and punishable.

39 However, if the medical treatment is not aimed at causing the patient's death, but rather at alleviating pain, although death is a possible or unavoidable consequence, such medical treatment is exempt from punishment (so-called 'indirect assisted suicide'). This is usually the case with the use of certain analgesics in terminally ill patients.

40 Due to the impunity of suicide, participation in suicide is not punishable. In this respect, the necessary punishable principal offence for participation does not exist. If a seriously ill person is given a lethal medication to administer to himself, this conduct is not punishable. The physician's duty to rescue after the patient's loss of consciousness is also ruled out, since the physician cannot be criminally liable if the self-determined patient chooses the freely responsible suicide.[11]

41 As a further life-shortening measure, treatment can be discontinued, constituting so-called 'passive' assisted suicide. If there is no medical indication for further treatment and it is in accordance with the patient's express will not to receive life-sustaining measures, it is even legally required to discontinue life-sustaining measures without penalty and thus allow the patient to die. Assisted suicide – by not initiating or discontinuing life-prolonging measures – is only permissible in accordance with the declared or presumed will of the patient, in order to allow dying to take its natural course in conformity with human dignity.[12]

42 The living will has become increasingly important. Even though the Federal Court of Justice has not applied §§ 1827 et seqq. BGB as a mandatory requirement in determining the patient's will, the prerequisites of §§ 1827, 1828 BGB must be observed.[13] Pursuant to § 1827 sub. 1 sent. 1 BGB, a patient who is capable of giving consent may specify in writing in advance which medical measures he consents to and which he prohibits.

---

[11] BGH 3.7.2019 – 5 StR 393/18, BeckRS 2019, 19646.
[12] BGH 15.11.1997 – 3 StR 79/96, BeckRS 1997, 865.
[13] BGH 10.11.2010 – 2 StR 320/10, BeckRS 2010, 29891.

2. Facilitating suicide as a recurring pursuit

In its ruling of 26 February 2020, the Federal Constitutional Court declared the – no longer valid – criminal offence of facilitating suicide as a recurring pursuit under § 217 StGB (former version) to be unconstitutional and void.[14] In its decision, the Federal Constitutional Court argues with the 'right to self-determined dying, which includes the right to commit suicide.'[15] Since the decision, the federal government has been examining the possibility of rewriting § 217 StGB. For institutions active in this field, further developments remain to be seen. **43**

V. Abortion

In addition to the pregnant woman herself, a physician or a third party can also be the offender of an abortion, cf. § 218 sub. 1 sent. 1, sub. 3 StGB. Physicians and thus also healthcare facilities that offer abortions must therefore keep in mind the special criminal risks. These can be avoided by fully complying with the legal requirements. **44**

§§ 218–219b StGB are an expression of the state's duty to protect unborn life. Since only intentional acts are punishable, negligent abortion is not punishable.[16] If necessary, however, criminal liability for negligent bodily harm to the patient must be considered. An abortion is also exempt from punishment if there is an exemption from punishment under § 218a StGB. Accordingly, the offence is not committed and the abortion is permissible under criminal law, if **45**

- the pregnant woman requests the termination of pregnancy and can prove that she sought counselling at least three days prior to the procedure (§ 218a sub. 1 no. 1 StGB),
- the termination is performed by a physician (§ 218a sub. 1 no. 2 StGB), and
- no more than twelve weeks have elapsed since conception.

Furthermore, the unlawfulness of the intervention does not apply if **46**

- a medical-social indication (§ 218a sub. 2 StGB) or
- a criminological indication (§ 218a sub. 3 StGB) exists.

Special risks of criminal liability for the physician arise from §§ 218b, c, 219b StGB if he violates medical duties incumbent upon him when performing an abortion. This is the case in the following situations: **47**

- the physician does not sufficiently assure himself that the prerequisites of a medical-social or criminological indication (§ 218a sub. 2, 3 StGB) have been established by another physician and nevertheless performs the termination (§ 218b sub. 1 sent. 1 StGB);
- the physician makes an incorrect determination about the indications according to § 218b sub. 2, 3 StGB against his better knowledge (§ 218c sub. 1 sent. 2 StGB);
- the pregnant woman is given insufficient opportunity by the terminating physician to explain her reasons for requesting that the pregnancy be terminated (§ 218c sub. 1 no. 1 StGB) or he is not given medical advice about the significance of the procedure, in particular about the steps in the procedure, its after-effects, risks, possible physical or psychological consequences (§ 218c sub. 1 no. 2 StGB);

---

[14] BVerfG 26.2.2020 – 2 BvR 2347/15, 2 BvR 651/16, 2 BvR 1261/16, 2 BvR 1593/16, 2 BvR 2354/16, 2 BvR 2527/16, BeckRS 2020, 2216.

[15] BVerfG 26.2.2020 – 2 BvR 2347/15, 2 BvR 651/16, 2 BvR 1261/16, 2 BvR 1593/16, 2 BvR 2354/16, 2 BvR 2527/16, BeckRS 2020, 2216.

[16] Prütting/Kessler StGB § 218a mn. 17.

- the physician has not convinced himself of the length of the pregnancy on the basis of a medical examination (§ 218c sub. 1 no. 3 StGB);
- the physician is both the advising physician and the physician performing the termination (§ 218c sub. 1 no. 4 StGB).

48 The offence contains various obligations to explain, advise and verify. § 219b StGB aims to prevent illegal abortions through the marketing of abortifacients.

49 The widely discussed ban on advertising for abortions under § 219a StGB (former version) was abrogated with effect from 19 July 2022.

VI. Breaches of the duty of confidentiality

50 According to § 203 StGB, the violation of the duty of confidentiality is punishable for physicians and other explicitly named professional groups: specifically, anyone who, as a member of the listed professional groups, discloses a secret that has been revealed or otherwise made known to him in his professional capacity without authorisation is liable to prosecution. This must be done intentionally. Physicians are named in § 203 sub. 1 no. 1 StGB as the first professional group for which the unauthorised disclosure of another's secret is punishable. This also seems appropriate, because the physician's duty of confidentiality is a core element of medical professional ethics. Without the physician's confidentiality, a relationship of trust between patient and physician would not be possible.

51 The physician's confidentiality is also protected at other points in the criminal proceedings: in criminal proceedings, medical documents are exempt from seizure and the physician has the right to refuse testimony pursuant to § 53 StPO.

1. Another's secret

52 Another's secret comprises facts which, according to the recognisable intention of the owner of the secret, are to be kept secret, are known only to a limited number of persons and for which the affected person has a justified interest in secrecy.[17] It is irrelevant what kind of facts are concerned and whether the disclosure is embarrassing to the affected person or detrimental to their social standing. Rather, this includes all information that the patient gives to the physician in connection with the treatment, as well as the patient's name and the fact that he is being treated at all. The concept of a secret is interpreted broadly.

53 It follows from § 203 sub. 5 StGB that the protection of the secret transcends the life of the bearer. The duty of confidentiality still applies after the death of the patient.

2. Physician as offenders

54 § 203 StGB is an offence, which can only be committed by a member of the professional groups listed in § 203 sub. 1 StGB, in particular by physicians, § 203 sub. 1 no. 1 StGB. The secret must have become known to the holder of the professional secret as a member of one of the professional groups – i.e. precisely in his capacity and function as a physician and not only as a private person. Whether the secret was revealed to him – i.e. precisely under circumstances from which his confidentiality obligation arises, such as during consultation hours – or otherwise made known to him is irrelevant, as long as the acquisition

[17] Prütting/Kessler StGB § 203 mn. 33.

has a functional connection with the activity as a physician.[18] Thus, the physician must also keep the secrets of patients who have not voluntarily sought treatment from him.

3. Disclose

Disclosure is any communication of a secret or a detail to a third party who had no or no comprehensive knowledge of it.[19] 55

The secret does not have to become public through disclosure; for the physician to be criminally liable, it is sufficient that he passes the information to a single person. The form is irrelevant. 56

It does not constitute a disclosure under § 203 StGB if the physician passes on secrets to third parties who would have come into contact with them anyway and who are themselves subject to confidentiality obligations (e.g. medical assistants, colleagues involved in treatment, nursing staff, physician's assistants and typists). This is explicitly regulated in § 203 sub. 3 sent. 1 StGB, so that the disclosure of secrets to professional assistants is not a punishable offence. This plays a significant role for the organisation of companies in the healthcare sector. 57

4. Unauthorised

The disclosure must also be unauthorised. This is the case if there is no consent of the patient, no exclusion of the offence according to § 203 sub. 3 sent. 1 StGB and no justification. 58

The patient can release the physician from the duty of confidentiality at any time and thus declare his consent to the disclosure of the secret to third parties. Regarding the question of criminal liability, giving this consent is in principle possible to do informally. It can therefore be given in writing, orally, but also impliedly by conclusive behaviour. In practice, a written release from the duty of confidentiality is always recommended in order to be able to provide proof of the release if necessary. Companies should instruct their employees, who are subject to the duty of confidentiality, accordingly. 59

In practice, secrets are often passed on carelessly. This is especially the case with relatives or other supposedly close persons of the patients. In any case, implied consent cannot be readily assumed. This applies all the more to other patients. 60

However, implied consent is obvious in cases where there is a compulsory division of labour, e.g. in a hospital. Here, it is usually assumed that upon admission to the hospital, the patient makes a conclusive declaration that he consents to the information flows usually associated with hospital treatment.[20] 61

In contrast, there is no implied consent in the case of the transmission of patient data and findings to an external billing office upon conclusion of a treatment contract.[21] The patient's consent must be obtained for this. In individual cases, this may also be done by a cooperating person pursuant to § 203 sub. 3 sent. 2 StGB. 62

If the patient is permanently or temporarily unable to give consent, presumed consent replaces the actual decision. It justifies the disclosure of a secret. The prerequisite for this – apart from the lack of an act of consent – are first of all the preconditions of consent, i.e. the presumed consenting person must be the owner of the legal interest concerned, authorised to dispose of it and capable of insight and decision. A typical case group is the 63

[18] BGH 28.10.1992 – 3 StR 367/92, BeckRS 1992, 3056.
[19] BGH 10.8.1995 – IX ZR 220/94, BeckRS 1995, 5641.
[20] Prütting/Kessler StGB § 203 mn. 57 with further evidence.
[21] BGH 30.04.1991 – VI ZR 229/90, BeckRS 2008, 15004.

patient who is admitted to hospital unconscious and whose relatives are informed about his physical condition. If it is impossible or disproportionate to obtain actual consent, it must be determined whether the patient would give his consent if he could have been asked beforehand, because the disclosure is in his interest. The interest is determined by his subjective preferences, i.e. his personal goals, wishes, needs and values. Recourse to presumed consent is therefore not possible if the holder of the legal interest has already refused consent or his contrary will is otherwise known to the offender. It does not matter whether his decision appears reasonable or comprehensible. Only if there are no indications of the particular interests of the affected person, a decision can be made based on what a reasonable third party would want.

64 Pursuant to § 203 sub. 3 sent. 2 StGB, disclosure by professionals, in this case in particular physicians, to external persons and third parties called in by them is not unauthorised insofar as this is necessary to employ the activities of the other persons involved. The prerequisite is that the disclosure is only made to the extent necessary to employ the other persons involved. It does not matter whether the use of the external third party is necessary as such, but whether the information that is given to the third party is actually necessary for the third party's activity.[22]

65 In practice, disclosure often takes place in connection with police or prosecutorial investigations, without the question of authorisation being sufficiently examined. Many physicians lack the awareness that confidentiality obligations also apply in such cases. Precisely so that the physician can resolve the conflict between questioning by investigating authorities and his confidentiality obligations, the Code of Criminal Procedure grants him the right to refuse testimony in § 53 StPO. If the physician does not make use of this right and discloses secrets without authority or justification, he is liable to prosecution if the other prerequisites are fulfilled.

5. Commitment errors

66 Pursuant to § 203 sub. 4 sent. 1 no. 1 StGB, anyone who, as a person named in paras. 1 and 2, has not ensured that another person involved, who reveals a secret of another person that has become known to him in the exercise of or on the occasion of his work without being authorised to do so, and who been formally put under the obligation to maintain secrecy is also liable to prosecution. The physician must therefore contribute to ensuring that other persons employed in his area of responsibility do not disclose secrets. To avoid this, it is at least necessary that the persons involved are required to sign a non-disclosure agreement.

VII. Issuance of incorrect health certificates

67 The issuing of incorrect health certificates can be committed by physicians (§ 13 BÄO (*Bundesärzteordnung*, Federal Medical Regulation)) or other licensed medical personnel (midwives, nurses, speech therapists, etc.) under § 278 StGB.

68 Health certificates are certificates that deal with the state of health or the course of illness of a patient. Health certificates include sick certificates, medical reports and certificates of incapacity for work. However, only incorrect written statements about another person are punishable.

[22] BT-Drs. 18/11936, 23.

The health certificate is incorrect if the statement or recorded facts about findings or expert conclusions do not correspond to the actual facts. Irrespective of whether the overall assessment is correct, the certificate is already incorrect if the physician certifies an individual finding untruthfully.[23] **69**

Contrary to the previous version of § 278 StGB, it is now no longer necessary that the incorrect health certificate be used for vis-à-vis a public authority or insurance company. Rather, the health certificate must have been issued for the purpose of deception in legal relations. This has the consequence that e.g. incorrect vaccination certificates for use in ordinary legal relations are now also covered by § 278 StGB. It is not necessary for the physician to have personally carried out the process of issuing the certificate. Rather, it is necessary that the physician outwardly recognises that he is responsible for the correctness of the content. **70**

With regard to the incorrectness of the health certificate, it is not necessary to act 'against one's better knowledge'; conditional intent is sufficient. **71**

In addition, § 277 StGB also punishes the unauthorised issuance of health certificates. The issuance of health certificates under the designation of a physician or another registered medical professional, without having the right to do so, is sanctioned. If health certificates are issued by companies in the healthcare sector, it must therefore be ensured from a compliance point of view that the correct issuer is involved and is also recognisable from the health certificate. **72**

C. Economic criminal law in medicine

The economic criminal law of medicine has gained considerable importance over the last years. As one of the economically strongest sectors in Germany, the healthcare sector offers many opportunities for at least a suspicion for a wide range of economic offences, not only because of the high turnover, but also because of the strong regulation, which nevertheless does not clearly prescribe every current individual case of treatment or interaction of service providers. **73**

Of great practical relevance are billing fraud (→ mn. 75 et seqq.), embezzlement (→ mn. 122 et seqq.) and corruption offences (→ mn. 133 et seqq.) – each with a different weighting in the context of defence or preventive counselling. **74**

I. Billing fraud

Billing fraud is not a special offence for physicians. Like fraud under § 263 StGB,[24] billing fraud is punishable, but the interpretation of the constituent elements of the offence is partly governed by special features shaped by case law. **75**

Understanding the different billing systems in the healthcare system is necessary to understand billing fraud. From these result different criminal law assessments of billing situations. **76**

[23] BGH 29.1.1957 – 1 StR 333/56, BeckRS 1957, 104707.

[24] For more general details see → Ch. 11.

1. Billing systems in the healthcare sector

77 Since a comprehensive presentation of all billing systems is not intended, the three most important constellations are presented below. These are liquidation according to the GOÄ (→ mn. 81 et seqq.), billing by the panel physician (→ mn. 87 et seqq.) and billing by the hospital, especially vis-à-vis the health insurance (→ mn. 91 et seqq.).

78 The type of insurance the patient has is also decisive. The German healthcare system offers different health insurance options for patients: the *gesetzliche Krankenversicherung* (statutory health insurance, SHI) is a compulsory insurance for all persons in Germany who are not classified as exempt from insurance or have no other entitlement to coverage in case of illness. It is offered by the health insurance funds. The *private Krankenversicherung* (private health insurance, PHI) can be taken out by insured persons with a private insurance company under certain conditions. Unlike SHI, freedom of contract applies in principle, so that a PHI does not have to accept a particular person and the amount of the insurance premiums does not (primarily) depend on the income of the insured person, but on the scope of the insured benefits and the individually insured risk.

79 Patients insured with the SHI do not pay for treatments covered by the SHI insurance themselves; instead, they present their SHI card, and the physician invoices the SHI for the rendered treatment. Patients insured with the PHI, on the other hand, generally pay for the treatment themselves; the physician invoices them for the rendered treatment; then the PHI patients submit the invoice with their PHI for reimbursement of the costs by their PHI. Depending on the insurance tariff, the full invoice amount or part of it will then be reimbursed. Civil servants and judges are generally insured with a private health insurance and are in particular entitled to *Beihilfe* (benefit). The benefit also reimburses part of the treatment services paid by the patient.

80 In some cases, SHI patients choose to pay themselves for treatments received (*Selbstzahler*, also see → mn. 81); this is the case when a desired treatment service is not covered by the SHI but the SHI patient nevertheless wants this treatment to be carried out by the physician. Those insured with the SHI can also take out 'private supplementary health insurance' (*Zusatzversicherung*) for certain services, such as private supplementary dental insurance or private supplementary hospital insurance.

a) Liquidation according to the German Medical Fee Index (GOÄ)

81 In the case of liquidation according to the GOÄ or private liquidation, the patient is usually a member of a PHI and/or receives a benefit. However, the patient may also be a 'self-payer' (*Selbstzahler*) – these are usually SHI patients who want a treatment to be carried out although it is not covered by the SHI and they are fully aware that they will not be reimbursed for the costs.

A treatment contract is concluded between the physician and the patient in accordance with § 630a BGB, which establishes mutual claims. A contractual relationship is established between the physician and the patient. There is no contractual relationship between the physician and the health insurance. Therefore, the patient pays the physician's fee directly or via a billing company to the physician and applies for reimbursement from his PHI or subsidy provider. The remuneration and service levels are basically the same.

82 The physician invoices the patient for the treatment rendered, which must comply with the requirements of the GOÄ. The GOÄ is mandatory law for all persons with PHI and those entitled to benefit. If there is a private supplementary insurance or if treatment at the patient's own expense has been agreed upon, billing according to the GOÄ can also be considered for patients with SHI.

83 The GOÄ contains a wealth of fee codes for individual treatments. Treatments may only be billed according to these. New treatment methods that are not yet covered by the GOÄ can be billed via so-called analogue numbers according to § 6 sub. 2 GOÄ. § 12 GOÄ specifies in detail what must be included in a proper medical bill.

84 Billing according to GOÄ can be done for both outpatient and inpatient services. In this respect, billing according to the GOÄ is possible, for example, both by a physician who treats outpatients in his individual practice and by a hospital physician entitled to issue medical bills.

85 Within the framework of private billing, the physician may, according to § 4 sub. 2 GOÄ, only bill for services that he has either personally performed or that have been performed under his professional supervision. Delegation of tasks to auxiliary staff is only possible under certain conditions.

86 In the private medical sector, the agreement of an elective physician's contract is possible. The purpose of such a supplementary agreement is that the patient has a right to highly personalised treatment by a specific elective physician (e.g. treatment by the head physician of a hospital). According to § 4 sub. 2 sent. 3 GOÄ, the latter can only bill for services that he himself or his permanent representative has provided. In addition, delegation to other physicians is permissible as long as the elective physician still provides the treatment's character.[25]

b) Billing by the panel physician

87 When billing is done by a panel physician, a treatment contract is concluded between the patient and the physician. However, the patient cannot be obliged to pay for the medical treatment received. The panel physician must turn to the Association of Statutory Health Insurance Physicians (SHIP Association) (*Kassenärztliche Vereinigung* – KV) for billing of his services. The SHIP Association is a public corporation and consists of the individual panel physicians as members. Only vis-à-vis the SHIP Association is the physician entitled to compensation, however, not for a certain amount, but rather to a certain share of the total remuneration.

88 The physician, who must first be registered as a panel physician within the SHIP Association, must evaluate the services he has provided himself and prepare a bill on his own responsibility, taking into account the uniform assessment standard and other guidelines. This bill is forwarded to the SHIP Association on a quarterly basis together with a so-called collective declaration. In the collective declaration, the panel physician explicitly assures, among other things, that all services were correctly stated in the invoices, correspond to the legal requirements and were provided personally or in compliance with the rules on delegation and substitution.

89 The SHIP Association first checks the bills for factual and arithmetical correctness. In individual cases, a plausibility check is then conducted on a random basis. Likewise, in individual cases, a random check of the economic efficiency is carried out.

90 On this basis, the SHIP Association bills its claim for compensation for all settlements to the health insurance funds. The SHIP Association receives the total compensation from the SHI on a quarterly basis. With the distribution of this total compensation, all services from SHI-accredited medical care are settled for the respective health insurance fund with discharging effect (§ 85 sub. 1 SGB V (*Fünftes Buch Sozialgesetzbuch*, Fifth Book of the Social Code)). The only creditor of the total compensation is the SHIP Association and not the individual physician. The total compensation is determined according to § 85 sub. 2

[25] BGH 20.12. 2007 – III ZR 144/07, BeckRS 2008, 1451.

SGB V. The amount of the total compensation as such says nothing about the specific share that the individual physician will later receive as compensation.

c) Billing by the hospitals vis-à-vis the health insurance funds

91 In order for hospitals to be allowed to provide hospital treatment that can be reimbursed by the SHI, they must be licensed. Approval is granted either through recognition as a university hospital according to federal legislation, inclusion in the hospital plan of a federal state or the conclusion of a care contract of the hospital with the federal state associations of health insurances and the Association of substitute health insurance funds, cf. § 108 SGB V.

92 Persons with SHI receive the benefits of the SHI as benefits in kind and services. In order for the SHI to be able to provide such services, it in turn concludes supply contracts with authorised service providers – in this case the authorised hospitals – which then provide the services to the patients. In principle, billing is then done between the hospital and the health insurance fund.

93 Hospital compensation is generally based on the Hospital Remuneration Act (*Krankenhausentgeltgesetz*, KHEntgG), cf. § 1 sub. 1 KHEntgG. The hospitals bill the health insurance funds on the basis of per-case flat rates, § 7 KHEntgG. Pursuant to § 17b of the Hospital Financing Act (*Krankenhausfinanzierungsgesetz*, KHG), a 'continuous, performance-oriented and flat-rate remuneration system' applies to the compensation of general hospital services. The basis for the compensation system is the German Diagnosis Related Group System (G-DRG-System), which codifies a DRG flat rate for each inpatient treatment. Basically, independent of the patient's length of stay, the amount of the DRG flat rate is based on the diagnosis, surgery and severity of the illness.[26] The compensation is lower for patients with lighter illnesses than for those with more severe illnesses that require more complex treatment. A certain range of duration is assumed regarding the length of the stay. Consequently, the same length of stay is remunerated regardless of whether the patient stays in hospital at the lower or the upper limit of the assumed range, making the actual length of the stay irrelevant in principle. If the length of stay is significantly longer or shorter, surcharges or discounts are usually applied. To enable billing, physicians document the diagnoses and treatments or select codes that already correspond to the treatment, which are then combined into DRGs using software.[27] Hospitals usually have coding specialists or entire departments for medical controlling that determine the DRG flat rate per case.

94 Since 2020, hospital compensation consists of per-case flat rates and a reimbursement of nursing costs. Accordingly, nursing staff costs are to be reimbursed independently of the flat rates per case.

95 The same costs as for SHI-patients are billed to private patients for general hospital services, but the private patient is the sole debtor of the hospital. Only vis-à-vis the PHI can the private patient claim reimbursement to the extent that his insurance contract allows. As a rule, however, the private patient assigns his claims vis-à-vis the PHI to the hospital, so that the hospital can settle the general hospital services directly with the PHI.

96 If an elective service agreement has been concluded, the patient is billed according to this agreement and regularly remains the debtor in this regard.

---

[26] https://www.bundesgesundheitsministerium.de/abrechnung-krankenhausleistungen.html (last accessed: 15.5.2025).

[27] MAH WirtschaftsStrafR/Tsambikakis § 31 mn. 12 et seqq.

2. Billing fraud in the healthcare sector

Billing fraud, as a specific type of fraud in the healthcare sector, first requires the prerequisites of § 263 sub. 1 StGB to be fulfilled: a deception about facts, an error of a human counterpart caused by it, an error-based disposition of assets by the counterpart as well as a pecuniary detriment.[28] Assessing whether the prerequisites are fulfilled with regard to the billing fraud in the healthcare sector raises considerable specificities especially with regard to the latter prerequisite. All these constitutive elements of the offence must be covered by the offender's intent. Additionally, the offender must have the intention to obtain an unlawful pecuniary benefit for himself or a third party. 97

a) Deception about facts

The first prerequisite, therefore, is a deception about facts. Facts for which a deception is conceivable are primarily the performance of the treatment itself (so-called fictitious treatments), its extent as well as the existence of certain preconditions, which are required for a treatment to be performed in the first place and its billing. The deception can happen expressly, impliedly or by omission, although an omission is only punishable, if there was an obligation to act – in this case to provide clarification on the correct facts. 98

In the case of billing fraud, however, the deception does not usually occur through the explicit statement of false facts, such as a medical treatment that does not actually exist, but through the billing as such, in which, for example, in the case of private payment, there are only fee codes and a brief description of the treatment, or in the case of billing by the hospital to the health insurance provider, there is only a code or flat rate per case that is supposed to cover the underlying medical treatment. According to case law, if this information is incorrect, this nevertheless constitutes a deception about facts. This is based on the assumption that the indication of a fee code or treatment code (impliedly) confirms the treatment facts required for its applicability.[29] Consequently, if the stated fee code is in fact incorrect, stating it constitutes a deception about the facts implied by it. Usually, however, it is particularly difficult to determine the only possibly correct facts pertaining to a certain medical bill and to correctly express the medical treatment actually performed in a medical bill. Oftentimes, different opinions or even disputes exist between treatment providers and payers about the correct billing method for treatment which has been performed. In these cases, it must be determined whether it is still possible to speak of a deception about facts (as in the case of fictitious treatments), or whether the billing reflects a different or incorrect legal opinion. 99

Especially in the case of alleged upcoding, assigning a higher code within the system of fee codes to a case, there are considerable uncertainties as to what the correct code must look like. Assigning a justifiable code to a certain case cannot constitute a deception about facts. Conversely, recording diagnoses that do not actually exist, or treatments that were not carried out or not carried out in this way can turn the subsequent billing into a deception. Especially in the private health insurance sector, the offence is often realised by non-compliance with the requirement of the personal provision of services. The collective declaration of the panel physician is intended to declare as a fact the compliance with all specifications regarding the provision of services, which raises doubts considering the complexity of the applicable social law. 100

The courts tend to assume that not only the specific facts of the treatment, but also the general conditions for the provision and billing of the treatment are declared by issuing a bill for it. Thus, for example, the involvement of a front man in the context of the estab- 101

[28] For more general details see → Ch. 11.
[29] BGH 25.01.2012 – 1 StR 45/11, BeckRS 2012, 6059.

lishment of a MCC is said to ultimately constitute a deception about the prerequisites for the authorisation of the MCC to provide panel medical treatment and thus about facts relevant to billing.[30]

102 Such extensive interpretation must be heavily criticised, because it attributes declaratory contents to the medical bill, which are not actually part of it. Nevertheless, it should be taken into account by both companies and criminal defence attorneys as established case law.

103 If faced with an unclear legal situation regarding the correct way of billing, an assessment should always be made, to determine whether pointing out the unclear legal situation and the legal opinion understood to be justifiable in the medical bill can serve to exclude a deception about facts.

b) Error of a human counterpart

104 A further prerequisite of fulfilling § 263 StGB is causing an error through a deception. Since only humans are able to be deceived, the deception must happen vis-à-vis a human person.[31] In the case of legal persons or associations of persons, the relevant person is the person acting for such legal person.[32] In the case of billing fraud, possible erring person are, depending on the specific billing and settlement system, in most cases either the clerk at the SHIP Association, the employee of the health insurer or the patient. If at the SHIP Association, the process of checking medical bills is fully automated and is carried out solely through the use of IT, no error of a human can occur and, consequently, only the offence of computer fraud pursuant to § 263a StGB can be fulfilled.

105 Regularly, such processes will not be fully automated. Rather, the relevant program will be run and monitored by a clerk. If the clerk is subject to a subjective misconception, he errs. If the clerk does not give any thought to the correctness of the information and thus lacks any conception, an error is ruled out. In particular, in cases of mass filing, if the clerk assumes that everything is in order (factual co-awareness), although there was a deception about facts in the declaration, according to case law, he does err.

106 Patients, who receive medical bills, rarely check the bills, especially if they submit them to their private health insurer and assume that the insurer will object if something is incorrect. However, the private health insurer was not present during the treatment and therefore – unlike the patient – cannot assess the performance of individual treatment steps. In criminal proceedings, it is not uncommon for patients to be examined with the aim of eliciting the statement from them that they trusted in the correctness of the invoice and assumed that everything was in order, i.e. that they erred according to case law.[33] The insinuation of an error in this case is doubtful, since it cannot be sufficient for the independent prerequisite of the offence to be based on a general conception.

107 Correctly, no error exists if the parties are in open dispute about the correct way of billing, e.g. in the system of fee codes. If the treatment provider and the payer are openly discussing about different opinions concerning the correct way of billing, it cannot be assumed that there is an error on the side of the payer.

c) Error-based disposition of assets

108 Fulfilling the offence further requires an error-based disposition of assets directly connected to a pecuniary detriment.

[30] BGH 19.8.2020 – 5 StR 558/19, BeckRS 2020, 27386.
[31] BGH 31.3.2004 – 1 StR 482/03, BeckRS 2004, 5411.
[32] BGH 27.3.2012 – 3 StR 472/11, BeckRS 2012, 10587.
[33] Cf. BGH 25.01.2012 – 1 StR 45/11, BeckRS 2012, 6059.

The required, error-based disposition of assets is made by the patient himself if billing happens according to the GOÄ. By paying the medical bill, the patient directly reduces his assets. If the hospital directly bills the health insurer, the competent employee of the health insurer disposes of the insurance's assets. As the disposition of the employee does not directly affect his own assets, the specificities of triangulation fraud need to be observed. These prerequisites are met, because the employee is authorized to dispose of the assets of the health insurer and is in a close relationship to it. 109

In the case of billing by the panel physician, an error-based disposition of assets is conceivable in two ways: payment of the total compensation by the health insurer to the SHIP Association or payment of the individual compensation by the SHIP Association to the deceiving physician. 110

The SHIP Association forwards the incorrect statements of the panel physician to the health insurer and claims the total compensation. Usually, however, the payment of the total compensation does not constitute a disposition of the health insurer relevant for the deception and the error, because the manipulation does, normally, not affect the amount of the total compensation. An exception is the billing of individual services within the meaning of § 87a sub. 3 sent. 5 SGB V, which are paid independently of the total compensation. Therefore, an error-based disposition of assets by the health insurer is regularly excluded. 111

Much more relevant in practice is the disposition made by the SHIP Association to the deceiving panel physician by quantifying the individual compensation claim. There is a dispute concerning who suffers a direct pecuniary detriment. Previously, it was assumed that due to the error of the clerk of the health insurer, the deceiving physician was assigned too high an amount of compensation points, and thus was entitled to an excessively high share of the total compensation, while the other (honest) physicians in the same SHIP Association received a lower share and thus their assets were reduced. More recent case law assumes a reduction in the assets of the SHIP Association.[34] As a corporation under public law, the SHIP Association is in a position to form assets, so that the total assets transferred by the health insurers are allocated as its own. 112

The prerequisites of triangulation fraud are also fulfilled in this case: according to previous opinions, the clerk makes dispositions of the assets of the panel physicians. Pursuant to § 85 sub. 4 sent. 1 SGB V, the clerk is statutorily authorised to distribute the total compensation and therefore makes dispositions of a part of the assets of the individual panel physicians.[35] According to more recent case law, the clerk makes dispositions of the assets of the SHIP Association, to which he also has the necessary close relationship. 113

d) Pecuniary detriment

The disposition of assets must have led to a pecuniary detriment. Whether there is a pecuniary detriment, is generally determined by comparing the total assets before and after the error-based disposition. If the balance of the assets after the disposition is negative, a pecuniary detriment is assumed (*Prinzip der Gesamtsaldierung*). A consideration directly received for the loss is factored into the balance and can lead to a compensation. This also includes the release from a liability, such as the obligation to fulfil the compensation claim. 114

As per case law, in medical criminal law the so-called strictly formal approach of social law applies to the pecuniary detriment. Accordingly, a medical treatment rendered has no economic value if not all requirements for its performance and billing were met, even 115

---

[34] BGH 19.08.2020 – 5 StR 558/19, BeckRS 2020, 27386.

[35] Fischer StGB § 263 mn. 79 et seq.

if it was rendered *lege artis* and the patient does not need any further treatment. The isolated non-compliance with the requirements leads to the loss of the right to compensation. Therefore, the payer is not released from an existing obligation.[36] Likewise, the rendered care service does not lead to compensation.[37] If the claim for compensation for a treatment is forfeited due to violations of social-law provisions, this assessment has to be transferred to criminal law in the interest of a uniform legal system. The treatment rendered can therefore not constitute assets protected by criminal law and, likewise, cannot be a relevant inflow of assets. Therefore, in the event of partial non-compliance with the requirements of social law, a pecuniary detriment is incurred despite the fact that the treatment was rendered *lege artis*. If the payer nevertheless pays for treatment that is provided but does not fully comply with social law requirements, the payer's assets are diminished. The only exceptions are cases in which social law exceptionally upholds a claim for compensation because only a purely regulatory specification was not complied with. In these cases, if this interpretation is transferred accordingly to the assessment under criminal law, there is no pecuniary detriment.

116 The same applies to compliance with the regulations of the GOÄ. In case of non-compliance, there is a pecuniary detriment even if the treatment was rendered *lege artis* and satisfactory and sufficient for the patient. If, for example, the reimbursement of expenses, such as the costs for medication, is claimed according to § 10 GOÄ without complying with the requirements of § 12 sub. 2 no. 5 GOÄ (i.e. attaching a corresponding receipt or other proof of the expense to the invoice if the stipulated value limit is exceeded), there is no entitlement to the reimbursement of the expenses. It is also irrelevant whether the expenses were nevertheless incurred and the patient was treated with the medication *lege artis*.

117 Such a formal interpretation does not reflect the nature of the offence of fraud as an offence against assets. This nature does not allow the economic value of the medical treatment to be ignored – irrespective of whether it is recognised under social law or in the context of private settlement. Rather, this interpretation – which has now also been confirmed by the Federal Constitutional Court[38] – violates the *ultima ratio*-principle that applies in criminal law. Nevertheless, as it is established case law, it must again be considered in entrepreneurial decisions.

e) Intent and intention to obtain an unlawful pecuniary benefit for oneself or a third party

118 The constitutive elements of the offence must be fulfilled with intent. An erroneously incorrect billing therefore does not constitute a billing fraud. In practice, however, in the case of systematically incorrect accounting, it will certainly require some effort to convince the public prosecutor or the court that there was an error, but no intent.

119 The offender must also have acted with the intention to obtain an unlawful pecuniary benefit for himself or a third party. The pecuniary benefit sought must be of the same substance as the pecuniary detriment caused, i.e., the reverse side of the pecuniary detriment.

f) Possible situations in practice

120 In everyday entrepreneurial activity, it will regularly be necessary to determine, who is criminally liable for a billing fraud: for physicians in private practice, who do their own billing, the answer is obvious. If, on the other hand, they hire an employee to do

---

[36] Cf. most recently BGH 19.8.2020 – 5 StR 558/19, BeckRS 2020, 27386.
[37] Cf. only BGH 5.12.2002 – 3 StR 161/02, BeckRS 2003, 420.
[38] BVerfG 5.5.2021 – 2 BvR 2023/20, 2 BvR 2041/20, BeckRS 2021, 12702.

the billing or if the hospital, represented by the management, does the billing through the accounting department based on the coding of the medical controlling department on the basis of the documentation prepared by the physicians, the answer becomes more complex. Generally, those who, technically speaking, prepare the invoice, do not have knowledge of any inaccuracies and do not fulfil the requirements of intent. It is imaginable that offenders, who commit the offence through another and who have superior knowledge (and will), such as the physicians preparing the documentation, may influence the billing. While rare in practice, commission by managing directors cannot be ruled out either. Experience shows that it is more common that the responsible staff is abetted by issuing corresponding instructions or aided (by omission) by tolerating or supporting (or in any case not preventing) inaccurate billing.

Oftentimes, the managing staff of a hospital will not have the necessary detailed **121** knowledge of correct billing and will, for good reason, delegate this task to the competent staff. If the suspicion of inaccurate billing is brought to the attention of the management, this must be investigated and, if required, necessary measures must be taken to prevent future inaccurate billing. Frequently, the question arises to what extent management has a duty to inform the payers if they subsequently learn of incorrect billing or even acts of fraud (e.g. by former employees or managing directors) that occurred without their involvement and without their knowledge. This issue has far-reaching consequences, because failure to comply with such a duty to inform could lead to a billing fraud by omission or to management aiding the offence by omission. In such situations, the course of action must be examined carefully in order to avoid any criminal liability on the part of the company's management.

II. Embezzlement, especially embezzlement by panel physicians

Next to billing fraud, embezzlement is a common offence in medical criminal law. **122** Damage to the assets of a natural or legal person by a person charged with safeguarding these assets is the characteristic injustice of embezzlement. Possible offenders are, for example, the managing directors of a PHI or the board of directors of a Chamber of Medical Practitioners. Ultimately, this is classic embezzlement, as it is also known from other areas of economic criminal law.[39]

Specifically for medical criminal law, the offence of embezzlement by panel physicians **123** was developed through case law. The central question of this offence concerns the extent to which the panel physician has an obligation to safeguard pecuniary interests. § 266 StGB distinguishes two different offences, the abuse of power to dispose of assets (sub. 1 alt. 1) and the breach of a duty to safeguard assets (sub. 1 alt. 2). Although it is disputed how the two offences relate to each other, in practice, it is generally only examined whether there has been a breach of the obligation to safeguard the pecuniary interests of another.

1. Obligation to safeguard pecuniary interests of another person

The offender must have a special relationship with the (potential) affected party, which **124** results from a prominent obligation to safeguard the pecuniary interests of another, i.e. which goes beyond the obligations applicable to everyone to safeguard the pecuniary

[39] For more general details see → Ch. 12.

interests of others.[40] A fiduciary duty can be established by law, by commission of an authority, legal transaction or by a de facto fiduciary relationship and must constitute a primary duty of the offender. The offender must have a certain degree of discretion in safeguarding the pecuniary interests of others, within the scope of which he can make decisions in his own responsibility.[41]

125 The Federal Court of Justice has concluded that the panel physician has an obligation to safeguard the pecuniary interests of the SHI.[42] The dogmatic reasoning behind this is controversial. In the past[43], the courts justified it by holding that the panel physician was the representative of the health insurer, as he could prescribe benefits in kind within the scope of his prescribing activities, which the patients were then entitled to vis-à-vis the health insurance fund. This judicature has since been discontinued. It was recognised that the panel physician does not act as a representative of the health insurer, but rather in the interest and on behalf of the patient.[44] Now, a duty to safeguard the patient's pecuniary interests is derived from the social-law requirement of economic efficiency pursuant to §§ 12 sub. 1, 70 sub. 1, 2 sub. 4 SGB V. The courts are of the opinion that the social law requirement of economic efficiency, which must be observed, creates a primary obligation for the panel physician to be considerate of the assets of the health insurer in the context of his prescribing activities.[45] The discretionary scope required for the existence of an obligation to safeguard pecuniary interests is assumed with the declaration by the panel physician that the eligibility requirements for the prescription of a medical remedy are fulfilled.[46]

126 This view is not convincing, because it is, at most, a secondary obligation in addition to the primary obligation to provide medical treatment to the patient.[47] Nevertheless, it is imperative to take into account the now established case law.

2. Violation of the obligation to safeguard pecuniary interests

127 For the offence of embezzlement to be fulfilled, a violation of the obligation to safeguard the pecuniary interests of another is required. To ensure that not every adverse breach of duty is penalised, the offender is only liable to prosecution if he is evidently in breach of duty.[48] In practice, an overall assessment is made, considering, among other things, the motives of the offender, the transgression of authority and the economic situation of the company. In simplified terms, this often involves the question of whether the action was justifiable from a business perspective or from the perspective of the person whose assets are to be safeguarded.

128 Examples of violations of an obligation in the context of embezzlement by panel physicians relevant in practice are:

- issuing medical prescriptions without a medical diagnosis[49];
- purchase of overpriced medical drugs in exchange for a turnover-based reimbursement[50] or of overpriced X-ray contrast agent, also in exchange for a reimbursement[51];

---

[40] BGH 29.1.2020 – 1 StR 421/19, BeckRS 2020, 3998.
[41] BGH 11.12.1957 – 2 StR 481/57, BeckRS 1957, 104835.
[42] BGH 16.8.2016 – 4 StR 163/16, BeckRS 2016, 16636.
[43] BGH 25.11.2003 – 4 StR 239/03, BeckRS 2003, 10717.
[44] BGH 29.3.2012 – GSSt2/11, BeckRS 2012, 13162.
[45] BGH 16.8.2016 – 4 StR 163/16, BeckRS 2016, 16636.
[46] BGH 16.8.2016 – 4 StR 163/16, BeckRS 2016, 16636.
[47] Cf. Prütting/Kessler StGB § 266 mn. 16.
[48] BGH 16.8.2016 – 4 StR 163/16, BeckRS 2016, 16636.
[49] BGH 25.11.2003 – 4 StR 239/03, BeckRS 2003, 10717.
[50] BGH 27.4.2004 – 1 StR 165/03, BeckRS 2004, 6163.
[51] BGH 25.7.2017 – 5 StR 46/17, BeckRS 2017, 121845.

- purchase of so-called consultation supplies in exchange for discounts in the form of the disposal of hazardous waste without disclosing this to the health insurer.[52]

Not a case of embezzlement by panel physicians is the prescription of at-home healthcare without the requirements of the healthcare measures being fulfilled, because the SHI has extensive supervisory options at its disposal.[53] 129

3. Pecuniary disadvantage

The serious breach of the obligation to safeguard assets must result in a pecuniary disadvantage to constitute embezzlement. Whether there is such a pecuniary disadvantage is determined by comparing the total assets before and after the wrongful act. If the assets are higher before the wrongful act, there is a pecuniary disadvantage. This adverse effect must extend specifically to the assets that the offender had an obligation to safeguard. 130

In cases of reimbursement, an adverse effect is always given if a fair market price was paid by the principal, but this price would have been lower without the commission transferred to the offender in breach of trust.[54] 131

4. Intent

The mentioned constitutive elements of the offence must be fulfilled with intent. 132

III. Corruption offences

Criminal law on corruption has become continuously stricter since 1997.[55] Since then, specific criminal offences and specialised prosecution offices have been created for corruption in the health sector. Corruption offences are regulated in §§ 299 et seqq. and §§ 331 et seqq. StGB. 133

1. Taking and giving bribes in healthcare sector (§§ 299a, 299b StGB)

Especially in the healthcare sector, cooperations are essential. It is not uncommon for hospitals to involve external physicians in their inpatient care, in order to be able to provide special expertise and outstanding treatment quality. Hospitals and physicians also cooperate with medical device and drug manufacturers to facilitate processes and jointly care for patients. In turn, the industry involves practitioners in the development and improvement of pharmaceuticals and medical devices, for example through participation in clinical trials and evaluations. Even if cooperations are considered necessary, there should be no legal vacuum for them. 134

The offender of § 299a StGB can only be a healthcare professional. It is therefore an offence which can only be committed by a specific group of offenders. The term healthcare professional includes physicians, dentists, veterinarians and members of so-called healthcare professions (including occupational and physiotherapists, speech therapists, midwives, nurses). Natural health practitioners and health craftsmen are not suitable offenders under § 299a StGB. Bribery under § 299b StGB can be committed by anyone. 135

---

[52] OLG Hamm 22.12.2004 – 3 Ss 431/04, BeckRS 2005, 12249.
[53] BGH 11.5.2021 – 4 StR 350/20, BeckRS 2021, 15100.
[54] BGH 23.5.2002 – 1 StR 372/01, BeckRS 2002, 5706.
[55] For more general details see → Ch. 10.

The commercial manager of a hospital can therefore be considered a suitable offender under § 299b StGB if he grants an advantage to a health care professional for the referral of patients. In the case of representation of the hospital by such a commercial manager within the framework of a cooperation, it must nevertheless be considered whether § 299a StGB may also be applicable, because the health care professionals who are at the centre of the cooperation must be considered. § 299a StGB is not automatically excluded if the relevant action is undertaken by a legal person.

136 Corruption offences in the healthcare sector are distinguished into a passive taking of bribes (§ 299a StGB) and an active giving of bribes (§ 299b StGB). For the passive taking of bribes, the member of a healing profession must demand, allow himself to be promised or accept a benefit. To bribe a member of a healing profession (active giving of bribes), he must be offered, promised or granted a benefit in connection with his professional activities. The object of the offence must be a benefit. A benefit is any improvement of the economic, legal or personal situation to which the offender has no legal claim.[56] Accordingly, both material and immaterial benefits are covered by the offence under §§ 299a, 299b StGB. It makes no difference whether the granting of a benefit was agreed upon contractually, because the conclusion of the agreement can already constitute a benefit. Moreover, before the conclusion of the contract, there was usually no entitlement to it. Possible examples of a benefit within the meaning of this definition are:

- compensation or other material advantages;
- remuneration;
- awards, commissions, discounts, reimbursement discounts and bonuses;
- shares of a company in the healthcare sector;
- providing items, such as medical devices;
- increasing the scientific reputation;
- granting of loans.

137 Benefits for third parties are also included. If benefits are granted, which lack the objective suitability to influence a specific healthcare decision (so-called socially-adequate gift), the offence is not fulfilled. Benefits are socially-adequate if they are not of serious interest to anyone. Otherwise, they would be suitable to influence the healthcare decision.

138 This understanding of the term 'benefit' is conceivably broad, so that the offence is only restricted by the element of an agreement to commit an unlawful act (*Unrechtsvereinbarung*). It is a prerequisite that at least a tacit agreement was made regarding the benefit as consideration for the unfair competitive advantage. The agreement to commit an unlawful act must concern the scenarios described in no. 1–3 – namely the prescription of medicines, remedies or health aides or medical devices (no. 1), the procurement of medication or health aides or medical devices which are designed for direct application by the member of the healing professions or one of their professional assistants (no. 2) or the supply of patients or samples and diagnostic data (no. 3).

139 No. 1 covers the prescription of medication, remedies or health aids or medical devices and means prescribing for the benefit of patients. The category of prescribing does not include cases of indirect influence in which (pharmaceutical) companies influence the prescription recommendations of medical professional associations or of advertising self-help groups.[57] However, a risk of criminal liability for pharmaceutical companies arises in cases where physicians prescribe medication as part of a so-called patient support programme, provided that an agreement on a commission has previously been concluded

---

[56] BGH 7.7.2005 – 4 StR 549/04, BeckRS 2005, 9205.

[57] Cf. Prütting/Kessler StGB § 299b mn. 15; Saliger/Tsambikakis MedStrafR-HdB/Tsambikakis § 14 mn. 57.

between the physician and the pharmaceutical company.[58] Within the meaning of no. 2, 'procurement' is to be understood as any act of acquisition. This also includes sub-actions such as ordering, acceptance or payment. However, only medications, remedies or health aids or medical devices intended for direct use by the health care professional or one of his assistants on the patient are included under procurement.[59] This scenario is relevant, among other things, if the physician is granted retroactive target discounts for medication he purchases.[60] According to the legislator's intention, the term 'supply' within the meaning of no. 3 is intended to correspond to the term 'allocation' in social and professional law (§ 73 sub. 7 SGB V as well as § 31 MBO-Ä (*Musterberufsordnung für Ärzte*, Medical Practitioners' Model Code of Conduct)), so that it is to be understood as any influence on a patient with the aim of influencing the patient's decision to choose a physician or other healthcare provider. The term is very broad. Problems can arise with cooperations between MCCs and hospitals, medical tourism, cooperations between hospitals and cooperations for the provision of laboratory services or samples and diagnostic data. For pharmaceutical companies, the scenario of the supply of samples and diagnostic data is of particular importance. This refers in particular to the forwarding of samples for the performance of laboratory tests.

In the subjective elements of the offence, the intent – at least in the form of *dolus* **140**
eventualis – must relate to the status as a healthcare professional, the preferential treatment in prescribing, procuring or supplying and the competitive situation as well as the unfairness.

Although both offences were introduced in 2016, there is hardly any case law and thus **141**
certainly no established case law on their interpretation. There is, however, a growing amount of discussion in legal practice and in literature. In scenarios that could fall within the scope of the provisions, it is therefore particularly advisable to consult a lawyer with experience in this area before making any business decisions.

2. Taking and giving bribes in commercial practice (§ 299 StGB)

In addition to taking and giving bribes in the healthcare sector, the offence of taking **142**
and giving bribes in commercial practice pursuant to § 299 StGB is also relevant for the healthcare sector. The offence is especially relevant if the offender lacks the status of a healthcare professional.

The two paragraphs of § 299 StGB each distinguish two different versions of the **143**
offence. While the respective no. 1 contains the so-called competition version, which criminalises unfair preferential treatment in competition, no. 2 stipulates the business owner version. It penalises the corruptive influencing of conduct by which the employee or agent simultaneously violates a duty towards their employer. § 299 sub. 1 StGB can only be committed by employees or agents of a company, whereas § 299 sub. 2 StGB can be committed by anyone.

Just like § 299a StGB, § 299 StGB in principle penalises demanding, allowing oneself **144**
to be promised and accepting a benefit. In this respect, reference can be made to the explanations of §§ 299a, 299b StGB. The benefit must be granted for an act in the course of commercial transactions; private acts or sovereign activities are not included.

Parallel to §§ 299a, 299b StGB, the person granting the benefit and the person receiving **145**
the benefit must have entered into an agreement to commit an unlawful act. In the context of § 299 sub. 1 no. 1 and sub. 2 no. 1 StGB, the advantage must be granted in return for

[58] Prütting/Kessler StGB § 299b mn. 17.
[59] Saliger/Tsambikakis MedStrafR-HdB/Tsambikakis § 14 mn. 61.
[60] Ulsenheimer/Gaede ArztStrafR/Gaede mn. 1346.

a future unfair advantage in competition. Competition must in turn relate to the purchase of goods or commercial services and is to be understood broadly. The preferential treatment is unfair if it is suitable to harm the competitor by circumventing the rules of competition and by eliminating the competitors.

146 Within the scope of § 299 sub. 1 no. 2 and sub. 2 no. 2 StGB the agreement to commit an unlawful act is structured in such a way that the benefit is granted in return for a future breach of duty. The violated duty must be incumbent on the employee or agent precisely vis-à-vis his employer.[61] An internal disturbance is not sufficient, as the breach of duty must be related to the purchase of goods or services. Consent of the company excludes criminal liability within the scope of the business owner version.

147 In the subjective elements of the offence, the intent – *dolus eventualis* is sufficient – must extend to the position as employee or agent, the existence of a business operation, the preferential treatment and the competitive situation as well as the unfairness. In addition, sub. 2 no. 1 requires the intention to act in competition.[62]

3. Accepting and granting benefits, taking and giving bribes (§§ 331 et seqq. StGB)

148 Among others in communal and university hospitals, there is a risk of fulfilling the offences in §§ 331 et seqq. StGB. The physicians employed there, who are in an employment relationship under public law, may be liable to prosecution under the classic corruption offences for public officials pursuant to §§ 331 et seqq. StGB. Due to their position as public officials, their actions are included in the protection of the integrity of the public service and the public's trust in it.

149 §§ 331 et seqq. StGB generally distinguish between taking (§§ 331, 332 StGB) and giving (§§ 333, 334 StGB) benefits. 'Taking' incorporates a criminal liability for demanding, allowing oneself to be promised and accepting a benefit, while 'giving' a benefit penalises the offering, promising and granting. Within accepting and granting benefits, a further distinction needs to be made considering whether the discharge of the duty was undertaken within its boundaries (§§ 331, 333 StGB) or in breach of the official duties (§§ 332, 334 StGB).

150 While the offences of taking a benefit (§§ 331, 332 StGB) can only by committed by a public official within the meaning of § 11 sub. 1 no. 2 StGB, everyone who grants a benefit to a public official is criminally liable (§§ 333, 334 StGB).

151 The criminal act and the definition of benefit are nearly identical to those applied in §§ 299, 299a and 299b StGB. Following this, benefits are in most cases material benefits, but can also be immaterial benefits, if their content is objectively quantifiable and provides an actual advantage to the public official.

152 Criminal liability in the cases of §§ 331 et seqq. also presupposes an agreement to commit an unlawful act, thus the substantive connection between the granting of a benefit and the discharge of a duty (in breach of the official duty), which must have the form of an agreement between the public official and the grantor. Systematically, the connection by an agreement to commit an unlawful act is identical to the one in §§ 299, 299a and 299b StGB. With regard to the discharge of the duty, for which the benefit is granted, it is not necessary that this duty is defined in the agreement in all detail. Rather, it is sufficient that it is recognisable and defined in broad terms as a concrete discharge

[61] Saliger/Tsambikakis MedStrafR-HdB/Tsambikakis § 14 mn. 195.
[62] Prütting/Kessler StGB § 299 mn. 21.

of official duties. Conversely, however, the granting of a benefit for the general discharge of duties is not sufficient.

153 Third-party benefits are also included in the criminal offences in §§ 331 et seqq. StGB. In addition to natural and legal persons, public bodies also qualify as recipients of benefits in this regard. Third-party funding, which has been acquired by physicians from third parties (pharmaceutical companies or manufacturers of medical products) to finance research at a hospital, also constitutes such third-party benefits.[63] In order to do justice to the dichotomy between the indispensable implementation of a wide variety of research projects and the duties of physicians under higher education law when acquiring third-party funding, the Federal Court of Justice solves this problem by interpreting the offence restrictively. Third-party funding is not covered by the offence of corruption if it has been acquired in compliance with the procedure provided for under higher education law. This is justified because compliance with the legally prescribed procedure ensures that the transparency of the allocation of third-party funding is sufficiently ensured. A restriction applies in the case of part-time positions held by public officials if the benefit is outside of an appropriate scope[64] or if the impression of venality is conveyed through deliberate concealment or non-transparency.[65]

154 From a subjective point of view, intent is required with regard to all objective elements of the offence – including being a public official.

155 If the acceptance of benefits was previously approved by the competent authority, the offence may be justified pursuant to §§ 331 sub. 3, 333 sub. 3 StGB. In cases of demanding a benefit, such an approval and, consequently, a justification of the offence are not possible. In hospitals, the competent authority will typically be the managing director or university president at the top of the administration, who then regularly delegates the authority to approve to the respective legal department. If the benefit has already been accepted, it can also be ratified retrospectively. In this case, it is necessary that the notification of the receipt of the benefit is given without undue delay and that the competent authority is fully informed.

D. Offences concerning medicinal products and pharmaceuticals

156 In addition to the offences included in the Criminal Code, other laws also define criminal offences, i.e. offences concerning medicinal products and pharmaceuticals. Such offences are primarily included in §§ 95 et seqq. AMG (*Arzneimittelgesetz*, Medicinal Products Act) and §§ 92 et seqq. MPDG.

I. AMG

157 Physicians regularly prescribe medicinal products to their patients without having any insight into their manufacture, development or distribution, so that responsibility

---

[63] BGH 23.5.2002 – 1 StR 372/01, BeckRS 2002, 5706.
[64] Ulsenheimer/Gaede ArztStrafR/Gaede mn. 1243.
[65] BGH 25.2.2003 – 5 StR 363/02, BeckRS 2003, 2884; OLG Hamburg 14.01.2000 – 2 Ws 243/99, BeckRS 2000, 1192.

diverges with regard to their use and the product itself.[66] Pursuant to its § 1, the AMG is intended to counteract this by ensuring the safety of medicinal products for the proper supply of the population with medicinal products. Such assurance is achieved through licensing requirements, regulations on development, production and sale, information obligations and the monitoring of medicinal products by pharmaceutical companies and authorities.[67] The AMG is primarily directed at pharmaceutical companies as manufacturers and distributors of medicinal products. Physicians must also observe the provisions of the AMG when they manufacture medicinal products, use them on patients or test the use of medicinal products on humans.

158 Medicinal products are substances or preparations made from substances which are either intended for use in or on the human body to cure, alleviate or prevent human diseases or disease symptoms (§ 2 sub. 1 sent. 2 no. 1 AMG) and which are used in or on the human body or administered to a human being to restore, correct or influence a physiological function (§ 2 sub. 1 sent. 2 no. 2 lit. a AMG) or to make a medical diagnosis (§ 2 sub. 1 sent. 2 no. 2 lit. b AMG). The AMG does not apply to veterinary medicinal products, cf. § 2 sub. 3 no. 1 AMG.

159 §§ 95 et seqq. AMG are so-called blanket criminal provisions. They do not themselves stipulate any prohibitions, but refer to such prohibitions in previous provisions of the AMG. Offenders under this provision can be physicians and pharmacists[68], but also pharmaceutical companies. §§ 95 and 96 AMG regulate criminal offences, while § 97 AMG specifies administrative offences. Since the offences under § 95 AMG are regarded as particularly worthy of punishment, they are sanctioned with the highest penalties of the AMG (prison sentence of up to three years or a fine). In addition to intentional acts, negligent acts (sub. 4) and attempts to commit an offence (sub. 2) are also penalised. In principle, the offences under § 95 AMG are abstract endangerment offences, and thus do not require a concrete violation of legal interests. The risk of such a violation of legal interests is sufficient. If a required action is not performed, the general rules for criminal liability by omission pursuant to § 13 StGB apply. In this respect, a guardianship relationship is required. In pharmaceutical companies, such a responsibility can arise from the performance of inspection and control duties. This mainly concerns the management level.[69]

160 § 95 sub. 1 no. 1 AMG prohibits the marketing and use of questionable medicinal products. The provision is directed at pharmaceutical entrepreneurs, wholesalers and pharmacists who come into contact with the medicinal product within the production and/or distribution chain. Placing a medicinal product on the market or using it after its expiry date does not fall within the scope of § 95 sub. 1 no. 1 AMG, as the manufacturer may only be obliged to do so within the shelf life of the medicinal product. However, placing a medicinal product on the market after its expiry date constitutes an administrative offence within the meaning of § 97 sub. 2 no. 1 AMG in conjunction with § 8 sub. 3 AMG.

161 § 95 sub. 1 no. 2 AMG sanctions the placing on the market and administration of medicinal products in violation of certain legal ordinances issued under § 6 AMG. This prohibition may be particularly relevant for pharmacists if they manufacture and place on the market medicinal products whose ingredients contravene the legal ordinances issued under § 6 AMG. Placing radioactive medicinal products on the market in contravention of § 7 sub. 1 AMG is penalised in no. 3. Whoever places medicinal products or active substances of significantly inferior quality (§ 8 sub. 1 no. 1 AMG) or falsified medicinal

---

[66] MAH MedR/Kügel § 17 mn. 56.
[67] MAH MedR/Kügel § 17 mn. 56.
[68] BVerfG 26.04.2000 – 2 BvR 1881/99, BeckRS 2000, 30108906.
[69] Saliger/Tsambikakis MedStrafR-HdB/Ufer § 16 mn. 71.

products or active substances (§ 8 sub. 2 AMG) on the market is penalised pursuant to no. 3a. In addition, no. 4, divided into three categories of offences, punishes trading medicinal products available on prescription only outside a pharmacy, dispensing medicinal products available on prescription only by legal persons or associations of persons to their members, and dispensing medicinal products available on prescription only upon prescription not by a pharmacy, in each case contrary to the provisions mentioned therein. The primary addressees of the offence in no. 5 are pharmaceutical entrepreneurs and wholesalers. It is prohibited to dispense prescription medicinal products, the dispensing of which is reserved for pharmacies, to others than those specified in § 47 sub. 1 AMG – e.g. other pharmaceutical companies, hospitals as well as physicians – or to obtain them as recipient (§ 47 sub. 2 AMG). However, a pharmacist who is active in the wholesale sector is also a possible offender.[70] Thus, both dispensing (sub. 1) and obtaining (sub. 2) prescription medicinal products is punishable. If the medicinal products in question are non-prescription medication, an administrative offence within the meaning of § 97 sub. 2 no. 12 AMG may be considered. The penal provision of § 95 sub. 1 no. 5a AMG is also primarily directed at pharmaceutical companies. If the company supplies or places medicinal products authorised for the conduct of abortions on the market to facilities other than those specified in § 47a sub. 1 AMG, this may lead to criminal liability.

The offences in § 96 AMG, which can only be committed intentionally, incur a lesser penalty. The maximum penalty is imprisonment for up to one year or a fine. As the lowest level, § 97 AMG sanctions the negligent commission of the offences specified in § 96 AMG as administrative offences (sub. 1). § 97sub. 2 to 2e AMG stipulate further administrative offences. **162**

II. MPDG

The Medical Device Law Implementation Act (*Medizinprodukte-Durchführungsgesetz*, MPDG) is a national law based on the EU 'Medical Device Regulation' (MDR) and the 'In-vitro Diagnostics Medical Device Regulation' (IVDR). The MDR and the IVDR are directly applicable in all Member States and do not require implementation. The regulations do, however, contain regulatory assignments for the Member States, which makes the establishment of a national law necessary. Within the framework of these regulatory assignments, the national legislator has made certain additions to the regulations. Among these are the criminal offences in §§ 92, 93 MPDG and the administrative offences in § 94 MPDG. **163**

The MPDG applies to devices within the scope of the MDR, IVDR and to products, which are not placed on the market as medical devices, but which are applied with the same purpose as medical devices (so-called 'fictitious' medical devices), cf. § 2 MPDG. **164**

A medical device within the meaning of Art. 2 no. 1 MDR is any instrument, apparatus, appliance, software, implant, reagent, material or other article intended by the manufacturer to be used for human beings for one or more specific medical purposes and which does not achieve its principal intended action by pharmacological, immunological or metabolic means, in or on the human body, but which may be assisted in its function by such means. The specific medical purposes, which must be fulfilled, are: **165**

- diagnosis, prevention, monitoring, prediction, prognosis, treatment or alleviation of disease,

[70] Saliger/Tsambikakis MedStrafR-HdB/Ufer § 16 mn. 61.

- diagnosis, monitoring, treatment, alleviation of, or compensation for, an injury or disability,
- investigation, replacement or modification of the anatomy or of a physiological or pathological process or state,
- providing information by means of in vitro examination of specimens derived from the human body, including organ, blood and tissue donations.

166 Medical devices – not in-vitro diagnostic medical devices – are divided into classes (I, IIa, IIb, III), taking into account their intended purpose, Art. 51 para. 1 sent. 1 MDR. This differentiation is relevant for criminal law, because the offences in § 92 sub. 3 MPDG and § 93 sub. 3 MPDG also differentiate between these classes. A classification of medical devices is undertaken according to the classification rules in Annex VIII of the MDR, cf. Art. 51 para. 2 MDR.

167 Even if in-vitro diagnostic medical devices in principle fulfil the legal definition of medical devices in Art. 2 no. 1 MDR, they are excluded from its application under Art. 1 para. 6 lit. a MDR. According to Art. 2 no. 2 IVDR, an 'in vitro diagnostic medical device' means any medical device which is a reagent, reagent product, calibrator, control material, kit, instrument, apparatus, piece of equipment, software or system, intended by the manufacturer to be used in vitro for the examination of specimens derived from the human body for the purpose of providing information. In vitro diagnostic medical devices are also divided into different classes A, B, C and D. The classification is done according to Art. 47 para. 1 IVDR according to the classification rules in Annex VIII of the IVDR.

168 In most cases, anyone can commit the criminal and administrative offences regulated in §§ 92 et seqq. MPDG, as long as they have committed the criminal act. If a legal person or an association of persons is targeted in the criminal or administrative offence, § 14 StGB and § 9 OWiG must be observed.[71] While the offences in § 92 sub. 1 to 5 MPDG penalize intentional as well as negligent commission, the commission of the offences under § 93 MPDG is only possible with intent. § 94 MPDG defines offences with a lesser degree of wrongdoing, which are, accordingly, penalised only as administrative offences.

169 Typical criminal acts of the offences are operating and applying, placing on the market, making available, putting into service and manufacturing. As far as these terms are not already defined in § 3 MPDG, the definitions in Art. 2 MDR and Art. 2 IVDR can be applied. With regards to the terms 'operation' and 'application', the definitions can be found in § 2 sub. 1 MPBetreibV (*Medizinprodukte-Betreiberverordnung*, Ordinance on the Operation of Medical Devices).

170 § 92 sub. 1 MPDG sanctions the application of questionable (no. 1 and 2) or falsified devices (no. 3), especially the operation and use of such devices. Sub. 2 sanctions the placing on the market or putting into service of devices that are subject to the provisions of the Radiation Protection Act (*Strahlenschutzgesetz*, StrlSchG) or legal ordinance issued on the basis thereof, or in the manufacture of which ionising radiation was used, in violation of Art. 120 para. 3 sent. 1 MDR. The offence in sub. 3 was established specifically for in vitro diagnostic medical devices, which corresponds with the offence in sub. 2. The offence in § 92 sub. 4 MPDG secures performance of the conformity assessment procedure laid down in Art. 52 MDR. The CE-marking obtained through the conformity assessment procedure is intended to ensure the recognisable marketability of medical devices throughout the European Economic Area.[72] § 92 sub. 5 MPDG again sanctions violations of certain provisions of the IVDR, which pertain to the conformity assessment procedure. Sub. 5 therefore corresponds to sub. 4 of the provision.

---

[71] For more details on this see → Ch. 4.

[72] Saliger/Tsambikakis MedStrafR-HdB/Gierok § 17 mn. 96.

CHAPTER 22
CAPITAL MARKETS LAWS

Table of contents

A. Introduction 558
  I. Scope of this section 558
  II. Overview of main sources of law 558
  III. Competent authorities 559
  IV. Sanctions framework and corporate responsibility 560
    1. General sanctions regime 560
    2. Corporate responsibility 561
    3. Capital markets compliance system 562
B. Market abuse regime 562
  I. Insider prohibitions 562
    1. Scope of applicability 562
    2. Definition of inside information 563
    3. Prohibited conduct 565
      a) Insider trading 565
      b) Unlawful sharing of inside information 566
    4. Sanctions 566
      a) Criminal law 566
      b) Administrative offence 567
  II. Market manipulation 567
    1. Prohibited conduct 567
      a) Manipulative trading 567
      b) Manipulative information 567
    2. Sanctions 568
      a) Criminal law 568
      b) Administrative offence 569
  III. Ad-hoc disclosure of inside information 569
    1. Publication obligation 569
      a) Inside information directly concerning the issuer 569
      b) Possibility to delay disclosure 569
      c) Timing, content and distribution of ad-hoc announcements 571
    2. Sanctions 571
      a) Criminal law 571
      b) Administrative offence 572
  IV. Maintenance of insider lists 572
  V. Directors' dealings 573
  VI. Closed periods 574
C. Further compliance obligations 575
  I. Recurring financial reporting 575
    1. Publication obligations 575
    2. Review and enforcement by BaFin 576
    3. Sanctions 576
      a) Criminal law 576
      b) Administrative offence 577
  II. Voting rights notifications 577
    1. Notification and publication obligations 577
    2. Sanctions 578

III. Rules on short selling ... 578
1. Disclosure obligations of net short positions ... 579
2. Prohibition of uncovered short sales ... 579
3. Temporary short-selling bans ... 579
4. Sanctions ... 580
D. Marketing of financial instruments ... 580
I. Prospectus requirements ... 580
II. Fraudulent conduct ... 581
1. General fraud ... 581
2. Capital investment fraud ... 581
3. Misleading advertising ... 582
4. Fraud-related to information on sustainability (greenwashing) ... 582
5. Sanctions ... 583
III. Inducing stock market speculation ... 583

A. Introduction

I. Scope of this section

1 This section describes the most relevant areas of potential corporate criminal liability in German capital markets law and introduces the main legal concepts. The presentation focuses on private sector companies that act as investors, trade financial instruments, or access the capital markets in order to raise funds. Excluded from the presentation are liability risks associated with activities regulated by banking and financial services laws (e.g., the performance of unauthorized banking business or embezzlement through granting of credit or in the course of asset management) as well as specific regulations for investment funds. In accordance with the scope of this handbook, this section does not address civil law liability such as civil prospectus liability and other forms of tort claims.

2 This introductory section continues with a brief overview of the primary legal sources, the competent supervision and prosecution authorities, and certain general rules and principles of the sanctions regime of German capital markets law. The main sections B. (→ mn. 18 et seqq.), C. (→ mn. 83 et seqq.), and D. (→ mn. 114 et seqq.) present the substantive prohibitions and legal obligations that can give rise to (criminal) liability. Section B. (→ mn. 18 et seqq.) describes the central regime on 'market abuse' (*Marktmissbrauch*) that mainly addresses insider prohibitions, market manipulation, and certain other obligations. Section C. (→ mn. 83 et seqq.) covers notification and disclosure obligations regarding financial statements and major shareholdings in publicly-listed companies. Section D. (→ mn. 114 et seqq.) deals with the marketing of financial instruments, in particular prospectus requirements and related fraudulent conduct, such as capital investment fraud.

II. Overview of main sources of law

3 There is no one legal act governing the behaviour in German capital markets and (criminal) responsibility. Rather, the relevant legal framework is comprised of an overlay of European legislation and German national laws and is scattered across numerous provisions in different areas:

- a central piece of applicable capital markets laws is the European Market Abuse Regulation (Regulation (EU) 596/2014) (**MAR**), which is directly applicable in Germany and all other EU Member States; the MAR seeks to establish a common regulatory framework on 'market abuse', which mainly consists of insider dealing, unlawful disclosure of inside information, and market manipulation, as well as measures to prevent market abuse in order to ensure the integrity of financial markets and enhance investor protection and confidence in those markets (cf. Art. 1 MAR);
- with respect to sanctions, the MAR is supplemented by the European Directive on criminal sanctions for market abuse (Directive 2014/57/EU) (**CRIM-MAD**), which seeks to establish a harmonized sanctions framework across the EU, but – as a directive – is not directly applicable in the EU Member States. It must be implemented through national legislation;
- in Germany, the MAR and CRIM-MAD are transposed and supplemented in particular by the German Securities Trading Act (*Wertpapierhandelsgesetz*) (**WpHG**), which includes the administrative and criminal sanctions provisions and additional obligations and prohibitions for capital market participants; the WpHG also transposes financial and other notification and public reporting obligations of the EU Transparency Directive (Directive 2004/109/EC on the harmonization of transparency requirements in relation to information about issuers whose securities are admitted to trading on a regulated market) (**Transparency Directive**);
- prospectuses are a key source of information for investors about financial instruments. These are mainly governed by the directly applicable European Prospectus Regulation (Regulation (EU) 2017/1129) (**Prospectus Regulation**), which has harmonized prospectus requirements for the public offering and listing of securities across the EU; the German Securities Prospectus Act (*Wertpapierprospektgesetz*) (**WpPG**) contains certain further provisions on the national level, in particular on liability for prospectuses under civil law (which is not covered by this chapter);
- besides the distinct laws and regulations governing capital markets, certain provisions of the general German Criminal Code (*Strafgesetzbuch*) (**StGB**) are also relevant for capital market activity, primarily general fraud (§ 263 StGB) and, more specifically, the criminal act of capital investment fraud (§ 264a StGB);
- further relevant provisions, in particular on criminal responsibility for financial statements (accounting fraud), are included in the German Stock Corporation Act (*Aktiengesetz*) (**AktG**) and the German Commercial Code (*Handelsgesetzbuch*) (**HGB**).

These core sources of law are supplemented by a large number of additional imple- **4**
menting acts, specifications, and guidelines issued by the competent authorities, which provide further details on a European and German level. Since this section only seeks to provide an initial overview for foreign practitioners, this level of law is not comprehensively listed or discussed, but occasionally referenced as relevant.

III. Competent authorities

The primary supervisory and administrative enforcement agency for capital markets **5**
laws in Germany is the German Federal Financial Supervisory Authority (*Bundesantalt für Finanzdienstleistungsaufsicht*, **BaFin**).[1] BaFin regularly publishes information on its supervisory practice and interpretation of applicable rules on its website. Among the central publications from a practical perspective are BaFin's 'Issuer Guidelines'

[1] https://www.bafin.de (last accessed: 10.10.2025).

(*Emittentenleitfaden*),[2] which contains valuable introductions and summaries of individual areas of capital markets regulations as well as answers to questions concerning their interpretation in specific scenarios. This publication is also available in the English language and is useful as a legal information source for issuers and all capital market participants.

6 On the European level, the European Securities and Markets Authority (**ESMA**) is the EU's financial markets regulator and supervisor. The primary responsibility of ESMA is the preparation of technical standards and implementation acts for the EU Commission based on existing EU directives and regulations (known as 'Level 2' measures). In addition, ESMA itself publishes guidelines, interpretations, and recommendations concerning EU directives and regulations ('Level 3' measures). Except for certain specific areas, ESMA does not act as a supervisor directly towards market participants.

7 While BaFin is vested with the general supervision of compliance with capital markets laws and responsible for sanctioning administrative offences, criminal violations are generally pursued by the competent local general prosecutors. Since many violations constitute administrative offences and, depending on the circumstances, criminal offences at the same time, there is a factual and legal overlay of competencies between BaFin and the general criminal prosecution authorities. In practice, this frequently results in proceedings in which both authorities are involved.

- Prosecution and sanctioning of administrative offences is generally conducted by BaFin (cf. § 121 WpHG in conjunction with § 36 sub. 1 no. 1 OWiG). In this case, BaFin is responsible for independent and autonomous investigations and takes the decision on the charges at its own discretion (cf. § 47 sub. 1 OWiG). If BaFin, through such proceedings or otherwise, learns about facts that give rise to the suspicion of a criminal offence, it is under a statutory obligation to report these to the general prosecution authorities without undue delay (§ 11 WpHG). This is one of the main sources for criminal complaints filed with the prosecutor's office.
- If the administrative offence at the same time constitutes a criminal offence, there is a general principle that only the criminal law applies (cf. § 21 OWiG). This is relevant, for example, when the same conduct constitutes an administrative offence in the case of negligence and a criminal offence in the case of willful misconduct (a frequent pattern in the capital market sanctions regime, as shown in → mn. 34 et seqq., → mn. 47 et seqq., → mn. 93 et seqq.). Consequently, if the prosecution of an administrative offence coincides with a criminal offence, the primary responsibility for the investigation rests with the public prosecutor's office. The public prosecutor's office is then also responsible for investigating the administrative offence. In these cases, an administrative offence is punished by the competent criminal court and not by BaFin (cf. § 45 OWiG).

IV. Sanctions framework and corporate responsibility

1. General sanctions regime

8 Violations of capital markets laws can constitute criminal or administrative offences. A frequent pattern is that a violation through willful misconduct results in a criminal offence (with the threat of imprisonment or a fine), whereas negligent or grossly negligent behaviour is sanctioned as an administrative offence, i.e., with an administrative

[2] https://www.bafin.de/EN/Aufsicht/BoersenMaerkte/Emittentenleitfaden/emittentenleitfaden_artikel_en.html (last accessed: 10.10.2025).

fine issued by BaFin. With respect to prohibitions under the MAR, the CRIM-MAD sets certain requirements for the sanctions framework in the EU Member States, which have been transposed in Germany through the WpHG (in particular §§ 119 and 120 WpHG).

Since the entry into force of the MAR and transposition of the CRIM-MAD, administrative fines for violations of capital markets laws can reach drastic amounts. A distinct element in this respect is that for companies the maximum fine amount can be linked to a percentage of a company's total annual turnover (e.g., 15 % for violations of unlawful insider trading), which can be very severe for large international enterprises. In addition, the administrative offence may be punished based on the economic benefit derived from the violation (e.g., up to three times of such amount for unlawful insider trading). The economic advantage includes profits made and losses avoided and may be estimated by BaFin. In each case, the highest variant will be used to determine the applicable range for the fine amount. 9

Further practical guidance can be found in BaFin's 'Administrative Fine Guidelines' (*WpHG-Bußgeldleitlinien*) in accordance with the WpHG (available in the English language as well).[3] These provide important details on how BaFin approaches the setting of fines in light of the broad ranges and different options available (→ mn. 97, 113). They also contain specific guidance on the potential calculation of fine amounts depending on the circumstances. BaFin differentiates between 'mild', 'moderate', 'severe', 'very severe', and 'exceptionally severe' offences and also considers mitigating or aggravating circumstances as well as the financial circumstances of the party concerned. 10

In this context, it should be noted that BaFin can also terminate administrative fine proceedings by negotiated agreement, i.e., in the form of a settlement. Such a settlement may accelerate the proceedings and reduce the fine amount. The procedure is exclusively based on BaFin's administrative practice and is unrelated to the statutory settlement process for criminal court proceedings pursuant to § 257c StPO. 11

Market participants should also be aware that decisions on measures and sanctions taken by BaFin in individual cases may be published by BaFin on its website in anonymized or non-anonymized form pursuant to § 123 WpHG ('naming and shaming').[4] An anonymized publication requires particular justification (i.e., an exceptional reason why the expected damage to the party concerned outweighs the public interest in the announcement, which generally applies in the case of private individuals). 12

2. Corporate responsibility

The CRIM-MAD requires the national laws of the EU Member States to ensure that legal persons may also be held liable for relevant capital markets offences committed for their benefit by certain qualified persons in their sphere. § 30 OWiG is generally viewed as a sufficient transposition of this EU requirement (for further details on § 30 OWiG → Ch. 4). This provision also provides for the application of the high (turnover-based) variable sanctions to legal entities mentioned above (§ 30 sub. 2 sent. 2 and 4 OWiG refers to the charges of the specific violations). 13

Most of the relevant capital markets regulations are directed at the relevant company, thereby fulfilling the requirement of § 30 OWiG for corporate liability for unlawful acts of a company's directors and officers. However, a case-by-case assessment is still required. For example, if a director conducts illegal insider trading for his or her own personal 14

[3] https://www.bafin.de/SharedDocs/Downloads/EN/Leitfaden/WA/dl_aktualisierung_bussgeldleitlinien_2018_en.html (last accessed: 10.10.2025).

[4] https://www.bafin.de/DE/Aufsicht/BoersenMaerkte/Massnahmen/massnahmen_sanktionen_node.html (last accessed: 10.10.2025).

benefit or violates the (personal) obligation of the submission of director dealings reports pursuant to Art. 19 para. 1 MAR (as opposed to the relevant company's obligation to publish such reports pursuant to Art. 19 para. 3 MAR), such behaviour may not give rise to corporate liability pursuant to § 30 OWiG.

15 In many cases, capital markets compliance is delegated to a certain extent within large enterprises. In this respect, corporate responsibility pursuant to § 30 OWiG in conjunction with § 130 OWiG can become relevant if capital market laws are violated by employees, and the internal supervisory and organizational measures are found to be insufficient (also → Ch. 4 for further details on the interplay between § 130 OWiG and § 30 OWiG).

3. Capital markets compliance system

16 In particular stock-exchange listed companies must have appropriate structures in place to ensure that all capital market rules, including the handling of inside information and disclosure requirements, are complied with at all times. Such a 'capital markets compliance system' usually consists of the designation of specific responsibilities, the implementation of rules and procedures, and documentation and training measures (→ Ch. 6). It must be tailored to the needs of the relevant organization and reflect the applicable legal framework in the individual case.

17 Similar requirements can apply to companies who have not issued listed securities, but regularly handle inside information relating to listed companies (e.g., advisors or publication media). In this context, institutional investors who regularly invest in listed financial instruments may have to establish proper systems as well, e.g., to comply with insider trading and shareholding notification obligations. In contrast, lower standards may apply to companies that deal with inside information only occasionally or incidentally through contact with other parties.

B. Market abuse regime

I. Insider prohibitions

18 A cornerstone of modern capital markets regulations is the prohibition on using private information advantages for the trading of financial instruments. Such prohibition aims at protecting the integrity of financial markets and confidence in securities prices. Two essential manifestations of this principle can be found in the prohibitions of insider trading, i.e., the use of certain material non-public information in conducting securities trades, and the restrictions on sharing inside information with others. These areas are both part of the broader framework of 'insider rules' of the MAR. If a company has issued listed securities, acts as investor or is otherwise engaged in trading on German capital markets, this is one of the most important areas of compliance with criminal liability risks.

1. Scope of applicability

19 The insider prohibitions of the MAR apply to a wide range of financial instruments. The definition of 'financial instruments' in the MAR (Art. 3 para. 1 no. 1) refers to the list of financial instruments contained in Annex I Section C of the EU Market in Financial

Instruments Directive (Directive 2014/65/EU) (**MiFID II**). This list comprises, among others, transferable securities (shares, bonds and others) as well as derivatives such as options, futures and swaps.

In addition, pursuant to Art. 2 para. 1 lit. a to d MAR, the relevant financial instrument must either 20

- already be admitted to trading on a 'regulated market' of a stock exchange (e.g., General Standard or Prime Standard of the Frankfurt Stock Exchange) or at least be the subject matter of a filed application for admission to trading on such a market (e.g., in case of an IPO); or
- already be admitted to trading on a multilateral trading facility (**MTF**) or be the subject matter of a filed application for admission to trading on an MTF; in the case of an MTF or organized trading facility (**OTF**), it is also sufficient that the relevant financial instrument is actually traded on such MTF or OTF even if no formal admission was granted/application for admission was filed. This category includes 'unregulated' segments of exchanges (e.g., the open market (*Freiverkehr*) of the Frankfurt Stock Exchange, including the 'Scale' segment) or other exchange-like private trading venues; or
- in price or value, depend on or have an effect on, the price or value of a financial instrument covered by one of the two categories above, including, but not limited to, credit default swaps and contracts for difference.

From a practical perspective, the following two points on the scope of the insider prohibitions of the MAR are worth noting: first, the insider prohibitions may apply to financial instruments even if the company that has issued the financial instruments has not actively initiated an admission to trading. This becomes relevant in cases where trading only takes place on relevant venues outside of the regulated market (i.e., MTF/ OTF), which can also be initiated by third parties, and therefore the issuer, especially in the case of a foreign company, may not even be aware of the trading. 21

Second, the insider prohibitions also apply to transactions which are performed outside of the trading venues that trigger the applicability of the MAR or even outside of any trading venue (Art. 2 para. 3 MAR). This means that, for example, a privately negotiated share purchase that is settled via direct transfer of the relevant shares from seller to purchaser can still give rise to illegal insider dealing even if it is executed outside of any exchange. 22

2. Definition of inside information

Given the importance of the prohibitions and obligations that are linked to the existence of inside information, it is essential to understand what constitutes 'inside information' within the meaning of the MAR. Pursuant to Art. 7 MAR, the relevant information must have the following characteristics: the information 23

1. is of precise nature,
2. has not been made public,
3. is directly or indirectly related to an issuer or financial instrument, and
4. if it were to be made public, would likely have a significant effect on the price of the relevant financial instrument.

The interpretation of the details of these characteristics varies from country to country within the EU. The following summarizes the main aspects for these elements pursuant to the administrative practice of BaFin (as presented in its Issuer Guidelines): 24

1. **Precise nature:** for the information to be of 'precise nature' it must reach a certain level of specificity such that it may be reasonably expected that the information will

have an effect on market prices. This means that very vague or general information is not sufficient. Pursuant to a decision of the European Court of Justice in the case Lafonta v. Autorité des marches financiers[5] it is not a requirement that the direction is known in which prices would go if the information were to become public. Further, the information must either refer to already existing facts or future events if one may reasonably expect that such events will occur. BaFin takes the view that a probability of more than 50 % is required ('more likely than not'). Intermediate steps of a protracted process (with an uncertain end-result) may itself constitute inside information if they fulfil these requirements. This was aspect introduced in the MAR based on a prior decision of the European Court of Justice in the case Markus Geltl v. Daimler AG[6].

2. **No public knowledge:** information 'has been made public' if it has been made available to a broad investing public and thereby to an indeterminate number of persons (irrespective of who distributed the information). For this requirement to be fulfilled, every interested market participant must have the possibility to access such information, but the access does not necessarily have to be free of costs (e.g., through broadly distributed publication media). However, if a publication channel only targets a distinct group of recipients, this is in general not sufficient.
3. **Direct or indirect relation to an issuer or financial instruments:** the information does not necessarily have to refer to facts and circumstances related to an issuer's sphere of activity or which *directly* affects an issuer or the financial instruments in question. Information with an *indirect* relation is sufficient, e.g., market data or information on macroeconomic conditions. BaFin's Issuer Guidelines contain further examples in this respect.
4. **Likely significant effect on the price:** pursuant to the MAR, a piece of information 'likely' has an effect on the market price of a financial instrument if the information is such that a 'a reasonable investor would be likely to use it as part of the basis for his or her investment decision.' BaFin assumes that the average investor has a basic knowledge of the stock market, decides on an objectively comprehensible basis of information and does not necessarily possess any special technical knowledge, but has a basic understanding of the practices of securities trading and corporate law. The additional requirement of 'significance' is intended to ensure that not every detail that may lead to a minor price movement is regarded as inside information. There is no precise quantitative threshold for what constitutes a 'significant' effect on the price (e.g., a percentage of the stock price). The requirement is assessed from an *ex ante* perspective, i.e., it is not decisive if the price has actually moved following a publication of information (but a significant change may be an indicator from an *ex post* perspective). The assessment also requires to take into account what other information is already publicly available and whether there is a certain expectation in the market in one direction or the other.

25 Whether certain specific information qualifies as inside information requires a thorough case-by-case analysis. BaFin's Issuer Guidelines outline typical scenarios in which inside information may become existent and provide practical guidance with respect to financial data, M&A transactions, personnel-related decisions and legal proceedings. They also contain a helpful list of specific examples for potential inside information. For publicly-listed companies it is important for ensuring compliance with all related obligations to constantly review whether a certain step (e.g., the preparation of a significant

[5] ECJ 11.3.2015 – C-628/13, ECLI:EU:C:2015:162 = BeckRS 2015, 80360.
[6] ECJ 28.6.2012 – C-19/11, ECLI:EU:C:2012:397 = BeckRS 2012, 81319.

M&A transaction) or significant event (e.g., a new material lawsuit or investigation by a public authority) fulfils the requirements of inside information.

3. Prohibited conduct

The two main prohibitions with respect to the existence of inside information and the dealing in financial instruments are the prohibitions of (1) insider trading and (2) unlawful sharing of inside information. The prohibitions themselves are contained in Art. 14 MAR which must be read in conjunction with Art. 8, which specifies unlawful insider dealing, and Art. 10, which specifies unlawful disclosure. 26

a) Insider trading

Art. 8 MAR states that 'insider dealing' arises when (1) a person possesses inside information and (2) uses that information to directly or indirectly acquire or dispose of financial instruments to which that information relates for his or her own account or for the account of a third party. In addition, it is prohibited to recommend another person to engage in insider dealing or induce another person to engage in insider dealing (known as 'tipping'). The purpose of the prohibition of insider dealing is to prevent the insider from taking unfair advantage to the detriment of third parties who are unaware of the relevant information. 27

An infringement of the insider dealing prohibition requires that the person is in possession of inside information at the time when the relevant transaction (e.g., purchasing or selling shares) is made, and, in addition, that the person has used the information as the basis for his or her decision on the transaction. This generally requires a causal link. However, under the MAR and based on a decision of the European Court of Justice of 2009[7] a presumption applies pursuant to which a person in possession of inside information who trades in financial instruments also uses such information for the purposes of such trading. This presumption may be rebutted. Art. 9 MAR lists certain scenarios for such a rebuttal, but a person can always establish a rebuttal beyond such list, i.e., if he or she can provide other evidence that there was no causal link in the individual case. 28

For large enterprises that regularly engage in trading activities (such as institutional investors and financial institutions) Art. 9 para. 1 MAR includes a possible rebuttal for companies that have established adequate and effective internal arrangements and procedures against insider dealing, in particular through the separation of the decision-making process regarding the entering into a transaction and knowledge about inside information (including, among others, 'Chinese walls'). Such structures are, e.g., used by financial institutions to separate the trading unit (which constantly performs transactions in listed securities) from the investment banking unit (which frequently obtains knowledge of inside information concerning stock-exchange listed companies in the course of their advisory business). 29

In addition, Art. 8 para. 5 MAR contains a specific provision for companies that conduct insider trading, pursuant to which individual persons who participate in the decision to perform a prohibited transaction on the account of the legal entity may also infringe the prohibition. 30

[7] ECJ 23.12.2009 – C-45/08, ECLI:EU:C:2009:806 = BeckRS 2009, 71428 – Spector Photo Group NV and Chris Van Raemdonck/Commissie voor het Bank-, Financie- en Assurantiewezen (CBFA).

b) Unlawful sharing of inside information

31 The prohibition against the unlawful sharing of inside information has the general purpose of limiting the number of persons who are in possession of inside information in order to thereby reduce the overall risk of prohibited insider dealing. According to BaFin, inside information is 'shared' for these purposes when the recipient is put into a position where he or she comes into possession of the information without any major difficulties. It is not necessary in such cases that the recipient actually perceives the information or recognizes that it is inside information.

32 Sharing of inside information with others is generally unlawful pursuant to the MAR, unless an exception applies. BaFin applies a case-by-case analysis taking into account the principle of proportionality. This means that the sharing of inside information with a third party always requires a legitimate purpose, must be necessary to achieve the purpose ('need to know' principle), and that the insider's interest in sharing the information outweighs the market's interest in limiting the private distribution of the information. Pursuant to BaFin, keeping the circle of informed persons as small as possible, entering into non-disclosure agreements and expressly highlighting inside information as such in relevant correspondence can be means to support the balancing of interests in the individual case. Announcing inside information publicly is not unlawful sharing, because the public disclosure results in the loss of the qualification as inside information.

33 The MAR further contains a distinct set of rules applicable to 'market soundings', which are primarily relevant for the preparations of large capital markets transactions, in particular the offering of newly issued securities, during which contact with potential investors is established in order to gauge general market interest for the evaluation of the prospects of a potential transaction. Art. 11 MAR stipulates certain formal requirements and obligations for theses sounding processes which, if adhered to, allow for the sharing of inside information in the course of such discussions, i.e., mainly the fact that a potential transaction is being prepared and the terms of a potential transaction that need to be discussed. Pursuant to Art. 11 para. 2 MAR, the rules on market sounding can also become relevant in the context of public takeover transactions.

4. Sanctions

34 Insider trading (and the recommendation/inducement to insider trading by another person) as well as the unlawful sharing of inside information constitute criminal offences in cases of willful misconduct (§ 119 sub. 3 no. 1, 2 and 3 WpHG) and administrative offences in cases of gross negligence (§ 120 sub. 14 WpHG) by the acting person.

a) Criminal law

35 The criminal offence of insider trading is punishable by monetary penalty or imprisonment of up to five years. Willful misconduct requires, among other factors, knowledge with respect to the facts and circumstances establishing the definition of inside information. The person must seriously consider that the relevant information has the potential to have a significant effect on prices. An accurate assessment of potential price effects is not necessary. An (intentional) attempt to commit insider violations is also sanctioned as criminal offence.

36 In addition, the unlawful sharing of inside information can constitute a violation of secrecy obligations under general corporate law, which is a criminal offence pursuant to § 404 AktG.

b) Administrative offence

For natural persons, the administrative offence may be punished with a fine of up to 5 million euros. For companies, the administrative offence may be punished with a fine of up to 15 million euros or, if higher, up to 15 % of the total turnover in the last year prior to the decision. In both cases (natural person or company) the limit can go up to three times the economic advantage derived from the violation. The 'naming and shaming' rules of § 125 WpHG apply. 37

II. Market manipulation

The prohibition on market manipulation is a central concept of the MAR, which gives rise to (criminal) liability risk for market participants. Market manipulation is a general concept that covers different acts and behaviours with the potential to distort the functioning and integrity of capital markets. Engaging or attempting to engage in market manipulation is prohibited pursuant to Art. 15 MAR. 38

1. Prohibited conduct

Art. 12 MAR further describes which behaviours can constitute market manipulation, whereby the two main categories are (1) manipulative trading and (2) disseminating false or misleading information. Art. 12 para. 2 MAR contains a list of examples of market manipulation, and Annex I to the MAR contains a non-exhaustive list of the indicators of manipulative behaviour. 39

a) Manipulative trading

It is prohibited to enter into a transaction, place an order to trade or behave in any other way that gives false or misleading signals as to the supply of, demand for, or market price of a financial instrument. This applies, in particular, if artificial trades are executed on the stock exchange. One example is that a trade does not result in a change of beneficial ownership, but rather involves a transfer and re-transfer of the same party ('wash sales'). Another case is when stock exchange trades are pre-arranged, i.e., market orders that are carried out based on a prior agreement between the buyer and seller that are not disclosed beforehand. Such trades give the false impression that the trade is the result of independent forces of supply and demand and can influence the market price. 40

BaFin analyses transactional and order data, carries out research and observes the market in order to detect cases of market manipulation. Stock exchange operators are obligated to prevent and detect market abuse. Market participants who professionally arrange or execute transactions relating to financial instruments are required to have systems in place to detect and report infringements. 41

b) Manipulative information

It is further prohibited to disseminate information through the media, including the internet, or by any other means, which gives, or is likely to give, false or misleading signals as to the supply of, demand for, or market price of, a financial instrument. 42

'Information' in this context is understood to be defined very broadly. In the view of BaFin, it not only comprises verifiable facts, but also value judgements, forecasts and rumours. It is not necessary for the information to be disseminated to the public or disclosed to a large group of persons. Nor does it not matter how the information is 43 disseminated. Dissemination via traditional communication channels is captured in the same way as dissemination of information via the internet, including websites, social media or anonymous blogs.

44 Based on general German criminal law principles, market manipulation can also be committed through an omission (cf. § 13 StGB) if an obligation to publish certain information is violated. This can be an obligation to publish inside information by way of ad-hoc release (→ mn. 52 et seqq.), financial statements (→ mn. 84 et seqq.), voting rights notifications (→ mn. 97 et seqq.) and other disclosure obligations. Pursuant to BaFin, a relevant omission requires that the information to be disclosed is not disclosed at all or that the disclosure is not done in a sufficient or timely manner.

45 The dissemination or withholding of information may constitute market manipulation if it (likely) sends false or misleading signals, in particular regarding the price of the relevant financial instruments. Information that constitutes inside information pursuant to Art. 7 MAR will often send signals of sufficient relevance due to its materiality (→ mn. 23 et seqq.). Therefore, false or misleading signals can be sent by issuers in particular through the failure to publish a required ad-hoc announcement (at all or in sufficient time). However, according to BaFin, information relevant for market manipulation can also be information that does not qualify as inside information. It is sufficient that there is a specific risk that a reasonable investor will be deceived by the information.

46 The general prohibition of market manipulation is complemented by a specific prohibition against the manipulation of reference values (Art. 12 para. 1 d MAR). Reference values (e.g., certain interest rates, such as the Euro Interbank Offered Rate – EURIBOR, or stock exchange indices, such as the DAX) are often a key factor for the pricing of many financial instruments. It is therefore important for the operation of capital markets to protect the integrity of these reference values. The prohibition covers the manipulation of the reference value itself as well as the transmission of false or misleading information regarding the reference value, the provision of false or misleading output data or any other action by which the calculation of a reference value is manipulated.

2. Sanctions

47 Market manipulation can constitute a criminal offence in cases of willful misconduct (§ 119 sub. 1 no. 1 WpHG) and an administrative offence in cases of gross negligence (§ 120 sub. 15 no. 2 WpHG).

a) Criminal law

48 According to BaFin, willful misconduct at least requires that the responsible person believes it is possible that he or she will make false or misleading statements or will send false or misleading signals, and also believes that a possible result of his or her actions will be an effect on prices, but accepts this consequence and still commits the offence.

49 For completion of the criminal act, it is further required that the market manipulation has resulted in an actual effect on the market price of the relevant financial instruments (*ex post* view). In this case, the criminal act may be punished with a monetary penalty or imprisonment of up to five years. However, an (intentional) attempt to commit market manipulation (i.e., without an actual influence on the market price) is also sanctioned as criminal offence. In this respect, general criminal law principles on attempts apply.

50 Significantly increased punishments apply pursuant to § 35 sub. 5 WpHG if market manipulation is committed on a commercial basis or in the capacity as member of a criminal organization or in connection with a work-related activity, e.g., for a supervi-

sory authority, a stock exchange or an investment services enterprise. In these cases, the punishment includes imprisonment of between one and ten years.

b) Administrative offence

For natural persons, the administrative offence can be punished with a fine of up to 5 million euros. For legal entities, the administrative offence can be punished with a fine of up to 15 million euros or, if higher, up to 15 % of the total turnover in the last year prior to the decision. In both cases (natural person or company) the limit may be raised to three times the economic advantage derived from the violation. 'Naming and shaming' rules of § 125 WpHG apply. **51**

III. Ad-hoc disclosure of inside information

Pursuant to Art. 17 MAR, 'an issuer shall inform the public as soon as possible of inside information which directly concerns that issuer'. This means, in principle, that any inside information directly concerning an issuer must immediately be published in a distinct announcement, which in Germany is known as 'ad-hoc announcement' (*Ad-hoc-Mitteilung*). The immediate public disclosure of inside information by an issuer is regarded as essential in order to avoid insider trading and misguidance of investors. **52**

1. Publication obligation

a) Inside information directly concerning the issuer

The obligation to publish inside information only applies to inside information within the meaning of Art. 7 MAR 'directly concerning the issuer'. Pursuant to the administrative practice of BaFin, this can be inside information originating from the company's area of activity (e.g., financial data) as well as external circumstances (e.g., the receipt of an unsolicited takeover bid or an important court decision). In contrast, pursuant to BaFin, potential inside information that may only *indirectly* affect an issuer includes, inter alia, general economic data, political events or natural disasters, change in the situation of a competitor, e.g., insolvency, or information which only relates to the financial instrument and not to the relevant company itself. These types of information can still qualify as inside information (resulting in the application of the insider prohibitions discussed in → mn. 19 et seqq.), but do not trigger an ad-hoc announcement obligation for the issuer pursuant to Art. 17 MAR. **53**

b) Possibility to delay disclosure

In certain cases, an issuer has a legitimate interest in keeping inside information confidential and not disclosing it to the market, at least temporarily. Therefore, Art. 17 para. 4 MAR provides issuers with the possibility to delay the publication of inside information if the following three requirements are met: **54**

1. immediate public disclosure is likely to prejudice the legitimate interests of the issuer;
2. the delay of the disclosure is not likely to mislead the public; and
3. the issuer is able to ensure the confidentiality of the information.

55 The following is a summary of the main aspects for these requirements pursuant to BaFin's administrative practice (as presented in the Issuer Guidelines based on guidelines issued by ESMA[8]):

1. **Legitimate interest of the issuer:** circumstances that are likely to prejudice the issuer's legitimate interests in BaFin's view arise, for example,
   - if the issuer is conducting negotiations, the outcome of which would likely be jeopardized by immediate public disclosure (e.g., with respect to M&A transactions, which in practice is the most common and relevant justification for delaying the disclosure of inside information);
   - if the issuer's financial viability is at risk and immediate public disclosure would jeopardize the conclusions of negotiations designed to ensure the financial recovery;
   - if inside information relates to a decision of the issuer's management that still requires the approval of another decision-making body of the issuer, provided that immediate public disclosure would jeopardize the correct assessment of the public and the issuer has arranged for the final decision to be made as soon as possible; or
   - if the issuer has developed a product or an invention and the immediate public disclosure of that information would likely jeopardize the intellectual property rights of the issuer.
2. **No misleading of the public:** circumstances in which the delay of disclosure of inside information can likely mislead the public in BaFin's view (based on ESMA guidelines[9]) include, for example,
   - if there is a material difference to previous public announcements;
   - if the inside information concerns the fact that the issuer's financial objectives are unlikely to be met, if such objectives were previously publicly announced;
   - if there are inconsistencies with the market's expectations to the extent these expectations are based on signals the issuer previously sent to the market, such as interviews, roadshows or any other type of communication organized by the issuer or with its approval.

   In addition, the issuer must not actively give any signals that contradict the undisclosed inside information.
3. **Confidentiality is ensured:** a delay of disclosure requires that confidentiality of the inside information is ensured. In order to ensure confidentiality, appropriate organizational measures must be taken, including the establishment of information barriers and the conclusion of confidentiality agreements.

56 The publication of inside information may only be delayed pursuant to Art. 17 para. 4 MAR if and as long as all three requirements above are met. Once a decision to delay disclosure has been made, the issuer must continuously observe compliance with these requirements, including ensuring confidentiality at all times. If this or another requirement is no longer fulfilled, the issuer is obligated to immediately publish the relevant inside information via an ad-hoc announcement.

57 Pursuant to Art. 17 para. 7 MAR, a sufficiently accurate market rumour may indicate that confidentiality is no longer ensured. In BaFin's view, this requires that the rumour has a 'kernel of truth' and indicates an information leak, which needs to be assessed on a case-by-case basis. The circulation of vague speculations or rumours without any substance is not considered to be sufficiently accurate. In the case of a sufficiently accurate rumour following a leak, the issuer may no longer respond publicly with a 'no comment'

---

[8] MAR Guidelines on delay in the disclosure of inside information (ESMA/2016/1478).

[9] MAR Guidelines on delay in the disclosure of inside information (ESMA/2016/1478).

statement, but is instead required to publish the inside information immediately, which is commonly made by a confirmatory reference to the rumours.

Lastly, the issuer must actively and explicitly resolve on the delay of the disclosure of inside information. If inside information is not disclosed as soon as possible and if no delay is resolved, this constitutes a violation of Art. 17 MAR, even if the requirements for a delay were met and the company could have delayed the disclosure. 58

c) Timing, content and distribution of ad-hoc announcements

The issuer is obligated to publish inside information pursuant to Art. 17 para. 1 MAR as soon as possible. In practice, this can mean that a decision on the existence of inside information and the initiation of the publication may be required very quickly. According to BaFin, this can require that a draft of a relevant ad-hoc announcement is already prepared in advance. However, BaFin is also of the opinion that usually legal advice can be obtained without violating the timely disclosure obligation. 59

Besides certain formal information about the issuer and the relevant financial instruments (such as name and ISIN), an ad-hoc announcement, which typically is similar to a short press release, must contain the inside information, including the date on which the circumstances giving rise to the information occurred. It must further contain an explanation of how the information is directly relevant to the issuer and how the information may likely have a significant effect on the stock exchange or market price. This means, e.g., in the case of an agreement, that the announcement contains the key points, such as the subject matter of the agreement, the contractual partner, the term of the agreement and its main rights and obligations, including the price. 60

Moreover, an ad-hoc announcement must not be used as a marketing instrument (Art. 17 para. 1 subpara. 2 sent. 2 MAR), i.e., it must be written in a neutral, informative way. This restriction is intended to make it easier for the public to quickly identify and process the most important information of the ad-hoc announcement. Therefore, e.g., if an M&A transaction is announced, the ad-hoc announcement is often published together with a press release which contains additional background information. 61

The ad-hoc announcement of inside information must be disseminated throughout the European Union (cf. Art. 2 para. 1 Regulation (EU) 2016/1055[10] in conjunction with § 3a WpAV (*Wertpapierhandelsanzeigenverordnung*, Securities Trading Notification Regulation). This usually requires the use of a specific service provider. Additionally, the issuer is obligated to provide access to ad-hoc announcements on its website for at least five years (cf. Art. 3 Regulation (EU) 2016/1055). 62

2. Sanctions

The obligation to publish an ad-hoc announcement of inside information can be violated in various ways, in particular if the required announcement is not made, is incorrect, is incomplete, is not made in the prescribed manner or is not made in due time. 63

a) Criminal law

Violations against the obligations to publish an ad-hoc announcement are not directly sanctioned under criminal law, but can constitute the criminal offence of market manipu- 64

[10] Commission Implementing Regulation (EU) 2016/1055 of 29.6.2016 laying down implementing technical standards with regard to the technical means for appropriate public disclosure of inside information and for delaying the public disclosure of inside information in accordance with Regulation (EU) No 596/2014 of the European Parliament and of the Council, OJEU of 30.6.2016, L 173/47.

lation (Art. 12, 15 MAR, → mn. 38 et seqq.). This particularly applies if inside information is not published at all or too late. However, market manipulation can also occur if the issuer has actively decided to delay the publication of inside information based on Art. 17 para. 4 MAR (→ mn. 54 et seqq.), but the legal requirements for such a delay are not (or no longer) met.

65 Additionally, the German Federal Court of Justice, in a decision of 2005, held that ad-hoc announcements that contain condensed financial information, for example, a typical overview table of profit and loss items or key performance indicators, can constitute a criminal offence pursuant to § 400 no. 1 AktG (misrepresentation or concealment of the situation of a company in presentations or overviews of the assets and liabilities).[11]

b) Administrative offence

66 Violations of the obligation to publish inside information constitute an administrative offence (§ 120 sub. 15 no. 6 to 11 in conjunction with sub. 18 sent. 1 WpHG). For natural persons, the administrative offence may be punished with a fine of up to one million euros. For companies, the administrative offence may be punished with a fine of up to 2.5 million euros or, if higher, up to 2 % of the total turnover in the last year prior to the decision. In both cases (natural person or company) the limit may be increased to up to three times the economic advantage derived from the violation. 'Naming and shaming' rules of § 125 WpHG apply.

67 Violations of the prohibition to use ad-hoc announcements for marketing purposes are subject to an administrative fine of up to 5 million euros (cf. § 120 sub. 18 sent. 2 WpHG).

IV. Maintenance of insider lists

68 In connection with the handling of inside information, Art. 18 MAR requires that an issuer (e.g., a company whose shares are listed on a regulated market of a German stock exchange) prepares and maintains a case-specific list of all individuals who have access to the relevant inside information. This is considered an important source for BaFin when investigating possible insider violations (cf. Recital 56 MAR).

69 Insider lists become most relevant when an issuer decides to delay the public disclosure of inside information pursuant to Art. 17 para. 4 MAR (→ mn. 54 et seqq.), e.g., during the preparation and negotiations of a significant M&A transaction. The issuer is not required to maintain a 'permanent insider list', i.e., a list of all persons who would, irrespective of an individual case, usually be expected to come into possession of inside information if any inside information comes into existence within the company.

70 The (case-specific) insider lists must be updated continuously and provided to BaFin upon request. The persons listed must be made aware of their legal obligations concerning the handling of inside information (in particular the prohibition of insider trading and unlawful disclosure), as well as of the legal consequences of violations. For each person the date and time when they obtained knowledge of the relevant inside information must be recorded on the list.

71 The obligation to prepare an insider list applies primarily to the issuer itself, but also to all persons acting on behalf or for the account of the issuer, which is broadly defined by BaFin to include most external service providers, such as legal, financial and tax advisors. For the issuer itself, it is sufficient to include one contact person for each service provider

[11] BGH 16.12.2004 – 1 StR 420/03, BeckRS 2005, 23 – EM.TV.

on its internal insider list. In turn, the service provider needs to include all internal individuals on its own list.

The insider list must be kept confidential and managed electronically in a specific table format. Commission Implementing Regulation (EU) 2016/347 provides further details of the format and provides a template for insider lists pursuant to the MAR. 72

Violations concerning the preparation and administration of insider lists constitute an administrative offence (§ 120 sub. 15 no. 12 to 16 in conjunction with sub. 18 sent. 1 WpHG). For natural persons, the administrative offence may be punished with a fine of up to 500,000 EUR. For companies, the administrative offence may be punished with a fine of up to one million euros. There is no turnover-based fine for violations of the obligations concerning insider lists. In both cases (natural person or company) the limit may be increased to up to three times the economic advantage derived from the violation. 'Naming and shaming' rules of § 125 WpHG apply. 73

V. Directors' dealings

Dealings in the shares of a publicly listed company by its managers are considered a valuable source of information to investors, and transparency about such dealings is also seen as a preventive measure against insider trading (cf. Recital 58 MAR). Against this background, Art. 19 MAR provides for the obligation of managers to notify their company at the latest within three business days when they carry out such transactions ('managers' transactions') (Art. 19 para. 1 MAR). In turn, the relevant company is obligated to publish the notification received within two business days upon receipt (Art. 19 para. 2 MAR). 74

The notification obligation of Art. 19 para. 1 MAR applies to 'persons discharging managerial responsibilities' (PDMRs). Pursuant to the MAR itself, this group comprises (a) members of the administrative, management or supervisory body, which will often be the board of directors, or, in the case of the typical German two-tier governance structure, the management board and supervisory board, as well as (b) senior executives who are not members of such bodies, but who have regular access to inside information and the power to take 'managerial decisions affecting future developments and business prospects of [the company]' (cf. Art. 3 para. 1 no. 25 MAR). Which senior managers, if any, fall within this second category below the board level, can only be determined in a case-by-case assessment. In its Issuer Guidelines, BaFin takes the view that – at least with respect to a German stock corporation (AG) with a two-tier governance structure, only a very small number of persons (if any) will fall in this category and notes that this might be more frequently the case in a one-tier governance structure. 75

In addition, and in order to prevent circumventions, the notification obligation also applies to 'persons closely associated' with persons discharging managerial responsibilities. Those are defined in Art. 3 para. 1 no. 26 MAR and include, among others, spouses and registered civil partners, dependent children and other relatives from the same household. 76

Art. 19 para. 6 MAR stipulates the required content of a notification, which must include, among other things, the identity of the manager and the type of transaction as well as the volume and price of the transaction. A separate regulation (Commission Implementing Regulation (EU) 2016/523) specifies a template that must be used for the notification.[12] 77

---

[12] https://www.bafin.de/SharedDocs/Downloads/EN/Formular/WA/fo_Art19_MAR_en.html (last accessed: 10.10.2025).

78 Persons discharging managerial responsibilities and persons closely associated with them benefit from a de-minimis threshold per year, which is set at 5,000 EUR by default, but may be increased to 20,000 EUR by the competent authority. This increase was resolved by BaFin with effect from 1 January 2020.

79 If a notification or publication of a 'managers transaction' is (intentionally or gross negligently) not made, is incorrect, is incomplete, is not made in the prescribed manner or is not made in due time, this can constitute an administrative offence (§ 120 sub. 15 no. 17 and 18 in conjunction with sub. 18 sent. 1 WpHG). For natural persons, the administrative offence can be punished with a fine of up to 500,000 EUR. For companies, the administrative offence may be punished with a fine of up to one million euros. There is no turnover-based fine for violations of the notification obligations concerning managers transactions. In both cases (natural person or company) the limit may be increased to up to three times the economic advantage derived from the violation. 'Naming and shaming' rules of § 125 WpHG apply.

VI. Closed periods

80 Art. 19 para. 11 MAR sets forth certain 'closed periods' which persons discharging managerial responsibilities are not allowed to trade in financial instruments of their company. The restriction applies to the 30 calendar days before the publication of an interim or annual financial report. Pursuant to ESMA and BaFin guidelines, the restriction may also apply to the publication of preliminary results if these already contain all key financial figures. The goal of this restriction is to prevent unlawful insider trading by managers who may become aware or receive information about the company's financial position in advance of the reporting which is not (yet) publicly known.

81 A practical issue is that the 30 day period needs to be calculated backwards, i.e., from the day of publication of the relevant financial results. Since the publication date can still change until the publication is actually made, managers can face some uncertainty regarding the formal start of the closed period. Therefore, internal capital markets compliance guidelines of listed companies sometimes use a fixed calendar day as a start date for an internal closed period, which goes beyond the requirement of the MAR. In addition, as a precaution, compliance guidelines of issuers sometimes also introduce closed periods in advance of the publication of quarterly earnings reports (which, for example, are required in Germany for companies listed in the Prime Standard of the Frankfurt Stock Exchange), to which the closed period under the MAR in Germany do not apply.

82 If a person discharging managerial responsibilities violates the trading restriction during a closed period (intentionally or grossly negligently), this can constitute an administrative offence (§ 120 sub. 15 no. 22 in conjunction with sub. 18 sent. 1 WpHG). For natural persons, this administrative offence may be punished with a fine of up to 500,000 EUR. For companies, this administrative offence can be punished with a fine of up to one million euros. There is no turnover-based fine for violations of the obligations concerning closed periods. In both cases (natural person or company) the limit may be increased to up to three times the economic advantage derived from the violation. 'Naming and shaming' rules of § 125 WpHG apply.

C. Further compliance obligations

Companies that have issued financial instruments admitted to trading on a regulated market of a German stock exchange are required to observe a number of ongoing compliance obligations, in particular disclosure requirements. These can be broadly divided into event-based announcement obligations (including ad-hoc announcements of inside information as described in → mn. 52 et seqq.) and recurring reporting obligations, in particular financial reporting. **83**

I. Recurring financial reporting

1. Publication obligations

Companies that have issued securities (in particular shares or bonds) or other financial instruments which are admitted to trading on a regulated market of a stock exchange in Germany are required to periodically publish financial statements and related reports. These obligations are have their European legal basis in the EU Transparency Directive and in Germany are governed by §§ 114 to 118 WpHG. The obligations apply to 'domestic issuers' (*Inlandsemittenten*), which are primarily companies incorporated in Germany (e.g., German stock corporations) and whose securities are listed in Germany, but can also include foreign companies if their securities are listed in Germany.[13] **84**

In particular, the law requires the publication of **85**

- comprehensive annual financial reports with audited financial statements within at least four months following the end of the relevant financial year (i.e., usually by 30 April) (§ 114 WpHG); and
- condensed half-year financial reports, for which interim financial statements for the first six months need to be prepared (but not audited) and which need to be published at the latest within three months following the end of the relevant financial period (i.e., usually by 30 September) (§ 115 WpHG).
- For a parent entity of a group of companies, the requirements apply with respect to consolidated financial statements (§ 117 WpHG). The WpHG and related regulations contain detailed provisions on the required content, format and language of the reports as well as publication modalities and related prior notifications.

In addition, companies subject to these reporting requirements have to publicly announce the date on which they plan to publish their annual and half-year financial reports and the internet address at which those will be accessible. **86**

Stock exchange regulations applicable at the local exchange where the securities are listed may impose further requirements regarding financial reporting beyond those contained in the WpHG. For example, companies whose shares are listed in the Prime Standard segment of the regulated market (*regulierter Markt*) of the Frankfurt Stock Exchange (*Frankfurter Wertpapierbörse*) have to publish quarterly earnings reports in addition to the annual and half-year financial reports pursuant to the WpHG. Violations of these requirements are not punished by BaFin, but by the relevant stock exchange (e.g., the Sanctions Committee (*Sanktionsausschuss*) of the Frankfurt Stock Exchange). **87**

---

[13] For further details, see the definition of 'domestic issuer' (*Inlandsemittent*) in § 2 sub. 14 WpHG and the related definitions.

2. Review and enforcement by BaFin

88 As financial statements are a key information source for investors, the German legal system relies on different mechanisms to ensure the correctness and integrity of financial information and reports, in particular when securities of a company are listed on the stock exchange. These include internal governance processes under applicable corporate law, audit requirements by independent accounting firms and outside monitoring by external institutions, such as BaFin with respect to the financial reporting pursuant to §§ 114 et seqq. WpHG described above.

89 Since 2022, following the collapse of Wirecard AG, BaFin has the sole authority and competence for reviewing the financial reporting of stock-exchange listed companies (§§ 106 to 113a WpHG). Pursuant to § 106 WpHG, BaFin is responsible for reviewing whether financial statements and reports, including underlying accounting records, comply with the statutory provisions and applicable accounting standards. Such a review of financial information is commonly referred to as 'enforcement' (of accounting rules).

90 BaFin is entitled to order an audit of financial statements if it has concrete indications of a breach of accounting provisions. However, BaFin may also order an audit without specific cause (known as 'random audit'). During its audit, BaFin has broad investigative powers, including the right to receive information, submission of documents and interrogation as well as access rights to offices and properties.

91 If BaFin has ordered an audit of financial statements, it may publish this on its website, stating the name of the company concerned and the reason for the order if BaFin considers this to be in the public interest. It may also publish information on significant procedural steps during its review as well as substantive findings. If the audit does not result in any objections, BaFin informs the company concerned accordingly. If the audit has been published in advance, the result of the audit ('no objections') is also published.

92 If the audit reveals that the financial reporting is incorrect, BaFin makes a formal determination of the relevant error. In addition, BaFin may determine how the financial reporting would have been presented without the error. Unless there is a lack of public interest in exceptional cases, BaFin will also publish the error, naming the company concerned and the main aspects of the audit.

3. Sanctions

a) Criminal law

93 The financial reporting requirements pursuant to the WpHG are not directly punishable under criminal law, except for the responsibility statement (*Bilanzeid*) by the directors, i.e., the required confirmation that, to the best of their knowledge, the financial statements and the management report give a true and fair view of the actual situation. Pursuant to § 119a WpHG, a false responsibility statement can be punished with imprisonment of up to five years or a monetary fine in the case of willful misconduct or up to two years or a monetary fine in the case of gross negligence.

94 If, during its audit of financial statements in an enforcement procedure or otherwise, BaFin becomes aware of facts giving reason to suspect a criminal offence has been committed in relation to a company's accounting, it is obligated to inform the competent prosecutor's office pursuant to § 110 WpHG. For listed stock corporations incorporated in Germany, criminal offences in relation to financial information can include, in particular, misrepresentation and concealment of a company's situation (§ 331 HGB and § 400 AktG). Falsification of documents, fraud and criminal offences relating to insolvency can also become relevant. Lastly, misrepresentations through financial statements of companies

listed on the capital market can, if the relevant requirements are met, also constitute the criminal offence of market manipulation pursuant to the MAR (→ mn. 44 et seqq.).

b) Administrative offence

Violations of the financial reporting requirements pursuant to the WpHG constitute administrative offences, which can be punished with a fine of up to 10 million euros or, if higher, up to 5 % of the total turnover in the last year prior to the decision or, if higher, up to twice the economic benefit derived from the violation. Non-compliance with procedural orders by BaFin during an enforcement process are also punishable as administrative offences. **95**

Violations of the legal requirements relating to the preparation of mandatory financial and non-financial reports for companies incorporated in Germany may also constitute administrative offences pursuant to § 334 HGB. In the case of a so-called 'capital-market oriented' corporation (*kapitalmarktorientierte Kapitalgesellschaft*), i.e., a company whose shares, bonds or other securities are publicly traded (cf. § 264d HGB), these violations may be punished for the acting individual with a maximum fine of 2 million euros or twice the economic benefit gained and (in conjunction with § 30 OWiG) for the relevant company with a maximum fine of up to 10 million euros, five per cent of the revenues or twice the economic benefit gained, whichever amount is higher (§ 334 sub. 3a HGB). **96**

II. Voting rights notifications

One further practically important compliance area outside of the MAR are major shareholding notifications, i.e., the obligation of investors to report their shareholdings and financial instruments if certain thresholds are exceeded or reached to BaFin and the relevant listed company. The relevant company is then obligated to publish such notifications. In Germany, these notifications are commonly referred to as 'voting rights notifications' (*Stimmrechtsmitteilungen*). This area is of high practical importance, as BaFin intensively scrutinizes violations and fines can be substantial even for incidents that may be perceived as minor. **97**

The basis for such obligations is the EU Transparency Directive. In Germany, the directly applicable requirements are contained in §§ 33 et seqq. WpHG. **98**

1. Notification and publication obligations

Natural persons and companies are obligated to disclose to BaFin and to the listed company their shareholding and financial instruments as soon as these reach, exceed or fall below one of the relevant thresholds as a result of an acquisition, sale or for other reasons within four trading days. The listed company is then required to publish this notification within three trading days (§ 40 WpHG). **99**

There are three different categories and various attribution rules to be taken into account when assessing voting rights notification obligations: **100**

1. **§§ 33 and 34 WpHG:** direct and indirect shareholdings with voting rights:
   - § 33 WpHG covers directly held shares with voting rights and stipulates the following thresholds: 3 %, 5 %, 10 %, 15 %, 20 %, 25 %, 30 %, 50 % and 75 %.
   - § 34 WpHG provides that voting rights attached to shares of a third party may be attributed to the person, subject to the notification obligation under certain

circumstances (e.g., if there is a parent-subsidiary relationship or in case of a trust agreement).

2. **§ 38 WpHG:** the same thresholds of § 33 WpHG (but starting only from 5 %) apply to direct and indirect holdings of financial instruments that allow the holder to acquire voting rights attached to shares (e.g., call options) or have a similar economic effect.
3. **§ 39 WpHG:** if the categories of §§ 33, 34 WpHG (shares) and § 38 WpHG (financial instruments) do not trigger a notification obligation individually, a notification can also be required if the relevant thresholds (starting from 5 %) are reached through aggregation of shareholdings and instruments (e.g., if an investor owns 2 % of shares and 3 % of call options).

101 Issuer have to publish their total number of voting rights pursuant to § 41 WpHG, which has to be used by market participants as basis for their calculations.

102 Detailed requirements for the trigger events, electronic format, deadlines and language for voting rights notifications are governed by §§ 33 et seqq. WpHG in conjunction with ancillary laws, such as the WpAV and BaFin's Voting Rights Notification Regulation (*Stimmrechtsmitteilungsverordnung* – StimmRMV).

103 BaFin has also published a dedicated chapter (Module B) on voting rights notifications and related obligations as part of its Issuer Guidelines, which covers a number of case scenarios and addresses many legal and practical questions.

2. Sanctions

104 Violations of the obligation of an investor to submit voting rights notifications are administrative offences pursuant to § 120 sub. 2 no. 2 lit. d and lit. e in conjunction with sub. 17 WpHG. The same applies to violations of the obligation for the company to publish received voting rights notifications, § 120 sub. 2 no. 3 lit. a in conjunction with sub. 17 WpHG.

105 For natural persons, this administrative offence can be punished with a fine of up to 2 million euros. For companies, this administrative offence may be punished with a fine of up to 10 million euros or, if higher, up to 5 % of the total turnover in the last year prior to the decision. 'Naming and shaming' rules of § 125 WpHG apply.

III. Rules on short selling

106 Short selling (*Leerverkauf*) refers to transactions that allow investors to speculate on decreasing market prices (in contrast to 'long' transactions, through which investors seek to benefit from increasing prices, e.g., when buying and holding a financial instrument). 'Short' selling is, for example, if an investor sells borrowed securities at a certain price with the intention to buy new securities later at a lower price to pay back the lender. If the market price of the securities decreases between the time of sale and the time when the investor has to buy the securities to pay back the lender, the investor can make a profit.

107 Short selling is regarded as valuable for increasing market efficiency, as it is one way in which negative information on a security can be reflected in the market price. Short selling can also be useful for hedging purposes. However, short selling transactions are associated with increased risks: in the example of borrowed shares, the investor at some point is obligated to pay back the lender, i.e., buy the securities, irrespective of the share price, which means even in a situation where the market price has significantly increased contrary to the investor's expectation. Since there is no limit to the price increase, the risk exposure is theoretically unlimited (in contrast to 'long' transactions, where the potential loss is limited to the full investment amount). Regulators are also concerned that short selling can exacerbate downward spirals of prices, thereby threatening financial stability, and may be used for abusive purposes together with the aggressive dissemination of false or misleading information ('short selling attacks').

Short selling of financial instruments is regulated on the EU level by Regulation (EU) No 236/2012 (**Short Selling Regulation**), which is also directly applicable in Germany. The Short Selling Regulation mainly covers two areas: (a) disclosure obligations for net short positions and (b) a general prohibition of uncovered 'naked' short selling. **108**

1. Disclosure obligations of net short positions

The Short Selling Regulation requires that in relation to shares issued by a company and sovereign debt instruments, net short selling, i.e., positions resulting from short selling or any other transactions to provide a financial benefit in the event of a decrease in price or value of the share or debt instrument (cf. the definitions in Art. 2 and 3 of the Short Selling Regulation), must be reported to the competent authority (in Germany: BaFin) if it reaches or falls below certain thresholds (cf. Art. 5 et seqq. of the Short Selling Regulation). The purpose of such notifications is to assist regulators in monitoring whether large positions pose systemic risk or are used for abusive purposes. **109**

For shares, the initial notification threshold is 0.1% of the issued share capital and then each 0.1% above that. In addition, a public disclosure requirement applies at 0.5% of the issued share capital. Details regarding the method of notification and disclosure are covered in Art. 9 of the Short Selling Regulation. The notification procedure in Germany is further specified in the German Regulation on Net Short Selling (*Netto-Leerverkaufspositionsverordnung*, NLPosV). **110**

2. Prohibition of uncovered short sales

The Short Selling Regulation contains a general prohibition (ban) of uncovered short selling in shares (Art. 12) and in sovereign debt instruments (Art. 13). Short selling is considered uncovered ('naked') if the short seller, when entering into the short sale, does not have any coverage for closing the short position when due. This situation creates the potential risk of settlement failure and market price volatility. In relation to shares, Art. 12 of the Short Selling Regulation in conjunction with an implementing regulation (Regulation (EU) No 827/2012) provide further details on the different options to obtain coverage, i.e., which types of agreements, arrangements and measures sufficiently ensure that shares will be available for settlement of the transaction (e.g., by having an enforceable claim based on a call option). **111**

3. Temporary short-selling bans

Art. 20 of the Short Selling Regulation provides the competent national authorities (in Germany: BaFin) with the right to issue a temporary ban of any net short selling (i.e., including through covered short sales) if they deem it necessary to address a serious threat to financial stability or market confidence. In the US, such a short selling ban was used in 2008 with the intent to prevent further stock price declines of banks during the financial crisis. In Europe, authorities in several EU Member States implemented broad temporary bans for one or two days in response to stock market declines caused by the outbreak of Covid-19. In Germany, the only short selling ban BaFin has ever implemented was aimed at addressing short-selling attacks on Wirecard AG in 2019. Art. 23 of the Short Selling **112**

Regulation also allows restrictive measures to be taken in the event of significant short-term declines in the prices of financial instruments.

4. Sanctions

113 Intentional or gross negligent violations of the Short Selling Regulation constitute an administrative offence (§ 120 sub. 6 no. 1 to 5 in conjunction with sub. 24 WpHG). This administrative offence can be punished with a fine of up to 200,000 EUR in case of failure to comply with notification/publication requirements and 500,000 EUR in case of prohibited (uncovered) short selling. There is no distinction between fines for individuals and companies.

D. Marketing of financial instruments

I. Prospectus requirements

114 Raising capital from a broad target group or the general public through the issuance or offering of new or existing securities, or other investment products, usually requires that some form of informational document is made available to potential investors as the basis for their investment decision, i.e. a prospectus. Prospectus requirements in Germany mainly depend on the type of financial instrument being issued or offered and the scope of the issuance/offering.

115 The most comprehensive and strictest prospectus requirements apply to transferable securities (in particular shares or bonds) that are listed or in the process to be listed on a regulated market of a stock exchange (such as in the course of an initial public offering (IPO) of a company or a capital increase). These types of securities are mainly governed by the European Prospectus Regulation.[14] Investment products that are deemed to not be transferable securities can still be subject to prospectus requirements pursuant to the German Capital Investment Act (*Vermögensanlagegesetz*, VermAnlG) or, in the case of shares in investment funds, pursuant to the German Capital Investment Code (*Kapitalanlagegesetzbuch*, KAGB). Generally, prior approval by BaFin is required before a prospectus may be published. Details pertaining to the circumstances requiring the publication of an approved prospectus (i.e., public offering and/or admission to trading on a regulated market of relevant instruments) as well as the required content of a prospectus are not covered in this section.

116 When a prospectus is required, offering or issuing the relevant investment products without publishing a prospectus constitutes an administrative offence. For example, a public offering of securities under the European Prospectus Regulation that is not accompanied by the publication of a prospectus can result in a fine of up to 700,000 EUR in the case of natural persons or, in the case of companies, 5 million euros or, if higher, 3 % of total revenues or, if higher, twice the economic advantage derived from the offence.

[14] The required content and presentation of prospectuses are specified by the EU Delegated Regulations 2019/979 and 2019/980 of the EU Commission, each dated 14 March 2019.

II. Fraudulent conduct

If information published in a prospectus or other marketing materials for financial instruments is false, incomplete or misleading, this can constitute a criminal act of capital investment fraud (*Kapitalanlagebetrug*) pursuant to § 264a StGB, which primarily seeks to protect the proper functioning of capital markets, or an act of general fraud (*Betrug*) pursuant to § 263 StGB, which primarily seeks to protect an individual from suffering damages. In addition, misleading advertising for financial products can be a criminal offence pursuant to § 16 UWG (*Gesetz gegen unlauteren Wettbewerb*, Act Against Unfair Competition). **117**

1. General fraud

If an investor suffered financial damage due to an investment in financial instruments that have been marketed with false or misleading information, the issuer or the relevant representative can be held criminally liable for fraud pursuant to § 263 StGB. In such circumstances, the German Federal Court of Justice has ruled that § 263 StGB takes precedent over § 264a StGB.[15] The type of investment is generally irrelevant, i.e., general fraud can be committed with respect to any financial instrument. **118**

General fraud pursuant to § 263 StGB requires: **119**

1. a deception of the facts by the offender,
2. which causes a misconception about the facts,
3. which results in a transfer of assets,
4. which, in turn, leads to a pecuniary loss by the victim of the deception or a third party.

In addition, the perpetuator must act with the intention of enrichment. **120**

Fraud can also be committed by representatives of a company, in particular managing directors or management board members, when preparing and approving prospectuses or other marketing materials to be published in connection with the offering of shares or other financial instruments of that company. The intention for enrichment does not need to relate to the representative itself. An intention to enrich a third party, i.e., the company, is sufficient. **121**

2. Capital investment fraud

Capital investment fraud pursuant to § 264a StGB does not require the deception of an individual person or the occurrence of a financial loss. It also does not require an intention for enrichment. It is sufficient that false or misleading information is used for the purposes of marketing an investment product. In this respect, it can be said that § 264a StGB applies 'earlier' than § 263 StGB. **122**

§ 264a StGB requires that the offender: **123**

1. made incorrect advantageous statements to a larger circle of persons or concealed disadvantageous facts,
2. in prospectuses, presentations or overviews of the asset condition,
3. with regard to the circumstances relevant to the investment decision,
4. in connection with the distribution of securities, subscription rights or shares intended to grant a participation in the results of an enterprise, or the offer to increase the contribution to such shares.

---

[15] BGH 29.10.2021 – 5 StR 443/19, NZWiSt 2022, 326.

124 Therefore, § 264a StGB – in contrast to § 263 StGB – does not apply to statements that are made individually to a person in a bilateral conversation or exchange. It also only applies to the specific investment products mentioned in the law and not to all types of financial instruments (as is the case with § 263 StGB).

125 Capital investment fraud can also be committed by representatives of a company, in particular managing directors or management board members, if they have contributed to the preparation of the erroneous prospectus, presentation or overview.

126 As mentioned above, as soon as the deception of a specific investor has occurred, § 263 StGB takes precedent. Since most cases are only notified to the prosecution authorities if investors actually suffered losses, historically, the significance of § 264a StGB in criminal law judgements has been rather low.

3. Misleading advertising

127 Someone who, with the intention of creating the appearance of a particularly favourable offer, advertises products or services through means of false statements in public announcements or utilizes misleading statements in communications directed at a larger circle of persons, can be held liable for the criminal offence of misleading advertising pursuant to § 16 sub. 1 UWG. This can also apply to the deceptive marketing of financial instruments, such as shares and other securities, including through prospectuses and other publications made in compliance with capital markets disclosure obligations.[16] In certain cases, the general administrative offences concerning misleading advertising in §§ 5 and 5a UWG can also be relevant.

4. Fraud-related to information on sustainability (greenwashing)

128 An increased awareness for sustainability and environmental, social and governance topics (**ESG**) has resulted in a stronger demand for 'green' investment products, i.e., investments in environmental-friendly assets that meet certain sustainability criteria. As a consequence, companies and asset managers face pressure to offer suitable investments and market them accordingly. If prospectuses or other marketing materials for financial instruments present these instruments as more sustainable than they actually are, this practice is commonly known as 'greenwashing'.

129 'Greenwashing' cases raise questions on the application of the relevant criminal provisions, such regarding (i) the distinction between wrong factual statements (which are captured by the criminal provisions) and mere expressions of opinions and beliefs (which are, as a rule, not captured), (ii) the requirement of § 263 StGB relating to a pecuniary loss (e.g., if the investment marketed with erroneous sustainability information still performs financially well) and (iii) the scope of relevant information for purposes of § 264a StGB (which, according to the German Federal Court of Justice[17] are only 'value-creating' factors that were historically understood to relate primarily to the profitability, security and liquidity of the investment and not necessarily other characterizations and qualifications, such as its effect on the environment).

130 In addition, new reporting requirements for large publicly listed companies on ESG matters (e.g., the non-financial report required in Germany pursuant to § 289c HGB that requires reporting on environmental, employment, social, human rights and anti-corruption matters) can also be a source of liability risk for false or misleading information.

---

[16] Cf. OLG Hamburg 19.7.2006 – 5 U 10/06, NJW-RR 2006, 1637.

[17] BGH 3.2.2022 – III ZR 84/21, NJW 2022, 1322.

This risk will continue to increase as new legislative measures are adopted that expand and further specify the sustainability-related reporting requirements in capital markets, such as the Corporate Sustainability Reporting Directive (CSRD)[18] and the Sustainable Finance Disclosures Regulation (SFDR)[19] in the EU.

5. Sanctions

General fraud pursuant to § 263 StGB carries a penalty of up to five years of imprisonment or a fine. In certain circumstances, the period of imprisonment can be up to ten years. Capital investment fraud pursuant to § 264a StGB can be punished with a fine or a period of imprisonment of up to three years. Misleading advertising pursuant to § 16 UWG can be punished with fines or a period of imprisonment of up to two years. With respect to the publishing of erroneous ESG-related information in the regular financial reporting, including the non-financial report pursuant to § 289c HGB (→ mn. 130). **131**

III. Inducing stock market speculation

Pursuant to § 26 BörsG (*Börsengesetz*, German Stock Exchange Act) it is generally prohibited to induce others on a commercial basis to enter into or participate in speculative stock exchange transactions by taking advantage of an investor's inexperience in such transactions. Such 'speculative stock exchange transactions' include purchase or sale transactions with a deferred delivery period aimed at making a profit from the difference between the agreed price and the market price existing at the time of delivery. In essence, this covers futures, options, contracts for difference (CFD) and similar transactions in financial markets. The prohibition is not restricted to transactions on German stock exchanges. **132**

This specific prohibition seeks to protect inexperienced (private) investors against the risk associated with such speculative transactions and can become relevant in cases of frivolous or fraudulent brokerage activities. Violations of the prohibition constitute a criminal offence pursuant to § 49 BörsG and can be punished with a period of imprisonment of up to three years. **133**

---

[18] Directive (EU) 2022/2464 of the European Parliament and of the Council of 14 December 2022.
[19] Regulation (EU) 2019/2088 of the European Parliament and of the Council of 27 November 2019.

CHAPTER 23
FOREIGN TRADE LAW

Bibliography: Achenbach, Verbandsgeldbuße und Aufsichtspflichtverletzung (§§ 30 und 130 OWiG) – Grundlagen und aktuelle Probleme, NZWiSt 2012, 321; Freund/Rostalski, Gesetzliche bestimmte Strafbarkeit durch Verordnungsrecht?, GA 2016, 443; Gehring, Aus dem Entwurf des Verbandssanktionsgesetzes für eine Neuauflage lernen, NZWiSt 2022, 437; Henssler/Hoven/Kubiciel/Weigand, Kölner Entwurf eines Verbandssanktionengesetzes, NZWiSt 2018, 1; Klindt, Arbeitsschutzrecht – die unterschätzte Compliance-Herausforderung, ARP 2020, 6; Niestedt/Lesko, Wirksamkeit der Russland-Sanktionen, UKuR 2022, 601; Pelz/Sachs, Übersicht über die neuen sektoralen EU-Russland-Sanktionen – Teil 1: Beschränkungen des Waren- und Dienstleistungsverkehrs, UKuR 2022, 9; Rostalski, Neben der Spur: Verbandssanktionengesetzgebung auf Abwegen, NJW 2020, 2087; Wiedmann/Will, Die Russland-Sanktionen der EU, RIW 2022, 173.

Table of contents

A. Introduction 586
B. Corporate criminal liability in foreign trade law 587
I. Principles of criminal 'liability' of corporations in Germany 587
II. Corporate liability under AWG 588
1. Reservation of statutory regulation 589
2. Blanket norms and legal definiteness 589
3. Applicability of the sanctioning norms of AWG in relation to persons 591
4. § 17 AWG: violations of arms embargoes 591
5. § 18 AWG: violations of the Dual-Use Regulation 593
6. § 19 AWG 595
III. Confiscation 596
C. Principles of AWG compliance 597
D. Selected practical problems 599
I. Export licences obtained through deception 599
II. EU sanctions using the Russia Sanctions Regulation as an example 600
1. Scope of application 600
2. Goods and technology-related sanctions 601
a) Dual-use goods/technologies 601
aa) Trade, service and financing prohibitions for dual-use goods/technologies 601
bb) Exemptions 601
b) Goods for technological enhancement in the defence and security sector, for use in oil refining and in aerospace 602
c) Maritime goods and technologies 602
d) Iron and steel products 602
e) Further prohibitions and export restrictions 602
3. Participation, investment and financing sanctions 602
4. Prohibitions in the area of capital markets 603
5. Prohibition of circumvention 603
6. Personal sanctions 603
a) Freezing 603
b) Ban on provision of resources 604

7. Criminal consequences of an offence under AWG 604
III. Growing importance of investment examination 605
1. Cross-sectoral audit procedure 605
2. Sector-specific examination procedure 606
IV. Growing importance of export controls of dual-use goods in surveillance technology 607

A. Introduction

1 Foreign trade law is an important regulatory instrument in international economic relations. The stipulations and prohibitions of the relevant legal provisions enable the state to assert its security, foreign policy, economic and trade policy interests and concerns through the relationship between the economic players.[1] However, according to the conception of such legislation and in the light of the need for an open economic system, state intervention should (of course) remain the exception. Put succinctly, AWG (*Außenwirtschaftsgesetz* – the German Foreign Trade and Payments Act) and its related statutory provisions thus represent the regulatory exceptions to the principle of free international economic trade. The exceptional character of state intervention in the free play between markets is stated *expressis verbis* in § 1 AWG and is presented in advance of the provisions of the law by way of clarification: 'The trade in goods, services, capital, payment transactions and other types of trade with foreign territories, as well as the trade in foreign valuables and gold between residents (foreign trade and payments) is, in principle, not restricted. It is subject to the restrictions contained in this Act or prescribed by ordinances issued on the basis of this Act.'

2 Legal sources of effective export control and its enforcement are provided in the legal acts of the EU, e.g. the Dual-Use Regulation, international law and national foreign trade law, which essentially consists of AWG and AWV (*Außenwirtschaftsverordnung* – the German Foreign Trade and Payments Ordinance).[2]

3 The stipulations and prohibitions under foreign trade law and their corresponding penalties generally result from a confluence of various national and international legal sources. This is one of the reasons why this area of law is considered complex. The legal field in question is also subject to a particular dynamism[3], which sees the legal framework being constantly adapted and supplemented in accordance with its meaning and purpose.

4 In the practice of corporate compliance, this area of law plays an important role, particularly in relation to manufacturing and trade. Especially in view of the far-reaching classification of economic goods as so-called 'dual-use goods', all relevant export control regulations subject to sanction need to be observed in corporate compliance. In addition,

---

[1] Such as was explicitly stated by the Federal Ministry of Finance in its online publication <https://www.bundesfinanzministerium.de/Web/DE/Themen/Zoll/Aufgaben/Aussenwirtschaftsrecht/Aussenwirtschaftsrecht.html> (last accessed: 2.12.2024): 'Foreign trade law regulates economic transactions with other states with special consideration of the concerns in the area of its own security, foreign, economic and trade policy. In order to be able to protect these effectively, there is a need for state intervention that can restrict foreign trade.'

[2] Leitner/Rosenau/Ahlbrecht, 1st edn 2017, AWG Vorbemerkungen mn. 1; Momsen/Grützner WirtschaftsSteuerStrafR-HdB/Meyer/Hüttemann § 37 mn. 13.

[3] BeckOK AußenWirtschaftsR/Schwendinger, 13. Ed. 1.8.2024, AWG § 17 mn. 13, which refers to the dynamic nature of the regulation of export lists as a consequence of constant 'change through advances in research and technology'.

the entire field of foreign trade in arms and military equipment is significantly shaped by export control regulations and the related administrative and licensing procedures.[4]

Furthermore, significant foreign trade law restrictions also arise in international commercial transactions and in M&A business[5] in the context of the so-called 'investment examination law'. 5

The establishment of a functioning compliance system that observes all applicable national and international rules of foreign trade and payments law is also of major importance in the fields of legal advice and defence for companies and managers confronted with relevant sanction proceedings: for example, as far as the law is concerned, the prosecution of certain administrative offences under the circumstances specified in § 22 sub. 4 AWG will not take place 'insofar as appropriate measures are taken to prevent a violation for the same reason'. Independent of this, compliance measures taken in advance of an infringement can have an exculpatory effect. This applies, on the one hand, with regard to the risk of imposition of a corporate fine due to some violation of AWG and, on the other hand, in relation to personal responsibility of managers who are responsible for the proper set-up of the business. 6

In terms of legal dogma, foreign trade law is a classic field within public commercial law. With regard to criminal compliance and legal defence in sanction proceedings, there is also a strong administrative 'accessoriness'.[6] Some of the primary features of foreign trade and payments law are notification obligations (§ 11 AWG), prohibitions subject to authorisation (§ 8 AWG), the corresponding procedures in applications to the Federal Office of Economics and Export Control ('BAFA') and by effectiveness reservations (§ 15 AWG). 7

B. Corporate criminal liability in foreign trade law

I. Principles of criminal 'liability' of corporations in Germany

In any consideration of the question of corporate criminal liability in German law, it is important at first to separate strictly the areas relating to the company's employees and managers from the company/corporation itself. From the German point of view, companies cannot make themselves liable to prosecution. Original criminal liability in Germany namely presupposes a determination of guilt.[7] Since companies cannot act and decide for themselves but are always legally present only in the person of their representatives, 8

[4] <https://www.bafa.de/DE/Bundesamt/Organisation/Aufgaben/aufgaben_node.html> (last accessed: 2.12.2024).

[5] See 'Referentenentwurf des Bundesministeriums für Wirtschaft und Energie – Siebzehnte Verordnung zur Änderung der Außenwirtschaft' (Draft Bill of the 17th Ordinance on the Amendment of the Foreign Trade and Payments Ordinance): 'Foreign direct investment is of great importance for economic development in Germany. At the same time, global geo-economic competition is steadily increasing. Concrete investment projects increasingly serve broader political-strategic interests. An effective investment appraisal instrument protects the security policy interests of the Federal Republic of Germany. It is of central importance in this regard that the state learns of potentially critical acquisition cases in good time. A case-by-case examination then ensures the appropriate balancing of entrepreneurial and security policy concerns.' https://www.bundeswirtschaftsministerium.de/Redaktion/DE/Downloads/P-R/referentenentwurf-siebzehnte-verordnung-zur-aenderung-der-aussenwirtschaftsverordnung.html (last accessed: 20.10.2025).

[6] Momsen/Grützner WirtschaftsSteuerStrafR-HdB/Meyer/Hüttemann § 37 mn. 29.

[7] Rostalski NJW 2020, 2087 (2088).

it is impossible from the outset to assign any condemnatory judgement to the company as a legal entity.

9 As a reaction to conduct that is subject to legal sanctions, only the criminal liability of individuals for unlawful acts within the organisation can be considered. From the point of view of the companies themselves, the 'only' risk is punishment in the form of a fine under the law on administrative offences.

10 There has more recently been an attempt to move away from the dogmatic objections[8] to a genuine corporate criminal law. In 2020, the German federal government presented a corresponding draft law providing for sanctions on corporations – the *Verbandssanktionengesetz* (VerSanG) ('Corporate Sanctions Act'). According to the explanatory notice given at the time, the aim of the bill was 'to place the sanctioning of corporations [...] on an independent legal basis, to subject them to the principle of legality and to enable appropriate punishment of corporation offences through an improved set of legal instruments'.[9] At the same time, the proposed bill was intended to 'promote compliance measures and provide incentives for companies to contribute to solving criminal offences by conducting internal investigations'.[10] The proposed bill, however, did not progress beyond the draft version. At the time of writing, the implementation of the Corporate Sanctions Act in Germany is also not being visibly advanced – although a renewed attempt to create such a law can be considered likely.[11]

11 Central to corporate responsibility in criminal offences are therefore still the existing sanction options against companies in the form of corporate fines (§ 30 OWiG)[12]. These do not presuppose any 'guilt' on the part of the company. Rather, a fine is imposed on the company if 'a responsible management person has committed a company-related offence'[13] – e.g. an offence under AWG. If the linkage offence was not committed by a management person, but by some other employee, a sanction against the company can be imposed only in the case of a breach of supervisory duty by the relevant management person (§§ 30, 130 OWiG).[14] In this case, it is not the AWG violation itself, but the lack of or inefficient implementation of compliance/organisational measures to avert such violations that is the linkage factor that would make the company liable for a fine.[15]

12 Against this background, the establishment and implementation of an effective compliance system will be imperative if liability under administrative offence law is to be avoided.

II. Corporate liability under AWG

13 As described above, criminal corporate liability, against the background of the Act on Regulatory Offences and in the context of unlawful conduct under foreign trade and pay-

[8] Discussed comprehensively in Rostalski NJW 2020, 2087.

[9] RegE 'Entwurf eines Gesetzes zur Stärkung der Integrität in der Wirtschaft', version: 16.6.2020, p. 1.

[10] RegE 'Entwurf eines Gesetzes zur Stärkung der Integrität in der Wirtschaft', version: 16.6.2020, p. 1.

[11] Gehring NZWiSt 2022, 437 (437); see the statement formulated before publication of the failed government draft bill in Henssler et al. NZWiSt 2018, 1 (6), which is still relevant: 'The question of introducing a criminal law for associations remains on the agenda for criminal policy regardless of this setback. This is ensured not least by the European Union, which in numerous criminal law-related instruments also calls for criminal liability of legal persons for offences attributable to them.'

[12] → Ch. 4 mn. 1 et seqq.

[13] Achenbach NZWiSt 2012, 321 (323).

[14] Achenbach NZWiSt 2012, 321 (323).

[15] cf. Achenbach NZWiSt 2012, 321 (323); Momsen/Grützner WirtschaftsSteuerStrafR-HdB/Meyer/Hüttemann § 37 mn. 94.

ments law, can be considered only if the responsible managers are themselves responsible for this unlawful conduct (§ 30 OWiG) or if there is a breach of supervisory duty by the management with regard to the unlawful conduct at the employee level (§§ 30, 130 OWiG). In both cases, an administrative offence or a criminal offence under AWG is required as a *linkage point* before a corresponding company fine can be imposed.

1. Reservation of statutory regulation

The relevant provisions on penalties and fines under foreign trade and payments law are derived from AWG. Neither the legal sources in the EU context (e.g. the Dual-Use Regulation) nor the sub-statutory legal sources, such as AWV, contain any criminal offence provisions for constitutional reasons: according to Art. 103 para. 2 GG, '[a]n act may be punished only if it was defined by law as a criminal offence before the act was committed'[16] This reservation of statutory regulation has the purpose of 'reserving the decision on the punishability of a certain act to lawmakers […].'[17] Accordingly, in the absence of a parliamentary act – which is neither an EU regulation nor the Foreign Trade Regulation – no sanctioning can take place.[18] **14**

In this respect, §§ 17 and 18 AWG, which contain the relevant criminal provisions, and § 19 AWG, which contains the provisions on fines under foreign trade and payments law, are authoritative and conclusive[19] as regards the specific sanctioning norms under foreign trade and payments law. **15**

2. Blanket norms and legal definiteness

The complexity of AWG and its sanctioning provisions is a result, in particular, from the fact that the content of provisions on criminal penalties and administrative fines can often be interpreted only by viewing them in context with the extra-legal acts referred to (EU regulations; legal ordinances).[20] They can accordingly be called blanket norms.[21] This regulatory method, which is used for the purpose of rendering legislation as effective as possible[22], often gives rise to certain concerns from the point of view of its legal definite- **16**

---

[16] BeckOK GG/Radtke, 56. Ed. 15.8.2023, Art. 103 mn. 23; cf. for applicability of Art. 103 para. 2 GG to the Administrative Offences Act BeckOK GG/Radtke, 56. Ed. 15.8.2023, Art. 103 mn. 19.

[17] BeckOK GG/Radtke, 56. Ed. 15.8.2023, Art. 103 mn. 23 – cf. also BVerfG 21.9.2016 – 2 BvL 1/15, NJW 2016, 3648 (3649): 'In its function as a requirement of legal certainty, Art. 103 para. 2 GG accordingly contains the obligation to clarify essential questions of punishability or exemption from punishment in the democratic-parliamentary decision-making process and to describe the preconditions for punishability in such concrete terms that the scope and area of application of elements of the offence can be identified and determined through interpretation.' – cf. also MüKoStGB/Freund, 4th edn 2022, AMG Vor § 95 mn. 54; BeckOK AußenWirtschaftsR/Schwendinger, 13. Ed. 1.8.2024, AWG § 17 mn. 6.

[18] cf. BVerfG 21.9.2016 – 2 BvL 1/15, NJW 2016, 3648 (3649): 'A penalty can be imposed according to Art. 103 para. 2 GG only on the basis of a formal law.'

[19] Momsen/Grützner WirtschaftsSteuerStrafR-HdB/Meyer/Hüttemann § 37 mn. 13.

[20] BeckOK AußenWirtschaftsR/Schwendinger, 13. Ed. 1.8.2024, AWG § 17 mn. 9.

[21] BeckOK AußenWirtschaftsR/Schwendinger, 13. Ed. 1.8.2024, AWG § 17 mn. 9, § 18 mn. 1, § 19 mn. 1; Momsen/Grützner WirtschaftsSteuerStrafR-HdB/Meyer/Hüttemann § 37 mn. 13 – see regarding definition of the term BVerfG 21.9.2016 – 2 BvL 1/15, NJW 2016, 3648 (3650): 'In the case of a blanket criminal law, lawmakers replace the description of the offence by referring to a supplement in the same law or in other – including some future – laws or statutory instruments which do not necessarily have to be enacted by the same legislative body'.

[22] BeckOK AußenWirtschaftsR/Schwendinger, 13. Ed. 1.8.2024, AWG § 17 mn. 9 et seqq., which refers to a 'high degree of flexibility', 'in order to be able to react quickly under criminal law to unforeseeable international crises'; see also in the context of § 17 AWG: Momsen/Grützner WirtschaftsSteuerStrafR-HdB/Meyer/Hüttemann § 37 mn. 16.

ness.[23] The argument of a lack of legal definiteness is not valid if the term is understood to mean a reduced 'comprehensibility' of the threat of sanctions.[24] It is sufficient when the content of the law can be reliably determined by way of interpretation and by also considering legal sources outside AWG.[25] In contrast, it is unconstitutional in the sense of the principle of legality of Art. 103 para. 2 GG (*nullum crimen, nulla poena sine lege*) if the legislature, by including other sources of law in the elements of the sanction provision, not only refers back to the source of law to concretise its sanction provision but leaves the decision on the criminal nature of certain conduct to the administration[26] – this is the case with so-called blanket provisions with a 'referral clause'.[27]

17 Doubts are sometimes raised about the constitutionality of § 17 sub. 1 AWG, because 'the lawmaker [...] precisely did not himself decide on the modalities of the offence in the formulation of the 'infringement' and thus comprehensively defined the elements of the offence'.[28] In contrast, § 18 sub. 1 AWG is considered to be an unproblematic blanket norm because it 'comprises an exhaustive catalogue of offences that the legislator considers to be worthy of punishment.'[29] However, the requirements of the principle of legality expressed in the quotations are too broad from the point of view of content.[30] In fact, Art. 103 para. 2 GG refers exclusively to sanction norms and not to the norms of conduct referred to by the sanctioning norms,[31] which in the case of § 17 sub. 1 AWG are concretised by the statutory instrument under § 4 sub. 1 AWG. Therefore, the demand that 'the punishable conduct should be defined as descriptively as possible by the penal legislator' is incorrect.[32] Rather, it is sufficient in principle if the punishability of violations of a certain type of behavioural norm[33] is defined – in this case, for example, the violation of prohibitions and stipulations that are legitimised by the legal interests defined in § 4 sub. 1 AWG.

18 On the basis of the aforementioned case law of the Federal Constitutional Court[34] and the principles asserted therein regarding the principle of legality and the separation of powers, concerns about the constitutionality of the Act actually arise because of the referral clause under § 17 sub. 1 AWG. It is stated there that punishment is due for 'whoever contravenes a statutory instrument [...] insofar as the statutory instrument refers to this penal provision for a specific offence [...]'. § 80 AWV contains such a referral clause in relation to § 17 sub. 1 AWG.[35] This is partly assessed as 'satisfying the constitutional requirement of definiteness'[36]. The opposite is in fact the case: with the referral in this case, the lawmakers did not necessarily and conclusively decide on the 'whether' of criminal liability himself but left the decision up to the executive. The executive decides on punishability by means of this referral. The same applies to the sanction specification

[23] Momsen/Grützner WirtschaftsSteuerStrafR-HdB/Rotsch § 2 mn. 16; BeckOK AußenWirtschaftsR/Schwendinger, 13. Ed. 1.8.2024, AWG § 17 mn. 10.

[24] BeckOK AußenWirtschaftsR/Schwendinger, 13. Ed. 1.8.2024, AWG § 17 mn. 10: 'Definiteness is counteracted by a high degree of complexity of norms and, in particular, also references.'

[25] BVerfG 21.9.2016 – 2 BvL 1/15, NJW 2016, 3648 (3650) (mn. 41).

[26] BVerfG 21.9.2016 – 2 BvL 1/15, NJW 2016, 3648 (3651) (mn. 47); MüKoStGB/Freund, 4th edn 2022, AMG Vor § 95 mn. 54.

[27] MüKoStGB/Freund, 4th edn 2022, AMG Vor § 95 mn. 54.

[28] BeckOK AußenWirtschaftsR/Schwendinger, 13. Ed. 1.8.2024, AWG § 17 mn. 13.

[29] BeckOK AußenWirtschaftsR/Schwendinger, 13. Ed. 1.8.2024, AWG § 17 mn. 13.

[30] cf. MüKoStGB/Freund, 4th edn 2022, AMG Vor § 95 mn. 61.

[31] MüKoStGB/Freund, 4th edn 2022, AMG Vor § 95 mn. 61; see regarding the separation of behavioural and sanction norms Rostalski, Alternativ legtimierte Verhaltensnormen, 2019, 8 et seqq. with other references.

[32] MüKoStGB/Freund, 4th edn 2022, AMG Vor § 95 mn. 61 (including the verbatim quote therein).

[33] Freund/Rostalski GA 2016, 443.

[34] BVerfG 21.9.2016 – 2 BvL 1/15, NJW 2016, 3648.

[35] Momsen/Grützner WirtschaftsSteuerStrafR-HdB/Meyer/Hüttemann § 37 mn. 13.

[36] Momsen/Grützner WirtschaftsSteuerStrafR-HdB/Meyer/Hüttemann § 37 mn. 21.

under § 18 sub. 1b no. 3 AWG. This also contains a referral clause that is, in the view of the present author, unconstitutional.

3. Applicability of the sanctioning norms of AWG in relation to persons

If the offender is German, §§ 17, 18 AWG apply even for offences committed abroad. In deviation from the general principle of territoriality[37] pursuant to § 3 StGB (*Strafgesetzbuch* – the German Criminal Code), an active principle of personality[38] under AWG is added to the exceptions under §§ 4 to 7 StGB codified in criminal law. Therefore, § 17 sub. 7, § 18 sub. 10 AWG represent an exception to the personal scope of application of general criminal law. They are linked to the perpetrator's actions and therefore do not apply to the participant.[39] 19

4. § 17 AWG: violations of arms embargoes

§ 17 AWG contains the most severe threat of sanctions. A violation of the norms of conduct referred to therein constitutes a criminal offence (§ 12 sub. 1 StGB)[40]: an infringement is punishable by imprisonment of not less than one year. Only misconduct in the form of recklessness is punished more mildly. Ordinary negligence is not punishable.[41] 20

The penalties under § 17 AWG relate to violations of arms embargoes.[42] 21

In its regulatory technique, § 17 sub. 1 AWG refers to 'infringements' against a legal ordinance according to § 4 sub. 1 AWG – i.e. a sub-statutory national source of law. This is, however, referred to only insofar as it serves the 'implementation' of a measure of economic sanctions decided by the Security Council of the United Nations (no. 1) or the Council of the European Union in the area of the Common Foreign and Security Policy (no. 2). This is equivalent to violations of enforceable rulings on the basis of such a regulation (sub. 1 clause 2). 22

Of central significance for the descriptive determination of unlawful conduct are thus the 'embargo provisions of the UN and the EU'[43] and Part 1 Section A of the Export List as an annex to AWV (the arms, ammunition and defence material list)[44]. The embargo provisions are 'activated' (in terms of criminal law) by the (national) implementing provisions by way of the ordinance, in that they are effectively implemented into national law by an amendment to the AWV – as an ordinance within the meaning of § 4 sub. 1 AWG.[45] Accordingly, criminal liability under § 17 AWG cannot arise before the 'effective conclusion of the respective implementation procedure'.[46] Likewise, the threat of sanctions does not cover any national regulation that goes beyond the scope of the implementation.[47] This is because the embargo provisions implemented in AWG must serve precisely the 23

---

[37] Walter JuS 2006, 870 (871).
[38] Müller-Gugenberger WirtschaftsStrafR-HdB Ch. 62 Auslandsgeschäfte mn. 62.35.
[39] WJS WirtschaftsStrafR-HdB/Hoffmann Ch. 24 mn. 151 et seq.
[40] Momsen/Grützner WirtschaftsSteuerStrafR-HdB/Meyer/Hüttemann § 37 mn. 13.
[41] GJW/Cornelius AWG § 18 mn. 1.
[42] Momsen/Grützner WirtschaftsSteuerStrafR-HdB/Meyer/Hüttemann § 37 mn. 13.
[43] Momsen/Grützner WirtschaftsSteuerStrafR-HdB/Meyer/Hüttemann § 37 mn. 13.
[44] Momsen/Grützner WirtschaftsSteuerStrafR-HdB/Meyer/Hüttemann § 37 mn. 20.
[45] Momsen/Grützner WirtschaftsSteuerStrafR-HdB/Meyer/Hüttemann § 37 mn. 13.
[46] Momsen/Grützner WirtschaftsSteuerStrafR-HdB/Meyer/Hüttemann § 37 mn. 13 (including the verbatim quote therein).
[47] Momsen/Grützner WirtschaftsSteuerStrafR-HdB/Meyer/Hüttemann § 37 mn. 13 (including the verbatim quote therein).

'implementation' of the resolution and CFSP legal acts designated in the sanction norm.[48] If they go beyond this, the nationally stipulated behavioural norm moves outside the area incriminated by § 17 AWG.[49]

24 In summary, the following can be considered as offences with reference to AWV:

1. the sale, export and transit of goods included in Part I Section A of the Export Control List from or through Germany or their transport to the designated embargoed countries using a ship or aircraft entitled to fly the German flag or bear the national identification mark of the Federal Republic of Germany (§§ 80 sub. 1 no. 1 AWV, 74 AWV (if applicable in conjunction with § 79 AWV));[50]
2. trade and brokering services in relation to goods indicated in Part I Section A of the Export Control List which are intended, directly or indirectly, for persons, entities or bodies in designated embargoed countries (§§ 80 sub. 1 no. 2 AWV, § 75 AWV (if applicable in conjunction with § 79 AWV));[51]
3. the import and acquisition of goods covered by Part I Section A of the Export Control List from the designated embargoed countries, as well as their transportation (§§ 80 sub. 1 no. 3, 77 AWV (if applicable in conjunction with § 79 AWV)).[52]

25 § 76 AWV regulates an exception to the prohibitions under § 74 sub. 1 and § 75 AWV.[53] According to this, the authority may in principle allow prohibited conduct in order to enable the export of non-lethal military goods intended exclusively for humanitarian or protective purposes, e.g. with regard to Syria or Belarus (§ 76 sub. 2 no. 1, sub. 15 no. 2a) AWV).[54]

26 With regard to the objects of the crime, the AWV refers to the goods under Part I Section A of the Export List. It should be noted here that this is not meant to cover only fully assembled goods, but in particular also disassembled components that 'can be reassembled with commonly used tools without a great deal of work.'[55] Even in such cases, namely a 'readiness for use' is to be assumed.[56]

27 Whether a certain conduct is to be considered as fulfilling, the requirements for an offence under § 17 AWG will generally be decided by the factual/technical question of whether a certain item is to be classified as a weapon, ammunition or armament material in the sense of the Export List Part 1 Section A.[57]

28 The sanction norm provides for more severe penalties for certain types of offences. According to this provision, the offender fulfils the conditions for this increased penalty if he commits the offence for a foreign intelligence service (§ 17 sub. 2 AWG) and commits the offence on a commercial and/or gang-related basis (§ 17 sub. 2 no. 2 AWG/§ 17 sub. 3 AWG). Less serious cases (§ 17 sub. 4 AWG) and 'only' reckless acts according to § 17 sub. 5 AWG result in a significantly reduced range of punishments.

29 The punishability of an attempt with regard to the intentional offences under § 17 AWG which are designed as crimes is specified under § 23 sub. 1 alt. 1 StGB.

---

[48] BGH 21.04.1995 – 1 StR 700/94, NJW 1995, 2174; Momsen/Grützner WirtschaftsSteuerStrafR-HdB/Meyer/Hüttemann § 37 mn. 18 et seqq.

[49] Momsen/Grützner WirtschaftsSteuerStrafR-HdB/Meyer/Hüttemann § 37 mn. 18.

[50] Momsen/Grützner WirtschaftsSteuerStrafR-HdB/Meyer/Hüttemann § 37 mn. 22.

[51] Momsen/Grützner WirtschaftsSteuerStrafR-HdB/Meyer/Hüttemann § 37 mn. 27.

[52] Momsen/Grützner WirtschaftsSteuerStrafR-HdB/Meyer/Hüttemann § 37 mn. 28.

[53] BeckOK AußenWirtschaftsR/Niestedt, 13. Ed. 1.8.2024, AWV § 76 mn. 1.

[54] Momsen/Grützner WirtschaftsSteuerStrafR-HdB/Meyer/Hüttemann § 37 mn. 29.

[55] OLG Düsseldorf 15.12.1983 – 1 WS 1053 – 1055/83, NStZ 1987, 565 in the transferable context of KWKG; also Momsen/Grützner WirtschaftsSteuerStrafR-HdB/Meyer/Hüttemann § 37 mn. 20.

[56] OLG Düsseldorf 15.12.1983 – 1 WS 1053 – 1055/83, NStZ 1987, 565 in the transferable context of KWKG; also Momsen/Grützner WirtschaftsSteuerStrafR-HdB/Meyer/Hüttemann § 37 mn. 20.

[57] Momsen/Grützner WirtschaftsSteuerStrafR-HdB/Meyer/Hüttemann § 37 mn. 20.

5. § 18 AWG: violations of the Dual-Use Regulation

The penalty for the non-qualified offence alternatives under § 18 AWG (which carries the threat of imprisonment for periods between three months and five years) is significantly reduced in comparison to the sanction for a violation of arms embargoes under § 17 AWG (carrying the threat of imprisonment for a period of not less than one year). 30

Apart from its regulations regarding arms embargos, the § 18 AWG comprehensively underpins the most important prohibitions under foreign trade and payments law with threats of sanctions.[58] According to sub. 1, violations of directly applicable legal acts of the EC and the EU regarding implementation of sanction measures within the framework of the CFSP are sanctioned.[59] Sub. 1a penalises a violation of certain individual interventions of foreign trade law – specifically acts in contravention of enforceable orders pursuant to § 6 sub. 1 sent. 2 AWG.[60] Sub. 1b sanctions infringement of stipulations and prohibitions in the context of the screening of investments. Sub. 1 no. 2 penalises violations of licensing obligations and enforceable orders based on the AWV. Violations of EC Regulation number 2368/2002 (Kimberley Process Certification Scheme for the International Trade in Rough Diamonds) are sanctioned under sub. 3, while infringements against EU Regulation 2019/125 (the so-called 'Anti-Torture Regulation'[61]) on trade in goods, capital punishment and torture, among others, are sanctioned under sub. 4 and sub. 5b. Sub. 5 sanctions violations of EU Regulation 2021/821 on dual-use goods. Sub. 5a sanctions unlawful conduct with regard to reporting obligations under the EU Regulation and its Implementing Regulation on restrictive measures in the face of acts undermining or threatening the territorial integrity, sovereignty and independence of Ukraine.[62] With the exception of criminal liability under Art. 5a, the mere attempt at any of the basic offences is also punishable, § 18 sub. 6. 31

The sub. 7 and 8 provide for an increased range of punishment for aggravating factors (*Qualifikationstatbestände*). This is the case if the offences are committed on behalf of a foreign intelligence service on a commercial and/or gang-related basis. With regard to sub. 1 and 1a, the aggravating factors are considered to include unlawful conduct that 'relates to the development, production, maintenance or storage of missiles for chemical, biological or nuclear weapons'. 32

Of particular practical relevance in this regard is the criminal penalty for violations of the Dual-Use Regulation under sub. 5.[63] The export of goods with 'dual use' is 'intensively examined' by the authorities in Germany.[64] 33

According to the legal definition in Art. 2 no. 1 Dual-Use Regulation, this examination and export control relates to 'goods, including data processing programmes (software) and technology, which can be used for both civilian and military purposes'. 34

---

[58] See for the following summary also GJW/Cornelius AWG § 18 mn. 2; BeckOK AußenWirtschaftsR/Schwendinger, 13. Ed. 1.8.2024, AWG § 18 mn. 1.

[59] See regarding the relevant ground for setting aside the penalty § 18 sub. 11 AWG for acts committed by the end of the second day following the publication of the act in the Official Gazette of the European Union and, in addition, lack of knowledge of the respective stipulation of prohibition.

[60] See regarding the relevant ground for setting aside the penalty § 18 sub. 12 AWG for acts committed by the end of the second day following publication of the relevant order and, in addition, lack of knowledge of the restriction.

[61] BeckOK AußenWirtschaftsR/Schwendinger, 13. Ed. 1.8.2024, AWG § 18 mn. 1.

[62] See regarding the relevant ground for setting aside the penalty § 18 (13) AWG if the report is made voluntarily and in full, if the offence is not discovered and if the subjective conditions for setting aside the sentence are met.

[63] GJW/Cornelius AWG § 18 mn. 2.

[64] Thus also *expressis verbis* stated by the Federal Ministry for Economic Affairs and Energy in its online publication, available at <https://www.bundeswirtschaftsministerium.de/Redaktion/DE/Dossier/ausfuhr-und-ruestungsexportkontrolle.html> (last accessed: 27.10.2025).

35 According to Art. 3 Dual-Use Regulation, the export of such goods is always subject to a permit if the goods are listed in Annex I of the Regulation. If the goods are exported without a permit, this constitutes a criminal offence according to § 18 sub. 5 no. 1 AWG. Art. 3 of the Regulation clarifies that the referenced list of dual-use items 'shall apply as amended from time to time'. Compliance with 'new' authorisation requirements, which may arise in the event of some change to the list, is thus mandatory immediately. From the point of view of the strictures under the Dual-Use Regulation, there can be no grounds for annulment of a penalty for offences committed during a transitional period, as provided for in the offence alternatives under § 18 sub. 1 and 1a AWG pursuant to § 18 sub. 11 and 12 AWG.[65]

36 Irrespective of the goods listed in Annex I of the Regulation, there may also be other licensing obligations within the meaning of the Regulation, or else an obligation to await the decision of the competent authority on whether certain goods are subject to a licensing obligation.

37 In this respect, there is a licensing requirement according to Art. 4 para. 1 Dual-Use Regulation if the exporter has been informed by the competent authority of more specific problematic (including only potentially) intended uses. Export without such a licence is punishable under § 18 sub. 5 no. 1 AWG.

38 If the exporter is aware of a problematic intended use of some item not listed in Annex I of the Regulation, he is obliged to notify the relevant authority (Art. 4 para. 2 sent. 1 of the Regulation). According to Art. 4 para. 2 sent. 2 Dual-Use Regulation, the authority in question is called upon to decide 'whether the export of these goods should be subject to authorisation'. If the exporter does not await a decision by the relevant authority or proceeds to export without a licence after informing the authority, he is liable to prosecution under § 18 sub. 5 no. 2 AWG.

39 The threats of punishment under § 18 sub. 5 no. 3 and 4 AWG refer to unlawful conduct in the context of brokering activities for transactions involving dual-use goods.

40 With regard to export licences, four licence types are to be distinguished according to Art. 12 Dual-Use Regulation. Besides the classic individual licence, there are also three special forms available to facilitate procedures. A general export authorisation by the EU serves the purpose of 'reducing the administrative burden on companies, especially SMEs, and regulatory authorities, while at the same time ensuring an appropriate level of controls on the items in question with the relevant destinations'.[66] Currently, Annex II, Sections A to H of the Dual-Use Regulation contain a total of eight EU General Export Authorisations within the meaning of Art. 12 sub. 1 lit. d Dual-Use Regulation. Within the scope of the provisions regarding export authorisations, exports are permitted without an individual licence.

41 In addition, there are a total of 18 general national export licences issued by the BAFA within the meaning of § 4 sub. 1 alt. 3 AWV, which also dispense with the need for an individual application.[67] These are the national general export licences provided for in Art. 12 para. 1 lit. c Dual-Use Regulation.

42 Finally, according to Art. 12 para. 1 lit. b Dual-Use Regulation, there are also global licences available (or collective licences according to the terminology of § 4 AWV), which can be useful especially in the context of effective realisation of industrial projects. This is to be understood as a license 'granted to an exporter for a type or category of dual-use

65 BeckOK AußenWirtschaftsR/Schwendinger, 13. Ed. 1.8.2024, AWG § 18 mn. 70.

66 Recital 19 of the Dual-Use Regulation (there also the citation).

67 See in this regard the overview at <https://www.zoll.de/DE/Fachthemen/Aussenwirtschaft-Bargeldverkehr/Genehmigungsarten-Bescheinigungen/Allgemeine-Genehmigungen/faq.html?nn=28572> (last accessed: 3.12.2024).

item which may be valid for export to one or more specified end-users and/or to one or more specified third countries.'[68]

According to the Commission's report to the European Parliament and the Council on the implementation of Regulation (EU) 2021/821 of 23 November 2021,[69] across Europe, national and EU general export authorisations covered only 15% of exported goods in 2019.[70] In contrast, 35% of the total value of approved exports was covered by global licences and 41% by individual licences.[71] At the same time, 20,300 individual licences were counted across Europe in 2019.[72] These figures provide an insight into the prime importance of the application process in the context of foreign trade with dual-use goods and the high practical significance of the sanction norms related to the application process. 43

6. § 19 AWG

The elements constituting an administrative offence under § 19 AWG include less serious infringements against foreign trade law compared to the provisions of criminal law.[73] Because of the fact that they are classified under the heading of administrative offences, mere 'operational errors', in particular, are removed from the area of criminal law and its punishments – as well as from the kind of condemnatory judgement associated with the determination of guilt under criminal law.[74] 44

Since § 18 AWG does not provide for criminal liability in the case of negligence,[75] the administrative offence also covers negligent wrongdoing (§ 19 sub. 1 AWG). This also includes negligent violations of the stipulations and prohibitions under the Dual-Use Regulation referred to in § 18 sub. 1, sub. 5 AWG. A corresponding sanctioning in the form of fines for violations of arms embargoes by way of ordinary negligence[76] is, in contrast, not regulated under § 19 AWG.[77] 45

Moreover, § 19 sub. 2 to 5 AWG primarily sanctions errors with regard to procedural and formal requirements under foreign trade and payments law.[78] 46

With regard to the elements of the administrative offence under § 19 sub. 3 to 5 AWG, § 22 sub. 4 AWG provides for a 'self-disclosure exempting from fines'.[79] This presupposes that the offence was *firstly* 'discovered by way of self-monitoring', *secondly* 'reported to the competent authority' and *thirdly* that 'appropriate measures are taken to prevent a repeat offence on the same basis'. 47

---

[68] Report of the Commission to the European Parliament and the Council on implementation of the Regulation (EU) 2021/821 of 23 November 2021, p. 13 (fn. 25) (<https://eur-lex.europa.eu/legal-content/DE/TXT/PDF/?uri=CELEX:52021DC0716&qid=1638033320359> last accessed: 3.12.2024).

[69] Report from the Commission to the European Parliament and the Council on implementation of the Regulation (EU) 2021/821 of 23 November 2021, p. 13.

[70] Report from the Commission to the European Parliament and the Council on implementation of the Regulation (EU) 2021/821 of 23 November 2021, p. 15.

[71] Report from the Commission to the European Parliament and the Council on implementation of the Regulation (EU) 2021/821 of 23 November 2021, p. 15.

[72] Report from the Commission to the European Parliament and the Council on implementation of the Regulation (EU) 2021/821 of 23 November 2021, p. 13.

[73] BeckOK AußenWirtschaftsR/Schwendinger, 13. Ed. 1.8.2024, AWG § 19 mn. 1.

[74] BeckOK AußenWirtschaftsR/Schwendinger, 13. Ed. 1.8.2024 AWG § 19 mn. 2 (including the verbatim quote therein).

[75] GJW/Cornelius AWG § 18 mn. 1.

[76] But see regarding negligent violation § 17 para. 5 AWG.

[77] BeckOK AußenWirtschaftsR/Schwendinger, 13. Ed. 1.8.2024 AWG § 19 mn. 2.

[78] BeckOK AußenWirtschaftsR/Schwendinger, 13. Ed. 1.8.2024, AWG § 19 mn. 2.

[79] Momsen/Grützner WirtschaftsSteuerStrafR-HdB/Meyer/Hüttemann § 37 mn. 96.

48 Although liability under the administrative penalty law is not the same as for a criminal penalty, the imposition of one or more regulatory fines can nevertheless have serious consequences beyond the penalty itself. Such facts 'may have an impact on an assessment of reliability in future licensing procedures and even lead to the loss of the status as authorised economic operator'.[80]

III. Confiscation

49 In addition to possible fines against corporations and personal criminal liability in the case of some wrongdoing subject to sanctions in the context of foreign trade law, further consequences must also be taken into account as part of corporate liability in the broader sense.

50 Confiscation in the case of criminal offences and administrative offences under AWG is regulated in the confiscation provisions found in the general part of the German Criminal Code (§§ 73 et seqq. StGB) and the German Act on Regulatory Offences (§§ 22 et seqq., 29a OWiG). § 20 sub. 1 AWG explicitly stipulates that confiscation is also to take place in the case of administrative offences under § 19 AWG. This is necessary since confiscation as a secondary consequence under the law of administrative offences can be considered only if expressly permitted by law (§ 22 sub. 1 OWiG).[81]

51 Furthermore, § 20 AWG expands the general confiscation as sub. 1 also allows confiscation to be ordered following a criminal offence based on negligence – in contrast to § 74 sub. 1 StGB – or an administrative offence.[82] Specifically, sub. 1 no. 1 provides for comprehensive seizure of objects that 'relate to the criminal offence or the administrative offence'. This includes all objects of the offence, 'e.g. the imported goods punishable under §§ 17, 18 AWG'.[83] Furthermore, according to sub. 1 no. 2, confiscation can be ordered for all objects 'which have been used or intended for the commission or preparation of the offence'.[84]

52 The 'confiscation of products, means and objects of the offence from other parties' – i.e. from third parties not involved in the offence – is possible under § 20 sub. 2 AWG in conjunction with § 74a StGB and § 23 OWiG.[85] Companies are regularly held liable for criminal offences from within their organisation by virtue of § 74e StGB/§ 29 OWiG, according to which acts by executive bodies and representatives that justify confiscation are attributed to the represented party – i.e. the company.[86]

53 Independently of the confiscation rules under AWG, the general confiscation rules provide for the confiscation of proceeds of crime (§§ 73 et seqq. StGB). This includes all 'economic benefits related to the execution of an export order'.[87]

54 In the case of sanctionable conduct on the part of a representative or executive entity of the enterprise within the meaning of § 30 OWiG or a breach of supervisory duty within the meaning of § 130 OWiG (in conjunction with § 30 OWiG), confiscation from

---

[80] BeckOK AußenWirtschaftsR/Schwendinger, 13. Ed. 1.8.2024 AWG § 19 mn. 2 et seqq.

[81] Leitner/Rosenau/Ahlbrecht, 1st edn 2017, AWG § 20 mn. 2.

[82] BeckOK AußenWirtschaftsR/Schwendinger, 13. Ed. 1.8.2024, AWG § 20 mn. 4; Erbs/Kohlhaas/Diemer, 243. EL 2022, AWG § 20 mn. 1.

[83] GJW/Cornelius AWG § 20 mn. 2 (including the verbatim quote therein), also: Erbs/Kohlhaas/Diemer, 243. EL August 2022, AWG § 20 mn. 1.

[84] Momsen/Grützner WirtschaftsSteuerStrafR-HdB/Meyer/Hüttemann § 37 mn. 100.

[85] BeckOK AußenWirtschaftsR/Schwendinger, 13. Ed. 1.8.2024, AWG § 20 mn. 4; Erbs/Kohlhaas/Diemer, 243. EL 2022, AWG § 20 mn. 1.

[86] Erbs/Kohlhaas/Diemer, 243. EL 2022, AWG § 20 mn. 1.

[87] Momsen/Grützner WirtschaftsSteuerStrafR-HdB/Meyer/Hüttemann § 37 mn. 100.

enterprises can also be effected in the form of association fines.[88] Since it is precisely the idea of confiscation of proceeds of crime that is the yardstick for assessment of the fine.[89]

C. Principles of AWG compliance

Particularly in export-oriented companies, trade compliance occupies a special place in their compliance management system. The background to this is the complexity and dynamics of this field of law and its application in practice (especially the reliable classification of dual-use goods, etc.), the severe sanctions and collateral consequences (including loss of reputation)[90] as well as the particular challenges to effective implementation of specific compliance rules, which often have to address the most diverse areas of company operations (from purchasing through construction and up to sales). 55

It is true that, in principle, there is no legally binding obligation to establish compliance measures under foreign trade law. It is, however, also clear that, simply in view of the risks of criminal prosecution and liability, 'companies [in no case] can avoid setting up an effective export control organisation.'[91] 56

The task of establishing a functioning compliance system in the organisation is primarily assigned to company management.[92] This means that the management is 'accordingly responsible for violations of the law by employees that could have been avoided through proper supervision, in particular in accordance with § 130 OWiG.[93] As a special feature of compliance with foreign trade law, a so-called 'person responsible for exports' must 'regularly' be appointed due to the special importance of export control for important EU goods.[94] This person should be '[a]s a member of the management [...] personally liable for the export control organisation'.[95] In the practical legal implementation of the non-delegable duties of the person responsible for exports, the function of the 'foreign trade or export control officer' has proven itself as a downstream function in the export control organisation.[96] This officer supports the export manager, who is often otherwise engaged with management tasks, with operational activities such as the 'classification of products, obtaining various export-relevant information, e.g. from the research & development, sales, shipping and finance departments'.[97] Often such officers will be granted comprehensive 'stop and instruction rights within the company' for compliance reasons.[98] 57

---

[88] Momsen/Grützner WirtschaftsSteuerStrafR-HdB/Meyer/Hüttemann § 37 mn. 100.

[89] Momsen/Grützner WirtschaftsSteuerStrafR-HdB/Meyer/Hüttemann § 37 mn. 100.

[90] cf. Momsen/Grützner WirtschaftsSteuerStrafR-HdB/Meyer/Hüttemann § 37 mn. 102: which speak of 'considerable liability risks and economic dangers for the company'.

[91] Momsen/Grützner WirtschaftsSteuerStrafR-HdB/Meyer/Hüttemann § 37 mn. 102.

[92] NSH/Beurskens GmbHG § 43 mn. 11.

[93] Rotsch Criminal Compliance/Moosmayer § 34 mn. 56 (including the verbatim quote therein); Klindt ARP 2020, 6 (8) – also Hümmerich/Lücke/Mauer, Arbeitsrecht, § 1 mn. 505 on the 'legal core' of compliance: 'Of course, the managing director or the board member himself must act in accordance with the law, but their duties go further due to their function, and cover not only their own actions but also the actions (and omissions) of all company employees'.

[94] Momsen/Grützner WirtschaftsSteuerStrafR-HdB/Meyer/Hüttemann § 37 mn. 102 (including the verbatim quote therein; on the requirements for designation, see in detail the 'Principles of the Federal Government for Examining the Reliability of Exporters of War Weapons and Armament-Related Goods', no. 2 p. 1; HML Corporate Compliance/Merz § 32 mn. 92.

[95] HML Corporate Compliance/Merz § 32 mn. 90.

[96] HML Corporate Compliance/Merz § 32 mn. 113.

[97] HML Corporate Compliance/Merz § 32 mn. 113 (including the verbatim quote therein).

[98] HML Corporate Compliance/Merz § 32 mn. 114 (including the verbatim quote therein).

58 The specific 'individualisation of responsibility'[99] under foreign trade law and the clear allocation of competences within the company for ensuring compliance with foreign trade regulations represents only one element of the compliance system. Art. 2 no. 21 Dual-Use Regulation defines 'Internal Compliance Programmes' (ICP), as 'ongoing effective, appropriate and proportionate policies and procedures that exporters put in place to promote compliance with the provisions and objectives of this Regulation and the terms and conditions of permits granted under pursuant to this Regulation, including due diligence measures to assess the risks associated with the export of the goods to end-users and end-uses'.

59 Suitable elements of such an ICP include 'clear instructions from company management'[100] (in particular a specific 'trade compliance policy') and the use of technical means (specific IT systems) to guarantee compliance with the appropriate and proportionate policies and procedures.[101] How exactly the ICP is to be designed depends on the company in question (its size, resources, organisational structure) and its foreign trade law commitment/risk profile. This is also made explicitly clear in Recitals 7 and 18 of the Dual-Use Regulation. Although, the compliance efforts of companies are to be supported by recommendations from the EU as the EU introduces 'guidelines for internal programmes for legally compliant behaviour'.[102] At the same time, however, the European legislator wishes to prevent a 'one-size-fits-all' approach.[103] According to the guiding principle of the Regulation, it is the exporter's responsibility 'to find his own solutions with regard to compliance and competitiveness.'[104] The guidelines are therefore, as already mentioned, only intended to support exporters.

60 A corresponding proposal is the EU Commission Recommendation (EU) 2019/1318 of 30 July 2019 regarding internal compliance programmes for the control of trade in dual-use items.

61 The Recommendation also takes the individual risk exposure of the company – measured in particular by the company's business activity on the one hand and '[the] product range, [the] clientele and [the] business activity' and its organisational structure including potential vulnerabilities on the other hand – as the starting point for a draft of an effective compliance system.[105]

62 Based on this, the Recommendation provides for the implementation of seven 'core elements' of an ICP that addresses the risks of trade in dual-use goods[106]:

63 *First*, the 'commitment of top management to compliance'. To implement this, it proposes, among other things, defining 'specific expectations in relation to compliance' and communicating the 'importance and value of effective compliance procedures'.

64 *Second*, the Recommendation requires the availability of 'sufficient organisational, human and technical resources' and their planned use as an indispensable prerequisite for developing and implementing effective compliance procedures.

65 *Third*, 'training and awareness raising' among company employees is recommended in order to inform them of their control obligations and to promote compliance.

---

[99] HML Corporate Compliance/Merz § 32 mn. 90.
[100] HML Corporate Compliance/Merz § 32 mn. 89.
[101] HML Corporate Compliance/Merz § 32 mn. 89.
[102] Recital 18 of the Dual-Use Regulation.
[103] Recital 18 of the Dual-Use Regulation.
[104] Recital 18 of the Dual-Use Regulation.
[105] Recommendation (EU) 2019/1318, L 205/19 (including the verbatim quote therein).
[106] Recommendation (EU) 2019/1318, L 205/19, see 'Annex EU Guidelines for an Internal Compliance Programme (ICP) for the Control of Trade in Dual-Use Goods'. The following points 1 to 7 have been taken from the Recommendation, with the following verbatim quotations also found in the Recommendation.

Fourth, the Recommendation describes the 'most critical element of an ICP' as the mandatory implementation of 'screening procedures' in relation to relevant business transactions for the purpose of preventing criminal transactions. Specifically, this means the monitoring and analysis of individual business transactions '[the] classification of goods, [the] assessment of business risk, [the] identification of and application for the relevant licences, and [the] post-licence control'. **66**

Fifth, in order to ensure an evaluation process aimed at the continuous development and updating of the compliance system, the Recommendation proposes regular and ad hoc performance reviews and audits of compliance with foreign trade law requirements at the operational level. The results of these procedures should then be brought to the attention of the decision-makers in the form of 'reporting' and, in the event of errors or weaknesses, corrected by way of appropriate measures. **67**

Sixth, the maintenance of 'adequate, accurate and traceable export control records' is recommended. Only in this way can the company's compliance activities be meaningfully demonstrated to the relevant authorities. **68**

Seventh, the Recommendation urges the physical protection of physical goods and information security with regard to software and technology in order to reduce the risk of theft of dual-use goods. **69**

Apart from the company-internal organisational measures, which are intended to exclude wrongdoing from within the company, the closest possible contact with the 'specialised authorities' is advisable from the point of view of foreign trade regulations and in order to ensure the most defensive error prevention strategy possible: 'Information on the list of goods' or project-related 'zero notices' (*Nullbescheide*) can be obtained from this source.[107] **70**

D. Selected practical problems

The following section highlights a number of legal issues of particular practical relevance and current legal policy developments with regard to corporate liability in German foreign trade law: **71**

I. Export licences obtained through deception

In the context of the requirement for the relevant permits, reservations under criminal law, there is a strict administrative accessoriness[108] in relation to the threat of punishment. A prerequisite for the offence is the absence of the relevant licence at the time of the act. **72**

It should be noted, however, that, according to the legal text of § 17 sub. 6 AWG and § 18 sub. 9 AWG, a situation where the permit was 'obtained by threat, bribery or collusion or by false or incomplete information' is equivalent to acting entirely without a permit. **73**

---

107 Momsen/Grützner WirtschaftsSteuerStrafR-HdB/Meyer/Hüttemann § 37 mn. 102 (including the verbatim quote therein).

108 Momsen/Grützner WirtschaftsSteuerStrafR-HdB/Meyer/Hüttemann § 37 mn. 29.

II. EU sanctions using the Russia Sanctions Regulation as an example

74 As a result of the political developments involving Ukraine and Russia that took place in 2014 (the presence of Russian troops in Crimea and the holding of a referendum on the annexation of Crimea by Russia), the EU, alongside other nations such as the US, began to impose sanctions against Russia. Russia's war of aggression against Ukraine, as well as its illegal annexation of the Ukrainian regions of Donetsk, Luhansk, Zaporizhzhya and Kherson, have led to a series of further EU financial and economic sanctions against Russia since 2022.

75 These sanctions are intended to weaken Russia's economic power and block its access to critical (information) technologies and markets. The EU expects this to significantly limit Russia's ability to wage war.[109] The sanctions relate in particular to export and import restrictions, restrictions in the area of capital markets, rating services, auditing and tax advisory services, as well as services in the areas of architecture and engineering, legal advice and IT consulting. Such EU sanctions regulations do not require national implementing acts; they are directly applicable in Germany.

76 Taking Regulation (EU) 833/2014 ('Russia Sanctions Regulation') as an example, the typical structure as well as the manifold sanction options are presented below:

1. Scope of application

77 The scope of application of the Russia sanctions corresponds to EU sanctions already known (e.g. against Iran or Belarus) and basically follows an approach characterised by the territoriality and personality principle. This means that the scope of the sanctions includes the territory of the EU, including its airspace, as well as aircraft and ships that are attributed to a Member State of the EU according to flag or register law. The scope of the sanctions moreover also covers (foreign) legal persons, entities and bodies in relation to transactions carried out in whole or in part within the EU.

78 In addition, the EU sanctions regulations also apply to persons who are nationals of a Member State, when acting inside and outside the territory of the EU, as well as to legal persons, entities and bodies incorporated or constituted under the law of a Member State, again whether acting inside or outside the territory of the EU. As a result, the legal entities concerned are also subject to the EU sanctions regulations in relation to transactions carried out in third countries (outside the EU).

79 Compliance with the EU sanctions regulations must be ensured by the entities concerned (natural or legal persons). Violations of EU sanctions regulations are punished as criminal offences or administrative offences under §§ 18 and 19 AWG.

80 In principle, the sanctions apply from the date they come into force. This can have a significant impact on a company's existing and new business relations. Some sanction regulations therefore make special allowances for existing contract clauses or settlement periods in order to enable the affected parties to complete existing contracts – if necessary by a certain deadline (e.g. Regulation (EU) No. 833/2014). In some cases, the existing contract clauses stipulates that an application for an exemption must be submitted by a certain date. Such applications must always be submitted via the ELAN-K2 export system.[110] It should be noted in this respect that in the event of any change in the essential

---

[109] Reactions of the EU to the Russian invasion of Ukraine <https://www.consilium.europa.eu/en/policies/eu-response-ukraine-invasion/> (last accessed: 3.12.2024); Niestedt/Lesko UKuR 2022, 601; BT-Drs. 20/3141 of 19.8.2022 no. 73, p. 52.

[110] https://www.bafa.de/DE/Aussenwirtschaft/Ausfuhrkontrolle/Embargos/Russland/russland_node.html (last accessed: 3.12.2024).

features of such an application (e.g. goods, number of items, value), such a project will be assessed by BAFA as a new export project. As a result, it is no longer possible to invoke the exemption clauses for existing contracts.

The EU sanctions against Russia at a glance: 81

2. Goods and technology-related sanctions

a) Dual-use goods/technologies

aa) Trade, service and financing prohibitions for dual-use goods/technologies. According to Art. 2 Russia Sanctions Regulation, it is forbidden to sell, supply, transfer 82 or export, directly or indirectly, dual-use goods and technologies, whether or not they originate in the European Union, to any natural or legal person, entity or body in, or for use in, Russia.

The prohibition under Art. 2 para. 1 Russia Sanctions Regulation is broadly defined. 83 An expected (military) end-use of the dual-use goods is in principle (no longer) relevant in this respect. Furthermore, Art. 2 para. 1 Russia Sanctions Regulation also prohibits deliveries to non-Russian customers within the EU when they in turn intend to make delivery to customers in Russia or with a final destination in Russia.

The ban on sales ensures that sales transactions are covered by the Russia Sanctions 84 Regulation even if the dual-use goods are not located within the EU but are stored in a country that is not itself covered by the scope of the Russia Sanctions Regulation.

This general prohibition is rounded off by Art. 2 para. 2 Russia Sanctions Regulation, 85 which additionally prohibits the direct or indirect provision of technical assistance, brokering services or other services in connection with dual-use goods, as well as the provision of financial resources or financial assistance in this context.[111]

bb) Exemptions. An exemption for the supply of goods and services involving dual- 86 use items is provided for in Art. 2 para. 3 Russia Sanctions Regulation for non-military purposes and for non-military end-users if the goods/technologies are in turn intended for humanitarian purposes, medical or pharmaceutical purposes, temporary exports by news media, software updates or use as a consumer communication device. The exporter must, however, notify the competent authority of the Member State within 30 days of the first export.

Art. 2 para. 4 Russia Sanctions Regulation provides for licensing possibilities for export 87 of dual-use goods/technologies. The Regulation allows namely the possibility of permits for transactions occurring in the context of intergovernmental cooperation in space programmes, for the operation, maintenance, reprocessing of fuel elements and civil nuclear cooperation, for maritime security and for civil telecommunications networks. Furthermore, these items may only be intended for use by non-governmental legal persons/organisations, for diplomatic missions of the EU, Member States and partner countries, as well as for transactions that have as their object the provision of cyber security and information security to natural and legal persons in Russia, with the exception of the Government of Russia and companies directly or indirectly controlled by it. There are strict deadlines for applying for such licences, and these can change with the respective revisions of the Russia Sanctions Regulation.

---

111 Pelz/Sachs UKuR 2022, 9 (10).

b) Goods for technological enhancement in the defence and security sector, for use in oil refining and in aerospace

88 Irrespective of the above-mentioned licensing options, there is a prohibition on the sale, supply, transfer and export of goods pursuant to Art. 2a, 3, 3b and 3c Russia Sanctions Regulation. The ban includes the technological goods listed in Annexes II, VII, X and XI, which may not be included in the dual-use list. These are, for example, microprocessors, computers, calculators, memory circuits, SRAM, analogue-to-digital converters, semiconductors, software, telecommunications equipment, sensors, lasers, marine and naval technology, equipment for oil production or oil exploration and for numerous goods for use in the aerospace industry. Again, it is also prohibited to provide financing or financial assistance related to the listed goods and technology and related technical assistance, brokering services or other services. As with dual-use items, there are also exemptions for existing contracts, some of which are subject to licensing.

c) Maritime goods and technologies

89 Art. 3f Russia Sanctions Regulation also prohibits the sale, supply, transfer and export of certain maritime goods and technology designated in Annex XVI. As with the previously mentioned prohibitions, the provision of direct or indirect technical assistance, brokering services or other services as well as financing or financial assistance related to the designated maritime goods and technology is also prohibited under this provision. Exceptions for existing contracts as well as options for obtaining authorisation are provided for in Art. 3f para. 3 and para. 4.

d) Iron and steel products

90 Art. 3g Russia Sanctions Regulation prohibits the direct or indirect import of iron and steel products (see Annex XVII) into the EU if they originate in Russia or were exported from Russia.

e) Further prohibitions and export restrictions

91 Art. 3d and 3e Russia Sanctions Regulation regulate landing, take-off and overflight bans on the territory of the EU for aircraft registered in Russia and for aircraft registered in another country but owned by Russian persons or companies.

92 Art. 3h prohibits the sale, supply, transfer and export of luxury goods listed in Annex XVIII (e.g. food delicacies, clothing, jewellery, vehicles, watches and art) with a value exceeding 300 EUR per item. The ban covers sales to Russian persons or companies as well as the use of these goods in Russia.

3. Participation, investment and financing sanctions

93 Art. 3a Russia Sanctions Regulation regulates the prohibition of equity participation, investment and financing in companies that are active in the energy sector, mining sector or in the extraction of stones and earths in Russia. Furthermore, it is also prohibited to provide securities services related to such activities. In this context, it is important to note that the prohibitions apply not only to Russian companies, but also to companies domiciled in third countries to the extent that they are engaged in business activities in the relevant sectors in Russia.

4. Prohibitions in the area of capital markets

Further comprehensive prohibitions apply in the area of capital markets, certain excerpts of which are described below. For example, according to Art. 5 Russia Sanctions Regulation, it is prohibited to directly or indirectly buy or sell transferable securities and money market instruments, to provide securities services or assistance in connection with their issue or to deal in them in any other way, if these securities and money market instruments were issued by persons, entities or bodies listed in Annexes III, V or VI (sectors of Russian credit institutions, defence companies or oil companies). 94

In order to place an additional burden on Russia's public financing, Art. 5a Russia Sanctions Regulation regulates a ban on trading in transferable securities and money market instruments issued after 9 March 2022 by Russia, its government or central bank, or a legal person/entity acting on their behalf. 95

Art. 5a Russia Sanctions Regulation, on the other hand, prohibits the direct or indirect agreement on business transactions with a legal person/organisation or entity established in Russia that is under public control. This also includes persons and legal entities with whom the Russian government or central bank has substantial economic relations or in which the Russian government or central bank holds a profit participation right. Annex XIX lists as examples the companies Rosneft, Transneft, Gazprom Neft, Amaz-Antex, Kamaz, Rostec (Russian Technologies State Corporation), JSC PO Sevmash, Opk Obronprom, the United Aircraft Corporation, Uralvagonzavod, Sovcomflot and the United Shipbuilding Corporation. 96

Further prohibitions regulated in the Russia Sanctions Regulation concern, inter alia, securities transactions and rating services (Art. 5e, f and j), debt capital (e.g. Art. 5 para. 6 or Art. 5a para. 2), deposit transactions and services in connection with cryptocurrency (Art. 5b para. 2), the exclusion of Russian credit institutions from SWIFT traffic (Art. 5h), cash (Art. 5i), public procurement and concessions (Art. 5k), support for public enterprises established abroad (Art. 5l), and the area of trust services (Art. 5m).[112] 97

5. Prohibition of circumvention

The prohibition of circumvention enshrined in Art. 12 Russia Sanctions Regulation, prohibits participation, when undertaken knowingly and intentionally, in activities with the purpose or effect of circumventing the prohibitions laid down in this Regulation. 98

6. Personal sanctions

Similar to Regulation (EU) 269/2014 ('Crimean Annexation Regulation'), the Russia Sanctions Regulation is focussed on natural persons.[113] 99

a) Freezing

Art. 2 para. 1 Crimean Annexation Regulation stipulates that all funds and economic resources of the persons affected that are located in the territory of the EU shall be frozen. The freezing of funds and economic resources also applies to economic resources of natural or legal persons, entities or organisations controlled by the persons/entities listed in Annex I. 100

---

112 Pelz/Sachs UKuR 2022, 49 et seqq.
113 Annex I Crimean Annexation Regulation.

101 Funds in the sense of the Regulation are financial assets and benefits of any kind, such as cash, cheques, deposits, securities, loans, etc.[114] Economic resources as defined in the Regulation are assets of every kind, whether tangible or intangible, movable or immovable, which are not funds but can be used to obtain funds, goods or services.[115]

102 According to the European specifications, freezing is understood to mean preventing the use of economic resources to obtain funds, goods or services.[116] Freezing therefore leads to a prohibition of disposal, i.e. a frozen object may no longer be sold, leased or encumbered or otherwise used as a source of income.[117]

b) Ban on provision of resources

103 Art. 2 para. 2 Crimean Annexation Regulation regulates a so-called prohibition on making funds or economic resources available to the persons and entities listed in Annex I. The consequence of the ban on making funds or economic resources available is that the persons or entities affected may not be granted access, either directly or indirectly, to funds or economic resources. Under European law, 'making available' is to be understood in a broad sense, as it '[…] does not refer to a specific legal qualification, but rather covers any act required under the applicable national law for a person to effectively obtain full power of disposal over the asset in question.'[118]

7. Criminal consequences of an offence under AWG

104 § 18 sub. 1 AWG stipulates imprisonment for a term of between three months and five years for anyone who violates an export, import, transit, transfer or transit, transfer, sale, acquisition, supply, provision, transfer or investment ban, any transfer or investment prohibitions or prohibitions on the disposal of frozen funds and economic resources. § 18 sub. 6 AWG also regulates the punishability of an attempted violation. Likewise, according to § 18 sub. 1 no. 2 AWG, violations of the relevant licensing obligations are punishable. If a violation has not been committed intentionally, but through negligence, this constitutes an administrative offence (§ 19 sub. 1 AWG), which according to § 19 sub. 6 clause 1 AWG is punishable with a fine of up to 500,000.00 EUR.

105 In view of the rapid pace of the implementation and adaptation of the sanctions, § 18 sub. 11 no. 1 AWG provides for certain exemption from the penalty. In this respect, a party will be exempt from punishment if it has acted up to the end of the second working day following the publication of the new statutory provision in the Official Gazette of the EU and was not aware of a prohibition or a requirement for a permit at the time of the act.

106 In this context, it should also be noted that, in the event of an infringement by an authorised person in the company (a managing director, executive, authorised representative, etc.), a corporate fine pursuant to § 30 sub. 1 no. 1 OWiG can be imposed. In these cases, the fine can be up to 10 million EUR for criminal offences (§ 30 sub. 2 OWiG) and up to 500,000 EUR for administrative offences (§ 19 sub. 6 AWG).

---

[114] Art. 1 lit. g Crimean Annexation Regulation.

[115] Art. 1 lit. d Crimean Annexation Regulation.

[116] https://www.bundeswirtschaftsministerium.de/Redaktion/DE/Downloads/U/umsetzung-der-russland-sanktionen-kurzuberblick.pdf?__blob=publicationFile&v=1 (last accessed: 27.10.2025).

[117] https://www.bundeswirtschaftsministerium.de/Redaktion/DE/Downloads/U/umsetzung-der-russland-sanktionen-kurzuberblick.pdf?__blob=publicationFile&v=1 (last accessed: 27.10.2025).

[118] CJEU ECLI:EU:C:2007:596 mn. 51.

The supervision of compliance with foreign trade law is according to § 130 OWiG one of the mandatory supervisory measures to be taken by a company. In this respect, there is also an obligation to comply with the provisions of foreign trade law.[119] **107**

III. Growing importance of investment examination

As one of the largest economies in the world, Germany is an attractive destination for foreign investors. In relation to such investments, the state must ensure that they do not have a negative impact on public order and security of the Federal Republic of Germany, for example because they would be harmful to the security of the FRG. The Federal Ministry for Economic Affairs and Energy ('BMWE') may accordingly subject any direct or indirect acquisition of a German enterprise or participation in such an enterprise by a non-EU citizen or entity to an examination on a case-by-case basis. The legal basis for such an examination is provided by AWG on the one hand and the AWV on the other. **108**

Within the scope of such investment monitoring, a distinction is made between a cross-sectoral and a sector-specific investment examination procedure. **109**

1. Cross-sectoral audit procedure

The cross-sectoral examination procedure generally applies to the acquisition of a German enterprise or shares in such an enterprise by a non-EU citizen who is also not registered in a Member State of the European Free Trade Association (EFTA). The inter-sectoral examination procedure is laid down in §§ 55 et seqq. AWV in conjunction with § 4 sub. 1 no. 4 and 4a, § 5 sub. 2 AWG. **110**

Pursuant to § 55 sub. 1 AWV, the BMWE may examine whether the direct or indirect acquisition by a third party is likely to impair public order or security in the FRG, another EU Member State or investment projects or programmes that are in the interest of the EU. An impairment of the justified interest of public order or security is likely to obtain if its adverse effect is sufficiently imminent in time and sufficiently severe. The BMWE must make a prognosis decision in this regard. **111**

§ 55a sub. 4 and sub. 5 AWV stipulates a notification obligation before a contract is concluded that has as its object the acquisition of shares in a company in the cases regulated in § 55a sub. 1 and 2 AWV. The thresholds of the notification obligations differ according to the object of the company. For example, in the case of companies engaged in a sector relating to critical infrastructure, the acquiring party must report the acquisition in accordance with §§ 56 sub. 1, 55a sub. 1 no. 1 to 7 AWV if it holds 10 % or more of the voting rights (cf. § 56 AWV). According to §§ 56 sub. 1 and 2, 55a sub. 1 no. 8 to 20 AWV, the party acquiring a company engaged in the field of critical technologies, such as semiconductors or artificial intelligence, must report the acquisition if it holds 20 % or more of the voting rights. As a default provision, § 56 sub. 1, sub. 3 AWV stipulates that in all other cases of direct or indirect acquisition of voting shares in a domestic company by a non-EU entity, notification must be made if the shareholding amounts to 25 % or more of the voting rights. **112**

Irrespective of the case groups regulated in § 55a sub. 1 and 2 AWV, there is no obligation to report the acquisition of or participation in a domestic company by a non-EU entity. However, even if there is no reporting obligation, an investor is free to apply in advance for a legally binding clearance certificate from the BMWE (§ 58 AWV). Such a **113**

---

[119] Wiedmann/Will RIW 2022, 173 (179).

clearance certificate enables the investor to obtain legal certainty at an early stage. The clearance certificate confirms to the acquiring party that there are no concerns regarding the aforementioned protected interests. In the absence of such a clearance certificate, the BMWE can initiate an *ex officio* investigation procedure up to five years after the contract under the law of obligations has been concluded.

114 The examination phase following the notification is divided into two sections. In the first examination phase, the BMWE has two months from the date of notification to examine whether to initiate the formal examination procedure by means of an opening decision (cf. § 14a sub. 1 no. 1 AWG). If the formal investigation procedure is not opened within this period, the clearance certificate for the acquisition pursuant to § 58 sub. 2 AWV is deemed to have been granted.

115 In the event that the Federal Ministry of Economics and Labour opens a formal investigation procedure, it will then have four months – after receipt of the complete documents – to review the acquisition or the participation in a so-called second investigation phase. In exceptional cases (particular difficulty, particular relevance for defence interests), the period of the second review phase may be extended by up to four months. The second review phase is concluded by the final decision of the BMWE to approve, restrict or prohibit the acquisition.

116 The legal transaction to be reviewed remains effective for the duration of the review but is subject to the resolutory condition of prohibition pursuant to § 15 sub. 2 AWG.

117 However, within the scope of the cross-sectoral and sector-specific review procedure (→ mn. 119 et seq.), a legal transaction intended to complete the acquisition is suspended (§ 15 sub. 3 sent. 1 AWG). This legal transaction is deemed to be effective from the time of its execution if the BMWE releases the acquisition or does not prohibit it within the time limits set forth in § 14a AWG after becoming aware of the conclusion of the contract, or if the release of the acquisition is deemed to have been granted (§ 15 sub. 3 sent. 2 AWG).

118 During the period of the suspended effectiveness of the acquisition, it is also prohibited – under penalty of a fine – to exercise certain executive acts (e.g. exercising voting rights) (§ 15 sub. 4 AWG).

2. Sector-specific examination procedure

119 The sector-specific examination procedure, on the other hand, will be applied if the acquisition entails a non-national – which also includes EU citizens – acquiring a German company or shares in a German company engaged in the field of defence technology (§§ 60 et seqq. AWV in conjunction with § 4 sub. 1 no. 1, § 5 sub. 3 AWG). Specifically, this concerns – according to § 60 sub. 1 no. 1 to 3 AWV – the acquisition of companies that produce goods indicated in Part I Section A of the Export List, goods from the field of defence technology or certain products with IT security functions. According to § 60 sub. 1 no. 4 AWV, the acquisition of a defence-related facility is also subject to sector-specific examination.

120 Any acquisition of a company through which a foreign investor reaches or exceeds 10 % of the voting rights in the company (§ 60a sub. 1 AWV) is subject to an inspection. In addition, an additional acquisition of voting rights exceeding a total of 20 %, 25 %, 40 %, 50 % or 75 % will also subject to inspection pursuant to § 60a sub. 2 in conjunction with § 56 sub. 2 AWV. In addition, the acquisition of a definable part of a business by a non-national is also subject to review under § 60a sub. 1a AWV. Finally, § 60 sub. 2 AWV contains a provision for transactions aimed at circumvention or wrongful arrangements that were made in order to circumvent an audit by the BMWE.

Within the framework of the sector-specific examination procedure, it is important to determine whether the acquisition of a German enterprise by a non-national is likely to impair the essential security interests of the Federal Republic of Germany (§ 60 sub. 1 AWV). The Federal Ministry of Economics and Technology has a margin of discretion in assessing this standard of review. 121

The examination itself corresponds to that of the cross-sectoral examination procedure. In the sector-specific review procedure, the BMWE is in charge. A prohibition or order requires the agreement of the Federal Foreign Office, the Federal Ministry of the Interior, for Construction and Home Affairs and the Federal Ministry of Defence (§ 13 sub. 2 and 4 AWG). 122

IV. Growing importance of export controls of dual-use goods in surveillance technology

In the context of the control of dual-use goods, the export of surveillance technology is becoming increasingly important. Export control is governed by the AWV as a national and the Dual-Use Regulation as a European legal framework. 123

The export list of the AWV indicates the goods (e.g. military equipment and dual-use goods) requiring a permit for export. 124

As early as 2015, Germany pioneered the introduction of a licence requirement for all activities that support certain information technology systems in third countries.[120] 125

The authorisation requirement applies to monitoring systems 'Law Enforcement Monitoring Facilities' and data retention systems pursuant to § 52b AWV. A Law Enforcement Monitoring Facility within the meaning of the AWV is any system that transmits information between providers and the criminal prosecution authorities, e.g. systems according to the 'ETSI ES 201 671' standard pursuant to number 5A902 lit. a of Annex AL to AWV. A data retention system is any system or device that records event data, such as telephone numbers, IP or MAC addresses. It does not include systems that serve the operation of a public network, quality management or billing of the provider according to the Note to number 5A902 of Annex AL to AWV. 126

It is necessary to obtain a licence if BAFA has informed the company intending to export that their technical assistance offered is intended for the development, manufacture, handling, operation, maintenance or repair of surveillance systems pursuant to number 5A902 lit. (b) of Annex AL to AWV. 127

In addition to the AWV, the Dual Use Regulation is of major practical importance in the area of surveillance technology because its scope of application has grown since 2009. 128

As soon as an item is listed in the Dual-Use Regulation, its export to third countries requires a licence. In a few exceptional cases, even the transfer of such goods to EU Member States also requires a licence. Furthermore, according to Art. 3 Dual-Use Regulation, the export of all goods listed in Annex I is subject to authorisation. 129

In the field of surveillance technology, the so-called State Trojan ('intrusion software') is listed in the Dual-Use Regulation according to number A4005 of Annex I of Regulation (EC) No. 428/2009. 130

This relates to any 'software' that has been specially designed or modified to circumvent 'protective measures' of a computer or network-enabled device. The software 131

[120] 'Vierte Verordnung zur Änderung der Außenwirtschaftsverordnung' (Fourth Ordinance Amending the Foreign Trade and Payments Ordinance) of 13 July 2015, press release of the Federal Ministry for Economic Affairs and Energy of 8.7.2015, (<https://www.zoll.de/SharedDocs/Downloads/DE/Vorschriften/Aussenwirtschaft-Bargeldverkehr/vierte_vo_aenderung_awv.html> last accessed: 3.12.2024).

must also be able to modify system or user data, enable external commands on foreign computers or extract data from a system. Explicitly included is the extraction of selected metadata and application content number 5A001 letter (j) of Annex I of Regulation (EC) No. 428/2009. Not included are debugging programs, tools for software reverse engineering or software for digital rights management.

132 Due to the broad definition of the offence, certain risks arise for companies that export IT security products. Software that enables so-called penetration tests ('pentests') serves to circumvent protective measures of a computer in the sense of 'intrusion software'. The pentest software would require approval if the templates used provoke reactions from the 'attacked' computer.

133 A further problem area is posed by programmes which, after export, can be misused to change or obtain user data, such as the developer tool 'interacts'[121]. The final link between production and circumvention is probably not present here. In this case, there is no intrusion software in the sense of the Dual-Use Regulation.

134 Legal uncertainty is increased by non-listed dual-use goods. The export of non-listed dual-use goods may be subject to authorisation under Art. 4, 5 and 10 Dual-Use Regulation. In this respect, the respective country of purchase or destination will be decisive, as will the intended use of the goods. The BAFA is responsible for examining export applications.

135 The European Union intends to create legal certainty for companies. The European Commission is currently drafting 'Guidelines for the Export of Non-Listed Goods for Digital Surveillance under Art. 5 of the EU Dual-Use Regulation'. The guidelines are to be made available to companies after the public consultation process has been concluded.[122]

---

[121] <https://www.csoc.de/bedrohung-durch-interactsh-control-panel-dns-hacker-nutzen-entwickler-tool-als-angriffswerkzeug/> (last accessed: 3.12.2024).

[122] <https://policy.trade.ec.europa.eu/consultations/guidelines-export-cyber-surveillance-items-under-article-5-regulation-eu-no-2021821_en> (last accessed: 3.12.2024).

CHAPTER 24
COMPETITION LAW

Table of contents

A. Introduction 610
B. Prohibition of agreements restricting competition (§ 1 GWB, Art. 101 TFEU) 612
I. Scope of application 613
II. Risks of cartel infringements 614
1. Risks related to competitor contracts (horizontal relationship) 614
a) Risks associated with participation in industry associations 616
b) Risks associated with cooperation between competitors (such as a joint venture) 616
c) Risks associated with tenders 616
2. Risks related to suppliers and customers relationships (vertical relationships) 617
III. Recent Bundeskartellamt cases 618
IV. Exemptions 618
C. Abuse control: abuse of dominance and other levels of market power (§§ 18, 19, 19a, 20 GWB, Art. 102 TFEU) 620
I. Abuse of dominance (§ 19 GWB, Art. 102 TFEU) 620
1. Dominance (§ 19 GWB, Art. 102 TFEU) 621
2. Abusive conduct (§ 19 sub. 2 GWB, Art. 102 sent. 2 TFEU) . 622
3. Recent Bundeskartellamt cases 624
II. Abuse of paramount cross-market significance for competition across markets (§ 19a GWB) 625
1. Scope of application (§ 19a sub. 1 GWB) 626
2. Intervention possibilities (§ 19a sub. 2 GWB) 626
3. Recent cases 627
III. Abuse of relative or superior market power (§ 20 GWB) 627
D. Public and private enforcement 628
I. Proceedings and intervention power 628
1. Administrative proceedings 628
2. Regulatory fine proceedings 629
3. Investigative powers 629
4. Right to be heard 629
5. Dawn raids 629
6. Settlement proceedings 630
7. Cooperation with other authorities 630
8. Investigation of violations of the Digital Markets Act (DMA) 630
II. Sanctions 631
1. Regulatory fines 631
2. Exclusion from public tenders 633
3. Criminal penalties 633
III. Leniency programme 633
1. Scope of application 634
2. Leniency requirements 635

3. Leniency proceedings 635
a) Extent of reduction 636
b) Marker requirements 636
c) Whistleblowing system 636
IV. Private enforcement 636
1. Binding effects of cartel infringement decisions 637
2. Disclosure 637
3. statute of limitation periods 638
4. Additional characteristics of cartel damage cases 638
a) Rebuttable presumptions 638
b) Calculation of damages 638
c) Pass-on 639
E. Merger control 640
I. Merger control regime 640
1. Scope of application 641
a) Turnover thresholds (§ 35 sub. 1 GWB) 642
b) Transaction value threshold (§ 35 sub. 1a GWB) 642
c) Exemptions 643
2. Substantive assessment 643
II. Consequences and sanctions 644
III. Merger control proceedings 645
F. Actions subsequent to sector inquiries 646
I. Requirement to notify mergers below § 35 GWB thresholds 646
II. Remedial measures 646

A. Introduction

1 In today's competitive commercial environment, it has become increasingly important for companies to understand and comply with the principles of competition law. Competition law seeks to promote fair competition and protects consumers, competitors and suppliers from anti-competitive practices. The goal of the legal framework is to ensure that companies compete on a level playing field and foster innovation, efficiency and stimulating the overall economy. Violations of competition law can lead to substantial regulatory fines, lawsuits and reputational damage. This chapter provides an overview of the liability risks associated with German and European competition law, alongside recommended best practices for compliance. Adhering to the applicable requirements not only helps avert significant monetary damage and reputational harm but also reflects a company's dedication to ethical behaviour and equitable business practices.

2 Corporate liability risks within the realm of competition law have traditionally been divided into three primary categories, which in Germany are stipulated in the Act Against Restraints on Competition (*Gesetz gegen Wettbewerbsbeschränkungen*, 'GWB') and at the European level by the Treaty on the Functioning of the European Union ('TFEU') and Regulation (EC) No. 139/2004 ('EU Merger Regulation'):

- prohibition of agreements restricting competition (→ mn. 10 et seqq.): prohibits agreements, decisions and concerted practices restricting competition between two or more independent undertakings (§ 1 GWB, Art. 101 TFEU);
- abuse of dominance and other levels of market power (abuse control, → mn. 38 et seqq.): prohibits unilateral abusive practices by dominant undertakings (§ 19 GWB, Art. 102 TFEU), undertakings with paramount cross-market significance (§ 19a GWB)

or undertakings with relative or superior market power (§ 20 GWB). German competition law recognises three distinct notions of market power.
- merger control (→ mn. 118 et seqq.): prohibits the implementation of concentrations subject to merger control without prior clearance (§§ 35 et seq. GWB, Art. 1 et seq. EU Merger Regulation).

3 The competent authority in Germany for the enforcement of these legislative measures is the *Bundeskartellamt* ('BKartA', Federal Cartel Office), based in Bonn. In addition to its powers in the three traditional areas mentioned in → mn. 2, the latest reform of the GWB (11th amendment, *Wettbewerbsdurchsetzungsgesetz*, 'GWB Competition Enforcement Act') equipped the BKartA with a new power: it can impose certain obligations on companies if it has concluded that such measures are required to protect competition following an assessment of the competitive situation in specific markets of a selected sector (known as 'sector inquiry'), even if no infringement of any competition laws was found (→ mn. 142 et seqq. for further details).

4 In recent years, the BKartA has lived up to its reputation as one of the most active competition law authorities deploying significant human and financial resources.[1] In 2024, the BKartA imposed regulatory fines for cartel infringements on a total of six companies/associations and one individual amounting to approximately 26 million EUR.[2] With regard to general abuse control, the BKartA initiated six proceedings in 2024.[3] In this area, the BKartA has also taken a leading role in monitoring dominant platforms in the internet economy and e-commerce sector. This is evident not least from the abuse proceedings against the so-called 'GAFA companies'[4] and most recently against PayPal,[5] as well as the latest sector inquiries.[6] In 2024, the BKartA also examined around 870 company mergers including eight formal in-depth investigations.[7]

5 The requirement for companies to put significant emphasis on competition law compliance arises from the eagerness of the BKartA and the European Commission at the European level to pursue violations and the often substantial regulatory fines that companies face if they infringe competition law. Under both German and European competition law, regulatory fines up to 10 % of the relevant company's total worldwide group turnover in the preceding business year may be imposed for culpable cartel infringements or the abuse of dominance, relative or superior market power (→ mn. 82 et seqq.). These regulatory fines have their legal basis in §§ 1, 19, 20 sub. 1-3, 20 sub. 3a, 20 sub. 5 GWB in conjunction with §§ 9, 14, 30, 130 OWiG and Art. 101 and 102 TFEU as well as Art. 23 Regulation (EC) No. 1/2003. The exact amount of the regulatory fines depends on the severity

---

[1] Approximately 450 staff and an annual budget of 60.6 million EUR in 2024, see BKartA, Annual Report 2024/25, p. 9, available at <https://www.bundeskartellamt.de/SharedDocs/Publikation/EN/Jahresbericht/Jahresbericht_2024_25.pdf?__blob=publicationFile&v=5> (last accessed: 12.10.2025).

[2] See BKartA, Annual Report 2024/2025 (→ fn. 1), p. 9.

[3] See BKartA, Annual Report 2024/2025 (→ fn. 1), p. 9.

[4] Commonly known as an acronym for Google (Alphabet), Apple, Facebook (Meta) and Amazon. Adding Microsoft to the list ('GAFAM') is a common variation of the term.

[5] In 2023, the BKartA initiated new proceedings against PayPal for potentially hindering competitors and restricting price competition through its terms of use. See BKartA, press release of 23 January 2023, available at <https://www.bundeskartellamt.de/SharedDocs/Meldung/EN/Pressemitteilungen/2023/23_01_2023_PayPal.html> (last accessed 21.5.2025).

[6] For example, the BKartA concluded its sector inquiry into non-search based online advertising in 2023 and its sector inquiry into scoring in the online retail sector in 2024, see BKartA, press releases available at <https://www.bundeskartellamt.de/SharedDocs/Meldung/EN/Pressemitteilungen/2023/31_05_2023_SU_Online_Werbung.html> and at <https://www.bundeskartellamt.de/SharedDocs/Meldung/EN/Pressemitteilungen/2024/19_06_2026_SU_Scoring.html> (both last accessed 12.10.2025).

[7] See BKartA, Annual Report 2024/2025 (→ fn. 1), p. 9.).

and duration of the infringement; they predominantly address cartel infringements, though they can also be applied to abusive unilateral conduct.

6 In German law, individuals may also face regulatory fines if they actively participated in the infringement or neglected their supervisory responsibilities within an organisation, as set forth in § 81 GWB and §§ 9, 130 OWiG. Legal representatives or individuals in managerial positions (including directors, officers and certain senior employees) bear responsibility for failing to oversee and prevent violations by subordinate staff, as specified in §§ 130, 30 OWiG, including in the area of competition law. Although the legislation does not mandate specific supervisory actions, case law, however, has inferred various measures deemed necessary, viable, and reasonable for adherence, typically encompassing employee selection, instruction, monitoring, and the enforcement of internal sanctions.

7 Moreover, individuals involved in the coordination of bids or the exchange of information on the conditions of bids during tenders (so-called 'bid rigging'), as defined under § 298 StGB, may even be subject to criminal penalties.

8 Beyond regulatory fines, companies infringing competition law must contend with further legal consequences. Particularly, in the area of cartel violations, private enforcement of follow-on damages claims has increased significantly in recent years (→ mn. 106 et seqq.). Moreover, agreements implicated in such infringements may be legally void and, consequently unenforceable.

9 Given the severe consequences and the vigorous enforcement activities of both the BKartA and the European Commission, adherence to competition laws often emerges as a main legal concern for companies. Many companies deploy considerable resources to the implementation of the required compliance programmes, designed around their specific operational structures and the unique risks pertinent to their industry sector, to forestall breaches of competition law and to heighten employee awareness of such risks. These measures can help companies to detect infringements, promptly terminate these infringements, and make timely decisions on leniency applications that could mitigate regulatory fines (→ mn. 93 et seqq.).

B. Prohibition of agreements restricting competition (§ 1 GWB, Art. 101 TFEU)

10 The prohibition of agreements restricting competition is governed by § 1 GWB, which establishes a general prohibition on all agreements, decisions, and practices between undertakings and associations of undertakings[8] that have as their object or effect the prevention, restriction or distortion of competition.

11 On European level, Art. 101 TFEU applies, whose wording since July 2005 is mirrored in § 1 GWB. However, there is one key difference: the EU prohibition requires (potential) effects on trade between EU Member States, whereas § 1 GWB applies only to German territory. The BKartA directly applies Art. 101 TFEU following from the parallel and decentralised enforcement of EU competition law pursuant to Regulation (EC) No. 1/2003. The interpretation of § 1 GWB must generally be in line with EU competition law, particularly EU precedents, practice, regulations and guidelines with regard to Art. 101 TFEU.[9]

---

[8] A body through which undertakings of the same general type coordinate their conduct on the market is referred to as an association of undertakings.

[9] The revised European Commission's Guidelines on the applicability of Article 101 of the Treaty on the Functioning of the European Union to horizontal cooperation agreements, C 259/1, 1 June 2023,

The BKartA has jurisdiction only over infringements that have effects on the German territory, but it tends to interpret this rule broadly, including indirect effects such as anti-competitive agreements concluded abroad by foreign entities.[10] 12

§ 1 GWB, Art. 101 TFEU is assessed in two steps, including – as step one (§ 1 GWB, Art. 101 para. 1 TFEU) – the assessment whether an agreement, decision or practice between undertakings has an anti-competitive object or actual or potential restrictive effects on competition (and is capable of affecting trade between Member States), and – as a second step (§ 2 GWB, Art. 101 para. 3 TFEU) – the assessment whether advantages produced by the relevant conduct offset the disadvantages for competition. Agreements that violate § 1 GWB, Art. 101 TFEU are automatically void. 13

I. Scope of application

The prohibition of agreements restricting competition applies to undertakings and associations of undertakings, including any entity that engages in economic activity, regardless of its legal status and the way in which it is financed.[11] The relevant determination is whether the entity engages in economic activity (known as the 'functional concept of undertaking').[12] For public law entities, liability depends on whether the activity in question can potentially be offered by private individuals on the market.[13] 14

In principle, any employee's conduct can give rise to a company's competition law liability, even if the employee is not a legal representative. 15

However, competition law ensures the economic freedom between independent undertakings. So the prohibition of agreements restricting competition does not apply within a single economic entity (e.g., between an undertaking and its 100 % subsidiary), considering the companies to be part of the same undertaking.[14] To establish a single economic entity, it is required that the controlled undertaking does not determine its market behaviour autonomously; rather, the controlling undertaking must exercise decisive influence over the controlled undertaking. Also with regard to parent companies exercising decisive 16

('European Commission's Horizontal Guidelines') provide detailed guidance to help companies assess whether their agreements fall inside the scope of Art. 101 TFEU and may benefit from the safe harbour and on how to 'self-assess' compliance with EU antitrust rules for research and development (R&D) and specialization agreements that fall outside the safe harbour as well as expanded guidance for information exchange and particularly with regard to sustainability agreements, mobile infrastructure sharing agreements and bidding consortia.

[10] For investigative measures outside Germany, the BKARTA depends on the assistance from other competition authorities. Particularly within the European Competition Network (ECN) framework, this cooperation between national competition authorities of EU Member States is comprehensively organised in the ECN+ Directive.

[11] Cf. ECJ 11.7.2013 – C-440/11 P, ECLI:EU:C:2013:514 – Commission/Stichting Administratiekantoor Portielje; ECJ 23.4.1991 – C-41/90, ECLI:EU:C:1991:161 – Höfner and Elser; ECJ 16.11.1995 – C-244/94, ECLI:EU:C:1995:392 – FFSA i.a.

[12] Cf. ECJ 23.4.1991 – C-41/90, ECLI:EU:C:1991:161 – Höfner and Elser; ECJ 16.11.1995 – C-244/94, ECLI:EU:C:1995:392 – FFSA i.a.; ECJ 11.12.1997 – C-55/96, ECLI:EU:C:1997:603 – Job Centre coop.

[13] Public authorities, public corporations or health insurances, which offer or demand goods or services on a market, can also be undertakings within the meaning of § 1 GWB, Art. 101 TFEU. Cf. BGH 26.10.1961 – KZR 1/61, BeckRS 1961, 105618 – Gummistrümpfe. Public authorities are not considered to be undertakings if the economic activity only serves its specifically sovereign, non-economic tasks. Cf. CFI 4.3.2003 – T-319/99, ECLI:EU:T:2003:50 mn. 35 – FENIN/Commission.

[14] Cf. ECJ 25.10.1983 – C-107/82, ECLI:EU:C:1983:293 mn. 50 – AEG/Commission; CFI 12.1.1995 – T-102/92, ECLI:EU:T:1995:3 mn. 51 – Viho/Commission. In recent EU case law, the focus is on the question of which company is liable for regulatory fines.

influence over their joint venture, these undertakings are considered to form a single economic entity.

II. Risks of cartel infringements

17 § 1 GWB, Art. 101 para. 1 TFEU prohibits agreements, formal or informal, between two or more independent undertakings that prevent, restrict or distort competition. This covers both horizontal agreements, between actual or potential competitors operating at the same level of the supply chain, and vertical agreements between firms operating at different levels, such as a manufacturer and its distributor. The guiding principle of § 1 GWB, Art. 101 para. 1 TFEU is that each company must determine independently its business strategy on the market, including the means it intends to use to implement that strategy and the conditions it intends to offer to customers (known as 'the postulate of independence').[15]

1. Risks related to competitor contracts (horizontal relationship)

18 Agreements between actual or potential competitors (horizontal relationships) may infringe the prohibition of agreements restricting competition if they have the aim or effect of restricting competition. 'Competitors' refers to all companies that compete with the company on the same geographic sales or purchasing market, as they buy or sell the same or comparable products or services. An undertaking can be considered a 'potential competitor' if it, within a short period of time, likely would undertake the necessary additional investments or other necessary switching costs to enter the relevant market on which the other undertaking is active. An agreement, which is intended to limit competition, is already sufficient to infringe the prohibition of agreements restricting competition without the need to identify market effects, since it is assumed that restrictions of competition by object have by their nature the potential to limit competition.[16] Therefore, the argument that such an agreement was never put into practice does not succeed. However, when examining whether a restriction of competition by object is involved, pro-competitive effects must also be taken into account.[17] Compared to those that limit competition by object, other horizontal cooperation agreements must be assessed based on their actual or potential impact on the market, including at least one of the competition parameters such as price, output, product quality, product variety or innovation.[18] The concept of agreements is broad and applies not only to written contracts but also to informal agreements known as gentlemen's agreements.

19 The most flagrant example of illegal conduct under Art. 101 TFEU is the creation of a cartel between competitors, which may involve an express or tacit agreement on price fixing (including individual pricing factors), quantities, production limits (quotas), capacities, market sharing (such as the promise not to attack certain customers or sales

---

[15] Cf. ECJ 28.5.1998 – C-7/95 P, ECLI:EU:C:1998:256 mn. 86 – John Deere/Commission.

[16] See e.g., ECJ 12.1.2023 – C-883/19 P, ECLI:EU:C:2023:11 mn. 106 et seq. – HSBC Holdings i.a./Commission; ECJ 20.11.2008 – C-209/07, ECLI:EU:C:2008:643 mn. 16 et seq. – BIDS; ECJ 6.10.2009 – C-501/06 P and others, ECLI:EU:C:2009:610 mn. 55 – GlaxoSmithKline/Commission i.a.; ECJ 4.6.2009 – C-8/08, ECLI:EU:C:2009:343 mn. 29 et seq – T-Mobile Netherlands and others.

[17] See ECJ 12.1.2023 – C-883/19 P, ECLI:EU:C:2023:11 mn. 139 et seq., 196 et seq – HSBC Holdings i.a./Commission.

[18] Cf. European Commission, Guidelines on the applicability of Article 101 of the Treaty on the Functioning of the European Union to horizontal cooperation agreements, COM(2023) 3445 final ('Horizontal Guidelines'), mn. 30 et seq.

territories of the other party, or not to exceed certain production quantities or quotas), and/or a collusion on product quality or innovation.[19] These agreements are considered as so-called 'hardcore cartel agreements', for which participants face high risks of detection due to leniency policies and regulatory fines, as well as follow-on damages claims from customers or suppliers.

However, even if such an agreement is not reached, the prohibition of agreements **20** restricting competition also covers concerted practices, which refer to a form of coordination in which practical cooperation is knowingly substituted for the risk of competition, without reaching the stage of a conclusive agreement.[20]

A concerted practice can, for example, involve two competitors exchanging compet- **21** itively sensitive information, revealing their market strategy, and also when facilitated by third parties.[21] In particular, the exchange of non-public information about current or future market behaviour (competitively sensitive information) is prohibited under competition law, such as information on pricing and pricing strategy (including price components and discounts surcharges), terms and conditions of contracts with customers and suppliers, sources of supply, production volumes and quantities (including capacities), costs (such as selling and manufacturing costs, including methods of costing), quality or other competition parameters such as timing, delivery and innovation, market sharing, customer allocation, business strategies, as well as conduct in tenders.[22]

Situations in which only one undertaking discloses strategic information to its com- **22** petitor(s) or one undertaking receives such information from its competitor(s) can also be considered an infringement under § 1 GWB, Art. 101 para. 1 TFEU: it is then presumed that the undertaking receiving the strategic information accepts the information and adapts its market conduct accordingly unless it responds with a clear statement that it does not wish to receive such information.[23] A one-time meeting during which competitively sensitive information was disclosed would be sufficient to constitute an infringement.[24]

In addition, the exchange of information regarding future market behaviour through **23** the public, known as signalling, can potentially infringe § 1 GWB, Art. 101 para. 1 TFEU.[25] This includes public announcements regarding price changes or list price adjustments. If such announcements are unavoidable, they should only be made to the public with little notice. Advance information for customers and suppliers should not be provided for those who are also competitors in the affected market.

Apart from clear infringements (such as the hardcore cartel agreements referred to), **24** several less restrictive agreements must be assessed carefully and may be exempted under

---

[19] Cf. European Commission's Horizontal Guidelines, mn. 366 et seq. In addition, agreements on other terms and conditions of business, such as delivery conditions, guarantee conditions, payment periods, interest, etc., are generally prohibited.

[20] See, e.g., ECJ 4.6.2009 – C-8/08, ECLI:EU:C:2009:343 mn. 26 – T-Mobile Netherlands and others; ECJ 31.3.1993 – C-89/85 and others, ECLI:EU:C:1993:120 mn. 63 – A. Ahlström Osakeyhtiö and others/ Commission.

[21] The strategic importance of non-public information depends on the aggregation/individualisation, age, market context and frequency of exchange.

[22] ECJ 4.6.2009 – C-8/08, ECLI:EU:C:2009:343 mn. 26 – T-Mobile Netherlands and Others; ECJ 5.12.2013 – C-455/11P, ECLI:EU:C:2013:796 mn. 36 – Solvay/Commission; GC 16.9.2013 – T-380/10, ECLI:EU:T:2013:449 mn. 37 – Wabco/Commission; see also in detail European Commission's Horizontal Guidelines, mn. 366 et seq.

[23] See ECJ 8.7.1999 – C-199/92 P, ECLI:EU:C:1999:358 mn. 162 – Hüls/Commission; ECJ 8.7.1999 – C-49/92 P, ECLI:EU:C:1999:356 mn. 121 – Commission/Anic Partezipazioni. This is particularly relevant for also just one-time participation in meetings (e.g., association meetings) during which competitors talk about their pricing strategy, cf. ECJ 4.6.2009 – C-8/08, ECLI:EU:C:2009:343 mn. 59 – T-Mobile Netherlands and others.

[24] ECJ 4.6.2009 – C-8/08, ECLI:EU:C:2009:343 mn. 59 – T-Mobile Netherlands and others.

[25] Cf. GC 2.2.2022 – T-799/17, ECLI:EU:T:2022:48 – Scania i.a./Commission.

the individual exemption if they lead to efficiencies being passed on to consumers or under an EU block exemption regulation ('BER') (→ mn. 37).

a) Risks associated with participation in industry associations

25 When participating in industry associations, during which representatives from different companies come together, it is permissible to exchange information on general, non-competitively sensitive topics unless the exchange leads to an unjustified coordination of the commercial behaviour of the companies. This includes legal and socio-political matters that could impact the industry as a whole (covering also joint representation of interests and lobbying), general economic issues like stock market prices and publicly available business or technology trends that all competitors and customers can access.

26 However, competitors exchanging information on cost increases arising from certain legal changes would, for example, constitute an exchange of competitively sensitive information infringing § 1 GWB, Art. 101 TFEU. Furthermore, any standards defined during association meetings must not exclude other companies from the market, and all interested parties should be able to participate and know the outcome.

27 Moreover, associations and third-party providers collect market data to publish market statistics, such as average prices or production volumes. Participation in the data exchange for the publication of market statistics is permissible under competition law if individual values of any particular competitor are not identifiable (such as by aggregating data from at least five participants), or if the data are sufficiently outdated to prevent inferences about a competitor's current business strategy.

b) Risks associated with cooperation between competitors (such as a joint venture)

28 The co-operating with competitors through, for example, a joint venture, can be permissible under competition law if information is only exchanged on a 'need-to-know' basis, meaning only the necessary information for the project's implementation and functioning in the specific project phase is shared. In most cases, the parties remain (potential) competitors outside of the cooperation, so sharing sensitive information beyond what is required is prohibited. To manage the risk of violating competition law, so-called 'clean teams' can be established during project planning in order to exchange competitively sensitive information to a limited extent. During the project implementation phase, additional confidentiality agreements, compliance training and guidelines can be implemented for that purpose.

c) Risks associated with tenders

29 Undertakings are not allowed to coordinate their bids or to share information on the conditions of their bids (known as bid rigging) during tenders.[26] This occurs, for example, when participants in a tender agree to submit identical bids (or to agree on minimum prices), eliminating price competition, or when they decide on which participant will offer the lowest price or bid for specific tender lots. However, certain forms of cooperation between two or more undertakings to submit a joint bid in a public or private procurement competition may be permitted.

---

[26] For more details on cooperation within bidding consortia, see European Commission's Horizontal Guidelines (→ fn. 9), mn. 347 et seq.

2. Risks related to suppliers and customers relationships (vertical relationships)

Prohibited agreements can also exist between companies that operate at different levels of the production or distribution chain, such as suppliers and purchasers, including independent dealers and service providers.[27] The parties to a vertical agreement need not compete with each other, as they operate in different markets (i.e., upstream or downstream in relation to the production or distribution chain). Such agreements, known as vertical restraints of competition, typically relate to the conditions under which parties can acquire, sell, or resell certain goods or services. Typical examples of vertical agreements include practices directed at distribution partners, such as influencing resale prices through fixed or minimum resale price maintenance ('RPM'), setting fixed or maximum rebates, or providing related incentives.[28] These are categories of severe vertical cases mostly resulting in high regulatory fines. Manufacturers or suppliers are not allowed to influence the prices that their customers or distribution partners charge their customers, except for non-binding recommended retail prices ('RRP') if customers or distribution partners remain free to decide on pricing without pressure.[29] Moreover, exclusive purchasing or supply obligations (i.e., more than 80 %) can also be considered a restraint of competition under § 1 GWB, Art. 101 TFEU, as well as best price guarantees or parity clauses by which a manufacturer undertakes to a particular customer not to offer more favourable conditions to other buyers or to always grant the buyer the most favourable conditions granted to other buyers.[30] In addition, agreements that restrict the territory or customers to whom the dealer may sell the contract goods can also infringe § 1 GWB, Art. 101 TFEU. 30

Selective distribution systems, mainly used for high-quality branded products, allow manufacturers to organise their sales by supplying dealers who meet certain selection criteria. The selection of authorised dealers must be based on qualitative criteria that are justified by the product's specific characteristics and are applied non-discriminately to all dealers willing to be admitted to the distribution system.[31] However, peculiarities arise regarding online sales within selective distribution.[32] Manufacturers are allowed to demand that dealers in the distribution system have a physical point of sale ('brick and mortar store') if it is necessary for objective reasons, thus excluding online-only dealers.[33] However, a general ban on internet sales for dealers who already have a brick and mortar store is considered a hardcore restriction under § 1 GWB, Art. 101 TFEU. 31

Competitors within supply relationships are allowed to exchange information that is strictly necessary for the implementation of the specific supply relationship but should avoid exchanging competitively sensitive information beyond that to comply with competition law. 32

---

[27] The competition law assessment of distribution agreements is essentially characterised by the Regulation (EU) No. 2022/720 to categories of vertical agreements and concerted practices ('VBER') and the Guidelines on vertical restraints 2022/C 248/01 ('Vertical Guidelines 2022').

[28] Cf. Vertical Guidelines 2022 (→ fn. 27), mn. 185 et seq.

[29] Cf. Vertical Guidelines 2022 (→ fn. 27), mn. 185 et seq.

[30] Cf. Vertical Guidelines 2022 (→ fn. 27), mn. 321 et seq., 356 et seq.

[31] Cf. ECJ 6.12.2017 – C-230/16, ECLI:EU:C:2017:941 – Coty; see also Vertical Guidelines 2022 (→ fn. 27), mn. 143 et seq.

[32] Cf. ECJ 13.10.2011 – C-439/09, ECLI:EU:C:2011:649 – Pierre Fabre; ECJ 6.12.2017 – C-230/16, ECLI:EU:C:2017:941 – Coty.

[33] Cf. Vertical Guidelines 2022 (→ fn. 27), mn. 155, 164.

III. Recent Bundeskartellamt cases

33 In recent years, the BKartA's cartel prosecutions have included different forms of cartels involving several sectors. In May 2025, the BKartA imposed fines totalling 10.5 million EUR on seven road repair companies for bid rigging and customer allocation.[34] Bid rigging by construction companies was also the subject of several fines imposed by the BKartA in 2023.[35] In 2024, the sectors affected included protective clothing, telecommunications, network technology, construction services and road repairs.[36]

34 In 2021, companies active in the sectors of steel and steel forging were prosecuted for exchanging competitively sensitive information.[37] In 2020, exchange of competitively sensitive information was also in the BKartA's focus when the authority fined companies active in the sector for plant protection products for price fixing,[38] the sector of vehicle registration plates for price fixing and distribution of projects,[39] and the sector of aluminium forging for price fixing.[40]

35 In addition, vertical price-fixing, in particular, is a common example of a hardcore cartel infringement that the BKartA consistently pursues and severely sanctions. In 2024, for instance, the BKartA fined companies for vertical price fixing agreements in the protective clothing sector and in the telecommunications and network technology sectors.[41]

36 Further, the BKartA has already flagged that § 1 GWB may apply to market behaviour influenced by collusive algorithms,[42] but it has not yet fined such behaviour.

IV. Exemptions

37 If an agreement or a concerted practice restricts competition pursuant to § 1 GWB, Art. 101 para. 1 TFEU, certain conduct can be exempted from the prohibition of agreements restricting competition:

---

[34] See BKartA, Annual Report 2024/2025 (→ fn. 1), p. 17.

[35] See BKartA, Annual Report 2023/2024, p. 18, available at <https://www.bundeskartellamt.de/SharedDocs/Publikation/EN/Jahresbericht/Jahresbericht_2023_-2024.pdf?__blob=publicationFile&v=5> (last accessed: 7.7.2025); See BKartA, case report of 15 February 2023 – B10-28/18, p. 1 (anticompetitive agreements regarding the awarding of road construction works), only available in German at <https://www.bundeskartellamt.de/SharedDocs/Entscheidung/DE/Fallberichte/Kartellverbot/2023/B10-28-18.html> (last accessed: 7.7.2025).

[36] See BKartA, Annual Report 2024/2025 (→ fn. 1), p. 16.

[37] See BKartA, case report of 10 February 2021 – B12-22/17, p. 1 (information exchange on costs, pricings and negotiations with suppliers and customers of steel forging companies), only available in German at <https://www.bundeskartellamt.de/SharedDocs/Entscheidung/DE/Fallberichte/Kartellverbot/2021/B12-22-17.html> (last accessed: 7.7.2025).

[38] See BKartA, case report of 21 October 2020 – B10-22/15, p. 1 (agreement on price lists, discounts and unit prices), only available in German at <https://www.bundeskartellamt.de/SharedDocs/Entscheidung/DE/Fallberichte/Kartellverbot/2020/B10-22-15.html> (last accessed: 7.7.2025).

[39] BKartA, case report of 29 May 2020 – B10-22/17, p. 2 (agreement on prices and discounts and on the distribution of two large projects), only available in German language at <https://www.bundeskartellamt.de/SharedDocs/Entscheidung/DE/Fallberichte/Kartellverbot/2020/B10-22-17.html> (last accessed: 7.7.2025).

[40] BKartA, case report of 3 February 2021 – B12-24/17, p. 2 (information exchange on strategical data and agreements on passing on cost increases to customers), available <https://www.bundeskartellamt.de/SharedDocs/Entscheidung/EN/Fallberichte/Kartellverbot/2021/B12-24-17.html> (last accessed: 7.7.2025).

[41] See BKartA, Annual Report 2023/2024 (→ fn. 35), p. 17; Annual Report 2024/2025 (→ fn. 1), p. 18.

[42] BKartA and the French Competition Authority, Working paper 'Algorithm and Competition', 6 November 2019, available at <https://www.bundeskartellamt.de/SharedDocs/Publikation/EN/Berichte/Algorithms_and_Competition_Working-Paper.pdf?__blob=publicationFile&v=3> (last accessed 21.5.2025).

- de minimis exemption for agreements that have limited market effects.[43] In general for horizontal agreements, the combined market share threshold of the undertakings concerned on any relevant markets affected not to be exceeded is 10 %, for vertical agreements the threshold is 15 %.[44] Moreover, a safe harbour rule applies to the cooperation of technology pools.[45]
- exemptions pursuant to § 2 sub. 2 GWB and EU block exemption regulations. Regulation (EU) No. 2023/1067 to certain categories of specialisation agreements ('Specialisation BER'),[46] Regulation (EU) No. 2023/1066 to certain categories of research and development agreements ('R&D BER'),[47] and Regulation (EU) No. 2022/720 to categories of vertical agreements and concerted practices ('VBER'), and Regulation (EU) No. 316/2014 to categories of technology transfer agreements ('TTBER'). For example, vertical restrictions that meet specific requirements, such as not qualifying for hardcore restrictions and market shares of not exceeding 30 % each, may be exempted from prohibition of agreements restricting competition under the VBER.
- individual exemption pursuant to § 2 sub. 1 GWB, which mirrors Art. 101 para. 3 TFEU on European level, for agreements producing pro-competitive benefits that outweigh their restrictive effects on competition. An individual exemption of § 2 sub. 1 GWB, Art. 101 para. 1 TFEU requires that the agreement meets four cumulative requirements:[48] the agreement must contribute to (i) improving the production or distribution of goods or contribute to promoting technical or economic progress (qualitative or quantitative efficiency gains), (ii) consumers must receive a fair share of the resulting benefits, (iii) restrictions must be indispensable to the attainment of these objectives, and (iv) the agreement must not afford the parties the possibility of eliminating competition in respect of a substantial part of the products involved.[49]
- exemptions for small or medium-sized enterprises ('SMEs') pursuant to § 3 GWB (i.e. agreements strengthening the competitiveness of SMEs).
- sector-specific exemptions, e.g., for certain (vertical) agricultural agreements (§ 28 sub. 1 and 2 GWB), certain agreements of companies ensuring public water supply (§ 31 sub. 1 GWB), and certain (vertical) agreements relating to the press sector (§ 30 sub. 1 GWB and § 30 sub. 2b GWB).

---

[43] This exemption is not applicable to serious cartel infringements, in particular as restrictions of competition by object.

[44] European Commission, Notice on agreements of minor importance which do not appreciably restrict competition under Art. 101 para. 1 TFEU, COM(2014) 291/01 ('De Minimis Notice'), no. 8a and b. De minimis agreements do not fall within the scope of ban of cartels (technically, no infringement to be exempted). See for horizontal agreements, European Commission's Horizontal Guidelines (→ fn. 9), mn. 41 and 42.

[45] European Commission, Guidelines on the application of Art. 101 TFEU to technology transfer agreements, COM(2014) 89/03, mn. 261. Under these circumstances, agreements do not fall within the scope of ban of cartels (technically, no infringement to be exempted).

[46] For more details on specialisation agreements, see European Commission's Horizontal Guidelines (→ fn. 9), mn. 172 et seq.

[47] From 1 July 2023 to 30 June 2025, a transitional regime applies to agreements in force on 30 June 2023 which do not satisfy the conditions for exemption established by the Regulation (EU) No. 2023/1066 but which satisfy the conditions for exemption established by the former Regulation (EU) No. 1217/2010. For more details on research and development agreements see, European Commission's Horizontal Guidelines (→ fn. 9), mn. 51 et seq.

[48] Cf. ECJ 13.7.1966 – C-56 and C-58/64, ECLI:EU:C:1966:41 p. 395 et seq. – Consten and Grundig/Commission; ECJ 17.1.1984 – C-43/82, ECLI:EU:C:1984:9 mn. 61 – VBVB and VBBB/Commission; see also European Commission, Guidelines on the application of Art. 81 para. 3 of the Treaty, COM(2004) 101/08, mn. 34; European Commission' Horizontal Guidelines (→ fn. 9), mn. 35 et seq.

[49] Cf. European Commission, Guidelines on the application of Art. 81 para. 3 of the Treaty, COM(2004) 101/08, mn. 34.

C. Abuse control: abuse of dominance and other levels of market power (§§ 18, 19, 19a, 20 GWB, Art. 102 TFEU)

38 German competition law also covers unilateral conduct by undertakings with market power. § 19 GWB prohibits abuse of dominance, which is similar to Art. 102 TFEU at European level. In 2024, the BKartA opened six new proceedings, compared with 19 in 2023.[50] However, unilateral conduct below the threshold of dominance can be subject to § 20 GWB or the newly introduced § 19a GWB, which makes German competition law stricter compared to Art. 102 TFEU.[51] The 10th amendment to the GWB ('GWB Digitisation Act'), effective from January 2021, updated and tightened regulations for undertakings with market power, specifically digital platforms, particularly by introducing the new § 19a GWB, which applies to 'undertakings with paramount cross-market significance' without requiring dominance. The GWB Digitisation Act bolstered the BKartA's capabilities by endowing it with broader investigative powers such as this proactive enforcement approach and specifically aimed to keep markets open within the digital economy, with its core focus on new regulations concerning the abuse of market power. § 20 GWB has also been revised for undertakings with relative market power in relation to depending on trading partners, including facilitating access to data and extending beyond small- and medium-sized undertakings to large undertakings claiming dependence. This also aims at digital platforms such as the GAFA companies.

39 Following the adjustments through the GWB Digitisation Act, German competition law now provides for three different concepts of market power (→ mn. 44 et seqq., → mn. 57 et seqq. and → mn. 66 et seqq.), which involve different behavioural demands. The BKartA's focus on online dominant cases[52] has increased due to the new regulations, especially for multi-sided platforms such as those of the GAFA companies.

40 Furthermore, § 21 GWB prohibits requesting a boycott of a third undertaking and other restrictive practices without requiring dominance.

41 Ultimately, in regulated industries such as electricity, gas, telecommunications, post and railway, special rules might apply, and the Federal Network Agency ('FNA') works with the BKartA to ensure compliance.

I. Abuse of dominance (§ 19 GWB, Art. 102 TFEU)

42 § 19 GWB prohibits the abuse of dominance by one or several undertakings. Similarly, on European level, Art. 102 TFEU prohibits the abuse of dominance by one or more undertakings within the internal market or a substantial part of it, which may have additional potential effects on trade between EU Member States. These provisions aim to prevent dominant undertakings from abusing that dominance and restricting competition, for example, by charging unfair prices, limiting production or refusing to innovate to the detriment of other market participants.

---

[50] See BKartA, Annual Report 2024/2025 (→ fn. 1), p. 9; Annual Report 2023/2024 (→ fn. 35), p. 9.

[51] Art. 3 para. 2 sent. 2 Regulation (EC) No. 1/2003 provides for that possibility.

[52] Cf. BKartA, case report of 17 July 2019 – B2-88/18 – Amazon, available at <https://www.bundeskartellamt.de/SharedDocs/Entscheidung/EN/Fallberichte/Missbrauchsaufsicht/2019/B2-88-18.html> (last accessed: 7.7.2025); BKartA 4.12.2017 – B6-132/14-2, BeckRS 2017, 143035 – CTS Eventim; BKartA 8.9.2015 – B6-126/14, BeckRS 2016, 1138 – Google; BKartA 22.12.2015 – B9-121/13, BeckRS 2016, 4449 – Booking.com.

The abuse of dominance pursuant to § 19 GWB, Art. 102 TFEU involves an objective concept. It concerns the conduct of a dominant undertaking that, on a market in which competition is already weakened due to the presence of that undertaking, employs methods that differ from those used in regular competition for products or services.[53] This conduct has the effect of hindering the maintenance or growth of competition in the market. However, identifying an undertaking or group of undertakings as dominant does not itself infringe § 19 GWB, Art. 102 TFEU. It simply means that the undertaking(s) in question have a responsibility not to impair genuine, un-distorted competition, regardless of the reasons for their dominant position.[54] 43

1. Dominance (§ 19 GWB, Art. 102 TFEU)

Dominance is established if an undertaking has economic strength in the relevant market, which enables it to behave independently of its competitors, customers and consumers, to an appreciable extent thereby preventing effective competition.[55] The assessment of dominance is dependent on the relevant product and geographical market being considered. The relevant product market includes all products that are interchangeable by suppliers and customers based on their characteristics, price and intended use. The geographical market is the territory in which undertakings supply and demand products, as well as the conditions of competition being homogeneous and distinct from neighbouring territories. 44

In German competition law, the concept of dominance is defined under § 18 GWB, which with regard to individual dominance applies when a company has no competitors or is not exposed to any significant competition or has a paramount market position in relation to its competitors. 45

When assessing dominance, several criteria may be considered under § 18 sub. 3 GWB. These include the undertakings' market share, financial strength, access to data relevant for competition, access to supply or sales markets, links with other undertakings, legal or factual barriers to market entry of other undertakings, actual or potential competition, ability to shift its supply or demand to other goods or commercial services, and the ability of customers or suppliers to switch to other undertakings. 46

However, market shares remain the most important criteria for assessing dominance. According to § 18 sub. 4 GWB, market dominance can be rebuttably presumed if the undertaking has a market share of at least 40 %. In EU law, courts generally presume dominance if the undertaking has a market share of at least 50 %.[56] When market shares exceed these thresholds, it can be challenging to rebut the presumption, even if possible in principle. 47

When assessing dominance in multi-sided markets and networks, § 18 sub. 3a GWB takes into account several criteria, including direct and indirect network effects, multi-homing, users' switching difficulties, economies of scale arising in connection with network effects, access to data relevant for competition and competitive pressure driven by innovation. 48

---

[53] ECJ 13.2.1979 – C-85/76, ECLI:EU:C:1979:36 mn. 91 – Hoffmann-La Roche/Commission; ECJ 3.7.1991 – C-62/86, ECLI:EU:C:1991:286 mn. 69 – AKZO/Commission; ECJ 19.4.2012 – C-549/10 P, ECLI:EU:C:2012:221 mn. 17 – Tomra Systems and Others/Commission.

[54] ECJ 16.3.2000 – C-395/96 P, C-396/96 P, ECLI:EU:C:2000:132 mn. 37, 38 – Compagnie Maritime Belge/Commission; ECJ 9.11.1983 – C-322/81, ECLI:EU:C:1983:313 mn. 57 – Michelin/Commission.

[55] See, e.g., ECJ 13.2.1979 – C-85/76, ECLI:EU:C:1979:36 mn. 38 et seq. – Hoffmann-La Roche/Commission; ECJ 14.2.1978 – C-27/76, ECLI:EU:C:1978:22 mn. 65 – United Brands/Commission.

[56] Cf. ECJ 13.2.1979 – C-85/76, ECLI:EU:C:1979:36 mn. 41 – Hoffmann-La Roche/Commission; ECJ 3.7.1991 – C-62/86, ECLI:EU:C:1991:286 mn. 69 – AKZO/Commission.

49 For intermediaries on multi-sided markets, § 18 sub. 3b GWB considers in particular the importance of the intermediary services for accessing supply and sales markets for the assessment of the market position. The BKartA used these criteria in its decisions 'CTS Eventim', 'Amazon' and 'Facebook'. In the case of 'Facebook', the BKartA found the company to be dominant in the social media networks market due to direct and indirect network effects resulting from the large user base, which lead to a user lock-in, enhanced appeal for advertisement customers and enhanced access to personal user data.[57]

50 In German and EU competition law, the concept of collective dominance is recognised. Collective dominance is considered when between two or more undertakings no substantial competition exists with respect to a certain type of goods or commercial services and when these undertakings jointly fulfil the requirements outlined in sub. 0 (§ 18 sub. 5 GWB). The undertakings must be linked in such a way that they adopt the same conduct on the market.[58] Collective dominance may be established through tacit collusion, an agreement or a concerted practice between several undertakings, whether or not infringing § 1 GWB, Art. 101 TFEU.[59] The 'Airtours' criteria of Court of Justice of the European Union (CJEU) are applied by German courts and the BKartA to determine collective dominance on a market.[60] § 18 sub. 6 GWB provides for a rebuttable presumption for collective dominance, applying to three or fewer undertakings reaching a combined market share of at least 50 %, or five or fewer undertakings reaching a combined market share of at least two-thirds.

2. Abusive conduct (§ 19 sub. 2 GWB, Art. 102 sent. 2 TFEU)

51 § 19 sub. 2 GWB, like Art. 102 TFEU, prohibits the abusive conduct of a dominant undertaking, mainly whether through exclusionary behaviour, targeting primarily the competitors of the dominant undertaking, or exploitative behaviour directed at the opposite market side. Exploitative abuse is considered when a dominant undertaking uses its market position to gain unjustified advantages, such as price abuse in relation to costs, price discrimination and unfair business conditions.[61] Exclusionary abuse is considered when a dominant undertaking uses its market position to hinder or exclude competitors, customers or suppliers, such as through tying practices, long-term exclusivity agreements, refusal to deal, denial of access to essential facilities or precursors, sales below cost price, price discrimination, fidelity rebates and margin squeeze.[62] § 19 sub. 2 GWB, comparable to Art. 102 sent. 2 TFEU, sets out specific types of abusive conduct within this context:

- unfair impediment of competitors (exclusionary conduct) and discrimination (no. 1). Examples of exclusionary conduct are practices to undercut competitor prices ('predatory pricing')[63], bundling, tying,[64] exclusivity provisions or loyalty rebates,[65] setting

---

[57] BKartA 6.2.2019 – B6-22/16, BeckRS 2019, 4895 – Facebook; confirmed by the Federal Court of Justice: BGH 23.6.2020 – KVR 69/19, GRUR 2020, 1318 – Facebook.

[58] ECJ 27.4.1994 – C-393/92, ECLI:EU:C:1994:171 mn. 42 – Almelo.

[59] ECJ 16.3.2000 – C-395/96 P, C-396/96 P, ECLI:EU:C:2000:132 mn. 44 – Compagnie Maritime Belge/Commission.

[60] See CFI 6.6.2002 – T-342/99, ECLI:EU:T:2002:146 mn. 56 et seq., 66 et seq. – Airtours/Commission.

[61] For more details see BBB AEUV Art. 102 mn. 44 et seq.

[62] For more details see BBB AEUV Art. 102 mn. 47 et seq.

[63] See e.g., ECJ 3.7.1991 – C-62/86, ECLI:EU:C:1991:286 – AKZO/Commission.

[64] See e.g., ECJ 14.11.1996 – C-333/94 P, ECLI:EU:C:1996:436 – Tetra Pak/Commission; CFI 17.9.2007 – T-201/04, ECLI:EU:T:2007:289 – Microsoft; GC 14.9.2022 – T-604/18, ECLI:EU:T:2022:541 – Google and Alphabet/Commission (Google Android).

[65] See e.g., ECJ 13.2.1979 – C-85/76, ECLI:EU:C:1979:36 – Hoffmann-La Roche/Commission; ECJ 9.11.1983 – C-322/81, ECLI:EU:C:1983:313 – Michelin/Commission.

unfair prices and conditions (such as price squeezing) or imposing supply and purchase restrictions ('refusal to deal') without any objective justification.[66] In addition, discrimination refers to the case when an undertaking directly or indirectly treats its customers, suppliers or competitors differently from similar undertakings without any objective justification.[67]
- exploitative abuses, such as excessive prices or terms and conditions (no. 2). This abuse refers to the conduct when a supplier or customer demands prices or other business terms that deviate from those that would most likely result from effective competition; in this context, particularly market practices of comparable undertakings in comparable markets with effective competition shall be taken into account.[68] A strict causal link between dominance and the abusive conduct is not required anymore for exploitative abuses.
- in addition, price or margin squeezes are addressed as a special case of exploitative abuse (no. 3). Typically, margin squeeze refers to cases when a dominant undertaking raises its wholesale prices so high that competitors cannot offer competitive retail prices.[69] The benchmark here is the undertaking's behaviour on comparable markets, not hypothetical competition. The differentiation might be objectively justified.
- access to essential facilities (no. 4). When a dominant undertaking refuses to supply another undertaking with a good or commercial service for adequate consideration, particularly to grant access to data, networks or other infrastructure facilities, provided that it is impossible for the other undertaking to operate on the upstream or downstream market for legal or factual reasons without the shared use of the infrastructure facilities, and the refusal threatens to eliminate effective competition on that market.[70] The refusal of the dominant undertaking might be objectively justified, for example, when it proves that shared use of the infrastructure facilities by another undertaking is not possible or not reasonable for operational (such as limited capacity) or legal reasons. In its recent decision 'Android Auto', the ECJ held that denying access to/interoperability with a digital platform developed by a dominant company to be used not only by itself, but also third parties, can constitute an abuse even if access to the relevant platform is not indispensable for the commercial operation of the company requesting access.[71]
- request for unjustified advantages ('tapping ban') (no. 5). For an abuse it might be sufficient to influence suppliers or customers without exerting pressure: a causal link between dominance and the abusive conduct is not required. In this regard, it is relevant whether there are given plausible reasons for the request and whether the advantage requested is proportionate to the grounds for the request.[72] Objectively unjustified commercial conditions can be, in particular, favours that are not performance related.

The list in § 19 sub. 2 GWB, Art. 102 sent. 2 TFEU of abusive practices is not exhaustive, 52
as denoted by the use of the term 'in particular' preceding it. Particularly, since the recent 'Towercast' decision of the Court of First Instance (CFI), which in principle recognises the

[66] Cf. e.g., ECJ 11.12.2008 – C-52/07, ECLI:EU:C:2008:703 – STIM; ECJ 25.11.2020 – C-372/19, ECLI:EU:C:2020:959 – SABAM.

[67] See e.g., ECJ 17.7.1997 – C-242/95, ECLI:EU:C:1997:376 – GT-Link/Danske Statsbaner; ECJ 24.10.2002 – C-82/01 P, ECLI:EU:C:2002:617 – Aéroports de Paris/Kommission.

[68] See e.g., ECJ 14.2.1978 – C-27/76, ECLI:EU:C:1978:22 – United Brands/Commission; ECJ 25.11.2020 – C-372/19, ECLI:EU:C:2020:959 – SABAM.

[69] See e.g., ECJ 17.2.2011 – C-52/09, ECLI:EU:C:2011:83 – Telia Sonera.

[70] See e.g., ECJ 26.11.1998 – C-7/97, ECLI:EU:C:1998:569 – Bronner; ECJ 6.4.1995 – C-241/91 P and C-242/91 P, ECLI:EU:C:1995:98 – Magill.

[71] ECJ 25.2.2025 – C-233/23, ECLI:EU:C:2025:110 – Android Auto.

[72] Cf. e.g., CFI 17.7.1998 – T-111/96, ECLI:EU:T:1998:183 – ITT Promedia/Commission.

abuse of dominance through a merger post the EJC's 'Continental Can' decision, market structure abuse has been revived.[73]

3. Recent Bundeskartellamt cases

53 In 2023 the BKartA initiated abuse of dominance proceedings against PayPal for its practices regarding surcharging rules and presentation in its user agreement that may foreclose competitors and restrict price competition.[74] Also in 2023, the BKartA conducted abuse proceedings in the food sector against Coca-Cola, particularly with regard to its rebate structure for food retailers and against Edeka in relation to the company's demands associated with the introduction of the Payback loyalty programme.[75]

54 In 2022 and 2023, with regard to general abuse control one focus of the BKartA was on the transport sector. In June 2023, the BKartA directed the German national railway company, Deutsche Bahn, to adjust certain practices and contractual clauses in relation to mobility platforms.[76] In 2024, the Düsseldorf Higher Regional Court largely confirmed the BKartA's ruling on abusive practices against Deutsche Bahn.[77] Moreover, in August 2022 the BKartA prohibited Lufthansa from terminating long-standing cooperation agreements (Special Prorate Agreements, or SPAs) with Condor, as such conduct would hinder Condor in competing on long-haul routes and thus infringe §§ 19, 20 GWB and Art. 102 TFEU.[78]

55 Moreover, in 2021 the BKartA closed abuse of dominance proceedings against Deutsche Post regarding its position in the delivery of addressed newspapers and magazines and its loyalty and exclusivity-based rebate system after the company modified its rebate system accordingly.[79]

56 Ultimately, the BKartA's prohibition decision against Facebook in 2019 was highly regarded in the area of the abuse of dominance.[80] The BKartA found an exploitative abuse in Facebook's practice of collecting and processing user data linked with data from different services, and for the first time, based exploitative abuse on a breach of the EU General Data Protection Regulation ('GDPR'). While the Düsseldorf Higher Regional Court dismissed the exploitative abuse claim, stating a lack of investigation into the terms

---

[73] ECJ 16.3.2023 – C-449/21, ECLI:EU:C:2023:207 – Towercast; ECJ 21.2.1973 – C-6/72, ECLI:EU:C:1973:22 – Continental Can.

[74] See BKartA, press release of 23 January 2023, available at <https://www.bundeskartellamt.de/SharedDocs/Meldung/EN/Pressemitteilungen/2023/23_01_2023_PayPal.html?nn=55030> (last accessed 21.5.2025).

[75] See BKartA, press release of 14.11.2023, available at <https://www.bundeskartellamt.de/SharedDocs/Meldung/EN/Pressemitteilungen/2023/14_11_2023_Cola.html?nn=55030> (last accessed 21.5.2025) and BKartA, Review of 2024 (→ fn. 7).

[76] See BKartA, press release of 28.6.2023, available at <https://www.bundeskartellamt.de/SharedDocs/Meldung/EN/Pressemitteilungen/2023/28_06_2023_FAQ_DB_Mobilitaet.pdf?__blob=publicationFile&v=3> (last accessed 21.5.2025).

[77] See BKartA, press release of 11.3.2024, available at: <https://www.bundeskartellamt.de/SharedDocs/Meldung/EN/AktuelleMeldungen/2024/11_03_2024_OLG_DB.html> (last accessed 21.5.2025).

[78] BKartA 29.8.2022 – B9-21/21, BeckRS 2022, 43567; also available (but only in German) at <https://www.bundeskartellamt.de/SharedDocs/Entscheidung/DE/Entscheidungen/Missbrauchsaufsicht/2022/B9-21-21.html> (last accessed 21.5.2025).

[79] BKartA, press release of 2.3.2021, available at <https://www.bundeskartellamt.de/SharedDocs/Meldung/EN/Pressemitteilungen/2021/02_03_2021_Pressepost.html?nn=55030> (last accessed 21.5.2025).

[80] BKartA 6.2.2019 – B6-22/16, BeckRS 2019, 4895, also available at <https://www.bundeskartellamt.de/SharedDocs/Entscheidung/EN/Entscheidungen/Missbrauchsaufsicht/2019/B6-22-16.pdf?__blob=publicationFile&v=1> (last accessed 21.5.2025).

of use in the event of functioning competition,[81] the Federal Court of Justice ruled that behavioural causality was not a necessary requirement for an infringement.[82] In addition to the Federal Court of Justice's decision in 2020, the ECJ confirmed the BKartA's position on matters of principle in 2023.[83]

In 2020, the BKartA opened new abuse of dominance proceedings against Facebook regarding the requirement of a Facebook account for the use of its Oculus virtual reality glasses and in 2021 expanded it under the new legal basis of § 19a GWB.[84] Ultimately, following abuse of dominance proceedings initiated in 2018 by the BKartA against Amazon and its German marketplace 'amazon.de', Amazon altered its worldwide terms and conditions for merchants in their favour.[85]

II. Abuse of paramount cross-market significance for competition across markets (§ 19a GWB)

§ 19a GWB establishes a new concept of market power and a proactive enforcement approach, which targets a specific group of undertakings operating digital platforms and multi-sided markets. 57

These undertakings may not currently be dominant but have the potential to become so due to their market position, resources and characteristics of the digital economy, such as network effects, data advantage and self-reinforcing effects resulting in market tipping. Thus, they may have the ability to expand into new markets, significantly influencing the business activities of third parties. While primarily addressing large gatekeepers and intermediaries such as the GAFA companies, smaller companies also might be caught by the provision, enabling the BKartA significant discretion. 58

§ 19a GWB operates as abuse control, allowing the BKartA to intervene preventively in markets that are not yet dominated. § 19a GWB does not directly prohibit conduct like the abuse of dominance in § 19 GWB, Art. 102 TFEU. But § 19a sub. 2 GWB enables the BKartA to prohibit conduct if it previously has determined that the undertaking has paramount cross-market significance through a declaratory order valid for five years. Hence, until the BKartA has issued two orders, one concerning the qualified addressees and the other concerning the conduct in question, no prohibition applies, and therefore, there is no risk for claims for injunctive relief or damages under civil law based on § 19a GWB. 59

§ 19a GWB and traditional abuse of dominance rules can be applied in parallel. The Regulation (EU) No. 2022/1925 on contestable and fair markets in the digital sector (Digital Markets Act, 'DMA') also aims to combat the power of market-dominant digital 60

---

[81] OLG Düsseldorf 26.8.2019 – VI-Kart 1/19 (V), BeckRS 2019, 18837. In March 2021, the OLG Düsseldorf has referred to the ECJ for a decision whether Facebook is abusing its dominant market position by unlawfully collecting and processing personal data (VI-Kart 2/19 (V)).

[82] BGH 23.6.2020 – KVR 69/19, GRUR 2020, 1318 – Facebook.

[83] ECJ 4.7.2023 – C-252/21, ECLI:EU:C:2023:537 = BeckEuRS 2023, 762357 – Meta Platforms and Others.

[84] For the time being, the BKartA does not raise any objections to the sale of the Quest 2 and Quest Pro glasses from Meta Platforms, Inc. (Meta) in Germany since, following the introduction of the Meta account, it is no longer necessary to log in with a Facebook account to use such glasses. See BKartA, case study of 23.11.2022, B6-55/20, available at <https://www.bundeskartellamt.de/SharedDocs/Entscheidung/EN/Fallberichte/Missbrauchsaufsicht/2022/B6-55-20.pdf?__blob=publicationFile&v=4> (last accessed 21.5.2025).

[85] See BKartA, case report of 17.7.2019, B2-88/18, available at <https://www.bundeskartellamt.de/SharedDocs/Entscheidung/EN/Fallberichte/Missbrauchsaufsicht/2019/B2-88-18.pdf?__blob=publicationFile&v=2> (last accessed 21.5.2025). The BKartA dropped its proceedings against Amazon on this basis.

companies and is applicable since 2 May 2023. The DMA overlaps in scope with § 19a GWB but is not congruent, particularly raising complex conflict questions in the future. The BKartA's orders pursuant to § 19a GWB may also prohibit practices beyond the DMA's scope, addressing even smaller platforms that do not meet the DMA's quantitative requirements.

1. Scope of application (§ 19a sub. 1 GWB)

61 The undertakings targeted pursuant to § 19a sub. 1 GWB do not need to be dominant in a specific market but must have paramount cross-market significance for competition across markets, which means that they must be active to a significant extent in multi-sided markets influenced by network effects, in which they have paramount cross-market significance for competition. For the assessment of paramount cross-market significance for competition across markets, the following non-cumulative criteria must be considered: market dominance, financial strength or access to other resources and inputs, vertical integration and activities on otherwise related markets, access to data relevant for competition, and relevance for third-party access to supply and sales markets and related influence on the business activities of third parties.

2. Intervention possibilities (§ 19a sub. 2 GWB)

62 § 19a sub. 2 GWB stipulates the conduct that can be prohibited for undertakings with paramount cross-market significance for competition across markets by the BKartA:

- self-preferencing when mediating access to supply and sales markets, in particular through preferential displaying or exclusively pre-installing its own offers (cf. EC's proceedings 'Google Shopping' and 'Google Android');
- restricting other undertakings' access to supply or sales markets where the undertakings' activities are of relevance for accessing such markets, in particular through the exclusive pre-installation or integration of the undertakings' own products or hindering other undertakings from advertising or reaching customers through other channels (cf. US lawsuit 'Apple v Epic Games');
- impeding competitors in adjacent markets in which the undertaking can rapidly expand its position even without being dominant (rolling up markets), in particular by tying and bundling;
- creating or appreciably raising barriers to market entry for other undertakings or impeding them in other ways by using certain data processing strategies, in particular by conditioning the use of one service upon the user's consent to the processing of data from other services of the undertaking or a third-party provider or by processing data relevant for competition received from other undertakings for purposes other than those necessary for the provision of its own services to these undertakings (cf. BKartA's 'Facebook' proceedings);
- restricting competition by refusing or impeding the interoperability of products or services or data portability;
- providing other undertakings with insufficient information about the scope, quality or success of the service rendered or commissioned, or otherwise making it more difficult for such undertakings to assess the value of this service; or
- demanding disproportionate benefits for handling the offers of another undertaking, in particular by demanding the transfer of data or rights not absolutely necessary for the purpose of presenting these offers or, by making the quality of the presentation of

these offers conditional upon the transfer of data or rights which are not reasonably required for this purpose.

Since there is no statutory prohibition, a subsequent second order of the BKartA is required to prohibit the conduct listed in → mn. 62. The BKartA can prohibit practices under § 19a sub. 2 GWB without having to prove any competitive harm. The decisive factor is based on whether the practices are objectively justified, which requires balancing the interests of free competition with those of the undertaking. The burden of proof for an objective justification of the respective conduct lies with the undertaking. 63

3. Recent cases

Since the enforcement powers of § 19a GWB came into effect, the BKartA has taken swift action against digital platforms, particularly the GAFAM companies. The BKartA concluded proceedings against Alphabet/Google (2020/2021), Meta/Facebook (2021/2022), Amazon (2022), Apple (2023) and Microsoft (2024), which have been found to have significant market power for competition across markets, resulting in the first declaratory orders issued under § 19a GWB.[86] 64

Moreover, the BKartA ended its proceedings against Alphabet/Google with regard to its data processing terms, particularly its ability to combine and process data from various services in October 2023 with binding commitments from Google.[87] The BKartA also ended its proceedings against Alphabet/Google with regard to Google Automotive Services and Google Maps Platform with binding commitments in April 2025.[88] In February 2025, the BKartA issued its preliminary legal assessment of Apple's 'App Tracking Transparency Framework' ('ATTF').[89] 65

III. Abuse of relative or superior market power (§ 20 GWB)

§ 20 GWB deals with exclusionary and discriminatory conduct by undertakings with relative or superior market power towards undertakings dependent on them, below the dominance threshold. The GWB Digitisation Act has extended the concept of relative market power to all undertakings that depend on their trading partners beyond the previous focus on small- or medium-sized undertakings. 66

Under § 20 GWB, dependency mainly refers to vertical relationships in which undertakings are dependent on other undertakings as suppliers or purchasers of goods or com- 67

[86] BKartA 30.12.2021 – B7-61/21, BeckRS 2021, 62514 – Alphabet/Google, confirmed as final by the court; BKartA 2.5.2022 – B6-27/21, BeckRS 2022, 47486 – Meta/Facebook, confirmed as final by the court; BKartA 5.7.2022 – B2-55/21, GRUR-RS 2022, 47485 – Amazon, confirmed by the Federal Court of Justice; BKartA 3.4.2023 – B9-67/21, GRUR-RS 2023, 9430 – Apple, confirmed by the Federal Court of Justice; BKartA 27.9.2024 – B6-26/23, BeckRS 2024, 34355 – Microsoft, confirmed as final by the court.

[87] BKartA, press release of 5.10.2023, available at <https://www.bundeskartellamt.de/SharedDocs/Entscheidung/EN/Entscheidungen/Missbrauchsaufsicht/2023/B7-70-21.pdf?__blob=publicationFile&v=3> (last accessed 21.5.2025). The BKartA is of the opinion that users were not given sufficient choice as to whether and to what extent they consent to the far-reaching processing of their data across services.

[88] BKartA, press release of 9.4.2025, available at <https://www.bundeskartellamt.de/SharedDocs/Meldung/EN/Pressemitteilungen/2025/04_09_2025_GAS_GMP.html?nn=52004> (last accessed 21.5.2025). The BKartA argues that both customers and competitors of Google were too severely restricted when interacting with those services.

[89] BKartA, press release of 13.2.2025, available at <https://www.bundeskartellamt.de/SharedDocs/Meldung/EN/Pressemitteilungen/2025/02_13_2025_ATTF.html?nn=52004> (last accessed 21.5.2025). In the BKartA's view, the ATTF may be prohibited under the control abuse provisions.

mercial services in such a way that sufficient and reasonable possibilities for switching to third parties do not exist, and there is a significant imbalance between the power of such undertakings and the countervailing power of other undertakings (relative market power), or horizontal relationships in which undertakings with superior market power dominate over small- or medium-sized competitors (superior market power).[90] Dependency can also apply to intermediaries on multi-sided markets to the extent that other undertakings are dependent on their intermediary services for accessing supply and sales markets in such a way that sufficient and reasonable alternatives do not exist (intermediation power).[91] Furthermore, dependency may arise if an undertaking relies on access to data controlled by another undertaking in order to carry out its own activities, even if such data have not yet been commercially traded (data dependency).[92]

68 § 20 GWB extends the prohibition of discrimination, exclusionary conduct and requesting benefits if such conduct lacks objective justification to the constellations referred to. Moreover, § 20 sub. 3 GWB provides examples of exclusionary conduct that undertakings with superior market power may exhibit, including, for example, not just occasionally offering goods or commercial services below cost price and implementing a cost-price squeeze.

69 Additionally, the GWB Digitisation Act introduced a new form of abusive conduct in relation to gatekeepers and digital intermediaries with superior market power, which unfairly impedes the independent attainment of network effects by competitors and in this way creates a serious risk of significantly restricting competition on the merits (§ 20 sub. 3a GWB). This new provision allows the BKartA to intervene to prevent market tipping and was first applied in a decision of 2021 by the Berlin District Court involving a market-leading online real estate platform.[93]

D. Public and private enforcement

I. Proceedings and intervention power

70 The BKartA can initiate investigations (*ex officio*) in cases of cartel infringements and or infringements of the abuse of dominance, relative and superior market power.[94] However, in practice, investigations are often triggered by leniency applications from involved parties (in cases of cartel infringements) or complaints from third parties, such as competitors, customers or suppliers who may use whistleblower lines.

1. Administrative proceedings

71 Administrative proceedings are used by the BKartA to enforce orders requiring undertakings to cease their infringements, see § 32 sub. 1 GWB, and for the European Commission see Art. 7 para. 1 Regulation (EC) No. 1/2003. In implementation of the Directive

---

[90] For more details see Bechtold/Bosch GWB § 20 mn. 11 et seq.

[91] For more details see Bechtold/Bosch GWB § 20 mn. 12b.

[92] For more details see Bechtold/Bosch GWB § 20 mn. 22a et seq.

[93] LG Berlin 8.4.2021 – 16 O 73/21 Kart, NZKart 2021, 463 mn. 37 et seqq. – Immobilien-Plattform, confirmed by KG Berlin 11.2.2022 – U 4/21 Kart, NZKart 2022, 215 mn. 12 – Tipping Gefahr.

[94] In the following, the explanations for the abuse of dominance (§ 19 GWB) also apply to the abuse of relative and superior market power (§ 20 GWB).

(EU) No. 2019/1 ('ECN+ Directive'), Germany revised the provisions of its administrative proceedings under §§ 54-62 GWB. The BKartA can issue orders under § 61 GWB in these proceedings, which can involve prohibition decisions and interim measures (§§ 32, 32a GWB), commitments (structural and behavioural) (§ 32b GWB), the disgorgement of benefits (§ 34 GWB) and the withdrawal of exemption (§ 32d GWB) against undertakings and associations of undertakings.

In Germany, abuse of dominance cases – in contrast to cartel cases – are prosecuted in administrative proceedings, which do not result in a regulatory fine as an ultimate sanction. Although regulatory fine proceedings including regulatory fines would be possible in this area under the legal framework, the BKartA typically either finds an infringement and issues a cease and desist decision (§ 32 GWB), or issues a commitment decision (§ 32b GWB), which are meant to enforce voluntary commitments without determining whether an infringement occurred, or closes proceedings due to lack of evidence. 72

§ 32a GWB further empowers the BKartA to impose interim measures in cases of urgent cartel, abuse of dominance or paramount cross-market significance for competition across markets cases. 73

2. Regulatory fine proceedings

The outlined administrative proceedings have to be distinguished from regulatory fine proceedings, which are governed by §§ 81-86 GWB. Regulatory fine proceedings often pertain very severe infringements (known as 'hardcore' infringements) and allow the BKartA to impose regulatory fines against undertakings, associations of undertakings and individuals pursuant to § 81 GWB. Additionally, under the new § 19a GWB, undertakings can be fined if they fail to comply with enforceable prohibition decisions issued based on § 19a sub. 2 and § 81 sub. 2 no. 2a GWB. The BKartA can use the powers available to prosecutors in criminal proceedings and those stipulated in the GWB. 74

3. Investigative powers

The BKartA has the authority to conduct various investigative activities in both administrative and regulatory fine proceedings. These powers include informal requests for information, mandatory requests for documents and information (with certain protections against self-incrimination), unannounced searches at corporate and residential premises (known as 'dawn raids'), and the scrutiny and confiscation of business documents, as well as the copying of data stored in electronic devices. 75

4. Right to be heard

Undertakings under investigation have the right to be heard at all stages of an investigation (§ 56 sub. 1 GWB). Typically, the BKartA will provide a statement of objections to which a response can be given before issuing a decision. The involved parties can request access to the files as necessary for the defence of their legal interests (§ 56 sub. 3 GWB). 76

5. Dawn raids

After a rather less-active phase of unannounced searches (dawn raids) during the Covid-19 pandemic (including only two dawn raids each in 2020 and 2021), the BKartA is 77 carrying out again an increased number of dawn raids in cartel cases.[95] Dawn raids usually require a court warrant, but in cases of imminent danger, searches are conducted even without a court warrant. Searches are conducted either at corporate premises or private premises. The BKartA can examine and seize or copy business documents and can copy entire hard drives and data stores in electronic devices. In the event of an unannounced search, employees should know exactly how to behave, such as to immediately inform the legal department or a legal representative, which should review the search warrant and stay in contact with the investigating BKartA officials, and to copy all seized documents and record the documents of which copies are made. Competition law compliance guidelines and competition law compliance trainings for employees may provide helpful guidance in the event of a dawn raid. Moreover, absolute secrecy should be maintained towards third parties about the search.

78 Since the GWB Digitisation Act and in implementation of the ECN+ Directive, § 59b sub. 3 no. 3 GWB provides for e.g. an obligation of the representatives or employees to co-operate in assisting the BKartA in the investigation of the facts (such as disclosure of information enabling access to evidence, explanations on facts or documents that might be connected to the subject matter and purpose of the search), the infringement of which can be fined, § 81 sub. 2 no. 11 GWB.

6. Settlement proceedings

79 The BKartA can offer informal settlement proceedings in which the undertakings, associations of undertakings and individuals can achieve an additional reduction of the regulatory fine of up to 10 % if they admit the facts they are accused of and accept the regulatory fine. Moreover, settlement proceedings can lead to a more concise decision, which can have advantages for potentially following claims for damages.

7. Cooperation with other authorities

80 The European Competition Network ('ECN') provides the setting for cooperation between the BKartA, other national competition authorities of EU Member States ('NCA') and the European Commission which includes, for example, the exchange of information and evidence. The cooperation possibilities between the BKartA and other NCAs have expanded pursuant to the ECN+ Directive and its implementation to the GWB. For example, the BKartA may assist other NCAs with their searches, interviews, the notification of preliminary objections and other documents, as well as the enforcement of decisions which impose regulatory fines in the German territory and vice versa. Moreover, the BKartA is represented in the International Competition Network ('ICN').

8. Investigation of violations of the Digital Markets Act (DMA)

81 Following the implementation of the 11th amendment to the GWB, the BKartA has been endowed with the authority to probe into potential infractions of Art. 5, 6, and 7 DMA by gatekeepers that have already been designated, § 32g GWB. The stipulations of the DMA are immediately effective and enforceable; adherence to them necessitates

[95] In 2023, the BKartA carried out a total of eleven dawn raids, three of which in the context of providing official assistance to other authorities (see BKartA, Review of 2024, press release of 19 December 2024, available at <https://www.bundeskartellamt.de/SharedDocs/Meldung/EN/Pressemitteilungen/2024/19_12_2024_Jahresr%C3%BCckblick.html?nn=55030> (last accessed 21.5.2025). In the peak years 2013 to 2016, there have been 15 to 18 dawn raids per year.

oversight by competition authorities. Consequently, the European Commission, which holds exclusive responsibility for the enforcement of the DMA, may benefit from the investigative capabilities bestowed upon national competition authorities.

II. Sanctions

1. Regulatory fines

In order to enforce infringements of competition law, primarily with regard to cartel infringements, the BKartA imposes regulatory fines in regulatory fine proceedings. Due to the GWB Digitisation Act, which implemented the ECN+ Directive, provisions on regulatory fines including a new turnover-based regulatory fine framework for certain infringements, and the codification of differentiated regulatory fine assessment criteria have been codified in §§ 81-81g GWB, while provisions on regulatory fine proceedings have been codified in §§ 82-86 GWB.[96] **82**

Regulatory fines for undertakings and associations of undertakings can range up to 10 % of the worldwide group turnover of the preceding business year, § 81c sub. 2 GWB.[97] This 10 % limit was interpreted by the Federal Court of Justice (*Bundesgerichtshof*, 'BGH') in its decision 'Grauzementkartell' in 2013 as a constitutionally compatible upper limit for regulatory fines, which contradicts the EU interpretation of a cap.[98] Following this decision, the BKartA issued guidelines for the imposition of regulatory fines (*Bußgeldleitlinien*) in 2013, recently updated by new guidelines issued in October 2021 ('BKartA's Fining Guidelines').[99] **83**

The BKartA calculates the regulatory fine based on a number of factors, including the gravity and duration of the infringement, the size of the market affected, the role of the undertaking during the infringement period, the degree of intent or negligence, the company's turnover, and any mitigating or aggravating factors.[100] Mitigating factors can include cooperation with the investigation or compliance efforts before – particularly if this enables the detection of the infringement – and also after the discovery of the **84**

[96] Although German competition law already complied with essential requirements of the ECN+ Directive, the following adjustments need to be made: expansion and alignment of the investigative powers of the German antitrust authorities; expansion of the sanctions regime for antitrust infringements, in particular for infringements of certain procedural rules and for infringements by associations of undertakings; strengthening of the procedural position of the antitrust authority in regulatory fine proceedings; and statutory anchoring of the leniency programme (BT-Drs. 19/23492, 56). In addition, the ECN+ Directive through cooperation with other national competition authorities of EU members states facilitates the BKartA to notify its decision to, and enforce payments of regulatory fines against undertakings, associations of undertakings and individuals without presence in Germany.

[97] The BKartA can estimate the amount of total turnover – which comprises the worldwide turnover of all natural persons and legal entities operating as an economic unit – for determining the statutory upper limit (§ 81c (5) second sentence GWB), particularly on the basis of consolidated (or provisional) annual financial statements.

[98] BGH 26.2.2013 – KRB 20/12, NZKart 2013, 195 mn. 50 et seq. – Grauzementkartell; cf. for the EU: ECJ 28.6.2005 – C-189/02 P and others, ECLI:EU:C:2005:408 – Dansk Rorindustri/Commission.

[99] BKartA, Guidelines for the Setting of Fines in Cartel Administrative Offence Proceedings ('BKartA's Fining Guidelines'), 11 October 2021, available at <https://www.bundeskartellamt.de/SharedDocs/Publikation/EN/Leitlinien/Guidelines_setting_fines_Oct_2021.pdf?__blob=publicationFile&v=1> (last accessed 21.5.2025).

[100] See BKartA's Fining Guidelines (→ fn. 98), mn. 14; § 81d GWB.

infringement (§ 81d sub. 1 sent. 2 no. 4 and no. 5 GWB) while aggravating factors can include previous violations or obstruction of the investigation.[101]

85 When it comes to calculating regulatory fines for associations of undertakings, generally the same rules apply as for individual undertakings. However, following the GWB Digitisation Act, the calculation base for associations of undertakings has expanded, as stipulated in §§ 81c sub. 4 and 81b sub. 2 and 3 GWB. If members of the association actively participated in the illegal activity, regulatory fines can now reach up to 10 % of the total turnover of all association members involved in that particular market and are no longer limited to the associations' turnover. However, there are exceptions for members who have already been fined or granted immunity from regulatory fines. In contrast to EU regulatory fine proceedings, German regulatory fine proceedings can be directed not only against undertakings and associations of undertakings, but also against certain individuals. Individuals, which legally represent the undertaking or are in managerial positions (including directors, officers and also certain senior employees) can be fined, either for being actively involved in the infringement or for failing to supervise and prevent infringements of lower-ranking employees, § 130 OWiG. Individuals can be fined up to 1 million EUR, the details depending on the quality of the infringement and the extent of the individual involvement, such as active participation or failure to supervise, as well as the financial circumstances, § 81c sub. 1 GWB and § 17 sub. 3 OWiG.

86 § 81a sub. 1 GWB provides that, pursuant to § 30 sub. 1 OWiG, the liability for regulatory fines is generally borne by the offending undertaking or the controlling parent company whose executive bodies or managers have committed the infringement themselves or through a breach of their supervisory duties, even if no proceedings are brought against an individual.

87 Furthermore, a parent company can be subject to regulatory fines for the illegal conduct of its subsidiary. To be considered liable in this regard, the parent company must be able to exercise a decisive role during the infringement period, which can occur not only in the case of wholly owned subsidiaries, but also in 50/50 joint ventures. The regulatory fine calculation is based on the group's total revenues. As a result, the parent company and its subsidiaries can be jointly and severally liable for regulatory fines imposed by the BKartA. Additionally, legal or economic successors can be fined under § 81a sub. 2 and 3 GWB.[102]

88 The regulatory fine imposed by the BKartA can be subject to review by the Higher Regional Court of Düsseldorf, which can reduce, uphold or increase the regulatory fine. If the company disagrees with the court's decision, it may appeal to the Federal Court of Justice. Since the BKartA's Fining Guidelines are not binding for courts, the latter can assess its own regulatory fines by balancing all circumstances of the case resulting in a higher regulatory fine up to 10 % of the worldwide group turnover of the undertaking concerned as the upper limit.[103] Thus, if addressees of an administrative order imposing a regulatory fine disagree with the amount determined by the BKartA, they might take a risk of facing an even higher regulatory fine on appeal.

89 The following table provides a selected overview of the maximum regulatory fines imposed by the BKartA for cartel infringements that have become final.[104]

---

[101] See BKartA's Fining Guidelines (→ fn. 98), Re: para. 14 Note 3; § 81d GWB. However, compliance efforts before the infringement cannot be taken into account if a person responsible for the management (such as a managing directors or a board member) was involved in the infringement.

[102] See e.g., ECJ 14.3.2019 – C-724/17, ECLI:EU:C:2019:204 – Skanska i.a.

[103] See e.g., OLG Düsseldorf 12.10.2017 – 2 Kart 1/17 (Owi), NZKart 2019, 59 – Tapetenkartell; confirmed by BGH 21.5.2019 – KRB 93/18, NZKart 2019, 562 – Tapetenkartell.

[104] Rounded figures. Table found in BKartA, Annual Report 2024/2025, p. 21 (→ fn. 1).

Year	Case	Total regulatory fines imposed in EUR
2024	Broadband devices	16 million
2023	Industrial construction services	3 million
2022	Expansion joints for bridges	7 million
2021	Steel forging companies	35 million
2020	Aluminium forging companies	23 million
2020	Plant protection products	158 million
2019	Quarto plates/Heavy plates	646 million
2018	Special steel	292 million
2014	Beer	318 million
2014	Sausage	80 million
2014	Sugar	282 million
2009	Coffee	163 million

2. Exclusion from public tenders

In addition, infringements of § 1 GWB, Art. 101 TFEU can result in exclusion from **90**
public award procedures under § 124 sub. 1 no. 4 GWB. This exclusion can last for up to three years from the relevant incident, according to § 126 no. 2 GWB.[105] The BKartA's and the European Commission's investigations of potential infringements can also lead to exclusion.

Contracting authorities are able to electronically access the BKartA's Competition **91**
Register (*Wettbewerbsregister*) to determine if a company may or must be excluded from the award process on account of specific economic offences, such as engaging in cartel practices. Since 2022, certain contract values even mandate contracting authorities to conduct such queries.

3. Criminal penalties

Since corporate criminal liability does not exist in Germany, only individuals who **92**
engage in anti-competitive agreements that are covered by bid rigging under § 298 StGB are liable for criminal penalties (for the principles of criminal liability see → Ch. 2).

III. Leniency programme

The BKartA has the ability to provide immunity or a reduction of regulatory fines to **93**
individuals, undertakings and associations of undertakings if they co-operate with the BKartA in uncovering cartels ('leniency'). On European level, the European Commission

105 In this context, the three-year time limit applies from the date of the decision in which the competent authority sanctioned the offending behaviour, rather than the beginning of participation in the cartel. ECJ 24.10.2018 – C-124/17, ECLI:EU:C:2018:855 – Vossloh Laeis GmbH/Stadtwerke München GmbH – on the interpretation of Art. 57 para. 4 lit. d) Regulation (EU) 2014/24, which corresponds functionally to § 124 sub. 1 no. 4 GWB.

also offers a leniency programme. In recent years, leniency applications have decreased both in Germany and the EU. In Germany, after a peak of 76 applications in 2015, only 17 were submitted in 2024.[106] This decline may be attributed to the implementation of a more decent compliance system, the risks associated with regulatory fines and tender procedures, and, most importantly, the increased threat of civil damages claims due to the implementation of the Directive 2014/104/EU ('Damages Directive') in 2017.

94 The rules for the leniency programme in cartel proceedings, including the standards set out for the reduction of regulatory fines as specified in Art. 17–23 ECN+ Directive, are stipulated in §§ 81h–81n GWB. In 2021, the BKartA published leniency guidelines ('Guidelines on the Leniency Programme'), which provide general administrative principles for the exercise of discretionary powers and the conduct of the leniency procedure.[107]

1. Scope of application

95 The leniency programme applies only to horizontal restraints of competition between actual or potential competitors in accordance with § 1 GWB, Art. 101 TFEU. However, the BKartA can also apply similar measures to vertical infringements of § 1 GWB, Art. 101 TFEU as stipulated in § 81d sub. 1 sent. 2 no. 5 GWB and § 17 sub. 3 OWiG. In the past, there have been cases in which the BKartA also granted regulatory fine reductions to those involved in vertical infringements who co-operated with the BKartA.[108] However, the immunity provided by the leniency programme does not extend to criminal penalties, such as those resulting for individuals from bid rigging, which is a criminal offence under § 298 StGB (→ mn. 92 seqq.). Since German law does not provide for corporate criminal liability, individuals are prosecuted by law enforcement authorities, while companies are prosecuted by competition authorities who coordinate their investigative efforts under § 82 GWB in these cases. Even if a granted immunity in cartel proceedings does not extend to criminal prosecution, the cooperation of the individual in the cartel proceedings must also be taken into account in such proceedings by way of not imposing or mitigating the penalty.[109]

[106] BKartA, Activity Report 2019/2020, p. 39; BKartA, Review of 2024, press release of 19.12.1024, available at https://www.bundeskartellamt.de/SharedDocs/Meldung/EN/Pressemitteilungen/2024/19_12_2024_Jahresr%C3%BCckblick.html?nn=55030 (last accessed 21.5.2025). European Commission: O. Dominte, D. Serban & A.M. Dima – 'Cartels in EU: Study on the Effectiveness of Leniency Policy', 8 Mgt. & Mkt. 529 (2013).

[107] BKartA, Notice No. 14/2021 on General Administrative Principles relating to the Exercise of Discretionary Powers in the Conduct of the Procedure for and Application of the Leniency Regime in accordance with §§ 81h to 81n GWB ('Guidelines on the Leniency Programme'), available at https://www.bundeskartellamt.de/SharedDocs/Publikation/EN/Leitlinien/Leniency_Guidelines_08_2021.pdf?__blob=publicationFile&v=6 (last accessed: 21.5.2025).

[108] For example, in the following decisions, the BKartA also took into account comprehensive cooperation and the settlement of proceedings in the case of vertical agreements when setting regulatory fines: decision against Bose on vertical price fixing (consumer electronics), BKartA 11.11.2021 – B10-23/20, case summary available at <https://www.bundeskartellamt.de/SharedDocs/Entscheidung/EN/Fallberichte/Kartellverbot/2021/B10-23-20.pdf?__blob=publicationFile&v=2> (last accessed: 4.6.2025); decision against Fond on vertical price fixing (school backpacks and school bags), BKartA 16.7.2021 – B10-26/20, case summary available at <https://www.bundeskartellamt.de/SharedDocs/Entscheidung/EN/Fallberichte/Kartellverbot/2021/B10-26-29_B2-130-18.pdf?__blob=publicationFile&v=2> (last accessed: 4.6.2025). See also BKartA, case report of decisions of 16.6.2015, 30.12.2015, 28.4.2016 and 2.12.2016 – B10-20/15, p. 2 (distribution of beer products through food retailing), available at <https://www.bundeskartellamt.de/SharedDocs/Entscheidung/EN/Fallberichte/Kartellverbot/2016/B10-20-15.html> (last accessed: 7.7.2025).

[109] This principle is stipulated in Art. 23 para. 2 and 3 of the ECN+ Directive.

The leniency application, when submitted for an undertaking, applies to all legal persons or associations of persons that constitute the undertaking at the time when the application is filed, as well as their current and former directors, managers and members of staff, based on § 81i sub. 2 sent. 1 and 2 GWB. It is important to note that the leniency application only benefits those who comply with the general leniency conditions stated in § 81j GWB. It is unclear from the statutory provisions whether an individual's leniency application would also benefit the associated undertakings or groups of undertakings, but it is unlikely to be accepted. **96**

2. Leniency requirements

In this context, it is important to differentiate between the following scenarios: **97**

- principally, a participant in a cartel is to be granted immunity from regulatory fines if it is the first to submit evidence that enables the BKartA in obtaining a search warrant for the first time, according to § 81k sub. 1 GWB. If the BKartA already has the ability to obtain a search warrant, and the evidence provided allows to prove the offence for the first time and the applicant is the first to apply for leniency, it is standard practice to grant immunity from regulatory fines under § 81k sub. 2 GWB.
- additionally, the BKartA has the discretion to reduce regulatory fines upon application if the applicant co-operates fully and submits evidence which, relative to the information and evidence already available to the BKartA, represents significant added value, as stipulated in § 81l GWB.

In order to receive full immunity or a reduction of regulatory fines, the applicant must fully disclose its participation in the cartel and terminate its participation immediately after submitting the application unless otherwise requested by the BKartA. The applicant must also co-operate fully by providing all accessible information, responding to requests for information, making sure supervisory and management bodies and other employees are available for questioning, not destroying or falsifying evidence, and not disclosing the filing or its content to third parties, § 81j sub. 1 no. 1-3 GWB.[110] From a practical point of view, the ability to provide information depends primarily on securing the electronic data of the requesting company. If the applicant has coerced others to participate in or remain in the cartel, immunity from regulatory fines will not be granted, § 81k sub. 3 GWB. **98**

3. Leniency proceedings

Leniency proceedings can be initiated by contacting the BKartA's Special Unit for Combating Cartels (*Sonderkommission Kartellbekämpfung*, SKK) or one of the Decision Divisions responsible for prosecuting cartels. Moreover, BKartA staff can accept leniency applications during a search. If the applicant meets the requirements for full immunity, the BKartA, upon request, issues an assurance that immunity will be granted conditional on the applicant's compliance with cooperation obligations. The decision on a reduction is communicated in the order imposing the regulatory fine. **99**

The European Commission also provides a leniency programme that allows companies to achieve immunity or a substantial reduction of regulatory fines by handing over inside evidence of cartels. In case an application for leniency to the European Commission covers more than three EU Member States as affected territories, the BKartA accepts a **100**

[110] The two latter requirements apply accordingly also during the time when the leniency applicant contemplated the making of a leniency application (except for disclosure to other competition authorities), § 81j sub. 1 no. 4 GWB.

summary application relating to the same cartel, but can require more information if, for example, this is necessary for the delineation or allocation of the case, § 81n GWB.

a) Extent of reduction

101 The extent of reduction in regulatory fines is determined on the added value of information provided by the applicant. This value is oriented to what the authority has already discovered itself or through the cooperation of other participants and the timing of the leniency application, § 81l sub. 2 GWB. The regulatory fine can be reduced by up to 50 %. In the case of multiple applicants, the order is based on timing of request and added value. The second applicant can be granted a discount of up to 50 %, the third applicant a discount of up to 30 % and each further applicant a discount of up to 20 % depending on the then-remaining possible added value.[111] The leniency programme allows subsequent applicants to step into the position of the previous applicant if the latter does not provide sufficient information.

102 A leniency application can be filed until the BKartA reaches its final decision, but the earlier the application, the better the chances of obtaining a greater reduction in regulatory fines.

b) Marker requirements

103 Leniency can only be granted upon application. However, it remains possible to declare the willingness to co-operate ('marker') securing a place in the queue for leniency, which persists until the submission of the full leniency application, § 81m GWB.

104 A marker requires minimal information, including the applicant's name and address, names of other cartel participants, products and territories affected, duration and nature of the offence, and a list of competition authorities receiving or having received leniency applications. The BKartA specifies a period within which the applicant must finalise its leniency application, regularly no more than eight weeks.[112]

c) Whistleblowing system

105 The BKartA provides a standardised whistleblowing system to enable anonymous tip-offs, as leniency applications have declined in recent years.[113] Also, inside knowledge or suspicion of a cartel may be reported anonymously to the European Commission via a whistleblower tool.[114]

IV. Private enforcement

106 In German civil courts, damages claims resulting from infringements of competition law, such as cartels or abuses of dominance, can be brought under §§ 33a sub. 1, 33 sub. 1 GWB. In recent years, there has been a significant increase in cartel infringements related follow-on damage litigation. Germany is now one of the most important jurisdictions in the EU for follow-on cartel damages claims resulting from cartel infringements. Particularly, the 9th amendment to the GWB in 2017, which implemented the Damages

---

[111] Cf. BKartA, Guidelines on the Leniency Programme (→ fn. 106), mn. 9.

[112] BKartA, Guidelines on the Leniency Programme (→ fn. 106), mn. 17.

[113] The BKartA's whistleblowing system is available at https://www.bkms-system.net/bkwebanon/report/channels?id=bkarta&language=eng (last accessed 21.5.2025).

[114] The European Commission's whistleblower Communication Tool is available at https://competition-policy.ec.europa.eu/cartels/whistle-blower_en, last accessed 21.5.2025.

Directive, and the plaintiff-friendly case law of the German Federal Court of Justice in recent years have contributed to the rise in lawsuits in Germany. In 2021 alone, there were 480 pending truck cases.[115]

In contrast to cartel damages claims, abuse of dominance claims are frequently brought on a stand-alone basis and do not necessarily follow an investigation and decision by the BKartA. In these cases, plaintiffs typically seek not just damages but are aiming to enforce certain conduct by the potential infringer, such as supply actions, to provide access to a distribution system or infrastructure or to continue contractual obligations. **107**

1. Binding effects of cartel infringement decisions

With regards to follow-on actions, German law provides for a binding effect for final decisions of the European Commission, the BKartA, or any other national competition authority in an EU Member State finding an infringement of competition law or the court pursuant to § 33b GWB.[116] The binding effect relates solely to the determination of the infringement, including the duration of the infringement.[117] The interpretation of an administrative order imposing a regulatory fine of the Commission with respect to the products concerned can be subject of questions referred to the European Court of Justice.[118] All other requirements, particularly regarding the causality of the damage and the quantification of the damage, need to be established subject to the standard rules on the burden of proof in German court proceedings. **108**

2. Disclosure

The disclosure provisions in Art. 5 and 6 para. 6 of the Damages Directive have been implemented with § 33g GWB.[119] § 33g GWB provides for civil law claims upon the disclosure of evidence and the provision of information, which are linked to the holding of evidence and information relevant for the assertion of a claim for damages. However, leniency statements and settlement submissions are not accessible to the disclosure claim, § 33g sub. 4 GWB. The defendant is also able to claim for disclosure of evidence needed to prove a pass-on defence under § 33g sub. 2 GWB. **109**

In a recent decision, the German Federal Court of Justice criticised overly high disclosure requirements and aims to enable the disclosure of confidential European Commission's decisions if the core of facts is accessible to evidence and it cannot be ruled out that the redacted information is likely to provide evidence of this.[120] However, not many claims for disclosure have been granted in Germany yet.[121] **110**

---

[115] See BKartA, Annual Report 2021/2022, p. 21, available https://www.bundeskartellamt.de/SharedDocs/Publikation/EN/Jahresbericht/Jahresbericht_2021-2022.pdf?__blob=publicationFile&v=3 (last accessed 21.5.2025.

[116] Binding effect can arise from final decisions of the European Commission, the BKartA, the German regional cartel authorities or the competition authorities of other EU Member States. The provision also applies to decisions taken by a court in another EU Member State acting as a competition authority and judicial decisions on appeals against the decisions of competition authorities.

[117] BGH 12.7.2016 – KZR 25/14, NJW 2016, 3527 – Lottoblock II.

[118] See ECJ 1.8.2022 – C-588/20, ECLI:EU:C:2022:607 – Daimler.

[119] § 33g GWB applies to all claims for damages on which an appeal was filed after 26 December 2016, § 186 sub. 4 GWB.

[120] BGH 28.6.2022 – KZR 46/20, NZKart 2022, 641 mn. 71 – Stahl-Strahlmittel.

[121] See, e.g., before § 33g GWB came into force, the LG Hannover 17.12.2020 – 13 O 265/20, NZKart 2021, 127 – Altbatterien-Kartell, had affirmed a claim to the disclosure of the confidential decision of the Commission regarding the battery recycling cartel. In other cases, the claim for the disclosure of (mostly contract) documents was rejected because the plaintiffs no longer had them at their disposal through their

3. statute of limitation periods

111 Statute of limitation periods are governed by § 33h GWB.[122] Infringements of the prohibition of agreements restricting competition and abuses of dominance are subject to a regular statute of limitation period of five years, which is dependent on knowledge (§ 33h sub. 1 and 2 GWB). More precisely, this statute of limitation period begins to run with the end of the calendar year in which the claim arose and the plaintiff obtained knowledge, or should have obtained knowledge without gross negligence, of the circumstances giving rise to the claim and of the fact that these constitute an infringement under § 33 sub. 1 GWB, as well as of the identity of the infringer and the infringement giving rise to the claim has ceased. In general, such claims can become statute-barred five years after the publication of the competition authority's decision. Moreover, irrespective of any knowledge or grossly negligent ignorance of the circumstances, claims under §§ 33 sub. 1 GWB and 33a sub. 1 GWB become statute-barred ten years following the date on which the claim arose and the infringement ceased (§ 33h sub. 3 GWB). However, the statute of limitation period can be suspended for the period of the competition authority's proceedings (§ 33h sub. 6 GWB).

4. Additional characteristics of cartel damage cases

a) Rebuttable presumptions

112 German competition law provides for two rebuttable presumptions in § 33a sub. 2 GWB. The first presumption is that a cartel results in harm, and the second presumption is that legal transactions with cartel participants regarding goods and services falling within the scope of the cartel in terms of product type, time period and geographic area were covered by that cartel.[123] However, the presumptions do not affect the amount of damages. The German Federal Court of Justice recognises the presumption of cartel-related damage in favour of buyers of potentially cartel-affected products based on a rule of experience.[124] In response to the 'Otis' ruling of the European Court of Justice, the German Federal Court of Justice has made it easier for courts to determine cartel involvement in their fact-finding process.[125]

b) Calculation of damages

113 The calculation of damages and the underlying data have become increasingly important in cartel damages proceedings. Although § 287 ZPO simplifies the procedures, the assistance of external economic expert witnesses is usually required to calculate the amount of damages. In most cases, an economic expert witness is called upon by the parties and the court for evidence.

own fault and, therefore, there was no information asymmetry to be compensated, see e.g., LG München 27.3.2020 – 37 O 18471/18, BeckRS 2021, 2231; LG München 19.2.2021 – 37 O 10526/17, NZKart 2021, 245 – LKW-Kartell (Spanien).

[122] § 33h GWB is also applicable to claims, if these arose before 27.12.2016 and were not time-barred on 9 June 2017 (§ 186 sub. 3 GWB).

[123] This provision only applies to claims that arose after 26 December 2016, § 186 sub. 3 GWB.

[124] See BGH 13.4.2021 – KZR 19/20, EuZW 2021, 988 – Lkw-Kartell II; BGH 11.12.2018 – KZR 26/17, NJW 2019, 661 – Schienen-Kartell I; BGH 28.1.2020 – KZR 24/17, NJW 2020, 1430 – Schienen-Kartell II; BGH 23.9.2020 – KZR 4/19, NZKart 2021, 44 – Schienen-Kartell V.

[125] The main points of the assessment of cartel involvement was shifted from the area of liability-creating causality to the area of liability-filling causality. As a consequence, full proof is no longer required, but the principles of § 287 ZPO apply, which facilitates fact-finding for the court. BGH 28.1.2020 – KZR 24/17, NJW 2020, 1430 – Schienen-Kartell II, which deviated from the former judgment (cf. BGH 11.12.2018 – KZR 26/17, NJW 2019, 661 – Schienen-Kartell I).

In court practice, the most common and recognised economic method for estimating excess revenue is through a comparative market approach, including regression analysis. This involves comparing the price development on the cartelised market with the counter-factual price development on the comparable, presumably free-of-cartels market.[126] If both parties present expert witness opinions with different results, the court can not reject the suitability of the opinion without intensive discussion and must still deal with all indications, including data basis, methodology and result.[127] **114**

c) Pass-on

Cartel damages may be suffered by both direct and indirect customers. Defendants can use the pass-on defence against direct customers' claims for damages, as damage to the purchaser of a product affected by a cartel is considered compensated if the purchaser has passed on the cartel-related price increase to its customers, § 33c sub. 1–4 GWB.[128] In favour of indirect buyers, under certain conditions, it is presumed that the price increase has been passed on to them pursuant to § 33c sub. 2 GWB. **115**

Legal hurdles for the pass-on defence are high, with court rulings setting strict requirements.[129] In its landmark ruling 'ORWI', the German Federal Court of Justice emphasised that defendants disputing the plaintiffs' damage from the perspective of benefit sharing must first present plausible general market conditions that suggest a pass-on of cartel-related price increases.[130] **116**

Furthermore, defendants must show and prove that the pass-on is not offset by any disadvantages for the plaintiff, such as a decline in demand that may compensate for the price increase.[131] A pass-on defence can be excluded for legal reasons in cases of scattered damages, in which the circle of persons involved is unmanageably large.[132] In such cases, a pass-on defence is not generally rejected but depends on a balancing process for the individual case, including an analysis of the sales market. **117**

---

126 See, BGH 13.4.2021 – KZR 19/20, EuZW 2021, 988 – Lkw-Kartell II. For examples of implementing the regression analyses, see e.g., LG Stuttgart 7.2.2022 – 53 O 275/21, NZKart 2022, 160 regarding the trucks cartel; LG Köln 9.10.2020 – 33 O 147/15, NZKart 2020, 618 regarding the sugar cartel; OLG Frankfurt 17.11.2015 – 11 U 73/11 (Kart), GWR 2016, 171.

127 BGH 13.4.2021 – KZR 19/20, EuZW 2021, 988 – Lkw-Kartell II. In a few decisions, the courts have adopted the damage estimate themselves pursuant to § 287 ZPO (without appointing an economic expert witness), see, e.g., LG Dortmund 30.9.2020 – 8 O 115/14 (Kart), BeckRS 2020, 25435 regarding the railway cartel; OLG Celle 12.8.2021 – 13 U 120/16, NZKart 2021, 581 regarding the chipboard cartel.

128 The provision applies to claims which did not arise after 26 December 2016, § 187 sub. 3 GWB.

129 See, e.g., BGH 28.6.2011 – KZR 75/10, NJW 2012, 928 – ORWI; BGH 23.9.2020 – KZR 4/19, NZKart 2021, 44 – Schienen-Kartell V.

130 BGH 28.6.2011 – KZR 75/10, NJW 2012, 928 – ORWI.

131 BGH 28.6.2011 – KZR 75/10, NJW 2012, 928 – ORWI.

132 In these cases the BGH assumes that cartel-related price increases have either not been passed on to subsequent sales levels or have been passed on to such a small extent or in such a fragmented manner that it is practically impossible to prove that they have been passed on. See BGH 28.6.2011 – KZR 75/10, NJW 2012, 928 – ORWI; BGH 23.9.2020 – KZR 4/19, NZKart 2021, 44 – Schienen-Kartell V; BGH 13.4.2021 – KZR 19/20, EuZW 2021, 988 – Lkw-Kartell II.

E. Merger control

I. Merger control regime

118 Merger control is an instrument of structural control, which is directed against the impediment of competition through external growth. Corporate transactions of certain size may require the approval of the BKartA or the European Commission prior to their implementation. The assessment of the concentration by the BKartA shall ensure that the concentration does not significantly impede effective competition in the market, in particular by creating or strengthening a dominant position. Merger projects subject to notification which are carried out in whole or in part without a prior clearance decision by the BKartA or expiry of the respective procedural deadline (so-called 'gun jumping') can infringe enforcement prohibitions, which can be subject to high regulatory fines.

119 Despite the limitations placed upon the concept of reportable transactions under the German merger control regime by the GWB Digitisation Act, which increased the national turnover thresholds from 25 million EUR to 50 million EUR and from 5 million EUR to 17.5 million EUR, it remains more comprehensive than other jurisdictions. German merger control covers non-controlling minority interests below 50 % and in some instances below 25 %. The BKartA continues to be highly active in merger control.

120 Most of the filed mergers are approved by the BKartA, but mergers may be prohibited, for example, if the merging parties are major competitors or if the merger would in other ways significantly weaken effective competition in the market. In 2024, the BKartA reviewed about 900 notified merger cases, ten of which were subject to the main review procedure, in which one merger was prohibited, two mergers were cleared, four merger projects were withdrawn and two merger proceedings are still ongoing.[133] Out of approximately 805 notifications in 2023, seven mergers have been examined in the main review procedure (so-called second phase), of which no merger was prohibited, two withdrawn and two cleared subject to conditions.[134]

121 The BKartA is particularly interested in cases of online markets in which e-commerce, data, platform intermediaries, network effects and online marketing play a more prominent role.[135] Furthermore, transactions in highly concentrated sectors, such as petrol stations, waste disposal and recycling, retail and food retail, hospitals, local newspapers, wholesale sanitary equipment and (mobile) telecommunications, among others, may potentially undergo an in-depth Phase II assessment (→ mn. 139 et seqq.).

122 In merger cases in which companies active in several Member States and reaching certain turnover thresholds ('Community dimension') are involved, the European Commission has jurisdiction. Mergers being examined at European level by the European Commission allow companies trading in different EU Member States to obtain clearance for their mergers in one go (the 'one stop shop'). Mergers below these thresholds can be reviewed by national competition authorities in EU Member States under the applicable national merger control rules. However, the BKartA is one of the most active Member State authorities in requesting referrals back from the European Commission to the

---

[133] See BKartA, Review of 2024 (→ fn. 7).

[134] See BKartA, Annual Report 2023/2024 (→ fn. 35), p. 9.

[135] This also applies for merger control, see e.g. the BKartA's proceedings B6-37/21 (available at <https://www.bundeskartellamt.de/SharedDocs/Entscheidung/EN/Entscheidungen/Fusionskontrolle/2021/B6-37-21.html>, last accessed: 7.7.2025) and B6-21/22 – Meta/Kustomer (available at <https://www.bundeskartellamt.de/SharedDocs/Entscheidung/EN/Fallberichte/Fusionskontrolle/2022/B6-21-22.html>, last accessed: 7.7.2025).

national level if the primary impact of the transaction is expected to occur in Germany (post-notification referrals), pursuant to Art. 9 EU Merger Regulation.

Furthermore, certain transactions may require additional regulatory approvals on European level aside from merger clearance. The expansion of regulatory procedures in investment control (Foreign Direct Investment controls, 'FDI'controls) and the introduction of control over third-state subsidies at European level (Foreign Subsidies Regulation, 'FSR') create additional obstacles in the area of corporate acquisitions, which are not covered by this chapter. 123

1. Scope of application

In contrast to the prohibition of agreements restricting competition and the abuse of dominance, merger control is applied in a preventive manner (*ex ante*). The German merger control regime requires a filing if the transaction is deemed a concentration within the meaning of § 37 GWB and 124

- the companies involved exceed the turnover thresholds of § 35 sub. 1 GWB; or
- exceed the turnover thresholds and transaction value threshold of § 35 sub. 1a GWB; or
- the acquirer is subject to a § 32f sub. 2 GWB decision, and the target exceeds the turnover thresholds mentioned therein/of § 32f sub. 2 sent. 2 GWB.

A concentration, as defined in § 37 GWB, pertains not only to the direct or indirect acquisition of control (solely or jointly), but also to the procurement of a minority interest. For instance, German merger control encompasses the mere acquisition of at least 25 % of either the capital or voting rights in another company, even if there is no assumption of control nor any significant influence over the target. 125

Furthermore, the procurement of a non-controlling minority shareholding below 25 %, which empowers the exercise of a significant competitive influence (directly or indirectly), even without control, can require notification. The attainment of significant competitive influence beneath the level of control necessitates the opportunity to participate in the decision-making regarding the undertaking subject to such influence. The acquisition of significant competitive influence is assumed in transactions wherein additional rights are conferred, like information rights concerning the operative business of the target, the right to appoint members of the management board, the board of directors or the supervisory board, or a de facto blocking minority during annual shareholder meetings. The competitive importance of this influence can arise from the fact that the purchaser is, or controls, a competitor of the target, or the purchaser or one of its group companies is involved in a significant vertical supply relationship with the target. Additionally, the acquisition of all, or a significant portion of, the assets of another undertaking constitutes a concentration. With regard to joint ventures, German merger control – in contrast to EU merger control – does not differentiate between full-function and non-full-function joint ventures. Therefore, joint ventures, which fail to perform functions of an autonomous economic unit on a lasting basis (so called 'non-full-function joint ventures'), must still be filed in Germany. 126

Concentrations, which are not subject to EU or German merger control,[136] do not need to be notified, nor is there an obligation to notify that the concentration has been put into effect. 127

---

136 Since the GWB Competition Enforcement Act came into effect in November 2023, following a sector inquiry the BKartA has been able to oblige companies to notify mergers that fall below the existing merger control thresholds.

128 If a concentration with a 'Community dimension' falls within the scope of the EU Merger Regulation, the BKartA has no jurisdiction (pursuant to the 'one-stop shop' principle), with exceptions such as the referral process. However, German merger control remains applicable if the concentration meets the EU turnover thresholds but is not relevant to the EU Merger Regulation, for example, in the case of non-full-function joint ventures.

a) Turnover thresholds (§ 35 sub. 1 GWB)

129 Mandatory pre-merger filings are required if the following general turnover thresholds (referring to the previous full business year) are met:

- combined worldwide turnover of all undertakings concerned exceeded 500 million EUR; **and**
- at least one undertaking concerned had a turnover in Germany exceeding 50 million EUR; **and**
- at least one further undertaking concerned had a turnover in Germany exceeding 17.5 million EUR.

130 The calculation of turnover figures includes the undertakings' turnover of the last completed financial year on a worldwide consolidated group basis, excluding intra-group sales and VAT. Transactions of the same parties concerning the acquisition of parts of a company during a two-year period are considered a single concentration to avoid circumventing the turnover thresholds.

b) Transaction value threshold (§ 35 sub. 1a GWB)

131 In addition, transactions that involve the acquisition of a company with low turnover in Germany, but substantial operations in Germany, are subject to merger control if they meet the following transaction value threshold:

- combined worldwide turnover of all undertakings concerned exceeded 500 million EUR; **and**
- in Germany,
  - the turnover of at least one undertaking concerned exceeded 50 million EUR; **and**
  - neither the target undertaking nor any other undertaking concerned exceeded 17.5 million EUR in turnover; **and**
- the value of the consideration for the transaction must exceed 400 million EUR; **and**
- the target undertaking must have substantial operations in Germany (local nexus).[137]

132 The transaction value threshold is not commonly used to determine the obligation to notify a proposed concentration. However, in 2021, the BKartA found that the proposed acquisition 'Meta/Kustomer' met the transaction value threshold,[138] which was ultimately confirmed by the Federal Court of Justice in 2025.[139] Also in March 2022, the

---

[137] Together with the Austrian Federal Competition Authority, the BKartA issued the 'Guidance on Transaction Value Thresholds for Mandatory Pre-merger Notification' in 2018, which was revised in January 2022, see <https://www.bundeskartellamt.de/SharedDocs/Publikation/EN/Leitfaden/Leitfaden_Transaktionswertschwelle_2022.pdf?__blob=publicationFile&v=2> (last accessed 21.5.2025).

[138] BKartA 9.12.2021 – B6-37/21, BeckRS 2021, 51840 – Meta/Kustomer.

[139] OLG Düsseldorf 23.11.2022 – Kart 11/21 (V), NZKart 2023, 35 – Meta (Facebook)/Kustomer. The OLG Düsseldorf dismissed Facebook's appeal against the decision by which the BKartA found that the merger had to be notified because the clearance had been granted in the meantime. But the appeal against the costs order was successful because the procedural fee would not have been incurred if the case had been handled correctly. The OLG Düsseldorf denied a notification obligation under § 35 sub. 1 GWB as well as under § 35 sub. 1a GWB, since for the latter it was a matter of Kustomer's activity in Germany and thus customers in Germany. In the opinion of the court, this activity was not significant.

BKartA reviewed a merger relating to driver assistance systems under the transaction value threshold and finally cleared it in Phase I.[140] In 2024, the BKartA cleared the first phase II proceedings which had to be notified due to the transaction value threshold.[141] However, in the recent proceedings 'Microsoft/Open AI', 'Microsoft/Inflection' and 'Edwards Lifesciences/JenaValve', the BKartA determined that it did not have jurisdiction to review the transaction as the target did not have substantial operations in Germany.[142] In February 2025, the Düsseldorf Higher Regional Court overturned two decisions of the BKartA ('Adobe/Marketo, Magento u. Frame.io'), because the target undertakings did not have substantial operations in Germany.[143]

c) Exemptions

Concentrations may be exempted from merger control if certain conditions are met. **133**

- For example, if the proposed joint venture does not generate turnover in Germany but both parties meet the prescribed turnover thresholds, it will not result in effects on the domestic market within the meaning of § 185 sub. 2 GWB (domestic effects clause) and, therefore, will be exempted.
- Cross-location concentrations of several hospitals or individual hospital specialties may also be temporarily exempted from clearance provided certain conditions are met, though they must be formally notified post-merger.

Additionally, the scope of assessment by the BKartA may be restricted if the de minimis market clause applies, if a market existing for more than five years with a total sales volume of less than 20 million EUR in Germany in the previous year is concerned (§ 36 sub. 1 no. 2 GWB).[144] Moreover, specific rules apply for the 'failing firm' defence in the press sector. **134**

2. Substantive assessment

In terms of substantive assessment, the BKartA uses the dominance test as its key standard example of the European significant impediment to effective competition ('SIEC') test.[145] Like the European Commission, the BKartA assesses whether a proposed horizontal, vertical or conglomerate merger would lead to a significant impediment to **135**

---

[140] See BKartA, press release of 21.3.2022, available at <https://www.bundeskartellamt.de/SharedDocs/Meldung/EN/Pressemitteilungen/2022/21_03_2022_Qualcomm_Arriver-Veoneer.html> (last accessed 21.5.2025).

[141] See BKartA, press release of 17.6.2024, available at: <https://www.bundeskartellamt.de/SharedDocs/Meldung/EN/Pressemitteilungen/2024/17_06_2024_Olink_Fischer.html?nn=49408> (last accessed 21.5.2025).

[142] See BKartA, press release of 15.11.2023, available at <https://www.bundeskartellamt.de/SharedDocs/Meldung/EN/Pressemitteilungen/2023/15_11_2023_Microsoft_OpenAI.html?nn=55030> (last accessed 21.5.2025); press release of 29.11.2024, available at <https://www.bundeskartellamt.de/SharedDocs/Meldung/EN/Pressemitteilungen/2024/29_11_2024_Microsoft.html?nn=55030> (last accessed 21.5.2025); press release of 20.2.2025, only available in German at <https://www.bundeskartellamt.de/SharedDocs/Meldung/DE/AktuelleMeldungen/2025/02_20_2025_JenaValve_Edwards.html> (last accessed 21.5.2025).

[143] See Higher Regional Court of Düsseldorf, press release of 26.2.2025, only available in German at <https://www.olg-duesseldorf.nrw.de/behoerde/presse/Presse_aktuell/20250226_PM_Beschluesse-VI-Kart-2_3_24-_V_/index.php> (last accessed 21.5.2025).

[144] The de minimis market clause does not apply to concentrations notifiable pursuant to the second set of thresholds provided by the GWB and with reference to markets in which the service is provided free of charge to users.

[145] For more details of the analytical approach taken by the BKartA, see the BKartA's Guidance on Substantive Merger Control of 29 March 2012, available at <https://www.bundeskartellamt.de/SharedDocs/Publikation/EN/Leitlinien/Guidance%20-%20Substantive%20Merger%20Control.html;jsessionid=364288A6C0D5698756382203489617E4.1_cid362?nn=3590470> (last accessed 21.5.2025).

effective competition, particularly through the creation or strengthening of dominance.[146] A transaction significantly impedes effective competition when the companies involved gain a scope of action that competition can no longer sufficiently control. Factors considered in the assessment include the market shares of the companies involved and their competitors, overcapacities on the market, access to competition-relevant resources (such as production sites, patents and distribution networks, etc.), barriers to entry the market and potential competitors, vertical integration, structural links to competitors and purchasing power of the opposite market side.

136 Generally, the BKartA prohibits concentrations that are expected to create or strengthen dominance, unless the undertakings concerned prove that the concentration will also lead to improved competition, which outweighs the disadvantages of dominance, such as efficiency gains passed on to consumers (as per § 36 sub. 1 no. 1 GWB).[147] In proceedings in which concerns are raised by the BKartA, undertakings can avoid a prohibition decision by offering commitments to address the competition concerns; this often involves selling part of the combined business to competitors (structural commitments).[148] In some cases, non-structural commitments, like offering early termination rights to large customers, waiving exclusivity agreements or license technology to another market player, have been accepted.[149] In principle, the BKartA grants clearance with conditions and obligations, but prefers conditions precedent, meaning conditions are satisfied before the concentration can be implemented (for example, 'upfront buyer solutions').

II. Consequences and sanctions

137 If a company implements a concentration without the required clearance by the BKartA or before the procedural deadline expires, it infringes the prohibition to implement a concentration (§ 41 GWB). This can result in severe consequences:

- regulatory fines up to 10 % of the worldwide group turnover of the undertakings concerned referring to the previous business year can be imposed on an undertaking or an association of undertakings, §§ 81c sub. 2, 81 sub. 2 no. 1 GWB;[150]
- individuals (for example, board members) can be subject to regulatory fines of up to 1 million EUR §§ 81c sub. 1, 81 sub. 2 no. 1 GWB;
- until clearance is granted, the merger is considered provisionally suspended and implementing any steps, such as transferring shares or assets, contracts or employees, is void under German law, § 41 sub. 1 sent. 2 GWB;

---

[146] The strengthening of a dominant position does not have to be significant, cf. BGH 12.1.2021 – KVR 34/20, NZKart 2021, 358 – CTS Eventim/Four Artists.

[147] In the practice of the BKartA, efficiency arguments have so far not played a major role. An example, in which the BKartA, however, examined and considered efficiencies positively is the 'Charité/Deutsches Herzzentrum Berlin' proceeding, see case summary of 7 July 2021 – B3-67/21, p. 7 et seq., only available in German at <https://www.bundeskartellamt.de/SharedDocs/Entscheidung/DE/Fallberichte/Fusionskontrolle/2021/B3-67-21.html?nn=3591568> (last accessed: 21.5.2025).

[148] For more details of the requirements to be met to clear an otherwise problematic concentration subject to conditions and obligations, see the BKartA's Guidance on Remedies in Merger Control of 30.5.2017, available at <https://www.bundeskartellamt.de/SharedDocs/Publikation/EN/Leitlinien/Guidance%20on%20Remedies%20in%20Merger%20Control.html;jsessionid=364288A6C0D5698756382203489617E4.1_cid362?nn=3590470> (last accessed 21.5.2025).

[149] See, e.g., BKartA 15.12.2011 – B7-66-11, BeckRS 2011, 141345 – Liberty Global Europe Holding B.V./ Kabel Baden-Württemberg GmbH.

[150] The BKartA regularly imposes regulatory fines (lately up to 4.5 million EUR) for closing notifiable transactions prior to clearance.

- in case of closing without obtaining prior clearance, the parties must be aware of 'gun jumping' risks, such as the exchange of competitively sensitive information between the participating undertakings which infringes § 1 GWB, Art. 101 TFEU and can lead to additional regulatory fines;
- regulatory fines can also incur for submitting incomplete or incorrect filings, §§ 81c sub. 3, 81 sub. 2 no. 3 GWB.

III. Merger control proceedings

The process for clearing mergers does not include specific legal deadlines for the notification of a concentration. Parties only need to demonstrate their good-faith intention to complete a well-defined concentration project in order to file a notification prior to the signing of transaction documents. The notification is submitted via a letter containing specific information required by § 39 sub. 3 GWB regarding both the concentration and undertakings concerned. No official filing form is required. It is important for the notification to be complete in order to begin the proceedings. The BKartA publishes all submitted filings, which includes both the parties' names and limited case information, on its website. 138

The majority of cases are concluded by the BKartA during its Phase I investigation within one month, having determined that the transaction does not cause any substantive competition problems in Germany. In such instances, the BKartA will issue an informal clearance letter. However, should indications of competition concerns arise that cannot be dismissed during Phase I investigation, the BKartA may initiate a formal in-depth investigation (Phase II investigation, main examination proceedings). In that case, the BKartA will inform the parties and extend its investigation by issuing a 'one-month letter'. The in-depth review can take up to five months from receipt of complete notification, but this period may be extended to six months if remedies are offered or even further with the parties' consent. During its investigation, the BKartA can request all relevant documents and business data from companies and associations of companies. It is therefore advisable to be cautious when preparing internal documents such as presentations to boards or investors, when outlining the impact of the transaction on markets, competitors and customers. If notifying parties fail to respond to a request of the BKartA, there is a stop-the-clock mechanism in Phase II proceedings. 139

Market surveys are regularly conducted to interview market participants such as competitors, suppliers and customers on specific topics that are not straightforward. Additionally, third parties with a significant economic interest may participate in the proceedings upon application and admission by the BKartA, which includes the right to be heard, submit comments, and access the non-confidential part of the file. 140

If the Phase II investigation confirms competition concerns, the BKartA determines the identified issues in a written statement of objections (or a draft prohibition decision). At the end of Phase II proceedings, the BKartA issues a published formal and reasoned decision on whether the concentration is prohibited or cleared (with commitments). The decision can be appealed before the Higher Regional Court of Düsseldorf. 141

F. Actions subsequent to sector inquiries

142 The enhancement of the BKartA's capabilities to implement actions following a sector inquiry, as delineated in § 32f sub. 2–4 GWB, was introduced through the latest reform of the GWB (GWB Competition Enforcement Act), which became effective in November 2023. This amendment empowered the BKartA to take action in the market(s) related to the economic sectors analysed in the sector inquiry, without the necessity of having previously identified a violation of competition law. The completion of a sector inquiry, culminating in a final report, is a requisite for such measures. The issuance of this report initiates a further 18-month period designated for any subsequent actions. Post sector inquiry, the BKartA may compel companies to notify mergers falling below the notification thresholds outlined in § 35 GWB (→ mn. 143), or it may identify 'significant and persistent distortions of competition' and implement corrective steps, which could, under especially stringent criteria, include ownership separation as a last resort (→ mn. 144 et seq.).

I. Requirement to notify mergers below § 35 GWB thresholds

143 Mergers that fall below the thresholds specified in § 35 GWB might still necessitate notification if, during a sector inquiry, the BKartA identifies indications suggesting that further mergers could substantially hinder competition within the pertinent sector, § 32f sub. 2 GWB.[151] In such instances, the BKartA is empowered to mandate companies to report all forthcoming mergers where the acquiring entity reports a turnover of 50 million EUR in Germany, and the target company has a turnover of 1 million EUR in Germany, for a duration of three years. The substantive assessment and the proceedings of these mergers adhere to the general principles of merger control (→ mn. 135 et seqq.). Also, the prohibition on implementing a merger remains applicable here, § 41 GWB.

II. Remedial measures

144 § 32f sub. 5 GWB explicitly outlines four scenarios in which competition may be adversely affected, namely in instances of unilateral supply or purchasing power (no. 1), barriers to market entry or exit, or limitations on the capacity of companies or on their ability to switch suppliers or purchasers (no. 2), uniform or coordinated actions (no. 3), or the foreclosure of input materials or customers through vertical relationships (no. 4). The impediment must be significant and persistent, meaning it must have been present for three years and is anticipated to continue for at least another two years. Moreover, the existing powers must be deemed inadequate for effectively and permanently addressing the issue upon an initial evaluation (prima facie). Such orders are issued to specific entities

[151] A comparable provision already existed – since the 10th and until the 11th amendment to the GWB – in § 39a GWB old version and has now been structurally removed from merger control. In January 2022, the BKartA began assessing the requirements for an extended notification obligation for future concentrations pursuant to § 39a GWB old version in the waste management sector with regards to Rethmann Group/Remondis. See BKartA, press release of 19 January 2022, available at <https://www.bundeskartellamt.de/SharedDocs/Meldung/EN/Pressemitteilungen/2022/19_01_2022_Remodnis_39a.html?nn=55030> (last accessed 21.5.2025).

that have significantly contributed to the impediment through their actions and their importance in the market structure. The entities in question have the right to contest this order.

Following the issuance of such an order, the BKartA may prescribe any behavioural **145**
or structural remedial measures deemed necessary to mitigate or eliminate the competition distortion. These measures can range from mandating access to data, interfaces, networks, or other facilities (no. 1), stipulations concerning business interactions (no. 2), the enforcement of so-called FRAND norms and standards (no. 3), the authority to impose contractual obligations (no. 4), prohibitions on unilateral information disclosure (no. 5), to, as a structural remedy, the financial or organisational separation of company or business units (no. 6), as detailed in § 32f sub. 3 sent. 7 GWB. Ownership separation, also a possible measure resulting from a sector inquiry, faces stricter criteria regarding the target entity and the nature of the impediment of competition as outlined in § 32f sub. 4 GWB. Appeals against any form of these measures are subject to a suspensive effect.

CHAPTER 25
PROTECTION OF COMMERCIALLY VALUABLE INFORMATION

Bibliography: Brockhaus, Das Geschäftsgeheimnis, ZIS 2020, 103, 109; Brodowski/Marnau, Tatobjekt und Vortaten der Datenhehlerei (§ 202d StGB), NStZ 2017, 377; Fuhlrott/Fischer, Verschwiegenheitsklauseln im Lichte des Geschäftsgeheimnisschutzes, NZA 2022, 809; Gramlich/Lütke, Die Strafvorschrift des § 23 GeschGehG – kein gesetzgeberisches Meisterstück, wistra 2022, 97, 101; Henseler, Datenhehlerei (§ 202d StGB) bei Rückerlangung von Kundendaten?, NStZ 2020, 258; Hiéramente/Wagner, Strafrechtliche Grenzen der Informationsbeschaffung über (ehemalige) Mitarbeiter der Gegenpartei eines Zivilrechtsstreits, GRUR 2020, 709; Hoeren/Münker, Die EU-Richtlinien für den Schutz von Geschäftsgeheimnissen und ihre Umsetzung – unter besonderer Berücksichtigung der Produzentenhaftung, WRP 2018, 150; Ohly, Das neue Geschäftsgeheimnisgesetz im Überblick, GRUR 2019, 441; Partsch/Rump, Auslegung der „angemessenen Geheimhaltungsmaßnahme" im Geschäftsgeheimnis-Schutzgesetz, NJW 2020, 118; Preis/Seiwerth, Geheimnisschutz im Arbeitsrecht nach dem Geschäftsgeheimnisgesetz, RdA 2019, 351; Rieks, Die Nebenklage – Terra Incognita des Wirtschaftsstrafverfahrens, NStZ 2019, 643; Rodatz/Judis/Haslinger, Meldepflicht im Immobiliensektor durch die neue Geldwäschegesetzmeldepflichtverordnung, NZWiSt 2021, 56; Schreiber, Das neue Gesetz zum Schutz von Geschäftsgeheimnissen – ein „Freifahrtschein" für Whistleblower, NZWiSt 2019, 332; Stam, Die Datenhehlerei nach § 202d StGB – Anmerkung zu einem sinnlosen Straftatbestand, StV 2017, 488; Stuckenberg, Der missratene Tatbestand der neuen Datenhehlerei (§ 202d StGB), ZIS 2016, 526.

Table of contents

A. Introduction 650
B. Violation of confidentiality obligations 652
I. Professional confidentiality obligations (§ 203 StGB) 652
1. The provision 652
2. Checklist 655
II. Official confidentiality obligations (§ 353b StGB) 655
1. The provision 655
2. Checklist 657
III. Breach of tax secrecy (§ 355 StGB) 657
1. The provision 657
2. Checklist 658
IV. Violation of secrecy of post and telecommunications 658
1. The provision 658
2. Checklist 659
C. Protection of trade secrets and intellectual property 659
I. Act on the Protection of Trades Secrets 660
1. § 23 GeschGehG 660
a) The provision 660
aa) The definition of trade secrets 660
bb) The *actus reus* of § 23 GeschGehG 663
cc) The *mens rea* 664
dd) Transborder cases 664
b) Checklist 665
c) Whistleblowing 666
d) Protection of freedom of press 667

2. Other provisions protecting trade secrets 667
II. Intellectual property 668
1. The protected works and rights 668
a) Copyrighted works 668
b) Related rights 669
2. Punishable acts... 669
3. Checklist 670
III. Patents, trademarks, and other publicly registered intellectual property 671
D. Illegal access to secret information 672
I. Illegal access to electronic data 673
1. § 202a StGB 673
a) The provision 673
b) Checklist 674
2. § 202d StGB 674
a) The provision 674
b) Checklist 675
II. Violation of privacy of the spoken word and of privacy of correspondence 675

A. Introduction

1 The protection of commercially valuable information is an important but difficult task for the legislator. The variety of information in need of protection and the vast array of possible threats require a multitude of provisions that cover a wide range of undesired acts but are concise enough to satisfy the criteria set out in the German constitution. As a consequence, the legal regime protecting secrets such as trade secrets (*Geschäftsgeheimnis*) is complex and multi-facetted. The criminal provisions protecting such secrets are laid down in the German Criminal Code (*Strafgesetzbuch*, StGB), the Act on the Protection of Trade Secrets (*Geschäftsgeheimnisgesetz*, GeschGehG), and the Act on Copyright and Related Rights (*Urheberrechtsgesetz*, UrhG). Some provisions, such as §§ 203, 353b, 355, 206 StGB, criminalise certain violations of confidentiality obligations, e.g. by lawyers or public officials, and are focusing on the specific role of the perpetrator (→ mn. 7 et seqq.). Other provisions, such as § 23 GeschGehG, §§ 106 et seqq. UrhG, are meant to protect the secret itself and are focusing on the content and its economic value (→ mn. 59 et seqq.). A further layer of protection is provided by §§ 201 et seqq. StGB. These provisions criminalise the unlawful access to (secret) information, including acts that infringe on the rights of the owner/user of the electronic data on which the information in question is stored (→ mn. 138 et seqq.).

2 Depending on the *modus operandi* chosen by the (alleged) perpetrator, multiple provisions might apply cumulatively.

3 **Example:**
Perpetrator P decides to steal trade secrets from company C. He uses tools to bypass the firewall and password-protection of C, copies a secret outline of a prototype on a cloud and then sells the copy to the mala fide competitor M. By illegally accessing the secret outline, P violates § 202a sub. 1 StGB (data espionage) as well as § 23 sub. 1 no. 1 GeschGehG (violation of trade secrets). By copying the outline, he violates § 106 sub. 1 UrhG (reproducing a copyrighted work). By forwarding the data to M, P violates § 23 sub. 1 no. 2 GeschGehG (violation of trade secrets) as well as § 106 sub. 1 UrhG again (distribution of a copyrighted work). M might be held liable

for handling stolen data, § 202d sub. 1 StGB, as well as under § 23 sub. 2 GeschGehG (violation of trade secrets).

The fact that multiple criminal provisions might apply in a specific case can have significant procedural implications. 4

- Some of the provisions require an explicit *request by the victim to prosecute* (e.g. § 203 StGB).[1] Such requests are time-barred (3 months upon knowledge of the criminal act and the identity of the perpetrator).[2] In the case of other provisions, the public prosecutor's office, even in the absence of a request to prosecute, is allowed to investigate if it deems there to be a special public interest in prosecution which calls for *ex officio* intervention (§§ 202a ff. StGB[3], § 23 GeschGehG[4]).
- Regarding some of the above-mentioned criminal provisions (e.g. § 23 GeschGehG, §§ 106 et seqq. UrhG, § 142 sub. 1 PatG), the victim of such offences is entitled to bring private prosecutions if the public prosecutor's office refuses to charge, cf. § 374 StPO. The downside of this procedural option is that the prosecutor might decide to terminate proceedings and request that the victim itself bring charges, which is a burdensome and rarely successful endeavour.
- The German Code of Criminal Procedure (*Strafprozessordnung*, StPO) entitles the victim of certain unlawful acts, inter alia § 23 GeschGehG,[5] to join as **private accessory prosecutor** (*Nebenkläger*). This allows the victim to be represented by counsel in the proceedings, to make statements, to request the taking of certain evidence and to appeal decisions that affect the victim, e.g. an acquittal on charges of a violation of trade secrets. The legal representative of the victim will then be able to be present during the criminal trial and make observations. It can also request certain measures to restrict access by the public to the relevant trade secrets in question (cf. § 172 no. 2 GVG).[6] The right to join as private accessory prosecutor also facilitates access to the case file (cf. § 406e sub. 1 sent. 2 StPO).

These differences regarding the procedural role of the victim are of significant relevance in day-to-day practice. From a defence perspective, one must consider multiple criminal provisions and their relevance for the investigation. Given that many of these acts require a request to prosecute, the defence will have to assess if such a request was made on time, by the correct person and in the proper form.[7] The procedural framework is even more important for the aggrieved party when considering if and when to file a criminal complaint or when it has to decide whether or not to engage in civil litigation or discussions for compensation of damages. 5

The following chapter will therefore not only provide an overview of the requirements and legal consequences of the individual provisions but also includes a checklist for each offence regarding the procedural specifics to consider in practice. 6

---

[1] See § 205 sub. 1 sent. 1 StGB.
[2] See § 77b StGB.
[3] See § 205 sub. 1 sent. 2 StGB.
[4] See § 23 sub. 8 GeschGehG.
[5] See e.g. § 395 sub. 1 no. 6 StPO.
[6] Cf. e.g. Rieks NStZ 2019, 643.
[7] Cf. e.g. BGH 12.5.2022 – 5 StR 398/21, NJW 2022, 2768.

B. Violation of confidentiality obligations

7 The German Criminal Code contains multiple offences for the violation of various confidentiality obligations. These obligations are founded in the professional role of the obligated person and accordingly, all offences only apply to a restricted group of possible perpetrators. This section provides an overview of the rules proscribing the violation of professional confidentiality obligations (→ mn. 8 et seqq.), it addresses the violations of official confidentiality obligations (→ mn. 29 et seqq.), especially the breach of tax secrecy (→ mn. 41 et seqq.) and closes with a brief look at violations of secrecy of post and telecommunications (→ mn. 49 et seqq.).

I. Professional confidentiality obligations (§ 203 StGB)

8 Several professions in the private and public sector are either legally sworn to secrecy or the public generally expects such secrecy because of the nature of the profession. A breach of this secrecy is punishable pursuant to § 203 StGB. The protection of the public trust in the confidentiality of these professions is, however, only a collateral goal of the provision. In the first instance, § 203 StGB protects the personal sphere of privacy and secrecy of the concerned individual, including legal persons. The offence safeguards the (constitutional) right of every person to decide on their own, when and to whom they disclose private information.

1. The provision

9 § 203 StGB generally covers two groups of **possible perpetrators**. Under sub. 1, the offence sanctions confidentiality breaches by professions which are either already legally obligated to keep information obtained from their patients, clients, etc. secret or are entrusted with especially private information because of the nature of the job.

10 This includes inter alia physicians, pharmacists and other medical professions (no. 1), professional psychologists (no. 2), lawyers, notaries, patent attorneys, auditors and tax advisors (no. 3) as well as agents of respective corporations even if they themselves are not licensed as lawyers etc. (no. 3a). § 203 sub. 1 StGB further covers marriage, family, education, youth and addiction counsellors (no. 4), abortion counsellors recognised under the Act on Pregnancies in Conflict Situation[8] (no. 5), state-recognised social worker and social educational workers (no. 6). Finally, no. 7 extends the professional confidentiality duties of medical professions, lawyers and tax advisors to persons that are involved in the financial part of their services and get therefore equally in touch with the same secrets. This includes members of a private[9] health, accident or life insurance company or private medical, tax consultant or lawyer invoicing services.

11 § 203 sub. 2 StGB further covers **public officials** and other persons with similar functions. The term 'public official' is defined in § 11 sub. 1 no. 2 StGB and includes not only civil servants but every person who has been commissioned to perform public administrative services, regardless of the organisational form chosen to perform such duties.

[8] *Schwangerschaftskonfliktgesetz*, SchKG.
[9] Members of public health insurances are covered by § 203 sub. 2 no. 1 StGB.

The term 'public official' therefore also includes employees of public health insurances as well as state banks and of private law corporations that are owned by public entities, like municipal utilities and public transport companies. 12

This broad definition raises questions where the state offers public services that are also provided by private institutions, e.g. state banks. While a breach of bank secrecy by an employee of a private bank constitutes only a contract violation, it is, if one were to follow the wording of the provision, a criminal offence for employees of a state bank. The Federal Court of Justice considers this to be an unjustified discrimination and thus excludes employees of state banks from the definition of 'public official'.[10] 13

§ 203 sub. 4 sent. 1 StGB extends the confidentiality obligations to other persons who themselves do not fall under § 203 sub. 1 and 2 StGB but work for such obligated persons. This includes professional assistants, persons working with the obligated person for the purpose of their professional training (e.g. apprentices, trainee lawyers and interns) and, since 2017, also other persons who are involved in the work or official duties of the obligated person ('other involved person', *sonstige mitwirkende Person*). This latest change to the provision is a reaction to the increasing outsourcing of support tasks like IT services, which by necessity includes the disclosure of secrets to externals. In distinction to 'professional assistants', other involved persons are not integrated in the corporate structure of the obligated person and do not take part in the specific service that warrants a confidentiality obligation.[11] 14

The provision further requires that the perpetrator must have learned of the secret in his or her professional capacity. Whether the perpetrator still has that capacity when he or she discloses the secret is, however, of no relevance. 15

§ 203 StGB protects **all secrets**, including, but not limited to secrets relating to a person's personal sphere of life and business or trade secrets. The law itself does not define the notion of 'secret'. It has, however, been defined by German courts:[12] a secret is an information which only a limited group of people knows of and has access to and that the person the information relates to does not want to disclose to further persons ('will to secrecy') and has a legitimate interest to do so ('interest in secrecy'). An information is thus not a secret if an indefinite group of peoples knows about it or can easily gain knowledge of it. 16

The law does not stipulate an exact number of people; this has to be determined on a case-by-case basis. As a rule of thumb, an information is no longer a secret if, from the perspective of the person concerned, it is irrelevant if a further person acquires knowledge of it.[13] 17

Whether there is a sufficient **interest in secrecy** must be determined objectively but from the perspective of the person concerned. The term 'secret' thus also includes facts about illegal circumstances (so-called 'illegal secrets').[14] A sufficient interest in secrecy can be lacking for petty secrets like favourite meals or vacation plans. In economic or business contexts, the existence of a sufficient interest in secrecy depends on whether there is a justified economic interest. 18

§ 203 StGB covers secrets of natural as well as of legal persons.[15] It does not matter if the secret relates to the person, e.g. the patient, client, etc., relying on the services of the perpetrator. Secrets relating to third parties, to whom the perpetrator owes no confiden- 19

[10] BGH 27.10.2009 – XI ZR 225/08, BGHZ 183, 60 = NJW 2010, 361.

[11] BT-Drs. 18/11936, 22.

[12] BGH 14.11.1963 – III ZR 19/63, BGHZ 40, 288 = NJW 1196, 449; BGH 10.5.1995 – 1 StR 764/94, BGHSt 41, 140 = NJW 1995, 2301.

[13] LK-StGB/Hilgendorf § 203 mn. 39.

[14] BGH 7.4.2005 – 1 StR 326/04, BGHSt 50, 64 = NJW 2005, 2406.

[15] MüKoStGB/Cierniak/Niehaus StGB § 203 mn. 31.

tiality, are also secrets if he or she learns of them in a capacity that establishes a confidentiality duty in general.[16] With regard to public officials, particulars about another person's personal or material circumstances which have been collected for public administration purposes are deemed to be equivalent to secrets.

20 The disclosure to professional assistants and those persons who work with the perpetrator for the purposes of their professional training does not even fulfil the objective elements of the offence (§ 203 sub. 3 sent. 1 StGB). As other involved persons are also under a duty of secrecy, a disclosure to them can be justified if it is necessary for the use of such services (§ 203 sub. 3 sent. 2 StGB). This includes, for example, the use of cloud computing services.[17] As the disclosure of secrets to involved persons is in itself not punishable, the legislator deemed it necessary to hold the obligated person to some extent liable for confidentiality breaches by these involved persons. The obligated person must therefore take the necessary precautions to ensure that involved persons are put under an obligation to maintain secrecy. This is not limited to involved persons with whom the obligated person has immediate contractual relations. Rather, the obligated person has to ensure that subcontractors on all levels are put under a secrecy obligation, e.g. by according contractual clauses with his immediate contractors.

21 A further, most relevant, form to exclude criminal liability for offences under § 203 StGB in practice is that the person concerned by the secret, e.g. the client, patient, etc., consents to its disclosure. **Consent** does not have to be given in writing and not even explicitly; it must be given before the disclosure and can be revoked any time. Consent has to be given by the person to whom the perpetrator is obligated to respect confidentiality, even if it concerns secrets of a third party.[18] Legal persons act through their agents and organs.

22 Examples of practical importance are the assignment of fee claims by physicians and lawyers and the handover of patient/client data in case of a sale of the office. In these cases, the physician, lawyer, etc. should obtain an explicit consent of the patient/client up front; otherwise he or she might be held liable pursuant to § 203 StGB.[19]

23 Furthermore, a disclosure can be justified if there is a **legal permission** or even **duty to disclose**, e.g. in the context of suspicious activity reports for money laundering[20] or with regard to the planning of certain serious offences (cf. §§ 138, 139 sub. 2, 3 sent. 2 StGB). The provision of § 203 StGB is of significant importance with regard to the issue of whistleblowing. Generally speaking, a whistleblower can be justified if he or she acted out of necessity (§ 34 StGB). Under the new law protecting whistleblowers, the German legislator included an additional layer of protection in § 35 HinSchG. The provision requires that the whistleblower reports a relevant infringement under the HinSchG (*Hinweisgeberschutzgesetz*, Whistleblower Protection Act) and follows its procedure and, in return, excludes liability for such acts.[21] The HinSchG does, however, neither apply to physicians and other health care professions nor to lawyers, patent attorneys and notaries (§ 5 sub. 2 no. 3, 4 HinSchG).

24 The **penalty** for offences under § 203 sub. 1 and 2 StGB is imprisonment for a term not exceeding one year or a fine. If the perpetrator acts for a consideration or with the intention of personal enrichment or the enrichment of another or the intention of harming

[16] Cf. MüKoStGB/Cierniak/Niehaus StGB § 203 mn. 27.

[17] BT-Drs. 18/11936, 22.

[18] Cf. MüKoStGB/Cierniak/Niehaus StGB § 203 mn. 86 et seqq.

[19] BGH 10.7.1991 – VIII ZR 296/90, BGHZ 115, 123 = NJW 1991, 2955; BGH 25.3.1993 – IX ZR 192/92, BGHZ 122, 115 = NJW 1993, 1638; cf. also § 49b sub. 4 BRAO (Federal Code for Lawyers); MüKoStGB/Cierniak/Niehaus StGB § 203 mn. 74 et seqq.

[20] Cf. e.g. Rodatz/Judis/Haslinger NZWiSt 2021, 56.

[21] For more details on the HinSchG, → Ch. 7.

another, the penalty is imprisonment for a term not exceeding two years or a fine (§ 203 sub. 6 StGB).

2. Checklist

There is a **limitation period** of three years (§ 78 sub. 3 no. 5 StGB) for the offence of § 203 sub. 1 StGB. If the conditions of § 203 sub. 6 StGB are fulfilled, the limitation period is five years (§ 78 sub. 3 no. 4 StGB). The offence is **prosecuted only upon request** (§ 205 sub. 1 sent. 1 StGB) within three months of knowledge of the act and the perpetrator(§ 77b sub. 1 sent. 1 StGB). 25

The fact that the offence is only prosecuted upon request by the victim is meant to offer an additional level of protection and guarantees that the victim him- or herself can decide whether to bring charges and to have a public trial. The fact that the public prosecutor's office is bound to the request by the victim – a request that can be withdrawn (§ 77d sub. 1 StGB) – also provides some flexibility to the victim for possible settlement negotiations with regard to damages. 26

The punishable duty to not disclose secrets corresponds with a **right to refuse testimony** in the different codes of procedure. Generally, a person covered by § 203 StGB is under no duty to disclose such secrets in judicial proceedings. The German Code of Criminal Procedure contains specific rules to guarantee that the right to refuse testimony on professional grounds is safeguarded if the professional is requested to provide testimony (§ 53 sub. 1 StPO) and the professional has not been released from their obligation of secrecy (§ 53 sub. 2 sent. 1 StPO). This protection also covers persons assisting such professionals (§ 53a StPO). The right of public officials to refuse testimony under certain circumstances is safeguarded by § 54 StPO. Despite the fact that professionals can be held criminally liable for a breach of secrecy and the fact that they have a procedural right to refuse testimony, German courts have stated that a testimony in violation of said rules can nonetheless be admissible.[22] 27

The confidentiality obligations are further safeguarded by a prohibition to seize evidence from persons that have the right to refuse testimony (§ 97 StPO). The protection is, in the view of the courts, not absolute and, inter alia, requires a professional secret of the accused.[23] 28

II. Official confidentiality obligations (§ 353b StGB)

§ 353b StGB protects official secrets (*Dienstgeheimnis*) and the public trust in the confidentiality of public authorities. While public officials are already possible perpetrators under § 203 StGB, § 353b StGB further requires a specific imperilment of important public interests. 29

1. The provision

§ 353b sub. 1 StGB covers public officials, persons entrusted with special public service functions, persons who discharges duties or exercises powers under the law on staff representation and European public officials as **possible perpetrators**. Employees of public or state-owned private businesses are also public officials if they perform public 30

[22] Cf. BGH 12.1.1956 – 3 StR 195/55, NJW 1956, 599; BGH 7.3.1996 – 4 StR 737/95, NJW 1996, 2435.
[23] Cf. BVerfG 27.6.2018 – 2 BvR 1405/17, 2 BvR 1780/17, NJW 2018, 2385 (2387) et seqq.

administrative services.[24] The entrustment of special public service functions requires a formal act of entrustment (cf. § 11 sub. 1 no. 4 StGB).

31 Pursuant to § 353b sub. 2 StGB, possible perpetrators are also persons who have *in concreto* been put under an obligation of confidentiality. This as well requires a formal act. It is not necessary that the perpetrator is still a public official when he or she discloses the secret as long as he or she has learned of the secret while being in such position.

32 The meaning of 'secret' is the same as in § 203 StGB.[25] § 353b StGB, however, does not require that the secret relates to another person, so that it also covers state and official secrets.

33 The provision can therefore cover a wider range of information such as internal memos, the existence of (criminal) proceedings or even an arrest warrant. Given the complexity of the modern administration and the need for privacy and data protection, the provision can therefore apply to many situations where public officials disclose internal information without the necessary permission.[26]

34 The imperative to keep an information secret can, in particular, arise from a general legal obligation. Public officials are, for example, generally obliged to keep all information they obtain during their work confidential (cf. § 67 BBG). § 353b StGB also covers so-called 'illegal secrets', i.e. information about illegal acts of public agencies.[27] In such a case it might, however, be standing to reason that the confidentiality breach does either not jeopardise important public interests (→ mn. 35) or is at least justified by necessity (§ 34 StGB) if no milder means are available to the perpetrator.

35 A breach of secrecy is only punishable pursuant to the provision if it jeopardises important public interests. An imperilment is not only possible if the breach jeopardises a specific public proceeding, like information about an open arrest warrant or about the offer of a competitor in a public tender. § 353b StGB also covers a mere collateral imperilment if the breach unsettles the public trust in the impartiality, incorruptibility or efficiency of the public administration.[28] Such determination requires, however, a cautious approach and should be interpreted narrowly as it is clear that the mere breach of secrecy should rarely be seen as seriously damaging the integrity of the administration.

36 The public announcement of even grave administrative misconduct, e.g. by the press or whistleblowers, does not suffice to warrant criminal punishment. The publication of deficiencies in the public administration can generally not jeopardise public interests.[29]

37 For public officials according to § 353b sub. 1 StGB, the possible **penalty** is imprisonment for a term not exceeding five years or a fine. Offenders who, by committing the offence, negligently jeopardise important public interests incur a penalty of imprisonment for a term not exceeding one year or a fine. Persons who are obliged to secrecy according to § 353b sub. 2 StGB incur a penalty of imprisonment for a term not exceeding three years or a fine.

38 The attempt is punishable (cf. § 353b sub. 3 StGB).

[24] Cf. MüKoStGB/Puschke StGB § 353b mn. 15 with further references.

[25] Cf. MüKoStGB/Puschke StGB § 353b mn. 21 et seq.; also → mn. 25 et seqq.

[26] For more examples cf. MüKoStGB/Puschke StGB § 353b mn. 29 et seq.

[27] BGH 8.11.1965 – 8 StE 1/65, BGHSt 20, 342 = NJW 1966, 1227; BVerfG 28.4.1970 – 1 BvR 690/65, BVerfGE 28, 191 = NJW 1970, 1498.

[28] BGH 19.6.1958 – 4 StR 151/58, BGHSt 11, 401 = NJW 1958, 1403; BGH 22.6.2000 – 5 StR 268/99, NStZ 2000, 596.

[29] Cf. BGH 9.12.2002 – 5 StR 276/02, BGHSt 48, 126 = NJW 2003, 979.

2. Checklist

The **limitation period** is five years for offences under § 353b sub. 1 sent. 1, sub. 2 StGB (§ 78 sub. 3 no. 4 StGB) and three years in case of § 353b sub. 1 sent. 2 StGB (§ 78 sub. 3 no. 5 StGB). The offence is only prosecuted upon authorisation (§ 353b sub. 4 StGB). The authorisation has to be given by the highest federal or *Land* authority, depending on which authority or agency the perpetrator worked for when he or she took note of the secret. **39**

§ 353b sub. 3a StGB creates a safe harbour for certain acts of aiding by members of the press (§ 53 sub. 1 sent. 1 no. 5 StPO). These acts are deemed not unlawful if they are restricted to the receipt, analysis, or publication of the secret. It does not exclude criminal liability for abetting an act of § 353b StGB. **40**

III. Breach of tax secrecy (§ 355 StGB)

Taxpayers are, by law, obliged to report detailed information on their occupational, economic and private affairs to the tax authorities. Therefore, they have far-reaching interest that the tax authorities keep their information secret and protect their right to privacy. While the tax secrecy, different to the postal and telecommunications secrecy, is not a constitutional right, it is codified in the Fiscal Code (§ 30 AO). The counterpart to this provision in the criminal code is § 355 StGB. The disclosure of information protected by the tax secrecy can thus also be justified if the disclosure was permitted under § 30 sub. 4, 5 AO.[30] **41**

1. The provision

Persons covered by § 355 StGB are public officials, persons entrusted with special public service functions, experts consulted by the tax authorities or courts and office holders in the churches and other religious communities under public law. The latter are included because Art. 140 GG, Art. 137 para. 6 WRV[31] grants religious communities under public law a right to raise taxes. Similar to what applies in the case of § 353b StGB,[32] it is only necessary that the public official learned of the relevant information in his official capacity. If he or she discloses the information later, after he or she has left that position, this can still constitute a punishable offence. **42**

The provision covers **two types of information** of another: personal data (§ 355 sub. 1 sent. 1 no. 1 StGB) as well as business and trade secrets data (§ 355 sub. 1 sent. 1 no. 2 StGB). **43**

The term **personal data** (*personenbezogene Daten*) shall be understood rather broadly. It covers not only economic information, but all information related to an identified or identifiable natural or legal person. § 355 sub. 1 sent. 1 no. 1 StGB is not limited to personal data of the taxpayer but also includes data of third parties. Inter alia, it thus protects the identity of persons filing a complaint for tax fraud.[33] The disclosed information does not need to be a secret. However, information for which there is no interest in secrecy or that is overt is not covered by § 355 StGB.[34] **44**

---

[30] For a detailed discussion cf. MüKoStGB/Schmitz StGB § 355 mn. 44 et seqq.
[31] *Weimarer Reichsverfassung*, Weimar Constitution.
[32] Cf. → mn. 29 et seqq.
[33] BFH 8.2.1994 – VII R 88/92, BFHE 174, 197 = DStR 1994, 1081; MüKoStGB/Schmitz StGB § 355 mn. 18.
[34] TK-StGB/Perron/Hecker StGB § 355 mn. 5.

45 **Business and trade secrets** (*Geschäfts- und Betriebsgeheimnisse*) in the sense of § 355 sub. 1 sent. 1 no. 2 StGB are all information that is known only to a limited group of people, is related to a business and for which the owner has an economic interest to keep it secret.[35] Different to the case of personal data, a punishable disclosure or use of business or trade secrets does not need to include information on the person the data refers to. It is sufficient that the business or trade secret itself is disclosed or used.

46 The information is only protected by § 355 StGB if the perpetrator has learned of it from a specific source: he or she needs to have gained knowledge of the personal data or business or trade secrets in an administrative proceeding, an audit procedure or judicial proceedings in a tax matter, in a criminal or regulatory fines proceeding on account of a tax offence or through an official communication by a revenue authority. This includes information that the official had access to but retrieved without authorisation to do so (§ 355 sub. 1 sent. 3 StGB).

47 The possible **penalty** is imprisonment for a term not exceeding two years or a fine.

2. Checklist

48 The **limitation period** is five years (§ 78 sub. 3 no. 4 StGB). The offence is **only prosecuted upon a request** by the official superior of the perpetrator or the person whose information has been disclosed (§ 355 sub. 3 StGB).

IV. Violation of secrecy of post and telecommunications

49 The secrecy of post and telecommunications is an explicit constitutional right under Art. 10 GG. The unlawful interception of information is punishable under § 202, § 202a StGB.[36] Information protected under the secrecy of post and telecommunications is, however, especially vulnerable to persons who can lawfully access it as they are providing services necessary to convey it. Under § 206 sub. 1 StGB, it is thus an offence to communicate without authorisation to another person facts which are subject to the secrecy of post or telecommunications, and which have become known to the perpetrator as the owner or employee of an enterprise which is in the business of providing postal or telecommunications services.

1. The provision

50 Only a selected group of persons can be **perpetrators** in the sense of the provision. § 206 sub. 1, 2 StGB can only be committed by owners and employees of enterprises that are in the business of postal or telecommunications services. While this is primarily meant to apply to enterprises that provide such services as their main business, e.g. mail carriers or internet or phone service providers, the scope of the provision reaches further: § 206 StGB does not require the intent to realise a profit or that the services are provided to an unlimited group of people.

51 It is thus subject to much debate if an enterprise may already fall under § 206 sub. 1, 2 StGB if it allows its employees to use the corporate email system for private purposes.[37]

---

[35] For details on the term of 'business and trade secrets' also → mn. 61 et seqq., 104 et seqq.

[36] Also → mn. 138 et seqq.

[37] Cf. OLG Karlsruhe 10.1.2005 – 1 Ws 152/04, MMR 2005, 178; LAG Berlin-Brandenburg 16.2.2011 – 4 Sa 2132/10, NZA-RR 2011, 342.

This question is of practical importance if such companies wish to access email accounts for an internal investigation without the employees' consent, cf. also § 26 sub. 1 sent. 2 BDSG.[38]

Pursuant to § 206 sub. 2 no. 3 StGB, an owner or employee of a postal or telecommunication enterprise can also be punished if he or she permits or encourages the communication of protected information by a third party, even if that person is not a person as defined in § 206 sub. 1, 2 StGB him- or herself. 52

§ 206 sub. 3 StGB extends the confidentiality obligations to persons who perform supervisory tasks over postal or telecommunications enterprises and subcontractors of such enterprises, who either provide the postal or telecommunications services themselves or are entrusted with the production or maintenance of facilities serving the operations of such services. 53

The provision only protects **information** that is covered by the constitutional right of secrecy of post and telecommunications. § 206 sub. 5 StGB further clarifies which information is meant to be protected. 54

For postal items this includes the content of the item, name and address of the sender and the recipient and where and when the item was sent. Telecommunication does not only include phone calls but also emails, chat messages, video calls, etc. The protected information includes the content, the participants of the communication, all traffic data (type of communication, phone number, IP address, time, place and length of the communication) as well as information about unsuccessful attempts of communication (§ 206 sub. 5 sent. 3 StGB). 55

In both cases – postal communication and telecommunication – § 206 StGB does not offer protection to communication that has not yet started or that has already ended.[39] Communication content and traffic data that is, for example, retrieved from the phone or computer of one participant of the communication after its end is therefore not protected. However, § 206 StGB does apply if information is retrieved from data stored on the servers of the telecommunications provider, even if this information is stored there permanently and if the recipient has already received the communication.[40] 56

The penalty for a violation of § 206 sub. 1 StGB is imprisonment for a term not exceeding five years or a fine. 57

2. Checklist

The **limitation period** is five years (§ 78 sub. 3 no. 4 StGB). The provision **does not require a request for prosecution** by an affected person and an investigation can therefore be initiated by the public prosecutor's office. 58

C. Protection of trade secrets and intellectual property

German law addresses the need to protect commercially valuable information in multiple ways. It protects trade secrets (→ mn. 60 et seqq.), un-registered (→ mn. 105 et 59

[38] Also → Ch. 16.

[39] Cf. BVerfG 2.3.2006 – 2 BvR 2099/04, BVerfGE 115, 166 = NJW 2006, 976; BVerfG 27.2.2008 – 1 BvR 370/07, 1 BvR 595/07, BVerfGE 120, 274 = NJW 2008, 822.

[40] Cf. BVerfG 27.2.2008 – 1 BvR 370/07, 1 BvR 595/07, BVerfGE 120, 274 = NJW 2008, 822.

seqq.) and registered intellectual property (→ mn. 128 et seqq.) in different and, at least in part, mutually exclusive ways.

I. Act on the Protection of Trades Secrets

60 This section deals with the protection of trade secrets in § 23 GeschGehG (→ mn. 61 et seqq.) as well as other provisions (→ mn. 104 et seqq.).

1. § 23 GeschGehG

61 The current provision of § 23 GeschGehG has been introduced in April 2019. Before the introduction of the Act on the Protection of Trade Secrets (*Geschäftsgeheimnisgesetz*, GeschGehG) intentional violations of trade secrets were punishable under the former §§ 17 et seqq. UWG and similar provisions in laws dealing with certain judicial persons. The former provision has now been replaced by § 23 GeschGehG. Impetus for the changes was the 'Directive (EU) 2016/943 of the European Parliament and the Council of 8 June 2016 on the protection of undisclosed know-how and business information (trade secrets) against their unlawful acquisition, use and disclosure' (hereinafter Directive 2016/943/EU). It introduced, inter alia, a European definition of the term 'trade secret' (Art. 2), a description of lawful acts such as independent discovery and creation or reverse engineering (Art. 3) as well as a determination of unlawful acts of acquisition, use and disclosure (Art. 4). Directive 2016/943/EU does not require the criminalization of such acts and focusses on injunctions (Art. 12), damages (Art. 14) and the proscription of certain standards for civil proceedings. The German legislator decided to create a specific law to transpose the directive and to add a specific provision criminalizing certain violations of the law. This leads to a rather complex structure of the criminal provision. The basis forms the definition of a trade secret in § 2 no. 1 GeschGehG. § 4 GeschGehG defines unlawful acts in the sense of Art. 4 Directive 2016/943/EU and § 23 GeschGehG determines that some of these acts shall be considered criminal if committed with the *mens rea* defined in § 23 GeschGehG.

a) The provision

62 In the following section we will provide a more detailed analysis of § 23 GeschGehG.

63 **aa) The definition of trade secrets.** § 23 GeschGehG is meant to protect trade secrets as defined by **§ 2 no. 1 GeschGehG**. The wording slightly differs – especially in lit. c) – from the definition contained in Art. 2 para. 1 Directive 2016/943/EU and is as follows:

64 Trade secret means an information

a) that is secret in the sense that it is not, as a body or in the precise configuration and assembly of its components, generally known among or readily accessible to persons within the circles that normally deal with the kind of information in question; it has an economic value because it is secret; and
b) that has been subject to reasonable steps under the circumstances, by the person lawfully in control of the information, to keep it secret; and
c) for which there is a legitimate interest in keeping it secret.

65 The law only protects a **secret information**. Information that can easily be accessed (e.g. on the internet or listed patents) might require protection but is not covered by § 2

no. 1 GeschGehG.[41] However, it has been clarified by German courts that a collection of data can be protected despite the fact that the data used to create the collection is itself publicly available.[42] The fact that the holder of the trade secret (see § 2 no. 2 GeschGehG) shares the information with others does not necessarily negate the secret nature of the information.

§ 2 no. 1 GeschGehG further stipulates that the information must also have an **economic value.**[43] This guarantees that the holder of secret information is not in a position to simply qualify a certain information as secret in order to receive the protection of the law. It must have an objective value warranting protection. The law does not, however, determine a specific threshold. The wording differs from the wording in Art. 2 para. 1 Directive 2016/943/EU in that it refers to an 'economic' value and not a 'commercial' value. This has led commentators to discuss whether the provision only covers information that has a 'positive value' and can be traded or if it also covers an information that, if known to third parties such as competitors, could have a damaging effect on the company that holds the secret ('negative value').[44] The wording of recital 14 of the Directive 2016/943/EU suggests that both interpretations are possible.[45] **66**

Examples of trade secrets are information regarding manufacturing processes, lists of clients and suppliers, calculations of costs, business strategies, business data, market surveys, prototypes, formulas, recipes, construction plans, algorithms, software, source code, personnel data, tender documents, etc.[46] **67**

From a practical perspective, the most relevant element of the definition is the requirement that the holder of the secret must have taken **reasonable steps to maintain the secrecy.** This requirement has been introduced in 2019 and was not part of the definition of a trade secret under the previously relevant §§ 17 et seqq. UWG. The different public prosecutor's offices in Germany took notice of this shift in the law and there is a tendency to refuse official criminal investigations if it cannot be shown in the criminal complaint that the (alleged) victim has taken the necessary steps to protect the trade secrets. It seems that this added requirement was welcomed by public prosecutor's offices as it gave them an opportunity to dismiss cases for which they sometimes deem civil litigation better suited. This creates an often-underestimated burden for the aggrieved party as it needs to provide – often on short notice – evidence regarding the suspicion of an offence (cf. § 152 sub. 2 StPO) as well as a – ideally quite detailed – description of the prior steps taken by the company to protect its secrets. An effective protection of trade secrets therefore requires preparation by management, legal, compliance, HR and IT in order to be prepared for the worst-case scenario of a criminal act under § 23 GeschGehG. The fact that the wording requires merely 'reasonable' steps indicates that the holder of the secret is not required to establish a 'perfect' protection of all secrets. It has been accepted by jurisprudence that the holder of the secret is allowed to determine the level of protection based on the level of relevance of the different trade secrets.[47] While a secret formula or **68**

---

[41] Cf. HOK/Harte-Bavendamm GeschGehG § 2 mn. 23 et seqq.; OLG Schleswig 28.4.2022 – 6 U 39/21, GRUR-RS 2022, 9007 mn. 42.

[42] Cf. BGH 23.2.2012 – I ZR 136/10, GRUR 2012, 1048 (1049).

[43] Cf. BT-Drs. 19/4724, 24.

[44] For the discussion see, inter alia, Brockhaus ZIS 2020, 103 (109); HKV StrafR-HDB VI/Reinbacher § 57 mn. 50; Köhler/Feddersen/Alexander GeschGehG § 2 mn. 45; HOK/Harte-Bavendamm GeschGehG § 2 mn. 37.

[45] → mn. 95 et seqq regarding the issue of protecting information on violation of the law by the holder of the secret.

[46] Cf. BT-Drs. 19/4724, 24; Köhler/Feddersen/Alexander GeschGehG § 2 mn. 19.

[47] Cf. OLG Schleswig 28.4.2022 – 6 U 39/21, GRUR-RR 2022, 404 (409) with further references; OLG Düsseldorf 11.3.2021 – 15 U 6/20, GRUR-RS 2021, 17483 mn. 38; Dann/Markgraf NJW 2019, 1774 (1775).

a secret recipe might require a sophisticated level of protection, less valuable secrets can be protected in different ways.[48] The holder of the secret is also permitted to take into account practical implications of such protection and balance the need for protection with the need to use the data by the company's employees.[49] The legislator expected – although possibly a bit optimistic – that most medium-sized and large companies would already have sufficient levels of protection in place, thereby implying that the threshold should not be too high.[50]

69 Commentators and courts agree that reasonable steps to protect a secret might involve a cumulation of different measures by the holder of the secret:

- **contractual measures** – the holder of the secret can establish protection of the secret by including confidentiality clauses in contracts with employees,[51] suppliers, clients, etc. Such clauses have been subject to judicial review and courts have clarified that an effective protection of secrets might require a sufficiently detailed description of the information in question and that catch-all-clauses could, depending on the circumstances, not be considered sufficient as a measure in the sense of § 2 no. 1 lit. b) GeschGehG.[52]
- **technical measures** – the most obvious steps to be taken by the holder are technical in nature.[53] This includes measures relating to IT security (firewall, password-protection, encryption) as well as IT rights management. It also includes a possible restriction of physical access to the premises or specific locations (e.g. servers, etc.).
- **training and awareness building** – other measures include, inter alia, guidelines for access to sensitive data (e.g. need-to-know principle, supervision, etc.), regular trainings, IT & Social Media Guidelines, pre-employment screening, guidelines on how to handle the (in-)voluntary departure of employees, etc.[54]

70 In order to take the necessary steps to ensure the protection of trade secrets, the holder of such secrets should make a careful and detailed risk assessment and determine the relevant secrets requiring protection.

71 The last element of the definition of a trade secret is included in § 2 no. 1 lit. c) GeschGehG. The German law requires that there be a **legitimate interest** in keeping the information secret. Since this element is not (explicitly) included in the definition of Art. 2 Directive 2016/943/EU this had led some commentators to question the conformity with EU law.[55] The element guarantees that not all secret information one could theoretically ascribe an economic value to are covered by the law.[56] It has also, in our view wrongfully, been interpreted as evidence that the German legislator intended to exclude information of violations of the law from the scope of § 2 no. 1 GeschGehG. Neither the legislative history of the provision nor the need for the protection of whistleblowers warrant such interpretation.[57]

---

[48] Cf. OLG Düsseldorf 11.3.2021 – 15 U 6/20, GRUR-RS 2021, 17483 mn. 38. BeckOK GeschGehG/Fuhlrott, 23. Ed. 1.3.2025, GeschGehG § 2 mn. 23 suggests a three-step approach; cf. also OLG Schleswig 28.4.2022 – 6 U 39/21, GRUR-RR 2022, 404 (409).

[49] Cf. OLG Schleswig 28.4.2022 – 6 U 39/21, GRUR-RR 2022, 404 (410).

[50] OLG Schleswig 28.4.2022 – 6 U 39/21, GRUR-RR 2022, 404 (409).

[51] Cf. Fuhlrott/Fischer NZA 2022, 809.

[52] Cf. ArbG Aachen 13.1.2022 – 8 Ca 1229/20, NZA-RR 2022, 178; Stück CCZ 2022, 163.

[53] Cf. Partsch/Rump NJW 2020, 118.

[54] Cf. BeckOK GeschGehG/Fuhlrott, 23. Ed. 1.3.2025, GeschGehG § 2 mn. 37 et seqq.

[55] Cf. Preis/Seiwerth RdA 2019, 351 (353) et seq.; Ohly GRUR 2019, 441 (444); Köhler/Feddersen/Alexander GeschGehG § 2 mn. 74.

[56] OLG Schleswig 28.4.2022 – 6 U 39/21, GRUR-RS 2022, 9007 mn. 91.

[57] For a detailed overview cf. BeckOK GeschGehG/Fuhlrott, 23. Ed. 1.3.2025, GeschGehG § 2 mn. 72 et seqq.

bb) The *actus reus* of § 23 GeschGehG. The provision penalises a multitude of different acts that are structurally different. It criminalises the original violation of the secrecy as well as acts that build on a first offence by the perpetrator or another person. 72

The most relevant provision in practice is **§ 23 sub. 1 no. 3 GeschGehG** which criminalises the unauthorised disclosure of a trade secret by an employee, director, manager, board member, intern, etc. The provision requires that the employee got access to the trade secret in his or her capacity as an employee and shared the information with a third party in violation of contractual obligations or instructions by the employer. 73

The provision explicitly states that the act of disclosure must have occurred while the employment relationship was still active. In other words, the fact that an employee has terminated the contract does not absolve him or her from the obligation set forth in § 23 sub. 1 no. 3 GeschGehG as long as the period of notice has not expired. Same holds true if the employer has terminated the contracted and has ordered (un-)paid leave. During this period, the employee is officially in a formal employment relationship and bound by the confidentiality obligations.[58] Once the employment relationship has formally ended, § 23 sub. 1 no. 3 GeschGehG ceases to apply even if the (former) employee is still contractually obliged to keep the information confidential. 74

Another relevant sub-provision is **§ 23 sub. 1 no. 1 GeschGehG** which criminalises an illegal access to a trade secret and refers to § 4 sub. 1 no. 1 GeschGehG. This provision is based on Art. 4 para. 2 lit. (a) Directive 2016/943/EU which states: 75

> 'unauthorised access to, appropriation of, or copying of any documents, objects, materials, substances or electronic files, lawfully under the control of the trade secret holder, containing the trade secret or from which the trade secret can be deduced'. 76

The provision applies to all perpetrators and criminalises behaviour by employees as well as outsiders, e.g. hackers.[59] The most important element of this sub-provision is the requirement that the secret information be stored on or contained in an information medium (e.g. electronic files, documents, etc.). This excludes all acts only targeting orally transmitted information even if the perpetrator decides to lay down such information in a medium.[60] The possible *modi operandi* are relatively wide as it encompasses unauthorised access and ways to secure future access. It is subject to debate whether the provision also covers forms of passive receipt of information or whether it requires an active behaviour by the perpetrator.[61] Whether the perpetrator acted without authorization requires a careful assessment on a case-by-case basis. 77

Employees of a company are normally authorised to access data they need to fulfil their assigned tasks.[62] The authorization often also requires that employees are allowed to make copies of documents or electronic files as this regularly facilitates their work. Whether or not they are granted permission to copy such data on private devices (e.g. use of a private phone or laptop when working from home, sending emails to a private email account) depends on the circumstances. In order to avoid ambiguity, it is recommended that these questions are explicitly addressed by guidelines, instructions, trainings, etc.[63] **Third parties** might have an implicit (e.g. service providers) or explicit (e.g. licence) contractual right to access or use the trade secret.[64] 78

---

58 Köhler/Feddersen/Alexander GeschGehG § 23 mn. 40; Hiéramente/Wagner GRUR 2020, 709 (710).

59 Cf. Hohmann/Schreiner StraFo 2019, 441 (442).

60 Cf. Hoeren/Münker WRP 2018, 150 (152).

61 Cf. Hiéramente/Wagner GRUR 2020, 709 (712) et seq.; OLG Frankfurt a.M. 27.11.2020 – 6 W 113/20, GRUR-RS 2020, 38662 mn. 32.

62 BT-Drs. 19/4724, 27.

63 Cf. Fuhlrott/Fischer NZA 2022, 809 (811) et seqq.

64 Cf. MüKoUWG/Hauck/Kamlah, 3rd end 2022, GeschGehG § 4 mn. 13.

79 The sub-provisions of **§ 23 sub. 1 no. 2 GeschGehG** and **§ 23 sub. 2 GeschGehG** are similar in nature. Both require a previous violation of the law. While the former deals with a prior violation by the perpetrator him- or herself (illegal access, appropriation or copying in the sense of § 4 sub. 1 lit. a) GeschGehG),[65] the latter stipulates that whoever uses or discloses a trade secret obtained by a criminal disclosure by another person is him- or herself subject to punishment.

80 § 23 sub. 2 GeschGehG allows for a criminal investigation into unlawful behaviour by a **competitor** if the competitor knowingly benefits from the criminal acts of another person who him- or herself committed an offence in the sense of § 23 sub. 1 no. 2, 3 GeschGehG. It is unclear whether this provision also applies if the competitor receives the trade secret through an intermediary without a deliberate decision by the perpetrator of the original offence. The existence of a specific provision (§ 4 sub. 3 GeschGehG), which § 23 GeschGehG does not refer to, suggests otherwise.[66]

81 The last sub-provision is **§ 23 sub. 3 GeschGehG**. It criminalises the betrayal of documents or instructions of a technical nature (formerly penalised by § 18 UWG).[67]

82 An important addition to these sub-provisions is **§ 23 sub. 7 sent. 2 GeschGehG** which complements the rules of aiding (§ 27 StGB) and abetting (§ 26 StGB). It stipulates that whoever attempts to induce or incite another to commit an offence under § 23 GeschGehG or declares their willingness or accepts the offer of another or agrees with another to commit or incite the commission of such an offence can be held criminally liable. These forms of attempted participation are normally only criminalised if the offence in question is a serious one in the sense of § 12 sub. 1 StGB.

83 **cc) The *mens rea*.** All the acts described above require **intent** on the part of the perpetrator. In addition, all sub-provisions require that an **additional subjective element** be fulfilled: this can be that the perpetrator acted in furtherance of the interests of a competitor,[68] self-serving or serving the interests of a third party or with the intention to damage the owner of the company.[69] The way the *mens rea* element is framed does not significantly restrict the scope of application of § 23 GeschGehG.

84 **dd) Transborder cases.** An effective protection of trade secrets also requires a level of protection from acts committed by perpetrators abroad. As is commonly known, the risks of industrial espionage are extremely high. The GeschGehG addresses this issue in two distinct ways.

85 The first measure to increase protection is **§ 23 sub. 7 sent. 1 GeschGehG** which refers to § 5 no. 7 StGB. This provision reads as follows:

86 Regardless of which law is applicable at the place where the offence was committed, German criminal law applies to the following offences committed abroad: […]
7. violation of the business or trade secrets of a business which is physically located within the territorial scope of this statute or of an enterprise which has its seat therein, or of an enterprise which has its seat abroad and which is dependent on an enterprise which has its seat within the territorial scope of this statute and which forms a corporate group with the latter; […].[70]

---

[65] Regarding a possible mens rea requirement cf. BeckOK GeschGehG/Hiéramente, 23. Ed. 1.3.2025, GeschGehG § 23 mn. 28 et seqq.

[66] For a contrary view cf. Gramlich/Lütke wistra 2022, 97 (101).

[67] BT-Drs. 19/4724, 41.

[68] Cf. OLG München 22.1.2004 – 29 U 4872/03, GRUR-RR 2004, 145.

[69] Cf. Gramlich/Lütke wistra 2022, 97 (100) et seq.

[70] The English version of § 5 StGB is taken from <https://www.gesetze-im-internet.de/englisch_stgb/englisch_stgb.html>, translated by Prof Dr Michael Bohlander, completely and regularly updated by Ute Reusch (last accessed: 27.10.2025).

This provision contains an exception to the general provision of § 7 StGB which restricts the applicability of German criminal law to acts committed abroad.[71] It allows the German authorities to prosecute acts as defined by § 23 GeschGehG by foreign perpetrators who acted from abroad. 87

Another measure to protect trade secrets in Germany is the definition of an **especially serious case** in § 23 sub. 4 no. 2 and 3 GeschGehG. It increases the maximum penalty to five years if the perpetrator of an offence under § 23 sub. 1 no. 2 or 3 or sub. 2 GeschGehG knew that the trade secret will be used abroad or if the perpetrator of an offence under § 23 sub. 1 no. 2, sub. 2 GeschGehG him- or herself uses the trade secret abroad. 88

It is subject to much debate how the term 'abroad' is meant to be understood in the context of the European Union. While the wording itself would suggest that any country that is not the Federal Republic of Germany (§ 3 StGB) is covered by this provision,[72] other commentators have suggested that a mere use in the European Union should be excluded from the scope of § 23 sub. 4 GeschGehG.[73] 89

b) Checklist

§ 23 sub. 8 GeschGehG determines that prosecution of an offence under § 23 GeschGehG requires either a **request to prosecute** (within three months of knowledge of the act and the perpetrator) or a determination by the public prosecutor's office of a special public interest in prosecution. There is a **limitation period** of five years (§ 78 sub. 3 no. 4 StGB). § 395 sub. 1 no. 6 StPO allows the (alleged) victim to join as **private accessory prosecutor**. This entails, inter alia, a privileged right to access the case file (§ 406e sub. 1 sent. 2 StPO), to be present at trial, to request the taking of evidence and to appeal certain decisions. It also allows the (alleged) victim to interfere if trade secrets are about to be discussed in open court and to request the exclusion of the public for a limited period of time and an order from the court obligating the persons present to observe secrecy (§§ 172 no. 2, 174 sub. 1, 3 GVG).[74] 90

A practical problem in cases involving trade secrets is the fact that § 374 sub. 1 no. 7 StPO entitles the victim to a **private prosecution**. The downside of this right is the corresponding option of the public prosecutor's office to decline bringing charges for such offences (§ 376 StPO) if it determines that there is no public interest in public prosecution. The law itself does not define the exact conditions for this determination. One therefore has to refer to the prosecutorial guidelines (*Straf- und Bußgeldverfahren-Richtlinien*, RiStBV) published by the Federal Ministry of Justice. No. 87 sub. 2 RiStBV stipulates that the public prosecutor's office shall investigate the matter if such assistance is necessary for the victim to establish the facts. It shall only decline to bring charges subsequent to such investigations. The RiStBV further contains a specific provision dealing with cases of violation of trade secrets (no. 260 RiStBV) which clarifies that a public interest shall only be declined in minor cases. 91

The above-mentioned procedural implications ought to be considered when determining whether to file a **criminal complaint** for suspected offences covered by § 23 GeschGehG. The advantages of a criminal complaint are, generally speaking, as follows: 92

- possibility of investigative measures by the public prosecutor's office such as searches (§§ 102 et seqq. StPO), seizures (§§ 94 et seqq. StPO), taking of witness testimonies (§ 161a StPO) or financial investigations and asset freezing (§§ 111b, 111e StPO);

---

[71] Cf. MüKoStGB/Ambos StGB § 5 mn. 5 et seqq.

[72] Cf. Köhler/Feddersen/Alexander GeschGehG § 23 mn. 84b; Gramlich/Lütke, wistra 2022, 97 (103).

[73] Cf. Hoeren/Münker/Bott/Kohlhoff GeschGehG § 23 mn. 100.

[74] Cf. Rieks NStZ 2019, 643. See also No. 260b RiStBV regarding the management of the case file and the protection of trade secrets.

- pressure on the alleged perpetrator/competitor to voluntarily compensate the victim and/or destroy copies of the trade secret;
- sanctioning of perpetrators.

93 The filing of a criminal complaint can also have disadvantages such as:

- constraints with regard to possible delays in (secret) investigations. The public prosecutor's office, an institution often burdened by a lack of resources, might refrain from investigations if the alleged perpetrator has been informed by the victim that the acts have been uncovered. This ought to be considered when deciding whether to request an injunction (§ 6 GeschGehG),
- risk of decisions by the public prosecutor's office to decline charges pursuant to §§ 170 sub. 2, 376 StPO,
- possible obstacle to a settlement with the alleged perpetrator/competitor if the public prosecutor's office affirms a special public interest in prosecution (§ 23 sub. 8 GeschGehG).

94 Given the complexity of such decision-making at an early stage of the proceedings it is recommended to conduct a thorough assessment that takes into consideration both the practices of the local public prosecutor's office and the amount and quality of available evidence.

c) Whistleblowing

95 The legislator has included one notable exception to the applicability of § 23 GeschGehG: § 5 no. 2 GeschGehG states that a person shall not have acted contrary to § 4 GeschGehG if he or she acted to protect a legitimate interest, notably for revealing illegal behaviour, professional misconduct or other wrongdoing if such action serves the protection of a public interest. It is accepted that the provision also excludes criminal liability if these criteria are fulfilled. The provision is meant to transpose Art. 5 Directive 2016/943/EU but differs from its (English) wording. This phrasing of the German provision has been subject to much controversy.

96 A first issue that commentators have been discussing vividly is whether **information regarding illegal activities** ought to be considered to be a trade secret in the sense of § 2 no. 1 GeschGehG and thereby protected by law. This debate focusses on two elements of the definition: some commentators question the economic or commercial value of such information; others deny that there is a legitimate interest in keeping such information secret. The commentators arguing for an inclusion of such information into the scope of the GeschGehG rightly note that the existence of § 5 no. 2 GeschGehG strongly suggests that such information can be considered a trade secret and that only this provision defines under which conditions the information can be disclosed.[75]

97 A second point of discussion is the question whether the provision also permits a **public disclosure** (e.g. to the press) or if it requires a prior use of internal channels or communication to the competent authorities. § 5 no. 2 GeschGehG is mute in this regard. While the explanation by the legislator might be understood as to require an appropriate form of disclosure,[76] such element was not formally included in the wording of the provision.[77]

98 Perhaps the most controversial element of § 5 no. 2 GeschGehG is its inclusion of '**other wrongdoing**' (*sonstiges Fehlverhalten*) – an element which is worded differently in Art. 5 Directive 2016/943/EU. The German legislator explained that this element should

[75] For an overview of the debate cf. BeckOK GeschGehG/Hiéramente, 23. Ed. 1.3.2025, GeschGehG § 2 mn. 72 et seqq. with further references.

[76] Cf. BT-Drs. 19/4724, 28; FS Merkel/Rönnau p. 909 (927).

[77] Schreiber NZWiSt 2019, 332 (336) et seq.

be understood as also covering unethical behaviour by the holder of the trade secret.[78] In this sense, § 5 no. 2 GeschGehG is broader than the official law protecting whistleblowers (HinSchG).[79]

99 The explanation to the legislative proposal mentions as examples child labour or hazardous conditions of production. The last example mentioned in the proposal highlights the possible practical implications of this provision for businesses in Germany. It notes that the provision should also cover systematic and unethical – not illegal – forms of tax avoidance. The law therefore suggests that disclosure of financially relevant information regarding business practices the person considers to be 'unethical' is legitimate and that the legal protection of such secrets is limited.[80] This led to a decision by the Higher Regional Court Oldenburg deciding that disclosure by an employee of business data regarding possible (legal) shipments of pharmaceutical products to the US that can be used in death penalty cases is covered by § 5 No. 2 GeschGehG.[81]

100 Given the rather broad scope of § 5 no. 2 GeschGehG, its importance for day-to-day business should not be underestimated.

d) Protection of freedom of press

101 It is worth mentioning that the legislator – in accordance with the Directive 2016/943/EU – clarified that the provisions protecting trade secrets shall not impinge the freedom of press as protected by Art. 5 para. 1 sent. 1 GG. This is highlighted in § 1 sub. 3 no. 2 GeschGehG and reiterated in § 5 no. 1 GeschGehG. A more concrete rule protecting the press was introduced in § 23 sub. 6 GeschGehG. The provision refers to the right of persons as defined by § 53 sub. 1 sent. 1 no. 5 StPO which mentions:

> **102** [I]ndividuals who are or have been professionally involved in the preparation, production or dissemination of printed matter, broadcasts, film documentaries or in the information and communication services involved in instruction or in the formation of opinion.[82]

103 In accordance with the jurisprudence of the German Constitutional Court,[83] such persons should be entitled to increased protection from criminal investigations. On the one hand, journalists should be able to receive information and to be able to protect their sources. § 53 StPO therefore limits searches and seizures. On the other hand, journalists should not themselves be targeted for criminal investigations for receiving, reviewing and possibly publishing certain secrets. With regard to official secrets, § 353b sub. 3a StGB already limits criminal liability for typical journalistic acts.[84] § 23 sub. 6 GeschGehG now contains a corresponding provision for private (trade) secrets.[85] A journalist might still be held liable for abetting the violation of the trade secrets act. If the journalist, however, passively receives documents containing trade secrets, he or she is entitled to review them and to publish them if deemed newsworthy.

---

[78] BT-Drs. 19/4724, 29.

[79] Cf. → Ch. 7.

[80] For a possible application of § 203 StGB → mn. 8 et seqq.

[81] OLG Oldenburg 21.5.2019 – 1 Ss 72/19, NZWiSt 2021, 30.

[82] The English versions of § 53 StPO is taken from <https://www.gesetze-im-internet.de/englisch_stpo/englisch_stpo.html>, translated by Brian Duffett and Monika Ebinger, updated by Kathleen Müller-Rostin and Iyamide Mahdi (last accessed: 27.10.2025).

[83] Cf. BVerfG 27.2.2007 – 1 BvR 538/06, NJW 2007, 1117.

[84] Cf. MüKoStGB/Puschke StGB § 353b mn. 60.

[85] Cf. BT-Drs. 19/8300, 15.

2. Other provisions protecting trade secrets

104 The protection of trade secrets via criminal law has a long tradition in Germany. Many laws containing the legal framework for the work of judicial persons include provisions specifically dealing with the protection of secrets. The most relevant provisions in practice in this regard are § 85 GmbHG, which addresses acts by directors of limited liability companies, and § 404 AktG, which addresses acts by members of the board of management and members of the supervisory board.[86] § 120 BetrVG contains a specific provision criminalizing violations with regard to trade secrets by members of the works council as well as representation of trade unions and employers' associations. All these provisions existed already before the implementation of the Directive 2016/943/EU and have not been amended. They have in common that they criminalise disclosure and exploitation but, contrary to §§ 4, 23 GeschGehG, not an illegal access to a trade secret. The terminology also differs in that these provisions refer to business and trade secrets (*Betriebs- und Geschäftsgeheimnisse*) instead of trade secrets which leads to the question whether the definition of § 2 no. 1 GeschGehG, especially the requirement of reasonable protection, applies.[87] Regarding the persons covered by these provisions an unauthorised disclosure or use of trade secrets can, depending on the circumstances, also amount to embezzlement (§ 266 StGB).[88]

II. Intellectual property

105 The main act on the protection of intellectual property is the Act on Copyright and Related Rights (*Urheberrechtsgesetz*, UrhG), which in §§ 106 et seqq. UrhG also includes multiple provisions on the criminal punishment of copyright infringements.

1. The protected works and rights

106 German law protects copyrighted works (→ mn. 107 et seqq.) and related rights (→ mn. 111).

a) Copyrighted works

107 The centrepiece of the UrhG's intellectual property criminal law is the term 'copyright-protected work'. According to § 1 UrhG, the UrhG only protects works in the literary, scientific and artistic domain, i.e. cultural creations. These terms must be interpreted broadly. § 2 sub. 1 UrhG exemplarily names certain kinds of works in the literary, scientific and artistic domain that thus enjoy copyright protection. This includes for example literary works, music, dance, architectural works, photographs and films. Since 1993, computer programs are also explicitly works that might receive protection. The list is not conclusive.

108 Technical achievements like inventions and economic organisation methods or systems like accounting systems are therefore not protected under the UrhG. However, only the invention, method, or system as such is not covered by the law; its representation in words, pictures or sound can be a 'work' under the UrhG.[89]

---

[86] See also § 331 sub. 1 HGB, § 151 GenG, § 19 PublG, § 315 UmwG, § 15 EWiVAG, § 53 SEAG.

[87] Cf. BeckOK GmbHG/N. Müller, 63. Ed. 1.2.2025, GmbHG § 85 mn. 26 et seqq.

[88] → Ch. 12.

[89] MüKoStGB/Heinrich UrhG § 106 mn. 5, Dreier/Schulze/Schulze, 7th edn 2022, UrhG § 1 mn. 6, see also § 1 no. 7 UrhG.

An additional requirement for a 'work' to fall under the protection of the UrhG is that it is the owner's own intellectual creation. The work must show a certain threshold of originality; the UrhG does not protect 'what everyone would have done this way'. The threshold is, however, not high; a modest level of intellectual creative activity is sufficient.[90] If the observer likes the work or if it is of any cultural quality is of no relevance. **109**

Protected works under the UrhG can thus be software and computer programs (cf. § 69a UrhG) and collections and databases, if they – by reason of the selection or arrangement of the elements – constitute the author's own intellectual creation (§ 4 sub. 1 UrhG). Translations, adaptions and transformations can enjoy their own copyright protection if the adaption shows the necessary threshold of originality by the adaptor. **110**

b) Related rights

The UrhG further protects several rights related to the copyright. These related rights guarantee protection not only of the creative author but also for facilitators of the work, that are not creative themselves. This includes inter alia the work of record and broadcasting companies and film studios. These entities have the exclusive right to exploit their methods of distribution (i.e. film, record, etc.). § 108 UrhG equates the unlawful exploitation of these rights with the unlawful exploitation of copyrighted works. **111**

2. Punishable acts

According to § 106 UrhG, it constitutes a punishable offence to unlawfully exploit copyrighted works by reproducing, distributing or communicating to the public a work or an adaption or transformation of a work without the rightsholder's consent and in manners other than those permitted by law. **112**

The three punishable acts are a mirror image of the basic rights of the author under §§ 15 et seqq. UrhG. It is the author's right alone to produce copies of the work ('reproduction', § 16 sub. 1 UrhG). Only the author is generally allowed to offer the original or copies of the work to the public or to put them into circulation ('distribution', § 17 sub. 1 UrhG). Finally, the author has the exclusive right to communicate his work to the public in non-material form ('communication to the public', §§ 19 et seqq. UrhG.). The communication of a work is deemed public if it is intended for a plurality of members of the public, whereby an exception is made for a limited group of persons who are personally connected either to each other or the perpetrator (§ 15 sub. 3 UrhG). **113**

Adaptions or other transformations of a work are not already a reproduction of the work and are thus not punishable as such. However, the distribution of an adaption or transformation is an unauthorised distribution of original work and therefore falls under § 106 UrhG.[91] **114**

An exploitation of a work does not fall under § 106 UrhG if the author has given his consent. Furthermore, the UrhG names a variety of statutory exceptions in §§ 44 et seqq. UrhG under which an exploitation is not unlawful. Most of these exceptions have very little practical relevance. Probably most relevant is the right of natural persons to make copies of a work for private use that does not serve commercial purposes. **115**

§ 107 UrhG penalises the unlawful affixing of a designation of authorship on an artistic work or to a copy of such a work. It thus does not protect the author's reproduction rights **116**

[90] So-called approach of the 'small coin', BT-Drs. IV/270, 38; BGH 21.11.1991 – I ZR 190/89, BGHZ 116, 136 = NJW 1992, 1316.

[91] MüKoStGB/Heinrich UrhG § 106 mn. 49.

but his right to be identified as the author of the work. The provision only applies to artistic works like paintings, drawings and sculptures and has little to no relevance in practice.

117 § 108b UrhG finally penalises the infringement of technical measures and right management information which are designed to prevent or restrict copyright infringements and where the infringement thus enables the unauthorised exploitation of copyrights. Pursuant to § 108b sub. 1 UrhG, it is a punishable offence to circumvent an effective technical measure without the rightsholder's consent to access a work or other subject matter protected under the UrhG. This includes the circumvention of copy protections by 'cracking'. Pursuant to § 108b sub. 2 UrhG, the unauthorised removal or alteration of rights management information affixed to a copy of the work and the distribution of such works with removed or altered rights management information constitutes a crime, if the perpetrator at least carelessly induces, enables, facilitates, or conceals an infringement of copyrights. § 108b sub. 3 UrhG penalises the production or distribution of devices to circumvent effective technical measures.

118 All offences under § 108b UrhG do only apply to acts with a commercial background and exclude from criminal liability the mere private use by the perpetrator. Both offences of § 108b sub. 1 UrhG do not constitute a punishable offence if the offence was exclusively committed for the private use of the perpetrator or of persons personally associated with the perpetrator. § 108b sub. 2 UrhG requires that the perpetrator acted on a commercial basis.

119 All offences are limited to exploitations on German soil, as intellectual property rights are territorially limited to the state that grants them.[92]

120 The penalty for offences under §§ 106 to 108 UrhG is imprisonment for a term not exceeding three years or a fine. The attempt is punishable. Where the offender acts on a commercial basis, the penalty is imprisonment for a term not exceeding five years or a fine (§ 108a UrhG).

121 For offences under § 108b UrhG, the penalty is imprisonment for a term not exceeding one year or a fine and, if the perpetrator acts on a commercial basis (§ 108b sub. 3 UrhG), imprisonment for a term not exceeding three years or a fine.

3. Checklist

122 The **limitation period** for offences under §§ 106 to 108, 108b sub. 3 UrhG is five, for offences under § 108b sub. 1, 2 UrhG three years (§ 78 sub. 3 no. 4, 5 StGB).

123 A **request for prosecution** is required unless the criminal prosecution authority regards *ex officio* action to be necessary on account of the particular public interest or the perpetrator is punishable under § 108a UrhG as he acts on a commercial basis (§ 109 UrhG). *Ex officio* action is generally necessary if the perpetrator has a criminal record, the (imminent) damage is significant or if the economic existence of the victim or the public safety or health is jeopardised (no. 261a RiStBV).

124 The victim of an offence under §§ 106 et seqq. UrhG may join the public prosecution as **private accessory prosecutor** (§ 395 sub. 1 no. 6 StPO). Independently from such an affiliation, the victim has generally the right to let a lawyer inspect the investigation files for him (§ 406e sub. 1 StPO) and can obtain additional information for a civil litigation against the perpetrator this way.

125 The offences are admissible for **private prosecution** (§ 374 sub. 1 no. 8 StPO). The public prosecutor's office shall raise public charges only if it is in the public interest (§ 376 StPO). Usually, this is the case when the violation of the intellectual property right is not

---

[92] BGH 3.3.2004 – 2 StR 109/03, BGHSt 49, 93 = NJW 2004, 1674.

only marginal considering the scope of the violation, the (imminent) economic damage and the enrichment sought by the perpetrator (no. 261 RiStBV).

Objects relating to an offence can be confiscated (§ 110 UrhG) and can already be seized during the investigations to secure a future **confiscation** (§ 111b StPO).[93] 126

If the perpetrator is convicted, the victim can ask for a public announcement of the verdict if he or she has a legitimate interest. This requires a weighing of the injured party's interest in satisfaction and rehabilitation as well as the public's interest in rectification against the offender's interest in resocialisation. Of particular importance are the type, extent and duration of the infringement of the intellectual property right, the extent to which the public has become aware of the offence and the reasonableness of the publication for the convicted person.[94] The victim has to file the application within one month after service of the final decision (§ 463c sub. 2 StPO). The manner of the publication is determined by the court, weighing the same interests as above.[95] 127

III. Patents, trademarks, and other publicly registered intellectual property

While the protection of the UrhG only relates to works in the literary, scientific and artistic domain, other certain kinds of intellectual achievements can be publicly registered in order to attain protective intellectual property rights. The registration has the effect that only the proprietor is entitled to use the registered invention etc. Consequently, there are also special criminal offences for the unauthorised use of registered intellectual property. 128

Public registers exist for inventions, designs, plants and semiconductors as well as for trademarks. Mostly parallel penal provisions can thus be found for patents (§ 142 PatG, 'Patent Act') and utility models (§ 25 GebrMG, 'Utility Model Act'), designs (§ 51 DesignG, 'Design Act'), plants (§ 39 SortSchG, 'Plant Variety Protection Act') and semiconductors (§ 10 HalblSchG, 'Semiconductor Protection Act') as well as for trademarks and related rights (European Union trademark and indications of geographical origin, §§ 143 et seqq. MarkenG, 'Trademark Act'). The following is a general overview of all possible offences. 129

Generally, the offences require that the protected intellectual property was previously registered with the relevant register. Only for trademarks, it is alternatively sufficient that the sign has acquired public recognition as a trademark within the affected circles (§ 4 no. 2 MarkenG). Whether the incorrect registration of a patent, design etc. in favour of a person who is not the creator already constitutes an offence of causing false (public) records under § 271 StGB is subject to debate.[96] 130

Punishable acts for (nearly) all offences are the manufacturing, offering, placing on the market and import of goods using the protected rights without authorisation of the owner. For patents, utility models and trademarks, the use of the intellectual property right alone is already punishable as well. With regard to designs, only the unauthorised use of the design is punishable. 131

---

93 Cf. → Ch. 5.

94 MüKoStGB/Heinrich UrhG § 111 mn. 4.

95 Dreier/Schulze/Dreier UrhG § 111 mn. 5; Erbs/Kohlhaas/Kaiser, Strafrechtliche Nebengesetze, 255. EL Januar 2025, UrhG § 111 mn. 6.

96 See BeckOK PatR/Stortnik, 26. Ed. 15.10.2022, PatG § 37 mn. 10; Beyerlein MittdtPatA 2003, 65.

132 The infringement of an intellectual property right assigned for Germany abroad does not fall under the offences as all intellectual property rights are territorially limited to the state that grants them.[97]

133 The possible **punishment** for all offences is imprisonment for a term not exceeding three years or a fine. The attempt is punishable. The **limitation period** is five years (§ 78 sub. 3 no. 4 StGB). The offence is **only prosecuted upon request**, unless the prosecuting authority deems there to be a special public interest in prosecution which calls for *ex officio* intervention. This is generally the case if the perpetrator has a criminal record, the (imminent) damage is significant or if the economic existence of the victim or the public safety or health is jeopardised (no. 261a RiStBV).

134 If the perpetrator acts on a commercial basis, the possible punishment is imprisonment for a term up to five years and no request for prosecution is required. In case of the violation of a trademark on a commercial basis or as a member of a gang whose purpose is the continued commission of offences under § 143 MarkenG, there is a minimum punishment of imprisonment for a term of three months.

135 The offences are **admissible for private accessory prosecution** (§ 395 sub. 1 no. 6 StPO) and **private prosecution** (§ 374 sub. 1 no. 8 StPO). The public prosecutor's office shall raise public charges only if it is in the public interest (§ 376 StPO). Usually, this is the case when the violation of the intellectual property right is not only marginal considering the scope of the violation, the (imminent) economic damage and the enrichment sought by the perpetrator (no. 261 RiStBV). Independently from an affiliation as private accessory prosecutor, the victim has generally the right to let a lawyer inspect the investigation files for him (§ 406e sub. 1 StPO) and can obtain additional information for a civil litigation against the perpetrator this way.

136 Objects relating to an offence can be confiscated and can already be seized during the investigations to secure a future confiscation (§ 111b StPO).[98] Confiscated items will normally be destroyed (§ 63 sub. 1 StVollstrO).

137 If the perpetrator is convicted, the victim can ask for a public announcement of the verdict if he or she has a legitimate interest. As with offences under § 106 UrhG, this requires a weighing of the injured party's interest in satisfaction and rehabilitation as well as the public's interest in rectification against the offender's interest in resocialisation. A legitimate interest exists in particular in the event of market confusion, uncertainty among customers caused by the offence and a consequent impairment and devaluation of the intellectual property right.[99] The victim has to file the application within one month after service of the final decision (§ 463c sub. 2 StPO).

D. Illegal access to secret information

138 While the provisions illustrated so far deal with the unlawful disclosure of secrets the perpetrator has rightfully learned of, the StGB also includes several offences that protect (secret) information against unauthorised access. The most important is the illegal access to electronic data (→ mn. 139 et seqq.), but the legislator has also criminalised violations of privacy of the spoken word and of privacy of correspondence (→ mn. 158 et seqq.).

---

[97] BGH 29.2.1968 – I a ZR 49/65, BGHZ 49, 331 = NJW 1968, 1042; BGH 16.6.1994 – I ZR 24/92, BGHZ 126, 252 = NJW 1994, 2888.

[98] Cf. → Ch. 5.

[99] GJW/Zimmermann PatG § 142 mn. 76.

I. Illegal access to electronic data

Although it is not the main aim of this chapter to discuss issues related to cybercrime,[100] it is important to understand the practical relevance of §§ 202a et seqq. StGB for the protection of commercially valuable information such as trade secrets. It is therefore worthwhile to provide an overview of the two most relevant provisions, § 202a StGB and § 202d StGB. Both provisions deal with the protection of electronic data (see § 202a sub. 2 StGB). 139

1. § 202a StGB

The most relevant provision that criminalises illegal access to electronic data is § 202a sub. 1 StGB which states: 140

> Whoever, without being authorised to do so, obtains access, by circumventing the access protection, for themselves or another, to data which were not intended for them and were specially protected against unauthorised access incurs a penalty of imprisonment for a term not exceeding three years or a fine.[101] 141

a) The provision

As is clear from the wording of the provision, the **data** (e.g. text documents, spread sheets, emails, software) is protected notwithstanding the exact content of the electronic documents. The information contained in the electronic document must neither be commercially valuable nor secret. Especially, there is no requirement that the information contained therein is a trade secret. 142

The provision criminalises access to such data without consent. This begs the question whose consent is relevant to the determination of a case of illegal access. The prevailing view is that § 202a StGB is meant to protect the **formal data secrecy.**[102] As a consequence, it is neither of importance who is benefitting from the commercial information contained in the electronic document nor is it relevant to which person the information contained therein refers. § 202a sub. 1 StGB is not a data protection provision *stricto sensu*. Application of the provision therefore requires a case-by-case determination as to which persons are entitled to access the data in question. 143

An easy example is the classic case of hacking: an outsider to a company is prohibited from accessing the data and can without question be a perpetrator of the criminal offence of § 202a sub. 1 StGB. An employee, on the other hand, is normally allowed to access data he or she requires for the work assignment. The fact that the employee is prohibited from sharing such information contained therein with third parties does not result in an illegal access to the data itself. An abuse of discretion will not automatically lead to a violation of § 202a sub. 1 StGB. If, however, the employee accesses data belonging to a co-worker and stored on a device to which, under normal circumstances, no access is granted, this can amount to a case of access without authorisation in the sense of the provision.[103] 144

---

100 → Ch. 17.

101 The English version of § 202a StGB is taken from <https://www.gesetze-im-internet.de/englisch_stgb/englisch_stgb.html>, translated by Prof Dr Michael Bohlander, completely and regularly updated by Ute Reusch (last accessed: 27.10.2025).

102 Cf. e.g. MüKoStGB/Graf StGB § 202a mn. 2; BT-Drs. 18/5088, 45.

103 Cf. MüKoStGB/Graf StGB § 202a mn. 24; for the complicated case of unauthorised access by an IT administrator see BGH 13.5.2020 – 5 StR 614/19, NStZ-RR 2020, 278 commented by Basar jurisPR-StrafR 4/2021; see also Klaas MMR 2022, 187.

145 To limit the scope of the provision and to avoid criminalization of day-to-day activities the provision also requires a **circumvention of access protection**. Such protection can be physical in nature, e.g. storage of a USB stick in a safe or a restricted area, or digital, such as passwords or other forms of encryption. The protection must, however, not be sophisticated but it must be established that the perpetrator circumvented the protection.

146 **Example:**
If a co-worker voluntarily gives away his password in order for the perpetrator to find a work-related document on the computer and the perpetrator misuses the password to read and copy private emails to a portable hard drive, such act does not qualify under § 202a sub. 1 StGB. If, on the other hand, the perpetrator 'guesses' the password and enters it in the absence of the co-worker, such act can amount to data espionage.

147 § 202a sub. 1 StGB requires **intent** in the sense of § 16 sub. 1 StGB.

148 The possible **penalty** is relatively low (maximum of three years of imprisonment or a fine). Currently and despite attempts to strengthen the provision, there is no specific rule determining a higher penalty for an especially serious case.

b) Checklist

149 § 205 sub. 1 sent. 2 StGB determines that prosecution of an offence under § 202a sub. 1 StGB requires either a **request to prosecute** (within three months of knowledge of the act and the perpetrator) or a determination by the public prosecutor's office of a special public interest in prosecution. There is a **limitation period** of five years (§ 78 sub. 3 no. 4 StGB).

2. § 202d StGB

150 A relatively new and heavily criticised[104] provision is § 202d sub. 1 StGB which penalises the handling of stolen data. It adds an additional layer of protection and clarifies that

> [w]hoever procures, for themselves or another person, supplies to another person, disseminates or otherwise provides access to data [§] 202a [sub.] 2 which are not generally accessible and which another person has obtained by an unlawful act for the purpose of personal enrichment or the enrichment of a third party or to harm another person incurs a penalty of imprisonment for a term not exceeding three years or a fine.[105]

151 It complements the rules of aiding (§ 27 StGB) and abetting (§ 26 StGB) an offence under § 202a sub. 1 StGB and penalises acts by an individual who is being involved after an illegal act of accessing the data has already occurred (e.g. a competitor buying stolen data).

a) The provision

152 § 202d sub. 1 StGB criminalises access to **'stolen' data**. The provision is not protecting the information stored on such data *per se*. Mere access to the information, e.g. by oral transmission of the content from a hacker to the perpetrator, is not supposed to be covered.[106] The scope of the provision is further limited by the fact that it is required

---

[104] Cf. Stam StV 2017, 488; Stuckenberg ZIS 2016, 526.

[105] The English version of § 202d StGB is taken from <https://www.gesetze-im-internet.de/englisch_stgb/englisch_stgb.html>, translated by Prof Dr Michael Bohlander, completely and regularly updated by Ute Reusch (last accessed: 27.10.2025).

[106] Cf. Hiéramente/Wagner GRUR 2020, 709 (714); see also OLG Stuttgart 15.11.2018 – 2 U 30/18, GRUR 2019, 422 (424) arguing that it suffices that information is provided on paper.

that the data is **not generally accessible**. This is meant to exclude acts of copyright infringement.[107] This has led commentators to question whether data sold on the dark net is covered by § 202d sub. 1 StGB.[108] The most important limitation contained in the provision is the fact that the data in question has been **obtained by an unlawful act** (see § 11 sub. 1 no. 5 StGB) committed by another person.

The most important provision the legislator had in mind is § 202a sub. 1 StGB. Acts of theft (§ 242 StGB) or fraud (§ 263 StGB) are also possible acts. The wording of the provision is, however, misleading in that it suggests a wide variety of criminal acts by another person could satisfy the criteria set out by the provision. The legislator has clarified though that such acts need to have violated the formal data secrecy,[109] thereby excluding certain acts covered by § 23 sub. 1 GeschGehG.[110] Furthermore, the German wording also suggests that the unlawful act cannot be identical with the act of granting access to the data,[111] thereby excluding inter alia acts already penalised under § 203 StGB, § 23 sub. 1 no. 3 GeschGehG, § 42 BDSG.[112] **153**

§ 202d sub. 1 StGB criminalises different types of behaviour. Most importantly, it criminalises **procuring access** to such illegally obtained data. The legislator has clarified that this requires coordination between the perpetrator and the person who has committed the prior unlawful act.[113] 'Stealing from the thief' does not qualify as an act of handling stolen data. The provision also covers supply and dissemination to another person as well as providing access to such data in other forms. **154**

§ 202d sub. 1 StGB requires **intent** in the sense of § 16 sub. 1 StGB. **155**

The possible **penalty** is relatively low (maximum of three years of imprisonment or a fine) and may be lowered if punishment for the prior offence is lower. **156**

b) Checklist

§ 205 sub. 1 sent. 2 StGB determines that prosecution of an offence under § 202d sub. 1 StGB requires either a **request to prosecute** (within three months of knowledge of the act and the perpetrator) or a determination by the public prosecutor's office of a special public interest in prosecution. There is a **limitation period** of five years (§ 78 sub. 3 no. 4 StGB). **157**

II. Violation of privacy of the spoken word and of privacy of correspondence

Pursuant to § 201 StGB, it constitutes an offence to make an audio recording of the privately spoken word of another or to intercept such word with a listening device without authorisation. Using such a recording or making it available to a third party is also punishable. **158**

§ 202 StGB protects a person's privacy as far as third parties are trying to access sealed or protected documents. This applies to letters in the first place but also to all kinds of documents that are protected by a sealed container. It is not necessary that the document **159**

---

[107] BT-Drs. 18/5088, 45 et seq.

[108] For the discussion cf. Henseler NStZ 2020, 258 (260); Stam StV 2017, 488 (489); Matt/Renzikowski/Altenhain StGB § 202d mn. 8.

[109] BT-Drs. 18/5088, 46.

[110] Brodowski/Marnau NStZ 2017, 377 (383); Matt/Renzikowski/Altenhain StGB § 202d mn. 6; cf. BVerfG 30.3.2022 – 1 BvR 2821/16, BeckRS 2022, 13689, mn. 21.

[111] Brodowski/Marnau NStZ 2017, 377 (382) et seq.

[112] Cf. NK-WSS/Reinbacher StGB § 202d mn. 1.

[113] BT-Drs. 18/5088, 47.

contains any secrets. It is not only a criminal act to open such letter or sealed container but also to take note of its content using technical means and without opening the seal.

160 The penalty under § 201 sub. 1, 2 StGB is imprisonment for a term not exceeding three years or a fine. A penalty of imprisonment for up to five years is possible if the perpetrator is a public official (§ 201 sub. 3 StGB). The attempt is punishable. The **limitation period** is five years (§ 78 sub. 3 no. 4 StGB).

161 For offences under § 202 StGB, the possible penalty is imprisonment for a term not exceeding one year or a fine, unless the act carries a penalty under § 206 StGB[114]. The limitation period is three years (§ 78 sub. 3 no. 5 StGB).

162 § 205 sub. 1 sent. 1 StGB determines that both offences are **only prosecuted upon request.**

---

[114] → mn. 49 et seqq.

Glossary

German – English

A

Abwickler	liquidator
Adhäsionskläger	ancillary plaintiff
Adhäsionsverfahren	adhesion proceedings
Aktiengesellschaft	stock corporation; public limited company
Amtsgericht	local court
Amtsträger	public official
Anfüttern (Korruption)	grooming
Angeklagter	defendant
Angeschuldigter	indicted accused; accused indictee
Anklageerhebung	indictment
Anknüpfungstat	underlying act
Anstifter	abettor
Anstiftung (§ 26 StGB)	abetting
Anwalt	attorney; lawyer
Arbeitsgericht	labour court
Auffangklausel	catch-all clause
Aufsichtsrat	supervisory board
Aufwendungen	expenditures
Auslieferung	extradition
Auslieferungsersuchen	request for extradition
Auslieferungsvertrag	extradition treaty
Aussage	testimony
Außenwirtschaft	foreign trade and payments
Aussonderung	separation
Auswärtiges Amt	Federal Foreign Office

B

Bande	gang
bedingter Vorsatz [also: *dolus eventualis* and → Eventualvorsatz]	conditional intent
Beendigung (der Tat)	termination (of the offence)
beiderseitige Strafbarkeit (Rechtshilfe)	double criminality
Beihilfe (§ 27 StGB)	aiding
Bereicherung	enrichment
Berufsrichter	professional judge

Berufung	appeal on points of fact and law
Beschlagnahme	seizure
Beschuldigter	accused person
Beschwerde	complaint
Beschwerdeverfahren	complaints procedure
Bestechlichkeit	taking bribes
Bestechung	giving bribes
Bestimmtheitsgrundsatz	principle of certainty
Betriebsrat	works council
Betrug	fraud
Beweis	evidence
Beweis durch Augenschein	evidence by inspection
Beweisantrag	motion to take evidence
Beweislast	burden of proof
Beweislastumkehr	reversal of the burden of proof
Blankettnorm	blanket norm
Bruttoprinzip (Einziehung)	gross principle
Bundesanstalt für Finanzdienstleistungsaufsicht	Federal Financial Supervisory Authority
Bundesanzeiger	Federal Law Gazette
Bundesarbeitsgericht	Federal Labour Court
Bundesfinanzhof	Federal Fiscal Court
Bundesgerichtshof	Federal Court of Justice
Bundesland	German State
Bundessozialgericht	Federal Social Court
Bundesverfassungsgericht	Federal Constitutional Court
Bundesverwaltungsgericht	Federal Administrative Court
Bundeszentralregister	Federal Criminal Records Register
Business Judgment Rule	business judgment rule
Bußgeld	administrative fine; regulatory fine
Bußgeldbescheid	administrative fining notice
Bußgeldleitlinien	guidelines on administrative fines; guidelines for the imposition of regulatory fines

C

Compliance	compliance
Compliance-Beauftragter	compliance officer
Corporate Governance	corporate governance

D

Daten	data
Delegierte Europäische Staatsanwälte	European Delegated Prosecutors
Delikt	offence
Dienstgeheimnis	official secret
Dreiecksbetrug	triangular fraud

drohende Zahlungsunfähigkeit	imminent illiquidity
Durchsuchung	search
Durchsuchungsbefehl	search warrant

E

ehrenamtlicher Richter	honorary judge
Einziehung	confiscation
Einziehung von Taterlangtem	confiscation of proceeds of crime
Einziehung von Tatobjekten	confiscation of objects of crime
Einziehungs- oder Nebenbeteiligte	confiscating party or secondary party
Einziehungsbeteiligte	party to the confiscation proceedings
Emittent	issuer
Entreicherung	loss of enrichment; disenrichment; loss of crime profits
Entschädigungsverfahren	compensation procedure
Entscheidung	decision
Erfolgsdelikt	offence of success
Erlaubnistatbestandsirrtum	justification error
Ermessensentscheidung	discretionary decision
Ermittlungsrichter	examining judge
Ermittlungsverfahren	preliminary proceedings
Erstellung des Jahresabschlusses	preparation of annual financial statements
erweiterte Einziehung	extended confiscation
etwas erlangen (Einziehung)	obtain something
Europäische Staatsanwaltschaft	European Public Prosecutor's Office
Europäischer Gerichtshof	European Court of Justice
Europäischer Haftbefehl	European Arrest Warrant
Eventualvorsatz [also: → bedingter Vorsatz and *dolus eventualis*]	conditional intent
Exequaturentscheidung	exequatur decision
externe Meldestelle	external reporting office

F

Fachanwalt	specialist lawyer
Finanzgericht	fiscal court

G

Garantenstellung	obligation to act
gebundene Entscheidung	bound decision
Gefährdungsdelikt	endangerment offence
Geheimnis	secret
Geldstrafe	monetary fine; pecuniary penalty
Geldwäschebeauftragte	Money Laundering Officer
Generalbundesanwalt	Federal Prosecutor General
Generalstaatsanwaltschaft	General Public Prosecutor's Office

Genossenschaft	cooperative
Gericht	court
Gerichtshof der Europäischen Union	Court of Justice of the European Union
Gesamtstrafe	aggregate sentence
Geschäftsführer	managing director
Geschäftsgeheimnis	trade secret
Gesellschaft bürgerlichen Rechts	civil law partnership
Gesellschaft mit beschränkter Haftung	limited liability company
Gewerbezentralregister	Central Trade and Industry Register
Gewerkschaft	trade union
Gläubiger	creditors
Gläubigerausschuss	creditors' committee
Gläubigerversammlung	creditors' meeting
Gremienentscheidung	joint decision
große Strafkammer	major criminal panel

H

Handelsregister	commercial register
Handlungsbevollmächtigter	authorised representative
Hauptverfahren	main proceedings
Hinweisgeber	whistleblower

I

Insolvenzgläubiger	regular insolvency creditors
interne Meldestelle	internal reporting office
interne Untersuchung	internal investigation
Irrtum	error; mistake

J

Jedermannsdelikt	everyone's offence

K

Kartell	cartel
Kartellabsprache	cartel agreement
Kausalität	causality
Kick-Back-Zahlungen	kick-back payments
kleine Strafkammer	minor criminal panel
Klimapflege (Korruption)	sweetening
Kommanditgesellschaft	limited partnership
Kommanditgesellschaft auf Aktien	partnership limited by shares
Kommanditist	limited partner
Komplementär	general partner
Korruption	corruption

Krankenversicherung	health insurance

L

Landesarbeitsgericht	higher labour court
Landgericht	regional court
Lebens- und Geheimnisbereich	sphere of personal life and privacy
Leerverkauf	short selling
Leichtfertigkeit	recklessness
Lieferkette	supply chain

M

Massegläubiger	preferential creditors
Meldung	report
mittelbare Täterschaft (§ 25 sub. 1 alt. 2 StGB)	indirect perpetration

N

nachrangige Insolvenzgläubiger	subordinated creditors
Nebenbetroffene	secondary aggrieved party
Nebenklage	accessory prosecution
Nebenkläger	accessory prosecutor
Nebenpflichten	collateral duties
Nebenstrafrecht	ancillary criminal law
Nettoprinzip (Einziehung)	net principle
Nullbescheid	zero notice

O

Oberlandesgericht	higher regional court
Oberverwaltungsgericht / Verwaltungsgerichtshof	higher administrative court
offene Handelsgesellschaft	general partnership
offene Stellvertretung	disclosed agency
Offizialdelikte	official offences
Opportunitätsprinzip	principle of opportunity; principle of discretion
ordentlicher und gewissenhafter Geschäftsleiter	prudent businessman
Ordnungswidrigkeit	administrative offence; regulatory offence
örtliche Zuständigkeit	local jurisdiction

P

personenbezogene Daten	personal data
Preisabsprache	price fixing
Privatklage	private prosecution
Prokurist	holder of a general power of attorney

Q

Qualifikationstatbestand	qualified offence; aggravated offence
R	
Rahmenbeschluss (EU)	Framework Decision
Rechtshilfe	mutual legal assistance
Regelbeispiel	presumptive example
Restrukturierung	restructuring
Restrukturierungsbeauftragter	restructuring commissioner
Revision	appeal on points of law
Richter	judge
Richtlinie (EU)	Directive
Risikoanalyse	risk analysis
Risikomanagement	risk management
S	
sachliche Zuständigkeit	subject-matter jurisdiction
Sachverständigenaussage	expert testimony
Sachverständiger	expert
Schöffe	lay judge
Schöffengericht	court that includes lay judges
Schuld	culpability
Schwarzarbeit	undeclared work
Schwarze Kasse	slush fund
Schwurgericht	criminal chambers for particularly serious crimes
Selbstanzeige	voluntary disclosure
Selbstgeldwäsche	self-laundering
selbstständige Einziehung	independent confiscation
sofortige Beschwerde	immediate complaint
Sonderdelikt	special offence
Sorgfaltspflichten	due diligence obligations
Spezialitätsprinzip	principle of specialty
Staatsanwalt	public prosecutor
Staatsanwaltschaft	public prosecutor's office
Stellvertretung	agency; representation; proxy
Steuerhinterziehung	tax evasion
Steuerpflichtiger	tax debtor
Stiftung	foundation
Strafantrag	demand for prosecution; request to prosecute
Strafanzeige	criminal complaint
Strafbefehl	summary penalty order
Strafe	penalty; sentence
Strafkammer	criminal panel
Strafsenat	criminal senate
Strafverfahren	criminal proceedings
Strafverfolgung	prosecution; criminal prosecution

Subventionsbetrug	subsidy fraud
T	
Tatbestandsirrtum (§ 16 StGB)	error of fact
Tatbestandsmerkmal	element of crime / of an offence
Täter	perpetrator
Täterschaft	perpetration; commission (of the offence)
tätige Reue	active repentance
Täuschung (Betrug)	deception
U	
Überschuldung	over-indebtedness
Unterlassung	omission
Unternehmen	enterprise; undertaking (esp. in competition law)
Untersuchungshaft	pre-trial detention
Untreue	breach of trust
Urkundenbeweis	documentary evidence
V	
Verbotsirrtum (§ 17 StGB)	error of law
Verbrechen	crime
verdeckte Stellvertretung	undisclosed agency
Verein	association
Verfahren	proceedings
Vergehen	misdemeanour
Vergleich	settlement
Verjährung	statute of limitations
verkürzte Steuern	understated taxes
Vermittlungsausschuss	mediation committee
Vermögensbetreuungspflicht (§ 266 StGB)	safeguarding duty
Vermögensschaden	pecuniary loss
Verteidiger	defence counsel
Verteidigung	defence
Verteidigungskosten	defence costs
Vertretung	representation
Verwaltungsgericht	administrative court
Vollendung (der Tat)	completion (of the offence)
Vollmacht	power of attorney
Vollstreckungssperre	stay of enforcement
Vorsatz	intent
vorsitzender Richter	presiding judge
Vorstand (Aktiengesellschaft)	management board
Vorstandsmitglieder	board members
W	
Wirtschaftskriminalität	white-collar crime

Z

Zahlungsunfähigkeit	illiquidity
Zeuge	witness
Zeugenaussage	witness testimony
Zulässigkeit	admissibility
Zuständigkeit	jurisdiction
Zuständigkeit in erster Instanz	original jurisdiction
Zwischenverfahren	interlocutory proceedings; opening proceedings

English - German

A

abetting	Anstiftung (§ 26 StGB)
abettor	Anstifter
accessory prosecution	Nebenklage
accessory prosecutor	Nebenkläger
accused person	Beschuldigter
active repentance	tätige Reue
adhesion proceedings	Adhäsionsverfahren
administrative court	Verwaltungsgericht
administrative fine [or: → regulatory fine]	Bußgeld
administrative fining notice	Bußgeldbescheid
administrative offence [or: → regulatory offence]	Ordnungswidrigkeit
admissibility	Zulässigkeit
agency [or: → representation]	Stellvertretung
aggravated offence [or: → qualified offence]	Qualifikationstatbestand
aggregate sentence	Gesamtstrafe
aiding	Beihilfe (§ 27 StGB)
ancillary criminal law	Nebenstrafrecht
ancillary plaintiff	Adhäsionskläger
appeal on points of fact and law	Berufung
appeal on points of law	Revision
association	Verein
attorney [or: → lawyer]	Anwalt
authorised representative	Handlungsbevollmächtigter

B

blanket norm	Blankettnorm
board members	Vorstandsmitglieder
bound decision	gebundene Entscheidung
breach of trust	Untreue
bribes	Bestechungsgelder; Bestechungsmittel
burden of proof	Beweislast
business judgment rule	Business Judgment Rule

C

cartel	Kartell
cartel agreement	Kartellabsprache
catch-all clause	Auffangklausel
causality	Kausalität
Central Trade and Industry Register	Gewerbezentralregister
civil law partnership	Gesellschaft bürgerlichen Rechts

collateral duties	Nebenpflichten
commercial register	Handelsregister
commission (of the offence) [or: → perpetration]	Täterschaft
compensation procedure	Entschädigungsverfahren
complaint	Beschwerde
complaints procedure	Beschwerdeverfahren
completion (of the offence)	Vollendung (der Tat)
compliance	Compliance
compliance officer	Compliance-Beauftragter
conditional intent	bedingter Vorsatz; Eventualvorsatz; *dolus eventualis*
confiscating party or secondary party	Einziehungs- oder Nebenbeteiligte
confiscation	Einziehung
confiscation of objects of crime	Einziehung von Tatobjekten
confiscation of proceeds of crime	Einziehung von Taterlangtem
cooperative	Genossenschaft
corporate governance	Corporate Governance
corruption	Korruption
court	Gericht
Court of Justice of the European Union	Gerichtshof der Europäischen Union
creditors	Gläubiger
creditors' committee	Gläubigerausschuss
creditors' meeting	Gläubigerversammlung
crime	Verbrechen
criminal chambers for particularly serious crimes	Schwurgericht
criminal complaint	Strafanzeige
criminal panel	Strafkammer
criminal proceedings	Strafverfahren
criminal senate	Strafsenat
culpability	Schuld

D

deception (fraud)	Täuschung
decision	Entscheidung
defence	Verteidigung
defence costs	Verteidigungskosten
defence counsel	Verteidiger
defendant	Angeklagter
demand for prosecution [see also → request to prosecute]	Strafantrag
Directive (EU)	Richtlinie
disclosed agency	offene Stellvertretung
discretionary decision	Ermessensentscheidung

disenrichment [or: → loss of enrichment]	Entreicherung
documentary evidence	Urkundenbeweis
double criminality (mutual legal assistance)	beiderseitige Strafbarkeit
due diligence obligations	Sorgfaltspflichten

E

element of crime / of an offence	Tatbestandsmerkmal
endangerment offence	Gefährdungsdelikt
enrichment	Bereicherung
enterprise [or: → undertaking (esp. in competition law)]	Unternehmen
error [or: → mistake]	Irrtum
error of fact	Tatbestandsirrtum (§ 16 StGB)
error of law	Verbotsirrtum (§ 17 StGB)
European Arrest Warrant	Europäischer Haftbefehl
European Court of Justice	Europäischer Gerichtshof
European Delegated Prosecutors	Delegierte Europäische Staatsanwälte
European Public Prosecutor's Office	Europäische Staatsanwaltschaft
everyone's offence	Jedermannsdelikt
evidence	Beweis
evidence by inspection	Beweis durch Augenschein
examining judge	Ermittlungsrichter
exequatur decision	Exequaturentscheidung
expenditures	Aufwendungen
expert	Sachverständiger
expert testimony	Sachverständigenaussage
extended confiscation	erweiterte Einziehung
external reporting office	externe Meldestelle
extradition	Auslieferung
extradition treaty	Auslieferungsvertrag

F

Federal Administrative Court	Bundesverwaltungsgericht
Federal Constitutional Court	Bundesverfassungsgericht
Federal Court of Justice	Bundesgerichtshof
Federal Criminal Records Register	Bundeszentralregister
Federal Financial Supervisory Authority	Bundesanstalt für Finanzdienstleistungsaufsicht
Federal Fiscal Court	Bundesfinanzhof
Federal Foreign Office	Auswärtiges Amt
Federal Labour Court	Bundesarbeitsgericht
Federal Law Gazette	Bundesanzeiger
Federal Prosecutor General	Generalbundesanwalt
Federal Social Court	Bundessozialgericht
fiscal court	Finanzgericht

foreign trade and payments	Außenwirtschaft
foundation	Stiftung
Framework Decision (EU)	Rahmenbeschluss
fraud	Betrug

G

gang	Bande
general partner	Komplementär
general partnership	offene Handelsgesellschaft
General Public Prosecutor's Office	Generalstaatsanwaltschaft
German State	Bundesland
giving bribes	Bestechung
grooming (corruption)	Anfüttern
gross principle (confiscation)	Bruttoprinzip
guidelines on administrative fines; guidelines for the imposition of regulatory fines	Bußgeldleitlinien

H

health insurance	Krankenversicherung
higher administrative court	Oberverwaltungsgericht / Verwaltungsgerichtshof
higher labour court	Landesarbeitsgericht
higher regional court	Oberlandesgericht
holder of a general power of attorney	Prokurist
honorary judge	ehrenamtlicher Richter

I

illiquidity	Zahlungsunfähigkeit
immediate complaint	sofortige Beschwerde
imminent illiquidity	drohende Zahlungsunfähigkeit
independent confiscation	selbstständige Einziehung
indicted accused; accused indictee	Angeschuldigter
indictment	Anklageerhebung
indirect perpetration	mittelbare Täterschaft (§ 25 sub. 1 alt. 2 StGB)
intent	Vorsatz
interlocutory proceedings [also: → opening proceedings]	Zwischenverfahren
internal investigation	interne Untersuchung
internal reporting office	interne Meldestelle
issuer (capital markets)	Emittent

J

joint decision	Gremienentscheidung
judge	Richter
jurisdiction	Zuständigkeit
justification error	Erlaubnistatbestandsirrtum

K

kick-back payments	Kick-Back-Zahlungen

L

labour court	Arbeitsgericht
lawyer [or: → attorney]	Anwalt
lay judge	Schöffe
limited liability company	Gesellschaft mit beschränkter Haftung
limited partner	Kommanditist
limited partnership	Kommanditgesellschaft
liquidator	Abwickler
local court	Amtsgericht
local jurisdiction	örtliche Zuständigkeit
loss of enrichment / of crime profits [or: → disenrichment]	Entreicherung

M

main proceedings	Hauptverfahren
major criminal panel	große Strafkammer
management board (stock corporation)	Vorstand
managing director	Geschäftsführer
mediation committee	Vermittlungsausschuss
minor criminal panel	kleine Strafkammer
misdemeanour	Vergehen
mistake [see also → error]	Irrtum
monetary fine [or: → pecuniary penalty]	Geldstrafe
Money Laundering Officer	Geldwäschebeauftragte
motion to take evidence	Beweisantrag
mutual legal assistance	Rechtshilfe

N

net principle (confiscation)	Nettoprinzip

O

obligation to act	Garantenstellung
obtain something (confiscation)	etwas erlangen
offence	Delikt
offence of success	Erfolgsdelikt
official offences	Offizialdelikte
official secret	Dienstgeheimnis
omission	Unterlassung
opening proceedings [also: → interlocutory proceedings]	Zwischenverfahren
original jurisdiction	Zuständigkeit in erster Instanz
over-indebtedness	Überschuldung

P

partnership limited by shares	Kommanditgesellschaft auf Aktien
party to the confiscation proceedings	Einziehungsbeteiligte
pecuniary loss	Vermögensschaden
pecuniary penalty [or: → monetary fine]	Geldstrafe
penalty [see also → sentence]	Strafe
perpetration [or: → commission (of the offence)]	Täterschaft
perpetrator	Täter
personal data	personenbezogene Daten
power of attorney	Vollmacht
preferential creditors	Massegläubiger
preliminary proceedings	Ermittlungsverfahren
preparation of annual financial statements	Erstellung des Jahresabschlusses
presiding judge	vorsitzender Richter
presumptive example	Regelbeispiel
pre-trial detention	Untersuchungshaft
price fixing	Preisabsprache
principle of certainty	Bestimmtheitsgrundsatz
principle of discretion	Opportunitatsprinzip
principle of opportunity	Opportunitätsprinzip
principle of specialty	Spezialitätsprinzip
private prosecution	Privatklage
proceedings	Verfahren
professional judge	Berufsrichter
prosecution; criminal prosecution	Strafverfolgung
prudent businessman	ordentlicher und gewissenhafter Geschäftsleiter
public limited company [or: → stock corporation]	Aktiengesellschaft
public official	Amtsträger
public prosecutor	Staatsanwalt
public prosecutor's office	Staatsanwaltschaft

Q

qualified offence [or: → aggravated offence]	Qualifikationstatbestand

R

recklessness	Leichtfertigkeit
regional court	Landgericht
regular insolvency creditors	Insolvenzgläubiger
regulatory fine [or: → administrative fine]	Bußgeld
regulatory offence [or: → administrative offence]	Ordnungswidrigkeit
report	Meldung
representation [see also → agency]	Stellvertretung

request for extradition	Auslieferungsersuchen
request to prosecute [see also → demand for prosecution]	Strafantrag
restructuring	Restrukturierung
restructuring commissioner	Restrukturierungsbeauftragter
reversal of the burden of proof	Beweislastumkehr
risk analysis	Risikoanalyse
risk management	Risikomanagement

S

safeguarding duty	Vermögensbetreuungspflicht (§ 266 StGB)
search	Durchsuchung
search warrant	Durchsuchungsbefehl
secondary aggrieved party	Nebenbetroffene
secret	Geheimnis
seizure	Beschlagnahme
self-laundering	Selbstgeldwäsche
sentence [or: → penalty]	Strafe
settlement	Vergleich
short selling	Leerverkauf
slush fund	Schwarze Kasse
special offence	Sonderdelikt
sphere of personal life and privacy	Lebens- und Geheimnisbereich
statute of limitations	Verjährung
stay of enforcement	Vollstreckungssperre
stock corporation [or: → public limited company]	Aktiengesellschaft
subject-matter jurisdiction	sachliche Zuständigkeit
subordinated creditors	nachrangige Insolvenzgläubiger
subsidy fraud	Subventionsbetrug
summary penalty order	Strafbefehl
supervisory board	Aufsichtsrat
supply chain	Lieferkette
sweetening (corruption)	Klimapflege

T

taking bribes	Bestechlichkeit
tax debtor	Steuerpflichtiger
tax evasion	Steuerhinterziehung
termination (of the offence)	Beendigung (der Tat)
testimony	Aussage
trade secret	Geschäftsgeheimnis
trade union	Gewerkschaft
triangular fraud	Dreiecksbetrug

U

undeclared work	Schwarzarbeit
underlying act	Anknüpfungstat
understated taxes	verkürzte Steuern
undertaking (esp. in competition law) [or: → enterprise]	Unternehmen
undisclosed agency	verdeckte Stellvertretung

V

voluntary disclosure	Selbstanzeige

W

whistleblower	Hinweisgeber
white-collar crime	Wirtschaftskriminalität
witness	Zeuge
witness testimony	Zeugenaussage
works council	Betriebsrat

Z

zero notice	Nullbescheid

Index

References in the following are to chapters and to the margin number of the chapter.

A

A1 certificate **19** 14, 112
ABC *see* anti-bribery and corruption
abetting **10** 67; **13** 83
abettor **12** 66
Abhilfemaßnahme **18** 101
Absatzkrise **15** 7
Absonderung
- *Absonderungsberechtigte* **15** 115
- *Absonderungsrecht* **15** 75
abstract endangerment offence **18** 143
Abteilung Cybercrime **17** 6
abuse alternative **12** 5, 7
abuse of dominance **24** 2, 42, 70
- cases **24** 72
- of undertakings **24** 42
abusive criticism **17** 97, 146
Abwickler **4** 25
accepting benefits **10** 26
- European official **10** 26
- public official **10** 26
accessory **5** 25, 28
active repentance **11** 154; **14** 15, 30, 32
- professional secrecy bearers **14** 44
Adhäsionskläger **2** 65
Adhäsionsverfahren **2** 65
ad-hoc announcement **22** 52
- content **22** 59
- distribution **22** 59
- timing **22** 59
ad-hoc disclosure
- inside information **22** 52
Ad-hoc-Mitteilung **22** 52
administrative fine **4** 4, 9, 89; **16** 8
- confiscation of financial benefits **4** 93
- LkSG **18** 142, 151
- penalty **4** 93
administrative law **20** 60
administrative liability **6** 10
administrative offence **4** 60; **22** 7, 47; **23** 13, 44, 45, 50
- for negligence **23** 104
- infringement **4** 137
- inside information **22** 66
- punishment for violation of EU sanctions **23** 79
administrative proceedings **24** 71
administrative sanction **4** 4
- addressee **4** 9
advisory board
- duty to file for insolvency **15** 43
affiliated enterprises **18** 48
AG *see Aktiengesellschaft*
agency
- disclosed **13** 52
- undisclosed **13** 52
aggravating factors **24** 84
agreement
- binding **12** 4, 8, 68
- collective **16** 115
- non-disclosure **21** 66
- Special Prorate Agreements **24** 54
- unlawful **10** 40, 42, 44, 53, 68, 75
agricultural agreements **24** 37
AI **17** 2
- models **17** 160, 161
- supported criminal offences **17** 2
- supported phishing campaigns **17** 2 used for criminal purposes **17** 159
aider **12** 66
aiding **10** 67; **13** 83
aiding after the fact **13** 89
aiding and abetting **2** 52; **11** 10; **12** 66; **13** 83
'Airtours' criteria **24** 50
AI systems
- developer's criminal liability **17** 164
- supporting law enforcement authorities **17** 159
Aktiengesellschaft **4** 10; **18** 37
AML *see* anti-money laundering
Amnesty International **18** 26
Amtsträger **10** 19
- Europäischer Amtsträger **10** 21

Anfüttern **10** 43
Angeklagter **2** 61; **3** 7, 73
Angeschuldigter **3** 7, 67
Anstifter **12** 66
Anstiftung **10** 67
anti-bribery and corruption policy **6** 43, 44, 94, 96
anti-corruption **6** 8
anti-money laundering **6** 8
- policy **6** 45
Anti-Money Laundring Authority **14** 127
Anti-Torture Regulation **23** 31
Antragsdelikt **17** 96
- *relatives Antragsdelikt* **17** 57
Anweisungen für das Straf- und Bußgeldverfahren **13** 59
appeal
- against administrative fining notice **4** 148
- on points of fact and law **3** 107
- on points of law **3** 112
Arbeitnehmerentsendegesetz **19** 121
Arbeitnehmerüberlassung **19** 12, 23
Arbeitnehmerüberlassungsgesetz **19** 113
Arbeitsschutzgesetz **19** 48
Arbeitszeitgesetz **19** 60
Area of Freedom, Security and Justice **9** 74
artificial intelligence *see* AI
asset **12** 14
- company **12** 15
- concrete threat **11** 56
- confiscation **5** 2, 35, 121
- damage-equivalent treat **11** 56
- disposal **11** 45; **12** 4
- disposal of assets **11** 111
- endangerment **12** 76
- illegally acquired **12** 14
- joint **12** 15
- loss **12** 39
- of another person **12** 14
- partnerships' **12** 15
- provisional securing **5** 123
- recovery **10** 81
- representatives' **12** 15
- seizure **4** 120; **17** 156
- shareholders' **12** 15
- third-party **12** 15
association
- board members **4** 28, 29
- board of directors **4** 28
- registered **4** 28
- with legal personality **4** 28
- without legal personality **4** 18, 33
Association of Statutory Health Insurance Physicians **21** 87
attempt
- abandon the attempt **13** 41, 42
attorney privilege **14** 35, 43
audio recording **25** 158
auditor
- safeguarding duty **12** 35
- special **13** 63
audit order **13** 62
audits **6** 78
Auffangtatbestand **12** 3
Aufwendungen **5** 96
Auslieferung
- Gegenseitigkeit **9** 30
- Spezialität **9** 35
Aussonderung
- Aussonderungsberechtigte **15** 115
Auswärtiges Amt **9** 6
author **25** 110, 111
- rights **25** 113
authorisation requirement
- data retention system **23** 126
- for monitoring systems **23** 126
authorized representative **4** 49
- chief **4** 50, 51
- trade **4** 50
- with general commercial power of attorney **4** 50, 52
authorship
- unlawful affixing of a designation **25** 116

B

BAFA handouts **18** 31
BaFin
- Administrative Fine Guidelines **22** 10
- *Emittentenleitfaden* **22** 5
- Issuer Guidelines **22** 5, 24
- *Stimmrechtsmitteilungsverordnung* **22** 102
- Voting Rights Notification Regulation **22** 102
- *WpHG-Bußgeldleitlinien* **22** 10
Bande **13** 46; **17** 110

bank
- private bank **25** 13
- state bank **25** 12
Bankrott **15** 87
bankruptcy **15** 87
Bannbruch **13** 84
bans on movement **13** 84
Basel Convention **18** 54
Beendigung **10** 76
Beihilfe **10** 67; **21** 79
benefit **10** 33, 93
- accepting **10** 17
- definition **10** 33
- financial **5** 30
- granting **10** 17
Berufsgenossenschaften **19** 59
Berufung **3** 107
Beschaffungsstrategien **18** 97
Beschlagnahme **3** 37
Beschuldigter **2** 61; **3** 7, 67
Beschwerde **3** 103
- *sofortige* **3** 103
Beschwerdeverfahren **7** 149; **18** 107
Bestechlichkeit **10** 48
Bestechung **10** 48
Bestimmtheitsgrundsatz **18** 69
best price guarantees **24** 30
Betriebsrat **7** 130
Betrug **11** 1; **12** 1
- *Kapitalanlagebetrug* **22** 117
Beweisantrag **3** 87
Beweislast **7** 122
Beweislastumkehr **7** 5
bid rigging **24** 7, 29, 92, 95
Bilanzeid **22** 93
blanket criminal provisions in the AMG **21** 159
blanket norms **23** 16
Blankettnorm **20** 1, 32
blockchain analysis **17** 152, 154
block exemption regulations **24** 24, 37
- R&D **24** 37
- specialisation **24** 37
- technology transfer **24** 37
- vertical **24** 37
bodily harm **20** 93, 125, 127, 135
- intentional **20** 109, 117
- negligent **20** 109
- serious **20** 117
bodily injury **20** 102, 130, 140
bonus payments **12** 10, 93
boycott **24** 40
branch office **18** 46
breach of fidelity alternative **12** 5, 10
breach of trust **12** 1, 48
- commission of and complicity in **12** 66
- negligence **12** 65
briber **12** 84
bribery **2** 35; **12** 83
- active **10** 83, 84, 96
- foreign or international officials **10** 62
- giving bribes **10** 48; **21** 136
- of international officials **10** 62
- of public officials **10** 5, 10, 91, 95
- of voters **10** 13
- passive **10** 83, 96
- taking bribes **10** 48; **21** 136
bribes **12** 82
- giving **10** 17; **12** 82, 85
- taking **10** 17; **12** 82
Bruttoprinzip **4** 97; **10** 81
Bundesantalt für Finanzdienstleistungsaufsicht see BaFin
Bundeskartellamt **24** 3
- *Sonderkommission Kartellbekämpfung* **24** 99
Bundeskriminalamt **17** 2
Bundeswehr **10** 27
Bundeszentralregister **13** 73
burden of proof **7** 106, 122
- reversal **7** 5; **8** 82
business and trade secrets **25** 43, 45, 46, 104
Business Judgement Rule **6** 8; **15** 18
Business Judgment Rule **12** 40, 94
business relationship
- termination **18** 103, 104
Bußgeldbescheid **4** 120
Bußgeldleitlinien **24** 83
Bußgeld- und Strafsachenstelle **13** 96

C

CAP *see* corrective action plan
capital market
- compliance **22** 15
- compliance system **22** 16
- offences **22** 13
- regulations **22** 14
capital markets laws **22** 3, 7
- competent authorites **22** 5

- violation **22** 8, 9
cartel
- between competitors **24** 19
- hardcore cartel agreements **24** 19, 24
- hardcore cartel infringement **24** 35
- infringement **24** 4, 70
cash pool
- crisis **15** 24
cash pooling **12** 98
catch-all clause **12** 3, 5
causality **13** 32; **20** 110, 118, 124, 129, 132
- general **20** 110, 116, 118
- individual **20** 118
- proof **20** 115, 119
- specific **20** 116
Central Cybercrime Contact Points **17** 6
central trade register **4** 112
CEO fraud **17** 115
child labour **18** 28, 53
Chinese wall **22** 29
civil servants **10** 46
climate litigation **18** 23
closed periods **22** 80
CLOUD Act **9** 72
cloud computing services **16** 28
clouds **17** 9, 124
CMS *see* compliance management system
CO *see* compliance officer
code of conduct **6** 31, 32, 33
- best practices **6** 38
coercion **17** 112
coercive measures **3** 37
collateral duties **12** 16
collective dominance **24** 50
collective labour law **19** 127
collegiate body **2** 37
commercial information **25** 1, 59
- protection against cybercrime **25** 139
commission
- taking of **12** 83
commitments **24** 71, 136
committee of spokespersons
- protection **19** 141
Committee of Sponsoring Organisations of the Treadway Commission **6** 20, 30
Committee on Anti Money Laundering **14** 124
communication services
- control **17** 17
Community dimension **24** 122
community dimension **24** 128
compensation
- for retaliation **7** 123
- for wrongful prosecution **3** 127
competition **21** 145
- register **2** 26, 88; **4** 87, 111; **10** 119; **19** 170; **24** 91
- significant competitive influence **24** 126
- significant impediment **24** 135
competitively sensitive information **24** 21
competitor
- cartel between competitors **24** 19
- contracts **24** 18
complaint
- immediate **3** 103
- ordinary **3** 103
complaints procedure **7** 149; **18** 107, 118
compliance **2** 2; **12** 86
- automated control mechanisms **6** 71
- capital markets **22** 15
- case **8** 19
- committee **6** 98
- controls **6** 58
- corporate **23** 4
- corrective action plan **6** 89, 90, 91, 92, 93, 95
- corruption prevention **10** 120
- department **8** 1, 16, 81
- due diligence obligations **18** 122
- foreign trade law **23** 107
- guidelines **6** 40
- health care sector **21** 2
- obligations **22** 83
- officer **2** 43
- organisation **8** 13, 14, 20, 21, 25, 32
- preventive measures **6** 28
- procedural controls **6** 66
- process-accompanying controls **6** 67
- risk assessment **6** 23
- risks **6** 24, 26
- roundtables **6** 52
- spot checks **6** 69
- structure **2** 37
- system **2** 72
- training **6** 53
- with environmental obligations **18** 15
- with human rights **18** 15

compliance management system **6** 4; **7** 2; **8** 8, 10, 78; **18** 30
compliance officer **6** 52, 98, 100, 101, 103; **8** 5; **18** 147
- safeguarding duty **12** 34
- tasks **6** 102
compliance programmes **24** 9
compliance violations **6** 84; **8** 8, 19, 70, 72, 86
- investigation **6** 72
- prevention **6** 41, 59
- remedial actions **8** 72
- risks **6** 28
compromising withholding taxes **13** 128
computer criminal law **17** 4
computer data
- preservation **17** 137
- search and seizure of stored computer data **17** 137
computer espionage **17** 39
computer fraud **17** 30, 73
computer sabotage **17** 58, 66, 69, 72, 74
concerted practices **24** 20
conclusive conduct *see* deception
conclusive declarations **11** 25
conferral **12** 8
- by commission of an authority **12** 8
- by law **12** 8
- by legal transaction **12** 8
- valid **12** 9
confession
- early confession **13** 79
confidentiality
- of public authorities **25** 29
- professional *see* professional confidentiality
- requirement **7** 100
confidentiality obligations
- official **25** 29
- of public officials **25** 34
- violations **25** 7
confiscation **2** 12, 58, 60, 69; **3** 97; **4** 95; **14** 38; **23** 50; **25** 126
- assets **5** 2, 5, 35, 121
- compensation procedure **5** 2
- confiscating party **2** 58
- cryptocurrency **17** 131
- extended **5** 12
- extended independent **5** 12
- from third parties **5** 60
- gross principle **4** 97
- money **5** 50
- non-netting rule **5** 36
- objections **5** 91
- of enterprise-owned property and rights **4** 109
- of profits **4** 87, 107
- order **2** 63
- proceeds **5** 21
- proceeds from tax offences **13** 91
- profits **5** 57
- requirement **5** 26, 30
- reward **5** 21, 41
- secondary party **2** 58, 59
- simple **5** 12, 13
- simple independent **5** 12
- spoils **5** 21, 31, 40, 41
- surrogate **5** 13, 21, 47, 57, 62, 82
- transferred spoils **5** 21
confiscation proceedings **2** 22, 62
- defence strategy **2** 63
- party **2** 58, 59, 61
consent **12** 44; **21** 10
- declaration **12** 44
- legal person **12** 46
- limited liability companies **12** 48
- majority shareholder **12** 48
- partnership **12** 50
- presumed **12** 45; **21** 9, 15, 63
- prior **12** 45
- risky transactions **12** 75
- stock corporation **12** 49
constructive notice **13** 70
consumer
- end **20** 93
- goods **20** 136, 153
- harm **20** 102
- interests **20** 137
- protection **20** 137, 164
contract
- bona fide **5** 69
- pending contracts **15** 110
Convention on Cybercrime **17** 18, 137
cooperative **4** 10, 31
- board of management **4** 31
copyright
- infringement **25** 117, 152
- punishable acts **25** 112
copyrighted works **25** 107
- distribution **25** 3

- reproducing **25** 3
- unlawful exploitation **25** 111, 112
copyright offences **17** 30
corporate citizenship **2** 2
corporate criminal law **1** 9 et seq., 18 et seqq.; **2** 5, 32; **4** 151; **12** 3; **23** 10
corporate criminal liability **1** 11 et seq., 17, 28; **9** 107 et seq.; **10** 6; **12** 100; **16** 9; **22** 1; **23** 8; **24** 92, 95
corporate defence **2** 33
- strategy **2** 81
corporate defender **2** 83, 102, 103, 104, 106
corporate responsibility **18** 5, 6, 14; **22** 8
Corporate Sanctions Act **6** 17; **23** 10
Corporate Social Responsibility *see* CSR
corporation
- 'capital-market oriented' **22** 96
corrective action plan **6** 89, 90, 91, 92, 93, 95
corruption **8** 85
- benefit **21** 136
- economic significance **10** 3
- healthcare sector **10** 12
- involving public officials **10** 14
- legal framework **10** 6
- meaning **10** 1
- offences commited in public office **10** 16
- passive **10** 11
- perpetrators **10** 17
- prevention **10** 120
- private sector **10** 7, 12, 110
- public sector **10** 7, 110
- scandals **8** 3
corruption offences **10** 6, 15
- against competition **10** 15
- public office **10** 15, 16
- sanctions **10** 69
COSO *see* Committee of Sponsoring Organisations
court
- administrative court **3** 14
- criminal court system **3** 11
- Federal Court of Justice **3** 14
- fiscal court **3** 14
- German court system **3** 14
- higher regional *see* higher regional court
- labour court **3** 14
- local *see* local court
- ordinary court **3** 14
- regional *see* regional court
- social security court **3** 14
- types **3** 15
creditor
- creditors' assembly **15** 120
- creditors' committee **15** 69, 102
- creditors' meeting **15** 69, 107
- file for insolvency **15** 99
- insolvency **15** 108
- involvement in insolvency proceedings **15** 120
- list **15** 74
- preferential **15** 115, 117
- preferential treatment **15** 92
- protection **15** 60
- regular insolvency **15** 115
- types **15** 115
- with preferential claims **15** 113
- with the right to separate satisfaction **15** 115
- with the right to separation **15** 115
crime
- against the state **3** 20, 21
- business **3** 20
- imprisonment **3** 18
- tax *see* tax crime
Crimean Annexation Regulation **23** 99
crimes of negligence **21** 17
criminal complaint **16** 10
criminal court
- organisation and jurisdiction **3** 11
criminal law
- computer criminal law **17** 4
- cooperation **17** 133
- corporate **2** 5, 32
- environmental *see* environmental criminal law
- food *see* food criminal law
- international **18** 26
- internet criminal law **17** 4
- IT *see* IT criminal law
criminal tax law
- procedural law **13** 93
- proceedings **13** 109
crisis **15** 1, 26
- cash pool **15** 24
- definition **15** 5
- detection **15** 3, 12

- early detection **15** 1, 4, 6, 8, 10
- early financial **15** 27
- late profit **15** 27
- liquidity **15** 7, 9
- management **15** 14, 16
- product and sales **15** 7
- profit **15** 7, 9
- stages **15** 7
- stakeholder **15** 7
- strategy **15** 7

crypto
- accounts **14** 130
- assets **14** 131
- service provider **14** 131
- theft **17** 43

cryptocurrency **17** 131, 151
CSR **18** 34
- initiative **18** 34

culpability **13** 39
cum/cum **13** 3
cum/ex
- cases **13** 5, 76
- complex **11** 10
- indictments **13** 4
- offences **11** 11
- proceedings **11** 8, 11; **13** 3, 81
- system **13** 82
- transactions **13** 2

customs
- border **13** 84
- fraud **13** 85
- investigators **13** 63
- violation **13** 84, 85, 87

cyberattack **17** 1
- threat situation **17** 2

cyberbullying **17** 144, 148
cybercrime **17** 13
- accusation **17** 7
- committed by means of information technology systems **17** 11
- cyber-specific offences causing damage **17** 57
- prosecution **17** 127
- protection of commercial information **25** 139

Cybercrime Division **17** 6
Cybercrime Federal Situation Report **17** 2
cybercrime objects
- information technology systems **17** 9

cybercrime offences **17** 30
- CEO fraud **17** 115
- cyber-grooming **17** 111
- cyberstalking **17** 103
- pornographic illustrations **17** 111
- relating to statements **17** 97
- skimming **17** 109
- special **17** 102

cybercriminal **17** 23
- activities **17** 2

cyber-grooming **17** 111
Cyber Resilience Act **17** 20
cybersecurity **17** 16
- strategy **17** 16

cyberstalking **17** 103

D

Damages Directive **24** 93
darknet **17** 123
data
- alteration **17** 64
- business **8** 39
- business and trade secrets **25** 43
- centres **16** 28
- collection **8** 94
- company **8** 62
- cross-border data disclosure **17** 16
- deletion **17** 61
- disclosure **17** 39
- electronic *see* electronic data
- encrypted **17** 48
- error **17** 129
- espionage **17** 42, 45, 51, 155; **25** 3, 146
- forgery **17** 129
- interception **17** 45, 46, 50
- IT criminal law **17** 31
- loss **17** 129
- manipulation **17** 49, 58, 69, 112, 139, 155
- of employees **16** 94
- personal **8** 54, 77, 94; **17** 9, 89, 95, 99, 145; **25** 43, 44, 45
- processing **8** 54
- publicly accessible data **16** 83
- special category **16** 36
- spying **17** 38
- stolen **17** 54; **25** 152, 154
- suppression **17** 62
- theft **17** 39, 151

data controller **16** 17, 18

- responsibilities **16** 30
- TOMs **16** 20
data dependency **24** 67
data of probative value **17** 122
- forgery **17** 141, 142
- suppression **17** 84
data privacy
- laws **6** 90, 92
- officer **6** 92
- violation **6** 92
data processing **17** 66, 67
- contract **16** 31
- operations **17** 66, 67, 70
- outside the EU **16** 35
data processor **16** 26, 27
- sub-processor **16** 33
data protection **6** 8; **8** 69
- management system **16** 1
- officer **16** 36, 50
- violation **17** 30, 89
data protection law **8** 77
- accountability **16** 8
- before GDPR **16** 67
- difference to criminal law **16** 7
- GDPR opening clause **16** 6
- violation **8** 67
data subjects' rights **16** 62
data transmission **16** 86
- consent **16** 100, 109
dawn raids **24** 75
DAX **22** 46
DDoS **17** 2, 70
- attack **17** 1
debtor
- preferential treatment **15** 93
deception
- about facts **11** 18
- by conclusive conduct **11** 19, 22, 24, 25, 29
- by express statements **11** 19, 20
- by omission **11** 25, 26, 29
- express statement **11** 29
decision
- bound **10** 52
- discretionary **10** 52
decisive influence **18** 60, 61
declaration of consent **12** 44
- legal person **12** 46
declaration of correction **13** 123
declaration of principles **18** 96
deepfakes **17** 162
de facto director **2** 39
de facto managing director **2** 39; **12** 11, 27, 96, 98; **15** 84; **19** 11
defence
- corporate *see* corporate defence
- costs **12** 89
- mandatory defence **13** 106
- strategy **8** 3
defence counsel **3** 9; **13** 104
- tax adviser **13** 104
defendant **2** 61; **3** 7, 73
Delikt
- *relatives Antragsdelikt* **17** 57
- *abstrakte Gefährdungsdelikte* **10** 68
- *abstraktes Gefährdungsdelikt* **18** 143
- *Äußerungsdelikte* **17** 30, 97
- *Beschädigungsdelikte* **17** 30
- *echte Amtsdelikte* **10** 17
- *elektronische Urkundsdelikte* **17** 30
- *Jedermannsdelikte* **10** 17
- *Offizialdelikte* **10** 110
- *Sonderdelikt* **20** 19
demand for penalty **16** 71
de minimis
- exemption **24** 37
- market clause **24** 134
Deutscher Corporate Governance Kodex **6** 9
Deutsche Rentenversicherung **19** 160
Diebstahl **12** 10
Dienstausübung **10** 28
diesel complex **11** 9, 120, 124
diesel scandal **11** 92, 100
digital economy **24** 38
Digital Markets Act **24** 60
digital platforms **24** 38
- GAFA companies **24** 38
Digital Services Act **17** 21
digital theft **17** 2
digital violence **17** 16
diligence of a prudent businessman **15** 89
direct economic link **13** 31
directors' dealings **22** 74
direct supplier **18** 62
- preventive measures **18** 98
discharge of a duty **10** 27, 28
disciplinary action **8** 80
disciplinary committee **8** 81

disciplinary measures **8** 14, 55, 72, 79, 80, 82
- admonition **8** 83
- demotion **8** 83
- dismissal of promotion **8** 83
- documentation **8** 82
- forfeiture of variable compensation **8** 83
- notice of termination **8** 83
- reduction of variable compensation **8** 83
- summary dismissal **8** 83
- suspension **8** 83
- withholding promotion **8** 83

discovery
- chance discoveries **8** 23
- e-discovery **8** 28, 36, 40

discrimination **24** 51
disenrichment **5** 111
disgorgement **5** 4, 18, 47, 107
- amount **2** 19
- criminal **2** 14, 20, 21
- order **2** 13

disposal
- assets **11** 45

dissemination **17** 100
dolus eventualis **12** 63; **13** 20, 33; **14** 33; **21** 140, 147
domestic issuer **22** 84
dominance **24** 44
donations **12** 42
doormat theory **13** 63
DORA **17** 20
double criminality **9** 16, 28, 53; **10** 108
Dreiecksbetrug **11** 60; **17** 116
dual-use
- exmination **23** 34
- export control **23** 34
- export of goods with **23** 33

dual-use goods **23** 4, 82
- authorisation **23** 134
- control **23** 123
- foreign trade **23** 43

Dual-Use Regulation
- export licence **23** 40
  - types **23** 41
- global licence **23** 42
- goods subject to permit **23** 35
- Internal Compliance Programmes **23** 58
- licensing requirement **23** 37
- surveillance technology **23** 130
- violation **23** 31, 33

dual-use technologies **23** 82
due diligence obligations **14** 80; **18** 9, 68
- appropriate manner **18** 31, 66
- compliance **18** 122
- environmental **18** 21, 64
- human rights **18** 64
- preventive measures **18** 71
- remedial measures **18** 71
- risk management **18** 71
- violation **18** 144
- vis-à-vis indirect suppliers **18** 112

Durchsuchung **3** 37
duty
- collateral **12** 16
- discharge **10** 26, 28
- elevated **12** 16
- grave breach **12** 43
- safeguarding **12** 16

E

EAW **9** 7, 10, 11, 17, 25, 31, 48, 60
- bars to extradition **9** 56
- deadline **9** 51
- enforcement **9** 60
- formal aspects **9** 50
- procedure **9** 51
- statute of limitation **9** 55

EAW Framework Decision **9** 9
ECN+ Directive **24** 71
ecocide **18** 26
EEA *see* European Economic Area
EEIG *see* European Economic Interest Grouping
e-Evidence **9** 85
EFTA *see* European Free Trade Association
eigener Geschäftsbereich **18** 60
Eigentumsvorbehalt **12** 17
Eigenverwaltung **15** 72
eingetragener Verein **4** 10
Ein-Mann-GmbH **4** 11
Einzelkaufmann **4** 9
Einziehung **2** 12; **5** 12; **13** 91
EIO **9** 7, 58, 65, 77
- Directive **9** 65, 78

elected officials
- bribery **10** 13

electronic data **25** 1
- illegal access **25** 139, 140
- protection **25** 139
electronic forgery offences **17** 30
electronic storage media **17** 124
embargo
- arms **23** 30, 31, 45
  - violation **23** 21
- countries **23** 24
- provisions **23** 23
embezzlement **2** 35, 41
employees
- accused **2** 106
- as potential witnesses **2** 111
- criminal liability **2** 34
- safeguarding duty **12** 33
employer **19** 8
endangerment
- abstract **20** 18
- concrete **20** 18, 40
- offence **18** 143; **20** 7, 18, 25, 69, 77; **21** 159
- serious **20** 77
end customer **18** 56, 58
Endkunde **18** 56
enforcement
- assistance **9** 1
- authorities **9** 93
- EU Member State **9** 106
- foreign judgments **9** 94
- foreign state **9** 104
- non-EU country **9** 106
- of German judgments abroad **9** 102
enriching **17** 54, 56, 94
enrichment **4** 79
- unjust **5** 47
enterprise
- affiliated **18** 48
- criminal liability **4** 3
- foreign **4** 16; **18** 46
- multicorporate **18** 48
- pre-enterprise **4** 14
- pre-incorporation **4** 14
- with limited liability **4** 11
Entleiher **19** 12, 117
Entreicherung **2** 21
Entschädigungsverfahren **5** 2
environmental code **20** 2
environmental criminal code **20** 2
environmental criminal law **20** 1
environmental criminal offences **20** 5
- air pollution **20** 51
- endangering proteced areas **20** 73
- releasing poison **20** 77
- soil pollution **20** 45
- unauthorised waste management **20** 7
- water pollution **20** 39
environmental goods **20** 18
environmental misconduct **6** 106
environmental offences **20** 1, 4, 5
environmental protection officer **18** 147
environmental, social, and governance *see* ESG
environmental standards **18** 26
EPPO **9** 76, 93
- Regulation **9** 93
Erfolgsdelikt **20** 7
Erfolgskrise **15** 7
Ermittlungsrichter **3** 29
ernsthaftes Einfordern **15** 50
error **13** 15, 37
- in thought **11** 37, 110
- of law **10** 55
ESG
- erroneous information **22** 131
- issues **6** 106
- matters **22** 130
- topics **6** 106; **22** 128
- violations **6** 106
ESMA **22** 6, 55
- guidelines **22** 55, 80
espionage
- computer **17** 39
- data **17** 42, 45, 51, 155; **25** 3, 146
- industrial **17** 2; **25** 84
essential facilities **24** 51
ethical
- behaviour **6** 20
- conduct **6** 47
- dilemmas **6** 52
- principles **6** 32
- requirements **6** 38
- standards **6** 34, 47, 48, 49, 54
EU Merger Regulation **24** 2
- concentration **24** 128
EURIBOR **22** 46
Europäische wirtschaftliche Interessensvereinigung **4** 47
European Arrest Warrant *see* EAW
European Competition Network **24** 80

European Cybercrime Centre **17** 6
European Delegated Prosecutors **9** 76
European Economic Interest Grouping **4** 13, 47
European Free Trade Association **12** 53; **23** 110
European Investigation Order **17** 136, *see* EIO
European Market Abuse Regulation **22** 3
European official **10** 22
European officials **10** 18, 21
European Preservation Order **9** 85, 88; **17** 135
European Production Order **9** 88; **17** 135
European Public Prosecutor's Office *see* EPPO
European Securities and Markets Authority *see* ESMA
EU-UK Trade and Cooperation Agreement **12** 53
EU-US Data Privacy Framework **16** 2, 35
evidence **3** 32
- by inspection **3** 32
- circumstantial evidence **13** 35
- digital evidence **17** 119, 122, 129, 130, 135
- motion to take **3** 87
exclusion
- issue-related reasons for exclusion **13** 62
- offence-related reasons for exclusion **13** 65
- personal reason for exclusion **13** 67
- reasons for exclusion **13** 61
exclusionary behaviour **24** 51
exclusionary conduct **24** 51
exclusion from public award procedures **24** 90
exclusion from the award of public contracts **18** 138
exclusive pre-installation **24** 62
execution proceedings **3** 114
exequatur decision **9** 97
Exequaturentscheidung **9** 97
existenzvernichtender Eingriff **15** 32
expenditure **5** 96
expert testimony **3** 32
exploitative abuse **24** 51
export
- authorisation **23** 129
- control **23** 2, 4, 123
- goods requiring a permit **23** 124
- licence **23** 40
- of goods with 'dual use' **23** 33
- of surveillance technology **23** 123
- types of licences **23** 41
- without licence **23** 37
external reporting office **7** 54
extradition **9** 1, 9
- admissibility **9** 18, 29, 39, 57
- bar **9** 26, 32, 35
- between EU Member States **9** 48
- case **9** 65
- documents **9** 14, 15, 16
- for fiscal offences **9** 30, 46
- for political offences **9** 26, 35
- in case of tax evasion **9** 3
- lack of reciprocity **9** 30
- mandatory reasons of refusal **9** 57
- optional grounds of refusal **9** 59
- prison conditions **9** 36
- procedure **9** 11
- proceedings **9** 20
- reciprocity **9** 30
- request **9** 2, 63
- requirements **9** 27
- rule of specialty **9** 35
- statute of limitation **9** 31
- third country request **9** 11
- to third countries **9** 25
- traditional **9** 49, 50
- treaty **9** 26, 45, 46
- waiver **9** 8

F
facts
- deception about facts **11** 108
fahrlässige Körperverletzung **20** 114
FCPA *see* US Foreign Corrupt Practices Act
Federal Cartel Office **24** 3
Federal Criminal Police Office **17** 2
Federal Financial Supervisory Authority **14** 124
Federal Foreign Office **9** 6
Federal Prosecutor General **3** 21
Financial Action Task Force **14** 5, 124
financial instruments
- marketing **22** 114
- misleading advertising **22** 127

Financial Intelligence Unit **14** 3, 46, 104, 127
financial reporting **22** 84
- publication obligations **22** 84
- sanctions **22** 93
Finanzkontrolle Schwarzarbeit **19** 146 et seqq.
fine
- administrative *see* administrative fine
- against a legal successor **4** 133, 134
- anonymous **4** 102
- assumption **12** 89
- corporate **2** 6, 7, 11, 23, 25, 26, 32, 55, 60, 62, 69, 96, 102; **23** 6, 11, 13
- cumulative **4** 100
- for misconduct **8** 7
- for tax crimes **13** 80
- isolated **4** 101
- limitation period **4** 123
- monetary **2** 7
- negotiated **2** 11
- regulatory *see* regulatory fine
  - notice **2** 62, 63
fingerprints **17** 120, 121
fiscal offences **9** 46
follow-on damage litigation **24** 106
food
- contaminated **20** 133, 136, 140
- export **20** 154
- placing on the market **20** 152
- production **20** 145
- spoiled **20** 136, 140
- transfer **20** 153
- treatment **20** 151
- wrongly labelled **20** 136
food crime **20** 140
food criminal law **20** 136, 140
- chain responsibility **20** 155
- obligations of the entrepreneur **20** 155
food entrepreneur
- auditing duty **20** 159
- information duty **20** 163
- investigation duty **20** 158
- traceability **20** 164
forced labour **18** 53
Forced Labour Convention **18** 53
foreign authorities **13** 69
foreign companies **18** 8
foreign counsel **9** 98
foreign direct investment **24** 123
foreign enterprises **18** 46
foreign judgments **9** 94
foreign national **9** 39, 47, 94, 102
foreign officials **10** 22, 62
foreign punishment **9** 108
foreign sentence **9** 97
- execution **9** 107
foreign state **9** 63
Foreign Subsidies Regulation **24** 123
foreign trade
- arms and military equipment **23** 4
- with dual-use goods **23** 43
foreign trade and payments **23** 1
- law **23** 6
foreign trade law **23** 2
- compliance **23** 107
- corporate criminal liability **23** 8
forgery
- electronic forgery offences **17** 30, 82
- of data **17** 129
- of data of probative value **17** 141, 142
- of documents **17** 141
forging of revenue stamps **13** 88
foundation **4** 10, 28
- board members **4** 29
Frankfurter Wertpapierbörse **22** 87
fraud **2** 35; **5** 15; **11** 1, 7, 14; **21** 97
- accounting-related **8** 85
- balance sheet **2** 35
- billing **21** 97
- capital investment **22** 117, 122
- CEO **17** 162
- computer **17** 30, 74, 80; **21** 103
- customs **13** 85
- deception about facts **11** 18
- general fraud **22** 118
- related to information on sustainability **22** 128
- sanctions **22** 131
- subsidy **11** 4, 13, 126
- triangular **11** 59; **17** 116
- triangulation **21** 113
freedom from self-incrimination **17** 121
freedom of association **18** 53
freedom of establishment **12** 51
freedom of expression **17** 97
Freiverkehr **22** 20
fremdes Vermögen **12** 14
functional concept of undertaking **24** 14

funding
- third-party **21** 153

G
GAFA companies **24** 4
GAFAM companies **24** 64
gang **13** 85, 90; **17** 110
- formation **13** 46
- member of a gang **13** 46
Garantenstellung **2** 36
GbR *see Gesellschaft bürgerlichen Rechts*
GDPR
- clarification obligations **7** 145
- information obligations **7** 145
Gefährdungsdelikt **20** 7
Geheimnis
- *Dienstgeheimnis* **25** 29
- *Geschäftsgeheimnis* **25** 1
- *Geschäfts- und Betriebsgeheimnisse* **25** 45, 104
Gehilfe **12** 66
Geldstrafe **9** 107
Geldwäschebeauftragter **14** 64
gemeinnützige Gesellschaften **18** 38
Generalbevollmächtigter **4** 50
Generalbundesanwalt **3** 21
general partner **12** 15
General Public Prosecutor's Office **9** 12
Generalstaatsanwaltschaft **9** 12
Genossenschaft **4** 10, 31
Gericht
- *Amtsgericht* **3** 14
- *Arbeitsgericht* **3** 14
- *Bundesgerichtshof* **3** 14
- *Finanzgericht* **3** 14
- *Landgericht* **3** 14
- *Oberlandesgericht* **3** 14
- *ordentliches Gericht* **3** 14
- *Sozialgericht* **3** 14
- *Verwaltungsgericht* **3** 14
German Corporate Governance Codex **6** 9
German court system **3** 14
German Diagnosis Related Group System **21** 93
German Federal Criminal Records Register **13** 73
German Money Laundering Act **14** 45
Gesamtstrafe **17** 34
Geschäftsbereich
- *eigener* **18** 60
Geschäftsführer **4** 27
Geschäftsleitung
- *sorgfältige* **15** 3
Gesellschaft bürgerlichen Rechts **4** 13, 14, 36; **18** 37
Gesellschaft mit beschränkter Haftung **4** 10; **18** 37
- *Vertretung* **4** 27
Gewerbezentralregister **4** 112; **19** 167
gift
- policy **6** 44, 94, 96
- socially-adequate **21** 137
giving bribes **10** 48
Gläubiger
- *Gläubigerausschuss* **15** 69
- *Gläubigerversammlung* **15** 69, 120
- *Insolvenzgläubiger* **15** 115
- *Massegläubiger* **15** 115
- *nachrangige Insolvenzgläubiger* **15** 115
global supply chains **18** 6, 15
GmbH *see Gesellschaft mit beschränkter Haftung*
GmbH & Co. KG **4** 13, 43; **12** 15
greenwashing **22** 128
Gremienentscheidung **2** 37
grooming **10** 43
gross principle **4** 97; **10** 81
- confiscation **4** 97
gross self-interest **19** 31
groundwater depletion **18** 28
Grundsatzerklärung **18** 96
guarantor position **17** 28
guidelines of professional societies **21** 19
gun jumping **24** 118

H
hacker attack **17** 1
hacker group
- Akira **17** 1
- ALPHV **17** 1
- Killnet **17** 1
hacking **17** 11, 42, 43
Haftung
- *allgemeine Geschäftsherrenhaftung* **2** 36
Handlungsbevollmächtigter **4** 50; **15** 35
harassment **8** 32
- sexual **8** 85

Hassrede **17** 21
hate comments **17** 147
hate speech **17** 21
Hauptverhandlung **3** 72
Hauptzollamt **19** 146
hazardous waste **20** 1
- illegal shipment **20** 31
- serious offence **20** 14
- unauthorised shipment **20** 11, 25
health
- damage **20** 110, 118, 137
- hazard **20** 136
- risks **20** 137
health insurance
- *private* **21** 78
- private supplementary **21** 80
- statutory **21** 78
higher regional court **3** 9, 14
- criminal senate **3** 11, 15
- jurisdiction **3** 16, 21
high-risk regions **18** 72
hindsight bias **12** 39
HinSchG **7** 3, 6, 7, 8, 11
- clarification obligations **7** 145
- information obligations **7** 145
- material scope **7** 19
- personal scope **7** 18
hinweisgebende Person **7** 3
hired-out employees
- protection **19** 112
hiring-out of employees **19** 12
- hirer **19** 12, 117
- lender **19** 12
homicide **20** 93, 102, 130
horizontal relationship **24** 18, 67
hospital compensation **21** 93
human dignity
- attacks **17** 146
- violation **17** 97
human rights **18** 5
- compliance **18** 15
- compliance in supply chain **18** 16
- dilemmas **18** 27
- due diligence **18** 34
- obligation of states **18** 14
- officer **18** 86, 147
- risks **18** 53
- statement **18** 95
- strategy **18** 95, 97
Human Rights and Business Dilemmas Forum **18** 27
human trafficking **18** 53

I
illegal employment **19** 77
illiquidity **15** 1, 5, 40, 46, 64, 81
- imminent illiquidity **15** 40, 58
- payment to shareholders **15** 31
immunity **24** 93
impunity **9** 32, 34; **12** 68; **14** 15, 32, 117; **21** 9, 40
in absentia **9** 38, 57, 101
income tax return
- corporate income tax return **13** 17
- personal income tax return **13** 17
independent proceedings **4** 114, 149
indirect perpetration **11** 119
indirect supplier **18** 63, 112
- definition **18** 113
- identification **18** 113
industrial espionage **17** 2
industry associations **24** 25
influence
- decisive **18** 60, 61
information
- commercial *see* commercial information
- inside *see* inside information
- of economic value **25** 66
- secret *see* secret information
information technology systems **17** 5
- attacks **17** 158
- objects of cybercrime **17** 9
- providers **17** 28
- remote searches **17** 125
- used for cybercrime **17** 11
initial access brokers **17** 2
initial public offering **22** 115
Inlandsemittent **22** 84
inside information **22** 23
- ad-hoc disclosure **22** 52
- definition **22** 23
- delay disclosure **22** 54
- publication obligation **22** 53
- sanctions **22** 63
- unlawful sharing **22** 31
insider lists **22** 68
insider prohibitions **22** 18
insider trading **2** 35; **22** 18

insolvency **15** 1, 7, 40, 72, 81
- administrator **15** 26, 84, 101, 102, 105
- application **15** 97, 100
- claw back **15** 112
- consumer insolvency **15** 89
- duty to file for **15** 1, 41
  - time frame **15** 41
- estate **15** 101, 113
- filing for insolvency **15** 61
- imminent illiquidity **15** 59
- intentional late filing **15** 44
- intentionally commited insolvency offence **15** 86
- management's criminal liability **15** 77
- management's duties **15** 40
- negligent late filing **15** 44
- offences **15** 77, 80, 81, 83
- payment restrictions **15** 60
- pending contracts **15** 110
- quota **15** 113
- reasons **15** 46
- remedy **15** 61
- subsidiary **15** 33

insolvency proceedings
- application **15** 97
- characteristics **15** 94
- court decisions **15** 104
- creditors' involvement **15** 120
- duties **15** 68
- duties toward creditors **15** 68
- duty to cooperation and information **15** 69
- in self-administration **15** 123
- main **15** 96, 103, 105
- preliminary **15** 96, 100
- reasons for initiation **15** 95
- shareholders' rights **15** 122

Insolvenz
- *allgemeine Auskunftspflicht* **15** 69
- *Insolvenzgläubiger* **15** 115
- *Insolvenzstraftaten* **15** 81
- *Mitwirkungspflicht* **15** 69
- *nachrangige Insolvenzgläubiger* **15** 115
- *Präsenzpflicht* **15** 69

Insolvenzreife **15** 7
Integrationslösung **9** 66, 83
intellectual property **25** 105, 128
- protection **25** 59

intellectual property rights
- territorial limitation **25** 119

interlocutory proceedings **3** 67
intermediation power **24** 67
internal investigation **6** 73; **7** 51, 74, 76, 88, 92, 95; **8** 33; **25** 51
- best practice **8** 43
- definition **8** 1
- interim measures **8** 91
- interviews **8** 42
- investigation plan **8** 33
- legal obligation **8** 5
- measure **8** 33
- scope **8** 33

internal reporting office **7** 47, 57
- requirements **7** 60

internal reporting process **7** 58
International Competition Network **24** 80
international cooperation
- data theft **17** 151

international officials **10** 11
- bribery **10** 62

internet criminal law **17** 4
Interpol **9** 11, 69
- Black Notice **9** 69
- Blue Notice **9** 69
- Commission for the Control of Interpol's Files **9** 22
- Purple Notice **9** 69
- Red Notice **9** 11, 20, 21, 23, 24
- Silver Notice **9** 69

interpreter **3** 78
intervention
- destructive **15** 32

investigating authorities **13** 94
investigation
- against executive body **2** 38
- internal **2** 2, 31, 96, 97
- mandate **8** 32
- measure **8** 13, 28, 32, 37
- of managers and employees **2** 23
- Phase I **24** 139
- Phase II **24** 139
- plan **8** 34
- preliminary *see* preliminary investigation
- report **8** 70, 71, 72, 74, 76
- team **8** 32, 35, 38, 41

investigation measures **13** 102
investigations **24** 70

involuntary manslaughter **20** 123, 125, 127
Irrtum **13** 15
- *Erlaubnistatbestandsirrtum* **10** 55
- *Verbotsirrtum* **10** 55
IT compliance **17** 7
IT criminal law **17** 3, 4, 5
- applicability of criminal law **17** 22
- case studies **17** 138
- data **17** 31
- fundamentals **17** 8
- outlook **17** 157
- practice **17** 118
- special features **17** 27
- typical offences **17** 30
IT criminal proceedings **17** 127
- cyberbullying **17** 144
IT forensic experts **17** 122
IT investigation measures **17** 123
IT offences **17** 118
- international cooperation **17** 132
IT security **17** 7
IT supply chain **17** 2
IT systems **17** 9
- attacks **17** 30
- disruption **17** 1
IT vulnerabilities **17** 2

J
JITs *see* joint investigation teams
joint controllers **16** 29
joint investigation teams **9** 84; **13** 3
joint venture **24** 28
judge **10** 24
- criminal **3** 17
- examining **3** 29
- honorary **3** 18; **10** 24
- honorary lay **3** 12
- lay **3** 9, 11, 18
- presiding **3** 80
- professional **3** 12; **10** 24
judgment **3** 93
Jugendarbeitschutzgesetz **19** 70
jurisdiction
- original **3** 15
- subject-matter jurisdiction **3** 15, 16
- venue **3** 15, 22

K
kapitalmarktorientierte Kapitalgesellschaft **22** 96
Kassenärztliche Vereinigung **21** 87
Kausalität **13** 32
- *generelle* **20** 116
- *konkrete* **20** 116
Kausalitätsnachweis **20** 115
KeyGen **17** 52
keyloggers **17** 42, 52
KG *see Kommanditgesellschaft*
KGaA *see Kommanditgesellschaft auf Aktien*
kick-back **12** 82
- payments **12** 58, 84
Klimapflege **10** 43
Kommanditgesellschaft **4** 13, 40; **18** 37
Kommanditgesellschaft auf Aktien **4** 10
- *Vertretung* **4** 26
Kommanditist **4** 40, 45
Komplementär **4** 34, 40, 43
Krankenversicherung
- *gesetzliche* **21** 78
- *private* **21** 78
Krise
- *Erfolg* **15** 7
- *Krisenfrüherkennungspflicht* **15** 4
- *Krisenmanagement* **15** 15
- *Liquidität* **15** 7
- *Produkt- und Absatz* **15** 7
- *Stakeholder* **15** 7
- *Strategie* **15** 7

L
labour
- child **18** 53
- forced **18** 53
law enforcement authorities
- cooperation **17** 17
Law Enforcement Monitoring Facilities **23** 126
Lebens- und Geheimnisbereich **17** 30, 36
Leerverkauf **22** 106
legal chatbot models **17** 161
legal entities **4** 10
- fine **4** 150
- sanctions **4** 150
legal person **3** 8
- declaration of consent **12** 46
legal personality **4** 9, 10

– partnerships **4** 13
legal remedies **3** 43, 99
– appeal on points of fact and law **3** 107
– appeal on points of law **3** 112
– complaint **3** 103
leichtfertige Steuerverkürzung **13** 112
Leichtfertigkeit **13** 116
Leiharbeitnehmer **19** 112
leniency **24** 93
– applications **24** 70
– guidelines **24** 94
– proceedings **24** 99
– programme **24** 93
licence
– export **23** 40
– global **23** 43
– individual **23** 43
– requirement **23** 125, 129
Lieferkette **18** 56
limitation period
– fine **4** 123
limited liability companies
– consent **12** 48
– safeguarding duties **12** 27
limited liability enterprise **4** 10
liquidator **4** 25, 27, 42
liquide Mittel **15** 22
liquid funds
– definition **15** 49
Liquidität
– *Krise* **15** 7
– *Plan* **15** 22
– *Prognose* **15** 21
liquidity
– forecast **15** 21, 47
– status **15** 47
liquidity plan **15** 22
local court **3** 14
– judicial body **3** 15
– jurisdiction **3** 16, 17
loss of crime profits **2** 21

M

main examination proceedings **24** 139
main hearing **3** 72
– chronology **3** 77
– preparation **3** 74
– secondary parties **3** 75, 77
main proceedings **3** 72
malicious software **17** 115
malware **17** 112
management
– criminal liability **2** 34
management board **4** 25
management responsibility **4** 55
management's duty
– controlling **15** 3
– diligence of a prudent business-man **15** 3, 14, 61, 136
– file for insolvency **15** 20
– monitoring **15** 3, 4, 20
– payment to shareholders **15** 29
– social security contributions **15** 28
– tax liabilities **15** 28
managing director **4** 27
man-in-the-middle attacks **17** 49
manipulation
– console manipulation **17** 79
– hardware manipulation **17** 79
– input manipulation **17** 75
– output manipulation **17** 79
– programme manipulation **17** 75, 76
manipulative information **22** 42
manipulative trading **22** 39, 40
marker **24** 103
market
– capital *see* capital market
– open market **22** 20
– regulated market **22** 87
market abuse
– insider trading **22** 18
– sanctions **22** 34, 47, 63
market manipulation **22** 38
market power **24** 2
market structure abuse **24** 52
Markt
– *regulierter Markt* **22** 87
Marktmissbrauch **22** 2
measure
– disciplinary *see* disciplinary measures
– remedial **8** 89
Meldekanäle **7** 10
Meldestelle **7** 10
– *interne Meldestelle* **7** 10
Meldung **7** 45
Menschenrechtsstrategie **18** 95
merchants **15** 83
merger **24** 118
– concentration **24** 124
merger control **24** 2, 118

– concentration **24** 128
– regime **24** 118
– reportable transactions **24** 119
Mindestlohngesetz **19** 105
misappropriation **12** 10
misappropriation of purpose doctrine **11** 58
misconception **11** 37
misconduct
– consequences **8** 7
– reported by whistleblowers **8** 19
– severe **8** 85
misdemeanour **3** 17
– imprisonment **3** 18
misleading advertising **22** 127
Missbrauchsalternative **12** 7
mistake in law **13** 39
Mitbestimmungsrecht **7** 130
mitigating circumstances **13** 79
mitigating factors **24** 84
mittelbarer Zulieferer **18** 63
mittelbare Täterschaft **11** 119
MLA *see* mutual legal assistance
money laundering **17** 155
– suitable objects for **14** 19
Money Laundering Act
– obliged entities **14** 48
– risk analysis **14** 67
– risk management **14** 60
– risk management system **14** 60
– Transparency Register **14** 98
Money Laundering Directive **14** 102
– Fourth **14** 46, 60, 102
– Fifth **14** 47, 100, 128
– Sixth **14** 126, 130
Money Laundering Officer **14** 64, 75
– responsibilities **14** 76
Money Laundering Regulation **14** 126
moratorium **15** 131
movement of goods **13** 84
multicorporate enterprises **18** 48
multilateral trading facility **22** 20
Mutterschutzgesetz **19** 66
mutual legal assistance **9** 1, 5, 6, 61, 63, 72; **13** 3; **17** 133
– incoming request **9** 2, 65
– Interpol **9** 69
– measures **9** 61
– outgoing request **9** 2, 67
– procedure **9** 62
– request **9** 2
– within the European Union **9** 73
– with third countries **9** 70

N
National Action Plan on Business and Human Rights **18** 6, 18
National Central Bureau **9** 12
national competition authorities **24** 80
National Cybercrime Cooperation Centre **17** 6
National Cybersecurity Agenda **17** 16
Nationale Cybersicherheitsagenda **17** 16
Nationale Kooperationsstelle Cybercrime **17** 6
natural persons **3** 7
Nebenbeteiligte **4** 143
Nebenbetroffene **2** 67
Nebenklage **2** 66
Nebenkläger **2** 66; **25** 4
Nebenpflichten **12** 16
Nebenstrafrecht **16** 10
ne bis in idem **3** 51, 63; **4** 128 et seqq.; **9** 20, 45, 57, 65, 80, 101
negligence **13** 34; **17** 33
negligent bodily injury **20** 114
nemo tenetur principle **16** 13, 14, 15, 120; **17** 121
net principle **4** 96
Nettoprinzip **4** 96
NGOs **18** 5, 26
NIS2 Directive **17** 19
nolle prosequi **13** 65
non-controlling minority interests **24** 119
non-full-function joint ventures **24** 126
non-governmental organisations *see* NGOs
non-hazardous waste
– illegal shipment **20** 36
non-invasive measures **21** 7
notification
– formal requirements **13** 65
– initiation of proceedings **13** 125
– of an audit order **13** 62
– of personal data breaches **16** 13
– of proceedings **13** 65
Nullbescheide **23** 70

O

obligation
- disclosure **13** 14
- report **13** 18
- special **13** 16

obligation to correct
- effected **13** 19

OECD Guidelines for Multinational Enterprises **6** 20; **18** 17, 18

offence
- abstract endangering **10** 68
- abstract endangerment **18** 143
- against competition **10** 82
- attempt **10** 73
- attempted **4** 62
- by omission **13** 16
- by public officials **10** 10
- capital market **22** 13
- commission of **12** 66
- committed by one act **17** 34
- completion **10** 75
- copyright **17** 30, 85
- cum/ex **11** 11
- cybercrime *see* cybercrime offences
- declaration **13** 10
- economic offences **21** 73
- electronic forgery **17** 30, 82
- endangerment *see* endangerment offence
- environment *see* environmental offences
- everyone's offences **10** 17
- fraud **11** 14
- genuine official offences **10** 17
- homicide **20** 93, 102
- IT **17** 118
- joinder of offences **17** 34
- multiple **4** 106
- official **10** 66
- of success **20** 7, 40, 47
- qualification **11** 77
- regulatory **2** 7
- relating to personal life and privacy **17** 30
- relating to statements **17** 30, 97
- special **2** 40; **11** 81; **13** 16, 128; **20** 19; **21** 75
- subsidy fraud **11** 126
- tax *see* tax offences

termination **10** 76
- unitary **4** 104

offene Handelsgesellschaft **4** 13, 38; **18** 37

Offenlegung **7** 107

öffentlicher Dienst **10** 16

officer
- chief sustainability **18** 147
- compliance *see* compliance officer
- data privacy **6** 92
- environmental protection **18** 147
- human rights **18** 147

official offences **10** 66, 110

officials **13** 63
- elected *see* elected officials
- European *see* European officials
- foreign *see* foreign officials
- international *see* international officials
- non-officials **10** 61
- public *see* public officials

oHG *see offene Handelsgesellschaft*

omission **13** 21

one-person enterprise **4** 11

Opportunitätsprinzip **4** 88; **13** 130

opportunity principle **13** 130

order imposing punishment **13** 97

orders **17** 137

organized trading facility **22** 20

other involved person **25** 14

over-indebtedness **15** 1, 5, 40, 55, 81

own business area **18** 60, 81, 87, 90, 94, 97, 99 et seqq., 107, 112
- preventive measure **18** 97

P

paramount cross-market significance for competition **24** 61

parent company **12** 98

parties to the offence **5** 28

partner
- general **4** 26, 40
- limited **4** 40

partnership
- civil law **4** 13, 36; **18** 37
- consent **12** 50
- general **4** 13, 38; **18** 37
- legal personalilty **4** 13
- limited **4** 40
- limited by shares **4** 10, 26
- limited partnership **18** 37
- safeguarding duty **12** 31
- with legal personality **4** 34

pass-on defence **24** 109
patents **25** 128
pecuniary damage **12** 55, 76
pecuniary interests **12** 16
pecuniary loss **11** 51, 52
penalty
- aggregated **17** 34
- determination of penalty **13** 77
- one **17** 34
- scale of penalties **13** 77
- surcharge **13** 71
- total **17** 34
perpetration **10** 66
perpetrator **5** 25, 28
personal data **16** 54
personality rights **17** 88, 97
personal life and privacy **17** 37; **25** 8
personenbezogene Daten **25** 44
phishing **17** 43, 45, 51, 83, 159
- AI-supported phishing campaigns **17** 2
- attack **17** 151
- campaings **17** 163
- emails **17** 162
place of action **17** 23
place of effect **17** 24
policy
- anti-bribery and corruption **6** 43, 44
- anti-money laundering **6** 45
- gift **6** 44
post and telecommunications
- violation of secrecy **25** 49
power of agency **12** 9
power of attorney
- holder of a general **15** 35
power of disposal **12** 68
Präventionsmaßnahmen **18** 94
preliminary investigation **3** 25
- commencement **3** 26
- completion **3** 44
preliminary proceedings
- legal remedies **3** 43
- termination **3** 49, 53, 64
prerequisite for trial **17** 37
preservation
- of stored computer data **17** 137
pre-trial
- custody **3** 130
- detention **3** 37, 42
preventive measures **18** 94
- in own business area **18** 97
- vis-à-vis direct suppliers **18** 98
price fixing **24** 19
price or margin squeezes **24** 51
principle
- of accessoriness **20** 3, 25
- of appropriateness **18** 70
- of certainty **18** 69
- of legality **3** 10
- of proportionality **8** 33
- of sovereignty **17** 124
Prinzip der Angemessenheit **18** 70
prior judicial decision **17** 127
privacy of correspondence
- violation **25** 158
privacy of the spoken word
- audio recording **25** 158
- violation **25** 158
privacy policy section **16** 39
private accessory prosecution **2** 66; **25** 135
private accessory prosecutor **2** 66; **25** 4, 90, 124
private individuals **13** 69
private prosecution **25** 91, 125, 135
probability prognosis **13** 67
probative value **17** 122
- forgery **17** 141, 142
- suppression **17** 84
- suppression of data of probative value **17** 84
procedural rules **16** 74
proceedings
- adhesion **2** 65
- administrative **24** 71
- confiscation *see* confiscation proceedings
- costs **3** 120
- cumulative **4** 148
- discontinuance of the proceedings **13** 107
- discovery proceedings **17** 153
- independent *see* independent proceedings
- joined **2** 61
- leniency *see* leniency proceedings
- main **2** 61
- objective **2** 62
- opening **3** 67
- secondary parties **3** 101
- taxation *see* taxation proceedings

proceed to trial **3** 67
procurement strategies **18** 97
product
- cosmetic **20** 136
- dangerous **20** 105
- defective **20** 93, 94, 95, 96, 98, 105
- development **20** 96, 97
- distribution **20** 95
- health-endangering **20** 94
- instruction **20** 103
- medicinal **20** 114
- production **20** 95, 99, 100
- recall **20** 96, 104, 108
- safety **20** 99, 101
- sale **20** 101
- sales stop **20** 108
- supervision obligation **20** 104
product criminal law **20** 90
product criminal liability **20** 95
production of data **17** 137
product liability **20** 90
- cases **20** 107
- criminal **20** 91
Produktkrise **15** 7
professional confidentiality
- duties **25** 10
- obligations **25** 8
professional misconduct **25** 95
professional secret **25** 28
prohibition of set-off **13** 31
Prokurist **4** 50; **15** 35
proof of causality **20** 115
prosecution
- private *see* private prosecution
- request for prosecution **25** 123, 133
prosecutor
- general local prosecutors **22** 7
- private accessory *see* private accessory prosecutor
prospectus **22** 3, 114
- Prospectus Regulation **22** 3
- requirements **22** 114
protection
- of commercial information **25** 1
protective measures **7** 113
public announcements **24** 23
public contracts
- exclusion from the award **18** 138
public institutions
safeguarding duty **12** 32
public officials **10** 18, 20, 44, 68, 111; **25** 11, 12
- bribery **10** 5, 10, 91, 95, 108
- corruption **10** 1, 14
- definition **25** 13
- gift **10** 121
- obligation to confidentiality **25** 34
- right to refuse testimony **25** 27
public prosecutor
- investigations **2** 1
- office **2** 11
public service **10** 16
- person entrusted with special public service functions **10** 18, 23, 26, 27, 45, 49, 50, 63
public tender **2** 26; **4** 111; **19** 172; **24** 90; **25** 35
purchase agreement **12** 17
purge **2** 108

Q
Qualifikationstatbestände **23** 32
quick freeze **17** 137

R
ransomware attack **17** 1, 2
Rechtfertigungsgrund **10** 47
Rechtsfehler **10** 55
Rechtshilfefreundlichkeit **9** 1
reciprocity **9** 54
recklessness **13** 116; **14** 34
reduction of regulatory fines **24** 93
Regelbeispiel **20** 14
regional court **3** 9, 14
- criminal chamber for particularly serious crimes **3** 11, 15, 20, 112
- criminal panels **3** 11, 112
- jurisdiction **3** 16
- major criminal panels **3** 15, 19
registered associations **4** 10
regulatory fine **2** 7; **4** 4; **16** 11
- notice **2** 11
- proceedings **24** 74
regulatory fines **24** 4, 74
- amount **24** 5
- guidelines **24** 83
regulatory offence **16** 118
related rights **25** 111
relationship
- contractual **12** 17

- expired legal **12** 11
- external **12** 7
- fiduciary **12** 4, 11, 12
- good **12** 85
- horizontal **24** 18, 67
- internal **12** 7, 9, 10, 11, 75
- invalid legal **12** 11, 12
- legal **12** 18, 37
- of trust **12** 1
- supplier and customer **24** 30
- vertical **24** 30, 67
- victim and perpetrator **12** 2

relative or superior market power **24** 66
remedial action **18** 100
remediation **8** 78
- measure **8** 23, 89, 90

remuneration **12** 92
report **7** 45
- documentation **7** 89, 92

reporting channels **6** 36, 59; **7** 40, 60, 77, 134
- external **7** 10

reporting obligation **14** 103; **16** 48
reporting office **7** 5, 10, 11, 14, 40, 54, 68
- centralised **7** 72
- decentralised **7** 70
- external *see* external reporting office
- follow-up measures **7** 95
- group privilege **7** 10, 76
- internal *see* internal reporting office
- minimum requirements **7** 60
- right of choice **7** 55

reporting option **7** 58
reporting system **7** 151
- central **7** 74
- decentralised **7** 71
- implementation **7** 129

representation
- fraudulent **15** 66

representative **4** 7, 20
- authorised **15** 35

Repressalien **7** 121
reprisal **7** 17
request to prosecute **17** 35, 37
requirement of confidentiality **7** 100
resale price maintenance **24** 30
restrictions of competition by object **24** 18
restructuring
- commissioner **15** 138
- court **15** 138
- plan **15** 125, 128

Restrukturierung
- *öffentliche Restrukturierungssachen* **15** 144
- *Restrukturierungsbeauftragter* **15** 138
- *vertrauliche Restrukturierungssachen* **15** 144

retaliation **7** 120
- compensation **7** 123
- damages **7** 123
- prohibition **7** 120

retention of title **12** 17
revenue authorities **13** 95
Revision **3** 112
Richter **10** 24
- *Berufsrichter* **10** 24
- *ehrenamtlicher* **10** 24
- *Strafrichter* **3** 17

Richtervorbehalt **17** 127
right of evocation **13** 99
right to refuse testimony **25** 27, 28
Risikoanalyse **18** 87
Risikomanagement **18** 80
risk analysis **18** 87
risk assessment **6** 8, 23, 25
- framework **6** 30
- guidelines **6** 30
- procedures **6** 20
- process **6** 25

risk country **18** 72
risk management **6** 20; **18** 9, 80
- monitoring **18** 86
- strategy **6** 107
- system **6** 9

risk sector **18** 72
risky transactions **12** 74
- consent **12** 75

Rückschaufehler **12** 39
rule of attribution (§ 14 StGB) **20** 19, 92
Russia Sanctions Regulation **23** 76

S

sabotage **17** 2
Sachverständigenaussage **3** 32
safeguarding duty **12** 5, 16
- auditors **12** 35
- breach **12** 37
- compliance officer **12** 34
- employees **12** 33

- lawyers **12** 36
- limited liability company **12** 27
- partnership **12** 31
- public institution **12** 32
- risky transaction **12** 75
- stock corporation **12** 20
- supervisory board **12** 22
- tax consultants **12** 35
- under different types of contracts **12** 17

sanctioning
- double sanctioning **4** 107

sanctioning companies **2** 6
sanctioning employees **6** 85
sanctions
- § 40 HinSchG **7** 53, 125
- against Russia **23** 74
- corruption offences **10** 69
- financing **23** 93
- for intent **4** 87
- for negligence **4** 87
- for violation of arms embargo **23** 30
- framework **22** 8
- fraud **22** 131
- goods and technology **23** 82
- investment **23** 93
- LkSG **18** 137
- market abuse **22** 34, 47, 63
- participation **23** 93
- personal **23** 99
  - freezing **23** 100
- short selling **22** 113
- voting rights notifications **22** 104

Sanierungspflicht **15** 15
Sapin II **6** 20
Schengen Information System *see* SIS
Schmähkritik **17** 146
Schöffen **3** 12
Schöffengericht **3** 9
Schuld **13** 39
Schwarzarbeit *see Finanzkontrolle Schwarzarbeit*
Schwarzarbeitsbekämpfungsgesetz **19** 82
Schwarze Kasse **12** 78
Schwurgericht **3** 15, 20
SE *see* Societas Europaea
search measures **3** 39
search warrant **17** 156
secondary participant **4** 143
secondary parties **3** 9, 31, 46
secrecy **25** 8
- bank **25** 13
- breach **25** 8, 27, 35
- consent to disclosure **25** 21
- interest in secrecy **25** 16, 18
- obligation **25** 20
- of post and telecommunication **25** 7, 49
- tax **25** 41
- will to secrecy **25** 16

secret **25** 16
- business and trade *see* business and trade secrets
- illegal **25** 18, 34
- of a person's personal life **25** 16
- official **25** 29, 32, 103
- of legal persons **25** 8, 19
- of natural persons **25** 19
- professional **25** 28
- trade *see* trade secrets

secret information **25** 65, 71
- holder of **25** 66
- illegal access **25** 138
- storage **25** 77

sector inquiry **24** 142
seizure **3** 41
Selbstanzeige **13** 47
Selbstgeldwäsche **14** 14
Selbstreinigung **2** 108; **18** 140; **19** 171
selective distribution systems **24** 31
self-administration **15** 72, 123
self-assessment taxes **13** 27
self-cleaning **18** 140; **19** 171
self-disclosure **19** 33
self-incrimination **16** 13
self-laundering **14** 14, 30
settlement **2** 20, 38
settlement proceedings **24** 79
shareholder
- duty to file for insolvency **15** 43
- influence **15** 35
- rights in insolvency proceedings **15** 122

shareholders' meeting
- right to control the management **15** 39
- right to monitor the management **15** 39

short selling **22** 106
- disclosure obligations **22** 109

- German Regulation on Net Short Selling **22** 110
- sanctions **22** 113
- temporary ban **22** 112
- uncovered short sales **22** 111
short-selling
- temporary bans **22** 112
Short Selling Regulation **22** 108, 109
SIEC test **24** 135
signalling **24** 23
single economic entity **24** 16
SIRENE Office **9** 12, 22
SIS **9** 12, 21
skimming **17** 109
slave labour **18** 28
slavery **18** 53
slush funds **12** 10, 78
small and medium-sized enterprises
- supply chain management **18** 34
small or medium-sized enterprises **24** 37
smuggling **13** 85
social adequacy **10** 44, 55
social engineering **17** 12, 115
social security contributions
- financial crisis **19** 26
- withholding **19** 1, 4
Societas Europaea **4** 10, 30
- administrative board **4** 30
- dualistic system **4** 30
- monistic system **4** 30
soldier **10** 27, 50
sole trader **4** 9
sonstige mitwirkende Person **25** 14
sonstiges Fehlverhalten **25** 98
Sorgfaltspflichten **18** 9, 65
Sozialadäquanz **10** 44
special public interest **17** 36, 57
sphere of personal life and privacy **17** 36
sponsoring **12** 42
sponsorship **12** 94
spying on data **17** 38
spyware **17** 49
Staatskasse **12** 89
Staatsschutzkammer **3** 20
Stadler ruling **11** 120
Stakeholderkrise **15** 7
stalking **17** 104
standard contractual clauses **16** 32
StaRUG **15** 125
statement on human rights **18** 95
statute of limitation periods **24** 111
Stellvertretung
- *offene* **13** 52
- *verdeckte* **13** 52
Steuerhinterziehung **13** 7
Steuerpflichtiger **13** 113
Steuerstempler **13** 23
Steuerzeichen **13** 23
Stiftungen **4** 10; **18** 38
Stimmrechtsmitteilungen **22** 97
stock corporation **4** 10, 25; **18** 37
- consent **12** 49
- safeguarding duty **12** 20
stock market speculation **22** 132
- induction **22** 132
Stop Ecocide International **18** 26
Strafantrag **3** 26
Strafanzeige **3** 26
Strafaufhebungsgrund **10** 47
Strafbefehl **3** 47
Strafkammer
- *große Strafkammer* **3** 15
- *kleine Strafkammer* **3** 107
Strafsenat **3** 15
Strafvollstreckungskammer **3** 116
Strategiekrise **15** 7
strategy crisis **15** 7
Strohgeschäftsführer **2** 39
subsidiary **12** 98
- insolvency **15** 33
- jeopardise subsidiary's existence **15** 32
subsidy
- definition **11** 132
- fraud **11** 13, 126
- under federal or state law **11** 133
- under the law of the European Union **11** 138
substantiated knowledge **18** 119
substantiierte Kenntnis **18** 119
Subventionen **11** 126
Subventionsbetrug **11** 4, 13
succession
- of an entity **4** 133
summary penalty order **3** 47
supervisory board
- duty to monitor management **15** 39
supplier
- direct **18** 62
- indirect **18** 63
supply chain **18** 56

– compliance with human rights **18** 16
– cooperation **18** 75
– global **18** 6, 15
– IT **17** 2
– labour abuse **6** 106
surveillance
– acoustic surveillance of private premises **17** 125
– foreign telecommunication surveillance **17** 134
– software **17** 125
– source telecommunication surveillance **17** 125
– telecommunication surveillance **17** 123, 125, 156
– total system surveillance **17** 125
surveillance technology
– Dual-Use Regulation **23** 128, 130
– export **23** 123
sustainability **18** 20

T
taking bribes **10** 48
Tatbestandsalternativen **12** 5
Tatbestandsirrtum **10** 55
Tatbestandsmerkmal
– *normatives* **10** 56
Tateinheit **4** 104; **10** 56; **13** 57; **17** 34
Täterschaft **12** 66
tätige Reue **11** 154
Tatmehrheit **4** 106; **17** 34
Täuschung **11** 19
tax
– evasion **8** 85
– investigators **13** 63
– proceedings
  – procedural law **13** 130
– understatement *see* understatement of tax
– understating of tax **13** 28
– VAT **13** 17
tax advantage
– for other reasons **13** 30
– large scale **13** 45
– other unwarranted tax advantages **13** 28
– unwarranted tax advantages **13** 7, 24, 60, 66, 115, 127
tax adviser **13** 104
tax assessment **13** 25
taxation bases **13** 13
taxation proceedings **13** 109
tax crime
– fine **13** 80
– of medium gravity **13** 80
– organised **13** 81
– petty **13** 80
tax estimate notice **13** 27
tax evasion **2** 35; **13** 7
– as a business **13** 79
– attempted **13** 32, 40
– limitation period **13** 58, 74
– on a serial basis **13** 79
– penalty interest **13** 60, 71
– presumption of intentional tax evasion **13** 38
– serious **13** 44, 76
– simple tax evasion **13** 75
tax fraud
– general minor tax fraud **13** 127
tax investigation unit **13** 100
tax offences **13** 84
– customs fraud **13** 85
– customs violation **13** 84
– other tax-related regulatory offences **13** 127
– participation **13** 83
– proceeds **13** 91
– regulatory tax offences **13** 111
– tax-evaded goods **13** 86
tax police **13** 100
tax return
– supplementary **13** 54
tax revenues **13** 7
tax secrecy
– breach **25** 41
tender **24** 7, 21, 29, 93
– public **2** 26; **4** 111; **19** 172; **24** 90; **25** 35
testimony
– expert **3** 32
– public officials **25** 27
– right to refuse **25** 27, 28
– witness **3** 32
theft **12** 10
– analogue **17** 2
– crypto **17** 43
– data **17** 39, 151
– digital **17** 2
third party
– *mala fide* **5** 115, 116

tipping-off ban **14** 120
trademarks **25** 128
trade secrets **25** 1
- definition **25** 61, 63
- freedom of press **25** 101
- other protection provisions **25** 104
- protection **25** 59, 68, 70, 84, 88
- protection against cybercrime **25** 139
- theft **25** 3
- violation **25** 3, 4, 91
- whistleblowing **25** 95
traffic data
- disclosure **17** 137
- information **17** 123
- real-time collection **17** 137
transaction value threshold **24** 131
transfer of sentenced persons **9** 94
transparency register **14** 97
Transparenzregister **14** 98
treasury **12** 89
treatment contract **21** 81
Treubruchsalternative **12** 10
trial **3** 72
- conclusion **3** 98
- duplication of trials **4** 128
- prerequisite **17** 37
turnover thresholds **24** 129
Typologiepapiere **14** 106

U
Überwachungssystem **15** 10
UK Bribery Act 2010 **6** 20
ultima ratio **16** 80
unbemakelter Vertrag **5** 69
understatement of tax
- large scale **13** 45
- reckless understatement of tax **13** 112
unethical behaviour **6** 44
unethical practices **6** 43
UN Global Climate Litigation Report **18** 24
UN Guiding Principles on Business and Human Rights **18** 16, 18
United Nations **18** 16
unlawful agreement **10** 40, 42, 44, 53, 68, 75
unlawfulness **13** 39
unmittelbarer Zulieferer **18** 62
Unrechtsvereinbarung **10** 40; **21** 138
unreliability, § 35 sub. 1 GewO **19** 166
Unterlassung **11** 25
Unterschlagung **12** 10
Untersuchungshaft **3** 37
Untreue **12** 1
unwarranted tax advantages **13** 7, 24, 28, 60, 66, 115, 127
upcoding **21** 100
upfront buyer solutions **24** 136
upstream loan **12** 99
US Foreign Corrupt Practices Act **6** 20
US Sentencing Guidelines **6** 20

V
value
- commercial **25** 66, 96
- economic **25** 66, 71, 96
- negative **25** 66
value-added tax *see* VAT
VAT
- inspection **13** 64
- non-payment or incomplete payment **13** 129
- returns **13** 119
VAT revenues
- compromising **13** 129
- impairment **13** 90
Verbandsgeldbuße **2** 7
Verbandssanktionengesetzes **6** 17
Verbot von Repressalien **7** 120
Verbraucherinsolvenz **15** 89
Verbrechen **3** 17
Verein
- *eingetragener* **4** 28
- *ohne Rechtspersönlichkeit* **4** 18, 33
Vergehen **3** 17
Vergleich **2** 20
Verjährung **13** 76
Verleiher **19** 12
Vermittlungsausschuss **7** 6
vertical relationship **24** 30, 67
Vertrag
- *Arbeitsvertrag* **12** 17
- *Darlehensvertrag* **12** 17
- *Kaufvertrag* **12** 17
- *Werkvertrag* **12** 17
Vertraulichkeitsgebot **7** 81, 100
Verwaltungsrat **4** 30
video surveillance **16** 57
Vollendung **10** 75
voluntary disclosure **13** 41, 47

– declaration of correction **13** 50
– exempting from regulatory fines **13** 121
– formal requirements **13** 54
– minor **13** 121
– minor differences **13** 56
– personal ground for exemption from punishment **13** 51
– reasons for exclusion **13** 61
– supplementary tax return **13** 54
Vor-GmbH **4** 9
Vorsatz **13** 33
– *bedingter* **10** 54; **13** 20
Vorstand **4** 28
– *Aktiengesellschaft* **4** 25
Vorstandsmitglieder **4** 28
Vorteil **10** 33, 93
Vorteilsannahme **10** 26
voting rights notifications **22** 97 et seqq.

W
wage
– minimum **19** 80, 105
– usury **19** 110
waste **20** 8, 32
– tourism **20** 11
– unauthorised management **20** 7
– unauthorised shipment **20** 25
– unlawful handling **20** 9
Wettbewerb
– *Straftaten gegen den* **10** 82
Wettbewerbsdurchsetzungsgesetz **24** 3
Wettbewerbsregister **4** 111; **10** 119; **19** 170; **24** 91
whistleblower **7** 1, 3, 4
– anonymous reporting **8** 16, 17
– identity **7** 101, 104
– retaliation **8** 18, 19, 55
whistleblower protection **7** 3, 4, 5, 111; **8** 16, 76
– burden of proof **7** 5
– exclusion of responsibility **7** 119
– internal **7** 112
– prohibition of retaliation **7** 120
– requirements **7** 113
whistleblowing
– of trade secrets **25** 95
whistleblowing system **6** 59, 60, 61, 62, 63, 64, 65; **7** 2, 3, 5, 12, 13, 59; **24** 105
– set up **7** 151
white-collar criminal law **12** 1
Wirecard **22** 89, 112
Wirtschaftsstrafkammer **3** 20
witness **3** 33
– potential **2** 111
– testimony **3** 32
work **25** 107, 108, 109
– copyrighted **25** 107
– distribution **25** 113
– exploitation **25** 115
– protected works **25** 110
– reproduction **25** 113
– unlawful affixing of a designation of authorship **25** 116
work safety **19** 44
works council **7** 130; **8** 36, 82
– co-determiantion right **7** 130
– protection **19** 129
– support during interview **8** 56, 58

Z
Zentrale Ansprechstellen Cybercrime **17** 6
Zeugenaussage **3** 32
Zulieferer
– *mittelbar* **18** 63
– *unmittelbar* **18** 62
Zusatzversicherung **21** 80